# OF BURMA'S FAMILY TREE

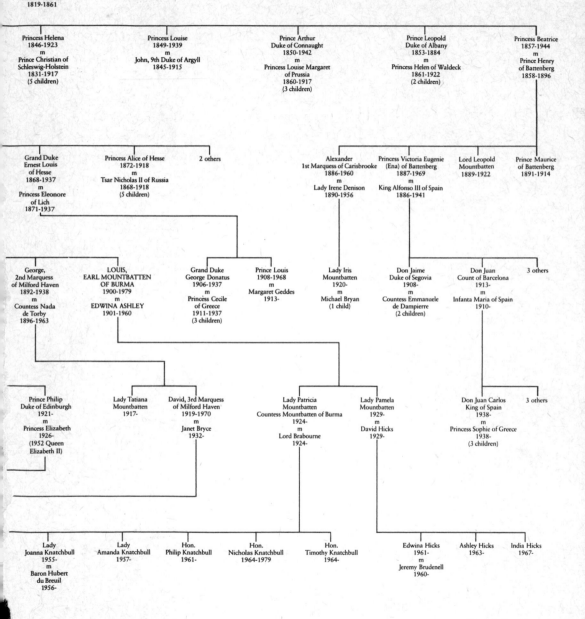

PRINCE ALBERT
OF SAXE-COBURG
AND GOTHA
1819-1861

Princess Helena
1846-1923
m
Prince Christian of
Schleswig-Holstein
1831-1917
(5 children)

Princess Louise
1849-1939
m
John, 9th Duke of Argyll
1845-1915

Prince Arthur
Duke of Connaught
1850-1942
m
Princess Louise Margaret
of Prussia
1860-1917
(3 children)

Prince Leopold
Duke of Albany
1853-1884
m
Princess Helen of Waldeck
1861-1922
(2 children)

Princess Beatrice
1857-1944
m
Prince Henry
of Battenberg
1858-1896

Grand Duke
Ernest Louis
of Hesse
1868-1937
m
Princess Eleonore
of Lich
1871-1937

Princess Alice of Hesse
1872-1918
m
Tsar Nicholas II of Russia
1868-1918
(5 children)

2 others

Alexander
1st Marquess of Carisbrooke
1886-1960
m
Lady Irene Denison
1890-1956

Princess Victoria Eugenie
(Ena) of Battenberg
1887-1969
m
King Alfonso III of Spain
1886-1941

Lord Leopold
Mountbatten
1889-1922

Prince Maurice
of Battenberg
1891-1914

George,
2nd Marquess
of Milford Haven
1892-1938
m
Countess Nada
de Torby
1896-1963

LOUIS,
EARL MOUNTBATTEN
OF BURMA
1900-1979
m
EDWINA ASHLEY
1901-1960

Grand Duke
George Donatus
1906-1937
m
Princess Cecile
of Greece
1911-1937
(3 children)

Prince Louis
1908-1968
m
Margaret Geddes
1913-

Lady Iris
Mountbatten
1920-
m
Michael Bryan
(1 child)

Don Jaime
Duke of Segovia
1908-
m
Countess Emmanuele
de Dampierre
(2 children)

Don Juan
Count of Barcelona
1913-
m
Infanta Maria of Spain
1910-

3 others

Prince Philip
Duke of Edinburgh
1921-
m
Princess Elizabeth
1926-
(1952 Queen
Elizabeth II)

Lady Tatiana
Mountbatten
1917-

David, 3rd Marquess
of Milford Haven
1919-1970
m
Janet Bryce
1932-

Lady Patricia
Mountbatten
Countess Mountbatten of Burma
1924-
m
Lord Brabourne
1924-

Lady Pamela
Mountbatten
1929-
m
David Hicks
1929-

Don Juan Carlos
King of Spain
1938-
m
Princess Sophie of Greece
1938-
(3 children)

3 others

Lady
Joanna Knatchbull
1955-
m
Baron Hubert
du Breuil
1956-

Lady
Amanda Knatchbull
1957-

Hon.
Philip Knatchbull
1961-

Hon.
Nicholas Knatchbull
1964-1979

Hon.
Timothy Knatchbull
1964-

Edwina Hicks
1961-
m
Jeremy Brudenell
1960-

Ashley Hicks
1963-

India Hicks
1967-

# MOUNTBATTEN

# MOUNTBATTEN

*Philip Ziegler*

*Alfred A. Knopf   New York   1985*

THIS IS A BORZOI BOOK
PUBLISHED BY ALFRED A. KNOPF, INC.

Library of Congress Cataloging in
Publication Data

Ziegler, Philip.
Mountbatten.

Bibliography: p.
Includes index.
1. Mountbatten of Burma, Louis
Mountbatten, Earl, 1900-1979.
2. Admirals—Great Britain—Biography.
3. Viceroys—India—Biography.
4. Great Britain. Royal Navy—Biography.
I. Title.
DA89.1.M59Z54   1984   941.082′092′4 [B]
84–48814
ISBN 0-394-52098-X

*Manufactured in the United States
of America*

# Contents

*Photographs*
Photographic inserts will be found following pages 98, 386 and 674. (Unless otherwise indicated, all photographs are from the Broadlands Archives.)

# Acknowledgements

I am most grateful to those members of the Royal Family and of the family of Lord Mountbatten who have been kind enough to talk to me about this biography and in some cases to allow me to read unpublished papers in their possession.

The Trustees of the Broadlands Archives – Lord Brabourne, Sir Rupert Hart-Davis and Sir Charles Troughton – invited me to write this book and, having done so, gave me unstinted encouragement and support while leaving me free to form my own impressions and draw my own conclusions. No author could ask for more.

The biographer of Lord Mountbatten is drawn into so many fields of specialist knowledge that he is bound to pillage the work of a multitude of scholars. To all those whose books and articles are cited in my notes I owe a debt of gratitude. It is invidious to pick out a few from among so many, yet it would be churlish not to express the obligation I feel to four historians in particular: Professor Michael Howard, the late Mr Ronald Lewin, the late Captain Stephen Roskill and Professor Hugh Tinker.

In the bibliography I list some two hundred people to whom I have spoken about Lord Mountbatten or with whom I have communicated in some way that has affected the contents of this book. Many of these have been prodigal of their time and hospitality. All of them I thank. Many others have assisted me along my way. The list is far from complete but I could not fail to mention the help given by Sir Antony Acland, Mr Kenneth Burns, Lord Egremont, Mr and Mrs Nicholas Fenn, Mr Douglas Hurd, Sir Kenneth Newman, Mr and Mrs Justin Staples, Sir Robert and Lady Wade-Gery.

Every researcher must be conscious of the debt he owes to those many librarians and archivists who make his work possible. Once again it is invidious to pick out individuals but I would like at least to refer to Sir Robin Mackworth-Young of the Royal Archives, Mr John Taylor of the National Archives of Washington, Mr Suddaby and Mr Sargent of the Imperial War Museum, Dr Ashton of the India Office Library, U Thaw Kaung of the National Library of Burma, Professor Eckhart Franz of the Hessisches Staatsarchiv, Mr Correlli Barnett of Churchill College, Cambridge, Professor Ravinder Kumar of the Nehru Memorial Museum, Dr R. K. Perti of the National Archives of India, Mr Douglas Matthews and the staff of the London Library.

The contribution of Mrs Travis and Mrs Chalk of the Broadlands Archives has been so great that they deserve not merely a paragraph but a page to themselves.

I am indebted also to my editor, Mr Richard Ollard, Mr Roger Schlesinger and Lady Elizabeth Bowes Lyon; to Mrs Carol Janeway of Knopf in New

York; to my agent Mrs Diana Baring; and to Mrs Wilber, who typed my illegible manuscript with dedication and miraculous skill.

Finally, my family endured five years' involvement with the affairs of Lord Mountbatten with equanimity. Above all, my wife Clare contributed hugely, both directly and through her perceptive understanding of the aspirations and frailties of mankind.

# *Foreword*

This is the official biography of Lord Mountbatten. The phrase requires some explanation. To me it has meant that I have my cake yet have eaten it too. I have been granted unrestricted access to the treasure-house of Mountbatten's personal archives at Broadlands and given all the help an author could hope for from those who knew him or who possessed relevant material. But no attempt has been made to exercise editorial control over what I wrote; Lord Mountbatten's family and trustees have saved me from many inaccuracies and provided invaluable testimony, but the decision as to what should or should not be written has been entirely mine. Most people, I believe, will feel this biography provides a generally favourable portrait of its subject, but it is far from hagiography. To suppress his weaknesses would have been to discredit the account of his formidable strengths. There is much in this book that would have caused Lord Mountbatten indignation or dismay; I hope that at the end he would have accepted that my portrayal is a fair one.

I could have written this biography in two, three or even four volumes – the material was rich enough. After much doubt I have finally settled for a single book. There were several reasons for this decision, not least that Mountbatten's career flowed in such a way that it was exceedingly difficult to know where to make the break: Combined Operations led logically to South-East Asia Command, SEAC to India. I have chosen, therefore, what was perhaps the line of least resistance. The result is massive but not, I hope, intolerably so.

OPPOSITE *Dickie as a naval cadet with his mother, Princess Victoria.*

# Part One

## 1900 - 1939

# CHAPTER 1

## *The Child*

ADMIRAL OF THE FLEET, the Earl Mountbatten of Burma, was a man who, for his own amusement, rarely took up any book unless it were one of genealogy, most especially one relating to his own forebears. During the reaches of the night in the Viceroy's House in Delhi, when his predecessors might have diverted themselves with the verses of Macaulay or the latest detective story by Mrs Christie, Mountbatten would relax over the tapestry of his ancestry, enumerating the generations that divided him from the Emperor Charlemagne and marvelling at the intricate web of cousinship which bound him many times over to the Wittelsbachs and the Romanoffs, the Habsburgs and the Hohenzollerns. His studies both gave him the satisfaction that attends the solution of a complex jigsaw-puzzle and gratified that pride in family that was one of the most prominent of his characteristics.

Only the least historically minded would deny that he had reason to be proud. The house of Hesse from which he sprang had for many centuries governed one of the most prominent if not powerful of German states. Philip the Magnanimous, a leading figure of the German Reformation, on his death in 1567 divided his lands between his four sons, but two of these fell by the wayside, to leave Hesse-Darmstadt and Hesse-Kassel surviving into the nineteenth century. The two royal houses of Hesse were celebrated for tolerance, patronage of the arts, and the despatch of their citizens as mercenaries to every corner of the globe. Both Hesses backed the losing side in the war between Austria and Prussia but, while Hesse-Kassel was annexed by Prussia, Hesse-Darmstadt survived under its own dynasty though as part of the Great Empire until the revolution of 1918. A Hessian, to judge by his national history, might be expected to be liberal, itinerant and combative. In none of these did Mountbatten deny his heritage.

Prince Alexander of Hesse, Mountbatten's grandfather, was the third son of Grand Duke Louis II and godson to the Tsar of Russia. When his sister married the Tsarevich, the future Tsar Alexander II, it seemed both sensible and in keeping with the national tradition that Alexander of Hesse should take service in the Russian army. He achieved distinction, had a regiment of the Lancers named after him and was awarded the Cross of St George. The

Tsar intended him as a husband for his niece and his future in Russia promised to be secure and prosperous. For Alexander, however, at this stage of his life at least, security and prosperity did not count for much. He fell in love with Julie Hauke, one of his sister's ladies-in-waiting, a Polish girl who, if hardly a nonentity, was not from a family sufficiently grandiose to justify so princely a match. The Tsar indignantly forbade the marriage. Alexander went to England to forget, remembered, returned to St Petersburg and in 1851 eloped with Julie to Warsaw and thence to Breslau where he married her.

This impetuous escapade effectively exiled him from Russia. It did little to improve his standing in his native Hesse. His elder brother, now Grand Duke Louis III, was almost as outraged as the Tsar, but felt that he could hardly let Alexander starve. An uneasy settlement was reached. Alexander was allowed to retain his status as a royal prince of Hesse; the defunct title of Battenberg – a pleasant town in the north of the Grand Duchy – and the quality of countess were conferred on his wife; any children of the marriage, though without claim to the throne of Hesse, would at least be of the same rank as their mother. Even this qualified disgrace did not last long. In 1858 Countess Julie of Battenberg was raised to the level of a Serene Highness and four years later the couple returned to Darmstadt. A new house had been born; royal, after a fashion, but bearing about it a faint aura of wildness and irregularity. 'I believe that the Battenbergs have always behaved somewhat peculiarly,' Himmler was to comment eighty years later, after reading the file that the Gestapo maintained on Mountbatten and his family.[1]

The Battenbergs had a palace in Darmstadt but their real home was Heiligenberg Castle, some ten miles south of the capital. Heiligenberg had been bought as a large farmhouse by the royal family in the early nineteenth century, and swelled significantly in the ensuing decades. By the time Alexander was installed it boasted twin towers, a ballroom and space for sixty or more people to stay, but the total effect was that of a villa built by a newly enriched industrial magnate rather than a feudal fastness. It was pleasant enough, though, and splendidly perched on the crest of a wooded hill, a good house in which to bring up children. Alexander and Julie had five of these, the second child and eldest son being another Louis, Mountbatten's father.

There had always been much to-ing and fro-ing between the courts of Great Britain and of Hesse, and this was intensified after the marriage in 1862 of the future Grand Duke Louis IV to Queen Victoria's daughter Alice. Young Prince Louis spoke German as his first language but was almost as much at home in English. He was a studious, sensible child, very conscious of his responsibilities as an elder brother. One of his few flights of fancy was his wish to become a sailor, an ambition in which he was encouraged by Queen

Victoria's son Alfred, a post-captain in the British Navy. Since there was no German fleet worth speaking of, it seemed to Louis self-evident that the British Navy should provide his career. His father was not so sure; there was nothing wrong with serving the British, but Hessians were soldiers. Louis could not be induced to change his mind, however, and in 1868 he set out for England.

Even for a member of a family as cosmopolitan and peripatetic as that of Hesse, to leave home at the age of fourteen and set off for a new life in alien surroundings must have been a daunting experience. There were to be many times in the next few years when he would question his decision. 'He was perhaps by nature the most German of us all, and was unspeakably attached to his native land,' wrote his sister Marie.[2] He never lost his slight German accent, or became completely assimilated with the people among whom he had made his life. To go to Hesse was to go home. Yet it was to Britain that his loyalty was due, and he never weakened in that certitude. From the moment that he took the oath of allegiance and joined the Royal Navy his dedication to his new profession and new country was unswerving.

Boys with foreign accents and royal connections, especially when they receive favoured treatment from the authorities, must expect to be viewed with some distaste by their contemporaries. That Louis endured such hostility and survived to become respected and even popular is a tribute to his doggedness and decency. His path into the Royal Navy was smoothed by privilege, his success within it was owed to merit. When he was appointed second-in-command of the battleship *Dreadnought*, William Redmond, in the House of Commons, suggested that this was the result of royal favour. The First Lord of the Admiralty replied briskly and correctly that Battenberg had been given the post because he was the man best qualified for it.[3] He was spectacularly successful as Commodore with the Mediterranean Fleet, but it was as Director of Naval Intelligence in the Admiralty that he established his claim to rise to the highest ranks. Hard work, efficiency and indifference to the cobwebs of sentimental traditionalism which enshrouded the machinery of Admiralty administration made him not only a new broom that swept clean but a constructive and thoughtful architect for the future. '. . . out and away the best man inside the Admiralty building,' the First Sea Lord, Fisher, described him.[4]

His personal life also prospered. In 1883 he became engaged to his cousin Princess Victoria of Hesse, eldest daughter of Grand Duke Louis IV, and thus married both into the main line of the Hessian royal family and the granddaughter of his new sovereign, Queen Victoria. 'She is such a lovely darling girl, as you know, and I am nearly off my chump altogether with feeling so jolly,' he wrote to the future King George V.[5] As well as lovely and darling,

Victoria was formidably intelligent and independent-minded. Radical in her ideas, insatiably curious, argumentative to the point of perversity, she leavened the somewhat doctrinaire formality of Prince Louis. That shrewdest of observers, Queen Victoria, was quick to perceive her quality, but also to detect a certain coolness and detachment, springing perhaps from her mother's early death and too much responsibility borne too young. Love must be exhibited as well as felt; she could never be too warm towards her husband, 'to whom, I think, a *little* more *tenderness* is due *sometimes*'.[6]

The Grand Duke was not gratified by his daughter's decision. Prince Louis was the progeny of a morganatic marriage; by the standards of European royalty or British aristocracy, he had little money; he lived abroad and would therefore remove Victoria to England and deprive the widower Louis IV of much-needed support. Victoria was left in no doubt that her father was displeased. She paid little attention, and would have had her own way even without assistance. As it happened, however, she found a powerful ally in her grandmother, who thoroughly approved the match. 'I am very glad she has found a person, kind, good and clever and whom she knows thoroughly well. Of course, people who care only for "gt matches" etc will not like it – But they do not make happiness. . . .'[7]

The relative penury in which the young couple set up house was never more than an inconvenience and, anyway, was quickly mitigated. On the death of his father in 1888, Louis inherited a substantial fortune, as well as the castle and estate of Heiligenberg. Victoria, too, was left several legacies, including one from Queen Victoria. They did not await any influx of wealth, however, before they launched their own family. Princess Alice was born in 1885, Louise in 1889 and George, the elder son, in 1892. Eight years then passed before, on 25 June 1900, their second son and youngest child was born. Mountbatten thereby performed a signal service to biographers, in that for the second half of each year at least his age was the same as that of the century.


Prince Louis of Battenberg, the future Lord Mountbatten, was born at Frogmore House, in the Home Park of Windsor Castle, at 6 a.m., 'a most vigorous baby who came kicking and shouting into the world'.[8] Queen Victoria took a keen interest in this latest great-grandchild, 'born under the shadow as it were of the castle', and urged that it should 'bear my name of whatever sex it may be'.[9] The Battenbergs got as near as they could by including Victor among the new baby's names, but the Queen then pressed for Albert to be added.[10] When the gold font was carried across from the Castle and the Dean of Windsor christened the baby in the drawing-room at

Frogmore, he was named Louis Francis Albert Victor Nicholas.* With a perversity characteristic of the British upper classes at the time, the child was never called by any of these. A nickname was *de rigueur* and the Queen suggested Nicky. This served for a while but caused confusion amid the plethora of Nickies at the Russian court, and recourse was had to Dicky, or, more frequently, Dickie. Dickie he remained for the rest of his life.

The christening was not without incident. The baby knocked off the Queen's spectacles with one hand and pulled at her veil with the other. 'He is a beautiful large child and behaved very well,'[11] she commented with some forbearance. She was, however, by no means the principal sufferer. A bucket of ice had been put under one of the chairs in an attempt to bring down the temperature of the room. The unfortunate Dean of Windsor settled on top of it, chilled his legs, and suffered a sciatic inflammation so serious that from then on he could only walk with the help of a stick.

'It is said that famous men are usually the product of an unhappy childhood,' wrote Winston Churchill, referring to the Duke of Marlborough but no doubt with his own experience in mind. Dickie disproved the rule: he was sometimes lonely but rarely felt real misery; by any standard he was a happy child. His first fond memory was of his nurse, a Welsh woman named Ellen Hughes. Dickie called her 'Ennen', because the double 'l' was difficult to pronounce. She went with the family to Heiligenberg and married there. Dickie attended her wedding in the parish church, clutching his pet rabbit. She was replaced by Sophie Becht. 'I hope you have made friends with Sophie,' Mountbatten wrote to his elder daughter when she visited Germany for the first time, 'thirty years ago I adored her.'[12] He spoke German from infancy, and was taught to consider Heiligenberg as a second home, and the royal house of Hesse a second family. As important as any of his nurses, however, was Nona Kerr, an impecunious admiral's daughter who in 1897 was engaged as lady-in-waiting to Princess Victoria. The role of lady-in-waiting, like that, at a humbler level, of 'companion', can be everything or nothing. In Miss Kerr's case it was everything. Endlessly patient, generous, obliging, and yet fully capable of protecting herself against her employer's periodic bouts of authoritarianism, Nona Kerr became an essential part of the family and a still point of security for Dickie in an itinerant and somewhat rackety existence.

Travel, indeed, was a major part of his life. To the peregrinations inevitably imposed upon the child of a naval officer, Dickie added an annual round of visits to the family in Germany and often Russia too. 1902, for

* There is some confusion about the order of the names. *The Times* of 18 July 1900 led with Albert – perhaps to please the Queen – but the form above seems to have been used thereafter.

instance, found him at Malta till the end of April, then at Heiligenberg for the summer, at other Hessian homes for the autumn and to Kiel for Christmas and the New Year. His childhood memories comprised a series of impressionistic snapshots: Gibraltar, where he crept downstairs to watch Lieutenant Walwyn eat his breakfast and marvel at the way his ears waggled as he chewed his bacon; the arrival of the circus at Heiligenberg and being allowed to move for the occasion to his sister Alice's bedroom overlooking the stableyard so that he could watch the performing animals even though confined to bed; Moscow, where his bedroom overlooked the Kremlin Square, with the great broken bell to his right and the giant cannon, Tsar Pushka, to his left.[13] Visiting Moscow sixty years later, Mountbatten ransacked the Kremlin in search of his old bedroom. Finally he tracked it down and announced in triumph that his bed had been here, the table there. As proof that he had found the right place, he pointed to the bell which still hung to the right of the window. The interpreter clucked apologetically but let the matter pass. Only later did he confess to a British diplomat that the bell had recently been moved.

Dickie's passion for machinery and gadgets of every kind was quickly evident. He was only three when his father announced that he had bought a car: 'We were the first of any branch of our vast family to own a petrol-driven motor-car,' Mountbatten noted proudly many years later. 'It had solid tyres.'[14] Two years later he was allowed to speak into a cylinder apparatus known as a phonograph; the sound of his own voice delighted him. When six he took his first flight in an airship, being pulled aboard at the last minute when it was discovered that the vessel was short of ballast. He did not succeed in arranging himself a flight in a true flying machine until the Frankfurt Air Show of 1909 – an experience which left him doubtful whether God had ever intended man to take to the air.

His first nautical recollection came from Hesse. When staying at Darmstadt in the autumn of 1903 he was fascinated by an oil-painting of an old wooden man-of-war on fire. 'The first conscious impact of art on me!' he noted seventy years later.[15] It was not to be followed by many others. Ships, however, were to fill his life. In February 1905 he went aboard the *Drake* at Portsmouth, and this was evidently not his first naval visit. 'I did like the *Drake* very much it is a nice ship it is the one ship which I like *too* much – I didn't like that other smelly ship.' He took with him his teddy-bear Sonnenbein. 'I did play lots with the bears and with Mackenzie a midshipman who I like very much.' He was greatly looking forward to being reunited with his father in the Mediterranean. 'We don't like London cause its so dirty as niggers in Africa.'[16] Later that year he visited his father's flagship at Gibraltar. He proved a headache to the officer responsible for his safety: 'If he was not up aloft, he was down in the stokehold getting as black as a sweep.' He would have fallen overboard and been drowned several times over if an able-seaman had not been appointed to watch his every move.[17]

Dickie was so much younger than his siblings that he was bound to be a solitary child. He found no problem in making friends with such children as he met, mainly the innumerable cousins scattered around Europe, but travelling as much as he did he had little opportunity to establish permanent relationships. His aunt Princess Anna remembered that, when the Battenberg children came to tea, Georgie and Louise sat sedately by the table, while Dickie settled in a corner, conducting an animated conversation with an invisible friend.[18] He learned to entertain himself and, in so doing, developed an imaginative streak that was to be allowed little scope in future years. The Grand Duke of Hesse once noticed him drawing a picture of a cow with an extraordinary head and five legs. He pointed out that this was hardly lifelike, whereupon Dickie said indignantly that it was not a cow, it was a 'Katuf'. The name was adopted for family use to describe any sort of fanciful animal.[19] His favourite reading fed his fancies; he loved the novels of E. Nesbit which were appearing about that time, as well as *Alice in Wonderland* and *Through the Looking Glass. The Wizard of Oz* was also a favourite, in part because the author, L. F. Baum, had the same initials as he had.

Pets were his most constant companions. His first and much-loved dog was a black rough-haired mongrel called Scamp, but Millie, a lamb given him at Heiligenberg when he was seven, was almost as dear to him. Millie satisfied his spirit of scientific enquiry by providing an illustration of the Pavlovian conditioned reflex at a date when Professor Pavlov was still formulating his theories. Far from being sure to go everywhere that Dickie went, the lamb was apt to dig in her heels and refuse to move. Her owner put a running noose in her lead, so that Millie choked if she refused to follow. Told that this was unkind, Dickie ceased the practice and instead tied the cord to one of Millie's legs. The gullible beast made choking noises as she was pulled along.

In January 1905 Dickie had his first brush with collective education. He began to attend classes at Macpherson's gymnasium. At the end of each class the boys would assemble for a patriotic sing-song. Dickie was not wholly confident of the words. 'Rue Britannia, Britannia rue the waves!' he would sing, an injunction that must have surprised anyone aware of his naval parentage. It was another four years before he attended a more formal establishment, Mr Gladstone's school in Cliveden Place. This institution in a sense left its mark. With two other boys Dickie played at leaning over the banisters on the first-floor landing, the object being to lean the farthest. Dickie won and toppled over, striking his chin on a wooden bench. A doctor was called, who stitched up the wound, but Dickie was left with a faint scar till the day he died.[20] Only a few months before, he had contrived to embed the catch on a dog-lead so deeply in the middle finger of his right hand that it had to be cut out. This too left a lasting scar. These were only the first of a long and melancholy catalogue of self-inflicted wounds. Dickie was a courageous but clumsy boy and he grew into a courageous but clumsy man. In the space of a single week three years later he contrived to cut himself to the bone in carpentry class, get hit in the eye 'in a petty fight', receive 'a good kick on my shin' while playing football, strain his hip in the course of the same game and 'chip a bit of skin off my finger' while trying to 'magnetize the form compass'.[21]

Nor did he show signs of outstanding intelligence. In his first termly order he came bottom in arithmetic, evidence of a weakness which was to dog him throughout his education and even threaten his prospects in the Navy. In most of the other subjects he was about two thirds of the way down the class; 'spelling weak, at times weird' was the comment on dictation. But he was never accused of not trying. 'Conduct excellent. Works well and is getting on,' was the overall comment. A diligent plodder, cheerful, willing, in no way remarkable, was the verdict of Mr Gladstone and his colleagues.[22]

The despatch of a child to boarding-school at the age of eight or nine was not a commonplace before 1914 but Prince Louis, now Commander-in-Chief of the Atlantic Fleet, was too uncertain about his future movements to make any other course practicable. In May 1910 Dickie was driven for the first time to Locker's Park School near Berkhamsted in Hertfordshire. Locker's Park was an orthodox, competently run preparatory school of the kind that was then proliferating all over Britain. Most of the boys were destined for Eton, Harrow, Winchester or one of the other traditional public schools, though there were usually a few who went to Osborne to begin life as naval cadets. The headmaster, Percy Christopherson, was decent, kindly and convention-al; the boys liked him and he liked them. Dickie could have done a great deal worse.

Adequately good at work and games, large for his age and well able to look after himself, he took to his new life with enthusiasm. 'I like the school very much,' he told his father, 'only we have such a lot of lessons';[23] and then again: 'I have never in my life had so many lessons as here. . . . We learn till our backs ake nearly every day.'[24] The other boys do not seem to have been particularly impressed by the fact that he was a Serene Highness, though the point was not lost sight of: 'Some of my nicknames are Batterpudding, 2 things beginning with a "p", prince and pig, also London Fire Brigade like LFB.'[25] He sometimes pined for his family and pets – 'In bed last night I felt awfully home-sick and cried'[26] – but such admissions were rare. The fact that they were not voiced suggests they were of little importance. Dickie was never the sort of stoic who would have hidden his unhappiness from those he loved. Throughout his life he made his feelings known.

Many years later, Mountbatten's mother talked to a friend about the upbringing of her son: '. . . she told me the secret of your success; I mean her cultivation of self-confidence and a belief that all things are possible, as being the most important qualities to encourage in childhood.' Her letters to her son are wise, understanding and tolerant. When Dickie was beaten she wrote that it was 'very unpleasant but generally necessary and deserved. . . . As long as you have done nothing really wrong and to be ashamed of, there is no actual disgrace in being "swished".' When the French master behaved unfairly she urged: 'Do not judge him too hardly for his fault and bear him malice for it. That he is a person you and the others cannot like is natural, only don't nurse your dislike for that would be unfair.' Honesty was essential at all times: 'Some people take a wrong pride in travelling first with a second-class ticket without being found out, but that is really cheating.' But she could be consoling too: 'All one's life is made up of pain and pleasure, meeting and parting, and I have always tried not to let my mind dwell on the sad things but to be grateful for the pleasant things I have had and to look forward to those that are coming, otherwise one's heart aches too much. You must try to do the same.' He did; he was always resolute in his determination to look on the bright side, forget failures, expect the best. At Locker's Park he must have taken comfort from the stalwart affection apparent in all his mother's letters: 'You know I love you very much, my dear boy, and it makes no difference in my feelings and thoughts if I am nearer or farther from you – and if you needed me much, I would come to you from anywhere. . . .'[27]

His career was as undistinguished as it had been at Mr Gladstone's. He began the term 'in a very half-hearted way', his first report said sternly,[28] but whatever childish malaise was responsible for his lacklustre start was quickly behind him and he was never again accused of failing to do his best. Arithmetic remained his weakest subject but in all others he fought his way doggedly upwards. By August 1912 he was first in Latin and English. 'He has maintained his high standard of industry. . . . His keen enthusiasm in work and games, his sense of humour and his modesty make him increasingly popular with boys and masters.'[29] Like half-heartedness, modesty was not to be a characteristic often ascribed to him. His mother rejoiced over his successes and was bravely nonchalant about his failures. To try was all-important: '. . . nothing makes Papa and me so happy as to see that our children are doing their best at work and are honest and brave. Cleverness is not the chief thing, it is the willingness to do right and the effort made for it that really counts.'[30]

Dickie was encouraged to be aware of his royal origins yet never to boast about them. When he went to Windsor for the funeral of Edward VII in May 1910, he was warned not to get so excited about it that he neglected his work; also 'I hope that you will not talk to the other boys too much about it'.[31] He was anxious to go to the Coronation the following year, if only for the pleasure of escaping a few lessons, but was too young to attend the Abbey ceremony. As a compromise he was invited to Buckingham Palace to watch the King and Queen lumbering away in the gold coach. His father led him around, introducing him to the various grandees. 'I remember him saying that the next man he was going to introduce me to was Field Marshal Lord Kitchener, the most famous man in the Army. He added that when war came (he seemed to expect it) he was sure Kitchener would be put in charge of the Army. I was immensely impressed with his magnificent uniform and piercing eyes.'[32]

As he advanced towards the top of the school, Dickie began to savour the delights of power. He quickly found that he was good at leading and that it gave him pleasure. The captain of a somewhat inferior cricket team, the 'little-little', was elected by the boys. Dickie was chosen. 'I am very glad as I like captaining the little-little better than playing in the little.'[33] His father missed no opportunity of pointing out that power carried responsibilities and that a leader must inspire and protect, not merely exercise authority. 'How grand your being head boy of C II and having some new boys to look after. This is the beginning of what you will have to do in the Navy – always looking after others who are younger and know less.'[34]

Parents and son alike took it for granted that Dickie's career was to be in the Navy. When he was sent a Coronation Medal his mother suggested a draft letter of thanks. 'I hope to wear it often when I am an officer in your Naval Service,' he was to say.[35] Even if there had been no other reasons, Dickie's hero-worship of his father would have led him to sea. At the end of 1911 Winston Churchill, then First Lord of the Admiralty, appointed Prince Louis Second Sea Lord. Fisher, who had just retired from the post of First Sea Lord, believed he should have been promoted still farther, to fill Fisher's own place as professional head of the Royal Navy. 'He is the most capable administrator in the Admirals' list *by a long way*,' he wrote to Churchill. As to accusations that he would be sympathetic to his native Germany, they were absurd: 'In reality he is more English than the English. . . .'[36] But the dogs of chauvinism were already yapping at Battenberg's heels. Horatio Bottomley, journalist and professional patriot, was quick to question the appointment. 'Should a German "boss" our Navy?' he asked indignantly. 'Bulldog breed or Dachshund?'[37] The contempt that Churchill felt for Bottomley's objurgations was shown a year later, when Prince Louis became First Sea Lord.

Dickie was finding that a father in high places was not invariably a passport to tranquil schooldays. Most boys were delighted by Prince Louis's triumph, especially since they were given a half-holiday to mark the occasion; but a schoolfellow called Walkinshaw 'had to grumble and insult Papa he called him a sea donkey and doesn't seem to honour the R.N. in the slightest'. The heroic course would no doubt have been to batter the outrageous Walkinshaw into apology, but, as well as being the larger of the two, he was a prefect and Dickie enjoyed a finely developed sense of hierarchy. 'I feebly remonstrated, only of course try the best I can, he is in authority and I have to obey.'[38]

Most boys would have felt the same. There was nothing heroic about Dickie's schooling, even by the modest standards of a preparatory school. He gathered no glittering prizes. He learned to box and flattered himself he could now defend himself against any bully, always excepting prefects. He learned to dance: 'I begin to like dancing fearfully – the waltz feels as easy as the two-step.' Otherwise his accomplishments were limited: he was a cheerful child, clumsy, mediocre at games and more dogged than brilliant at work, talkative, friendly, trusting, generally popular but not among those who would have been voted most likely to succeed. He was, in fact, an ordinary little boy.

# CHAPTER 2

## *The Cadet*

THE ROYAL NAVY before the First World War was not merely the greatest fighting force afloat but had been so since far beyond living memory and assumed that it would remain so for eternity. It was the Senior Service of what was taken by its inhabitants, and most of the rest of the world as well, to be the richest and most powerful of nations. The best is apt to assume itself perfect, and the Navy found it hard to conceive that it could be improved in any significant respect. It was, indeed, intensely professional, performing what it was taught to do with skill and dedication. What it was taught to do, however, did not invariably take account of the latest technical or political developments. The Navy was not dangerously out of date but it despised the *avant garde* and looked inward at its own operations with monomaniac if often justified satisfaction.

To be a naval officer was to belong to an exclusive elite, self-perpetuating in that well over half its members were the sons of former or serving naval officers. Almost all were born gentlemen, many came from aristocratic families. They were not particularly rich; the members of any Guards and most cavalry messes would have boasted far larger private incomes than their naval counterparts. This enhanced the ineffable superiority of the latter. Conservative, authoritarian, honourable, narrow-minded, totally loyal to his Service and his country, the average naval officer not merely reflected the values of the British upper classes but enshrined them with peculiar lustre. He did not question these values any more than he doubted the tenets instilled in him during his training; imagination and divine discontent were not qualities esteemed aboard a British warship. The naval officer knew that he was right. He quite often was.

Though later entry was possible, the most usual practice was for aspirant naval officers to go to the Royal Naval College at Osborne at the age of twelve or thirteen and continue to Dartmouth a couple of years later. Osborne was built on the site of the stables of Queen Victoria's house in the Isle of Wight, a fact that was believed by the boys to be responsible for the hay-fever and pink-eye that plagued many of them. The cadets wore uniform, of a heavy cloth that never kept its shape, and boots and starched collars were compulsory.[1] Everything was done at the double, whether or not there was need for hurry, and the discipline was military. 'The limited time allowed them for saying their prayers and brushing their teeth', wrote a former master drily, 'made for neither godliness nor cleanliness.'[2] To toughen the boys in mind and body was a constant preoccupation. 'You were right when you said it would be cold,' Dickie wrote to his mother ruefully, 'for, in spite of the fires, everywhere it is nearly freezing, especially washing and having plunge in the morning.' He slept in his socks, since his feet had nearly frozen during the night.[3]

He passed in fifteenth out of eighty-three, his best subjects being English and German, with arithmetic as usual the worst. The Exmouth term, as his intake was called, was not outstandingly distinguished, though the future Admiral Scott-Moncrieff and three rear-admirals made a respectable tally of naval magnificos. They arrived in May 1913. As part of the initiation ceremonies each boy had to undergo some ordeal; Dickie's was to climb the flagstaff and sing 'A Life on the Ocean Wave' while aloft.[4]

Because his father was First Sea Lord and of royal blood, Dickie found that he was something of a celebrity. 'All my term greatly pity me, because I have without the least exaggeration been asked over 100 times my name, whether I was a prince; our Cook's name (the only thing I refuse) etc. I get pointed at, have my cap knocked off. . . . However I am now so used to this I don't mind it much.'[5] The teasing seems to have been reasonably good-natured. Anthony Combe, at Osborne at the same time, remembers that there was great interest among the other cadets at a prince of the royal house being one of their number,[6] while the future Admiral Parham, one term Dickie's junior, looked wonderingly at the brass plate on top of the Prince's sea-chest, which had specially small writing to accommodate the 'Serene Highness'.[7]

Occasionally malice crept in. An old enemy from Locker's Park, John Scott, also an admiral's son, had come to Osborne a term ahead of Dickie and took pleasure in tormenting him. Egged on by the other boys, Dickie challenged Scott to a fight, and won. It was generally considered a crime to strike a boy from a senior term, but Scott was disliked by everyone and the victor was hailed as a hero. 'Everyone asked "Did you fight Scott?" "Yes." "Did you lick him?" "I think so." . . . and then I was patted very hard on the back, and told that they gave me leave to kick and fight him whenever I liked (which I don't).'[8]

Violence was part of the life of English schools and Osborne, with its military traditions, was no exception. For giggling in bed Dickie was rapped so hard over the knuckles with the edge of a steel ruler that he bore the mark a week later. For a worse offence a cadet might get '5 with a lanyard on the hand and sometimes 3 on the hand and 3 on the stern sheets'. The ultimate sanction was a public flogging. Barthorpe ran away and paid the penalty. 'We

were all marched into our places and then it began. He could only stand 7 so
the doctor said. I had a splendid view. He squealed and struggled rather like a
rabbit when you pick it up by its ears. It was awful fun.'[9]

Dickie was an active boy with varied interests. He learned the kettle-
drums at two shillings a lesson and was proud to be able to play a roll after
only his second practice. He had a passion for model aeroplanes and asked
that his Christmas present from his aunt the Tsarina (a generous £5) should
be spent on a new model which worked by compressed air like a torpedo and
would fly up to a mile.[10] Anything connected with wireless telegraphy
fascinated him and he spent happy hours with a friend near Bridport, trying to
pick up broadcasts from the Eiffel Tower on a primitive crystal receiver.[11] He
was not unpopular but was felt by some to be rather stand-offish, doing
almost everything with his three particular cronies – Stopford, Bradford and
Graham. His sense of humour did not endear him to everyone. He went out
for the day with the parents of a boy called Ross and took out a boat with
Ross and his younger brother. The latter could not swim and so was supposed
always to wear a life-jacket. When they came back to shore Dickie went ahead
and broke in on his friends' parents with a distraught expression on his face.
'I'm so sorry, Mrs Ross,' he stammered. 'I didn't realise he couldn't
swim. . . .'[12]

As for any schoolboy, holidays were more important than the terms,
though Dickie's were exotic beyond the ken of the normal English naval
family. The summer of 1913 was particularly poignant in his memory
because for the last time it brought him together with his ill-fated Russian
cousins. All the family were there: Alice, his beautiful elder sister who had
surmounted the handicap of deafness to marry the genial, soigné Prince
Andrew of Greece; Louise, now twenty-four, with austere, almost medieval
features, who had disgraced herself by refusing to marry the loathsome King
of Portugal – a decision which her mother found eminently reasonable but
which caused deep offence to George V, who hated to see a good alliance
going to waste; Georgie, a lieutenant in the battle-cruiser *New Zealand* and a
dashing figure to his younger brother. The Tsar and Tsarina and their five
children came to stay in Hesse and there was an immense family party with
picnics, dancing, riding and endless games, the children chattering away to
each other in English, French or German as the mood took them. Dickie
convinced himself later that he had fallen in love with his cousin Marie of
Russia. Certainly she was of his age and, from the photographs, appears an
irresistibly attractive child.

At the time, though, it was his Christmas holidays that seemed to Dickie
the more memorable. On Boxing Day 1913 he went to stay with his brother
Georgie, who was on duty aboard the *New Zealand* in Devonport dockyard.

Georgie took the enraptured cadet all round the yard, including a visit to the battleship *Centurion*: 'I was very proud wearing my naval uniform,' Dickie recorded many years later.[13]

In July 1914 he was in the *New Zealand* again for the naval review. He was allowed to trail along behind the Captain during his inspection of the mess-decks and seems generally to have been indulged. 'We had a sham fight in the afternoon and I was in A turret, Georgie's. He let me train and elevate the 12″ guns. . . . It was great fun. I am sure I did for the Lord Nelson and Drake! . . . We then steamed back to Cowes. I steered the ship on the way back, partly.'[14]

'Whatever is happening about this German affair?' Dickie asked his father a few days later. 'I hope war doesn't break out or anything. You won't be able to have your holiday unless it is cleared up soon, will you?'[15]

The outbreak of war on 4 August made little immediate impact on the naval cadets. Everyone knew that the war would be over in six months, probably less, so there was no chance of joining in the fun. For Dickie it was sobering to reflect that many of his relations would be fighting on the other side, but no doubt they would all have a good laugh over it once peace was restored. Georgie was in danger; but for a fourteen-year-old war meant the chance of glory, not death or maiming. The most noticeable consequence was that civilians took over many of the duties normally carried out by naval officers, with disastrous results so far as standards of drill were concerned. It took the sinking of three cruisers with 1200 drowned to bring home to the cadets that war was more than an exciting game. Among the dead were some who had been cadets at Osborne in Dickie's time. The following month another cruiser went down, taking with it an Osborne doctor, Surgeon-Lieutenant Custance. 'I really loved him,' wrote Dickie. 'He was about the only officer I really did like here. . . . When I heard the news . . . my head sort of swam, but cleared after I had run round Collingwood in the cold air several times. That night I cried myself to sleep. I suppose he is happier where he is, but still. . . .'[16]

Worse was to happen. In wartime Britain everything German was abused, innocent shopkeepers had their windows smashed, dachshunds were kicked by passers-by. Spies were suspected everywhere and when the *Goeben* and the *Breslau* slipped through the net and made their way to Turkey it was at once assumed by those with a taste for conspiracy that a senior British naval officer must have assisted them. '. . . people hear only that a British admiral is a German spy so they hit upon Papa as being the most likely as a German by birth and that he is at the Admiralty.'[17] No one at Osborne fully believed it, yet boys are gullible: Prince Louis *was* by birth a German, the Germans *had* achieved inexplicable success, there was no smoke without fire. . . . Dickie found himself looked at with suspicion. The unkindest cut came when his best friend, Stopford, called him a German spy. Only Graham stayed faithful to him and even he showed signs of wavering. 'Do not let these things bother you,' wrote his old headmaster from Locker's Park. 'Just go ahead as you are doing now, and I have not a shadow of doubt that you will never have any lack of good friends of the right stamp.'[18] The advice was no doubt sound, but one may doubt whether it gave much consolation to the hurt and bewildered boy.

Dickie's ostracism never amounted to persecution and it was short-lived. Even before Prince Louis was driven from office at the end of October, the tide of opinion had turned. The Navy was solidly behind its First Sea Lord; no one with any knowledge of the matter considered the accusations even worth rebutting. Prince Louis's resignation was a matter for sympathy, not rejoicing. But whatever the reactions of his fellow cadets, the destruction of his father was for Dickie an appalling and unforgettable experience. The story of his marching out to the flagstaff at Osborne and standing there alone, at attention, with the tears streaming down his face, is almost too picturesque to be credible, yet it would have been a characteristic gesture, flamboyant but undoubtedly sincere. The recollection of his contemporary G. S. Hugh-Jones is equally striking. Hugh-Jones commiserated with him on his father's dismissal. 'It doesn't really matter,' replied Dickie, with some nonchalance. 'Of course I shall take his place.'[19] The nonchalance, one can safely assume, was put on. The ambition was not.

For the rest of his life Mountbatten would say that it was the wrong done to his father that fired his determination to succeed. Thirty years later, in South-East Asia, Bernard Braine looked at the photograph of Prince Louis on Mountbatten's desk and said: 'Sir, he was a greatly wronged man.' 'Yes, he was,' replied Mountbatten softly. A moment later he put his hand on Braine's shoulder and said: 'I have only one ambition – I want to go back to sea and then to become First Sea Lord.'[20]

It would be wrong to take such protestations at face value. If the wish to avenge his father had not existed, Mountbatten would have found some other reason for striving to reach the top. But the pain which he suffered in the autumn of 1914 was inexpungible. From then onwards the office of First Sea Lord was to possess almost sacred significance. No other dignity, however glorious, could satisfy his need.


In January 1915 Dickie moved on to the next stage of his naval training, the Royal Naval College at Dartmouth. His weight, he recorded scrupulously in his diary, was 7 stones 1½ pounds; his height 5 feet 5½ inches; his size in

collars 13½; his size in hats 6⅝. He delighted in details of this kind and was
to record them throughout his life. Everything seemed on an intimidatingly
large scale after the comparative intimacy of Osborne. 'This is an enormous
place, almost like a palace,' he told his mother. 'We are all quite lost in it, and
as we are apparently not going to be shown round, we will have to find out
things for ourselves.'[21] He reported faithfully on his first night:

> The Captain gave us a speech on the quarter deck after prayers, and
> then we had to turn in. I was about half-way down my rank, and
> when we got outside it was literally a race, in which I gained to be
> about 6th. I then bounded into the dormitory, tore off my clothes,
> shoved on a towel and dashed into the bathroom. . . . I then just had
> time to run off the rusty water in the tap, fill my mug, give one scrub
> with my brush, and fly back through the passages, nearly last. . . . I
> went to sleep shortly after ten, and slept well. In the morning I woke
> up with the first notes of the old reveille in my ears. I was out of bed
> with my pyjamas off and my towel on just as the bugle ceased. I then
> simply flew for the bathroom and was second to get into the plunge.
> The plunge is not sunk into the ground like the Osborne ones are, but
> stands up and has only about 2 ft 6 ins of water in, so I kind of slid in
> with my mouth open. Alas, I swallowed a mouthful before I realised
> it was salt water. Then I hurried off to wash, once more raced up to
> the dormitory, where I dressed as fast as I could and yet I was only
> just out within 3 seconds of the time the Cadet Captains gave us. We
> then had cocoa at about 5 minutes past 7, and then dashed off in the
> vain hope of finding the right classroom.[22]

In many ways life went on as at Osborne. There was the same sharp
discipline. Dickie was caught talking in the dormitory and was given a day's
total silence as a punishment. To avoid a second day of the same he 'accepted
one with a birch rod, bare stern, after plunge. Whopping mark.'[23] The bullying
of juniors went on too. Cadet Captain Standleby made Dickie slave for him,
lay out his clothes, do up his boots, even brush his hair. He seemed to take
especial pleasure in tormenting the son of a former First Sea Lord, beat him
for a trifling offence and said next time it would be 'three bare stern with
cow-hide'.[24] Dickie's close friends remained the same, though in June 1915 a
new acquaintance appeared on the scene – 'a jolly decent chap called
Lambe'.[25] Thus he met for the first time Charles Lambe, who was to become
his closest friend and eventually succeed him as First Sea Lord.

Games were taken with great seriousness but, although Dickie seems not
to have disliked them, they earned him no distinction. Running was disastrous. He came last in the heat for the 100 yards: 'Most of my buttons had

come off my shorts and in the middle my shorts opened and I shuffled in my step trying to close it again.' With no such excuse he still came last in the 220 yards, though he managed fourth out of six in the quarter-mile.[26] He played cricket and rugby with similar lack of success. At shooting he got a bull with his first shot but then did worse and worse: 'I don't seem to be shooting at all well here.' Fencing was the only sport at which he gained credit. He came second in the sabre and won a pewter mug for his pains.

Homosexuality was likely to exist at any institution where a lot of boys were cooped up together but seems to have been a minority sport at Dartmouth. It was not to Dickie's taste. He wrote disapprovingly to his mother that people were becoming 'too swinish for words'. They hinted at nasty things during meals or in bed. 'Some people in the other dormitory have even begun to do filthy things, I have heard.'[27] This could have been eyewash to allay a parent's fears, but in his private diary he recorded his dismay when his friend Bradford was accused of having gone into a hut 'with the swinish gang . . . and done nasty things with them'. Dickie stoutly denied the truth of the charge and, sure enough, Bradford was able to prove that he had been forced into the hut against his will.[28] Dickie himself seems to have been more interested in the Admiral's fourteen-year-old daughter, Rosamond Palmer. He haunted their house and made her a catapult. 'Had the first half hour with Rosamond alone,' he recorded proudly, though the time seems to have been devoted more to catapults than to romance.[29]

He was confirmed in November 1915: 'Felt as though I wanted to cry after the laying on of hands. . . . Played Clumps after tea.' A fortnight later he went to Holy Communion. 'It was very wonderful!'[30] The exclamation sounds more dutiful than heartfelt and religious experiences vanish henceforth from his diary. His strongly practical brain rejected any phenomenon that he could not at least partially explain and docket. His interest in the workings of the natural was insatiable, but the supernatural he rejected. Flying saucers might exist, but if they did they must be susceptible to rational investigation. A deity who by definition could not be investigated was irrelevant. He did not think seriously enough about religion to classify himself an atheist – was, indeed, always to style himself a believer in some sort of prime cause – but God did not play a large part in his reflections. There was always something more immediate to think about.

The main difference between Osborne and Dartmouth was that the war had come that much closer. At the end of their course the cadets would join the Navy. Even before that moment there seemed to be the possibility of action. Shortly after the start of Dickie's first term the boys were told that German armed trawlers were in the vicinity and might open fire on the College. Instructions were given for evacuation. 'I have decided that if the alert is sounded by day and I am near our block I shall seize my greatcoat and rug. I have put my greatcoat on a peg near the door for the occasion. I intend if it is cold giving my rug to any poor chap who may be in need of it.' At night he put warm clothes in a bag under his bed; the idea was generally approved and soon most of the boys were doing the same.[31]

During his first holidays Dickie was allowed to join Georgie in the *New Zealand*. They steamed off Heligoland, guarding the edge of a large minefield. It was a daunting experience, for the weather was rough and Dickie was frequently sick. To make matters worse he had stomach-ache and received a bad blow in the back while playing hockey in the wardroom. Nothing could dampen his zeal, however – 'I am having the time of my life' – and when he got back to Dartmouth he had 2000 sea miles behind him.[32] The trip kindled another life-long passion. A rich friend had given Prince George a portable projector for 35mm films. Georgie borrowed films from a local cinema and showed them to the ship's company. Dickie was allowed to help. He loved the cinema already; this exercise in do-it-yourself was to lead in due course to the founding of the Royal Naval Film Corporation.[33]

His other holidays were those of any fifteen-year-old boy from the upper or upper-middle classes. With foreign travel impossible he stayed mainly at his parents' house on the Isle of Wight: messing about in boats, helping his mother shop or garden, reading *The Prisoner of Zenda*, Stephen Leacock, *The Scarlet Pimpernel*. During a Christmas season in London he saw *The Merchant of Venice*, Ruby Miller in *A Little Bit of Fluff* ('screamingly funny') and D. W. Griffith's *Birth of a Nation* ('Too wonderful. The Ku Klux Klan was splendid'). He found a white kitten, called her Flavia and treated her rough, giving her constant baths and shooting at her with an air-gun from 100 yards' range: 'Hit her once. She hardly noticed it.'[34] The loss of his job and of the income from his investments in Russian platinum mines meant that Prince Louis was short of money, and several of the servants were given notice. They were never really poor, though, and in July 1915 they bought a new Wolseley car called a Stellite. It once got up to 37 m.p.h. and Dickie was allowed to drive it, though not at such hectic speed.[35]

In September 1915, after less than a year at Dartmouth, rumours began to fly around that the course was to be curtailed; with luck they would be at sea by the following Easter. Then came better news still. 'Isn't it grand, isn't it splendid!!!?' Dickie wrote to his mother. 'I suppose Papa will have told you by now that we are going to sea in January. This has far surpassed my faintest hopes.' He was at once filled with good resolutions; in particular, to work extra hard at the practical tasks like engineering, seamanship, navigation and at signals which, curiously, in view of his later career, had proved his weakest subject. This might mean that his academic results suffered but 'a few places in exams will not make much difference.'[36] Best of all, his father told him that he was to go as a midshipman to Beatty's flagship *Lion*, and Stopford and Bradford would probably accompany him.[37]

Within forty-eight hours hopes had been dashed; some clerk had bungled, Exmouth term was, after all, not to go to sea till April. 'How beastly it is to think we have got to stay here another term,' Dickie wrote disconsolately. 'It is the worst term in the whole year, too.'[38] He would have been more miserable still if he had known that he was to be one of the seventy-two cadets who went on to the Naval College at Keyham. Keyham was the Navy's engineering college but recently the curriculum had been broadened to include naval history, seamanship and other subjects. For all Dickie cared, it could have specialised in ballet or bibliography. 'It is too hopeless and sickening! . . . The war may be over before we get to sea, and we get no medal and don't even see a shot fired in earnest.'[39]

As it turned out, Keyham was a turning point in his fledgeling career. In spite of a bad tobogganing accident, which led to his taking the final examinations with an ankle in plaster, Dickie had done reasonably well at Dartmouth. He came fourteenth in the final order before the examinations, had expected to improve his position by a place or two and, in spite of his handicap, still managed to come through in the first eighteen. He ended, therefore, more or less where he had begun. Keyham marked a dramatic improvement. To his own amazement and delight he passed out top overall. Nobody could have accused him of lacking confidence before, but he did not have the habit of excelling. Now he realised that it could be done, he would never again be satisfied with anything less. No amount of success, however, could compensate for the fact that he and the other cadets were 'crawling about the dusty parade-ground on our bellies with fixed bayonets at the time Jutland was going on'.[40] To miss the war's greatest naval battle by a few months seemed an intolerable privation to a belligerent boy of about sixteen, made worse by the fact that British losses were reported long before it became clear that Jutland, though tactically a draw, was strategically a victory. 'Some quite choice expressions were used by us,' he told his mother, 'because if the admiralty had only stuck to their original plan some of us would have been in for the fun.'[41]

His mother wrote to congratulate him on his triumph at Keyham and took advantage of the occasion to put on paper some of the feelings which she could never convey when they were face to face:

> That both of our boys have worked and done so well as naval cadets makes us very happy, for it is not only the actual places you have taken in your final tests we are thinking of, but more even that both

Georgie and you have never given us a moment's worry by your general life and conduct as cadets – for after all, to do well at one's work may be due a great deal to the natural gifts one has been born with, but to have come through the many temptations that assail a boy in his school life so well as you have done, is a sign of a good character, and that is your own doing, therefore a better thing in our eyes than the highest place in exams. I have seen, my dear child, how steadily you have struggled against your faults, and with what good success and I know how difficult such a struggle is, for many of your faults are mine, too. The 'black pig' who when you were a little fellow would at times look nearly as big as yourself, has remained a little starved object, whilst you have grown, and your good qualities have developed, and this has made me more happy than you can perhaps quite understand.

Now your school life is near its end, and the bigger, more responsible life of an officer in the Service is beginning, may God help and strengthen you my very dear boy, and never forget that we love you very dearly and have been young ourselves once, and shall be able to understand the difficulties outside and in yourself which you may meet in your new life, and if we can help by word or deed will always do so.[42]

# CHAPTER 3

## *Junior Officer*

THOUGH NO ONE REALISED IT at the time, Jutland had been the last great set-piece battle of the kind which the Royal Navy felt to be its destiny. For Dickie Battenberg the First World War was to consist of rare moments of excitement set in a waste of monotonous patrolling, constantly alert against the possibility of action, yet knowing that such action was unlikely to occur.[1] At least he was close to the heart of things. He joined the *Lion*, Beatty's flagship, as a midshipman on 19 July 1916 and was employed as 'doggie' – A.D.C., messenger and general dogsbody – to the Captain, Chatfield. Thus he quickly came to the attention of one of the men who was to have the greatest influence on his career.

The *Lion* was a battle-cruiser of 26,000 tons. Life for a junior midshipman was never restful and frequently a torment. Tradition dictated that he was the lowest form of life; ill-luck had it that the sub-lieutenant in charge of the gunroom was a malevolent bully who delighted in making things worse than they would anyway have been. Beatings were inflicted for the slightest peccadillo. If the sub-lieutenant shouted, 'Breadcrumbs,' every 'wart', as the junior midshipmen were called, had to stop his ears with his fingers. The last to do so was beaten. If he then shouted, 'Cancel breadcrumbs,' and any midshipman removed his fingers, he was beaten for listening. On the order 'Provide bumf!' the wart had to rush to the W.C. and return with a handful of lavatory paper. Last home was beaten. If 'Angostura trail!' was called, the wart was blindfolded and made to crawl along a trail of bitters smeared on the deck. For any deviation from the trail, he was beaten. Such practices were silly and slightly degrading but did no harm unless the sub-lieutenant exercised his authority with too much relish.[2] In the *Lion* he did. Dickie got at least his share of the punishment; a contemporary remembers him taking eighteen strokes without a murmur.[3] Some years later in the *Repulse* a midshipman came up to him and said: 'I think, sir, you know my frater.' When he realised that the brother in question was the sadistic sub-lieutenant from the *Lion*, he had to restrain himself from kicking the midshipman down the gangway.[4]

He may sometimes have invited retribution. Another contemporary in the *Lion* remembers him on arrival as disconcertingly self-confident, knowing all

42

the answers and obviously determined to succeed.[5] The discipline, the gunroom bullying, the hard work must quickly have curbed any over-exuberance. And he thrived on the treatment. When it seemed at the end of the year that he was likely to be transferred, he wrote in dismay to his father to urge him to intervene. 'You can't imagine what hell it would be changing. . . . We are the one and only ship for a Midshipman to be in. . . . I do so hope you succeed. It means such an awful lot to me.'[6]

Like every junior officer, Dickie hero-worshipped Beatty, whom he felt to be the pattern of chivalry. As Chatfield's doggie, he was usually on the fore-bridge tending the voice-pipes and thus close to the Admiral. He was there on 19 August when a clash with the German fleet seemed imminent. At the last moment Jellicoe signalled Beatty, ordering him to stay in touch but not to engage. 'I thought Beatty was going to blow up; he blasphemed and cursed and said the most terrible things.'[7] The midshipmen had been sent below to have a meal before action. Dickie found time to write to his mother. Later 'I tore up the letter as I was ashamed of its sentimentality'. The day was not wholly without incident all the same. Two of the attendant destroyers were sunk and the *Lion* herself was missed by three torpedoes and narrowly escaped hitting a mine. 'I think you will agree that my experiences are more than dull and commonplace,' he wrote with satisfaction.[8]

Beatty replaced Jellicoe as Commander-in-Chief of the Grand Fleet in December 1916 and Pakenham took his place. He did not endear himself to the Fleet by ordering that Christmas festivities should be kept to a minimum. He would not wish anyone a merry Christmas because only children should be merry. But he was still well-liked, wrote Dickie charitably. 'He always says "good morning" to Ordinary Seamen and Boys, and does physical drill in a stiff shirt at 6 a.m. on his bridge.'[9] One of the officers he brought with him was Dickie's brother, Prince George. George had recently married Nada de Torby, a daughter of the Grand Duke Michael of Russia, and the home they had established near Rosyth was Dickie's refuge when away from his ship. Prince George was more brilliant than his younger brother. James Watt, after twenty years at Osborne, pronounced him to be the cleverest and the laziest boy he had every taught.[10] He was endlessly inventive, though his ingenuity was more likely to be devoted to increasing his own comfort than to the best interests of the British Navy: his cabin contained a thermostat linked to fans and radiators, electric lathe-motors to provide hot water and a primitive Teasmade. Dickie adored, envied and admired him, and was determined that, if he could not keep up with him by sheer intelligence, he would do so by hard work.

*

The Admiralty rarely let two brothers serve in the same ship and Dickie was now transferred to the flagship of the Grand Fleet, the *Queen Elizabeth*, based at Scapa Flow. 'The midshipmen work much harder here than in the *Lion*, and the Gun Room (*entre nous*) is much happier,' he told his mother. 'Although . . . I would not let any of the Grand Fleet Fellows know, I do prefer this life up here.'[11] He had only been in his new ship for a few months when the King decided that the name of the royal house should be anglicized and that the various Tecks, Holsteins and Battenbergs who were British citizens should do the same. In June 1917 Prince Louis took the title of Marquess of Milford Haven – 'Arrived Prince Jekyll, Departed Lord Hyde' he noted drily in Georgie's visitors' book. George himself became Earl of Medina and the family name was translated directly into English as Mountbatten. According to one report, Dickie first heard of this when the newspapers arrived in the wardroom of *Queen Elizabeth* where he was dining as a guest.[12] It seems hardly likely that he was given no prior warning but no letter on the subject survives. At all events, he treated the matter 'as a huge joke and laughed uproariously'. He told his mother it was the only sensible thing to do. 'Of course Dickie had to ask me hundreds of questions about Peers and their positions and families, and whether he and Louise could marry whoever they liked without the King interfering, and whether his sons would be plain Mr or Hon'ble.'[13] One point which had been tacitly agreed was that the new peers would not play an active part in the House of Lords[14] – a point which caused Dickie no concern since, although as the younger son of a marquess he bore the courtesy title of Lord Louis Mountbatten, he was not a member of the Upper House. He remained 'Lord Louis' till he was ennobled in 1946 and many addressed him as such till the day he died, but for the sake of simplicity it is as Mountbatten that he will henceforth appear in these pages.

Another branch of the family fared worse. 'How awful about what has happened in Russia,' Mountbatten wrote in March 1917. 'I suppose Uncle Nicky is quite safe, though I can't understand why he has abdicated, if they are not going to form a republic, but become a constitutional monarchy. . . . It says Aunt Alix is under guard, so I suppose she is all right, also Aunt Ella and the cousins.'[15] Mountbatten's Russian relations were linked in his mind with summer and sunshine, the most enchanted of childhood memories. Their murder was not only a family tragedy but a blow to the structure of his life. If the Russian royal family could fall so finally, what fate might not threaten the other royal heads of Europe?

The experience that most pleased Mountbatten at this period came when he was posted away from the *Queen Elizabeth* for two months to the submarine

K6. This was part of a scheme to broaden a midshipman's training. Mount-batten exulted in the opportunity. The wardroom, he told his mother, was

> a grand and sumptuous compartment, in the centre of which you really can stand up without bumping your head. It looks for all the world like a tuppenny tube, except that in place of umpteen adver-tisements . . . they are bedecked with gaily coloured pictures of semi-nude females out of *La Vie* [*Parisienne*]. . . . That department has been turned over to me, as has also our 'garden'. This is a wonderful piece of 'terra' of sorts, dug and sown in March with all manner of vegetables . . . cabins have no bulkheads but curtains. Bath is a LONG one at least 3 ft long!!! The WC is the most wonderful contraption of valves you have ever seen.[16]

'Snotty, your first duty is to provide drinks for the officers and your second duty is to do whatever Mr Frary [second-in-command] tells you, otherwise he will kick your behind,' was the Captain's somewhat brusque admonition. Mountbatten was not discomfited. Frary at first was unim-pressed by this tall, thin figure, who lolled about eating chocolates, but at the end of the two months he realised that the newcomer had acquired a complete knowledge of the working of a K-boat and 'wrote a marvellous essay on the subject'.[17]

Mountbatten now decided that a life under the ocean wave was his manifest destiny. He wrote to his father setting out the advantages of a career in submarines: the extra four shillings a day – 'rather an important factor for me' – longer periods of leave, more rapid promotion. It was true that the casualty rate was higher than in other ships, but that was because they were 'practically the Only People Who Fight'. In other ways the crews were as safe, or safer, as well as being healthier. 'It is the greatest honour to be alive and to be able to get into the greatest and most efficient Service of the Greatest Navy the world has ever seen,' he quoted grandiloquently from *Blackwood's Magazine*. 'Will you let me have that honour?'[18] Lord Milford Haven was not hostile to the idea in principle, but felt that for the sake of his son's career Mountbatten should first spend time in a small surface vessel.[19]

Mountbatten's interests widened in other ways. He conceived the idea of starting a ship's magazine, got together a group of officers to help him, cajoled an autograph letter out of the Commander-in-Chief, wrote several of the articles and made a profit of £11 on the first issue. By the time he left the ship the *Chronicles of the Queen Elizabeth* were on their fourth number and going strong.[20] He also wrote a short story and had it accepted by *Sea Pie*, a naval magazine – 'very excellent . . . quite one of the best that has ever come into our hands'. The judgement does not reflect well on other contributions; the story, published under the title 'Soapy – The Tale of a Dog,' was a sentimental piece about a cocker spaniel on board a battleship, which was distinguished neither in style nor in content. His *nom de plume*, 'N.O.', appeared once more under a story in the *Royal Magazine* called 'The Sense of Smell' – an unpretentious naval story about a midshipman in a P-boat who captured an enemy submarine more or less single-handed. Mountbatten was paid eight guineas but the next story was rejected as being too amateurish and he evidently decided that he had better things to do.[21]

His experience was further broadened when he attended a short torpedo course in H.M.S. *Terrible* at Portsmouth and, in July 1918, paid a visit of ten days to the army in France. The Front itself almost remained unvisited, since the boils from which he suffered much at this period suddenly ran rampant and induced a high fever. As a result he had only two days with the front-line troops, visited Poperinghe and Ypres, came under artillery fire, and was confirmed in his conviction that the Navy had the happier lot in war as well as peace. By now he had done a stint as senior midshipman and had been promoted to sub-lieutenant. It was time to take the next step in his career as prescribed by his father. On 13 October 1918 Mountbatten joined H.M.S. P31.


P31 was a tough, stubby vessel, excellent at speed in rough weather, designed for escort and anti-submarine work. Mountbatten's first hint that he might join her had come in April, when a friend had written enthusiastically to say that he was shortly to be posted and would thus leave a vacancy on board. 'It is a ripping little ship and will suit you down to the ground. Awfully nice captain too.' A special delight was that ships of this class needed frequent boiler cleaning and refitting, which meant extra leave, at least two weeks every four months: 'you really get more than that because all the boats down here are always having collisions. . . . We are at sea now arseing about the Channel doing bugger all as usual.'[22]

Within a few weeks of Mountbatten joining P31 the end of the war meant that the enemy ceased to be the Germans and became those powers-that-be determined to cut down the Navy to a more economic size. His ship was among those in which the crew was supposed to be reduced to the level of Care-and-Maintenance but the Captain boldly decided to keep her in full commission. Mountbatten was alone in charge when it was announced that the Port Admiral would arrive to inspect the ship in fifteen minutes. Fifty-one men were crowded into the boiler-room, fifty-one dinners were hurriedly concealed, a suitably small gang was left visible, mainly occupied in painting the boiler-room door so as to make access difficult. Mountbatten contrived to keep the Admiral on the jetty, from where he claimed the finer points of the ship could best be appreciated. Questions about the ship's condition were evaded; when the Admiral asked directly whether she was yet in Care-and-Maintenance, Mountbatten replied that she was not exactly so but was the next thing to it – an answer he justified to himself on the grounds that the ship moored alongside was indeed in that condition. If the Admiral had discovered the rest of the crew in the boiler-room, Mountbatten proposed to tell him that they were members of a secret society who had been allowed to meet there because of their anti-Bolshevik principles.[23]

In January 1919, after several weeks during which Mountbatten had been left in command of P31, a new captain arrived. Lieutenant-Commander T. G. Carter, Mountbatten wrote insouciantly, 'is quite a good sort and does what I tell him, which is the main point'.[24] It is doubtful whether Carter would have seen the relationship in quite the same light. Indeed, one of Mountbatten's most vivid recollections of Carter's captaincy was an occasion when a spring broke and the Captain bellowed through a megaphone: 'First Lieutenant, you're a bloody fool!' Mountbatten claimed subsequently that the irritation he felt at this taught him never to abuse an officer in front of his men – a precept which some who served under him would hold to have been more honoured in the breach than the observance.[25]

Carter appears to have attached no importance to the episode. 'A most zealous and efficient executive officer who has shown much tact in dealing with men,' he summed up in his official report.[26] Mountbatten never got a bad report in his life. 'A very promising young officer,' Chatfield had said about his time in the *Lion*;[27] 'earnest, industrious, and highly intelligent', was the verdict of the officer responsible for engineering instruction in the *Queen Elizabeth*.[28] Yet he was still generally thought of as a slogger who would go far but lacked the fire of greatness. One contemporary remembered that, when the other midshipmen were fooling around in the gunroom, he seemed always to be writing up his notes.[29] Admiral Jerram recollected one of the naval instructors in the *Queen Elizabeth* rating Mountbatten as being well below average for intelligence and stressing that only by hard work could he hope to keep abreast.[30] P31 gave him his first taste of independence. He relished it. Given a chance to use his initiative, he grasped it eagerly, not always displaying his enterprise in ways which would have appealed to his superiors if they had known of them. When it seemed that P31 might be denied a place in the peace celebrations, he asked Princess Mary to tell her father the King how badly she wanted to visit a P-boat, and actually contrived it so that the King himself expressed a wish to come on board. P31 was duly present at the Peace River Pageant on the Thames on 4 August 1919.[31]

*

The ceremony proved to be his swan-song. A few weeks later P31 was ordered
to the Baltic. She sailed without Mountbatten, who in October 1919 went as
an undergraduate to Cambridge.

With broad-mindedness unusual at that period, the Admiralty had concluded that some of those whose training as cadets had been cut short by the
war should now complete their education at university.

'Oh, show me how a rose can shut and be a bud again!' Kipling urged
these belated recruits to academe:

Hallowed River, most gracious Trees, Chapel beyond compare,
Here be gentlemen sick of the seas – take them into your care.
Far have they come, much have they braved. Give them their hour of play,
While the hidden things their hands have saved work for them day by day:
Till the grateful Past their youth redeemed return them their youth once
    more,
And the Soul of the Child at last lets fall the unjust load that it bore![32]

Mountbatten was nearer the bud than most of the young naval officers
who went to Cambridge with him, but he did not find the transition
altogether easy. Confined to his college, Christ's, for some minor offence, he
wrote in indignation to a friend: 'Oh, it's unbearable. After over 3 years
actually at sea in this Blessed War, having been Executive Officer of my own
ship responsible for the discipline of her 60 men, I come to this place during
the B....y Peace and get treated worse than a snivelling school kid.'[33] Such
outbursts were rare, however; on the whole he enjoyed himself greatly at
university.

Work did not figure prominently among his preoccupations. He once
recorded that he was writing an essay on Byron up to 1.30 a.m.;[34] and he had
evidently read enough not merely to pass his own examination with credit but
also coach a friend up to the required standard;[35] but other aspects of life
concerned him more. He indulged in the usual undergraduate follies, hurling
the coals from a blazing fire into the street to the considerable danger of
passers-by and joining a mob of students who besieged the rooms of the
Junior Dean, the Rev. Mr Burnaby, demanding tickets for a lecture supposedly to be given by Dr Marie Stopes on sexual problems. Yet he was not
conspicuously uproarious. He refused to join the Committee of the Cambridge Naval Temperance Society, which drank only beer and whisky, 'not
wanting to be gated every night for the mad escapades they expected me to
organize'.[36] He was more likely to be found dining noisily but less riotously
with his cousins Bertie – future Duke of York and King George VI – and
Harry – future Duke of Gloucester – who were installed in a house a little way
outside the town.

It was as a debater that he entered most vigorously into university life. He started his career in the Milton Society, a group confined to Christ's College, where he spoke 'at every debate I have attended, but have not overdone it'. From there he graduated to the Junior Acton Club, where he spoke in defence of the modern novel – a contribution which can hardly have been based on profound knowledge of its subject – and finally began to speak in the Union itself. He made his name in a debate on the reduction of expenditure on armaments, arguing passionately that a strong army and navy were essential until the League of Nations was well established. At that time 'we should turn our fleet – lock, stock and barrel – to work with it'.[37] His side lost, but only because the naval undergraduates mistook their port for their starboard and went through the wrong lobby. For the first time Mountbatten experienced the intoxication of feeling an audience stirred by his words: 'It's one of the most wonderful sensations in the world, and I can quite understand people going mad on it.'[38]

Largely as a result of this performance, Mountbatten was invited to stand for the Committee of the Union, a rare distinction for a freshman, let alone a naval officer. He accepted and was elected, coming fourth out of fifteen candidates. Next term he led for his side in the Inter-Varsity debate on a motion proposing that the time was now ripe for a Labour government. He opposed the motion: 'It was useless to deny that Labour Government meant government by a class as much as if all "those rotten dukes" held the reins. We should be ruled by sectional interests, by any workers with a "bleat on". . . . It might be ready in the future to assume power, but, for the present, ignorance of foreign politics made the experiment dangerous.'[39] Mountbatten got Winston Churchill down to speak, and the motion was defeated by the satisfactory margin of 651 votes to 265. 'Is an exponent of terse naval English,' commented the President of the Union on his performance. 'A gift of slang too. He can be most effective at confuting an opponent out of his own mouth. He had a difficult time in attacking Labour, because (rumour has it) his sympathies ran strongly that way.'[40]

A disadvantage about debating societies was that they cut into the time available for social life. Mountbatten had discovered the delights of susceptibility. He first fell in love with the leading lady of a musical revue he saw in Edinburgh. He bombarded Phyllis Elaine with chocolates and invitations but she had little time for a callow midshipman, cut her engagements without compunction and finally threw him over at the last moment on the grounds that her mother was ill, only to be found later dining with a senior officer. 'Mother is mythical,' noted Mountbatten sadly in his diary.

By mid 1919 he had lost his heart to half a dozen girls, often two at once. His mother watched indulgently. 'It doesn't matter how often you are in that state as long as somewhere in your heart you keep the knowledge of the difference of a love that is merely based upon strong attraction, and that other love which I hope may come to you only later on and which is one of head and heart together for a girl you will want to make your wife.'[41] Mountbatten had already been convinced such a love had come to him. His choice was Peggy Peyton, the daughter of a retired Indian army colonel. 'She is a ripping girl,' he told his mother, whom he usually kept posted about his more serious affairs, 'about the best pal I've ever had in the female line of that age, and I do love her most frightfully.' Mountbatten dreamed of marriage – 'We are cut out for each other. She'd make a splendid wife for anybody and in many ways an ideal one for me'[42] – but they could not possibly afford it, and before Lady Milford Haven had any reason to fear for her son's future Colonel Peyton intervened to end the relationship. 'I have been very miserable of late about Peg, and she has been as bad, but we've settled down to the position of occasional letter writing friends.'[43]

By the time he was at Cambridge his taste had turned to something more sophisticated. Audrey James was the prettiest debutante of her season, with £4000 a year and a reputation for being rather fast. 'She has got the wee-est and most perfect eyebrows under the sun, marvellous grey eyes, and the most kissable mouth that God ever made,' gushed an enraptured Mountbatten. He fell in love with her photograph in the *Tatler*, secured an invitation to a dance which he knew she was to attend, monopolized her all night, dashed back to Cambridge to write an essay and attend a lecture, was back in London in time for tea and another dance, and managed to keep going without sleep for eighty hours. He planned to take her to the Oxford and Cambridge rugby match with a party including Prince Henry, but at the last moment the King decided to attend. 'Harry is so young, he can't stand up to his father like I can,' commiserated Prince Albert with all the hauteur of an elder brother. 'Of course, he ought to have told him he had a party of his own. He doesn't understand, like you and me, the trouble it is to get these girls to do anything, otherwise he wouldn't have let the King spoil it all.'[44]

The next few weeks were hectic. Miss James was attracted by Lord Louis but had no intention of letting her many other admirers off their strings. Sometimes she seemed wholly devoted to him, at others was clearly more concerned with someone else. One day 'Audrey did not turn up and I left in a rage'; the next 'Audrey was outstandingly nice to me'. He was besottedly in love, felt a day wasted in which he did not meet her and would undoubtedly have performed less creditably in his Cambridge examinations if she had not left on a trip to New York. 'It's no earthly good preaching to me about Audrey,' he told Peter Murphy. 'I have never been so completely struck "stupid" (you'll like that word) in all my little life before.'[45]

It was Peter Murphy who had organized Audrey James's meeting with Mountbatten. Mountbatten and Murphy had first met in the rooms of Christopher Glenconner and had immediately taken to each other. Murphy was highly intelligent, bilingual in French and fluent in Russian, Italian and German, well read, a pianist in the Gershwin style who was competent enough to be offered an engagement at the Café de Paris. He had been in the Irish Guards and had a wealthy mother who allowed him enough money to live in comfort but not luxury; since luxury was what he liked, he tended to look to the very rich for friends. In return for their favours he provided wit and excellent company; he was a generous, tolerant and amiable man who gave as much pleasure as he received.

> I immediately felt he was different [he wrote of Mountbatten], not only from the other young naval officers, but from the other under-graduates at Cambridge. Physically he was strikingly good-looking, with knock down charm, second only to that popular idol, the Prince of Wales himself. We were soon in earnest conversation and although it was evident that he lacked culture and had read little, he had a quick, wide open, enquiring mind and could carry on a vivacious and interested conversation. . . .
>
> I was really astonished to find a member of the Royal Family so free of prejudice and reaction, with such a genuinely receptive, progressive outlook. I helped him to start reading intelligent books and papers. I tried to get him to take an interest in music, which he enjoyed, though his tastes were simple. In art his outlook was hopelessly conventional, but in politics he was certainly no reactionary.[46]

Mountbatten was socially in a state of some confusion. From his mother he had inherited egalitarian instincts, yet also a strong sense of caste. He could simultaneously deplore the fact that the University Pitt Club consisted mainly of 'snobs and little Eaton [*sic*] boys', yet rejoiced that one met there 'a lot of really nice fellows of one's own class'.[47] He was hungry for new ideas, congratulating himself on having met 'a most interesting Labour M.P. (moderate views, unfortunately)'.[48] Peter Murphy was his key to a new world. Strongly left-wing himself, he opened Mountbatten's eyes to what he believed to be the inherent flaws in the capitalist system. Mountbatten himself was pragmatic and unphilosophical, disinclined to concern himself with abstract concepts. He did not prove an apt pupil in this respect, or a convert to any doctrinaire theories of socialism. Yet his instinctive sense of what was fair was alerted by Murphy's preaching; he learned to view the shibboleths of his class with suspicion and to question their values; he was never to close his mind to radical ideas however startling they might appear to him. Intensely elitist, proud of his royal birth, he was yet more genuinely democratic than many of those who might have dismissed him as a member of an obsolete ruling caste.

That Mountbatten should have so articulately left-wing a friend at Cambridge was a matter of little concern to anyone except himself. As he grew into positions of greater responsibility, however, the politics of those around him became of wider interest. Murphy was distrusted by many of the officers who surrounded Mountbatten and it was frequently suggested that his influence was malign and damaging to the national interest. In 1952 he was denounced as a Communist agent. While not believing a word of it, Mountbatten felt that he had to ask the Security Service to investigate his friend. They did so, and concluded that there was no reason to believe that Murphy was a member of the Communist party, still less that he was working actively on its behalf. They also reported that he was homosexual and had been so for many years.

This was no news to Mountbatten; the matter had always seemed to him of little importance. On one occasion he was told that his naval servant was homosexual. 'Of course,' he replied. 'All the best valets are.' The fact that Murphy was constantly around his house, however, and that he also enjoyed the company of flamboyant homosexuals like Noel Coward, inevitably fed rumours that he shared their tendencies. The point, to the biographer, is of considerable significance. In spite of the popular belief that the Royal Navy thrived on rum, sodomy and the lash, the second at least of these was viewed askance by the authorities. To be caught red-handed was the end of one's career; even to be the subject of rumour was an impediment to promotion. If, as *Private Eye* has stated,[49] Mountbatten was a practising homosexual, he was risking everything he valued most to indulge a fleeting appetite. In that case his character was wholly different from anything delineated in this biography.

As a boy there is no reason to believe that he viewed homosexual relationships between his contemporaries with anything except slightly priggish dismay. When he first met Peter Murphy and might have fallen victim to his charms, he was besottedly in love with a series of girls; one of Murphy's principal attractions, in fact, was that he provided access to Audrey James. For the first few years of his married life Mountbatten was preoccupied with his wife. All his naval contemporaries who have expressed an opinion on the subject – and some worked very close to him – state emphatically that they do not believe the stories to be true. The only direct testimony to the contrary seems to be based on self-deception. As an old man, Mountbatten liked to have young and attractive people around him who would listen to his stories and keep him company. Like many people, especially when elderly, he expressed affection by touching, and would often lay a hand on the arm or shoulder of the person to whom he was talking. Observing Mountbatten with his hand on the arm of an attractive young man, the less charitable observer leapt to an agreeably scandalous conclusion. The fact that the arm would more often belong to an attractive young woman was neither here nor there. In fact Mountbatten preferred the companionship of young women to young men – his riding companions were almost invariably female – but their sex was not a matter of great importance to him. Sex itself was not a matter of great importance to him.

He would not have been pleased to have heard this said about him. In 1975 the *Daily Mirror* published articles about a homosexual ring centred on the Life Guards' barracks in London. Mountbatten was told that his name had been mentioned in this connection. 'I refused to take this seriously,' he recorded in his diary, 'and I said I might have been accused of many things in my life but hardly of the act of homosexuality.'[50] To Sir Robert Scott, in a similar context, he remarked: 'Edwina and I spent all our married lives getting into other people's beds.'[51] In this he did himself less than justice. He conducted at least two protracted love-affairs outside his marriage, to the apparent satisfaction of both parties, but he was never promiscuous. Though he liked to imagine himself a sexual athlete, he seems to have had in fact only slight enthusiasm for the sport. He loved the company of women, sought their affection and had an almost irresistible urge to use them as confidantes, but his energies were channelled into his working life. If asked to choose between seduction by the most desirable of houris and a conversation about service matters with a person of influence, he would unfailingly have chosen the latter. Never would he have sacrificed his career for lust. To suggest that such a man was actively homosexual seems to be flying not merely in the face of the evidence but also of everything we understand about his character.

# CHAPTER 4

## Royal Tours

AT THE END OF DECEMBER 1919 Mountbatten was in London for a dance at Lady Ribblesdale's. The Prince of Wales came up to him and asked whether he would like to accompany him in the *Renown*. 'Of course I nearly jumped out of my skin for joy and to be quite candid Audrey slid completely out of my mind.'[1]

From the moment he had heard that in March 1920 the Prince of Wales was to visit Australia and New Zealand, Mountbatten had been dreaming that he might go too. Indeed, he did more than dream, and pulled every string at his disposal, successfully involving his fellow undergraduate Prince Albert as an ally. His formal role was that of flag-lieutenant to the head of the royal party, Rear-Admiral Halsey, but in practice he was to serve as A.D.C., companion and nanny to the Prince.

Up to that time Mountbatten had seen little of his cousin David. The Prince was six years older and invested with the aura of a future monarch. His charm was a byword; less well known were the uncertainty, the brooding introspection, the selfishness and the frivolity which were eventually to destroy him. Suspicious of any courtier put about him by his father, he responded warmly to the presence of this hero-worshipping relative, whom he himself had invited and with whom he found he could relax in complete security. 'He is such a dear boy,' he told Mountbatten's mother, 'and so marvellously sympathetic and understanding. We have become the closest friends possible, and I may say we are quite devoted to each other. . . . He is a very exceptional boy, though he is still only a boy, although a very advanced one, and I have had to sit on him slightly once or twice, but only in the spirit of being his best friend and he appreciates that and was grateful!!'[2]

Mountbatten was indeed quick to appreciate anything that came to him from his wonderful new friend. 'Mamma dear,' he wrote to his mother,

> you've no idea what a friend David is to me – he may be 6 years older but in some respects he's the same age as me. How I wish he wasn't the Prince of Wales, then it would be so much easier to see lots and lots of him. He's such a marvellous person and I suppose the best friend I've ever had. I've seen all his letters from home. His father's

might be the letters of a Director of some business to his Assistant Manager and even his mother seems so stiff and unnatural, and Mamma, he was quite surprised in some ways when I told him how much I loved you all, although of course he says that with parents like you, it's very different. He's only had one 'mother', though he'd be the last person in the world to admit it, and that is his great friend Freda Dudley Ward, who is so nice, and about whom you have probably heard – Oh, such wicked lies.

She's absolutely been a mother to him, and he has brought all his troubles to her and she has comforted and advised him, and all along he has been blind, in his love, to what the world was saying. She, sensible creature that she is, is trying to shift the friendship to a more platonic and casual footing . . . and he is rather miserable but is beginning to see that it is best so. They do overwork him out here. Why even *I* get so tired I don't know what I'm doing at times. He does so want to meet Papa and you away from his – as he calls them – 'rotten' family.

David's is a rotten life and he's so wonderful about it all. He's only got 2 fellows on his staff that he's really fond of – the Admiral and Godfrey Thomas. The others are more for 'self' than 'him'. I don't know if I've ever told you before exactly what friends David and I are. I have told him more about myself and he has told me more about himself than either of us ever have told anyone in our life before.[3]

The *Renown* sailed on 15 March. One of Mountbatten's duties was to keep an unofficial diary of the tour. Admiral Halsey had originally suggested he undertake this task, though he cannot have realised quite what he was starting. Mountbatten concentrated on the lighter side of the tour and produced a chronicle which, though often amusing, was rarely discreet. It was to be the source of much embarrassment. When Alan Lascelles joined the Prince's staff later in 1920 he found the office in turmoil. Scotland Yard were on the telephone, anguished conclaves in progress in every corner. Gradually he discovered that the official photographer with the party had absconded with one of the twenty copies of the diary that the proud author had had printed on the ship's press. The culprit was eventually tracked down to Kettner's restaurant where he was bargaining with an American journalist, the diary on the table in front of him. The asking price was £5000.[4]

In the first few weeks Mountbatten paid most attention to the japes and jollities with which the party diverted themselves. Colonel Grigg turned on the wrong tap and flooded Godfrey Thomas's cabin. 'This was considered such a good joke that Sir Godfrey was again flooded out before dinner.'[5] One of the private secretaries saw the light of a steamer overtaking the ship: 'On closer inspection this proved to be our own stern light.'[6] On 1 April Mountbatten, Lord Claud Hamilton and Piers Legh were urgently summoned on deck to observe some sharks chasing a whale. When questioned, a petty officer replied, ' 'e 'adn't seen no sharks, but 'e 'ad seen the calendar'.[7] Crossing the line gave rise to all the usual excesses. The Prince was treated roughly enough but Mountbatten fared worse – being given a double dose of a noxious concoction called 'number five', lathered in black, purple and white and ducked sixteen times.[8] A young officer doubted how much the Prince and his party enjoyed such frolics. One evening polo on chairs was organized in the wardroom, with tablespoons as mallets and a cricket ball. 'Not a bad form of rag when in the mood for it,' commented the future Admiral Willis, 'but . . . I fear H.R.H. and Staff were rather bored.'[9]

The serious business began when the *Renown* arrived at New Zealand. Wherever he went, the Prince was greeted by a remarkable show of loyalty. At Wellington the crowds were so dense that many people were swept along with the royal cortège and several injured by the motor-cars. Mountbatten found it impossible to emulate the rest of the staff and stare stonily ahead, leaving all the responses to the Prince. 'I always try and catch as many people's eyes as I can and nod and smile and even wink at schoolboys, because – well, I don't know why, but I don't know how one can drive through a crowd of people without paying any attention.'[10] The only serious problem came with the railways, since the engine-drivers chose this moment to strike for higher pay. At Auckland the strikers showed good will by gathering to cheer lustily at the Prince's arrival. Their loyalty, however, did not extend to taking the royal train out the following day.[11]

The Prince of Wales was proving restive under the demands made on him by the enthusiastic New Zealanders. At Reefton he caused offence by failing to attend a Returned Soldiers' Dance; two days later he refused to open a club for a similar group of veterans.[12] The schedule was indeed a gruelling one, but that did not excuse his bad manners or his display of pique when a bag of confetti burst and emptied down his neck. Mountbatten was responsible for much of the organization, and did it well, but it was tacitly accepted by the rest of the staff that his most important function was to keep the Prince contented and on the rails. This did not prove easy, since Mrs Dudley Ward was sorely missed. 'With all these hundreds of people round him he is as lonely and homesick as can be and is HATING this trip!' reported Mountbatten.[13] Things did not improve notably in the Australian phase of the journey. At Gilgandra the crowd was indignant that he could not be bothered to get out of bed to greet them when the royal train went through early in the morning. To show their disapproval they 'counted out' the Prince, a local ritual by which an unpopular person was made the object of a chant: 'One, two, three, four, five, six, seven, eight, nine, ten, OUT!' On the return journey, however, the Prince appeared on the platform, made a speech and was ceremonially counted in again.[14]

Mountbatten himself was not universally approved. Dudley North, another member of the Prince's staff, objected to his habit of bursting into the dining-room and shouting, 'Hurry up, David!' to his cousin – 'In this ship, in company, please remember that he is our future King.'[15] Others resented the fact that the Prince patently preferred Mountbatten's company to theirs, and grumbled about the special treatment which this very junior officer was accorded. Mountbatten was hurt, since he felt he was taking endless pains to ensure he remained in his proper lowly position. 'At the bottom of it all is – as the Admiral told me – jealousy that David should happen to like me more than they consider he ought to like a distant cousin.'[16] His colleagues cannot have been made any happier by a story in *The Bulletin* which commented on the stuffiness of the royal entourage. 'The least likeable is Lord Claud Hamilton. Lord Louis Mountbatten, with all his solid pride, has many good points. Officially a member of the gunroom, he is rarely among the "snotties" but ambles in the rear of his relative, whom he alone addresses as David. Mountbatten . . . is more phlegmatic than Edward, and neither the juiciest cocktail nor the Cleopatra of all flappers can lure him from his post of royal watch-dog.'[17] Nor did the young Keith Murdoch do him a good turn when he described him as 'a charming character and exceedingly good-looking fellow to boot. . . . Lord Louis is the Prince's special chum, and though he has to . . . attend zealously on his exacting admiral, he finds sufficient time off to be a great deal in his cousin's company.'[18]

Politics in Australia were in a turbulent phase. W. M. Hughes, the Prime Minister, had broken with his socialist colleagues and formed a national government in 1917. His apostasy, as his former allies saw it, caused much bitterness, and labour relations were particularly inharmonious. There was some nervousness about the reception the Prince might receive, but in fact the enthusiasm proved as intense as it had been in New Zealand. Immense crowds gathered everywhere and, though they greeted the royal entourage with some ribaldry – Mountbatten being hailed with cries of 'Oh, Percy, where did you get that hat?' – their loyalty was obvious. To see or, better still, touch the Prince was their ultimate ambition. On 28 May he shook hands with more than 20,000 people and was black and blue from the affectionate pats which his future subjects lavished on him as he walked among them.

The Prime Minister was a constant subject for derision in Mountbatten's diary. At a ball in Melbourne he had first refused to take part in an official set of Lancers, then at the last moment decided that he would like to after all. Chaos ensued but 'it was worth it, for Mr Hughes danced a little set of Lancers all by himself, and really, the remainder of the dancers hardly worried him'.[19]

Hughes would not have been pleased if such titbits had appeared in an American paper; nor would the inhabitants of Geelong where 'The naval guard was really rather pathetic. . . . Some of the men had their caps on the back of their heads, looking even more untidy than a liberty man can do ashore.' The Lieutenant-Commander seemed dazed, the mayor dropped his 'h's; as for the official reception party, 'Most of them seemed dippy; for although H.R.H. spoke to them frequently he never once got an intelligent answer.'[20] Such tetchy comments are not typical of the diary, which on the whole was good-humoured and as inclined to ridicule the author as anyone else. It was a young man's production, though, with little sympathy for the feelings of those who might be overawed by the occasion.

So the trip wore on. At Ballarat the Prince was presented with a pair of satin pyjamas and told they were for use on his honeymoon; in Brisbane he was given a koala bear which wept so piteously for its former owner that it had to be returned with a polite note; in Sydney the royal party ran amok at a party given by some local grandees called Walker – the Admiral dressed up as a Chinaman, the Prince was involved in a pillow fight, the carpets were drenched with water, and Mrs Walker, with tears in her eyes, was reduced to appealing for peace. At Canberra a stone was laid in the centre of the future capital; nothing else was visible except two or three tin shanties and an embryo power-station. The visitors were doubtful whether there would ever be much more but kept this heresy to themselves. The Prince complained that the stone was not laid flat but was told it was the spirit-level which was at fault; it had been used by his father nineteen years before and had been resurrected for this occasion.[21]

Immense distances were travelled by train. The Prince could hardly sleep at all, which frayed his temper; Mountbatten slept like a top, which made his cousin still crosser. On the journey from Sydney to Perth the train was derailed. Dudley North was standing by the bar and was drenched in Benedictine and cherry brandy while the Minister of Works caused great pleasure by being trapped in the lavatory. The Prince was discovered, reported the *Western Mail*, 'reclining amid the wreck of the costly compart-ment, smiling and smoking a cigar'.[22] He emerged from the wreck looking notably cheerful and remarked: 'Well, anyway, at last we have done some-thing which was not on the official programme.'[23]

On the journey home Mountbatten, with help from the official cinema-tographer, busied himself making a film of manoeuvres at sea which could be used for the teaching of signals. Halsey applauded his initiative and his report on the project was forwarded to the Admiralty. In due course Mountbatten was summoned to expound his ideas and the film was sent to H.M.S. *Excellent* for further consideration.[24] Mountbatten's recollection is that he later received a letter from the Admiralty stating baldly: 'Their Lordships are unable to see any useful application for cinema films for instructional purposes in the Royal Navy.' Many years later he tried to track down a copy in the Public Record Office: 'In view of the fact that my idea was taken up by the Admiralty, who have since spent many millions of pounds on instructional films, you can imagine how much value I place on this particular letter.'[25] It had long vanished from the files.

The *Renown* returned to Portsmouth on 11 October. Before they had even reached Australia the Prince had decided that he must have Mountbatten's companionship on the next long journey to India and Japan. Mountbatten urged his father to agree: 'My gunnery courses are so secondary compared to seeing the world like this.'[26] At the time it seemed that one trip would follow the other with an interval of only a month or so, and Lord Milford Haven agreed without too much hesitation. In the event a year elapsed, a circumstance which could have been damaging to Mountbatten's career but in fact worked out well. For the first three months of 1921 he did a sub-lieutenants' course at Portsmouth, from which he emerged with the top position which he was beginning to feel was his by right. Then, unexpectedly, when he had hoped to go on leave, he found himself in command of a platoon of naval stokers sent north to quell disorder should the strike in the coal-mines lead to trouble. None of the men had handled a rifle before so their usefulness in case of crisis was uncertain, but he gave satisfaction to the military authorities: 'very keen, trustworthy and energetic', recorded his senior officer, Captain Gibson.[27] They were moved to Aintree, near the Grand National course, and for three days lived on bully beef, dry bread and water and slept on the asphalt floor of a disused bicycle-shed in army blankets swarming with fleas. The cold was appalling and they worked sixteen hours a day. 'Thank God I'm not in the Army! They deserve all the pay they get, poor fellows.'[28]

His passion for Audrey James seemed undiminished. He feared she would distract him from the sub-lieutenants' course but, on the contrary, 'She has given me the incentive to work. . . . I could never have believed that I was ever going to love one small woman so much. Every time I see her she has grown more wonderful.' Yet within six months all was over. Miss James dithered and fretted and refused to make up her mind. In the end the Prince of Wales himself told her that a straight answer was overdue. Forced to commit herself, she decided to remain single. Peter Murphy sought to revive the relationship.

'No, it is hopeless, Peter,' Mountbatten answered. 'I wouldn't have her back if she came and implored me . . . even if she did change her mind again, I should live in constant dread of the same thing happening. Also I *was* too young to really think of getting married.'[29] Miss James swiftly transferred her affections to the wealthy scion of a great cotton family – exchanging a coat of arms for the arms of Coats, as some humorist put it. Mountbatten too did not go long unconsoled. His letter to Peter Murphy had been written shortly after a stay on the Vanderbilts' yacht. Among the guests was a certain 'Edwina Ashley (such a nice girl)'.

On 25 June 1921 Mountbatten joined H.M.S. *Repulse* to serve out the three months which remained before the Prince of Wales left for India. A few weeks later Lord Milford Haven came aboard to spend a week as the guest of the Captain, Dudley Pound. It was his longest period at sea for many years and he enjoyed it thoroughly. He suffered from a bad chill during the last three days, but seemed fully recovered by the time his son saw him off at Inverness before going on to Dunrobin to stay with the Duke of Sutherland. The following day a message reached Dunrobin that Milford Haven had died after a heart attack. He had been in poor health for a long time and had lost much of his zest for life, but the suddenness of the blow was stunning. His son still had total faith in his father's wisdom and, indeed, omnipotence. With departure only just over a month away, however, and his brother George out of the country, he had too much to do to brood on his loss. He told a friend in the *Repulse*, Andrew Yates, that he was glad he was going to be so rushed 'as he hadn't dared to try and realize what had happened yet'. He left his ship almost immediately. 'I wish we weren't losing Dick,' wrote Yates to his grandmother, 'as he is very popular, and an excellent Officer, though I don't suppose will ever compare with his Father.'[30]

The Prince of Wales's visit to India was undertaken against the advice of many of those best qualified to comment. In 1919 new constitutional measures should have heralded an improvement in Anglo-Indian relations, but the introduction of trial without jury for those accused of political crimes, coupled with the massacre at Amritsar the same year, more than undid any possible advantage. At the end of 1921 the mood was still sombre; the Prince would certainly encounter hostility and possibly his life would be in danger. But such thoughts did little to dampen Mountbatten's enthusiasm. 'Tomorrow we arrive in India,' he wrote in his diary for 16 November:

> I am not by nature incurably romantic but there is something rather
> wonderful, rather thrilling at the idea of setting foot for the first time

in a country which genuinely belongs to the Far East. India is a country one has heard about, read about, even dreamt about, but up to the present I have found it hopeless to conceive what it is like in real life. The next four months ought to show me. We are going to traverse India from East to West, and then from South to North, with a trip to Burma wedged in between these two tours. Finally, we double on our tracks and return to the West – Karachi.

It was not long before they encountered the hostility of the Indians. At Allahabad the streets were deserted and a ceremony at the university was boycotted by the students. At Benares it was the same story. At Peshawar the Governor was so alarmed that, to the Prince's fury, he sneaked him into the palace by an unadvertised short-cut. Sir Herbert Russell, who wrote an ingratiating and cliché-ridden account of the tour, declared smugly that the extremists bore the signs 'of sheepishness and shamefacedness as though born of the realization that they had not really been playing the game towards the royal visitor',[31] but the Prince had no such illusions. 'I must tell you at once', he wrote to the King, 'that I'm very depressed about my work in British India as I don't feel that I'm doing a scrap of good; in fact I can say that I know I am not.'[32] Mountbatten had little sympathy for the nationalists' aspirations: 'rude young cubs', he called the students at Benares, and when a taxi-driver in Madras charged a demonstrator he noted with relish that the victim was left 'a somewhat shapeless mass in the road'.[33] Such brash comments make ironic reading when one considers Mountbatten's future role in the sub-continent.

Mountbatten described the other members of the staff to Edwina Ashley. Piers 'Joey' Legh was 'rather rude and superior'; Godfrey Thomas 'I quite like but don't altogether trust'; Lord Cromer was 'loquacious but not very sagacious'; Newport, the Surgeon-Commander, was nice but 'not quite the type of gentleman one used to get in the executive branch of the Navy'. 'Fruity' Metcalfe, recruited from the Indian Army, was 'the nicest fellow we have. Poor, honest, a typical Indian cavalryman.' And finally himself, 'Dickie, a little brute you once met in a yacht, whom you can kick if you like'.[34]

The Prince of Wales, in some ways more perceptive than Mountbatten, realized that all was not well between his young cousin and the rest of his staff, and did what he could to improve relations. They were 'not only nice to him but recognise him as my *personal* A.D.C.', he told Lady Milford Haven.[35] But his own infirmities he could not cure. 'David goes through his "black" phases more often than ever now, poor chap,' noted Mountbatten.[36]

'It was my impression at the time', wrote the Prince of Wales many years later, 'that [Dickie's] interest in the manifold problems of India was confined to that part of the country bounded by the white boards of polo fields.'[37] The comment was not wholly unfair. Mountbatten was stirred and excited by his new experiences but, though his mind was too lively to ignore the social, political and economic problems of the sub-continent, his attention was principally focused on more immediately seductive topics. Of these there was no doubt which was the most pressing. 'I've gone completely dippy about Polo, which in my opinion is the best game in the world,' he wrote to Prince Albert.[38] He had his first game at Jodhpur when he was called in to replace an absent player. The game was of a high standard, and during the first half he never got close to, let alone hit, the ball. Then, in the last chukka, 'to my own intense surprise, I actually hit the ball three or four times'.[39] A lifetime's passion had taken root. The future General Messervy somewhat unkindly told him that the only proper way to mount a polo pony was to run up from behind, take a flying leap and vault into the saddle. Only when the tyro had met disaster several times did Messervy admit that he only used the technique himself on one particularly tranquil and trusted pony.[40] Mountbatten would probably still have tried the manoeuvre even if he had known the truth, but his horsemanship did not match his courage. Few who watched those early games believed he would make even a competent player. It was to take several years before he could prove that intense and skilfully applied effort could be a substitute for natural ability.

Mountbatten's diary reveals little sense of serious dedication. The innumerable new sports which India had to offer engaged his attention above all. On the day that he first played polo he also stuck his first pig, spearing the boar triumphantly after a fifteen-minute run. With the Maharaja of Bharatpur he hunted black buck from a Rolls-Royce, twisting and turning at fifty miles an hour over the most impossible country: 'If Rolls ever need an advertisement they ought to have an account written of what that car did.' In Nepal he shot his first tiger and, in recording the fact, exhibited one of those flashes of disarming self-perception which recur throughout his life: 'Naturally I was frightfully pleased but I am afraid that I talked a good deal too much about the whole question and as to the possibility of it being mine or Joey's tiger, which was silly of me and I am sure could not have added to my popularity with the others.' At Patiala he shot a panther, though his pride dwindled when he discovered that the animal had been removed from a zoo and doped. 'They had originally laid out a rare and valuable black panther as well, but when they heard that David was not shooting they returned it to the zoo and revived it.'[41]

Mountbatten relished the extravagance and exoticism of the Princely States: the sedan-chair at Bharatpur, 'slightly larger than a Pickford's furniture van, slung between two enormous elephants . . . gorgeously caparisoned in blue and gold'; the fire-eaters of Bikaner; the Khyber Pass, which he had been more keen to see than anything else in India. Occasionally, though, the diet became too rich for his palate. At Udaipur three hundred pigs were maintained at the palace and the finest boars matched against leopards in a nearby arena. Mountbatten watched such an encounter with interest (the boar won), but commented disapprovingly: 'I regret to say that even when there is a famine in the town the pigs are not neglected – there are times when I do sympathize with the Bolsheviks.'[42]

As in Australia, huge distances were covered by train; four trains, in fact, to accommodate the retinue. Mountbatten's cabin was twice as large as the one he had enjoyed in the days of P31. He would gaze at the infinite vastness of the Indian night, lit every hundred yards by the guttering torches of peasants who guarded the line in a cordon that stretched thousands of miles across the continent. Next door the Prince would be tossing fretfully; complaining about the noise, the rocking of the train; inveighing endlessly against the coldness of his parents, the cruelty of being separated from the woman he loved. Yet his energy was astonishing. At Rangoon Mountbatten was forced to play four sets of tennis with him in the noonday sun; then, when he flagged, the Prince took on the Admiral and finally spent an hour and a half practising on the polo ground. 'I've never seen anybody take so much exercise on so little food, as he only eats biscuits for lunch.'[43]

In Madras Mountbatten found time to visit a protegée of his sister Louise, the Russian-born Baroness de Kuster. He always derived satisfaction from exploring the opinions of cranks and eccentrics – if a leader of the Theosophical Society can properly so be described – and was admirably open-minded about the Baroness's revelations. She knew the Prince well on the astral plane and was able to tell his cousin in strict confidence that his last incarnation had been as Akbar. Mountbatten duly passed this on: 'David was not over-pleased at the idea of having been a black man!' Mountbatten was fascinated by the theory of reincarnation but worried that 'all souls occupying the bodies of Theosophists last came from some King or famous man. None has ever appeared under the humble name of Smith or Jones.'[44]

In general he far preferred the semi-independent Indian states to the more predictable and rigidly formal British India. Delhi, however, with its pomp and splendour, struck a romantic chord. In 1922 Viceroy's House was still comparatively modest. A special pavilion had been built in the grounds for the Prince of Wales and most of his staff were in tents around him; the tents, however, were sumptuous and the army of gorgeously dressed servants more than made up for any deficiencies of decor. The same accommodation problem occurred in Kandy, ancient capital of Ceylon, where Mountbatten with some disdain surveyed the King's Pavilion: 'It is rather a hopeless house, for although it contains many large and airy reception rooms, there is an entirely inadequate supply of sleeping apartments.'[45] Twenty-two years later he was to make the same building his official residence.

From Ceylon the expedition moved on to Japan. Mountbatten was immediately and lastingly impressed by what he saw. 'Next to our own service I have never seen such fine ships,' he wrote on arrival at Yokohama. 'Any one of them could have taken us on, on equal terms. . . . I received the impression that here was a power to be reckoned with.'[46] The official doctrine about the Japanese was that they were 'mere copyists of western techniques and equipment, and rather inferior copyists at that'.[47] The officers from the R.A.F. team training the Naval Air Service confirmed the view; the Japanese did not make good pilots. Mountbatten was unconvinced. He contrived to visit their newest battleship, the *Mutsu*. The British naval attaché had previously been refused permission to go aboard and Mountbatten would probably have fared no better if it had not been assumed that he was an innocuous minor royal with no expert knowledge or interests. In the fortunate absence of the Japanese Commander, Mountbatten was allowed into almost every part of the ship and admired greatly what he saw.[48] 'As regards Japan from the point of view of a world power,' he summed up at the end of the tour, 'my visit has been an eye-opener to me as regards her resources, her ships, her army.'[49]

He was ready for any new experience. Duck-catching in butterfly-nets promised at least to be energetic but in fact proved disappointing; the ducks zoomed blindly along a narrow ditch and all the hunter had to do was lower his net towards the surface of the water. Fishing with cormorants at Kyoto was more stimulating. But it was shopping for a kimono at Mitsukoshi, the Harrods of Tokyo, which provided the most memorable experience:

> On arrival . . . we were met by the manager and an assistant, who conducted us to a private room. . . . Here we were given armchairs and offered cigarettes. Presently a little geisha girl came in with Japanese tea, which she set before us. After another ten minutes' wait the manager returned with the sales manager and several heads of departments to whom I was introduced with much bowing on both sides. We then discussed the weather. As we had by now been at least quarter-of-an-hour in the shop . . . I asked whether they would let me see some ladies' kimonos. This was a blunder and a very tactless one. I could see that they were pained that I should have introduced such a sordid subject into our delightful little breakfast party. They shrugged their shoulders and called for the little serving girl who now brought in some European tea, which I politely drank. I again

ventured to remind them of the reason for my visit. This time the girl was sent for cakes, which we all ate with chopsticks.

Presently one of the managers went out and returned some five minutes later with two assistants carrying a box. 'Good,' I thought, 'the kimonos at last.' Of course I was mistaken. It was a large camera and tripod which they unpacked and proceeded to erect. I had begun to realise that the best thing I could do was not to refer to the painful subject of the kimonos again but take an interest in whatever else they brought. . . .

When the kimonos did start arriving it was a case of 'thick and fast, they came at last'! I was bewildered. I was completely swamped. . . . The simple looking ones cost fortunes, others that looked complicated would be one quarter the price.

Choosing the kimono took an hour; then came the *obi*, or sash; the silk socks with the separate big toe; the string that fastened round the *obi*. Mountbatten had arrived at the shop at 8.30 a.m.; he left at noon.[50]

From Japan the party made for home. For Mountbatten the tour had been an enthralling experience. Beyond the discovery that Japan was a powerful country and India an attractive one, he experienced no dramatic new revelations, but he enjoyed himself immensely and he learned how to handle a wide variety of human beings in a still wider variety of circumstances. He came back a wiser and more tactful man. He also came back engaged to Edwina Ashley. For this alone it had been one of the most important occasions of his life.

# CHAPTER 5

## *Edwina*

EDWINA WAS THE DAUGHTER of Wilfrid Ashley, a Conservative Member of Parliament who was a grandson of the reforming Earl of Shaftesbury but himself a strikingly illiberal reactionary. He was to embarrass his daughter by his insistence that all socialists were subversive and that the totalitarian regimes of Europe offered the best hope for the future. More important, Edwina was the grand-daughter of Sir Ernest Cassel. Cassel had been born in Cologne, son of a Jewish money-lender and small-time banker. In a career as remarkable as that of any Rothschild, he battled his way to immense fortune and, through his role as private banker and financial adviser to the future Edward VII, lodged himself in the innermost temples of the Establishment. He was one of the richest and most powerful men in Europe. His wife had died in 1880 and when Edwina's mother, his beloved only child Maud, followed her in 1911, he lost much of his zest for business and, indeed, for living. Edwina became his principal interest and in 1919, when she was seventeen years old, she came to live with him in Brook House, his massive mausoleum in Park Lane.

A lesser girl might have been daunted by the sombre splendours of Brook House, but Edwina was indomitable. Highly intelligent without being intellectual, elegant and vital rather than conventionally beautiful, she blazed in London society with a fierce brilliance which alarmed some and dazzled almost all. Restless, egocentric, intolerant, she was rarely a comfortable person to be with yet, equally, was never boring. Her passion for the syncopated rhythms of the age reflected something deeper in her personality. In almost the only piece of verse which he is known to have written, and of which he was inordinately proud, Mountbatten apostrophized her:

> Oh female of ridiculous dimensions
> Your proclivity for dancing is absurd
> Though your terpsichorean effort far surpasses
> All the animated annals of the world.[1]

Her proclivity for dancing, for hectic pleasure, was indeed extravagant, if not absurd, and she rejoiced in the attention earned by her talents and her position as Cassel's favourite grandchild. She was one of the most sought-after girls in London.

When Mountbatten first met her at a ball at Claridge's given by Mrs Cornelius Vanderbilt in October 1920 she was being vigorously wooed by the Duke of Sutherland, and Mountbatten himself was still embroiled with Audrey James. They met occasionally that winter but it was not until they were in the same party at Cowes in August 1921 that they really took notice of each other. From that moment the pace was furious. Mountbatten quickly decided that this was the girl for him; Edwina was little slower in responding. It is possible to view their mutual attraction cynically, as an alliance in which great fortune on one side was to be balanced against royal blood on the other. But, significant though such considerations might have been, they were also overwhelmingly in love and made this evident to all around them. When Edwina's *enfant terrible* of a younger sister, Mary, rose to her feet in the dining-room of the Highland Hotel, Strathpeffer and announced to all present, 'This dazzling gentleman and my sister are courting. Let's drink to their health!' she did not endear herself to either party but said nothing that was not known to all their friends.[2]

When Lord Milford Haven was visiting his son in the *Repulse* he asked who would be staying at Dunrobin. Mountbatten mentioned Edwina Ashley. 'I've met her,' said his father. 'There's a really intelligent and beautiful girl. I hope you'll marry someone like her.'[3] A few days later Lord Milford Haven was dead. 'You know, it's funny, and I can't explain exactly,' Edwina wrote in consolation, 'but I felt all along as if it were my *own* loss along with yours, and am unhappy with you.' When he replied, Mountbatten told her how much his father had liked her: 'So you see, Edwina, that your sympathy is all the more precious.'[4] A week later Edwina got back to Brook House to find that her grandfather had had a heart attack and had died without recovering consciousness.

Ernest Cassel left £7.5 million. Brook House and £30,000 a year were left to his sister for life and then to Edwina, and his favourite grand-daughter also got the lion's share of the residue, £2.3 million. Mountbatten's pay at the same period was £310 a year and his income from dividends provided an additional £300.[5] This was as much as, or more than, most of his naval friends but the disparity was still striking. To neither, however, did this seem an obstacle to their marriage. Only the fact that they were both in mourning prevented Mountbatten proposing before he left for India, and even so he contrived to make his feelings clear. '*How* glad I am you didn't wait till June to tell me everything,' wrote Edwina.[6] The letter he wrote to her on his last night in London shows how far matters were already settled:

My own beloved Darling, when you get this we will have been parted
for the last time for a long while, and so I want to tell you that you
will be truly *ever* in my thoughts, and you will be my 'guiding spirit'
throughout. Don't think of eight months as a long while, Darling,
but please just think of next June. . . . I shall try very hard to be
worthy of your great love, though darling – it is difficult for a poor
sinner like me to look up to such a wonderful, wonderful girl. . . . I
am such a ridiculously lucky chap and I don't believe you realise it at
all. Write to me sometimes darling, as I shall be lonely and your
letters will be such a help. . . . The tour is about 246 days long – so
when you get this you can already scratch off one day and call it 245!
So you see the time is already passing and soon we will be together
again, darling, and then! – what bliss!

> Bless you Edwina, my own darling,
> I just love you with all my heart.
> Your very own Dickie.[7]

The while was not to be so long as he had feared. Within a few weeks of his
departure Edwina had decided that a visit to India to stay with the Viceroy,
Lord Reading, would be an appropriate step in her education. Mountbatten
was ecstatic. 'I need you so badly. You just don't know what a difference your
coming out to India is going to make. It's going to help me and strengthen me
and give me fresh courage. It's one of the most wonderful things you have ever
done in your life.'[8] He was in a fever of excitement, fretting over the minutiae
of her journey, what she should bring, where she should stay: 'Please be very
careful what sort of food you eat and above all what water you drink.' 'To
expose your head to the Indian sun, even on a cloudy day, is to court disaster.
. . . Nothing short of a topee is any good . . . between 9 a.m. and 4 p.m.'[9]
Throughout their married life he was to overwhelm her with admonitions and
instructions, most of which Edwina ignored. She disliked fuss and detail; to
Mountbatten they were a staple of life.

The Prince of Wales suspected that an engagement was imminent. 'He
liked Audrey,' Mountbatten told Edwina, 'but thoroughly disapproved of her
and was largely instrumental in breaking it off.'[10] Edwina, on the other hand,
had won his full approval. When the couple were reunited at Delhi he did all
he could to foster the liaison, even putting his sitting-room at their disposal.
Nevertheless, Mountbatten's exuberant happiness gave him fresh cause for
moping: 'That it should be his best friend, he says, will make his loneliness
seem more complete in contrast.'

While at Mysore Mountbatten had consulted a celebrated prophet,
Professor Coomaraswamy, who obligingly told him that he would marry

young and that the marriage would be the happiest event of his life. Since the Professor also predicted that his visitor would excel at polo, Mountbatten's cup was full.[11] He needed little encouragement. 'I asked her if she would marry me, and she said she would,' was the diary entry for 14 February 1922 – a somewhat bald comment which he embellished next day by remarking that it was 'probably the most momentous statement that I am ever likely to make'. He had promised his mother that he would take no irrevocable step before he left for India, and Edwina's arrival left him in doubt as to what he should do. He wrote to Lady Milford Haven:

> I have made up my mind that each person knows within himself when he is old enough to marry. I am now.
>
> I have never really sown any wild oats, and as I never intend to, I haven't got to get over that stage which some men have to. I am also sufficiently certain of myself this time to feel happy. Mama – we want to get married just as soon as we can when we get back.
>
> Mamma darling, please don't think I have forgotten either you or Louise or any of the others of the family at home in my joy. I know how sad you still are at the loss of Papa, and indeed ever will be – as we all of us shall – but I do suggest that he who while living approved of Edwina would want us to be happy. . . . I am quite certain in my own mind that Papa is smiling down on Edwina and me.[12]

In Delhi nobody was surprised and almost everyone delighted. A large silver cup was filled with champagne. Seventeen people drank half of it and Mountbatten was called on to drain what remained. He met the challenge. 'I felt very ill all today,' he noted ruefully, 'and it is the last time I shall ever do anything of the sort.'[13] If Lady Milford Haven had any doubts she quickly suppressed them. 'I am really and truly happy at it,' she wrote enthusiastically.[14] Only the Viceroy's wife struck a discordant note. Apologetically she wrote to Colonel Ashley: 'I hoped she would have cared for someone older, with more of a career before him.'[15]

Even a peripheral member of the royal family could not marry without great pother. The King's consent had to be obtained; the Prince of Wales's wish to stand as best man must be approved by the high priests of protocol. Prince Albert was conscripted to help. 'It is a great responsibility to arrange somebody's wedding,' he grumbled, 'especially when both bridegroom and best man are at the other end of the world. But most of the big things in life have been done like that.'[16] The engagement was supposed to be a secret; and, though everyone seemed to know about it, the official announcement was still hailed with a fanfare of publicity. The couple revelled in it all. 'I hear that in

London our engagement was announced on the posters in red type four feet high side by side with the Armstrong murder case,' Edwina wrote exultantly. 'Isn't it swell!'[17]

The Prince's party got back on 21 June 1922, and proceeded in state carriages to Buckingham Palace. 'Edwina was on the balcony of Bath House,' noted Mountbatten.[18] He was involved at once in a fury of preparations. A cornucopia of presents was emptied before them: cuff-links for a regiment of shirts, buttons for a battalion of waistcoats, cigarette-boxes for every table in every house they could ever hope to inhabit. The Prince of Wales gave them a silver globe with the tracks of the two royal visits engraved upon it; gold George II wine-coolers came from other members of the royal family. There were eighteen fans, ten blotters, a pair of shooting stockings and a cut-glass bottle containing water from the River Jordan.

The wedding took place less than a month after Mountbatten's return, on 18 July, at St Margaret's, Westminster. It was suitably magnificent. The royal family was present in mass, fourteen hundred guests were invited to the reception, a crowd of eight thousand was beginning to form outside the church by 5 a.m. Mountbatten, to his great delight, was created K.C.V.O. to mark the occasion. The wedding-cake had little lifebuoys on it, and tiny lifeboats hanging from silver davits. The Prince of Wales submitted to much banter about the date when he could be expected to follow his cousin as a bridegroom. For the public the wedding provided a glorious opportunity for vicarious day-dreaming; the *Yorkshire Post* devoted thirteen full columns to the story and the national dailies did not fall far behind. Whether one believed with the *Star* that it was the wedding of the century or preferred the more sober judgement of the *Daily Telegraph* that it was merely the wedding of the year, there is no doubt that it was a considerable occasion.

The Mountbattens spent the first nights of their honeymoon at Broadlands, Colonel Ashley's country house near Romsey in Hampshire, staying in bed until lunchtime and venturing outside the grounds only to see a film of their wedding at a Southampton cinema. Then it was the Ritz in Paris and, by car, to stay with King Alfonso and Mountbatten's cousin Queen Ena of Spain. Here the Grand Cross of Isabella the Catholic was added to the K.C.V.O. and Mountbatten saw his first bullfight. The matador was 'exceptionally marvellous', but 'the first part with the horses is quite revolting'.[19] A pilgrimage to Germany was an essential part of the itinerary; Mountbatten was never to tire of revisiting favourite scenes from his past and introducing them to new generations. It was the first time he had been to Hesse since before the war and he found that the palace of Wolfsgarten had shrunk to half its size. His beloved Heiligenberg was in a sad state of disarray and much altered.[20] It was now that he found that the press might not always be as kind to him as when he was a dashing bridegroom. 'That the Mountbattens should choose to stay in Germany, for part of their honeymoon, is surely a *faux pas*,' sniffed the *Daily Mail*.[21] 'True, his lordship is of wholly German parentage, and his wife is half German, but Prince Louis of Battenberg . . . had severed all connections with the Fatherland.' In fact he had retained Heiligenberg till 1920 and only sold it then with reluctance. The transaction proved a disaster, since inflation had set in before the purchase price was paid and reduced it to a pittance. By the time the honeymooners arrived, £50 bought 26,000 marks and Mountbatten was able to get his sister Louise a fur stole for just over two guineas.

For most couples the honeymoon would now have been over, but Mountbatten knew that never again would he get the chance of six months' holiday without serious detriment to his career. On 28 September they set out aboard the *Majestic* for the United States. They occupied a sumptuous suite for which they paid only the price of a single cabin, thus exemplifying the curious rule that the poor are rarely the recipients of largesse while unto the rich is given what they could perfectly well afford to pay for themselves. Mountbatten took instant delight in the brash, vibrant, enthusiastic society of New York. They were fêted by the Jerome Kerns and Douglas Fairbanks – 'Fairbanks was recognised and mobbed everywhere,' noted Mountbatten wistfully;[22] taken to baseball games and the Ziegfeld Follies. The sightseeing tour across the United States that followed was recorded painstakingly in Mountbatten's diary. What was missing in colourful detail – the view 'beggared description'; in the Adirondacks 'the foliage was too lovely' – was redeemed in statistics – the Grand Canyon was 'an average 13 miles wide, 1 mile deep and 200 miles long'. To the *New York Sun* Mountbatten confided that the Canyon was 'the most wonderful thing scenically that I know', adding, 'and I suppose I've seen about 85% of the wonderful scenery of the world'[23] – a proud boast for a man of twenty-two.

They reached Hollywood on 18 October, stayed at the Fairbankses home Pickfair, and were entertained by Charlie Chaplin. With him and Jackie Coogan they made a film: 'It was fascinating work. Edwina and I are "lovers" in it.'[24] Mountbatten's valet Thorogood was recruited to play the butler. Chaplin became a life-long friend. 'He is the most loveable, shy and pathetic little man and yet so full of humour that he can keep one amused by the hour,' Mountbatten told his mother.[25] Shooting was frequently delayed while the amateurs tried to stop laughing at Chaplin's antics. The enterprise made nobody's reputation but gave great pleasure to everyone concerned. The American newspapers reported that 'personages in exalted positions' in

London were less than pleased by these exploits,[26] but nobody said a word to the Mountbattens to indicate dissatisfaction.

The American press had a field-day with their exotic visitors. The 'close relation of the King of England' and 'the richest heiress in the world' proved an irresistible source of copy; and 'they are both attractive, too', added the *Washington Herald*, 'and quite human, and natural and likeable; which made us all that much more interested. . . .'[27] Mountbatten's views were quoted on every subject: on prohibition, 'Quite all right, but I would not want it in England'; on the U.S. Navy, 'one of the finest bodies of men in the world'; on hospitality, 'The word must have been coined here in America.'[28] Quick-thinking, responsive, with charm and unaffected enjoyment of the whole proceeding, Mountbatten handled the press with a skill that rarely betrayed him. The American journalists, however, tended to lard his comments with adornments such as 'rippin'', 'my eye' or 'bah jove'. He complained about this to one reporter, who agreed that in reality he talked like a regular guy. 'And I am a regular guy, or at least I try to be. For the love of Mike, don't make me talk like a bally English dude or say I wear a monocle. Why, if I wore a monocle, I couldn't remain in the navy half an hour.'[29]

Inevitably, they were asked their views on marriage and divorce. 'I think the greatest happiness is found when the husband works at his career and his wife looks after the home and children,' said Mountbatten firmly, while another paper quoted him as saying, 'Career for Lady Louis? Why, she's going to be my wife, career enough!'[30] His wife was content to go along with this description of her role; she 'was not faintly interested in feminism'; indeed, on one occasion, 'Scrubbing floors, dishwashing and cooking, says Lady Mountbatten, are her long suits.'[31] Both were insistent that Mount-batten was a serving naval officer with a job to do. A reporter remarked to him that he did not now need to work. 'His smiling features twisted into an expression of disgust and his eyes snapped as he replied, "I have a most profound contempt for men who do nothing. I always shall work."'[32]

That he was sincere in this was obvious to everyone who knew him. He set out his problem to his father-in-law, Colonel Ashley.

> If I retire, what am I to do? I have enough money to carry on in the navy very comfortably as a bachelor, though I will not deny that I have, at present, nowhere near enough to support a wife. This has been the subject of considerable argument between Edwina and me. I would be perfectly willing to go into business and try to make enough, but that is where she disagrees with me as she would prefer me to work for practically none in the navy, where I do stand a chance of making a name for myself if I work hard, than to try and increase her considerable fortune.[33]

In this conviction that her husband's place was in his beloved Navy, Edwina never wavered. She was not always the most conscientious of naval wives, but she submitted to many inconveniences and restrictions on her liberty in support of his career.

How that career would develop seemed uncertain as their protracted honeymoon drew to a close. They returned to England on 9 December 1922. Mountbatten had expected to be back a month earlier at least. The plan was that he should join H.M.S. *Truant*, a destroyer attached to the Signals School. Then the *Truant* was sent for refit and its captain, Commander Joel, cabled that she would not sail before mid January. Mountbatten was ecstatic. 'I am having the most wonderful time,' he replied, 'and will not therefore disguise my joy at the extra time this gives me.'[34] The last few weeks were as good as any. 'Really I see no reason why Alfonso's wish to us of "a perpetual honeymoon" should not come true,' Mountbatten wrote to his wife.[35] But his future as a sailor was by no means as secure as he imagined. The Royal Navy which he hoped to rejoin was a beleaguered service. On the day war ended it boasted sixty-one battleships to the American thirty-nine, ninety cruisers to the American nineteen. The true disparity was not as great as these figures suggest, but the British Navy was still by far the most powerful force afloat. With peace, however, fierce financial cuts were decreed. In 1919 the notorious 'Ten Year Rule' was imposed, directing that Service estimates should be based upon the somewhat questionable assumption that the Empire would be involved in no major war during the next ten years. The Admiralty accepted that Great Britain could not hope to do more than maintain a fleet as large as that of any other power. In 1920 a scheme was introduced for cutting numbers by offering gratuities in exchange for early retirement. It failed. Sir Eric Geddes, the First Lord of the Admiralty, was told to use more drastic methods, and in 1922 the 'Geddes Axe' fell with dread effect. 350 lieutenants were to be retired; fifty-two per cent of the officers from Mountbatten's year would have left the Service before the end of 1923.[36]

One of the factors allegedly considered when deciding which officers should survive the holocaust was whether they had private means. By such a criterion Mountbatten was an obvious victim. During his absence in America, King George V sent for his brother Georgie, who had succeeded his father as Marquess of Milford Haven, and explained the policy of the Admiralty. Milford Haven asked whether Mountbatten should do a job. 'Every young man must work,' said the King. Then he would merely do somebody else out of a job in civil life, and perhaps do it badly into the bargain, Georgie argued. If he was an efficient naval officer, he should surely continue in that function.

The King professed himself convinced and said he would speak to the First Lord.[37] Whether this somewhat *simpliste* argument in fact proved so effective must be open to question. Chatfield, who was one of the committee responsible for deciding which officers must retire, was asked by the future Admiral Backhouse why the wealthy Mountbatten had escaped the axe. 'You don't understand,' Chatfield replied. 'The only way it is possible for us to work on this committee is not to consider the individuals, but to think of the good of the Service. I know Mountbatten and I consider it for the good of the Service for him to stay.'[38] If there had been any royal intervention – and the Prince of Wales also claimed to have influenced the decision – Chatfield was not prepared to admit it.

There was some feeling in the Navy that Mountbatten 'should sacrifice his professional ambitions in favour of a less fortunate officer of corresponding rank'.[39] From Mountbatten's point of view, the weakness in this argument was that the less fortunate officer was also less capable. He believed that not merely was he an exceptionally competent officer but that he was destined to get to the top and would do the Navy great service by so doing. To renounce such a destiny in the interests of charity would to his mind have been ignoble and absurd.

Even though his position might be secure, his future was not likely to be particularly easy. His trips with the Prince of Wales, his glamorous marriage, his frolics in Hollywood, had not escaped attention among his colleagues, and much of the comment had been unfavourable. By those who had not worked with him he was considered a playboy. Even those who knew him suspected that he had grown swollen-headed and would no longer make a good member of a team. Gilbert Stephenson, Captain of the *Revenge*, which the Admiralty eventually preferred to the *Truant* as Mountbatten's next ship, felt that Mountbatten would not look to him for praise or blame; 'he wouldn't care a tuppenny cuss what I thought of him'. Stephenson asked the Admiralty to remove Mountbatten's name from the list of those who were to join the *Revenge*. The Admiralty refused, 'and of course nobody was more grateful than I was that they hadn't',[40] commented Stephenson long afterwards.

In his attitude he reflected the vague unease with which many naval officers contemplated Mountbatten at that period. Viewing Mountbatten's career as a whole, there can be no doubt that his wealth and connections were helpful to him. In the few critical years after he rejoined the Navy they were an impediment. To establish himself once more in the race to the top he had not merely to do as well as his contemporaries but conspicuously better.

# CHAPTER 6

## *Signals Officer*

EARLY IN 1923 an international fleet was in the eastern Mediterranean policing an uneasy truce between Greek and Turk. The Lausanne Conference was achieving nothing, a Turkish attack seemed imminent, Britain's allies were disinclined to help her meet it. 'War means at least a week in the Bosporus,' Mountbatten told Edwina, 'bombarding and evacuating British civilians and our army.'[1] H.M.S. *Revenge* was one of the battleships with this force. Mountbatten joined her at Constantinople on 14 January, carrying with him 220 kilograms of luggage as opposed to the not ungenerous allowance of 150. 'I arrived with very little luggage, no Rolls-Royce cars and (let us pray) no "publicity",' he wrote virtuously.[2] Subsequently he was apt to say that he had met with some hostility from his fellow officers, but there is no evidence of this in his contemporary writings: 'The officers seem nice,' he told Edwina, 'the men seem happy and the jobs I am going to take on are both interesting and pleasant.'[3] Nevertheless, he had arrived in a mood of gloom. 'I am not sure that it is not a good thing that I am joining a big ship in such a rotten place. . . . No one can say I "wangled" that!'[4]

His job was to be in charge of about half the fo'c'sle division and a 15-inch gun-turret, which meant he was responsible for some 160 men. He treated this task with exemplary seriousness, preparing a book in which each man had a full page to himself giving particulars of his career and background. These facts he memorised, matching them with the face until he was confident that he had personal knowledge of every man in his command. It was a technique he was to use all his life; good public relations certainly, but stemming from genuine interest in and a sense of duty towards those who served under him. He was anxious that *his* gun or *his* division should outshine every other, and at one time offered prizes to his turret's crew as an incentive for good shooting, desisting only when it was pointed out that this was unfair to other officers who could not afford to do the same.[5] 'A most enthusiastic and zealous officer,' reported Commander Sedgwick. 'His zeal is apt at times to make him put the good of his Division before that of the ship, but he will grow out of this.'[6]

His zeal extended beyond his work. He flung himself into every activity:

introduced mah-jong and got all the officers to play it; wrote a script for and
directed a black-and-white Pierrot show – 'Please get me a couple of plain
glass eyeglasses . . . and a selection of some half-dozen or so little mous-
taches,' he asked Edwina.[7] From Douglas Fairbanks he secured a print of
Fairbanks's new film *Robin Hood*; he persuaded C. B. Cochran to transcribe
the musical accompaniment, designed an instrument to simulate the noise of
arrows whipping through the air, rigged up the quarterdeck as a theatre and
gave three performances for the Fleet. The Admiral attended the final evening.
'The show was the most wonderful success: both machines ran perfectly, the
band were wonderful and I was in constant communication with them
through a Voice Pipe. I was very happy.'[8]

Yet he counted the days till he might return to England. 'Very lonely and
sad today,' he wrote in his diary. 'Wrote a 24 page letter to Edwina.'[9] A
fortnight later H.M.S. *Malaya* sailed for home. 'Oh! Why can't we go home
too? It's 61 days since I left Edwina and seems like 61 months!'[10] At one time
it appeared he might be transferred home for a signals course before the
*Revenge* herself returned. Edwina was enlisted to canvass Beatty's support.
'He was *awfully* nice and I am sure he will always do anything he can for you,'
she reported, but the upshot was that Mountbatten would do better to serve
out his full tour. 'I must say it would be silly to do anything to make you
unpopular, and far better wait for the next [course] if it was going to cause
any difficulty.'[11] Within a few weeks of this letter word came that *Revenge*
would be back with the Atlantic Fleet by the end of April – 'A mad night in the
wardroom in consequence of the news.'[12]

Leonard Wincott, ringleader in the Invergordon Mutiny, Communist and
long-term resident of Moscow, paid tribute to Mountbatten's popularity. It
had nothing to do with his royal connections, Wincott said. 'He was an officer
who had set out to show the right way to lead and develop his men. . . . He
was . . . advanced in his ways of dealing with the lower deck that adored him,
whilst he on his part respected them. When he left the *Revenge* . . . he received
such a send-off from the men that I doubt if any captain ever was so
spontaneously or sincerely bid *bon voyage*.'[13] With great pleasure Mountbatten in 1973 showed this passage to the Prince of Wales. He was sceptical,
though, about the small importance Wincott attached to his royal blood. 'I
don't mind betting', he told Prince Charles, 'that when you have done as long
at sea you will be a greater legend than your old great-uncle seems to have
been – and for the same reasons.'[14]

Captain Stephenson, too, had become one of Mountbatten's most fervent
admirers. 'Directly I saw the man at work I realized how tremendously
intelligent he was, how full of life and vivacity. He had the gift of getting on
with people; people, in other words, wanted to do what *he* wanted them to

do. . . . He was, in fact, the most successful of all my officers when handling difficult men.'[15] Yet though his contemporaries realised he was able and industrious, they had no sense that he was destined for particular renown. 'No more a high-flyer than anyone else,' commented a fellow naval officer, Charles Hughes Hallett, though he admired Mountbatten's enterprise. Hughes Hallett went with him to the reception at Holyrood for the Crown Prince of Sweden and Mountbatten's sister Louise, who had married the Crown Prince in November 1923. Mountbatten decided that the long line of cars would cause tedious delays, filched a sheet of paper from the palace, wrote himself a pass, and waved it triumphantly at the police as he swept to the head of the queue.[16]

What finally turned out to be more than eighteen months in the *Revenge* ended in August 1924 with ritual revelry: 'At the Commander's instigation 4 fellows tried to take my trousers off and failed. . . . Very, very sad at leaving.'[17] There now began the long and sometimes wearisome process of training as a specialist signals officer at the signals school at Portsmouth and the naval college at Greenwich. The Mountbattens settled at Adsdean, a large, ugly, mainly Victorian house about twelve miles from Portsmouth, which was taken initially for nine months but was to remain their base until Edwina inherited Broadlands just before the war. She furnished it with style, there was a polo practice-ground, a golf-course, three tennis-courts, eight hundred acres of shooting, room for twenty guests or so; it was an ample, comfortable establishment on a scale by no means rare in Britain in the 1920s and 1930s, yet lavish compared with the homes of most of Mountbatten's naval colleagues. From Adsdean and Brook House Mountbatten conducted a furious pursuit of pleasure, in which every moment that was not dedicated to work seemed to be spent at meals, on the dance-floor or in one of the sporting activities appropriate to the British gentry. Yet work never suffered; Mountbatten would rush to London at the end of a day in Portsmouth, dine and dance away the night, then be driven back in his Rolls-Royce which had been fitted with a collapsible seat to allow him to sleep in transit, often arriving at Adsdean only just in time to change and drive on to the signals school. It was a regimen made possible only by the prodigal expenditure of wealth, but which demanded great stamina and devotion to duty.

During these years polo began to bulk large in Mountbatten's mind: 'the main recreational interest of my life', he wrote in old age. 'I had immense happiness playing and being with other polo players.'[18] He was not naturally a good horseman and he had done little serious riding before he took a month's course in military equitation with the Life Guards in 1923. He could afford expensive ponies, but the best ponies are only in part a substitute for a player's skill. It took endless practice, coaching by experts, and a scientific study of his weaknesses before he became a first-class player. Even then his greatness was as a captain; his teams were always better than the sum of their parts. The 'Bluejackets' achieved results to which no naval players had aspired before and twice almost carried away the Inter-Regimental trophy, playing against teams which were theoretically in a far higher class. Their success was the fruit of many hours of discussion and practice. No detail was ignored: 'Mountbatten insisted on our calling to each other for passes by our christian names,' recorded Robert Neville; 'by the inflection of our voices we used to interpret what was in the caller's mind and act accordingly. . . . He was the perfect captain, both on and off the field. . . . He inspired his team-mates. . . . On the field he never got rattled or bad-tempered. And no matter how silly one was he was always forgiving and encouraging.'[19]

He was not content with mastering the existing techniques of the game but determined to improve and refine them. He devised and patented an oval-shaped head to the polo stick which gave 'loft and length' and, over the years, brought in many hundreds of pounds in royalties to the Royal Naval Polo Association. Dissatisfied with the existing books on polo, he decided to write his own and recruited Peter Murphy to turn his product into lucid English. *Polo* by 'Marco' has been the polo-players bible for many years and was translated into Spanish and French. Nothing stood in the way of success. When he wanted Robert Neville for his Adsdean team and found he was to be posted to the Atlantic Fleet, he persuaded Admiral Keyes to invent the post of 'Port Adjutant, Portsmouth' and assign Neville to it.[20] Some of his contemporaries felt that he pursued success too vigorously, was too professional in his approach to what was only a game. Mountbatten could never understand such arguments: whatever one did, work or play, the object was to excel.

Those who complained that Mountbatten took polo too seriously might have been mollified if he had done badly or, at least, less well on his signals courses. He did not oblige. 'To my surprise', he came out top of the signals course.[21] The surprise, one suspects, was perfunctory. 'Hard working', 'energetic', 'very keen' were epithets that occurred monotonously in every report for the period, but there were also shrewder and more perceptive comments. 'Appears anxious to reach higher rank by his own merit rather than through his social advantages,' was one such judgement. 'A young officer of outstanding ability. . . . Will make some enemies as he is inclined to suffer fools badly,' was another.[22]

*

After a few months with the Reserve Fleet in the battleship *Centurion*, Mountbatten at the beginning of 1927 went back to the Mediterranean Fleet. He was to be there for eight of the next ten years, arriving as a young officer of promise, leaving as a man certain to get very near if not to the top of his profession. The British Mediterranean Fleet was still the largest maritime unit in the world; it and the Home Fleet provided the most sure ladder up which the ambitious young officer could climb towards glory. Chatfield believed the Mediterranean was the heartland of the Royal Navy, 'a great strategic centre for naval warfare and always will be so long as navies count in the world'.[23]

The Commander-in-Chief was Roger Keyes – 'a fine fellow but is not blessed with much brains', in Jellicoe's opinion.[24] He was fanatical in his support of polo and encouraged the more skilful practitioners to play regularly at the expense of their work – not to mention of their colleagues, who had to perform the extra duties. Charles Lambe, who himself adored polo, referred to Keyes's 'iniquitous favouritism' in recalling a cruiser in the middle of exercises and sending his barge for one of the team.[25] This may refer to the same incident as was described by Mountbatten to Robert Neville. Seeing a signal demanding the immediate return of a certain Lieutenant Alexander-Sinclair, Mountbatten claims he stormed off to Keyes 'and told him I could not remain captain of his team if he was going to subordinate fleet practices to polo'.[26] Mountbatten was apt to recall what he wished had happened rather than the less colourful reality. This is not one of his most convincing anecdotes. Apart from the fact that he himself was not above manipulating the details of naval discipline in the interests of polo, an officer of twenty-eight who berated his Commander-in-Chief so roundly would have been imperilling his career. Mountbatten was ready to risk his future on certain issues, but never on one as trivial as this. Indeed, in 1928 he was more than half inclined to agree with Keyes's comment that 'polo brought out all the qualities needed by officers in destroyers, submarines and now in the air. I had never met a keen, dashing polo-player who was not also a good officer.'[27]

The Fleet Wireless Officer, to whom Mountbatten acted as assistant, was Lieutenant-Commander Minter, a man of greater amiability than application. When he was passed over for promotion at the end of 1927 he wrote to his 'horribly competent R.H.M. [right hand man]' commiserating with him on backing the wrong horse.[28] From Mountbatten's point of view the horse could not have been a better one. He was left in peace to do not merely his own work but his superior's as well. 'This weekend is saving my life,' he wrote while in Cyprus. 'I had eye-ache, head-ache and generally overtired feelings when I arrived.'[29] The previous three weeks he had been up till 1 a.m. every morning, preparing a set of twelve two-hour lectures for midshipmen and junior officers.[30] He thrived on the regimen, protesting only when others

failed to appreciate his efforts. He wrote in despair to his friend Andrew Yates
just before he left for Malta:

> No one will ever believe I work.... I am quite sure that anybody who
> notices † after my name in the Navy list* either thinks that the King
> ordered it to be put there because he thought it looked pretty or that I
> bribed someone at the Admiralty to let me go to Greenwich for 6
> months, so as to have a rest cure at Brook House.... If I do come out
> to Malta and work like a beaver people won't believe it, and if I am
> seen on the polo-ground, they will say 'I told you so.'
>
> After all, Andrew, what's the good? Let the world think what it
> likes so long as I can satisfy my conscience and my immediate
> chiefs.[31]

The world had some excuse for its doubts. The Mountbattens had
installed themselves in the Casa Medina, a small but pleasant villa in
Guardamangia, where they held court in considerable style. The run-of-the-
mill naval officer rarely penetrated its gates, it being regarded by them as a
redoubt for polo-players, other smart cronies and senior officers.[32] This
aloofness was little resented; nor was there ill-feeling over the Mountbattens'
enjoyment of a sixty-six-ton yacht, fast cars and other appurtenances of rich
living; but such trimmings were not easily reconciled with the reality of a
conscientious and hard-working officer. Mountbatten came from a different
world. 'Travelling with Dickie is always full of incident,' Charles Lambe told
his mother. 'One never can tell who will suddenly discover his identity and
start to treat him as if he was second only to the Prince of Wales.'[33]

Mountbatten would have been well content to remain with the Mediterranean Fleet until he eventually succeeded as Fleet Wireless Officer. For an
ambitious signals officer, however, a stint at the signals school at Portsmouth
was an obligation. By July 1929 the Mountbattens were back at Adsdean and
Lord Louis, now a Lieutenant-Commander, was in charge of wireless instruction (W.I.). Almost without knowing it, he had taken a critically important
step in his career. He had initially been offered the chance of running the naval
experimental staff (A.I.) – a plum job of high technical interest, at which most
signals officers would have grasped. Mountbatten was nervous of commit-
ting himself to too rigorously specialist a task. When his friend Geoffrey
Burghard, who had been offered the relatively unfashionable task of chief
instructor, showed that he coveted the other post, Mountbatten proposed

* Sign indicating the officer had passed a specialist signals course.

and organized an exchange. By so doing he escaped the designation as an 'expert' which might have impeded his future progress. Twenty-five years later Burghard wrote to congratulate him on his appointment as Fourth Sea Lord. 'I suppose all this comes of exchanging A.I. for W.I. with you a long time ago,' he added wistfully.[34]

Mountbatten proved a superb teacher. Peter Dawnay, who was taken by him through the technical side of the Long Signal Course, was overwhelmed by the lucidity with which he expounded these arcane and complex subjects. 'He also made it amusing and fun, which was a great thing in a course which was a hard grind for students.' No effort was too arduous if it would help a young officer who genuinely wanted to get on. He knew the value of cultivating certain eccentricities, always prefacing his remarks when he turned to the blackboard with a sonorous, 'Watch me – Observe!'[35] He revelled in his skill. 'Great fun!' he noted after he had lectured to the Staff course at Greenwich for an hour, and answered questions for a further hour and a quarter. 'It went (apparently) very well and I was told by several people it had been the best lecture they had heard.'[36] The captain of the signals school considered him a lecturer of exceptional ability: 'Full of ideas, most of which are excellent. . . . He has a great future in the service.'[37]

He did not merely teach the established syllabus, he reformed it. The student at that period was required to work from a variety of handbooks in which basically similar radio circuits were described diagrammatically in a confusing medley of styles. Mountbatten set up a drawing-school to produce simple standardized diagrams of every circuit, and made sure that they were incorporated, with his own explanations, in the new edition of the *Admiralty Handbook of Wireless Telegraphy*. The drawing-school was his most jealously guarded preserve; he visited it four times a day and took intense interest in all the work in progress. His standards were high: 'Well done, but . . . ,' was the almost invariable preamble to any comment. One Saturday in 1930 he broke his collarbone playing polo. The staff of the drawing-school prepared with some relief for a week or two free of his supervision. By 9 a.m. on Monday he was on the telephone from his bed giving detailed instructions for each man. At noon he rang again for a progress report.[38]

The most significant and lasting memorial to Mountbatten's time at Portsmouth was 'BR 222', a technical description of every wireless-set in use in the Royal Navy which drew together information from a plethora of disparate sources and reproduced it in a standard and relatively simple form. He felt colour-printing was essential to make clear the functions of the various circuits and ran foul of the authorities, who deemed such extravagance unjustifiable. Here the advantages of private means were manifest; Mountbatten bought a colour-printer himself and only later convinced the

Admiralty that it was both necessary and economical. Private means helped again when the Keeper of Stationery, J. F. Haynes, objected to the use of loose-leaf notebooks. Mountbatten discovered that Haynes was President of the Camping Society of Great Britain and arranged for his members to be allowed to camp beside the Test at Broadlands the following summer. The objections to the loose-leaf notebook were not renewed. (A later edition of this handbook, *The User's Guide to Wireless Equipment*, is still in use.)[39]

Mountbatten was prone to claim exclusive credit for achievements that should properly have been shared with others. His endless energy and ingenuity, his refusal to accept that anything was sacrosanct or impossible ensured, however, that his own personal contribution was astonishingly large and varied. He had only to arrive in an institution to plan its reorganization – usually to the improvement of the body concerned but by no means always to the satisfaction of the existing incumbents. It was typical of him that, within a few weeks of his arrival in the *Revenge*, he had devised a new form on which all the information about any given man could be entered. This proved so successful that the Commander-in-Chief recommended it to the Admiralty and it was eventually adopted for the whole Navy.[40] To the signals school he made one final contribution – a tie in delicate shades of grey and blue, known disrespectfully as 'Blue blood and grey matter.'[41]

Into the crowded life of an instructor he managed to fit a flying course at Hamble. 'Did four spins getting into and out of them myself,' he recorded proudly in February 1930. A fortnight later he went solo.[42] He was a brave, resourceful but not particularly skilful pilot. As he became more senior, he was to cause consternation to many professional airmen by insisting on taking over the controls of the aircraft in which he was flying and demonstrating his ancient prowess.

In August 1931 Mountbatten was back in the Mediterranean as Fleet Wireless Officer, either aboard the Fleet flagship or, when in harbour, at the Commander-in-Chief's headquarters in Malta, the Castille. He was already celebrated within the signals world; with this appointment he established himself as a leading contender for the biggest jobs the Navy had to offer. Royer Dick, who was Fleet Signals Officer and slightly senior to Mountbatten, observed with rueful admiration the maelstrom of activity which was unleashed. Although he was mildly to resent the legend which credited Mountbatten with the feat of having single-handedly transformed the Fleet's wireless communications from an antiquated and inefficient curiosity to a dazzling miracle of modern skills, he recognized his subordinate as a magnificent technician and the outstanding signals officer of his generation.[43]

Others were less charitable. Admiral Jerram, then Chatfield's secretary, felt that the new broom was altogether too keen to sweep clean and that a proliferation of paper was more the mark of Mountbatten's stewardship than any greatly increased efficiency.[44] Anything Mountbatten did was accompanied by a certain amount of flamboyant fuss, but most observers agree with Dick rather than Jerram: 'An outstanding officer of exceptional ability,' read his first report; 'outstanding' and 'invaluable' recur in all its successors.[45]

He made it his business to visit every ship in the Fleet, and tried to know personally every officer and telegraphist. For ships and individuals alike he kept a card on which accomplishments and failures were noted. These he would study as he darted from ship to ship in his private motorboat, convincing everyone he visited that he knew everything about his affairs. Peter Murphy once asked the victim of such an inspection whether he had been surprised at the extent of Mountbatten's information. 'No,' was the answer. 'We had always suspected we were his favourite ship and his detailed knowledge confirmed this. That is why we try especially hard to do well for him.'[46] His personal staff at the Castille listened in to much of the Fleet signalling, and any misdemeanour was at once denounced; as a result the discipline and accuracy of operators rose dramatically. But he did not make himself unpopular by such methods; on the contrary, the communications staff in each ship prided themselves on their accomplishments and entered vigorously into the competitions which he introduced, comprising the coding and decoding of signals over a wide range of subjects.[47] In return for their efforts Mountbatten defended them fiercely. Paymaster Lieutenant Tighe had the temerity to post some signals ratings away from the Fleet, and found himself assailed by a furious Fleet Wireless Officer. 'Leave my Telegraphists alone! They are no business of yours. Everything that goes on to do with *my* personnel is *my* business. Don't mess around with them as though they are pawns on a chessboard!'[48]

Training too improved dramatically. He opened a drawing-office modelled on the one he had started at Portsmouth, and arranged for specialist officers to give lectures at the signals training centre.[49] At weekends he would take a group of midshipmen out in his yacht for eating, bathing and a limited allowance of alcohol. From time to time he would monitor the radio transmissions from the ships in Valletta harbour so that on Monday he could startle the various telegraphists by his knowledge of their iniquities.[50]

Shortly after his return to the Mediterranean the Atlantic Fleet mutinied at Invergordon in protest against cuts in pay. There was known to be discontent in the Mediterranean Fleet too but, fortunately, this was dispersed on its summer cruise. Mountbatten was quick to check all wireless communications to ensure that no illicit messages were passed from ship to ship.

Through his telegraphists he got the impression that there might be trouble unless the various elements of the Fleet were kept apart, and on 29 September he explained his fears to Chatfield's Chief of Staff. 'Important talk with C.O.S. re situation in Med Fleet,' he noted in his diary. Subsequently he referred often to an interview he said he had had with the Commander-in-Chief himself. Chatfield asked why nobody else had had the courage to warn him about the danger of mutiny. Mountbatten replied that all the other officers were afraid to put their career at risk. 'He would not want to buy his promotion by silence. What he did care was that the C.-in-C. should know the truth.'[51] The interview may have taken place, but it is surprising that Mountbatten did not mention so memorable an encounter in his diary. Certainly Michael Hodges, his close friend and Assistant Fleet Wireless Officer at the time, did not substantiate Mountbatten's recollection of events. 'I never felt that we were close to mutiny,' he wrote. 'I never heard, nor did you tell me, of any attempted communication between what you call "mutineers".'[52]

In August 1932 the Prince of Wales and his brother Prince George visited the Mediterranean Fleet. Charles Lambe, in attendance on the royal party, was terrified at the prospect. 'I know some simple thing which I ought to have foreseen will occur to mar the smooth working of the visit,' he wrote. 'Luckily Dickie will be there, but sometimes he makes things more complex and therefore less smooth!'[53] The Prince of Wales wrote to Chatfield to suggest that 'Dickie could help you to draw up the kind of programme that I should like. . . . I know that his job on your Staff is a very important one, but I would be grateful if you could let him look out for me as Naval A.D.C.'[54] The visit almost ended in disaster when the two Princes were flown off H.M.S. *Glorious* to disappear into an unexpected wall of fog which enveloped the Fleet. 'I suppose a Commander-in-Chief has seldom been in a less enviable position in history,' remarked Chatfield.[55] Fortunately the fog cleared and all else went to plan: 'Dickie was a great help and he has extraordinary energy and fixed everything so well,' wrote Prince George appreciatively.[56]

In November of the same year Chatfield's successor as Commander-in-Chief, William Fisher, decided that every man in the Fleet must be able to hear King George V's inaugural Christmas broadcast. For this a special receiver had to be built, connected to transmitters in the *Royal Oak*. The design was that of the technically brilliant Lieutenant Robinson, but the impetus came from Mountbatten and it was he who would have been responsible if things had gone wrong. In fact all went exceedingly right, so much so that private receivers throughout Malta and Gozo could hear the King as well.[57] This was the sort of challenge which delighted Mountbatten. His success encouraged him to push on with a plan for transforming the silent film-projectors on the ships of the Fleet into sound-projectors, so that they could show the new sound-films. The cost of a new projector was £800 a ship, far beyond their resources; with Robinson's help Mountbatten devised a scheme for converting silent receivers to sound at a cost of £60 a time.[58]

Mountbatten's idea of relaxation was to turn to other work. At the weekly dances he would habitually arrive with a large party, then slip away at about ten to spend a couple of hours in his study before going to bed.[59] He was wistfully aware of the cultural interests of Charles Lambe or Peter Murphy, yet had little wish to emulate them. But, even leaving polo to one side, his life in Malta was not austerely professional. The Casa Medina had not been available for this tour but Edwina had secured a group of small houses on the other side of the same narrow lane, run them into one and produced a stylish and comfortable home. Whenever she was in Malta she filled the house with friends. Her sister's yacht, the *Lizard*, long, sleek and with a top speed of thirty-two knots, was a constant diversion. There was bathing and hectic outings in the motor-boat, travel, amateur theatricals. Cars gave much pleasure. In 1932 Mountbatten bought a new Chrysler Six which proved a great success. 'The M.G. fell to bits in 6 months and cost twice the money. What *is* the matter with English cars?'[60] But it was his work that was the centre of Mountbatten's life.

Before he left the job he organized an elaborate display to exhibit the miracles of modern communications. There were three sessions, one attended by the Commander-in-Chief and all his staff. The C.-in-C. was invited to put some question to the Admiralty (he asked about the weather) and got his reply almost instantaneously. In a session on radio discipline Mountbatten showed how it was possible to identify every ship by the nature of its call-sign. Finally there was a demonstration of a communications room during a Fleet action. A rocking platform was brought on to simulate the bridge of a destroyer, and a signalman in a sou'wester added verisimilitude to the narrative. The performance provided a crown to a highly satisfactory passage in his career, success which had been officially recognized when he was promoted to Commander at the end of 1932: 'Stupendous!' he recorded in his diary. 'Shoals of congratulatory signals.'

At the foot of the recommendation which led to this promotion Chatfield added: 'He must not be allowed to confine himself to the Wireless Dept. any longer.'[61] Fleet Wireless Officer was indeed to be Mountbatten's last specialist post. Before he took to the wider stage, however, he was sent to Paris to do an interpreter's course. It was intended as something of a holiday, a reward for good and arduous service, but Mountbatten would not have been what he was if he had treated it as such. He took a flat with French servants, read only French books and newspapers, talked only French, kept his diary in French,

even had his business letters translated into French before they were sent on
from London.[62] On 16 January 1934 he took his interpreter's examination in
London. Pausing hardly to draw breath, the following day he began a course
at the tactical school at Portsmouth. It was the final preliminary before he
took up his first independent command.

# CHAPTER 7

## *Rising Star*

'VISITED CAPTAIN (D)* and asked if I could go to his flotilla. He said "Yes, *Daring*." Marvellous!' was Mountbatten's laconic diary entry for 2 May 1933. Three days later he sneaked a look at his future command. 'Visited *Diana* and *Daring*. Lovely ships.' He had reason to be pleased. *Daring* was one of the most modern of Britain's destroyers; 1350 tons with a crew of 140 and a top speed of over thirty-eight knots. 'She is even more marvellous than I had imagined possible,' he told his mother exultantly, 'and when you see her you will realise that she is a complete small cruiser.'[1]

Mountbatten had to wait more than ten months before his new appointment was officially announced. He was, the *Daily Express* then told its readers in that staccato style that was already its trademark, 'one of the best liked of our minor royalties, tho' rarely seen by the British public'.

> 33. Lean face. Good teeth. Wavy hair.
>
> Married rich, elegant Edwina Ashley.
>
> Intelligent. Invents ingenious military gadgets. Plays a pretty game of polo, emitting peculiar naval shriek when excited but never losing his temper or emulating expletive exploits of military poloists.
>
> Smokes cigarettes: prefers a pipe.
>
> Drinks whisky: prefers lemonade.
>
> Eats his way thru banquets: prefers a chunk of bread, a slab of cheese.[2]

His flotilla commander – Captain (D) – was H. T. Baillie-Grohman, who at that time had hardly met Mountbatten. Baillie-Grohman was alarmed lest his new Captain would live so extravagantly that other officers would either feel humiliated or face pauperism. 'So I had a private word first with Lady Mountbatten [*sic*] on this point, and later with Dickie, with the result that they always lived modestly . . . for which I was grateful. They were most understanding.'[3] Reality was not quite as Captain (D) imagined. Mountbatten summoned his officers and told them that he was very rich, enjoyed

---

* The D signified command of a flotilla of destroyers.

living well and proposed to go on doing so. He did not think it fair, however, that they should be asked to pay more than their basic mess-bills, and he would bear any extra cost himself. Such a gesture could have seemed offensively patronizing; it is a tribute to the officers' tolerance and Mountbatten's patent good will that it was well received.[4]

The world of the destroyer was jealously exclusive and the officers of *Daring* had doubts about a Captain who was not merely a flamboyant social figure but also a signalman. 'We need not have worried,' one of them recorded. Mountbatten proved 'a fine seaman, of tireless energy, intense curiosity and unremitting drive. . . . In addition he was very human and approachable. . . . We were a thoroughly happy Wardroom under him and this atmosphere radiated throughout the ship, so that not only were we a happy ship but an intensely active and confident one.'[5] The new Captain had prepared for his role with habitual thoroughness. Months before he took over he had asked for a list of the ship's company with individual details of each man, and when the company mustered on the first Sunday he spoke to each man as if he had known him for years. It was a stunning *tour-de-force* and the men relished it.[6]

Mountbatten's reputation as a capable Captain with panache worthy of his destroyer's name quickly spread through the Mediterranean Fleet. He was particularly proud of executing fast and accurate sternboards – in layman's language, going backwards – up the narrow and winding Sliema creek in which *Daring* had her moorings. The first time he took the ship out under his own command the Commander-in-Chief, William Fisher, 'The Tall Agrippa' as he was known, came out in the *Daring* to watch a gunnery exercise and then insisted on remaining on the bridge while Mountbatten performed this demanding feat. All went well. 'It is a strange feeling controlling 38,000 horses at 12 knots backwards,' Mountbatten told his mother. 'It is a new form of "thrill" and although I've had some narrow squeaks, I've also had a "manoeuvre well executed" for the way I brought her in.'[7]

He was not to enjoy the delights of *Daring* for long. Of the two hundred or so destroyers in the British Navy nearly half were more than twelve years old. He had been lucky to get a modern ship as his first command; soon his luck turned when he was ordered to take *Daring* to Singapore and there exchange her for H.M.S. *Wishart* before returning to the Mediterranean. 'One of the most tragic days of my life,' he noted in his diary on 17 December 1934. 'I handed over my beloved *Daring* after 8 months in command and took over the *Wishart* . . . smaller, years older and not even so clean between decks.' She had in fact been launched in 1919 and was two hundred tons lighter and five knots slower than her predecessor. Within a few weeks, though, any regrets at these shortcomings had been forgotten. H.M.S. *Wishart*, in Mountbatten's eyes, had become the most desirable ship in the British Navy. She was called after an eighteenth-century admiral, whose anyway undramatic career had been prematurely blighted by unwise support for the losing side in politics, but Mountbatten found a nobler namesake. 'Our ship is named after the Almighty himself,' he told the company, 'to whom we pray daily: "Our father wishart in Heaven. . . ." '

The fierce competitiveness which had found relatively little scope while he had been Fleet Wireless Officer now had full rein. *Wishart* must be the best destroyer in the Fleet. He was a strict disciplinarian, driving his men to the limits and sometimes, they felt, beyond; insisting on the highest standards in every aspect of life aboard. 'I hope you will enjoy your life here,' he addressed a new recruit. 'It is a smart flotilla and *Wishart* is the smartest ship in it. I expect her to be seen to be the smartest at all times. In all activities I expect her to be first!'[8] He could have been the most disliked commander in the Fleet; instead, as he had done when Fleet Wireless Officer, he enthused his men with his own will to succeed. It was the first time that his powers of leadership had been exercised to the full. They proved instantly compelling.

H.M.S. *Wishart* did become the best destroyer in the Fleet. The traditional jousting-ground between the various ships was the annual regatta. In September 1935 *Wishart* swept the board and won the coveted title of 'Cock of the Fleet.' It was not achieved without strenuous efforts. 'Away with all whalers at 0540,' read a typical diary entry; then followed a full day's gunnery exercises, and the whalers were out again at 8 p.m. Their style was inelegant – like a drunken water-beetle, somebody described it – but notably effective. Mountbatten installed metronomes in each boat and devised a new, shorter stroke which enabled him to increase by nearly a quarter the number of strokes rowed per minute. When in sight of other ships traditional methods were used, the secret weapon being reserved for practice in seclusion. His methods demanded great physical exertion but paid off when *Wishart*'s boats won every race. The officers were driven even harder than the men. When their bottoms blistered, Mountbatten produced tins of a loathsome gooey substance which had to be boiled and slapped, still piping hot, on the affected parts. But when the groaning victims returned to the wardroom they found their Captain's guest, Noel Coward, waiting for them, with dry Martinis ready and the promise of entertainment later. For the men there were films, entertainments, sing-songs, a ship's band trained by Peter Murphy. Serving in *Wishart* might be arduous, but it was fun as well.

Months before the regatta Mountbatten had told Baillie-Grohman that *Wishart* would not only be Cock of the Fleet but would win the water-polo and the cricket competitions as well. When he received his flotilla commander's congratulations, he was mildly hurt that Baillie-Grohman failed to refer to this bold prediction. A letter from the sailor he revered above all others in the Mediterranean Fleet more than consoled him. 'You had a great victory,' wrote Andrew Cunningham, 'and it is a great personal triumph for yourself. . . . It is always very difficult to get a Chatham crew really going but when one succeeds they go all out. They are not responsive to just any sort of Blarney, they are much too intelligent.'[9] *Wishart*'s crew had been got going, and they rejoiced in it. Their newspaper, the *Wishart News*, triumphantly proclaimed:

> He trained each crew to make it best.
> On each man's shirt he pinned a crest.
> His infectious spirit did the rest.
> Our Captain!     Our Regatta!

It was not only in games that the *Wishart* excelled. She won the gunnery trophy, scoring twice as many hits as the next contender. Baillie-Grohman somewhat ungraciously commented that the rate of fire seemed slow. Mountbatten retorted that, if a rate-of-fire competition were introduced, he would abandon accuracy and win that too. Similarly, when the style of *Wishart*'s rowing was criticized, he said that his men rowed to win. If a *concours d'élégance* were introduced, they would adapt accordingly and add that cup to their collection. 'He is not the natural possessor of great tact,' commented Baillie-Grohman in his final report, generously adding, 'although well above the average in this respect.'[10]

His flamboyance caused as much disquiet as his tactlessness. To have Noel Coward to stay, to entertain Norma Shearer and the King of Spain was not what the staider officers expected. Going out to dinner, he would take off his shoes and socks, roll up his trousers and be towed on water-skis. More annoying still, he never fell in. His polo ponies, his large green motor-yacht, his high-speed jolly-boat, his grandiose cream-coloured motor-cars with silver semaphoring signalmen on the bonnet and the registration number LM – it was all amusing enough, no doubt, but was it quite the thing? Yet such idiosyncrasies were part of the complex that made the *Wishart* Cock of the Fleet: 'It was not surprising that a ship's company whose captain shed so much glamour should consider itself a cut above all others.'[11]

He never believed that anything in *Wishart* could not be improved. He invented a new torpedo-grab designed to replace the old-fashioned method of recovering torpedoes by means of a sling. It was tried out at the torpedo school but not considered to be much use at sea.[12] The 'Mountbatten Station-Keeping Equipment' had a longer run for its money, though it too had its critics. This gadget, adapted from a French original, was designed to make it easier for ships to preserve their distance when advancing in line abreast. There were those who argued that such a device was irrelevant in modern warfare, where assaults in line abreast during a set-piece battle no longer took place. In 1935, however, this was far from established doctrine. A more common ground for complaint was that, though it might be useful for an amateur destroyer commander (which many of Mountbatten's peers considered him to be), any old-school professional could judge better by eye alone.[13] Andrew Cunningham cautiously commented that there was 'definitely a lot in it, though whether it is good for mankind in general and Service mankind in particular to have too many mechanical aids I am not prepared to venture an opinion'.[14] The Station-Keeping Equipment was eventually installed in three classes of destroyer and found some champions, though it never achieved the universal acceptance that Mountbatten felt was its due.

Cunningham at that time was Rear-Admiral, Destroyers. Once, when *Wishart* was temporarily out of action, Mountbatten was invited to watch the manoeuvres from the bridge of Cunningham's ship, the *Coventry*. He never forgot the experience. 'I watched this absolute wizard handle 36 ships entirely by himself,' he wrote later. 'In spite of his rather red and watery eyes he always saw everything first. . . . It was the greatest one-man performance I have seen on the bridge of a ship.'[15] It seemed at that time as if Cunningham's skills might soon be used in battle. In the autumn of 1935 Italy invaded Abyssinia. Mountbatten's flotilla was left behind at Malta while the rest of the Fleet set off for Port Said, and Edwina was recruited by the local radio station to broadcast news-bulletins relayed from London. The Prince of Wales had passed on to Mountbatten the Foreign Office's guess that there was a fifty-fifty chance of the Italians bombing Malta. 'I shall send [Edwina] away', Mountbatten told his mother, but when the time came she flatly refused to be evacuated.[16]

At the end of the year Mountbatten was despatched to Bizerta to liaise with the French Navy and port authorities. It proved a disillusioning experience. The French were haunted by the spectre of trouble with the large Italian population and determined to avoid any signs of active co-operation with the British. Mountbatten was allowed ashore only after promising to wear 'some clothes that did not look too obviously English and to speak only French'. The French Admiral refused to allow an interpreter into the meeting, while the dockyard superintendent insisted on serving the refreshments himself and kept all his experts in the next room so that they could answer any question without knowing the identity of their interlocutor. 'What his servants and staff officers must have thought of their chief's movements can only be conjectured,' commented Mountbatten drily, 'but it is doubtful whether these tactics are more likely to have allayed than aroused suspicion.' What was more worrying was that only the vaguest outline was available of plans for harbour defences and the like, not through the demands of secrecy but because 'the French had no concrete War Plan and did not seriously contemplate ever having to put these arrangements into operation'.[17]

It was almost time to leave the Mediterranean. Early in 1936 Mountbatten visited London for the funeral of King George V and took advantage of the occasion to sound out the authorities about his future movements. He was to do a tour at the Admiralty, he was told, though in what capacity it was not yet decided. On his return to Malta he was summoned by Admiral Fisher and found Fisher's successor designate, Dudley Pound, and Admiral Backhouse from the Home Fleet also present. The object of these dignitaries was to cross-examine Commander Mountbatten on Britain's future strategy and developments in London. Luckily, as he told Edwina, because of 'my new mania for meeting interesting people', he was able to report conversations with Eden, Baldwin, Chatfield and the French Chief of Naval Staff, Durand-Viel, and to give Fisher 'some useful information'. 'Anyway, I was thoroughly in my element, laying down the law to the 3 senior Admirals, as you can imagine.'[18] It was a taste of things to come.

He left on a high tide of glory. Baillie-Grohman told him in confidence that his name had been put forward for promotion to Post-Captain, even though he was not yet in the 'zone' from which such recommendations could properly be made. 'I gather I am the only officer in this huge fleet to have been selected for this signal honour, and am quite overcome.'[19] There might well still be years to wait but phenomenally early promotion seemed certain. James Somerville, Cunningham's successor, strongly endorsed the recommendation: 'An exceptionally capable and gifted officer and an excellent leader of officers and men.'[20] Mountbatten left *Wishart* with all due ritual, rowed ashore by the officers while the men turned out and cheered. He went to Tiger Point to watch his ship leave harbour, was recognized and cheered again. 'Very sentimental moment. Really sad,' he wrote in his diary,[21] but the future held too much excitement to allow of more than a moment's mourning.

Mountbatten returned to a London ablaze with gossip about his cousin, who had succeeded his father as King Edward VIII. In the period since the royal tours the two men had grown apart. Mountbatten's closest ally among the royal princes was George, now Duke of Kent; the King found his former 'best friend' boringly wrapped up in his career and a little pompous. He complained that Mountbatten always seemed to be asking for some favour. They

were still fond of each other, however, and some time in the early 1930s
Mountbatten prepared for his cousin a list of eighteen unmarried European
princesses, ranging from the thirty-three-year-old Alexandra of Hohenlohe-
Langenburg to Princess Thyra of Mecklenburg-Schwerin, who was a mere
fifteen. When he went to England for George V's funeral he drove directly to
Fort Belvedere and went with the new King to St George's Chapel, Windsor.
'Talked with David till 3 o'clock in the morning,' he noted in his diary. 'Very
satisfactory.'[22]

It is hard to imagine the source of the satisfaction. He had already met Mrs
Simpson several times in the Mediterranean and the two had sized each other
up with cautious and qualified approval. The Prince, Mountbatten told his
mother, had been as friendly as ever: 'I have also made friends with the lady so
as to help keep the influences on him in the right direction.'[23]

> Dickie [commented the lady] belonged to a breed unfamiliar to me.
> . . . [He] bubbled with ideas on every conceivable subject – housing,
> relieving unemployment, new strategies of attack in polo, or how to
> cure the chronic maladies of the British Exchequer. The more
> baffling these problems were to the experts, the more convinced
> Dickie was that he had a fundamental contribution to make and was
> determined to make it. He bombarded the Prince with pamphlets,
> books, and clippings, all carefully annotated or underlined and all
> urgently commended to the Prince's attention.[24]

It can safely be assumed that one of the baffling problems to which he felt
able to contribute was the Prince's marriage; the nature of the contribution is
less certain. Mrs Simpson at one time felt the Mountbattens to be the nearest
approach to allies among the royal family. 'I am lying here making all sorts of
*wise* decisions,' she told Edwina at the end of November. She was determined
to leave England and 'soon the charming people, the man in the street and the
lunatics will forget me, and all will be well once more'.[25] It seems that
Mountbatten played with the idea that the British public might be persuaded
to accept at least a morganatic marriage. Through the unlikely intermediacy
of John Strachey, then a Communist supporter, he made overtures to Claud
Cockburn, editor of *The Week*, and asked whether Cockburn would agree to
publish some 'inside information of a particularly sensational character'
which might influence public opinion in the King's favour. Cockburn
accepted, not because he cared for the monarchy but because he enjoyed a
row and thought Mountbatten sounded 'a bonny fighter who ought to be
encouraged'. When the time came, however, the messenger arrived with a
disappointingly slender package. Inside all it said was: 'The situation has
developed too fast.'[26]

As late as 7 December 1936 Mountbatten was still putting himself forward as a loyal supporter of the King. 'I can't bear to be sitting here doing nothing to help you in your terrible trouble,' he wrote from Brook House.

> If you want me to help you, to do any service for you or even to feel you have a friend of Wallis's to keep you company you have only to telephone.
>    I don't want to be a nuisance but I hate to feel that there is nothing I can do to help except to bite people's heads off who have the temerity to say anything disloyal about their King – and there are practically none who do so – at any rate in my presence.[27]

There is a strong feeling of 'my monarch right or wrong' about this letter, yet the evidence suggests that his feelings were at the best ambivalent. Though he saw the King half a dozen times, he does not seem to have had any serious discussion with him between 30 September, when they travelled down from Balmoral together – 'Long and interesting talk with David' – and the lunch at Fort Belvedere on 10 December, when all four brothers assembled for the final confrontation. 'Dickie down at the Fort all day where chaos reigns,' Edwina wrote in her diary. 'Everyone completely sunk except the King who remains fairly calm and cheerful.'[28] Mountbatten was called on to provide a destroyer for his cousin's departure; 'Long talk to Bertie,' he noted that evening. In the interval he was, as he told the King, 'sitting here doing nothing', excluded from his cousin's innermost councils, half relieved and half resentful at his exclusion.

His most reliable source of information was Charles Lambe, who was now assigned to the King as A.D.C. At Buckingham Palace Lambe found that the subject was taboo – 'There was nobody to speak to except Dickie.'[29] Lambe shared Mountbatten's loyalty to the monarch, but not his affection for an old friend and cousin. He felt Edward VIII might prove a disastrous king, and unequivocally deplored his association with Mrs Simpson. He must have made Mountbatten fully aware of the impending crisis. From the U.S.A. Noel Coward appealed to Mountbatten to take some step which might check the 'degrading and horrible publicity'. Could not the King be persuaded to make some statement which would 'squash finally these idiotic rumours'? Coward recalled how he had told the first-night audience at *Cavalcade* that 'it was pretty exciting to be English'. 'I can only feel now, in the midst of all this scandal and vulgarity, that it's bloody uncomfortable to be English!'[30] Mountbatten sympathized, but he can have had little doubt that any statement by the King would exacerbate, not quash, the scandal.

His own view of the King was less rosy than might have been deduced from his protestations of devotion. He still liked to think of Edward VIII as his best friend, but had been disgusted by the King's callous abandonment of his former mistress, Freda Dudley Ward. Over the years he had begun to recognise the futility and wilfulness which made the King unfit to rule; even the celebrated charm was now in tatters. Mrs Simpson he liked and was amused by, but he had concluded that she would never sit happily on a throne. She had got off to a bad start when she had first gone to stay at Adsdean and brought with her a cold chicken from Fortnum and Mason's. Edwina, who flattered herself that her Austrian chef was among the best in Europe, was not enchanted by the gift. 'I can't understand why he wants to *marry* the woman,' was old Lady Milford Haven's comment, and her son saw no reason to dissent.

But as important as his disillusionment with Edward VIII was Mountbatten's new respect for the future King George VI. In the past he had seen the Duke of York through the eyes of the Prince of Wales – 'Dear old Bertie', honest, loyal, a little stupid. Only as the crisis deepened and the abdication became more likely did he begin to appreciate the integrity and radiant decency which were to make the unfashionable younger brother so much better a monarch than the more glamorous Prince of Wales would ever have been. Mountbatten and the Duke of York were together at Fort Belvedere as Edward VIII was preparing for his final departure. The Duke was agonized, arguing his inadequacy for his new role: 'I've never even seen a State Paper. I'm only a Naval Officer, it's the only thing I know about.' Mountbatten's reply was as characteristic as it was sincere. 'This is a very curious coincidence,' he said. 'My father once told me that, when the Duke of Clarence died, your father came to him and said almost the same things that you have said to me now, and my father answered: "George, you're wrong. There is no more fitting preparation for a King than to have been trained in the Navy." '[31]

On 11 December Mountbatten set down his thoughts on paper:

My dear Bertie,
    Heartbroken as I am at David's departure and all the terrible trouble he has brought on us all I feel I must tell you how deeply I feel for Elizabeth and you having to shoulder his responsibilities in such trying circumstances.
    Luckily both you and your children have precisely those qualities needed to pull this country through this ghastly crisis. You will have the sympathy of all except a few extremists (be they Communists or Fascists) who may use this opportunity to stir up trouble.
    On all hands in the Admiralty one hears the profound satisfac-

tion of the Navy expressed at having once more a Sailor King – as the
1st Sea Lord remarked today, the first King to have fought in a naval
battle.*[32]

Mountbatten has been accused of abandoning King Edward VIII and
switching allegiance to his brother with indecorous haste. Certainly he was
never one to hitch his wagon to a star unless he was first satisfied that it was
unlikely to sputter out into eternity. He did, however, do his best to remain
loyal to old friendships. Without consulting anyone outside the family, he
volunteered to go to Candé to act as best man at the Duke of Windsor's
wedding. He always believed that this offer was refused only because the
Duke had already invited his equerry, 'Fruity' Metcalfe, to do the job. In fact
the Duke, distressed that he was not able to have his two brothers as
supporters, announced that he was damned if he would invite anybody
connected with the royal family.[33] What happened then is hard to establish.
An extract survives from a letter written to the Duke by Mountbatten on 5
May 1937.

> You will have heard that although I succeeded in fixing a date for
> your wedding that suited Bertie, George, etc, other people stepped in
> and have produced a situation that has made all your friends very
> unhappy. I have made several attempts to get matters put right, but at
> present, I cannot even accept your kind invitation myself. I haven't
> quite given up all hope yet, though my chances don't look good. I'll
> write again when I know finally.[34]

Without knowing the background, it would be rash to attach too much
significance to this passage, but the obvious implication is that at one point
King George VI and the Duke of Kent proposed to attend their brother's
wedding but were over-persuaded by 'other people' – presumably politicians
and courtiers. An embargo was then placed on any member of the royal
family going to Candé, and Mountbatten accepted the ruling, though under
protest. The first part of this hypothesis seems implausible; though George VI
may have played with the idea it is highly unlikely that he ever committed
himself to attendance on a certain date. The second is more probable. It
would no doubt have been heroic if Mountbatten had ignored the ukase and
set off for Candé, but he was a serving officer and a naval A.D.C. to the new
King. To defy orders, so as to be present at a ceremony of which he himself
anyway overtly disapproved, would have been as much foolish as chivalrous.
What would have happened if the Duke of Windsor had accepted his offer to

* The First Sea Lord was wrong. James II fought at the battle of Lowestoft and William IV at
Cape St Vincent.

be best man and the ban on attendance had subsequently been imposed is a different matter. It was fortunate for Mountbatten that his cousin's trucu-lence spared him a painful struggle with his conscience.

Shortly after his visit to London for King George V's funeral Mountbatten wrote in high excitement to Edwina to tell her that he was to be posted to 'the best job in the Admiralty, the famous Plans Division, the *corps d'élite* of the Naval Staff'.[35] He had previously been asked to come to the Naval Air Division, he told her, but had been advised to turn it down. Ten days later the job had fallen through, no vacancy existed. He was to go to the Air Division after all. 'This would suit me even better,' he announced[36] with that infinite capacity for looking on the bright side of things that marked him in every field of endeavour.

Second thoughts were, in fact, best. For a young officer with a name to make in Whitehall, the Naval Air Division was as promising a berth as could be desired. Ever since the Smuts Committee had recommended a unified air service in 1917, the Navy had been seeking to gain control of its own planes and pilots. In 1924 an uneasy compromise recognized that the Fleet Air Arm was part of the Royal Air Force, but that the Navy should have some control of the personnel. With this the sailors had to remain content, though their dissatisfaction deepened as it became clear that in the United States and Japan ship-borne aircraft were to remain firmly under the command of the Navy. When Chatfield became First Sea Lord in 1933 he dedicated himself to securing the same treatment for his own Service. 'Of all the battles with which I was faced,' he wrote, 'there was only one which gave me real anxiety – namely, control of the Fleet Air Arm.'[37]

By the time Mountbatten arrived at the Admiralty in July 1936 battle had been rejoined. In April Sir Thomas Inskip had been asked to carry out an enquiry into the problem. Before he could report, however, Samuel Hoare took over as First Lord. Unfortunately for the Admiralty, Hoare had been Secretary of State for Air from 1922 to 1927 and, though politicians could reasonably be expected to change their principles with their departments, it sometimes took a little time. Potent allies were needed from outside. Winston Churchill, now the most significant figure outside the Government, was an obvious target for recruitment. Two months before Mountbatten joined the Air Division, Churchill had promised that he would do what he could to help.[38] He had to be kept up to the mark, however, and this became the particular responsibility of the new recruit. In March 1937 Mountbatten sent the former First Lord an eleven-page memorandum arguing that the Admiral-ty should have control of the Fleet Air Arm and should provide its entire personnel, who would be trained by the Air Force but would then join shore establishments of the Navy. The Air Force, it was handsomely conceded, should remain responsible for all anti-aircraft defence.[39] Churchill forwarded the memorandum to Inskip, who was by now launched on a second, more fundamental enquiry.

There were other strings, too, which Mountbatten was able to pull on behalf of the Admiralty. 'Took Portal and Graham to see David re F.A.A.,' read the diary for 13 October 1936 – Reggie Portal being Mountbatten's immediate superior, Assistant Director of the Air Division and brother of the future Air Marshal; Cosmo Graham the Deputy Director; David, King Edward VIII. Three days later it was: 'David telephoned re Baldwin and F.A.A.'; on 6 November: 'David rang up re F.A.A. After discussion with Admiral Nasmith [the Second Sea Lord, who chanced to be dining at Adsdean] rang up C.N.S. [Chief of Naval Staff] and finally David again. Things are moving.'

Things were moving, but it was not till July 1937 that Inskip submitted his final report. By that time Hoare in his turn had moved on, to be replaced by Duff Cooper. 'I will take the closest possible interest in the conduct of our case, and will give my evidence just as if I had remained at the Admiralty,' Hoare promised Mountbatten.[40] He was as good as his word. The Inskip recommendations kept Coastal Command under the Air Force but otherwise gave the Navy almost all it wanted. The Secretary of State for Air protested, but Hoare supported Cooper and the Admiralty won the day.[41] Mountbatten's contribution to the debate was not of crucial importance but he had still played a useful part, far more than could have been expected from an officer of his seniority. His work in the Air Division was rewarded by promotion to Captain in June 1937. 'Promoted at 37.0. Average age 42–5. Some Lt Cdrs to Cdr over 37!' he recorded exultantly.[42]

He by no means confined himself to the duties of his own department. He was a pioneer in the long struggle to induce the Navy to adopt the Typex enciphering machines, which were already in use with the R.A.F. It was largely due to his approach to the Controller, Admiral Henderson, that five of these machines were obtained from the R.A.F., but the Admiralty Signals Department resented any suggestion that they should adopt equipment championed by another Service, and dragged their feet when it came to extending the system. It was not till 1942, under pressure from the Americans, that Typex became a commonplace in the Royal Navy.[43]

Results also came slowly with another of Mountbatten's crusades: the adoption of the Oerlikon gun by the Royal Navy. Sometimes Mountbatten

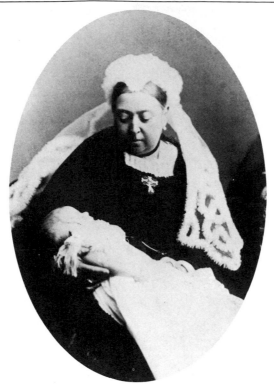

ABOVE *Queen Victoria and Mountbatten.* BELOW *Dickie's father and mother, Prince Louis and Princess Victoria of Battenberg, photographed in 1906.*

ABOVE LEFT *Dickie in his first sailor suit, with his favourite teddy-bear, Sonnenbein, on the balcony of his parents' London home, 70 Cadogan Square.* ABOVE RIGHT *A naval family: Dickie in a sailor suit and Georgie as a cadet with their father, Prince Louis, aboard HMS* Drake *at Gibraltar.* BELOW *Aboard the Russian imperial yacht* Standardt. *Dickie is seated in front of (from left to right) the Tsar, the Grand Duke of Hesse, Prince Sigismund and Prince Waldemar of Prussia.*

A Christmas card from four of Dickie's Russian cousins, Olga, Tatiana, Marie and Anastasia, and a postcard to Dickie from his Aunt Alix, the Tsarina, with a picture from the front of a similar card.

ПОЧТОВАЯ КАРТОЧКА.

Для письма.   Для адреса.

*Happy Xmas*
*dear Dick*
*fr. Olga.*

*Tatiana.*

*Marie.*

*Anastasia.*

1915.

Оберъ-офицеръ 11-го гусарскаго Изюмскаго
генерала Дорохова

ХРИСТОСЪ   ВОСКРЕСЕ!

ВСЕМІРНЫЙ ПОЧТОВЫЙ СОЮЗЪ. РОССІЯ.
UNION POSTALE UNIVERSELLE. RUSSIE.

1910.

POSTKARTE. ПОЧТОВАЯ КАРТОЧКА. CARTE POSTALE.

*Wishing Dicky dear a happy*
*Easter. So sorry you had*
*still to walk on crutches &*
*can imagine how it bores*
*you. — Cousins are well have*
*many lessons, work in the hospi-*
*tal, visit the wounded. Work in*
*the snow — cut ice with the sailors.*
*Anna plays quite well now on the cello*

Пасхальная заутреня.

LEFT *The four Battenberg children in 1910. From left to right, Alice, Louise, Georgie and Dickie.* BELOW *Mountbatten as First Lieutenant, with the air of ineffable self-confidence that impressed some and irritated others.*

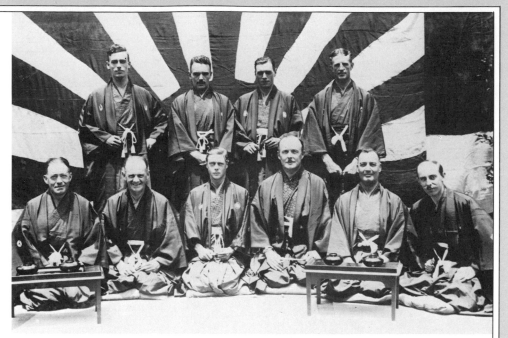

ABOVE *The Prince of Wales and his staff in Japanese dress. From left to right, standing: Mountbatten, Hon. B. Ogilvy, Sir G. Thomas, Captain 'Fruity' Metcalf; seated: Captain North, Admiral Halsey, the Prince, Surgeon-Commander Newport and Hon. P. Legh.* BELOW LEFT *Trinidad, 1920: tennis with the Prince of Wales. The Prince's energy daunted even the usually indefatigable Mountbatten.* BELOW RIGHT *Mountbatten carrying on his shoulders the Duke of York, future King George VI, during their time at Cambridge.*

*Edwina Ashley: (left) in 1919,
and (below) looking relaxed at
the time of her engagement.*

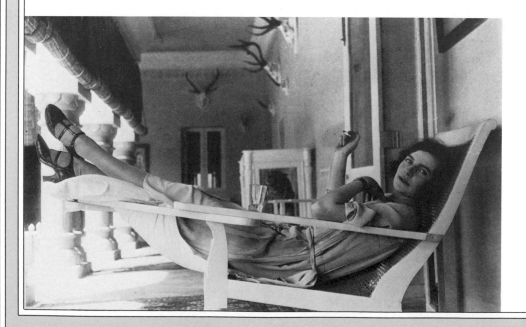

*Mountbatten arrives for his wedding with his best man, the Prince of Wales.*

*The honeymoon couple visit Cecil B. De Mille's studio in Hollywood.
Charlie Chaplin is between De Mille and Edwina.*

RIGHT *Mountbatten and Edwina with Charlie Chaplin during the filming of* Nice and Friendly, *the film they made together in 1922.* BELOW *Edwina shakes hands with the legendary Babe Ruth while the Mountbattens watch a baseball game in New York during their honeymoon.*

ABOVE *Adsdean: a large, mainly Victorian house near Portsmouth.*
BELOW *Yola Letellier, Patricia and Edwina.*

TOP *The Shrimps polo team. From left to right: Mountbatten, Charles Lambe, Teddy Heywood-Lonsdale, Tufty Courage.* ABOVE *Polo at Valetta. Mountbatten on Maltese Cat, one of his favorite ponies.*

LEFT *Douglas Fairbanks and Mountbatten with slightly apprehensive wives held aloft.* BELOW *Mary Pickford and Douglas Fairbanks on holiday at Adsdean.*

RIGHT *Peter Murphy.*
BELOW *A fancy-dress party at Malta—costumes provided by Douglas and Mary Fairbanks.*

ABOVE *On the bridge of HMS* Wishart *in 1935.* BELOW *The Mountbattens on a rooftop in Malta.*

*Mountbatten (above) at Adsdean with Prince Philip and Patricia, and (below) with Princess Elizabeth for the Coronation Review.*

LEFT *The Prince of Wales and Mrs Simpson aboard HMS* Wishart *at Cannes in 1935. To the left are Mrs Fitzgerald and Lord Sefton; to the right, Mrs Buist.* BELOW *The Mountbattens with their two daughters, Pamela and Patricia, in 1938.*

claimed credit beyond his due; in this case historians have sought to deprive him of credit which was rightly his. In particular, Captain Stephen Roskill has questioned the value of his contribution, pointing out, quite correctly, that Mountbatten played no part in the concluding stages of the negotiations.[44] This, however, was at the end of 1939. It was not till after the outbreak of war that the Director of Naval Ordnance agreed that it was 'vitally necessary to take immediate steps to secure at once the rights to manufacture Oerlikon guns . . . in England and elsewhere'.[45] Mountbatten had seen the need for such steps more than two years before.

Oerlikon was a Swiss gun with a rate of fire superior to the half-inch Vickers, and firing a shell able to penetrate the armour on a U-boat. Mountbatten was first shown a film of the Oerlikon in action in February 1937 by Antoine Gazda, a representative of the Zürich-based manufacturer who was himself partly responsible for the gun's development.[46] Mountbatten was at once impressed by its potential, but found that the Gunnery School Experimental Department was wholly wedded to Vickers. Through his friend Peter Du Cane, a senior executive of Vospers, he arranged for an Oerlikon to be installed in a motor torpedo boat which Vospers were developing for the Admiralty. Tests were highly satisfactory but, though the Admiralty took the boat, they removed the Oerlikon and replaced it by a Vickers half-inch gun.[47] Mountbatten was indignant and complained to Backhouse, the First Sea Lord. 'Many thanks too for having mentioned me to Admiral Sir Roger Backhouse,' Gazda wrote in gratitude.[48]

Mountbatten did not let the matter rest with a mere mention. On 8 July 1938 he took Gazda to see Sir Kingsley Wood, the Air Minister. Four days later Backhouse called to discuss the matter. In December Mountbatten took Gazda to the Admiralty. 'He has introduced the Oerlikon gun to Admiralty notice,' was a point mentioned with approval in Mountbatten's annual report.[49] He became famous for his championship of the weapon; G. F. Wallace, a technical officer in the Air Ministry who was at the heart of the controversy, wrote that 'the story of Mountbatten's sponsoring of the Oerlikon was known and discussed all over Whitehall'.[50] Fame, indeed, sometimes verged on notoriety. The future Lord Adeane was told by his chief, John Knox, that he had seen in the Admiralty a long memorandum extolling the virtues of the Oerlikon. On it a senior officer had written: 'It is quite obvious Captain Mountbatten has an interest in selling this gun.'[51]

Antoine Gazda wrote in triumph to Mountbatten in May 1939 to report that the Admiralty had at last ordered 500 Oerlikon guns. 'It is due to your advice and appreciation of the value of this sort of gun that my previous two-and-a-half years' work to perfect this model for the Admiralty has succeeded.'[52] That the Royal Navy would have obtained the Oerlikon gun

just as soon without Mountbatten's intervention seems unlikely but cannot be disproved; that they would have got it a great deal earlier if they had heeded his prescience is incontrovertible.[53]

A cause as precious to Mountbatten as the Oerlikon gun was the acquisition of films to show on naval ships at sea. Thanks partly to his efforts, many ships of the Royal Navy were now equipped for sound projection but the supply of films was erratic and their quality indifferent. Mountbatten determined to set up a body which would put this right. First he despatched Noel Coward to the Mediterranean and Home Fleets to establish what sort of films the men would like to see. The results were disconcerting. All his own favourites – Westerns, Douglas Fairbanks, Marlene Dietrich, naval stories – were disliked by the lower deck; what they wanted to see were films starring George Formby, Jessie Matthews, Jack Hulbert and Cicely Courtneidge and other such homespun heroes.[54] Undismayed, Mountbatten proceeded to tackle the industry. Royal patronage, lavish entertaining and a disconcertingly accurate knowledge of his subject were his weapons.

Andrew Cunningham went to a lunch given by 'young Louis Mountbatten' at Brook House in October 1938. 'He gets the Duke of Kent to preside and gets a couple of the Admiralty Board to come. After lunch, and under the influence of the distinguished company and lashings of booze, the film gentlemen just promise everything.' This particular lunch had been for Jack Warner, 'the biggest film man in America . . . (and a good chap I think)'. By the end of lunch he was ready to offer the films free of charge, but Mountbatten insisted that the Navy must pay something. 'A most amusing lunch, and incidentally a very good one: half a dozen footmen in red and blue livery; and we ate off silver plate, etc, etc – that's the way it's done.'[55]

In April 1939 Mountbatten's efforts culminated in the inauguration of the Royal Naval Film Corporation (R.N.F.C.). A grand dinner was held aboard H.M.S. *Ark Royal* at Portsmouth. The Duke of Kent had to drop out at the last moment but his speech was pre-recorded and proved a great success. More serious was the absence of most of the ship's company, since a sudden war alarm had meant they were at action stations. Mountbatten persuaded the First Lord, Lord Stanhope, to refer to this in his speech so as to avoid giving any impression that the men had no interest in the proceedings: 'This caused Fleet Street sensation and P.M. had 1st editions called in.'[56] Lord Stanhope was far from pleased, but it meant more publicity for the R.N.F.C.

The man who would have rejoiced most at the launch of the new enterprise was not there to witness it. George Milford Haven, Mountbatten's elder brother, had left the Navy some years before and made a profitable career in business. Then, in December 1937, he fell and broke his thigh. The bones took a long time to mend but there seemed no serious cause for worry

when Mountbatten left for Jamaica to captain an English team in an international polo tournament. It was at the end of January 1938 that he telephoned his sister-in-law, Nada, and heard that cancer had been diagnosed. Georgie was dying. To abandon the tour would have provoked much publicity and the doctors insisted that Georgie should not know about his condition. 'I can't get Georgie out of my mind night or day,' Mountbatten told his mother, 'and am utterly miserable and wretched to be prevented from returning at once. . . . Mama dear, I've been just like a baby. I cry myself to sleep almost every night, a thing I haven't done since Papa died.'[57]

He returned at the end of February to find his brother still alive, cheerful and uncomplaining but in intense pain. For the next six weeks Georgie clung on, often wandering in his mind but assured by all around him that he was well on the way to recovery. He died at noon on 8 April. 'The sweetest natured, most charming, most able, most brilliant, entirely lovable brother anyone ever had is lost. Heartbroken,' was Mountbatten's entry in his diary.

Georgie left £72,000, an ample fortune for the time. Mountbatten felt some responsibility for his son, David, but the new Marquess of Milford Haven was safely launched on a naval career and his place in English society was established and secure. Prince Philip, son of Mountbatten's sister Alice and Prince Andrew of Greece, posed more of a problem. Andrew was now living in the South of France, unable to return to Greece and not really belonging anywhere else, causing no trouble but not contributing much, either in ideas or fortune, to his son's future. His wife, Princess Alice, though an altogether more serious personality, was equally ill-equipped to look after the interests of her son. Her thoughts turned more naturally to matters spiritual than material, and she was in bad health. Prince Philip was left stateless, nameless and not far from penniless. George Milford Haven and his mother had taken upon themselves the duty of seeing him through school and into the Navy. When George died his brother accepted the charge.

The Duke of Edinburgh was sometimes resentful of the general assumption that he had been brought up by the Mountbattens. 'I don't think anybody thinks I had a father,' he once remarked. 'Most people think that Dickie's my father anyway.'[58] Even after George Milford Haven's death he was more likely to stay with his grandmother, now installed in a grace-and-favour establishment in Kensington Palace, than with the Mountbattens in Brook House. Nevertheless, he was often with his uncle and spent frequent weekends at Adsdean. Almost the first time he went there was with David Milford Haven. The two boys were in a rebellious mood and had just decided that it was absurd to call senior officers 'Sir'. Unfortunately, the First Sea Lord was also at Adsdean that weekend and embarrassment seemed likely until Mountbatten quelled the threatened mutiny. No offence was taken on either side; not long afterwards Mountbatten wrote to Edwina: 'Philip was here all last week doing his entrance exams for the Navy. He had his meals with us and he really is killingly funny. I like him very much.'[59]

Perhaps the most important contribution that Mountbatten made to his nephew's upbringing was to persuade him not to go into the Air Force but to stick to family tradition and join the Navy. Apart from anything else, the change probably saved Prince Philip's life: his ambition was to be a fighter pilot and he would have achieved that aim in time to fight in the Battle of Britain, with all the appalling risks that would have entailed. Instead he went to Dartmouth and was a cadet there when Mountbatten attended the King and Queen and the two princesses on a visit to the naval college in the Royal Yacht, *Victoria and Albert*. 'Philip accompanied us and dined on board,' Mountbatten noted in his diary on 22 July 1939; and then with satisfaction the following day: 'Philip came back aboard V and A for tea and was a great success with children.' It is hard to believe no thought crossed his mind that an admirable husband for the future Queen Elizabeth might be readily available.

By the time of the Dartmouth visit war was imminent. Mountbatten dreaded it yet had believed it inevitable since Hitler first revealed the scale of his ambitions. His cousin Prince Louis of Hesse was at that time serving as Cultural Attaché in the German Embassy in London.

> I agree entirely with you [wrote Mountbatten in May 1937] that we must at all costs avoid a war between any European countries as this is bound to spread.
>
> I am glad you realize that if Germany gets involved in a European war she will find herself against us and that can only end in the same result as 1918, only with far more horror for Germany, and incidentally the rest of the world this time.
>
> You and Berthold [of Baden] are the only Germans I have met in recent years who seem to realize that although our present Government may give the impression that we would never go to war with you, in fact, if Hitler pushes us beyond a certain point, no British government could survive that did not accept his challenge and fight.
>
> . . . the only way to avoid the horrors of a second world war is for the Nazis to cease their present policy, both internally and externally, which can only end in a world war. In fact peace lies solely in the hands of the Nazi leaders. . . .
>
> Thank God I'm not a German.[60]

Junior captains in the Royal Navy, if they have political opinions, are normally expected to keep them to themselves. Even if they do not, nobody is likely to pay them much attention. Mountbatten, if only because his social connections led him into a world where men of power and influence were constantly encountered, was in a different class. His closest friend on the political scene was Anthony Eden. Eden had resigned from the Government in February 1938 in protest at the proposed settlement with Mussolini over Italy's invasion of Abyssinia. Mountbatten had been on his polo tour of the West Indies at the time but as soon as he got back he warmly congratulated his friend on his action. 'I was the more gratified at this', wrote Eden many years later, 'because as you had been away I could not be sure what your opinion was, though I hoped it would be the same as mine and Bobbetty's [Lord Cranborne, later Lord Salisbury].'[61] Some months later, when Eden was staying with Cranborne in Dorset, the two men drove over to Broadlands to consult Mountbatten about a letter they were planning to send to *The Times*. 'It may seem strange that I should seek advice in that way,' Eden remarked later, 'but he and I were friends. We were of the same generation, and we were among the few who took exactly the same political view at the time in the Czech crisis.'[62]

Mountbatten remembered the meeting vividly – somewhat too vividly, in fact, since he was apt to claim that it was as a result of it that Eden resigned from the Government. As a man of German descent, he said he could see the situation more realistically than any Englishman. Unless the Government made clear the circumstances in which it would fight, Hitler would continue to believe that we posed no serious threat. Since the Chamberlain Government seemed anxious to befog rather than clarify the issue, war must be inevitable. He supplied Eden regularly with copies of Claud Cockburn's *The Week*, which took a view of the Fascist dictators even more disapproving than that held by Mountbatten. 'I wish that *The Week* were more often wrong,' wrote Eden. 'The clouds continue to gather. I can see no signs of their being dispelled and wonder anxiously when they will burst, this year, next. . . .'[63]

Duff Cooper – First Lord of the Admiralty since 1937 – was another minister in whom Mountbatten felt confidence and who, also, had long been a personal friend. Mountbatten wrote to him about the promotion prospects of a young officer and the Chief of Naval Staff saw the letter. It should have proceeded through the usual channels, 'so you will probably be getting a raspberry from him', wrote Cooper cheerfully. 'I didn't, of course, tell him that I had asked you to approach me directly on any subject you liked.'[64] As the crisis over Czechoslovakia deepened, Duff Cooper became more and more certain that the policy of appeasement would triumph again. Mountbatten was less certain. In September 1938 he had the pictures and silver from

Brook House packed up and sent down to Adsdean. The precaution proved
unnecessary. Chamberlain flew to Munich, abandoned the Czechs and
returned proclaiming he had won peace with honour. Duff Cooper resigned
on 1 October 1938 and Mountbatten applauded his courage:

> I expect it is highly irregular of me, a serving naval officer, writing to
> you on relinquishing your position as First Lord, but I cannot stand
> by and see someone whom I admire behave in exactly the way I hope
> I should have the courage to behave if I had been in his shoes, without
> saying 'Well done'. . . . Your going at this time is a cruel blow to the
> Navy; none knows this better than I, who enjoyed to a certain
> measure your confidence. A great friend of mine has just written
> from Paris: 'Until yesterday I did not think that one solitary states-
> man of the four powers who sold Czecho-Slovakia could possibly
> emerge with honour from the crisis, but yesterday your First Lord
> emerged with great honour.'[65]

By the time he wrote this letter Mountbatten had left the Admiralty himself.
His final report was particularly shrewd. 'He possesses a naive simplicity
combined with a compelling manner and dynamic energy,' wrote Cosmo
Graham. 'His interests incline mainly towards the material world and he is,
therefore, inclined to be surprised at the unexpected; he has been so successful
in that sphere that he does not contemplate failure. His social assets are
invaluable in any rank to any Service. His natural thoroughness is extended to
sport. Desirable as it is to avoid superlatives, he has nearly all the qualities and
qualifications for the highest Commands.'[66] Three months' leave were
followed by a series of short courses designed for senior officers on the brink
of high responsibilities. With monotonous regularity he excelled. 'The only
fault I can find with him is that he is inclined to be a little over-enthusiastic on
any subject about which he is particularly keen . . . ,' commented Admiral
Kennedy-Purvis – a criticism almost as inevitable as the excellence against
which it was contrasted.[67]

He served briefly on the Admiralty Board which interviewed potential
Dartmouth cadets. The experience provided him with some of his favourite
anecdotes: the boy who, when asked what he knew about Egypt, said that
there was something called 'The Spink', which he believed to be a sharp,
triangular object in the shape of a woman; the other boy who had expected to
be asked the number of the taxi he came in. 'Well, do you know it?' asked
Mountbatten, anxious to oblige. 'No.' 'Why ever not?' 'Because I didn't come
in a taxi.' Mountbatten delighted in questioning the candidates on why there

was a clutch between motor and propeller in a motor-boat but none in an aeroplane – not expecting that the candidate would know the answer but curious to see how he would set about the problem. He seems to have played his part with humanity and some imagination. A young and obviously nervous would-be cadet was asked by the chairman where he lived. 'I live at Brighton; where do you live?' was the reply. The chairman huffed and puffed and wanted to reject the candidate for blatant impudence. Mountbatten pleaded that the boy had obviously been advised by his father not to be intimidated but to treat the interview as a kind of conversation. He had his way, and the boy survived to make a naval officer.[68]

But such activities, though interesting enough, were for Mountbatten only marking time till his next real job could begin. On 22 October 1938 he went to Newcastle to take his first look at H.M.S. *Kelly*. Six days later *Kelly* was launched.

## CHAPTER 8

# *The Marriage and the Man*

FROM THE OUTBREAK OF WAR in 1939 the current of public affairs swept Mountbatten along with such irresistible force that it becomes increasingly hard to trace the development of the private man. At this point in his life, when he is poised on the threshold of great enterprises, it seems appropriate to say something of his family and domestic life; of his personality and of the factors which had shaped it.

Mountbatten was not sexually demanding, nor did he make ambitious emotional demands on others. He was sentimental rather than passionate. What he sought from matrimony was close comradeship, loyal support, affection. By nature he was monogamous; ready, indeed eager, to give total devotion; craving it in return. At first his marriage seemed to conform to all his hopes. Though their life together ranged socially from the active to the hectic, the Mountbattens were content with each other's company. When Mountbatten had influenza, Edwina would sit by his bedside reading him Agatha Christie's *The Murder on the Links* or some similar entertainment. 'Dined alone with Edwina,' read a diary-entry for December 1923, 'and read aloud, as usual, afterwards.' Most evenings they would dance; in restaurants or night-clubs, perhaps; with parties of their friends; or just by themselves at home. When they were separated, Mountbatten moped. 'I loathe dancing without Edwina,' he noted after he had made a dutiful appearance at the Commander-in-Chief's dance. A few days later he stood in for a friend on duty so as to avoid having to go to a ball given by the Governor of Gibraltar.

His devotion was redoubled at the birth of his elder daughter in February 1924. The *Revenge* was at Madeira at the time and the telegram with the news was a reason for champagne in the officers' mess, beer for the petty officers, 'too, too thrilling'. 'My dear, dear darling little mother,' he wrote to Edwina:

> I could hardly hold myself in when I got the wireless message this morning saying that our daughter had been born. For a few days past I felt convinced it would be a girl and was praying it would be as I think it's so much much nicer to have a daughter as one's first child. That I am a father I simply cannot believe, and oh! my dear, I am so

excited I can hardly wait until I come home to see her. It *is* thrilling, isn't it, my dear?

Bless you sweet – if anything could make me love you more dearly than I already do, it will be our baby. I think it's just so wonderful that I feel quite *drunk* about it.[1]

To celebrate he went gambling. He put his money on 0, his daughter's age, and won. Then he backed 13, which he thought was her birthday. 14 came up; in fact she had been born early on the morning of 14 February. Back in London, he hurried to Brook House to see the baby 'who is to be called Jean or Patricia, and fell in love with her'. She was Patricia, and he remained in love with her throughout his life. The only jarring note was struck by the Prince of Wales, who complained how hard it was to think of his friend as a father. 'You see, I'm getting quite an old bachelor now, and a more confirmed one each year, tho' I suppose I'll have to take the fatal plunge one of these days, tho' I'll put it off as long as I can 'cos it'll destroy me.'[2]

The Mountbattens had expected to have about £20,000 a year after tax but soon found that their income would be much larger. 'Edwina and I are in that heavenly state when we don't really fuss and worry about money, which is my own and which is her own, and who is paying for what,' wrote Mountbatten to his mother when he waived his share in a legacy in favour of his brother.[3] They spent their money lavishly. Brook House was maintained in the grandest style, with Mountbatten relishing every item of their conspicuous expenditure and Edwina more amused than irritated by his obsessive love of detail. His letters from abroad abound with butlers and under-butlers, footmen and grooms – 'There is also the question of giving Tucker a blue livery coat and white waistcoat . . . (this will make you laugh at me, won't it, Snoopsie?).' At considerable expense his bedroom was remodelled to resemble an officer's cabin; at the press of a switch the hum of ventilation-fans could be heard; a 'porthole' at the back led into a disused shaft which had been converted into a diorama of Valletta harbour. The scene could be viewed by day or moonlight, and the model ships would flash messages to each other. Mountbatten was so entranced by his conception that he held an open day for the press. Much publicity ensued. 'I agree that it looked like an advertisement for me,' wrote Mountbatten contritely, 'which is unfortunate as it was allowed to be done solely as an advertisement for the designer.'[4]

Adsdean was run with similar splendour. Without Edwina's humanizing hand, visitors might have found it too regimented for perfect comfort. Every evening guests were provided with a long docket on which they were required to state what they wanted to do the following morning and afternoon. Another docket listed available cars, ponies and such like. The two dockets were then married up, one set for the butler's pantry, one for the stables and one retained by Mountbatten. Almost any activity, or lack of activity, was acceptable; only irresolution caused offence.[5] House-parties were large and usually glamorous; film stars and members of the royal family, admirals and politicians mingled with the old cronies to whom the Mountbattens remained loyal. At first they were inclined to be circumspect about their entertaining. When Douglas Fairbanks and his wife Mary Pickford arrived in London, Mountbatten was anxious to repay the hospitality they had been given in Hollywood but nervous about the King's reactions. He asked his mother to sound out George V: 'I am sure – bigoted though he is with his early Victorian ideas – he cannot want us to be such super-snobs as to ignore them altogether. Anyhow, they go almost everywhere in society, as you know, when they come over here.' Lady Milford Haven considered the right answer would be a dinner at Brook House followed by a small dance. None of the royal princes should be invited but 'I am willing to dine with you that night if you think it would please the Fairbanks and look polite.'[6]

Even in 1924 such scruples seemed a little exaggerated; within a few years the Mountbattens were mixing princes and entertainers with equanimity. Noel Coward was a regular visitor at Brook House, Adsdean and in Malta. Once Edwina invited a Lieutenant Wood to a party and received a polite reply to the effect that 'he would rather not accept on a Sunday'. Coward scribbled on the back of the letter:

Lieutenant Wood is never bored
On days devoted to the Lord.
He feels himself to be at one
With God the Father, God the Son,
(And tho' he'd rather die than boast)
Also with God the Holy Ghost.

Altho' he never drinks nor smokes
And shrinks from questionable jokes,
Altho' he won't indulge in sports
And entertains no carnal thoughts,
Lieutenant Wood is *never* bored
On days devoted to the Lord.

This doggerel got Mountbatten into trouble many years later when he read it on a radio programme celebrating Noel Coward's seventieth birthday. A listener rebuked him sternly: 'Not only was it absurd that a man in your position should have been seen and heard in public making a fool of himself in a ridiculous gesture towards a rather decadent member of a not generally very highly regarded profession, but in your pathetic attempt to exalt that Bumkin, you even stooped so low as to blaspheme against the Holy Trinity.'[7]

The Bumkin sometimes gave sound advice. In 1932 Mountbatten reported from Malta that Coward was 'disgusted at the size my tummy had got to' and had put him on a diet: 'No potatoes, no bread or pastry (only Ryvita), no butter, no sugar, chocolates or sweets etc. In a fortnight it reduced my tummy girth by an inch and in a month I expect to be lovely and slim.'[8]

Though Mountbatten fretted about the size of the household bills ('Darling, please don't worry about the accounts . . . life is far too short,' wrote Edwina[9]), he rarely resisted the temptation to buy some expensive toy. His Rolls-Royces were fitted with a wealth of gadgets, and the registration number was LM 0246 – the LM either standing for Louis Mountbatten or for London Mayfair followed by his ex-directory telephone number. He introduced a new streamlined bonnet which so outraged Rolls-Royce that they withdrew their warranty; eventually the quarrel was patched up and something close to Mountbatten's design was accepted as standard. (This particular car achieved its apotheosis when it was resurrected to drive Fleur Forsyte to her wedding in the television version of *The Forsyte Saga*.[10]) His speed-boats were equally flamboyant; in 1925, driving his 450 h.p. racing motor-boat *Shadow II*, he covered eighteen miles in twenty-seven minutes and won by three seconds over Claude Graham White's *Gee Whiz*. It was the first time Mr White had been beaten in British waters.[11]

It amused him to be considered an arbiter of fashion. 'He is faultlessly groomed,' wrote *The Outfitter* approvingly. 'His mahogany-brown shoes are well worthy of comment.' With the Prince of Wales and Lord Westmorland, he pioneered a tail-coat with broad lapels breaking exceptionally high – 'This adds height to the figure and width to the chest.' But most of his innovations were designed to cut down the time needed to dress. Zips for trousers were one speciality. This might 'become one of the most important developments of men's fashions since knee breeches' wrote *London Life*.[12] Then there were ready-tied elastic shoe-laces, braces permanently stitched to the trousers, a buttonless waistcoat that pulled over the head like a jumper. He could undress, bath and dress again in two minutes, though only with the second-by-second co-operation of his valet.[13] To be incorrectly dressed caused him distress, though he did not elevate the matter into a religion. During one weekend with the Sassoons at Trent a schoolboy fellow-guest appeared for dinner in white tie and tails. Mountbatten explained that the Duke of York had specially asked for dinner-jackets to be worn. Aghast, the boy admitted he had no dinner-jacket. Mountbatten slipped away, to reappear, a little late for dinner, wearing tails.[14]

The Mountbattens lived amidst a plethora of pets. Wherever they went they would acquire miscellaneous fauna; some indigenous, others, as in the case of the anteater from Brazil, as exotic as the Mountbattens themselves. There was a chameleon called Gandhi; a lion-cub called Sabi; two kangaroos produced by Edwina from the Far East – 'Great fun and trouble putting kangaroos to bed'; a mongoose; a bushbaby called Bozo, which swung wildly around the chandeliers and eventually died from drinking a bottle of liniment; Rastas, the honey bear. Rastas was a particularly endearing character. Once during a luncheon party in Malta, Mountbatten exiled him from the house. Twenty minutes later the parquet floor of the hall began to heave and a triumphant Rastas emerged, having burrowed his way back under the front door in search of his master. The Mountbattens genuinely loved their bizarre menagerie, but enjoyed too the contribution that the animals made to their own image as dashing, adventurous, above all different.

It seemed that life could hardly hold more, yet the idyll proved more apparent than real. Once the first delights of matrimony had worn off it became evident to both of them that, though they complemented each other admirably in many, perhaps most, respects, in others they were woefully incompatible. Restless, dissatisfied, rapacious for new experience, it is unlikely that any one man could have given Edwina all she needed. Certainly her husband proved inadequate. His failure was not solely, or even primarily, physical. Edwina rebelled fiercely against the fetters of domesticity. Mountbatten's vision of an ideal marriage was of a relationship so close that every confidence was shared, no private fancies pursued. He longed to possess and to be possessed. The vision filled his wife with horror. She valued above all her independence and her privacy: independence to do what she wanted when she wanted; privacy in which to pursue her own development unobserved. She rejected Mountbatten's confidences, shunned the heart-to-heart confessions which were his delight.

The clumsiness and tactlessness that once had seemed so charming now became irritants; sharply alive to every nuance of her own sensitivity, Edwina rarely stopped to reflect that her husband might have feelings too. His affection sometimes moved her but too often it provided a new cause for irritation. A proud spirit, she was doomed to live alone in a fortress whose walls Mountbatten could never breach, whose existence, indeed, he never more than dimly suspected. Mountbatten's letters were expressed in affectionate, sometimes cloyingly sentimental terms. Edwina's responses were more brittle and less heartfelt, catalogues for the most part of weekends and dances: 'A *marvellous* new fox-trot called "In a Silver Canoe" which you'll be mad about!!! has just come out. Quite divine.'[15] Her husband's verbose and complex planning letters were briskly dismissed: 'You don't for a moment expect me to do all the things you mention in your letters . . . do you?'[16]

Increasingly they fretted each others' nerves, Edwina withdrawing ever more in angry isolation, Mountbatten baffled and reproachful. To be alone together, once a source of delight, became a peril to be avoided. Peter Murphy was enlisted as something close to a third member of the marriage: an essential emollient, good-humoured, tactful, fond of both parties, too intelligent to become involved in the ever more frequent rows. References to him in both their diaries are so frequent that it seems he almost took up residence in their houses. To the children, indeed, he appeared part of the family. Yet even Murphy could not be everywhere.

In September 1924 the couple went to New York. Minor vexations, tolerable when Mountbatten was occupied with his career, proved more painful when on holiday. Edwina became impatient. On the eve of their return to England she announced bluntly that she would not be coming. It was the first of many temporary desertions. Gossip began to spread and was embroidered busily even after her return. 'Went to see David at St James's Palace,' noted Mountbatten in his diary. 'He had a queer story about Edwina.'[17] Their lives diverged. When in England, Mountbatten more and more often stayed at Adsdean during the week, working or playing golf, tennis and polo with his naval cronies, while Edwina remained in London, reappearing at weekends with large house-parties. From Malta she would leave on adventurous expeditions around the globe, doing her bit as a naval officer's wife on her return, but rarely doing it for long. 'Lovely to see the old girl again,' Mountbatten would note wistfully, or, 'Divine having the old girl back.'[18]

Early in 1928 a divorce action was threatened in the United States in which Edwina was to be cited as co-respondent. Beaverbrook was called in to help. 'If threat is serious it is a matter of utmost importance that suit should be stopped,' he cabled the New York lawyer Paul Cravath. 'Our money resources are sufficient or if money is of no use we will offer immense social influence in support of plaintiff.'[19]

The gossip was damaging to Mountbatten's career as well as to his pride. 'A Royal Spanking For Gay Lady Mountbatten,' proclaimed the *San Francisco Chronicle* in banner headlines above a full-page story. Queen Mary was said to be displeased at her behaviour, in particular at the fact that she had danced a Charleston with Fred Astaire. In punishment the Queen had 'caused this vivacious lady's husband to be blackballed from the Royal Yacht Squadron, the very stronghold of British aristocracy'.[20] In fact, the King thought strongly that Mountbatten *should* be a member of the Squadron and was incensed at his rejection, particularly when this happened a second time.[21] It was a humiliating rebuff for Mountbatten, but his wife's adventures were only partly to blame; more important was the tactlessness of his proposer, Lord Beatty, and the feeling of certain members that the candidate was a rackety young man with a weakness for showing off in fast motor-boats.

Gossip linked Lady Louis's name with many men but in the late 1920s she became associated almost exclusively with Laddie Sandford, a rich, polo-playing American of the type for which the word 'cad' seems to have been invented. To the outside world Mountbatten appeared to observe this liaison with the same tolerant indifference as he had shown towards her other affairs; only to Edwina did he admit that Sandford had been 'the cause of pretty well all the unhappiness I have known'. Even then, he grasped touchingly at his wife's offer of renewed friendship and shared confidences: 'I offer you all my sympathetic understanding about Laddie, and will really . . . try to feel nicely about him always.'[22] For a man often accused, and with some reason, of arrogant self-confidence, his humility and readiness to admit his own inadequacies in his relationship with his wife are constantly astonishing. He wrote to her from H.M.S. *Warspite* in 1927:

> I want you to know that no action, however small, of yours, passes unnoticed by your spouse and that he is more grateful than he probably shows for the hundred and one little thoughtful acts by which you make life so very pleasant for him. The interest you take in my humble efforts at polo and the encouragement you have given me to play as often as possible . . . have made a wonderful difference in my life.
>
> If I could in any way alter my character and nature to be less selfish and more thoughtful I should be a very happy chap. I should like to be able to wait until you have gone to sleep at night, sleep without snoring, steal out of bed without waking you up, sit up late and dance late with you, knock off making plans, writing chits and discussing servants. I should love to feel I really wasn't a snob, and that I wasn't pompous. . . .
>
> I wish I could drive a car like Bobby Casa Maury, play the piano and talk Culture like Peter . . . shoot like Daddy . . . play polo like Jack. I wish I knew how to flirt with other women, and especially with my wife. I wish I had sown many more wild oats in my youth, and could excite you more than I fear I do. I wish I wasn't in the Navy and had to drag you out to Malta. I wish I had an equal share of the money so that I could give you far handsomer presents than I can really at present honestly manage. In other words – I would like to feel that I was really worthy of your love.
>
> . . . I have properly let my pen run away with my thoughts, but I

am different from you in that I must unbottle my feelings to someone, and in my case this could only be to you who are so much more than a mere wife and lover to me. You see, my sweet, you happen to be my first, principal and truest friend. That's why I love you so.[23]

Such cries from the heart would melt Edwina, and she was periodically assailed by pangs of conscience. 'I feel I've been such a beast,' she wrote after one leave during which she had conspicuously lavished more attention on Laddie Sandford than on her husband. 'You were so wonderful about everything, and I do realise how hard it all was for you, altho' I know you think I don't. I feel terribly about it all.'[24] But good resolutions soon wore off, irritants returned to the forefront. For Mountbatten one hazard was that, though Edwina demanded full independence for herself, she betrayed fierce jealousy if her husband seemed to be coming under the influence of another woman. A trial of strength would ensue in which Edwina would seek either to take over the relationship or to end it. Once Mountbatten flew to Paris to spend a weekend with a particularly favoured girl-friend only to discover that Edwina had arrived the day before and removed her to a spa in another country. He protested with unusual vigour and was sharply snubbed for his pains. 'I have never in any way tried to pinch her from you. . . . She must decide for *herself* how much she wanted to see you, and altho' I know she's very fond of you . . . she has got other people in her life, quite outside of her friendship for me, which has nothing to do with my being your wife. . . . I don't want our friendship spoiled . . . by this ridiculous attitude you have been taking up: jealousy, hurt feelings, and all over nothing.'[25]

Yola Letellier, the subject of this letter, was Mountbatten's closest female friend from the time they met in 1926 until his death. He first saw her in Deauville, enquired who she was, and was told, as he thought, that she was '*la femme de l'hôtelier*'. He was distressed at the thought that so beautiful a girl should be married to a mere hotel-keeper, but persisted in seeking an introduction. His broad-mindedness was rewarded when he found that her husband was in fact Henri Letellier, and Mayor of Deauville. Their friendship was close, yet relaxed and emotionally undemanding. Strikingly attractive, good company, an excellent dancer, she was somebody with whom Mountbatten could legitimately feel proud to be seen in public; she offered affection and uncomplicated companionship of a kind that he was often denied at home. Edwina was wise enough to make her into a friend; she once told her husband that she liked Yola very much but that he was not to marry her if ever he found himself a widower.

The birth of their second daughter, Pamela, in April 1929 eased things for a while. The birth, premature and in Barcelona, proved a difficult one and

Mountbatten became almost hysterical with anxiety. He telephoned the King of Spain and despatched more than forty telegrams within twenty-four hours, summoning gynaecologists, nurses, relatives and friends from all over Europe. Edwina suffered a haemorrhage and was afraid that the baby might be still-born. 'I was far too worried fearing for her own life,' Mountbatten told his mother. 'I was so relieved that I wouldn't have cared if it had been a baby kangaroo as long as she was all right.'[26] For a time the couple were drawn closer together. 'I think it takes sometimes a crisis like this to make one realise just how much one cares for a person,' wrote Edwina. 'I don't think there can be anything *seriously* wrong if we feel like I think we both did, during this last week.'[27] The effects soon wore off. Mountbatten, perennially optimistic, was convinced that this time they were reconciled for ever, but within a year his wife was on her travels again. In 1931 the news that she was to visit the Mexican city of Cuernavaca – at that time celebrated as a place where divorces could readily be obtained – filled the American papers with stories that this spelled the end of her marriage. 'We all turned it into a marvellous joke,' reported Edwina, 'and the following day appeared a long denial, *very sweet*, saying . . . that we were really one of the ideal couples noted for our connubial bliss!!'[28] It seems unlikely that Mountbatten fully enjoyed the joke.

Next came the British press. On 20 May 1932 'that vulgar socialist Sunday paper *The People*', as Mountbatten called it, published a story under the headline: 'Society shaken by terrible scandal,' which could only be interpreted as meaning that Lady Louis was having an affair with the negro singer Paul Robeson and that the couple had been caught red-handed. '3 months gossip to the effect that I had been exiled from England for 2 years as a result of my association with a colored man (Robeson) whom I have never even met!!!!' wrote Edwina indignantly in her diary.[29] A recent biography has suggested that she in fact knew Robeson and that he had often been a guest at parties in the Mountbatten penthouse above Brook House.[30] Even if one accepts that she lied in her private diary and that she was prepared to perjure herself, it seems inconceivable that none of the many fellow-guests who must have witnessed Robeson's presence was ready to testify to that effect in court. *The People* were reported to have spent £25,000 trying to find evidence that the pair had met on at least one occasion. They failed, and were reduced to making a grovelling apology, conceding that there was no truth in their columnist's allegations. The royal family rallied behind the injured parties: the Mountbattens lunched at Buckingham Palace the day after the hearing – the King and Queen were charming, according to Edwina's diary[31] – and the Prince of Wales gave a party for them at York House a few days later.

The scandal emphasised vividly the need for caution, but it did not heal

Mountbatten's marriage. He found much consolation in his children. To Patricia and Pamela their mother was the tinkle of a charm bracelet, a whiff of scent, a quick goodnight kiss. It was their father who sat on their beds, chatted about the day's events, taught them how to tie bows, read to them *Emil and the Detectives*, *The Phoenix and the Carpet*; the Babar books in French (as much to improve his French as theirs). In theory he was reading them to sleep, in practice he would often fall asleep himself. He invented games for them: a typical one, called 'pencil golf', involved tracing blindfold the course of a ball on a golf-course which he had previously drawn for them. He would join them for breakfast, though he could rarely stay for more than five minutes: a fried egg was neatly cut in half and then disposed of in two mouthfuls.

He never preached, and practised a morality based more on common-sense than any programme of ideals. When Patricia, aged eleven or twelve, was caught smoking in the shrubbery, he reproached her with being so stupid. If she really wanted a cigarette that badly she should have asked him. It was wrong to do it secretly or to lie about it. 'I don't believe God will strike you dead if you lie, but people won't rely on you and in the end you won't be clever enough to remember what you said before and you'll be caught out.' Similarly, when Pamela lied about stealing chocolates, it was her silliness which he complained about. Lying might sometimes be forced on one but nearly always caused more trouble in the end. 'Everyone is allowed to tell one lie in their lives. Don't waste it on chocolates.'

The girls' nanny resented this gloss put upon her more simplistic ortho-doxy, and complained to Edwina that Lord Louis was upsetting the children. Edwina's jealousy of any other woman in her husband's life extended to her children. She did not wish to dominate them, or even to play a larger role in their lives, but she resented it if her husband showed signs of filling the gap himself. In particular, she was suspicious of the close relationship that was growing between Mountbatten and his elder daughter. She took nanny's side, and for a while he was almost banished from the nursery. Time did not make the affection between father and daughter any more acceptable to her. Even when Patricia was grown-up his meetings with her had to be contrived with discretion, the two conspiring to ensure that Edwina should not suspect that a relationship existed from which she was excluded.

That his wife's infidelity, and the scant regard which she paid to his feelings, made Mountbatten deeply unhappy must be plain to anyone. That it had another effect is at least possible. The biographer is well advised to hesitate before playing amateur psychologist but it does not seem unduly venturesome to suggest that the sense of inferiority and failure which Edwina's behaviour instilled in him was in part responsible for the furious ambition with which he dedicated himself to his career in the fifteen years after his marriage began. He would show her that, even if he could not satisfy a wife, he could still impose himself upon the Royal Navy. Out of humiliation arose a new and more potent pride.

That his ambition was intense and naked could be attested by anyone who knew him. His comment when a young seaman fell overboard from H.M.S. *Warspite* and was drowned is typical of his single-mindedness. 'What an opportunity for anyone to earn an Albert Medal. Wish I'd been on deck.' Many people might have had this thought, most would have dismissed it with slight shame, few indeed would have inscribed it in their diary.[32] By 1939 any illusion that he was just a talented playboy had long vanished; the qualities which were to enable him to realize his ambitions were apparent for all to see. A procession of senior officers had paid tribute to his energy, his dedication, his flexibility of mind, his powers of leadership, his charm, his phenomenal memory, his determination. The praise sometimes contained a faint flavour of censoriousness, as if the writer found something unsporting, unEnglish, about this determination to master every detail, to come out best, but there was, too, a note of affection towards a man who was well liked by officers and worshipped by his men.

It was not all praise. His impulsiveness was often a cause for comment; Mountbatten did not merely leap before he looked but leapt before he even knew whence he was leaping. His judgement was often held in question. The vanity which was to become so powerful as his career developed to some extent possessed him already. Rank, titles, honours held extravagant significance for him; his own talents and achievements he viewed with inordinate satisfaction. (About his physical appearance he was curiously modest. Until old age he retained a belief that he could divest himself of his identity with his decorations. When a girl-friend asked him whether, as Supreme Commander in South-East Asia, he would not find it embarrassing to visit a chemist's shop in Kandy to buy her some urgently needed feminine requisites, he replied with patent sincerity that there would be no problem – 'No one will recognise me without my uniform.')

Yet he was aware of and ready to admit to his failings. For a headstrong man he was remarkably ready to listen to advice or to admit that he had acted rashly; sometimes he would make the same mistake next day, but his contrition was a sign of grace. His vanity and pride were sources of worry to him. 'I fear I have all the makings of a snob,' he told his mother, 'but am very lucky for two reasons – firstly having married a wife whose only form of snobbery is a desire to know successes on the stage, cinema, business or art. . . . Secondly, having discovered my weakness for myself I can actually see myself giving way, and so find it fairly easy to pull up, with the result that I have become far less of a snob instinctively, and really in my heart of hearts no longer set one quarter of the store I did on uniforms, functions, decorations etc.'[33] He never did pull up, but he always tried.

Apart from polo and his family there was little to divert him from his profession. His intellectual resources were limited. Beyond the books he read to his children and a rarely indulged affection for P. G. Wodehouse, he did not often venture beyond official papers. A friend once accused him of being a *Reader's Digest* man, preferring a précis, even though over-simplified, to the complex and confusing subtleties of profound debate. He went frequently to the theatre but rarely had strong opinions about what he saw. When he did his taste was erratic: Shaw's *St Joan* he hated, *The Constant Nymph* was 'a wonderful show', *The Seagull* 'V.G.'. He loved bold, noisy tunes but serious music meant little to him. *Die Walküre* was 'Lovely but four hours' – a reasonable qualification, some may think – while of *Aida*, 'To my mind it does not compare to any of Wagner's operas'. Gilbert and Sullivan he relished. Of pictures he was barely aware; the one he liked best was Wright of Derby's 'The Iron Forge,' and that because it hung at Broadlands. The cinema was his favourite art form; Fred Astaire, Rita Hayworth, later Grace Kelly and Shirley Maclaine his preferred stars; the *avant garde* was viewed with suspicion. Left alone of an evening, he would probably devote himself to genealogy. Failing that he might work on some new gadget: 'Made a Squish Squash board. Practised the Charleston' was the entry for one solitary evening; 'Designed a Valve Buzzer Circuit' was another. He was the least reflective of men.

Politics meant little to him except as the means to some particular end. Edwina was predisposed to admire all things of the Left. 'It's fascinating being here again and seeing the progress everything has made since 1929,' she wrote from Moscow at the height of the Stalinist purges. '. . . it's gone ahead by leaps and bounds . . . I gather shorter hours, higher wages, *and* lower prices (not only from what Intourist tell one!!) and the people on the whole are contented, and the young ones happy and enthusiastic.'[34] Mountbatten was more pragmatic and less gullible. He too was inclined to favour the Left, but from a generous if vague conviction that the poor and deprived ought to be given a better chance, rather than commitment to any ideology. His deep dislike of Fascism was an over-riding factor; whoever opposed it was his friend. Robert Bruce Lockhart lunched with him in October 1936 and talked of affairs in Spain. 'He is very frightened of a Fascist triangle and thinks it will be very bad for us. He would prefer a left-wing victory in Spain – even Communist.'[35]

Religious speculation was as alien to him as political philosophizing. 'Today was Easter Sunday and so all of us once more trickled off to church and all that sort of thing,' was the extent of his fervour in 1922.[36] When his daughter Pamela had a religious phase after confirmation he was mildly disquieted and urged her not to take it too seriously. But he was temperate in his lack of faith. When his sister Alice was thinking of joining a religious order he wrote to his mother that he would

> willingly see her adopt the Shinto religion if she felt that way. I do believe in the Soul and in trying to live an honest, upright life, but my only reason for clinging to the Church of England is that that is the religion I was brought up in and is probably as good as any. It is nice to have a church one can go to for the big moments of one's life, marriage, one's children's baptism, etc. . . . Otherwise I fear I bother very little about religion, except to 'think my prayers' for a few seconds every night.[37]

Religion was almost the only field in which he played a part without total commitment and enthusiasm. Into every other pursuit he hurled himself with an abandon that was always invigorating, sometimes alarming. He demanded the highest standards from himself and from everyone else. Yet his professionalism was not cold or calculating, he got enormous pleasure out of everything he did and communicated it to all around him. If people genuinely wanted to get on, to achieve success in some activity, however trivial, Mountbatten would go to endless pains to help them – at polo, at trigonometry, at amateur theatricals. He was a kind man who liked to make other people happy. If he hurt them it was by insensitivity, never malevolence, and he sought to put things right as soon as he perceived his blunder. Generous in money, still more so in time and effort, he gave much to life and did not exact more than a fair return.

OPPOSITE *On the bridge of* Kelly *during the long journey home under tow in May 1940.*

# Part Two

## 1939 - 1946

# CHAPTER 9

# Kelly I

SHORTLY AFTER HE TOOK COMMAND of H.M.S. *Daring* in 1934, Mount-batten employed some local plumbers to link up a basin in his cabin to the ship's hot-water system. Mr A. P. Cole, at that time in charge of destroyer refits in the Malta dockyard, discovered what was going on, mistakenly assumed that the ship's bottom was being tampered with, and protested to the Rear-Admiral. Mountbatten protested with equal vigour against this unwar-ranted invasion of his cabin, demanded an apology and, after a characteristic outburst of temper, turned on an equally characteristic display of charm. Cole was invited aboard for a drink and the two men became firm friends.[1]

When Mountbatten got back to London he found Cole in charge of destroyer design. At this time the finishing touches were being put to the design of the 'Tribal' class, and Mountbatten contributed several ideas to the construction of the bridge, including recessing the fore-end, the fitting of a weather-shield and a rearrangement of the instruments.[2] Cole accepted the ideas with enthusiasm and in April 1938 Mountbatten went to Thorneycrofts to attend trials of the new model. 'Wonderful ship. My bridge a great success,' he noted with satisfaction.[3] By this time the new 'Javelin' class of destroyer was far advanced. Mountbatten's bridge was adopted with only minor modifications, and he eagerly supported Cole's more important structural innovations, which were frowned on by some of the more conservative spirits in the Admiralty. 'It was a case of perfect collaboration between Naval architect and Naval officer over the whole period of design; to the advantage of both,' Cole described the relationship.[4]

H.M.S. *Kelly*, the first of a new flotilla identical in all important respects to the *Javelin*, was laid down in August 1937 at the Hawthorn Leslie yards on the Tyne. She was to carry six 4.7-inch guns and two quintuple torpedo-tubes, and her two boilers were to develop 40,000 shaft horse-power giving a speed of thirty-two knots. The low silhouette and single funnel distinguished the J and K classes from earlier destroyers, but the most revolutionary feature was the construction of the hull on a 'longitudinal system' intended to give greater strength. *Kelly* was to be leader of a new 5th Destroyer Flotilla which would eventually include the *Kingston, Kimberley, Kelvin, Kashmir, Khar-toum, Kandahar* and *Kipling*.

Mountbatten did not formally become Captain of the *Kelly* until 27 June 1939, but long before this date he was absorbed in his future command. In the autumn and winter of 1938 P. W. Burnett, First Lieutenant designate, found himself deluged by letters advising him what books and papers he should read, what courses he should attend, whom he should call on, what orders he should prepare – 'I would much like to see your complete draft in the first case.' By the following spring their correspondence was ranging over every detail of the ship's planning. 'I am afraid I have not been able to find any alternative storage for potatoes,' apologized Burnett. 'The best solution would be to move the oilskins . . . out of the Decontamination Store,' replied Mountbatten. He was concerned about the provision of a plug for his electric razor, a drying-room for towels, the colour of the ceremonial awning – 'I have every reason to think that we may be employed from time to time on special duties which would make this desirable.' Nothing was too small to engage his attention; the size of the bookshelves in his cabin was prescribed to the nearest half-inch.[5]

During the summer of 1939 Mountbatten visited the other ships in the flotilla which were now under construction, and had several of the future commanding officers to stay with him so that they could get to know each other and discuss their plans. The Mountbatten Station-Keeping Equipment was naturally to be installed in all the new destroyers, and the engineer officers, wherever possible, were despatched to the Admiralty Fuel Experimental Station to learn the best use of boilers in support of this system. The crew was completed in July and everyone who joined met the Captain within the first few hours. Mountbatten would have already mastered his dossier and left each man with the impression that he had been selected as an individual and would be judged as such.[6] The junior officers, from the day of their arrival, were made to feel that their contribution would be vital to the successful running of the ship.

Mountbatten's initial address to the crew, through its adoption word for word by Noel Coward in his film *In Which We Serve*, has entered national folk-lore. 'In my experience,' he began, 'I have always found that you cannot have an efficient ship unless you have a happy ship, and you cannot have a happy ship unless you have an efficient ship. That is the way I intend to start this commission, and that is the way I intend to go on – with a happy and an efficient ship.' It was splendid public relations, but his words also reflected a genuine concern for the welfare of his men. He expected total loyalty from them, but he offered it in return, and did his best to understand and sympathize with their weaknesses as well as to appreciate their strengths. 'I have had a difficult time with my love-sick doctor,' he told Edwina, 'who can't eat and finally came to see me in despair, having been weeping in private in his cabin ever since he was parted from his bride.' Patiently Mountbatten explained that all married men felt like this, that even after eighteen years he himself 'was just as upset but tried not to show it', that for the sake of doctor, wife and crew it was essential that he should come to terms with his misery. Perhaps surprisingly, the treatment worked.[7]

The *Kelly* was formally handed over on 23 August. By that time war was imminent. Mountbatten decided that things were moving too fast to allow for the usual tempo of commissioning the ship. 'The Captain was certainly some guy,' wrote Able-Seaman Sidney Mosses, 'he cleared the lower deck, gave us a big pep talk and explained the situation and how we were going to do in three days what would normally take three weeks. Some hope! He must be quite good, we did it.'[8] The most remarkable feature for Mosses was that officers and men alike buckled down to the task. When the time came to repaint the ship in its drab wartime colours, nobody was excused duty except the cooks. Mosses remembered seeing the Captain over the side with a group of ratings, splashing away vigorously. The ships of 5th Flotilla all used a light mauve-pink paint, the inspiration for which had come from a Union Castle liner which Mountbatten had noted was hard to pick out against the skyline. The Naval Stores Department made it up specially, and even called it 'Mountbatten pink'. The uncharitable said that the idea had originated with someone else and that, anyway, in certain lights ships so painted stood out with embarrassing clarity.

'We had just been fitted up with a Hen Coop on the foremast, a thing called RADAR,' wrote Mosses. Mountbatten had somehow contrived to procure this primitive piece of equipment from an experimental Swordfish aircraft which had been permanently grounded. The flotilla navigator, Maurice Butler-Bowdon, recorded that this proved a boon in action, the only drawback being that, as it was fixed rigidly to the mast, the ship had to be pointed towards the contact before any bearing or range could be obtained.[9]

On 3 September 1939 Mountbatten was lecturing to officers and petty officers about his Station-Keeping Equipment. A slip of paper was handed to him and he glanced at it. At this point in his lecture, he remarked, he usually said: 'Now I have given you the basic principles of operating my gear. If war should at this moment break out, you know enough about it to work it.' He paused for effect. 'Well, war has at this moment broken out.'[10] Two days earlier he had received a letter from his mother which set out sentiments he fully shared but would have hesitated to express with such magniloquence:

> The motto Papa and I chose when he got his arms as a peer, will guide
> me as I know it will guide you: 'In Honour Bound'. . . . We who come
> from an old stock of a privileged family, that has not had to worry

over material existence, has inherited that sense of duty towards our
fellow men, those especially whose nation we belong to, and who
look to us instinctively for example and guidance.

I know that you feel this too, more than ever in times like these.
Let us live or die honourably. I am proud, with the old feelings of our
ancestors, that you my son once more are called to such high service.
My love for you and my pride in you are too deep for selfish worries
or repining.[11]

Mountbatten described this as 'the finest letter any son ever had from his
mother'. To Edwina he wrote in terms less heroic: 'So the war has started with
all its horrors and destruction. In August 1914 I was thrilled, excited and
pleased – now I have a home and family to think of and I'm worried.'[12] There
was to be little time to spare for the luxury of worry in 1939, when it seemed
that the Royal Navy was bearing the burden of war almost single-handed.

The Second World War was a very different affair from its predecessor, which
Mountbatten had greeted with such excitement. No senior sailor anticipated
a great set-piece battle on the scale of Jutland. Germany possessed large and
powerful vessels but their role was to be confined to rapid sorties. The most
dangerous enemy weapons were the magnetic mine and the submarine,
together posing a threat which came close to severing Britain's supply-lines.
The war against the U-boat, Churchill declaimed, was 'hard, widespread,
bitter, a war of groping and drowning, a war of ambuscade and stratagem, a
war of science and seamanship'.[13] In this war it was the destroyer, that tough,
speedy yet alarmingly vulnerable maid-of-all-work, which played the leading
part.

The *Kelly* was in battle against the U-boat, or thought she was, within
days of the outbreak of war. '2 torpedoes from enemy submarines missed us
by 40 yards,' wrote Mountbatten in his diary on 4 September. 'Seen by 8 of
my men. . . . We attacked. . . . Burnett was sure it was a submarine and oil
came up.' To his wife he was a little more cautious. They had had a narrow
escape from being sunk by one submarine and had sunk another, he thought.
'But one can never be certain.'[14] One can still not be certain forty-five years
later, but the evidence suggests that no German submarine was within fifty
miles of the spot at the time the incident occurred. Certainly none was sunk.
Nothing was easier than for sailors, particularly those fresh to submarine
warfare, to identify imaginary hazards and credit themselves with victories
over the chimera which they had conjured up. The Admiralty was more
conservative. In March 1940 the Director of Anti-Submarine Warfare was

chased from his office by Churchill for estimating that only nineteen sub-marines had been sunk instead of the far higher total claimed publicly by the Prime Minister. The true total was fifteen.[15] The *Kelly*'s 'kill' was not even logged by the Admiralty as a probable. Mountbatten was always prone to believe the best, and not merely where the Navy was involved. 'Haven't the R.A.F. been doing magnificently?' he wrote to his daughter Patricia. 'I can assure you that the figures which the B.B.C. gave out . . . are most cautious and conservative – as indeed they should be.'[16]

When Mountbatten had hinted to his First Lieutenant that he expected *Kelly* to be used for formal purposes, he had in mind a visit which the King proposed to pay to Belgium. The war put paid to that but another royal occasion soon offered. On 12 September the *Kelly* was despatched to Cherbourg to collect the Duke and Duchess of Windsor from their exile. Randolph Churchill was assigned by his father, now First Lord of the Admiralty again, to welcome the former King. The Windsors were waiting in the Admiral Commandant's office with three dogs and a mountain of cardboard boxes. 'Dickie is a striking figure,' wrote the Duchess, 'and thus encountered on the Admiral's lawn, he personified at once the majesty and tradition of the British Navy. In his wake clattered and clanked another martial figure, Randolph Churchill, in the uniform of a lieutenant of the 4th Hussars.'[17] To the Duke Churchill's appearance was rendered less martial by the fact that his spurs were upside down. Mountbatten made a brave attempt to persuade the Duchess that the deck of his destroyer should not be defiled by the ramshackle luggage of the royal refugees, but was quickly borne down by its unyielding owner.

On the way to Cherbourg Mountbatten had called the senior officers together and warned them not to be over-impressed by the Windsors' charm. He seemed to fear, remembered Lieutenant Dunsterville, that the officers might be seduced into thinking that the wrong brother was King. He had little cause for worry; the Duchess remained discreetly below while the Duke plagued the Navigating Officer on the bridge with idiotic questions: 'Where are we, Pilot?' 'How do you know?' 'But how do you know which buoy it was?' It was with considerable relief that Mountbatten deposited his visitors with all their impedimenta on the quayside at Portsmouth and was free to go back to the war.[18]

'I wish I had a definite job like you,' the King wrote to him wistfully. 'Mine is such an awful mixture, trying to keep people cheered up in all ways, and having to find fault as well as praising them.'[19] For the first few weeks of the war the *Kelly*'s 'definite job' was vague enough, operating from Plymouth against submarines which everyone believed were there but rarely seemed to be where they were expected. At least the flotilla was beginning to take shape.

On 20 September H.M.S. *Kingston* joined *Kelly*; a month later the *Kandahar* arrived from the Clyde. Mountbatten was now in practice as well as theory 'Captain (D)5', commander of the 5th Destroyer Flotilla, the 'Fighting Fifth' as he christened it. Then, towards the end of October, the flotilla was moved to the north, reaching its base at Scapa Flow on 5 November.

Even before they reached Scapa they had been sent on a mission which promised to be tricky diplomatically as well as militarily. The *City of Flint* had been captured by the German pocket battleship *Deutschland*, a prize-crew was installed, and the cargo boat, with many British merchant seamen aboard, was on its way back to Germany, slipping down the Norwegian coast and sheltering wherever possible within territorial waters. Mountbatten was despatched to intercept her, and picked a position where shallow waters would force her to venture out into the open sea. On arrival they were met by a Norwegian gunboat which warned them to keep outside the three-mile coastal zone. Mountbatten complied, blandly calling in German to the Norwegian captain: 'Please give my compliments to my cousin, Crown Prince Olaf.'

After forty-eight hours on patrol the *Kelly* made a quick dash to Sullom Voe to refuel. On the return journey Mountbatten made what two at least of his officers felt to be an elementary and inexplicable mistake, aiming to intercept the *City of Flint* at a point which logic suggested she would have passed already. Dunsterville and another lieutenant remonstrated, but Mountbatten would not be moved, saying that he was convinced that this was where she would be found. If he had been right it would have been a brilliant feat; as he was not, the *City of Flint* was soon far ahead and safely back into Norwegian waters. Mountbatten, Dunsterville remembers, later took the two officers aside and apologized for not heeding their advice.[20]

Another setback quickly followed. Racing for home in high seas, *Kelly* turned abruptly, was hit by a great wave and heeled over fifty degrees to starboard. All the boats, davits and guard-rails on the starboard side were carried away, one stoker was washed overboard and drowned, another sailor, also swept overboard, was miraculously thrown back a few seconds later, bruised, dazed but otherwise undamaged. Cole wrote to commiserate with Mountbatten on the 'dreadful experience' which had befallen *Kelly*. 'The general opinion here is that the combination of sea and speed could quite conceivably have caused your terrific roll (which I believe is almost a record), and that very few ships would have survived it.'[21] Cole legitimately congratulated himself on the excellence of *Kelly*'s design, but the question remains whether it should have been exposed to such a test. The *Kelly* was proceeding at twenty-eight knots through a sea in which half that speed would have seemed more appropriate. Emergencies demand desperate remedies, but by

3 November it was clear that the *City of Flint* was lost. If Mountbatten had a purpose in pushing on at such reckless speed, it is not apparent. It seems more likely that, as was his wont, he was ordering full steam ahead out of sheer impatience to reach wherever he was heading to start on something else. The impulse was laudable but in the circumstances should have been curbed. He was lucky to escape as lightly as he did.

The *Kelly* limped back for repairs and the strengthening of her bottom for future forays into the Arctic. 'Where is your Lord Louis Mountbatten?' enquired Lord Haw-Haw, the Irish-American propagandist, on Berlin Radio. 'You mustn't imagine we don't know. We do. He is on the Tyne. But he will never leave it.'[22] Two days later he left it. Repairs had barely been completed when news came that a British tanker, the *Athol Templar*, had been attacked and was sinking off the mouth of the river. With another destroyer, the *Kelly* was despatched to the rescue. Mountbatten, who suspected that the tanker had been mined and not torpedoed and that any precipitate rush to the scene would lead to his destroyers suffering the same fate, questioned the order to the Flag Officer, Tyne, Rear-Admiral Maxwell. Maxwell checked with the Commander-in-Chief and was told the order stood. Mountbatten raced down the Tyne and then, more gingerly, steamed towards the burning tanker. An anchored mine grated along *Kelly*'s bottom, bumping heavily under the fore-bridge, the engine-room, the wardroom and then, when it seemed as if the ship had miraculously escaped, hitting the propellers and exploding. The stern was wrenched several feet out of line, and the *Kelly* left wallowing helplessly.[23] Worst damaged were the Captain's quarters: 'Had to dismantle all my cabin. Very sad,' noted Mountbatten in his diary.

By midnight the *Kelly* was back in dry dock again, this time for a stay of eleven weeks. It was ten days before Christmas, but most of the men had used up their free passes and spare money while the ship had been under repair over the previous weeks. Lady Louis stepped in and offered to pay the return fare for any member of the crew who wished to go home. It was a gesture which won much affection for her and for her husband. For skilful handling of men as well as real sympathy for human frailties, it would, however, be hard to better Mountbatten's treatment of the stoker who panicked when he felt the mine knock against the bottom of the boiler-room, deserted his post and fled to the deck. Mountbatten first of all rubbed in to the unfortunate man the penalty for such cowardice; then summoned the ship's company.

Out of 240 men on board this ship [he told them], 239 behaved as they ought to have and as I expected them to. . . . One did not. I had him brought before me a couple of hours ago, and he himself informed me that he knew the punishment for desertion of his post could be death. You will therefore be surprised to know that I propose to let him off with a caution, one caution to him and a second one to myself, for having failed in four months to impress my personality and doctrine on each and all of you to prevent such an incident from occurring. From now on I will try to make it clear that I expect every one of you to behave in the way that the 239 did, and to stick to their post in action to the last. I will under no circumstances whatever again tolerate the slightest suspicion of cowardice or indiscipline, and I know from now on that none of you will present me with any such problems.

I want to make it clear to all of you that I shall never give the order 'abandon ship', the only way you can leave the ship is if she sinks beneath your feet.[24]

Nobody is fearless, but Mountbatten throughout his life accepted physical risks with an equanimity, even enjoyment, which few could match. Partly this was lack of imagination; he did not have the urge or even the ability to conjure up gruesome images of what might happen if a shell struck here, a torpedo there. His temperament – equable, optimistic, extrovert – was ideally suited for hazardous enterprises. After a close shave, where other men would brood and bottle up their fears, Mountbatten, noted Peter Murphy, 'could not stop talking about each incident and would bore us all by repetition for two or three weeks. Having talked the horrors out of his system, he dismissed the incident so completely from his mind that he never mentioned it again.'[25] Nor, indeed, thought of it again. Not for Mountbatten the anguished recollections and uncertainties of the small hours. He slept soundly, woke refreshed, and met each new horror on its merits. A tranquil mind may not be the most important quality of a great warrior, but it is a pre-requisite. Mountbatten enjoyed it in abundance. It is the more to his credit that it did not blind him to the problems of others less well endowed.

At the beginning of March 1940 the *Kelly* had concluded her repairs and was at sea again. This time she stayed there a little longer but at dawn on 9 March, in a raging snowstorm, she was in collision with another British destroyer, H.M.S. *Gurkha*, and emerged with a long gash torn in her bows. The fault was *Kelly*'s; the officer of the watch could have avoided the accident if he had reacted with sufficient speed. Mountbatten treated this dereliction with striking charity, and was more irked by the fact that, through no fault of anyone, *Kelly* became a laughing-stock in the Fleet. 'The ever efficient Mountbatten', recorded Admiral Ewing, 'had given orders to his radio operators that should they ever hear an explosion they should immediately send out a signal "Have struck a mine." '[26] The signal in fact sent was, 'Have

been hit by mine or torpedo. Am uncertain which' – a message which
Mountbatten had arranged should automatically be transmitted to avoid the
possibility of the ship sinking with no hint reaching the Admiralty as to what
its fate had been. Unfortunately, Mountbatten had not allowed for the
possibility of a collision. From *Gurkha* came the cheerful response: 'That was
not mine but me.'

So it was back for another six weeks' repairs. 'I do hope you will be able to
do something great, don't you?' wrote his daughter Pamela on 30 April. 'But
in doing so I do hope your beautiful *Kelly* will not get too much damaged,
though I expect she will.'[27] By the time she wrote the letter the beautiful *Kelly*
was already on the way to Norway. She arrived there for the final stages of a
botched and ill-conceived campaign. The Germans had got there first,
established air supremacy, and repelled with dispiriting ease all efforts to
restore the situation. The *Kelly*, with a mixed force of French and British
vessels, was now despatched to embark what could be salvaged from General
Carton de Wiart's forces, which had landed in Namsos a fortnight earlier and
were still pinned down in the area of the port. 'In the course of that last endless
day,' wrote Carton de Wiart, 'I got a message from the Navy to say that they
would evacuate the whole of my force that night. I thought it was impossible,
but learned a few hours later that the Navy do not know the word.'[28]

'I took the four destroyers by echo sounds and asdics and at 0445 hurried
them into the entrance to Namsos fjord,' recorded Mountbatten.[29] A quarter
of an hour later the fog lifted – unfortunately, since it frustrated the first
attempt to bring off the Allied troops; fortunately, since rocks were
revealed directly ahead. Mountbatten took the destroyers back into another
fog-bank 'for bed and breakfast', but this in its turn lifted, leaving them
exposed to attack from the air. They found a third bank, but their masts
protruded above the shallow carpet and H.M.S. *Maori* was hit by bombs. So
it went on till evening when the destroyers and transports ventured back into
the fjord. This time they reached Namsos, to find the whole town ablaze.
*Kelly* was first in and took off 229 French *Chasseurs Alpins*, whom she ferried
to one of the transports. The whole Allied force was embarked. Then it was
back down the fjord and out to sea, under ferocious attack from the air. The
French destroyer *Bison* was hit in the magazine and exploded; H.M.S. *Afridi*
stayed to pick up survivors, was hit in her turn and eventually capsized. The
*Kelly* was constantly assailed and destroyed at least one German dive-
bomber. 'It was a tremendous undertaking to embark that whole force in a
night of three short hours, but the Navy did it and earned my undying
gratitude,' wrote Carton de Wiart.[30] 'What a party – but what luck it was no
worse,' was Mountbatten's terser comment.[31]

Less than a week later came the *Kelly*'s most celebrated exploit. A flotilla of destroyers led by Mountbatten was designated to accompany the cruiser *Birmingham* in quest of a group of German mine-layers believed to be at work off the Dutch coast. They were three miles from the *Birmingham* when an escorting aircraft reported a submarine ahead, which he had forced to dive. *Kelly*, accompanied by the *Kandahar* under Commander Robson, set off in pursuit. Mountbatten claimed to have picked up traces of the U-boat on his hydrophone; Robson was sceptical but dutifully joined the hunt. After a quarter of an hour, however, Robson grew anxious as the *Birmingham* vanished over the horizon. 'I think it is time we were going,' he signalled. 'Give it another twenty minutes,' was the response.

Twenty minutes yielded nothing, and the two destroyers, now joined by H.M.S. *Bulldog*, set off in pursuit of the main force. Robson was just congratulating himself on this uneventful ending to what he felt to be an ill-judged enterprise when to his consternation *Kelly* began to signal to *Birmingham* with a bright Aldis light. One message read: 'How are the muskets? Let battle commence.' Thus to advertise one's presence seemed to Robson the height of irresponsibility. Retribution swiftly followed. A torpedo hit *Kelly* on the starboard side under the bridge, blasting a fifty-foot hole in the side, tearing open the for'ard boiler and enveloping the ship in a cloud of smoke and steam which rose several hundred feet into the air. David Milford Haven, Mountbatten's nephew, was on the bridge of *Kandahar* when the explosion happened. '*Kelly* has gone,' he said in horror. Milford Haven wanted to stay and search for survivors, but Robson was a disciple of Warburton-Lee, whose doctrine it was that for one destroyer to stay at the scene of another's destruction would compound the original disaster. Both men took it for granted that the *Kelly* had sunk and that there could be few if any survivors.[32]

In fact *Kelly* was crippled but survived. Twenty-seven men were killed, many more injured. No power was left, and only emergency lighting. She was listing badly to starboard and in danger of foundering at any moment. *Kandahar* was by now far out of sight but the *Bulldog*, which had been lying behind, appeared out of the darkness. Within an hour of the explosion the *Kelly* was under tow; 'I consider that the handling of the *Bulldog* was a supreme display of seamanship,' wrote Mountbatten in his official report.[33] With the starboard gunwale awash and only limited hand-steering possible, *Kelly* proved cumbersome to tow but somehow limited progress was made. The night's excitements were still not over, however. At about 1 a.m. a German motor-torpedo boat emerged from nowhere, rammed the *Bulldog* at full speed, ricocheted, advanced on the *Kelly* with pom-poms blazing and clearly out of control, mounted the starboard side of the British destroyer and swept down it, carrying away boats and guard-rails. Finally she disappeared

into the darkness, ruined but with guns still firing, presumably to sink. Undismayed by this bizarre happening, *Kelly* battled on. The *Kandahar* reappeared. 'Is Captain (D) alive?' signalled Robson. 'Yes. You are not in command of the flotilla yet!' replied Mountbatten triumphantly. The *Kandahar* came alongside and took off *Kelly*'s injured and any personnel not needed to keep the ship in action.

It took ninety-one hours to tow *Kelly* back across the North Sea, and at any moment it seemed possible, if not probable, that she would sink. 'Damage control' had always been a subject to which Mountbatten paid particular attention and the training he had given his crew paid off handsomely. He set his torpedoes to safe and fired them, abandoned all the depth-charges and surplus ammunition, cut adrift the boats – in fact, shed all the top weight that could be spared. Still the ship seemed unstable, with a long, low, heavy roll which threatened to capsize her at any moment. As a last desperate measure, Mountbatten sent off all remaining members of the ship's company except six officers and twelve men. 'On returning to harbour,' he wrote with pardonable pride to his wife's cousin Lady Brecknock, 'the designer of the *Kelly*, A. P. Cole, carried out certain calculations, which showed that if I had not removed the surviving ship's company . . . the ship would undoubtedly have gone over before we got her back.'[34]

Even with two tugs, progress was slow, and the battered little convoy with its solicitous destroyers hovering around provided a tempting target for the German Dorniers, which launched frequent attacks during the hours of daylight. Two German submarines were also reported to be in the vicinity. Admiral Layton in H.M.S. *Birmingham* suggested that the risks involved in taking the shattered ship any farther were too great for the salvage value; the best course would be to scuttle *Kelly*. According to Mountbatten, his reply was brusque: 'I do not require your services any more, thank you. I will get home by myself if you will spare me a tug.'[35] It seems probable that in fact his tone was less peremptory, but the effect was the same. Layton was reluctant to order a captain to abandon a ship against his will, and the tow went on.

'After many vicissitudes we reached the Tyne in the evening,' was Mountbatten's diary entry for 13 May, 'and were towed to the accompaniment of cheers all up the river.' He dined aboard the *Kandahar* and then, 'I went as I was, no luggage, unshaven and filthy, to the Station Hotel and after 91 hours in tow a real bed was heaven.' A salvage officer who inspected the *Kelly* next day said that it would be impossible to imagine a vessel being more badly damaged and surviving. To bring her back to port had been a feat not merely of courage but of consummate seamanship.[36] It would be six months or more before the ship would be ready to sail again, and there could be no question of keeping the crew together for so long. Mountbatten mustered the

men and sadly said goodbye. 'All volunteered to remain on or come to any other ship with me.'[37]

The *Kelly* should not have been where she was when the attack took place. The purpose of the expedition had been to harass enemy mine-layers. Mountbatten allowed himself to be diverted in fruitless search of a U-boat. He then dallied too long in pursuit – 'One should never lose visual contact with one's own forces at night' was an axiom for destroyer commanders which Robson, at least, held sacred. Finally, he had compounded his errors by making conspicuous and unnecessary signals. A report prepared for the benefit of the Commander-in-Chief, Home Fleet concluded that Mountbatten had blundered into a trap.[38] Even if that attributes too much cunning to the Germans, it is evident that he contributed largely to his own undoing.

From the ensuing disaster he won glory. The return of the *Kelly* in circumstances of almost impossible difficulty was an epic of skill and heroism. In economic terms it might have been as cheap to scuttle the ship and rebuild from scratch; for the morale of the crew, of the Navy, even of the nation, the difference was inestimable. Mountbatten's feat caught the imagination of the public; it also caught the imagination of Winston Churchill. When Mountbatten was mentioned in despatches in recognition of his achievement, Churchill minuted that surely this gallant young officer was worth a D.S.O. The First Sea Lord referred the matter to the Commander-in-Chief, Home Fleet, who replied that many other destroyer captains were more worthy of the honour.[39] The Duke of Kent also intervened with no more result. 'If the King's brother cannot get his cousin the same decoration as every other Captain (D) has been given, then the powers working against me must be very strong indeed,' wrote Mountbatten bitterly. From Beaverbrook came the sinister message: 'Tell Dickie that Winston warned me that Forbes means to break him.'[40]

Forbes was the Commander-in-Chief of the Home Fleet, and he did not mean to break Mountbatten; indeed, it would be more true to say that Churchill meant to break Forbes. He did, however, think that Mountbatten's reputation was inflated and accepted Hughes Hallett's verdict that the heroism would not have been necessary but for the initial blunder. When the First Lord argued that Mountbatten's feat in bringing back the *Kelly* was sufficiently remarkable to deserve a decoration, Forbes replied 'that owing to a series of misfortunes – mine, collision, torpedo – *Kelly* had only been to sea 57 days during the war, and that any other captain would have done the same in bringing the ship home'.[41] In this he was less than fair. Mountbatten's achievement had indeed been extraordinary; but Forbes's reluctance to recommend a man for an award when the justification for it stemmed from his own misjudgement does not seem unreasonable. Certainly it did not amount

to victimization. This Mountbatten found hard to accept. 'There is never smoke without fire,' he told his wife darkly in a letter describing the resentment felt by everyone in *Kelly* at this slight to their Captain. 'Please promise me *not* to show my letter to anyone – not even . . . Lady Pound. If you like to learn up the arguments by heart and make out you got them from any of my officers direct – I cannot see there is any harm in that.'[42]

Though Mountbatten did not know it, the interest taken in his career by Winston Churchill was to prove to be worth a dozen D.S.O.s. The Prime Minister believed that this dashing and courageous young officer was being unfairly held down by stick-in-the-mud admirals who had no idea how to fight a contemporary war. That belief was to stand Mountbatten in good stead when his career took its next and decisive turn.

# CHAPTER 10

# Kelly II

EVEN WHILE H.M.S. *Kelly* was limping back to the Tyne, the Germans struck in the west. Within a few days Belgium and Holland had been overrun; a few days later the French Army was broken, its will to resist almost extinct. To Mountbatten this came as no surprise. At the end of 1939 he had written to Eden about the disastrous state of French morale. Eden replied consolingly. 'From all accounts the temper of the French people seems to be satisfactory . . .', he wrote. 'There is certainly nothing in our present information to justify the alarmist point of view expressed in the documents you enclosed.'[1] Mountbatten was unconvinced. Perhaps his first letter had been slightly too alarmist, he accepted, but he still felt that 'the strong likelihood of France not being able to hold out another Winter, if as long, should be taken very strongly into account'.

> I know you will treat this letter as very confidential [he concluded] since I suppose it is hardly my place to write to you in this strain; however, now that Leslie [Hore-Belisha] has left, you appear to be the only man of our generation in the Cabinet and I often wonder whether the older Generation will ever be brought to realise that this war is not a 1914 Edition slightly brushed up, but something so fundamentally different that it must be tackled in a completely different way unless we are to be sunk by an enemy who realises to the full the very changed conditions.[2]

It is small comfort to be proved right, if what one is predicting is disaster. As the British Army streamed back from Dunkirk and German invasion seemed not merely possible but imminent, the disaster was close to being complete.

Mountbatten's first concern was for his family. Anybody of prominence in the war against Nazi Germany had reason to fear for his dependents. A family of recent German origin like his own was bound to be doubly vulnerable. Worst of all, Edwina's Jewish blood meant that she and their daughters would be prime targets for elimination if Britain were conquered. The children at least must be put out of danger.

For Mountbatten the disruption of family life was the worst part of the war. 'I miss you very much, my darling daughter,' he wrote to Patricia, '– more than you probably realize. . . . It's funny that it requires a war to make one fully realize all that one's family and home mean to one. In peace-time one takes them so very much for granted.'[3] When she went off to boarding-school and shamefacedly admitted to feeling homesick, he wrote that, if one was fond of one's home, this was inevitable. 'I am now and always have been subject to fits of homesickness. I can hardly bear to think of Adsdean, its green fairways, flowerbeds and woods, and lovely rides.'[4] To exile his children three thousand miles across a submarine-infested ocean was a daunting prospect, but neither he nor Edwina doubted that it was essential. 'The sooner they leave the country the happier we shall both feel,' he wrote to his wife as the Battle of Britain continued overhead.[5]

Mountbatten would have preferred his wife to seek safety too, but did not delude himself that there was any prospect of persuading her to do so. The imminence of war had given Edwina the chance to harness to useful purpose the formidable energy and organizing power which she had inherited from her grandfather. Within the St John's Ambulance Brigade her talents were quickly recognized; by mid 1940 she was organizing the ambulance training centre; by autumn of the following year she had become Deputy Superintendent of the Nursing Division. She knew that her work was important and that she did it supremely well. Nothing would have induced her to abandon it. 'You will be very proud of your mother when the full story comes to be written of all that she has done and is doing every day . . . ,' wrote Mountbatten to Patricia. 'When most of the other "Society" people (the Tatlerocracy) have left London . . . she is carrying on with her nursing and St John's Ambulance work and goes down into all the bombed areas to work among the victims and is a real heroine.'[6]

His first idea was that Edwina and the children should charter a small boat, moor it at Salcombe in Devon, and escape to Madeira and thence to the United States when the Germans landed. 'I implore you not to wait too long,' he wrote on 17 June 1940.[7] Then he abandoned this somewhat hazardous venture and got the children passages in the liner *Washington*, which sailed with a cargo of evacuees on 4 July. Soon he was writing regularly to them – 'How I envy you being in New York. It is the most thrilling city in the world, isn't it?'[8] Mountbatten was much attracted by America and Americans, but he shared too the superiority which a race at war felt towards a mere observer, and realized how baffled his daughters must be by customs and manners which were strange to them. 'Don't get too snuffy about the Americans,' he wrote to Patricia, 'because it only makes one unhappy to look down too much on the land that is giving one hospitality. It is true that they are different from us, but who is to say who is the better? We like to think and hope we are, but what do you suppose they think? So I am glad that you conceal your thoughts from them.'[9]

Distance in no way diminished his concern for his children's happiness and proper upbringing. He urged Patricia to read the novels of Jeffrey Farnol and, with some qualifications, Dornford Yates: 'Mr Yates is rather "precious" and rather a snob and his English seems very much less good to me at 40 than it did at 20, and yet he writes about "our sort of people" so well (now I'm being a snob).'[10] In case the snobbery might be contagious, he arranged for her to receive the *New Statesman*: 'It is such a very sensible paper with advanced liberal views,' and beautifully written as well. Soon he was writing to enquire how she enjoyed it – 'I find they are in agreement with my views 5 times out of 6.'[11]

He was concerned above all that his daughters should be equipped to deal with a world which would be fundamentally different from anything they had known before. He wrote to Pamela to explain that, with tax at seventeen shillings in the pound and reduced dividends on which to pay taxes, they were already far poorer than before the war. But nevertheless:

> By comparison with most other people we are very lucky and who cares if one drives in a Ford or a Rolls-Royce so long as one still has a car or whether one has a couple of £30 hacks or 15 £300 polo ponies so long as one still can ride?
>
> But if the war goes on long enough . . . then the whole world will be very much poorer and we shall all have to set to and work hard to rebuild it into a better and happier place and for that reason alone I am glad that you and Patricia are keen to improve your knowledge of languages and typing and English composition, etc, because a woman can help best by being good at the secretarial and accountant side of business. There won't be room for any idle people in the post-war world . . . and so I am glad that you and Patricia are learning to become useful people when you grow up, not only so that you can earn your own living if we end up that poor – but because I know you will both want to play your part in the reconstruction of the world.
>
> By all means get all the fun out of life too – ride as much as possible, go to museums, plays and cinemas – but remember that in the years to come your chief pleasure in life will be in honest work. I have certainly found it my chief pleasure.[12]

Their own style of living was sharply diminished. Brook House was closed, the furniture and pictures stored in the country – fortunately, since a direct hit in November 1940 destroyed much of the Mountbattens' penthouse. Broadlands had been requisitioned for use as a hospital. 'We have both always felt that so large a house should be used for the public good . . . ,' Mountbatten told Patricia. 'One wing is being kept back for the family, which will be ample.'[13] After a period without a London base they rented a small house in Chester Street for seven guineas a week. It was to be some time before Mountbatten spent more than the occasional night there.

With the *Kelly* lodged back in the yards on the Tyne, Mountbatten moved south-east to Immingham, at the mouth of the Humber. Although he worked a twelve-hour day, either in his office or at sea in one of the ships of the 5th Flotilla, it was a relatively tranquil period. Almost every day he managed to break for a couple of hours, to play golf, walk or visit the new naval cinema he had set up. 'By getting away for a short while once in every day I manage to keep fresh and fit,' he told Patricia.[14] Others found his cinema outings less refreshing. For one of his captains, Trevylyan Napier, the seats were too hard, the heat fearful, 'the sound arrangements went wrong constantly, and the whole thing stopped six times for an average of at least ten minutes'.[15] The Navigating Officer, Butler-Bowdon, was dragged there willy-nilly and went to sleep after the first ten minutes. 'I realized that to watch a film was a complete relaxation for him,' he wrote wonderingly. Butler-Bowdon lived in one of a row of twelve railwaymen's cottages. Once Mountbatten dropped him off after a visit to the cinema, and slowed the car in front of the wrong door. Butler-Bowdon explained that he lived farther on. 'But Pilot, there can't be more than one house here!' exclaimed Mountbatten incredulously.[16]

But the centre of action had moved south. In October 1940 Mountbatten and his flotilla were transferred to Plymouth. His pleasure was redoubled when he heard that Admiral Tovey was to replace Forbes as C.-in-C., Home Fleet; Forbes, Mountbatten told the King, disliked him 'for talking too much and not being sufficiently humble'.[17] The next two months provided almost constant action. He had barely settled in before he was despatched in the *Javelin* at the head of seven destroyers to help the battleship *Revenge* bombard Cherbourg. The destroyers fired 801 rounds in three and three-quarter minutes and then screened the *Revenge* for a further quarter of an hour. Not until *Revenge*'s last salvo had been fired did the Germans realize that it was not an air-raid and stop firing upwards.[18]

A few days later Mountbatten, searching for enemy destroyers off Brest, found himself assailed not merely by E-boats and Dorniers but by two British Blenheim bombers. One of the bombers subsequently crashed; the contrite pilot of the second met Mountbatten the following day and pleaded inadequate briefing. Mountbatten passed the story to the King, but asked him to keep it to himself; one day, when the time came for the Navy to renew its claims on Coastal Command, he promised that the matter would be revived.[19]

On 28 November, again in the *Javelin*, Mountbatten took his flotilla in search of some German destroyers which were said to be attacking coastal traffic. As was his wont, he was moving at full speed, and the resultant noise, coupled with the enemy's superior radar, gave the Germans ample warning of his approach. 'Closed to 1000 yards and turned to engage,' recorded Mountbatten. 'Our shots went over the German and theirs over me. After two salvoes our torpedoes were reported ready and Torps sang out "Swing to Port to Fire." At that moment 2 torpedoes hit us and our after-magazine blew up. . . . Maddening to be put out of action but lucky to escape with 50 killed [in fact 46] and bow and stern blown off.'[20] Hans Bartel, Captain of the German destroyer *Karl Galster*, recorded that they had had four minutes' warning of the attack; the British destroyers 'obviously only observed the German destroyers at a very short range of a few hundred metres and therefore were too late to alter course'.[21]

German technical superiority gave them a marked advantage but Mountbatten's conduct of the operation was much criticized. When the British flotilla burst upon the German destroyers, Mountbatten had three possibilities before him: to go straight on and engage the Germans in a gunnery duel, which would have avoided any serious risk of being torpedoed; to turn slightly to starboard, which would have enabled the British destroyers to use their torpedoes but risked quickly losing contact with the speedier German vessels; or to swing ninety degrees to port, thus turning on to a parallel course with the Germans but exposing his own ships to the maximum danger of being torpedoed as they turned. In his account of the action Anthony Pugsley, Commander of *Javelin*, 'said to Lord Louis "Straight on at 'em, I presume, sir?" To my dismay he replied: "No, no. We must turn to a parallel course at once, or they will get away from us." '[22] To Pugsley this seemed a disastrous mistake, leaving *Javelin* exposed, and throwing the guns off target so that the chance of loosing off another better-directed salvo was lost. By day the manoeuvre might have been permissible; by night, when the first few salvoes at point-blank range could be all-important, it was clearly an error. Henry King, the Captain of the *Kashmir*, felt that the turn to port 'made everything much more difficult at 0500, after a night of high-speed manoeuvres and alterations of course. The Officers and Ships' Companies were all tired as the ships of the Flotilla were on the go almost every night. Captain (D) [Mountbatten] did not go out so frequently.'[23]

The powers that be, mulling over the affair in tranquillity, concluded that Mountbatten had been at fault. The Commander-in-Chief, Plymouth criticized the adoption of 'line of bearing' rather than 'line ahead' in the assault and said searchlights should have been used; the Director of Operations (Home) concurred and considered that time had been wasted manoeuvering for position when the British destroyers should have gone straight for the enemy and engaged them with all weapons; the Director of Trade and Staff Duties commented, 'The night action organization of the flotilla does not appear to have been up to the required standard'; while the Vice Chief of Naval Staff concluded: 'It is elementary that one should open fire first at night.'[24]

It is easy, in the calm of the study, to find fault with decisions taken with only seconds for deliberation and in the full fury of action. Mountbatten himself did not accept the criticisms. In his view to have used 'line ahead' would have been cumbersome and contrary to the latest and most enlightened doctrine. To have held on, as Pugsley suggested, would have meant running past the German ships. Searchlights would in no way have helped. He had not done the wrong thing, but the right thing too late: 'In retrospect I recognise that I should have turned earlier and fired torpedoes earlier and I must take the blame.'[25] It is impossible to prove that any of his critics would have done better on the night, or that their theories were more correct. Nevertheless, an action in which a superior British force was left with its flotilla leader crippled and almost sinking while the Germans escaped with superficial damage cannot be described as creditable. The weight of naval opinion is that Mountbatten blundered.

Once again he extracted a measure of triumph from disaster. Patricia read the press reports and wrote excitedly: 'I am so pleased to see you "have got a reputation of being a brilliant and able officer". . . . Nobody could want more. . . . It was a pity it was such a lovely new ship, but I am delighted to see you paid the German destroyers back for it all.'[26] The naval correspondents pointed out that, if only the *Javelin* had not been disabled and the British flotilla left leaderless, 'the results might have been very different'.[27] More important, Churchill invited Mountbatten to Chequers, congratulated him, and 'staggered me by asking my reactions to being appointed to the Admiralty as . . .'.[28] In his diary he left the details of the office blank, but it seems that it must have been that of Vice Chief of Naval Staff, a critically important post which would have represented dramatic promotion. The suggestion, he told Patricia, was 'so flattering I can hardly believe it – but said I would prefer to remain at sea (if I had the choice) and finish off their destroyers'.[29] When Dudley Pound repeated the offer, he made the same reply: he would go where he was sent but he would feel it a sacrifice to accept.

The sacrifice was not exacted. The First Sea Lord, no doubt anyway less enthusiastic than the Prime Minister about this somewhat irregular appointment, let the matter drop. Mountbatten may have felt slight disappointment, but relief must have been predominant. 'At the present moment,' he told Patricia, 'I have undoubtedly the finest job of anyone aged 40 in the whole Navy, and everyone envies me.' To the King he described his job as a lovely one, 'either in command or second-in-command of every offensive operation planned against the German Atlantic forces'.[30] He loved his work and, however important his duties at the Admiralty might have been, he thought them well lost if he could remain on active service.

Life became still better early in December when *Kelly* put to sea again. On the first day the engineer failed to hear an order, with the result that the ship rammed the S.S. *Scorpion* and had to return to dock for repairs to her bow, but this was a fleeting if familiar setback. Communications streamed in from former members of *Kelly*'s crew anxious to rejoin: from D. S. Olden: 'I am very desirous of joining the happy ship again'; from four ratings in H.M.S. *Nigeria*: 'we feel we would be much more happy on the *Kelly* again'; from Stoker Lynn: 'The disaster which overtook the *Kelly* has in no way diminished my faith in the ship or her captain'.[31] Some of these were solicited; two men in Guy Grantham's new cruiser applied for a transfer and admitted on being asked that they had only done so on receipt of a letter from Mountbatten.[32] More of them were not. Many could not be spared from their new jobs. Out of a crew of 260, 170 had never been to sea before 'and so get seasick whenever it is rough, poor things – but they'll get over it'.[33] A month of ferociously intensive training was enough to see the *Kelly* back at Plymouth, this time as part of the Western Approaches Striking Force.

On 31 December Dunsterville burst into his Captain's cabin to report that he had just intercepted a Reuter message saying that Mountbatten had been awarded the D.S.O. 'I can't write to thank A.V. [Alexander, the First Lord of the Admiralty] – nor can you – but try and say a word of appreciation next time you see him,' Mountbatten wrote to Edwina. 'I have an awful feeling if it hadn't been for your large blue eyes, I should never have got it anyhow.'[34] Tovey's appointment had perhaps more to do with it than Edwina's blue eyes, but at least in terms of action seen and dangers survived Mountbatten deserved the honour. It made a heartening start to 1941. A fortnight later the *Kipling*, *Kashmir* and *Jersey* rejoined their leader; the 5th Flotilla was in action again.

Towards the end of March Mountbatten seized the bridge voice-pipe and informed his startled crew: 'We are now going to intercept the two battle-cruisers *Scharnhorst* and *Gneisenau* and also four cruisers of the Hipper class, with destroyer screen. . . . After breaking through the destroyer screen, we will torpedo the battle-cruisers and the cruisers, then will intercept the destroyers and hope to take one back as a prize to C.-in-C., Western

Approaches. I know I can depend on each and every one of you.' His flamboyance did not conceal the fact that, if he had intercepted the German ships, *Kelly*'s chances of survival would have been slight. The crew were unruffled. 'If he had said "*Kelly*'s got wings," and we were going to the North Pole, we'd have believed it, because everything he said, we always seemed to do it.'[35] Indications were that the battle-cruisers were heading for St Nazaire, but Mountbatten concluded that Brest was a more likely destination and set course accordingly. For this somewhat risky initiative he was rebuked by his Commander-in-Chief and told that, if the ships were in fact at St Nazaire, he would risk losing command of his flotilla. Instead, his guess proved right; the cruisers were at Brest but, fortunately for *Kelly* and her crew, were safely inside by the time the 5th Flotilla reached the vicinity.

In April 1941 the 5th Flotilla was despatched to reinforce Andrew Cunningham's desperately hard-pressed Mediterranean Fleet. The previous month the Italian fleet had been routed at the Battle of Matapan, but Rommel was now driving the British forces towards Cairo and on 6 April the German armies began their advance through Greece. They had established air super-iority over the central Mediterranean and Malta was besieged. It was there that *Kelly* arrived at the end of April, taking the berth which had until recently been occupied by the aircraft-carrier *Illustrious*. A seventy-bomber raid was in progress when the *Kelly* docked. Commander Simpson met Mountbatten with a message and was asked what the usual procedure was in such a case. He explained that anyone not required to man the guns took refuge in the rock shelters. Mountbatten clearly felt this was a poor idea and stood, looking admiringly at his ship, as a stack of bombs fell nearby. When the dust had settled he walked with Simpson to the shelter, took delivery of his message and watched his visitor retreat. On the fly-leaf of his copy of the book in which Simpson had told this anecdote Mountbatten wrote triumphantly: 'As soon as Simpson had left the shelter I returned to the *Kelly*.'[36]

Mountbatten decided that half the ship's complement should sleep in the shelters each night that *Kelly* was in port. When it came to the point, however, he could not face the possibility that the ship might be hit while he was safely ashore. He alone stayed with the *Kelly* every night. He wrote to his old friend Robert Neville to describe the situation:

> On average we have four daylight air-raids and two night raids. About sixty aircraft came over the Grand Harbour together, bombs whistle down and all of us have had many narrow shaves. . . . I won't pretend it's fun. It's altogether different when the ship is at sea and 'alive', to being a sitting target. But the morale of my chaps is really magnificent and has never showed up better. . . .

I have had the mortification of seeing two of our fighters shot down as I was watching the raid from our quarter-deck. We have lost three fighters this week, and so far as I know, the only certainties shot down are by A.A. fire, though the fighters think they got one. . . . I hope to God something gets done about this soon. It ought to be a cracking good show in the air here with our best chaps instead of our worst and most inexperienced. The Hun sent their famous Yellow Maize Squadron here, realising what a focal point this is, and they just butcher our young fighter pilots.

The best man out here is the new Lieutenant Governor, Sir Edward Jackson. The people like Bobbie – he is a religious maniac and prays aloud after dinner, invoking the aid of God in destroying our enemies. This is highly approved of by the Maltese, who have the same idea about God, but I would prefer an efficient Air Force here.[37]

The inadequacy of the air support, explicable enough given the strain to which the Air Force was being subjected in Africa, Greece and at home, seemed unforgivable to the battered victims in Malta. Mountbatten wrote to protest to the Vice Chief of Naval Staff, Vice-Admiral Phillips. German superiority was such that the enemy could lay mines at the mouth of the Grand Harbour whenever they chose to do so. The only mine-sweeper had been sunk, so the destroyers were constantly being denied entrance to their port or, worse still, bottled up there as the air-raids raged above them. 'Candidly, I hated this, and but for your having impressed me with the vital need to stay at Malta as long as it was tenable, I should have begged to be sent to Alexandria until the new sweeper arrived.'[38] Cunningham at least was sympathetic. He told Mountbatten that three weeks at Malta was as much as any sailor could put up with and that the Kelly would be relieved after that for a short break at Alexandria, 'though I warn you there is no rest for destroyers in the Mediterranean'.[39]

On one occasion when they had extricated themselves from Valletta they were sent to bombard Benghazi, which was being used by the Germans to supply Rommel's army. They inflicted much damage but did not fully satisfy Cunningham. 'I was a little disappointed with the 5th Flotilla,' he told Dudley Pound. 'They were dive-bombed by moonlight and legged to the Northward. If they had gone South in accordance with their orders I think they would have picked up 4 ships which arrived at Benghazi next day.'[40] Retribution arrived quickly. The Kelly did indeed leave Malta after three weeks but the short break at Alexandria was not to be part of their programme. On 20 May the Germans began an all-out assault on the island of Crete, which the British had hoped to retain after the fall of Greece. The initial attack was by air, but they would have to reinforce by sea. The primary task of the Navy was to stop any such landing, the second to lend the Army a hand by bombarding suitable targets ashore. Mountbatten viewed the prospect with some distaste. 'I realized that if we were to be used as a "striking force",' he told Patricia, 'we stood a good chance of being sunk in the process,'[41] so he packed a suitcase with essential uniforms and deposited it at Malta, to ensure that he would have something to wear if he survived without his ship.

To Admiral Cunningham fell the miserable task of sending his Fleet to Crete, though aware that air cover would be minimal or non-existent. He knew that he would be consigning a large part of the force to destruction. Afterwards Mountbatten asked him what his feelings had been. 'I felt', Cunningham replied, 'like going out in a destroyer into the thickest of the bombing and getting killed.'[42] For the 5th Flotilla the already monstrous problems were then compounded. Early on 23 May Cunningham was told that the cruisers *Gloucester* and *Fiji* had been sunk and that the battleships were empty of short-range ammunition. He felt that he had no option but to recall them. Too late a corrected version of the deciphered signal was produced. The word was not 'empty' but 'plenty'. Cunningham believed that if he had known the truth and kept the battleships in action, the destroyers might have been saved. The subsequent end of the *Prince of Wales* and the *Repulse* suggests that he was over-sanguine, but certainly the decision to withdraw the big ships made more certain the fate of the 5th Flotilla.[43]

At 4 a.m. on 23 May, *Kelly* and *Kashmir* were asked by General Freyberg to bombard the German-held airfield at Maleme. The operation was a success. Butler-Bowdon later asked an army officer who had been on the scene whether they had contrived to hit the airfield but not the British troops. 'Have no worries,' was the reply, 'we cheered like hell when we saw the gun flashes from seaward and then when the shells landed right on target and none landed in our own lines.'[44] The bombardment made possible the recapture of the airfield, fleeting though this victory proved. Two caiques crammed with German troops were also sunk by the *Kelly*. The sacrifice, therefore, was not in vain; but that it was to prove a sacrifice Mountbatten, for one, felt certain.

By first light *Kelly* and *Kashmir* were retreating helter-skelter. Within ten minutes high-level bombing had begun. At 8 a.m. twenty-four Junkers dive-bombers came into sight. 'Christ, look at that lot,' exclaimed Mountbatten as the first wave prepared to dive. He remained completely calm as they came down in waves of six, three on *Kelly*, three on *Kashmir*. 'Things happened very fast,' remembered Sidney Mosses, 'the ship twisting and turning, the noise of the guns, the smoke, turning hard to starboard when I saw that the ship's side was folded up like a sardine tin, right up to the pom-pom, over and over she went, thought this is it, and over we went still going at full speed, remember seeing the funnel go into the sea.' *Kashmir* was hit first and disappeared in two minutes, *Kelly* was hit shortly afterwards at the foremost end of the after-superstructure. Within thirty seconds she had turned turtle to port, the propeller still swinging round in the air. She capsized with all guns firing and everyone at their action stations.[45]

The last view anyone had of Mountbatten before the *Kelly* went down was standing on the bridge, clinging on to his beloved Station-Keeping Gear in case he was swept away before he judged the time ripe for him and the ship to part.

> I felt I ought to be the last to leave the ship [he told Patricia], and I left it a bit late because the bridge turned over on top of me and I was trapped in the boiling, seething cauldron underneath. I luckily had my tin hat on, which helped to make me heavy enough to push my way down past the bridge screen, but it was unpleasant having to force oneself deeper under water to get clear. Then I started swallowing water. I knew I'd be finished if I couldn't stop this so I put my left hand over my mouth and nose and held them shut. Then I thought my lungs would burst. Finally I began to see daylight and suddenly shot out of the water like a cork released.[46]

Almost the first thing he did was to jettison his tin hat, an action he regretted when the Germans machine-gunned the survivors. Then he and the First Lieutenant, Lord Hugh Beresford, began to rescue the men on the surface who were either weak swimmers or too badly hurt to fend for themselves. They dragged them to the nearest raft or Carley float, deposited them in comparative safety and then swam off to look for others in the oily waters around the wreck. From the float Mountbatten called for three cheers as the *Kelly* finally went down, then led what was left of his crew in a bedraggled rendering of 'Roll Out The Barrel!'

With the German Air Force rampant overhead and German-occupied Crete the only land within reach, it seemed that Mountbatten's war must end in a prisoner-of-war camp or Davy Jones's locker. Then H.M.S. *Kipling*, another member of the 5th Flotilla who had dropped out of the action earlier with defective steering and was now hurrying to rejoin her fellows, appeared over the horizon. With gallantry and consummate seamanship her Captain, St Clair-Ford, succeeded in picking up the survivors of *Kashmir* and *Kelly* and evading the German bombers.

Exhausted, bruised, half-blinded by oil, overwhelmed by sadness at the loss of his ship and so many of his men, Mountbatten kept going, first directing the overall rescue operation in his role as Captain (D), then looking after his injured while St Clair-Ford resumed command and took the *Kipling* safely to Alexandria. Lawlor, *Kelly*'s coxswain, had been badly burned and the doctors predicted that there was not much hope that he would survive. 'I can remember while the doctor was giving me a blood transfusion, Lord Louis said to me: "Now, Lawlor, I want you to liven yourself up, and remember your honeymoon when you get home. And above all, you've got to avenge those burns sometime." Then he went round talking to the other wounded, though he was hit himself. . . . In three months I may be fit to go to sea again,' Lawlor said fifteen months after the sinking, 'and I feel if I go back to sea, he is the man I'd want to go with.'[47]

The *Kipling* arrived in Alexandria twenty-four hours later. Mountbatten was ashore in the first boat, to be met by 'the cheery grinning face of our nephew Philip who had come to meet me. He roared with laughter on seeing me and when I asked him what was up he said, "You have no idea how funny you look. You look like a nigger minstrel!" I had forgotten how completely smothered we all were in oil fuel.'[48] Prince Philip's must have been one of the few cheerful faces in Alexandria that day. Mountbatten cabled his wife: 'Once again all right but this time heartbroken.'[49] Three cruisers and five other destroyers had been lost in the Battle of Crete. Not all the gallantry could conceal the fact that British armed forces had suffered yet another defeat. Even Mountbatten's prescience in leaving a suitcase full of clothes in Malta was not rewarded; the R.A.F. had absent-mindedly flown it back to England.

He spent the next few days staying with the Commander-in-Chief. Andrew Cunningham was 'kindness itself', Mountbatten later remembered. 'I had lost more than half my officers and ship's company and was naturally feeling very sad. Cunningham made me feel that their loss had been worthwhile, and that the Navy had never put up a finer show.'[50] Mountbatten's reverence for the Commander-in-Chief was undiminished; his enthusiasm was not wholly reciprocated. 'I like and admire Mountbatten,' Cunningham had told Dudley Pound when offered either Lord Louis or John Edelsten as Chief of Staff, 'but he is very junior still and I doubt if he is as sound as Edelsten.'[51] Their few days of cohabitation did not allay his doubts. Another destroyer officer who was staying in the house noticed the Commander-in-Chief's irritation at his guest's ebullience. At dinner the day after Mountbatten had left for England, Cunningham, in expansive mood, turned to his remaining guest and said: 'The trouble with your flotilla, boy, is that it was thoroughly badly led.'

The judgement was a harsh one and was probably affected by the jealousy which many senior officers felt for Mountbatten. He was glamorous, he was rich, he was royal, he had connections far grander than they could boast, he seemed to regard himself as the equal of men far senior to him. He was, they felt, something of a puppy, and, like all puppies, needed to be kept in check. Yet this resentment does not invalidate Cunningham's conclusion. Mountbatten was not a good flotilla leader, or wartime commander of destroyers. It is perhaps not too fanciful to equate his performance on the bridge with his prowess behind the wheel of a car. He was a fast and dangerous driver. His maxim was that, if you were shaping up to pass and saw another car approaching, it was always better to accelerate and press on. Usually this worked, but if it did not the casualty list was likely to be formidable. His daughter Pamela remembered how, driving up from Adsdean in the staff bus, the servants would point out black stains on the road: 'Look, his Lordship's skid-marks!'

If a destroyer could leave skid-marks, *Kelly* would have disfigured every sea in which she sailed. Mountbatten was impetuous. He pushed the ship fast for little reason except his love of speed and imposed unnecessary strain on his own officers and the other ships in the flotilla. He allowed himself to be distracted from his main purpose by the lure of attractive adventures. Above all he lacked that mysterious quality of 'sea sense', the ability to ensure that one's ship is in the right place at the right time. Mountbatten was as good a captain as most and better than many of his contemporaries but among all his peers who have expressed an opinion the unanimous feeling is that, by the highest standards, he was no better than second-rate.

To say this is in no way to disparage his qualities of leadership, the loyalty and devotion he inspired among all who sailed with him. His farewell address to what was left of his crew showed him at his best.

> I have always tried to crack a joke or two before, and you have been friendly and laughed at them. But today I am afraid I have run out of jokes, and I don't suppose any of us feel much like laughing. The *Kelly* has been in one scrap after another, but even after we have had men killed the majority survived and brought the old ship back. Now she lies in fifteen hundred fathoms and with her more than half our shipmates. If they had to die, what a grand way to go, for now they all lie together in the ship we loved. . . . We have lost her, but they are still with her. There may be less than half the *Kelly* left, but I feel that each of us will take up the battle with even stronger heart. . . . You will all be sent to replace men who have been killed in other ships, and the next time you are in action remember the *Kelly*. As you ram each shell home into the gun, shout 'Kelly!' and so her spirit will go on inspiring us until victory is won. I should like to add that there isn't one of you I wouldn't be proud and honoured to serve with again. Goodbye, good luck, and thank you all from the bottom of my heart.[52]

The night before Mountbatten left Alexandria, what was left of the *Kelly*'s officers gave him a farewell dinner – 'but with more gaps than places it was a sad affair'.[53]

# CHAPTER 11

# Combined Operations:
# The Adviser

MOUNTBATTEN COULD HAVE REMAINED with the Mediterranean Fleet, building up a new flotilla from the relics of the 'Fighting Fifth'. In some ways that is what he would most have enjoyed, but he knew that it was time for a move. 'It seems incredible to think that my two years – such happy though adventurous years – should already be up this summer,' he wrote to Patricia in April 1941. 'I am glad, though, that they left me where I was so long – I should not really have liked the idea of sitting at an office desk in war. My one hope now is for something much bigger. I fear it is impossible to imagine anything much better.'[1] Something bigger had in fact already been suggested. Admiral Syfret, Naval Secretary to the First Lord, had written to offer him command of the newest large cruiser. Mountbatten temporized; it was a flattering offer but there might be still better prospects. He told Syfret that he would like to consult him in person when the *Kelly* returned for her next boiler-clean, and wrote to Edwina: 'Above all I'd like to get in a word with A.V. [Alexander] before seeing Syfret if you can get him to lunch. . . . If you see A.V. – *par hasard* – you might find out what he wants me to do. A cruiser, or better an aircraft-carrier for a year might be a grand education.'[2]

The *Kelly*'s boilers would never need cleaning now, so his lunch with A. V. Alexander would take place earlier than he had expected. Cunningham decided to take advantage of his return to London to send a furious protest about the way the Middle East had been starved of air support. Miles Lampson, British Ambassador in Cairo, saw Mountbatten the day before he left and was in no doubt about the relish with which he would deliver the message; 'being who he is,' noted Lampson, 'he has access to everyone and is not in the least afraid of our good Prime Minister or anyone else'.[3] The Ambassador may have over-estimated Mountbatten's insouciance, but certainly he was more likely than most to stand up to Winston Churchill.

The journey back took fourteen tedious days, with delays at Lagos and in the Gambia. For Mountbatten, longing to play his part in the capital and to resolve the uncertainties of his future, the time dragged painfully, but he used the hours profitably, sightseeing, enquiring into the Nigerian economy and the state of its Navy, attending a meeting of the chiefs. The latter complained that they had to pay income tax of two shillings in the pound. With some asperity Mountbatten retorted that his own level of tax was now nineteen shillings and sixpence in the pound. Ah yes, said the chiefs, not to be taken in by so obvious a ruse, but if you want another sixpence, all you need do is print another pound note. *We* can't do that.[4]

Once back in London, he was quickly given his chance to pour out to the Prime Minister the woes of the Mediterranean Fleet. Churchill listened benignly, then put both his hands on Mountbatten's shoulders and said, 'My boy, I can't tell you how glad I am to see you back safely,' a response gratifying in its warmth, even if imprecise on how the deficiencies in aircraft were to be made up.[5] His interview with Arthur Tedder, then responsible for aircraft production, proved little more rewarding. 'Dickie Mountbatten pressed me hard on the subject of air support to the Navy and Army in Greece, the Aegean and Crete,' the Air Marshal recorded. Even if the aircraft and pilots had been available, Tedder argued, there were no forward bases from which they could have operated.[6] At least Mountbatten was able to extol to all and sundry the merits of Andrew Cunningham, 'for I was fanatically devoted to him and all that he stood for'.[7]

Mountbatten's hesitation in accepting Admiral Syfret's offer of a cruiser now proved justified, for he was offered command of the aircraft-carrier *Illustrious*. It was the *Illustrious* which had preceded *Kelly* in the Grand Harbour at Valletta, and had seemed the chosen target for every marauding German aircraft. She had survived, though sorely damaged, to slip away through the Suez Canal to the United States, where she was being repaired in the yards of Norfolk, Virginia. She was not expected to be ready until November, but the Prime Minister felt it would be useful if this dashing and well-connected young sailor were to go out before it was really necessary, to make propaganda and cultivate useful contacts.[8] Lady Louis was to go as well, on a goodwill tour to thank the American Red Cross for all their help. Nothing could have pleased them more, for it meant that they would be temporarily reunited with their daughters. For Mountbatten it was bound to be professionally absorbing. His spirits could hardly have been higher when he flew out of London on 26 August 1941 with his two trunks, a suitcase and tin-helmet case.

Almost the first thing Mountbatten did in the United States was hasten to Virginia to visit the *Illustrious*. There were many old acquaintances among the crew, and a handful of officers from the *Kelly* whose transfer Mountbatten had organized. The first visit was made memorable by the fact that he was mauled by the ship's mascot, a goat. His daughter delightedly sent him a cutting of the Ripley 'Believe It Or Not' column, syndicated throughout the United States, reporting that the gallant captain had survived many battles without a scratch only to be severely bitten aboard his own ship. 'I am afraid you really never will live that story down!' concluded Patricia.[9] For Mountbatten, goat or no goat, it was love at first sight; no ship could rival the *Kelly*, but he knew that together he and the *Illustrious* would do wonderful things.

His tour of the United States turned into a triumphal progress. Everywhere he was fêted by the rich and the powerful. Among his lectures to huge and enthusiastic audiences was one at Annapolis to a thousand midshipmen. Many years later he remarked how hard it had been to speak to so many hungry young men *before* lunch. 'If you had asked for volunteers to serve with you in the *Illustrious*,' was the comment of one of his audience, 'you would have had a thousand American midshipmen.'[10] Twice he dined at the White House, the first time talking to the President until half past one in the morning. They played some of Noel Coward's records, and Mountbatten presented Roosevelt with a copy of Coward's latest hit, 'London Pride'. 'Riveting' was his description of the evening, an unilluminating summary of what must have been an interesting conversation.

For his visits to the more sensitive military establishments, Mountbatten travelled under the somewhat permeable alias of Louis Mountain; for the rest of the time he was subjected to the full fury of the American publicity machine. This fate delighted him; more than forty press photographers were welcomed aboard the *Illustrious* at his first visit. He met almost everyone who counted in the American naval establishment – Admiral King, the Commander-in-Chief of the Atlantic Fleet; Colonel Knox, the Secretary of the Navy; Admiral Stark, the Chief of Naval Operations – and briefed them fully if somewhat tendentiously on the state of the war in Europe. A visit to the U.S. Pacific Fleet at Pearl Harbor was soon to prove of unexpectedly topical interest. He was appalled by the inadequate preparations against surprise attack and told his daughter Patricia of his forebodings when he saw her in New York a few days later. He went out in Admiral Halsey's flagship, the *Enterprise*, was transferred to the destroyer *Balch*, and took part in an attack by the destroyer squadron on the U.S. Fleet.

He was particularly effective with the press. In mid October he met the leading American columnist Walter Winchell. Winchell talked for two hours. When he had run dry

> Mountbatten went into action, with all his charm and personal experience of active service [recorded an unidentified observer]. He did more in half an hour to make Winchell appreciate the attitude of a typical officer in the Royal Navy towards the war than ten million

words of print could ever achieve. . . . I have seen Mountbatten in action on several occasions since he arrived in the United States, and, in my opinion, he has done more than anyone else to instil and to encourage American admiration for Britain. Naturally his duties to the Navy come first, but it is a thousand pities that he was not permitted to remain in this country until the *Illustrious* leaves next month, so that he could fulfil the various important engagements made on his behalf which would have enabled him to use his dynamic personality in putting across a real life story of the Navy in action.[11]

Mountbatten's visit was cut short abruptly when he flew back to Los Angeles from Pearl Harbor to be met by a message from the naval attaché ordering him to fly at once to Washington for an urgent briefing. Apprehensively he obeyed, to be told that his posting to the *Illustrious* was cancelled; instead he was to return to London to take up some post connected with Combined Operations. 'We want you home here at once for something which you will find of the highest interest,' read Churchill's personal telegram, while in a message to Harry Hopkins, Roosevelt's most intimate adviser, apologizing for the abrupt removal of his guest, the Prime Minister explained that he was needed for 'a very active and urgent job'.[12] To Mountbatten it seemed that no job could be more active or urgent than the command of H.M.S. *Illustrious*. He had long had his own ideas about Combined Operations and in any other circumstances would have been happy to get a chance to put them into action, but now he had set his heart on commanding a big ship and was bitterly unhappy at being called on to renounce it. 'There is not only the real grief of losing my lovely ship with all my friends in her,' he told Edwina, 'but with my somewhat snobbish career complex, to see my chances of doing a "Beatty" being knocked on the head means more to me than I'd like to admit to others. . . . I am more and more "homesick" and miserable as time goes on and for the first time in my life apprehensive about my new job – what do I know of soldiering? I wish I had my dear old *Illustrious*. I know I'd have done marvels with her!!!'[13]

With some temerity Mountbatten replied that he would need a week to settle important outstanding engagements but would fly back on 18 October. The Prime Minister was not pleased – 'More than 12 days have been wasted,' he minuted. 'He should come at once'[14] – but since one of the engagements was a final dinner at the White House, it was felt that the extra delay was permissible. Mountbatten was more concerned about his farewell visit to the *Illustrious*. He felt that he was letting down those officers from the *Kelly* whom he had induced to join her, and had no intention of leaving America without taking a proper farewell of them.

He was preceded to London by a letter to the First Sea Lord from Admiral Stark:

> I want you to know that he has been a great help to all of us, and I mean literally ALL.
>
> His knowledge of his profession, his keen observation of our methods, his frank statements of his thoughts of them, his telling us of the British Navy methods . . . his sincerity, frankness and honesty have not only won our liking, but also our deep respect.
>
> There is not the slightest doubt in my mind that his visit has been genuinely beneficial to the United States Navy. If he carries back to you anything that will be nearly so helpful to you as what he leaves with us, we shall be very glad.
>
> We regret to see him go, as there is more we would have liked to work out along with him, but we are glad that circumstances have suddenly arisen which will enlarge his field of usefulness.[15]

Roosevelt's comment to Churchill was terser but equally emphatic: 'Mountbatten has been really useful to our Navy people.'[16]

He returned by way of Lisbon, where he visited the economic adviser to the Ambassador, David Eccles, whom he planned to recruit for his new office.

> Yesterday I had a real treat [Eccles told his wife]. Louis Mountbatten walked into my office and said, 'We must have a talk'. . . . I'd always heard he was the best of our younger sailors, but I never suspected he was quite outstanding on *any* subject. People say complimentary things about semi-royalties to show they know them, and instinctive- ly one discounts such praise. In this case no one has said enough to me. This man *knows* how to fight and wants to fight. . . . It is the first time I've ever met an officer of whom I could say this in the full meaning of 'Knowing how to fight *our* war in the conditions of the war *as it is*, and even *as it may be*. . . .' This is an extraordinary man with the *instinct* and the *industry* necessary for modern warfare.[17]

Combined Operations may be said to have begun when the first soldier was transported to an enemy shore by a naval crew. Before the days of mechanical warfare and rapid communications, however, the question was one of providing enough boats to land the men on a usually undefended beach. Only in the First World War, when the difficulties of forcing a landing against an alert and well-armed enemy became a serious consideration, did the need for special techniques to overcome the problem become apparent. The Gallipoli campaign, in which Vice-Admiral Keyes was Chief of Staff to the naval Commander-in-Chief, proved bloodily that the traditional methods of dumping troops on the beaches and leaving them to get on with it could no longer be employed with any hope of success. At Zeebrugge in 1918 Keyes had a chance to put into practice some of the lessons he had learned so painfully at Gallipoli, and did so with striking success. The science of Combined Operations had been born.

It did not thrive between the wars. The first specialist flat-bottomed landing-craft were developed, but with limited enthusiasm; only nine were in existence by 1938. A sub-committee of the Chiefs of Staff was set up in 1937 to consider the various problems but, though its conclusions were sensible enough, little was done to implement them. By the outbreak of war Great Britain was as ill-equipped to put an army ashore in the face of opposition and to maintain it once landed as it had been in 1918.[18] Meanwhile, the rapid development of air power had made the traditional techniques of amphibious warfare still more irrelevant. This deficiency did not seem significant to those in charge of British strategy; at a meeting of the Chiefs of Staff on 15 December 1939 the then Colonel Macleod, one of the original apostles of Combined Operations, argued the case for greatly increased numbers of landing-craft. Churchill, who was present as First Lord of the Admiralty, remarked that he could see no need for such facilities except possibly in support of Finland against Russia.[19] Yet even Macleod's proposals were hardly *avant garde*; Mountbatten attended a lecture which he gave to the naval war college in December 1938 – 'Out of date!' he commented tersely.[20]

The fall of France left Britain confronted by a European coastline either hostile or neutral. The first preoccupation was to avert the threat of invasion but eventually re-entry to the Continent would be necessary. Suddenly the need for Combined Operations was all too obvious, and on a scale far vaster than anything contemplated in the past. Lieutenant-General Bourne, Adjutant-General of the Royal Marines, in June 1940 was appointed Commander of Raiding Operations and adviser to the Chiefs of Staff on Combined Operations. This selection had the advantage that the Marines, logically the ideal unit for commando action, were closely involved with Combined Operations from the start. Against this was the fact that the new organization was considered by the Admiralty and, indeed, the rest of Whitehall to be little more than an exotic naval by-blow.

Churchill wanted something more independent and more grandiose. He resurrected the hero of Zeebrugge, his old friend Admiral of the Fleet Lord Keyes, now nearly seventy, to build up a powerful new force. 'We have suffered greatly in the first war from "dug-outs",' commented Ian Jacob, 'and here was the same tendency to bring back men for jobs which they would have been ripe to undertake twenty-five years earlier.'[21] The reaction of the military leaders ranged from scepticism to outrage: 'Roger Keyes intrigued himself into the position of Director of Combined Operations in spite of the protests of the Chiefs of Staff,' Pound told Cunningham.[22]

In fact Keyes did not do too bad a job. He established Combined Operations in a separate headquarters in Richmond Terrace and placed it firmly on the Whitehall map. Minor raids were carried out on the French coast and a start made on training troops and landing-craft personnel for more substantial landings. Five thousand men were organized into ten commandos, ready for action. Mountbatten was being less than fair when he told Captain Roskill that he had inherited 'absolutely nothing' of value from his predecessor.[23] But what there was was far from perfect. Alan Brooke, visiting the Combined Operations training centre at Inverary in September 1941, found 'the training far too stereotyped to fit in with varying conditions of our possible operations; still thinking much too small in all our plans'.[24] Far too often Keyes would look to his contemporaries and cronies when a post needed filling: 'If Roger Keyes goes on pulling out these retired officers and giving them spot jobs on what is essentially a young man's business,' wrote Admiral James, 'there will be a lot of gnashing of teeth.'[25]

But Keyes's greatest failure was one of personal relationships. Partly this was due to Churchill's weakness – of which Mountbatten was one day to be the victim – for appointing people without properly defining their responsibilities or hierarchical position. Keyes was clear that he was solely responsible to the Minister of Defence – who happened to be also Prime Minister – on all matters concerned with Combined Operations. The Chiefs of Staff were equally certain that Keyes was their servant, with limited responsibilities for training and conducting minor raids but none for large-scale amphibious operations. The differences, with good will, could have been reconciled, but Keyes despised the Chiefs of Staff. Where tact and dexterity were called for, Keyes was obstinate and arrogant. 'It is really a terrible business having Roger Keyes mixed up with the business as D.C.O. . . ,' wrote Dudley Pound. 'I am sorry to say it but I firmly believe that the only thing he cares for is the glorification of Roger Keyes.'[26]

The dispute came to a head in the autumn of 1941. The Chiefs of Staff insisted that Keyes's duties should be re-defined, and that his title of 'Director' should be changed to that of 'Adviser'. Keyes reacted furiously, bombarding Churchill with letters abusing his 'craven-hearted' advisers, and demanding a personal interview with the Prime Minister. Churchill backed the Chiefs. 'Your title of "Director" does not correspond to the facts,' he told Keyes. 'The responsibility for advising the Defence Committee and the War Cabinet can only be with the Chiefs of Staff.' Keyes continued to bluster and on 4 October

Churchill told him bluntly that he was arranging for his relief.[27] Dudley Pound greeted the news with jubilation: 'He never had much brain and what he has got left is quite addled.'[28]

For Mountbatten, therefore, Keyes's most significant legacy was one of bitterness. The Chiefs of Staff – indeed, almost all the principal military figures of the day – viewed Combined Operations with distrust if not dislike. With some reluctance they accepted its existence, but only in a subordinate role, with limited powers and equally limited ambitions. Any attempt to assert itself, or play a part outside its restricted sphere, should be sharply checked. This was to prove a formidable handicap in the coming years. So also, though more fleetingly, was Keyes's popularity among many of those who served him. With all his failings he was a big man, decent, honourable, able to command affection and loyalty. 'You were both our Tall Ship and the star we steered her by. It is rather hard for us soldiers to be bereft of both,' wrote Brigadier Haydon after Keyes's dismissal.[29] Such men felt that he had been unfairly treated and were quick to look for failings in the upstart who had replaced him. Lord Lovat, one of the more dashing of the young commando officers, compared Keyes for his qualities of leadership with Churchill, Smuts and Carton de Wiart – 'In Montgomery and Mountbatten, the inner qualities were not apparent.'[30]

Keyes himself was characteristically generous. 'Dickie Mountbatten is a splendid fellow,' he wrote to Churchill, 'and a live wire with lots of drive. He always makes a study of anything he undertakes and will do everything in his power to overcome the difficulties of executing amphibious operations. I will do all I can to give him a good start.'[31] But he would have been superhuman if he had not believed that he could have done the job better himself. Mountbatten was a most able staff officer, he wrote, 'but what is wanted is someone with the guts to make big decisions'.[32] That *he* had such guts, and nobody else in the war machine, was his firm belief. Again and again he complained that he had been dismissed for claiming certain powers and that then those powers had been lavished on Mountbatten. 'I am still very attached to Winston,' he told Ismay. 'I can't think why, for he has given me a very raw deal and has now added insults to injury for I hear he has given Mountbatten all that he agreed to allow the Chiefs of Staff to take away from me.'[33] He wrote this letter on 30 October, when Mountbatten was only a few days back in England. At that time he had no grounds for his belief that his successor was to inherit not merely his empire but an improved version of it. Time was to prove him right.

*

When Mountbatten returned to London on 25 October 1941 he had time only for a hurried lunch with his mother before he drove to Chequers. 'P.M. gave me staggering orders on my new job,' he noted in his diary. At first he had pleaded that he should be allowed to return to the *Illustrious*. 'You fool!' stormed Churchill. 'The best thing you can hope to do there is to repeat your last achievement and get yourself sunk.' Then he went on to expound the greatness of the task. Mountbatten was to mount a programme of raids of ever-increasing intensity. But his main object was to be the invasion of France. For this he must create the machine, devise the appliances, find the bases, create the training areas, select the site for the assault. 'You are to give no thought to the defensive. Your whole attention is to be concentrated on the offensive.'[34] The orders were indeed staggering; and if the scope of Mountbatten's responsibilities did not correspond exactly with that envisaged by the Chiefs of Staff, then what matter? No member of the Chiefs was present at the meeting.

Commodore Mountbatten, as he now became, to all intents and purposes took over his new task before the end of October. It was another three weeks, however, before the rumours that Keyes was on the way out and had been replaced by a young and untried naval captain were officially confirmed. Public reaction – at any rate, as manifested in the press – was enthusiastic. Keyes was a hero, but he was also seventy; Mountbatten had become something of a hero too, and he had youth, panache, glamour. The country desperately wanted to be assured that it would one day be able to forsake its defensive role and hit back at the Germans; Mountbatten's appointment showed that the Government was doing something about it.

Mountbatten's new directive had been issued on 16 October 1941.[35] His responsibilities were defined under four heads:

Under the general direction of the Chiefs of Staff you will:-

(a) Act as technical adviser on all aspects of, and at all stages in, the planning and training for combined operations.

(b) Be responsible for co-ordinating the general training policy for combined operations for the three Services. You will command the Combined Training Centres and Schools of Instruction.

(c) Study tactical and technical developments in all forms of combined operations varying from small raids to a full-scale invasion of the Continent.

(d) Direct and press forward research and development in all forms of technical equipment and special craft peculiar to combined operations.

So far as planning large-scale operations or even small raids was concerned, Mountbatten's role was confined to giving technical advice 'from their inception to the point when they are finally approved'. Only in the case of 'raids on a very small scale' carried out by Special Service troops was Mountbatten to appoint the force commander and retain responsibility for the detailed planning. Important though these functions were, they obviously fell a long way short of the absolute authority which Keyes had dreamed of and which the Prime Minister had hinted might be Mountbatten's. The new Adviser was not discomfited; the future for Britain's striking forces could only be one of immense expansion and he was confident that within it he could carve out a satisfactory empire for himself. 'You will be amused to hear that my great gloom and depression has now disappeared,' he told Patricia, 'and that I am enthusiastic about this mad job, and may even be able to contribute personally towards speeding up the war. Anyway, it is all very thrilling and exciting.'[36]

For anyone with less ebullience, Mountbatten's youth and lack of rank would have been a daunting handicap. Not merely was he replacing an elderly Admiral of the Fleet; his first Chief of Staff was fifty-seven and one rank senior to Mountbatten even after the latter's promotion; almost all the other important jobs in the organization were held or would be given to men with considerably more experience and established reputation. 'It is going to be difficult but not impossible to keep my end up,' he wrote, and again a few days later: 'I seem constantly to be attending meetings with people I never in my life expected to sit at the same table with on duty, or taking the Chair at other meetings at which I always seem to be the youngest person in the room.'[37] That the situation gave rise to little difficulty is in part a tribute to Mountbatten's tact and discretion, but so also does it reflect well on the senior officers who accepted this young officer's elevation above their heads with cheerfulness and generosity. That there was some grumbling is certain; that this was never translated into an attempt to sabotage or even embarrass Mountbatten in the conduct of his office is equally evident.

Those at whose table Mountbatten had least expected to sit were the Chiefs of Staff. Mountbatten knew that, while the Chiefs had not resisted his appointment, the initiative had come from Churchill. He anticipated scepticism, perhaps even hostility, from these distinguished and conservative potentates. The scepticism, indeed, existed; the hostility did not. He was perhaps fortunate that, when he first encountered the Chiefs, General Dill had not yet been replaced as Chief of the Imperial General Staff by the more acerbic and intolerant Alan Brooke. Dill was a sad and sick man, knowing that his days at the head of the Army were numbered. He made Mountbatten welcome with a generous consideration that was typical of his nature. So, too,

did the Chief of Air Staff, Charles Portal. Mountbatten remembered that
when he attended his first meeting Portal told him not to be concerned that he
was so much junior to everyone else. 'It's not so bad; all we want is
professional competence and knowledge and co-operation. Don't let yourself
be pushed about; if you have a point of view, you are fully entitled to express
it.'[38]

Perhaps not surprisingly, the most serious doubts among the Chiefs about
Mountbatten's promotion were held by his own Service. Dudley Pound, the
First Sea Lord, approved of, even admired, his young colleague but he had a
strong sense of propriety and belief in the hierarchical principle. Destroyer
captains of forty-one should not suddenly be translated to Whitehall and
expect to be treated as an equal by full admirals or generals. Pound would not
oppose Mountbatten, but he would constantly be looking for evidence that
the Adviser on Combined Operations was getting above himself – worse still,
that he was trespassing on what properly should be the preserve of the Royal
Navy. Any such infringement would be repelled.

From the point of view of his subsequent career at Combined Operations
it was fortunate that Mountbatten began his term in a position of unequivocal
subordination. Mountbatten 'is young, clever and determined', wrote Admiral James, 'and I am glad to say his position vis-à-vis the Chiefs of Staff is
regularised and many of the difficulties experienced in the past should
vanish.'[39] If Churchill had tried to thrust a second Keyes on to the Chiefs he
would have been fiercely opposed; as it was, they had time to get used to the
new incumbent before Mountbatten was given his next step upwards. He
attended his first Chiefs of Staff meeting on 28 October, appearing for a single
item and saying only that he had no objection to the Inspector of Infantry
visiting commando establishments – a point on which Keyes had been more
truculent.[40] 'Very nice,' was his somewhat pallid comment on the proceedings. From then on he attended Chiefs of Staff meetings once a week or so,
whenever an item concerning Combined Operations was on the agenda. It
cannot be said that he swept all before him. In early December he pleaded that
more landing-craft were needed for training purposes, to be told that none
could be spared from operations; three weeks later two more of his ideas were
rebuffed – the first that markings on R.A.F. planes should be changed so that
aerial photographs could be obtained for Operation BONUS without security being jeopardized; the second that a sum of money should be distributed
among the inhabitants of the Norwegian island of Vaagso to compensate
them for damage done during Operation ARCHERY. Both these proposals,
it was felt, would set dangerous precedents – a criticism that was often to be
levelled at Mountbatten's ideas over the next two years.[41]

His appearances at the Defence Committees of the Cabinet were similarly in a prudently low key, though he caused a mild stir at his first meeting by going initially to the wrong place and almost arriving after the Prime Minister.[42] All in all, he had got away to a discreet and well-ordered start to his new career. By so doing he made it much easier for Churchill to extend the scope of his duties as soon as an opportunity offered.

# CHAPTER 12

# *Combined Operations:*
# *The Chief*

MOUNTBATTEN BEGAN as he intended to continue. He never devoted less than twelve hours a day to his work and at first often slept in the office, starting in the early hours of the morning and toiling through till midnight or later. The Embassy in Washington had recommended that he should be given a holiday of at least fourteen days before he began his new job – 'a very good joke', commented Mountbatten, 'as I can hardly spare 14 hours off'. In theory he recognized how important it was that no one should be required to survive without an occasional break, and, indeed, instituted a system by which members of his staff were required to state the day they proposed to take off and then to certify that they had done so. When it came to his own practice, however, he fell down sadly; if he managed to spend one night a fortnight at Broadlands he was doing well, and even then his visit was usually linked to the inspection of some Combined Operations enterprise in the neighbourhood.[1]

By early December his work bore fruit in a fundamental reorganization of what must have been the most rapidly expanding part of the British war machine. In a revised directive[2] it was accepted that Mountbatten had a dual role; as Adviser, when he dealt with Chiefs of Staff or force commandos, and as 'Commodore Combined Operations' for administrative command, whether of raiding forces or of longer-term, large-scale operations. It was as Commodore Combined Operations that he was responsible for the incredible multiplicity of problems connected with equipping and training an armada for eventual landing on a hostile coastline.

The most pressing need was to strengthen the centre so that Combined Operations' rapidly swelling empire did not dissolve into unco-ordinated fragments. When Mountbatten took over Combined Operations Head-quarters (C.O.H.Q.), its total staff, including typists and messengers, was twenty-three, a number which could be seen as proving Keyes's healthy dislike of bureaucracy or, more convincingly, illustrating his inability to cope with any kind of administrative problem. Keyes's vision of C.O.H.Q., John Hughes Hallett commented, never went beyond planning for 'a bigger and better Zeebrugge-type raid'.[3] Even for this the present organization was pitifully inadequate. Rebuilding had to start almost from scratch. Mountbatten began by splitting C.O.H.Q. roughly into two halves, for administration and for operations. The first half consisted of a predominantly naval staff which dealt with personnel, material and ships, and worked closely with the Admiralty – so closely, indeed, that it was sometimes difficult to distinguish between the two.

It was on the operational side that the inter-Service nature of Combined Operations became apparent. Mountbatten believed fervently that ventures in which sailors, soldiers and airmen were required to co-operate closely could succeed only if those concerned not merely planned together but lived together, played together and forgot, not their skills, but their individual loyalties and patterns of thinking. Those who worked in C.O.H.Q. were not considered as representatives of the Navy, Army or Air Force, and any attempt to behave as such – to establish separate messes or even Service cliques within the messes, to argue the case for an individual arm when priorities for a particular operation were being discussed – was taken as evidence that the offenders were unfit for their present work. Attitudes formed over centuries cannot lightly be discarded. Inter-Service rivalries and suspicions persisted. The naval contingent were usually the worst offenders. Arthur Marshall, who served in C.O.H.Q. as a major in charge of security, remembers that the regular naval officers felt themselves an élite, superior to the amateurs of the R.N.V.R. and, *a fortiori*, all lesser mortals from other Services. They treated C.O.H.Q. as a ship, always going up the gangway to their cabin rather than the stairs to their room.[4] But Mountbatten did his best to curb such tendencies and to a great extent succeeded; the sailors on his staff might air their nautical fancies but, if it came to a showdown with the Admiralty, their loyalties were usually with the organization for which they worked.

The operational side of C.O.H.Q. fell broadly into four parts: planning, intelligence, training and communications. Planning in its turn was quickly subdivided to cope with the very different requirements of small raids which were to take place within the next few weeks, and full-scale invasion that might be two or three years away. Intelligence was concerned not so much with the collection of information as with knowing where information was available, drawing on the sources as required and processing the results for the benefit of the planners. Training, though co-ordinated in C.O.H.Q., took place in those parts of the British Isles where landscapes existed to test the arcane skills required of the would-be invader. The greatest concentration of such bases was in Scotland, and in time the Hollywood Hotel at Largs became a centre from which the training areas were administered. The communications section grew most rapidly of all, a committee which had been set up by the Chiefs of Staff to report on 'Communications in Combined Operations' being transferred bodily to C.O.H.Q. and made the basis of a new inter-Service organization.

To man this plethora of new establishments a large number of officials had to be found. Within six months the staff of C.O.H.Q. grew to over four hundred. A high proportion was recruited personally by Mountbatten. He had an extraordinary talent for attracting personnel. When he found that naval cadets almost always put destroyers down as their first choice and mentioned Combined Operations, if at all, towards the bottom of the list, he toured the cadet schools. He would speak of his time in the *Kelly* and urge them to try for destroyers; the next best thing, he would say, was Combined Operations, which also guaranteed plenty of close action. 'The result was that almost everybody put down their first choice as destroyers and their second choice as Combined Ops. There were only a few vacancies for destroyers, and so we scooped the rest of the cream of the officer entry.'[5] Not everyone felt that the results were equally happy when it came to filling the more senior posts. Robert Henriques, the novelist, styling himself 'Meego', touched on this when he wrote of Mountbatten after he had endured a fierce denunciation of his own arrogance and tactlessness while standing to attention studying his accuser's 'excessively handsome profile'.

> From this aspect the only weak feature of this most genuine of War Lords – the not small, but smallish eyes, too close together by only a fraction – was inevident; and the face represented for Meego all that he would always covet of power, personality and assurance; and ambition justified; a vast ambition that was not reprehensible, because it exactly coincided with public interest; an imperial ambition, superbly equipped for any conquest, armed with a quick, logical mind and an even swifter intuition, with no weakness, except a total inability to judge men correctly, whether they were his cronies or his subordinates, and yet with the power to command an uncritical loyalty from almost everyone; an ambition rather sad to see in an age that offered it too little scope.[6]

A 'total inability to judge men correctly' is a serious weakness in any leader, most of all in a leader charged with rapidly building up a large and complex organization. Mountbatten's record in Combined Operations gives some support to the accusation. He did not feel at ease unless supported by those whom he liked and trusted, and to a greater extent than at any subsequent stage of his career he indulged this frailty by recruiting old friends to fill the more important posts. Hugh Dalton, the Minister for Economic

Warfare who was also responsible for the Special Operations Executive – an organization whose work in the fields of subversion and sabotage brought it into contact and sometimes rivalry with C.O.H.Q. – was told that Mountbatten had 'surrounded himself with a group of his personal friends, most of whom are not very good at their jobs'.[7] As a generalization this seems unjustified. Most of the appointments were good ones. An exception might have been the critically important position of Chief of Staff. Mountbatten wanted to appoint Robert Neville, one of the most honourable, decent and courageous of men but not cut out for a taxing and complex administrative role. Mountbatten's invitation, Neville himself believes, was an example of loyalty overcoming good judgement. Fortunately, Neville could not extricate himself from his duties at the Admiralty and instead recommended Wildman-Lushington, a fellow Marine and highly capable staff officer.[8] Another controversial selection was that of the Marquis of Casa Maury as head of intelligence. Casa Maury was a rich, glamorous racing-driver who had been a conspicuous member of the Mountbattens' set before the war. His appointment stirred up some resentment among the career officers, and he was often dismissed as a decorative playboy. Others defended him, however, Hughes Hallett, for one, believing that Casa Maury did his work 'with astonishing despatch, displaying considerable skill, artistry and imagination'.[9] He could not fairly be called a failure; what was certain, however, was that only exceptional success could redeem in some people's eyes the stigma of having got his job on the old-boy network.

Many other posts were filled only on professional grounds. Hughes Hallett, the naval adviser, was picked because he was already at work on anti-invasion measures. Vice-Admiral Theodore Hallett and General Drew, in charge of training, were also well qualified for their work. But other old friends of Mountbatten found refuge in the innumerable crannies in which Combined Operations abounded. One was fitted up with a job at 'one of our places in Amersham. Took me all day to find out we had one,' confessed Mountbatten.[10] Peter Murphy was hired to consider the political implications of the various operations and advocated sending in political officers with the assault troops to get across 'specific messages' to the local populations. He does not seem to have been notably effective, while his left-wing associations and Irish birth caused alarm to those charged with security.[11] Harold Wernher, George Milford Haven's brother-in-law, was brought in to organize the supply of material and labour for the myriad needs of Combined Operations. Unlike Murphy, he *was* notably effective, but at the price of making himself detested; the general verdict on his performance, wrote Bernard Fergusson in his history of Combined Operations, was that 'he certainly got things done, but they would probably have got done anyway, and he built up untold animosity for C.O.H.Q. by his arrogance and tactlessness'.[12]

But it was Mountbatten's circus of scientists who aroused the gravest doubts among the professionals. Mountbatten believed unusual needs called for unusual means; he greatly respected intellect, was amused rather than outraged by conduct which might be deemed contrary to good order, enjoyed the company of people who could tell him how things worked. He prized his scientists highly. Geoffrey Pyke, the most maverick and in some ways most talented, came first. 'Mountbatten thinks he chose me,' Pyke told Solly Zuckerman. 'He's wrong. I chose him because of the way he had devised new tactics for playing polo.'[13] Pyke subscribed to no academic discipline, but had a brilliant if unbridled imagination and a gift for asking the right questions. Then came J. D. Bernal, Professor of Physics at London University, an intemperate left-winger who had made his name in Whitehall by his attacks on the organization of Civil Defence and had been recommended to Mountbatten by Sir Henry Tizard. Bernal in his turn introduced Solly Zuckerman, South African born, more accustomed to the vagaries of primates than of professional soldiers, but with a brilliant and restless intelligence that questioned everything and frequently discovered under an encrustation of traditional dogma a truth that at first seemed heretical but was soon accepted as self-evident. Zuckerman was offered the rank of Group Captain. Mountbatten urged him to refuse it. 'The most they would make you is an Air Vice-Marshal and then you'd have to say "Yes, Sir" to an Air Marshal. And you don't even call me "Sir".'[14] That the scientists were worth their keep is today obvious. At the time they gave ammunition to those who wished to deride C.O.H.Q. as a resort of cranks and Communists. 'I lunched with C.C.O. [Chief of Combined Operations],' noted Evelyn Waugh in his diary, 'arrived rather tipsy, found the house a nest of Communists and behaved rather badly.'[15] The other guests were J. D. Bernal and Geoffrey Pyke.

Mountbatten rejoiced in accusations that his organization was established on eccentric principles. 'The only lunatic asylum in the world run by its own inmates,' was his favourite description. 'H.M.S. *Wimbledon* – all rackets and balls,' was a more acerbic comment.[16] He was excited and amused by the work himself, and wanted others to be so too.

> It was fun serving under Mountbatten [wrote a member of his staff].
> I don't mean that there was anything frivolous – though I've heard
> dyed-in-the-wool Admiralty wallahs use that very word. But it was
> *fun* in the sense that, though we were all deadly serious and – well,
> yes, dedicated, I suppose you can call it – we had something then that
> we hadn't had since we were kids, a sense of being in on something

not only tremendously exciting, and tremendously important, but something – this is the point – *tremendously full of surprises.*[17]

C.O.H.Q. also worked. 'The Combined Operations organisation has made tremendous strides,' wrote Churchill's Chief of Staff 'Pug' Ismay in March 1942, 'and unlike the old days is functioning in complete accord with the Service departments and Home Forces.'[18] With astonishing speed an organization sprang up capable of supporting the myriad demands that were to be made on it. Mountbatten concerned himself with every aspect, from the exact siting of the sentry-boxes so that the occupants would not find themselves in a draught, to the chain of command between the Defence Committee of the Cabinet, the Chiefs of Staff and the Adviser himself. But the task was not accomplished without extravagance – indeed, at no time would Mountbatten have been a proper person to turn to if an economical solution was desired. The motto of C.O.H.Q., Arthur Marshall once remarked, should be 'Regardless' – meaning regardless of effort, regardless of risk, and regardless of cost.[19]

Disregard of expense and the innate urge to build an empire led to over-staffing and the invention of superfluous functions. To Lord Lovat, coming from the austere north, C.O.H.Q. seemed 'honeycombed with rooms filled with every branch of the Services, including the powder-puff variety, who looked elegant in silk stockings. ... There was said to be a fair proportion of drones among the inmates.'[20] Yet to Major Hasler, quite as much a warrior and enemy to the bureaucracy of Babylon, the organization was 'highly efficient, hyperactive'.[21] Elegance need not denote idleness or incompetence. Both men had a case; and, Mountbatten being what he was, efficiency and extravagance went hand in hand.

The organization was not built up without a prolonged and occasionally bitter struggle. Navy, Army and Air Force had been trained for generations to survey each other with suspicion and be on their guard against any encroachment on their prerogatives. C.O.H.Q. posed a threat to all three simultaneously. Bernard Fergusson has told how men seconded to Mountbatten's staff were sometimes nobbled by senior officers in their own Service and encouraged to put their traditional loyalties first.[22] Captain Robson, who had been put in charge of naval training, was criticized by several admirals who could see no point either in Combined Operations or its chief. One even told him that landing a force from the sea was 'only a boating operation', though he recanted most handsomely after witnessing the invasion of North Africa.[23] Such hostility was not often overt; most people accepted that C.O.H.Q. was a fact and did their best to make it work. But latent suspicion survived, as did a conviction that Combined Operations was untidy, irregular, and should be wound up as soon as it had fulfilled its most immediate function. Nor was this a prejudice of backward-looking admirals only – it was General Ismay who, when the time came to re-think the structure late in 1943, minuted: 'All these loose ends like S[pecial] O[perations] E[xecutive] and C.O.H.Q. are anomalous and tiresome.'[24]


Viewed in broad terms, the tasks of Combined Operations fell into two main categories: raids on the coast of German-occupied Europe and preparation for an eventual invasion. In theory the first was complementary to the second; in practice it sometimes seemed that the demands which the raids entailed on limited resources made the two almost irreconcilable. There were some who argued that raiding Europe was a futile diversion of effort, but the generally accepted judgement was that, pinpricks though such enterprises might be, they raised public morale, maintained an offensive spirit among the troops, compelled the enemy to deploy large forces in defence of the coastline and occasionally achieved useful results in the destruction or capture of key facilities.[25] Since anyway the principle of raiding was insisted on by Churchill and eagerly supported by Mountbatten, the merits or demerits of the policy were not much debated.

To the Army it was evident that the coasts represented two front lines: the Channel was no-man's-land, raids on the Continent differed in no important respect from attacks across the trenches in the First World War. Clearly they were an Army responsibility. It was equally obvious to the Navy that, since such operations were sea-borne and the forces to be used ought properly to be Marines, theirs must be the predominant voice. C.O.H.Q. was in a way invented to escape from this dilemma. But there were other groups quick to resent trespass by Combined Operations on what they felt to be their preserve. The Special Operations Executive at first claimed that it should handle small raids employing less than thirty men, and it was not until Mountbatten conferred with Hugh Dalton early in 1942 that the two organizations agreed to co-operate rather than squabble over demarcation.[26] The Secret Service in its turn complained that raids on the Continent interrupted their operations and disturbed vital channels of information. Mountbatten remained politely sceptical and the Chiefs of Staff eventually decided that the Admiralty should arbitrate if there seemed to be a clash between the interests of the two bodies.[27]

It was not till May 1942 that Mountbatten's responsibilities for raiding were finally spelt out. Combined Operations had the tasks of identifying the target, preparing a draft plan, agreeing it with the commanders-in-chief involved, and submitting it to the Chiefs of Staff. If it was approved, force commanders were then appointed to produce precise orders, these in their turn were agreed with the commanders-in-chief and once more returned to the Chiefs of Staff for final approval. The procedure was cumbersome and, if followed in detail, would have rigidly circumscribed Mountbatten's freedom of action. As it was, an almost surreptitious streamlining occurred – the force commanders, for instance, usually working within C.O.H.Q. Only rarely did the demands of bureaucracy prove a serious impediment.[28]

The first raid to take place after Mountbatten's appointment was on Vaagso, an island off the coast of southern Norway. The targets – enemy shipping and a few small industrial concerns – were of trivial importance, the forces employed almost equally inconsiderable, but it was the first operation in which all three Services were truly interwoven in planning and execution. Within its limitations it was a total success. In February followed a raid on Bruneval, an operation even smaller in scope but this time designed for a specific purpose: the capture of a German radar installation. 'It seems rather silly to crow over this relatively unimportant affair when so much is going awry elsewhere,' commented Admiral James, 'but even a tiny success lightens up the dark clouds.'[29] Then in March came the still minor but more important raid on St Nazaire, to destroy the dry dock which it was feared might otherwise shelter the German battleship *Tirpitz*. To achieve this, a super-annuated destroyer was packed with explosives and rammed the lock gates. She went up the following day, killing well over four hundred Germans. British casualties, too, were heavy, but the dry dock was not repaired before the end of the war and the *Tirpitz* was denied its possible asylum.

Mountbatten delighted in the planning of these adventures, took an interest in every detail and fretted obsessively while they were in progress – 'Anxious day waiting for news of Raid on St Nazaire'.[30] The more outrageous the methods used, the more he relished them. At one time a raid on Brest was being discussed, involving the landing of tanks and the rolling of depth-charges into the dry dock. Horrified by this prospect, an officer on his staff, Captain Norris, said flippantly to a friend: 'Let's forget about all this nonsense and catch the 5.15 from St Malo!' Mountbatten overhead this and, much struck by the idea, at once called for a plan which involved hijacking a train, putting on a fake guard and driver and taking it into the harbour.[31]

An operation as small as any of those described, and which did not take place until the end of 1942, illustrates well the degree of his interest. Operation FRANKTON was intended to disrupt blockade-running between Germany and Japan by sending Marines in small boats sixty-two miles up the Gironde to fix limpet mines to cargo boats in the docks at Bordeaux. Mountbatten sanctioned the venture with reluctance, since he felt it unlikely that any of the twelve participants would return. For the same reason he vetoed the inclusion in the group of Major Hasler, commander of the Royal Marine boom patrol detachment. A man of his experience was too valuable to lose. Hasler protested. At a meeting at C.O.H.Q. he pleaded that he could not continue to command the unit if he let less experienced men go off on the first expedition. Mountbatten canvassed the views of everybody present. With one exception they all felt Hasler should stay behind. Hasler assumed that the day was lost when Mountbatten suddenly smiled and said: 'Well, much against my better judgement, I'm going to let you go.'

The final rehearsal was a disaster. Mountbatten found Hasler drowning his sorrows in the canteen and asked for details. Mournfully they were supplied. 'Splendid!' said Mountbatten. 'You must have learnt a great deal, and you'll be able to avoid making the same mistakes on the operation.' When the time came only two canoes reached Bordeaux but four German ships were damaged, two of them severely.[32] Hasler was one of the only two survivors to get back to Britain. The impression derived from the story, as so often in the early days of Combined Operations, is one of amateurishness redeemed by courage and a bold spirit of improvisation. The cost to the Germans in damaged shipping can hardly have justified the effort and casualties on the British side, but such an equation does not give the whole picture. The Naval Attaché in Stockholm reported his Vichy colleague as stressing the great effect that such raids had on French morale.[33] The British were similarly heartened. And, of no small importance to Mountbatten, the impact on the Prime Minister was as strong as that on any of his fellow countrymen.

Churchill approved strongly of Mountbatten's conduct of affairs. He considered that his selection had been amply justified and that the time had now come to move on to the next stage. On 4 March 1942 Mountbatten was summoned to lunch at Downing Street where 'he told me I was to be Chief of Combined Operations, to sit as the fourth Chief of Staff and have the acting ranks of Vice-Admiral, Lieutenant-General and Air Marshal'.

In telling Mountbatten what he had in mind, Churchill was pre-empting the views of his chief advisers. There were considerable doubts about the wisdom of the move, particularly so far as the First Sea Lord, Dudley Pound, was concerned. He wrote to the Prime Minister to say that the Navy was disturbed because they believed the advice of the Admiralty was being ignored.

If Mountbatten is made an acting Vice-Admiral, it will be attributed to one of three things:

(a) That it is on my advice. I am afraid I feel so strongly that it is wrong that I cannot shoulder this responsibility and, if I did so, it would reduce confidence in my leadership.

(b) That it has been done contrary to my advice. Naturally, I could not say this and consequently people must be left to think what they like, and I am very much afraid that it would be taken as another supposed case of your overriding my advice.

(c) That it is his Royalty. This would naturally do him harm in the Service.

Apart from the above, the Service will not understand a junior Captain *in a shore appointment* being given three steps in rank*. . . .

The question of his rank will not make the slightest difference to the weight which is given to the opinions he expresses at the Chiefs of Staff meetings. . . .

I must apologize for writing at such length, about what may appear a small matter. It is only because I feel the reactions will be so great that I have done so.[34]

Churchill was not put out by Pound's opposition. In a note to the Chiefs of Staff written the day after the First Sea Lord's letter he formally set out his wishes: 'The Chief of Combined Operations will attend meetings of the Chiefs of Staff as a full member whenever major issues are in question and also, as heretofore, when his own Combined Operations, or any special matters in which he is concerned, are under discussion.' To this he added in manuscript a minatory postscript; the Chiefs were welcome to discuss the matter among themselves, 'but I trust they will find themselves generally able to agree'. To Ismay he was even blunter; the Chiefs could discuss the details of his proposal if they cared to, 'but I cannot have the plan seriously affected'.[35]

Alan Brooke, who had taken over from Dill as Chief of the Imperial General Staff at the end of 1941, made it plain that this interloper had been foisted on the Chiefs. He felt that Mountbatten was doing a good job at Combined Operations and had no particular objection to the titles with which he was to be adorned, but it seemed to him that his membership of the Chiefs of Staff Committee – even as qualified by Churchill – was a waste of time, and that the present system gave him all the representation he could reasonably require. There is no evidence that knowledge, or, at least, suspicion, of Brooke's attitude disturbed Mountbatten deeply, but it must have caused him some apprehension. A member of his staff noticed how Mountbatten, 'who ordinarily stood in awe of no man but the King', approached Brooke with considerable caution and was ready to abandon a

* Two steps would appear more accurate.

project at once if he knew the C.I.G.S. was likely to oppose it. 'Mountbatten would if necessary fight the Admiralty and the First Sea Lord to the last ditch but not the C.I.G.S.'[36]

For Combined Operations the new appointment was a cause for unequivocal rejoicing. 'My own reaction', recorded John Hughes Hallett, 'was one of exhilaration, almost exultation. At one stride our organisation had penetrated the very centre and citadel of Power. We were now to work for a man with access to all the secrets, and for one who could, and would, be an advocate at top level for any plan.'[37] Mountbatten was equally jubilant. To Churchill he stressed that after the job was over he must be allowed to return to his substantive rank and command of a big ship; with his future in the Navy thus secure, he settled down to exploit his new opportunities. 'I am now going about wearing a Vice-Admiral's stripes and feeling very self-conscious,' he told Patricia. 'The youngest Vice-Admiral since Nelson was Lord Beatty who became one at 44. Does that stagger you or (as the Americans say) does that stagger you? Although the Army and Air Force are pressing me to get Lieutenant-General's and Air Marshal's uniforms, I am, at present, too shy and plead insufficient coupons.'[38]

To Leo Amery, then at the India Office but listened to by Churchill on defence questions, it seemed that Mountbatten's appointment was a presage of a further reorganization which would leave the Chief of Combined Operations as 'supreme Chief of Staff'.[39] His view was not shared by Alan Brooke and his colleagues, who were reluctant to admit that the new recruit was in any way their peer. Mountbatten's slow progress towards *de facto* if never *de jure* status as a full member of the Chiefs of Staff can be charted in the minutes of their meetings. At first he was listed below the line with the experts called in to attend for a specific item. On 16 March for the first time he climbed above the line but was still 'present for Items 9 and 10'. On 20 March, with Churchill in the chair, he appeared with no such qualification – perhaps because it was felt that any meeting at which the Prime Minister presided must be occupied exclusively with 'major issues' and so involved Mountbatten's attendance throughout. During April and May a confused secretariat described Mountbatten's participation as the mood took them – sometimes as a full member of the committee, sometimes not. It was only in the high summer that any attempt to distinguish between him and the other Chiefs was finally abandoned.

During these early days at Combined Operations, Mountbatten had little time for any activity outside his duties. He made one enjoyable exception, however. In July 1941 he and Edwina had gone with Noel Coward to the cinema.

Afterwards, wrote Coward, 'Dickie told whole story of the sinking of *Kelly*. Absolutely heart-breaking and so magnificent. He told the whole saga without frills and with a sincerity that was very moving. He is a pretty wonderful man, I think.'[40] Coward now conceived the idea of making a propaganda film about life on a British destroyer which would be modelled on the *Kelly*. Mountbatten took to the idea with delight; discussed every detail of the scenario; took Coward to call on the First Lord and the Minister of Information, Brendan Bracken; paid frequent visits to Denham Studios; and invited the King and Queen to inspect work in progress. He was involved in the casting even of the minor roles. Bernard Miles was summoned to a studio in London so that some unspecified dignitaries could see a film about the Home Guard in which he had played a part. As he waited nervously, Mountbatten, Coward and the novelist Clemence Dane, who had written the script, swept in and settled at the front. They watched the Home Guard film twice. As they left, Mountbatten glanced at Miles and said, 'You'll do.' 'High praise, dear boy!' murmured Coward. Mountbatten was equally concerned about the extras – deciding that they were so unseamanlike in their appearance that he recruited two hundred convalescent patients from the naval hospital at Haslar.[41]

Noel Coward always insisted that he had taken care not to model his hero too closely on Mountbatten. 'My Captain (D) is quite ordinary, with an income of about £800 a year, a small country house near Plymouth, a reasonably nice-looking wife (Mrs not Lady), two children and a cocker spaniel.'[42] This was disingenuous; though the Captain's social background might be different, in every particular his conduct and mannerisms when on board were modelled on Mountbatten. Two or three of his speeches to the crew were provided by Mountbatten verbatim.[43] The Admiralty firmly denied that *In Which We Serve* was based on any particular destroyer, but no one took the disclaimer seriously. Nor was Mountbatten at great pains to maintain the fiction. Mrs Roosevelt dined at Buckingham Palace in October 1942, to meet Mountbatten:

> . . . contriving to look as handsome and dashing and glamorous as his reputation. After dinner we adjourned to the cellar bomb-shelter, where we were shown the Noel Coward film *In Which We Serve*, which had just been completed. Mountbatten, of course, was model and inspiration for this film's principal character; he distracted us only slightly by keeping up throughout the screening a running fire of comments upon the experiences which had served as basis for the film's plot.[44]

The *Daily Express* in September opened a public debate on whether it was proper for Coward to play the role of Lord Louis Mountbatten.[45] The Ministry of Information began to waver. Mountbatten dined with Brendan Bracken so as to stiffen his resolution. 'Dickie's militant loyalty, moral courage and infinite capacity for taking pains, however busy he is, is one of the marvels of this most unpleasant age,' wrote Coward. 'I would do anything in the world for him.'[46] The militancy was displayed when a senior civil servant in the Ministry of Information took exception to the making of a film which featured the sinking of a British warship. It must never be shown abroad, he told the Admiralty. It was back to Bracken again, Mountbatten waving the letter and demanding that the unfortunate official should be summoned. 'Dickie went off like a time-bomb,' Coward described the meeting, 'and it was one of the most startling and satisfactory scenes I have ever witnessed. I actually felt a pang of compassion for the wretched official, who wilted under the tirade like a tallow candle before a strong fire.'[47]

When Noel Coward came to write the autobiography from which the last passage is taken, he sent a draft to Mountbatten for his comments. 'You may not realise it,' replied Mountbatten, 'but I have been greatly criticised, chiefly among my brother officers, for being a party to the making of a film which was apparently designed to boost me personally.' Coward's present text might support such an impression. Could it not be changed in such a way as to indicate that 'my co-operation over this film was based on the understanding that it was not to be recognisable as the story of my own ship and certainly not as my own story?'[48] In fact it is hard to find any naval contemporary of Mountbatten who does not feel that *In Which We Serve* was a splendid piece of propaganda which did good for the Service. Its putative hero had to put up with some mild ridicule, but nothing stronger. Mountbatten himself never tired of seeing it. He went to a preview on 27 September, a performance at C.O.H.Q. on 15 October, the screening seen by Mrs Roosevelt on 23 October and at least a dozen others over the next decade. His pride in it was justified.

Mountbatten always attributed his vendetta with Beaverbrook to a shot in the film in which a copy of the *Daily Express*, dated 1 September 1939 and bearing the headline 'There will be no war this year', was pictured sinking in the sea. Beaverbrook turned on Mountbatten at a dinner-party given by Averell Harriman in October 1942 and accused him of ingratitude and self-glorification: 'You and Coward have gone out of your way to insult me and try to hold up the *Daily Express* to ridicule!' Mountbatten pleaded that he had tried to persuade Coward to cut out this scene, but Beaverbrook would have none of it: 'I shall never forgive you for this piece of disloyalty. From now on, you watch out. You will live to regret the day that you took part in such a vile attack on me!'[49]

The protracted campaign which the Beaverbrook newspapers waged against Mountbatten will recur at several points of this narrative. To attribute it wholly or even in large part to this trifling cause does, however, seem unwarrantable. The full fury of the *Express*'s denunciations of Mountbatten did not become apparent until much later and then seems to have related more to his attitude towards imperialism than to any personal grievance. The two men were still corresponding on affectionate terms as late as the spring of 1944.

# CHAPTER 13

# SLEDGEHAMMER *and the Americans*

In JUNE 1941 the Germans invaded Russia. 'Isn't it grand news that the Russians are fighting on our side,' wrote Mountbatten to Pamela. 'The original Bolsheviks murdered most of our relations and I never thought the day would come when I would welcome them as allies, but we must on no account let the Nazis win, must we?'[1] It is striking how, in his letters to his wife and children, Mountbatten almost always referred to the enemy as 'the Nazis' or 'Hitler'. The fact that Britain was at war with the country of his parents, where he had so many friends and relations and had passed such happy holidays, must have been unpalatable. By speaking always of Germany's leaders or ruling party, he rendered slightly less distressing the fact that the two countries which meant most to him were involved in total war. His loyalties were never strained – Mountbatten felt himself one hundred per cent British and committed to British victory – but he told himself that the German people were misled and that their hearts were not truly in the fight. David Astor, who was working in C.O.H.Q., had kept in touch with émigré German friends who had gone into exile because of their political views. The Security Service disliked this connection and denounced him to the C.C.O. Mountbatten sent for Astor and asked whether the charge was true. Astor said that it was, and that he would have been ashamed if he had dropped his former friends. 'Quite right,' said Mountbatten approvingly, and left it at that.[2]

The entry of Russia into the war created urgent problems. Opinions differed as to whether or for how long the Russians would be able to resist the German invasion. Mountbatten was among the more optimistic; to a junior colleague he 'said openly that he thought the pattern of 1812 would be repeated'.[3] In any case, no one doubted that everything possible should be done to sustain them. This meant that supplies had to be diverted from national needs to the Russian front; still more, the concept of armed landings on the Continent took on new urgency. Previously anything more substantial than a raid had seemed a remote, almost visionary, prospect; now it became apparent that a massive diversion, even though premature and tactically unjustifiable, might have to be mounted to relieve the pressure on Britain's new ally. Something between a raid and a second front – a hybrid previously ruled out as strategically unsound – began to be envisaged.

On 7 December 1941 came the Japanese attack on Pearl Harbor and the entry of the United States into the war against Germany. There was no longer any question of *if* the Allies would one day be able to launch a second front, the only problem was how soon. With a speed astonishing to the older, less flexible societies of Europe, the gigantic strength of the United States adjusted to the needs of war. The acquisition of this ally set Mountbatten a new challenge. In C.O.H.Q. he had created the first truly integrated headquarters, where the pure doctrine of amphibious warfare was preached without reference to the shibboleths of any individual Service. Now his aim became an international headquarters, where Americans and Canadians would work alongside Britons, Frenchmen or any other ally, with loyalty to a common cause and effort raised above the national interest. It was a dashing and generous concept, peculiarly well suited to Mountbatten's temperament. Some months passed before he could take even the first steps towards its realization; but from the moment it became certain that American forces would play a part in the re-conquest of Europe, he knew that this must be the future of C.O.H.Q.

It is a testimony to Mountbatten's work in his first six months at Combined Operations that by the time the first Americans surveyed his fledgeling organization they found something to admire and support. He had taken over a directorate with little executive authority and only small resources in men and material. By the spring of 1942 he controlled an important command which enjoyed a virtual monopoly in the skills of amphibious warfare. He had established himself firmly in his new role. Chips Channon, whose awe-inspiring naivety about himself contrasts curiously with his shrewdness about others, sat next to him at dinner in April. 'I . . . found Dicky much grown in stature since he took up his highly important, indeed vital command. But he remains simple and unaffected, and only when I talked of his nephew, Prince Philip of Greece, did his sleepy strange eyes light up with an affectionate, almost paternal light.'[4]

So marked, indeed, was his growth in stature that it seems Churchill at least briefly considered appointing him to a yet more important post. It was well known – best known of all to the First Sea Lord – that Churchill had lost confidence in Dudley Pound and was itching for a change. Andrew Cunningham came home from the Mediterranean in 1942 to find Pound in great distress. 'He told me that Winston was thinking of getting rid of him and putting Mountbatten in as First Sea Lord!! Naturally I told him to glue himself to his chair.'[5] Pound took his advice and stuck it out for another fifteen months, when ill-health forced him to retire. Ismay, who knew

Churchill's mind as well as anyone, had no suspicion that any such move was in question and doubted afterwards whether the Prime Minister could have been serious – 'He may well have teased Pound himself, but not more than that.'[6] Pound certainly took it seriously, however, and it was always difficult to be sure when a Churchillian whim might not become reality. Mountbatten himself, as much in the dark as Ismay, claimed afterwards that he would have refused the appointment 'on the same grounds that Bruce Fraser gave in 1943, namely that A.B.C. [Cunningham] was such an obvious choice to the whole Navy that they would not understand him being by-passed for this appointment, and certainly not for a "dip-down" like me'.[7] Whether he would in fact have had the fortitude to reject promotion was not put to the test; the idea was still-born and the temptation spared him.

That Churchill could have conceived such an idea, however, illustrates how far Mountbatten had established himself as a member of the team charged with the running of the war. Though Brooke was sometimes less than enthusiastic when Mountbatten aired his views on higher strategy, there was no escaping the fact that the voice of the Chief of Combined Operations was going to be heard with increasing force whenever Allied action against the Continent was in question. In March 1942, even as Mountbatten was easing himself into his new responsibilities, this issue came dramatically to the fore. The Director of Plans, arguing that the coming summer was likely to be decisive on the Russian front, pleaded that the British should be prepared to launch a force across the Channel sufficiently large to relieve the pressure on their allies. To achieve this end, it was calculated that eight to ten divisions would have to be landed on the European coast. That such a force might be lost, or that its assembly might disrupt preparations for a more permanent and substantial invasion the following year, was held to be neither here nor there. If the Russian front collapsed, then the prospects of a second front in 1943, or 1944 for that matter, would be remote indeed.[8]

When such an operation could be launched and at what target it should be directed were matters of great concern to the Chief of Combined Operations. On the first point Mountbatten insisted that the Allies could not have a sufficiently large force of landing-craft assembled before July 1942 at the earliest. This had been his message from the moment he took over Combined Operations. A fleet of specialized landing-craft was a pre-requisite of a successful invasion. It was not enough to imagine that barges or other such craft could be cobbled up to meet the new need and entrusted to crews with little experience of amphibious operations. A wide range of landing-craft was going to be needed for a variety of precise ends, each one manned by personnel trained in their particular speciality. There had to be landing-craft large and landing-craft small; craft for men and for machines; heavily or lightly armoured; carrying rockets, carrying searchlights, carrying tanks or guns; landing-craft that could tackle walls or cliffs, act as bridges or ramps. A new science and a new industry were called for, and in the spring of 1942 both were in their infancy. Even worse, if such few vessels as were already available were withdrawn for attack on France, they could not be used for training the men who would man the generations of craft planned for the future. No one knew better than Mountbatten that if the plan for limited re-entry to the Continent – styled SLEDGEHAMMER – was ever made reality, it would not merely cost the country dear in men and equipment but would seriously dislocate the build-up for the great invasion that was his main responsibility.

His view on this subject was generally accepted, though not necessarily fully taken into account. On the other issue – the site of SLEDGEHAMMER – he was less successful. Planning for this operation had been referred to the Combined Commanders and Mountbatten's colleagues on this body, Sholto Douglas, the head of Fighter Command, and Bernard Paget, the Commander-in-Chief, Home Forces, argued strongly for a landing in the Pas de Calais. There were geographical reasons for such a course; a landing between Le Touquet and Boulogne would be 150 miles closer to the Rhine than a beach-head in Normandy and only 130 miles from the great port of Antwerp. The Seine and the Somme would not confront the invaders on their logical line of attack. Such arguments, however, assumed a landing which would be followed by a powerful and sustained advance. Their application to SLEDGEHAMMER was uncertain. The decisive argument for the Pas de Calais was that the short Channel crossing offered the possibility of providing air-cover for the assault. To draw the German Air Force into action and destroy all or part of it would achieve as much to help the Russians as the landing itself. Against this Mountbatten and his C.O.H.Q. experts argued that the coast was too heavily defended, the ports too shallow, the entrances too narrow, it would be too easy for the Germans to reinforce the threatened areas. Only if the invasion were moved west of Le Havre to the Baie de la Seine in Normandy would there be any chance of putting a force ashore without appalling carnage, still less of sustaining it once landed.

The dispute came to a head in the Chiefs of Staff Committee on 28 March[9] when the Joint Report of the Combined Commanders was put forward. Paget and Douglas argued the case for the Pas de Calais. Mountbatten did not rule this out categorically, but 'he was not yet in a position to say that a landing on the scale proposed in the Pas de Calais was a practicable operation'. Even if it were executed, re-embarkation would be extremely difficult; 'the operation in the Cherbourg Peninsula should be examined in further detail'. Brooke, while disliking both variants of what he felt to be a thoroughly undesirable operation, summed up decisively against C.O.H.Q. 'The Pas de Calais area was the only place in which the military object could be achieved. In no other area could this be done and operations in other areas were not practical military propositions.'

In his diary for that evening Brooke noted that Mountbatten 'was still hankering after a landing near Cherbourg, where proper air support is not possible. Finally I think we convinced him sufficiently to make his visit to Chequers that evening safe.'[10] In a codicil added later Brooke remarked that Mountbatten's visits to Chequers were always perilous as 'there was no knowing what discussions he might be led into and . . . let us in for'. In their ebullience, wide-ranging imagination and appreciation of the dramatic, Churchill and Mountbatten were well matched, and together would work themselves into a fury of what Brooke felt to be dangerous fantasy. Mountbatten was loyal, and dutifully requested briefings on every subject which it seemed likely would be raised, but as 'it was not easy to predict what he might be asked, it was not possible to guard against all eventualities'. The Monday mornings after a Chequers weekend, when Mountbatten would tell the Chiefs of Staff what had transpired between him and the Prime Minister, sometimes produced unpleasant surprises.

On this occasion Mountbatten was far from convinced by the reasoning of Brooke or the Combined Commanders. He stuck to his contention that any invasion, be it a hurried expedient like SLEDGEHAMMER or full-scale re-entry to the Continent (in the end OVERLORD, then styled ROUNDUP), must avoid the Pas de Calais if it were to succeed. The relationship between his championship of Normandy and the eventual decision to launch the invasion proper in that area is hard to establish. Mountbatten himself was wont to claim that the two were intimately linked, that the decision to invade in Normandy represented the victory of his arguments over the school of Paget and Douglas. He described in vivid detail a meeting of the Chiefs of Staff at which the Combined Commanders argued vigorously for the Pas de Calais, and he, speaking from his seat as a Chief of Staff rather than a Combined Commander, 'shot their plan down in flames'. The records of the Chiefs over this period provide no evidence of this dramatic encounter, a fact which Mountbatten explained to Captain Roskill by claiming that 'the minutes rather blurred over the clash'.[11] Hughes Hallett's independent account of a meeting at which two at least of the Chiefs were present is similar to Mountbatten's.[12] Some such debate there must have been, though its precise forum and significance is uncertain.

Certainly, when the Chiefs of Staff considered the matter again they ruled that the 'responsibility for planning Operation ROUNDUP should be brought into line with that for Operation SLEDGEHAMMER, i.e. it should be transferred to the C.-in-C., Fighter Command and the Chief of Combined

Operations'.[13] Certainly, by May 1942, Admiral Ramsay, recently appointed naval commander of the invasion fleet, was speaking of Normandy as the agreed landing area, whichever operation was in question.[14] Certainly, too, one of the principal preoccupations of C.O.H.Q. was to devise some means by which air support could be provided for a landing as far afield as Normandy.[15] As will be seen (p. 214 below), it was at a meeting presided over and stage-managed by Mountbatten that the choice of Normandy was finally accepted by all those responsible. It appears, therefore, that the Pas de Calais was the approved landing site when SLEDGEHAMMER was conceived, that opinion subsequently moved in favour of Normandy, and that, long before the invasion took place, it was taken for granted that the latter was the only possible target. To attribute this change of heart exclusively to the preaching of Mountbatten and C.O.H.Q. would be over-generous; to deny them considerable credit must surely be unreasonable.

As the American build-up in Britain developed, so increased attention had to be paid to their views. Early in April 1942 General Marshall, the Chief of Staff, U.S. Army, came to London to compare notes with the British Chiefs of Staff on how the Allied strategy was to develop. With him came a trusted staff officer, Al Wedemeyer, who cast a shrewd if sometimes suspicious eye over the assembled dignitaries. Brooke, he concluded, was articulate, sensitive, 'one who would nibble away to gain his ends'. Pound was 'a gentleman, courteous, a twinkle in his clear blue eyes, small in stature, large in his grasp of humanity and at times rather taciturn'. Portal he judged to be a notch above the other members of the hierarchy 'so far as character and all-round intellectual capacity were concerned'. At first he dismissed Ismay as insincere, 'a smoothie', a 'Mr Fix-It', but later he decided that he had integrity and moral courage.

> Mountbatten was by all odds the most colorful on the British Chiefs of Staff level. He was charming, tactful, a conscious gallant knight in shining armor, handsome, bemedaled, with a tremendous amount of self-assurance. Because of his youthfulness which was emphasized by his appearance, it was obvious that the older officers did not defer readily to his views. They were careful, however, to give him a semblance of courteous attention. After all, he was a cousin of the King and, no doubt about it, a great favorite of the Prime Minister.[16]

In the course of his meeting with the Chiefs of Staff, Marshall was invited to visit the various Service Ministries, and chose to go first to C.O.H.Q. On 10 April the call was duly paid. Wedemeyer was again in attendance and, in spite of his impressions of the day before, was expecting to meet something of a playboy. Instead, though he thought the entourage at C.O.H.Q. contained 'the most peculiar people', he told Marshall afterwards that he was struck by Mountbatten's 'great enthusiasm and imagination'.[17] Marshall felt the same. With some prompting by Mountbatten, he was induced to say that he would like American officers to join C.O.H.Q. and operate as part of an international headquarters. Mountbatten eagerly grasped at a proposal which reflected his own aspirations. The same day the Chiefs of Staff took up the suggestion and formally invited American planning officers to join in the work of C.O.H.Q.[18] Within a month Brigadier-General Lucian Truscott and eight other American officers were at work in Richmond Terrace.

Marshall's visit was doubly useful. Enthusiastic about all he had seen, he asked what more the Americans could do to help. The C.C.O. replied promptly: 'Telegraph today to double every British order for landing-ships and landing-craft and take over the new orders yourself.' Then he took a piece of paper and sketched out the rough plan of an L.C.I. (L) – Landing-Craft Infantry (Large) – the basic tool of the amphibious operation, which could transport two hundred troops in reasonable comfort and land them on an enemy beach. Design and build three hundred of them, he asked, half for the British, half for the Americans. From Harry Hopkins, with whom he stayed at Chequers, he wanted even more. A thousand barges from the Port of London would make a useful back-up to an invasion force, yet the engines to propel them were not available. These, too, the Americans were asked to provide. Marshall and Hopkins listened with equanimity to what even Mountbatten admitted was a tall order, and promised to do their best. Their best was more than good enough.[19]

The following month General Eisenhower came to London, as a senior planner from the War Department in Washington, and also attended a meeting with the Chiefs of Staff. Asked to give his views on a future invasion, he said that he felt the first step must be to name a commander. 'That man must be given every bit of power that both governments can make available to him' – whether in planning or the requisitioning of men or equipment. Brooke asked him whom he would suggest should fill such a role.

In America [said Eisenhower] I have heard much of a man who has been intensively studying amphibious operations for many months. I understand his position is Chief of Combined Operations and I think that his name is Admiral Mountbatten. Anyone will be better than none; such an operation cannot be carried out under committee command. But I have heard that Admiral Mountbatten is vigorous, intelligent and courageous, and if the operation is to be staged originally with British forces predominating, I assume he could do the job.[20]

A slightly embarrassed silence was broken by Brooke, who said: 'General, possibly you have not met Admiral Mountbatten. This is he, sitting directly across the table from you.' Reporting on the meeting to Marshall, Eisenhower remarked that Brooke did not seem over-impressed by the idea of a single commander for the invasion force. He stuck to his guns, however, and, not surprisingly, was given a warm reception when he called on C.O.H.Q. the following day. Mountbatten, recorded Eisenhower, believed that his particular mission was 'to develop the training and tactical doctrines applying to the assault echelon'. He argued with particular fervour for the large landing-craft, maintaining that only if enough men could be put ashore simultaneously on a wide enough front would the coastal defences be overwhelmed.[21]

Eisenhower quickly became Mountbatten's close ally, agreeing with him not only about the need to invade on a wide front, but also on the crucial importance of a highly trained assault force under a single commander which would be first ashore along the whole front. On this Mountbatten found himself in a minority among his compatriots. General Paget, with whom he was frequently at variance, took the line that the whole thing was a lot of stuff and nonsense; any competent soldier should be able to jump out of a boat and fight his way ashore, and any competent corps commander could ensure that troops fit for such a role were in the vanguard. 'In view of the British insistence that only through the immediate appointment of a single supreme commander can planning for this operation receive the necessary impetus,' mused Eisenhower, 'it is quite impossible to uncover the reasons why they do not see the same necessity in this particular case. I fear that some interservice jealousies or politics may be involved.'[22]

Eisenhower's relationship with Mountbatten was put on an official plane in June 1942, when it was decreed that the two men should deal with each other on all matters concerned with the training of forces intended for use in operations on the Continent. Such formalization was hardly necessary, however; what mattered more was that they respected, liked and, above all, trusted each other. A typical if trivial illustration of Mountbatten's sympathy for Eisenhower came a few weeks after the latter's posting to Britain. A chain-smoker, Eisenhower concluded that he would be unable to attend any meal where the King's health was toasted and smoking forbidden before that moment. Mountbatten insisted that he should come to a banquet given at C.O.H.Q., and promised that smoking would present no problems. As soon as the soup was cleared, Mountbatten proposed the health of the King and the President, then called loudly: 'Now, General, smoke all you want.'[23]

Eisenhower proved a useful ally on many fronts. In July 1942 'Wild Bill' Donovan, founder of the American intelligence service, the O.S.S., wished to place a liaison officer within C.O.H.Q. Mountbatten was doubtful about the wisdom of having representatives of too many separate American agencies milling around London, but told Eisenhower he would accept the officer if Marshall felt it desirable. His friend moved firmly in his support. 'The Combined Operations staff is not, repeat not, a subversive organisation,' he cabled Washington, and the idea was quashed.[24]

With Marshall's support, Eisenhower continued to press for Mountbatten to be put in charge of SLEDGEHAMMER and the eventual invasion. 'Here is where Lord Louis fits in,' he told Marshall at the end of July. 'I should like to see him assigned, with the bulk of his staff, as the assault *Chief of Staff*. ... I think there is little need to point out the several advantages of the scheme. ... No other trained land-sea-air staff exists, and already there is good American representation on it. Moreover, the individuals in the group are *friends*, and work in a single building of their own (no small item).'[25] Marshall responded enthusiastically, and Eisenhower returned to the charge with Ismay, urging that Mountbatten at once be assigned to this work.[26] It does not seem that the Chiefs of Staff gave the American proposal any serious consideration; certainly, it ran counter to the accepted doctrine of the time. Though Eisenhower was still bombarding Ismay with solicitations on behalf of his friend as late as the end of October,[27] the British remained deaf. It was not until April 1943 that a command was set up to run the invasion, and C.O.H.Q. as such played no part in the new organization. The Americans were not alone in thinking that Mountbatten was to some extent penalized for his youth and lack of seniority. Victor Cazalet told Hugh Dalton that the C.C.O., 'though a great pet of the P.M., is still being completely held up by the three Services, the Heads of all of which are very jealous of him'.[28]

Nevertheless, it seems that the reluctance of the Chiefs to go along with Eisenhower's proposal stemmed not from doubts about Mountbatten's ability or the desirability of making any such appointment but from their determination not to be rushed into any course which might make more likely major action against the Continent in 1942 or even early 1943. British and Americans were agreed that Europe must be invaded and the German Army defeated; they also agreed that Britain was the base from which the main effort must be launched. At that point, however, thinking diverged. The British favoured a war of attrition, a campaign in the Mediterranean to precede the invasion proper, a laborious build-up of resources for the final assault. The Americans were bent on a quick and ferocious knock-out blow, sceptical of British motives in urging the prior clearance of the enemy from North Africa, displeased at the idea that they should mass their forces in

Britain if there was to be no action for many months. If the American armies in Europe were to stand idle, it might be better to reverse the accepted policy of 'Germany first', and use their strength to drive back the Japanese.

Marshall had left London after his talks in April in the firm belief that an invasion of the Continent would take place within a year and that SLEDGE-HAMMER was still an active possibility for later in 1942. On the latter point, at least, the Chiefs of Staff had grave reservations. When the Combined Commanders reported on the material problems involved in mounting SLEDGEHAMMER, the Chiefs listened sympathetically and ruled that, while preparations should continue, there should also be plans made for a major raid which, by implication, would take SLEDGEHAMMER's place. On 1 June Mountbatten urged that a formal decision to bury the operation should be taken, since it would be incompatible with an invasion in the first half of 1943.[29] The Chiefs of Staff, presumably loath to go back on something which had so recently been agreed with the Americans, continued to insist that the operation should be prepared, even though it was never to be executed. To this Mountbatten took exception. He

> held the view strongly that it would be very wrong to mount an Operation which we had no chance of carrying out. There was always the danger that, if the Operation were mounted, we might be ordered to carry it out. . . . He suggested that no military advantage would be gained by carrying out large-scale exercises in 1942 and by the assembly of craft and troops for this purpose. If it was essential to mount an Operation, he suggested that it should be one which could be mounted without prejudice to training and capable of being carried out.[30]

As the most consistent opponent of SLEDGEHAMMER, yet also the military leader most dedicated to the offensive, Mountbatten seemed the obvious person to sell to the Americans the unpalatable fact that there was little hope of any major action in Europe in 1942. At the end of May Churchill telegraphed Roosevelt to report that 'preparations are proceeding ceaselessly on the largest scale'. So far so good, but the message went on: 'Dickie will explain to you the difficulties of 1942 when he arrives.' Worse still, there were references to the battle in North Africa, with a clear implication that it was there that the most important engagements would be fought in the forthcoming months.[31] The telegram caused alarm in Washington, particularly to the Secretary-of-War, H. L. Stimson. Were the British reneging on their commitment to attack across the Channel? What extravagant diversions were being proposed? Most alarming of all, would President Roosevelt stand firm against the blandishments of Mountbatten, followed, as they were shortly to be, by a visit from Churchill, the arch-magician himself?[32]

Mountbatten believed that he got on particularly well with Americans. So, on the whole, he did. His particular brand of flamboyance, his ruthless professionalism, sometimes jarred on his fellow countrymen. Across the Atlantic they seemed more acceptable. But he did not always enjoy the Americans' confidence. He laboured, said Michael Adeane, a future royal private secretary who at that time was assistant to the C.O.H.Q. representative in Washington, under the twin burdens of being British and being royal.[33] On both these counts he merited suspicion; on the latter a touch of incredulity. Al Wedemeyer, in particular, viewed his coming with some dismay. Wedemeyer, wrote Adeane in 1942, would never see a British officer without a witness. Mellowed by time and discretion, his published memoirs still reflect this mood. Though Mountbatten was only 'John the Baptist laying the groundwork for the great strategic evangelist Winston Churchill', his presence was still enough to cause disquiet. 'Now we had an extremely articulate Britisher endeavoring to raise bogies about the hazards of a cross-Channel operation.' When Mountbatten spent five hours closeted with the President, Wedemeyer was near despair: 'After all, I had been exposed to his charm, plausibility and enthusiasm when I was in London.'[34]

Hughes Hallett, who credits Mountbatten with a six hours *tête-à-tête* with Roosevelt, records that the C.C.O. emerged elated, convinced that the President now shared the British point of view.[35] The report which he gave Churchill of their conversation reflects no such optimism.[36] Roosevelt seemed to accept Mountbatten's thesis that there were not enough landing-craft available to mount SLEDGEHAMMER on a scale which would force the Germans to withdraw troops from the Russian front, but still insisted that the British should be prepared to make a landing if German morale were to crack during the autumn. He was resolutely opposed to sending 'a million American soldiers to England on the off-chance of ROUNDUP being on in the Spring of 1943' and demanded firm guarantees that the Allies would attack during the winter or, at the latest, before 1 April. On the other hand, he was more sympathetic than many of his advisers to Churchillian ideas for landings in North Africa. Mountbatten had reason to be modestly encouraging when he saw the Prime Minister on his return to England (since he flew back overnight from Montreal, went to Chequers the same evening, was kept up till 4 a.m., was back in his office for a meeting of the Chiefs of Staff at 9.30 a.m. and worked through till 9.30 p.m., he had reason to be sleepy too) but certainly there were no grounds for ebullience. Nor did Churchill see things differently. When he in his turn got to the White House on 21 June there was, reported Stimson, 'a good deal of pow-wow and a rumpus'. The Prime Minister, it seemed, was disturbed 'by some casual remarks the President had made to Lord Mountbatten some time earlier about the possibility of having to make a "sacrifice" cross-Channel landing in 1942 to help the Russians'.[37]

The remarks might have been rather less casual if Mountbatten had not been able partially to appease the President with an account of the great raid that was planned for later in 1942. The target was to be Dieppe.

# CHAPTER 14

# *Dieppe*

WITH THE POSSIBLE EXCEPTION of the partition of India, no episode in
Mountbatten's career has earned him as much harsh criticism as the raid on
Dieppe. It is the only point on which he showed himself invariably on the
defensive. Whether the affair was in fact the out-and-out failure which many
believed it to be, and, if it was, how much responsibility should properly be
attributed to Mountbatten are questions which can be answered only if one
has decided what it was supposed to achieve. Yet this fundamental question
proves extraordinarily difficult to answer. Brian McCool, the Principal
Military Landing Officer, was interrogated by the Germans for two days after
his capture. At the end he was asked: 'Look, McCool, it was too big for a raid
and too small for an invasion. What was it?' 'If you can tell *me* the answer,' he
replied, 'I would be very grateful.'[1] The Chiefs of Staff might have made a
better shot at answering, but the confusion would not wholly have been
dissipated. And in this imprecision about objectives lies one reason why
Dieppe was doomed to failure before it was even launched.

The concept that more and larger raids should follow the minor successes
of Bruneval and St Nazaire was accepted by April 1942.[2] What is more
difficult to establish is how it was accepted that such a raid could also make an
important contribution towards relieving pressure on the Russian front and,
in the minds of some people, could by extension be considered a substitute for
SLEDGEHAMMER. Obviously it was no such thing. A raid lasting less than
a day, however large the forces involved and important the target, could not
replace a landing of eight to ten divisions and the establishment of a
bridgehead that would be held for several weeks, perhaps months, and might
conceivably become permanent. But the idea that it could achieve at least
some of the objects of SLEDGEHAMMER grew in attractiveness as
SLEDGEHAMMER itself became more and more remote. When Mountbatten explained to the Chiefs of Staff on 5 May 1942 that SLEDGEHAM-
MER could not take place before 15 August, he stressed that the raid on
Dieppe, then planned for the end of June, would compensate for the delay.[3] A
month later, when SLEDGEHAMMER had tacitly been abandoned, he
argued: 'This made it all the more important to do at least one more big raid.'[4]

Alan Brooke played with the idea of some uneasy compromise by which two divisions would maintain themselves ashore for a week or so, but the Prime Minister thought little of the idea.[5] By the middle of the year the raid on Dieppe – Operation RUTTER – was all that was left to satisfy the Americans and Russians of British aggressive intentions against the Continent. As Colonel Stacey, in the official history of the Canadian Army, said of the final decision to revive the operation towards the end of July, there was 'no evidence that the Russian situation was actually a large direct factor in the decision to revive the Dieppe project, but the news that a large distracting raid in the West was again in prospect was welcomed by the British Prime Minister'.[6]

But there was another justification for the raid. It was official doctrine in the middle of 1942 that the invasion could not succeed unless the Allies secured two or three major ports. Churchill, supported by Mountbatten, believed that much could be done to sustain the landings over sheltered beaches, but the more othodox military were dismayed at the prospect of an invasion force cut off from its support by rough weather. The operation was therefore designed to establish whether a major port could quickly be captured in something close to working order. In this sense it was a dress-rehearsal for invasion – a 'reconnaissance in force' as Brooke and later Churchill styled it,[7] in which the techniques of Combined Operations were tried out in the most testing of circumstances.

The project was first put before the Chiefs of Staff in the middle of May, though the target committee at C.O.H.Q. had been working on the details since early April. Mountbatten put up his ideas against a background of mounting irritation with the cumbrous machinery of inter-Service planning. Infuriated by the insistence of the Commanders-in-Chief that they alone should be responsible for plans affecting units under their command, he pleaded in July that 'he should be vested with the executive responsibility for mounting and launching the next large-scale raiding operation'. Brooke ruled that, while the C.C.O. should be responsible 'for the marshalling and launching of large-scale raids', his powers should end when it came to the 'actual execution of the raid to the extent of signing the operation orders'.[8] Whether Mountbatten would have been the ideal man to assume supreme control of the planning and execution of the raid on Dieppe may be open to question; what can hardly be doubted is that things would have gone better if some competent individual had been vested with such powers. The probability of muddle, uneasy compromises and botched execution was latent in the operation from its conception.

On 23 May Brooke and Mountbatten spent three hours with Churchill discussing the Dieppe raid and the prospects for invasion. The Prime Minister, said Brooke, 'was carried away with optimism at times and established lodgments all round the coast from Calais to Bordeaux with little regard to strength and landing facilities'.[9] Dieppe was accepted by all concerned to be an ideal target for an exploratory foray. Its defences were strong but, as was fondly hoped, not too strong. There were plenty of barges and small craft sheltering there whose destruction would add point to the operation. It was close enough to England to allow passage under cover of summer darkness. And, finally, it was not a port which would be relevant in the case of real invasion.[10] It was agreed that C.O.H.Q. should be charged with all detailed planning. Solly Zuckerman's first task on joining the organization was to establish the number of nights in a month in which conditions would be suitable. 'It took a month or so, working on tides, wind forces and directions and moonless nights. In the end I proudly presented the results to Mountbatten with the words "Well, it turns out that there never will be a night suitable." '[11]

It was soon clear that the finer tactical points alone were in Mountbatten's bailiwick. C.O.H.Q.'s plan for the main assault was promptly matched by a rival project prepared by the planners of Home Forces.[12] The two varied in one vital particular: C.O.H.Q. envisaged flank landings a mile or two from Dieppe and a pincer movement on the port; Home Forces were in favour of a frontal assault on Dieppe itself. As Commander-in-Chief, Eastern Command, General Montgomery attended the first joint meeting and dismissed the plan for a flank attack as the work of an amateur. If it was a fact that assault troops would be able to remain ashore only for fifteen hours, there was no hope that a flank attack could surmount the various obstacles and reach the port. A frontal attack offered the only prospect of success. Haydon and Hughes Hallett, who represented C.O.H.Q. at this meeting, were borne down by Montgomery's superior fire-power, but Mountbatten resumed the engagement at the next meeting on 25 April, arguing that 'success' in terms of the occupation of the port was not of the first importance; what mattered was to try out landing techniques and to prove that the port *could* have been occupied if it had been essential to do so. Montgomery was not impressed. He pointed out that current intelligence suggested a frontal attack would succeed without too much difficulty, and that, if the Allies failed to take Dieppe, the operation would ever after be represented as a failure.[13]

When Mountbatten accepted the arguments for a frontal attack it was implicit in the plan that any such landing would be preceded by a heavy air bombardment. Strict rules governed the bombing of targets in occupied Europe that might affect the local populations, but the Chiefs of Staff recommended that the restriction be waived on this occasion. On 1 June Churchill agreed. Then, within a few days, the position was reversed. At a meeting on 5 June, with Montgomery in the chair and Mountbatten hob-nobbing with Roosevelt in Washington, the designated Force Commander, Major-General Roberts, argued that bombing would block the narrow streets of Dieppe and make it impossible for the tanks to advance. Leigh-Mallory, the Air Force Commander, was equally ready to abandon a preliminary air attack, since he felt that the target was so small that most of the bombs would fall inland or in the sea.[14] By the time Mountbatten got back, the decision to proceed without a prior air attack had become irrevocable.

The invaders would therefore have to rely on whatever artillery support the Navy could supply. Mountbatten had long been urging that a battleship should be made available for this purpose. Dudley Pound, mindful of the recent destruction of the *Prince of Wales* and *Repulse* by Japanese air attack, rejected the idea: 'Battleships by daylight off the French coast? You must be mad, Dickie!'[15] Baillie-Grohman, who had been appointed Naval Commander for the operation, was dismayed when he heard of this ruling and pleaded that a couple of cruisers at least should be made available. He was told that this too had been rejected.[16] Brigadier Truscott was informed that cruisers could not be risked in such restricted waters.[17] All that would be on the spot to support the landing was a group of destroyers with guns of relatively small calibre.

Mountbatten could be forgiven for feeling something close to despair as he surveyed the final plans submitted to the Chiefs of Staff in mid June. Not merely had he lost on the issues of the flank attack, aerial bombardment and the support of a capital ship but also, instead of the Marines and commandos whom he had proposed should make up the assault force, there had been substituted Canadian troops whose courage and zeal were not in question but who had never had experience of an amphibious or, indeed, any other operation. This was, said Mountbatten, 'a high-level political decision, and not one in which I was involved'.[18] When Antony Head, who had joined Combined Operations in the summer of 1942, complained that the plan to land tanks on the beach without a prior bombardment was fundamentally unsound, the matter was referred to Montgomery. Head was told that he was talking nonsense.[19] A C.O.H.Q. proposal that obsolescent tanks should be filled with explosives and used to blast a hole in the sea wall was rejected by the Force Commander, who put his faith in 'Bangalore Torpedoes man-handled up the beach'.[20] The Canadian soldiers paid the price when no single torpedo achieved its aim.

It could be argued that in such circumstances Mountbatten should have disavowed the whole affair. Such a step would have shown remarkable moral courage, if not a dangerous degree of insubordination. Mountbatten did not contemplate it, mainly because he would not have accepted that the enterprise *was* doomed to failure. Like Montgomery, he believed that a frontal attack would succeed, even though at a high cost. If he had foreseen the carnage and failure that lay ahead he would indeed have been in a moral dilemma; as it was he observed events with regret but reasonable confidence.

Mountbatten missed the first dress-rehearsal at Bridport on 13 June but it was so patently a *débâcle* that the operation was postponed, and a second rehearsal fixed for 23 June. This went better, and it was decided that the landing should take place on the first suitable day after 24 June.[21] Promptly the weather deteriorated. A fortnight later Churchill summoned Mountbatten and Hughes Hallett to the Cabinet Room for a final review of prospects. Suddenly he turned on Hughes Hallett and demanded to know whether success could be guaranteed. Brooke, who was also there, interrupted and told Hughes Hallett not to reply. 'If he, or anyone else, could guarantee success, there would indeed be no object in doing the operation. It is just because no one has the slightest idea what the outcome will be that the operation is necessary.' Churchill grumbled that this was no moment to be taught by adversity, but subsided when Brooke retorted that in that case he had better forget about invading France.[22]

A week later the weather was still bad, and two of the vessels involved in the operation were bombed and put temporarily out of action. It was decided to cancel the operation. A raid on Alderney had recently met the same fate, an operation against Bayonne had been aborted. Morale at C.O.H.Q. was low. Everyone concurred that it would be impossible to mount any other major operation in 1942. Then in the course of a post-mortem on RUTTER at C.O.H.Q. Mountbatten, to use his own words, 'made the unusual and, I suggest, rather bold proposal that we should remount the operation against Dieppe'.[23] The initial reaction was dismay, as it was when he raised it with the Chiefs of Staff and then the Prime Minister. So many people now knew the target at which RUTTER had been aimed that it would only be prudent to suppose the Germans knew it too. Exactly, retorted Mountbatten; if there was one target we might be expected *not* to attack, it was Dieppe. The knowledge of our intentions could be kept to a tiny group. It was: the Defence Committee was never consulted, the First Sea Lord kept the First Lord of the Admiralty in the dark, and Ismay vividly recalled the indignation of the Vice Chief of the Imperial General Staff, General Nye, when he first heard of the operation after the troops had landed.[24] The gamble worked: though many of the participants in the raid thought otherwise at the time, it is clear from captured documents that the Germans had no inkling what was about to happen.[25]

Operation JUBILEE, the re-christened RUTTER, took place on 19 August 1942. Mountbatten spent the previous day at the ports of embarkation. 'He struck me as a grand guy and very full of fight,' recollected a U.S. Ranger, Corporal Franklin D. Koons, 'he made us all laugh and we were very cheerful.'[26] To the Canadians he began his harangue: 'I was on destroyers in the early part of this war, and I know what it felt like when some admiral who'd been sucking his teeth ashore for months came aboard to tell us how to fight. I'm not going to tell you how to fight, because you know how.'[27] Then he went back to Uxbridge to spend what little was left of the night with Leigh-Mallory. He was up by 3 a.m.: 'Great air battle,' he wrote in his diary. 'Many casualties and some successes.' By the following day the successes were hard to find.

There is no need to describe in detail the events of that unhappy day. To the west of Dieppe, Lovat's commandos successfully captured and destroyed a German battery; to the east a similar operation partially gained its objective; but the main assault on the beaches of Dieppe itself met resistance far more fierce than had been anticipated. Many of the Canadians in the landing-craft were casualties before they even got ashore; those men and tanks that landed were pinned down and never reached the town. By the end of the day sixty-eight per cent of the Canadians and twenty per cent of the commandos who had landed were dead or wounded; two thousand prisoners and nearly a thousand dead were left behind when the battered armada turned for home. Mountbatten was able to tell the War Cabinet next day that nearly two-thirds of the raiding force had returned, but this figure merely illustrated how many of the men had failed even to get ashore.

That Dieppe taught the Allies many important lessons is indisputable; whether they were worth the price that was paid for them is less easy to establish. What the raid did was to remove any illusions that invasion would be easy, that all that was necessary would be to decant an army on to a beach and leave it to get on with the war. It may fairly be said that nobody who remembered Gallipoli should have needed so elementary a reminder, but nations at war have all too often had to re-learn lessons forgotten from earlier conflicts. If there had been no Dieppe, and the invasion proper had been conducted with similar insouciance, the bloodshed would have been on a scale many hundreds of times greater, the course of the war might have been turned. 'Except for Dieppe and the work of your organization,' wrote Eisenhower, 'we would have been lacking much of the special equipment and much of the knowledge' needed for the invasion.[28]

The first and most important moral drawn from Dieppe was that the

Allies could not rely on capturing a usable port in the early stages of an invasion. 'Well, if we can't capture a port, we will have to take one with us,' Hughes Hallett is supposed to have said as he returned from the battle. The genesis of 'Mulberry', the portable harbour, will need examination in the next chapter, but the events of 19 August gave it the greatest stimulus. Second, Dieppe showed that a preliminary bombardment was essential and that far greater fire-power was needed in support of the troops. The destroyers, hampered by smoke-screens and themselves under attack from the German batteries, were too inaccurate and too lightly armed to blast the German machine-guns and light artillery into silence. The invasion forces would be accompanied by capital ships and rocket-ships capable of coming close in shore and showering the enemy positions with a cascade of devastating projectiles. Third, it was at last accepted that *ad hoc* arrangements for landing-craft would not suffice; a permanent naval assault-force would in future be maintained, and would play an indispensable role in the invasion.[29]

Dieppe also yielded dividends which are harder to evaluate yet whose existence is demonstrable. In his *Bodyguard of Lies*, Anthony Cave Brown suggested that the Dieppe raid was originally planned by Churchill to persuade the Americans that SLEDGEHAMMER would fail and was rein-stated as part of a deception operation to convince the Germans that the Allies were about to invade the Continent.[30] The latter object was in fact achieved. The Germans were satisfied that when the invasion proper came it would be aimed at a major port, and that such an invasion might well be imminent. They were persuaded to mass their forces along the Atlantic wall, rather than to build up a strong mobile reserve. 'Strategically,' wrote Churchill, 'the raid served to make the Germans more conscious of danger along the whole coast of Occupied France. This helped to hold troops and resources in the West, which did something to take the weight off Russia. Honour to the brave who fell. Their sacrifice was not in vain.'[31]

But need so many brave have fallen, and who was responsible for the blunders that cost their lives? In his memoirs Field Marshal Montgomery claimed that the two worst mistakes were the substitution of commandos for paratroops and the cancellation of the preliminary air bombardment – both decisions taken at the meeting of 5 June 1942 at which he himself was in the chair.[32] Mountbatten prompted his former Chief of Staff, Wildman-Lushington, to write to him pointing this out. He then copied Lushington's comments to Montgomery under cover of another letter, congratulating him on 'a truly magnificent contribution at the highest level to military literature on command in war. You will have received many tributes about your book, but I imagine fairly few from those who had to take a knock in it!'[33] 'I return Lushington's letter,' Montgomery replied loftily. 'I don't recall him. He is obviously a little man.' As to the question of the knock Mountbatten had been given – 'don't worry about that. It is a nothing compared to the "knocks" I gave myself!!'[34] Mountbatten had the last word in what otherwise might have become a somewhat irascible correspondence. 'Thank you for your typical letter . . . ,' he wrote. 'Of course, I do not worry about the "knocks" for, as Lushington points out, the records show that your assertions were not correct, and I notice you do not contest this! I would have loved to have got some of the "knocks" which you gave yourself.'[35]

In his recent biography of Montgomery, Nigel Hamilton has claimed that the 'real reason for disaster' was neither of the two causes put forward by the subject of his book but 'Mountbatten's promise of naval support artillery that never came'. In a strikingly intemperate attack on Mountbatten – 'a master of intrigue, jealousy and ineptitude, like a spoilt child he toyed with men's lives with an indifference to casualties that can only be explained by his insatiable, even psychopathic ambition' – he alleges that the C.C.O. 'stressed again and again that it was the primary duty of the naval destroyers to provide amphibious artillery support for the troops and tanks as they landed – an emphasis which, tragically, was taken at face value by Brooke, Montgomery and the senior army commanders. Only Mountbatten and his naval advisers could know that, in the face of hostile coastal batteries and attacked by a Luftwaffe air fleet deliberately enticed into the battle above Dieppe, his destroyers had no possible hope of providing effective artillery support.[36]

It is difficult to find chapter and verse to support this accusation. Mountbatten never doubted that the Hunt class destroyers were inadequate for the role in which they were cast – otherwise he would hardly have plagued Dudley Pound to provide a battleship or, at least, a cruiser. There is no indication in the official records that he 'stressed again and again' that destroyers could do all that was needed of them. Equally, he was as surprised as anyone else that they proved so inadequate.[37] The reason for their failure was not so much retaliatory action by the Germans – which was anticipated – as the strength of the defences and the skill with which enemy guns were entrenched in the cliffs around the town. 'The destroyers, of course, did their best to give gun support at Dieppe but the Hunts' guns do not fire a heavy enough broadside,'[38] Mountbatten told Admiral Dewar. He knew the size of the broadside before the operation; what he did not know was the target at which they would be firing.

If Mr Hamilton wanted a stick with which to beat Mountbatten, he would have done better to dwell on the faulty appreciation of the German fortifications. Dieppe represented a failure of British intelligence. When Baillie-Grohman asked Mountbatten who would provide him with up-to-date intelligence, 'a very foreign looking officer in Wing Commander uniform was indicated'.[39] Whatever success Casa Maury may have enjoyed at other stages of the war, there is no doubt that at this point he forfeited the respect of his fellow officers. 'I was soon to find him utterly useless,' wrote Baillie-Grohman. The official battle summary placed first among the causes of failure the 'absolutely mistaken estimate of the extent of the German defences'.[40] Information about the numbers of German troops proved more or less correct, but their quality and their deployment were woefully misconstrued. There were excuses – last-minute troop movements, hurried work to reinforce the defences of all the Channel ports after reports of an Allied naval build-up – but the intelligence failure remains. 'It seems impossible to avoid the conclusion', wrote Colonel Stacey, the Canadian official historian, temperately, 'that from the beginning the planners under-rated the influence of topography and of the enemy's strong defences in the Dieppe area.'[41]

Other agencies than C.O.H.Q. were involved in the collection and interpretation of intelligence, but Casa Maury was Mountbatten's man and the shortcomings of his department were ultimately Mountbatten's responsibility. He cannot be acquitted of adding to the problems that faced the luckless invaders at Dieppe. On the whole, however, the weakness was one of organization rather than of individuals. Too much can be made even of this. 'All three Services were deployed and co-operation among them was at a high level,' wrote the American historian of Combined Operations, Colonel Clifford. 'There was a Joint Command, and it worked well.'[42] But though the Joint Command made the best of a bad job, its position was never a happy one. 'My own feeling about the Dieppe raid', wrote Montgomery in one of his less tendentious moments, 'is that there were far too many authorities with a hand in it; there was no one single operational commander who was solely responsible for the operation from start to finish, a Task Force Commander in fact.'[43] Colonel Stacey reached a similar conclusion: 'So far as any one individual had general authority over the operation, it was the Chief of Combined Operations, Lord Louis Mountbatten, but obviously even his powers were circumscribed. The fact is that the Dieppe plan was the work of a large and somewhat indefinitely composed committee. . . . There were a great many cooks, and this probably had much to do with spoiling the broth.'[44] Mountbatten, to pursue the analogy, was like a *chef de cuisine* who had no control over the heating of the ovens or the timing of the service, who had to respect the independence of the pastry cook and the man in charge of the roasts, whose main role indeed, it sometimes seemed, was to supervise the printing of the menu. It was an unrewarding task, and one may doubt whether anyone would have performed it with great distinction.

This was to cause him much chagrin over the next few months – indeed, throughout his life. P. J. Grigg, the Secretary of State for War, was enraged when he saw the raid described in the press as a 'commando operation', and tried to take advantage of the affair to wrest control of the commandos from Combined Operations. He appealed to Churchill, who had some sympathy with the Army's feelings, but made it clear that the commando system was here to stay. He had no wish to kill it off, wrote Grigg with resignation, merely to take it over. 'I gathered . . . from what you said to me yesterday that you are not prepared to consider taking the control away from C.C.O. and I do not therefore pursue the matter.'[45]

Thus far Churchill supported Mountbatten, but he was shaken by the high cost of the operation and the equivocal attitude of the C.I.G.S. Brooke and Mountbatten dined at Chequers on 29 August. 'I was absolutely dumb-founded', Mountbatten later wrote to the C.I.G.S., '. . . when you made your very outspoken criticism of the manner in which the Dieppe raid was planned. I had meant to come and see you about it after leaving the dining-room but, before I could do so, the Prime Minister sent for me on the terrace and said: "I heard the C.I.G.S. complaining that the planning was all wrong for the Dieppe show: what did he mean?"' Mountbatten protested that, step by step, he had followed the procedures laid down by the Chiefs of Staff. He may have doubted the system's wisdom but he had conscientiously done his best to make it work. The issue, he concluded,

> is fundamental so far as my own position and the work of my organisation is concerned. I shall very much hope that after reading the account of the planning arrangements . . . you will feel able to withdraw your criticism and assure me that the planning was, in fact, done with due regard to the Army's special responsibilities.
>
> If however you should still feel that the arrangements for planning were unsatisfactory, I should have no option but to ask the Minister of Defence for a full and impartial enquiry into the planning and execution of the raid and the conduct of all concerned.[46]

Brooke presumably mollified Mountbatten in a personal interview; there is anyway no trace of a written reply. Churchill continued to brood, however, and just before Christmas Ismay wrote to report that the Prime Minister was again asking questions about the operation: 'It may be that adverse criticisms have reached his ears, or again, it may be that he wishes to ensure that false deductions have not been drawn from the results. . . . Yet again, it may be that his mind is harking back to the incident at a dinner party at Chequers when the C.I.G.S. made a number of allegations which you afterwards cleared up with him, and which were never reported to the Prime Minister himself.'[47] Mountbatten took the hint in Ismay's final sentence and responded with a précis of the full report on Dieppe. Churchill subsided again. If he had been

hearing adverse criticism, one of the most likely sources was Lord Beaverbrook, who took the deaths of so many young Canadians as a personal wound
and associated it with other grievances he was accumulating against Mountbatten. Increasingly, any comment in the Beaverbrook press on Mountbatten's conduct of affairs was accompanied by a reference to Dieppe: 'Don't
trust Mountbatten in Any Public Capacity . . . ,' Beaverbrook wrote darkly
to his son, Max Aitken, in 1958, 'he said he took full responsibility for
Dieppe.'[48] It was Beaverbrook more than anyone else who kept alive the
belief that Dieppe was one of the blackest pages in Mountbatten's history.
That there was a little substance in the allegation should be apparent from this
chapter; that the guilt was shared with many others, and should more
properly have been attached to the machine than to any individual who
controlled or failed to control it, seems to be a not over-generous verdict.

# CHAPTER 15

# *The Road to* OVERLORD

IF THE ROLE OF COMBINED OPERATIONS fell roughly into two parts – raiding the coast of Europe and preparing for invasion – then Dieppe, that uneasy compromise between the two, marked the moment at which the emphasis switched from the first to the second. To some who did not properly understand the functions of C.O.H.Q. it seemed, indeed, as if that organization had lapsed into stunned inactivity. Churchill himself was not guiltless. In October 1942 he had stated that 'he wished the Chief of Combined Operations to intensify his small-scale raids, as he was certain that the Germans were being worried by them'.[1] Then he reappeared from Washington in mid 1943 protesting that nothing had been done and that the Americans were complaining. Mountbatten retorted with some irritation that the Combined Operations Command had been more than fully occupied 'forging the amphibious weapon which is now about to go into action'. In spite of this, twenty small-scale raids had been carried out; twelve mounted but not executed – usually because of adverse weather; and thirty-eight planned but not actually mounted – almost always because the essential landing-craft had been removed to take part in other, more important operations.[2] The Prime Minister, Mountbatten told the Chiefs of Staff with some relief, had agreed that the American criticism was most unfair.[3]

In fact the raids that had been carried out did not amount to much. The showpiece was to have been an attack on the Channel Islands, certainly on Alderney, possibly on Guernsey and Sark as well. It was being planned at the end of 1942, but even then there was some scepticism about the raids taking place – 'it now appears extremely unlikely that Home Forces are in agreement about the desirability of their capture', wrote Antony Head, 'and, even less likely, that they will disgorge the necessary troops for their capture'.[4] Mountbatten presented the plan as a diversionary operation designed to discourage the Germans from switching forces to the Mediterranean. His proposals were savaged in the Chiefs of Staff Committee: 'the present plan was unsound', said the C.I.G.S. An attack on Alderney would be worthless unless as a complement to landings on the mainland.[5] Brooke fulminated in his diary against Mountbatten 'who was again putting up wild proposals disconnected with his direct duties. He will insist on doing the work of force commanders. . . . Both Portal and I were driven to distraction.'[6]

One of Brooke's recurrent worries was the propensity of the C.C.O. and the Prime Minister to cook up extravagant schemes together. One such idea, which Brooke did not block but in which he had little faith, was 'Project Plough', a plan dreamt up by Geoffrey Pyke to equip small groups with fast, armoured, fighting snow-vehicles and infiltrate them into northern Norway. This project was to be developed by the Canadians. Lieutenant-Colonel H. R. Johnson was put in charge of the project and quickly fell out with Pyke. Mountbatten called a meeting of Pyke, Johnson, and another Canadian, Lieutenant-Colonel Robert Frederick, who had put in a report somewhat critical of the plan. Johnson began by protesting that he was interested in taking part only if it was certain that the operation would really take place. 'Mountbatten did not comment on Johnson's stipulation. He simply sat silently, and it soon became obvious . . . that the Chief of Combined Operations had turned his thoughts into more absorbing channels. Finally, he appeared to have reached an inner decision which greatly satisfied him, and, returning his attention to Johnson, called the meeting to an end.' That night Frederick was put in charge of the operation. He was amazed but delighted. It was, said the historian of the expedition, inescapably Mountbatten's choice, and a brilliant, daring and unorthodox one. As time was to show, it also worked.[7]

Project Plough combined all the elements that appealed to Churchill: dash, the unexpected, the use of novel gadgets. He was constantly goading Mountbatten into fresh ventures. Why was nothing being done to attack the *Tirpitz* while she was at Trondheim, he asked in February 1943. 'It seems very discreditable that the Italians should show themselves so much better in attacking ships in harbour than we do. What has happened to the chariots and to the diving mines? . . . It is a terrible thing that this prize should be waiting, and no one able to think of a way of winning it.'[8]

Urged on by Churchill on the one hand, curbed by the Chiefs of Staff on the other, the raiding policy of Combined Operations was bound to consist largely of false starts. Another complicating factor was the attitude of the Free French. Mountbatten at first had serious reservations about de Gaulle. He told Hugh Dalton early in 1942 that 'there was very little difference between him and the Vichy Generals'. The Free French should be told to get rid of their Fascists: 'He hoped that we were in touch with the French workers, from the pink trade unionists to the Communists.' When Dalton agreed with him Mountbatten waxed still more radical, denouncing the followers of the Comte de Paris and the 200 Families. 'Our conversation thus ended in an atmosphere of enthusiastic political agreement.'[9] But Mountbatten was sufficiently realistic to accept that, whatever de Gaulle's political views, he was a force that had to be reckoned with.

His insistence on the independence of the French units under his command was a constant source of friction. He wanted a totally French commando unit to be formed, about whose use he should always be consulted. Mountbatten said that there could only be such consultation if the unit were used by itself; in the case of larger operations the Free French leader would be informed, as now, at the last moment.[10] De Gaulle was far from satisfied, and insisted that he should be warned in advance of any raid on French soil. Robert Henriques was summoned to the C.C.O.'s office, to find de Gaulle already there, refusing to accept a cigarette or even to sit down. Mountbatten, in French, told Henriques what de Gaulle wanted. Eighteen people already knew in advance of every raid, said Henriques. It might be safe to increase the number to nineteen, but only if the information went no farther.

> 'You hear that, *mon général*,' said Mountbatten. 'You will not mind giving me that guarantee?'
>
> De Gaulle, with his face and voice expressionless, answered, '*Je connais la guerre.*'
>
> 'Naturally, *mon général*,' Mountbatten said politely, 'but that is not an answer to my question.'
>
> '*Je connais la guerre.*'
>
> Mountbatten, exquisitely courteous, persisted. . . . But de Gaulle would say nothing else, and indeed had said nothing else throughout the whole interview. After repeating three times that he knew, that he understood war, he stalked out.[11]

Security within C.O.H.Q. itself was not always immaculate. Some months later Henriques drafted a report highly critical of the Americans and submitted it to Mountbatten. As always he was impressed by the speed with which the C.C.O. grasped the essential points: 'When Mountbatten's thoughts were let loose on a precise subject such as this it was as if a famous pack of hounds from the cream of the Midlands were hunting for a lost scent.' But the contents of the report were somehow leaked to the Americans. 'It was characteristic of Mountbatten', wrote Henriques, 'that, once again, he understood instantly the situation and all its implications; that he never attempted to suggest that the leakage was anywhere but in his own personal office.' Instead, he turned to Henriques 'with his invincible charm and asked what he should do to help restore the situation'.[12]

Mountbatten won the confidence of his staff by his readiness to accept responsibility and his ability to get things done. Leo Amery met him for the first time in February 1942. He was at the time 'much worried about the

departmental instinct for passing on responsibility and avoiding bold decisions'. Lord Louis, he commented, 'is the kind of man who ought really to be
made more use of in this war'.[13] Harold Wernher, in 1944, bemoaned the fact
that his proposals for rehabilitating the French ports had not been pushed
with real vigour: 'That is where I miss you so,' he wrote to his former Chief,
'because you would have gone straight to the Supreme Commander and put
the case to him.'[14] Mountbatten always knew the right string to pull, and
never flinched from pulling it.

He was adept in what would now be called 'man-management'. General
Haydon, indignant about being kept in the dark over the re-scheduling of the
raid on Dieppe, and dissatisfied on other grounds, wrote to 'state my
conviction that my position on your staff has become intolerable'.

> On official grounds I have found no difficulty in writing this letter,
> because everything I have said is based on fact and on absolute
> conviction.
>      On every personal ground it has been the most difficult letter to
> put to you. I owe you promotion, I owe you a decoration, and I owe
> you countless kindnesses. From all these points of view I would have
> given much to let things slide and do nothing. Feeling as I do, you
> would have been the first to pillory me if I had.[15]

Mountbatten saw Haydon the same day and the next morning his Vice
Chief wrote: 'You are – you know – a very difficult person to deal with.
Yesterday I felt angry, sore and hardly-done-by. Today I feel a worm for ever
having harboured any of those feelings. I really do. It is all most disconcerting
but, in any case, thank you very much for being so completely
understanding.'[16] There were to be many occasions in Mountbatten's career
when angry visitors arrived in his office spoiling for a row and left baffled,
charmed and, on the whole, content.


When Mountbatten told Churchill that many raids had never got beyond the
drawing-board because the landing-craft were needed for other areas, he had
in mind particularly the demands of Operation TORCH. With SLEDGE-
HAMMER to all intents and purposes dead and the Americans insistent on
action in 1942, an invasion of French North Africa became the obvious
priority. The decision was taken on 28 July and the same day Mountbatten set
up five teams within C.O.H.Q. to plan the five different landings that were
envisaged. A week later Mountbatten saw Eisenhower, who had by then been
appointed Allied Commander-in-Chief, and offered him all the help that his
organization could give, whether in men, material or expertise.

One of the more valuable gifts with which Mountbatten endowed the expedition was the headquarters ship. It may seem obvious today that a massive and complex amphibious operation needs to be controlled from a vessel which remains offshore after the landing, which is not liable to be removed to take part in some naval operation, and into which all the communications from land, sea and air are channelled. In the 1930s, when Mountbatten claims he first discussed the matter with his Assistant Fleet Wireless Officer, Michael Hodges, the idea was hardly in embryo.[17] The first major operation at which the deficiency seems seriously to have been felt was the ill-fated attack on Dakar in 1940. 'Seldom have I felt so impotent as during this expedition,' wrote General Irwin, 'when I was separated from my forces and tied to any naval operations which might become necessary.'[18] The commander of any such enterprise, he urged, must retain his independence from the fleet.

The idea was taken up by C.O.H.Q., and worked on by Hodges. Mountbatten cajoled the Ministry of War Transport into surrendering H.M.S. *Bulolo*, a former Australian passenger ship of 6400 tons, which his signals staff then took to bits and reassembled as a floating command and communications centre. The work was completed in the summer of 1942, by which time a second headquarters ship, H.M.S. *Largs*, was being put together. Both ships were made available to Eisenhower, though full use was not made of them. General Patton, in particular, scorned the amenities of *Bulolo* and insisted on supervising the operation from the American flagship *Augusta*. To the unconcealed delight of the C.O.H.Q. representatives, retribution struck. *Augusta* disappeared from the landing beaches to repel a threatened French sortie, and it was forty-eight hours before Patton joined his men ashore.[19]

The loan of these ships and, still more, of landing-craft and trained men for the African landings denuded the Combined Operations Command of much which it needed to prepare for the invasion proper. A fortnight before TORCH took place Mountbatten reported in some alarm to the Chiefs of Staff that he was losing all his landing-craft except those designed for tanks and all his trained landing-craft crews. However dire the emergency, it would be impossible to revive SLEDGEHAMMER before March or April 1943, and difficult by then.[20] Brooke, who anyway had no intention of reviving SLEDGEHAMMER, was sympathetic; Churchill less so. 'We must be careful not to make heavy weather over the manning of landing-craft . . . ,' he wrote blithely. 'We could not possibly afford to tie up a large mass of men indefinitely waiting for the chance of a big cross-Channel operation. . . . In trying to be perfect you will spoil the whole thing.'[21] The Prime Minister seemed to be reviving the old heresy that, provided the landing-craft existed, any able-bodied seaman would be fit to man them. Mountbatten was appalled by this nonchalance. 'For a cross-Channel operation, a prolonged and thorough naval training is essential,' he retorted. If this was neglected, the invasion would either be a disaster, or more probably would not start at all, through the refusal of any reputable naval officer to command the force.[22] With the Prime Minister's grudging acquiescence he appealed to the Minister of Labour, Ernest Bevin. The Navy had had more than its share of manpower, he was told, and all the spare men were needed for the Army that would one day invade France. If there were no crews for the landing-craft, was the reply, the Army would never get to France. Bevin took the point, and agreed that in future the personnel for landing-craft should be found from the Army's allocation.[23]

One source of recruits, for commandos as well as landing-craft, was the Royal Marines. When General Bourne, a Marine himself, took over Combined Operations, it seemed that his Division would provide the backbone of the new amphibious forces. Under Keyes, however, the Marines fought shy of losing their independence and most of the Division remained in unhappy isolation in Wales. From this seclusion Mountbatten, supported by his old friend the Marine Robert Neville, tried vigorously to woo them. For some time they resisted his blandishments; then Colonel Bruce Lumsden took his battalion over to Combined Operations. The rest followed. Early in 1943 the Division was disbanded, its infantry battalions reorganized as commandos and many of the other units transferred to landing-craft.

Laboriously Mountbatten began to rebuild his invasion armada. The easiest solution would have been for the units lent by C.O.H.Q. for the North African landings to return to the United Kingdom, but it was soon clear that they were still needed in the Mediterranean. In January 1943, at Casablanca, a conference was held to decide future Allied strategy. Mountbatten flew there in a converted Liberator. 'I slept on the floor,' noted Brooke ruefully, '. . . and had Dickie Mountbatten sleeping next to me. I did not find him a pleasant bed companion, as every time he turned round he overlay me, and I had to use my knees and elbows to establish my rights to my allotted floor space!'[24] The C.C.O., as always, slept maddeningly well, and emerged at Casablanca bouncing with energy and enthusiasm. He had reason for his confidence. The contribution that C.O.H.Q. had made to the North African landings was acclaimed by everyone; his precious headquarters ship H.M.S. *Bulolo* provided the communications for the conference; his planners were easily the best equipped with facts, figures and ideas. 'Well, it was a good party for Combined Operations!' he said proudly to General Macleod, his representative on the Joint Planners. 'Sir, the party *was* Combined Operations,' was the equally proud reply.[25] But the faint ambiguity about Mountbatten's status persisted. Harry Hopkins noticed the confusion when a photograph was wanted of Churchill with the Chiefs of Staff, 'because nobody seems to know who makes up the Chiefs of Staff . . . and I think there were two or three in that didn't belong there'.[26]

Brooke found Mountbatten an uneasy bedfellow in the conference room as well as on the floor of a Liberator. After much debate, the Chiefs of Staff in London had decided that Sicily should be the next target for an Allied landing, and Brooke had finally talked Marshall into accepting this decision – 'One might say we came, we listened and we were conquered,' wrote Wedemeyer ruefully.[27] Mountbatten, however, hankered after Sardinia, since an attack on Sicily would take three months longer to prepare and he felt it important to keep the Germans on the run. On 21 January 1943 Mountbatten and the Joint Planners returned to the charge: 'Peter Portal and Pug Ismay were beginning to waver,' wrote Brooke, 'and dear old Dudley Pound was, as usual, asleep with no views either way.'[28] Brooke quashed the mutiny and insisted that the Americans must be given no chance to renege on their acceptance of the British strategy. Mountbatten was not giving up so easily, however. The following day he lunched with Hopkins and reopened the question – his zeal, it may be felt, oustripping his loyalty to his colleagues on the Chiefs of Staff. 'Mountbatten claims all the younger officers in the British lay-out agree with this [the desirability of attacking Sardinia], but the big boys on the Chiefs of Staff have over-ruled their subordinates,' recorded Hopkins. 'Mountbatten always gives you the impression of being a courageous, resourceful, fighting man, but I fancy the British Chiefs of Staff push him around pretty much. At any rate, he cautioned us not to say anything about his urging the attack on Sardinia instead of Sicily.'[29]

His plotting gained Mountbatten nothing; Sicily was to be the target and Operation HUSKY the code-name for its invasion. The decision taken, he flung himself and his organization into its preparation. In June 1943 the Chiefs of Staff gave him permission to attend the landings; at last he was to see something of an operation which he had helped to mount.[30] Mountbatten flew to the Mediterranean for last-minute conferences with Cunningham and Eisenhower, Supreme Commander for HUSKY as he had been for TORCH. He was with Eisenhower on the eve of the landings, waiting anxiously for the first news. It came in a news flash from the B.B.C., introduced as a bulletin from the Supreme Commander. 'Thank God!' said Eisenhower. '*He* ought to know.'[31] Then Mountbatten was off with Cunningham to visit the British landing areas: 'Only saw 3 bombs drop on beaches. 2670 ships and major craft afloat and hundreds of minor craft.'[32]

The following day he went ashore to stay with Montgomery and enjoy his first taste of the war on land:

We came to a long, narrow village which had a main road running through the centre, where it forked. Monty was sitting beside the driver; his A.D.C., I and my staff officer, Brigadier Antony Head, were sitting in the back. Suddenly there was a rat tat tat of machine guns and we saw a Messerschmitt flying down the main street gunning all the vehicles. All of us at the back immediately flung ourselves down, but not so Monty who sat bolt upright and didn't even turn his head to look at the Messerschmitt. As luck would have it we reached the fork just before the aircraft reached us; we went down the right hand fork and the aircraft went down the left hand fork and so we were missed. But Monty never turned a hair and didn't seem to be afraid.[33]

Much had gone wrong in the planning and execution of TORCH but this had mattered little because of the fragility of the opposition. Mistakes over HUSKY would have been more expensive. There were very few. The invasion was well-planned and well-executed and the contribution of the Combined Operations organization was of the first importance. Many of the landing-craft were prepared for the operation at Troon and sailed out by crews specially trained for the ocean navigation of their vulnerable vessels. An order for landing-craft armed with anti-aircraft weapons was received and supplied. The lessons of Dieppe were applied and craft armed with rockets and 4.7-inch guns supported the landings. The two headquarters ships played a vital part in co-ordinating the innumerable different facets of the operation. 'All in all, HUSKY was an enormous success,' concluded Bernard Fergusson, 'and Mountbatten was much too human to suppress his delight at the part C.O.H.Q. had played in it.'[34]

The invasion of Sicily was not the only important decision reached at Casablanca. General Haydon had observed the North African landings on behalf of C.O.H.Q. and had reported to Mountbatten that 'there is a lack of a strong guiding hand and someone has got to take a grip *now* – sort out the tangle that has resulted from the rather haphazard approach to the problem and set people on the right road. . . . We *cannot* do it – it must be done by General Eisenhower or a very senior representative.' Mountbatten passed on the report to Eisenhower, who was delighted: 'Both his critique and letter echo just what I have been thinking.'[35] The command structure for HUSKY worked better but, more important, thought was given to the eventual invasion of Western Europe. It was still too early, it was felt, to appoint a Supreme Commander, but there was immediate need for a Chief of Staff to this as yet mythical being who would be in charge of the organization of any major cross-Channel operation.[36] So the concept of COSSAC – the Chief of

Staff to the Supreme Allied Commander – was born. Lieutenant-General Morgan was selected to fill the slot and took up his task on 13 April. His appointment had an immediate impact on the work of Combined Operations – indeed, it marked the beginning of the gradual retraction of that body.[37] Mountbatten's empire was still enormous, but the creation of COSSAC set a limit to its sphere of influence.

Setting a limit to the sphere of influence of C.O.H.Q. was nothing new. Nine months before the appointment of COSSAC had been conceived, Mount-batten had asked that he should be designated as one of the authorities responsible for the preparation of the invasion plan. Brooke retorted sharply that this was out of the question. 'The C.C.O. had not been shown on this level because he was not one of the force commanders. His responsibility in the preparation of the plan would be confined to the provision of technical advice on all aspects of the assault.'[38] Mountbatten did not pay scrupulous attention to this definition of his role, but the main thrust of his activity was directed towards the logistic support which an invasion force would need, rather than the conduct of that force in battle. To assess the value of the Combined Operations organization in the build-up for invasion is difficult, but no one can doubt that its contribution was multifarious and, in some sectors, of critical importance. The growth of its activities was evident and dramatic, so also was the number of its detractors – both those who argued that it was doing the wrong thing, and those who conceded that the thing was worth doing but claimed that it was being tackled with extravagant disorder. Whether in the achievement itself, or in the provocation which it constituted for the critics, the personality of Lord Louis Mountbatten was of the first importance.

> I do congratulate you so very much [wrote King George VI] on the success you have made of C.O. despite all the obstacles you have met and the heavy opposition you have fought both on the administrative side and in Active Operations!! . . . Why should it be so difficult to get other people to understand the supreme value of Combined Opera-tions, after the way you have shown that it can, will and does work when properly organized and you have troops trained for it?[39]

The heaviest opposition came from his own department, the Admiralty. Partly this was for the very reason that it *was* his own department – the urge to take Dickie down a peg or two proved irresistible to many senior naval officers; partly it reflected the fact that the Admiralty was the most conserva-tive of the three Services; but the main factor was that the armada of landing-craft which Mountbatten was accumulating impinged directly on territory the Admiralty considered its own. By June 1943 the twenty-two landing ships which had existed eighteen months before had risen in number to 113; the landing-craft and barges from 509 to 3979; the number of naval personnel trained to man the craft from 4970 to 38,209.[40] Not surprisingly, the Admiralty looked with alarm and jealousy on what they regarded as a rival establishment, and resolved to assert control over its nautical elements.

The opening shots were fired by the Commander-in-Chief, Home Ports, who as early as June 1942 urged the importance of landing-craft coming under the Navy for administration and discipline. Mountbatten promised to consider the matter but did so, if at all, with little urgency.[41] Admiral Daniel, the senior sailor in Combined Operations – 'That maaaster of Negation' as Churchill once described him[42] – now joined the battle on the side of the Admiralty – an unkind cut from one whom Mountbatten had hoped might prove an ally. In November the Chiefs of Staff accepted in principle that the assault fleet was too large to be controlled by the C.C.O.[43] Mountbatten could only consent. Principle, however, took some time to translate into practice and it was August 1943 before the Admiralty formally took charge of the invasion fleet and its bases. The transfer almost coincided with Mountbatten's departure from Combined Operations.

But landing-craft and the personnel to run them were far from being the only contribution made by Combined Operations to the invasion. A plethora of gadgets, some trivial, some of immense importance, owed their development in part or in entirety to the efforts of Mountbatten and his men. It is rarely possible to state exactly where any idea originated but the enthusiasm of the Prime Minister and of Mountbatten contributed greatly to such ideas being considered, tested and often brought to fruition. Churchill was relentless in the barrage of questions which he levelled at his advisers. What about sea-borne bridges for landing tanks at the top of cliffs, he asked. They were already being worked on in C.O.H.Q., replied Ian Jacob, Ismay's deputy. Then what about quantos? This was one of his unhappier efforts. 'I think there must have been some mistake which, I imagine, arose from the peculiarity of American speech,' wrote Jacob firmly. 'There is no such thing as a quanto. The article you describe is a pontoon.'[44]

Mountbatten matched the Prime Minister in his relish for new and improbable devices. An impertinent staff officer wrote a Belloc-ian poem on the subject which the Chief of Combined Operations – who, for a man of striking self-esteem, was surprisingly ready to laugh at himself – cherished and frequently quoted:

Mountbatten was a likely lad,
A nimble brain Mountbatten had,
And this most amiable trait:
Of each new plan which came his way
He'd always claim in accents pat
'Why, I myself invented that!'
Adding when he remembered it,
For any scoffer's benefit,
Roughly the point in his career
When he'd conceived the bright idea,
As 'August 1934'
Or 'Some time during the Boer War.'[45]

He was indeed prone to claim in his more expansive moments that he had 'invented' this or that; more often, however, he would maintain with greater justice that without his backing and energy the project would have withered on the drawing-board.

Probably the most important of these was Mulberry, the artificial harbour, without which it is hard to see how the invasion could have succeeded. 'The first time I heard this idea tentatively advanced was by Admiral Mountbatten in the spring of 1942,' wrote Eisenhower. 'At a conference attended by a number of service chiefs he remarked: "If ports are not available, we may have to construct them in pieces and tow them in." Hoots and jeers greeted his suggestion, but two years later it was to become reality.'[46] The idea had not sprung that instant from Mountbatten's head; he himself attributed the original conception to Hughes Hallett, while Hughes Hallett said that an engineer called Guy Maunsell had shown him plans for an artificial breakwater as early as 1940.[47] Churchill's celebrated minute of May 1942 – 'They must float up and down with the tide. The anchor problem must be answered. . . . Let me have the best solution worked out. Don't argue the matter. The difficulties will argue for themselves'[48] – was a stimulus to a debate that was already raging and was, anyway, far removed from the final solution to the problem: 'One of those pontifical generalities thrown out with a whiff of cigar smoke,' as Vice-Admiral Hickling unkindly described it.[49]

The factor which made Mulberry work was the sinking of ships to compose a breakwater. Captain Hussey, who in 1941 had been put in charge of a committee to investigate the project, attributed this refinement to Mountbatten; 'without your brainwave there could have been no harbour and a certain catastrophe'.[50] At the time ships were scarce and the need for an artificial harbour not generally accepted. By 1943 there were more ships to spare and Dieppe had demonstrated brutally that it would be exceedingly difficult if not impossible to secure a major port in the opening phases of an invasion. The idea was revived, Hughes Hallett claiming that it came to him while listening to the singing of the anthem in Westminster Abbey in June 1943.[51] Whatever the relevance of Mountbatten's earlier ideas to the development of Mulberry, his contribution at this stage was of great significance. When Colonel Steer-Webster, the Director of Experimental Engineering at the War Office, was summoned to C.O.H.Q. to expound the various approaches to the problem, Mountbatten listened patiently, agreed which scheme seemed best, drove Steer-Webster to Downing Street, paraded him at a meeting of the War Cabinet, and secured a general blessing for the plan.[52] Even after the appointment of General Morgan as COSSAC he continued to champion the idea. His enthusiasm and vigorous rebuttal of all the counter-arguments were more than anything else responsible for its final acceptance at the RATTLE Conference at Largs in June 1943.[53]

It was one thing to land vehicles in the artificial harbour, another to get them off the beaches. A committee under C.O.H.Q. chairmanship worked out a scheme for hundreds of miles of flexible steel and concrete mattress to be prepared and laid on the softer parts of the beach. Mountbatten's zest for the dramatic led him to champion a glorified version of this – 'Swiss Roll', a monstrous drum of flexible roadway propelled by rockets on each side. At its first trial Swiss Roll ran amok and chased a group of distinguished admirals and generals into the sea. At the subsequent post-mortem it was decided that, though the device offered possibilities for harmless fun, its practical value was too doubtful to make it worth pursuing.

Once ashore, the vehicles had to be supplied with fuel. As early as June 1942 Mountbatten told the Chiefs of Staff that 'the supply of petrol, oil and lubricants would prove a limiting factor, if not *the* limiting factor, on the size of the Force that could be landed and operated in France'.[54] One reform which C.O.H.Q. championed was the substitution of the tougher and larger American jerrican for the flimsy four-gallon containers traditionally used by the Army. The latter leaked under rough treatment – a weakness which was both wasteful and hazardous to the vessels that carried them. The Army objected to the change but in the end were overborne, and twenty million jerricans were produced for the British forces.[55]

This would not be a complete answer, however. 'Very drastic new methods would require investigation,' Mountbatten told the Chiefs of Staff, 'such as, for example, laying pipelines from ports to forward distribution depots.'[56] Two months before he had proposed an even more drastic method to Geoffrey Lloyd, who was Minister in charge of the Petroleum Warfare Department.[57] Mountbatten had gone to Salisbury Plain for a demonstration of flame-throwers – weapons, incidentally, whose development Lloyd ascribed largely to the encouragement of the Chief of Combined Operations, a man of 'immense ability, drive and imagination'. After the show was over Lloyd asked casually whether there was anything else his visitor would like done. 'Well,' Mountbatten replied, 'could you lay a pipeline across the Channel?'[58] Predictably the experts declared that the project was impossible, and then began to look for ways to accomplish it. Tests were conducted across the Medway, then across the Bristol Channel. There were many teething troubles and expensive mistakes, but in the end PLUTO, acronym for Pipe Line Under The Ocean, was successfully put into operation. At its peak it was delivering more than a million gallons of petrol a day to France.

Mountbatten encouraged the scientists on his staff to indulge their fantasies, with the comfortable assurance that there would be plenty of people able and willing to prove them unsound if in fact they were so. Pyke was particularly fecund. 'Pyke's Uphill Rivers' was one such chimera which came to nothing; eight-inch pipes running from ship to land, which would simultaneously carry stores and water to the front line.[59] Most splendid of his dreams, however, was the iceberg/aircraft-carrier, christened Habbakuk* after the fifth verse of the first chapter of that prophet's book: 'Behold ye among the nations, and regard, and wonder marvellously: for I work a work in your days, which ye will not believe though it be told you.' Aircraft-carriers made of ice, unsinkable, cheap to manufacture, easily repaired after bombing by the pouring of water into the craters, were indeed a tempting prospect. They would solve the difficulty of providing air cover for landings far from the mainland of Britain; at a time when aircraft-carriers were in short supply, they would be of immeasurable help in the U-boat war in mid-Atlantic. Ice was notoriously fissile, yet Pyke perfected a compound of paper-pulp and sea-water that was almost as strong as concrete and was called Pykecrete.

Pyke pursued his project with ferocious zeal. Zuckerman recalled a meeting with him at a flat in Albany where he was recovering from an illness. Mountbatten, Harold Wernher, Bernal and Tom Hussey were also there, grouped around the bed in which

> Pyke was sitting up, looking with his strange beard, like some jaundiced Christ. Mountbatten tried to assure him that work was proceeding as fast as it possibly could. Pyke was not satisfied. 'Without faith', he kept protesting, 'nothing will come of this project.' 'But I have faith,' replied Mountbatten. 'Yes,' said Pyke, 'but have the others got faith?', and turning to Harold Wernher he asked solemnly: 'Have you got faith, Brigadier?' Poor Wernher did not know what to say, but before he could utter a word, the C.C.O.

* Or, as Bernard Fergusson pointed out, more correctly Habakkuk.

had chipped in with the remark: 'Wernher's on my staff, to see that I am not over-lavish with my own faith.'[60]

The next step was to enthuse the Prime Minister. Mountbatten sent him a memorandum in December 1942 extolling the wonders of this new creation which would 'abolish the aeronautical disadvantages of the sea'. Not only would it serve as an aircraft-carrier, it would transport vast quantities of goods 'in ships immune to bombs, mines, torpedoes'. If power to freeze the water was short, then Habbakuk could be manufactured by natural freezing in north Canada or Russia. Churchill's backing was essential if the Allies were not to 'miss the use of a decisive weapon for want of a little foresight and the expenditure of a few thousand pounds'.[61] The Prime Minister was predictably enchanted, but he failed to impress his scientific adviser, Professor Lindemann, who surveyed the scheme with uncaring scepticism and finally reported: 'I have so little belief in this project that I have agreed with Mountbatten that I should no longer remain a member of his Committee.'[62] The Chiefs of Staff took the possibility seriously enough to authorize further study, Stafford Cripps lent the idea his support, and a model of Habbakuk, sixty feet long, thirty feet wide, twenty feet deep and weighing one thousand tons, was built on Patricia Lake in Canada.[63] In the end, however, all would depend on the attitude of the Americans, who alone could provide the huge quantities of steel that the project demanded. The scene in which Mountbatten expounded the merits of Habbakuk to the Combined Chiefs of Staff in Quebec was one of high comedy. Two lumps of ice were carried in, the second being of Pykecrete. Mountbatten borrowed a revolver and fired at the first, which shattered into splinters. Then he fired at the second. The block of ice remained unmarked, the bullet ricocheted, nicking the leg of Admiral King, the redoubtable American Chief of Naval Operations, and embedding itself in a wall. Outside, the staff officers, who knew how strained the atmosphere had grown in the earlier discussions, anxiously speculated whether King had shot Brooke or Brooke King.

The Americans, however, were not to be persuaded. Habbakuk posed alarming technical problems. Even if it worked, it would not be ready before 1945, by which time there would be a superfluity of conventional aircraft-carriers. Long-range petrol-tanks for fighter aircraft and the acquisition of bases in the Azores further weakened the argument.[64] The First Lord of the Admiralty, A. V. Alexander, who had never liked the scheme,[65] supported the American position. Even Churchill lost heart when he realised that the ships would cost £6 million or more as opposed to the budgeted £1 million, let alone Mountbatten's 'few thousand pounds'. What was needed was something cheap, which would be available within a few months.[66] In January

1944 came word that the Americans had finally interred the project.[67] With hindsight it is evident that it deserved no better fate, and yet it had a splendid simplicity which commands admiration. Mountbatten always maintained that, of Habbakuk and Mulberry, it was Mulberry which was the more outrageous concept. Only the fact that it was carried out made it generally acceptable. If the war had lasted another three years, if aircraft-carrier production had lagged, if the Azores had remained closed to the Allies, perhaps Habbakuk too would have come to seem unsurprising. As it was, it remained fantasy, and Mounbatten's association with it was taken as further proof of his innate romanticism.

Mountbatten had always been an exceptionally hard worker. In the *Kelly* he had often spent three or four days at a stretch with only a few moments' sleep snatched at odd intervals. As a destroyer captain, however, his bouts of intense activity were interspersed with occasional passages of calm; even at Immingham he had usually managed to take an hour or two off each day and a day or so each fortnight. His regime was leisurely compared with his tempo of life at Combined Operations. On a typical day in London he would work sixteen to eighteen hours: starting on his papers before six, working through at the office till nine or ten at night, taking more papers home and continuing till past midnight. On top of this came the demands posed by the Prime Minister, who enjoyed Mountbatten's company and used him ruthlessly as a stimulant and sounding-board. On 24 April 1942, for example, he was summoned in late afternoon, 'drove fast to Chequers, Oliver Stanley the only other guest; talked till 0315; worked with P.M. till 0345'. Three days later he was called away from dinner to 10 Downing Street for another lengthy session. When he visited the innumerable stations in his command, his pace was no more tranquil: 'I've just finished a very hectic two-days tour,' he told Pamela after a foray to the Clyde, 'and I have inspected 8000 men and visited a corresponding number of ships, camps and air-stations. I made no less than 16 speeches – nearly as much as Mummy seems to do on her trips.'[68]

In April 1943 his health cracked. While on a brief visit to Broadlands he contracted pneumonia. For two days he made light of it, then his temperature rose to 103° and remained there for several days. Mountbatten himself was convinced that his white blood corpuscles had multiplied alarmingly and that only treatment by the new wonder drug, penicillin, saved his life. The doctor who treated him observed no increase in the white corpuscles, and said that, anyway, penicillin had been administered in such small quantities as to make little difference. Mountbatten was naturally strong and recovered with rest and conventional treatment. Dr Brooks, however, confirmed that Mountbatten was dangerously debilitated by overwork, and that if he had neglected his condition for another twenty-four hours he might well have died.[69] It was several weeks before he was fully back to work and even then he was cutting short the convalescence recommended by his doctor. He learned by his experience, however, and never again neglected the early symptoms of disease. He did not become a hypochondriac, but he treated his health with the utmost seriousness and summoned a doctor for causes that to others sometimes seemed trivial. It could be that his first serious illness since adolescence made an important contribution to the good health he enjoyed for almost all his life.

By the time Mountbatten was in harness again, General Morgan had taken over as COSSAC. If Mountbatten felt any regrets at an appointment which he knew must severely limit his own responsibilities he did not show it. His only critical comment was one of disappointment that Morgan had not been given greater powers; if the Chief of Combined Operations was worth a seat with the Chiefs of Staff, then surely the same must be true of the man charged with organizing the vast complexities of the invasion? The relationship between the two men was defined by the Chiefs of Staff in terms that emphasised that Mountbatten's role was no more than advisory. Small-scale raids would continue to be dealt with by the C.C.O., but 'if such an operation is connected with the larger Channel operation, he will work under your directions. In either case he will consult you at all stages. You will consult the Chief of Combined Operations on all aspects of and all stages in, the planning and training for combined operations across the Channel.'[70]

Such an arrangement offered limitless possibilities for misunderstanding and ill-feeling. That none arose says much for the tact and commonsense of General Morgan, who knew how much Mountbatten had to offer him and had no intention of allowing false pride to stop him soliciting it. It also says much for the generosity of the C.C.O. that he offered Morgan, without equivocation, every facility at his disposal. Mountbatten was sometimes, and not unfairly, accused of being over-zealous in the protection of his own powers and status. But he was never ungenerous. Morgan was there, he was a fact of life, and Mountbatten was going to do all he could to help him. COSSAC needed experts to reconnoitre possible invasion beaches. No such units existed except in Combined Operations. 'We therefore asked the Chief of Combined Operations for help,' wrote Morgan, 'which was, as ever, gladly and enthusiastically given. Virtually he put at our disposal the planning and intelligence sections of his own headquarters, than which nothing better could be imagined.'[71]

It was both in recognition of the newly defined role of Combined Operations, and because of its enormously increased strength – nearly fifty thousand strong – that Mountbatten in May 1943 reshaped his Command in such a way as to delegate much responsibility for executive action that hitherto had rested in his hands. The Vice, Deputy and Assistant Chiefs of Combined Operations – respectively a soldier, airman and sailor – were to have their titles altered to Military, Air and Naval Chiefs of Staff. 'I propose', wrote Mountbatten, 'that the Heads of Services should be empowered to deal at their own discretion with all matters concerning their own Service.'[72] Churchill was dubious about the wisdom of such a move. 'Pray take care to maintain the position of the C.C.O. and his Command intact,' he minuted. 'I trust that the integrity of the Inter-Service Organisation of C.O.H.Q. will be preserved and that the reorganisation will not split your Staff too rigidly into their separate Services.'[73]

Six months before, Mountbatten would have been more preoccupied by the same considerations. By the summer of 1943, however, he accepted that Combined Operations as an independent entity must be a dwindling force. From now on it was COSSAC and the forces charged with the invasion that would bear the burden. C.O.H.Q. had still much experience to impart and skills to teach, but as an originating force its bolt was largely shot. Mountbatten himself was beginning to think beyond his present job to the command of a big ship of which Combined Operations had deprived him.

He had, however, one signal service to render first. Many critical questions remained to be answered before planning for the invasion could progress much farther. The scale and targets of the preliminary bombardment were still debated. Many sceptics were not yet convinced that an artificial port was a practical possibility. Most important of all, though it does not seem that many of those in supreme authority had doubts about the proper answer, no formal decision had yet been taken as to the choice between Normandy and the Pas de Calais. There was need for a prolonged high-level study period at which all these questions could be thrashed out and a clear directive given to COSSAC.

'From this appalling quandary', wrote General Morgan, 'we were rescued by the Chief of Combined Operations, always a leader of progressive thought, and somewhat of an *enfant terrible* to his more elderly *confrères*. He presented us with the opportunity to uproot the whole wrangle from the arena of London, where surroundings were inimical both materially and psychologically to open-minded consideration of any bold departure from established precedent, to an entirely fresh setting.'[74] Mountbatten invited Morgan, Paget, commander of the British Home Forces, the American General Jacob Devers, Admiral Little from Portsmouth, Leigh-Mallory, the C.-in-C. Fighter Command, and anyone else who was intimately concerned with the running of the invasion to the C.O.H.Q. training base of Largs in

Scotland. It was, he told Montgomery with unconvincing modesty, 'my humble personal attempt to get a move on with OVERLORD'.[75] Harold Wernher said that RATTLE, as the Largs conference was called, was a deliberate attempt on Mountbatten's part to rally support for Morgan in his future task. He saw his job as being 'not only to transfer the loyalty of all his men to his successor – or successors; he had, also, to gather in the various independent units, and to unite them with Combined Operations – in spirit, at any rate, so as to form one coherent Invasion Planning Force'.[76]

Mountbatten was in the chair – by no means unused to finding himself by eight years the youngest officer at the table. RATTLE was a masterpiece of presentation, a 'sort of psychological Motor Show', Bernard Fergusson described it.[77] Twenty generals were present, eleven air marshals and air commodores, eight admirals, five Canadians, fifteen Americans. H.M.S. *Warren*, where the conference was held, was the former Hollywood Hotel in nautical disguise. 'The showmanship could not have been excelled,' wrote Morgan gratefully. Nothing was neglected. 'As there were suspected to be savage breasts among us, the pipe band of the local Home Guard appeared at intervals to rend the atmosphere with the indigenous substitute for music. Even the weather was apparently cajoled into giving us perfect days.'[78] But behind the flummery business of deadly significance had to be transacted. Mountbatten and Morgan were determined that the conference should not end before agreement had been reached on the place and method of invasion. At the end of the first day they were near despair. By the end of the second day they knew that they were winning. When the Largs Conference ended, they had won. The shape of OVERLORD was established, and in all essentials it was the plan that C.O.H.Q. had mulled over and aimed towards over the previous twelve months.

When the conference was over Mountbatten flew back to London with Harold Wernher. Wernher said that he thought RATTLE had been in many ways the supreme achievement for C.O.H.Q. and for Mountbatten himself. But, he said, the end of Mountbatten's activities was in sight, because more and more the commanders in the field would take over the conduct of operations. 'I therefore advised Mountbatten to look for another job.'[79] The advice was superfluous; Mountbatten had already worked it out for himself.

Yet when the time came in August 1943 for him to leave Combined Operations, he did so with the feeling of dissatisfaction that accompanies a job half, or perhaps three-quarters, done. 'I should like to take this opportunity to congratulate you on the wonderful advance the Combined Operations made under your able guidance,' wrote Brooke. 'Successes achieved in landing operations during the last year are in no small measure due to the energy and to the organising power which ['you' omitted?] instilled into everything connected with Combined Operations.'[80] But he would not be there to see the landing operation that really counted; when the invasion came, Mountbatten was six thousand miles away, dependent for his information on the news bulletins and the reports of his friends.

His contribution was not forgotten. In the wake of the invading armies the Prime Minister visited France, accompanied by Smuts, General Arnold, Brooke, Admiral King and General Marshall. From the train on their return from Normandy they sent the former Chief of Combined Operations a telegram:

> Today we visited the British and American armies on the soil of France. We sailed through vast fleets of ships with landing-craft of many types pouring more and more men, vehicles and stores ashore. We saw clearly the manoeuvre in process of rapid development. We have shared our secrets in common and helped each other all we could. We wish to tell you at this moment in your arduous campaign that we realise that much of this remarkable technique and therefore the success of the venture has its origins in developments effected by you and your staff of Combined Operations.[81]

Ismay wrote to add his congratulations. 'If anyone had told us two years ago that we could throw ashore a million men, two hundred thousand vehicles, and three-quarters of a million tons of stores, across open beaches, in none too favourable weather, in thirty days, we would have dubbed him mad. So that's a great feather in your cap, Dickie.'[82]

Compliments cost nothing and the biographer is usually well advised to treat them with discretion. In this case, however, it is impossible to doubt that they were weighed and fully intended. To Mountbatten it was 'the nicest telegram of my life'. 'I wonder if anyone', he wrote, 'has ever had the fantastic luck to receive so nice a telegram signed by the six greatest war leaders on the field of battle?'[83] He might also have wondered, and no doubt privately did so, whether anyone had ever done so much to merit such a message. Given the scale of the operation and the immensity of his contribution, it is a reflection that could be forgiven him.

# CHAPTER 16

## Quebec

MOUNTBATTEN AT THE AGE OF FORTY-THREE was still far younger than many of those he commanded and all of those with whom he worked on equal terms. He had, however, matured during his time at Combined Operations. He still believed that he could conquer the world, but he appreciated more clearly than heretofore that circumstances would impose certain temporary restrictions on his progress and that it might be wisest to accept these with good grace. He was still impetuous and occasionally imprudent, but years of working closely with susceptible and sometimes jealous senior officers had taught him the necessity for discretion. He had become more adept in the pursuit of power and the manipulation of those who controlled it. He knew how to get things done and how to ensure that other things were not done instead. The limitations on his skills were to become obvious over the next two years, but he was now a political operator of formidable ability.

He was also a master of his craft. He had never needed conversion to the principles of Combined Operations, but he now espoused them with fanaticism. He knew as much about the techniques of amphibious warfare as any man alive, but to him his job meant far more than that. From Maeterlinck's *The Life of the Bee* he had learned to value highly 'the spirit of the hive'; the concept of a group of people working closely together in harmony, all contributing, drawing strength from unity; a team rather than individuals; soldiers, sailors and airmen, British and Americans. It was this dream which he had tried to realize in C.O.H.Q. He had gone far towards achieving his end. He was destined to face the same challenge on a grander scale. For the moment, however, his thoughts were concentrated on his return to the Royal Navy.

In August 1943 he set sail with the Prime Minister and the Chiefs of Staff in the *Queen Mary*. Their destination was Quebec, where Roosevelt and the American Chiefs of Staff were to meet them. The conference was designed to hammer out the grand strategy for the wars against Germany and Japan, and much of the trans-Atlantic journey was devoted to meetings at which British plans were perfected and the last details sorted out. One hundred and fifty officers were in the party, of whom twelve came from Combined

Operations.[1] Mountbatten was a constant participant but his principal preoccupation was to stalk the First Sea Lord and press him for a date at which he could return to sea. Pound proved evasive, and when cornered was not forthcoming. Mountbatten was disappointed but not discouraged. In the meantime he concentrated on winning support for Habbakuk and Mulberry. Professor Bernal, who had been included in the party, was unleashed on Churchill. 'The Prime Minister has taken the most enormous personal interest in the artificial harbours,' Mountbatten reported with satisfaction.[2] He was less successful in persuading Brooke to press his projects on the Americans. 'To Hell with Habbakuk!' said the C.I.G.S. unkindly. 'We are about to have the most difficult time with our American friends and shall not have time for your ice-carriers.'[3]

Another member of the British party was Orde Wingate. Wingate had won a reputation as a latter-day T. E. Lawrence by his exploits behind the enemy lines in Ethiopia and then in Burma. His courage, imagination, braggadocio and messianic zeal were calculated to appeal strongly to the Prime Minister, who in July had recommended to the Chiefs of Staff that Wingate should be promoted to overall command of the Army in South-East Asia. 'There is no doubt that in the welter of inefficiency and lassitude which has characterised our operations on the Indian front, this man, his force and his achievements stand out.'[4] The Chiefs were far from convinced that this would be a rational appointment, but made no objection when Churchill insisted on taking Wingate with him to Quebec as a token of British resolve to reconquer Burma. Mountbatten was sufficiently impressed by Wingate's quality to ask him to give the Combined Operations team an hour's talk on his adventures behind the lines.[5] Wingate was 'an absolute born military genius with a mystical fire about him', wrote Mountbatten after his death.[6] His comments were not always equally flattering when the obligations of the obituarist did not lie upon him, but he appreciated Wingate's spirit and was not as repelled as some by his arrogance and his eccentricity.

On 15 August, when the conference was well advanced, Mountbatten and the Chiefs of Staff lunched with Churchill. Afterwards the Prime Minister invited Mountbatten to stay behind. He spoke about South-East Asia, and asked whether the C.C.O. would be prepared to go out there to try to pull things together. Mountbatten assumed, or professed to assume, that a brief visit of inspection was being suggested. He would go where he was sent, he said, but what he *wanted* was to go to sea again. Churchill snorted with indignation. 'Go to sea! Don't you understand that I am proposing you should go out as Supreme Commander?' Mountbatten asked for time to think it over and fled from the room. He went to Ismay for reassurance and advice. 'I feel as though I have been pole-axed,' he began.[7]

The situation in South-East Asia was such that reassurance was indeed in order. In April 1942 the British had been chased from Burma. Only the skill of their commanders had saved them from total destruction. The British, or largely Indian, Army was inadequately equipped and feebly led. The Royal Air Force was pitifully weak, the intelligence services barely noticeable. They had no conception how to fight in the jungle, but instead clung to the roads and were invariably outflanked or taken in the rear. Their Chinese allies were ill-disciplined and prone to pursue their own, private interests; the Burmese were at best apathetic, more often hostile. The disorganized rabble that straggled across the frontier into India had not been merely defeated, it had been routed and humiliated.

India lay open, but with their lines of communication stretched and supplies running short the Japanese hesitated to press on. Laboriously Wavell, British Commander-in-Chief in the Far East, tried to build up a capacity to resist and then to strike back but, starved of trained troops and modern equipment, plagued by the need to maintain security in India itself, he could make little headway. When a limited offensive was begun in the Arakan Peninsula on the Burmese coast, the British commanders seemed to make all the same mistakes as in the previous campaign. By May 1943 a battered and demoralized army was back where it had started from, and could count itself lucky to have escaped at all. The only units to have acquitted themselves with any credit were Wingate's Long Range Penetration Groups, their successes being made to look more significant and brilliant by the abject failure of the orthodox forces.

General Irwin, the corps commander responsible for the ill-fated Arakan offensive, was now brusquely recalled. 'The very limited operations carried out this year', he wrote in mid April, 'have disclosed the lamentable fact that the Army is not yet sufficiently trained or efficiently led to take on the Japanese on even superior terms in numbers or material.'[8] When Mountbatten spoke to him in September he was no more cheerful. He said that morale was disastrous. British troops believed the Japanese to be invincible. His own batman 'reported back to the General that he had been shattered at the loss of all *esprit de corps* among the wounded and sick'. Irwin went on that 'he did not see how any unit at present in the front line could be counted on to hold in the event of the Japanese much-heralded "march on Delhi", much less stage an advance'.[9] Auchinleck, the Commander-in-Chief in India, was almost equally gloomy. In July he warned against any premature offensive. Nothing could be done with the present resources.[10] Angrily Churchill grumbled that the commanders on the spot seemed determined 'to magnify the difficulties, to demand even larger forces and to prescribe far longer delays'. What was needed, he concluded, was the appointment 'of a young, competent soldier, well trained in war, to become Supreme Commander and to re-examine the whole problem of the war on this front so as to infuse vigour and authority into the operation'.[11]

Mountbatten occasionally remarked that the best moment to take over a job was when things were at their worst. His timing in the case of South-East Asia could hardly have been more perfect. The new Fourteenth Army under General Slim was in fact already on the road to recovery; intensive training was in progress, morale was rising. The blackest moment was past. But the situation still seemed dismal enough to satisfy any but the most demanding of pessimists. Numerically the six divisions in India and the three American–Chinese in the north slightly outnumbered the five or six Japanese divisions then in Burma, but the latter had the advantage of internal communications and crushing superiority in the techniques of jungle warfare. There were more Allied than Japanese aeroplanes in the sector, but here again the enemy equipment was immeasurably superior and would remain so for several months. The Japanese fleet dominated the Bay of Bengal. Above all, the Japanese knew they were destined to win; the British were still half-convinced they would lose. Confidence was being rebuilt, but it was an arduous process. Whether Slim could have done it alone must remain uncertain. An ally was on the way.

Mountbatten was far from being the first choice for this assignment, though his name has been one of the earliest canvassed. The idea of a Supreme Commander was mooted in May 1943, though the Chiefs of Staff did not formally endorse the idea till June.[12] Its most energetic champion was Leo Amery, the Secretary of State for India. Wavell was a spent force, Amery telegraphed Churchill on 31 May, and the Prime Minister should appoint 'an immediate Supreme Commander and consider the possibility of Mountbatten'.[13] At the time Churchill was unconvinced that such an appointment was desirable and 'brushed aside my suggestion of Mountbatten, which Brooke had definitely liked, on the ground that his health is bad and that he was not big enough'.[14] It was largely American pressure, and the failure of Wavell to establish any sort of working relationship with the American commander of the Chinese armies in Burma, General Stilwell, that led Churchill to change his mind. Roosevelt agreed that the new slot should be filled by a British officer, and the hunt was on.[15]

The first candidate was Sholto Douglas, but he was detested by the Americans and vetoed by Roosevelt.[16] The American Chiefs of Staff countered with Tedder or Cunningham, but Eisenhower considered Tedder irreplaceable in the Mediterranean and Cunningham was unenthusiastic: 'an unattractive job' he deemed it.[17] Brooke persisted that Cunningham would be the best man and in the end it was Churchill who quashed the idea: 'I do not think that a sailor is well qualified for a command of this character. The sea-faring and scientific technique of the naval profession makes such severe demands upon the training of naval men, that they have very rarely the time or opportunity to study military history and the art of war in general.'[18] Admiral Sir James Somerville was then suggested, but he too was a sailor through and through, and the Americans viewed him with little enthusiasm. Other names put up at one time or another included General Sir Henry Maitland Wilson, General Sir George Giffard, Lieutenant-General Sir Henry Pownall, Lieutenant-General Sir Oliver Leese and Air Marshal Slessor – 'all the names submitted by the Chiefs of Staff were very ordinary' observed Ismay with some hauteur.[19]

So the situation rested when the *Queen Mary* steamed towards Quebec. It is hard to see why the possibility of Mountbatten had not already come back into Churchill's mind. The value he attached to the C.C.O. is apparent in the remark he addressed to Eden when it was suggested that most members of the Quebec party should fly the Atlantic together: 'I don't know what I should do if I lost you all: I'd have to cut my throat. It isn't just love, though there is much of that in it, but that you are my war machine. Brookie, Portal, you and Dickie. I simply couldn't replace you.'[20] At some point in the voyage, at all events, he seems to have concluded that Mountbatten's health, youth, stature and other deleterious features were not, after all, factors of the first importance. He summoned Ian Jacob and General Hollis and asked them who they thought should be the new Supreme Commander. Jacob suggested Giffard; Churchill looked sceptical, then 'with a face like a naughty schoolboy produced Mountbatten's name'.[21]

The matter was quickly concluded. The Chiefs of Staff were acquiescent if unenthusiastic. Mountbatten was 'as likely to make a success of the job as any junior officer', commented Dudley Pound, and no more senior candidate was available.[22] 'What he lacked in experience he made up in self-confidence,' was Brooke's verdict. 'He had boundless energy and drive, but would require a steadying influence in the nature of a very carefully selected Chief of Staff.'[23]

When the question was put in London, Churchill's deputy Attlee and Eden made a last plea for Cunningham,[24] but Churchill would have none of it. All earlier doubts were forgotten; Mountbatten was the master of Combined Operations and his appointment would 'command public interest and approval, and show that youth is no barrier to merit'.[25] Neither Attlee nor Eden was disposed to fight further on such an issue, and it was left to Churchill to try the idea on the Americans.

They proved to be less qualified in their approval than the British.

Marshall and Eisenhower were predictably delighted, but it was more remarkable that the anglophobe Ernest King found Mountbatten the most impressive officer at the Quebec conference.[26] Wedemeyer noted that, when Mountbatten visited Washington when the conference was over, everyone he met found him 'gracious, charming, democratic'.[27] His nomination was 'unanimously approved' by the Americans, Pound told the First Lord; 'I think that the U.S. were very gratified by the interest which we were taking in Far Eastern operations'.[28] The only discordant notes were struck by those elements of the press and political world which would have looked with disgust at the appointment of any British officer to command American troops. The Patterson papers denounced the selection of 'a princeling', whose preferment to MacArthur demonstrated the powerful influence the reactionary British still exercised in Washington; while Representative Jessie Sumner from Illinois said that it was part of a British plot to oust Admiral Leahy and keep MacArthur from the highest military command.[29]

The President's son, Elliott Roosevelt, recorded a curious conversation which he claimed to have had with his father. The account is suspect, if only because it is supposed to have taken place at Casablanca, eight months before Mountbatten's possible appointment was mentioned to the Americans, but in its essentials it has the ring of truth. Certainly it presaged many of the difficulties which were to arise between the Allies in South-East Asia. Roosevelt says that he saw his father

> grinning at some secret thought. 'What's it, Pop?' 'Thinking of Mountbatten,' he answered. 'You know why Winston has Mountbatten here with him? It's so that I can be filled up to the ears with arguments about how important it is to divert landing-craft to South-East Asia.' I looked my astonishment and incredulity. 'Sure!' he went on. 'Burma. The British want to recapture Burma. It's the first time they've shown any real interest in the Pacific, and why? For their colonial empire!' 'But what's that got to do with Mountbatten?' 'He's their choice for Supreme Allied Commander of a brand-new theater – South-East Asia.' 'But what about Europe?' I asked. 'What about the cross-Channel deal?' 'Don't worry. Mountbatten has a lot of charm, a lot of persuasion, but I doubt strongly he'll be able to show enough to convince Ernie King.'[30]

On 24 August 1943 Churchill sent telegrams to the Prime Ministers of South Africa, Australia and New Zealand, announcing the new appointment.

> Mountbatten has unique qualifications in that he is intimately acquainted with all three branches of the Services, and also with amphibious operations. He has served for nearly a year and a half on

the Chiefs of Staff Committee, and thus knows the whole of our war
story from the centre. I regard this as of great importance on account
of the extremely varied character of the South East Asia front by land
and sea. Mountbatten is a fine organiser, and a man of great energy
and daring. His appointment has been cordially welcomed by the
President, and by the American Chiefs of Staff, and was hailed with
delight by Soong, on behalf of the Generalissimo.[31]

It was hailed with something less than delight by certain people who
would have a powerful influence on the course of Mountbatten's service in
South-East Asia. P. J. Grigg, the Secretary of State for War, roamed Washington denouncing the selection of this aristocratic playboy.[32] Andrew
Cunningham, with a bile that ill became his greatness, wrote that he
much regretted Mountbatten's promotion. 'It rather defeats me how he can
imagine he is the man for the job. It is the end of his service career. A political
job, of course. . . . It is a poor business but I think most people in the service
have just laughed.'[33] Auchinleck, too, was disappointed, since he had hoped
that he would be put in command of operations in Burma. 'He was surprised
and somewhat upset at Dickie Mountbatten's appointment as Supreme
Commander,' wrote Somerville; 'the Auk is a bit conservative, and does not
like innovations of this character.'[34]

Outraged conservatism; the jealousy of senior officers passed over in
favour of a comparative youngster; resentment at a selection which some felt
was made because of royal connections or political pull; genuine doubts
about the ability of this novice to fill the role assigned to him: all these
coloured reactions to the appointment. Yet the most common response was
one of satisfaction; Mountbatten might be unproven but his qualities were
what were needed in the present situation; he was uncontaminated by failure;
in his very lack of experience lay hope for the future. Oliver Harvey, Eden's
private secretary, summed it up when he recorded in his diary that Mountbatten had been appointed with Wingate as 'a good second'. 'People here are
doubtful of Mountbatten being up to this but the P.M. and the Americans are
het up on it. Mountbatten–Wingate is at least a refreshing contrast to
Wavell–Auchinleck.'[35]

Mountbatten had good reason to feel cautious as he took his first glance at his
new command – 'such a hot potato', Ismay described it, 'that nobody
particularly wanted to hold it'.[36] He sought reassurance from the Chiefs of
Staff. Portal told him frankly that he would have preferred Tedder or Douglas
but that, these being ruled out, the Chief of Combined Operations was his
first choice. Pound substituted Cunningham for the two airmen but gave the

same endorsement. Amery assured him that Brooke too was enthusiastic.[37] Mountbatten would have preferred to hear that he was thought by everyone to be the ideal man for the job, but this was good enough. To doubt for long was not in his nature, and he accepted with unquestioning optimism the assurances of those who told him that he would receive all the support which had been lacking in the past. Harold Wernher found him in 'a highly delighted state of mind'. He warned the new Supreme Commander that he would be low on the priority list for men and materials, but the warning was brushed aside.[38] 'It's grand. They have promised me everything!' he told General Macleod with sublime naivety.[39]

His mood, to judge by his letters to members of his family, was one of awestruck exultation. 'You have probably heard', he told his elder daughter, who had now returned from America and joined the female element of the Navy, the WRNS, 'that there are at present two American Generals who are Supreme Allied Commanders for the Mediterranean and Pacific respectively called Eisenhower and MacArthur. Well, the President and Prime Minister have picked a chap with the same surname as Wren Mountbatten to be the Supreme Allied Commander to South East Asia. . . . Can you beat it? I still feel stunned.' A few days later he wrote again: 'My task is probably the biggest and most difficult which any Englishman has been given in war. To reconquer Burma, Malaya, the Dutch East Indies and all the places in which the British Empire's present forces received an unparalleled series of defeats on land, at sea, and in the air. Particularly as no one seems to have done anything about it until now!'[40]

To Churchill Mountbatten poured out his gratitude and his excitement.

> I have never really thanked you properly for giving me the finest chance any young man has ever been given in war. I had been hoping to get back in a humble way into the fight at sea; such a dazzling prospect as you have held out to me had never for one second entered my head. I could not at first bring myself to believe that the Chiefs of Staff in agreeing to this appointment were activated by any motive other than loyalty to you. All three, and Pug [Ismay] have now convinced me that they are ready to back me from their own convictions. All this has now begun to make me feel that your decision in this case may turn out to be as right as it has certainly been in all other cases. You can imagine how stimulating and encouraging this is for me.
>
> Finally may I say that I would not have felt competent to take this on if I had not had the rare privilege of being allowed to sit for 18

months at the feet of the greatest master of strategy and war this
century has produced. Nor have I overlooked your method of
applying the spur to the sluggish war horse.[41]

His tripartite role gave him particular pleasure. 'It is the first time in
history that a Naval officer has been given supreme command over land and
air forces,' he told Edwina. 'It will mean another stripe.'[42] This promotion, to
full Admiral, caused some dismay in the Admiralty, where Pound stressed
that the rank should be acting and unconfirmed.[43] Churchill concurred,
ruling for some reason that the new Supreme Commander should be known
as Admiral Mountbatten and not Admiral Lord Louis Mountbatten.[44] Prince
Philip was vastly amused at his uncle's fresh elevation.

What are they going to make you? Acting Admiral of the Fleet or
something? You had better be careful, . . . before you know what you
will have the prospect of 40 years without promotion in front of you.
What a thought! As a string-puller, of course, you've practically lost
all value, you're so big now that it might smell of nepotism (just to
make sure I had the right word, I looked it up in the dictionary, and
this is what it says: undue favour from holder of patronage to
relatives, originally from Pope to illegitimate sons called nephews).[45]

The Chiefs of Staff put their feet down, however, when the question arose
of promoting Mountbatten in the other two services as well. He was already
an honorary Lieutenant-General and Air Marshal, they said, and that was
enough. He had got the ranks to help his work in Combined Operations and,
though they would not now seek to remove them, promotion would imply
that 'Supreme Commanders in other theatres should also have honorary
ranks in other Services'.[46] Since Mountbatten was the only British Supreme
Commander and likely to remain so, the prospect of a flood of such spurious
appointments seemed remote; but the issue was not disputed. Mountbatten
kept the honorary ranks he already enjoyed.

He gloried in the splendour and significance of his new role, but he was
closer to being daunted by it than by any earlier challenge. To Edwina he
admitted that, the more he thought of the job, the more alarmed he became.
Was there no chance that she could come out to join him?

I really don't know how I will be able to do this job without you. I've
got so used to leaning on you and hearing your brutally frank but
well-deserved criticism. But above all you have been such a help with
all the people I have to deal with. Then again, I have grown so
completely to rely on the family background for rest and relaxation. . . .

> Wouldn't it be romantic to live together in the place we got
> engaged in, and in a job which is really more important in the war
> than our host's was. . . .
>
> Please don't think I underestimate the importance of your job – I
> am just being a very selfish husband who would like to have his wife
> with him!![47]

Lady Louis had excellent reasons for saying that she was needed where
she was. In August 1942 she had become Superintendent-in-Chief of the St
John's Ambulance Nursing Division and she was doing work of great value.
Even if she had not been, however, it is doubtful if she would have relished a
role in South-East Asia in which she had no real purpose except to cosset
her husband. She did not share or understand his need for companionship.
C.O.H.Q. had won a reputation for the bevy of glamorous young women
who were employed there; their function, it was unfairly said, less obvious
than their decorative value. Mountbatten rejoiced in the dashing image thus
bestowed upon him, but what he wanted most was the society of a single
woman in whom he would have complete confidence. It was the lack of this
which he feared in South-East Asia; the responsibilities he would accept
with alacrity but the loneliness of high command was a terror which he faced
with deep reluctance.

He departed to a plethora of good advice and exhortation. 'You have the
devil of a job,' said Montgomery. 'If you can, by your energy and enthusiasm,
shake India out of its lethargy you will have done something no one has ever
been able to do before.'[48] MacArthur was more precise. 'Tell him that he will
need more Air!' he urged Air Marshal Goddard. 'And when you have told him
that, tell him again from me that he will need *more Air*!!' Here he thumped the
table and almost shouted: 'And when you have told him that for the second
time, tell him from me for the third time that he will need still MORE
AIR!!!'[49] But the most relevant counsel came from General Morgan,
COSSAC, whom Mountbatten had asked for a treatise on 'What a Young
Supreme Commander should know'. Morgan, among other things, urged
him always to remain at his proper level. In Combined Operations he had
been able somehow 'to strike the complete octave by being a Chief of Staff at
one end of the scale and the coxswain of a landing-craft at the other'. Now he
must get into the stratosphere and stay there. He must at all costs get away
from Delhi. And he must remember Kipling's line: 'And the epitaph drear: "A
fool lies here, who tried to hustle the East."'

> You may think this is rather a dismal note on which to finish, but I do
> it deliberately, because I do ask you above all things to spare yourself
> as much as you can. For some time past you have driven yourself

much too hard, even according to European standards. If you do that in the East, you will definitely kill yourself.[50]

Mountbatten noted this last piece of advice. Probably he accepted that it was wise. But if he believed that he would follow it, he deluded himself absurdly.

# CHAPTER 17

## *Supreme Command*

MOUNTBATTEN LEFT NORTHOLT AIRPORT on 2 October 1943. He stopped at Baghdad, to find that the British Ambassador had for some reason dragged the Regent back from Jerusalem to receive a highly important personal message. Mountbatten said he had no wish even to see the Regent, let alone give him a message, whereupon the Ambassador implored him to invent something. Mountbatten rose to the occasion, and duly reported that 'the King was counting the days to the Regent's visit to Buckingham Palace'. The Regent was much touched by this special mark of attention. At dinner the Prime Minister, Nuri, drew Mountbatten aside and asked whether he had brought his driver with him. 'Which driver?' asked Mountbatten, uncertain whether a golf-club or a chauffeur was in question. 'The famous one, of course,' answered Nuri, leaving Mountbatten none the wiser. 'No' seemed a safe answer in any case.[1]

On 6 October he arrived in Delhi. 'I could not help getting a certain thrill at the moment when we crossed the coast of India,' he wrote in his diary, 'to feel that it had fallen to me to be the outward and visible symbol of the British Empire's intention to return to the attack in Asia.' There was some way to go – Mountbatten's Command included Burma, Ceylon, Siam, the Malay Peninsula and Sumatra; with the exception of Ceylon and a strip of territory in Burma along the Chin hills and in Arakan, the whole of it was in enemy hands – yet he had no doubt that he would carry out his directive and clear the Japanese from the area. Faridkot House, a maharaja's palace in New Delhi, had been put aside for his lodgings. Assuming that he would wish to be near his Commanders in Chief, those in charge of office accommodation had located Admiral Somerville and the naval staff on the ground floor and General Giffard and the Army staff on the second, leaving the Supreme Commander sandwiched in between. Mountbatten at once set to work to evict them: 'it really was essential', he wrote, 'that I and my sixteen officers of Major-General's rank (!) should all be housed in one block'.[2] To others it seemed a first, ominous sign of how he proposed to run his new empire.

He quickly remembered Morgan's advice to escape from Delhi. He found the atmosphere of the capital smug and stultifying. Social life continued

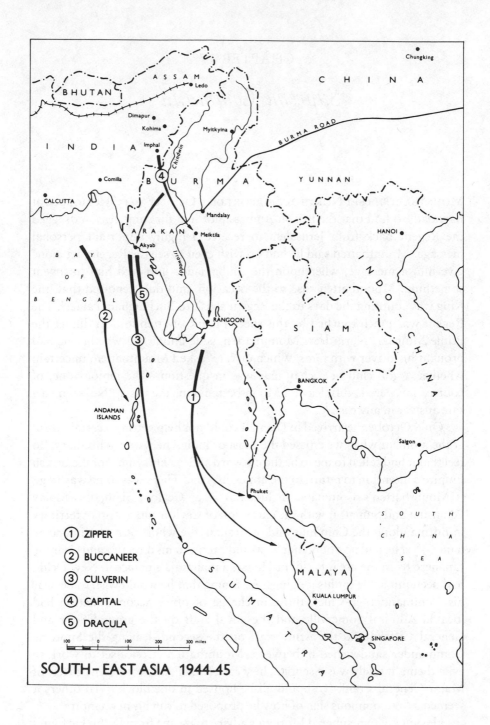

1 ZIPPER

2 BUCCANEER

3 CULVERIN

4 CAPITAL

5 DRACULA

100   0   100   200   300 miles

SOUTH-EAST ASIA 1944-45

merrily as if there was no war in Asia. On his first day an A.D.C. asked whether he had got a book. 'Why, have you run out of detective stories?' asked Mountbatten, to be told a visitor's book was in question. Twelve people had already called and left cards. No social callers were to be received, he ruled; and when Bapsy Pavry, an eminent Parsee lady who was later to become Marchioness of Winchester, insisted that there must be some time in the future when he could make time for her, he replied that he would see her on 31 March 1947. Miss Pavry had the last laugh, however, for by then he was back in Delhi as Viceroy, and she was on the spot to collect her due.[3] The headquarters itself was infested by a horde of under-employed cleaners, messengers, etc. left over from the civilian administration, who gave the place an air of sloppy indolence. Security was lamentable. 'An Indian boy about four feet high (whom I suspect of being a Japanese spy in disguise) comes into my office every day to try and sell me chocolates and cigarettes.' Try as they would, the A.D.C.s and sentries could not keep him out; in the end it was Mountbatten who got rid of him by forcing him to unpack his entire stock outside in the passage.[4]

There was every reason to expect trouble between the old India hands, who were disposed to think the newcomers brash, ignorant and tactless, and Mountbatten's staff, who looked expectantly for signs of slothfulness and inefficiency. Friction there certainly was: 'But Mountbatten and I worked very well together,' wrote Auchinleck, 'and I think we stopped it.'[5] The initial exchanges were frosty, however. Montgomery warned Mountbatten that 'the Auk' was 'a curious bird. The basic trouble there is an "inferiority complex", and he goes on the defensive very quickly. Possibly you have discovered this!!'[6] He had. At their first meeting Mountbatten found that Auchinleck 'seemed already to have built up an icy barrier between us'. He could hardly bring himself to mention Mountbatten or his office: 'he would say, "This matter must be settled by the Supr ... I mean Adm ...", then having come to a complete stop he would turn to me and say, "I mean, this is a matter *you* must settle."' After dinner the first night he took Mountbatten aside and stressed that all the troops in India must remain under his sole command; he alone would be responsible for selecting and training the forces for S.E.A. Command.[7] 'It doesn't sound as if Mountbatten had got on too well with the Auk,' wrote the Supreme Commander's Chief of Staff, General Pownall, in his diary. 'The former effervescent and dynamic, the latter very mulish at times and, like a mule, without warning and over very minor matters. I wouldn't say his nose is out of joint but he cannot exactly relish a Supreme Commander coming to sit down in what is so very much his parish.'[8]

Auchinleck, however, was too big and generous a man to allow pique to

stand in the way of doing what he felt to be his duty. Possibly nervous about
future ructions, Amery wrote to him to say he was sure that 'the Viceroy,
Mountbatten and yourself will be a great and indivisible trinity'.[9] 'Mountbatten and his staff (which is a healthy and growing child) are settling down,'
replied Auchinleck, 'but naturally have still to depend on us for much
information and help. We are, I think, giving them of our best and will
continue to do so while I have any say in the matter.'[10] Once the initial reserve
had worn off, he treated Mountbatten with consideration and even affection;
'absolutely first class', Mountbatten described him in February 1944. 'Every
week he becomes more friendly and more helpful.'[11]

Wavell, the third member of Amery's great trinity, was equally co-
operative. The Viceroy had been in favour of Mountbatten's appointment
from the start, 'if he has a level-headed C.G.S. to check any wild ideas'.
Boldness, he felt, was needed. The present Commanders-in-Chief were
painfully cautious – 'I pointed out many times that the Japanese would never
have invaded Malaya or got anywhere if they had planned on our conservative lines.'[12] Viceroy and Supreme Commander surveyed each other with
amused and baffled respect, so dissimilar in temperament and style that
they were almost beings of different species, yet each recognizing the quality
of the other. It was not to be the last time that their contrasting characteristics were vividly exhibited.


The organization of South-East Asia Command and the powers and responsibilities of its different elements gave rise to so great a pother, such endless
recriminations, that it is sometimes easy to overlook the fact that the principal
campaign was against the Japanese. To put the problem in a sentence: no one
knew precisely – or, it sometimes seemed, even approximately – what a
Supreme Commander was supposed to do, or how he was supposed to do it.
The difficulties that arose from this failure to define Mountbatten's role were
clearly less significant than the battles of Arakan and Imphal. For a biography
of Mountbatten, however, they provide a vivid illustration of his strengths
and weaknesses, his priorities, preoccupations and ways of working. For this
reason, even more than their intrinsic curiosity, they deserve some examination.

There were generally held to be two models a Supreme Commander could
follow: that of Eisenhower or that of MacArthur. Unfortunately, this dicho-
tomy meant different things to different people. It could mean that, as with
Eisenhower, the Supreme Commander would be responsible to the Combined Chiefs of Staff of Britain and the United States, rather than, like
MacArthur, responsible to one of the national Chiefs of Staff on all but the

most grandly strategic issues. On this point the Americans insisted on the Eisenhower solution, and got their way.[13] It could, on the other hand, mean that, as with Eisenhower, the Supreme Commander would have three semi-independent Commanders-in-Chief, each with his own planning staff, rather than, like MacArthur, force commanders controlled by an integrated central staff. He could either be a chairman of a committee, or a commander who truly commanded. It was in this second sense that the main protagonists used the terms, and it was this debate which gave rise to so much acrimony and misunderstanding. It would have been fairer to Mountbatten if it had been settled in advance.

Mountbatten's contention was that he had originally intended to be an Eisenhower but that the Chiefs of Staff had insisted he must be a MacArthur and Churchill had reinforced their view. 'I cannot possibly evade that responsibility,' he told his naval Commander-in-Chief, Admiral Somerville. 'On the other hand I fully see the dangers of attempting to become a Dictator and am grateful to you for pointing them out.'[14] With such support it might be thought that the Supreme Commander's thesis would inevitably prevail. When it came to the point, however, his ground proved unsure. Cunningham took over as First Sea Lord from the ailing Pound – 'I have heard that he has a special hate against Dickie,' Somerville told his wife[15] – and at once disavowed whatever his predecessor might have said on the subject. Brooke and Portal were at the best equivocal. Churchill had certainly urged Mountbatten to take his senior officers by the scruff of the neck and harry them into action, but it is unlikely that he gave any thought to the problems of organization implicit in his proposition. Only the Americans were fully aware of what they were recommending, and their views were coloured as much by doubts about the existing British Commanders-in-Chief as by belief in the merits of the MacArthur system.[16]

General Pownall, Mountbatten's Chief of Staff, had been encouraged by Brooke to see himself as a benevolent uncle, curbing the headstrong excesses of a nephew who had prematurely succeeded as head of the family.[17] Such was his usual role, but when it came to Mountbatten's relationship with his Commanders-in-Chief he chose to egg on his master rather than restrain him. 'There is no doubt who is in *command* of the whole show,' he wrote in his diary. ' "Supreme Commander" means just that – he is not just the chairman of a committee.'[18] He encouraged Mountbatten to set up a powerful central planning staff. This dismayed the Commanders-in-Chief, who saw themselves being by-passed, rather as if Churchill had chosen to rely on Ismay, Jacob and Professor Lindemann and ignore the Chiefs of Staff.

Mountbatten's most vulnerable point was the size of the organization which he was creating. Somerville complained to Ismay that 'the machine has

# SOUTH-EAST

BRITISH CHIEFS OF STAFF

SUPREME COMMANDER
S.E.A.C.
Admiral Lord Louis Mountbatten

DEPUTY SUPREME COMMANDER
1 Lieutenant-General Stilwell till October 1944
2 Lieutenant-General Wheeler

CHIEF OF STAFF
1 Lieutenant-General Pownall (to December 1944)
2 Lieutenant-General Browning

DEPUTY CHIEF OF STAFF
1 Lieutenant-General Wedemeyer till October 1944
2 Major-General Fuller

C. IN C. EASTERN FLEET
1 Admiral Somerville till August 1944
2 Admiral Fraser till November 1944

C. IN C. EAST INDIES FLEET
3 Vice-Admiral Power

C. IN C. ALLIED LAND FORCES
1 General Giffard till October 1944
2 Lieutenant-General Leese till July 1945
3 Lieutenant-General Slim

G.O.C. IN C. 14th ARMY
1 Lieutenant-General Slim till July 1945
2 Lieutenant-General Dempsey

# ASIA COMMAND

COMBINED
CHIEFS OF STAFF

AMERICAN CHIEFS OF STAFF

COMMANDING GENERAL
C.B.I. THEATER
1 Lieutenant-General Stilwell till
   October 1944
2 Lieutenant-General Sultan
  (for Burma and India only)

CHIEF OF STAFF TO
GENERALISSIMO CHIANG KAI-SHEK
1 Lieutenant-General Stilwell till October 1944
2 Lieutenant-General Wedemeyer

ALLIED AIR C. IN C.
1 Air Chief Marshal Peirse till November 1944
[2 Air Marshal Garrod deputized till February 1945]
3 Air Chief Marshal Park

G.O.C. IN C. 12th ARMY
(formed May 1945)
Lieutenant-General Stopford

run away and is gathering momentum daily'. The latest addition was a
banquet manager masquerading as a subaltern.[19] Ten days after this letter
was written, but evidently before it was received, Ismay wrote: 'I do wish you
could stop Dickie collecting staff in this crazy way. I have implored him not to
make the same mistake as he made as C.C.O. (where incidentally he did a
damn fine job). . . .'[20] When Al Wedemeyer, Mountbatten's American Deputy Chief of Staff, visited London, he was told that Mountbatten had been
extravagantly loyal to his old supporters from Combined Operations: 'He
created posts on our staff to permit their advancement and not in keeping
with the requirements from the viewpoint of the work to be accomplished.'[21]
Cunningham even raised the matter with the Chiefs of Staff and Mountbatten
was informed that 'until after the defeat of Germany, he should curtail his
requirements and make greater use of the existing staffs of his Commanders-
in-Chief'.[22] The Supreme Commander was deeply hurt. 'In spite of an
undeserved reputation to the contrary,' he told Lambe, 'I dislike large staffs
and have done everything in my power to keep my own staff down.'[23] He
wrote to Brooke to report that, anticipating the views of the Chiefs of Staff, he
had conducted the most searching investigation and found that his staff was
not merely fully employed but grossly overworked. He went on to thank
Brooke for advising him to set up his own 'Small Separate War Staff', which
was functioning admirably. Brooke's reply was notably non-committal:
'Delighted to hear that you also have been uneasy about your Staff getting too
big. . . . With the present man-power situation we must all cut Staffs to the
very minimum.'[24]

The Chiefs of Staff contrived to avoid ruling on whether Mountbatten
should have his own independent planning staff. When Mountbatten, briefly
back in London, attended a meeting of the Chiefs, the minutes record a
discussion of striking indecisiveness. 'On the one hand, it was suggested that
his task was rather to co-ordinate operations of the various Commanders-in-
Chief under his control. On the other it was pointed out that ultimate
responsibility for his theatre rested with him; and it was clearly within his
powers to overrule the advice of his Commanders-in-Chief if he thought fit.'
The Chiefs of Staff then added a bland hope that 'consultation and co-
operation on the spot' would avoid the need for constant reference to higher
authority.[25]

Somerville was feeling anything but co-operative, his rage fuelled by
certain officers on Mountbatten's staff who seemed to delight in couching any
dictum from Supreme Headquarters in terms as provocative as possible. 'The
madhouse is worse than ever,' he told his wife. 'I had a long talk with
[Mountbatten] yesterday when he tried to convince me that his Staff was
really much too small, that he was only doing this and that because the P.M.

insisted. I'm afraid I believe very little of what he said.'[26] To Ismay he complained about his adversary's 'bare-faced lobbying': 'If you have a good case, then you should rely on the normal channels.'[27] Coming as it did in a private letter to Churchill's chief staff officer, the charge appears a trifle disingenuous. On 9 June he wrote a formal letter to the Admiralty, protesting at Mountbatten's attempt to set up a MacArthur-style organization and preference for the advice of his own planners to that of the Commanders-in-Chief.[28] The justification for this somewhat extreme action which he later gave suggests an imbalance not far removed from paranoia. Mountbatten was seeking 'a form of absolute control usually exercised by dictators', he was determined to be in personal charge of every important issue, 'it was essential someone should put on the brake and I appeared to be the only one willing and able to attempt this'.[29]

Pownall chanced to be in London and on this occasion urged Mountbatten not to take up the challenge. If he appealed to the Chiefs of Staff, Cunningham would be certain to back Somerville and the question would have to be referred to Churchill, who had more than enough on his plate at the moment. After all, it was only another six weeks before Somerville was to be replaced; his successor, Bruce Fraser, might take the same line but would undoubtedly be easier to deal with.[30]

The advice was excellent, but Mountbatten felt that he could not let an official complaint to the Admiralty go unanswered.[31] He wrote to his wife to report that he had just been spending seven hours working on his riposte to Somerville. 'I have had the painful duty to "tick him off" by a letter to him and a telegram to the C.O.S. Committee. Really, life is difficult!'[32]

It got no easier. The Chiefs of Staff had no intention of being drawn into the squabble. Mountbatten had to be content with a mere acknowledgement and a sharp note from Ismay. For his private information, he was told, the Chiefs of Staff 'are very preoccupied with live problems of first importance, and feel they cannot spend time on legalistic disputations. The precise clarification of your powers, which are much the same as those which have been worked satisfactorily by other Supreme Commanders, seems to them unnecessary.'[33] With that he had to rest content.

It was Charles Lambe, now Director of Plans in the Admiralty, who brought belated peace to the scene. Early in July he lunched with Somerville and told him that he had always been in favour of the Eisenhower formula. He offered to go to SEAC Headquarters to try to sort out the mess.[34] Exactly what he said to Mountbatten will never be known; Lambe merely records that he persuaded his friend to disband his staff and to revert to the Eisenhower system of command.[35] Next day the Supreme Commander told Philip Mason, then serving on his staff, that he was still convinced that the

MacArthur system was best. However, he went on with disarming honesty, Lambe had pointed out that to quarrel with two successive naval Commanders-in-Chief would gravely damage his chances of becoming First Sea Lord. The only way to ensure that Fraser did not become as inveterate an enemy as Somerville was by giving way on the matter of planning staffs. Mountbatten took the point and despatched Mason post-haste to Somerville's headquarters, in case the 'cantankerous old bugger' had changed his ground. He had not. Somerville was delighted: 'Wanted to help him. Young naval officer. Always anxious to help a young naval officer. Very promising young naval officer. Full of energy. But then he got these ridiculous ideas which wouldn't work. Anyway, it's all over now and I'm glad.'[36] Somerville was told that Mountbatten's main concern was the indignation of his War Staff when his decision was revealed to them. 'He therefore expressed the hope that when the matter came up for discussion at the forthcoming conference of Commanders-in-Chief at Kandy I should not appear to be outwardly too pleased.'[37]

Mountbatten did nothing by half measures; if forced to change course he did so with good grace, even with ebullience. It took him little time to convince himself that he had been privately in favour of the new arrangements all along. On 5 August he attended a meeting of the Chiefs of Staff and told them, no doubt to their considerable relief, that he had amalgamated his War Staff with the planning staffs of the Commanders-in-Chief.[38] Three months later he was writing to Somerville who had replaced Sir John Dill as representative of the Chiefs of Staff in Washington: 'I know you will be delighted to hear that the Joint Planning Staff works a fair treat, and since their introduction there have been no more arguments with the Commanders-in-Chief.'[39] To Lambe he used the same expression; the new staff not only worked a fair treat but was the 'one very great success' of the last few months.[40]

The question of the planning staffs was at the heart of Mountbatten's difficulties with his Commanders-in-Chief, but other issues caused almost as much ill-feeling. Largely it was a question of personalities. The Supreme Commander had been encouraged by Churchill and others to view his new colleagues with impatience if not contempt. He was afraid, Dill told him, 'that your most senior British Commanders in all Services may be a bit . . . old and a bit too experienced for the tasks you will want them to perform. . . . Your difficulties in this regard, if you have any, might be very great because you are younger and you were junior to them all.'[41] That Mountbatten was senior to these venerable grandees went without saying; the extent of his control and of their autonomy was more obscure. He himself firmly believed that he had been given authority by the Chiefs of Staff to dismiss them if they did not give satisfaction. He overestimated the strength of his position. Pound died before the matter could be put to the test, but Brooke's behaviour at the time of the dismissal of Giffard and Leese did not suggest he had given Mountbatten *carte blanche* to remove his Commanders-in-Chief.[42] Portal later denied that he had offered any such powers.[43] On the other hand, Mountbatten arrived with all the authority of someone who had been – to all intents and purposes – a Chief of Staff, as well as a protégé of the Prime Minister and a man much heeded in Whitehall. His position may not have been as strong as he represented it, but strong it undoubtedly was.

Air Marshal Peirse was least likely of the three Commanders to cause him trouble. Peirse had been sceptical about the need for a Supreme Commander in the first place. His doubts were strengthened by the fact that Mountbatten was an international commander only on land; the 10th U.S. Air Force was kept effectively under the orders of the Supreme Commander's American Deputy, General Stilwell.[44] This Mountbatten resolved to remedy, and Peirse backed him loyally. 'I could always rely on his support for determined and vigorous policies,' wrote Mountbatten in the Personalities Report, which he prepared for submission to the King.[45] He was impressed enough to ask Portal for a six months' extension when Peirse's original posting ran out early in 1944. But then things began to go wrong. The Air Marshal's protracted affair with Lady Auchinleck became a flagrant scandal, the neglect of his duties while cavorting with her in Kashmir lost him the respect of his own officers. When Portal in his turn suggested that Peirse's term of office be still further extended, Mountbatten refused, declining even to keep him on for two or three months after his designated successor, Leigh-Mallory, was killed when flying out to take over. It was the end of Peirse's career.

The Air Commander was a mere eight years older than Mountbatten; General Sir George Giffard was a veteran of fifty-eight. General Stilwell had refused to put his American and Chinese forces under a commander whom he believed to be timid and inept. Giffard in fact was neither of these things; he was an honourable and kindly gentleman, thoroughly competent, but never a firebrand and now grown slow and prudent. All his instincts told him to defend his prerogatives against the incursions of an inexperienced naval overlord, and, although his courtesy softened the impact, a collision was in the end inevitable.[46]

Mountbatten told Dill that he agreed his Commanders-in-Chief were too old for the job, 'but I must say that Giffard and Peirse have been so loyal and helpful to me that I feel it is better to carry on a bit longer'.[47] He conspicuously failed to say as much about his third Commander-in-Chief, Admiral Sir

James Somerville. Somerville was eighteen years Mountbatten's senior; a
naval officer of great courage and distinction, charming, humorous, outspoken, irascible and with a strong sense of hierarchy. It was inevitable that
he would resent the incursions of this whipper-snapper, equally inevitable
that Mountbatten should be on his guard against slights or patronage.

In fact both men started with the best intentions. Shortly before Mountbatten arrived in Delhi, Somerville summoned his staff and told them that the
arrangement had *got* to work, 'anyone who put a spanner in the works would
be for the high jump'.[48] He sent a friendly telegram to the new Supreme
Commander who replied humbly: 'Quite the most terrifying part of the task
which has been so unexpectedly and undeservedly allotted to me was the
prospect of having a great Naval Commander-in-Chief within the South East
Asia Command. . . . If I may say so, there is no really senior Naval Officer of
my acquaintance who I feel would be so ready to play with an Officer whose
naval experience is so very immature by comparison.'[49]

The honeymoon did not last long. So ambiguous was their relationship
that there would have been ructions even if the two men had been wholly
unassertive. To Somerville it was *his* fleet, placed within SEAC for certain
limited purposes but otherwise independent and responsible only to the
Admiralty. 'You ask what Dickie has to do with the E[astern] F[leet],'
Somerville wrote to his wife. 'Well, all that happens is that certain ships are
placed under his orders for specific operations but he has nothing to do with
operations to protect our communications or operations against enemy
surface forces.'[50] To Mountbatten it was equally *his* fleet. 'You will be
provided', read Churchill's directive, 'with a battlefleet of sufficient strength
to engage any force which the Government consider the Japanese might be in
a position to disengage from the Pacific theatre.'[51] Charles Lambe pointed out
that the sentence should really have read: 'The Naval Commander-in-Chief
will be provided . . .', but the damage was done.[52] Not till mid November did
the Admiralty formally consider whether the Eastern Fleet did or did not form
part of SEAC; not till the Cairo Conference at the end of that month was a
decision reached.[53]

To make matters worse, the decision then made proved strikingly indecisive. 'For all purposes of SEAC,' ruled Churchill, 'the Naval C.-in-C. and all
his forces are under the Supreme Commander.' The Admiralty were not to
issue 'over-riding orders to the Eastern Fleet obstructive of the purposes of the
Supreme Commander'.[54] Relations between the Supreme Commander and
the Naval C.-in-C., Cunningham told Churchill hopefully, must be 'inter-
preted with elasticity and good will'. Where conflicts over responsibilities
arose, they must be settled 'in a spirit of give and take'.[55] Neither of the
protagonists was disposed to be elastic or to give an iota, and to embroil

things still further both were convinced that they had won. At Cairo, Mountbatten told Ismay, 'the First Sea Lord gave a specific ruling which, curiously enough, Somerville did not wholeheartedly appear to accept. . . . He has always unconsciously misread the directive, largely I think through wishful thinking'.[56] 'I am glad that a decision has been given . . . ,' wrote Somerville to Cunningham, 'since I am quite positive that the efforts now being made to centralise everything . . . will lead to tremendous overloading and consequent inefficiency. It is quite clear, however, that this decision has not been well received by Dickie.'[57]

Trouble next arose over Mountbatten's wish to visit vessels of the Eastern Fleet, in the same way as he inspected Army and Air Force establishments. Somerville was enraged when he received a draft memorandum about the procedure to be followed on such visits: 'This was so royal in character and in certain respects so much a departure from ordinary custom that I returned the memorandum with certain suggestions couched as politely as possible.'[58] When Mountbatten wanted to visit a ship she always seemed to be engaged in trade protection and therefore outside his Command, or to be on the point of leaving for the Pacific.[59] Somerville offered to welcome him aboard any ship, but only as a guest; Mountbatten found the proposal less than alluring. 'He has already stated that as a matter of principle he does not want the officers and men to be led to believe that I have any official position over the Naval Establishments in Ceylon or the men of war in the harbours of Ceylon.'[60]

Cunningham found himself required to arbitrate. His judgement, largely drafted by Charles Lambe, was more sympathetic to Mountbatten than Somerville can have hoped or expected. 'I think you must give the Supreme Commander a little rope,' he wrote. Strictly speaking, he had no right to visit ships not under his orders for amphibious operations, but 'I think you must look at his difficulties. As you know well, the American conception of a Supreme Commander is very different to ours; in their view he is really a Commander.' Somerville, of course, must fix the modalities for such occasions but 'I have told Mountbatten that I expect you will invite him to visit some ships or establishments'.[61]

This matter of naval visits was by no means the only cause of dissension. When the Eastern Fleet bombarded Japanese targets, Somerville claimed that the fleet was not under SEAC and so *he* should issue the communiqué; Mountbatten retorted that the target was, and so *he* should.[62] Somerville insisted that he alone should decide whether clandestine operations involving the use of naval vessels should take place; Mountbatten maintained that he should be consulted before cancellation.[63] 'The squabble was mainly parochial,' wrote Somerville's secretary, Alan Laybourne, 'and a number of matters were quite trivial. In fact they both behaved like schoolgirls at times.'

On the issue of Mountbatten visiting ships of the Eastern Fleet, Laybourne told Somerville roundly that he thought he was being stupid: 'I couldn't see what the hell it mattered.'[64] With equal vigour Charles Lambe told Mount-batten that he ought to accept Somerville's offer to receive him aboard as a guest. 'The whole thing seems to me to be childish in every way.'[65] So perhaps it was, but to men under continual strain it is not surprising that small things should sometimes bulk large. Both Somerville and Mountbatten were big men; in their relationship with each other they merely demonstrated what should anyway be well known – that greatness and pettiness go often hand-in-hand.

# CHAPTER 18

## *The Americans and China*

MOUNTBATTEN'S TRIBULATIONS in the running of South-East Asia Command have taken us far beyond that point in his story when he first arrived in the area as Supreme Commander. In fact, after barely a week in Delhi he was on the move again to visit China, a country which was not in his command yet whose existence and needs were radically to affect the conduct of his campaigns.

China had been at war with Japan for seven ruinous years. Immense tracts of the country remained free, but the economy and administration were chaotic and the writ of the head of state, Generalissimo Chiang Kai-shek, ran only in the central and southern parts of the country. Even there the provincial governors enjoyed something close to autonomy, while in the north the Communists were in control. The Chungking Government of Chiang Kai-shek was as much preoccupied with the threat from their Communist compatriots as from the Japanese invaders. There was little to stop the latter from occupying as much more Chinese territory as took their fancy, if they had the incentive to do so or the troops to garrison the newly conquered areas. What they could not do was spare the resources to knock China out of the war altogether. The campaign tied up a significantly large proportion of the Japanese air and land forces and this, together with a hazy conviction that one day China would serve as a base from which the attack might be carried to the enemy homeland, convinced the Americans that it was a paramount Allied interest to keep China in the war. This view was reinforced by the long history of American involvement in China, religious and military as well as economic, which lent a romantic, semi-proprietorial flavour to the policy of the United States towards her Asian ally. It is not too much to say that the Americans regarded China with the same sort of jealous possessiveness and conviction that they alone understood her problems as the British did imperial India.

This dedication to China was responsible for a fundamental difference of opinion between Britain and the United States about the purposes of the campaign in South-East Asia. As a Supreme Commander responsible to both Governments, Mountbatten found himself in the unfortunate position of having to pursue two separate and, in essence, incompatible policies. The British required him to liberate Burma as a stepping-stone towards the more significant Malaya and Singapore and the recapture of all the former colonial empire, Dutch and French as well as British. To the Americans these aims were irrelevant if not mischievous. 'U.S. forces and resources are committed to the China–Burma–India area for the purpose of assisting China,' stated the American Chiefs of Staff bluntly.[1] The significance of Assam and North Burma was that they provided bases from which supplies to China could be ferried by air across the mountains loosely known as 'the Hump', and eventually, it was hoped, by road. Operations in South-East Asia should be restricted to what was needed to clear North Burma and thus improve communications with China. Imperial adventures were to be eschewed. SEAC, joked the Americans, stood for Save England's Asian Colonies; and they were determined that their resources should not be squandered in an enterprise so unprincipled as well as wasteful.

General Joseph Stilwell, Mountbatten's American Deputy Supreme Commander, enjoyed a separate existence as Chief of Staff to Generalissimo Chiang Kai-shek and commander of the Chinese troops in Burma and Assam. His role within the new Command, as the Americans saw it, was to safeguard Chinese interests and curb any British tendency to pursue their national objectives. He believed fervently in the policy to which he was pledged: whatever the Americans and British might achieve, he told the British Chiefs of Staff, 'the final battle with the Japanese must be fought on land through China'.[2] It was inevitable that he should have differences of opinion with a British Supreme Commander; the personality of Stilwell ensured that these were pursued with the utmost virulence and rancour.

Stilwell was a fine commander of fighting troops; courageous, resourceful, a bold and inspiring leader. His horizons were limited, however; his administrative skills negligible; and he was possessed by a consuming and acidulous misanthropy. Not for nothing was he known to all as 'Vinegar Joe'. The world was against him and he revenged himself with black bile and an excoriating tongue. An enemy of imperialism, he listened avidly to the wisdom of his political adviser John Paton Davies – 'Britain can be a first-class power only as it has the empire to exploit. Imperial role . . . means association with other peoples on a basis of subjugation, exploitation, privilege and force.'[3] – and took it as a basis for his conduct. From Washington Marshall urged him to be a little more co-operative, and General Handy insisted that, even if he would not join in the singing of 'God Save the King', at least he should stand up when it was played.[4] Yet his anglophobia was matched by his equally stark contempt for the China which he had been appointed to serve – 'A one-party government supported by a Gestapo and headed by an unbalanced man with little education.'[5] Indeed, Stilwell despised every race except his own, and most Americans as well.

Mountbatten was aware of the problems that would be posed by his deputy. In his capacity as commander of the Chinese troops in Burma, Stilwell had refused flatly to serve under General Giffard, on the grounds that the British Commander-in-Chief was dedicated to a policy of inactivity. This problem was uneasily resolved when Stilwell agreed to come under the operational control of Giffard's subordinate, Slim, at least until his forces reached a certain point in Burma – 'I would fight under a corporal as long as he would let me fight.'[6] General Marshall was to write to Mountbatten to excuse Stilwell's intransigence: 'He wants merely to get things done without delays.... Impatience with conservatism and slow motion are his weakness – but a damned good one in this emergency.'[7] Mountbatten was more than half inclined to agree with Stilwell's assessment of his Commander-in-Chief and was as impatient as the American with conservatism and slow motion. He believed that he would be able to strike up a good working relationship with his deputy and resolved that one of his first visits must be to Chungking, to pay his respects to Chiang Kai-shek and his formidable wife and to have his first meeting with Stilwell on ground where he supposed the latter would feel at ease. He was aware that it might be his last meeting as well. T. V. Soong, Chiang Kai-shek's brother-in-law and Foreign Minister, had already accosted him in Delhi and told him with much satisfaction that the Generalissimo had lost all confidence in his American commander, and that Stilwell's appointment as Deputy Supreme Commander would have 'disastrous irrevocable repercussions'.[8] Then on 12 October 1943 came a telegram from Churchill to report that Stilwell's position in Washington was 'fairly weak and it seems most probable that Generalissimo's wishes will lead to Stilwell's removal'.[9]

Mountbatten flew to Chungking on 16 October. At the last moment it was learned that Japanese fighters were on the lookout for the Supreme Commander and so the flight over the Hump was postponed till darkness, causing a delay of five hours. The arrival was correspondingly late and several Chinese generals were kept hanging about at the airport. 'I was highly distressed at this unintentional discourtesy,' wrote Mountbatten in his diary, but the experts who accompanied him assured him that he could not have made a better start. 'Face' had been gained; the Generalissimo himself would have admired the ploy. Lieutenant-Colonel Dobson, a Chinese scholar, was less pleased when Mountbatten, after a barrage of courtesies, allowed himself to be pushed into dinner ahead of General Ho Ying Chin. Dobson complained that the Supreme Commander had yielded too quickly and Mountbatten recorded and for the rest of the visit we had the most wonderful and strenuous battles as to whether my host should precede me into meals or not, and I only gave in just before we reached the point of physical violence. This, evidently, is the height of good manners! . . .

After dinner I wanted to read some papers, but as they had put in an expensive porcelain light bowl, which obscured the light to such a degree that one could not read, I asked Dobson to remove the shade. He held up his hands in horror, and said this would be considered as having drawn attention to their lack of hospitality in not having produced an efficient light, so we stayed in semi-darkness all the evening, feeling frightfully polite.[10]

At 12.30 the following day T. V. Soong told Mountbatten that Stilwell was definitely to go. Within a few hours, however, the decision was reversed; Stilwell was reconciled with the Generalissimo and still in office. The role of Mountbatten in this volte-face is obscure. He saw Stilwell the same afternoon and was subsequently to claim that he had asked him whether he wanted his job back. When Stilwell said that he did, Mountbatten promised to bring this about, and then sent a message to Chiang Kai-shek through T. V. Soong to the effect that no Chinese army in SEAC would be allowed to engage the Japanese except under Stilwell's orders.[11] This cannot be correct, if only because Mountbatten did not see Soong between his meeting with Stilwell and the latter's reconciliation with the Generalissimo. Neither his diary nor his report to the Prime Minister indicates that he intervened personally to any marked effect.[12] It is more likely that various enemies of Soong felt he was becoming too powerful and chose the issue of Stilwell's dismissal – for which he was notoriously eager – as one on which to discredit him with the Generalissimo. Mountbatten's contribution seems to have been no more than a message to Chiang Kai-shek by way of the American, General Somervell, to the effect that he would be sorry if the Chinese forces were put under a new commander when operations were about to begin. He was satisfied with the outcome, however. 'Although I think he will be a very difficult man to work with,' he told Churchill, 'I am glad that he is not being sacked immediately on my arrival, as I am quite certain that the American forces out here would have felt that I had been the cause.'[13]

Mountbatten's first interview with Chiang Kai-shek took place the following day. The Generalissimo kept him hanging about for fifteen minutes in his ante-room, whereupon Mountbatten, enjoying the new game of 'face', in his turn delayed while he slowly searched for the personal letter from the King which he had brought with him from London. His Chinese aides were reduced to hysterical alarm by this impiety: 'I have never come across such awesome reverence as they showed towards the Generalissimo. I very much doubt whether devout Christians could show any more reverence for Our Lord if He were to appear on earth again.' Whether because of or in spite of Mountbatten's calculated disrespect, all went swimmingly. Mountbatten admired Chiang Kai-shek – 'He is a most arresting person – far the most impressive Chinese I have ever seen' – and still more so his wife: 'She has a beautiful figure and the most lovely legs and feet imaginable.' Mountbatten, who in such circumstances agreed with the March Hare that butter could never do any harm provided it was the *best* butter, explained how, as a young and inexperienced officer, he had felt it essential to rush to Chungking to 'lean on the wisdom and experience of the best and most renowned soldier of our generation. . . . I made a few more complimentary remarks of this type which, had they been made to me, would have made me squirm, but they went down like a dish of hot, green tea with the Generalissimo.' Madame Chiang Kai-shek, who acted as interpreter, responded with enthusiasm. When Mountbatten told her how heavily he would rely on her for help, she replied that 'if there was one thing she prided herself on it was being a fine judge of human character, and she had already made up her mind to become my firm friend'.[14]

The visit did not produce much except generalized good will, nor was it intended to. Chiang pressed for a guarantee that the supplies ferried to his aid over the Hump would never fall below ten thousand tons a month. Mountbatten replied that operations in Burma would occasionally make a shortfall inevitable but that in the long run China would benefit by the reopening of a land link over the mountains. 'I trust you,' said the Generalissimo simply – an observation which his subsequent conduct did not totally endorse.[15] Chiang Kai-shek also agreed that Mountbatten could carry out covert operations in Siam and Indochina, the second of which had not been assigned to SEAC, but here too the accord proved illusory. At the time, it seems, the Generalissimo believed Indochina was indeed part of Mountbatten's bailiwick; within a few weeks the Americans were reporting significant differences of opinion between the British and the Chinese about Mountbatten's right to send agents into areas within the Chinese zone of influence.[16]

Mountbatten set off from Chungking on 20 October in a glow of good will: 'I must say I left the Chiang Kai-sheks with a real feeling of affection and regard, and I am sure that this is reciprocated since I was told on my return that he had been ringing up constantly to make certain that I had arrived back safely.'[17] Addressing him as 'My dear Great Friend', Chiang Kai-shek wrote to King George VI to assure him that complete agreement had been reached on the need to co-operate in the war against Japan.[18] Roosevelt wrote enthusiastically to tell Mountbatten how well he had been told the talks had gone. 'I am really thrilled over the fact that for the first time in two years I have confidence in the personality problems in the China and Burma fields – and you personally are largely responsible for this.'[19] From London Lord Beaverbrook, who had earlier advised Mountbatten on the tactics he should adopt, echoed the praise: 'If your conquest at Chungking is as permanent as it appears to have been complete, then I shall feel that I have had some part in the most important Combined Operation since the Fall of Jericho.'[20]

There is no doubt that the Supreme Commander had made a strong and favourable impression on the Chiang Kai-sheks. Equally the slight scepticism in Beaverbrook's letter proved to be justified. The lasting effects of Mountbatten's conquest of Chungking, though real, were not as substantial as he had hoped. The cautious Pownall assessed the situation correctly: 'I hope this optimism is justified but I don't suppose he is any better judge of Orientals than I am. No doubt he did better than the dour Wavell on a similar occasion two years ago but I fear that Mountbatten's enthusiasm is carrying him away somewhat.'[21] Chinese courtesy and the blandishments of Madame Chiang Kai-shek had indeed left Mountbatten with the impression that he had gained more than in fact was the case. General Grimsdale, the military attaché in Chungking, called on Edwina Mountbatten in London and spoke in glowing terms of all her husband had accomplished:

> The only thing he feared was that you'd been slightly taken in by Madame and that you mustn't be too influenced by her references to your wonderful eyes!!! As the same technique is used on each distinguished Englishman and American who arrives, and he has watched it with interest for three years, including our dear old John Dill. He said he'd mentioned it to you nervously, not wishing in any way to disparage the beauty of your eyes!! but felt he should utter a word of warning.[22]

After a private meeting with the Generalissimo on 19 October, Mountbatten noted cryptically in his diary that 'a certain special difficulty appears now to have been resolved'. Probably this relates to covert activities in Siam and Indochina, but it might refer to the discussion which undoubtedly took place about General Stilwell and his future role. Stilwell himself believed Mountbatten had pleaded his case vigorously and was in part at least responsible for his retention by the Generalissimo. His initial view of his Supreme Commander was a rosy one; 'Louis is a good egg,' he wrote to Marshall, in one of those Bertie Wooster phrases that occasionally lard the letters of this least Wodehousean of generals.[23] His main concern was that Mountbatten should prove more ready to fight than had been the case with his predecessors. At first he thought he had found the champion he desired. 'Admiral, I like working with you,' he told the Supreme Commander one evening in New Delhi, 'you are the only Britisher I have met who wants to fight!'[24] The compliment was the less impressive for having been paid in almost identical terms to two British generals, Slim and Festing, but Mountbatten relished it. 'I feel you should know', he wrote to Dill, 'that all the British I have met have the lowest possible opinion of his intellect and co-operativeness, and I am told that 90% of the Americans hate his guts. Nevertheless, he and I are getting along surprisingly well and so far I have no complaints about his relationships with me, and have every intention of trying to make a success of them.'[25]

The honeymoon did not last long. By January 1944 Stilwell was writing: 'The Glamour Boy is just that. He doesn't wear well and I begin to wonder if he knows his stuff. Enormous staff, endless walla-walla, but damned little fighting.'[26] As the year wore on his diary entries became more splenetic. Mountbatten was 'a fatuous ass'; 'childish Louis, publicity crazy'; a 'pisspot'. Stilwell's anglophobia became all-consuming: 'The more I see of the Limeys, the worse I hate them'; 'the bastardly hypocrites do their best to cut our throats on all occasions. The pig-fuckers.'[27] When face-to-face with Mountbatten, however, he remained correct, even affable. Though the Supreme Commander found his deputy increasingly difficult to deal with, he had little conception of the hatred which apparently seethed beneath the crabbed exterior.

Though the other Americans on Mountbatten's staff shared Stilwell's suspicions about the tendency of the British to advance their imperial interests at the expense of the Americans, the atmosphere at Supreme Headquarters was markedly harmonious. Mountbatten made his first priority the creation of a truly international staff who would put the interests of their Command ahead of that of their country or their Service. Complete success could never be achieved, but he got a great deal closer than most people would have thought possible; closer, probably, than any other commander could have done. The Supremo became a symbol of Allied co-operation, his car bedecked with the flags of the national forces under his command, the various sections of his headquarters manned by a skilfully balanced blend of British and Americans.

In this campaign he was most actively supported by his American Deputy Chief of Staff, Albert Wedemeyer. Wedemeyer had been initially dismayed when he was selected for the post; partly because he thought South-East Asia likely to be something of a backwater; partly because, though he had been favourably impressed by Mountbatten when he had seen him at work in C.O.H.Q., he doubted how well they would get on in partnership. Eisenhower did something to reassure him. 'Lord Louis', he told Wedemeyer, 'is occasionally belittled by people who think they know more about war than he does, but in my honest opinion he has a lot on the ball and you will find that you are under a man you can respect in every way. Moreover, he is a man who will listen to advice and soak it up.'[28] Wedemeyer's remaining doubts were quickly settled. He found Mountbatten 'intelligent, amenable and apparently willing and anxious to get on with the job'. He had been told by some British colleagues that the Supreme Commander could be devious, but 'only on one occasion did he assume that I would go along with him when he had no right to do so'. The two men worked happily together: 'I abhorred sycophants and I soon discovered that Mountbatten was of like mind.'[29] The Supreme Commander for his part praised his colleague lavishly. Wedemeyer, he told Brooke, had arrived with the reputation of being anti-British but was now beloved by all. 'He is 100% loyal and straightforward.'[30]

Even more anxious to co-operate than Wedemeyer was General Raymond 'Speck' Wheeler, Principal Administrative Officer and already well versed in the logistical problems of the area. Wheeler, wrote Mountbatten, 'is one of the nicest men I have ever met'.[31] He was also one of the most emollient, and was to do valuable work as a go-between when Anglo-American relations in SEAC became strained over the integration of the American 10th Air Force with the other units under the British Commander-in-Chief. For the first few months of Mountbatten's Supreme Command, the 10th Air Force remained outside the system. Major-General George Stratemeyer was responsible not to Peirse but to Stilwell. This could have been no more than an administrative inconvenience but, given the personality of Stilwell, it threatened to prove disastrous. When the Japanese advanced against Fort Hertz, Mountbatten told the 10th Air Force to fly in reinforcements. Units of the 4th Burma Regiment were embarked and already in the air when Stilwell countermanded the instruction and ordered the planes back to base. The Supreme Commander was not notified till twenty-four hours later. As it turned out, the Japanese attack proved superficial and no harm was done, but the risks of the same thing happening in more dangerous circumstances could not be ignored.[32]

Mountbatten grew impatient. He urged Dill in Washington to do all he could to get the system changed; 'it is quite unacceptable to me', he complained, 'to have a subordinate officer like Stratemeyer with an independent directive which absolutely prevents my controlling the U.S. Air Force'.[33] He proved to be pushing at an open door.

At the Cairo Conference in November 1943 Mountbatten got ready agreement from Marshall and General Arnold, Commanding General of the U.S. Army Air Force, that if he wanted to amalgamate the 10th Air Force with the rest of his Command he would be free to do so.[34] Fortified by this knowledge, he pressed vigorously for immediate integration, but Stilwell on principle, and Stratemeyer out of loyalty to his superior officer, resisted stoutly. Mountbatten was not prepared to delay further. On 11 December he told the recalcitrant generals that he proposed to issue a directive placing Stratemeyer directly under the command of Peirse. When they said that they wished to protest to Washington he refused to allow them to do so directly but forwarded their arguments accompanied by his own rebuttal. 'It is time we had a showdown . . . as to who is in command of this party,' he noted in his diary. 'I do not believe the U.S. Chiefs of Staff will reverse my decision. I know it is really essential for the future conduct of the war.'[35]

The directive was duly promulgated.[36] Mountbatten at once concerned himself with mollifying Stratemeyer – not too difficult a task since the American had in the past expressed himself an enthusiast for integration. 'Old Strat has played so loyally and enthusiastically with the British all along,' commented Wedemeyer.[37] He was appointed deputy to Peirse. 'If I have judged your character correctly,' wrote the Supreme Commander, 'you will throw yourself enthusiastically into the new set-up. . . . I feel confident that you will do great things in the coming fighting.'[38] His confidence was justified. Stratemeyer worked loyally under Peirse and the integration caused no problems. There were still to be many complications over the aircraft assigned to the supply of the Chinese forces across the Hump, but Mountbatten's control of the 10th Air Force was unquestioned.

# CHAPTER 19

## *Monsoon, Malaria, Morale*

AND THEN THERE WERE THE JAPANESE: five divisions in Burma with a sixth on the way under the overall command of the formidable Field Marshal Terauchi. There were some 350,000 Japanese in South-East Asia, of whom half were in Burma soon after Mountbatten took over his command. The numbers were not enormous, in theory dwarfed by the total force of Allied troops in India, but such comparisons were illusory. Relatively few of the Indian troops were available for operations against the Japanese, and those troops that were at Mountbatten's disposal had a long and dismal record of defeat behind them. The Japanese, initially content to sit it out on their extended perimeter and let the enemy lose their will to fight, were now planning an attack into Assam and the overthrow of the Indian Government, to be replaced by a puppet administration. The only field in which the Allies were beginning to establish superiority was in the air, and even there the advantage was still precarious.

Mountbatten had thus accepted a formidable challenge in undertaking not merely to hold the Japanese but to destroy their armed forces. He identified three factors which must be set right before he could engage the Japanese forces with a certainty of success: monsoon, malaria and morale, a list the order of which varied according to the exigencies of the moment. Over all these a vast advance was made in the first nine months of his Supreme Command.

The belief that it was impossible to fight during the monsoon was held by the Japanese as well as the British. From May to October, therefore, except for desultory skirmishes, the war closed down. Mountbatten considered that this would slow up his campaign intolerably, and that the perils of engaging in battle under the appalling conditions of the monsoon would be more than made up by the advantages of surprise. Even before he left London he had set the experts to work on the special equipment that would be necessary to operate such a policy. On his way back from Chungking he called in on Slim's headquarters and told the staff bluntly that he would expect them in future to fight on, whatever the weather. Slim was delighted, some of the other officers outraged, and General Giffard, when he was told what had been said, dismissed it as a piece of empty braggadocio.[1] That he was wrong was demonstrated some nine months later, when Slim acted on his new instructions and exploited ruthlessly his victory at Imphal against the stricken Japanese. Mountbatten's determination to fight through the monsoon, wrote Brian Kimmins, the Director of Plans at SEAC, 'hitherto considered impossible, and in the face of much contrary advice, was the major factor in the defeat of the Japanese in this theatre'.[2] That is pitching it somewhat high – the control of the air was surely a more decisive factor – but it was still a critically important and bold decision.

It could not have been practicable if the war against malaria had not already been in great part won. The health of the 14th Army – as the Eastern Army was soon to be christened, under its commander General Slim – was still calamitously bad when Mountbatten arrived in South-East Asia. Sir Ronald Adam, the Adjutant-General, had warned Mountbatten what to expect. Malaria, he said, 'is almost a greater enemy than the Japanese in the fighting zones of the East'.[3] The statistics suggest that this was over-generous to the Japanese. During the monsoon of 1943, for every wounded man admitted to hospital there were 120 sick, from dysentery and other tropical diseases too, but in most cases suffering from malaria.[4] Improved medical discipline and attacks on the malarial mosquito were beginning to change the situation, but a fresh injection of energy from the top was urgently needed. This Mountbatten provided. He was horrified by the inadequacy of the hospitals which he found on his first visit to the Arakan and began a vigorous onslaught on the Indian administration to secure better facilities. From his wife he demanded an immediate reinforcement of seven hundred nurses, and he pleaded with Brooke to expedite their arrival.[5] With a diligence that Edwina would have admired, he toiled around every military hospital he could visit, praising where praise was due, rebuking slovenliness or poor hygiene, noting deficiencies of staff or equipment and agitating to have them made good when he got back to his headquarters. He did not always enjoy such work. 'Why doctors insist on taking me to see the most sick-making operations I shall never understand,' he complained. 'I really can't bear to see someone's stomach being cut open and all their guts being pulled out, but it is difficult to refuse what is evidently regarded as a great privilege.'[6] His efforts were rewarded. By the end of 1944 the proportion of sick to wounded had fallen to twenty to one and by the end of the war was only six to one; the malaria rate, which was eighty-four per cent of the army strength in 1943, fell to thirteen per cent by 1945.

Visiting a hospital in Secunderabad, he was startled to find that five consecutive patients had not even got as far as the front line before collapsing with neurotic complaints. 'I could not imagine anybody getting shell-shocked until they had been shelled,' he commented.[7] Discoveries of this kind confirmed his belief that there was something seriously wrong with the morale of the British Army. It came as no surprise. 'All my spies tell me that the tails of our forces in India are fairly well down,' he had told Lambe a month before he left.[8] Already things were improving, but Mountbatten was convinced that only a taste of victory would complete the process, and he did not believe that victory could be achieved unless the British first realized that the Japanese were not invincible, that physically and mentally they were no better equipped for fighting a jungle war than the Indians or Europeans who opposed them. The British had begun the war complacent and vainglorious; they had swung to black defeatism; now they must be restored to the determination that they would win.[9]

One reason for their dejection was their belief that nobody in Britain took any interest in their existence. The phrase 'the Forgotten Army' seems to have been coined by a *News Chronicle* war correspondent some time in the summer of 1943, but the idea behind it had long had currency among the soldiers.[10] Their view was confirmed by the Ministry of Information, who concluded that the mass of the public was largely indifferent to the war in the East.[11] Mountbatten was determined that this should not persist. He pleaded with Beaverbrook to make the campaign better known[12] and urged Eden to

> bring the Far East more into the political limelight in England. Do you think that the creation of a political post within the Government, for the sole purpose of directing Far Eastern affairs, would help to bring this about? Might the solution be in having a second Parliamentary Secretary in the Foreign Office ... ? Such an appointment would underline in Chinese and American minds that we are coming back to the East.[13]

Eden showed little enthusiasm for this solution. The machinery was already there; it was only a question of making it work.[14] Nor was Churchill impressed by what he felt to be Mountbatten's premature crusade to increase public knowledge of his command: 'I cannot too strongly emphasise the importance of damping down all publicity about this theatre for at least 3 months.'[15] Otherwise great things would be expected, and hope inevitably disappointed. But it was not only at home that the 14th Army felt themselves neglected. 'There is a general feeling ...', reported General Adam, 'that G.H.Q. India does not know and does not care about the British troops.' He was the first staff officer of any seniority who ever visited them.[16] 'The distance from Delhi to N.E. Assam is the same as from London to Leningrad,'[17] wrote Auchinleck apologetically, but this was not much consolation to the men in the jungle.

Mountbatten, therefore, could not rely on much help from outside in his battle to hearten the British troops. He was not discomfited; indeed, as so often, he made a virtue out of what seemed a disadvantage. You think you are the Forgotten Army, he told the troops. Don't kid yourselves, there was nothing to forget, nobody ever even heard of you. But this was not going to last. Great things were going to happen. New material and reinforcements were pouring in. It would be a stiff fight but victory was on the way. This message he hammered home on every occasion. Whenever he could escape from his desk – which happened far more often than some of his staff officers felt desirable – he would take off for the front line, travelling frequently in discomfort and considerable danger, determined to visit, if he could, every outpost, however remote, however small. Michael Edwardes was serving in a forward unit which only a few hours before had been driving the Japanese before them. Mountbatten erupted in their midst. Everyone was tired and dirty, the Supreme Commander spick and span:

> Yet the impression he gave was not that he had just arrived from a comfortable base headquarters but that, somehow, he had managed to slough off the sweat and dirt to which everyone else had succumbed. He brushed aside the officers and the general 'bull' of a commander's parade, told the soldiers to break ranks, and began to confide his thoughts and hopes to them. It was a masterly performance, and at least one sceptical soldier . . . went away convinced that great events lay in the hollow of Mountbatten's hands.[18]

His technique was almost invariable. First the officers would be fallen in, at double intervals so as to make each conversation private. He would question each man on his background, and with his astonishing memory would usually be able to find some point of contact. An A.D.C. would note down the particulars of every man he spoke to, so that next time he met him he would be forewarned and any decoration or promotion suitably recognized. Sometimes the system broke down and Mountbatten was left looking a little foolish; far more often it worked perfectly and the officer was amazed and delighted by the relationship he had established with his Supreme Commander.

Then the officers would fall back and the other ranks would cluster round. A soap-box would appear and Mountbatten climb on it to address them. He spoke briefly and informally, giving the impression that he was taking his audience into his confidence. The Japanese were vulnerable, he would insist; not denizens of the jungle but city-dwellers, and short-sighted city-dwellers at that. He would mention what the King had said to him, what Churchill had said, and leave them feeling that here was a man who could get things done, a 'Commander who was going to take a grip on things', 'a real go-getter'.[19]

There were some bizarre incidents among his visits. At Comilla his talk was disturbed by a colony of crows. Someone threw a stone at them but they were quickly back again. 'Finally a team consisting of two Lieutenant-Generals, one Air-Marshal, one Major-General, one Air-Commodore and three A.D.C.s kept up a constant bombardment of the tree, and under this somewhat disturbing influence I continued my speech.' When he visited 607 Squadron it was the constant coming and going of aircraft that disrupted his address. In the end he gave up. 'I was only trying to convince you that we will eventually have enough resources to ensure our victory,' he told his audience, 'and the sight we see today on this airfield is better proof of that than anything I could tell you.'[20]

On the Indian troops his impact was particularly dramatic. He mastered a few phrases in Urdu and would walk through the ranks, trying them on every twentieth soldier or so, and hoping the reply would not demand any further linguistic effort. The technique was almost always successful, though set-backs occurred. *'Tumhare noukari kitni hi?'* he asked one man. The Indian looked politely baffled. Mountbatten repeated the question. 'Oh, you want to know how many years service I have,' came the reply in impeccably accented English. 'I have twelve years service, sahib.'[21] The Indian troops were more impressed than the British by his royal blood; he was the cousin of the King-Emperor and as such invested with some shreds of divinity himself.

The American units he visited were less certain what to expect. In January 1944 he found his way to one of their Long Range Penetration Groups called 'Galahad'. The men were curious to see the 'glamour boy' in person, and assumed that, since he was staying with them for the night, 'that exalted and fastidious personage would require "a baaath, you know, old boy"'. With great difficulty they borrowed a white bathtub from a British hospital and installed it in a tent. The Supreme Commander made use of it with satisfaction but, far from exalted or fastidious: 'We found him to be friendly, unostentatious, soldierly in appearance, sensible, kind and considerate of our problems, and concerned about what the future would hold for Galahad.'[22]

Lieutenant-Colonel Cochran of the U.S. Air Force flew Mountbatten from Gwalior in a light aircraft. Mountbatten explained he hadn't flown for several years and asked if he could have a go. Cochran ceded the controls. 'Taking off, the first thing he did was a ground loop. He had big feet and got them all over the pedals, and the plane went spinning around. I yelled at him, "Get your feet off the brake!" . . . He said, "Which is the brake?"' With a certain amount of help from Cochran and a wing scraping the runway, Mountbatten at length became airborne. 'He flew around for an hour and a half, and every once in a while he would turn round to me, nod and grin, congratulating himself. All the time I was wondering, "How is he going to land it?"' Disaster was avoided but only just – the landing was a rough one. Cochran soon received a charming letter apologizing for so nearly destroying his aircraft.[23]

Mountbatten knew that he was supremely good at raising the spirits of the men of his Command, and got great pleasure from doing so. He enjoyed also the promotion of himself and SEAC to the outside world, though regularly professing distaste for self-advertisement. Asking Wildman-Lushington to help the journalist and politician Tom Driberg prepare a profile of the Supreme Commander, he found it necessary to explain: 'You will remember that throughout our time together I had a firm policy that there should be no personal publicity, or at all events that it should be damped down as far as was reasonably possible.' However, the situation was now so critical that 'some dignified personal publicity . . . seemed necessary'.[24] No one was deceived by such disclaimers. Charles Lambe wrote him a word of warning. Press communiqués had recently been issued as coming from 'Admiral Mountbatten's Headquarters'. Lambe said that Eisenhower had been asked what sort of man MacArthur was. 'You will notice', answered Eisenhower, 'that our communiqués from Algiers go out from A.F.H.Q. In the South-West Pacific, on the other hand, communiqués are issued as from General Mac-Arthur's Headquarters. That is the kind of man he is.'[25] Mountbatten had already told Somerville that he deplored MacArthur's practice and had given orders that his name was not to appear in communiqués or press hand-outs.[26] Mysteriously, however, his orders continued to be ignored. Such behaviour could readily be justified: SEAC desperately needed to gain confidence and the glory of being commanded by a glamorous hero was a useful element in the process. To his enemies, however, it was all part of his gluttonous appetite for publicity. Andrew Cunningham went to see *Burma Victory*, the film about the British reconquest of the country, and admired it greatly. 'But the Supreme Commander and his staff, and Slim and his staff, doing film-star work made me physically sick.'[27]

Flamboyant himself, Mountbatten did not always appreciate it in others. A Canadian major-general met him near the front line wearing a stetson and pistols in holsters. When they encountered a file of African soldiers the general tossed his hat in the air and drilled it with bullets from his pistol. The Africans cheered loudly. 'That's the way to lead men, isn't it, Admiral?' blustered the Canadian. 'No,' said Mountbatten coldly. A few moments later the general's jeep came so close to the Japanese lines that the occupants had to take shelter in a ditch. The Supreme Commander was not amused, and the general lasted only a few more weeks.[28]

Mountbatten's efforts to promote his Command were not conducted single-handed. As Deputy Chief of Staff in charge of information (and civil affairs, against the day when there were reconquered territories to administer), he had taken on a retired Air Chief Marshal, Philip Joubert. Joubert initially had doubts; the responsibilities seemed ill-defined and also: 'When I was Commander-in-Chief, Coastal Command, for the first time, Lord Louis Mountbatten was a Lieutenant-Commander at the Admiralty, and it appeared to me that our relationship, him as Supreme Commander and I as a member of his staff, was likely to be difficult.' A particularly cold autumn day in Britain convinced him that such difficulties could and must be overcome. He was in charge of public relations – telling the rest of the world what SEAC was doing; information – telling SEAC itself what was going on; and psychological warfare. 'It was a most interesting and valuable conception which only just failed to be a resounding success.'[29]

Under the heading of 'information' Mountbatten's principal contribution was to secure the services of Frank Owen, the brilliantly successful young editor of the *Evening Standard*, to start a daily newspaper, *SEAC*, for the whole command. P. J. Grigg, the Secretary of State for War, disliked the appointment and stirred Churchill into opposition by pointing out that Owen was contemplating standing as an independent candidate in a by-election and was thus a proven enemy of the Government. Mountbatten stuck to his guns. If the Prime Minister had sufficient confidence in him to appoint him Supreme Commander, he maintained, then 'he must have enough confidence to let me pick my own staff. I made an absolute issue of the matter, and won.'[30] *SEAC* proved a spectacular success. 'It is hard to say what the troops appreciated most,' wrote Joubert, 'Owen's pungent leading articles that frequently got him – and me – into trouble with the War Office, the sports news, or the "Jane" strip-cartoon.'[31]

Owen's indiscretions caused frequent turmoil in Whitehall, as also did Mountbatten's other ideas for the promotion of himself and his Command. In May 1944 the Chiefs of Staff ruled out the possibility of broadcasts to the troops by the Supreme Commander on Forces Radio.[32] Churchill came to the rescue and argued that, 'in the special circumstances which prevailed in the SEAC', occasional broadcasts could be permitted provided that the text was cleared in London first.[33] The Chiefs yielded but took their role as censors seriously; later that year Brooke was criticizing Mountbatten's Christmas broadcast on the grounds that it should place 'more emphasis on the hard work necessary to defeat Japan and on the strenuous time ahead, and less emphasis on the subjects of leave, repatriation and amenities'.[34] Mountbatten pleaded that this procedure led to unnecessary delays and cipher traffic, but Brendan Bracken replied blandly that the Prime Minister attached so much importance to what men of such eminence might say that he felt it only right he should be warned in advance.[35]

'During the winter of 1943–44,' wrote the Supreme Commander in his Report,[36] 'great improvement in morale became evident.' The mere creation of the Command had done something to restore confidence. Mountbatten fostered the new sense of unity by designing an emblem which everyone would wear and every document carry. His first idea was for a rising sun transfixed by a sword but this was abandoned when it was pointed out that anyone captured by the Japanese when wearing such a device would inevitably be executed. Instead he sketched out a phoenix, symbol of renascent strength. The troops christened it the 'pig's arse', but it was none the less popular for that.[37] It was one more symbol that they belonged to a new and potentially victorious army. When Mountbatten toured Arakan in December 1943 he was vastly encouraged by the new spirit shown by the men in the front line.[38] He was not deluding himself. A year later General Adam visited the Command. 'I can confirm the very high morale of your Army,' he told the Supreme Commander. 'In fact, I have not seen higher morale anywhere.'[39]

To the three 'ms' of monsoon, malaria and morale Mountbatten was soon to add a fourth problem – India. He knew how totally he depended on the sub-continent for communications, man-power and supplies, knew too that the Japanese would be quick to exploit any disaffection through the renegade Indian National Army and its leader Subhas Chandra Bose, and was convinced that his security lay in keeping India as contented and prosperous as could be contrived. With famine imminent, he believed that a large relief programme was essential. He found it difficult to communicate this sense of urgency to Whitehall, mainly because of the obduracy of the Prime Minister who, as he remarked to Wavell, regarded sending food to India merely as 'appeasement' of the Indian nationalists.[40] In April 1944 the situation became so critical that he told the Chiefs of Staff, 'unless arrangements were promptly made to import wheat requirements, he would be compelled to release military cargo-space in favour of wheat'.[41] The threat worked, though it was another two months before the Chiefs agreed to free enough shipping to help with the Indian famine.[42]

In such activities he had the blessing and support of the Government of India. It was another matter when he urged the expansion of the Indian economy to help supply military needs. All his proposals ran up against apparently insuperable obstacles; when he requested, for instance, that the manufacture of parachutes should be increased from 35,000 to 200,000 a month, he was told that this would divert cloth from the civilian market and increase earning-power without providing extra goods on which the money could be spent. 'I suspect that behind all this is an unexpressed, possibly even subconscious desire to keep India as a market for British manufactured goods after the war.'[43] He commissioned his old friend Peter Murphy to mount a study into the problems of the Indian economy but got little satisfaction from the result. Any major expansion, said Murphy, was blocked by 'an immense wall of prejudice, backed by vested interests at home', but the situation was such that haphazard reforms would be worse than useless. The alternatives were to overthrow the system or to live with it; since Mountbatten could not do the first, he must adopt the second. 'Seriously, Dickie, be *careful* what you embark on.'[44]

Mountbatten met the same opposition over the Assam railways but this time overcame it. The railway line to Ledo, on which the British forces in Burma and the supply shuttle across the Hump to China depended, had been designed by the tea industry to carry 600 tons a day. By the end of 1943 the figure had been increased to 2800 tons, but this was deemed to be near capacity. Three times as much was needed. Without consulting anyone in the Indian Government, Mountbatten invited a team of American experts from Persia to assess the situation.[45] At a conference on 23 October General Somervell promised an immediate increase of fifty per cent if American railway engineers were put on the job. Mountbatten insisted that the offer must be accepted unless the present management could do as much by April 1944. The representatives of the Indian Government, backed by Auchinleck, refused to give any such guarantee, but equally opposed American participation; American methods would not work, they said, and even if they did the resultant inflation would be unacceptable.[46]

Mountbatten now set out to circumvent the opposition, though trying to conceal the fact that he was doing so. He asked Brooke to bring pressure on Auchinleck, 'though I am particularly anxious that my telegram sent should be based entirely on Somervell's evidence and that this private letter of mine should in no way be quoted'.[47] Churchill was recruited to play the same role with the Viceroy: 'Please don't make my situation more difficult by saying *I* asked you to do this – say Somervell converted you.'[48] By 6 November Auchinleck had agreed that the Americans should be called in.[49] The results were dramatic. Within six months Pownall was able to tell the Chiefs of Staff that the daily load would shortly reach 8000 tons and that even during the worst of the monsoon it would not fall below 6000. 'The improvement', he stated, 'was largely due to the better management introduced by the U.S. engineers.'[50]

By the spring of 1944 Mountbatten's forces were ready to engage the Japanese in battle. It remained to decide what sort of battle should be fought.

# CHAPTER 20

## *The War of the Codewords*

THE RECONQUEST OF BURMA was an important and well-contrived victory, sufficiently glorious in Mountbatten's eyes for him to assume 'Burma' as the territorial appendage to the viscountcy he was granted at the end of the war. It is a curious paradox that the nature of the victory was so different from the vision he had conceived on his arrival; that, if it had been offered him then, he would have dismissed it as second best – almost, indeed, undesirable.

'They have provided me with everything!' he had announced after Quebec.[1] To Slim he was more specific: 'We're getting so many ships that the harbours of India and Ceylon won't be big enough to hold 'em!'[2] It was ships that were indispensable if he was to perform his role as he intended. His skills lay in the world of amphibious warfare and it was by seaborne assault that he believed the Japanese should be defeated, the alternative being a painful war of attrition in the Burmese jungle – 'going into the water to fight the shark', as Churchill memorably described it.[3] The Chiefs of Staff planners heartily endorsed the view. To recapture southern Burma and Rangoon would be 'a small strategic gain for the expenditure of great effort . . . the recapture of Singapore before Rangoon is a full and correct application of sea and air power. It will electrify the eastern world and have an immense psychological effect on the Japanese.'[4] To electrify the eastern, and indeed the western, world was much to Mountbatten's taste.

There were formidable obstacles. The American General Everett Hughes summed it up pithily in his diary: 'Something wrong in Burma! . . . British want to go to Singapore, U.S. to China.'[5] Roosevelt was convinced that the British were obsessed by the wish to reconquer Singapore and had no intention of helping them to do so; and, since the Americans would have to supply much of the equipment needed for a large maritime operation, their approval was essential. Stilwell knocked on the head any possibility that the American Chiefs of Staff might champion the British cause against their President when, in Washington in November 1943, he was asked his views of his Supreme Commander's plans for an amphibious operation and replied that 'he was unable to offer anything except criticism'.[6] American support would only be forthcoming for an operation that would patently help relieve the pressure on the Chinese. And since even Churchill conceded that the British must 'regard ourselves as junior partners' in the war against Japan, stern limits were inevitably placed on Mountbatten's more ambitious projects.

Nor was Mountbatten's support in Whitehall as solid as he might have wished. The Chiefs of Staff believed priority must be given to the campaign in Europe. Brooke opposed any attempt by the Prime Minister to strip the Mediterranean of ships so as 'to equip Mountbatten for ventures in Sumatra'.[7] Even before he left London the Supreme Commander had seen himself deprived of his allocation of landing-craft in favour of an operation in the Dodecanese. They were restored after protest, but only grudgingly and, as it turned out, not for long.[8] Indeed, at first it seemed that Mountbatten might find more support in Washington than London. In November 1943 Dill warned the Chiefs of Staff that the new Supreme Commander had made a great impression on the Americans and that any policy he might advocate which had the backing of Stilwell would be likely to gain acceptance. The qualification, however, proved more significant than the original premise, since any policy which did not contribute directly to the opening of the China road was unhesitatingly opposed by Stilwell.

Churchill's favoured operation was CULVERIN, the capture of north Sumatra, which would outflank the Japanese in Burma and make possible an attack on Singapore – the TORCH of the Indian Ocean, he described it.[9] 'I was, and of course still am, extremely keen on this operation,' Mountbatten told the King,[10] but it did not take close examination to establish that greater resources would be needed than were at present available.[11] The plan was pursued in a desultory way, Mountbatten suggesting that Brian Horrocks be appointed Force Commander and Brooke countering with an offer of General Stopford,[12] but there was an element of fantasy about the enterprise. It can have come as no surprise to Mountbatten when, on his return from Chungking, he found a telegram reporting that no further resources could be provided. Without repining, he put CULVERIN temporarily behind him and looked around for fresh targets which could be tackled with the forces he now possessed.[13]

He arrived at the conference at Cairo armed with plans for operations during the dry season of 1943–4. These included an advance along the Arakan coast towards Akyab, further progress by Stilwell's three divisions and the Chinese in the north, supporting operations by Wingate's Long Range Penetration Groups and, most cherished by Mountbatten, a mini-CULVERIN called BUCCANEER involving an amphibious attack on the Andaman Islands. 'The Andaman Islands? Where are they?' Elliott Roosevelt asked his father. 'To hear Churchill talk you'd think they were the most strategic point this side of his beloved Balkans. Oh, they're in the Bay of Bengal, off southern Burma. From the Andamans, they figure they'll be able to attack Rangoon.'[14]

On 23 November 1943 Mountbatten formally expounded his plans to the assembled dignitaries in Cairo. 'He made an excellent presentation of his problem,' noted Admiral Leahy, 'which I believed would be solved by his energy and aggressive spirit.'[15] Unfortunately, there were factors that made it improbable that any clear-cut decisions would emerge. The most immediately apparent was the presence of the Chinese. Churchill had a taste of what lay ahead when the Generalissimo called shortly after his arrival. Mountbatten was the only person present except for the official interpreter, Madame Chiang being ill. The Prime Minister said he would return the call next day at noon. 'The Generalissimo is delighted, and says when will you call?' asked the interpreter. Churchill tried again. 'Tell His Excellency that when the sun is at its zenith I will come.' This needed repeating and earned the reply that Chiang Kai-shek would expect the Prime Minister at tennish. 'I never get up as early as that!' exclaimed Churchill, now thoroughly alarmed, and the unfortunate interpreter was treated to a lecture on the subject of the sun being at its zenith not at tennish but at twelveish. Mountbatten made sure that the ever-reliable Colonel Dobson was in attendance when the return call was paid.[16]

After Mountbatten had explained his plans at the plenary session, the Chinese were asked their views. They remained politely non-committal, though they made it clear they would make their participation conditional upon an amphibious operation taking place in the Bay of Bengal.[17] Chiang Kai-shek seemed gradually to be raising his terms, so the meeting was suspended and Mountbatten sent to speak to him privately. Mountbatten tried to explain that the counter-proposals the Chinese were putting up had been considered as part of a plan for an attack on Mandalay and abandoned as impracticable. 'To prove that we had worked it out in great detail, I showed him a marked map and full technical details. The old boy's eyes glistened. He said, "I like this plan, we will carry it out." I repeated very patiently that the plan was not possible and gave exact reasons. However, he defeated me by saying "Never mind, we will carry it out all the same." '[18]

Three times during the Conference Chiang Kai-shek was talked into saying he would co-operate with an advance into central Burma accompanied by an airborne attack on the airfield at Indaw; three times he qualified his agreement to the point of making it worthless. 'I am delighted that the Prime Minister and President . . . are at last being given first-hand experience of how impossible the Chinese are to deal with,' wrote Mountbatten. 'They have been driven absolutely mad.'[19] When the conference was over he flew to Ramgarh, headquarters of the Chinese in India, to continue his talks with the

Generalissimo. Chiang Kai-shek at once conceded everything that was asked of him. 'I feel that we have now actually become friends,' he told the Supreme Commander, while Madame Chiang reinforced his words by assuring Mountbatten that in China friendship was rarely given, and once given was regarded as sacred. Relieved but sceptical, Mountbatten returned to Delhi. 'I must say that this job is enough to turn my few remaining hairs completely grey,' he wrote in his diary. 'I could not have believed so difficult a job would have been invented for anybody and those who envy me my job (if there are any) must be mad.'[20]

Almost as unfortunate as the presence of the Chinese was the absence of the Russians. From Cairo Churchill and Roosevelt moved on to Teheran to confront Marshal Stalin. 'It was *crazy* to have the Cairo Conference before the Teheran one,' wrote Edwina sympathetically, 'as the latter must of necessity have upset so many decisions taken at the former. Poor you.'[21] Stalin promised to enter the war against Japan as soon as Germany was defeated but demanded as a *quid pro quo* more energetic moves by the Allies in Europe. The British Chiefs of Staff, always dubious about the merits of BUCCANEER, began to consider whether the resources Mountbatten needed for the operation would not be better employed elsewhere. To make matters worse, the Supreme Commander chose this moment to send in revised estimates, raising the number of troops he would need for a successful operation to 50,000.

The immediate result of this ill-timed request was that he forfeited the support of Winston Churchill. When Ismay explained that only 18,000 men would actually be involved in the assault, so that the proportion of attackers to defenders would be 3½ to 1, the Prime Minister grumbled that to suggest so substantial an advantage was necessary was 'the grossest libel ever uttered against our soldiers'.[22] Even after Mountbatten had shown that the Americans worked to the same formula, Churchill would go no farther than: 'Noted. There is no doubt that a steam hammer will crack a nut.'[23]

President Roosevelt, however, had gone unwisely far in promising Chiang Kai-shek that there would be some sort of amphibious operation to accompany TARZAN, the main offensive in Burma.[24] An embittered battle now took place in the Combined Chiefs of Staff, the British insisting BUCCANEER was impracticable in view of other commitments, the Americans maintaining that the political damage to relations with China if it were cancelled was too serious to contemplate. 'This may lead to [the Generalissimo] refusing to carry out his part of the Burma campaign,' noted Brooke. 'If he does so, it will be no very great loss.'[25] In the end Roosevelt gave way. Churchill rang Ismay in jubilation. 'He that ruleth his spirit is greater than he that taketh a city,' he proclaimed. Ismay was baffled, till Churchill explained that BUCCANEER had been cancelled. 'If I had given a thought to the bitter disappointment which Dickie Mountbatten would feel at yet another postponement of his offensive against the Japanese, I would have capped his quotation with another quotation from Proverbs. "Hope deferred maketh the heart sick."'[26]

Mountbatten bore the bad tidings gallantly. Wavell found him 'more tired and depressed' that he had ever seen him,[27] but he rallied quickly and told Brooke that, though everyone in SEAC was 'absolutely heartbroken about the decision',

> we remain in good heart and have our tails [up] and intend to fight as hard as our resources will permit.
>
> Although many people are gloomy as to the effect that this cancellation of operations may have on morale out here, I must certainly admit in the light of everything that I have heard, I cannot help agreeing in my heart of hearts with the decisions you have made.[28]

CULVERIN and BUCCANEER had perished. TARZAN was in peril. A satirist in SEAC headquarters hymned the sequence of events:

> Plan followed Plan in swift procession
> Commanders went, commanders came
> While telegrams in swift succession
> Arrived to douse or fan the flame.[29]

Undeterred, Mountbatten settled down to devise yet another plan that would suit what was left of his resources. This time it was to be PIGSTICK, a landing in the Mayu Peninsula intended to cut Japanese communications with its garrison at Akyab. He hoped that this would prove substantial enough to persuade Chiang Kai-shek to co-operate and asked Stilwell to tell the Generalissimo what was proposed. Retribution was swift. The Chiefs of Staff told the Prime Minister that they were 'much disturbed' that the Supreme Commander had thus jumped the gun on an operation 'which had not yet been approved, and which required resources which might be needed for operations of higher priority'. A week later Mountbatten was told that his three fast tank landing-ships must be returned to take part in the Italian campaign. He hurriedly recast his plans on the basis that at least the slow tank landing-craft would be left him. It was Andrew Cunningham who drove home the final knife when he proposed in the Chiefs of Staff on 31 December that 'Admiral Mountbatten should be told that there was no chance of keeping these two ships'.[30] 'PIGSTICK has become PIGSTUCK,' reported

Churchill laconically to Roosevelt.[31] With it passed the last hope that the Chinese would help make TARZAN a reality.

Mountbatten gained sympathy for his setback but little more material comfort. Writing to condole, Portal went on to suggest that further disappointments lay ahead. 'The fact is that we have not the resources to prepare alternative plans for two entirely different strategies, and it looks to me at the moment as if the role of the SEAC theatre may remain a secondary one.'[32] Even the King tempered his regrets with the proviso that he felt it essential to finish the battle for Rome before concentrating on the East, 'and so really do you'.[33] Mountbatten really did, but he still allowed himself a few days of melancholy. To Brooke he recapitulated all his woes and ended:

> I am sorry to write in this gloomy strain but I cannot possibly talk like this to my Staff since to them I have to keep up an optimistic and enthusiastic front and one has to blow off steam on somebody!
>
> Whatever you do to us I shall continue to make bricks without straw, but please remember that without straw bricks are very fragile![34]

The next exercise in brick-making was quickly under way. Road communications with China through north Burma, Mountbatten argued, would take absurdly long to establish. The main force of SEAC would meanwhile stand idle. The supply of China should therefore be left to the Air Force, while the rest of his forces should make a real contribution to the war against Japan and thus help release the pressure on China by swinging south through Sumatra. During January 1944 his planners put the finishing touches to a revised and more economical CULVERIN to take place in November or, at the worst, in April 1945.[35] Mountbatten decided to entrust the presentation of his case to his Deputy Chief of Staff, General Wedemeyer, in the belief that an American would get a better hearing in Washington. The AXIOM mission, as it was hopefully christened, left on 5 February. 'Over 100 of our staff, British and American, male and female, came to see Al and his team off,' Mountbatten told his wife. 'John Keswick said it was like the departure of a football team . . . with cries of "Don't come back without the Cup, boys!!"'[36]

For the Supreme Commander it seemed the last throw. He told Lambe, who was now appointed Captain of what had once been Mountbatten's aircraft-carrier:

> If the decision goes against us I think you should let me go back to the *Illustrious* and find another ship for yourself. You might also send out the waxwork which I hear Madame Tussaud's has made but which at present is naked for lack of coupons. It could have my

Admiral's uniform and sit at my desk and carry out the deception policy against the Japanese as well as I could.[37]

To imagine that a war-machine which had just failed to accommodate a minor operation like PIGSTICK could now undertake a full-scale invasion of the nature of CULVERIN was evidence, if evidence were needed, of Mountbatten's indomitable optimism. In London Wedemeyer found Churchill enthusiastic but the Chiefs of Staff more than sceptical. The project, said Brooke, must be 'tested by one essential question – what would it contribute to the shortening of the war against Japan?' By this criterion, it failed.[38] Wedemeyer appealed to Churchill. 'I anticipate difficulty in my homeland', he wrote on 15 February, 'with regard to our recommendation that the Ledo road project should be discontinued. . . . I would appreciate your support in this regard.'[39] But in the last resort Churchill was not prepared to overrule his military advisers. The AXIOM mission must manage as best as it could in Washington with no help from Whitehall.

It stood no chance. Stilwell, alarmed to find his *raison d'être* thus challenged, had not merely argued against the policy at SEAC headquarters but had sent his own mission to Washington to sabotage his Supreme Commander's efforts. Such behaviour could be justified by his double role as Chiang Kai-shek's Chief of Staff; what was unforgivable was that he never warned Mountbatten of his intentions.[40] In fact his exercise was unnecessary. Even before the AXIOM team arrived, the American Chiefs of Staff had recommended that offensive operations in north Burma should be redoubled and plans for an assault against Sumatra abandoned.[41] Wedeyemer argued the contrary, but neither he nor Mountbatten's adviser from the Foreign Officer, Esler Dening, did their case any good by overstating it: in London Wedemeyer had claimed that Admiral King would never allow a British fleet into the Pacific when the contrary was known to be true, while Dening caused 'hoots of merriment' when he tried to justify CULVERIN on the grounds that, without it, Mountbatten's staff would be left unemployed.[42]

Mountbatten was distressed though not wholly surprised by the failure of the mission; he was outraged at what he regarded as Stilwell's treachery. He demanded his deputy's dismissal.[43] Marshall at once despatched Stilwell to Delhi to apologize, and Stilwell dutifully 'ate crow' in the presence of Wildman-Lushington as well as the Supreme Commander. He showed them Marshall's telegram, which made it clear that he would hold his job only on Mountbatten's sufferance. The latter's response was generous:

> On this I came forward in as friendly a fashion as I could and fully accepted his apology and said that my chief regret at the various actions he had recently been taking behind my back was that they

made the outside world think that we did not trust each other or work in close harmony.

He was kind enough to say: 'I must have been mad not to take you into my confidence in the same way as you have always done to me, and I want you to know that I have always trusted you completely and I shall continue to trust you in the future.' After that we metaphorically kissed each other and went ahead and ironed out all the difficulties which had been cropping up since his departure.[44]

Brooke found time to send Mountbatten a telegram of commiseration, 'to let you know how much I feel for you in all your disappointments since you took up your present job. I can so well realise all you must have been going through.'[45] Churchill alone refused to accept that the decision was final. At the end of March 1944 he returned to battle with furious complaints that he was being kept in the dark and insistence that the maritime strategy should be pursued: 'All preparations will be made for amphibious action across the Bay of Bengal against the Malay Peninsula and the various island outposts by which it is defended, the ultimate objective being the reconquest of Singapore.'[46] Wearily, the Chiefs of Staff renewed the argument. Their trump-card was that nothing could be done without American help and such help was not forthcoming.[47] Brooke wrote irritably to Dill:

> In South East Asia Command we have Dickie who is determined to do something to justify his supreme existence. He is therefore naturally doing all he can, and using all possible arguments and propaganda to bring about a Culverin Policy. His outlook fits in well with that of the P.M. and they encourage each other by periodic personal wires. Here again the trouble might be overcome if it was not for the fact that the P.M. after creating Dickie and his command is loath to see its wings clipped and reduced to a creature crawling about in Burma.[48]

From London Dening reported early in April that the Chiefs of Staff were obdurate and would resign rather than yield on military grounds. 'On the other hand, they will probably have to give way if he insists on political grounds.'[49] Mountbatten knew Churchill well enough to be sure this was something he would never do. Somerville noted in his diary that CULVERIN still had 'priority in the mind of the S.A.C.', but for the next few months at least it was to be little more than a nagging and reproachful shadow. The pressures of reality made sure of that.

# CHAPTER 21

## *Imphal*

IT WAS THE JAPANESE who rescued Mountbatten from this hectic inactivity. Burma, for them, was by no means the remote and relatively unimportant battlefield which many Americans and, indeed, British conceived it. It was, the Japanese premier, General Tojo, once told the Prime Minister of Siam, 'a bulwark of defence for us in the Indian area', a zone whose strategic importance was far too great for it to be abandoned.[1] The Japanese were conscious of the build-up of Allied power in India and the threat implicit in the creation of the South-East Asia Command. By October 1943 an increased budget had been allocated for the transit of Japanese troops through Siam.[2] Japan had taken Burma with only four divisions; a fifth arrived late in 1943; two more in January 1944; by the end of March the total was eight.[3] The Japanese were clearly preparing to strike first or, at least, to react fiercely to any Allied advance.

Through the breaking of the Japanese diplomatic and military ciphers Mountbatten was aware in general and sometimes in striking detail of their resources and intentions. Though the organization was not fully established in Delhi until June 1944, a special liaison unit had already been operating for several months, and the Supreme Commander received MAGIC (diplomatic) and ULTRA (naval and military) material from the moment of his arrival.[4] It is difficult to assess how useful this was. General Wedemeyer considers that, though it was undoubtedly of considerable value, it was less so in South-East Asia than in some other war zones. The Japanese Army did not make as much use of enciphered communications with its headquarters as, for instance, the German; while the naval signal traffic, so all-important in the Pacific, was in this area of minor interest.[5] General Giffard distrusted, or perhaps dis-approved of, information obtained by cipher-cracking, and relied on it as little as possible. Mountbatten, on the other hand, was enchanted by the novelty and eager to promote its use. The fact that he enjoyed a clear picture of the evolving Japanese command structure in Burma and the reinforcement of its armies was to help him considerably in measuring the extent of the threat when the enemy attacked early in 1944.[6]

By January of that year the Japanese had assessed the dangers of an Allied assault and concluded that there was still time to pre-empt it. 'It has been found', read the Weekly Intelligence Report of the Vice Chief of the General Staff, 'that the British Indian army is not suited to jungle warfare. Accordingly, the real offensive for the recovery of Burma will be two-pronged, launched simultaneously in the India–Yunnan area and the Thailand–Indochina area; this campaign will require naval co-operation and the necessary preparations are not yet complete.'[7] By striking at Assam, the Japanese believed that they would sever communications between the 14th Army and Stilwell's Chinese forces in the north, and prepare a bridgehead from which the British hegemony in India could be destroyed. This would effectively rule out the possibility of any amphibious operations being mounted from Indian bases.

In February 1944, almost on the day that the AXIOM mission left to persuade London and Washington of the need for a maritime strategy, the Japanese made the debate largely academic by attacking in Arakan. Mountbatten had visited the area a few weeks before, getting to within a thousand yards of the enemy lines.[8] 'Yesterday Louis Mountbatten came round to see us and did us all a power of good,' General Lomax told his mother. 'He spoke amazingly well to the men, who were delighted to see him. He has a great personality.'[9] The corps commander, General Christison, no man for flattery, told Mountbatten after the battle that 'many officers and men I have spoken to have stated that your very heartening visit to the Arakan was an important factor in keeping fighting spirit and morale going through a critical three weeks'.[10]

The first reports from the Arakan indicated dismally that the familiar *débâcle* was to be repeated. British units had been by-passed, outflanked, stranded where it seemed they must either scuttle in headlong flight or admit defeat and surrender. They did neither, but stood their ground and fought. The defence of the Administrative Box, in which 15 Corps rallied around its headquarters, relied on the air for its supplies and held the enemy at bay, signalled the birth of a new strategy and the end of the myth of Japanese invincibility. 'Hold on and you will make history,' was Mountbatten's message.[11] They held on, and they did. Starved of supplies, threatened by a renewed British advance, the Japanese retreated with 5000 out of the original 8000 invaders dead. 'We expect very shortly to be able to announce a great victory,' Mountbatten told Edwina, 'thanks to the really magnificent morale and courage of our men. Last year they ran like hell under very similar conditions, so I feel that SEAC has justified itself.'[12]

One critical difference between the two Arakan campaigns was the vastly increased Allied air-power, which made the support of units behind the Japanese lines a possibility. There was also, however, an equally significant change in spirit among the troops. Christison had pledged that, if air support was guaranteed, he would not retreat but stand firm and provide an anvil against which the reserve forces – the hammer – would smash the Japanese. 'Mountbatten later claimed that he was the initiator of these tactics and had ordered them to be used,' wrote Christison in his unpublished memoirs.[13] 'What he had done was to endorse them and make them possible.' The comment was a fair one. The Arakan was Christison's battle, perhaps Slim's. The Commander-in-Chief, Giffard, and still more the Supreme Commander were remote, almost stratospheric figures. Once Mountbatten had agreed the strategy in its broadest outline and ensured that the materials to support it were available, his task was largely one of exhortation.

He found this withdrawn posture a troublesome one to maintain. In December 1943 his Chief of Staff took strong issue with him for issuing 'an outrageous personal minute interfering with the purely land side of the future Burma campaign'. Pownall remonstrated sternly with the delinquent Supreme Commander:

> I told Mountbatten frankly he had gone completely off the rails and he had no right to go about things the way he had done. I said I'd been warned in London that I should have difficulty in keeping him on the rails, and here he was completely off them. . . .
>
> I'm bound to say Mountbatten took all this amazingly well, indeed he cried '*Peccavi*' and apologized. I hope that in the future I shall only have to wag my finger at him, and that he'll be more careful.[14]

That the effects of this magisterial rebuke wore off was shown when Pownall's successor General Browning made precisely the same complaint. 'Dickie has been interfering in your battle again,' Browning told Christison. 'I've told him he must not and he is going to come and apologize to you. Don't be nice to him, he's so keen he'll only do it again!'[15]

There were times, however, when the Supreme Commander's intervention was tolerated, indeed actively sought, by his commanders. On 5 March 1944 Slim wrote to Mountbatten about 15 Corps' success in the Arakan. He went on to say: 'I think we are in for something even more serious on 4 Corps front, where our dispositions are not quite so favourable for meeting it. . . . I am very anxious to reinforce that front if I possibly can. As you know, transportation and maintenance are a great headache.'[16] Two days later battle began on the Imphal plain.

Though both Mountbatten and Slim had known that something was brewing on the borders of Assam, neither of them had expected the attack to come so soon or in such force. Nor did they realize how far the campaign in the Arakan had been a deception operation, designed to tie up the British reserves far from what was intended to be the real killing-ground. Slim's plan had been to retreat in an orderly fashion. General Scoones's 4 Corps would then make a stand at Imphal and the encircling Japanese would themselves be encircled and destroyed as relief came from the west. Inconsiderately, the Japanese had attacked too soon and too vigorously to allow this to work out. 4 Corps was almost overrun, all its reserves engaged. Some seventy miles north Kohima was in peril, and with it the railhead and supply-depot of Dimapur. Disaster was close, and Slim believed it could be averted only by flying in reinforcements from the Arakan. Mountbatten alone was in a position to make the necessary aircraft available, and he was temporarily out of action.

A few days before, when visiting Stilwell at his forward headquarters, the Supreme Commander had been driving himself in his jeep along a jungle track. A bamboo was pushed aside by the front wheel and sprang back violently, hitting him in the left eye. 'It took a certain amount of moral courage', wrote Mountbatten, 'to feel and see if my left eyeball was still in its socket, as I could not believe after such a blow that it could still remain there. My relief at finding it still in place was tempered by my finding that I was completely blind in the left eye. I put a first-aid dressing on and drove on.'[17] He was flown to Ledo, where there was, fortunately, a distinguished American eye-specialist, Captain Scheie, who diagnosed a serious internal haemorrhage but said that the eye should recover if subjected to no kind of strain. Mountbatten spent five days with both eyes bandaged, in agonizing pain which was made worse by the bad news pouring in from the Imphal plain. Then he overruled the doctor's protests, discharged himself and flew to Slim's headquarters at Comilla. He knew that in so doing he was risking permanent damage to his eye, but even the certainty that he would blind himself would not have kept him any longer from the action. At 10 a.m. on 14 March 1944 Mountbatten, still in considerable pain and unable to read or write, landed at Comilla to be told of the desperate need for thirty transport aircraft. The problem was that almost all the transport aircraft in the area were American, earmarked for the supply of China. He had made a switch of these planes during the Arakan operations, but it had taken ten days to obtain the prior approval of Stilwell and the Combined Chiefs of Staff. Half as long a delay would be fatal in the battle for Imphal.

The following day, from Delhi, Mountbatten cabled the Chiefs of Staff. 'The dangers of Japanese success and the magnitude of the defeat we may inflict on them are both greater than in the case of the Arakan.' Unless he was ordered to the contrary, he proposed to divert aircraft from the Hump on 18 March.[18] The Chiefs quickly urged agreement on their opposite numbers in

Washington and Churchill weighed in with a personal telegram to Roosevelt: 'The stakes are pretty high in this battle, and victory would have far-reaching consequences.'[19] The Americans agreed, though they were not ready to accept Mountbatten's further request that in future he should be allowed to divert aircraft from the Air Transport Command without reference to the U.S. authorities.[20] He had already taken agreement for granted and ordered all preparations to be made; by 19 March the air-lift was at work. 'He saw the urgency at once,' recorded Slim, 'and, on his own responsibility, ordered thirty Dakotas . . . to join Troop Carrier Command – a decision which earned my gratitude and played a major part in the result of the battle.'[21] The move was not made quite so much on Mountbatten's sole responsibility as Slim's phrase suggests but he still acted with determination and courage.

Certainly General Giffard could not have been relied upon to perform a similar rescue operation. 'I am desperately worried over the way the situation got out of control during the week I was away,' Mountbatten told Edwina on 20 March, and, ten days later: 'If the Battle of Imphal is won it will be almost entirely due to Dickie over-riding all his Generals!'[22] This ebullient comment was made in the heat of the moment, but his criticism of Giffard was something he held to and eventually acted on. As early as 5 March he had asked his Commander-in-Chief to start moving reinforcements by road and rail to Imphal, yet ten days later no steps had been taken.[23] Little in war is black and white – there were reasons for keeping the troops where they were, reasons for doubting the seriousness of the threat to the Imphal plain – yet Giffard's fellow Commanders-in-Chief united in condemning his inactivity. Peirse supported the Supreme Commander in a letter to Portal, while Somerville noted in his diary: 'the General is slow and I think it is correct that it was the S.A.C.'s personal pressure which resulted in a division being moved to the Imphal area in time to prevent it being over-run by the Japanese'.[24]

This incident brought to a head ill will that had long been simmering between Mountbatten and Giffard; the only surprise is that the explosion had been so long in coming. 'The S.A.C. is certainly volatile, enthusiastic and impatient,' wrote Somerville, 'whereas the General is stolid, critical and generally sound, though I agree he lacks speed of thought and action.'[25] Pownall blamed Giffard for complacency and a failure even to try to communicate with his Supreme Commander.[26] His immediate reaction to a new plan 'is always one of negation', commented Peirse. 'He has consistently adopted the attitude to Mountbatten that not only is he his adviser, but when he says that something cannot be done the matter is final.'[27] When the Supreme Commander put forward plans for following up what it was now clear was going to be Slim's emphatic victory at Imphal, Giffard blocked them all: the men were not available, nothing could be done during the monsoon.

Early in May, knowing that the Commander-in-Chief was tired and ill, Mountbatten tried to persuade him to retire on medical grounds; 'but he is such a straight and upright old gentleman', the Supreme Commander told Edwina, 'that he would not agree to any such subterfuge'.[28] Mountbatten had already got Brooke's agreement to his dismissing Giffard if it proved necessary, and now he did so. 'The trouble is we all like him. . . . He is, however, non-aggressive, a non-co-operator, and unwilling to recognise me as the one responsible for the Burma campaign.'[29]

At the beginning of May Scoones reported that the air-lift to the besieged garrison at Imphal was still leaving it dangerously short of food and ammunition. Simultaneously Mountbatten was instructed to return to the Middle East the seventy-nine transport aircraft which had been borrowed at the start of the Arakan offensive. Slim insisted that this would make impossible the position of the British forces in Imphal, and Mountbatten ruled that no aircraft were to leave without his permission. From the Chiefs of Staff he won a reprieve; first to 24 May and then to mid June. Once again Churchill proved a potent ally. 'Let nothing go from the battle that you need for victory,' he telegraphed. 'I will not accept denial of this from any quarter, and will back you to the full.'[30]

The Americans on Mountbatten's staff greeted with some derision the suggestion that more aircraft should be withdrawn from the route to China to help supply a garrison which was considerably larger than the force that was besieging it. The size of the Japanese force was in fact underestimated, but there is still no doubt that the British force in Imphal was numerically stronger than the Japanese. Wedemeyer clamoured for more activity: 'The battle in those areas may be described as being fought passively on a day-to-day basis, countering enemy blows.'[31] Mountbatten was unperturbed. He knew from the ULTRA intercepts that the Japanese around Imphal were short of supplies, and accepted Slim's thesis that it was best to let them wear themselves out and then destroy them when the monsoon cut off their retreat. He issued a directive stating that the road from Kohima to Imphal should be opened by mid July: 'I was grateful to him', wrote Slim, 'for not being stampeded by more nervous people into setting too early a date.'[32] Dorman-Smith, Governor of Burma in exile, heard the Supreme Commander addressing a meeting of senior officers: he was 'absolutely brimming over with confidence', arguing that it did not matter how far the Japanese advanced; in the end they would be destroyed.[33]

It was with General Scoones at Imphal that Mountbatten encountered his first unwounded Japanese prisoner, a deserter. The Supreme Commander asked him what sort of treatment he expected to receive and was told: 'Good treatment, the same as your prisoners receive from the Japanese.' Only a day

or two before Mountbatten had been told of a team of muleteers working for
the West Yorkshire Regiment who had been captured by the Japanese. They
were tied up by their hands to trees and flogged into insensibility; then, when
they came to, bayoneted to death. 'This is only a sample of the many atrocity
stories I am beginning to collect. One day I hope to catch some of the Japanese
responsible and put them on trial.'[34] Mountbatten could never bring himself
wholly to forgive the Japanese for their behaviour towards their prisoners – a
feeling that was redoubled at the end of the war when he met the survivors
from the forced-labour and concentration camps.

It was the end of April before Mountbatten's injured eye ceased to trouble
him seriously, and the pain and inconvenience, coupled with the need for
constant, gruellingly uncomfortable and dangerous travel, and worry over
the outcome of the campaign, did something to dim the verve that normally
characterized his performance. Dorman-Smith might find him 'brimming
over with confidence', but Wavell was more perceptive when he observed that
'what with the Japs, the P.M. and the Americans', Mountbatten had lost 'that
first fine careless confidence that caused my predecessor to call him the Boy
Champion'.[35] Noel Coward stayed with him when the Battle of Imphal was at
its height, and behind the sunburn and the enthusiasm 'detected a strain in his
eyes'.[36]

One trouble was that, though Slim and Mountbatten were convinced that
the battle was progressing satisfactorily and that the destruction of the
Japanese Army was becoming daily more certain, to others the position
seemed very different. Wedemeyer was in Washington in June and reported
that, in the Arakan and around Imphal and Kohima, the British were on the
defensive and 'looking forward to the monsoon so that they can de-emphasize
operations'.

> The entire attitude of the British has been apathetic, which has put
> the Americans in a difficult position on the staff of SEAC. Mount-
> batten's attitude has been fine, aggressive and enthusiastic, but
> between him and the troops who execute his directives are comman-
> ders who emasculate his directives and who are so anxious to prove
> that they have been right the past two years that they intentionally do
> not follow the orders the Supreme Commander gives them.[37]

The only place where there was any real activity, claimed Wedemeyer,
was in the north, where Stilwell's Chinese and Americans had made a sudden
and unexpected dash in mid May to capture the air-strip at Myitkyina.
'Whoops! Will this burn up the Limies!' was Stilwell's triumphant diary
entry.[38] The feat was a remarkable one, though made less useful by his failure
to complete the job by taking the town. In London and Washington the

people who criticized Slim's apparently leisurely approach were given a fresh stick with which to beat the 14th Army and its Supreme Commander. Mountbatten was irritated by Stilwell's failure to keep him posted about his plans, but did not feel the humiliation and anguished rage his deputy had hoped for. Indeed, his comment to his daughter was notably bland: 'Isn't the news of the capture of Myitkyina airfield great? It is one of my most interesting fronts, commanded by my deputy General Stilwell.'[39]

The visit to Stilwell's headquarters which had so nearly cost Mountbatten an eye had been undertaken primarily to convince the irascible American that General Wingate's latest adventure was likely to be helpful to him in his advance. It was not a contention that was easy to maintain. The Supreme Commander had felt himself bound to do something with the Long Range Penetration Groups – 'Mountbatten considers himself personally charged by the P.M. to look after Wingate's interests,' commented Pownall[40] – but what the something should be was difficult to decide. Once TARZAN was abandoned and it became clear that there would be no significant Chinese advance from Yunnan, there seemed no particularly useful role for him to play. Wingate, of course, would never accept such a conclusion: 'Wingate worried me,' recorded Mountbatten in his diary for 5 January 1944, 'heaven knows I have a big load these days.'

In his fiercely partisan account of the Chindit leader, General Tulloch claims that Mountbatten never told Wingate directly what limitations would be placed on his future activities but allowed him to continue to train his troops for an operation which nobody intended to mount.[41] There is some truth in this – Mountbatten usually shrank from quarrels and confrontations – but he also believed that the Special Force could be used in the end with some, if not great, advantage. Wingate, however, sometimes stung him into unwontedly intemperate response, as was shown when he complained that his Special Force was being given no credit by the official news machine:

> Has it occurred to you that your assumption that people are going to try and belittle or conceal the doings of your party, makes it all the more difficult for me to ensure that they get the correct measure of credit? For instance, your letter was quite unsuitable for circulating to Air Headquarters. . . . In future, I suggest that when you consider a direct report to me is necessary, that this should be written entirely objectively without any note of bitterness being allowed to creep in. If you wish to let off steam, I don't mind your doing so in a covering letter which no one else sees, but if you mix vituperation and factual

accounts, it merely means that the factual accounts cannot be
circulated.

Your astounding telegram to Joubert has made me realise how
you have achieved such amazing success in getting yourself disliked
by people who are only too ready to be on your side.[42]

This letter was written two weeks after Wingate's special force at last
went into action. By 10 March 9000 men and 1100 animals had been landed
far behind the Japanese lines.

The landing was soon followed by the death of Wingate in a flying
accident. The enthusiasm which Mountbatten had originally felt for Wingate
and his ideas had long been tempered by scepticism: 'my mind was in step
with Bill Slim all the way through', he told Ronald Lewin many years later,
and Slim's view was that, though the Special Force might be useful in certain
circumstances, in Burma in 1944 it was more trouble than it was worth.
Nevertheless, Mountbatten's penchant for the heroic, the eccentric and the
larger-than-life ensured that he never wholly lost his admiration for this
remarkable man. 'I cannot tell you how much I am going to miss Wingate,' he
told Edwina. 'Not only had we become close personal friends but he was such
a fire-eater, and it was such a help to me having a man with a burning desire to
fight. He was a pain in the neck to the generals over him, but I loved his wild
enthusiasm and it will be very difficult for me to try and inculcate it from
above.'[43]

The loss of Wingate did nothing to ease the inexorable pressure on the
Japanese. On 22 June the relieving force at last broke through. The siege of
Imphal was lifted, the Japanese Army shattered, the battle all but won. 'It is
the most important defeat the Japs have ever suffered in their military career,'
Mountbatten told his wife, 'because the numbers involved are so much
greater than any Pacific Island operation.'[44] At a conservative estimate the
Japanese 15th Army lost 30,000 men between mid March and mid June.[45] It
was not till 10 July that the enemy ordered a general retreat, and by that time
only shreds of their Army survived.

It remained to decide what should happen next. In early May Mountbatten had cabled the Chiefs of Staff to ask for a 'clear-cut and up-to-date
directive'.[46] Brooke's opinion was already clear-cut. The campaign was a
wasteful nuisance. The time had come to define the Supreme Commander's
responsibilities 'so as to bring to an end, if possible, the continued pressure to
increase our commitment in Burma'. If Brooke had realized the scale of the
approaching victory he would perhaps have been less chilling in his dis-
couragement; as it was, Churchill protested that it was deplorable that our
forces should be left with no operation to carry out in the autumn and winter

of 1944.[47] A fortnight later Pownall flew to London and painted a rosy picture of events around Imphal: the Japanese would be exterminated, 'the morale of our own forces was excellent, and after a time they came to regard fighting the Japanese as a superb form of big-game shooting'.[48] On 3 June the new directive was issued. Emphasis was still to be put on communications with China but Mountbatten was required, so far as was consistent with this main objective, 'to press advantages against the enemy by exerting maximum effort . . . during the current monsoon period'. The 14th Army was therefore given *carte blanche* to press on, but there was no mention of possible amphibious operations; if Slim could not reconquer Burma overland, then he would have to sit it out on his present lines. To Mountbatten and to Churchill it was a profoundly unsatisfactory conclusion. Neither intended to accept it. 'When history comes to be written,' Ismay told Pownall, while the debate was still raging, 'I believe that the waffling that there has been for nearly nine months over the basic question of our strategy in the Far East will be one of the black spots in the record of British Higher Direction of War.'[49]

# CHAPTER 22

# *The Road to Rangoon*

THE NINE MONTHS AFTER THE BATTLE OF IMPHAL provide a curious echo of the nine months before it: Mountbatten's hopes for an ambitious operation were first raised high, then dashed, and compensation was found in a victory which at first had been neither wanted nor expected.

By the middle of 1944 Mountbatten had transferred his headquarters from Delhi to Kandy in Ceylon, some 1600 miles to the south and nearly 500 miles farther from the battlefield in Burma. The move was a manifestation of his wish to adopt a maritime strategy and not allow his forces to be bogged down in the Burmese jungle. The change had been foreshadowed several months before the Command was even established, the Chiefs of Staff recommending in June 1943 that the new Supreme Commander's head-quarters should be outside India, probably in Ceylon.[1] At that time Churchill favoured Calcutta, on the grounds that Ceylon was too far from the battlefield,[2] but by the autumn he had come round to the idea of at least an alternative headquarters in Ceylon: 'Lord Louis Mountbatten should operate from whichever best suited his purposes at the moment.'[3] Mountbatten himself had no doubt that he wanted to escape from Delhi as rapidly and permanently as possible: 'I want to make sure that my staff can stand on their own feet. . . . It will be a good thing to get away from the social and political atmosphere of a large capital.'[4] A reconnaissance party came back reporting that Kandy would suit his purposes admirably, and plans were set in train.

Somerville, who loathed wartime Delhi even more than did Mountbatten and liked the idea of Kandy's proximity to the Fleet's main base at Trinco-malee, enthusiastically backed the move,[5] but there was opposition to overcome. The Americans deplored what they saw as a flight from reality.[6] Auchinleck believed the move would 'complicate and delay the course of business'.[7] Giffard and Peirse grumbled that they would be too far from the fighting and would have to spend interminable hours travelling between Delhi, Kandy and the front line. Even the British Chiefs of Staff began to have doubts.[8] Mountbatten was unperturbed. Calcutta was 'over-crowded, famine-ridden, and full of objectionable troubles'. The choice was between

Delhi and Kandy, and of these Kandy was better climatically, geographically and politically.[9] The move must go on.

On 13 April 1944 Mountbatten returned to the capital from Assam. 'Why is it', he mused, 'that in Delhi there always seems to be a somewhat negative atmosphere, whereas at the front everyone is full of dash and go?' Two days later the move began, by air and four special trains. Army Group headquarters was to be four miles north-east of Kandy, Air Command four miles north-west.[10] Mountbatten took over the imposing King's Pavilion as his residence and a lavish array of huts sprang up at his headquarters in the Botanical Gardens. 'Kandy is probably the most beautiful spot in the world, and a delightful place in which to work,' wrote the Supreme Commander with satisfaction.[11]

The headquarters soon became a byword for elegance and luxury. A perpetual *fête champêtre*, Peter Fleming found it, while Carton de Wiart was reminded of the court of Napoleon's formidable adversary, the Archduke Charles.[12] Ralph Arnold was overwhelmed by the 'prodigious number of shiny staff cars' and the way everybody looked 'sleek, smart and prosperous'. 'I felt that the atmosphere of Kandy was a bit too grand for me,' he concluded.[13] The standard of living was said to be so high that Ismay feared the junior officers might run into debt.[14] Much of this was fantasy, or the pardonable envy of those compelled to live in discomfort and danger. Kandy was well laid out and maintained; the messes were comfortable; the food good: but it was nothing very remarkable. The equivalent American headquarters might have lacked the style, but it would certainly have been more opulent. Yet it could fairly be said that Kandy was remote from the sordid business of battle: 'the peace and quiet and lack of all direct contact with the war . . . do not appeal to me', decided Somerville.[15]

A more serious criticism was that Kandy was grossly over-staffed. Mountbatten started with the best intentions. The grand total involved in the move, he calculated, would be 4100, as opposed to the 26,000 Eisenhower was supposed to be taking to Rome.[16] But, somehow, by the time the move actually took place the total had risen dramatically. 'It does make one wonder', wrote Admiral Layton, Commander-in-Chief in Ceylon, 'if it is right that one Commander should collect together 7000 able-bodied men and women to plan and supervise operations the scale of which is not yet settled.'[17] It was not long before the tally was near 10,000. At a time when manpower was desperately short, the Chiefs of Staff frowned on what seemed to them marked extravagance. The last straw for Brooke came when Mountbatten asked for a senior officer to act as his representative in Delhi. 'As both Peirse and Giffard are stopping there surely either one or other of them could represent you far better than an additional Lieutenant-General who in his turn will build up another large staff to assist him?'[18]

In other ways, too, the headquarters was not run economically. The airstrip which Mountbatten had carved out of the mountains nineteen miles from Kandy would have been of uncertain value even if the weather had not ensured that it was notoriously unreliable. The caravan which he had had built in the Colombo workshops was no more lavish than that of other commanders, but it was too rarely used to be a justifiable expense. Only the most fanatical of Mountbatten's admirers would deny that Kandy could have performed the same function with less liberality in men and money.

It could not, however, have been Mountbatten's headquarters. If his panache, enthusiasm, flamboyance were thought desirable in the interests of morale, then they had to be paid for. Mountbattens do not come on the cheap. The appearance of Kandy was as much part of Mountbatten's image as the galaxy of flags on the bonnet of his jeep; the photographs always available for admirers; the three portraits in his office at the King's Pavilion – Churchill, Eisenhower and King George VI. It was a superbly effective piece of public relations; and though it irritated some it exhilarated and encouraged many others. Kandy was an efficient headquarters, but it was also an expertly contrived theatrical entertainment. Mountbatten's misfortune was that his failure to win acceptance for his maritime policy meant that the value of Kandy in its first capacity was never put fully to the test.

Mountbatten's arrival at Kandy found him hoping that the powers-that-be might yet relent. Dening reported from London that the Chiefs of Staff were at last seriously alarmed at the way the Americans were playing their own game in South-East Asia, and realized that the time had come to evolve a British strategy.[19] He raised Mountbatten's hopes to little purpose; in fact, the familiar debate was still raging between the Chiefs, who wanted a policy based on Australia and the support of MacArthur's left flank, and Churchill, who hankered after his invasion of Sumatra.[20] At one point Churchill played with the idea that Mountbatten himself should take over MacArthur's left flank. 'I don't know how that is to be brought about,' mused Pownall, 'unless Mountbatten is to come *under* MacArthur, on which our C.O.S. seem quite firm. Moreover, for an operation which is essentially naval I doubt if the Admiralty would accept Mountbatten as its commander. Since he has never commanded a big ship they think little of him as a commander in any sense – so prejudiced are they.'[21]

The Supreme Commander was meanwhile meditating a new approach to the problem. In July he came forward with two plans: CAPITAL, for the advance of the 14th Army to Mandalay and eventually southwards towards

Rangoon; DRACULA, for an amphibious and airborne assault on Rangoon in January 1945. Originally these were put forward as alternatives, with the 14th Army remaining passive if DRACULA were adopted, but after protests from Slim and Giffard it was agreed that the mainland advance should continue whatever happened, at least as far as Mandalay. Lambe was enlisted to argue the cause of DRACULA and put forward a rather tepid plea for some kind of combined operation, even if 'only a little one'. On 3 August Mountbatten set off for London himself. 'I hope you will have a successful visit . . . and that you will get all you want,' wrote Auchinleck. 'I do not think it will be easy if past experience goes for anything.'[22]

During his absence Stilwell, to the general surprise, decided to live up to his title of deputy and take command at Kandy. The announcement, remarked Barbara Tuchman, aroused at headquarters 'the emotions of Rome awaiting Alaric the Hun'.[23] He found the atmosphere displeasing and the endless meetings almost intolerable – 'terrible', 'dumb', 'crappier than usual', 'I never felt at ease in such make-belief acts!'[24] His dissatisfaction was amply reciprocated. He was judged to be 'pathetically at sea'. 'All my senior staff, British and American,' wrote Mountbatten, 'reported to me on my return that he had been quite incapable of taking charge or giving any useful directions at Theatre level.'[25]

Meanwhile in London a promising start was made. Brooke agreed resignedly that *something* had to be done in Burma, and that of the various possibilities the attack on Rangoon seemed best.[26] Cunningham was the only dissentient, arguing that the forces allocated to the attack on Rangoon were 'too light' and the proposed assault by river 'wishful thinking'. Mountbatten, not unreasonably, retorted that on every other occasion his demands had been criticized as extravagant. This time he was determined to depend as far as possible on his own resources.[27] The trouble was that, though he might have the men and aircraft for DRACULA, he did not have the landing-craft or the resources to exploit whatever initial success he might achieve. The critical debate took place on 8 August. Mountbatten had to counter on the one hand Churchill, who still hankered after the invasion of Sumatra, on the other the Chiefs, who wanted the real weight put behind a Pacific strategy. Eden was his only dependable ally, championing the attack on Rangoon as the best chance of finishing the war in Burma quickly and freeing British forces for action elsewhere.[28] He suggested that Australian troops might add substance to the landing – a will-o'-the-wisp dreamed up by Mountbatten which was quickly extinguished in Canberra.[29]

Mountbatten started the day 'very unhappy', noted Eden; he ended it 'very content'.[30] Ten days later Brooke recorded a final interview with the Supreme Commander, 'to discuss our plan for the capture of Rangoon which is based on our being able to start withdrawing the 6th Division from the European Theatre on 1 October. It is a gamble, but I believe one worth taking.'[31]

The Americans seemed to be the only people capable of upsetting the applecart of DRACULA. In Washington in June Wedemeyer had warned that he would oppose any enterprise of this kind unless satisfied that it would make a '*timely* contribution' to the opening of the China road.[32] A month later Mountbatten reported that for the first time there was 'an absolute Anglo-American split' in his staff on the issue of where the next offensive should be.[33] At the Second Quebec Conference in September the Americans proved at the best lukewarm about DRACULA, but were prepared to stomach it, provided that the advances in the north and centre of Burma were not starved of resources as a result. Six extra divisions, it was concluded, would in this case be needed, to be found partly from India, partly from forces withdrawn from the campaign in Italy. Mountbatten, Pownall wrote in his diary, was in 'the seventh Heaven of delight. He is so very simple-minded. For my own part, and in his position, I wouldn't get over-excited, or unduly pleased, until I was plumb certain of the resources.'[34]

Once again the sceptics proved correct. Plans for DRACULA had been based on the assumption that the Germans would be defeated well before the end of 1944; optimistic in August and September, this thesis was patently nonsensical by early October. At a Cabinet meeting on 2 October Churchill pronounced that the diversion of forces from Europe required for DRACULA could not now be justified; the operation must be postponed till after the 1945 monsoon.[35] Brooke claims that ten days later he was still having to curb the Prime Minister's desire to withdraw troops from Italy for the attack on Rangoon – 'He was mainly influenced by his desire to do something for Mountbatten.'[36] Churchill's second thoughts cannot have been strongly held; DRACULA in its full glory was dead and word of its demise had already reached Mountbatten. 'I believe the blighters at home have gone back on all their promises . . . ,' he told Edwina. 'I am in such despair that I have written Anthony a long letter.'[37]

His letter to Eden summed up all his feelings about the campaign in South-East Asia. A failure on the part of the British to reconquer at least one colony before the end of the war would 'irretrievably impair our prestige in the Far East'. Yet this would be the result of the cancellation of DRACULA, not to mention a 'catastrophic effect on the morale of this Command'. The main objective of an advance by land must be to open an overland route to China, a goal which even most Americans conceded was now irrelevant to the war against Japan: 'So I have in fact been ordered to do precisely what I recommended should not be done, in order to satisfy a national ambition which has now become out-of-date; and the whole British war effort against Japan . . . is to be bogged down in Northern Burma.' DRACULA was said to be postponed only until November 1945, yet it seemed more likely that it would be January 1946 before the resources would be made available. Meanwhile the Americans criticized the inadequate British contribution: 'If we are condemned . . . to paddle about in fever-ridden jungles and swamps in North Burma for another 14 months or more, what are now malicious distortions of the case may come to be perilously near the truth.'

> You know me well enough to believe me when I say that it is not for reasons of personal ambition . . . that I am so upset at the turn that events are taking. . . . As I told you when I got this job, I have no military ambition, and indeed I hope to go back to the command of a ship at the end of the war. But so long as I remain responsible for the forces in this theatre, I feel it very keenly that hundreds of thousands of British soldiers, sailors and airmen should be made to feel that they have fought out here for years, under unbelievably appalling conditions, largely in vain.[38]

In mid October Mountbatten took off for a further conference at Cairo, hoping against hope that the tide could be turned and DRACULA resurrected. He arrived to find the Prime Minister still in Moscow and, being anxious to meet Stalin, at once suggested he should fly there to join the party. An alarmed 'Most Immediate' telegram from Moscow vetoed the idea; such a visit, since Russia was not at war with Japan, might cause endless political reactions. Nor did he do much better once Churchill finally arrived. 'It is too funny . . . ,' recorded Mountbatten, with what must have been hollow laughter, 'meeting again at the same place . . . as last November . . . asking for some help and assistance to our theatre, in almost the same terms as last year.'[39] It was not forthcoming; he should press on with his offensive by land; if he could manage some mini-DRACULA with what resources he had available and a few scrapings from India, then so much the better. Mountbatten had to console himself with Eden's report of what Churchill had said to him on the way to the airport: 'I give Dickie full marks; we gave him a lousy job, and we have given him absolutely no help ever since he has been there, in fact the reverse, but nevertheless he has kept the show running and always turns up smiling, whatever we do to him. We really must try and help him all we can in the future.'

> I record the above [wrote Mountbatten] since it is so rare that one ever hears anything directly encouraging in this way: it is nice to know that one's masters appreciate one's difficulties.[40]

And so it was back to Kandy and the drawing-board. His woes were made all the greater when the demolition of his plans for amphibious operations was made a reason for suggesting that he reduce his staff. Brooke told Wavell that the headquarters was 'hopelessly overgrown',[41] and there were even suggestions by the planners that the Supreme Commander should now accept reality and move to Calcutta.[42]

It also happened that, for a variety of reasons, Mountbatten within a few months parted company with his Deputy Supreme Commander, his Chief of Staff, his Deputy Chief of Staff and all three Commanders-in-Chief. Stilwell's departure was the most conspicuous. The two men had long been in fundamental disharmony. Mountbatten characteristically assumed that, in spite of their differences, Stilwell still cherished affection and respect for his Supreme Commander. Stilwell was equally sure that Mountbatten viewed him with loathing. Both were wrong. Their relationship, however, had grown progressively more strained during July and August over Stilwell's treatment of Wingate's Special Forces after the death of their commander. Stilwell had never rated their prowess highly, but this was no excuse for the callous indifference with which he kept them in the field long after they were due to be recalled and the hostility he displayed towards them and their new commander, Brigadier Lentaigne.

Eventually the Supreme Commander was forced to intervene to point out that they had already served a month longer than the period Wingate had considered the maximum they could be expected to endure.[43] Stilwell was asked to arrange for their immediate withdrawal from the battle. When Stilwell spoke contemptuously of the unit, Mountbatten was so enraged that he sent General Wedemeyer to his deputy's headquarters to demand an apology. It was forthcoming, though grudgingly and not in writing.[44] Nor was Stilwell made more popular at Kandy by a 'March of Time' film called *Background Tokyo*, which concentrated exclusively on his campaign and gave the impression that no other forces were engaged in Burma. 'The South East Asia Command is not referred to,' Mountbatten told Churchill, 'but I am told there are two pictures of myself being social with Madame Chiang Kai-shek!'[45]

There was therefore little grief when, in October 1944, the Generalissimo made his accustomed demand for Stilwell's removal and this time got his way. 'The sheriff has caught up with me and I have been yanked out,' Stilwell told Auchinleck lightly,[46] but his resentment was sharper than his words suggest, and Mountbatten was one of the people he blamed for his humiliation. In this he was unfair. 'Most Englishmen,' Mountbatten told him, 'as you yourself undoubtedly know, find you a difficult man to deal with, but, with the exception of the trouble over Lentaigne . . . I can testify that I have found you both easy and helpful in all matters which I raised in person direct with you.'[47] It was generous of him not to refer to the AXIOM mission as well. 'I was sorry to see Stilwell go,' he told Roosevelt, 'not only because I personally like him, but because it meant that I lost my beloved Al Wedemeyer.'[48]

Stilwell's job was divided into the three parts it should always have been. General Wheeler replaced Wedemeyer at Kandy, General Sultan took over the campaign in north Burma, while Wedemeyer himself moved to Chungking. Mountbatten had high hopes that this last posting would lead to a new readiness to co-operate on the part of Chiang Kai-shek, and a good start was made when the Generalissimo agreed that, in the changed circumstances in Assam and Burma, Chinese troops could now serve under a British general.[49] But the honeymoon did not last long; it could hardly be expected to, for, as Wedemeyer said in his memoirs, he was now in the position of competitor for American favours, and must protect Chinese interests at the expense of SEAC.[50] This Mountbatten found hard to accept. The trouble about their relationship, Wedemeyer remarked after he had been a few months in China, was that 'you still think of me officially as your D.C.O.S. and expect the same reaction to your proposals'. He would promise personal loyalty and straightforward dealing. 'What you cannot expect is complete agreement to your proposals when actually my own actions and yours are determined on Government levels.'[51]

Somerville was the first of the three Commanders-in-Chief to depart. Bruce Fraser was installed by early September 1944. 'I like him so much,' wrote Mountbatten. 'What an improvement on his predecessor.' Fraser showed himself mercifully indifferent to those 'points of principle' that had so bedevilled the relationship between Somerville and Mountbatten; in no time, wrote his Flag Lieutenant, Vernon Merry, 'that whole terrible atmosphere of tension and hostility just melted away'.[52] By the end of November, however, Fraser had moved on with many of his ships to form the new Pacific Fleet. Admiral Power was entrusted with what was left of the East Indies Fleet, though this rump, with its landing-craft and crews, was numerically far larger than the Pacific splinter-group and was also more closely integrated with the rest of South-East Asia Command than Fraser's or Somerville's fleet had ever been.[53] Churchill had insisted that the new post should be filled by an officer who would work in the closest harmony with Mountbatten[54] and Power filled the bill admirably. 'Mount B is easy, and we should hit it off well, I am quite sure,' Power told Cunningham. The Supreme Commander, he said, was going to almost embarrassing pains 'to keep me in the Kandy picture and not to step off his mat'.[55] Mountbatten for his part was equally enthusiastic about his new Commander-in-Chief, though he could never entirely escape the suspicion that the Admiralty had 'transferred their affections to the British

Pacific Fleet'.[56] When Power was appointed to the acting rank of Admiral, Mountbatten's congratulations were delivered with especial fervour, 'because at one time I feared that they were deliberately trying to keep your part of the Fleet . . . at a lower level of importance than Fraser's'.[57]

Next to go was Peirse. Portal originally hoped to send Sholto Douglas as a replacement,[58] then switched to Leigh-Mallory. In his letter welcoming the latter Mountbatten spelt out the conditions for his appointment, notably that 'you entirely accept the fact that I am the S.A.C. in fact as well as in name, and not in any sense a co-ordinating chairman of a committee', and that 'although I will normally take your view on all air operations, I have the over-riding right to reject your views'.[59] It is interesting to find these issues still preoccupying Mountbatten as late as August 1944. In fact, Leigh-Mallory was killed before he could take up his new post. His successor, the New Zealander Keith Park, does not seem to have received a similar ultimatum; possibly Mountbatten knew enough of him to be sure that no displays of independence were likely.

Giffard had been dismissed in May but was at his post till October, his relationship with the Supreme Commander curiously more tranquil than at any time previously. Pownall was looking for a successor in June and identified Oliver Leese as the best candidate 'but he is now heavily committed in Italy'.[60] At one time Mountbatten played with the idea of dispensing with an Army Commander-in-Chief and doing the job himself; he claims that Brooke suggested this to Pownall but the proposal hardly bears the hallmarks of the C.I.G.S.'s thinking. In the end Leese was disengaged from Italy and took over a more extensive command which involved control of the Chinese–American forces as well as the 14th Army.[61] 'I can't tell you how grand it is to have Oliver out here . . . ,' wrote Mountbatten to Montgomery. 'Since it was obviously impossible to pull you away from your battle, it is wonderful being able to get your principal disciple, to carry on your doctrine.'[62]

Last and least desired loss was that of the Chief of Staff, Henry Pownall. At times he had played the nanny too energetically and his judgement was not always impeccable, but Mountbatten had grown to depend on his commonsense, honesty and total loyalty. His health, however, was frail, and by early September it was clear that he could not last much longer. Brooke suggested that Slim might replace him, a proposal Mountbatten rejected brusquely; Slim was indispensable where he was; besides, he was unsuitable for such work, 'his line is command, and he does it very well'. He had previously suggested Generals Swayne or Nye; if both these were still unavailable he would 'have recourse to Lushington. I do not wish this as I think it inappropriate, but if the Army cannot from their resources assist me with a suitable Chief of Staff I see no other alternative.'[63]

Mountbatten was still smarting under the rebuffs of Cairo when he wrote this letter, and its somewhat sour note can therefore perhaps be excused. Brooke did not excuse it. 'I do not consider that you have any reason to imply that the Army is not wishing to assist you,' he wrote. 'I have suggested a name for your consideration of an officer I consider . . . eminently fitted for the appointment. I cannot accept that he is unsuited but am prepared to agree if you state that he cannot be spared from his command.' Lushington, he said, was wholly inappropriate; instead he proposed General Browning. 'I wish to make it quite clear that I am prepared to assist to the utmost in providing you with a suitable Chief of Staff. I do however take exception to the tone of your telegram which fails entirely to take into account the fact that there are other active fronts beyond South East Asia which have to be catered for, and also to your lack of consideration for other people's requirements.'[64]

The final outcome was a happy one. Though Pownall feared that Browning might be 'rather nervy and highly strung' for the job of restraining Mountbatten,[65] he brought to South-East Asia qualities of energy and boldness that were badly needed at that stage of the campaign. He arrived in mid December: 'It is grand value having a young man like Boy [Browning] as my new Chief of Staff,' commented Mountbatten, 'he is only three years older than me' – a deliberately casual comment which none the less reveals how arduous it must have been constantly to order around men his senior by a decade or more.[66] In March 1945 it was rumoured that Browning had been killed in a plane crash. 'It was not until I was faced with the prospect of your having been extinguished', wrote Mountbatten, 'that I realised how very much you had come to mean to me in these last few weeks, and what a tremendous difference you have made to the whole command.'[67]

When Mountbatten returned from Cairo in October 1944 he still believed something might be saved from the wreck of DRACULA. 'I am making every effort to scrape together sufficient forces to start amphibious operations,' he told Roosevelt on 20 November.[68] 'I do hope you can start those amphibious operations,' replied the President. 'Those people in China are having a truly hard time.'[69] The message can only have produced wry smiles in Kandy, following as it did an unequivocal declaration from Washington that no additional landing-craft or other such facilities could be made available.[70] 'I am afraid that these continual postponements are Hell for you,' wrote Eden sympathetically. 'If it is any comfort, we are in lots of trouble here too, what with Greece and all!'[71]

What was of greater comfort was that in all the sectors – the north, where the Chinese army from Yunnan and the American–Chinese forces under General Sultan were inexorably clearing the road to China; the Arakan, where Christison too was pushing forward; and, above all, in the centre, beyond Imphal – the Japanese were in retreat. On 16 December Mountbatten flew low over the battle-front:

> Beneath us was a most inspiring sight – an army in hot pursuit of a beaten enemy. . . . Down the River Chindwin an endless stream of D.U.K.W.s and other craft were carrying soldiers; along the track on the river bank lorries and motor vehicles of all types were ploughing on in an endless stream like the traffic leading to Epsom on Derby Day. Alongside them marched the infantry in single file, interspersed with mule trains. It is just one vast forward surge, and one of the most exhilarating sights I have ever seen.[72]

Conditions were appalling, yet they were far worse for the Japanese, starved of supplies and transport, inadequately prepared to resist the ravages of malaria. It was now that the efforts that had been poured into hygiene and combating the mosquito began to pay full dividends; we have succeeded, wrote Mountbatten proudly, in turning the notoriously disease-ridden Kabaw Valley into 'a reasonably healthy and safe place for our troops to operate in'.[73]

Yet Mountbatten still could not accept that this was the right way to reconquer Burma. Slim's instructions were ambivalent. He was to occupy north Burma. If in so doing the Japanese forces had been so badly mauled that the way was open to Mandalay and Rangoon, he was to push on. If not, he was to hold the enemy and 'withdraw troops for more profitable operations'.[74] Before the point was reached when a final decision had to be made came victory in the north. 'Following for President, Prime Minister and Combined Chiefs of Staff,' telegraphed Mountbatten on 22 January 1945. 'The first part of order I received at Quebec has been carried out. The land-route to China is open.'[75] The news caused satisfaction and some mirth in Washington. General McFarland telephoned General Hull to suggest that an acknowledgement should be sent. How about, suggested Hull, 'noting with satisfaction the great accomplishments which you have carried out reluctantly'? That's right, agreed McFarland. Let's say, 'We are relieved to find that despite your reluctance you have finally accomplished what we were interested in!'[76] The final congratulatory message was expressed with greater decorum and less frankness.

The opening of the road should have meant that larger forces were freed to aid the 14th Army in its drive south. The reverse proved true. For one thing, with his land-link to India now assured, Chiang Kai-shek lost interest in the Burma campaign. For another, Roosevelt had not been exaggerating when he said that the Chinese were having 'a truly hard time'. A fierce Japanese offensive was threatening the air-base at Kunming and as early as November 1944 Wedemeyer had announced that he must withdraw two divisions and supporting air-combat groups from Burma. When Mountbatten protested, the Chiefs of Staff ruled that such a move was essential, and Carton de Wiart, Britain's military representative in Chungking, agreed that the demand was reasonable. 'I do not think you are fair to the Generalissimo,' he wrote, '. . . if you put yourself in his position, what else could you do?'[77]

This was only a beginning. Wedemeyer, now viewing Asian strategy through new spectacles, told Chiang Kai-shek early in January 1945 that 'the center of strategic gravity should shift east into China rather than south to Rangoon'. A week later he was 'prepared to recommend that the entire Chinese Army in India' should return to its homeland.[78] In March Mountbatten flew to Chungking to try to persuade the Generalissimo to modify his stand. He found his ally obdurate; no Chinese troops would operate south of Mandalay. In that case, said the Supreme Commander, let them all be withdrawn as quickly as possible so as to relieve the British and Indians of the burden of supplying them. The campaign in central Burma was so far advanced that he could face the loss of the Chinese troops with equanimity, but to provide the planes to transport them home was another matter. It would be still more difficult to manage without the U.S. 10th Air Force. Churchill appealed to Marshall's 'sense of what is fair and right between us' to ensure that Mountbatten was not stripped of his air support.[79] The appeal was heard; it was pledged that the 10th Air Force would not be transferred until the monsoon broke in June or Rangoon was captured.

Though the situation had temporarily been saved it was evident that, with the withdrawal of the American–Chinese forces to China and a term set to the participation of the 10th Air Force, the Americans would henceforth play a much smaller role in SEAC. General Wheeler privately urged that they should disengage entirely.[80] To this Mountbatten would have been resolutely opposed. He believed in the international status of his Command, not just as a reflection of its real power but as a concept of peculiar value. The alliance was not the sum of its parts; two and two made five at least. He would have pressed for American representation in his headquarters even though no solitary technician or fighting man remained outside it. Yet the strains on the alliance grew every day. General Sultan assured Marshall that his relationship with the Supreme Commander was still 'on a very frank and cordial basis. . . . There is absolutely no friction of any kind evident at this time.' But he feared that British and American interests might soon diverge: 'I foresee further problems after Burma has been cleared of the Japanese and SEAC advances towards Malaya.'[81]

That moment was fast approaching. In Arakan a small but highly successful amphibious operation captured Akyab. Christison had assembled his force more quickly than had been expected and was in a position to attack before the press corps was in position. Frank Owen, who was even more conscious than the Supreme Commander of the desirability of ample publicity for the Command's first seaborne assault, urged delay. Mountbatten seconded his efforts and signalled Christison that a cyclone was threatening: 'But having turned over responsibility to Force Commanders, leave final decision to them.' Christison took the Supreme Commander at his word and pushed ahead – there was no cyclone (which would have been a freakish rarity at that season), little publicity and total military success.[82] Mountbatten certainly pressed for delay on grounds that were more political than military, but bore no grudge when Christison put the latter first and ignored the Supreme Commander's overtures.

By now the extent of Slim's victory in the centre was becoming apparent. Operations in Burma, wrote Brooke in mid January, 'have taken quite a different turn, and there is now just a possibility of actually taking Rangoon from the north'.[83] Confident that Mountbatten would somehow hold together the air support essential for his sustained advance, Slim pushed on boldly towards Mandalay and Rangoon. It was evident that it was going to be an exceedingly close thing if the capital were to be reached before the monsoon broke. If the advance faltered, the 14th Army would be bogged down in the jungle, possibly bereft of the support of the American Air Force. In mid March Slim proposed a mini-DRACULA – a sea and airborne landing at Rangoon which would secure the port and take the Japanese in the rear. Mountbatten delighted in the idea; Oliver Leese did not. The honeymoon between the Supreme Commander and his new Commander-in-Chief briskly ended. Leese at first rejected the idea out of hand, then grudgingly agreed to it in principle but did his best to whittle it down.[84] On 10 April Mountbatten flew to Leese's headquarters and personally countermanded the Commander-in-Chief's instruction that no parachutists should be used in the operation.[85]

Mandalay fell on 20 March. 'Such is the frailty of human nature', wrote Air Vice-Marshal Vincent in the first draft of his memoirs, 'that the Supremo and General Leese . . . were both "hurt" that we had done the triumphal entry and not they. It was apparently resented that those who were actually responsible had taken the credit.'[86] The remark was dropped by the time the book was printed, whether because Vincent decided it was uncharitable or libellous it is hard to say. Certainly the lack of publicity which Vincent attributed to the Supreme Commander cannot fairly be blamed on him; he was upset at the little attention paid to the victory by the British papers, due mainly to the superior attraction of the advances of Patton and Montgomery in Europe.[87] He himself visited Mandalay two days after its occupation: 'It was sad to see the ground where David and I played polo burned black as a result of the battle,' was the only comment he made which expressed less than complete satisfaction with the way things had gone.[88]

And so the race for Rangoon was on. Mountbatten believed that it was of the first importance that the airfield at Toungoo north of the city should be captured by 25 April so that close air-support would be available for the landing on 1 May. Slim was doubtful but agreed that the Supreme Commander should visit General Messervy, who had succeeded Scoones in December 1944, and urge him on. On 18 April Mountbatten flew to Meiktila and saw Messervy:

> He thought it would be impossible to get there [Toungoo] before the first week in May, but I told him that I would personally take responsibility for his getting anything up to 3000 men killed in an attempt to speed up the advance, and he promised to go down that afternoon to the forward elements of the 5th Division, and stick a sharp spur into them.[89]

Toungoo was taken on 22 April, with relatively light loss of life.

Three days before the landings were due Mountbatten was prostrated with a vicious attack of amoebic dysentery. He retreated to bed but held the most important meetings in his room and was constantly in touch by scrambler telephone. 'Supremo is holding up very well . . . ,' Browning told Brooke, 'and it has by no means got him down. It does however enable me to exercise an increasing control upon him!'[90] For the first time Kandy operated as it was intended, in the role of headquarters controlling a combined operation. From ULTRA sources Mountbatten learned that the puppet Burmese Government was busy securing its line of retreat; that Japanese civilians were being turned into volunteer units to help defend the city; finally, that the code-books were being burned and the machines smashed.[91] Still, it was expected that anything up to 40,000 Japanese would defend Rangoon. Only when aircraft flew over the city a few hours before the landing and saw the sign 'Japs gone' triumphantly scrawled on the roof of the prison was it realized that the enemy had fled; DRACULA would meet with no resistance. Slim's nearest men were still some thirty miles to the north; but though they had lost the race, it was they, wrote Mountbatten, who 'had really won the battle; for if their rapid advance had not forced Lieutenant-General Kimura to evacuate the port, DRACULA ... would have met with severe opposition'.[92]

> I can't tell you how thrilling the race to Rangoon has been [Mount-batten wrote to Patricia]. Unless we could capture the port by the monsoon we should get the 14th Army bogged down and confined to a single tarmac road which could easily be held by the Japs, and further the storms would be so bad we couldn't do a landing.
>
> If we landed before the 14th Army was within 50 miles from the City, the defences could be so strong as to resist the assault. You can imagine what a thrill the race was.
>
> The first day it was OK to carry out the landing was also the day on which the monsoon broke, as it is a fortnight early this year. We watched the monsoon predictions advance with horror in a race with the 14th Army, and we won out after more than a year's constant advance by a few hours!![93]

# CHAPTER 23

## *The End of the War*

SLIM HAD BARELY BEEN GIVEN a chance to wear his laurels before an attempt was made to wrest them from him. The bizarre imbroglio, during which he was first dismissed by Leese and then not merely reinstated but promoted to take Leese's place, has now been reconstructed in most of its detail, but still inspires a degree of incredulity in the reader.

The incident took place against a background of increasing irritation between Leese on one side and the Supreme Commander and the other Commanders-in-Chief on the other. Browning's explanation for the ill-feeling was that Leese fancied himself a second Montgomery, but lacked the talent.[1] Montgomery himself was in part responsible for this illusion. Mountbatten, he told Leese, was 'a most delightful person but I fear his knowledge of how to make war is not very great!! You ought to go out there as his Army C.-in-C. and keep him on the rails!'[2] Leese therefore expected to be undisputed master in his own house but, instead, found Slim in control of the battlefield and he himself, as Browning told Brooke, serving 'a Supreme Commander who is an outstanding leader . . . and possesses a sounder and quicker brain'.[3] He reacted with piqued insubordination. In May 1945 he not only rejected out of hand a proposal of Mountbatten, but did so in an offensive telegram which he then copied to all and sundry. He earned and duly received a fierce rebuke: 'A stupid, vain and dangerous man,' Mountbatten told Edwina, 'and like all bullies, collapses when really stood up to.'[4] For a few weeks things settled down.

On 3 May Leese came to Kandy, where Mountbatten was still in the throes of his amoebic dysentery. He announced that Slim was a tired man, who deserved relief and was, anyway, not proficient at amphibious warfare. He should be left behind to conduct mopping-up operations in Burma, while the 14th Army was handed over to General Christison, who had made a success of the landings at Akyab and was better qualified to handle the next phase, a maritime invasion of Malaya. Mountbatten was surprised at the suggestion that a victorious army and its general should be so quickly separated, but did not rule out the idea. The tone of the interview can only be surmised, but General Browning, who was present, told Brooke: 'The Supreme Commander informed Oliver that he could not countenance any change which might carry the slightest indication that Slim was being removed from his Command. He informed Oliver that he should handle the matter extremely carefully, that he had the highest opinion of and confidence in Slim, and that he would not consider anything which might affect Slim's future.'[5]

Furnished with what was apparently a clear directive, Leese flew on to Akyab to see Christison. 'Dickie', he told him, 'has felt for some time that Slim has become a very tired man, and I must say I agree.' Mountbatten had decided that Slim should be relieved. 'I wanted Dickie to see him and do it himself, but he refused, and said it was my job as his immediate superior.'[6] Christison was to take Slim's place. And so Leese went on his way, leaving an exultant if surprised Christison behind him. When he reached Slim's head-quarters, his greeting was: 'Before we talk of anything else, I must tell you that I have decided to give Christison command of the 14th Army. . . . I do not consider you capable of planning a large-scale amphibious operation; so I do not think it would be fair either to the 14th Army or yourself to leave you in command of it.' With the consciousness of a good job done, Leese then telegraphed Brooke with the news of his doings and returned to his head-quarters, leaving Slim, as he imagined, 'thinking it over' and 'at heart happy'.[7]

Slim was far from happy, and as the news spread among his officers fury mounted. 'Oliver "Twist" and Mountbatten must be out of their minds,' wrote Jim Godwin, a member of Slim's staff. 'I never trusted that affected, silk-handkerchief-waving guardsman.' Slim decided he could not accept the proffered post and must retire or find a job elsewhere. Mountbatten later told Brooke that he was 'very worried when he saw what was happening, and was intending to take the matter up with Leese'.[8] While he was still hesitating, however, a thunderbolt arrived from Whitehall. Brooke was astonished at Leese's telegram. The Commander-in-Chief had no business even to discuss the matter with Slim; no change could be countenanced except on Mount-batten's personal recommendation.[9] Mountbatten hurriedly summoned Leese to Kandy and told him that Slim's dismissal must be reversed. Accord-ing to Browning, Leese was contrite and agreed that he had not carried out his instructions, but the confusion 'will inevitably make for friction between . . . the two Commanders'.[10]

With the blood of one Commander-in-Chief already on his hands, Mountbatten was not unnaturally reluctant to dismiss another. Brooke, however, left him little choice; Leese had lost the confidence of his subordin-ates and must go. He suggested that Slim should take Leese's place and Stopford replace Slim.[11] Christison saw Leese on 5 June at Calcutta. 'I gather I'm carrying the can for Dickie over this,' he remembers his former Com-mander-in-Chief remarking. If there was any can, it was Leese who had made it for himself. His considered judgement was more generous. 'On no account do I want you to think that I am blaming Mountbatten for what happened,' he wrote in 1973. 'He certainly gave me no authority to sack Slim.'[12]

Mountbatten, debilitated as he was by amoebic dysentery, had acted with unusual irresolution. At another time, Leese would have left Kandy on 3 May with instructions so precise that even a man of his arrogance would hardly have transcended them; the Supreme Commander would have moved more quickly to repair the damage and not awaited an outraged telegram from Brooke; Mountbatten would have himself concluded that Leese's position was untenable and called for his dismissal. The episode did not show him at his best. Yet it did nothing to poison his relationship with Slim. There were those who said that Mountbatten was jealous of Slim, determined that there should not be 'two Kings of Burma'.[13] On the contrary, each man valued the other highly, knowing his own abilities but knowing, too, that the other had complementary strengths which were essential for success. Mountbatten always believed that Slim was one of the finest soldiers of his generation and was to pull every string to ensure that he was appointed C.I.G.S., against the inveterate opposition of Montgomery and others. He visited Slim many years later when the Field Marshal, as he had then become, was on his death-bed. When Lady Slim entered the room to say that it was time to leave she heard her husband murmur: 'We did it together, old boy.'[14] Their partnership won the war in Burma.

With victory in Burma assured, attention turned to the future battlefield, and a new cause for dissension among the Allies was uncovered. After some havering, French Indochina had eventually been included with Siam within the Generalissimo's sphere of influence. When he first visited Chungking Mountbatten took up this question and got Chiang Kai-shek to accept that SEAC forces would be free to invade either country if they were in a position to do so first, and that in the meantime they could carry out necessary 'pre-operational activities'. This was the so-called 'Gentleman's Agreement'; as with so many similar accords, when it came to the point the gentlemen were not at all clear to what they had agreed. Mountbatten insisted that the only limit on his freedom was an undertaking to tell the Chinese what he was doing; Wedemeyer maintained with equal certainty that every operation must obtain the Generalissimo's clearance in advance.[15] In so doing he was acting partly to protect what he saw as legitimate Chinese interests, partly out of suspicion of British motives. Mountbatten was convinced that the best way to procure the defeat of the Japanese in Indochina was by involving the French as actively as possible; the Americans, on the other hand, were far from reconciled to the restoration of the French colonial empire and reluctant to agree to any commitment that might make that end more likely. Since most of Mountbatten's projected operations in Indochina involved some degree of French participation, Wedemeyer viewed them with little enthusiasm. To Mountbatten this seemed like treachery. While on his staff, he told Eden, Wedemeyer had enthusiastically backed operations in Indochina; now 'he seems to think it his duty to try and upset all the arrangements which he had subscribed to before'.[16] The Americans were no less offended. 'There must be an extraordinary importance to the clandestine operations being carried out by Mountbatten in Indochina', remarked Marshall, 'to justify the possible creation not only of ill will but of a feeling that there is a lack of good faith.'[17]

The rights and wrongs of the dispute are impossible to establish, depending as they do on recollections of who said what and surmises as to what they meant by it. Both men seem to have behaved with unnecessary rigidity. Wedemeyer was in a difficult position, caught, as he once put it, 'betwixt and between, a mediary acting for a British lion and the Chinese dragon. Both of you puff steam and growl at me, and purr like kittens at each other.'[18] The British Chiefs of Staff backed Mountbatten, though without much enthusiasm. 'I admit to having some sympathy for Wedemeyer's point of view . . . ,' wrote Ismay. 'The one thing that must be avoided at all costs is friction between your command and his.'[19] Friction there was, but no worse, thanks not so much to the good sense of the two protagonists as to the rapid development of the war which made their squabble irrelevant.

Against this acrimonious background it was a relief for Mountbatten to meet an American who seemed disinclined to question his motives. General MacArthur had begun by resenting the creation of SEAC, and fearing that Mountbatten would prove a threat to his own independence of action. This, however, was long forgotten, and Mountbatten was greeted with flattering enthusiasm when he visited Manila. 'I had a long and interesting conversation with MacArthur,' he recorded in his diary; 'Or, to be more precise, I listened to a fascinating monologue, and found the same difficulty in trying to chip in as I have no doubt most people find in trying to chip in to my conversation.'[20] The next two days MacArthur devoted almost exclusively to his visitor. Mountbatten's initial good impression was fortified:

> Contrary to popular conception, he gives the impression of being a rather shy and sensitive man, who regards compliance with the needs of publicity as a duty. . . . He does not look at all fierce or commanding until he puts his famous embroidered cap on. As we went out together to face the photographers, and he pulled his cap on, his whole manner changed. His jaw stuck out, he looked aggressive and

tough, but as soon as the photographers had finished, he relaxed completely, took off his hat, and was his old charming self. . . .

. . . I fully admit I am completely under his spell: he is one of the most charming and remarkable characters I have ever met, and so sympathetic and friendly towards the South East Asia Command.[21]

A British liaison officer, Colonel Wilkinson, wrote of MacArthur: 'He is shrewd, selfish, proud, remote, highly-strung and vastly vain. He has imagination, self-confidence, physical courage and charm, but no humour about himself, no regard for truth and is unaware of these defects. He mistakes his emotions and ambitions for principle. With moral depth he would be a great man: as it is he is a near-miss.'[22] It is tempting to speculate how far Mountbatten's enthusiasm was based on recognition of strengths and weaknesses similar to his own. Enough in Wilkinson's harsh judgement can, with some verisimilitude, be applied to MacArthur's fellow Supreme Commander to make the parallel a plausible one. The most profound difference between the two men was that Mountbatten was a far more generous being. He was not selfish, not remote; vain certainly, but not possessed by cold arrogance; ambitious, but with a saving commonsense which told him that his own aggrandizement was not the end-all and be-all of existence. He was endearingly able to laugh at himself. Though the truth in his hands often suffered a sea-change, he was genuinely surprised and upset when instances of this were pointed out to him. He was impetuous and easily misled, as could be seen in his judgement of MacArthur, but these weaknesses were founded on good will, a dislike of half-measures, a determination to act vigorously and for what he felt to be the best. It is doubtful if MacArthur's opinion of his visitor was as flattering as Mountbatten's of his host; in Mountbatten's warm-hearted susceptibility lies the most marked difference between their characters.

The next move after the reconquest of Burma was to be a major amphibious invasion of Malaya. At last the demands of the war in Europe made possible an operation of the kind which Mountbatten had been appointed to command. ZIPPER was to be his apotheosis as Supreme Commander. Originally it had been intended to precede the attack on Malaya by the seizure of the small island of Phuket off the west coast of Siam. This limited operation, inevitably code-named ROGER, was acceptable to the Americans, who were still doubtful whether the larger forces needed for ZIPPER could properly be spared.[23] On reflection, however, Mountbatten decided that it would nevertheless be better to strike directly at the main objective. He would capture

Singapore before the end of 1945, he told Eden, 'provided that the light fleet-carriers which were provisionally allotted to me are not sent to the Pacific. So I am feeling very optimistic.'[24]

His proviso was a trifle disingenuous. The Admiralty, as he well knew, were set on sending the carrier-force to join Fraser's Pacific Fleet. 'We turned down Mountbatten's attempt to steal the light fleet-carriers,' Cunningham wrote in his diary with some satisfaction a week later.[25] When Mountbatten got back to London in July he was told by the Fifth Sea Lord, Admiral Troubridge, that the decision to remove the carriers had been taken by Cunningham alone, even though Fraser had said that there was time for them to take part in ZIPPER before they were needed in the Pacific.[26] Emboldened by the admission, Mountbatten raised the matter in the Defence Committee of the Cabinet. 'He is always trying this method of putting pressure on the Admiralty,' grumbled Cunningham. 'I said I would look into it.'[27] The First Sea Lord later taxed Mountbatten with disloyalty in introducing this issue into such a forum, to which Mountbatten replied that there was no point in discussing it in the Chiefs of Staff since Brooke and Portal would inevitably accept Cunningham's opinion on a naval matter. 'I gave him a pretty good doing,' concluded Cunningham, 'but promised to put his name in on my recommendation for R[ear]-A[dmiral] next batch.'[28]

Mountbatten in the end had to do without his carriers, but a worse threat to ZIPPER existed. On 8 June P. J. Grigg announced that service abroad for the soldiers of SEAC would be cut from three years, eight months to three years, four months. Without consultation and with almost no warning, Mountbatten was deprived of some of the skilled personnel most badly needed for the forthcoming operation. For once the Chiefs of Staff were solidly behind him: 'It looks much like an electioneering dodge,' wrote Cunningham.[29] Mountbatten protested vociferously to Ismay about this 'stab in the back'. 'The 32,300 officers and men who get home earlier . . . will presumably be delighted, but the million odd men in the Navy, Army and Air Forces . . . who are now condemned to inactivity, will moulder and rot.'[30] Mountbatten attributed the measure, in part at least, to active malevolence on the part of Grigg. 'He doesn't like you,' Pownall had warned him some time earlier. 'Now when P.J. doesn't like someone, he does not neglect an opportunity to stick in a knife.' 'As you know, my weakness is to think that everybody likes me,' replied the Supreme Commander wistfully, 'but this does not extend to the Secretary of State for War.'[31] But though Grigg's ill will may have added some savour to his announcement, it seems most unlikely that it was responsible for it. The decision was, as Cunningham surmised, a political one, taken largely to win advantage in the approaching election.

The loss of the veterans forced Mountbatten to delay ZIPPER by a month.

In July 1945 he flew to Berlin to attend the Potsdam Conference which followed the end of the European war. General Marshall took him aside and revealed to him in the strictest secrecy that the United States had evolved an atomic bomb and proposed to drop it in early August. This must mean the rapid end of the war. That evening Churchill broke the same news. 'He advised me to take all necessary steps to compete with capitulation as soon after this date as possible. I therefore sent a telegram to Boy Browning to take all the necessary steps, without of course being able to give him the reason.'[32] If ZIPPER was to take place at all, it seemed that it would not be in the face of effective opposition.

When Churchill had finished with Mountbatten, he invited him to call at Downing Street next time he was in London. 'We will talk about your future, as I have great plans in store,' said the Prime Minister. Mountbatten was less excited by the prospect than he might otherwise have been. Some time previously he had asked Peter Murphy to prepare an analysis of the likely result of the General Election that was then imminent. Murphy had predicted an overwhelming victory for Labour, and all Mountbatten's instincts told him that his friend was right. 'It was a mournful and eerie feeling,' he wrote in his diary, 'to sit there talking plans with a man who seemed so confident that they would come off, and I felt equally confident that he would be out of office within 24 hours.'[33]

Though it saddened Mountbatten to think that the Prime Minister, to whom he owed so much, was about to face his downfall, the setback to the Conservative party caused him neither regret nor surprise. Unlike Edwina, who still saw herself as a committed supporter of the left-wing, he prided himself on being non-political – a stance which both represented his real feelings and was imposed on him as a naval officer and a member of the royal family. He was, indeed, singularly unconcerned with political theorizing. A pragmatist in all things, he accepted cheerfully whoever his leaders might be, and judged them by the speed with which he could persuade them to adopt his favoured course and their energy in pursuing it once adopted. Nevertheless, his egalitarian instincts and generalized belief in progress told him that it was time for a change. Something had to happen to accommodate the aspirations of the returning soldiers, sailors and airmen and, though Mountbatten was not sure precisely what it might be, he felt that it was more likely to come from the Labour party than the Conservatives. On neither personal nor political grounds did he find difficulty in accommodating himself to the new Government; in the four days that he spent in London after the Potsdam Conference, he contrived to have conversations with Attlee, Alexander, Bevin, Cripps, George Hall, Isaacs, Lawson, Lord Nathan, Pethick-Lawrence, Lord Stansgate and Tom Williams. He encouraged the King to look on the bright side of matters. 'You will find that your position will be greatly strengthened,' Mountbatten told his cousin, 'since you are now the old experienced campaigner on whom a new and partly inexperienced Government will lean for advice and guidance.'[34]

Mountbatten was dining at Windsor on 6 August. 'Everybody was in good form as the atomic bomb had just fallen,' he wrote in his diary. He would have been prescient indeed if he had foreseen even a tithe of the consequences that were to flow from this cataclysmic happening. At the time it represented only a short-cut to the ending of the war, a measure which he never doubted saved literally millions of lives, most of them Japanese. A week later he was alone with Attlee when a secretary burst in with the news that the Japanese had surrendered. Churchill telephoned him an hour later. 'Well, Dickie . . . I hope that you have made all plans and that you are ready to send your first aeroplane into Singapore tomorrow. Mind you, I no longer have the right to talk to you like this, but speak as a friend who hopes we will press on quickly.'[35]

The first problem was whether to cancel ZIPPER. The expeditionary force had to get to Malaya somehow and nobody could be quite certain whether all the Japanese forces would obey the surrender order, so it was decided to let the fleet sail to schedule, though stripped of some of its trimmings. On 9 September the Allied forces went ashore, a double landing in the Port Dickson area and over the Morib beaches at Port Swettenham. The planning of ZIPPER has been criticized with some justice and, less reasonably, it has been maintained that if there had been armed resistance the invading forces would have met with a bloody reverse. Censure relates mainly to the breakdown of communications, and the choice of a site near Port Swettenham, which would have led to the landing becoming bogged down and being exposed to counter-attack. The point about the communications can be quickly dismissed. Communications on the Morib beaches were deplorable – at one point the only link between land and sea was through an advanced observation-post of the naval artillery – but this arose because the naval Force Commander had elected to remove H.M.S. *Bulolo*, the communications headquarters ship, so as to provide himself with a comfortable base when he attended the surrender ceremony at Singapore. By definition this could not have happened if fighting had still been going on.[36]

The choice of landing-site was more culpable. Mountbatten himself visited the Morib beaches in 1972 and was amazed by the apparent firmness of the sands, concealing soft mud below. 'I can hardly blame the people who gave me the intelligence,' he concluded.[37] Blame there must be, however. The Combined Operations Pilotage Parties – known as COPP or, more informally, 'Mountbatten's Private Navy', had sent a team ashore but certain key officers had failed to return. Brave men doing a difficult job under conditions of appalling discomfort and danger,[38] they had nevertheless given a clean bill of health to beaches that should have been shunned. The armour sank axle-deep into the sands below low-water mark even before it confronted the worse hazard of the mangrove swamps ahead. 'Beach turned out to be far worse than anticipated,' wrote the Force Commander, Ouvry Roberts, in his diary. 'On the beaches we found that 47 vehicles were bogged and drowned.'[39]

What is in question is not a disaster but a potentially costly setback. The Japanese would have been taken by surprise. Successful deception operations had so reduced their anyway limited resources that only one battalion of low-calibre and lightly armed infantry was available to resist the landings. If these troops had got into position in time they would still have been pushed aside, even without the help of armour. The landing at Port Dickson some thirty miles away went without difficulty and would quickly have relieved whatever pressure there was on the other beach-head. Nevertheless, setback there might have been, and many lives lost. For this somebody must be held responsible.

At the lowest level it must be the reconnaissance parties who so misjudged the beaches. At a higher level General Roberts has no doubts: 'I accept the responsibility as mine. I made the plan. I never thought of what would happen below low-water mark. I should have. Lack of experience, I suppose.'[40] In the last resort, however, the Supreme Commander would have taken the credit for victory and borne the blame for defeat. Outright defeat there would not have been, but for the sake of his reputation it was just as well that the landings were made without opposition.

Mountbatten had other things on his mind. The problem of prisoners-of-war was a pressing anxiety. The Japanese prisoners were bad enough. The Supreme Commander visited a camp in India and was dismayed by their surliness and ill discipline: 'When I think of the way the Japanese overwork their Prisoners-of-War, and flog them at the slightest excuse, I am horrified to think that when the Japanese are the Prisoners-of-War and we are the jailers, they seem to get the better of us.'[41]

This could easily be remedied. The plight of the Allied prisoners was more troublesome. MacArthur insisted that he must take the Japanese surrender in Tokyo on 2 September before surrenders could be accepted in the outlying territories, and the British Chiefs of Staff had told Mountbatten that he must conform to this directive.[42] Meanwhile, however, Allied prisoners-of-war were in the last stages of malnutrition and in fear of their lives from vengeful guards. Officially nothing could be done before 2 September, but in practice aid was parachuted into many of the camps. 'I have been going into the question of our Prisoners-of-War and it seems we here have been rather caught with our trousers down,' Mountbatten had told Ismay a fortnight before. Edwina must come out to advise. 'Perhaps you could obtain the P.M.'s blessing – verbally – as I would not like him to read in the papers she'd come out! . . . She *really* does know her stuff and can help.'[43]

She really did and could. Already in March and April she had completed a gruelling 34,000-mile tour of the area, working with such total dedication that her two A.D.C.s finished up in hospital. On 23 August she had reappeared, operating often far ahead of the Allied forces in areas where she had no idea whether she would encounter dissident Japanese, rebellious nationalists or miscellaneous brigands. She was with Mountbatten when they visited the notorious Changi jail only a few hours after liberation. The impatient prisoners, awaiting the invasion, had christened him 'Linger-longer Louis'. He arrived, as one prisoner, Russell Braddon, remembered, 'in his tropical whites, and never did a man look more glittering, glamorous and splendidly handsome'. He stepped on to his traditional soap-box. 'I'm sorry I didn't get here sooner,' he began. 'Oh, I know what you called me. So now I'm going to tell you exactly why I lingered so long.' And, simply and convincingly, he told them of the obstacles that had prevented an earlier victory. 'It was a magical moment.'[44]

The timing of the surrender was not the only issue on which Mountbatten began to doubt his first impressions of MacArthur:

> I am sure that your views coincide with mine [he wrote], namely, that it will be the greatest mistake to be soft with the Japanese. The fact that you have been prevented from inflicting the crushing [defeat] . . . will, I fear, enable the Japanese leaders to delude their people into thinking they were defeated only by the scientists and not in battle, unless we can so humble them that the completeness of defeat is brought home to them.
>
> Normally I am not a vindictive person, but I cannot help feeling that unless we really are tough with all the Japanese leaders they will be able to build themselves up eventually for another war.[45]

In a letter to Carton de Wiart he went even farther, arguing that the war should have continued until the Emperor had arrived in Manila to surrender in person. This might have involved two or three more weeks' fighting, even more atomic bombs, but 'it would have destroyed for all time the feudal and militaristic structure of Japan, which now looks like being saved'.[46] MacArthur saw things differently. In particular, he considered that the surrender of swords was an archaic practice, likely to lead to loss of face and a breakdown in discipline. To Mountbatten this seemed an argument for, rather than against, the exercise. He insisted that in his zone swords should be surrendered by all senior officers in formal ceremonies in front of their men, and distributed the spoils among his own officers and selected beneficiaries at home. The process did not give satisfaction only to the British: Lee Kuan Yew described the 'final humiliation of these little warriors' as 'one of the greatest moments of the history of South East Asia'.[47]

Inevitably there were large areas where the Japanese had to be used to maintain order, even after the surrender, but Mountbatten only reluctantly had recourse to their aid. When it was proposed that commendation cards should be issued to certain former enemy soldiers who had done good work in helping the Allies, Mountbatten ruled categorically that in no circumstances should any form of commendation be issued to any Japanese. Richard Kirby came to Kandy as a member of the Australian War Crimes Commission. He argued the case for leniency. 'I'd be more stern than that,' said Mountbatten. 'If I had my way I'd shoot about twenty of them – you've got to do something to satisfy the bloodlust. Then, I'd officially kick about 200 or 300 of them in the arse in front of all the rest, and I'd let them go back to their countries with reprimands. And that would be the end of the whole show, old man.'[48] The American General Arnold found him particularly vengeful about the Japanese royal family. He thought they were all morons, inbred and degenerate, wrote Arnold in his diary. He says 'the royal family should all be liquidated. He knows them personally.'[49]

SEAC's own formal surrender ceremony took place at Singapore on 12 September. After the signing, Mountbatten ordered the Japanese to withdraw. 'I have never seen six more villainous, depraved or brutal faces in my life,' he wrote in his diary. 'I shudder to think what it would have been like to be in their power. When they got off their chairs and shambled out, they looked like a bunch of gorillas, with great baggy breeches and knuckles almost trailing on the ground.' In the middle of the formalities the Chinese representative pulled out a camera and began to photograph the proceedings: 'Not even Hollywood, had they been called upon to stage such a ceremony, could have thought up the idea of a Chinese delegate taking pictures.' After the ceremony the Supreme Commander drove two miles back to his headquarters 'through densely packed crowds to one never-ending thunderous wall of cheers. . . . I think it is a remarkable demonstration of the delight of the people of Singapore to find the British back once more.' At a less emotional time Mountbatten might not have been so tendentious in his explanation of the crowd's enthusiasm; in the moment of victory, however, he may fairly be pardoned some looseness of political analysis.

'To receive the unconditional surrender of half a million enemy soldiers, sailors and airmen must be an event which happens to few people in the world,' Mountbatten reflected. 'I was very conscious that this was the greatest day of my life.'[50] He had, indeed, come a long way since he had first arrived at Delhi nearly two years before. Yet the most taxing period of his time as Supreme Commander still lay ahead.

# CHAPTER 24

## *Post Surrender Tasks*

TO BE A SUPREME COMMANDER is by definition a lonely task; for Mount-batten the solitude was peculiarly painful. More than ever he craved female companionship: 'I do feel the need of opening my heart to a woman and not another man when I'm worried,' he told Patricia.[1] Towards the end of the war it seemed that his relationship with his wife might be revitalized when Edwina's established lover married. Mountbatten's letter to his wife was characteristically generous:

> I must tell you again how deeply and sincerely I feel for you at this moment when, however unselfish you may be about A.'s engage-ment, the fact that it is bound to alter the relationship – though I feel convinced not the friendship – which has existed between you, is bound to upset you emotionally and make you feel unhappy.
>
> You have however still got the love and genuine affection of two chaps – A. and me – and the support of all your many friends.
>
> You have only one more bad patch in front of you – the week A. gets married. After that they will presumably live a year or two abroad, and when next you meet I feel the difficulties will have disappeared. . . .
>
> A. always knew that I had accepted the fact that after the war you were at liberty to get married and I could not let either of you get the impression that anything I had ever done had stood in the way.[2]

The possibility of divorce had occurred to Mountbatten on many occa-sions over the previous years. Should Edwina not be allowed the liberty she seemed to crave; might he not be happier by himself or remarried to someone more amenable, more indulgent to his needs, more relaxed? The thought was never very seriously pursued, however, and he would have been disconcerted and distressed if Edwina had been the one to propose it. However imperfect their marriage, both parties knew that the other possessed certain qualities that could hardly be found elsewhere. Each respected profoundly the other's abilities. The economic and social arguments were formidable enough but what kept them together was, above all, their belief in the family and their conviction that they were a unique partnership and that life could never offer the same possibilities, the same excitement, in other company. It was an alliance as much as a marriage. Their love for each other sometimes wavered, but the attachment between them remained unbreakable.

Edwina was touched by the kindness and affection of her husband's message. 'As well as helping so tremendously at what must be a difficult time in my life,' she wrote, 'it has made me realise more than ever before how deeply devoted I am to you and what very real and true affection as well as immense admiration I have for you.'³ When they were reunited in the spring of 1945, each made a real effort to rebuild their marriage.

> I am so glad that you felt as happy as I did about our new-found relationship [wrote Mountbatten]. I have always wanted to have you as my principal confidante and friend, but so long as A. was yours – it made it literally impossible for me. I hope you didn't mind my mentioning about my girl-friends – it was only to show you that they never have meant to me what A. meant to you, and so can never come between us, provided you no longer make difficulties about my seeing them, within reason, as you were apt to do in the old days!!⁴

But there was an element of make-believe about such musings. Mountbatten must have known that his wife was incapable of the sort of intense yet cosy relationship which was his ideal. For 'principal confidante and friend' he looked more and more to his elder daughter Patricia, a girl of mature wisdom and loyalty. He was endlessly preoccupied with her welfare and development, intellectual and social as well as emotional. She wrote to say that she disliked smart London life and preferred the middle-classes. 'It is nice that you don't miss . . . the social life of a London season because I do feel most of that is past,' replied her father; 'on the other hand I do hope you are keeping in touch with the political side of life.' As he had once recommended the *New Statesman*, he now prescribed a course at the feet of Peter Murphy – 'I can't tell you what a help he can be.'⁵

He was less pleased when she said she had decided not to take a commission in the WRNS but did not force the issue too hard, no doubt calculating that, as was the case, she would come round to the idea in the end. He was far more insistent that Patricia should come out to South-East Asia. His daughter was dutiful but had no intention of being pushed about. 'I do want to come and am doing what I can,' she told him, 'so relax a bit and don't feel you have to write me incitements in every single letter, so that I don't forget about it! Be original and write me one letter without telling me what a unique opportunity it is!'⁶ She came in the end, sensibly refusing to serve in her father's shadow at Kandy but instead securing a posting to New Delhi.

Trying to persuade Edwina that it was desirable for their elder daughter to come to Asia, Mountbatten stressed 'what a difference it would make to me to have someone I could talk to about family matters, or rather any matters well away from "shop". Peter of course helps a bit but we do always end up with shop.'[7] Peter Murphy's role on Mountbatten's staff was one which caused confusion and even distress to those who prized hierarchical good order above all else. He had been smuggled out under the auspices of the Political Intelligence Department of the Foreign Office to act as a kind of odd-job man: 'I am dealing so much with every sort of non-military question,' explained Mountbatten, 'that I would have to devil out for myself long and involved papers that come to me with requests for decisions if I did not have Peter to turn the whole thing over to and produce a short, concise summary with proposals.'[8] While the fighting was on, Murphy's importance was trifling; when attention turned to the civil government of the reconquered territories there were those who maintained that his influence was over-powerful and malign. Certainly he spoke always for liberality and an attitude of cautious welcome towards the new nationalists, but Mountbatten would have reached that conclusion without assistance. Murphy's value was that he was a trusted friend with whom Mountbatten could totally relax.

There were not many others. On Christmas Eve 1943 he drove with another old friend, Bunnie Phillips, to spend the evening with Peter and Janey Lindsay. 'We sat till the small hours of the morning playing the gramophone and telling stories. I had never realised what a relief it was to get away from one's staff, however much one likes them, and go to a private house and spend an evening with friends of one's own set.'[9] 'One's own set' was not a snobbish verdict – there were many other people in SEAC of impeccable social credentials – but it represented a degree of intimacy based on old acquaintance, common interests and assumptions, a scale of values unquestioned and largely unstated yet for all that of paramount importance to its members. Mrs Lindsay was the heart of the set – 'I only have one friend I can gossip with about non-serious matters and that is Janey.'[10] Christmas Eve 1944 was again spent with her, this time with Prince Philip and Boy Browning. The Singhalese cook, overawed by the occasion, took refuge in drink and served dinner cold, late, and back to front: Christmas pudding at midnight, turkey at 1 a.m. Nobody minded, least of all Mountbatten – it was one's own set.[11]

Prince Philip's ship had stopped briefly at Colombo. When he was in London he usually stayed with the Mountbattens. In March 1942 he and David Milford Haven dined and then borrowed the Vauxhall so as to tour the night-clubs before returning to spend anything left of the night on camp-beds in the dining-room. At 4.30 a.m. they ran into a traffic-island, destroyed the car and returned with their faces cut and bleeding: 'So, after facing death many times over at sea', mused Mountbatten, 'they got their first wounds in a London blackout.'[12] In spite of such contretemps, he strongly approved of his nephew and had long felt that he would make the ideal husband for Princess Elizabeth. When war broke out Philip was still a Greek citizen and therefore technically a neutral. He should be sent to a ship on the China station, Mountbatten suggested to George VI.

When Greece joined the war Mountbatten feared that the King of Greece would expect Philip to join the Greek Navy – a painful prospect, since he spoke hardly any Greek – but this turned out not to be the case. On the contrary, the King's main preoccupation was the same as Mountbatten's and he pressed the young Prince's claim to Princess Elizabeth's hand with undiplomatic zest. 'We both think she is too young,' George VI told Queen Mary. 'I like Philip. He is intelligent, has a good sense of humour and thinks about things in the right way. . . . We are going to tell George [of Greece] that P. had better not think any more about it for the present.'[13] To Mountbatten too he urged prudence. 'I have been thinking the matter over since our talk,' he wrote on 10 August 1944, 'and I have come to the conclusion that we are going too fast.' Mountbatten was to see the King of Greece at Cairo later that year, and George VI was anxious that they should talk only of Prince Philip's application for British citizenship, not the possible marriage. 'I am sure this is the best way of doing this particular operation, don't you? though I know you like to get things settled at once, once you have an idea in mind.'[14]

Mountbatten on the whole curbed this inclination when the talks took place in Cairo, though he contrived to say a word to his nephew on the subject. 'Philip entirely understood that the proposal was not connected with any question of marrying Lilibet,' he told his mother, '. . . though there is no doubt that he would very much like to one of these days.'[15] Indeed, he urged his sister, Princess Alice, not to mention the matter to the King and Queen. 'The best hopes are to let it happen – if it will – without parents interfering. The young people appear genuinely devoted and I think after the war it is very likely to occur.'[16]

Parents were one thing, uncles evidently another. Mountbatten could not resist lending a helping hand from time to time. Prince Philip occasionally revolted. 'Please, I beg of you, not too much advice in an affair of the heart, or I shall be forced to do the wooing by proxy.' He was more acquiescent about his uncle's forays into political education and was somewhat indignant when Mountbatten suggested that he would never get round to reading the copy of Bernard Shaw's *Intelligent Woman's Guide to Socialism and Capitalism* which he had sent him. Such doubts suggested he was 'antagonistic to the principles of Socialism'. He was not in the least so, but he was suspicious of abstract theorizing:

What I want to know is, what is the present Labour Party in England going to do about it, how are they going to set about it, given the present conditions in England and the world. If that programme offers a reasonable chance of success in improving the present conditions of England and the world and it does not entail extra-democratic political powers, then I shall be convinced. If not, it means that I shall turn not to the old system but to some other system that offers a better solution.

Don't forget you are attempting to educate me politically for a certain job, and a little knowledge is a dangerous thing, if not worse than none at all. There is still another aspect and that is that for this particular job it is not only necessary to know reasonably intimately the two opposing creeds but every other credo that may be attempted in the future.[17]

'I hope this letter is to your liking,' Prince Philip concluded, 'and you can amuse yourself wondering what you are going to do with your Pygmalion next.' Galatea was presumably what he had in mind, but he must have known well how inapt the analogy was; not even in his most sanguine moments can Mountbatten have believed that his nephew was his creation. He did, however, take pride in the commonsense and open-mindedness that his protégé was displaying.

The gradual maturing of the love between Prince Philip and Princess Elizabeth was one of the two things that brought pleasure to his last, most troublesome year in South-East Asia. The other was the engagement of Patricia. On 19 September 1947 Mountbatten dedicated a copy of his South-East Asia Report:

> To Captain the Lord Brabourne, the Coldstream Guards, who as
> A.D.C. to SACSEA held my hand sucessfully during the first half of
> 1946, and held my daughter's hand even more successfully during
> the second half of 1946.

Patricia had doubts whether John Brabourne was the man for her; Mountbatten had none. Even though he believed that his adored daughter's marriage would cost him her companionship, he never ceased urging her to take the plunge. But what would happen, she asked, if in a few years she fell madly in love with someone else. 'I know you,' he replied. 'It won't happen. Your sense of duty won't let it happen.' They married, with great pomp, on 26 October 1946 and lived happily ever after. 'Sad without Patricia,' was the comment in Mountbatten's diary next day.

When the couple returned from their honeymoon Patricia, who was used to hearing from her father at least once a day, expected a letter or telephone call. Nothing happened. After three days she rang in some alarm to ask what was wrong. Was he ill? No, said Mountbatten. 'I've taken an important decision. Life's different now. John must be the most important person for you. I must step down. Our relationship must alter.' Patricia said that this was absurd, they were no less fond of each other because she was married. 'Oh, do you really mean that?' said Mountbatten, enormously relieved, and at once he came round rejoicing.

The marriage not merely proved Mountbatten right by being entirely successful but rewarded his virtue by making him happy too. The ancient cliché for once came true; he had not lost a daughter but gained a son. John Brabourne – tough and subtle under a cloak of disarming amiability; devoted to and admiring of his father-in-law, yet never a worshipper; a shrewd businessman who exercised highly professional skills while ostentatiously flying amateur colours – gave Mountbatten everything which his father-in-law had missed by having only daughters as children. It was a relationship which contributed enormously to his happiness during the rest of his life.

Such solaces were needed, for the end of the war had brought Mountbatten not merely new responsibilities but also new vexations. The first was the problem of the war honours. On 11 December 1945 he received a telegram offering him a barony in the New Year's Honours. He was dismayed: as the son of a marquess and member of the royal family, his precedence was already far higher than that offered him, and the fact that the new rank would allow him to take his seat in the House of Lords offered no comfort. He told Edwina that there were other rewards he would prize far more highly: 'I would gladly have the Garter *instead* if deemed worthy of it. For God's sake be tactful about that. The Order of Merit would be the next best.'[18] When he found that Alexander and Montgomery were to be made viscounts, he was outraged; to fob off the Supreme Commander in South-East Asia with a lesser honour would be an insult both to the man and to his command. 'If the King calls upon me to accept a Viscountcy in the National Interest I suppose I shall have to bury my feelings and accept – subject to minor conditions such as continuing to call myself Lord Louis Mountbatten, and having a special remainder to Patricia – and if I am offered a Barony it lets me out with a clear conscience and I shall definitely refuse in the interests of SEAC.'[19] In the end he played for time, saying that he felt it would be inappropriate to accept an honour while men were still fighting and dying in the farther-flung reaches of his Command. The excuse was accepted, and the King had been put on warning that for Mountbatten it was a viscountcy or nothing.[20] The viscountcy duly came, and was garlanded with a cluster of other honours. In a crowded five weeks in June and July 1946 Mountbatten was given an Honorary LL.D. at Cambridge and made an Honorary Fellow of Christ's College, given an Honorary D.C.L. at Oxford, made a member of the Mercers' Company, awarded the Freedom of Romsey, invested as a Commander of the Legion of Merit at the American Embassy, driven in state to the Guildhall to receive the Freedom of the City and a Sword of Honour, and admitted to the Vintners' Company. In the course of the next three months he was awarded the Grand Cross of the Order of George I, took his seat in the House of Lords, received the Freedom of the Grocers' Company, was installed as Grand President of the British Empire Service League, became an honorary member of the Cambridge Union and, on 29 August, 'Patricia and I went to see me at Madame Tussaud's'. Finally, in December he was invested with the Garter – other recipients being Brooke, Portal and Montgomery. There could be no question now that he was among his peers.

His indifference to his viscountcy, except in so far as he felt unfairly discriminated against without it, was genuine. In May 1946 he wrote to the King to urge a peerage for Auchinleck – 'The man who made my victory in Burma possible. . . . I would gladly and willingly stand down in favour of him if only one can be spared for this theatre. He is a great man.'[21] In the event Auchinleck refused the honour. Mountbatten reacted very differently when an attempt was made to strip him of his honorary ranks in the Army and Air Force. It was Portal who fired the sighting-shot, pointing out that the appointments dated from his time as Chief of Combined Operations and were irrelevant to his duties as Supreme Commander.[22] On the contrary, they had been of the greatest help, retorted Mountbatten, but if the Chiefs of Staff felt he should resign the commissions, he would of course do so. Then came his most devastating riposte. 'There is one small point,' he concluded. 'While staying with the King at Windsor over the Bank Holiday, I consulted him as to whether I should take any steps about these ranks. His Majesty said that he would like to think the matter over. . . . I wonder therefore if you would be so kind as to clear the matter with the King.'[23]

On the same day Mountbatten wrote to the King about what he described as this 'uncalled for and ungracious act'. It had been suggested that Mountbatten as his next job should be responsible for a new Inter-Services Staff College; for this role the three ranks would be invaluable. Apart from this, the award of high honorary ranks was a prerogative of the King and he should have been consulted first – 'They would never have dared to take this step if Winston was still Prime Minister.' The King, Mountbatten suggested, might argue that the Supreme Commander had 'earned the right to retain these ranks since he is the only man in English history ever to hold these commands for nearly four years'. It would make it easier, Mountbatten concluded somewhat disingenuously, if it was not known that he himself had protested, since then the King's decision would seem more unbiased.[24]

It may be doubted whether George VI was wholly convinced by his cousin's arguments, but he was still moved to action. At the end of August Alan Lascelles, the King's private secretary, wrote to Portal to suggest that no precipitate decisions should be taken, certainly none before Mountbatten's final return from the East. Even then he might find himself doing work which would make the three ranks a useful asset.[25] The Chiefs knew when they were beaten; three days later Portal wrote to Mountbatten to say that he and Brooke had agreed to drop their proposal that the honorary commissions should be resigned.[26]

It would indeed have been somewhat unjust if Mountbatten had been reduced in honorary rank just at a time when his actual responsibilities were increased. At Potsdam it had been agreed that, once the fighting was over, South-East Asia Command should be widened to include French Indochina, Java, Borneo and the Celebes. On 14 August 1945 this decision was implemented. The Combined Chiefs thus added half a million to the million square miles for which Mountbatten was already responsible. The population of the enlarged Command totalled more than 128 million. In addition to this there were 122,000 Allied prisoners-of-war to be tracked down and succoured and nearly three quarters of a million Japanese to be rounded up and eventually repatriated. The whole area was devastated by war, internal and external communications had largely broken down, civil administration was almost non-existent, the collapse of the Japanese had created a power vacuum which was rapidly being filled by nationalist groups of varying degrees of respectability. Somehow Mountbatten had to restore order, rebuild the economy and apparatus of civil government, and prepare the area for a return to its former masters or some other, as yet unspecified, destiny.

The Supreme Commander's new headquarters in Singapore, where he moved in the autumn of 1945, was a bedlam of different interests. At a luncheon on 28 September he was astounded to count 'between 60 and 70 people, all of whom appear to be living in Government House, and very few of whom I remember inviting. . . . It is like the Dorchester Hotel and I only hope that the uninvited guests will pay their bills!'[27] On a typical evening in Kandy – which for two months Mountbatten maintained in tandem with his headquarters in Singapore – he noted that as midnight struck

I had General Sena Narong waiting to sign the final agreement with the Siamese in the dining-room. . . . In one corner of the lounge the Governor of Burma and his staff were having final discussions with Aung San, Tin Tut and U Ba Pe over the final agreement which I was about to sign with them. In another corner Brian Kimmins had laid out an enormous plan of the Municipal Buildings in Singapore and . . . was busy going through the ceremonial for the surrender. In yet another corner . . . the Director of Intelligence and one of the Saigon Control Commission were drafting a reply to an unsatisfactory signal. . . . Luckily the French and Dutch Commanders-in-Chief had by this time returned to their respective houses and the party from Tokyo were drinking quietly in the only free corner.

If Hollywood had attempted to stage such a scene . . . I am afraid it would have been regarded as burlesque.[28]

It was hardly surprising that the average 450 telegrams a day with which his headquarters had had to deal in wartime soon rose to 920. Since this increase coincided with the demobilization of many of the most experienced personnel, a sense of hectic strain permeated Singapore. 'This place is hell!' wrote Mountbatten feelingly to Eisenhower.[29]

He needed urgently to establish his attitude towards the burgeoning nationalist movements which had sprung up in the shadow of the Japanese occupation and now thrived in the sunshine of liberation. Mountbatten was influenced by two main considerations. The first was practical and military: it was his job to maintain stable government and he could not do that by waging civil wars which he lacked the resources to conduct. If the independence movements were too strong to ignore, then the only course was to come to terms with them. The second was personal and idealistic. He believed that people should be allowed as far as possible to control their own destiny. The territories of South-East Asia might not yet be ready for full independence, but the aspirations of their peoples could not be ignored. It must be made clear to them that the former imperial powers accepted that they were on the road to self-government. Both these considerations led him to take up positions which, to the more conservative of those who served under him, seemed radical and misguided.

Brian Kimmins, himself far from starry-eyed about the capacity of the former subject races to rule themselves, summed up the situation well. Some critics, he wrote, labelled Mountbatten as 'too inclined to the left, too ready to listen to upstart leaders in the emergent liberation forces. It would be fairer, I think, to say that he recognized more quickly than many that the old status quo could never be restored.'[30] The critics were not necessarily wrong-headed. Recognizing the emergent liberation forces often meant abandoning more traditional and conservative elements which had loyally supported the colonial rulers in the past. There was a body of moderate opinion among the local inhabitants that might have rallied to a determined attempt by the returning Western powers to reassert their full authority. It can be argued, indeed, has been argued, that South-East Asia would now be a more prosperous and contented area if such an attempt had been made and had succeeded. In the conditions of the post-war world, however, it is impossible to believe that a debilitated West could have sustained any such campaign, or a resurgent East have allowed it to attain a lasting victory. In the words of the official historian F. S. V. Donnison (himself no devotee of Mountbatten): 'It is difficult to feel that the development of events after the military period has not increasingly vindicated the soundness of Admiral Mountbatten's largely intuitive estimate of the vitality of the nationalism he encountered.'[31]

Some accused Mountbatten of being an unconscious servant of international Marxism, probably under the malign influence of Peter Murphy. Mr Ulius Amoss, who ran an organization in the United States known as International Services of Information, went still farther and announced that he had positive evidence that Mountbatten was himself 'deeply involved with the Communist Party'.[32] Certainly Mountbatten was not scared of the word, nor was he inclined to label nationalist movements Communist merely because they adopted left-wing policies and were hostile to the West. Sometimes this led him to controversial conclusions, as when he told Carton de Wiart that the Communist Chinese were 'not Communists in the Russian sense at all, and that their territory is far more justly and competently administered than that of the Central Government. Consequently the word "Communist" can no longer be used as a bogy, particularly not by the Labour Government (strong though its dislike of *real* Communism is).'[33] In Malaya, at least, he proved to have been naive in his assessment of the political philosophy of the independence movements. He erred, however, not because he was 'soft on Communism', still less because he had any sympathy for it, but from an over-readiness to assume the best of those with whom he had dealings.

His policy was founded largely on empirical considerations; until almost the end of the war he believed that he faced a protracted and bloody struggle to drive the Japanese from South-East Asia and that he would need all the help that he could get from the local nationalists. But he was still consistently liberal in his leanings. When, in Burma, his civil advisers wanted to extend the scope of the death penalty to cover the failure to surrender firearms, Mountbatten insisted that an intent to use the firearms in a way which would itself have incurred the death penalty must first be proved. Since such an intent was virtually impossible to establish, the matter dropped.[34] 'I am sorry,' he ruled in April 1944, 'but I am quite unable to agree to any extension of whipping in Burma during the time I have any authority in the matter. We are by way of fighting this war of progress and enlightenment [*sic*], whereas this measure would be extremely reactionary.'[35] 'I hope you will not wish me to impose any political censorship,' he wrote to Dorman-Smith. '. . . I feel confident that you will agree with me that freedom of the press is one of the freedoms for which we are fighting.'[36] He refused to accept that, because a citizen of some territory occupied by the Japanese had indulged in political or even military activities against the Allies, he should be punished as a criminal.

> The guiding principle which I am determined shall be observed is that no person shall suffer on account of political opinions honestly held, whether now or in the past, even if these may have been anti-British, but only on account of proven crimes against the criminal law or actions repugnant to humanity.[37]

His views on the future of the countries in his Command struck some of his colleagues as alarmingly socialistic. Dorman-Smith remarked that it was most undesirable that foreigners should own millions of acres of Burmese soil. Mountbatten agreed, but felt that no Burmese should do so either. He had the same opinion about industry: '. . . we must beware of allowing powerful vested interests to arise. . . . It would be a thousand pities if our seven years' custodianship were to result in our handing the country over, not to the people of Burma, but to a handful of landowners and . . . industrialists.'[38]

Sometimes it seemed to him that his socialist masters in London were as blind to these fundamental truths as his benighted subordinates in South-East Asia. Edwina fed his fears. 'Bevin is behaving like the *worst conservative diehard*,' she wrote indignantly from London. At least Tom Driberg was coming that evening 'so I'll get the Leftist views on Java, etc'.[39] In September 1945 Lawson, the Secretary of State for War, briefly visited the area. He had been briefed by Bevin on no account to get involved in local politics. He was left little option. Mountbatten, assuring his visitor that he was a socialist 'just like you', called in all his major-generals from the various regions and in no time had the Secretary of State endorsing his policies. 'I was quite sad to see the old boy off,' he noted in his diary. 'He has done a grand job out here.'[40]

Lawson had come out partly to quell an incipient mutiny among troops idling in the transit-camps awaiting repatriation. In January 1946 four thousand R.A.F. men at Selatan struck because of what they considered to be unreasonable delay in their return to Britain. Keith Park drafted a statement condemning the 'agitators' who had fomented this trouble. Mountbatten suggested certain changes:

> It is of course perfectly true that these people are led and directed by people who are practised in organising demonstrations of this nature; but I cannot help feeling that unless grievances (real or imaginary) are very strongly felt to exist, agitators would never be capable of achieving any success.
>
> It therefore seems to me to follow that as long as this feeling of grievance exists, those men who are in a position to lead and advise the people . . . must inevitably command a measure of loyalty and admiration. Instances such as the beating-up at night of men who had returned to duty are the obvious work of a rowdy, hooligan element; I think that it would be unwise to saddle the serious-minded leaders with the misdeeds of the rough elements, by lumping them together in the name 'agitators'.[41]

The naivety, as some would see it, the fair-mindedness, as surely all would grant, of such an attitude was characteristic of Mountbatten's dealings with his great empire. Mountbatten, said Lee Kuan Yew, 'exemplified the kind of liberal British tradition trying to meet a new human situation with a great sense of anticipation . . . of what is to come in this region'.[42] He won the hearts of the Burmese, said Ne Win. 'He removed their distrust of the British. They were used to very different people in Burma and it was such a contrast the way Mountbatten treated them.'[43] It was not surprising that a man who created such response among the Asian subjects of the still powerful Raj should be looked at askance by some of his compatriots. The reputation that he gained in South-East Asia was to stand him in good stead in India not much more than a year later.

# CHAPTER 25

# *Burma*

IN ONE PART of South-East Asia Command the problems of peace impinged long before the war was over. As Burma was liberated, Mountbatten found himself responsible not only for law and order but also the reconstruction of the economy and the civil administration. To help him in this work he had the Civil Affairs Service (Burma) or C.A.S.(B). But though C.A.S.(B) had wide powers, it had no right to make decisions with long-term political implications. These fell to the Government of Burma in exile in Simla, under the direction of the former and still titular Governor, Sir Reginald Dorman-Smith.[1]

It is easy to deride Dorman-Smith as a reactionary blimp, and Mountbatten was apt to do so after the two men fell out in mid 1945. He seems, however, to have been a man of liberal leanings, to the extent of having incurred Churchill's anger for 'talking a lot of nonsense about our handing over Burma'.[2] At first Governor and Supreme Commander got on famously. 'I have great confidence in Lord Louis, who seems to see very much eye to eye with us and who really does take a very deep interest in the political as well as the military problems . . . ,' wrote Dorman-Smith in May 1944. 'He is keen on winning the peace as well as the war.'[3] They met in Kandy five months later. Dorman-Smith had set out his views in a paper which he rather patronizingly described as 'short enough to enable even soldiers, sailors and airmen to read it'. Mountbatten, while protesting that the subject was no concern of his, 'waxed enthusiastic and launched into the realms of politics with gusto'.[4] Still the love-feast went on. The Supreme Commander told his guest that he was so delighted with the Governor of Burma that he had asked Oliver Stanley, the Secretary of State for the Colonies, to produce a similar being for Malaya. 'I only hope that Oliver can produce someone who by nature thinks along Mountbatten's lines,' commented Dorman-Smith, 'as he is a very determined man who knows what he wants and will not be satisfied until he gets it!' Mountbatten was no less enthusiastic. Dorman-Smith, he noted, 'has first-class ideas on the future of Burma, and we see eye to eye on all Burma questions'.[5]

It did not last. The two men got on well while there was nothing in Burma to govern but, once real issues instead of theorizing were involved, a power struggle developed. 'Damn it all, I'm *governing* Burma – not he, whatever his title,' wrote Mountbatten indignantly when Dorman-Smith retreated in pique to Simla rather than broadcast a speech to the Burmese people prefaced by the words 'Admiral Mountbatten has invited Sir Reginald . . .'.[6] The parallel with Somerville's refusal to allow Mountbatten to visit ships of his fleet except as a guest is obvious, but this time Mountbatten was the would-be host.

It was the Burma National Army, or B.N.A., which provided the *casus belli*. The B.N.A. had been set up by the Japanese to assist in the war against the former colonial rulers. They proved uncertain allies. From as early as 1943 there were rumours that their leader, Aung San, was disaffected with his new masters and was contemplating secession, and in early April 1945 the Japanese Ambassador in Rangoon reported the 'vexing' news that the B.N.A. had revolted and taken to the jungle.[7]

Through the breaking of the diplomatic ciphers Mountbatten knew that the Japanese were disturbed by this development. He knew, too, that they were drawing consolation from reports that the British were not enlisting the B.N.A. as allies but instead disarming them and treating them with some disdain.[8] Opinion in the British camp was divided between those who felt that the members of the B.N.A. were patriots, who had committed no crime and should be welcomed as allies for military reasons if no other, and those who saw them as ill-disciplined and treacherous terrorists to be treated with suspicion if not hostility. Mountbatten, advised by the experts of the para-military Force 136 who had encouraged the B.N.A. to change sides, was strongly of the former view. Dorman-Smith inclined to the latter. In February 1945 Oliver Leese ruled that arming Burmese guerrillas was more dangerous than useful and should be stopped.[9] Mountbatten promptly overruled him. 'Due to an oversight by my Staff,' he blandly informed his Commander-in-Chief, 'you were not informed that I reserve political decisions to myself. . . . The advice which you have received does not fit into the broad policy for Burma which I have decided upon.'[10]

The following month Mountbatten's 'broad policy' was considered by the India Committee of the Cabinet, with Dorman-Smith present.[11] They disliked the prospect of co-operation with the B.N.A. but, since Mountbatten based himself firmly on the military need to gain the support of powerful guerrilla groups, they saw no option but to agree. The race to Rangoon was on, and the B.N.A. could make the difference between success and failure. They passed on their conclusions to the Chiefs of Staff, who on 30 March gave Mountbatten permission to make use of the B.N.A., though stressing that he should give them no chance to present themselves as a future government.[12] To this Mountbatten cheerfully acceded, but he, the Chiefs of Staff and the Cabinet Committee were all deluding themselves if they imagined that enlisting the B.N.A. as allies would not inevitably put them in a powerful position when it came to establishing the structure of post-war Burma.

Now the breach with Dorman-Smith and, indeed, a growing distinction between policy propounded in London and practice in the field in Burma became more apparent. On 16 May Slim, with Mountbatten's blessing, met Aung San at Meiktila. He was immediately impressed, found him a realist, honest and patriotic – 'I have always felt that, with proper treatment, Aung San would have proved a Burmese Smuts,' he wrote long afterwards.[13] The curious thing about Dorman-Smith's attitude was that he conceded all the virtues detected by Slim and later Mountbatten. 'Aung San', he wrote in mid 1945, 'is the most important figure in Burma today. Everyone appears to trust him and to admire him. . . . His troops adore him and will do anything he says. . . . He has no ambition.'[14] Yet he failed to draw the same conclusion and accept Aung San as a man to back. He was influenced above all by the hostility towards the rebel leader shown by the group of Burmese who had accompanied him to Simla and to whose support he felt committed – 'we must not neglect those who have stood by us in very great adversity'.[15]

Mountbatten had signally failed to convince the interim Conservative Government that his attitude towards the B.N.A. was the correct one. When he argued that any young Burman of spirit could have been expected to accept the Japanese offer of independence, Eden commented, 'Surely we should not boost these people so much. They will give great trouble hereafter.' 'I cordially agree,' replied Churchill.[16] With the Labour ministers he did better, though not as well as he would have liked. Pethick-Lawrence, Secretary of State for India and Burma, endorsed the Supreme Commander's recommendation that the B.N.A. should be integrated with the loyal Burmese forces, but hedged his approval with provisos about the need to guard against Aung San enjoying any privileged status.[17] In so saying he came closer to Dorman-Smith's position than to Mountbatten's. On 16 May Mountbatten had recommended to the Governor that Aung San should be told that members of his self-styled 'Provisional Government' might be included in the advisory council that would be set up when civil government was restored.[18] Dorman-Smith, outraged, flatly refused to offer any such undertaking; 'it would be a disaster to give even semblance of recognition to Aung San or any organisation styling itself Provisional Government while legitimate Government still exists'.[19]

It is not necessary to be a student of colonial history to recognize the classic confrontation between the traditionalist, who believes that one should put one's trust in old and loyal friends, and the progressive, who wishes to come to terms with what he is certain will prove to be the government of the future. It is easy to feel sympathy for the traditionalist, difficult not to conclude that in the circumstances of the post-war world the progressive has again and again been shown to have the sounder judgement. The clinching argument for the progressive is that, fairly or unfairly, the old and loyal friend will be dismissed as an Uncle Tom, an imperialist puppet, by all the more dynamic forces in his own society. To support him may postpone by a few years the inevitable victory of the new opposition, but it will also ensure that the victory, when it comes, is more embittered and hostile to the former colonial power than would otherwise be the case. In the summer of 1945 Mountbatten was championing the progressive cause against the Governor, most of the Civil Affairs Service, and strong elements in Whitehall. It is impossible to prove that things would have gone better in Burma if he had been allowed a free hand. The murder of Aung San came too soon to show whether he would have become a Smuts, as Slim and Mountbatten believed, or a Soekarno, as Dorman-Smith felt was certain. But in supporting the claims of the old-style politicians from Simla the Governor was backing a horse that was bound to lose.

The victory parade in Rangoon on 15 June 1945 found a contingent of the B.N.A. goose-stepping through the streets to tremendous applause from the crowds. 'I am sure', wrote Mountbatten, 'that having Aung San and his Army take part in this Review, will have done more to prevent strife and civil war and to establish friendship, than anything I could have done.'[20] To Admiral Power, on the contrary, it seemed an unhappy gesture, especially when 'that treacherous warrior Aung San' attended the reception at Government House, still in the uniform of a Japanese general.[21] Later that day Mountbatten held a press conference and was assailed by American journalists asking about plans for censorship, curfews and other aspects of authoritarian rule – 'It is horrifying to think that the American and Indian press evidently still regard us as merely Imperial monsters, little better than Fascists or Nazis.'[22]

The next two months were devoted to trying to establish an accord between the various parties so that civil government could get off to a smooth start. The task was made easier for Mountbatten by the fact that he had got rid of Philip Joubert and Major-General Pearce, his Chief Civil Affairs Officer. Joubert and Pearce, even more than Dorman-Smith, had advocated taking a strong line with the B.N.A. Pearce fulminated to Dorman-Smith about 'the wilfully blind preconceptions and pre-emptive conclusions of that Heaven-inspired politician Dicky M. I deliberately say his inspirations were heavenly because they certainly did not come from having both feet firmly on the earth.'[23] While Pearce remained in charge of Civil Affairs it was certain that the Supreme Commander's policy would not be conscientiously applied. The new Chief Civil Affairs Officer, Major-General Rance, was Mountbatten's man; a 'progressive and high-minded officer' as the Supreme Commander described him, who shared the view that it was essential to work with the Burmese activists.

The discussions went smoothly. Dorman-Smith at first got on well with Aung San and agreed that he should be made one of the two Deputy Inspector-Generals of the Burma Army. But now a new cause of dissension arose. With the greater part of Burma liberated, the Governor began to feel that it was time he took back his former powers. Mountbatten argued that more time was needed: the police must be retrained, the loyalty of the Army assured, disarmament of the insurgent groups completed; communications restored. Dorman-Smith was unconvinced, though he paid tribute to the Supreme Commander's anxiety 'not to hand us a baby which will be bound to die. . . . There can be no doubt but that Mountbatten is extremely interested in every problem connected with Burma. He appears to enjoy the political problems, which, by and large, are, I think, being handled in the right way.'[24]

So far, so amicable; but the temper changed when Mountbatten argued that the end of the war actually made the return to civil government more difficult. His new responsibilities meant that he would have less resources to devote to Burma. 'You can imagine how nice it would be for me if I could shelve all my Burma troubles on to your shoulders,' he protested, but unless a way could be found of running the country without military help this seemed a remote possibility.[25] This was too much for Dorman-Smith. He refused to come to Kandy for a further conference and threatened resignation unless a date in the near future was fixed for his taking over.[26] He gained his point. When the two men met in Kandy in September it was agreed that military rule would end the following month.

The conference of 6 September was Mountbatten's last chance to exert his civil authority as Supreme Commander. He used it to quell the serious suspicions which had arisen among the men of the B.N.A. about the terms of their integration with the regular Army. Aung San found him friendly, almost avuncular. 'You must decide to be either a Churchill or a Wellington,' Mountbatten told him. 'You cannot be a soldier and a political leader at the same time.'[27] 'The mission was a success,' Aung San's deputy announced to the press. 'We were treated very cordially.'[28] Aung San himself paid tribute to the 'transparent fairness and high-mindedness' of Mountbatten, which, he said, augured well for the future. But the Supreme Commander failed to convince Whitehall that Burmese suspicions would never be allayed until a time-limit was fixed at which direct rule by the Governor would end.[29] When Mountbatten formally handed over on 16 October he did so with good grace

but in the dissatisfied conviction that the job was only half done. In later life
he was apt to say that he had only made one mistake in his life, when he agreed
to hand over the government of Burma before the time was ripe.

One of the strongest cards in Mountbatten's hand was that there were
practically no troops in Burma who could be relied on to suppress Aung San
and his followers if need arose. Traditionally the British had depended on
Indian troops to keep order but Auchinleck had served notice that this could
not continue.[30] Mountbatten put the point squarely to Dorman-Smith in
January. 'Said the Supremo, "You must so govern the country that there will
be no rising." "By that you mean", said I, "that I must hand over power to
Aung San!" Mountbatten did not deny the implication. I replied that I had no
intention of doing any such thing.'[31] What Dorman-Smith *did* intend was less
certain. He was in an unenviable position. Pethick-Lawrence was urging him
to take a strong line with Aung San, leader of 'a single party with marked
Fascist leanings';[32] yet it became more and more evident that Aung San was
not merely the most powerful man in Burma but also the hero of everyone
except a small group of largely discredited veterans. 'I hear [Dorman-Smith]
is accusing me of having been too progressive – he need never fear being
accused of that himself,' wrote Mountbatten balefully. 'I am building up the
evidence against him carefully, and may have to recommend his removal if he
brings the country once more to the verge of turmoil.'[33]

In February 1946 a crisis almost occurred when Dorman-Smith telegraphed the Secretary of State in London for permission to arrest Aung San on
a charge of murder. The Burmese leader had been concerned in the execution
of an Indian headman who had organized resistance to the Japanese. His
guilt, if it had come to a trial, would have turned on the validity of the excuse
that at that time he was serving the occupying power. He might well have
been convicted, but it is hard today to find a Burmese of any political
complexion who doubts that his arrest would have led to revolution.[34] On the
grounds of expediency there was therefore a strong case for doing nothing.
Mountbatten held that this was also desirable on the grounds of justice, since
evidence sufficient for Aung San's arrest had not yet been assembled. Even if it
had been, he would still have held that equity demanded an acquittal. 'Where
would we be today', he asked Bunnie Phillips, 'if we had shot Field Marshal
Smuts and General Botha for doing just what General Aung San has been
doing?'[35] In his turn he telegraphed London to urge that no arrest be made.

As you may imagine [Dorman-Smith wrote to Pethick-Lawrence]
Mountbatten's intervention did not go down well with me. I looked
upon it as a quite unwarranted interference in the political affairs of
Burma. . . . The plain fact is that here we are reaping the fruits of his

policy towards AFPFL [Aung San's party] and bitter fruits they are. Had Mountbatten faithfully followed the directive sent to him by the Cabinet and the Chiefs of Staff much of our trouble would not have arisen.[36]

So matters dragged on unhappily, the Governor grumbling about Mountbatten's left-wing policies which had ruined his chance of securing stable government in Burma; the Supreme Commander reviling Dorman-Smith's inept conservatism which had destroyed all that had been achieved in the months before he took over. In London things had swung in Mountbatten's favour. In March 1946, when Pethick-Lawrence was out of the country, Attlee took over his responsibilities. 'As soon as I began to read Pethick's papers I realised we would have to change our line,' recorded the Prime Minister. 'The new policy could be described as following Mountbatten instead of Dorman-Smith.'[37] Mountbatten urged Attlee to dismiss the Governor before he involved the British in a major war in Burma,[38] and his advice must surely have been an important contributory factor in the Government's decision to replace Dorman-Smith when he fell ill in August 1946. In his place was put Mountbatten's protégé General Rance. The Supreme Commander urged the new Governor not merely to take a new course but ostentatiously to cut loose from the old one. The Burmese, he wrote, 'know that Reg's idiotic and vacillating policy was the worst piece of work ever done for Burma, and that his illness is the merest excuse to sack a glaring failure!! . . . If you whitewash him, you're sunk!'[39]

The ultimate vindication of Mountbatten's policies would have been Aung San's emergence as a wise and benevolent statesman. He was murdered, along with most of his ministers, before he had a chance to prove himself. The feud between Mountbatten and Dorman-Smith lingered on. On 2 January 1969 *The Times* quoted the former Supreme Commander as saying that he had made a tremendous error in handing over to civil government: 'If I had held on to the government myself, Burma would still be in the Commonwealth; but I turned it over to people who mucked it up.' A week later he received a letter from Dorman-Smith's solicitors stating that their client's views were in advance of those of the British Government and he was merely carrying out official policy. They asked for an apology and correction in *The Times*. No apology was made, no correction published, no further action taken. For the sake of the two men's reputations it is fortunate that the matter never went farther – but it would have made an interesting case.

# CHAPTER 26

# *The Return of Empire*

IN THE OTHER COUNTRIES of Mountbatten's territory the 'Post Surrender Tasks', as he called his official report to the Combined Chiefs of Staff,[1] began at the time his title suggests. This did not mean, however, that there were no commitments made or positions taken before the Japanese surrender. In Malaya and Singapore, in particular, the situation was one of extreme complexity.

The first and most urgent problem was that Malaya boasted a vigorous resistance movement to the Japanese, whose members were largely Chinese and often Communist.[2] The decision to support such movements had in effect been taken as long ago as August 1943, when the representatives of Force 136 established contact with the guerrilla leaders.[3] Mountbatten sought to regularize the position. In particular, he favoured support for the extreme left-wing Malayan People's Anti-Japanese Union (M.P.A.J.U.), which he judged was a genuine nationalist movement, as opposed to those who looked to the Chinese in Chungking for leadership. He was backing the group most likely to support the advancing Allies, and could thus justify his stand on military grounds, but he underestimated the degree to which Communist control of the M.P.A.J.U. made it unlikely that its members would ever work harmoniously with a colonial government, however liberal. At a ceremony in Singapore after liberation the Supreme Commander presented medals to a large gathering of resistance leaders. The ceremony was much photographed. Mountbatten's critics alleged that the resulting pictures were of great value to the British security forces for the identification of the terrorist leaders in Malaya's long-drawn-out civil war.

The second complicating factor in Malaya was that almost all the effective resistance fighters had been Chinese. The predominantly Malay police, though disaffected with the Japanese, had on the whole collaborated with them. Relations between Chinese and Malays, never happy, were now disastrously bad. Mountbatten was concerned by this, and anxious to build up the concept of a united Malayan state and people. When a draft Directive on Policy towards Malaya, which had been sent to him for comment, recommended special measures to protect Malay interests against the more resourceful and economically aggressive Chinese, he argued that nothing would be worse for harmony between the communities: 'our objects should be to break down racial sectionalism in every way open to us, politically, economically and socially, and to endeavour to substitute for it the idea of Malayan citizenship'.[4] Though he was too pragmatic to deny the necessity when the moment came, he regarded the eventual separation of Malaya and Singapore as the defeat of his aspirations.

In January 1946 the Labour Government proposed to announce the setting up of a Legislative Council which would have a built-in official majority and limited powers. Mountbatten greeted this timid concession to progress with some dismay. Surely, he argued, a small *unofficial* majority, circumscribed as it would be by the overriding authority of the Governor, would not present too great a risk. More important, any such step must be presented as a temporary expedient; otherwise 'it will be considered to be a constitution autocratically imposed from London . . . and, as such, will be stigmatised as a return to the old type of Colonial Government'.[5] He suggested that a Royal Commission should be set up to visit Malaya and establish the wishes of the people. Such a procedure had already been considered and dismissed as too slow, said the Colonial Secretary, George Hall; the White Paper made it clear that no final decisions about the constitution were being taken at the present stage.[6] With this Mountbatten had to rest content.

Liberation was followed by inflation and near famine. The labour force, finding itself denied the prosperity which it had assumed would follow the return of peace, grew restless. A rash of strikes afflicted the country. Where these were in pursuit of higher wages or better conditions, Mountbatten endured them with equanimity as 'a normal democratic procedure';[7] but where they were manifestly political and designed to embarrass the Government different considerations came into play. He was not prepared to allow the security of his base to be jeopardized or the administration of the country rendered impossible.

His liberal instincts pulled him one way, his responsibility for good order another. Most of his advisers said that he inclined too far towards the former. Major-General Hone, the Chief Civil Affairs Officer, complained that the Supreme Commander approached any such issue 'with a determination to follow too lenient a course'.[8] Slim was one of the few who thought he got it right. 'What nonsense they all talked,' he grumbled as he left a meeting devoted to Malayan affairs. 'Supremo?' hazarded Slim's A.D.C., John Brabourne. 'Good God, no!' said Slim. 'Only two people talked sense. One was Supremo, the other me.'

It was the arrest of Soon Kwong, one of the more militant of the Chinese leaders, that provoked the first serious confrontation between government and opposition. A court of British officers had convicted him, but the legality of the proceedings was dubious and Mountbatten on 25 January 1946 told the G.O.C. Malaya, General Messervy, that the man must be released, otherwise his imprisonment would smack of 'preventive arrest, which was contrary to my policy'.[9] Before any such action could be taken, however, a twenty-four-hour general strike was called, specifically to secure Soon Kwong's release. Mountbatten curbed the zeal of the police, who wanted to arrest all the strike leaders – 'I could not imagine anything more disastrous than to make martyrs of these men' – but simultaneously cancelled the release of Soon Kwong 'as I could not accept doing this under duress'.[10] The strike proved to have little popular support and Soon Kwong was quietly released a fortnight later.

The next challenge was to be a second general strike on 15 February, the anniversary of the fall of Singapore to the Japanese. 'Whether the proposal was to celebrate the day as one of mourning and shame, or as one of rejoicing,' commented Mountbatten, 'the intention to discredit the British administration was clear. I refused to allow processions to take place.'[11] The military authorities pressed to be allowed to arrest the organizers of the strike and thus frustrate their plans. This Mountbatten refused, but he reluctantly agreed that up to fifty of the trouble-makers could be deported if it could be proved that they were Chinese nationals. A warning to this effect was published on 13 February, two days before the strike was due. The following day ten Chinese were arrested and their names recommended to Mountbatten for deportation.

To the dismay of his advisers, Mountbatten refused to agree. Insufficient warning had been given; the Chinese would be punished under an ordinance published after their offence had been committed. The most he would accept was that the ten men should be held temporarily in gaol. Browning wrote to tell his Supreme Commander how profoundly wrong he thought this decision. Mountbatten was unperturbed. A military regime, he answered, had above all to avoid any action which could seem dictatorial. 'I consider I am going a long way in authorizing the detention of the agitators and undesirable characters . . . for, after all, this smacks of the notorious 18B Regulations in in the U.K. [permitting internment without trial]'[12] From this position nothing would move him. 'There was no rancour or bitterness in our exchanges,' commented Hone, 'but a straightforward and understandable clash of opinions on a matter of great importance to both.'[13]

He caused further disquiet among his advisers when he announced that the Viceroy had agreed to Nehru visiting Singapore as representative of the Congress Party. The visit was supposed to be an investigation into the conditions of the Indian minority in Malaya, but the conservatives took it for granted that the Indian leader would stir up trouble. The initially hostile reactions of the Commanders-in-Chief came close to mutiny when Mountbatten announced that he proposed to treat his visitor as if he were prime minister of an independent India.[14] Dorman-Smith, when asked to receive Nehru in Burma, had refused to do so; that, felt the Commanders-in-Chief, was the way to cut a rebel down to size.

Mountbatten now sent for Brigadier Chaudhuri, Messervy's Chief of Staff, and put him in charge of arrangements. 'I was very impressed by Lord Mountbatten's efficiency,' wrote Chaudhuri, 'and the care he had taken to see that the whole trip was a great success.'[15] Some staff officer had taken it upon himself to rule that no official transport could be made available for Nehru; Mountbatten did not bother even to countermand the order, but put his personal car at his visitor's disposal.[16] On arrival Nehru was taken to Government House for tea. 'I told him that I would impose no restrictions on his movements or programme, and give him every assistance.' Nehru was only asked to avoid any formal ceremony at the memorial to the dead of the Indian National Army; to this he agreed, though he slipped away quietly the following day and left his personal wreath.[17]

Next the two men set off together for the Indian Y.M.C.A. 'The sight of the Pandit seated by the Supremo's side', wrote S. K. Chettur, the Agent for the Indian Government in Singapore, 'was rightly acclaimed by the entire populace . . . as a signal mark of honour, and popular enthusiasm reached the pitch almost of frenzy. . . . I took off my hat to Lord Louis. . . . It showed the fine imaginative sensibility for which Lord Louis is so justly famous.'[18] What had been intended by some as an anti-British demonstration was transformed into a celebration of Anglo-Indian amity. Edwina met them at the Y.M.C.A. and polite exchanges were developing when

> a roar as of a dam bursting fell upon our ears, and the crowd burst through every door and window of the Y.M.C.A. In no time they were upon us. Edwina was the first to be knocked down, and disappeared under the mob. The Pandit screaming 'Your wife; your wife; we must go to her,' linked arms with me and together we charged into the crowd in an endeavour to find her. Meanwhile she had crawled between the people's legs, and had come out at the far end of the room, got on a table, and shouted to us that she was all right.[19]

Eventually the party escaped into a kitchen and barricaded the door with a table from which Nehru addressed the crowd. 'That was an unusual introduction,' remarked Nehru afterwards.[20]

When they got back to Government House Mountbatten was enraged at the mismanagement of the visit to the Y.M.C.A. and the scratches all over his brand-new car. Edwina quietened him with the aid of a stiff drink and assurances that Nehru himself was delighted at the way things were going. She was right. When he returned for dinner their visitor was conspicuously affable, and on the way home he told Chaudhuri that 'he had not enjoyed an evening with English people so much since he had come down from Oxford more than thirty years ago'.* That he was sincere seems certain. The Mountbattens out to please were a formidable combination; when they genuinely liked and admired the person whom they wished to charm, the effect was irresistible. Nehru left Government House in the conviction that he had met an English couple whom he could trust and who understood and sympathized with the needs of India. When he landed in Burma on his return journey, Aung San asked him what impression he had formed of the Supreme Commander. Nehru deliberated before replying: 'A very noble specimen of British imperialism.'[21]

Mountbatten's satisfaction would have been complete if he had known of Dorman-Smith's reaction. 'Nehru's reception by Mountbatten', the Governor wrote to Pethick-Lawrence, 'has not been without embarrassment to me. He apparently treated Nehru as a MOST IMPORTANT PERSON and went out of his way to pander to him.' Nehru's plane visited Rangoon on the way back – due to engine trouble, said the R.A.F.; out of a wish to embarrass him, Dorman-Smith suspected.

> Criticism has been levelled at me ... [wrote the Governor] that whereas Mountbatten treated Nehru with that regard which impelled him to entertain him at Government House and to travel about with him in a motor car, I took no notice of him. The fact that I was not in Rangoon when Nehru arrived is irrelevant. Had I been there I am bound to admit that I would not have thought of asking him to stay the night with me, having been unwilling to receive him in Burma in the first place.[22]

By the time Nehru had come and gone, Lord Killearn had arrived as Special Commissioner for South-East Asia. A fortnight later, on 1 April 1946, Singapore and the Malayan Union were restored to civil government. The following month Malcolm MacDonald took over as Governor-General. Certain residual responsibilities remained for SEAC but, effectively, Mountbatten's task in Malaya was over.

*

* A surprising observation, given that Nehru had been at Cambridge.

Siam took less time and trouble. For the last two years Mountbatten had been presiding over a joint headquarters of which the British section was at war with Siam while the American was not. Hostilities, however, had never been conducted with noticeable energy and early in 1945 the Regent of Siam offered to bring over his army to the Allied side and asked for arms. 'It was sufficiently unusual to be offered command of the enemy army in war,' commented Mountbatten, 'but to be asked to equip it as well, seemed a shade over the odds.'[23] The Siamese were advised to bide their time, but contacts between the dissidents (who seemed to comprise the vast majority of the ruling class) and the agents of Force 136 remained close. By June Mountbatten was recommending that the Free Siamese Movement be armed and trained,[24] and when in September a Siamese military mission arrived in Kandy, they came as friends. They were, however, not wholly sure of their reception. Observing that the presiding general had difficulty sitting down because of his vast ornamental sword, Mountbatten asked a waiter to remove it. The general blanched. At the end of lunch Mountbatten asked him to stay behind. The general grew whiter still. Only when he left did the Supreme Commander realize that his visitor had thought his sword had been confiscated in token of surrender and that he himself was being retained as a hostage.

The Americans were suspicious of British intentions. The U.S. Ambassador to China, Patrick Hurley, was not convinced by Eden's assurance that he wanted to see a fully independent Siam: 'I feel that if we do not move forward in this matter the British will succeed in out-manoeuvring us . . . and in gaining some measure of control.'[25] Mountbatten, for one, had no such intention. He regarded Siam as an attractive diversion from his real responsibilities and was preoccupied mainly by the problems of the King, pitchforked from the school-room into the role of head of state. Ananda was in fact nineteen but seemed five years younger. Mountbatten arrived to be greeted by this 'frightened, short-sighted boy; his sloping shoulders and thin chest hung with gorgeous diamond-studded decorations; altogether a rather pathetic and lonesome figure'.[26] He put himself out to set his host at ease. His attitude, said his Director of Plans, Denis O'Connor, was 'the perfect mixture of respect to the King and a fatherly attitude to the small boy at his side'.[27] Mountbatten cross-examined the King and found that he knew nothing of royal procedures and had not even read *The Prisoner of Zenda*. 'I then told him as tactfully as I could how our King managed his affairs of state and he took it all in with pathetic gratitude.' Next day they drove together through Bangkok. The King sat immobile, looking nervously straight ahead. Mountbatten leant across and suggested he acknowledge the cheers of the crowd by saluting or bowing. The King was much struck by this advice and at once acted on it, thereby no doubt breaching the rules of a millennium of royal etiquette but noticeably increasing the enthusiasm of the people.[28] 'The poor King hadn't got a clue,' Mountbatten told Patricia proudly, 'but he has now after your father took him in hand.'[29] It did him little good; the following year King Ananda was mysteriously murdered.

Indochina and the Netherlands East Indies presented the last two serious problems in Mountbatten's Command; different, in that both regions were former colonies of Britain's allies, which were now open for the taking by whoever could first grasp the instruments of government. Towards both countries Mountbatten's attitude was broadly the same: that the colonial power should return but should respect the ambitions of the local independence movements. More by chance than policy, he proved more sympathetic towards the French in Indochina than towards the Dutch in the East Indies.

Since his arrival in South-East Asia Mountbatten had maintained that Indochina was of great importance as a Japanese supply-route and that, without French help, it would prove extravagantly difficult to reconquer. No covert operations could be mounted unless the former colonists co-operated.[30] Throughout 1944 he argued this case vociferously.[31] At least he wanted French representation on his staff and acceptance of the offered support of a *Corps Léger d'Intervention* which would infiltrate the area in advance of Allied landings.[32] The British Government were ready to agree, but encountered the determined opposition of the Americans. Roosevelt in particular disliked the idea of handing Indochina back to the French, and even at the beginning of 1945 would go no farther than to say that it was a matter to be settled when the war was over.[33] Mountbatten was able to win agreement that a mission under General Blaizot should come to Kandy and the *Corps Léger* get as far as India, but that was the limit to his achievements.[34]

At the Potsdam Conference it had been agreed that Indochina should be divided into two spheres of influence. North of the Sixteenth Parallel the Japanese would surrender to Chiang Kai-shek, south of it to Mountbatten. The Supreme Commander subsequently stated that he had made plans to occupy the whole country and had earmarked the 26th Indian Division for Hanoi.[35] If he had carried this through successfully, the post-war history of Vietnam might have been different. It would, however, have been a formidable task. As in Malaya, the most effective resistance had come from the Communists and, particularly in the north, they were best placed to fill any power vacuum left by the Japanese surrender. They would certainly have opposed reoccupation by Allied forces. Whether Mountbatten would have been allowed to use Indian troops to crush the Communist Viet Minh and whether his strength would have been sufficient to restore order to the whole province is at least doubtful. Nor would the Americans have been pleased. Mountbatten had already agreed with Marshall that the division of the country involved no serious problems.[36] The Americans were convinced that the Viet Minh were misrepresented patriots. 'Forget the Communist bogey,' was the advice of the American intelligence service. 'V.M.L. [the Viet Minh League] is not communist, stands for freedom and reforms from French harshness.'[37] Mountbatten to some extent shared this opinion. But he felt that the favour which the Americans were showing towards the nationalist movement was in this case being manifested in victimization of the French. To Wedemeyer he wrote in protest about the murder of a French officer by the Viet Minh. As he died, an American standing nearby remarked: 'I guess I am now a neutral.'[38]

The Chiefs of Staff, aware that the future of Indochina was likely to prove messy and painful, tried to remain disengaged. Mountbatten's instructions were that he should occupy no more of the area than was necessary to secure control of the Japanese forces. The rest of the south could be left to the French. Unfortunately, the French were too thin on the ground to restore order by themselves, and the Viet Minh had no intention of remaining quiescent until their former rulers returned in force. On 2 September 1945 there were riots in Saigon and a massacre of the French was narrowly averted. 'The Annamites ... have started to give trouble ...,' Browning warned Brooke. 'The last thing we want is to get Douglas Gracey and his Indian division embroiled ... before the French reach F.I.C. [French Indochina] in sufficient strength to do their own work.'[39]

The last thing happened. On 17 September the Viet Minh proclaimed the independence of the Republic of Vietnam.* Slim, who happened to be in Saigon, reinforced Mountbatten's order that the British and Indian troops should occupy themselves solely with the Japanese,[40] but on 21 September General Gracey judged that, if he did not act, total chaos would ensue. In effect he proclaimed martial law throughout the whole of southern Indochina. Two days later he backed a French *coup d'état* in Saigon. 'Your General Gracey has saved French Indochina!' General Leclerc told Mountbatten gratefully.[41]

His General Gracey had also acted in defiance of his clear directive. In his biography of Leclerc, Adrien Dansette claimed that only Leclerc's intervention with Mountbatten saved Gracey from immediate recall.[42] This seems unlikely. Mountbatten was surprised by Gracey's behaviour and his first

* Though a case can be made for dating the formal proclamation either earlier or later.

response was to remind the errant general of his instructions,[43] but at a meeting in Singapore on 23 September he spoke in defence of what had been done. He was not wholly convinced of the wisdom of the decision, but Gracey had acted courageously and in good faith and he supported him with the Chiefs of Staff.[44] To them he pointed out that his directive should be reviewed. On 1 October he got his answer: he was to act in support of the French throughout the whole of southern Indochina.[45]

Mountbatten's preoccupation now became to induce the French and the Viet Minh to negotiate a settlement. To Colonel Cédille and General Leclerc he repeatedly emphasized that to crush the Viet Minh by force of arms would not merely be morally questionable but would tax the French to the uttermost. 'If only the French will be reasonable and come forward with an imaginative offer, the war in French Indochina can be over . . . ,' he told Tom Driberg. 'I can assure you that if I was left as free a hand in F.I.C. and N.E.I. [Netherlands East Indies] as I was left in Burma, I could solve both these problems by the same methods; though it is heart-breaking to have to leave the political control to other nations when we are really in military control.'[46] Subsequent history suggests that he was right in his estimate of the military problem but over-optimistic about the readiness of either party to accept a compromise. Himself convinced that every dispute could be solved by rational argument, and almost as ready to listen to the arguments of others as to propound his own, he found it hard to believe that anyone could hold views with such fanatical fervour that they would not modify them by an iota. To be a reasonable man in a world of extremists is to court constant disappointment; luckily for Mountbatten, he had reserves of optimism sufficient to ensure that he emerged ebullient from every setback.

Even though the British were now committed to supporting the French, Mountbatten tried to play as minor a role as possible. On 2 October, when forced to use Japanese troops to help keep order, he told the Chiefs of Staff that: 'We shall find it hard to counter the accusations that our forces are remaining in the country solely in order to hold the Viet Minh Independence Movement in check.'[47] All Mountbatten could do was present British activities as palatably as possible. 'I was most distressed to see you had been burning down houses; in congested areas too,' he wrote to Gracey. If they were really necessary, could not such unsavoury jobs be left to the French? No, replied Gracey; the French did not understand minimum violence and would have burnt not twenty but two thousand huts.[48]

In the short term, at least, Gracey's measures succeeded. By early 1946 order had been restored and the French had assumed responsibility for military matters; on 4 March Indochina was excluded from SEAC.[49] In *The British in Vietnam* George Rosie has argued that the British should not have become involved in executing a pro-French policy in Indochina. Gracey was the main villain, but as Supreme Commander Mountbatten was also implicated.[50] Others maintain that, in fact, British intervention made little difference; the Viet Minh were still weak in the south and it would have been relatively easy for the French to dislodge them.[51] What is certain is that, if Mountbatten had been master of his own actions, things would have been different. In 1972 Leclerc's former A.D.C. told Mountbatten how clearly he remembered the Supreme Commander urging Leclerc

> not to fight but to try and make friends, to establish the same policy as we had in Burma and Malaya, that we had come to liberate them from Japanese occupation and to give them their freedom, if that is what they would like, within the Commonwealth. He said I added that this would mean a great saving of lives, money and ill-will, and would strengthen France's position in the Far East in a way that a war, even if successful, never could.
>
> He reminded me that Leclerc had given long and anxious thought and then had said that he was a soldier and he had come out to fight, and fight he would.[52]

And fight he did. Whether Mountbatten could have coerced or cajoled the French into negotiation, and whether, if he had, the Viet Minh would have co-operated will always be uncertain, but, surveying the bloody carnage that is Vietnamese history since 1945, it is hard not to feel that it would have been worth a try.

The Netherlands East Indies – the future Indonesia – presented problems superficially similar to those of Indochina: an ally anxious to reclaim its colony but lacking the strength to do so single-handed; an independence movement determined not to be reclaimed; a Supreme Commander with obligations towards the former, sympathy for the latter and an overriding wish not to get caught in crossfire between the two. The Indonesians, however, were more firmly entrenched than the Vietnamese; the Dutch weaker than the French. For both these reasons Mountbatten's problems were to prove more painful and protracted in Indonesia* than Indochina.

At first he thought there would be few problems. Dutch intelligence was abysmally out of touch; there might be a little scattered opposition to their return, it was confidently stated, but there was no nationalist movement of

---

* I did not call Indochina 'Vietnam' since this would have excluded Laos and Cambodia. No such considerations apply in the case of Indonesia, and the name is, anyway, less of a mouthful than 'Netherlands East Indies'.

any consequence.[53] Nor did SEAC's own sources do much better; seven officers parachuted into Java on 8 September 1945 reported that few of the people had any interest in political movements.[54] Only when Edwina returned from a foray to the prisoner-of-war camps, where she had talked, among others, to Laurens van der Post, who had spent the last two years imprisoned there, did Mountbatten realize that he had to deal with a powerful movement whose leader, the dynamic and ingenious Dr Soekarno, had already proclaimed Indonesia an independent republic.

As in Vietnam, Mountbatten's instructions were to secure control of the Japanese and repatriate the Allied prisoners-of-war. As in Vietnam these instructions could be interpreted in many ways. Van der Post believed that there was a choice between waging a bloody war on behalf of the Dutch and persuading the two parties to negotiate. Only one thing stood between the British and a disastrous commitment in South-East Asia: 'the Supreme Commander's intuitive assessment of the situation'. He possessed an 'almost extra-sensory perception of what was hidden around the dangerous corners or coming up unseen below the horizon'.[55] He was to need it all.

From the beginning Mountbatten insisted to the Dutch Lieutenant-Governor General, Dr van Mook, that he was determined to remain outside the conflict and that the Dutch should open negotiations with the more influential of the Indonesians, led by Dr Soekarno.[56] To the Dutch, Soekarno was not merely a rebel but a traitor who had collaborated with the Japanese. Nevertheless, van Mook proved ready to listen to advice. At a conference in Singapore Mountbatten put himself between the Lieutenant-Governor and the Dutch Admiral Helfrich 'and worked on them like mad throughout dinner'.[57] By the time the evening was over van Mook was ready to make overtures to the Indonesians. He was promptly disowned by his Government, the Dutch Ambassador in London going so far as to say that if any Dutchman negotiated with Soekarno he should be tried for treason.[58]

The British commander in Indonesia was General Christison. 'I am afraid you are in for a very sticky time,' Mountbatten warned him.[59] According to Christison, Mountbatten told him of the time his father had been hounded from office in the First World War.

> Ever since that disgraceful episode, I have lived determined to get to the top and vindicate his memory. Nothing and no one; I repeat, nothing and no man, will ever be allowed to stand in my way. This Dutch East Indies business looks very tricky. I don't want to have responsibility for it directly. Will you take it on for me? I know you'll do it well and I'll back you all I can. I just don't want to fall down at the last jump after all I've been through.[60]

In another account Christison attributed a similar *démarche* to General Browning.[61] The words were recollected many years later and neither record is convincing. Mountbatten was capable of appalling frankness, but it would have been unlike him to try to avoid responsiblity, particularly since, like it or not, it would be attributed to him in the end. Indeed, to Lawson and to Brooke he emphasized that he was involved in every decision being taken in Indonesia. Nevertheless, he knew that the British occupying force was being given a singularly unattractive task and he must have made it clear that its first priority was to avoid unnecessary entanglement. 'Characteristically,' wrote Christison, 'in the event and in the unpleasant actions I had to take, Lord Louis backed me to the hilt.'[62]

Christison's orders were to occupy only the key areas and make no attempt to pacify the whole country. To the Dutch this was a betrayal of Britain's duty to a loyal ally. To the Indonesians it was a cloak behind which the British planned to reintroduce the Dutch Army and destroy the republic. At Sourabaya there was savage fighting; Brigadier Mallaby was murdered as he toured the city with the more moderate of the Indonesian leaders, trying to secure a truce, and something close to civil war broke out. Mountbatten's problems were made worse by Nehru's insistence that Indian troops should not be used to repress the Indonesians. 'Why we should accommodate the Dutch who are playing the role of an aggressor and dominating power in Indonesia, I do not know,' Nehru told Auchinleck.[63] The Americans added to the pressure by ruling that American vessels were not to be used to ferry Indian troops from Bangkok to Java.[64]

Mountbatten had considerable sympathy with Nehru's point of view. Encouraged by Browning and Leese's Chief of Staff, General Pyman – 'Strongly advised S.A.C. to knock van Mook for six'[65] – he had concluded that the main stumbling-block to a peaceful solution in Indonesia was Dutch intransigence. The Dutch were even worse than the French, he told Tom Driberg. 'They have been reviling Christison for meeting . . . Soekarno, and yet they were getting on splendidly with [him] until there was interference from the Hague.'[66] As a result of his private approach to Prince Bernhard, Colonel Frowein came out to see what was going on. Mountbatten stressed that, with Indian troops on the way out, it was more than ever important that the Dutch should come to terms with the Indonesian leaders. When Frowein made his report in The Hague there was some discontent, one minister remarking that it was odd to find Mountbatten playing the game of Professor Laski (Chairman of the Labour Party and prominent critic of intervention in Indonesia).[67] On the whole, however, the visit had a good effect. The new Dutch Commander-in-Chief, General Spoor, proved more amenable than his predecessor and the attitude of his men towards the Indonesians became less intransigent. Mountbatten still had reservations, however, warning Bernhard 'that you are always likely to find one or two over-enthusiastic officers . . . who will feel it is their duty to try and kill as many Indonesians as possible'.[68]

Though the soldiers on the spot shared Mountbatten's view, in Whitehall the feeling was that it was in Britain's best interests to support the Dutch. The violence of the Indonesian rebels, in particular Mallaby's murder, was much criticized in the United Kingdom. Mountbatten asked Murphy to prepare a brief which would

> knock on the head once and for all the confused idea that if you can label an Independence movement Fascist you can marshal world opinion on your side. . . . Perhaps we should distinguish between Soekarno's lot, who are obviously educated Left-wing leaders, and the extremists, whom they themselves condemn. . . . Perhaps it might be a good thing to label them 'Trotskyists', and plug this as a new line, since presumably everybody will combine to condemn Trotskyism.[69]

Edwina, meanwhile, lobbied vigorously, contriving to talk on the subject to Lawson and Bevin as well as Attlee. 'They are not prepared to toe the line to the present Dutch attitude much longer,' she replied optimistically. '. . . I think your stock is very high on all sides.'[70] The trouble was that nobody in London gave the problems of this remote and little-known region high priority. Gradually a policy evolved, however. Brooke visited the area in December 1945 and stoutly backed Mountbatten's line. If the Dutch would negotiate with the Indonesians on the basis of some sort of dominion status, then the British would co-operate in keeping the key areas of the country peaceful; if not, they would confine themselves to disarming and repatriating the Japanese. The Dutch accepted this *Diktat* with comparative equanimity. 'I think the Conference did good and that Dickie ran it very well,' reported Brooke. 'There is no doubt that during the last few years he has come on in a most astonishing way.'[71]

By April 1946, when Mountbatten paid a farewell visit to Indonesia, the situation had to some extent settled down. The tactful withdrawal of Soekarno in favour of the more emollient Sjahrir had eased the progress of negotiations. Dutch forces had been reintroduced in considerable numbers without any too conspicuous incidents. But the latent problems were still daunting. When Mountbatten mentioned casually to the Acting Lieutenant-Governor General that he would be seeing Dr Sjahrir, there was an explosion of protest. Mountbatten was unperturbed; he would never have contemplated coming to Java, he said, except on the understanding that he would meet the Indonesian leaders. He saw Sjahrir that evening at Laurens van der

Post's house and took a fancy to him – 'Archie Kerr's description of him as "a spaniel whom one expects to jump on one's lap and lick one's face if petted", cannot be bettered.'[72] The Dutch reaction was predictably hostile, the local newspaper greeting Mountbatten's arrival with a violent personal attack and a parliamentary commission announcing that all the trouble in Indonesia had been due to him. 'These are valuable "Recommendations",' he told Peter Murphy.[73] He left Indonesia in the conviction that the outcome would not be a happy one: 'The gap between the Dutch and Indonesians is widening again,' he reported regretfully to the Chiefs of Staff.[74]

Britain's contribution to the return of the Dutch to Indonesia was not quickly forgotten. In 1964 the then British Ambassador in Djakarta, Andrew Gilchrist, referred to lingering rancour at 'British armed intervention in support of Dutch colonialism'.[75] One of Mountbatten's staff was rash enough to pass it upwards, marked 'an excellent despatch, which should be read in full'. Angrily Mountbatten minuted: 'I regard this as an uneducated schoolboy's views in schoolboy language!'[76] He wrote to the Foreign Secretary to protest and to ask that the section of his report dealing with post-surrender tasks should at last be published. He had to wait another five years, but a reading of it and of the many papers which have subsequently become available suggests that his irritation was justified. If to be abused by both sides is evidence of impartiality, then certainly he deserves more praise than blame.

Laurens van der Post quotes Dr Sjahrir as saying when the British troops left Indonesia: 'You introduced to our country by your personal qualities some traits of western culture our people here have rarely seen before from white people: I mean your politeness, your kindness, your dignified self-restraint.'[77] One suspects that his aim was as much to rebuke the Dutch as praise the British; to President Truman he complained that the British had reimposed Dutch rule on the Indonesians.[78] The Dutch for their part accused the British of 'strengthening the hands of the Indonesians to the detriment of the Netherlands Government's position',[79] while in the *New York Herald Tribune* Sumner Welles claimed that Indonesian–Dutch relations had been prejudiced by 'the ineptitude of Great Britain's participation in the liberation of the islands'.[80] The wide range of the criticism indicates Mountbatten's achievement. He did not solve the crisis in Indonesia – no one in his position could have done so – but he did avert disaster. He maintained a measure of peace over a critical period and gave time for passions to calm and for the Dutch and Indonesians to negotiate. That the opportunity was thrown away was not his fault; that it existed at all was a tribute to his statesmanship.

\*

In another way, too, Mountbatten was frustrated in his last few months as Supreme Commander. His experience in South-East Asia had reinforced the lessons he had learned in Combined Operations, that the closest possible integration between the three Services was essential. In June 1946 he had a meeting with the Chiefs of Staff and argued vehemently that a combined headquarters for South-East Asia should be kept in being in Singapore. The most that the Chiefs would agree was that General Stopford should act as a stop-gap Supreme Commander till November, and should then hand over to a committee. 'What made this idiotic retrograde step virtually unworkable', wrote Mountbatten, 'was that the Naval Commander-in-Chief was to have his Headquarters in Hong Kong. . . . Thus the First Sea Lord was able to achieve his much cherished object of keeping the Navy as far apart from the other two services as possible.'[81]

Mountbatten had lobbied vigorously in favour of his ideas. Lawson was known to be in favour of a combined headquarters, and the King was recruited to see the Labour politician on his return from his Asian tour and urge him into battle.[82] In the Defence Committee Bevin pronounced himself an ally. Even Attlee, when Mountbatten taxed him with it later, said he personally agreed. But it was not an issue on which a Prime Minister was likely to overrule the united voices of the Chiefs of Staff. The matter could not be put right until the Chiefs themselves recommended it, and this was not to be expected under the present management.[83]

By the time that the Chiefs had thus consigned Mountbatten's Supreme Command to the scrap-heap, his immediate post-war work was almost done. 'I can honestly say that I shall have cleared up my theatre and completed my tasks,' he told Ismay, 'with the exception of what looks like a long-drawn-out but ever decreasing commitment in the Netherlands East Indies.' For the sake of his various successors, if for no other reason, it was time for a change; how would it be for them to 'find themselves having to work indefinitely alongside the man who used to do all their jobs single-handed?'[84] The truth was that he had had more than enough of South-East Asia and was itching for a return to England and the Navy. 'I sincerely hope that they are going to let me come home for the Victory Parade,' he wrote to Alan Lascelles in April 1946, 'and I hope even more that they will find a successor for me and not send me back again.'[85] The successor was not forthcoming but his final wish was granted. His departure was celebrated with great *réclame*; at one farewell dinner a baby elephant appeared, carrying an illuminated sign which read 'Goodbye Supremo!'[86] On 30 May 1946 Admiral Mountbatten – to give him the acting title he was now about to lose – left Singapore for London. The Supreme Command was dead.

# CHAPTER 27

## *Marking Time*

WHEN GENERAL POWNALL LEFT South-East Asia at the end of 1944, after fifteen months as Mountbatten's Chief of Staff, he found time to write a character-sketch of his former Supreme Commander. It is a critical commentary, harshly so in some respects, but acerbity can be forgiven a man who has worked for so long and so hard in so debilitating a climate and with deteriorating health. It is on the whole fair and perceptive. It deserves quotation – slightly pruned but at length.

Pownall started by commenting on the hostility Mountbatten encountered from many people in London.

> Perhaps it is just because they are at a distance that the criticism continues. They do not come under his charm of manner – that is one of his greatest assets; many is the time I have gone in to him to have a really good showdown, and prepared for a first-class, perhaps final, row. But it never comes to that stage, because his manner was always so admirable when one found fault with him. He would always accept, indeed seem to welcome criticism. He would apologise, promise to mend his ways, be grateful for correction; and then, so soon afterwards, go and do the same thing again.
>
> His actions and behaviour viewed from a distance were often infuriating; even if his actions were correct he contrived to put them in an unfavourable light, or at least cause intense irritation, to a recipient of his communications. . . . There is no question in anyone's mind but that Mountbatten has great drive and initiative, very necessary qualities for high command. He is apt however to 'leap before he looks', he is too impulsive by far, and putting the engine back on to the rails is pretty near a whole time job. His acceptance of responsibility is much to be admired; he has plenty of moral courage in that regard, yet not enough to allow him to face calmly an unpleasant interview, a difference of opinion with a Commander-in-Chief, not even to remove an unsatisfactory Staff Officer when that is plainly needed. He is too fond of a 'quarrel by proxy'. For he hates a

row and wishes to be popular and well thought of, and indeed is almost pathetically surprised when he learns that there are people who do not care for him and his ways.

To him, to meddle in detail is a relaxation of the mind: he is never so happy as when designing a badge, arranging the seating for a conference, or worrying over some question of flying a flag. Indeed to relieve him of detail, in the sense that a Chief of Staff should take detail off a Commander, is largely fruitless. For, relieved of detail, he will invent other detail for himself and fuss everybody about, unnecessarily, on some stupid ploy. Better that he should be led to deal with detail connected with his job, than irrelevancies of his own invention.

He cannot take No for an answer. Professionally it is often necessary to fight against the Noes, but when it is a matter of a little personal inconvenience or acceptance of a slightly lower standard in something that does not really matter, that is quite a different thing. For he is undoubtedly conceited, that comes natural to him, perhaps the outcome of his birth and antecedents. To be humble is not in him.

His output is tremendous. In speech he talks too much himself, his meetings are overlong because he likes talking instead of hearing, weighing and deciding, and he likes a good big audience to hear what he has to say. Many is the battle I have had to fight about overlong, overcrowded meetings, but he takes them that way and it has been hard to persuade him otherwise. In letters and telegrams he is prolific – he is always emitting them, not always well judged in phrase, or properly considered before despatch. He has promised so often that he will never, never, send off a letter dictated over night without reading it carefully in the morning. I trust that he will remember his promises, but I am not certain, for 'Repentance oft before, he swore'.

Specialists have an easy time selling themselves or their wares to him. The arrival of an expert in this or that was always followed by a commotion which took several days to subside, and he was, at any rate at first, too ready to form an extra branch or section of the Staff to deal with a particular stunt in detail. His grandiose ideas always led him to increase his staff unnecessarily and to upgrade them. Although he laid down the admirable principle that his staff should be small, he was one of the worst offenders in suggesting additions, nor do I ever remember his doing anything but welcome warmly an addition suggested by another person.

One of his best points is his way with troops; that is quite admirable. He looks the part; he says the right things, and he's the

King's cousin – at heart the troops are snobby to that extent. His strongest point is his resilience, and that I admire enormously. He has had many disappointments and frustrations; but whatever his private feelings he has never failed to 'come again' and to conceal from others the fact that he was saddened. The capacity to come again is a most necessary trait in a Commander in War. I believe only a young man is thus capable, just as the elderly boxer in the ring cannot stand punishment. In sum, he has the necessary qualifications for high command. Stripped of his lesser, but serious weaknesses he can become a great man, but he must learn to see things as they are, not merely as he would wish them to be.

Let me finish by adding that he has always treated me with the greatest kindness and consideration; ready to lend an ear to advice; courteous and friendly; appreciative of my coming, a much older man, to help him in the very great difficulties which beset him. Yet we are not, never could be, real friends; our upbringings, surroundings, ways of thought are too different. 'His people are not my people.' But I have a respect for his good qualities which is very high.

With all his natural advantages, and the experience he is now getting, he will surely play a big part in the post-War Empire, and he is qualified to do so. If he will but apply his mind successfully towards improving himself there is very little that he cannot achieve.

Mountbatten was shown this piece in 1967. His reaction was generous. 'I am not at all surprised to read what he has written about me,' he commented, 'because I always had the impression that this was what he felt. He was one of the nicest senior officers I ever had any dealings with.'[1]

In the eighteen months since Pownall's departure Mountbatten had borne taxing and multifarious responsibilities and had matured in exercising them – 'he has come on in a most astonishing way', Alan Brooke had commented.[2] Yet through these gruelling years he had preserved the spirit of a boy, with all that this implied in the way of impetuosity, energy, enthusiasm, the urge to find out how things worked and the readiness to question accepted principles. His technique had matured yet his temperament was unchanged. He remained startlingly naive; incapable of concealing his intentions; childishly triumphant in his displays of what he hopefully took to be low cunning. He was inept as an intriguer: 'an elephant trampling down the jungle rather than a snake in the grass', as Peter Thorneycroft was to describe him.[3] His ambition remained consuming and his efforts to conceal it were unavailing.

When on the point of promotion at the end of 1945 he wrote to Robert
Neville:

> I would be most grateful if you could find out for me, very discreetly
> and without indicating your reasons, the following information.
> What age (in years and months) were Beatty and Nelson on promo-
> tion to Rear-Admiral and Vice-Admiral? If these are not the youngest
> promotions, within recent times, what younger promotions have
> there been?[4]

His fierce energy led him to involve himself in many matters which his
professional advisers felt should not have been his concern. 'When called to
order,' wrote General Pyman, 'he justifies his interference on the ground of
the political aspect. . . . Partly because practically every military matter out
here has a political aspect, and partly because of his tremendous charm of
manner, it is extremely difficult to establish a cast-iron case where he has
really been naughty.'[5] This note of exasperated affection is often struck by
those who worked for him; and Pyman, as well as Pownall or Browning,
would readily have admitted that Mountbatten's interference was capable of
having unexpected and sometimes beneficial results. His energy provided the
fuel for his obsessive love of detail. His Comptroller of Administration,
Admiral Jerram, called him an 'inspiring leader of boldness and imagination',
but fully supported Pownall's complaint that he fussed endlessly over trivia:
he 'could not relax when there was no operational activity on which to
concentrate his attention', but took refuge in the delights of protocol or
costume.[6]

If he had been the sort of man who could relax with Trollope or even a
crossword-puzzle, such complaints might not have been levelled at him, but
he read little outside official documents. His passion remained the cinema.
The Viceroy decided to show a film when Mountbatten was staying with him
and secured a copy of *Casablanca* – 'a typical film story of the sentimental-
thriller type', as he described it in his diary. After it was over Wavell told his
guest how bored he had been.

> He is a great film fan and was horrified. He apparently has one most
> nights – 'so much easier and quicker than reading a novel', he urged.
> 'But I seldom read novels,' I said. 'But what do you read then for
> relaxation? From your writing it is obvious that you do read
> sometimes.' I replied that I read biographies and poetry, rather than
> novels. 'But don't you like musical films?' 'I fear I am not musical.'
> 'But you don't need to be musical to enjoy musical films, with just

cheerful songs and dancing.' He is still youthful and I am afraid received the impression that I was a cheerless killjoy.[7]

'Supremo overworks himself to an almost alarming extent,' Arthur Power told Cunningham.[8] To keep in the air as many military and diplomatic balls as was required of him would have taxed any Supreme Commander. Mountbatten's energy and unwavering concentration never flagged, but his A.D.C.s sometimes paid the price in his explosions of temper. For these he would disarmingly apologize in advance: 'I'll have been spending the day with people I can't afford to lose my temper with, and I'll just be letting off steam.' Sometimes he would apologize the following day as well, but as often as not the incident would have passed from his mind. Any trifle might kindle an outburst. Once, in Singapore, Government House was turned upside down because the Supreme Commander demanded sardines in the early hours of the morning. He got them – but removed from their tin. He was outraged by this solecism and demanded redress; but no more sardines were to be found. In the end the wretched steward had laboriously to pack the sardines back into the tin again – a process which reduced him to a rage little less imposing than that of the Supreme Commander.

Yet beneath the tantrums, the vanity and the impetuosity Mountbatten had learned new wisdom in South-East Asia. His judgement of men and measures was more sure, his manipulation of events more adept. He had accumulated a whole new armoury of skills, acquired an understanding of political issues which few men of his career had enjoyed. He was a far more rounded and formidable figure; ready, as Pownall had said, to 'play a big part in the post-War Empire'.

In March 1946 the Mountbattens paid an official visit to Australia. It proved to be a triumphal progress. In Canberra, Melbourne, Sydney, Brisbane the streets were packed with enthusiastic crowds: 'She's a beaut, but he's more beaut,' was one comment called from the crowd which Mountbatten found 'hot-making' but privately cherished.[9] At Melbourne he had to make nine speeches in three days, and as the same distinguished figures featured at almost every function even he found the task wearing.[10] It was still worse at Brisbane, where he was required to make two speeches at the same dinner. The chairman offended him by making 'a very foolish speech' in which he urged everyone to forget the horrors of war and remember only the bright side – the comradeship and the pleasant adventures.

This was more than I could take, so I stood up and disagreed violently with him, asking everyone to remember the lousy side of

war, so that there should be no fear of the real . . . horrors being
forgotten and conditions being created again where another war
would be possible. This, as might be expected, caused considerable
consternation.[11]

At Sydney their reception was particularly enthusiastic. They drove in
state down the racecourse and even the bookmakers left their stands to watch
them go by. One enterprising bookie laid ten to one that Edwina would get
out of the door first, 'and was taken up by several people who did not seem to
realize what a gentleman I was!'[12]

Apart from a brief (and unsuccessful) negotiation with the trade union
leaders responsible for holding up Dutch shipping in Australian ports, no
business of any significance was transacted. The Duke of Gloucester, however, was about to retire as Governor-General and suggested that his cousin
would be the ideal person to take his place. The Australian Prime Minister
informally made the same proposal. Cunningham in London, his interest
sharpened by the fact that he was the British Government's candidate for the
job, watched sardonically. 'One must always wonder what he's up to next,'
he noted in his diary. 'Is he after the Governor-Generalship?' And then a few
days later: 'Dickie in Australia, I see. I have no doubt talking a lot. Still, he has
the film star technique and would make an excellent Governor-General.'[13]

No remarks could have shown more clearly how Cunningham misunderstood his younger colleague. Mountbatten had no desire but to return to the
Navy. Late in 1945 he had dined aboard H.M.S. *Cumberland*. 'It made me
feel so homesick dining on board ship again,' he wrote in his diary.[14] Leaving
to one side his ambition to become First Sea Lord and wipe out the stain on his
father's honour, it was on board ship that he felt happiest and most at home.
If he had been told it was indispensable in the national interest that he should
govern Australia, then he would have done so; but it would have been with
deep regret. 'There is a terrific lot of nonsense being talked by senior officers
about . . . the certainty that the country will want me to do some big job,' he
told Charles Lambe. 'In my own mind I am sure that this is wrong.'[15] In May
he asked A. V. Alexander if he could have a command afloat, and was told an
aircraft-carrier squadron was a possibility.[16]

There were plenty of other 'big jobs' being suggested. Lord Kemsley
wanted him to be Prime Minister.[17] One of his staff officers believed he was
playing his cards carefully so that if the royal family were forced into
abdication he might become President.[18] The King, more realistically, felt he
should become 'a sort of Chief of Staff to the Minister of Defence' – an idea
that was sensible enough but, as both Lambe and Mountbatten said, five
years too soon.[19] Churchill took it for granted that Mountbatten would move

on to things, if not higher, at least as high. 'Tell me, Pug,' he asked Ismay, 'what's all this about Dickie wanting to be a midshipman again?'[20] But a midshipman, or at least a Rear-Admiral, was exactly what Mountbatten did want to be.

On the whole the Navy wanted it too. Cunningham told Lambe he thought Mountbatten was 'a good chap', who ought to be back in the Navy in peacetime,[21] and if that was Cunningham's view no lesser sailor was likely to contradict him. But some senior admirals were not wholly happy when it was suggested that the former Supreme Commander might serve under them. Algernon Willis, the Commander-in-Chief in the Mediterranean, refused to take Mountbatten for the First Cruiser Squadron, saying that there was only room for one prima donna in any Fleet, and he was it.[22] Mountbatten's future was still uncertain when he got back to London in June 1946, but there was more than enough to occupy him, with holidays at home and abroad, ceremonial occasions and the preparation of the official Report on his period as Supreme Commander.

Mountbatten never doubted that his reputation would survive any calumny and emerge unblemished in the eyes of posterity, but he was not above giving the eyes of posterity a little help. He took enormous pains over his Report, the *Apologia pro vita sua* not only of *a* Supreme Commander but of *the* Supreme Commander, for his work is a hymn to the virtues of the office as well as the officer. The first draft was prepared by Major J. H. Money and the work was then taken in hand by Peter Murphy. According to Murphy, the 'maddening and rather muddled' Major Money had arranged the Report so illogically and expressed it so clumsily that it needed rewriting almost from scratch.[23] According to Money, his own perfectly fair and sensible first draft was first reduced to total confusion by Murphy and then peppered with errors and distortions – the object of the second exercise being to eliminate 'the chops and changes, mistakes and improvisations, which marked the whole campaign'.[24] Colonel Zvegintzov, one of Mountbatten's Planning Staff, made the same point when he commented in verse:

> I must confess to some surprise,
> Nor did I really realise
> Until the document I scanned,
> How really well we planners planned.
>
> Each Jap offensive, it appears,
> We had forestalled by several years,
> I wonder how the blighters dared
> To think they'd find us unprepared.

Banzai! Good Show! Well done each 'CinC'
And yet I cannot help but think,
If all was right and nothing wrong
Why did the darned thing take so long?

The jibe is not unjustified; the bland and well-worked surface of the
*Report to the Combined Chiefs of Staff*[25] does indeed gloss over a multitude
of doubts and setbacks and suggests an atmosphere of omniscient self-
confidence at Supreme Headquarters that can rarely have existed. Such is the
way of official despatches, however, and in this respect the Report seems no
worse a specimen than others. Certainly it is not an exercise in personal
vainglory; 'owing to the almost complete absence of ego', wrote one reviewer,
'it would seem that it has been written by an observer rather than a
Commander who, faced by almost insuperable difficulties, brought the
operations to such a successful conclusion'.[26] This is perhaps a little strong;
Mountbatten's presence broods over the entire saga. But so it should. The
Supreme Commander was the hero of the story; the fact that he was also the
author could not be expected to reduce his role to nullity.

With the bulk of the Report behind him, and a rich harvest of accumulated
leave successfully garnered, Mountbatten at the end of 1946 prepared to
attend a Senior Officers Technical Course at Portsmouth. It was to be his
gateway back into the Royal Navy. When the appointment was announced he
was speculating eagerly about his subsequent posting. And yet perhaps he had
some suspicion that his naval career might not run smoothly. 'I really want to
go back to the Navy, as you know,' he had written to Edwina from Karachi
early in 1945, 'and don't like the idea of governing . . . but if it ever became
unavoidable I know that you would make the world's ideal Vicereine!'[27]

OPPOSITE *The Mountbattens driving through the streets of London on the way to*
*the Guildhall, where Mountbatten was to receive the freedom of the city.*

# Part Three

# 1946-1948

# CHAPTER 28

# *'The Most Important Journey'*

WHEN MOUNTBATTEN VISITED INDIA with the Prince of Wales in 1921, the long march to independence was already under way. Sullen, hostile crowds, student boycotts, nervous and omnipresent police showed that the march was unlikely to be a tranquil one. And yet, since far back in the nineteenth century, successive generations of British politicians had at least paid lip-service to the idea that India was part of the British Empire because this was in the best interests of the inhabitants, and that as soon as they were fit to do so they would be free to decide their own form of government. Some had believed what they said; others had felt that any such moment must be impossibly far away, a phantasmagoria designed to lull the appetites of local nationalists without causing serious disquiet to the hard-headed merchants who were making a good thing out of India.

If a time had to be picked when phantasmagoria became reality it would be 1917, when Edwin Montagu in the House of Commons stated categorically that the aim of the British Government was to establish India as an independent democracy within the Empire. The following year Montagu and Lord Chelmsford prepared their celebrated Report which reiterated that responsible self-government, first in local and then in national affairs, was the British objective in India. A federation of more-or-less self-governing provinces, around a centre responsible for such matters as communications and defence, was the projected pattern – 'but the last thing we desire is to attempt to force the pace'.[1] The troubled India which Mountbatten discovered on his first visit to the sub-continent showed that, so far as Gandhi and the Indian National Congress Party were concerned, the pace could not be fast enough.

The 1920s and 1930s were marked by campaigns of civil disobedience, usually passive, sometimes fiercely violent. Under the surface swell a tide of independence was flowing, marked not so much by institutional changes as the erosion of the British will to govern, the acceptance by even the most reactionary that the end of the Raj lay not centuries but decades away. Yet those who sought to impede the process had legitimate weapons with which to do so. In India nothing is simple, little straightforward, and nowhere was this more true than in the freedom movement. Freedom from what and movement to what goal? The erratic, almost casual growth of the Empire in India had meant that some forty per cent of the land-space of India was not properly British at all, but consisted of a plethora of states responsible not to the Indian Government in Delhi but to the British Crown. How were these Princely States to be fitted into the jigsaw of independent India?

And what of the Muslims? To those who looked for chicanery in British policy towards India, their case seemed striking. Here, said the Hindu nationalist, was a minority which for many generations had lived in harmonious synthesis with the other groups of the sub-continent. Wilfully, the British had fomented a sense of separatism by giving the Muslims their own electorates and encouraging their individual culture and sense of history. There is enough truth in the accusation to give it some plausibility – 'divide and rule' is a traditional expedient of imperial powers – but many years after the system of separate electorates had been imposed Hindu and Muslim were still united in their opposition to the British and support for a greater India. Muslim separatism was never a British creation, nor can the limited encouragement which they gave it have made the difference between its survival and extinction.

In 1935 came what should have been the next great step in India's peaceful march to independence. Though Churchill blithely described it as 'a gigantic quilt of jumbled crochet work, a monstrous monument of shame built by pigmies',[2] the Government of India Act, 1935 was a perfectly sensible piece of legislation which set up eleven British–Indian provinces with limited autonomy. It was a logical stepping-stone in the direction of a federal India in which the Princely States would take part, but it was a stepping-stone which ignored the aspirations of the Indian political leadership. It gave the Princes a right of veto over the future federation and encouraged their separatist ambitions in a way which was unacceptable to nationalist leaders who, anyway, saw the Maharajas and Rajas as an irritating feudal anachronism. It reserved to the Viceroy and provincial governors powers which any patriot must feel intolerably great. And yet in spite of, indeed because of, its imperfections, it prepared the way for the triumph of Congress at the forthcoming elections in British India. That triumph proved a step on the path to partition and the massacres. Since its foundation the National Congress had been the voice of independence, demanding self-government for a unified India that would make no distinction between Hindu and Muslim. Mahomed Ali Jinnah, who was to become unquestioned leader of the Muslims in British India, began his career as a loyal member of Congress. Only when effective power began to seem more than a distant dream did the polarization of politicians and voters into Congress and Muslim League begin to pose a serious threat to unity. Not until 1936 did Jinnah argue that only if Hindu and

Muslim were organized separately could they understand and work with each other; not till the year after that did he formulate the dread concept of a Muslim 'nation'. Even then a united, independent sub-continent was still the aim of all the Indian leaders, but more and more they were forming policies from a sectarian rather than a pan-Indian point of view.

In 1936 Lord Linlithgow arrived as Viceroy, pledged to launch the Indian federation during his time in office. Honourable, decent, without guile, he was ill-equipped to cope with the mercurial temperaments and infinite subtlety of the Indian leaders – 'heavy of body and slow of mind', Nehru described him uncharitably, 'solid as a rock and with almost a rock's lack of awareness'.[3] He struggled hopefully but achieved little. By the time the war began attitudes had grown still more rigid, the Hindus determined to accept no settlement that would shatter the unity of India, the Muslims equally resolute that they must have the substance if not all the trappings of a separate state, both agreeing only that the British must go and go quickly.

The war changed everything and nothing. Willy nilly, the Indians found themselves part of a conflict in whose direction they played no part. Congress condemned an 'imperialist' war and pulled its representatives out of the various provincial governments. With Japan's entry into the war and the overrunning of Burma, the threat of Indian dissidence became far more alarming. Pressed by the Labour and Liberal members of his coalition Government, and by his American allies, Churchill reluctantly conceded that some step should be taken to break the deadlock. 'I hate Indians,' he petulantly remarked to Amery in 1942. 'They are a beastly people with a beastly religion.'[4] Mountbatten told Wavell that India was the Prime Minister's blind-spot and that he was 'most unreasonable and riding for a fall over it'.[5] But once Churchill had agreed that Stafford Cripps, the austere socialist Lord Privy Seal in the coalition Government, should visit India to find a basis on which independence could be granted after the war, he stood back and allowed his colleague to do his best.

The Cripps mission in its turn foundered. Cripps made a significant step forward when he committed the British Government to a policy of complete independence for India, inside or outside the Commonwealth as its new rulers might desire. Congress, however, was not going to be satisfied with jam tomorrow, while the British were not prepared to surrender any significant degree of control with the Japanese at the gates of India. When Mountbatten took over as Supreme Commander at the end of 1943 a campaign of civil disobedience was in progress and the Congress leadership, including Gandhi, was behind bars.

By then, too, Linlithgow had departed and Wavell become Viceroy. Generous of mind, artistic by temperament, a gallant soldier and fine leader of men, Wavell was no more capable than his predecessor of reconciling the irreconcilable and juggling with the different desires and demands of the Indian leaders. Taciturn, cautious, wholly without political guile, he won the respect of Gandhi, Nehru and Jinnah but neither their affection nor their confidence. He could not convince himself, let alone others, that his negotiations were likely to reach an acceptable conclusion. Probably not even the craftiest political operator could have done much better at such a time. As the Japanese threat dwindled, so Whitehall's anxiety for a rapid settlement was appeased. Other problems appeared more urgent; Churchill's doubts about the need for change once again became apparent. Wavell called a conference at Simla to establish an executive council which would be representative of all Indian interests; but though he marched his negotiators up to the top of the hill, he soon found that no basis for agreement existed, and marched them down again. To induce the Congress and the Muslim League to co-operate, he told George VI, 'reminds me of one of my childhood puzzles – a little glass-covered box with 3 or 4 different coloured marbles which one had to manipulate into their respective pens by very gentle oscillation; just as the last one seemed on the point of moving in, some or all of the others invariably ran out'.[6]

From Kandy, and later from Singapore, Mountbatten watched the Viceroy's travail with sympathy but a tinge of exasperation. What struck him most forcibly was what Lord Listowel later described as the 'abject and humiliating thraldom' in which Wavell was held by London.[7] He was genuinely shocked when Wavell told him that he had not been allowed to have an informal talk with Gandhi, and could not understand why the Viceroy had not simply conducted his conversation first and only subsequently reported it to Whitehall.[8] But that was not Wavell's way.

In the summer of 1945 the Labour Government came to office, dedicated to the rapid withdrawal of British power from India. Lord Pethick-Lawrence was technically to be in charge of whatever negotiations were necessary; but in fact Cripps and the Prime Minister, Clement Attlee, took over the responsibility. In March 1946 a Cabinet mission visited India. Its first preoccupation was still to establish a federal India, yet it arrived in a sub-continent divided as never before. In the recent elections Congress had swept the board in all the predominantly Hindu provinces, while the League had won almost every Muslim seat. Polarization was complete. Against this background the mission did extraordinarily well to reach a position where the Muslim League had accepted in principle a plan for a federation, while Congress had moved some way at least in the same direction. There negotiations stuck. 'It looks as if,' Wavell wrote gloomily to Mountbatten, 'after many weeks of bargaining, the Congress were going to run true to form and turn down yet another offer. What will happen next is uncertain, but it will certainly be difficult and unpleasant.'[9] Ironically, Congress would have accepted with relief in 1947 the terms that they rejected in 1946, but by that time it was too late – the Muslim League would settle for nothing less than the creation of an independent Pakistan.

What happened next was indeed 'difficult and unpleasant'. The Muslim League called on its followers to observe 16 August as 'Direct Action Day' in protest against Hindu intransigence. In Calcutta action became massacre; in three days more than twenty thousand people were killed or seriously injured in communal rioting. In chain-reaction, similar though lesser outbreaks of violence occurred throughout East Bengal and Bihar. The Punjab needed only a spark to explode with a fury that would dwarf the horrors of Calcutta. Worst of all, there was evidence that, under the pressure of sectarian passion, discipline in the administration and the police, even the Army itself, was beginning to crumble. A sense of impending catastrophe was in the air. It was evident that something must be done with desperate urgency, but what that something should be remained unclear.

Wavell had shot his bolt. 'I have tried everything I know to solve the problem of handing over India to its people, and I can see no light,' he told Mountbatten. 'I have only one solution, which I call Operation Madhouse – withdrawal of the British province by province, beginning with women and children, then civilians, then the army.'[10] If this were unacceptable, he reported bluntly to the Cabinet, the only alternative would be to reinforce the Indian Army with four or five divisions from Britain and prepare to rule the sub-continent for another fifteen years. This would, he knew, be unacceptable to a Labour – or, indeed, any other British – Government. But his first proposition was received with equal disfavour. He was 'frankly pretty defeatist by then', commented Attlee.[11] In Cabinet Wavell's plan was dismissed as 'a policy of scuttle unworthy of a great Power'.[12] The counsel was of despair and must be rejected.

A new initiative was necessary. George Abell, Private Secretary to the Viceroy and one of the wisest and most experienced of Indian administrators, told the Cabinet that he estimated that there was one chance in ten of an acceptable agreement between the Indian leaders.[13] Attlee was more optimistic; he told the King that he put the odds at six to four against success. Whatever the chances, however, the attempt had to be made, and Wavell was not the man to make it. Attlee looked around for a successor and had what he later described as 'an inspiration'. 'Dickie Mountbatten stood out a mile. Burma showed it. The so-called experts had been wrong about Aung San, and Dickie had been right.'[14]

*

Mountbatten had, in fact, first been suggested as a replacement for Linlithgow by Leo Amery in the summer of 1942.[15] Nine months later he had again
been put forward by Sir Ralph Glyn.[16] In 1946 his name must have been very
much to the fore. He had every qualification that could be required. In
South-East Asia he had proved himself a liberal and de-colonizer. As a popular
hero, his nomination would assuage the fears of some, at least, of the
imperialists. The appointment of the King-Emperor's cousin would appeal to
the Indian Princes. He had already established an excellent relationship with
Nehru, and Krishna Menon had told Cripps that his selection would be most
acceptable to the Congress leadership.[17] He was 'an extremely lively, exciting
personality', said Attlee. 'He had an extraordinary faculty for getting on with
all kinds of people. . . . He was also blessed with a very unusual wife.'[18]
Attlee's only doubt was whether he would accept.

It has been suggested that Mountbatten's reluctance to become Viceroy
was as much feigned as that of the Speaker who has to be dragged protesting
to the Chair of the House of Commons. All those who were close to him at the
time agree that this was not the case.[19] Directly after his first meeting with
Attlee he went round to see his old friend Charles Lambe and said he did not
want to go. Lambe maintained that he must; nobody else could do the job.
Back at the Senior Officers Course he told Royer Dick what was in the wind.
He was, said Dick, in 'considerable distress of spirit'. 'I do hope you are
feeling less depressed now,' his daughter Patricia wrote to him. 'I did feel so
very sorry for you.'[20] It was not the unpleasantness of the task or the
probability of failure that deterred him – if anything, such considerations
were an incentive to accept – but the fact that he had set his heart on returning
to the Navy, had accomplished it with some difficulty and was now robbed of
his desire. It had not been easy to convince his naval superiors that he should
be allowed to return after his time as Supreme Commander; would it not be
more difficult still after another two years and another job ashore?[21]

But, though genuine, Mountbatten's reluctance was also extremely useful. 'I fortunately find myself in a pretty strong position,' he told Wavell,
'since I do not think any of the Cabinet can be under the illusion that I wanted
this job.'[22] Though he did not dictate his terms to the Government with quite
the forthrightness he sometimes suggested, there is no doubt that he was given
greater liberty in making his arrangements and writing his own instructions
than had traditionally been allowed to even the most magnificent of Viceroys.
His first condition – which he put in a letter to Attlee shortly after his first
interview at Downing Street on 18 December – that he would go to Delhi only
'at the open invitation of the Indian parties' – was admittedly soon dropped as
being impracticable,[23] but otherwise he got his own way to a remarkable
extent.

The most striking example of this arose over Mountbatten's insistence that a firm date must be fixed for the handing over of power. Without such a proviso, he maintained, the Indians would never believe that he had in reality come to end and not to perpetuate the vice-regal system.[24] He was not alone in perceiving this. Wavell had unavailingly made the same demand and, many years later, Attlee remembered: 'I decided that the only thing to do was to set a time-limit and say – "whatever happens, our rule is ending on that date".'[25] In his recent biography of Attlee, Kenneth Harris has pointed out that the need for a deadline was discussed in the Cabinet's India Committee before Mountbatten was even offered the Viceroyalty.[26] The credit for the idea is therefore not uniquely Mountbatten's. But, though accepting the need for some vague goal like 'the middle of 1948', Attlee opposed any more precise commitment on the grounds that it could prove a serious embarrassment as the time drew near.[27] Wavell supported him, arguing that, even if a date were to be fixed, it should be left until after Mountbatten arrived and had summed up the situation.[28] To Mountbatten this would have defeated the object of the exercise; if he was to win the confidence of the Indian leaders he *must* bear with him the guarantee of his rapid disappearance. He stuck to his point and won; the final instructions read:

> The date fixed for the transfer of power is a flexible one to within one month; but you should aim at 1 June 1948 as the effective date for the transfer of power.[29]

It is less clear whether he won over what later in life he would refer to as his 'plenipotentiary powers'. In 1968 Vice-Admiral Brockman questioned Mountbatten's use of this phrase, and said that he had never heard it referred to during Mountbatten's time as Viceroy. 'It is quite true that I only mentioned this to Pug Ismay and he strongly advised that I should not mention it to anybody else at all,' replied Mountbatten. 'The only person who tumbled to the situation was Panditji [Nehru] himself, who realised what had happened within a week.' When Brockman was still politely sceptical Mountbatten retorted, 'It is a pity that Attlee, Cripps, Ismay and Nehru are all dead.' The discussion was graven on his memory, 'and I am quite prepared to put in a signed statement, if necessary going to a Commissioner of Oaths. I do not personally believe it will be any use searching the Cabinet records because there was no secretary in the room to make any notes.'[30]

In this last point he is certainly correct. Neither in the Cabinet records nor in Attlee's correspondence is there any mention of special powers. Nor, if by the phrase 'plenipotentiary powers' is meant the liberty to act at one's discretion, without reference back to a home Government (and there is nothing else it can mean, if it is to have any real significance), did Mountbatten avail himself of such a freedom. On the contrary, not only did he submit to London his draft plan for a settlement, but when he needed to modify it he himself flew to London to present his case. It seems probable that the words were used in the course of discussion, but unlikely that they held any precise legal implications. Rather, they expressed what undoubtedly was true: that Mountbatten enjoyed a discretion far wider than any Viceroy had known since the invention of the telegraph had brought Whitehall to within a few minutes of New Delhi.

Mountbatten also pressed for the removal of Pethick-Lawrence as Secretary of State and his replacement by someone with whom he could work more easily. Attlee needed little convincing; he found Pethick-Lawrence prolix and argumentative and was glad to let him go.[31] 'I suggested Billy Listowel,' Mountbatten later explained, 'because I already knew him and knew that he was deeply steeped in India and I thought would be an easy person to deal with.'[32] Listowel in fact was an afterthought. Stafford Cripps had disconcerted Mountbatten by offering to accompany him to India, a well-intentioned proposal which dismayed the future Viceroy – 'I don't want to be ham-strung by having to bring out a third version of the Cripps offer!!!' he told George VI.[33] To Attlee he was more diplomatic. 'The presence of a man of his prestige and experience', he told the Prime Minister, 'could not fail to reduce me to a mere figure-head.'[34] He ingeniously escaped from the quandary by suggesting that the most useful thing Cripps could do would be to go to the India Office and act as a rear-link in London.[35] 'You certainly had a brainwave in asking Cripps to take on the I.O.' wrote the King approvingly. 'I should never relish the idea of having him either on my staff or staying in my house.'[36] In the event Cripps stayed where he was and the experienced and amenable Listowel was called on to see out the last days of the India Office.

Mountbatten insisted on, and was granted without argument, the right not merely to pick his own staff but to superimpose it on the existing administration in Delhi. His most important acquisition was Churchill's former Chief of Staff, General Ismay. Mountbatten went to ask him what he thought about the new assignment. Ismay's reaction was that it was 'one of the most delicate and perhaps distasteful assignments imaginable, but that it was difficult to see how he could refuse'.[37] Mountbatten had planned to ask him to join the party but he found Ismay so jubilant about a trip to Australia which was to take place the following month that he did not have the heart to suggest it. Next day, however, Ismay proposed it himself: 'If you are going out to play the last chukka twelve goals down, count me in on your team.'[38] His title was to be 'Chief of the Viceroy's Staff', a position intended to be akin to the French *Chef de Cabinet*. 'My opinion of your new boss has gone up,' wrote Alan Lascelles in some surprise. 'I know that you, throughout the war, never hesitated to hit him over the head, hard and often, whenever he deserved it, and it is greatly to his credit that the first person he should ask to help him now, is yourself.'[39] Lascelles's surprise was itself surprising. It was not necessary to know Mountbatten well to be aware that a readiness to hit him over the head from time to time would be considered not a handicap but an important recommendation.

Sir Eric Miéville, for long a Private Secretary to the Viceroy, was also recruited to serve as 'Principal Secretary'; Mountbatten had no idea what role he was to play but liked and trusted him and felt sure he would be useful. Various old hands from South-East Asia were to come along: Brockman as Personal Secretary; Alan Campbell-Johnson as Press Attaché; Peter Murphy as Peter Murphy. Cripps, prompted by Nehru and Krishna Menon, recommended that the present Private Secretary, George Abell, should be replaced as soon as possible. Mountbatten approved what he had heard of Abell, reckoned that his experience would be indispensable and insisted that he should stay.[40]

Mountbatten's last preoccupation was his naval career. If he was once again deprived of the chance to do what he really wanted, he should at least be left on the Active Flag List, so that his future employment would not be put at risk. This too was agreed; his old York aircraft, which he had used as Supreme Commander, was put at his disposal; it was accepted that he should not be bound by the rigid formality of former Viceroys – 'my wife and I would wish', he wrote, 'to visit Indian leaders, and representative British and Indian people, in their own homes and unaccompanied by staff; and to make ourselves easier of access than the existing protocol appears to have made possible'.[41] No one, it was clear, was going to stop *him* seeing Gandhi.

It was not till 11 February 1947 that Mountbatten formally accepted the office of Viceroy, and even then there was a last-minute contretemps over the text of the announcement. Attlee showed him what he proposed to say and asked for his comments. Mountbatten said that he felt it was too long, and in particular contained a paragraph gratuitously offensive to the Indians. Attlee appeared annoyed and Ismay explained that it had already been agreed by the Cabinet. Mountbatten said he was sorry to hear it, but his view remained the same. The announcement was made without the questionable paragraph.[42] Mountbatten was lecturing at the Joint Services Staff College when the statement was released. Rear-Admiral Douglas-Pennant added the news to his speech of thanks. There were cheers and clapping. 'It is not a matter for applause, I assure you,' said Mountbatten drily.[43]

Wavell had been given no hint what was in the air when he was in London, nor was he told of his fate until 13 February, after the negotiations had been going on for nearly two months. He took the news with characteristic dignity and generosity. 'An unexpected appointment,' he noted in his diary; 'but a clever one from their point of view; and Dickie's personality may perhaps accomplish what I have failed to do.'[44] 'They've sacked me, George,' Wavell said to Abell after he had digested the news. 'I think they're probably right, don't you?'[45] Mountbatten himself felt that his predecessor had been shabbily treated. 'I hope you will not mind my mentioning this,' he told Attlee, 'but I am sure you will understand how much happier I should feel in succeeding a man I admire so much, if his services were to receive high recognition.'[46]

When Mountbatten agreed to go to India he won himself a formidable enemy. Winston Churchill was never wholly to forgive what he considered a personal as well as a national betrayal. In the House of Commons he confined himself to attacking the Government. Was Mountbatten, he asked, 'to make a new effort to restore the situation, or is it merely Operation Scuttle on which he and other distinguished officers have been dispatched? . . . I am bound to say the whole thing wears the aspect of an attempt by the Government to make use of brilliant war figures in order to cover up a melancholy and disastrous transaction.'[47] To his friends he made no secret of the fact that, though he condemned the Government for their policy, he blamed Mountbatten too for lending himself to its execution.[48]

The debate in the Commons, with the Government in a massive majority, could end in only one way; in the House of Lords a defeat for the official policy was on the cards. Lord Templewood, who initiated the debate, argued in particular that the imposition of a time-limit was a breach of faith, imperilling the peace and prosperity of India. The voice of the doubters was predominant in the argument that followed, until Lord Halifax, a former Viceroy and a Tory, pleaded with the House not to accept the motion condemning the Government. He would not say that their policy was right but 'the truth is that for India today there is no solution that is not fraught with the gravest objection, with the gravest danger'. In such circumstances, he concluded, unpalatable though he might find it, 'I am not prepared to condemn what His Majesty's Government are doing unless I can honestly and confidently recommend a better solution.'[49] His intervention proved decisive, and Lord Templewood withdrew his motion.

Churchill was not the only one to ask what Mountbatten was going to India to do. He must be given a clear directive, noted George VI in his diary. 'Is he to lead the retreat out of India or is he to work for the reconciliation of Hindus and Moslems?'[50] The answer was that nobody knew; Ministers hoped for reconciliation but expected retreat. Mountbatten's instructions, which were very similar to the Prime Minister's earlier statement and incorporated all the points on which the new Viceroy had laid such emphasis, were set out in a letter addressed to him by Attlee on 18 March.[51] 'It is the definite objective of His Majesty's Government', stated the letter boldly, 'to obtain a unitary Government for British India and the Indian States, if possible within the British Commonwealth.' So far, so good, but then began the qualifications. The plan could not be imposed, only negotiated; 'there can be no question of compelling either major Party to accept it'. If it was clear by 1 October that such negotiations had proved abortive, then Mountbatten was to report back on what steps must be taken to transfer power by 1 June 1948 or within a month or so of that date. Somehow the Indian rulers must be induced to work with each other and with the British in the search for a settlement. 'The keynote of your administration should therefore be the closest co-operation with the Indians and you should make it clear to the whole of the Secretary of State's Services that this is so.' Finally, he was to do all he could to keep the Indian Army intact and maintain 'the organisation of defence on an all Indian basis'. Keep India united if you can; if not, try to save something from the wreck; whatever happens, get Britain out was the essence of Mountbatten's orders.

Mountbatten had hoped to confer with Wavell before setting off, so that he could discuss any unsuspected pitfalls with the Ministers in London. This proved impossible, and he had to settle for a brief handover in New Delhi. Departure was fixed for 20 March. He had been able to make few preparations before the formal announcement a month before, so the final weeks were impossibly crowded with meetings, briefings, fitting of clothes and uniforms, injections, interviews and a welter of farewells and miscellaneous celebrations. He said goodbye to his mother at Broadlands on 17 March. Lady Milford Haven was now eighty-three and, though she was still strong, each time that he left her for more than a few days he felt that it might be for the last time. She had been deeply opposed to her son accepting the appointment: 'Damn! Damn!' she had exclaimed when the offer was first spoken of – the only time Patricia had ever heard her swear. Now, as Mountbatten kissed her, he remarked lightly: 'Well, I'll be back in a few months.' 'You won't,' said his mother. 'You'll be there for years, if you come back at all.' The same note of foreboding was struck by many – both informed and uninformed. 'I wonder if they will come back alive,' speculated Noel Coward after one of the many farewell parties that were crowded into that final month.[52] Mountbatten wondered the same thing. 'We shall be incredibly unpopular,' he told Peter Howes, a naval officer on his staff, 'and the odds are we shall end up with bullets in our backs.'[53]

The last word belongs to Stafford Cripps:

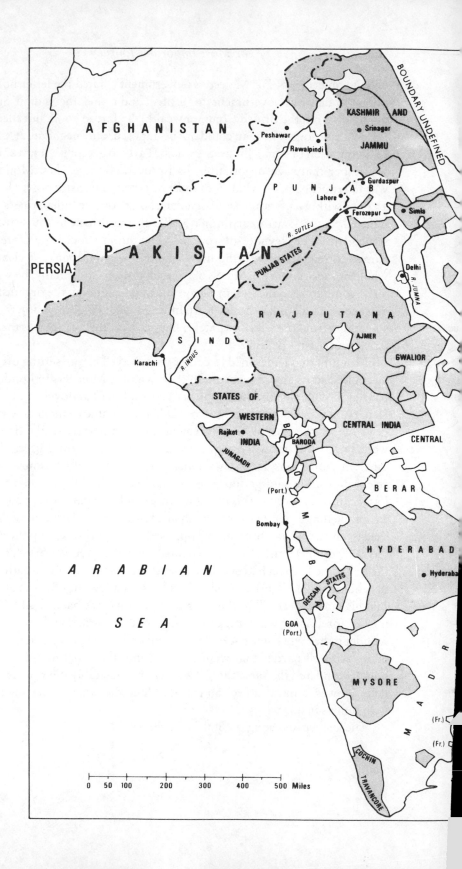

AFGHANISTAN

KASHMIR AND

Peshawar

• Srinagar

Rawalpindi

JAMMU

P  U  N  J  A  B

Gurdaspur

Lahore •

• Simla

PAKISTAN

• Ferozepur

Delhi

PERSIA

R. SUTLEJ

R. JUMNA

PUNJAB STATES

R  A  J  P  U  T  A  N  A

AJMER

S  I  N  D

GWALIOR

Karachi •

R. INDUS

STATES  OF

WESTERN

CENTRAL INDIA

CENTRAL

Rajkot •

BARODA

INDIA

JUNAGADH

BERAR

(Port.)

Bombay •

HYDERABAD

• Hyderaba

DECCAN  STATES

A  R  A  B  I  A  N

GOA
(Port.)

S  E  A

MYSORE

(Fr.)

(Fr.)

COCHIN

TRAVANCORE

0  50  100      200       300       400      500  Miles

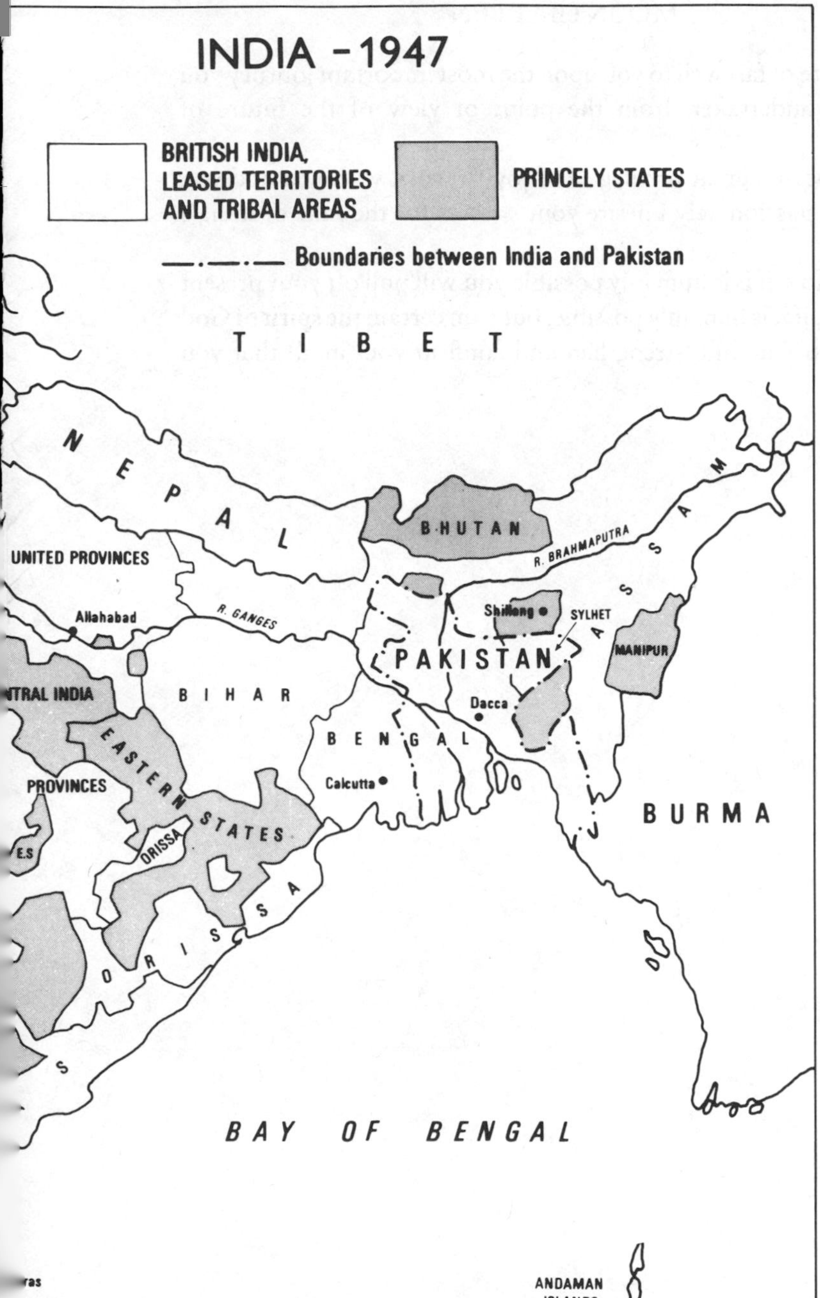

# INDIA - 1947

BRITISH INDIA,
LEASED TERRITORIES
AND TRIBAL AREAS

PRINCELY STATES

—.—.— Boundaries between India and Pakistan

T I B E T

N E P A L

B·H U T A N

UNITED PROVINCES

R. BRAHMAPUTRA

A S S A M

Allahabad

R. GANGES

Shillong ●   SYLHET

MANIPUR

PAKISTAN

NTRAL INDIA

B I H A R

Dacca
●

CENTRAL INDIA

EASTERN

B E N G A L

PROVINCES

Calcutta ●

STATES

ORISSA

E.S

O R I S S A

BURMA

S

BAY   OF   BENGAL

ras

ANDAMAN
ISLANDS

0

This is a note of farewell to you upon the most important journey you have ever undertaken from the point of view of the future of humanity.

It has been a great privilege and joy to work with you and you know how passionately I desire your success for the sake of India's future.

. . . I know if it is humanly possible you will pull off your present plans. I say, if it is humanly possible, but I am certain the spirit of God will be with you and 'strengthen and confirm you' in all that you do.[54]

# CHAPTER 29

## *The End of Unified India*

THE MOUNTBATTENS ARRIVED AT DELHI in the afternoon of 22 March 1947. They were driven by open landau with cavalry escort to Viceroy's House, the Lutyens palace that was to be their home and headquarters. There the Wavells met them at the head of the great red-carpeted sweep of steps. Mountbatten bowed, Edwina curtsied, for there could only be one Viceroy at a time and the job would be Wavell's till he left Delhi the following morning. This one evening was left to them to discuss the monstrous catalogue of problems that was now being handed on to the new incumbent.

The state entry into Delhi provided Mountbatten with his first taste of the pomp and circumstance that encompassed the Viceroy in all his doings. Diminished though it was by the ease of communication with Whitehall, a Viceroy's authority was still enormous. If it had dwindled, however, the magnificence had not. With its vast halls, acres of exquisitely tended garden, regiment of servants, Viceroy's House was the Versailles of southern Asia; a building created to impose; a shrine of the man-god who was sent from far across the sea to wield terrible power over the Indian peasant. Mountbatten loved it, even when he laughed at it. 'I still can't get used to being treated like an Emperor,' he told Patricia. 'I find you have to hold ladies' hands very firmly while they make a deep curtsey as they seem to steady themselves on your hand and are apt to pull themselves up by it. Occasionally I try to help them up with a tug but the result is rather like Bob's strong mother giving Angie [Laycock] a leg-up and throwing her clean over her horse, as the ladies come whistling up much quicker than they expected and aren't grateful!'[1] He only took exception to the grandeur when it impeded his freedom of action, as when police tried to escort him when he went on a morning ride, or he decided to pay a visit to Simla at short notice. 'It would take three days to organize,' said the Comptroller. 'I will travel light, with a minimum of staff,' said the Viceroy. 'In that case, I can just manage it,' said the Comptroller. And so 'a mere skeleton staff of 180 officers and servants accompanied me. And I, in my innocence, had vaguely thought it would be rather like ordering a jeep to drive to Dimbula [his bungalow near Kandy] for the weekend.'[2]

Splendour mingled curiously with austerity. The Mountbattens ruled

363

that, because of the near-famine in some parts of India, rationing would be imposed in Viceroy's House. Helpings were so small that the hungrier members of the staff sought invitations from the Ismays, where they could be sure of a square meal. In another respect, too, the aspect of entertaining changed. 'Dickie and Edwina have both got off to a magnificent start,' reported Walter Monckton, adviser to the Nizam of Hyderabad. 'His sincerity, frankness and charm are obvious enough but I think it is also understood that he won't be b—d about (as we used to say in the Royal West Kent Regiment). Moreover Viceroy's House is wide open, socially and politically, to people who would never have found their way here before – particularly the Indians in that category.'[3] There was nothing new in the idea of receiving Indians at Viceroy's House, but the Mountbattens cast the net farther. Every week they held two garden parties, three or four luncheons for thirty, two or three larger dinners, 'at which I have made it a rule that not less than 50% of those present must be Indians'.[4] Not all the British guests took kindly to this innovation. Pamela overheard one English lady saying to another: 'It makes me absolutely sick to see this house full of dirty Indians!' Mountbatten repeated the remark at a meeting of provincial governors, and 'invited their co-operation in sending home anybody who expresses sentiments of this type'.[5]

Open diplomacy was, so far as possible, the order of the day; writing from Hyderabad, Monckton noted that he could follow the progress of negotiations as easily from the columns of *Dawn* or the *Hindustan Times* as in private talks with Ismay or the Viceroy.[6] Yet openness did not exclude a degree of manipulation, even chicanery, which would have been inconceivable to either of his immediate predecessors. Mountbatten was well aware that certain of his advisers felt that his tactics sometimes verged on the unethical, but believed that sleight of hand was justifiable to achieve the greater good; the lie direct was to be avoided, the lie circumstantial might be acceptable. Ian Scott, his Deputy Private Secretary, remembered the Viceroy looking up after proposing a certain course of action and catching the expression on his and Abell's faces: 'I know what you're thinking. Wavell would never have done it. Well, I'm not Wavell, and I will!'[7]

Only a man of phenomenal strength and energy could have kept up the pace that Mountbatten set himself. 'I can rarely *start* my paper work before 11 p.m.,' he told Patricia, 'and often don't finish with Ronnie [Brockman] till after 1 a.m. and then read on in bed till 2 or 3. I can't last much longer at this rate but I've got to stick it a bit longer.'[8] A strenuous but not exceptional night found an emergency meeting finishing at 1.15 a.m., Brockman departing at 2 a.m., Mountbatten reading for a further hour, and leaving at 7.15 a.m. on a hurried provincial tour. 'SEAC – even in the hectic days of Kohima and

Imphal – was a rest cure.'[9] The only way he could survive was by ruthless concentration on the essential issues; on Easter Sunday he told Patricia that he was rejecting appeals against the death-sentence at the rate of four a day without even having time to read them.[10] Yet on those issues to which he gave his full attention his clarity of mind and capacity to absorb and digest were formidable. Abell remembers late one night handing him a thick dossier and saying that, as it would take two hours even to glance through, there was no chance of his studying it before next morning's meeting. Mountbatten was non-committal, but by the next morning he had identified the key issues and decided how they should be handled.[11]

His wife was an invaluable ally, both through the reputation she won in the world of health and welfare, of which she had made herself the queen, and through the rapport which she established with the Indian leaders and, still more, their wives. Her close relationship with Nehru did not begin until the Mountbattens were on the verge of leaving India, but Gandhi was touchingly fond of her, and her courage, spirit and total dedication won the admiration of all who observed her in action. For Mountbatten, however, she was not a comfortable companion. Fiercely competitive, she had always operated before in a different sphere to her husband: now she found herself outshone, and hated the experience. She was determined to match him: if the Viceroy had three files to work on, she must have four; if he worked to 1 a.m., she must work to 1.30. Her health was poor, her nerves on edge. At the best of times she was quick to take offence; now it was necessary to think twice at least before saying anything to her. Her husband, who found it hard to think even once, was perpetually in trouble. 'The last two days have been pretty good Hell,' Ismay told his wife. 'Both Dickie and Edwina are dead tired, nervy as they can be, and right across each other. So that in addition to my other troubles, I have been doing peace-maker and general sedative. . . . It's very wearing for them, and for me.'[12]

His solace was his daughter Pamela, who had accompanied her parents to Delhi. Every morning at 6.30 father and daughter would ride together. For the Viceroy it was probably the only moment of the day – a day of eighteen hours at least – in which he was not concentrating exclusively on the problems of his task. If he managed to snatch another hour or so, late at night or on a Sunday afternoon, it would usually be devoted to work on his beloved family tables – a web of relationships over several centuries, which every day grew more intricate as he sought for that comprehensiveness which is the genealogist's dream.

While they still retained some reservations about the intentions of the British Government, the Indian leaders – at least so far as Congress was concerned – quickly concluded that Mountbatten was to be treated as a friend. Not all his British subordinates were so easily converted. Auchinleck commented on the bad treatment Wavell had received and went on: 'There is little comment, other than scurrilous, so far about his successor, who in spite of his great record is not really known to India.'[13] The old India hands were sceptical about the wisdom of imposing on them this brash, impetuous amateur who could not be expected to understand the subtleties of the task he was so blithely undertaking. Those who saw him in action were quickly reassured about his professionalism and acute political sensitivity. John Christie, Joint Private Secretary to the Viceroy and a Wavell man to his fingertips, remarked that, whatever he might feel about his hero's dismissal, 'the choice of his successor had been brilliant'.[14] With a determined good will that owed much to Ismay and Abell, old hands and new men settled down to work together. Mountbatten was served with total loyalty, even though those concerned knew they were toiling towards their own extinction. He was to need all the loyalty he could command.

Some Indians were at first sceptical. P. C. Joshi, General Secretary of the Communist Party of India, assured the faithful that the British had no real intention of leaving: 'A Tory Field Marshal goes, but a Tory Admiral, accompanied by one of the cleverest imperialist generals, Ismay, both Mr Churchill's favourites, comes.'[15] Other Indians, less disposed to think the worst of the British, nevertheless doubted that their departure could really be so imminent. The first indication that Mountbatten's Viceroyalty was to be different from all others came at the swearing-in ceremony on 24 March. Traditionally the Viceroy on this occasion was mute but resplendent; Mountbatten yielded not one whit of the splendour but addressed his audience, reiterating that power was to be transferred by June 1948. 'I am under no illusion about the difficulty of my task,' he concluded. 'I shall need greatest goodwill of the greatest possible number and I am asking India today for that goodwill.'[16] Though the issue was of relatively small importance, the fact that he was able and willing thus to defy precedent showed well the strength of his position. Not merely did he enjoy greater independence from Whitehall, the deadline by which power had to be transferred liberated him largely from dependence on the Indian leaders. As he was to tell Jinnah, his position was very favourable 'compared with the Cabinet Mission and others who had been sent out to find a solution to India's future, as I did not have to obtain prior acceptance from the Indian parties to the course I intended to recommend'. He would, of course, he added reassuringly, 'not recommend any solution which was patently unacceptable'. Jinnah, the Viceroy recorded, 'seemed pleased with these remarks'.[17]

The swearing-in was barely over before Mountbatten embarked on the series of interviews with Indian leaders which he planned as a first step in the process of carrying out his mandate. The meetings each lasted about an hour, took place in the Viceroy's study (which had been painted light green, a colour Mountbatten felt less forbidding than the sombre wood panelling favoured by his predecessors) and were recorded immediately they were over. Mountbatten's recollections of his conversations were not always reliable, but in this case the immediacy of the reporting as well as the importance of the theme inspire confidence in their accuracy. He planned to see representatives of all the main elements in Indian life – Christians and Parsees as well as Hindus and Muslims; businessmen and academics as well as politicians – but he quickly decided where the real power lay and who his principal targets must be. For the Hindus they were Nehru, Gandhi and the Congress Party 'boss', Sardar Patel; for the Muslims Jinnah alone would take the decisions that mattered, though his right-hand man, Liaqat Ali Khan, also deserved attention.

'You know Nehru,' Wavell had written, 'quixotic, emotional, socialistic.'[18] Mountbatten had taken greatly to Nehru when they first met at Singapore. He admired the charm, intelligence, radicalism tempered with wordly-wise sophistication; he believed – quite wrongly – that he understood the way Nehru's mind worked and – quite rightly – that Nehru responded warmly to his affection and respect. 'Pandit Nehru struck me as most sincere,' he began his record of their first meeting. After that they talked as much as anything of Jinnah, of whom Nehru spoke with mingled respect and loathing. When Mountbatten mentioned the Commonwealth, Nehru said he did not see how India could remain within it, and yet seemed to be casting around for some formula that might make it possible. There was room for manoeuvre, the Viceroy felt, both on this issue and on the central question of the future shape of India. Partition was not something Nehru was prepared to contemplate, in their first few discussions at any rate, but the relationship between the centre and the provinces, and the right of the provinces to associate with each other on grounds of politics, propinquity or religious faith, were open to endless gradations.[19]

In Jinnah Mountbatten found no such flexibility. Nehru had presented him as a monster of negativism, a man who would agree to nothing because it might split his followers if he did. In this he underestimated his adversary. Jinnah used negativism to achieve positive ends; by saying no he inexorably closed all avenues except the one leading to the only affirmative he would accept – an independent Pakistan. He paid his first visit to Viceroy's House on 5 April – 'My God, he was cold!' Mountbatten exclaimed as the Muslim leader left the building.[20] His sister, who some weeks later had tea with

Edwina, responded with equal frostiness when her hostess remarked how pleased she had been to find that at Lady Irwin College a class of fourteen Hindu and two Muslim girls had elected one of the Muslims as head girl. 'Don't be misled by the apparent contentment of the Muslim girls there,' Miss Jinnah said. 'We have not been able to start our propaganda in that College yet.' By this time any illusions Mountbatten might have fostered about the possibilities for reconciliation between the communities had so far withered that, when the remark was reported to him, he commented: 'I might add that the Hindus are nearly as bad, and that the determination, from the highest to the lowest in the land, to make out that the opposite religionists are devils incarnate as well as crooks, makes any sensible solution appear out of the question.'[21]

When Mountbatten invited the Jinnahs to dinner, *The Statesman* reported the fact with the cryptic comment, 'Other riot news on page 4'.[22] The Viceroy was never to gain any pleasure from his meetings with Mr Jinnah – a form of address that he continued to use in his most private and informal engagement diary when every other Indian was given a first name or bare surname. Mountbatten argued endlessly the case for a unified India. Jinnah 'offered no counter-arguments. He gave the impression that he was not listening.' It was more than an impression; to all intents and purposes he was *not* listening; he had made up his mind. His attitude was an affront to Mountbatten's conviction that everyone was susceptible to reason. Until he had met Jinnah he had not thought it possible that 'a man with such a complete lack of sense of responsibility could hold the power which he did'.[23]

At their meeting on 18 April the Viceroy tried a different tack. He professed to see the logic of Jinnah's arguments for partition, but pointed out that the same considerations applied to the two huge provinces of the Punjab and Bengal, where Muslims and Hindus existed in more or less equal numbers. If India must be partitioned, so must they. Jinnah was distressed. Bengal and the Punjab, he said, benefited too much by their unity. To divide them would not only be to weaken Pakistan, but to destroy peaceful and harmonious entities to no good purpose. How true, retorted Mountbatten; Jinnah had restored his conviction that India too should not be divided. 'I am afraid I drove the old gentleman quite mad, because whichever way his argument went I always pursued it to a stage beyond which he did not wish it to go.'[24]

Though it was gratifying to score debating points, Mountbatten soon realized that they served no real purpose. Jinnah would fight for the inclusion of Bengal and the Punjab in Pakistan, but if this proved impossible he would accept their partition rather than lose his independent state. Indeed, he would probably have sacrificed the two provinces altogether if he could have had

Pakistan on no other terms. At first he does not seem to have resented Mountbatten's attitude; Chaudhuri Muhammad Ali refers to him as speaking in 'unusually warm terms' about the Viceroy's integrity and good will.[25] But it was not long before this anyway limited enthusiasm dwindled; by the time Montgomery saw him towards the end of June Jinnah was freely speaking of his hatred of Mountbatten, who, he said, was in the pocket of Nehru.[26]

Jinnah had warned Mountbatten that Gandhi wielded vast power but had no responsibility; he could make agreement impossible but would agree to nothing.[27] Mountbatten accepted the essential correctness of the comment but was still fascinated and delighted by Gandhi's personality. The Mahatma called on 31 March, and stayed two and a quarter hours; again on 1 April, for two hours; again on 2 and 3 April. Wavell had quickly grown irritated by the time spent on his inconclusive conversations with a man he regarded as at the best evasive, at the worst a charlatan. Mountbatten, on the contrary, said he was ready to spend ten hours with him if necessary. 'He is deeply impressed with him,' noted Alan Campbell-Johnson, 'and thinks he is still of the first importance.'[28] 'An old poppet,' was the Viceroy's affectionate if not wholly adequate description of his visitor.[29]

There was indeed real warmth on both sides. To the first interview Gandhi brought his honorary grand-daughter Manu, and asked if she could ramble around the garden. 'Certainly,' said Mountbatten; then turning to Manu: 'All this is yours. We are only trustees. We have come to make it over to you.'[30] The answer enchanted Gandhi, but he remained sceptical about the underlying intentions of the British Government. 'The dawn of freedom has appeared,' he wrote grandiloquently, 'but we do not feel the glow of its sunrise. . . . We are trembling between hope and fear. Our hearts are filled with doubt.' He went on to express somewhat more prosaic arguments about the effect on negotiations of British commercial interests in India.[31] About Mountbatten, however, he had no reservations. He was, said Gandhi, a famous naval commander, but, while he did not believe in non-violence, he still 'assured me that he believes in God and always tried to act according to his conscience'. The people should therefore trust in the Viceroy's honesty of purpose.[32]

It did not take Mountbatten long to conclude that Gandhi was committed to the concept of a united India and that any step in the direction of partition would be resolutely opposed. It was with this in view that on 1 April Gandhi put forward a plan which he had aired from time to time in the past; that Jinnah be invited to form an interim central government. Congress, said Gandhi, should be prepared to accept government by the Muslim League if by so doing they could ensure the unity of their country. Mountbatten, encountering the idea for the first time, found it bold, imaginative, splendidly far-fetched. He saw in it, as he had seen in Habbakuk, the iceberg aircraft-carrier, the appeal of the outrageous yet remotely feasible. In his staff meeting he described the proposal as 'undoubtedly mad, except for the fact that Gandhi's amazing personal influence . . . might induce Congress to accept it' (in the final record the word 'mad' was watered down to 'wild').[33]

The plan never had the remotest chance of success. All Mountbatten's advisers told him that such an administration would be unworkable and the Congress leadership rejected it with alacrity. Gandhi, however, had inter-preted the Viceroy's open-minded interest as a pledge of support and felt betrayed when his proposal was not taken up officially. He did not blame Mountbatten personally but felt that the staff at Viceroy's House had shown themselves antagonistic. He withdrew from the negotiations; physically, for a few days, to Bihar, psychologically for the critical period in which the decisions were made. His was the strongest voice against partition, and his silence eased the process of negotiation. There were some who saw in this a master-stroke by Mountbatten, eliminating a force which he foresaw would make things difficult in the future.[34] Such an interpretation of events credits the Viceroy with too much cunning and too clear an idea of where he was going. By mid April he was becoming sure that some sort of partition was inevitable, but what form it would take and how it would be achieved remained obscure. He would have felt it premature to eliminate *any* factor from the complex equation that was taking shape.

Sardar Patel was the Tammany Hall boss of the Congress Party: tough, unscrupulous, knowing, a pragmatist concerned with the realities of power, indifferent to abstract theorizing. Nehru and he viewed each other with suspicion and some distaste, most of the time, however, remembering that they were indispensable to each other. Mountbatten found Nehru vastly the more sympathetic, but felt surer of his ground in discussion with Patel. At their first meeting the Viceroy recorded that Patel was 'most charming',[35] but later encounters were not always so harmonious. Some time after his meeting with Patel of 24 April, Mountbatten added to the record a note of a sharp dispute which he explained he had omitted before 'to avoid inflaming British Staff opinion against him [Patel]'. Mountbatten objected to the tone of a memorandum Patel had circulated, Patel flew into a rage, Mountbatten reciprocated and insisted Patel withdraw the memorandum, Patel refused, whereupon Mountbatten said that either Patel must leave the Government or he would resign as Viceroy. 'Patel suddenly realised that I meant business and completely collapsed,' from thenceforth he was 'respectful and helpful'. The detail of this set-to would be more convincing if it had been recorded at the same time as the rest of the interview but, even though Mountbatten's victory may not have been as conclusive as he later represented it, there seems no doubt that there was some sort of confrontation and that Patel emerged with an enhanced view of the Viceroy's determination.[36] The two men on the whole worked harmoniously together – a fortunate circumstance for Mountbatten, since, unlike some of the other Indian leaders, once Patel had been convinced that a certain course was logically necessary he would pursue it with indifference to the ideological objections that might be raised by others.

'The spirit of the hive' that Mountbatten had evoked in South-East Asia was equally fostered in Viceroy's House. The staff meetings were the heart of the hive, the innermost conclave in which Mountbatten, Ismay, Miéville, Abell, Ian Scott, Christie, Erskine-Crum, the Conference Secretary, and a few others would review the events of the last twenty-four hours and consider future policy. For Mountbatten they provided an invaluable sounding-board on which he could try out any idea that had been put into his head; confident that one of those present would demolish it if that was its proper fate. The old India hands present would each speak for the area they knew best: Abell for the Punjab, Scott for the future Pakistan, Christie for Bengal. The most conspicuous omission was Hindu or Muslim representation; their absence made frank and objective discussion easier but also sometimes gave the deliberations the aspect of a *Hamlet* not merely without the Prince of Denmark but with a cast confined to Rosencrantz, Guildenstern and the grave-diggers. It was only when V. P. Menon, the subtle and experienced Reforms Commissioner and confidant of Sardar Patel, joined the group that any real insight into day-to-day Indian thinking was vouchsafed its members. The price that was paid for Menon's inclusion was the conviction of the Muslims that the Viceroy's staff was prejudiced against their cause.

Whether in staff meetings, in Cabinet or in dealings with his provincial governors, Mountbatten stuck out for the same liberal and libertarian principles as he had championed in South-East Asia. Fred Burrows, former trades union official and now Governor of Bengal, deplored the fact that the Communist Party could not be outlawed:

> Personally I feel it would be most disastrous to declare the Communist Party illegal [replied the Viceroy] as this would have all the aspects of a Fascist action. You will remember that not even during the war years in Great Britain was the Communist Party declared an unlawful association, and I cannot believe that it is ethically sound in time of peace to ban a political party which is not openly engaged on subversive activities.[37]

One of the first and most troublesome of Mountbatten's problems was posed by the handful of soldiers from the Indian National Army who remained in jail. Congress claimed that these were political martyrs; patriots, misguided perhaps, who had put Indian independence before their oath of allegiance, had deserted to the Japanese and were now being victimized for their love of their country. General Auchinleck and the other military leaders argued that, on the contrary, these men were convicted not for their principles but for brutal crimes against civilians or their fellow soldiers. To release them would not only be to defy justice but would destroy the morale of the Army. Wavell had limited his successor's freedom of action by supporting Auchinleck and vetoing discussion of the question in Cabinet. With a motion in the Assembly demanding acquittal, that line could no longer be held.

Mountbatten worked on both parties and found that both British soldiers and Indian politicians were disconcertingly ready to admit the force of the others' argument, but coupled this broad-mindedness with an obdurate refusal to concede an inch. Auchinleck in particular was 'more difficult to deal with than I can remember at any time since October 1943'.[38] Confrontation came at a meeting at Viceroy's House on 2 April. It provided a remarkable demonstration of Mountbatten's persistence, agility of mind and persuasive powers. The issue, he believed, must be settled before it was discussed in the Assembly; the irreconcilable must be reconciled. Jinnah, perhaps, would have withstood him, but men of generosity and good will like Auchinleck and Nehru stood no chance. Little by little he cajoled them from their rigid stance on points of principle to a discussion of practicalities: yes, Nehru supposed he *could* stress in the Assembly that the crimes committed were civil and not military; yes, Auchinleck grudgingly agreed, he *might* accept that the Chief Justice should take a new look at the sentences. In the end a precarious compromise was patched up and acted on by the Viceroy with a speed that precluded any second thoughts.[39] 'I think your success over the most difficult I.N.A. problem is really remarkable, and I do most heartily congratulate you on it,' wrote Cripps.[40] Mountbatten did not underestimate his achievement. To Patricia he wrote of his 'unbelievable triumph . . . I achieved the miracle of effecting a compromise . . . and Nehru got the motion withdrawn at the end of a heated debate without my having to use my veto!'[41] 'Nothing like blowing your own trumpet, is there?' he asked wrily at the end of another letter a week or so later. 'A family failing I fear!!'[42]

A sense of hectic urgency was instilled in those early weeks. He arrived convinced that by fixing June 1948 as the date for the transfer of power he had set himself an impossibly hurried task; by the time he first paused to take breath he had satisfied himself that he could not afford to wait so long. 'The situation is everywhere electric,' wrote Ismay, as little prone to panic as

anyone on earth, 'and I get the feeling that the mine may go off at any moment
. . . the inter-communal hatred is a devouring flame.'[43] 'If we do not make up
our minds on what we are going to do within the next two months or so, there
will be pandemonium,' he wrote grimly a few days later. 'If we do, there may
be pandemonium.'[44] Some of the more cautious members of Mountbatten's
entourage were still not wholly convinced. Against the desirability of speed,
argued Eric Miéville, must be put the importance and permanence of
whatever solution was arrived at. Mountbatten did not deny that the decision
must be the right one; but to arrive at no decision might be worst of all.[45]

Under a burden of responsibility and hard work which would have
crushed most mortals, Mountbatten thrived. 'Everyone was just as gloomy
and pessimistic when I came out in October 1943,' he told his mother, 'and I
was wildly enthusiastic and optimistic then, and I am again now, with no
sounder reasons than then. It certainly is the most fascinating job anyone
could wish for.'[46] He revelled in the pace, the excitement, the feeling that he
was in control of great events. He was never depressed, never regretful about
past setbacks, never fearful over future challenges. If sometimes in the
night-watches he had moments of anxiety, no trace of it showed when he met
his staff next day – it is probable that, in fact, he had slept peacefully while
others would have tossed in anguish at their awful task.

He was to need all his optimism, for whatever he decided would cause
distress or fury among some of those affected. By the end of March he was
already putting forward an alternative to the Cabinet mission's plan –
partition with certain powers reserved to a central authority and India
divided into three units: Hindustan, Pakistan and the Princely States.[47] He
quickly realized that this would satisfy nobody. 'At this early stage I can see
little common ground on which to build any agreed solution for the future of
India,' he reported sombrely.[48] But in a negative sense common ground or,
perhaps more correctly, absence of common ground was emerging. Not only
was a truly united India inconceivable, it was becoming more and more
apparent that, with the possible exception of Gandhi, all the Hindu leaders at
least tacitly accepted that this was so. D. V. Tahmankar, Sardar Patel's
biographer, put the crucial date as 8 March, two weeks before Mountbatten
arrived, when the Working Party of Congress approved a resolution which
envisaged the division of the Punjab.[49] Nehru himself told Michael Brecher
that partition had become inevitable a year before it happened.[50] Mountbatten's first few weeks contain an element of play-acting, with everyone
except Jinnah mouthing the appropriate sentiments about Indian unity, yet
all except Gandhi privately knowing that the cause was lost. At the staff
meeting on 11 April Mountbatten conceded that there was no possibility of
shifting Jinnah from his position, and that without his agreement unity could

only be imposed on India by force of arms. He retained an open mind, he said, but the time had come to work out the details of an alternative strategy. Ismay was deputed to prepare a plan for the partition of India.

Revisionist Indian historians see Mountbatten as a 'crafty diplomat' who 'manipulated' the innocent Indian politicians: 'Thus many Indian leaders ended up stating the impossibility of a united India without an unparalleled civil war, while Mountbatten pretended himself to be completely open on the question of the country's partition.'[51] Such reasoning both exaggerates the Viceroy's cunning and assumes he was indifferent to his directive from the British Cabinet. Independence for a united India was the solution which would have won him the greatest credit with the Labour Government. Ministers had by no means abandoned this goal. 'If Jinnah doesn't face up to it now – well I give up hope!' Cripps wrote to Amrit Kaur on 4 March. 'You must be patient for a little and try and clear away every possibility of anything preventing him in joining.'[52] Mountbatten discovered the truth more quickly but it was a solution imposed on him. Partition was a defeat, to be accepted with reluctance.

> When and if the time came for this plan to be announced [Mount-batten was recorded as saying] he wanted a most careful preamble to be written making it clear that his view had all along been completely impartial; that it was only when it became apparent that the reten-tion of any form of a united India would start civil war that he had regretfully been obliged to give up this ideal; and that he had therefore chosen a means which gave the choice of their future, as well as the somewhat primitive democratic machinery could allow, to the Indian people themselves.[53]

The decision in principle was made; it remained to work out a plan which would be acceptable in practice to everyone concerned.

# CHAPTER 30

## *The Plan*

THE THREAT OF UNBRIDLED VIOLENCE between Muslim and Hindu loomed over those critical weeks. Not only would the toll in human lives have been fearful, the atmosphere in which negotiations were being conducted might have become so embittered that further progress would have been impossible. On 8 April the Viceroy suggested to Jinnah that he should join with the Congress leadership in an appeal to all Indians to avoid provocative acts that might lead to bloodshed.[1] Jinnah made no objection and, since the Congress leaders had already said that they were in favour of such a declaration, the matter seemed almost concluded. In India, however, nothing was so simple. A draft was quickly agreed, but when Jinnah found that it was to be signed not only by Gandhi but by the President of Congress, Acharya Kripalani, he took offence, arguing that it would belittle the Muslim League if he were to associate his name with such an 'unknown nobody'. Nehru in his turn took offence and said that it was for Congress to decide who would sign on their behalf.[2] For a day or two it seemed possible that the declaration would perish unpublished, but commonsense prevailed and everyone agreed that Mountbatten should settle the matter. The appeal was issued over the names of Jinnah and Gandhi.

One of the areas which seemed most likely to slip into chaos was the North-West Frontier. The province was an anomaly in that, though more than nine-tenths of the population were Muslim, they had returned a Congress government in the elections of 1945. If India were to be partitioned, there was obvious scope here for disastrous controversy: as a Muslim state, the League had no doubt that it should form part of Pakistan; with a Congress government, the Hindu leaders felt that it should remain with India. Since the elections the tide of opinion had flowed strongly against Dr Khan Sahib's Congress administration, to the extent that, when Nehru announced his intention of paying the province a visit in October 1946, the Governor, Olaf Caroe, urged him to stay away because of the disorder his presence would stir up. Nehru took this as evidence of Caroe's hostility towards Hinduism and the Congress Party, and when he paid his visit and was met by stones and insults he assumed that the demonstrations had been organized by the

375

Governor to weaken the present administration. In this he was unfair, but not grotesquely so; Caroe had deep knowledge of and affection for all things Muslim and this was reflected in his attitude towards his Ministers and the opposition, however much he strove to be impartial.[3]

Impartial or not, Caroe was a victim of the pressures of his office – 'terribly tired and strained', Ismay found him when he visited Peshawar in April.[4] That he was in a somewhat over-emotional condition is suggested by the letter he wrote to his wife after he had met Mountbatten in Delhi:

> For the first time in years I feel I have met with a man I love. . . . He is splendid. He has great beauty of appearance, captivating charm, a living quick mind that attunes with mine, and a deep and living patriotism, based on knowledge of what is great and divine. . . . I have found the Leader of my prayers, and feel I could follow to the death.[5]

The tribute is the more remarkable in that the Viceroy had told Caroe frankly that, while he would back him as far as he could, he could not guarantee that circumstances would allow him to keep the Governor in office. 'I like him immensely,' he told Listowel, 'and in my opinion he is a very competent, loyal and honest official,' but if he had lost the confidence of the Congress Party and by his presence was impeding a settlement, it would be for the greater good that he should go.[6]

On 21 April Mountbatten himself visited the North-West Frontier, one of the only two provincial visits he managed to find time for during his Viceroyalty. A vast crowd of Pathans, all supporters of the Muslim League, had gathered to make their views evident to the new arrival. The previous night the garden of Government House had been invaded and a shot fired through the windows; the mob now seemed more noisy than aggressive, but a false move would have been enough to turn its mood and send it surging through the inadequate police guard to sack the buildings and massacre any Congress Ministers they could find. Caroe advised that a personal appearance by Mountbatten would be more likely than anything to appease them. Edwina, who was in the party, insisted on accompanying her husband and together they clambered up the railway embankment to confront the crowd. Caroe described the scene:

> The Viceroy, not resplendent in stars and orders, but a fine figure always, wearing a green bush-shirt of Burma provenance – there were not wanting those who noted that this was the right colour for a *Haji* [one who has made the pilgrimage to Mecca] – brought his hand to the salute and stood facing the crowd. The moment was dramatic,

the gesture superb. The atmosphere changed. Cries of *Pakistan zindabad* died away, and I heard more than one voice of admiration.[7]

It did not need a demonstration to convince Mountbatten that the situation in the province was one of exceeding delicacy. Somehow the will of the people must be established before the government of the Frontier could be allowed to adopt any irrevocable stance over partition. He decided that, given the state of local politics, a referendum would be more satisfactory than fresh elections. To this the main obstacle was Nehru, who must privately have recognized that the result was likely to be the loss of the province to Congress. He summed up his feelings about the problem and Mountbatten's part in solving it in a note which he wrote in early June. The Viceroy, he said,

> is obviously playing and going to play an important part. . . . I have no doubt about his sincerity and bona fides and desire to do the right thing. . . . He realizes the difficulties of the Frontier problem and wants to do everything in his power to solve them. I think he will prove helpful. He is convinced, however that . . . a chance must be given to the Frontier people to decide themselves by means of a referendum. He has definitely committed himself to this, and he cannot get out of it without grave injury to his own prestige and impartiality. He would probably prefer to resign than to face such a situation.[8]

Nothing would have suited Nehru worse than Mountbatten's resignation, and he accepted the referendum without much demur. His price was that it should be administered by a Governor whom he believed to be truly neutral. Caroe must go. Caroe went – ill-health being the formal reason, and 'on extended leave' rather than dismissed. Dismissed he had been, however, and the fact caused him lasting distress and transitory bitterness. Any grievance he might have had against the Viceroy quickly passed, however; in later life he freely conceded that his departure was necessary for the future of the province. Mountbatten for his part paid tribute to Caroe's gallant acceptance of the inevitable: 'if you had not behaved as a very great gentleman', he said, 'it would have been impossible to carry through the referendum'.[9] Caroe returned the compliment. 'I can only say,' he summed up, 'that to me personally, then and later, Mountbatten behaved with honour and sincerity, and an attitude that I can only describe as royal.'[10]

Trouble on the Frontier was only one of the factors lending urgency to the deliberations in Delhi. On 17 April Mountbatten told the Secretary of State that a decision had to be made in the near future 'if we are to avert civil war and the risk of a complete breakdown of the administration'. He expected to have a plan ready within ten days, to send Ismay home with it by the end of the month and to call together a conference of Indian leaders at Simla on 15 May.[11] The first part of this exuberant schedule was fulfilled, even though at the cost of some attention to detail. 'We have made almost innumerable alternative drafts,' Ismay told his wife, '. . . but it is impossible to get Dickie to go through them methodically. He is a grand chap in a thousand ways but precision of thought and writing is not his strong suit.'[12] Each formula was designed to achieve the same thing in a different way; to partition the country yet to save as much as possible from the wreck, some form of Supreme Defence Council being the vestigial centre from which it was hoped that one day a Federal India might emerge. A special committee consisting of the Viceroy, Ismay, Abell and Miéville was set up to thrash out the details of the plan, and make sure that the various Indian leaders would find it acceptable.

The plan which Ismay presented in London on 3 May provided for partition, with Bengal and the Punjab having the option of being split between India and Pakistan, joining in entirety with either state, or going it alone. The position of the Princely States was left obscure, the implication being that it would be for them to decide their own future. It was inherent in such a scheme that India and Pakistan might in the end prove to be only the two largest units in a patchwork of more or less viable independent states.[13] To British Ministers, committed to the precepts of self-determination, this seemed eminently proper. Mountbatten had urged the Cabinet to consider and approve the plan within ten days at the most. They took only a week. Such amendments as they made were mainly at the behest of the parliamentary draftsmen who wished to clarify a few obscurities. Their changes certainly made more evident the right of the different parts of India to decide their own future, but no fresh element was introduced.[14] The only new point that appeared likely to cause disturbance was the proposal that the North-West Frontier should also be allowed to opt for independence – and to Mountbatten and his advisers it seemed that this was as likely to distress the Muslim League as Congress. 'Everything is going well at home,' reported Miéville. 'Our proposals have been generally accepted and indeed improved in many ways by the draftsmen at home.'[15]

By 10 May, when the amended plan was returned, Mountbatten had retreated to Simla. 'After averaging 17 hours a day for 6 weeks I'm just about worn out,' he told Patricia, 'and must recuperate before the meetings have to start on Pug's return.'[16] He invited Nehru and Krishna Menon to stay with him, hoping to spend three tranquil days walking, talking and doing the minimum of business. Mountbatten's intention was to release the text of the plan only twenty-four hours before the meeting of the Indian leaders, now fixed for 17 May, and thus to give them the minimum of time to argue and suggest amendments. At the last moment, however, he had second thoughts and decided to show the paper to his guest. 'I had a hunch Nehru wouldn't like it,' he told Patricia.[17] To those of his staff who objected that it was unfair to give the draft to one party and not the other he replied that the issue was too important for such niceties to be observed. Anyway, it was Congress who were likely to object, not the Muslim League.

Mountbatten gave the paper to Nehru to read as he was going to bed. At midnight Krishna Menon was woken by his distraught leader. 'He was almost beside himself and said that this plan was very far from what he had expected and was quite unacceptable.'[18] He kept Menon up till 4 a.m. mulling over the enormity of the proposals. Next morning came what the Viceroy referred to laconically in his diary as 'Nehru bombshell'. A letter from the Indian leader was laid in front of him:

> The whole approach was completely different from what ours had been [wrote Nehru], and the picture of India that emerged frightened me. In fact much that we had done so far was undermined and the Cabinet Mission's scheme and subsequent developments were set aside, and an entirely new picture presented – a picture of fragmentation and conflict and disorder, and, unhappily also, of a worsening of relations between India and Britain.[19]

Nehru viewed partition as an evil, but an evil which had to be faced in the interests of securing independence. That India should be still further balkanized, with the provinces and Princely States permitted – almost, it seemed to him, encouraged – to go their separate ways, was intolerable.

Mountbatten was stunned. The issue, he thought, had already been cleared up. 'We are naturally a bit rattled,' wrote Miéville from Simla with commendable restraint. 'After talking to Nehru we found to our amazement that whereas he had more or less accepted our plan as taken home by Pug, he had completely switched round on the redraft from London. . . . What has happened I really do not know.'[20] The plan 'had been cleared in principle with the 5 main leaders', Mountbatten told Patricia. 'Then the India Office and Cabinet redrafted it.'[21] Faced with what seemed to them Nehru's volte-face, it was not surprising that they looked for an explanation in the changes that had been introduced in the draft while it was being considered in London. Yet it is hard to believe that these not insignificant yet minor amendments can have had more than a peripheral effect. The surprising thing seems not so much that Nehru rejected the amended plan as that it should ever have been expected he would approve the original. Nehru had 'more or less accepted' the plan, said Miéville; it had been 'cleared in principle', said Mountbatten. Such phrases cover limitless possibilities for misunderstanding. Miéville had seen Nehru on the afternoon of 30 April and 'went through the draft statement with him',[22] but it is not clear exactly what the statement contained, nor whether Nehru was given a chance to study a draft at leisure. It does not seem that anything on paper was left with the Congress leader and H. M. Patel, Indian representative on the Partition Council, is confident that Nehru was vouchsafed only the haziest sketch of what was in the wind.[23] Nehru himself subsequently maintained that he had only been shown a short note dealing mainly with the partition of Bengal and the Punjab.[24] The full truth is unlikely ever to be known, but it is painfully obvious that, given Nehru's propensity for believing what he wanted to believe and Mountbatten's for hearing what he wanted to hear, a genuine misunderstanding could easily have arisen between them. It is hard otherwise to explain V. P. Menon's conviction that Nehru would find the plan unacceptable as soon as he had been given a chance to consider it properly. Nor does Nehru's outburst to Krishna Menon suggest that he was even in part prepared for the proposals. Too much had been assumed on both sides. 'It is clear the whole of this sorry postponement has been due to over-trustfulness and impatience,' wrote Christie in his diary on 14 May. 'The Lord needs George [Abell] or Ismay to steady him.'[25]

An Indian historian, Y. Krishan, has recently suggested that the plan was put forward with the intention that it should be rejected: 'It can be explained away only as a tactic to browbeat the opposition to India joining the British Commonwealth.'[26] This 'sinister interpretation', as Krishan himself describes it, argues a cunning in the Viceroy which was wholly lacking. For Mountbatten it was one of the worst blows he had suffered in his life. Not only did it seem that British policy was once more in ruins, but he had endured a personal and most humiliating rebuff. He had sent Ismay to London with a virtual guarantee that the plan would be acceptable to the Indian leaders; on this basis he had insisted that it be handled with the utmost despatch; now it had been rejected out of hand and, what was more, rejected by the man with whom he felt that he had established a special relationship. For a few hours he was as close to despair as he had ever been. Then his immense resilience reasserted itself. The fact that he had anticipated Nehru's opposition became a matter for congratulation: 'Imagine the scene if I'd not discovered this first!! . . . The "hunch" which so often saved me in South East Asia saved me again.'[27] With only the most cursory tear for the spilt milk around him, he settled down to seeking a new and more satisfactory solution. By the time V. P. Menon dined at Viceregal Lodge that night, 'Lord Mountbatten had completely regained his buoyant spirits and good cheer'.[28]

It was V. P. Menon who brought into the debate the fresh element that made progress possible. After telling Patricia about his fortunate hunch, Mountbatten had ended his letter: 'I think I can get Congress back into the Commonwealth!!! Hush!'[29] By almost miraculous sleight of hand, the destruction of Mountbatten's plan was turned into a triumphant ploy to keep India in the Commonwealth. Less than forty years later it is possible to wonder how membership of this diffuse and disparate body can have so transformed the situation in the eyes of Indians and British alike. In 1947 the Commonwealth was much more coherent and like-minded, flourishing within a strong framework of economic and military rights and obligations. Today one can see that the inclusion of India, Pakistan and eventually a host of other nations diluted if it did not destroy the original concept of the organization. In 1947 it seemed that admission to the Commonwealth might transform the future of India and Pakistan.

It was not a new idea; it had, indeed, been mooted ever since the Balfour Report was adopted by the Imperial Conference of 1926. Towards the end of 1946 V. P. Menon had discussed with Sardar Patel the possibility of India joining the Commonwealth. To do so, he argued, would ensure a peaceful transfer of power, speed the pace of independence and make it easier for British civil servants and soldiers to stay on in an independent India.[30] Patel, most pragmatic of men, would have been content to accept Menon's advice provided that the balance of advantage was in India's favour; but Nehru saw membership of the Commonwealth as an infringement of India's independence and the Constituent Assembly passed a resolution that India was to become a sovereign republic.

Not all the British favoured accepting India into the Commonwealth. General Nye, the Governor of Madras, argued cogently that to do so would saddle Britain with strategic and economic burdens that would certainly be onerous and might prove intolerable.[31] In Whitehall many civil servants felt the same.[32] Mountbatten, romantic, internationalist, fervent believer in the symbolic significance of the Crown, could not but see things differently. He looked beyond the cosy inner circle of the white Commonwealth to a wider union, which would embrace a polyglot variety of creeds and colours and yet preserve the essential values of democracy and individual freedom and work closely together as a coherent group in world affairs. Today the vision is to some extent discredited; twenty years ago it was almost a truism; in 1947 Mountbatten was ahead of his time. Whether it did or did not work out in practice, it was a noble vision and one which demanded political courage and imagination if it were to be carried through.

Mountbatten told Krishna Menon that he 'was one of those sentimental fools who would always try to help any nation that wanted to be in the

Commonwealth'.[33] The rulers of some of the Princely States hoped that, provided they expressed themselves eager candidates for admission to the Commonwealth, the Viceroy would help them achieve independence. Mountbatten was tempted but refused; he would do nothing to splinter still farther the unity of the sub-continent. Yet he spared no other effort to help the Commonwealth cause. When Whitehall informed the Indians that in future their students would not be admitted to the Imperial Defence College or similar bodies, Mountbatten protested indignantly to the Prime Minister. Auchinleck pointed out that the practical effects would be small, since few Indians were eligible for the courses and those that would be were, anyway, badly needed in their homeland. That was not the point, explained Mount-batten, who then gave the Commander-in-Chief an outline of one of the plans he was currently considering. 'A feature of this scheme was the almost immediate offer of . . . Commonwealth status to India.'[34]

He never lost sight of the issue as the negotiations struggled on. 'Towards the achievement of this objective,' wrote the Indian historian Manmath Nath Das, 'he revealed a steely determination, and often resorted to dubious diplomacy. It was a stunning performance. . . .'[35] To the economists he pointed out the preferential advantages that India would enjoy; to those concerned with defence he stressed the benefits that Commonwealth mem-bership would confer on Pakistan, the crippling loss to the Indians if they were deprived of similar assistance. He told Krishna Menon that he had 'received the strictest instructions not to make any attempt to keep India within the Commonwealth' – a blatant untruth that he justified to London on the score of 'tactics'.[36]

In spite of this, there had been no mention of the Commonwealth in the plan Ismay took to London. Mainly this was because Mountbatten believed, with good reason, that it would be unacceptable to Nehru.[37] But when confronted by what he felt to be the enormity of the British plan, Nehru became more flexible. Patel proved still less of an obstacle.[38] When Menon suggested that, if India and Pakistan were both to accept Commonwealth membership, the unity of the sub-continent would to some degree be pre-served, independence could therefore be granted more rapidly, and the right of Bengal, the North-West Frontier or other states to opt for independence would be at the worst left implicit, and with luck excluded altogether, Nehru grasped eagerly at the life-line. Mountbatten for his part both found the proposal intrinsically attractive and saw in it a chance of extricating himself from the disastrous position in which his negotiations seemed to have landed him. By the evening of 11 May a new basis for the transfer of power had been hammered out and Nehru and Patel had agreed that it was acceptable in principle. '. . . We shall get what is called "Dominion Status", which is said to be more or less equivalent to independence,' wrote Rajendra Prasad, with endearing vagueness.[39] At 9 p.m. Mountbatten sent a telegram to Ismay in London, setting out the case for an early transfer of power on the basis of Dominion status, with both India and Pakistan joining the Commonwealth. If the plan was to work, he said, he was convinced that the grant of independence would have to be made during 1947.

> The advantages which would accrue to India through an early transfer of power and remaining within the Commonwealth are obvious enough. I consider that the main advantages which the United Kingdom would gain are briefly:
>
> (a) The terrific world-wide enhancement of British prestige and the enhancement of the prestige of the present Government.
>
> (b) The completion of the framework of world strategy from the point of view of Empire defence.
>
> (c) The early termination of present responsibilities, especially in the field of law and order.
>
> (d) A further strengthening of Indo-British relations which have enormously improved since the statement of 20 February.[40]

It was Mountbatten's impetuosity which had landed him in his present quandary, but it is difficult to praise too highly the energy and resilience with which he recovered from it. To switch horses in mid-stream is notoriously a manoeuvre to be avoided, but if one horse dies under you there may be no alternative. Mountbatten had performed the trick with no more than a nasty splashing, and had brought the second horse to the other bank. It remained to convince Whitehall that he had acted wisely. The British Cabinet was disconcerted. They had received a plan sent them by the Viceroy with the assurance that it would be acceptable to the Indian leaders, had considered it with exemplary speed, and had made only the minimum of amendment. Now they were told that the plan had been abandoned and another substituted, which they were expected to approve almost as soon as they heard of it. Not unreasonably, they protested. The situation, they told Ismay, was so confused that either a ministerial mission must fly to Delhi or Mountbatten return to London. Ismay did not find it hard to guess what Mountbatten's reaction would be to the arrival of Cripps in Delhi at such a moment. He rejected the alternative out of hand and urged Mountbatten to return to London.[41]

The Viceroy's first reaction was to bluster: nothing would be gained by his return; the Cabinet knew his recommendations; they must take them or leave them; if they left them, he would resign.[42] V. P. Menon and Lady Mountbatten did not have too much difficulty in persuading him that the Cabinet were within their rights – indeed, were showing themselves remarkably tolerant. A hectic forty-eight hours were devoted to ensuring that this time there would be no misunderstandings. Jinnah refused to sign any document but indicated general assent. Mountbatten felt sure he would present no problem. About the Congress leaders he was less confident. Nehru persisted in viewing the new plan as 'a continuation of the Cabinet Mission's Scheme with suitable variations to fit in with the existing situation',[43] and since it was clearly nothing of the sort, the possibility of some sudden recantation could not be ignored. Subject to everyone else accepting the plan as a final settlement, however, Nehru committed himself in writing to general agreement. That was good enough for Mountbatten. On 18 May he set off for London.

With hindsight it is easy to see that the British Cabinet could not possibly have rejected, or even substantially amended, any plan put forward by the Viceroy and accepted by both Congress and the Muslim League. At the time the immense strength of his position was less apparent. He did not expect rejection but feared that he might be given some rough treatment by resentful Ministers. He had no cause for concern. At the crucial meetings of the India Committee and the Cabinet,[44] Mountbatten's exposition of the problem was listened to sympathetically and his suggestions were accepted with alacrity. Attlee, in his final summing up, 'paid tribute to the remarkable skill and initiative which the Viceroy had shown in his conduct of these difficult negotiations'. It was essential, he said, that Mountbatten 'should be given a large measure of discretion to amend the details of the plan, without prior consultation with His Majesty's Government'.[45] As a vote of confidence it could hardly have been more enthusiastic.

There was one caveat. Herbert Morrison stressed that there would be no hope of getting the necessary legislation through Parliament before the summer recess unless the Opposition co-operated. Attlee assured him that such co-operation had been promised, provided that it was certain that the Indian leaders found the plan acceptable. It was up to the Viceroy to convince the Conservative leaders that this time he had got it right. On 20 May he had a first meeting with Churchill, Eden, John Anderson and Lord Salisbury. It went well, and the following day Churchill telephoned him to say that in principle the Opposition were prepared to help the legislation through. Mountbatten was summoned for further discussion and found the Leader of the Opposition still in bed. Churchill, recorded the Viceroy:

> was extremely pleasant about what had been achieved in India in a short while. But he was extremely vitriolic about my predecessor.
> He said that he hoped to get Indian matters dealt with on a

bi-party basis. If I could achieve Dominion status for both Hindustan and Pakistan, the whole country would be behind us, and the Conservative Party would help to rush the legislation through.

When Mountbatten said that Nehru had committed himself to Dominion status provided that power was transferred in 1947, but that Jinnah was still hanging back, Churchill was amazed: 'By God, he is the one man who cannot do without British help!' He sent a personal message to the Muslim leader, pointing out the perils for Pakistan in any hesitation. 'Finally he suggested that if I were appointed Governor General of Hindustan and Governor General of Pakistan, I might adopt the title "Moderator", which at one time had been suggested by the late President Roosevelt, instead of the title "Viceroy".'[46]

Though Churchill no doubt had reservations which he did not voice, it seems that the unexpected possibility of India's accession to the Commonwealth had at least temporarily reconciled him to the grant of independence. This benign mood was not to endure for long, nor was there any shortage of Conservatives hostile to the Viceroy's activities from the start. The view that Mountbatten was betraying the principles of empire, destroying a noble heritage in a search for easy popularity, was not held only by blimps and reactionaries. It was to gather force after the massacres that followed partition, but already there were many who looked askance at the pace and, still more, the direction of events. General Wedemeyer chanced to visit London a few weeks after the Viceroy had returned to India and wrote to warn his former Supreme Commander of the ill people spoke of him.

There were one or two people who told me that you were slightly pinko or at least a Leftist Liberal. I do not believe this. I think your conception of evolving political and economic structures that will give all deserving peoples equal opportunities economically and the chance to participate intelligently in the government has been misinterpreted. I have made an earnest effort to acquire objective knowledge concerning Marxian ideologies, their interpretation and implementation by Lenin and Stalin. I think all Americans and Britishers must do this. But I am absolutely certain that you do not agree to the basic tenets of Karl Marx and that you do not visualise abrogating personal freedom for which mankind has struggled so many thousands of years.[47]

The significance of the colours in Wedemeyer's political spectrum is not easy to fathom. Mountbatten would have felt no shame if accused of being 'slightly pinko', still less 'a Leftist Liberal'. He was not remotely a Marxist, however, viewing any ideology with suspicion and abhorring totalitarianism. There were indeed those on the right wing of British politics who denounced him as Communist or, at least, the tool of the extreme left. Such accusations were flimsy even by the standards of political invective. His policy towards India was dictated by pragmatism and not principles; he could see no other course of action that could succeed. He did believe also in the principles of democracy and self-determination, but that was by the way. He had been given a mandate by his Government and was carrying it out in the best way he could. If in the course of his work he made political enemies at home then that was to be regretted — for Mountbatten never took lightly the hostility of others — but provided no reason for doubting the correctness of his actions. His reputation as a dangerous radical was firmly established, however, and was to do him some harm in the future.

On 31 May Mountbatten and Ismay returned to Delhi. 'A long flight with Mountbatten was an experience which I was careful not to repeat,' wrote Ismay ruefully. 'The idea of a reasonable degree of comfort never entered his head. Speed was all that mattered.'[48] The same was true of the forthcoming negotiations. Mountbatten was determined to drive them forward at a pace which would make it impossible for anyone to have second thoughts or fuss overmuch about the details. At 10 a.m. on 2 June Nehru, Patel and Kripalani for the Hindus, Jinnah, Liaqat Ali Khan and Abdur Rab Nishtar for the Muslims, and the Sikh Baldev Singh met with the Viceroy to receive copies of the British Government's statement, 'Immediate Transfer of Power'. Mountbatten told them that he did not expect an instant response, but that the broad outline of the plan was already well known to everyone present and he would expect his answer before midnight. He got what he wanted, but only just. Congress made points about the proposed plebiscite in the North-West Frontier Province and the right of one Dominion to leave the Commonwealth though the other did not, but they were not argued with great conviction. Jinnah said that he could accept nothing without the authority of the Council of the All-India Muslim League and that this would take a week to assemble. Did Jinnah support the plan personally? asked the Viceroy. Yes. Was he justified in recommending to the Prime Minister that he should go ahead and make the announcement as planned? Yes. Would Jinnah at least nod his head when Mountbatten said that he was satisfied with the assurances he had received from the Muslim League? A reluctant yes. Knowing that this was the best he could hope for, Mountbatten decided to carry on. The leaders met again early on 3 June. The plan was accepted.

*HMS Kelly (top) carrying out her first full-power trials in August 1939, and (middle) in dry dock with a hole ripped in her side by a German torpedo.* ABOVE *HMS* Javelin *with bow and stern blown off, November 1940.*

LEFT *Mountbatten with his WREN daughter Patricia at Broadlands.* BELOW *Casablanca, 1943. 'Pug' Ismay and Mountbatten stand behind Churchill and Roosevelt.*

ABOVE *Arrival in India,
October 1943. From left to
right: Mountbatten, General
Sir George Giffard, Air Chief
Marshal Sir Richard Peirse,
General Sir Claude Auchinleck. Mountbatten (right)
with Generalissimo and
Madame Chiang Kai-shek
on a visit to Chinese troops
in India and (below) with
General 'Vinegar Joe' Stilwell
at Kandy.*

*The Supreme Commander (above) addressing an Indian Air Force contingent at a station near the front line and (below) reading the Surrender Address from the steps of the Municipal Building in Singapore. From left to right: Admiral Power, General Slim, Mountbatten, Lieutenant-General Wheeler, Air Chief Marshal Park.*

LEFT *A visit to General MacArthur at Manila. With his cap on, noted Mountbatten, 'his jaw stuck out, he looked aggressive and tough.'* BELOW *The Mountbattens with a group of schoolboys during their visit to Australia in* 1946.

ABOVE *Greeted by the Wavells on arrival at Delhi on 22 March 1947. Pamela Mountbatten is at far left.* BELOW *With Gandhi on the terrace of Viceroy's House.*

RIGHT *Edwina Mountbatten and Nehru share a joke outside Viceroy's House. Admiral Brockman is in the background.* BELOW *At a formal banquet with Rajkumari Amrit Kaur (the Minister of Health) and his successor as Governor-General, C. Rajagopalachari.*

ABOVE *The Viceroy behind his desk in Delhi.* RIGHT *The Mountbattens in 1946 enjoying a brief holiday in New Zealand.*

ABOVE *The press conference of 4 June 1947. Sardar Patel stands beside the Viceroy, and in front sit V. P. Menon, Eric Mieville, General Ismay, George Abell and Ian Scott.* BELOW *The return from India. Mountbatten stands between the Duke of Edinburgh and Mr Chetty, the Indian Finance Minister, with the Prime Minister, Clement Attlee, Edwina and Krishna Menon to their left.*

*Mountbatten (above) with Marshal Tito during a naval visit to Yugoslavia in June 1952 and (below) with General Eisenhower at SHAPE.*

*Mountbatten (top) with his sparring partner, Admiral Carney, on a visit to Naples and (above) with Prince Charles and Princess Anne on a beach in Malta in 1954.*

ABOVE *Six Admirals, representing the six Allied Navies under his command, pull the Admiral's Galley on Mountbatten's departure from the Mediterranean in December 1954.* LEFT *The First Sea Lord, on a visit to Woomera in 1956, concentrates with characteristic intensity on the job in hand.*

Mountbatten (left) with
Admiral Rickover at the
controls of the nuclear
submarine Skipjack in October
1958 and (below) preparing to
aqualung in the Mediterranean
near Leghorn.

ABOVE *The Defence Council in* 1964. *From left to right: Solly Zuckerman; Mount-batten; the Minister of Defence, Peter Thorneycroft; Permanent Under-Secretary, Henry Hardman; the two joint secretaries; First Sea Lord, Admiral Luce; Minister of Defence for the Royal Navy, Lord Jellicoe; Chief of Air Staff, Air Chief Marshal Elworthy (partially obscured); Minister of Defence for the RAF, Hugh Fraser; Chief of the General Staff, General Hull.* BELOW *Churchill, Admiral Somerville and Mountbatten receive honorary degrees at Oxford.*

*Mountbatten takes the salute as C.D.S. for the last time. Behind him are ranged his successor, Field Marshal Hull, Admiral Luce, General Cassells and Air Chief Marshal Elworthy.*

ABOVE *The Head of the Immigration Mission meets Archbishop Makarios in Nicosia.*
BELOW *Mountbatten in Washington in November 1961 as Chairman of the NATO*
*Military Committee meets President Kennedy and General Lemnitzer at the White House.*

I may say that 2nd/3rd June was the worst 24 hours of my life [Mountbatten told Patricia]. I gave the leaders the plan at 10 a.m., said I required the answers of this Working Committee by midnight and got 3 unsatisfactory answers. [He described the various objections and his tactics for circumventing them.] Believe it or not, the plan went through without a comma being changed. The night before things had looked so black that I was wondering if I'd have to resign and come home! Though I never let on to anyone that I was so worried. I never do, I hope.[49]

The statement was duly made in London and the following day Mountbatten gave an audience for three hundred journalists from India and all over the world. It was, said Campbell-Johnson, 'the most brilliant performance I have ever witnessed at a major Press conference'.[50] Speaking without notes, Mountbatten spent three-quarters of an hour expounding the background and the details of the plan, and then dealt with more than a hundred questions, ranging from rabid abuse to searching requests for amplification of the finer points. The Viceroy answered them all with courtesy, confidence and extreme quick-wittedness. Sometimes he was surprisingly frank, as when he was asked whether the States would be free to opt for independence as members of the Commonwealth. When paramountcy lapsed, he replied, the States could do what they wished, but they could not enter the Commonwealth as Dominions. Was he certain that Congress, the Muslim League and the Sikhs, deliberating at leisure and in full session, would honour the undertakings of their leaders? 'I am the person who is carrying the responsibility of going ahead with this business. If I have gone ahead it is because I feel that that was the right thing to do. . . . I have taken, if you like, the risk in doing so but I have spent the last five years in taking what you might call calculated risks.' Again and again he hammered home what he believed to be the essential message. It was the Indians who had wanted independence, it was the Indians who had made partition inevitable, it was the Indians who must now make it work. 'Every time you ask me whether I am going to decide a question for you I say "No". If you put the same question in a second and third way, I still say my answer is "No". I am quite sincere when I say that you have got to make up your minds.'[51]

The most startling piece of information provided at the conference was delivered casually, almost as if a passing thought, and was not even included in the excerpts telegraphed to London. 'How long will "His Excellency" stay as "His Excellency" and thereafter as Governor-General?' he was asked. 'That is a most embarrassing question,' he replied. 'I think the transfer could be about the 15th of August.'[52] There is little evidence that this or any other precise date had been established beforehand with his advisers, with Whitehall, or with the Indian leaders. In mid May he had told Jinnah that he proposed to recommend that the transfer of power should 'take place as soon as possible – preferably by 1st October'.[53] In London he had said nothing to suggest that he was by then thinking of an even earlier date. In one of his more picturesque accounts of the proceedings, Mountbatten claimed that the date came to him as by inspiration, the only reason for 15 August being the somewhat tenuous one that it was the anniversary of his appointment as Supreme Commander.[54] This is contradicted by his own retrospective despatch in which he states that 15 August was agreed with the Indian leaders in the first days of June.[55] No trace of such conversations is to be found in the copious records. Writing to Patricia on 11 June, Mountbatten said that when he first proposed 15 August, 'even my own staff was horrified and kept saying "It can't be done! It can't be done!" When Nehru heard it, he is reported to have said, "I can't believe it!" '[56] At what moment or by whom this revelation was made to Nehru remains obscure. What at least is clear is that he and Jinnah had accepted that this or something close to it was to be the date before the news was broadcast to the world. In London Leslie Rowan, Attlee's Private Secretary, remarked that it would prove extremely difficult to get the legislation through on time. 'Accept Viceroy's proposal,' the Prime Minister minuted laconically.[57]

Whatever the circumstances, the deed was done, and within a few days it had become accepted by everyone. The choice proved unfortunate for reasons that the Viceroy could hardly have predicted. 'The astrologers are being rather tiresome,' Mountbatten reported.[58] 15 August was inauspicious for so significant an event. Whatever Nehru's private views of necromancy, he had no wish to offend public prejudice, yet to change the date would invite ridicule as well as cause inconvenience. Fortunately, midnight on 14 August would still be a suitable moment. The Constituent Assembly was summoned for late in the evening of 14 August. At the stroke of midnight it would take over power. India would be free.

Some of the most searching questions posed at the press conference had come from Devadas Gandhi, the Mahatma's son. Mountbatten knew that Gandhi could overthrow the still fragile basis for a settlement if he chose openly to oppose it. His support was not needed, neutrality would be enough, but could that be guaranteed? Krishna Menon warned the Viceroy that the Mahatma was in an unhappy and emotional mood and that some feared he might denounce the agreement at the prayer-meeting he was to hold on the evening of 4 June. Mountbatten asked Gandhi to call at any time before the meeting, and an hour before it was to begin he duly appeared. Mountbatten devoted all his energies to persuading his visitor that every element in the new arrangement had in fact been inspired by Gandhi, that it was he who had insisted that the people of India should decide their own destiny, that the plan should properly be called the 'Gandhi Plan', not, as some papers styled it, the 'Mountbatten Plan'.[59] It seems unlikely that Gandhi was convinced by this line of argument, but intelligence and subtlety are not necessarily sure guards against flattery. 'He put his case', wrote Gandhi's biographer, 'with a skill, persuasiveness and flair for salesmanship which the author of *How to Win Friends and Influence People* might well have envied.' His efforts were successful. 'The British Government is not responsible for partition,' Gandhi told his prayer-meeting. 'The Viceroy had no hand in it. . . . If both of us – Hindus and Muslims – cannot agree on anything else, then the Viceroy is left with no choice.'[60] Partition was tragic but inevitable; the agreement must be implemented as best it could.


'The biggest crime and the biggest headache', said Ismay, was the breaking up of the Indian Army.[61] Mountbatten would have agreed wholeheartedly. So long as he was responsible for law and order, he told Liaqat, nothing would induce him 'to take one step that would imperil the efficiency of the Army'.[62] In the British Cabinet he argued the same way: the unity of the Army was essential – 'He thought that the Indian leaders themselves would sooner or later realize that the retention of the Indian Army under central control was vital.'[63] The Muslims knew that in due course he would realize that one army and two countries was an impossibility; they only hoped that the revelation would come sooner rather than later, since the shorter the time left for dismemberment, the less chance there was that Pakistan would secure a fair share of the equipment. Mountbatten's reluctance to set the work in train was seen by Jinnah as fresh proof of his partiality to the Hindu cause, a sign of his determination to cripple the new state from its inception.[64]

Mountbatten accepted the inevitable sooner than the Commander-in-Chief. Even to hint at the possibility of a divided Army, said Auchinleck, would cause a drastic breakdown of morale. If the operation were to be undertaken it would take several years, during which time India would have no defence against external aggression.[65] The Viceroy could hardly ignore the advice of his senior professional adviser, but he knew well that, if the impossible had to be done, it got done. 'There is no evidence', wrote Auchinleck's biographer, John Connell, 'to show that, after April 25, the Commander-in-Chief was consulted again as to policy: he was simply given his instructions, and told to carry them out. This is not to be construed as a deliberate affront either to Auchinleck or to the Armed Forces which he commanded; but it was the expression of an extraordinary and unpre-

cedented revolution in fundamental attitudes on the part of the Viceroy.'[66] In
mid June the Armed Forces Reconstitution Committee – Auchinleck's
euphemism to avoid the use of the word 'partition' – was set up to unmake the
omelette of the Indian Services and ensure that, by the date of the transfer of
power, two Armies, Navies and Air Forces existed; one Muslim, one Hindu;
one in Pakistan, one in India. To manage the operation Mountbatten called in
the Governor-Designate of East Bengal, Sir Chandulal Trivedi, who combined the attributes of being a former Secretary of the Defence Department, a
confidant of Nehru and Patel and a close friend of Liaqat Ali Khan. It was
V. P. Menon who suggested the appointment – 'I then had the brainwave of
sending for Trivedi,' was Mountbatten's characteristic announcement of the
news to London.[67]

One item was saved from the wreck of a unified Army. From 15 August
Auchinleck would become Supreme Commander. His role would be nebu-
lous, with no operational control over any unit except those moving from one
Dominion to the other, but his very existence seemed to offer some hope of
continuity. He would be responsible to the Joint Defence Committee, a body
on which both Governor-Generals (or, as Mountbatten then hoped, the one
common Governor-General) and both Ministers of Defence would sit. To
Mountbatten it seemed that this body could prove the ultimate guarantor of
law and order in the sub-continent and provide a sign pointing the way
towards future federation. In so thinking he over-estimated the appeal of
reason in a continent beset by fear and hatred.

The Army broke up in awful bitterness. When Ismay told an old friend, a
senior officer in the Indian Army, that he had come to help India achieve
independence, the man said: 'We soldiers have trusted you for forty years,
and now you are going to betray us.' With that he walked out of Ismay's
room, and out of his life.[68] It cost Auchinleck more than distress. Mountbatten was blamed by the Muslim League for his tardiness in putting in hand
the division of the Army; Auchinleck, who, left to himself, would have
advanced far more slowly if at all, paradoxically became the object of extreme
suspicion on the part of Congress. It was probably true to say that the
Commander-in-Chief, like most British Army officers, preferred Muslims to
Hindus; but Auchinleck, the most honourable of men, would if anything have
been spurred into taking the side of the Hindus by his knowledge of this
predilection. Unfair though it might be, however, Nehru and, still more, the
Defence Minister Baldev Singh had lost all confidence in him, to the extent
that they were on the point of refusing to accept him as Supreme
Commander.[69] Mountbatten managed to stave off so awkward a confrontation, but the knowledge of the rankling disaffection did not boost his
confidence in the Joint Defence Committee.

Just as the partition of the Army was getting under way, the Chief of the Imperial General Staff, Field Marshal Montgomery, arrived in Delhi. His visit permitted Mountbatten to make the sort of gesture he most relished. The Viceregal servants wore his personal insignia, 'M of B', set within the Garter. For Montgomery of Alamein, also a member of the Order of the Garter, the 'B' was changed to 'A'.[70] Montgomery was delighted. 'He and Dickie together are a scream,' wrote Ismay. 'They both concentrate on their "ego" and on their own personal views and achievements – so discussion becomes a bit confused.'[71] On the subject of the armed forces, however, some communication was achieved, and the Field Marshal had at least one talk with Auchinleck in which he tried to make the Commander-in-Chief more ready to accept the destruction of his beloved Army.

And so the stage was set for the final act.

> Magnificent [wrote Cripps]. We have been thinking of you hour by hour, and what you have accomplished has exceeded even our expectations and hopes. I know you have a very tough job ahead but I hope you have now got out of the dangers of a land-locked harbour on to the High Sea where the storms will be easier to ride out.[72]

The message was kindly meant and Mountbatten no doubt appreciated the nautical metaphor. He may also, however, have remembered the fate of *Javelin* and *Kelly* and reflected that storms were not the only perils that could afflict a vessel on the high seas.

# CHAPTER 31

## *The Working-out*

JINNAH HAD NO SOONER GIVEN his unenthusiastic yet all-important nod of acquiescence at the meeting of 3 June than Mountbatten produced and threw on to the table copies of a document which he had caused to be prepared called *The Administrative Consequences of Partition*. With a precision that was all the more devastating for its matter-of-fact presentation, the paper set out the gigantic and complex problems that would have to be solved if two nations were to emerge from one. Mountbatten's intention was to stop the Indian leaders arguing about the past and to compel them to address themselves urgently to the future. In this he was at least partly successful. 'The severe shock that this gave to everyone present', he wrote, 'would have been amusing if it was not rather tragic.'[1] The tragedy lay in the fact that neither Congress nor Muslim League had given more than a passing thought to what lay ahead. To them the winning of independence and the decision to divide the country had been an end in itself; now they saw that it was only a beginning.

Speed was all-important. The administrative machine and the instruments of law and order had run down alarmingly over the last few years as experienced British personnel had been withdrawn without replacements being made available. There were many Indian public servants of the highest calibre, but not enough to carry the burden of independence. With the approach of partition, erosion gave way to disintegration. The Army, the police, the judiciary found themselves faced with brutal dismemberment. Traditional loyalties lapsed, new and as yet unformed allegiances took their place. Nothing was certain except that everything would change. The period Mountbatten had left between the decision to partition India and the transfer of power, in a sense ludicrously short, seemed also alarmingly long. To keep the machine of a united India running while simultaneously stripping down the engine and reconstituting it in two parts proved a task of horrifying difficulty. Ten years would not have been long enough to do the job properly; ten weeks was almost too long. Mountbatten had a calendar prepared with a page for each day bearing the dread reminder, 'X Days left to prepare for the Transfer of Power.' Like shopping days before Christmas, the leaves slipped away with alarming speed.

By 5 June the leaders had already met three times to discuss the problems. 'Both sides were still very anxious to obtain my services as arbitrator in all matters of dispute,' reported the Viceroy.[2] He was determined not to play this part. As judge he would inevitably have affronted one or other party and quickly undermined his position. He must remain above the fray. Unless he could maintain his reputation for impartiality, his usefulness would disappear. Gandhi urged him to choose whichever of the parties he felt was right, and support it to the full. 'You have to make your choice at this very critical stage in the history of this country. If you think that Qaide Azam Jinnah is, on the whole, more correct and more reasonable than the Congress, you should choose the League as your advisers.'[3] Mountbatten saw his role very differently. He must not choose either side. Hindus and Muslims alike scrutinized his every action for evidence that he was favouring the other party. An article in *Dawn* alleged that he was discriminating against the Muslims by providing military supervision for the referendum in the North-West Frontier Province but not in Sylhet, a district of Assam. 'My God, the fellow is right!' exclaimed the Viceroy, and provided troops for Sylhet too.[4] Casual enquiries about the hill stations in Assam, made on behalf of the putative Governor, Lord Killearn, who was concerned for the health of his small children, led to panic-stricken surmise on the part of Congress that Britain was planning to hand over Hindu territory to Pakistan. Here again hurried explanations put the matter right.[5] But a predisposition on both sides to scent treachery could not invariably be allayed. Both Congress and the Muslim League accumulated a dossier of instances in which they felt that the British were discriminating against them. Though Mountbatten personally was rarely involved, the status of the Viceroy was such that nothing the British did or were alleged to do in India could fail to affect his reputation.

If by reason of personalities alone, it was inevitable that the Muslims should have the greatest doubts about his integrity. Mountbatten had arrived in India with an impressively open mind, anxious to treat both parties with equal consideration and to make as close a friend of Jinnah as of Nehru. The Muslim leader defeated his intentions. Nehru could be egocentric, temperamental, perverse, but he was warm-hearted, charming, always ready to respond generously to a generous gesture. He liked and admired Mountbatten and made his feelings clear. Jinnah eschewed the generous gesture, treated the Viceroy with cold suspicion. Ismay said of a message which Jinnah addressed to the Viceroy that: 'It was a letter I would not take from my King or send to a coolie.'6* Nehru might lose his temper, but he would never have been guilty of gratuitous offensiveness.

Mountbatten had far closer links with the Congress party than with the Muslim League. V. P. Menon was among his closest advisers, and provided a constant line of communication with Sardar Patel. Krishna Menon was another ally.

> I fully appreciate all that you say about Krishna Menon [Mountbatten told Listowel]. I was aware that he is *persona non grata* in many circles at home, and I would not say he is popular or entirely trusted here. But he has been of the very greatest help to me. . . . Fortunately, I made his acquaintance some years ago in England, when he was very much an outcast because of his Left-wing views and activities. He has never forgotten this, and I have found him a valuable contact between Nehru (whose complete confidence he has) and myself, and through him I have been able to be particularly well-informed about the trend of Congress thought and opinion.[7]

The Viceroy had no such lines into the Muslim League; his closest relationship was probably with the Nawab of Bhopal, who was close to Jinnah but not an intimate – if any intimate existed of that most detached of men – and was anyway preoccupied with his role as Chancellor of the Chamber of Princes.

Mountbatten was accused of injustice in that he consulted Nehru while the first plan for the transfer of power was still in draft, but gave Jinnah no similar opportunity. He could reply that he was confident Jinnah would accept the draft but had doubts about Nehru. To this the Muslims would retort that the complaisance of the League was no reason for giving Congress an advantage denied to their rivals. But the decision to show the plan to Nehru, it could be pleaded, was taken at the last moment, and only because he happened to be staying at Simla. Precisely, the Muslims would reply. And why was he staying at Simla, and Jinnah not? To this the only honest answer was that Jinnah would probably have refused even if invited and that his presence would anyway have ruined what was intended to be a few days of pleasant relaxation. The fact remained, however, that Nehru had been unfairly privileged for little reason except that Mountbatten found him sympathetic; the fault perhaps was Jinnah's but the Muslim League had some reason to think themselves hardly used.

---

* The letter was apparently received on 28 June. The only letter from Jinnah of appropriate date recorded in *The Transfer of Power* or to be found in the Broadlands Archives was despatched on 24 June. Though cool in tone and disagreeable in content, it does not seem to merit such strong condemnation.

It was against this background of brooding ill will that the Viceroy battled to keep government going during the period before the transfer of power. It was a hazardous and wearying process, with both parties perpetually on the verge of resignation. The Interim Government was kept in being for an uneasy few weeks until the passage of the Indian Independence Bill freed Mountbatten to set up what were in effect two separate Cabinets and administrations for what were to be the future India and Pakistan. 'My worst headache to date,' Mountbatten described it,[8] and there were times when he was almost punch-drunk from the constant battering of the turbulent politicians. On the evening of 2 July Krishna Menon came to see the Viceroy, 'all tense and exclaiming triumphantly, "I think I have prevailed on Congress not to resign." All I could summon up by way of acknowledgement was to say "Really". My mental process was to dismiss the whole matter as being only yesterday's crisis.'[9]

Almost any issue provided fuel for a row. At a Cabinet meeting Mountbatten obtained agreement that there should be a general moratorium on high official appointments until the administrations had been divided, and that if any had to be made it should be left for him to decide whether they should be submitted to the Cabinet. Nehru then said he wished to pick a few ambassadors straight away; this, of course, was no concern of Pakistan. Liaqat took exception; Pakistan, he said, would not wish to see an ambassador appointed to Moscow. This proviso was rendered mischievous by the fact that Liaqat knew Nehru intended his own sister, Mrs Pandit, for the post. Nehru complained that such interference was intolerable; Liaqat responded with equal heat; Nehru threatened resignation. 'Pandemonium then broke loose and everyone talked at once.' Mountbatten eventually secured silence and protested: 'Gentlemen, what hopes have we of getting a peaceable partition if the very first discussion leads to such a disgraceful scene as this?' He closed the debate and said that he would decide the matter personally in due course. Then he surveyed the angry and resentful politicians. 'I am not going on with the next item until I see a row of smiling faces in front of me,' he declared. The tactic worked, everyone laughed and the tension was eased; but though tact and good humour could get over many temporary difficulties, they could do little to relieve the hostility and suspicion that ruled between the two parties.[10]

When Hindu and Muslim occasionally united, it was usually in frustration of one of Mountbatten's wishes. The Viceroy was anxious that both the new Dominions should carry the Union Jack in the upper canton of their flags. Nehru said that his Congress followers already felt too much was being done to pander to the British – the minutes of the Indian sub-committee appointed to consider the question of a national flag make it clear that Mountbatten's suggestion was not even considered.[11] Jinnah, more ingeniously, argued that it would offend religious feeling to have a Christian cross alongside a Muslim crescent. Mountbatten accepted defeat. No such disillusionment could dispel his conviction that good will and commonsense would triumph in the end. When asked at his press conference whether certain practical arrangements would continue after partition, he remarked that the last place anything similar had happened had been Ireland.

> After the division between Northern and Southern Ireland was complete, you will be surprised to hear that the Irish had not finished making all their agreements. Among others, there was no agreement over the railways. But do you think one train stopped on that account? They ran on. The General Managers rang each other up and said they would go on the basis of a standstill agreement. Gradually agreements were built up. The world is really a sensible place once you get the anger out of it, and unless I have a completely wrong estimate of the Indian character, India will be sensible too.[12]

So far as the officials working out the nuts and bolts of partition were concerned, India *was* sensible. At the highest level this was less true. The machinery there was the Partition Committee, later styled the Partition Council, with two members of Congress, two of the League, and Mountbatten in the chair, to see fair play rather than to arbitrate. Chaudhuri Muhammad Ali, a future Prime Minister of Pakistan and one of Mountbatten's harshest critics, regularly attended these meetings. 'Mountbatten,' he wrote, 'who made a superb Chairman, was determined not to let a deadlock develop, and used his ingenuity and resourcefulness to keep things moving.'[13] A typical instance arose over the Government printing-presses. There were six of these, but all in Delhi, and Sardar Patel flatly refused to allow even one to be moved to Karachi – 'No one asked Pakistan to secede!' Mountbatten said he found this 'a shocking spirit in which to start partition', but Patel was obdurate. Mountbatten thereupon promised that Britain would give top priority to providing a printing-press for Pakistan.[14] 'To anyone who knew the critical condition of industrial production in Great Britain at this time, the offer meant nothing,' wrote Muhammad Ali cynically. 'It would take a few years for the printing-press to reach Pakistan. But because Mountbatten made the proposal sound so convincing, he succeeded in creating an illusion of a solution, and the Partition Council was able to resume its work.'[15]

'There is no let-up in the negotiations with the parties,' Mountbatten told Sir John Colville, the Governor of Bombay, 'and every day something fresh occurs which almost threatens to break down our slender basis of agreement.

So far I have managed to jolly them along, but it is not an easy task.'[16] His greatest single contribution was to persuade the politicians that most of the work should be done by the civil servants, thus introducing into the picture some of the commonsense which the politicians so conspicuously failed to show. H. M. Patel, the Cabinet Secretary, and Chaudhuri Muhammad Ali were deputed to control a network of expert sub-commmittees which would divide up the sub-continent's resources on an equitable basis and ensure that partition did not mean a breakdown of communications between the two new countries. A tribunal was set up to arbitrate in cases where Patel and Muhammad Ali reached deadlock. Jinnah supported the British lawyer Sir Cyril Radcliffe as Chairman of the tribunal but Congress opposed the appointment; 'apparently', reported Mountbatten, 'under the impression that he is a Conservative and therefore likely to favour the League!' These objections – interesting for the view which it suggested Congress held of the Conservatives – cannot have been seriously felt; in the same letter Mountbatten was reporting that Radcliffe had been accepted by everyone as Chairman of the Boundary Commission.[17]

From the moment partition on the basis of Commonwealth membership became a probability, Mountbatten had assumed that the transition period would be made easier by India and Pakistan initially choosing the same Governor-General. Though he publicly insisted that nothing be said to prejudge the issue, he privately took it for granted that the first incumbent of the dual office would be himself. Nehru had expressed his wish for this as early as 17 May.[18] Jinnah had floated the idea of two Governor-Generals, with Mountbatten or some other representative of the Crown acting as a supreme mediator between them, but he had not pursued the idea and it was generally supposed that he had abandoned it as constitutionally improper as well as unworkable. Mountbatten was already making plans for carrying out the new task when ominous signs began to suggest that Jinnah might have other ideas. At a meeting on 23 June he was obstinately reluctant to name a Governor-General but insisted 'that whatever decision he reached would not be taken on the grounds of not wanting the Viceroy, in whom he had implicit trust and confidence'.[19] Mountbatten correctly deduced that this unwonted good will could only be a preamble to a particularly harsh rebuff.

On 1 July the rebuff came. 'Saw Mr Jinnah who suggested himself as G G Pakistan,' recorded the Viceroy's diary laconically. His report to London of 4 July was more expansive and showed clearly how angry and disappointed he was at being robbed of an appointment which he was not only convinced would best have served the interests of India but would also have crowned his achievements as Viceroy. Jinnah is 'suffering from megalomania in its worst form', he commented. When Mountbatten pointed out that the Muslim leader's powers as Prime Minister would be far greater than as Governor-General, Jinnah retorted: 'In my position it is I who will give the advice and others will act on it.' Mountbatten argued that only with a common Governor-General did Pakistan stand any chance of securing its fair share of the national assets. Jinnah was unmoved. 'I asked him "Do you realise what this will cost you?" He replied sadly, "It may cost me several crores of rupees in assets," to which I replied somewhat acidly, "It may well cost you the whole of your assets and the future of Pakistan." I then got up and left the room.'[20] According to Chaudhuri Muhammad Ali, who was present at this encounter, the Viceroy 'belaboured Jinnah with arguments and appeals and bluster. . . . Jinnah bore this onslaught with great dignity and patience.'[21] The account is not unconvincing; Mountbatten clearly lost his temper and Jinnah's impassivity would only have fuelled his indignation.

Now Mountbatten was in a quandary. Previously he had taken it for granted that he would stay as Governor-General of both Dominions or of neither. He had told Patricia on 11 June that he was still waiting for Jinnah to invite him to take on the office — 'I won't stay unless he does — so it's once more touch and go if I'm here for several years or until 15th August.'[22] To remain as Governor-General of India alone would, he felt, identify the supreme British authority in the area as the servant of one country and thus destroy Britain's reputation for impartiality as well as his own. 'He fears the loss of objective status will be a crippling handicap to his usefulness and may well dissipate the good will he has won from Hindu and Moslem alike,' recorded Campbell-Johnson.[23] Yet the Indians still wanted his services, and to refuse them on the ground that Pakistan did not feel likewise would be to cause quite unmerited offence. What was more, his Muslim advisers assured him that Pakistan too would welcome his taking on the Governor-Generalship of India.[24] Jinnah confirmed that, even if he did take on the task in New Delhi, the Pakistanis would wish him to remain as Chairman of the Joint Defence Committee.[25] Auchinleck went so far as to say that few British officers would be prepared to stay on if Mountbatten left.[26] The Viceroy's distress and confusion of mind is shown in his letter to Patricia.

> Your poor old Daddy has finally and irretrievably 'boobed' and I've now landed myself in a position from which I cannot conceivably extricate myself with honour.
>
> Either I accept to stay with the Dominion of India and be for ever accused of taking sides . . . or I let down the Congress leaders. . . . Mummy feels I should preserve my reputation for impartiality and go on 15th August. The others feel I cannot let down Nehru and must stay. In both cases I'm in the wrong. In fact I've at last made a mess of

things through over-confidence and over-tiredness. I'm just whacked and worn out and would really like to go.

I'm so depressed darling, because until this stupid mishandling of the Jinnah situation I'd done so well. It has certainly taken me down many pegs.[27]

Unable to decide for himself on the best course, he despatched Ismay to London to canvass the views of King, Government and Opposition. To Attlee he displayed the same unwonted humility as to Patricia: 'I do not want to conceal from you that I consider the whole of this situation to be my fault,' he wrote. He should have anticipated the possibility of Jinnah's decision, and established the position in advance; now, whichever way the decision went, he would seem to have let someone down.[28] He can have had little doubt of the final solution. When the Cabinet discussed the question on 7 July, only Cripps emphasized that, by becoming the servant of one of the two countries he had previously ruled, he would damage his position and reputation. Everybody else felt that the balance of advantage was heavily in favour of his staying on: 'In the interests of the new Dominion of India, he ought to complete the work he had started with such distinction: if his services were lost at this stage, the whole policy embodied in the Indian Independence Bill might be endangered.'[29] Ismay was despatched to Chartwell to establish the views of Churchill and secured an equally emphatic endorsement of acceptance: 'Lord Mountbatten might be of great help to the Hindustan Government in the next year or so and in Mr Churchill's opinion he ought not to withhold that aid.'[30] Finally, the King was also recruited to urge his cousin to take on the job.[31] Mountbatten was already more than half convinced that he both ought and wanted to become the first Governor-General of an independent India. He required no further encouragement.

I can never begin to tell you how difficult the job is now [Mountbatten told Patricia at the end of June], far, far worse than before June 3. Dear old V. P. Menon . . . came to me a couple of days ago (I was looking rather worn out and haggard). He said he thought all the leaders had gone neurotic and that Nehru was heading for a breakdown. He said, 'The only man who can hold India now is Your Excellency. If you break down too all will be lost, everyone on both sides hangs only on you.' Unfortunately that is true and I get so worn out by the scenes and squabbles about partition, I really get harassed and depressed at times and dare not show it to anyone for it's only by a tremendous show of optimistic confidence I keep them all together.[32]

That no man is indispensable is a truism; yet at that moment in India Mountbatten had as much right to think himself so as any great man at a turning-point in history. The strain told; almost one might say that the strain of concealing the strain told most of all. It called for a colossal and enduring exercise of will, not merely to drive himself to the verge of breakdown but to remain outwardly calm and ebullient when everything seemed to be going wrong. 'A stinking day,' wrote Christie in his diary. 'No sign of rain. . . . H.E. at 20 to 5 started spitting blood over not having seen the Partition Council papers. These, however, had been put in front of him before lunch!' And the following day: 'H.E. looks tired and it shows itself by his talking round the point.'[33]

Yet only people as close to him as Christie detected the signs of exhaustion. On 17 July the Mountbattens gave a silver-wedding dinner-party for ninety-five guests. Jinnah and Nehru were there, all the members of the Cabinet, many of the Princes. There was Indian dancing and music; the Viceroy was totally at ease, obviously enjoying himself, without an apparent care in the world. An American diplomat, George Merrill, and the Governor of the United Provinces, Sir Francis Wylie, 'decided one evening when we were watching Lord Louis and his consort in action that in all history no revolution had perhaps ever been put through with so much grace'.[34]

What was to prove the harshest and bloodiest phase of the revolution was now to begin. By the end of June the Provincial Assemblies of Bengal and the Punjab had voted for partition. Mountbatten never doubted that this was a prescription for disaster, acceptable only because no alternative was conceivable. 'The more I look at the problem of India,' he told the Secretary of State, 'the more I realise that all this partition business is sheer madness. . . . No one would ever induce me to agree to it were it not for this fantastic communal madness that has seized everybody and leaves no other course open.' On Bengal he said, 'I have no doubt myself that unity is necessary,' yet when he asked the Governor, Sir Frederick Burrows, whether he was still sitting on a barrel of gunpowder, he got the reply: 'Good Lord, no, we got off that a long time ago and are now sitting on a complete magazine which is going to blow up at any time.'[35] As for the Punjab, that was still worse. 'An agreed partition of the Punjab appears to me virtually impossible,' wrote Evan Jenkins, the experienced and prudent Governor.[36] In Bengal, for the most part, the problem was that of awarding tracts of land to one side or the other; in the Punjab the task was still more complex; every village, every house almost, seemed to provide grounds for argument.

The Sikh community, some fourteen per cent of the total population, made the situation immeasurably more difficult. Their faith had elements of both the Hindu and the Muslim; they felt themselves closer to the former mainly because of their deep fear and hatred of the latter. Traditionally warlike, schooled to survive, they were bloodthirsty when aroused, and were aroused easily. If any large part of what was traditionally held to be Sikh territory – above all, their sacred city of Amritsar – were handed over to Pakistan, no one doubted that there would be violent disorder. Already there was murder and arson on a scale so menacing that both Nehru and Jinnah urged Mountbatten to take drastic steps to restore order. When Mountbatten refused to impose martial law – not out of squeamishness but because the Governor assured him that it would merely make things worse – he was abused in Cabinet by representatives of Congress and the League alike. 'Nehru, as usual, completely lost control of himself and demanded the sacking of every official, from the Governor downwards, that same day. I had to reprimand him publicly for this irresponsible suggestion.'[37] To Jenkins the most sinister feature was that neither the police nor the Army could be relied on to quell disorder. Themselves contaminated by communalism and deprived of most of the British officers who would have remained neutral in the conflict, they were beginning to abet, if not actually indulge in, violence directed at their religious enemies.[38]

Mountbatten took the situation seriously but not tragically. In April Jenkins had warned him that, if partition were imposed on the Punjab, it would take four divisions from outside the province to restore order.[39] Since partition would not be imposed but agreed with both parties, the Viceroy felt that such calculations need not be found too disturbing. If violence were met firmly, he believed, it could be controlled. It was Mountbatten's view, Attlee told the Cabinet, that 'the only hope of checking widespread communal warfare was to suppress the first signs of it promptly and ruthlessly, using for this purpose all the force required, including tanks and aircraft'.[40] Mountbatten gave the same message even more categorically to Maulana Azad, the only Muslim member of the Congress hierarchy. 'I shall see to it that there is no bloodshed and riot,' Azad recalled Mountbatten declaring. 'I am a soldier, not a civilian. Once partition is accepted in principle, I shall issue orders to see that there are no communal disturbances in the country. If there should be the slightest agitation, I shall adopt the sternest measures to nip the trouble in the bud. I shall not use even the armed police. I will order the Army and Air Force to act and I will use tanks and aeroplanes to suppress anybody who wants to create trouble.'[41] Whether or not the words were correctly quoted, this was his belief. It was not to be long before the Viceroy and his advisers – Indian as much as British – were to discover how tragically mistaken they were about the nature and the magnitude of the threat.

Some of the harshest criticism of Mountbatten's attitude towards the impending violence came from those Muslims who complained that, in spite of his proud words about tanks and aeroplanes, he did nothing to restrain the Sikhs when it was clear that they were bent on mischief. In fact something was done. In response to the threatened violence, the Punjab Boundary Force was set up, a supposedly neutral body which would maintain a unified military command in the whole area. The idea was a good one, its execution was to prove less successful. But in any case it would have been hard-pressed to cope with the plans of the Sikh leaders for sabotage and murder. Intelligence reports made it clear that Master Tara Singh and his colleagues were plotting the assassination of Jinnah as well as certain dramatic acts of sabotage. Jinnah and Liaqat Ali Khan immediately demanded the arrest of the conspirators; Sardar Patel argued that any such step would exacerbate rather than assuage the trouble; Mountbatten was personally in favour of strong measures but felt that the authorities on the spot must be consulted first. The matter was referred to Jenkins who in turn consulted the Governors-Designate of East and West Punjab, Sir Chandulal Trivedi and Sir Francis Mudie. The three men were unanimous in holding that, while there might have been a case for such preventive arrests in the past, it was now too late. To arrest Tara Singh would provoke an immediate explosion; to leave him at liberty was the lesser risk.[42]

Meanwhile the two new countries were taking shape. Mountbatten at first was inclined to favour the Muslim League proposal that the work of dividing the Punjab and Bengal should be left to teams from the newly-founded United Nations backed by expert assessors from the two communities.[43] Nehru feared the delay involved and the uncertainty as to what stray Pole or Swede might be imposed on them. In the end it was agreed that one man should be Chairman of the Boundary Commission for both the Punjab and Bengal, with a casting vote to be used in the case of dissension between the representatives of the League and Congress who were to advise him. The holder of this terrifying responsibility was to be nominated by the British Government. They selected Sir Cyril Radcliffe, a lawyer of great intelligence, probity and an intellectual toughness that was to enable him to withstand almost intolerable pressures. Mountbatten had known him when he was Director-General of the Ministry of Information during the war and had been struck by his ability.[44] By 8 July he was in India and at work. He was resolved to prepare his award, however rough and ready, by the time of the transfer of power.

For Mountbatten the arrival of Radcliffe meant relief from a potentially monstrous burden. From now on he could legitimately claim that the dismemberment of Bengal and the Punjab was no concern of his. Radcliffe was installed not in Viceroy's House but in a separate house on the Viceregal estate, and the two men ostentatiously kept each other at arm's length.

Mountbatten wished neither to influence nor to be informed of the progress of Radcliffe's deliberations. He had the greatest difficulty in persuading the Indian leaders that this was in fact the case. On 9 August Nehru sent the Viceroy a secret letter, enclosing a memorandum about the irrigation system of the Punjab, which he suggested should be passed on to Radcliffe. 'I hope you will agree', Mountbatten replied, 'that it is most important that I should not do anything to prejudice the independence of the Boundary Commission, and that, therefore, it would be wrong for me even to forward any memorandum, especially at this stage.'[45] Two days later it was the turn of the Muslims. Liaqat Ali Khan wrote to Ismay to protest about the alleged award of Gurdaspur to East Punjab 'on political grounds'. Ismay replied that to the best of his knowledge no award had yet been made and that it was, anyway, nothing to do with the Viceroy.[46] When the Maharaja of Patiala brought a delegation of Sikh officers to press their views on the Punjab boundary, Mountbatten refused even to see them but sent them packing to make their case to the Boundary Commissioners.[47]

By the end of July there was room for guarded optimism. Though their assurances were hedged around by qualifications, both Congress and the Muslim League had stated that in principle they would accept Radcliffe's award. Violence was alarmingly evident, yet Jenkins and the other experts believed that, provided the lines of partition were accepted by the leaders, order could be maintained without too much difficulty. There would inevitably be displacements of population, but these would be on a relatively minor scale and spread over a long period. It seemed reasonable to hope that Independence Day would be celebrated in an atmosphere of tranquillity and followed by a period of painful but at least generally peaceful reconstruction. One problem, however, remained unsolved and was now demanding the most urgent attention: the future of India's Princely States.

# CHAPTER 32

## *The Princely States*

As THE BOUNDARIES OF BRITISH INDIA had gradually extended in the first half of the nineteenth century, an increasing number of Princely States had entered into treaty arrangements with the new power, under which they accepted the presence of a British Resident in their capitals and a degree of subordination to the Raj, but were not absorbed into the colonial bloc. These States for the most part remained loyal to Britain during the Mutiny, and it was in recognition of the debt owed them by the British that Queen Victoria in her proclamation of 1858 declared: 'We shall respect the rights, dignity and honour of Native Princes as our own.' By 1947, 108 rulers sat in the Chamber of Princes, and twelve representatives of a further 127 lesser States. Altogether there were 565 separate States ranging from Hyderabad or Kashmir – equal in area and population to a considerable European power – to petty principalities smaller than the estates of the Dukes of Sutherland or of Atholl; some immensely rich, some impoverished and without resources; some models of good administration, some primitive or ruled according to the whim of a ruler who might be cruel and corrupt as well as inefficient.

What was to happen to these States in an independent India? There were two schools of thought. The first argued that the relationship between the British Government in India and each Princely State was peculiar to those two entities, and that the rights and responsibilities of the paramount power would lapse as soon as British rule in India came to an end. This was the traditional Whitehall view, emphasized by the Butler Committee and reiterated in Cabinet at a meeting attended by Mountbatten in May 1947. 'As soon as Dominion status was granted to British India, paramountcy would come to an end. The States would then become fully independent and would be free to negotiate new agreements if they thought it desirable to do so.'[1] Against this there were those who held, as Nehru's father Motilal had done in 1928, that such a policy reflected the determination of the British to 'convert the Indian States into an Indian Ulster'.[2] Gandhi told Mountbatten that the Princes were the creation of the British, small chieftans built up as allies to weaken Indian resistance to the Empire. 'He considered it wicked of Sir Stafford Cripps not to have recommended the turning over of paramountcy to the Central

Government.'[3] If Mountbatten in any way encouraged the Princes to stand out for their independence, he would in the eyes of Congress be deliberately sabotaging the new state of India by balkanizing its rightful territory and allowing artificial and undemocratic anachronisms to flourish at its expense. The Muslim League in reality felt little different, though the fact that there were few among the Princes who could be expected to accede to Pakistan gave them the opportunity to make things difficult for Congress by holding forth about the right of the States to decide their own destiny.

Mountbatten's instructions left him ample room for manoeuvre; he was to urge the more reactionary rulers in the direction of democracy, and assist them all 'in coming to fair and just arrangements with the leaders of British India'.[4] In so far as he had thought at all about the problem, it was to assume that it would easily be regulated once the fundamental decisions about the transfer of power had been taken. He was personally sympathetic to the Princes, several of whom he numbered among his closest Indian friends. As cousin to the King-Emperor as well as Viceroy, he felt a particular responsibility to a group of people who attached such significance to their ties with the Crown of England. But he was not sentimental about feudal relics, which he recognized would fit uneasily into post-Imperial India. He would do what he could for them, but they must not be allowed to impede the greater good of a peaceful and permanent handover. In Cabinet he had talked vaguely of treating the States as Napoleon had dealt with the kingdoms and duchies of Germany, welding them into larger and more viable units which could then negotiate their own arrangements with independent India.[5] Once he had arrived in India, the hectic pursuit of a settlement acceptable to Congress and the Muslim League drove all minor considerations from his mind. Though Conrad Corfield, the Political Adviser responsible for the States, repeatedly urged him to concentrate on the Princes, Mountbatten was not to be deflected: 'It proved impossible', wrote Corfield despairingly, 'to distract his attention from British Indian problems.'[6]

In a speech in the Constituent Assembly in 1949 Sardar Patel claimed that, in exchange for Indian acceptance of partition, Britain had agreed to withdraw within two months and not to interfere in the question of the Indian States: 'We said, "We will deal with that question. . . . The Princes are ours and we shall deal with them." '[7] There is no evidence that Mountbatten accepted this somewhat over-simplified statement of the position – indeed, his intense activity in the last few weeks before independence shows that the problem was very evidently not one for India alone – but the course of events in his first two months made it inevitable that the voice of Congress would sound loudest in his mind when at last he addressed himself to the problem.

He saw three courses open to him. He could ignore the problem and allow the States to negotiate for themselves after independence; adopt the Napoleonic tactic of creating new nations out of the existing units; or work towards their accession to India or Pakistan. The first was temptingly easy, but would either leave the States at the mercy of an independent India, or threaten the disintegration of the sub-continent into a chaos of separate countries. The second should have been initiated ten years earlier at least if it was to get anywhere before independence. That left only the third, and it was to this that Mountbatten was to devote his energies, first seeking to extract from India reasonable terms that would ensure that the rulers retained their privileges and a modicum of independence, then cajoling or bullying the rulers into acceding to India or Pakistan on the proffered terms. By so doing, he believed, he would honour Britain's treaty obligations towards the States and yet avoid the disaster of a fragmented India. He was immeasurably aided in his task by India's decision to remain within the Commonwealth – a step which made accession far more palatable to those rulers who cherished their association with the Crown.

The prospects for extracting a decent offer from Patel did not at first seem promising. The Sardar told Mountbatten that the problem was unimportant, since after the transfer of power the people would rise, overthrow their rulers and rally to independent India.[8] Nehru was equally intemperate, declaring: 'I will encourage rebellion in all States that go against us.'[9] Once again it was V. P. Menon who found the formula which offered a chance of reconciliation. If the rulers would accept that for the purposes of defence, foreign affairs and communications they would come into the Indian Union, then their remaining rights would be protected, their privy purses left inviolate: 'In other matters, we would scrupulously respect their autonomous existence.'[10] To Mountbatten this was all, indeed more than, he had expected. 'If I can get all the States in on the wonderful terms I have been able to obtain for them,' he told George VI, 'I shall have carried out your instructions to do what I could to see fair play for the Princes.'[11]

Conrad Corfield took a different view. He did not doubt that the eventual future of most if not all the States lay within a united India, but he felt that the Viceroy was doing the Princes a grave disservice by urging them to accede before the transfer of power. If paramountcy was first allowed to lapse, the Princes would be in a stronger position when it came to negotiating terms for their merger with India. His arguments were not accepted. Mountbatten, Corfield wrote,

ceased to listen to the political department from the day he made his bargain with Vallabhbhai Patel about promoting a limited adherence, which I could not support. Mountbatten told me that he had succeeded in persuading Patel to limit adherence to defence, external affairs and communications. I pointed out that he had agreed to use his influence as the representative of the paramount power to recommend a bargain which could not be guaranteed after independence. . . . V. P. Menon was virtually his political adviser from that date.[12]

When Mountbatten emphasised that the rulers' link with the Crown was protected by India's membership of the Commonwealth, Corfield asked whether accession could be revoked if India subsequently decided to become a republic. Mountbatten replied 'that he felt sure that the cabinet would accept this and I could assure the rulers accordingly. But I felt unable to do so!'[13]

Corfield went to London with Ismay in May 1947 to discuss the lapse of paramountcy with the India Office. He told Mountbatten of his intentions. 'I don't think he understood, and I did not explain, what the lapse of paramountcy would mean,' he told Leonard Mosley with disconcerting frankness. 'My job was to look after the interests of the Princely States. It was no part of my job to make things easier for India.'[14] Mountbatten could hardly be expected to take a similar view of his own responsibilities. When Corfield flew back to Delhi by the plane that was to take Mountbatten to London the following day, he carefully kept away from Viceroy's House. From then on, he noted, Mountbatten 'viewed me with some suspicion'.[15] The suspicion was merited. Corfield settled down systematically to obstruct what he knew to be the Viceroy's policy, pleading subsequently that in so doing he was carrying out the instructions he had received in London. 'Whether H.M.G. had formulated any other policy for the so-called Princely States I do not know,' he wrote. 'If they did, I had no inkling of it from Mountbatten.'[16]

He had some justice on his side. Opinion in London had not evolved at the same speed as the Viceroy's. When Mountbatten sent to Whitehall the text of his speech to the rulers which he planned to deliver on 25 July, civil servants minuted that it was inconsistent with the Prime Minister's assurance that the States would be entirely free to decide their own future. 'The impression is given that the Viceroy condones pressure on them to accept.' Horace Rumbold, Assistant Secretary at the India Office, said that Mountbatten should be warned that he might be creating 'grave embarrassment' for the British Government. Attlee approved a telegram telling the Viceroy he was going too far. In particular, his statement that the States must accede before 15 August was inconsistent with what had been said in Parliament. Mountbatten's reply was decidedly cross. 'I am afraid you have completely misunderstood the purport of my speech and object which I am trying to achieve.'

What he was aiming for was to make the States see the advantages of accession. If they missed their chance now, Britain would never again be in a position to assist them. 'I am trying my very best to create an integrated India which, while securing stability, will ensure friendship with Great Britain. If I am allowed to play my own hand without interference I have no doubt I will succeed.' Whitehall went into alarmed retreat. 'The Viceroy seems to me to be handling the States question with his usual very great skill,' minuted Rumbold. 'While it is true that, in some respects, he may be going just a little beyond what was said in Parliament, I think it would be a mistake not to allow him the free hand he desires.' Listowel concurred and told Mountbatten so in almost grovelling terms, expressing his 'great satisfaction' at the 'amazing measure of success' Mountbatten had achieved.[17]

Abandoned by London and outgunned in Delhi, Corfield had no chance of success. At a stormy meeting on 13 June, Nehru claimed that Corfield and the Political Department were acting in a way highly damaging to Indian interests. He charged them with misfeasance and demanded a judicial enquiry. 'I saw Jinnah looking at Lord Mountbatten as though waiting for him to intervene and protect his Political Adviser,' wrote Corfield. 'But nothing was said.'[18] In this he seems to have been unfair. The minutes record that the Viceroy supported Corfield by saying that he was doing no more than carry out the policy of the Secretary of State.[19] He did so without much enthusiasm, however, and, when V. P. Menon complained that Corfield was trying to persuade the Nawab of Bhopal and others of the Princes to make a last-minute stand against accession, his sympathies were largely with his Hindu adviser.[20]

One thing on which Nehru and Jinnah agreed was that a States Department should be set up to work out standstill agreements and take over from Corfield's Political Department all relations that did not involve the exercise of paramountcy. 'I am glad to say that Nehru has not been put in charge . . . which would have wrecked everything,' reported Mountbatten. 'Patel, who is essentially a realist and very sensible, is going to take it over.' Even better, V. P. Menon was to be Secretary.[21] Corfield derived less satisfaction from this appointment. He argued that no new department should be set up until after 15 August, since otherwise the rulers would assume it was taking over the role of the former imperial power. Once again he was overruled. He was ordered to organize a conference at which Mountbatten would expound to the Princes the advantages they would reap from immediate accession. He obeyed, but arranged to leave his job and India two days before the Princes assembled. 'I boarded the plane', he wrote, 'with a feeling of nausea, as though my own honour had been smirched and I had deserted my friends.'[22]

Patel had accepted the terms under which the rulers could accede on the understanding that all, or virtually all, the Hindu States could be prevailed upon to rally to India. V. P. Menon had told Patel some time before that the Viceroy's help would be essential if this were to be achieved: 'Apart from his position, his grace and his gifts, his relationship to the Royal Family was bound to influence the rulers.'[23] Mountbatten accepted the responsibility. From the moment the bargain with Patel was struck, he devoted himself to bullying or cajoling the rulers into accession. His letter to the Maharaj-Rana of Dholpur illustrates how far he was prepared to push them.

> If you accede now you will be joining a Dominion with the King as Head. If they change the Constitution to a republic and leave the Commonwealth, the Instrument of Accession does not bind you in any way to remain with the republic. It would appear to me that that would be the moment for Your Highness to decide if you wish to remain with India or reclaim full sovereign independence.
>
> I know that His Majesty would personally be grieved if you elected to sever your connection with him whilst he was still the King of India now that it has been made clear that this would not involve you in accepting to remain within a republic if this was unacceptable to you when the time came.
>
> I too will be grieved if I find that Your Highness refuses to accede before the 14th August, since I shall bitterly feel the fatal isolation of an old friend; and it would be sad that you or your illustrious family would travel without any diplomatic privileges unless Your Highness were able to set up legations or consulates in various parts of the world. . . .
>
> You asked me what I thought India would do to Dholpur if you did not accede. To the best of my knowledge and belief they will do nothing; that is precisely the trouble – nothing whatever will be done and your State will remain in complete isolation in the centre of an indifferent India.[24]

To Mountbatten accession was so self-evidently to the benefit of the rulers and so important for the future of India that he would have believed any measure of persuasion justified. Corfield and others with similar loyalties, on the other hand, felt that the Viceroy was misusing the vast authority which his office and his royal connections bestowed on him. In the first draft of his memoirs Corfield described a conversation with a minister from one of the Princely States who had been subjected to the full blast of Mountbatten's salesmanship – 'he now knew what Dolfuss felt like when he was sent for to see Hitler: he had not expected to be spoken to like that by a British officer: after a moment's pause he withdrew the word "British" '.[25] Corfield later excised this passage, but it deserves quotation as illustrating the bitterness expressed by some of those who felt themselves to be the Viceroy's victims.

The Chamber of Princes assembled on 25 July, Mountbatten splendid in full uniform with an imposing array of orders and decorations which outshone even the most highly decorated of the potentates who confronted him. Twenty-five of the major ruling Princes and seventy-four States' representatives were present. He spoke without notes, 'the apogee of persuasion', V. P. Menon described his speech.[26] It was, indeed, one of his most impressive performances: at times eloquent, at times informal, even casual; palpably the words of a man who believed what he was saying; hammering home with all his might that this was an opportunity that would never be repeated, that their internal autonomy would be protected, that the bargain was so advantageous to the States that even now he was not certain he could persuade the Indian Government to accept it.[27] His control of the meeting never faltered; he sensed precisely when to curdle the blood with fearful prophecies, when to relieve tension with a joke. The representative of one Maharaja claimed to have no instructions from his ruler as to what to do. Mountbatten picked up a glass paperweight which happened to be in front of him. 'I will look into my crystal,' he declared, 'and give you an answer.' Ten seconds of dramatic silence followed, then the Viceroy pronounced solemnly: 'His Highness asks you to sign the Instrument of Accession.'[28]

Intensive lobbying of the individual rulers followed. On 1 August Mountbatten held a luncheon for some of the leading Princes. By the time it was over, he knew that only a handful of recalcitrants was still outstanding. 'I have been making unbelievable progress with the Princes,' he told Patricia. 'I gave a lunch to the 22 in Delhi and all agreed to announce their accession to India that afternoon. . . . It may not be realised at home but I am in the act of bringing off a coup second only to the 3rd June plan, and sincerely hope that by 15th August I shall be able to turn over power to only 2 central Governments for the whole of India.'[29]

Among those who stood out, however, were some of real importance. The Nawab of Bhopal, Muslim ruler of a Hindu state, was an old friend of Mountbatten as well as being a responsible and statesmanlike figure. He told his friend Sher Ali Pataudi that, when he heard Mountbatten was to come to India as Viceroy, he rejoiced that all would now be well with the Princely States. Instead the Princes had been betrayed. He himself had resigned as Chancellor of the Chamber of Princes because he was determined to preserve the independence of his State.[30] 'I suppose', wrote Mountbatten, 'I have spent more time on Bhopal's case than on all the other States put together, because he is such a charming and high principled man that it would be a tragedy if he were to wreck his State by failing to come in now.'[31] As the date of independence grew closer and Bhopal found himself more isolated, he began to waver. He threatened to abdicate in favour of his twenty-three-year-old daughter, tried to negotiate a standstill agreement without actually acceding, then finally succumbed. He told Patel that 'throughout I have been treated with consideration and have received understanding and courtesy from your side',[32] but he never saw Mountbatten again.

One by one the other doubters followed suit. The Maharaja of Indore blustered and threatened, but in the end despatched the Instrument of Accession to the States Department by the ordinary post. The *dewan*, chief minister, of Travancore produced files of press cuttings to illustrate the wickedness of Congress and the impossibility of acceding to such an entity. 'I advised him to follow the example of Lord Balfour,' reported Mountbatten, 'and not to read the newspapers if he is going to let himself get upset in this way.'[33] Jodhpur was a Hindu State with a Hindu leader, but adjoining Pakistan, and the young Maharaja tried to play off Jinnah against Nehru by securing from the former a list of special concessions which would be granted him if he rallied to Pakistan. V. P. Menon bought his accession by offering similar terms himself, but not before the Maharaja had caused a stir by pulling out a pistol concealed inside a fountain-pen and threatening to shoot Menon with it. The pistol was presented to the Viceroy and eventually passed on by him to the conjurors' society, the Magic Circle, of which both Mountbatten and the Maharaja were members.[34]

In two critically important cases, however, Mountbatten failed to get his way; the problems caused thereby were to plague him throughout his time as Governor-General and, in the case of Kashmir, to embitter relations between India and Pakistan up to the present day. Hyderabad was India's largest State with a population of nearly sixteen millions. As with Bhopal, a Muslim dynasty ruled a largely Hindu state, but Hyderabad was far better equipped to go it alone in genuine independence. The Nizam enjoyed the backing of Jinnah, who warned the Viceroy that, if Congress tried to bring pressure on Hyderabad to accede, 'every Muslim throughout the whole of India' would rise as one man to defend the sanctity of its frontiers.[35] The French, too, were reported to be playing with the idea of recognizing Hyderabad's independence, though the Americans promised to hold off until the negotiations for accession were over.

The Nizam's most potent ally, however, was an English lawyer with a distinguished record in public life, Sir Walter Monckton. Monckton was the Nizam's Constitutional Adviser and, though Mountbatten realized that this precluded any attachment to the Viceregal staff, Ismay and the Viceroy were still anxious that he should be available to lend a hand from time to time.[36] Monckton told the Nizam that he had been friends with Mountbatten, Ismay and Miéville for many years. He had been keeping closely in touch and would do all he could 'to see that the new Viceroy understands the vital part that Indian India must continue to play'.[37]

When Monckton heard that Patel had been put in charge of the States' problem he commented gloomily that his policy could be summed up in a sentence: 'He intends, if he can, to inherit the rights, but not the obligations of the Paramount Power.'[38] Given his loyalties, it was inevitable that the negotiations which Monckton conducted with Mountbatten and Menon in Delhi should sometimes be stormy. Mountbatten said repeatedly that, if the Nizam did not accede, his State would be ruined and his throne lost. Monckton retorted that this was intolerable blackmail; if Hyderabad were pushed too far it would go down fighting and kindle a civil war all over India. At one point Mountbatten threatened to pull all the British troops out of Hyderabad before independence, thus leaving the Nizam practically defenceless. Ismay and Abell protested that this would be a breach of faith; Mountbatten heard them out, nodded acceptance and dropped the idea.[39] He was convinced that, if only he could get to see the Nizam, he would make him see reason; but the Nizam was conspicuously reluctant to receive him, and the rebuff involved if the Viceroy had turned up uninvited and failed to get an audience was too damaging to contemplate.[40]

There was an element of bluff in Monckton's attitude. 'We have got to make terms with Congress some time because we live land-locked in the heart of Hindustan,' he told the Nizam. 'Congress will never again offer such good terms as we should get now.'[41] Unfortunately, no such sense of realism existed in Hyderabad, where the Nizam was in the power of a fanatical Muslim movement working in close contact with Jinnah himself. Attitudes hardened on each side. When Monckton came to Delhi a few days before the transfer of power, Menon refused to make any sort of standstill agreement unless Hyderabad first acceded. When Monckton said that this was contrary to British pledges, Menon retorted that the Indian Government would not consider themselves bound by any such undertaking. Mountbatten, according to Monckton, then remarked that no doubt Congress would lay themselves open to much criticism, 'but one had to face the facts, and criticisms from the world would not deter them'.[42]

Monckton now drafted a letter to Churchill, Salisbury, Eden and Butler which, he told Ismay, had been sent to London and would be despatched if the improper pressure on Hyderabad was not relieved.

I have been reading Ciano's Diary and I am bound to say that the present exhibition of power politics seems an exact replica of those in which Hitler indulged.

It may well be that you will not hear from me again upon this matter apart from a short message to let you know that the German tactic on the old European model has been adopted in India. But I rely on you in the name of our old friendship to see to it that if this shameful betrayal of our old friends and allies cannot be prevented, at least it does not go uncastigated before the conscience of the world.[43]

Mountbatten would certainly have felt ill at ease at such a letter being sent to the Conservative leaders, but there is no reason to think that he knew of its existence. By the time Ismay saw the draft on 10 August the Viceroy had anyway concluded that there was no hope of accession before the date of the transfer of power and was concentrating on gaining time for more negotiations later. This he achieved. An extension of two months was agreed by the Indian leaders, and Mountbatten's offer of his services in future conversations was gratefully accepted. It was not everything, but at least a disastrous breakdown had been averted.[44]

Kashmir was the obverse of Hyderabad: a largely Muslim state with a Hindu ruler, bordered largely, though not exclusively, by what was to become Pakistan. To Mountbatten it was as obvious that Kashmir should accede to Pakistan as Hyderabad to India, the only possible alternative being that the State should be partitioned, with the smaller, Hindu section of Jammu going one way and Kashmir proper the other. Congress leadership would for the most part have acquiesced in either of these results, but the problem was bedevilled by the emotional involvement of Nehru, himself a Kashmiri Brahmin. The leader of the popular front in Kashmir, Sheikh Abdullah, a close friend of Nehru, had been imprisoned by the Maharaja, and Nehru was anxious to visit the capital, Srinagar, to put things right. Patel, who saw Nehru ending up inside a Kashmiri jail, tried to dissuade him. 'Nehru had broken down and wept, explaining that Kashmir meant more to him at the moment than anywhere else.'[45] The Viceroy was then appealed to and conveniently recalled that he himself had a long-standing invitation to visit the Maharaja which he was on the point of taking up.

Mountbatten and Ismay arrived in Srinagar on 15 June. The message they bore was that the Maharaja should establish the will of his people and then accede to India or Pakistan according to their wishes. If the choice was for

Pakistan — as surely it would be — Patel had assured Mountbatten that the Indian Government would not object.[46] The Maharaja, however, disliked the prospect of accession to Muslim Pakistan even more than to Congress India. Shiftless and indecisive, he was resolved to defer any decision for as long as possible, secretly hoping that he might emerge in the end with unfettered independence. 'In his heart,' wrote his son, the Yuvaraj, 'my father still did not believe that the British would actually leave.'[47] The visit got off to a poor start. The Maharaja had installed a bell under the table which he could press when the point in the state banquet had been reached at which the band should strike up 'God Save The King'. Mountbatten's long leg touched it off half way through the chicken curry, the band struck up and the startled guests struggled to their feet. The Viceroy was enchanted by this effect, the Yuvaraj collapsed in schoolboy giggles, the Maharaja was not amused. Things got no better. 'Instead of taking advantage of Mountbatten's visit to discuss the whole situation meaningfully . . . ,' commented the Yuvaraj, 'he first sent the Viceroy out on a prolonged fishing trip . . . and then — having fixed a meeting just before his departure — got out of it on the plea that he had suddenly developed a severe attack of colic.'[48] Mountbatten had to return empty-handed to Delhi, to confront a Nehru bitterly disappointed that his friend was still imprisoned. 'However, I think he was pleased at the Maharaja and Prime Minister agreeing not to make any independence declaration for the present and agreeing to give serious consideration to joining one or other Constituent Assembly as soon as the picture about Pakistan was a bit clearer.'[49]

That was the limit of his achievement. The Maharaja continued to procrastinate and by 15 August nothing had been concluded. Some Pakistanis have seen in Mountbatten's failure to persuade the Maharaja into choosing Pakistan more evidence of his supposed partiality for India. It would be as sensible for the Indians to blame him for his failure to talk the Nizam of Hyderabad into accession. Possibly, if he had known that the Maharaja would still be dithering in two months time, still more if he had realised how damaging the issue of Kashmir was to be to future relations between India and Pakistan, he might have been more forceful, have breached the door of the Maharaja's bedroom, have refused to take 'no' or 'perhaps' as an answer. It is unlikely, though, that such an interview would have achieved anything; the Maharaja had real problems and was resolved not to accept the Viceroy's solution for them.[50] And so Kashmir joined Hyderabad as one of the unresolved issues that the newly independent countries would have to sort out for themselves.

Even with these two great exceptions, and a few trivial ones, Mountbatten had achieved an astonishing measure of success. 'Against all the probabilities,' wrote H. V. Hodson in his classic study, 'the overwhelming majority of

States had joined the new Dominions, and the constitutional chaos and insur-
rectionary violence that might have followed the total lapse of paramountcy
had been averted.'[51] About the energy and skill which he deployed there can
be no question. There are those who doubted whether the cause was as good as
the weapons used. 'It is horrible that we should have encouraged the Rulers to
believe in our promises up to such a short time ago and should then leave them
without the resources to stand comfortably on their own feet,' wrote Monckton to Leo Amery. 'It is still worse that they should feel that, in spite of
loyalty, they are being left at the mercy of those who have proved in the past to
be our enemies and theirs.'[52] Horrible it may have been, and the subsequent
history of India's treatment of the Princes makes it no less so, but neither
Monckton nor anybody else could suggest a better course. The British were
not able to provide the rulers with 'the resources to stand comfortably on
their own feet', or do other than leave them at the mercy of the Indian
Government. To have washed his hands of the whole affair and left it to the
rulers to make what arrangements they could with the Central Government
after the transfer of power would have been the easy way out for Mountbatten. In some people's eyes it would have left him with a less tarnished
reputation. He himself felt, however, that it would have represented a
shameful shirking of responsibility. He had satisfied himself that accession
was in the best interests of the rulers and, though their subsequent history was
far less satisfactory than he had hoped, there is no reason to think that it
would have been any better if no such agreement had been negotiated.
Probably it would have been far worse.

'Perhaps the princes were doomed to extinction anyhow, but that they
should have been coaxed and driven to the slaughter-house by the shepherd
they trusted most is what adds poignancy to the scene.'[53] Chaudhuri Muhammad Ali's bitter comment reflects the point of view of many Pakistanis. Yet
Mountbatten saw no slaughter-house; rather, he would have described
himself as a shepherd leading his charges to a fold to protect them from the
wolves that would have attacked them if they had remained in isolation. The
wolves got them in the end, but Mountbatten did at least procure them a few
years of reasonable prosperity. He may be blamed for not foreseeing their
eventual fate, but his distress and indignation when the Indian Government in
the end renounced its agreements show how little he had expected such a
conclusion. He may be called naive but of duplicity he can be acquitted. It was
George VI, the King-Emperor himself, who with his usual commonsense put
the matter into perspective. 'I am so glad', he wrote, 'that nearly all the Indian
States have decided . . . to join either one or other of the Dominions. They
could never have stood alone in the World.'[54]

# CHAPTER 33

# *Independence*

THE SITUATION HERE is indescribably difficult [Mountbatten wrote to General Nye early in July]. It is not unlike a military operation. D Day on June 3 saw us ashore on the beaches; the Partition Council's decision on the partition of the Armed Forces was the battle of the break-out, and we must try to get across the Rhine before the 15th August. After the 15th August all the 'postwar problems' will loom as great out here as they did in Europe. The enemy still has a kick left in him too![1]

The crossing of the Rhine now lay ahead and the troops were on the point of collapse. With reports flowing in of mounting violence in the Punjab, grappling from dawn till long after dusk with the problems of dividing India, watching the days slip away from the threatening calendars on the wall, it is no wonder that the staff in Viceroy's House sometimes felt they would never survive to hail the coming of independence. 'It is almost impossible to describe the atmosphere in which we have been living or the strain to which everyone has been subjected,' Mountbatten told Listowel.[2] Miéville was seriously ill with thrombosis, Ismay in bed with dysentery, Brockman, too, was an invalid. Mountbatten rode the storm, to the outward eye ebullient and vigorous as ever. Only those who worked in his intimate circle detected the exhaustion which overcame him if for an instant the pressure was relieved. He would relapse into blank and battered silence, then spring alive again when the next crisis burst around him. It was not an atmosphere in which cool and considered judgements could be hoped for; it says much for Mountbatten's stamina that any judgement was brought to bear at all.

Meanwhile Radcliffe was drawing near the end of his task. He knew only too well that his had been a butcher's, not a surgeon's, operation. Since his Hindu and Muslim colleagues had disagreed on almost every controversial issue, he had been forced to take most of the decisions himself, and, though he had done his best to reconcile the demands of race, tradition and economic necessity, it was realised by everyone that his awards would cause anguish to many millions of people on one side or other of the new frontier and appear deeply unsatisfactory to both Governments. The only hope that Mountbatten could see was that the rulers of India and Pakistan respectively would be sufficiently impressed by the indignation shown by the other party to realize that they themselves could not have been so badly treated as they had first supposed.

On 9 August, with less than a week to go before the transfer of power, word came that the award of the Punjab Boundary Commission might be presented to the Viceroy that very evening. This confronted the Viceroy with a problem of presentation which up till then he had been ignoring. Should the awards be made public as soon as they were received, or held up for a few days until the celebrations of independence were over? Abell argued the merits of immediate release; this would enable troops to be moved into the affected areas before the transfer of power and avoid any possible accusation of jiggery-pokery if it became known that the Viceroy had suppressed the news for his own ends. Other advisers suggested that the proper day would be 14 August, when any chagrin at the awards would be swallowed up in the euphoria of liberation. Mountbatten favoured a third possibility – that no announcement should be made until 16 August, when the celebrations were over. To do otherwise, he believed, would be to mar what should be a day of rejoicing and reconciliation – a risk potentially more serious for the new Dominions than the administrative inconvenience of not knowing exactly what their frontiers were at the moment they gained independence.[3] Jinnah saw a less altruistic motive behind Mountbatten's behaviour. He told Sir George Cunningham, future Governor of the North-West Frontier Province, that the Viceroy had promised him he would arrest the Sikh leaders at the same time as the awards were announced. By deferring the announcement till after the transfer of power, he allowed the responsibility to fall on somebody else, in effect had made sure the Sikhs remained at liberty.[4] The accusation would have been more convincing if Mountbatten, on the unanimous advice of the experts from the Punjab, had not reluctantly given up his plan to arrest the Sikhs some days before it was agreed to defer the announcement of the awards.[5]

By the time of the staff meeting on 12 August there was still no decision on tactics. Details of the awards were beginning to filter through and it was announced at this meeting that the Chittagong Hill Tracts were likely to be given to Pakistan. The population of this remote territory was mainly Buddhist or Animist and, though no systematic attempt was made to establish their views, the more vociferous elements at least were in favour of union with India. The reasons for Radcliffe's award, which as in every case he kept firmly and wisely to himself, seem to have been that economically the area was dependent not on Indian Assam but on the Pakistani part of Bengal. When

V. P. Menon heard what was proposed, there ensued what Christie described
as 'a quite unexpected flare-up of communal bias'.[6] The award lacked 'all
sense of justice, equity and propriety', declared the All-India Congress Committee. The decree was 'ineffective, infructuous and incapable of execution in
international consciousness'.[7] Next day Patel followed up with a letter of
peculiar ferocity. He called the award 'monstrous . . . a blatant breach of the
terms of reference', and said that he had urged the tribesmen to resist
amalgamation with Pakistan by force if necessary.

> The one man I had regarded as a real statesman with both feet firmly
> on the ground, and a man of honour whose word was his bond, had
> turned out to be as hysterical as the rest . . . [reported Mountbatten].
> Candidly I was amazed that such a terrific crisis should have blown
> up over so small a matter. However, I have been long enough in India
> to realise that major crises are by no means confined to big matters.[8]

Even before Patel's explosion, Mountbatten had concluded that, if so
moderate a man as Menon reacted with such indignation, the rest of the
Congress Party would prove far more violent. He foresaw an Independence
Day marred by rancour, Nehru boycotting the ceremonies, India born in an
atmosphere not of euphoria but angry resentment. The evening of the staff
meeting he sent Christie and Campbell-Johnson to call on Radcliffe and ask
him to postpone the delivery of the awards till after the transfer of power.
They met with a cool reception. 'C.R. refused flat – too many people know it's
ready,' Christie noted in his diary. The awards for Bengal and the Punjab were
already complete; only the demarcation line for Sylhet, in Assam, remained to
be drawn. Eventually Radcliffe conceded that there was no need to deliver the
awards one by one; he would hand over the complete package on 13 August,
by which time the Viceroy would be on the point of leaving for the
Independence Day celebrations in Karachi. 'Back to H.E. who had had a
couple,'* Christie went on. 'Didn't like it but swallowed it.'[9]

All went to plan. The awards arrived too late for study and were placed, so
far as is known unlooked-at, in the safe at Viceroy's House. The leaders of
India and Pakistan were summoned to a meeting on 16 August to hear the
details. The celebrations could take their course undisturbed. Extraordinary
importance has been given by some to this decision to withhold publication
for three days. '. . . millions of people died or lost everything as a result,'
wrote Leonard Mosley. 'This is a matter for Mountbatten's conscience.'[10] It
is certainly possible to criticize the decision. What can be presented as a wise
resolve to launch the new Dominions in an atmosphere of good will can be

---

* If Christie was right, the occasion must have been most unusual. Mountbatten drank little
alcohol and almost never showed the effects of drinking.

seen less charitably as a vain man's determination to let nothing mar his moment of glory. Since Mountbatten, like most people, was impelled by a complex of motives, which he rarely sought to analyse, one may assume that both elements played some part in shaping his conclusions. It is difficult, however, to see how the postponement can have cost a single life, let alone 'millions'. Though no one realized it at the time, the announcement of the frontiers was to provoke vast movements of population from one new country to the other, and it was the flood of refugees across territory occupied by hostile inhabitants which provoked the bloodiest massacres. This phenomenon would have been no less marked if it had begun on 12 or 13 August – or even 9 August when, theoretically, some of the awards might have been available – rather than 16 August. Indeed, if anything, it might have been expected that the extra three days would have allowed the Boundary Force time to mass its resources in the most seriously threatened areas – though the Force in fact was to prove so inadequate that its earlier deployment would have made little difference. Mosley's contention that 'A prior report would have given millions of Hindus, Sikhs and Muslims a chance to pack their bags and leave', provokes the query 'Prior to what?' It was the report itself and the consequential migrations which did the damage – a few days one way or the other would have made no difference.

A yet more serious crime has been laid to Mountbatten's charge by certain Pakistani writers, and is still cited from time to time today. It is alleged that Mountbatten delayed the publication of the reports so as to allow himself an opportunity to consult Nehru and amend the awards in India's favour. India's indignation at the award of the Chittagong Hill Tracts to Pakistan – an unchanged feature of the reports when they were eventually published – may have been a factor in making up Mountbatten's mind to keep the reports to himself till after independence. The proponents of the 'conspiracy' theory maintain, however, that Mountbatten's wish to tamper with the awards relating in particular to Gurdaspur and Ferozepur in the north Punjab was the real cause for his decision.[11]

The main evidence supporting the charge against Mountbatten consists of maps left among Jenkins's papers which eventually were inherited by the Pakistani Government. These showed the demarcation line in the Punjab as sent by George Abell to the Governor under cover of a letter dated 8 August. The line announced on 16 August differed to a minor but significant extent in India's favour. From this it was immediately deduced that Mountbatten had used the intervening week to secure the changes insisted on by his Hindu friends, to whom, after independence, his allegiance would be solely due.

The facts seem to be as follows. Jenkins had pressed the Viceroy to give him as much warning as he could of the terms of the award so that troops could be moved to the areas where trouble was likeliest. Mountbatten told Abell to do what he could.[12] Abell applied to Radcliffe's office and was given a rough-and-ready version of the award for the Punjab while it was still undergoing final adjustments.[13] 'There will not be any great changes from this boundary,' he remarked, a comment the correctness of which depends on the definition of the word 'great'.[14] Subsequently a telegram was despatched with the message 'eliminate salient'. Jenkins deduced correctly that this related to the area of Ferozepur and amended his map accordingly. He felt no particular surprise since, as he recorded twenty years later, he had never taken the map to be more than a rough guide. He thought it inconceivable, he stated, that Mountbatten had any hand in altering it.[15]

Both Ferozepur and Gurdaspur contained Indian and Muslim populations of roughly equal size and a case could have been made for dividing them on several different bases. In the case of Ferozepur, the area awarded to India contained certain important head-waters in the Indian area of the Punjab which were vital for the irrigation of Bikaner. Gurdaspur was essential to India if the Amritsar district was not to be isolated. The Pakistanis betrayed no surprise or indignation at the decision comparable to that shown by the Indians at the decision on the Chittagong Hill Tracts; Justice Mohammad Munir, a member of the Boundary Commission, said that he had been certain from the start that it would be awarded to India.[16] Subsequently it was alleged that Mountbatten had awarded Gurdaspur to India so as to make possible land communications with Kashmir. The argument is ingenious, but suggests remarkable prescience on the part of the Viceroy, who anyway at the time was still engaged in trying to ensure that the Maharaja of Kashmir acceded to Pakistan.

Some tenuous support is lent to the allegations over Ferozepur by Kanwar Sain, Chief Irrigation Engineer of the state of Bikaner at the time of the transfer of power. Word reached Bikaner that the Ferozepur head-waters were to be awarded to Pakistan. The Maharaja telegraphed Mountbatten, asking him to receive Sain and his Prime Minister, Sardar Pannikar, who thereupon flew to Delhi. Abell said that the Viceroy was far too busy to see visitors, but eventually allowed them five minutes at 9 a.m. on 11 August. Pannikar had hardly begun to speak before Mountbatten interrupted and said that the matter was no concern of his. Radcliffe reported to the British Government, not to the Viceroy. In that case, said Pannikar, Bikaner would go back on its decision and accede to Pakistan. Mountbatten changed colour but said nothing. That evening the visitors heard that the announcement had been deferred for several days, and when the award was announced all proved to be well. Sain states that Justice Munir told him Radcliffe had changed his mind on this issue, and had done so after a conversation with Mountbatten.[17]

None of this provides strong ground on which to base so grave an accusation. To argue that Mountbatten tampered with the awards is to suggest that Radcliffe, a man of monumental integrity and independence of mind, meekly allowed his recommendations to be set aside by somebody who had no official standing in the matter. 'Sir Cyril has informed me that his award of the 13th August was the result of his own unfettered judgment and that at no stage was any attempt made by the Governor-General to influence his decision,' was the text of a projected statement which Radcliffe had seen and approved.[18] It would suggest too that Mountbatten risked his reputation and all he had achieved in India for little advantage. It is inconceivable that he was seriously daunted by Pannikar's bluff; he must have known that neither economically nor politically was the Maharaja of Bikaner – one of his closest allies among the Princes – in a position to recant and opt for Pakistan.[19] It is easy to believe that Nehru pressed him to amend the awards, far harder to find any reason why he should have succumbed to the pressure. Even Liaqat Ali Khan, who must have known as much as any Pakistani about the course of events, stated categorically that he did not doubt Mountbatten's probity over the partition line.[20]

Yet a nugget of uncertainty remains. In his diary for 9 August John Christie wrote: 'George tells me H.E. is in a tired flap and is having to be strenuously dissuaded from asking Radcliffe to alter his awards.'[21] Thirty-five years later he could throw no further light on this. Nor can Sir George Abell, beyond assuming that, whatever had inspired his original remark, it must have referred to some conversation between the Viceroy and Ismay.[22] Ian Scott, Deputy Private Secretary, believes that it is possible that Mountbatten might have gone along with a suggestion from Nehru over Ferozepur.[23] Mountbatten himself, when told by Ismay that the Pakistani Foreign Minister was making great play with the discovery of the maps among Jenkins's papers, replied: 'I am fairly satisfied that there can be no evidence in Jenkins's file to support any accusation that the award was tampered with.'[24] The comment is certainly not an admission of guilt, but it is not the rousing affirmation of innocence that might have been expected. Possibly he thought that any such affirmation could be taken for granted. Yet Philip Noel-Baker, the Secretary of State for Commonwealth Relations, hardly gave the Viceroy an unequivocal acquittal when he told Attlee in February 1948 that Radcliffe had indeed altered his awards at the last minute, 'but we have no knowledge that this was done on the advice of Lord Mountbatten'.[25]

The most likely explanation seems to be that at one point Mountbatten, under pressure from Nehru, did contemplate asking Radcliffe to amend the awards. It would have been in character for him to have discussed this possibility freely with Ismay and others, and the gossip that might have been

thus generated would have been more than enough to raise suspicions among
the Muslims. In the end, however, commonsense and the counsels of Ismay
must have convinced him that the risks were too great; the game was not
worth even a small part of the candle. He may have been guilty of indiscretion, but not of the arrant folly as well as dishonesty of which his enemies
accused him.

And so the last days slipped away before the transfer of power. With his
insatiable appetite for details, Mountbatten took an interest in every aspect of
partition and continued to be apprised of more of them than would have
seemed possible for any mere mortal. His overriding concern was that
Independence Day should pass off successfully, if possible without clash
between Muslim and Hindu, at all costs without tension between the British
and their former colonial subjects.

> It is important that the Union Jack should not be much in evidence on
> that day [he wrote to Colville], as we must avoid all possible risk of
> insult to it. Plans for one or two local ceremonies have come to my
> notice which seem to suggest that there may be a ceremonial
> lowering of the Union Jack and its replacement by the National flag. I
> hope you will somehow be able to secure that this does not happen
> anywhere in your Province. Nehru entirely agrees that there should
> be no lowering of the Union Jack, which should not appear at all on
> the 15th August.[26]

The exigencies of the soothsayers, which had meant that India would
become free at midnight on 14 August, allowed the Viceroy to attend the
ceremonies at Karachi on the same day and still be back in Delhi for the
critical moment. The Mountbattens flew to Karachi on 13 August and drove
in state to Government House. Colonel Birnie, Jinnah's Military Secretary,
told them that the crowds were noticeably thicker than those which had
greeted Jinnah when he made a similar entry a few days before. Less
agreeably, he also reported that a plot had been discovered to throw a bomb
into Jinnah's open car during the state procession the following day. The
police saw little hope of arresting the conspirators before the procession took
place. Jinnah was ready to go through with it, if the Viceroy concurred. This
was not the sort of challenge Mountbatten could resist; he at once agreed that
the arrangements should be unaltered.[27] The inevitable state banquet had
then to be endured. 'Supposed to be no speeches but Mr Jinnah read one and I
had to make one without warning,' noted Mountbatten in his diary. No one
present could have detected that he had been taken by surprise. 'For ten

minutes the appropriate phrases and thoughts flowed from him in smooth sequence,' wrote Campbell-Johnson. 'He is a born raconteur, and his informal but quick-firing eloquence is ideally adapted to after-dinner speech-making.'[28] Mountbatten sat between Jinnah's sister and the Begum Liaqat Ali Khan. These ladies enjoyed themselves mocking the credulous Hindus, who had allowed astrologers to dictate to them when they could begin life as an independent nation. The joke rebounded on them, according to Mountbatten, when it was realized that Jinnah had forgotten the rules of Ramadan and a luncheon-party he had planned for the following day had hurriedly to be cancelled.[29]

Next morning Mountbatten addressed the Pakistan Constituent Assembly. It says something about his attitude towards the two Dominions that, while he had worked and re-worked his speech in Delhi, he accepted Christie's draft for Karachi and professed himself too tired to do more than tinker with it.[30] The result was eloquent but impersonal: a dutiful tribute to Mr Jinnah, an appeal for an end to violence, an affirmation that this was not the parting of the ways but the start of a new relationship. Then came the procession; Jinnah and Mountbatten side by side, Edwina and Miss Jinnah in the car immediately behind them. To drive for three miles through dense crowds, knowing that every window, every group of figures, might conceal an assassin, would have tested the nerves of anyone. Mountbatten and Jinnah passed the test with aplomb, neither betraying by the slightest gesture that the occasion was anything but one of relaxed euphoria. 'Bomb attack reported never materialised,' noted Mountbatten briefly in his diary. With an unusual display of emotion, Jinnah placed his hand on the Viceroy's knee when they reached their destination and thanked God that he had brought his visitor back alive. 'I retorted by pointing out how much more serious it would have been if he had been bumped off.'[31]

So it was back to Delhi to launch the other part of the sub-continent into independence. 'At the stroke of the midnight hour, when the world sleeps, India will awake to life and freedom,' Nehru proclaimed grandiloquently in the Legislative Assembly. At the stroke of the midnight hour, Mountbatten was in his study in what had almost ceased to be Viceroy's House, alone except for Campbell-Johnson.

> Mountbatten was sitting quietly at his desk. I have known him in most moods; tonight there was an air about him of serenity, almost detachment. The scale of his personal achievement was too great for elation, rather his sense of history and the fitness of things at this dramatic moment when the old and the new order were reconciled in himself, called forth composure.

Quite deliberately he took off his reading-glasses, turned the keys on his dispatch boxes and summoned me to help tidy the room and stow away these outward and visible signs of Viceregal activity. Although there was a whole army of servants outside, it never occurred to either of us to call them. Only when all the papers had been put away and his desk cleared were they called in.[32]

The stage was set for Nehru and Rajendra Prasad, President of the Constituent Assembly, to issue a formal invitation to Mountbatten to serve as first Governor-General of independent India and to submit to him a list of the new Cabinet. Mountbatten had played some part in shaping the first Indian Government. At a staff meeting on 28 July V. P. Menon had told the Viceroy that he was worried lest the Cabinet should contain too many old political warhorses to whom Nehru felt he owed a debt of loyalty. Mountbatten promised to talk to Nehru about this and stress that though, as Governor-General, he would have to accept whatever advice he was given, he did have a right to know what was planned in advance and to express his views.[33] The extent of his influence was shown by the case of Baldev Singh. Believing Baldev and Auchinleck would never work together, Mountbatten had persuaded Nehru not to appoint the Sikh as Defence Minister as had originally been proposed. Then Auchinleck and Baldev were reconciled; worse still, Nehru selected as substitute for the Defence portfolio a man whom Burrows described as being 'so low that a snake could not crawl under his belly'. Mountbatten now hastened back to Nehru, ate his words and said Baldev was after all right for the job. The Sikh was duly appointed.[34]

Some mystery surrounds the appointment of Sardar Patel. V. P. Menon came in alarm to the Viceroy to report that Nehru proposed to exclude the Sardar from his Cabinet: 'This will start a war of succession in the Congress and split the country.'[35] Mountbatten spoke to Nehru, and Patel was appointed. So much is clear. But Sarvepalli Gopal, Nehru's biographer, dismisses as nonsense the idea that Mountbatten's intervention was necessary. When Nehru on 1 August formally invited Patel to serve, he went on: 'This writing is somewhat superfluous because you are the strongest pillar of the Cabinet.'[36] Either Nehru had suffered a most dramatic conversion, or Menon was panicking unnecessarily. The latter seems more probable. Nehru had little liking for Patel but he must have known that to rule India without him would have been almost impossible – the more so if he had driven his rival and colleague into opposition.

Ceremoniously Nehru handed over to Mountbatten the envelope containing the list of his first Cabinet. It contained only one surprise – that it contained nothing. Either by oversight or because the list had not yet been properly typed, the envelope was empty.

Within a few hours the official celebrations had begun. In their hundreds of thousands the peasants had flocked from the surrounding countryside into what was already an over-populated city. 'Never have such crowds been seen within the memory of anyone I have spoken to,' wrote Mountbatten.[37] When the new Governor-General and his wife drove from the Durbar Hall, where Mountbatten had sworn in the Ministers, to the Council Chamber, and then back to what was now Government House, four guards of honour of a hundred men each and an army of policemen were barely able to keep the vast throng at bay. '*Jai Hind*' – Long Live India – was the usual refrain, but when the official coach was near shouts of '*Mountbatten ki jai,*' '*Lady Mountbatten ki jai*' and even '*Pandit Mountbatten ki jai*' drowned the rest of the hubbub. By evening, when they sallied forth again, having attended a monster children's party in the afternoon, the crowd had swelled to something between a quarter of a million and six hundred thousand (most Indian statistics are similarly uncertain). Long before the coach had reached the grandstand where the flag was to be hoisted, it had become immobile in the ocean of humanity. What was supposed to be a military parade had been swamped by the cheerful, all-pervading mob. The ceremony was cut short and the carriage began to creep back to Government House, the mounted body guards frantically trying to clear a path without trampling the spectators underfoot or starting a panic as people pulled away from the horses' hooves.

It was an enormously happy occasion; yet one accident, one trivial outbreak of violence, could have provoked catastrophe. The state carriage, inching its way back from the ceremony, drew upon itself interest so overwhelming that it seemed at times as if it must vanish under the great wave of humanity around it. The Mountbattens alone would have ensured that the coach was the central attraction of the day; as if this was not enough, Nehru, unable to get back to his own car, joined the party and sat cross-legged upon the hood. 'Meanwhile refugees who had fainted or had been almost crushed under the wheels were pulled on board and we ended with four Indian ladies with their children, the Polish wife of a British officer and an Indian pressman who crawled up behind.'[38] Campbell-Johnson met the pressman the following day; he was notorious for his extreme left-wing views, but that did not stop him shaking the Press Attaché by the hand and exclaiming: 'At last, after two hundred years, Britain has conquered India.'[39]

To end the day, three thousand people came to an evening party at Government House. They stayed till 2 a.m. Mountbatten can hardly have slept for more than eleven or twelve hours in the previous three nights, he had been the focus of unremitting public attention, he had made four major speeches, conducted negotiations of great importance, enjoyed hardly a moment of waking relaxation. Somehow he kept going, concealing his exhaustion, endlessly charming. At last it was over, India and Pakistan were well and truly free, the first part, at least, of his task was accomplished. 'I have never experienced such a day in my life,' he concluded his report.[40]

His speech to the Constituent Assembly was an apologia for his conduct of the negotiations. He spoke of the terrifying communal violence, the threat of anarchy, which had led him to fix so early a date for the transfer of power; and stressed once more that partition was made necessary by the will of Hindus and Muslims and was decided on the lines they had dictated. The wise and realistic leaders of India

> have placed me in their debt for ever by their sympathetic under-standing of my position. . . . They agreed from the outset to release me from any responsibility whatsoever for the partition of the Punjab and Bengal. It was they who selected the personnel of the Boundary Commissions including the Chairman; it was they who drew up the terms of reference; it is they who shoulder the responsi-bility for implementing the awards. You will appreciate that had they not done this, I would have been placed in an impossible position.[41]

The most significant passage of his speech, however, came when he spoke of his own future. 'From today,' he said, 'I am your constitutional Governor-General and I would ask you to regard me as one of yourselves, devoted wholly to the furtherance of India's interests.' It was a phrase that was noted in Karachi and confirmed the worst suspicions of the Pakistanis. Yet it should have come as no surprise. When Jinnah had chosen to become his own Governor-General he had made it inevitable that Mountbatten must espouse the cause of India. The Governor-General might do his best to ensure that the Pakistanis got fair play, but his best was circumscribed by the fact that he was the servant of the Indian state. In his speech Mountbatten described the nature of his new role. He also laid down its period. In April 1948, he said, he would ask to be relieved of his post and to leave India.

Soon there was to be doubt and questioning, but on 15 August 1947 nothing was heard but the paeans of praise. 'I still can't believe that you have pulled it off,' wrote Ismay. 'It is the greatest *personal* triumph for you and Edwina of modern times – far more so than winning a great battle or even a great campaign. I confess that I had not much hope that you'd do the trick when I volunteered for the team; but I was absolutely positive that NO ONE ELSE IN THE WORLD could do it.'[42] For the moment Ismay spoke for almost every Briton. They had been seduced by the glamour and the style, the entry of the two new countries into the Commonwealth, the spontaneous explosion of affection for the old imperial power. They would have echoed enthusiastically the terms of Attlee's telegram of congratulations:

> My warmest thanks to you on this day which sees successful achievement of a task of an unexampled difficulty. The continual skill displayed in meeting every difficulty has been amazing. Your short tenure of Viceroyalty has been one of the most memorable in a long list. In this message of thanks I include Edwina, Ismay and other helpers.[43]

Two days later Mountbatten wrote to his wife:

> My Darling,
>     I've written to thank so many people for their help in finding the right solution for India, but so far I've not written to the person who helped me most.
>     The enclosed telegram from the Prime Minister – who is under no illusion as to the part you played – helps me to remedy this; and surely no husband in history has had the proud privilege of transmitting a telegram of appreciation from the Prime Minister to his wife.
>     I'm very proud to be that exception.
>     I'm deeply grateful too, for the way you've helped to keep me on the rails in certain matters in which I'm very apt to go off them.
>     Thank you, my pet, with all my heart.[44]

'Indian Independence Day,' wrote Leo Amery in his diary. 'Wrote to Dickie and wished him well. It is all starting so much better than one dared hope at one time.'[45] Even the ranks of the most traditional Conservatives could scarce forbear to cheer, even Churchill briefly believed that all had not been for the worst. Mountbatten was raised in rank from Viscount to Earl, taking the title Earl Mountbatten of Burma. Lord Killearn wrote to Ismay to say how well deserved he felt the honour was. 'He, and Edwina, are simply *terrific*,' he wrote. 'And no other living man could have got the thing through. . . . It has been a job supremely well done.'[46] The only outcry against this further honour came from its unwilling recipient – Lady Mountbatten herself. 'Mummy is in despair at another blow of fate,' Mountbatten told Patricia, 'for she disapproves *so much* of all these nonsensical titles. . . . I pointed out that it was at least a double recognition of our work together, and this bucked her up.'[47]

In India, too, the hysterical fervour of the crowds was matched by the more considered eulogies of the statesmen. Nehru praised Mountbatten publicly whenever occasion offered, but perhaps the most remarkable tribute came from the more phlegmatic Sardar Patel.

> You were good enough to call me a stern realist, and it is as such that I make bold to say that, when the history of the six months of your Viceroyalty comes to be written, it cannot but accord to you the major share of the credit for the manner in which the manifold difficult tasks have been accomplished and for the transformation which has been made in Indo-British relationship during these fateful months. India and Indians have always been quick to respond to understanding and sympathy. Both Britain and India must congratulate each other that in you they at last found one so abounding in these virtues, essentially a man of speed and action, frank and painstaking and genuinely sincere and anxious to deliver the goods. The only regret of ours is, and of the future historian will be, that we should have had the benefit of your wise council [sic] and the privilege of your able guidance at a much earlier date.[48]

The true dimensions of Mountbatten's achievement will need to be assessed a little later, when the immediate after-effects of the transfer of power had worked off and the shape of the future was becoming clearer. For the moment he was buoyed up by an immense wave of affection and admiration; as dramatically the hero of the hour as any military commander and yet one who had worked through patient negotiation and affection. He was to be allowed only a few days to bask in the warm glow of glory before he found himself thrown back into a crisis so hectic as to leave him no time for self-congratulation and so desperate as to make him question the reality of his accomplishment. The hour was his, however. The trumpet-blast that gratified him most had come not from Briton or Indian but that sagest of commentators, Walter Lippmann, writing in the *Washington Post*.[49]

> Perhaps Britain's finest hour is not in the past. Certainly this performance is not the work of a decadent people. This on the contrary is the work of political genius requiring the ripest wisdom and the freshest vigour, and it is done with an elegance and a style that will compel and will receive an instinctive respect throughout the civilized world. Attlee and Mountbatten have done a service to all mankind by showing what statesmen can do not with force and money but with lucidity, resolution and sincerity.

# CHAPTER 34

## *The Massacres*

THE ROLE OF GOVERNOR-GENERAL in an independent Dominion can be as important or as trivial as that of the constitutional monarch on whose behalf he acts as Head of State. Depending upon circumstances, the Governor-General may be little more than a decorative figurehead, opening bazaars and greeting foreign potentates, or a major force in the shaping of foreign and domestic policy. When he has recently stepped down from a position close to that of absolute ruler, and his Government is preoccupied with enjoying and demonstrating its independence, it might be anticipated that he would rarely be allowed to trespass beyond the limits of the purely formal. Mountbatten believed that his relationship with Nehru was sufficiently close to ensure that behind the scenes his advice would often be asked for and sometimes heeded, but he neither expected nor desired that he would perform a more overt role. He looked forward with some satisfaction to nine months or so of relative tranquillity in which he would play the elder statesman and leave the hurly-burly of executive government to those who had fought so long for it. Within two weeks it became apparent that no such dispensation was to be allowed him.

Radcliffe's awards were sent to the leaders of the two new countries at 2 p.m. on 16 August. Three hours later Liaqat Ali Khan, Nehru and Sardar Patel, and Baldev Singh for the Sikhs gathered in the Council Chamber of Government House. It quickly became clear that Radcliffe had proved his impartiality. Everyone was displeased. Liaqat was outraged over the allocation of Gurdaspur to India, Patel equally put out at the loss of the Chittagong Hill Tracts to Pakistan. 'It is quite clear to me', reported Mountbatten, 'that if we had not brought the leaders together to hear each others' indignation and thus regain their sense of proportion, we might have had as serious a blow-up as V. P. Menon feared.'[1] As it was, he was able to argue convincingly that India could not have done so badly if Pakistan were so disaffected, and Pakistan could have nothing to complain about in a solution that caused India such dismay. The leaders were sufficiently impressed to accept the awards under protest and to agree that they should immediately be published.

It was at this point that the Punjab fell apart. Only an insane optimist would have supposed that the announcement of the new frontiers would bring to a halt the violence which had been mounting over the previous weeks. Even a pessimist like Jenkins had presumed, on the other hand, that if the lines of partition were accepted by both parties things would gradually settle down; there might be some movement of population over the next few years, but for the most part Muslims and Hindus, even Sikhs, would continue to co-exist in reasonable harmony. The pessimists proved over-optimistic. Incidents multiplied in the last few days before the transfer of power. In East Punjab Sikhs were alleged to have raped Muslim women and paraded then naked through the streets before murdering them; in West Punjab a Muslim mob surrounded a Sikh temple and burnt it to the ground with all its occupants. Such atrocities may have been grossly exaggerated, may never have taken place at all, but the rumours were enough. Fear fed on hatred, hatred on fear. On both sides of the frontier, thousands, hundreds of thousands, eventually millions of peasants concluded that their lives were in peril, that they could find safety only by abandoning their homes and fleeing to the homelands which had been so arbitrarily called into existence. On both sides of the frontier the new citizens of India and Pakistan looked with hatred at the river of refugees flowing across their land and determined to avenge the wrongs being done to their compatriots. Trains packed with refugees were set upon and their passengers massacred; those who fled on foot ran the gauntlet of bands of murderers. Each incident provoked a new wave of refugees, each wave of refugees generated its own crop of bloody incidents.

Too late the Indian and Pakistani leaders realised what horrors had been unleashed. At a meeting of the Joint Defence Committee Mountbatten persuaded the two Prime Ministers to discuss what could be done to check the violence. Liaqat and Nehru went to Amritsar, in the heartland of the Sikhs, and jointly appealed for peace; they set but nets to catch the wind – their visit may have done some good, but hardly enough to be noticed in the tornado of evil. Civil government had broken down. Inexperienced new Ministers struggled to compete with problems which would have perplexed the strongest of administrations. The police split upon communal lines; either lay low or actively helped the progress of destruction. All that was left was the Army, and the Army too was gravely weakened by the ravages of partition and infected by the plague of communalism.

The Punjab Boundary Force, under Major-General Rees, seemed to offer the best if not the only hope for the restoration of order. Fifty-five thousand strong, mainly British-officered and composed of troops such as Gurkhas who were not emotionally involved in the disturbances, the Force for a time

was admired by Muslim and Hindu alike. 'The hard truth is that without the
. . . P.B.F. the slaughter and terror would have been desperate and completely
out of control', wrote Rees to Auchinleck, 'and it would almost certainly
develop that way if any attempt were made to withdraw us before things have
a chance of settling down.'[2] Mountbatten backed him to the full. Yet it was
clear within a few days of independence that the slaughter was out of control.
Things would certainly have been worse without the Force, but they were so
awful with it that the distinction seemed hardly perceptible. Some had been
doubtful from the start. Penderel Moon, a former private secretary to the
Governor of the Punjab and now based in Bahawalpur, was told by a Sikh
major on his way to join the Force that 'he was utterly sceptical of its capacity
to maintain order. He thought that a large proportion of the troops would be
infected by the communal virus and prove unreliable.' Moon himself thought
the Force far too small to be any good; barely numerous enough even to
maintain security in the districts of Amritsar and Lahore.[3]

By the last week in August the leaders of India and Pakistan had each
decided that the Force favoured the other side and was, anyway, impotent to
affect the course of events. The first charge was convincing evidence that Rees
was doing his job; the second showed that he could not do it well enough. At a
meeting of the Joint Defence Committee on 25 August Mountbatten had hotly
to defend the Force against criticism of its conduct and to oppose proposals
that it should be broken up and reconstituted on national lines. He foresaw
the risk that such independent armies would not only fail to co-operate but
might even clash in something close to civil war. Reluctantly, however, he
was brought to accept that, if both Governments had lost their confidence in
the Force, it became more a liability than an asset.[4] Separate forces might
not enforce the peace with such impartiality, but at least they would know
what they were doing and could be relied on to obey the orders of their
officers. On 29 August a Joint Defence Committee meeting at Lahore agreed
that the Force should be disbanded. With its disappearance Mountbatten's
last operational responsibility had ended. He was now free to perform his
function as Governor-General in the manner he felt most appropriate. He
made his intention manifest in his decision to take a long-delayed holiday
in Simla. With Edwina he went there directly from Lahore.

'Lazed in bed all morning,' was his triumphant diary entry for the start of
his holiday. It was the first time he had been able to say as much since he had
left England, and it was to be the last for several weeks. The crisis had been left
behind him but its clamour reverberated in his ears. On 31 August the
Mountbattens had a farewell party for one of the A.D.C.s, Flight-Lieutenant
Beaumont, before he left for Delhi and England. The train was held up and a
hundred Muslims on board were butchered, the only survivor being

Beaumont's bearer who was successfully concealed under the seat. The following day came the news that the Viceroy's Treasurer and his wife, who had been thirty years in Viceregal service, had been murdered in another train to Delhi. Worse still, violence was taking grip of the capital itself. If the seat of government fell prey to the chaos of communalism, what could survive?

On the evening of 4 September the Mountbattens went round for a drink at the Christies' home.

> He took me out on to the front lawn and said he would like my advice [wrote Christie in his diary]. V. P. Menon had telegraphed to say that the situation was now completely out of hand and he had better come down to Delhi. How far could he go in gripping matters for them instead of making them do it themselves? I said I thought they had stage-fright: it was the first time they had faced the footlights. They were badly in need of support from him, but he mustn't *appear* to be gripping matters himself.[5]

There is some obscurity about Menon's appeal. He himself claimed he had discussed the idea with Sardar Patel beforehand and had been assured that not only did Patel think it a good idea but that Nehru would certainly feel the same.[6] Nehru's secretary M. O. Mathai, on the other hand, claims that neither Nehru nor Patel had authorized Menon's message. Both men were furious when they heard that the Governor-General was on the way, but agreed that 'the only thing left to do was not to embarrass Mountbatten and do something gracious to associate him with the handling of the developing situation in Delhi which Menon had exaggerated enormously'.[7] Mountbatten was sufficiently impressed by Mathai's evidence to agree that 'though V. P. Menon misled me into believing that both the P.M. and his deputy wished me to return to Delhi, he had in fact consulted neither'. This, he felt, accounted for the fact that Nehru and Menon were both ill-at-ease when they came to see him on his return.[8]

Though Menon may have acted without authority, he certainly had not exaggerated the desperate danger of the situation. Nor did Nehru and Patel appear reluctant to involve the Governor-General in their activities. When Mountbatten, after a brief period for reflection, proposed that an Emergency Committee be set up to deal with every aspect of the troubles, the Indian leaders agreed with alacrity on the understanding that he would be the chairman. 'Within the general framework of Cabinet policy,' read the terms of reference of the new group, 'the Emergency Committee will issue all the necessary executive orders to meet the current emergency. The Emergency Committee has been given by the Cabinet overriding authority and priority in dealing with the emergency.'[9] The powers could hardly have been more sweeping, and Mountbatten, after the briefest possible hesitation, exercised them with a will. He was back in Delhi on the evening of 5 September, the Emergency Committee was set up the following morning, it met for the first time at 5 p.m. on 6 September, and at 8 p.m. the following evening completed its third meeting which lasted a total of eight hours and in the course of which forty directives had been issued. 'I am sure that we did more business and set more wheels turning in the first three days, than would otherwise have been done in several weeks,' he wrote with justified pride.[10]

The Emergency Committee interfered in almost every field of national life. Plans were made for the requisitioning of civilian transport, the harvesting of crops in areas abandoned by the refugees, the protection of foreign diplomats, the guarding of trains, the collection of corpses, injections against cholera, distribution of newspapers. At each meeting the Minister responsible reported on progress made since the directive had been issued. It was the sort of operation at which Mountbatten excelled; he engrossed himself in the detail yet never lost sight of the broad strategy. Somehow he found time to concern himself with myriad issues and personalities. When the High Commissioner for Pakistan, 'who is, I concede, in a particularly dangerous position', tried to escape from Delhi, Mountbatten decided that his presence in the capital was essential and sent one of his staff to the airport to drag the wretched man off the aircraft which he had already boarded.[11] The Map Room in Government House was prepared according to his meticulous specifications. He detailed the number and nature of the maps, the composition of the graphs, the arrangement of the telephones – 'If there is to be a large crowd visiting the Map Room it is for consideration whether a North Entrance should not be opened as a special Map Room entrance, and whether special Map Room passes should not be issued.'[12] General Rees, at liberty now that the Punjab Boundary Force had been closed down, was called in to run a small military staff operating within Goverment House.

Once they had accepted his leadership, Nehru and Patel supported him in every decision, however repugnant some of them may have been.

> Nehru has backed me to the hilt all through the past week [Mountbatten reported]. I have also been able, I hope, to act as a source of consolation to him. He has come suddenly to see me alone on more than one occasion – simply and solely for company in his misery; to unburden his soul; and to obtain what comfort I have had to give. He has lately written me two or three letters indicating that he does not know why he is writing, except that he feels he must write to someone to get his troubles off his chest.[13]

The two men already liked and trusted each other; in these hectic weeks they grew into complete mutual confidence and deep affection. Mountbatten never forgot that Nehru was the most important man in India, the one man whose disappearance could overnight destroy what little order remained. When the Prime Minister casually remarked after dinner that a threat to assassinate him had been uncovered, Mountbatten immediately rang up General Rees and instructed him to increase the guard on Nehru's house and on no account to pay any attention to what the Prime Minister might say himself about his own security. 'I warned Nehru that the greatest ill-service he could do India at this moment was to allow himself to be bumped off.'[14]

With the demise of the Boundary Force, collaboration between India and Pakistan grew tenuous. The Prime Ministers met from time to time, but it was as much to bicker acrimoniously as to discuss what needed to be done. Almost the only regular liaison was through the Joint Defence Council, where Mountbatten found himself in the awkward predicament of playing the part of neutral chairman while self-evidently the servant of one of the two parties. He managed it with grace and retained, if not the confidence of the Pakistanis, at least their acceptance. Jinnah knew that no Indian or Pakistani would be as well qualified to regulate the rival interests, that the Council was on the whole more likely to protect than to assail the essential interests of Pakistan, and that Mountbatten was the only man who would both feel some sense of obligation to Pakistan and stand a chance of imposing his will on the Indians. In this calculation he was to prove justified. One of the Governor-General's first steps after he returned to Delhi was to send Ismay to see Jinnah in Karachi, 'to explain to you in detail what is being done as I feel that conditions in both East and West Punjab are similar, and it would probably be advantageous if both our governments moved on similar lines'.[15] Not all his efforts could make the lines converge, but that they continued roughly in parallel owed much to his initiative.

While Mountbatten struggled to check the violence, his wife was doing heroic work to mitigate its consequences. With the Minister of Health, Rajkumari Amrit Kaur, and a handful of dedicated and usually exhausted supporters, she toured the refugee camps, organizing, inspiring, consoling, bullying the apathetic and resentful inhabitants into following the rules of hygiene, galvanizing the bureaucrats into activity by her energy and fierce determination. Working seventeen or eighteen hours a day, constantly on the move in the intense heat and under conditions of extreme hardship, in danger from infection as much as from fanatics on both sides of the conflict, she allowed nothing to deter or deflect her. Not merely did she gain the respect of those with whom she worked; by her compassion and warmth she won the love of all those victims of the violence with whom she came in contact. In such circumstances her immense qualities were all-apparent; the restless discontent, the jealousy, that had made her so uncomfortable a wife, faded into insignificance. As Vicereine she had done great work to help her husband's cause; during the massacres she achieved miracles for India and humanity.

> We are now under a far greater pressure than at any time since we came out here [Mountbatten told Attlee on 12 September]. Nevertheless I honestly feel that we are all beginning to get a grip on a wellnigh desperate situation, and I feel we shall pull through all right if none of my vital ministers are bumped off – a factor which is not impossible of fulfilment with the fear-crazed half-mad crowds of people roaming the streets of Delhi.[16]

Mountbatten never lost heart. In a report to Whitehall Ismay drafted: 'We are hanging on by our eyelids and it is certainly not more than even money against complete chaos.' Mountbatten amended this to read: 'The general position is more grave than you evidently appreciate and we are only now beginning to turn the corner.'[17] Ismay's phraseology was the more picturesque, but Mountbatten's was the voice of resolute optimism; only if buoyed up by optimism could the battered relics of government have found the spirit to carry on. Yet the road seemed endless. 'Took Emergency Committee of Cabinet for a 5 hour flight over Punjab,' Mountbatten noted in his diary for 21 September. Campbell-Johnson was among the sightseers.

> Today we saw for ourselves something of the stupendous scale of the Punjab upheaval [he recorded]. Even our brief bird's-eye view must have revealed nearly half a million refugees on the roads. At one point during our flight Sikh and Muslim refugees were moving almost side by side in opposite directions. There was no sign of clash. As though impelled by some deeper instinct, they pushed forward obsessed only with the objective beyond the boundary.[18]

With so few troops available who could be relied on to act impartially, Mountbatten was tempted to use those British units that remained in India. There was a British Brigade in Delhi which could have done invaluable work in guarding hospitals and other institutions. Auchinleck resolutely opposed any such action. British troops should be used, if at all, only to protect British lives. 'I have not pursued this matter,' Mountbatten told the King.[19] He did, however, manage to persuade Auchinleck that volunteers from the British units should be allowed to help in the running of the refugee camps.

Auchinleck was convinced that the solution to the problem was to take stronger measures against the Sikhs. He was particularly incensed when the

Government withdrew its ban on the wearing of 'Kirpans', or ceremonial swords. This measure proved, he said, that the authorities were 'afraid to deal with the Sikhs as they should be dealt with . . . the present policy of half-measures and appeasement . . . is in my opinion worse than useless and is fraught with the gravest danger for the future'.[20] Mountbatten had no illusions about the leading role the Sikhs had played in provoking and carrying out the massacres. He was determined, however, to avoid anything that could look like discrimination against one section of the population. Even if he could have carried the Indian Government with him, he knew that to treat the Sikhs with particular harshness would be to leave them with a grievance that it would take decades, perhaps centuries, to eradicate. This was no way to build the new India; and through the carnage and the smoke of burning villages Mountbatten was looking ahead to a time of reconstruction and reconciliation.

Somehow the violence was confined largely to the Punjab. Throughout the sub-continent communities of Muslims and Hindus co-existed uneasily, yet trouble was averted. In Bengal, traditionally the scene of the most ferocious communal rioting, the credit belonged largely to Gandhi. The Mahatma had moved to Calcutta before Independence Day and taken up his residence in the poorest quarter of the city among the Untouchables. When trouble began and threatened to spread, he declared a fast unto death which was to end only if sanity returned. The violence died away and Bengal remained tranquil. 'My dear Gandhiji,' wrote Mountbatten. 'In the Punjab we have 55,000 soldiers and large scale rioting on our hands. In Bengal our forces consists of one man, and there is no rioting. As a serving officer, as well as an administrator, may I be allowed to pay my tribute to the One Man Boundary Force.'[21] To Campbell-Johnson he estimated that Gandhi had brought about by moral persuasion what four divisions would have been hard pressed to achieve by force.[22]

'I've never been through such a time in my life,' Mountbatten told Patricia at the end of September. 'The War, the Viceroyalty were jokes, for we have been dealing with life and death in our own city.'[23] He was justified in his use of the past tense, for the worst was over. As the two populations painfully disengaged, so the points of friction became less numerous. Protection for the trains and refugee columns grew more efficient; the forces of security expanded while the numbers of the fugitives dwindled. The re-opened railways began to draw away the army of refugees which had descended on Delhi, meetings of the Emergency Committee became less frequent. By 2 October Mountbatten could tell Robert Neville that the Government had 'just about restored law and order, in the Punjab at least'.[24] By early November the flow of refugees across the frontier had almost ceased.

Sporadic outbreaks of violence still occurred and threatened to provoke wider uproar, but the authorities quickly restored order. The Punjab was bleeding and ravaged, but it was now time to begin the work of rehabilitation.

How many lives were lost can never be established with any pretence at accuracy; the records were inadequate to begin with and were usually lost in the mass migration. 'A million dead' was the propagandist's slogan, but none of those who have made any attempt to base their calculations on serious analysis of the sources of information puts the figure so high. G. D. Khosla estimates 4–500,000;[25] Ian Stephens 500,000;[26] Humphrey Trevelyan 'less than a quarter of a million';[27] Chandulal Trivedi, first Indian Governor of the Punjab, 225,000.[28] Probably the most systematic attempt to work out a correct figure was that of Penderel Moon, who suggested the most likely total was 200,000.[29] Even if this is nearest to the truth, it is catastrophic enough. India is a country inured to tragedy on the grandest scale. The Bengal famine of 1943 is believed to have cost one and a half million lives – a figure which not even the most determinedly gloomy of commentators has suggested as the price of the Punjab massacres. But human suffering is not to be counted in statistics; the partition of the Punjab caused untold misery to several million refugees and left a scar of pain across the surface of Mountbatten's Indian achievement.

At a speech in India House when he was on a visit to London in November, the Governor-General sought to minimize the scale of the disaster. 'Only' a hundred thousand people had died, he said, only a small part of the country had been affected. 'I was horrified at Dickie's speech,' Ismay told his wife. '. . . It seems to me immaterial whether one hundred thousand or a million have actually died: or whether only 3% of the country is in turmoil. The essential facts are that there is human misery on a colossal scale all around one and millions are bereaved, destitute, homeless, hungry, thirsty – and worst of all desperately anxious and almost hopeless about their future.'[30]

Mountbatten would not have disagreed. Though he continued to argue that the massacres must be judged with due sense of proportion, he never pretended that they were less than a fearful blemish on his achievement.

Was he – indeed, was anyone – to blame? That he was taken by surprise is demonstrably true. At his first meeting with Clement Attlee, Mountbatten told the Prime Minister he had never supposed 'that the Indians could achieve self-government without the risk of further grave communal disorders'.[31] What he had failed to anticipate was the massive and panic-stricken exodus from both sides of the new partition line. He was asked about this at his press conference on 4 June and had replied that he foresaw no such movement 'because of the physical difficulty involved. . . . But I equally think that a measure of transfer of population will come about in a natural way, that is to say, people will just cross the boundary or the Government may take steps to transfer populations.'[32] People did just cross the boundary, but there was nothing 'natural' about that monstrous pilgrimage. Yet if Mountbatten was taken by surprise, so too were all the experts: Hindu, Muslim or British; civil servants, soldiers or politicians. No one had contemplated the immensity of the problem; no one therefore had proposed measures that might have mitigated the damage. 'My country has gone mad!' exclaimed a distraught Nehru. He spoke of the bloody violence, but he could as well have been referring to the movement of population which fuelled it. Panic is perhaps a kind of madness; its consequences, anyway, will rarely be foreseen by rational men planning the future in the calm of their sequestered offices. In the words of that most rational of men, V. P. Menon:

> It has been said that if a planned exchange of population had been arranged before the transfer of power, the communal holocaust would have been avoided. But could there be any question of an exchange of population between two sides which had agreed and publicly announced that they would retain their respective minorities? Indeed, the Congress was definitely against any exchange of population.[33]

If that was the official policy, who can blame those responsible for partition for their failure to plan for the opposite to happen?

The gravest charge against Mountbatten is not that he failed to foresee the consequences of partition, but that by his precipitate rush to independence he created the circumstances in which such consequences became more probable. At its most extreme, the accusation has it that he allowed his anxiety to return to his career with the Royal Navy to distort his judgement; that he had allotted only a few months to the task of dividing India and was not prepared to devote more time to it, whatever the cost in human life. This is patently absurd. Mountbatten knew that his task as Viceroy was the most important he would ever undertake and that posterity would judge him by it. For him to imperil his success for the sake of a more rapid return to sea would argue a sense of proportion so distorted as to cast doubts upon his sanity. It was not even as if his naval future were at stake; he had Attlee's categoric assurance that he could return to the Navy in June 1948. When writing to Patricia about the possibility that he might stay on as Governor-General, he remarked, 'so it's once more touch and go if I'm here for several years or until 15th August' – a comment that does not suggest he regarded even this deadline as sacrosanct.[34] Peter Murphy wrote to tell him how glad he was that the communal carnage had boiled up only after the British had handed over, and how he wished it had happened after Mountbatten's own departure. 'I agree,' the Governor-General replied, 'but only provided it had happened well after my departure and not two or three days after. In fact, I do not know how I could have faced the situation if I had arrived home on the 16th August to read of this appalling massacre.'[35]

If Mountbatten blundered he did so in good faith. But did he blunder? Some maintain that if he had proceeded at a less breakneck speed the worst consequences of partition could have been averted. There would have been time to prepare people for the idea of partition, to persuade them to stay put; if they insisted on moving, then the migration could have been planned with deliberation, troops and police drafted to the danger-spots, convoys of refugees organized and protected. There would always have been disorder but the mass carnage might have been averted. The counter-argument is that Mountbatten was playing from a weakening hand. The British elements in the Army, the police and the civil service were being rapidly run down, already reduced to a skeleton in certain critical sectors, and it was becoming every day more clear that in the rising swell of communal bitterness the Hindu and Muslim elements could not be relied upon to administer the law with impartiality. Once the principle of partition had been accepted, it was inevitable that communalism would rage freely. The longer the period before the transfer of power, the worse the tension and the greater the threat that violence would spread. Today it was the Punjab, tomorrow Bengal, Hyderabad, any of the myriad societies in the sub-continent where Hindu and Muslim lived cheek by jowl. Two hundred thousand dead could have become two million, even twenty million.[36]

Since the other approach was never tried, no one can state with certainty that it would have proved more or less successful. What is however evident is that those people who, from their position or their special knowledge, speak with authority on the subject agree that delay could only have provoked a far worse catastrophe. Ismay was an old India hand, as close as anyone to the centre of the action, a man of determinedly independent mind. He was harrowed by the horror of the massacres and wrote to his wife of his mission's 'grim and total failure'. 'The only consolation is that looking back over the last six months, I would not have changed, in essentials, a single decision that we took.'[37] To Mountbatten he wrote of a conversation he had just had with a man who had insisted that the adminstration in India could have held the position for several more months at least. 'You, and all of us who were with you, were not blind to the dangers of rushing things, but we were completely convinced that every day's delay was fraught with the utmost danger; and we felt that the wisdom of your decision was absolutely vindicated by events.'[38]

Ismay was perhaps too close to the formulation of the policy to be dispassionate. What about those members of the Viceregal staff in Delhi who were professionals of the Indian Civil Service, in no sense Mountbatten's men? George Abell believes that the massacres could only have been worse if there had been further delay.[39] Conrad Corfield, who had every reason to criticize Mountbatten, welcomed the accelerated transfer of power: 'Ever since I had attended the first meeting of the Governor-General's Council when the politicians were members, it was clear that the Crown had already lost control. Subsequent events in British India had proved it. There was, therefore, no time to waste.'[40]

In the provinces the view was no different. Evan Jenkins was as opposed to the idea of partition as any man, but in the end he accepted that there was no other solution and that it had best come quickly.[41] Penderel Moon, at the time a Minister in Bahawalpur State, believed that nothing could have averted the conflagration, 'on the other hand by lack of decision and dilly-dallying it might easily have been made far worse than it actually was. The vigour and speed with which Lord Mountbatten acted had at least the merit of confining it to the Punjab.' To argue that to have stuck to the original time-table would have meant that the province would have been brought under control before partition 'rests on the false premise that the means and the time were available for controlling and tranquillizing the Punjab'. Moon even argues that it is lucky Mountbatten did not foresee the coming catastrophe. 'Had he done so, he might have fumbled and faltered, casting about vainly for means of avoiding it while the whole country drifted into civil war.'[42] Humphrey Trevelyan, for long Joint Secretary to the Government of India, made the same point. 'The critics' argument is based on the wholly unwarranted assumption that, whereas two to three hundred thousand lost their lives, delay would have saved them all, or nearly all. If anarchy had spread over the whole of India, as might well have happened, it would have been for the British the ultimate shame. . . . The Punjab massacres were appalling but how much more terrible the loss of life would have been if your decision had gone the other way.'[43] Some Indians today believe that Mountbatten's precipitation helped to fuel disaster, but the only surviving civil servant who was close to the centre of the action, H. M. Patel, Indian representative on the Partition Council, believes that every day's delay would have added to the toll in lives.[44]

That the Congress leaders, who themselves did so much to advance the date for the transfer of power, should have defended the decision subsequently can hardly come as a surprise. It would be tedious to quote the many pronouncements made by Nehru and Sardar Patel. The last word can perhaps be left to C. Rajagopalachari, who was to replace Mountbatten as India's first Indian head of state. 'If the Viceroy had not transferred power when he did,' he said, 'there could well have been no power to transfer.'[45] That, in a sentence, is the case for Mountbatten.

Jinnah was a dying man. It is conceivable that, if the Viceroy had played for time, the disappearance of this great champion of partition would have transformed the situation. It seems more likely that by 1947 the campaign for an independent Pakistan had gained such momentum that no individual's death could have affected it. The question is, anyway, of no practical importance. Mountbatten did not know and could not have known of his adversary's failing health. The decision to divide India was inevitable by the time he arrived in India. Only the British Government could have aborted the causal chain that led to partition and the massacres. Perhaps they should have defied world opinion and their own principles, vastly reinforced their presence in India, resolved to sit it out until a truly united and independent India became a possibility. If they had done so, they would have had to have found another Viceroy. Mountbatten did not go to India to maintain the power of the Raj, and would never have taken on the task. The job he was given to do instead he did supremely well.

# CHAPTER 35

## *Kashmir and Hyderabad*

THOUGH MOUNTBATTEN, MENON AND PATEL between them had tied up most of the loose ends among the Princely States before the transfer of power, three had obstinately avoided any neat solution. Two of these, Kashmir and Hyderabad, had rarely been far from the minds of the negotiators; the third, Junagadh, had almost entirely escaped their attention yet was to prove the most immediately embarrassing.

Though small by comparison with the giants, Junagadh had 700,000 inhabitants. It sprawled among the Gujarati states on the north-west coast of India, its boundaries so ill-defined that no one knew with certainty which areas were part of its territory and which belonged elsewhere. The Muslim Nawab, an eccentric who loved dogs with such fervour that he spent a fortune on the marriage of two of his favourites and proclaimed an official holiday in their honour, ruled over a predominantly Hindu population, a situation similar to that of Hyderabad. Junagadh, however, did not possess the resources to claim convincingly that it could go it alone, and its geographical integration with its Hindu neighbours made its destiny as part of India seem certain. Or so it was assumed, until Muslim League politicians took office shortly before the transfer of power. Egged on by Jinnah, they first procrastinated, then at the last moment acceded to Pakistan.

Mountbatten felt personally betrayed. The Nawab himself had not attended the meeting of the Chamber of Princes but his *dewan* had given every indication that the state would accede to India. Now the policy had been reversed and a solution imposed which defied the principles of geography, economics and the will of the people. Yet it could not be denied that the Nawab had acted, however injudiciously, within his rights.

For the Indian Government the problem was particularly vexatious. If they acquiesced in Junagadh's move, then they would be in no position to protest if the Nizam of Hyderabad decided to follow the lead of his co-religionist and take his state into Pakistan. Yet if they intervened by force or brought extreme economic pressure to bear, they would be sanctioning similar action by Pakistan in the case of Kashmir, as well as earning themselves much discredit in the eyes of the world. Mountbatten saw the incident as a cunning ploy to lure the Indians into precipitate action which they would subsequently regret;[1] probably the Pakistani tactics owed more to opportunism than deep guile, but the risks for India were no less serious. The Governor-General concentrated his energies, therefore, on curbing those hot-heads who wanted to send the Army at least into the areas to which Junagadh's title was uncertain. Sardar Patel was particularly vociferous, while V. P. Menon threatened to resign and take up arms 'to fight on behalf of the wronged states inside Junagadh against their oppressors'. At a Cabinet meeting on 29 September the clamour for some sort of military operation became almost irresistible. Mountbatten held to his view.

> I pointed out that, if the 'strong line' included entering Junagadh (i.e. Pakistan) territory, a senseless act of aggression, for which India would have to pay the price before the world, would have been committed. I said that all the high international prestige which India had achieved, all the Ambassadors and Embassies we had established abroad, and all the Corps Diplomatique which we were so assiduously collecting in Delhi, would become a liability instead of an asset, for we should assuredly lose our international position if we were to prove ourselves to be nothing more than out-and-out aggressors.[2]

In his efforts he was supported with embarrassing fervour by the British Chiefs of Staff of the Indian Services. Alarmed that an invasion of Junagadh and perhaps even war with Pakistan seemed imminent, these officers wrote a joint letter to the Cabinet, stating that the armed forces of India were in no position to undertake a serious campaign and that British soldiers could not take part in any operation which would involve clashes with another Dominion. Movements of troops should at once stop, they said, and the issue be settled by negotiation.[3] 'This letter seemed to us very extraordinary,' Nehru protested to Mountbatten. The Chiefs of Staff appeared to be saying that they would not carry out any policy with which they disagreed. 'That is a position which hardly any Government can accept.'[4] The Governor-General in fact sympathized with the views of the Chiefs of Staff, but he disapproved strongly of the way they were trying to impose them on the Government. He called in the three officers and sharply rebuked them. The paper was withdrawn, and Auchinleck wrote to Nehru to plead that the offending commanders had been under great pressure and had acted with the best intentions.[5] To make sure that such incidents did not recur, a Defence Committee of the Cabinet was set up. Mountbatten was asked to act as its first chairman and agreed to do so. Militarily the appointment made sense, but it undermined whatever standing was left to the Governor-General as

neutral chairman of the Joint Defence Committee. The Pakistani belief that
Mountbatten was as Indian if not more Indian that the Indians was reinforced
– a development that was gravely to limit his usefulness when more serious
conflict threatened over Kashmir.

Meanwhile he continued his efforts to restrain his Government. At the
beginning of October he coaxed Nehru into informal discussions with Liaqat
Ali Khan. Nehru argued that no attempt had been made to establish the
wishes of Junagadh's people; India would abide by the results of an election
or plebiscite if it were conducted fairly. Mountbatten supported him. The
same would apply to any state, he emphasised. India would never try to force
a state to join it against the wishes of the population. 'Pandit Nehru nodded
his head sadly; Mr Liaqat Ali Khan's eyes sparkled; and there is no doubt that
the same thought was in each of their minds: "Kashmir!" '[6]

The way seemed open for Pakistan to withdraw, having extracted the
maximum political advantage from what they must have realized would turn
into an unprofitable commitment. Still they played for time, however. Indian
patience, never notable, now wore very thin. A Provisional Government of
Junagadh was set up in Bombay and, though it was not officially recognized
by the Indians, it became a focus for revolt within the state. The Nawab fled
the country, the State Council began to have second thoughts about its
accession to Pakistan, and on 8 November the *dewan* appealed to India to
take over the administration of the country before it collapsed in chaos. The
invitation was accepted with alacrity. Mountbatten was tactfully left in the
dark. By the time he discovered what was afoot, troops were already on the
move.[7] All he could achieve was the despatch of a conciliatory telegram from
Nehru to Liaqat Ali Khan. It did not receive a conciliatory reply. The
Pakistanis argued that Junagadh, having legally acceded, was now part of
their country, and India had committed aggression. Though the referendum
held in February 1948 showed an overwhelming majority for accession to
India, legally Pakistan was in the right.


Junagadh was the curtain-raiser for the two main dramas that were to follow.
Ever since his failure to pin down the Maharaja, Mountbatten had continued
in a desultory way to try to persuade the Kashmiri Government to consult its
people and join whichever country proved more popular. The transfer of
power merely increased the need for a solution. On 10 October he saw the
*dewan* of Kashmir and told him that, while there was no legal objection to
Kashmir acceding to India, 'if they did so against the wishes of the majority of
their population, it would not only mean immense trouble for Kashmir, but
might well involve trouble for the Dominion of India'. Whatever was to be the

future of Kashmir, a plebiscite must be the first step. That night he told Nehru and Patel of the discussion, 'and they both accepted what I had said'.[8]

The Maharaja continued to vacillate. Possibly he had deluded himself that independence for Kashmir might still be achieved, possibly he was holding out for more favourable terms. When Ismay tried to bring pressure on him during a visit to Srinagar, all he would talk about was polo at Cheltenham in 1935 and the prospects of his colt in the Indian Derby.[9] He suffered the usual fate of those who hesitate too long. Sporadic violence, begun sometimes by Muslims, sometimes by Hindus, had been growing in frequency and intensity; then on 24 October came invasion by Pathan tribesmen from the North-West Frontier. It was taken for granted by every Indian that the Pakistan Government had not merely acquiesced in the attack but had inspired and organized it. Every Indian was probably right.

When the new Defence Committee met under Mountbatten's chairmanship on 25 October, it was clear that there was little to oppose the advance of the tribesmen. Muslim elements in the Maharaja's army had rallied to the invaders and, slaughtering and burning as they went, the Pathans were already within a few days of the capital. As H. V. Hodson has pointed out,[10] Mountbatten's new function meant that he was virtually acting as Prime Minister on issues like Kashmir when the important decisions were made not in Cabinet but in the Defence Committee. To him fell the task of deciding whether and how this dangerous incursion should be checked. Reinforcement by land would be impossibly slow. If India was to intervene it would have to send troops by air. Aeroplanes were earmarked for the operation, troops put on the alert, and V. P. Menon posted off to Srinagar to find out what was going on.

> Kashmir affects me in a peculiar way [Nehru was to write some time later to Edwina Mountbatten]; it is a kind of mild intoxication – like music sometimes or the company of a beloved person. For years and years I could not visit Kashmir because of prison, etc, and the desire to come here again became a passion and an obsession. It is not just the beauty of the scene, though I love beauty and beautiful things, but even more is the very air of Kashmir which has something mysterious and compelling about it.[11]

Indian foreign policy over the next decade was to be distorted and to some extent bedevilled by Nehru's devotion to his ancestral land. Before the Pathan invasion it is possible that he could have reconciled himself to Kashmir's accession to Pakistan; from the moment that India became involved in a rescue operation it became ever less probable that he would agree to anything of the sort. He continued to pay lip-service to the idea of a plebiscite which would ascertain the true wishes of the inhabitants but, consciously or unconsciously, he was going to do all he could to ensure that no such test took place. If Mountbatten had realized the depth and passion of his Prime Minister's determination, he might have managed matters differently; as it was, his tactics were of immeasurable aid to those elements in the Indian Government who were to seek to retain Kashmir at whatever cost over the coming years.

Kashmir, Mountbatten insisted, must accede to India before it would be proper for Indian troops to intervene in its defence – 'This was the only basis on which Indian troops could be sent to the rescue of the State.'[12] Such a step should be temporary, conditional upon an eventual referendum to establish the wishes of the people, but the Maharaja must sign a properly drafted Instrument of Accession and India accept it. Though other members of the Defence Committee were doubtful whether this preliminary was really necessary, the Governor-General got his way. V. P. Menon, who had returned from Kashmir with reports of the Maharaja's virtual abnegation of all responsibility, was sent back armed with this ultimatum: accede, and rescue would be on the way in a few hours; hesitate, and all would be lost.

It is hard to understand why Mountbatten attached such importance to immediate accession. 'There had been no necessity for this,' argued a future Canadian Ambassador to India, Escott Reid. 'An independent state has the right to ask a friendly country to send it help to repel an invader; a friendly country has the right to accede to the request.'[13] If there had been no accession, the Indian presence in Kashmir would have been more evidently temporary, the possibility of a properly constituted referendum have become more real. By exaggerated legalism the Governor-General helped bring about the result he most feared: the protracted occupation of Kashmir by India with no attempt to show that it enjoyed popular support. The embittered hostility of Pakistan and the disapproval of the United Nations followed inexorably from this state of affairs.

It did not take V. P. Menon long to secure the necessary signature from the panic-stricken Maharaja. He was back in Delhi by the evening of 26 October, and the formality of acceptance by the Indian Government was quickly disposed of. The air-lift could proceed. For Mountbatten this came as a vast relief. There were many British citizens living in and around Srinagar who would have been a tempting target for the Pathans. Auchinleck had pleaded to be allowed to send British troops to protect them. Mountbatten was convinced that this would be improper. 'Those people will be murdered and their blood will be on your head,' said Auchinleck accusingly. 'I shall have to take that responsibility,' was the reply, 'but I could not answer for what might happen if British troops became involved.'[14] The thought of what might occur if the Pathans broke through to Srinagar could not have been easy to live with in the unsettling days before the rescue party took to the air.

Once the decision to intervene was taken, Mountbatten involved himself totally in the work of making it effective. 'The mantle of the Governor-General fell from him and he assumed the garb of the Supreme Commander,' a member of his staff was quoted as saying.[15] Pakistani sources claimed to have seen him at the airport, supervising the loading of men and weapons into the hundred-odd aircraft assembled to ferry the force to Kashmir. It seems unlikely that his control was as close as that, but he certainly played a prominent part. 'Messervy [now Commander-in-Chief in Pakistan] came up from Pindi for a talk . . . ,' wrote George Cunningham in his diary. 'He was in Delhi two days ago and was surprised to find Mountbatten directing the military operations in Kashmir. M.B. is daily becoming more and more anathema to our Muslims, and it certainly seems as if he could see nothing except through Hindu eyes.'[16]

The Governor-General could justifiably feel pride in the outcome of his operation. The improvised air-lift worked with astonishing smoothness; planning began on 25 October; the green light was given on the evening of the following day; troops were in the air at dawn on 27 October; the airport at Srinagar was secured a few hours later; and Indian forces were in contact with the advance-guard of the invaders some twenty miles from the capital before nightfall. So well did everything go, indeed, that ill-disposed observers asserted that it could not possibly have been organized at the last minute. There must have been a plot which the Pathan incursion had done no more than expedite. So persistent was the rumour that the three British Chiefs of Staff found it necessary to issue a joint statement affirming that nothing had been prepared in advance.[17] The records of the Defence Committee and Mountbatten's reports to London confirm that this was true.

The deed done, Mountbatten made his first priority the avoidance of war with Pakistan. Jinnah at one point ordered his army to march on Kashmir, and it was only the refusal of his British Commander-in-Chief to act without Auchinleck's approval that gained time for second thoughts. In the end Jinnah suspended action and agreed to meet Mountbatten and Nehru at Lahore. The Governor-General was delighted to accept, but when he tried to recruit his Prime Minister for the mission he found the sternest opposition. It would be another Munich, said V. P. Menon. Sardar Patel was still more emphatic. 'For the Prime Minister to go crawling to Jinnah when we were the stronger side and in the right would never be forgiven by the people of India.'[18] Nehru alone found the idea of such a visit acceptable. Mountbatten asked Gandhi why his Ministers were so reluctant for their Prime Minister to visit Lahore. Was it a question of prestige? He himself 'would be prepared to go to see anyone, anywhere and at any time, if it would help the public interest'. Gandhi said that he felt just the same. 'Of course, you are a great man,' replied Mountbatten, in a moment of unguarded self-revelation.[19]

Nehru agreed to go, fell ill, recovered, flew into a rage at an ill-judged statement by the Pakistan Government, and in the end grudgingly agreed that Mountbatten could go to Lahore with no escort except that of Ismay. 'Dickie and I had 3½ hours with Jinnah, but did not get very far,' commented Ismay. 'It is a fantastic and maddening situation.'[20] It is difficult to see where they could have got. Even if Mountbatten had been able to negotiate freely on behalf of his Government, there was no question of India withdrawing its troops from Kashmir. Nor was it reasonable to expect that they should, with the Pathans still poised at the gates of Srinagar. As for the Pakistanis, there was as little question of their withdrawing the tribal invaders. Jinnah did at least admit some responsibility for their activities when he said that, if the Indian troops were removed, he would pull out the Pathans. 'I expressed mild astonishment at the degree of control that he appeared to exercise over the raiders,' Mountbatten commented drily.[21] But though Jinnah's comment clarified the issue it did not help towards a solution. The most that can be said for the Lahore Summit is that the prospect of a serious conflict between India and Pakistan seemed somewhat more remote once it was over.

> All my efforts during these last hectic days may yet be brought to naught [Mountbatten reported]. If this happens, and open war results, I shall be clear, in my conscience, that I have done all I could to stop it. I must add that I remain confident that open war will not be declared, but unless an agreement can be reached, undeclared war may gradually develop.[22]

This was not the end of Mountbatten's efforts to promote direct discussions between the Indian and Pakistani leaders. The last three months of 1947 were marked by sporadic meetings, each of which at the time seemed to offer some small advance towards a negotiated settlement, each of which was followed by a revulsion towards violence as some insulting letter or new atrocity disturbed the fragile compromise. Gradually the Governor-General came to accept that he could achieve little. The New World had to be invoked, if not called into existence, to redress the balance of the Old. The New World found its manifestation, shining and unsullied, in the form of the United Nations. Idealistic, international, progressive, dedicated to the cause of peace, the United Nations Organization was irresistibly attractive to Mountbatten. He regretfully conceded that at first it was unlikely to be fully effective, but he had no doubt that it was the duty of the great powers to strengthen its machinery and encourage its moral influence. World government might be a distant prospect, but it was a dream which he would have felt it cowardly to dismiss.

The United Nations had two possible roles in Kashmir: to keep the peace and to supervise a plebiscite. Nehru at first saw little to be said for either activity; unless the United Nations could be enlisted to help drive out the invaders, their function would be irrelevant to the real issues. Mountbatten for his part felt that the organization had much to offer. The need for an international peace-keeping force seemed particularly urgent, since as the year petered out the beleaguered Indian garrison in Kashmir found itself under ever more severe pressure, and the temptation to launch a counter-attack on Pakistan itself became harder to resist.

> When first I suggested bringing UNO into this dispute [the Gov-ernor-General told Nehru] it was in order to achieve the object I have quoted above – *to stop the fighting* and to stop it *as soon as possible.* What has happened since then has only served to reinforce my views, and to increase the urgency.
>
> I do not know in what form you are drafting the actual reference to UNO. But from these Cabinet Minutes, I have gathered the impression that at present the main object seems to be to argue the case in New York.
>
> Surely the main object should rather be to bring UNO here at the earliest moment – to get a team nominated, to come out and deal with the business and help to *stop the fighting*, within a matter of days? Can we do nothing to hasten this object?[23]

Nehru's reply was far from conciliatory;[24] indeed, so close did Mountbatten believe the two Dominions had come to war that he appealed to Attlee to fly out to meet the Prime Ministers. Attlee confined himself to a letter exhorting moderation and India duly referred the issue to the United Nations. To that extent Mountbatten could congratulate himself, but the way in which India made the gesture did much to undo its usefulness. If Pakistan did not stop its aggression, said the Indian Government, they might be compelled, in self-defence, to strike against Pakistani territory. 'I have pointed out to Nehru that international bodies like the Security Council do not like working with a threat of this nature hanging over their heads,' wrote Mountbatten sadly;[25] but by that time the damage was done.

After this unpromising start, it was not surprising that the Indian delega-tion got less satisfaction than it had expected from its appeal. By the beginning of February Nehru was telling Mountbatten that it had been a grave mistake to pin any faith in the United Nations. 'I asked him how he could feel this in view of all that he stood for in international ethics, and the belief of [sic] arbitration instead of force. He replied that UNO had been a great disillusionment to him, for it was clearly an American racket.'[26] The inept presentation of the Indian case as opposed to the skilled professionalism, both legal and oratorical, of the Pakistani representative, Zafrullah Khan, was a factor in India's lack of success, but Kingsley Martin, on a visit to Delhi, assured the Governor-General that American ideas on global strategy did indeed bulk large in the affair. Pakistan was believed to be staunchly anti-Communist, India was at the best ambivalent; naturally the United States felt that the former's case over Kashmir should be given a favourable hearing. As for the attitude of the British delegation, Martin felt that this reflected the personality of Philip Noel-Baker, a man of intelligence and charm but 'on matters of high policy weak as water'.[27]

Mountbatten was thoroughly alarmed by the increasing anti-Western and even anti-British feeling in Delhi. He had already been pressing Whitehall to secure some concessions to the Indian point of view. The first move, he felt, must be an instruction to Pakistan from the Security Council that the Pathan invaders were to be withdrawn. Even if this could not be achieved, the British delegation should be seen to be working towards that end. His own influence on the Indian Government had dwindled. 'During the last two months, I have pressed Nehru almost to the point of distraction.'[28] He told Kingsley Martin that it must be made clear to Noel-Baker that the British attitude was 'endangering the whole structure of good will between Britain and India'.[29] He had already done his bit to bring enlightenment to the errant Noel-Baker by giving a visiting junior minister, Patrick Gordon-Walker, a brief prepared by his staff extremely critical of British policy towards Kashmir. Noel-Baker was offended and asked Ismay to warn Mountbatten that this was a most improper way for a constitutional Governor-General to behave. 'No bones were broken,' remarked Ismay.[30] Certainly Mountbatten seems scarcely to have noticed the rebuke – a month later he was still doughtily defending India's interests. He telegraphed Attlee personally to warn him that there was a real risk of India concluding that Russia was its best friend and adjusting its foreign policy accordingly.

> Mr Attlee gave his view that Russia's aim was to prevent a settlement of the Kashmir issue, and then bring about anarchy and chaos throughout the sub-continent. I later replied that I could not believe that Russia would consider her interests so well served by this, as by the emergence of a strong, stabilised India, activated by a deep feeling of gratitude and admiration towards Russia.[31]

Mountbatten continued to press the British Government to be more friendly towards the Indian case. He had some success. By 20 March Nehru was prepared to admit that he was reasonably satisfied with the way things were going at the United Nations. 'I told him that I claimed practically the whole credit for this change, as I had been working very hard to obtain it. He smiled and said "I suspected as much." '32 A fortnight later the Security Council set up a commission to visit the sub-continent and mediate between the two parties. Neither Pakistan nor India was satisfied by this conclusion, but at least the possibility of war had become less likely. A final solution seemed as remote as ever.

When Mountbatten saw Malcolm MacDonald and Arthur Henderson at the beginning of the year he told them that he believed that the partition of Kashmir was the only answer. 'He had not personally been able to advocate this, because he would have been hounded out of India immediately.'33 There were those who held that, if he had pressed this solution on the Maharaja from the start, the whole imbroglio could have been avoided.34 This probably underestimates the talents of the Maharaja when it came to procrastination. At all events, the opportunity, if it ever existed, was missed. Shortly before he left India Mountbatten tried again. V. P. Menon was asked to prepare a plan for dividing the state and it was discussed in principle with Nehru. Liaqat Ali Khan was due to visit India and Mountbatten intended then to confront the two leaders with his proposal.35 Liaqat fell ill, however; the visit was postponed; another opportunity slipped by. Mountbatten left India with the sore of Kashmir still running, and Pakistan's fury over events in Hyderabad destroyed any immediate hope of a compromise. 'I believe that, in the end, good sense will prevail,' the Governor-General had written in December 1947, 'and the two Dominions will be placed in the position where they can concentrate their money and their efforts on economic planning, industrialisation and internal welfare, instead of frittering them away on a useless struggle in Kashmir.'36 He would have expressed himself less confidently six months later. Once again he had learned painfully that reason and good will could not always prevail when prejudice and national pride were ranged against them.


The lesson of Hyderabad was not dissimilar. The Nizam and his Ministers, influenced by an extremist Muslim group, the Razakars, and convinced that India was too preoccupied with Kashmir to devote much time to their problem, rejoiced that they had survived the transfer of power with their independence inviolate and schemed to perpetuate this happy state after their period of grace had expired. The more rational elements among the Muslim leadership, which most of the time included the Nizam himself, recognized that some sort of a deal would have to be done with India, but the grasp of the fanatics was strong enough to ensure that the voice of reason was rarely heard. Mountbatten always believed that, if only he personally could get through to the Nizam, all would be well. He may have been right. The Muslim ruler felt for the cousin of the King-Emperor a respect and trust which he would never have extended to mere Hindu politicians. He could not escape from his advisers, however, and thus the Governor-General was forced to negotiate at second hand, for the most part with moderate men whose word was regularly disavowed by their principals in Hyderabad.

Mountbatten's instinct was to play for time. The Muslim minority could be educated into the belief that it would be in their best interests to do a deal. 'I must say that I did not share Lord Mountbatten's optimism,' wrote V. P. Menon, but the Congress leaders were prepared to give the Governor-General a chance to bring this errant chicken home to roost.[37] 'I think His Excellency will succeed in persuading his Government to refrain from blockading or any other obviously improper pressure,' Monckton reported to the Nizam at the end of August, but that did not mean 'that the State can look forward with equanimity, if negotiations fail, to a quiet life, in which no indirect pressure will be put upon the State to accede'.[38] What both Monckton and Mountbatten were groping towards was a treaty which would enshrine the reality of accession in a formula designed to convey an impression of Hyderabad's independence. The nearer they got to a solution acceptable to the Nizam, the more certain it was that they would incur the disapproval of Patel; the nearer they came to Patel's requirements, the less likely it was that the Nizam would impose it on his fanatic fringe.

In October it seemed that a solution might be in sight. Mountbatten devised an imposing document with no heading to indicate that it was an Instrument of Accession but most of the relevant terms contained within it. If he could get the Nizam to sign it, he was sure Patel would not resist for long. 'I would then write: "I accept this Instrument on behalf of the Government of India" and it would then become an Instrument, and India could look upon it as an Accession, and Hyderabad as an Agreement.'[39] The attempt foundered on the intransigence of both parties. Mountbatten made a last-minute telephone call to Monckton in Hyderabad to try to avert a complete breakdown. They spoke in French in case the line was tapped; the connection was anyway inadequate; the call was periodically interrupted by the voice of John Brabourne in London reporting that Mountbatten had just become a grandfather: the problem of Hyderabad can rarely have seemed more intractable.[40]

Something at least was saved. 'By a miracle I've tied up Hyderabad – anyway for a year – and thus avoided the risk of trouble and possibly even Civil War in the South,' Mountbatten wrote in triumph to Patricia.[41] It was indeed something of a miracle to have persuaded the Indians to accept the prolongation of the standstill agreement by a further twelve months. All the Nizam conceded in return was a promise that he would in the meanwhile not accede to Pakistan. Nevertheless, the Razakars staged a riot in Hyderabad and the delegation travelling to Delhi to sign the agreement was delayed by several days and then demanded various changes to the agreed form of words. Mountbatten 'for once was not his usual amiable self', wrote V. P. Menon.[42] He refused to allow any changes to the main agreement and only minor adjustments of wording to the collateral letters. It was still a satisfactory result for Hyderabad, however; 'This, therefore, is your day, Walter,' Mountbatten wrote to Monckton.[43]

The Governor-General's hope that Hyderabad was 'tied up for a year' soon proved over-sanguine. The Indians claimed that the Muslims were repressing and persecuting the Hindu majority; the Nizam's Ministers complained that India was fomenting trouble and waging economic war. Both had some reason for their protests. Mountbatten at first doubted whether he had any role to play. Intelligence reports quoted the Nizam as saying that the Governor-General was no friend of Hyderabad and that he was anyway powerless to help. Since the Nizam had lost all faith in him, Mountbatten told Monckton, 'I therefore think it best that the negotiations should take place . . . in August or September after I have gone'.[44] This unusual mood of abnegation did not last long. The Nizam changed tack and urged him 'as a member of the Royal Family of England' to help conclude a permanent settlement.[45] Meanwhile incidents multiplied. A *de facto* blockade of Hyderabad by the Indian authorities began to threaten the structure of the state.

Mountbatten had no idea how far things had gone until Monckton returned from a visit to London. A short time before, he had written in his usual friendly terms to say that he was on the way back to Hyderabad in the hope that his presence might give the Nizam the courage to stand up to his extremists.[46] He arrived in Hyderabad on 24 March, rapidly summed up the deteriorating situation, and stormed indignantly to Delhi. He saw Mountbatten the day after his arrival.

> H.E. was very upset about my having declined to stay or dine with him after our fifteen years of intimate friendship. I told him that I could not stay in his house and at the same time attack him publicly as I should have to do if there was a showdown. . . . I said that there was now an economic boycott in full force in spite of all the assurances he had given me about no improper pressure. These were the very methods against which we had fought two wars. . . . If after the assurances he had given, H.E. became a party to them, I would

attack him publicly by every means in my power, and would go back to Hyderabad, and fight such a policy to the end.[47]

Monckton laid about Nehru with equal vigour, telling him that 'coercion by pressure direct or indirect was wrong and wicked'. The Prime Minister mildly replied that he knew nothing of any blockade. He was in no hurry over Hyderabad, which was bound to fall into place in due course.[48] Mountbatten took the same line. If there were any blockade it must have been applied on the initiative of the officials on the spot; V. P. Menon and Patel as well as Nehru had denied absolutely that they knew anything of it, still less had ordered it. 'I can't believe that these three trusted friends would have intentionally deceived me. . . . We were all equally upset and furious.'[49] Whether or not the Indian leaders were disingenuous is unlikely ever to be established. Mountbatten certainly was taken by surprise, and hurt by Monckton's personal attack.

But the activities of his own Ministers caused Mountbatten concern. In mid March he discovered that military plans existed for the invasion of Hyderabad; to make matters worse, the operation had been christened under the code-name of his beloved POLO. He took up the matter with Nehru, who professed surprise that Mountbatten did not know of the project already. This was a contingency plan, no more, prepared against the eventuality that there might be a massacre of the Hindus in Hyderabad. Mountbatten greeted these comfortable words with some scepticism: 'I told him that it was my impression that Ministers were seriously contemplating trying to put this plan into effect . . . irrespective of any massacres and I said that I would take an extremely poor view of any such action.' Absurd, said Nehru; he would never be a party to such a move.[50] Perhaps he was sincere, but the subsequent history of Hyderabad does not inspire much confidence.

Monckton and Mountbatten were soon back at work trying to patch up a settlement. It was indeed the principal preoccupation of Mountbatten's last months in India and his negotiating skills were rarely shown to better advantage. He was endlessly patient, conciliatory, understanding, yet knew when the moment was ripe for tough words. When the Nizam's Premier, Mir Laik Ali, said that his ruler would rather be shot than accede to India Mountbatten retorted that 'if Hyderabad was occupied by an Armoured Division there would be very little shooting'. It would be a bloodless victory and the Nizam would die only if he chose to throw himself under a tank. More probably he would end up living in a small house in straitened circumstances.[51]

He could be as harsh with his own Ministers. After endless negotiation a package of reforms for Hyderabad had been agreed which would set it on the path to constitutional government, and thereby, as the Governor-General saw it, to eventual accession to India. At this point he received a letter from Sardar Patel, who was lying ill at Dehra Dun. He was perturbed, wrote Patel, to find that Mountbatten was still trying to devise a formula which would satisfy everybody. The proper, indeed the only, course for India was to break off negotiations and tell the Nizam bluntly that immediate accession alone was acceptable as a solution.[52] Mountbatten, furious, demanded an interview with Nehru.

> The Governor-General said that he thanked God he would be a free man in a fortnight's time. He was also an honest man. He would be able to say what he liked and he would say what he thought. If war came between India and Hyderabad this would be the result of Sardar Patel's deliberate effort against those which he himself, Pandit Nehru, Sir Walter Monckton, Mir Laik Ali and Mr Menon had been making. Such a war would bring about the slaughter of tens of thousands of innocent Muslims, beginning in Delhi. Everything that Mahatma Gandhi had stood for would be gone. . . . He never thought that the day would come when he would be glad to leave India. He could be far more dangerous than people apparently thought. Surely Mr Patel and Mr Menon could not have imagined that he would be a party to breaking off negotiations with Hyderabad as was advocated by Sardar Patel? A situation had now been reached where Pandit Nehru would have to make a straight choice between Sardar Patel and himself.[53]

Nehru listened sympathetically to this outburst, but he knew – as Mountbatten did too, except in moments of outrage – that there was no way in which he could overrule Patel on such an issue. The fact was that, as Mountbatten told the Nizam, the Indian people were strongly opposed to the relative moderation of its leaders; an attack on Hyderabad would be vastly popular.[54] Patel must be induced to accept the deal with Hyderabad. Monckton set out the facts bluntly to the Nizam. 'Patel and an important group in the Cabinet are against any compromise,' he reported. 'Mountbatten, Nehru and Menon want a compromise. Without Mountbatten's drive it is doubtful whether the other two could carry the day.'[55] On 13 June the Governor-General flew to Dehra Dun to say goodbye to Patel, who was still confined to bed after a heart-attack. He showed the invalid the proposed terms for Hyderabad. Patel rejected them as being absurdly over-generous. Then, at the end of the visit, he said that India owed Mountbatten so much that he deserved anything as a token of its gratitude. The Governor-General promptly asked for acceptance of the Hyderabad agreement. To his amazement Patel briefly hesitated, then signed the document. When Mountbatten passed on the news to Monckton the following day, he 'could scarcely believe that India could be so generous and flew back, overjoyed, to Hyderabad'.[56] The Sardar had acted on an impulse of uncharacteristic sentimentality, but he was not wholly blinded by affection. 'You can take it from me,' he told H. M. Patel after the Governor-General had returned to Delhi, 'the Nizam will never accept.'[57]

It seemed to Mountbatten that he had achieved the near-impossible. He reckoned without the feeble cunning of the Nizam. Further changes were demanded from Hyderabad. The Governor-General knew that he could extract no more from Patel; there was nothing between acceptance and rejection. 'I cannot bring myself to believe that it is Your Exalted Highness's intention to reject this settlement which it has taken so many hours and so much effort to reach,' he wrote to the Nizam in a last, despairing appeal. It availed nothing. Monckton arrived back in Hyderabad at 6.30 a.m. on 17 June. At 1.15 p.m. he sent the laconic telegram 'Lost.'[58] 'I am inclined to agree with you when you said that those whom the Gods wish to destroy they first make mad,' Mountbatten wrote to Monckton, 'for surely only madness could have prevented Hyderabad grasping the hand of friendship which Nehru was holding out.'[59] Four days after the message from Monckton, Mountbatten left India. Fourteen months later Indian troops moved into Hyderabad.


The affairs of these three Princely States illustrate well the reality, yet also the limitations, of Mountbatten's influence on the Indian Government. In each case he advocated a policy which did not appeal to his Ministers. He called for patience, compromise, negotiation at a time when passions ran high and more bravura gestures were what the Indians wanted. No other foreigner would have been listened to with such attention. His strictures on their conduct were accepted with good temper, his point of view pondered on and taken into account. But for him it is likely that there would have been war between India and Pakistan before the end of 1947; it is almost certain that India would have attacked Hyderabad in the first half of 1948. Yet ultimately he did not get his own way. Junagadh was taken over in circumstances of, at the best, doubtful legality. Kashmir was not partitioned, nor were its peoples allowed to decide their future. Hyderabad was occupied by force of arms. When the Indians believed that their essential interests were involved, then Mountbatten could do little to shift them.

CHAPTER 36

# *The Governor-General and his Government*

IN DUE COURSE Prince Philip and Princess Elizabeth became engaged. Whether or not their betrothal owed anything to the machinations of Mountbatten, it gave him great satisfaction, on grounds personal as well as dynastic. He believed that the two were calculated to make each other extremely happy, but, even if he had been less certain of this, the fact that the heiress to the throne of England was to marry his nephew, and one who bore the name of Mountbatten, would have delighted him. He took much credit for the match and showed himself keenly interested in every detail of the wedding and the future *ménage*. To his nephew, indeed, it sometimes seemed that the interest was too keen. 'I am not being rude,' Prince Philip wrote – half but by no means entirely in jest – 'but it is apparent that you like the idea of being the General Manager of this little show, and I am rather afraid that she might not take to the idea quite as docilely as I do. It is true that I know what is good for me, but don't forget that she has not had you as Uncle *loco parentis*, counsellor and friend as long as I have.'[1]

There were some among the more traditional courtiers who took less lightly than Prince Philip the threat that Mountbatten might set up as General Manager to the royal couple. Such a take-over might, they held, imperil the future of the monarchy. Mountbatten was unsound, and his notoriously left-wing wife was worse. He would preach the doctrine that the institution should be modernized, made more relevant – whatever that might mean. No doubt with the best intentions, he would thereby destroy the basis of hallowed tradition on which the monarchy rested. This vision of Mountbatten as radical iconoclast was exaggerated, but it is easy to see how the courtiers would have viewed apprehensively the future influence of this unpredictable and disconcertingly heroic figure. Some people believed that General 'Boy' Browning was installed as Comptroller and Treasurer to the young couple specifically to keep Mountbatten at bay. As his former Chief of Staff, it was argued, Browning would be on his guard against unwarranted incursions and nobody would know better how to thwart them. The theory

457

would be more convincing if it had not been Mountbatten who had recommended Browning to Prince Philip, and in the warmest terms: 'Boy has drive, energy, enthusiasm, efficiency and invokes the highest sense of loyalty and affection in his subordinates. His judgment in all matters that he understands is absolutely sound, and he would sooner die than let his boss down . . . he is not a "yes man" or even a courtier and never will be. He will fearlessly say what he thinks is right. . . . Frankly, Philip, I do not think you can do better.'[2]

Mountbatten could rarely resist giving advice, and when the potential recipient was husband to the future Queen resistance became impossible. Fortunately Prince Philip did not allow his pride to prevent him accepting such advice as he felt was good. Most of it was excellent. Tom Driberg wrote to warn Mountbatten that there was considerable feeling in the Labour Party against any lavish allowances being made to the Prince on his marriage, or undue extravagance over the ceremony itself. Mountbatten replied, promising that he would pass on the comments.

> You can rest assured that he thoroughly understands this problem and indeed he spoke to me about it when I was home in May. I am sure he is entirely on the side of cutting down the display of the wedding, and his own personal feelings are against receiving any civil list for the very reasons which you give. I have, however, persuaded him that it is essential he should take something. [Philip had virtually no money beyond his pay; his] tiny little two-seater made a big hole in his private fortune, and except when travelling on an officer's warrant he usually goes Third-class by train. [Philip did not mind this but] as a future Prince Consort, however, I think you will agree that Third-class travel would be regarded as a stunt and a sixpenny tip to a porter as stingey. . . . It really amounts to this: you have either got to give up the Monarchy or give the wretched people who have to carry out the functions of the Crown enough money to be able to do it with the same dignity at least as the Prime Minister or Lord Mayor of London is afforded.[3]

The royal wedding was fixed for 20 November 1947. Mountbatten was anxious to attend, but, as he somewhat vaingloriously told the King, the whole Government was leaning on him to such an extent that he might have to cry off at the last minute.[4] The conflict over Kashmir was at a dangerous stage. Mountbatten was inclined to feel that his failure to attend the wedding would emphasise and thus exacerbate the danger. His wife believed that the situation was so critical that he would rightly be accused of desertion if he left his post.[5] 'Edwina has been dreadfully tiresome lately,' Ismay told his wife. 'There have been daily scenes about Dickie's decision to go home for the wedding. Personally I think it's advisable on every count. It's good for the Govt of India because it will show them that they can do without him: It's good for Pakistan because it will show them that he is not as they charge – the Supreme Commander of the Kashmir offensive: and it's good for Dickie himself as he badly needs a change.'[6]

The Governor-General was back at his post on 24 November – 'Lovely to be home,' he noted in his diary. As Viceroy he had had few opportunities to visit India outside the immediate trouble spots; now he amply made up for it. In the seven months that remained to him he visited Jaipur and Bombay; Gwalior; Bikaner; Bhopal, Nagpur and Madras; Allahabad; Dehra Dun; Lucknow and Cawnpore; Calcutta and Orissa; Assam, Trivandrum, Travancore and Cochin; Udaipur; Mashubra and Simla; Patna; Mysore, Ootacamund and Bangalore; Jodhpur and Bundi; Chavil; Baroda. He inspected factories and power-stations; visited schools and universities; laid foundation-stones; opened hospitals; received honorary degrees; endlessly extolled the virtues of a united country and the wonders that the future would hold if only all Indians would work harmoniously together. He delighted in what was to be almost the last fine flourish of princely India: processions of pompous elephants; palatial splendour; the traditional diversions of the rulers – tiger-shooting in Gwalior, fishing in Mysore, the celebrated sand-grouse of Bikaner. Nor were humbler pursuits despised; at Ootacamund: 'Golf course lovely. They cut a tree down to make it easier for me!'[7] It was a world which he had helped to destroy; but the inevitability of its passing made its attractions no less seductive.

He made innumerable speeches and he was interminably spoken at. This last was the most arduous part of the proceedings. He could imbibe flattery in lavish doses, but even he was abashed by the oration of the Mayor of Calcutta. 'Within your veins', he was told, 'courses in rich pulsation Royal blood. . . . By fingers that were deft and arms that were strong, you have laboured to raise a twin edifice. We look upon Your Excellency to unite your handicrafts by a bridge of Peace, a bridge of Delight.'[8] There were more enjoyable moments. The antique Maharaja of Kapurthala spoke at a state luncheon, declaring how fortunate India had been to have such an outstanding and brilliant couple as Viceroy and Vicereine, the best India had ever had. After continuing in this strain for some time, he invited everyone to rise and drink the health of Lord and Lady Willingdon.[9]

Occasionally Mountbatten left his territories. Lahore was strictly business – for negotiations with the Pakistanis – but even there ceremony was oppressive. 'Funny seeing ladies curtsey to him and not to me – but quite right,' he commented after an evening with Jinnah.[10] Burma was pleasure. The Mountbattens visited Rangoon in March 1948, the official reason being the handing over of King Theebaw's throne, returned to Burma as an independence present from its former occupiers. It can have come as a surprise to no one that Mountbatten took advantage of the occasion to lecture the new rulers on the dangers of their foreign and domestic policies, which seemed designed to alienate every foreigner, Communist or capitalist, from East or from West. Viewing the later history of Burma, it cannot be maintained that much attention was paid to his strictures, but he was heard with courtesy and received with affection.[11]

It is almost true to say that, whenever the Mountbattens were not being entertained, they were entertaining. During their fifteen months in India they had 7605 guests to luncheon, 8313 to dinner, 25,287 to garden-parties and other such receptions.[12] In terms of liveries, silver, and other manifestations of splendour, they received in the grandest style, but they had a disconcerting habit of proclaiming periods of austerity to mark their solidarity with the sufferings of the Indian peasantry. When Lord Listowel stayed at Government House during the massacres, he was regaled with 'cabbage water masquerading as soup, one piece of spam and potato, a biscuit and a small portion of cheese'.[13] He sceptically enquired afterwards whether the menu had been specially contrived in his honour. His suspicions were unjust.

Apart from travel, the duties of a more-or-less constitutional Governor-General allowed Mountbatten a little time to enjoy himself. Riding, polo practice, golf, were once more possible. He patronized amateur theatricals with enthusiasm.

> If only I wasn't Governor-General but just a grass-bachelor sailor I would have had the most wonderful time here [he wrote to Patricia from Simla]. An exceptionally lovely Anglo-Indian girl, leading lady of the second play, attracted me more than any girl for years. And as luck would have it I absolutely clicked with her. I just saw enough of her on the stage after the show and sitting opposite her after the Club dinner to know we could have had a wonderful time. She came round to ask for my autograph and managed to get her hand over mine long enough to indicate what she felt! Isn't it maddening I just can't do anything about it. She was just my cup of tea.
>
> Pammy was amused but luckily I don't think Mummy noticed anything.[14]

*

Mountbatten had clear ideas about his role as Governor-General, though circumstances frequently forced him – not always unwillingly – to step beyond its limitations. One thing he was determined that he was *not* was a representative of British interests in India. When Mr H. Rowan Hodge from Calcutta asked to see him, Mountbatten said he would be delighted to receive him socially, but not in his official role. Hodge asked his views on membership of the Bengal Club. Mountbatten said that he felt it essential either that Indians should be admitted on the same basis as Britons or the name changed to 'United Kingdom Club'. Hodge 'asked if he might quote me when talking it over with the members, since they had wanted to know what my views were officially. I replied: "Certainly not; if they cannot make up their own minds without official advice from the constitutional Governor-General of India, then God help them!" '[15]

For different reasons he also refused to act as chairman of the Partition Council, which continued to exist after the transfer of power. To do so, he felt, would inevitably lead to his losing all standing with one side or the other. When he went to London for the royal wedding he was disconcerted to find how far it was assumed that this had already happened, that he was irrevocably pro-India and anti-Pakistan. Wavell saw him on 20 November and found him 'voluble as ever and full of confidence and personality'.

> He has very much gone over to the Congress side, as was, I suppose inevitable in his position; says Jinnah has become an impossible megalomaniac, and that Nehru has shown himself a really great man. He thinks Liaqat the only man on the Muslim side who has shown sense and some statesmanship, which about tallies with my judgment. But Liaqat is a sick man and may collapse, which will leave Pakistan barren indeed. The bitterness of feeling between Hindu and Moslem is worse than ever before and neither side trusts or believes the other about anything.[16]

Churchill treated him more roughly, producing 'such a tirade against the Congress party and my Government as would have seemed quite incredible if his views on the subject were not fairly well known'. He said the Muslims were Britain's friends, and that it was terrible that an Englishman and a cousin of the King should now support Britain's enemies against them. 'He accused me of having planned and organised the first victory of Hindustan (he refused to call it India) against Pakistan by sending in British trained soldiers and British equipment to crush and oppress the Muslims in Kashmir.' His considered advice to Mountbatten was to get out quickly 'and not involve the King and my country in further backing traitors'.[17]

As servant of the Indian Government, it was inevitable and proper that

Mountbatten should take the Indian side. Certainly he was prejudiced in their favour and sometimes unfair in his references to Pakistan. He did, however, do his best to ensure that Pakistan got a fair deal after partition. Even the most fanatical Muslim could hardly deny him credit over the division of the cash-balance. In the middle of December 1947 approximately fifty-five crores of rupees – say £30 million pounds at the exchange rate then prevailing – remained to be transferred from India to Pakistan. In view of the state of near war which existed over Kashmir, India suspended payments. Mountbatten did his best to persuade his Ministers to change their minds and stigmatized their behaviour as unwise, unstatesmanlike and dishonourable.[18] When this availed nothing, he involved Gandhi in his battle. The Mahatma was about to embark on a fast in an attempt to end communal violence in Delhi. He added the issue of the cash-balances to those that must be righted before he would eat again.

Pyarelal, Gandhi's secretary and future biographer, was supposed to attend a reception at Government House the day the fast began. He asked to be excused but Gandhi insisted on his attending. 'Mountbatten will probably want to discuss the fast with you. It would be worthwhile getting his reaction at first hand. In any case, you will be able to report whether any drinks were served!' Pyarelal duly attended and was assured that the Governor-General was strongly in favour of the fast. 'I was again struck by his innate courage and the boldness of his imagination,' wrote Pyarelal. 'When I reported this to Gandhiji, he was delighted. "Have I not often said," he remarked, "that one must be a great warrior fully to appreciate the power that is non-violence!"'[19]

On the fifth day of the fast the Mountbattens visited Gandhi. 'It takes a fast on my part to bring the mountain to Mohammed,' observed the Mahatma. Mountbatten explained that the visit was more than personal; he wanted the world to see that he supported Gandhi in his objective.[20] The Government could hardly withstand such pressure. They capitulated and announced that the fifty-five crores would be transferred immediately. 'The best news in three months,' Mountbatten described it.[21]

It is a curious commentary on human nature that, while Mountbatten survived this and similar episodes with his popularity and influence undiminished, Auchinleck for far less offence lost the confidence of the Indian Government. The Commander-in-Chief struggled nobly to be impartial. 'Our position as a neutral body trying to partition the Armed Forces to the equal advantage of both Dominions is not . . . exactly an easy one,' he wrote in September. 'I think any fairminded person would acknowledge that the work has been well done.'[22] Fair-minded people were hard to find in India in 1947. Patel in particular told Mountbatten that it was unbearable to see

Supreme Headquarters 'acting as the advanced outpost of Pakistan'. Mountbatten protested that Auchinleck's integrity was beyond dispute and that the staff of Supreme Headquarters were at pains to act impartially. 'They may think they are acting impartially,' retorted Patel, 'but as they are all mentally completely pro-Pakistan, they are in fact out to help Pakistan at every turn.'[23]

It is interesting to speculate whether things would have been different if Slim had replaced Auchinleck, as Montgomery had suggested in April 1947. Mountbatten had replied that there could be no question of replacing the Commander-in-Chief before the transfer of power, and that, anyway, Slim was surely destined to be next Chief of the Imperial General Staff.[24] The question came up again when Montgomery visited Delhi in June. Montgomery argued that no officer with an Indian Army background could be acceptable as C.I.G.S. and became indignant when Mountbatten persisted that Slim was obviously the best man for the job. Subsequently, Mountbatten related, he persuaded Attlee that Slim should be appointed. Attlee overruled Montgomery's opposition, and insisted that Slim should be recalled from retirement. 'This is out of the question,' Mountbatten quotes Montgomery as saying, 'I have already told Crocker that he is going to succeed me.' 'Well, untell him!' replied Attlee laconically.[25]

If Montgomery had had his way and Slim been pushed into what he undoubtedly hoped would prove a backwater, Mountbatten's task might have been easier. Auchinleck was no less honourable than Slim but he was less agile in mind and tractable in manner. Slim would have encountered the same prejudices, but would have known better how to circumvent them. As it was, Supreme Headquarters was embittering rather than improving relations between India and Pakistan and Auchinleck's presence was damaging the standing of Britain in Indian eyes. Montgomery had no doubts about the proper solution.

> It is my opinion that Auchinleck's usefulness in India has finished. He is 63; he has spent all his life in India under a previous regime; he is too old to readjust himself to new ideas which he dislikes in his heart.
>
> He is viewed with suspicion by the senior officers of the Indian army. . . .
>
> I personally consider that if you want military matters to run smoothly and efficiently in India you will have to remove Auchinleck; I further consider that if you do *not* do so you will have trouble. . . .
>
> I would tell Auchinleck to retire and recommend him for a G.C.S.I., nothing more.[26]

Mountbatten's answer to this ungenerous proposal was that he agreed the Supreme Command should close down but not that Auchinleck should be fobbed off with a G.C.S.I.: 'Auchinleck's Indian career has been a singularly long and fine one, and I have the Prime Minister's permission to ask him if he would wish to have a peerage.'[27] To Attlee he had said that it could only be a matter of days before the Indian Government demanded Auchinleck's recall. 'I want him to go while he can still go with a reputation as the greatest Commander-in-Chief the Indian Army has had for many years. If he holds on, he will lose that reputation.'[28]

On 26 September Mountbatten embarked on what he described as 'probably the most difficult letter that I have ever had to write in my life'. He described to Auchinleck the resentment of the Indians at the presence in Supreme Headquarters of 'a man of your very high rank and great personal prestige and reputation'. He had tried to persuade them that their suspicions about Auchinleck's impartiality were wholly unjustified. Now the issue was about to be raised in the Joint Defence Council. Auchinleck had often told him in the past how gladly he would fade from the picture if this would help matters. 'Bitter though it is for me to say so, I sincerely believe that the moment has arrived for me to take advantage of your selfless offer.'[29] Ismay wrote to support the Governor-General. 'I feel as strongly as I have ever felt anything in my life that you in a big way, and I in a much smaller way, are now in a completely impossible position by reason of our lack of power.'[30]

That Auchinleck's first reaction was one of resentment is hardly surprising; that he soon concluded that Mountbatten was indeed proposing the best course is a tribute to his generosity as well as his good judgement. At first he took the line that the end of the year was the earliest it would be possible to close Supreme Headquarters without confusion and hardship.[31] At a painful interview on 7 October Mountbatten argued that everyone, including the British Chiefs of Staff, felt that swifter action was called for.

> After a very long discussion in which he was most friendly and reiterated his complete trust in my friendship, he finally said: 'I will go and close down my Headquarters whenever you think it right; I leave it to you.' I said: 'How about the 15th November?' At this he looked very sad and said: 'The last reunion of my old Regiment takes place on the 20th November, it will be sad missing that. . . .' I am afraid my heart melted towards him, and I said: 'All right, make it the 30th November, and I'll support you to the best of my ability.' He really seemed quite touchingly pleased about this.[32]

To the Pakistanis the premature closure of Supreme Headquarters was but one more illustration of Mountbatten's malign partiality. The Governor-

General had 'invariably supported any stand taken by the Indian leaders . . . supported the Indians over the division of stores, and paid no attention to Auchinleck's expert advice'.[33] What more likely than that he would seize the first chance to drive the Supreme Commander from office? More temperately, Brigadier Desmond Young said that Mountbatten's worst mistake was 'not only to consent to splitting the Indian Army but also to insist on accelerating the process. The ideal would have been to retain the Army intact under Field Marshal Auchinleck for two years from Independence Day to assist the two Governments impartially in the maintenance of order.'[34] Mountbatten would have accepted the truth of this, but to maintain a united Army when both its component elements were determined to assert their independent existence was an ideal not readily achieved. Once the decision to partition India was taken, the choice was between a chaotically disintegrating united Army or two more-or-less coherent separate forces. To move as rapidly as possible from the first to the second seemed to offer the best chance. Mountbatten might have kept Supreme Headquarters alive for a few more months, might even have bolstered Auchinleck's tottering authority, but to have done so would in no way have preserved the unity of the Indian Army.

Mountbatten had hoped that the Joint Defence Council might eventually be expanded to consider the defence of India and Pakistan against external threats. He found it hard to raise enthusiasm for the subject: 'Pakistan's enemy is our friend' was more the attitude of the Indian leaders. Morris Jones, the constitutional adviser on his staff, prepared a paper arguing the case for some more permanent structure, perhaps based on the Australia–New Zealand defence agreements. If Mountbatten read the paper at all, he certainly failed to act on it. Probably he realized that the time was unpropitious.

The Defence Council itself was due to expire on 1 April 1948. Mountbatten had hoped that its existence might be prolonged, perhaps for ever. Some months before he had pleaded that it should be constituted with another chairman, but both Indians and Pakistanis had been anxious that he should continue to serve.[35] Now he urged that at least the two Prime Ministers, accompanied by other Ministers, should meet every month or so to discuss problems of common interest.[36] When Mountbatten left India this was almost the only relic of the old federal dream which still existed. It did not long survive his departure.

'If you decide to go, let us go together,' Ismay had told Auchinleck. 'I haven't yet tied Dickie down to a definite date.'[37] He had originally proposed that he should stay on until the end of 1947, and as that date approached he became more and more certain that he did not wish to extend it farther. 'It is only natural that the Government of India should regard themselves as having proprietary rights over you, their Governor-General,' he wrote to Mountbatten, 'and you told me yesterday that you yourself accepted this position.'[38] The trouble was that he could not view things the same way; he still felt himself the servant of the British Government; his heart was as much with Pakistan as with India, perhaps even more so. Mountbatten knew that in staying on for four months after independence Ismay had already done as much as duty or friendship could demand. He valued his integrity and wisdom more than that of any other adviser, but agreed without too much demur to his departure.

> I can't pretend to have been happy these last few months . . . [Ismay told Mountbatten]. But I am damned proud to have been associated with you in the making of history; I am damned grateful to you for having taken me with you, and for having been so patient with and kind to me: and whatever has happened, or whatever may happen, I am convinced, first that you did the only possible thing, and secondly that *no-one* else could have done it.

Mountbatten, he said, should not stay in India long after April 1948; it would be bad for India and bad for him. Progressively he should take more of a back seat.

> Even when you preside [over the Defence Committee], take things a bit easier; sit back and let the Committee ventilate all their views before you sum up. You are the best Chairman of a Committee – except for Neville Chamberlain – with whom I have ever worked: but you are so eager, so anxious to get clear-cut decisions, so amazingly quick in the uptake, that you are sometimes apt to be impetuous in your summing up and, worse still, not to give every member of the team an innings. Bradman wins matches by making a hundred or so himself on every occasion: but if the tail-enders don't get a knock now and then, the Australians will have a poor side when Bradman retires!
>
> Finally – to complete the catalogue of crime! – I suggest that you should do your utmost to order your arrangements well ahead and then to stick to your programme as closely as possible. . . . Uncertainty is always demoralising. Forgive me, Dickie, for pointing out these very insignificant shortcomings so frankly. They are such a drop compared with your ocean of virtues: courage, industry, drive, vigilance, magnetism.[39]

Mountbatten would not have considered that forgiveness was called for; constructive criticism from those whom he respected was never taken amiss.

Acting on the advice was another matter. His tendency to take upon himself responsibilities that should have been exercised by his Ministers was not complained of only by Ismay. 'H.E. seems to have an itch to be prodding his Government,' wrote Christie. 'He must be careful not to overdo it'; and then a month later: 'I find it difficult to understand what is happening. Either H.E. is encouraging the submission to him of departmental business, or the present Government is self-confessed absolutely helpless to carry on its own business.'[40]

For a man who prided himself on his progressive views, Mountbatten's influence on his Government was decidedly conservative. In economic matters he preached caution, the avoidance of steps that might frighten away foreign investment, a moratorium on nationalization until such time as there were enough efficient managers to run the industries. He promoted the interests of traditionally minded civil servants like V. P. Menon or Girja Shankar Bajpai, who could be relied on to view the shibboleths of socialist planning with scepticism if not distaste. He was, as Sarvepalli Gopal has remarked, temperamentally close to Nehru but in ideology far more like Patel.[41] Within a week of the transfer of power he had written a long letter to Nehru and Patel urging the need for provident planning; he was afraid, he told Campbell-Johnson, that 'stern economic realities' might be swamped by political considerations.[42] Nine months later his line was unchanged; he told an eminent English resident, Sir Percival Griffiths, with some pride, that 'whenever Nehru or Patel produced any unacceptable ideas, he never told them that it could not be carried out, but merely warned them of the value of a sense of timing'.[43]

He was concerned that Britain should continue to play the leading role in the development of the Indian economy, and in particular that the United States should be kept at bay. In September 1947 a proposal was put forward for sending a group of specialists from the United Kingdom to help India in its industrialization programme. Mountbatten strongly supported the scheme; Sir Terence Shone, the first British High Commissioner in India, was sceptical whether the time was ripe. 'I told him that in my opinion Mr Grady had been sent here for one purpose only as U.S. Ambassador,' Mountbatten recorded, 'and that was to sell the American Industrialisation to the Indians at the earliest possible moment. . . . Unless the British offer was received by the Indians before the American offer, there would be a good chance that we should be too late altogether.'[44] Mr Grady for his part complained to the State Department that Mountbatten was warning the Indians against the perils of dollar imperialism. 'I have waited patiently for a hand of co-operation from the British but it has never come,' he reported wistfully. 'The British are not happy about the strong position which we have in India, or about the weak position that they have.'[45]

It was not anti-Americanism that dictated Mountbatten's attitude so much as his wish that nothing should disturb the growth of the still fragile Commonwealth ties. Another example which he cited to Griffiths of his influence on Indian policy was that 'no precipitous action had been taken in regard to leaving the Commonwealth'.[46] Only three weeks before the interview Nehru had told Attlee that he favoured 'close and intimate friendship' with Britain rather than a more formal link. Such friendship, he said, was possible 'because the change in British policy, and more particularly the presence and activities of the Mountbattens, had enabled Indians to forget the heavy legacy of British rule'.[47] Mountbatten's own view was that the reality of the Commonwealth was far more important than its precise form; provided that its members believed in its existence and its value, then they could call it anything they liked. 'While I appreciate the point made at home that you are either in the Commonwealth or out of it,' he told Rance, 'there is much to be said for investigating whether a somewhat looser form of association is possible. . . . I am convinced that the British Empire must move with the times.'[48]

In January 1948 the American newspaper *P.M.* credited Mountbatten with a plan for changing the nature of the Commonwealth to enable India to be part of it while ceasing to be a Dominion.[49] The Governor-General's tendency to think aloud, quite regardless of the presence of journalists, had no doubt inspired a report which, though premature, reflected Mountbatten's thinking. It was not till 6 February that Vernon Erskine-Crum produced a paper arguing that allegiance to the Crown was likely to prove the factor that might drive India out of the Commonwealth. He suggested two categories of membership – Dominions which owed allegiance to the Crown, and Republics which accepted it as a symbol of unity. Mountbatten, who had been personally responsible for the initiation of the study, approved its conclusions. After all, he pointed out, the Commonwealth already contained one anomaly in Eire. An institution so flexible could easily accommodate some more.[50]

By the end of the month the paper had been discussed informally with Nehru and was ready to be sent to London. 'Although there has been a lot of staff discussion and thinking on the subject,' wrote Campbell-Johnson, 'it is very much Mountbatten's own document, characteristically bold, direct and original.'[51] Mainly it dealt with nomenclature: the fact that the word 'Dominion' alarmed new recruits to the Commonwealth was no reason why the word 'Republic' should deter the long-established members. A Commonwealth by any other name would serve no less useful a purpose. The counter-argument was that, if the formal structure of so amorphous a body was too much weakened, nothing would be left but a community of interests. If that in its turn proved to be illusory, as seemed sure to happen at some point or other, the insubstantial pageant would fade for ever. Mountbatten saw the risk as clearly as anyone else, but he believed that his overriding priority was to keep India in the Commonwealth. It is reasonably certain that but for him this would not have happened. Whether Britain, India, the Commonwealth or, indeed, the world was the better for his success is a question to which it is still too early to find a conclusive answer.

# CHAPTER 37

## Farewell to India

EARLY IN 1948 the Mountbattens spent a few days touring in Bhopal and Madras. The Governor-General arrived back in Delhi with his two daughters at 2.30 p.m. on Friday, 30 January and soon went out riding. When they returned they were met with the news that Gandhi had been shot while presiding over a prayer-meeting at Birla House, his temporary Delhi home. Before Mountbatten had changed and reached his car, it was confirmed that the Mahatma was dead.

Campbell-Johnson went with the Governor-General to Birla House. Mountbatten 'was very tense, and spoke in short, staccato sentences'.[1] His immediate preoccupation was lest Nehru also should be at risk. Only two days before, men carrying bombs had been arrested while he was addressing a meeting at Amritsar. Beyond that, Gandhi's murder threatened incalculable perils. Not merely had India lost its most revered leader, the loss itself could provoke disaster. 'We had been told that the assailant was a Muslim,' wrote K. M. Munshi. 'This opened up a ghastly prospect; the next day rivers of blood would flow both in India and Pakistan.'[2] As Mountbatten arrived at Birla House he heard a loud cry: 'It was a Muslim who did it!' Furiously he rounded on the speaker, 'You fool, don't you know it was a Hindu?' 'How can you possibly know?' Campbell-Johnson whispered to him. 'If it wasn't we are lost anyhow,' replied the Governor-General.[3] Mercifully the facts justified his words; the assassin proved to be a Hindu fanatic who felt that Gandhi had betrayed his people.

Mountbatten found most of the Cabinet already at Birla House, dazed and almost incoherent with grief. Unity of purpose and quick action were essential if the nation was to be steadied. Nehru and Patel had recently been on bad terms, and were now sitting in opposite corners of the room surrounded by groups of their friends. With characteristic opportunism Mountbatten saw how the tragedy might yield at least one dividend for India. He beckoned to the two men to join him and told them that the last wish Gandhi had expressed to him was that he should do all in his power to bring them together and keep them friends. The two men nodded and embraced in silence.[4]

'Like an elder member of the family,' wrote Patel's biographer D. V. Tahmankar, Mountbatten took the situation in hand.[5] He persuaded Nehru and Patel that they must broadcast jointly to the nation that evening so as to make manifest that the Government was in full control. His first proposal was that the body should be embalmed and carried around India on a funeral train, as a means of reinforcing the Mahatma's message of reconciliation and love. Nehru and Patel liked the idea, but Gandhi's secretary Pyarelal insisted that he had always wanted to be cremated within twenty-four hours of his death as became an orthodox Hindu. Surely in the circumstances this rule might be relaxed, asked the Governor-General. Pyarelal was inflexible. Gandhi had told him: 'Even in my death I shall chide you if you fail your duty in this respect.' 'His wishes shall be respected,' said Mountbatten.[6]

The crowds which attended Gandhi's funeral were comparable in size with, perhaps even larger than, those which had assembled some six months before on Independence Day. A way was with difficulty kept open for Mountbatten and his staff and family to reach the funeral pyre on the Raj Ghat, but it did not take long to realize that, if the pressure of the multitude surrounding the site continued to grow, all the dignitaries at the front would themselves be immolated. He walked around the pyre, urging those in the front three or four rows to sit down and thus provide a solid obstacle to those behind; but for this, recorded General Chaudhuri, 'a great many V.I.P.s and distinguished Indians might have been pushed into the fire'.[7] As the flames rose up, however, the pressure of several hundred thousand Hindus continued to grow more intense. Mountbatten stood up and surveyed the gathering 'as though appraising a military situation'. 'We must go now,' he said quietly. Linked in a human chain, his party struggled after him. The crowds did their best to make a way for him and in his wake an exodus began.[8]

'I had become so fond of dear old Gandhi that his assassination was a real personal blow as well as an immense anxiety,' Mountbatten told his mother.[9] He never fully understood the Mahatma – probably no Englishman could – but he warmed to his charm and felt instinctively that here was someone great, of wholly different greatness to anyone he had met before, and for that reason more remarkable. Mountbatten had a great capacity for wonder and an appreciation of quality in whatever form it came. 'What a remarkable old boy he was,' he wrote to Mabel Strickland in Malta. 'I think history will link him with Buddha and Mahomet, and the Indians include Christ in this classification.'[10]

The Governor-General's presence at Gandhi's funeral was not universally applauded. General Nye, the Governor of Madras, who accompanied him to the pyre, showed him a letter that had been received by a young Welsh Guards

officer serving on his staff. The A.D.C.'s father, a retired Regular Army
officer, was outraged to hear of Governor-General and Governor sinking so
low as to honour the corpse of a man whose proper end would have been on
the gallows.[11] Mountbatten told his old friend Stewart Perowne that he had
heard that the West End clubs had been rocked to their foundations at the
thought of the King's representative sitting on the ground amidst a crowd of
natives – and in uniform too. 'I wonder what the old fogies imagined would
have happened had I absented myself. Really, I despair of anybody in England
ever understanding the form out here.'[12] A vague unease at the Governor-
General's activities, a feeling that he was not behaving in a way wholly
becoming for a representative of the King – so recently a representative of the
King-Emperor – was found in circles more sophisticated than the traditionalist recesses of clubland. On 24 June 1948 the *News Chronicle* carried a
photograph of Edwina embracing the Governor-General designate, Rajagopalachari. Alan Lascelles cut it out for the King's inspection. 'It is, I fear,
having a wide circulation in London today,' he noted gloomily.[13]

Lady Mountbatten's friendship with Pandit Nehru was to give rise to
more enduring criticism. After Gandhi's murder Mountbatten urged the
Prime Minister to come to live with them at Government House where
adequate security could be more easily maintained.[14] Nehru refused, but with
the death of the man who had so strongly influenced him he began to see more
and more of the Mountbattens and to draw from them some of the moral
sustenance which he had used to derive from the Mahatma. Their effect on
him was subtle but pervasive:

> I am afraid New Delhi and more specially you and Dickie have
> civilised me too much – and you have humanised me a little also [he
> wrote to Edwina in June]. The humanising part I welcome but the
> civilising process is not so welcome, however desirable it might be.
> The wild animal in me, tame though it has grown, resents it and I
> long to break away. I remember when I was not so tame, and had
> greater freedom of action, though within a limited sphere. I was
> rather like a flame burning myself and scorching others, and obli-
> vious of both. The flame grows dim and smoky and the bright point
> which gave me faith is no longer there.[15]

In the Mountbattens Nehru found companions who were not only
congenial but secure. They had no axes to grind in India, no relations to
advance, no home-towns to favour, no covetous eyes on the succession. They
might see things differently, but their view was as nearly objective as Nehru
was likely to hear. The Prime Minister respected their judgement, had
absolute confidence in their good will, drew comfort from their support. 'I

want someone to talk to me sanely and confidently, as you can do so well,' he wrote in April, 'for I am in danger of losing faith in myself and the work I do. . . . What has happened, is happening, to the values we cherished? Where are our brave ideals?'[16]

This letter was addressed to Edwina but applied to both of them. A month later it would have been different. On 13 May 1948 Nehru drove with the Mountbattens to spend a few days with them in the country near Simla. 'Suddenly I realised (and perhaps you did also)', he wrote nearly ten years later to Edwina, 'that there was a deeper attachment between us, that some uncontrollable force, of which I was only dimly aware, drew us to one another. I was overwhelmed and at the same time exhilarated by this new discovery. We talked more intimately, as if some veil had been removed, and we could look into each other's eyes without fear or embarrassment.'[17]

So began a relationship that was to endure until Edwina Mountbatten's death: intensely loving, romantic, trusting, generous, idealistic, even spiritual. If there was any physical element it can only have been of minor importance to either party. Mountbatten's reaction was one of pleasure. 'Please keep this to yourselves but she and Jawarhalal [sic] are so sweet together,' he wrote to Patricia, 'they really dote on each other in the nicest way and Pammy and I are doing everything we can to be tactful and help. Mummy has been incredibly sweet lately and we've been such a happy family.'[18] He liked and admired Nehru, it was useful to him that the Prime Minister should find such attractions in the Governor-General's home, it was agreeable to find Edwina almost permanently in a good temper: the advantages of the alliance were obvious. Nor did Nehru feel that his love for Edwina need in any way diminish his respect and affection for her husband. On the contrary, it heightened it; the Prime Minister and Edwina seemed sometimes to be almost conspirators in ensuring that Mountbatten got all that he wanted out of life and was not made to feel excluded from their relationship. Nehru wrote to thank her for a suitably inscribed silver cigarette-box. 'For your private ear I might tell you, provided you do not tell Dickie, that the spelling of my name was all wrong. I make no grievance of it. Indeed in a way I like this mistake which makes the inscription characteristic of Dickie; who has thus far failed to grasp completely how my name should be written or pronounced.'[19]

Though Mountbatten knew how close the relationship was between Nehru and his wife, and Edwina knew that Mountbatten knew, they were for several years reticent about discussing the matter except by veiled references. Then in 1952 Edwina wrote to ask Mountbatten to keep Nehru's letters for her.

You will realise that they are a mixture of typical Jawaharlal letters full of interest and facts and really historic documents. Some of them have no 'personal' remarks at all. Others are love letters in a sense, though you yourself well realise the strange relationship – most of it spiritual – that exists between us. J. has obviously meant a very great deal in my life, in these last years, and I think I in his too. Our meetings have been rare and always fleeting, but I think I understand him, and perhaps he me, as well as any human beings *can* ever understand each other. . . .

It is rather wonderful that my affection and respect and gratitude and *love* for you are really so great that I feel I would rather you had these letters than anyone else, and I feel you would understand and not in any way be hurt – rather the contrary. We understand each other so well although so often we seem to differ and to be miles apart. You have been very sweet and good to me, and we have had a great partnership. My admiration and my devotion to you are very great.[20]

Mountbatten did understand and was not hurt – indeed, this letter repaired the only injury that the relationship had done him, that sometimes he had felt himself not merely excluded but kept in the dark.

I am glad you realise that I know and have always understood the very special relationship between Jawaharlal and you, made the easier by my fondness and admiration for him, and by the remarkably lucky fact that among my many defects God did not add jealousy in any shape or form. I honestly don't believe I've ever known what jealousy means – universal as it seems to be – and if it concerns the happiness of anyone I'm as fond of as you, then only my desire for your happiness exists. That is why I've always made your visits to each other easy and been faintly hurt when at times . . . you didn't take me into your confidence right away.[21]

There is an element of self-deception in this letter. There had been times when Edwina's behaviour with other men had caused Mountbatten sharp pain – pain that was certainly akin to jealousy. Nor did his wife's relationship with Nehru leave him entirely unmoved; after Edwina's death he asked his daughter Pamela to look first at Nehru's letters, so fearful was he that he might find among them some proof that the love between the two had not been as platonic as he had imagined. Yet for the most part he felt not even a tremor of regret. He had never hankered after an exclusive relationship with his wife; he was happy, proud almost, to open it to a man he esteemed so highly. To call it a triangle, or Mountbatten a complaisant husband, would be to belittle a relationship that was enriching to all concerned.

When he had originally agreed to stay on as Governor-General, Mountbatten had suggested that he should leave India in April 1948. 'There has been every sort of pressure from every sort of person to stay not less than one year,' Mountbatten told Monckton, 'in fact most people want us to stay five and some even ten years.'[22] Such extravagant, and perhaps not wholly sincere, proposals he found easy to resist, but when Nehru approached him early in 1948, 'with his rather engaging and shy smile', and urged him to stay as long as possible, he found it harder to say no. A few days later Rajagopalachari took up the charge and pleaded that, since Nehru had now lost his principal supporter and friend in Gandhi, it was more than ever important that Mountbatten should stay on to sustain him. Both for the sake of India and of his own naval career, Mountbatten was convinced that any extension of his mandate must be a short one. On the other hand, he was anxious not to rebuff his Indian friends altogether. The Constituent Assembly was due to finish its work some time in June; his birthday fell on 25 June; his eighty-four-year-old mother set great store by family anniversaries and he had promised to be home by that date if humanly possible. 21 June was put forward as the date for his departure and, with some reluctance, accepted by his Ministers.[23]

'Poor Dicky,' wrote Auchinleck sardonically, 'his job gets no easier and yet I see he has "allowed" himself to be "persuaded" to stay on till June. I wonder what is really in his mind?'[24] It is unnecessary to look farther than his conviction that he was performing a task of the first importance which nobody else could do as well. He was not indispensable, but he felt himself to be almost so; it was in part this apprehension of impending indispensability that led him to insist on quick retirement. In England word raced around that he was to stay on for many months, years perhaps. 'Those rumours about my staying on with my "lousy" Indians are not quite right,' he told Robert Neville, 'for I only agreed to extend my time from mid-April to 21 June. . . . I must say I take a dim view of your epithet; which is that frame of mind that really almost lost us India altogether!!!'[25]

It would have been unlike him if he had not sought to regulate the affairs of India before his departure. No issue was too important, no detail too trivial to escape his attention: from the identity of the next Governor-General – he thought that it should be Sardar Patel[26] – to the question of whether Government House should eschew alcohol under the new dispensation – pointing out that 'if they went dry when putting up distinguished foreigners, and when giving parties to the Corps Diplomatique, this would be regarded as very poor hospitality'.[27]

His political testament was enshrined in a document which he sent to Nehru, Patel and Rajagopalachari on 19 June 1948.[28] 'I am not for one moment expecting you to be guided by this memorandum,' he wrote with unconvincing modesty, 'for it would be gross conceit if I were to try and continue to influence the Government of India after my departure. On the other hand, I have done so much thinking about the future of India that I felt it would not be right not to put some of my thoughts down on paper before leaving.' Then followed a ragbag of recommendations, almost all of them sensible and practical, which in their mixture of the significant and the trivial, the strategic and the tactical, are wholly characteristic of their author.

*Cabinet Reconstruction.* Reshuffles were desirable at frequent intervals if ministers were not to grow stale and overworked. 'I think that every nine or twelve months or so the Prime Minister should consider whether changes would not be profitable.'

*Cabinet Ministers' Portfolios.* No one man should handle too many. 'I do, with all respect, suggest that it is asking too much of the Prime Minister to expect him to hold the Foreign Affairs portfolio as well.'

*Junior Ministerial Posts.* 'I have looked in vain for a younger generation who can eventually take the place of the present generation of political leaders.' Junior Ministers should be appointed with the specific intention of training them for high office.

*Ministerial Backing of Civil Servants.* Ministers must support their civil servants and defend them against public strictures.

*Appointment of Ambassadors and Governors.* These should sometimes at least be selected from the civil service. 'I do not think the importance of Ambassadors and Governors being chosen not only for their own qualities but also for those of their wives is yet fully appreciated in India.'

*Future of the Princes.* After the French Revolution the aristocracy turned against the Government and made no contribution to public life. The same would happen to the Princes unless they were made to feel that their services were required.

*Economic Policy.* 'The recent statement on the Government's economic policy has indicated an intention to move in the general direction of Socialism. I suggest that the timing of any such policy will require very careful handling; otherwise it will be a case of "more haste less speed".'

Nothing must be done to discourage foreign investment: 'Prospects in India are not so attractive that there are large corporations waiting anxiously for the opportunity to invest.' Private businessmen could not be allowed to exploit the people or establish monopolies but they should still be made to feel that the long-term prospects were sufficiently encouraging to induce them to plough back their profits. Nationalization should be taken slowly. The Government should study the example of Sweden 'where they have advanced very slowly towards socialism, and after 20 years are still in the process of achieving it, but in the most successful manner imaginable'.

*Holidays.* All ministers should be made to take them regularly.

*New Constitution.* Work on this should advance slowly. The present constitution could easily be amended, a new one might be taken as a sacred text and thus be unnecessarily rigid.

*Cost of Living.* 'I have been an ardent opponent of decontrol ever since I first heard the word mentioned.' Controls should carefully be examined to see which needed to be reinstituted.

*Press Conferences.* 'General Press Conferences about nothing in particular should be avoided. . . . My own experience has always been that to talk freely and frankly to press correspondents and give them the full story, prefacing of course certain parts of the conversation with the remark that "This is off the record", is the best method.'

*Official Secrets Act.* Secrecy about Cabinet matters appeared to be non-existent. The Act should be applied more strongly, the police called in to investigate its breach and offenders prosecuted.

*Corruption and Nepotism.* This was on the increase. 'The undue lowering of the standard of living among the higher wage groups . . . is likely to lead to a lowering of their normal standards' of probity.

*Air Conditioning.* If the Government was to function properly in Delhi this was essential not only in offices but also in the bedrooms of the more important Government servants.

*Oil.* Exploration should be pressed forward. 'To me it seems quite incredible that there should be oil to the north and west of India, and oil to the east of India, but no oil has been found in India apart from Assam.'

The list is as interesting for what was missing as for what was included. Another man would have written of the principles of democratic government, individual freedom, justice, the rule of law. This was not Mountbatten's way. Partly he said nothing because he took it for granted that the Indian leaders would continue to conduct themselves in a manner he would approve, but far more his silence reflected his indifference to abstract concepts. What interested Mountbatten was how things worked, the nuts and bolts of government, not the philosophical theories that underlay it. Air-conditioning and proper attention to the wives of Ambassadors were his prescription for a successful India; in so far as dogma was mentioned it was to be questioned and usually deplored.

His last reflections duly transmitted, it remained only to depart. This involved fêting, both popular and private, on a scale reminiscent of Independence Day itself. For the first time since an attempt had been made on Lord Hardinge's life in 1912, a Governor-General drove along the Chandni Chowk, the highway of old Delhi. Then Mountbatten progressed through dense and tumultuous crowds to the site of Gandhi's funeral pyre, where a quarter of a million Indians awaited him and a quarter of a million more sought admittance. Vast crowds are not unusual in Delhi, and an Indian crowd is easily moved to enthusiasm, but no European can ever have been acclaimed in such a manner.

So ended the nine months of Mountbatten's Governor-Generalship. They had not been without setbacks, and those who argued that he should never have taken on the task once it was evident that he would be Governor-General of India alone had something with which to support their case. He had lost the favour of the Pakistanis – been reviled, indeed, as the man who had robbed them of Kashmir and done all he could to ensure that India came better out of the division of the sub-continent's assets. He had lost favour at home too. At the end of his Viceroyalty he had been everyone's hero; in the carnage that followed, however, those who had initially deplored the grant of independence had been fortified in their convictions. Mountbatten was to return home to find that some abused him as an impetuous blunderer, a few even held him a traitor.

But he had won and was to retain the love of India. The affectionate farewell of the Delhi crowd was not lightly awarded to an Englishman, nor did its fervour fade. Mountbatten – or, rather, the Mountbattens, for she had become almost as much loved as he – were national heroes and would never be able to revisit the country without being welcomed accordingly. In his speech at the last of the banquets given in their honour, Nehru spoke for his people.

> You came here, Sir, with a high reputation, but many a reputation has foundered in India. You lived here through a period of great difficulty and crisis, and yet your reputation has not foundered. That is a remarkable feat.
>
> [Speaking of the reception they had enjoyed in Delhi that morning] I do not know how Lord and Lady Mountbatten felt on that occasion, but used as I am to these vast demonstrations here, I was much affected, and I wondered how it was that an Englishman and

Englishwoman could become so popular in India during this brief
period of time. . . . A period certainly of achievement and success in
some measure, but also a period of sorrow and disaster. . . .
Obviously this was not connected so much with what had happened,
but rather with the good faith, the friendship and the love of India
that these two possessed. . . . You may have many gifts and presents,
but there is nothing more real or precious than the love and affection
of the people. You have seen yourself, Sir and Madam, how that love
and affection work.

It is difficult for me or anyone to judge of what we have done
during the last year or so. We are too near to it and too intimately
connected with events. Maybe we have made many mistakes, you
and we. Historians a generation or two hence will perhaps be able to
judge what we have done right and what we have done wrong.
Nevertheless, whether we did right or wrong, the test, perhaps the
right test, is whether we tried to do right or did not. . . . I do believe
that we did try to do right, and I am convinced that you tried to do the
right thing by India, and therefore many of our sins will be forgiven
us and many of our errors also.[29]

# Part Four

## 1948 - 1965

# CHAPTER 38

## *Return to the Navy*

MOUNTBATTEN IN 1948 was among the most immediately impressive of living mortals. Still aged only forty-eight, his glamour, good looks, great wealth and royal blood were now crowned by an aura of success and worldwide fame. His effect on some women at least was dramatic. He kissed Barbara Cartland's cheek. 'A streak of fire ran through me as if I had been struck by lightning. It was a definitely painful yet ecstatic sensation. From a woman's point of view the power was devastating. From the moment Dickie fixed his eyes on her, spoke to her in that deep, amazingly attractive voice . . . she was his.'[1] Others less privileged than Mrs Cartland still found the impact of his personality almost overwhelming. He radiated ineffable self-confidence, invulnerable to the pin-pricks of lesser beings whose hostility was dismissed as founded on base, if natural, jealousy. Golden boy had become superman, and nothing seemed beyond his powers.

Beneath this formidable carapace things were different. Those who knew him best realized that his proud, sometimes arrogant awareness of his qualities hid a raw vulnerability. It was fostered by his wife. Since they had been reunited after the end of the campaign in South-East Asia she had proved a magnificent partner in his work but a termagant in his marriage. Physically and emotionally it had been a difficult period for her and she showed her distress by waging psychological warfare against her husband. Her jealousy was ferocious – of his office, his achievements, his women friends, his relationship with Patricia. She struck out fiercely and he reacted with bemused and injured affection. In June 1949 he wrote to her from his ship after a particularly fraught few days in Malta, in which a quarrel had been provoked by his blurting out the news of his promotion to Vice-Admiral with what seemed to his wife clumsy tactlessness.

> Although I did not do anything unkind intentionally I fear that my own misery made me a poor companion and a thoughtless one who must have caused you pain. Believe me, darling, I never never want to cause you any pain because I always have been and I always will be far too fond of you for that.

If I have avoided having talks with you I am sure it is the sub-conscious wish to avoid another scene which has hitherto followed my attempt to 'have things out'. . . . When we had that row in the boat yesterday . . . I became so violently unhappy that I really felt physically sick, and greedy as I usually am I could eat no lunch, and talkative as I usually am I could find nothing to say.

Let me begin by criticizing myself. I am terribly self-centred and rather conceited and full of the vainglory of uniforms and decorations. I am bad with women as a whole and of course particularly bad with you. . . . I believe that early failures caused me to despise myself – and to feel (perhaps without justification) that you shared this view of myself. . . .

. . . do please believe me when I say that the one thing I've always looked for is complete family love and friendship. That love and friendship can grow and become the most vital thing in the lives of the 4 of us provided we do not start trying to impose restrictions on one another or harbour unkind thoughts.

There had been discussion as to whether they should meet again in a few days in Cyprus. Mountbatten had felt a longer parting might be wiser.

But then the old, old miracle happened, you pressed my hand and caught my eye and gave me that divine smile which I like to think you give to no one else . . . and I kissed the back of your hair and the old heart fluttered in the same ridiculous way in which it has fluttered for 28 years, ever since I first met you . . . and I realised that if you came to Cyprus in that mood, my mood would meet you far more than half way and we could have a wonderfully happy time. . . . The real proof that you believe in me and do understand my position, my feelings and my love for you will be a cable saying that you have finally made up your mind to come and join me in Cyprus and that we'll never have another cross word and trust each other to have a freedom which can only exist when there are real bonds of affection.[2]

Edwina could nearly always be relied on to respond to an appeal of this kind. 'Affectionate thanks sweet letter,' read her cabled reply, 'so looking forward Cyprus fond love dear Vice Admiral.'[3] But no reconciliation could eliminate altogether her resentment at the close affection between her husband and her elder daughter.

What I should do without Patricia I can't think [he told his mother]; she has been the best and truest friend any father could ever wish for. It is fun finding a child grow up and feel that they resemble oneself so closely, except that, luckily for her, she has a much nicer character than me. If I had had such a nice character and friendly disposition I should never have been a Supreme Commander or a Viceroy.[4]

Their relationship had to be conducted in strict conspiracy. Patricia would address her regular letters to her mother and send separate letters to her father in his ship. 'Don't thank me too much for letters,' he told her, 'as Mummy doesn't know how often or how long I write.'[5] But, deep though his affection was, it remained unblemished by jealousy. When the news came that Patricia was to have a second baby, Mountbatten rejoiced, even though it deprived him of a visit from her. 'As I am just about as self-centred as John [Brabourne] and probably even more successful in making other interests revolve round my own, I am constantly surprised to find that your interests always come first when they are in conflict with mine.'[6] The greatest stroke of good fortune that Mountbatten enjoyed was that Patricia married a man whom he liked immensely, respected, and came to consider almost as the son he had never had. Though doubtful of the wisdom of Lord Brabourne's decision to enter the world of the cinema, he supported it vigorously and got as much pleasure out of his success as did either his son-in-law or his daughter. He wrote to offer his opinions when Brabourne was still hesitating over his choice of a career.

> You alone must make up your mind what you want to do. I strongly recommend you to adopt the old 'Staff College' procedure which I invariably adopt on all my problems official or private.
>
> First make up your mind what your OBJECT is . . . then put down the possible courses which achieve the object. Usually only one course will *really* achieve it, but if there are more than one then put them all down.
>
> I do not know what you will put down as your object. If you were certain of financial security it might be 'Public Service' or 'Political Fame' or 'To follow in your father's footsteps'. But can you be sure of economic security? [If Britain faltered economically he might have only his personal ability to depend on, in which case] your object would be 'To ensure your ability to provide for wife and family by your own work and without private means.' [If he used the private means he now enjoyed to make himself able to earn money, he would also be equipping himself] to fill any job – either in politics or as a governor – in fact to be a leader.
>
> Think it over John, and talk it over with Patricia and then make up your own mind and stick to it. I'll support you whatever your decision for I have unbounded faith in you.[7]

Mountbatten's own 'object' was a subject for discussion for many people. When he returned from India he was at the peak of his powers. His energy and forcefulness were unimpaired but they had been bridled by the disciplines of taxing diplomacy. He was never to lose his impetuousness or his dynamism, but in 1948 these dangerous qualities were better controlled than at any other moment. Those who divined the grandeur of his ambitions yet did not know him well wondered what new fields there could be for him to conquer. Politics seemed hardly his forte. Massive wealth was his for the taking, but he had enough of it already and would never have been content with a career in business. Governor-Generalships he had already rejected. To administer the disintegration of what was left of the Empire would have been a mean task for the liberator of India. Minister of Defence? Ambassador in Washington? Such speculation was far wide of the mark. Mountbatten was as resolved as ever to return to the Navy. 'I feel that your decision to go to sea is not only becoming and natural to you,' wrote Churchill, 'but also in harmony with what is due to your great position – hereditary and self-made.'[8] Mountbatten's 'object' was simple – it was to succeed his father as First Sea Lord. Only one course would achieve that end – his return to the Navy. The time had come for Attlee to honour his promise and set him back in his proper place in the naval hierarchy.

'Reported to Naval Secretary, First Lord and First Sea Lord and said I wished only to go where they wished to send me.' Mountbatten's diary entry for 25 June 1948 does less than justice to the attention he had devoted to his future over the previous three months. The Duke of Edinburgh rang the first alarm-bell when he wrote on 10 April to report a conversation he had had with the First Sea Lord, John Cunningham, who had succeeded his namesake Andrew in 1946. Cunningham was concerned to know whether Mountbatten 'could resist the pressure to take on some other political job long enough to make it worth his while giving away one of the plum junior flag jobs'. Reassured on this, he was still uncertain whether the right posting would be as Commander-in-Chief in the West Indies or C.S.1. (Commander of the First Cruiser Squadron) in the Mediterranean.[9]

This letter galvanized Mountbatten into frenetic activity. 'Your stream of letters has been pouring in and unless I do something I see no prospect of stemming the flood,' wrote his nephew despairingly two months later.[10] All the regular advisers were called in for consultation. The Cruiser Squadron was more relevant from the point of view of his future naval career but, Mountbatten told Ismay, 'John Cunningham is second only to Andrew Cunningham in his desire to do me down'. In the Mediterranean Fleet 'there were enough tireless busybodies about to cause mischief . . . the one way my enemies could wreck my career would be to create trouble between the Senior Flag Officers and myself'.[11] An independent command in the West Indies, on the other hand, carried no such risk but was considered by some to be a dead-end job, disqualifying its holder from further promotion. The King was for the Mediterranean, where 'the Fleet is a going concern';[12] Edwina was not so much for the West Indies as against a return to Malta.[13] Brockman and Goodenough were for the West Indies,[14] Ismay for the Mediterranean. The latter put the anguished debate in perspective when he commented '. . . my final advice is that you should do whatever you yourself think best, both on public as well as private grounds. I have not the slightest doubt that you will be First Sea Lord, whichever course you take.'[15]

In the end John Cunningham ruled that Mountbatten was to take over the First Cruiser Squadron. The Mediterranean Fleet in 1948 was one of the most powerful naval forces afloat, and the Cruiser Squadron was the only permanent unit in the Royal Navy containing four large ships. The job therefore was of considerable importance, but insignificant compared with the awe-inspiring responsibilities of Viceroy or Supreme Commander. Mountbatten was not even Second-in-Command of the Fleet, being junior to Vice-Admiral Douglas-Pennant as well as the Commander-in-Chief. In the order of precedence in Malta he was ranked thirteenth. The transition must have been a tricky, if not a painful, one but both Mountbattens accomplished it with signal grace. 'I am desperately anxious to avoid publicity as far as possible once I get to Malta,' Mountbatten told his old friend Mabel Strickland, proprietor of the *Times of Malta*.[16] At all costs he was determined to play an inconspicuous role. Indeed, he made a virtue of necessity, welcoming the appointment, as he told Peter Murphy, because it would mean that he would 'get his backside kicked by senior naval officers. . . . He felt he was becoming impossible and needed this. And the funny thing is that I am sure he meant it.'[17] He asked his old friend Geoffrey Norman, then Chief of Staff, to let him know at once if he began to throw his weight around; above all, 'Please stop me if I start to cross the bows of the Commander-in-Chief.'[18]

He was fortunate that the Commander-in-Chief was Arthur John Power, who had served under him in South-East Asia and was notably well disposed: 'embarrassingly kind and thoughtful', Mountbatten called him.[19] He was apt to address Mountbatten as 'sir', in absent-minded recollection of SEAC; Mountbatten punctiliously 'sirred' him back; and when the Duke of Edinburgh joined the Fleet all three men could be observed 'sirring' and deferring to each other with great éclat. Power had recently married a shy and asthmatic girl who was decidedly unsure of herself in her new grandeur. Edwina warmed to her, took endless pains to support and encourage her, and contrived to push her always into the leading role without seeming either patronizing or obsequious.

The Mountbattens' determination to remain unobtrusive was helped by the fact that they were far poorer than they had been when last in Malta. Income tax was still nineteen shillings and sixpence in the pound, and Edwina's pre-war income of £45,000 after tax was now only a tenth of that amount. 'We are hopelessly overdrawn and mortgaged,' Mountbatten told Edwina's cousin Felix Cassel. Their commitments made it inevitable that they should live on an expensive scale. 'My Private Secretary has estimated that Edwina and I between us would need a minimum of two high-class secretaries and two or three stenographers to compete with the public side of our lives, quite apart from what I do in the Navy.' Edwina's money was mainly tied up in a family trust and Monckton had advised them that the Government might be prepared to give facilities for a Private Bill to break the trust 'provided that it could be shown to be sufficiently in the public interest for the matter to be raised in this form'.[20] To Stafford Cripps Mountbatten remarked that the only alternative was for Edwina and him to divorce and live in sin. 'Stafford said that the Government would go to great lengths to avoid our having to take such a step; so that is always a threat to hold over them.'[21]

A full-blooded campaign was now launched, Cripps and Attlee enlisted, the King asked to lend his support on the grounds that Mountbatten had taken over many of the representational duties of the Duke of Kent.[22] A Personal Bill was introduced and passed by the House of Lords, but Tory opposition was threatened and a Bill which would apply to anyone finding herself in Edwina's position – the Married Woman (Restraint upon Anticipation) Bill – was introduced in its stead. The Mountbatten case, said Oliver Stanley, was 'the least deserving of the cases which are going to come up under this procedure'. Forty-seven Tories voted against the Bill. The opposition had nothing to do with the merits of the case, said Woodrow Wyatt in the House of Commons, but was 'based entirely upon personal, political animosity against a member of another place who was a very fine Viceroy but who happened to carry through a policy in which he believed and in which Hon. Gentlemen on the other side did not believe. This is the way in which they are attempting to pay him out.'[23]

The debate was a disturbing reminder to Mountbatten of the ill will he had earned himself. There were other such testimonials, typical of which was the Christmas message from Lieutenant-Colonel Liddell of Pitlochry, wishing that: 'Admiral Lord Mountbatten of Burma (and Chaos) may be reminded of the unsavoury and disgusting part he played in India in diminishing British influence and Imperial preference.' Lord Beaverbrook was hardly more temperate, and through his newspapers was capable of doing greater damage.

'I regard Mountbatten as the biggest menace to the Empire,' he told Tom Driberg. 'He has perpetrated one outrage after another. He was responsible for the present position in Burma. His conduct in Malaya is indefensible. He damaged the Dutch suzerainity in Indonesia, thus weakening the whole Middle East [*sic*] structure.' As for India, he had handed it over to a group of incompetents and was responsible for the terrible massacres. 'He should never be given power or authority.'[24]

Power and authority were just what the Labour Ministers seemed anxious to give him. In February 1949 Jowitt, the Lord Chancellor, came to Malta and invited him to join the Government as Minister of Defence as soon as his term with the Cruiser Squadron was over.[25] Mountbatten refused the offer without hesitation. He had no intention of destroying his cherished career for a sojourn in a job that would certainly be temporary and probably unpleasant into the bargain. Anyway, he was enjoying his new life far too well to wish to leave it. Any initial awkwardness quickly wore off, the 'tireless busybodies' out to wreck his career proved to be vain chimeras, the Navy had welcomed him back and he rejoiced in their welcome. 'I can't tell you how much fun it is being back again,' he told Neville.[26] Brockman thought that the history of Mountbatten and the First Cruiser Squadron could be summed up in a few words: 'a wonderful holiday after nine years flat out'.[27] It was more than that, yet the holiday element was never far away.

He took again to polo with an ardour quickened by his long abstinence. 'Can you influence Dallas to try and pick Marine officers for the Mediterranean Fleet who are potential polo players?' he asked Robert Neville. 'Of course any such move must be kept very secret.'[28] But a new passion entered his life which almost supplanted polo. Underwater swimming or, better still, fishing was his new interest. A strong swimmer with excellent lungs, courage and endless curiosity, he was well equipped to explore the exotic world of submarine life. After months of practice he could dive and hit a fish with a harpoon-gun at a range of twenty feet. He was immediately preoccupied with the need to shoot more and bigger fish than anybody had done before. He often succeeded.

Their comparative poverty did not involve noticeable discomfort. Their house in Malta cost only £600 a year but to staff it they had three cooks, six stewards, the coxswain and two Marine drivers, a valet, a butler, a house-keeper, two housemaids and two charwomen – nineteen in all, 'and yet we are not too grossly overstaffed', Mountbatten told Edwina. 'I fear you think I'm very spoilt wanting a valet and I do admit I am, but if one is working hard it does help if there is a second man in the house who can look after my clothes.'[29] They settled in the Villa Guardamangia, across the road from their old Casa Medina, after a long stint in the Hotel Phoenicia while their house was being refurbished, an air-raid shelter blown up, statues and summer-houses removed from the garden, and bougainvillaea trained to grow around a six-feet-high statue of Mercury wearing a bowler hat which defied the attentions of the demolition men.[30]

One suggestion for Mountbatten's future had been that he should be put in charge of a group of ships and sent around the world as an itinerant ambassador. Though his world was that of the Mediterranean, his work with the Cruiser Squadron was not wholly incompatible with this proposal. Mountbatten adored the foreign tours, loving the excitement and colour and relishing the consequence which he eschewed in Malta. 'I suppose I oughtn't to get a kick out of being treated like a Viceroy/Supreme Commander when my position is now that of the junior admiral in the fleet,' he told Patricia, 'but I'd have been less than human if I hadn't been affected by the treatment I received at Trieste.'[31]

When the Squadron visited Navarino, it was a family affair. The King and Queen of Greece came to dinner aboard and Queen Frederica made Mount-batten an apple-pie bed. 'Am anxious to know how you slept last night please?' was the cable that arrived next day. 'Very well,' came the reply. 'My faithful steward having no confidence in Queens searched my bunk success-fully before I turned in.' 'I don't believe it,' retorted the Queen indignantly, but she underestimated the conscientiousness of Mountbatten's steward.[32] Six months later Mountbatten had his revenge when staying with the Greek royal family. 'Put packet of brown sugar in Freddy's bed,' read his diary. But such jollities were only frills on the political purpose that could be served by naval visits. In January 1949 Mountbatten was staying with the King of Greece when the Government fell. The King was attracted by the possibility of installing a strong right-wing Government under Field Marshal Papagos, and Mountbatten was asked by the British Ambassador to preach the cause of democracy. This he willingly did. Whether his words made any difference cannot be proved, but Papagos was still out of office when Mountbatten came back to the country a year later.

His visit to Beirut caused less controversy. '. . . without equal in the three years I have been here,' the British Minister reported. '. . . the exploits of Admiral Mountbatten during the War, the outstanding part he has played in the history of our times, as well of course the fact that he is a member of the Royal Family, made of this visit an occasion of especial and signal signi-ficance. It has been said in some Lebanese quarters that this visit was worth twelve months work by the Information Section.'[33] The President of the Lebanon so took to his visitor that he pressed him to accept a fine Arab stallion as a present. Mountbatten asked if he could treat the President as a friend. The President was gratified. 'Then I claim the privilege of a friend in refusing the gift.' 'But I hoped every day you rode it you would think of me!' 'I would only ride it once a week and I want to think of you every day. Give me a photograph of the horse and I will hang it in my cabin.' The President gave way. 'Game, set and match to Daddy!' Mountbatten reported triumphantly to Patricia.[34]

At Tripoli Mountbatten was taken by the British Administrator to lunch with the Grand Qadi and the Mufti.

'We are deeply honoured', they said, 'that Britain should have sent her greatest man, next only to the King, to Tripoli at this moment, for you alone can solve our difficulties.'

'I am only here as a simple sailor with my squadron.'

'But you liberated four hundred million people in India. Think what a relatively small and easy task it would be for you to give only one million of us Arabs your freedom.'

'I am back in the Navy and . . . cannot possibly help you.'

'We can nevertheless hope that having come here you will not overlook our problems and will arrange a speedy settlement.'

'I repeat, it has nothing to do with me. My visit is purely naval.'

'Will you at least permit us to regard your visit as a fortunate omen for the Arabs?'

'You can regard it as any damned thing you please, it won't make any difference!'

The Administrator remarked afterwards that, as the British Government was almost certain to give the Arabs what they wanted, Mountbatten would get the credit and be hailed as a national hero.[35]

The Duke of Edinburgh joined the Mediterranean Fleet in October 1949, and for the first month lived with his uncle and aunt at the Villa Guardamangia. It gave Mountbatten great pleasure to have him there, yet to begin with the relationship was an uneasy one. Prince Philip was 'very busy showing his independence', and sometimes did so with some brusqueness. Neither uncle nor nephew was the most emollient of men and clashes were frequent. 'The trouble about not having a real son of one's own but only a couple of nephews and a son-in-law is that however much one may like them they will never feel the same way about the older generation if one isn't their real father, not that I blame them tho' it makes me feel a bit sad at times.' Perhaps his eldest grandson, Norton, would fill the gap, he suggested rather wistfully to Patricia.[36] A few weeks later he felt more cheerful. A *modus vivendi* seemed to have been established. 'Philip is right back on 1946 terms with us and we've had a heart-to-heart in which he admitted he was fighting shy of coming under my dominating influence and patronage!'[37] That problem having been aired and regulated, the two men found each other excellent company and co-existed harmoniously.

Towards the end of November Princess Elizabeth arrived to join her husband. After a few days with the Governor at his official residence she moved into the Mountbattens' house, where she and Prince Philip were to live for a month while their own home was being got ready. For Mountbatten, familiarity with royalty not only did not breed contempt but enhanced its splendour. He never ceased to delight in his intimacy with the British royal family or to boast about it with almost childlike naivety; it was a standing joke in Whitehall that he could never leave a meeting without murmuring that he was expected at the Palace. To have the heir to the throne staying in his house would have been a pleasure in any case; it was an added satisfaction that he found he liked her enormously as a person. 'I don't think I need tell you how fond I've become of her,' he told Patricia; and then again: 'Lilibet is quite enchanting and I've lost whatever of my heart is left to spare entirely to her. She dances quite divinely and always wants a Samba when we dance together and has said some very nice remarks about my dancing.'[38] And yet he was never quite certain that his affection was reciprocated. Prince Philip had told him that 'she used NOT to like me' and the thought lingered to torment him. Patricia was commissioned to find out tactfully whether Princess Elizabeth really liked him or not – a task that might have taxed her ingenuity if she had addressed herself to it. In fact Mountbatten must have known well that the future Queen enjoyed his company, but he craved to be told so by somebody else.

21 April was Princess Elizabeth's birthday. Peter Howes, Mountbatten's Flag Captain, organized a group of young officers into an impromptu choir. At 8.45 a.m. the Princess's telephone rang. When she answered, she heard a spirited rendering of 'Happy Birthday to You' accompanied by some of the band of the *Liverpool*. 'Lilibet was wildly excited and kept saying, "Oh! Thank you, thank you! That was sweet but who are you?" ' The response was the second verse harmonized by the officers' Glee Club, and then a refrain on the bagpipes. Mountbatten interrogated Howes suspiciously as to who could have dared behave so cheekily, then decided that it had been a great success and claimed the credit for himself. Her maid, who had been in the room at the time, 'told me Lilibet first went white, then quite red, and ended up with tears in her eyes. . . . I think she's so sweet and attractive. At times I think she likes me too, though she is far too reserved to give any indication.'[39]

*

For Mountbatten, though, it was his success in command of the Cruiser Squadron that would make or mar his time with the Mediterranean Fleet.

The 'enemies' whom Mountbatten believed were out to wreck his career may have been phantasmagoria, but there were plenty of naval officers who would have rejoiced to see him make a fool of himself. He approached his junior officers in a mood of uncharacteristic humility, admitting freely that his knowledge of equipment and tactics was out of date and welcoming help and correction. But he soon showed that his appetite for work was undiminished, he learned rapidly, and it was only a matter of weeks before he was laying down the law with his usual vigour.

His officers had viewed his arrival with some apprehension. His predecessor, Rear-Admiral Symonds Taylor, had been relatively easy-going. From the moment Mountbatten took over it was clear that he intended to get things done, and to get them done quickly. He inspected his own somewhat cramped quarters, expressed himself well satisfied, but complained that there was not enough light and air. 'Clear those blanked-off scuttles!' The Executive Officer of *Newcastle*, Edward Blundell, said that they had been trying to get this done for over a year. At the other end of the ship a hundred ratings were crowded into accommodation little more spacious than that enjoyed by the Admiral – yet their scuttles were blanked-off as well. Mountbatten inspected the mess-decks and ruled that their scuttles must be given priority. 'Then you'll leave your cabin?' 'Certainly not! Get the mess-decks done and have mine done at the same time.' The work was in hand within three days.[40]

He had expected to be 'rusty and out of touch', he told Patricia seven weeks after he took up his command, but he found that the Squadron was composed of very young men, average age under twenty-one, and that they were learning the job together. He had been to sea every week and had already flown his flag in every ship in the Squadron. He had entertained over a hundred of his officers individually, 'but have another 110 names to learn as soon as I can'. Everyone was enthusiastic and eager to raise the standard of efficiency. 'I could not love this job more and had almost forgotten what fun life at sea is.'[41]

Mountbatten's interests ranged beyond the Mediterranean. 'What do you think about Flying Saucers?' he asked Patricia. He had been discussing the phenomenon with Peter Murphy. They were

> both convinced that they come from another planet but we mutually and independently came to the conclusion that they were not 'aeroplanes' with silly little almost human pilots but are themselves the actual inhabitants: Martians, Venusians, Jupiterians or what have you. Why should life in another planet with entirely different

conditions in any way resemble life on our planet? Their inhabitants
might be 'gaseous' or circular or very large. They certainly don't
breathe, they may not have to eat and I doubt if they have babies –
bits of their great discs may break away and grow into a new
creature. The fact that they can hover and accelerate away from the
earth's gravity again and even revolve round a V2 in America (as
reported by their head scientist) shows they are far ahead of us. If
they really come over in a big way that may settle the capitalist-
communist war. If the human race wishes to survive they may have to
band together.[42]

His interest in the subject was so keen that he tried to persuade the editor
of the *Sunday Dispatch* to put a team on to sifting the reported cases and
pursuing the more promising. He again put forward his theory that the
mysterious objects not merely came from outer space but were the inhabitants
rather than their flying-machines. 'I know this sounds ridiculous,' he added
apologetically, 'and I am relying on you . . . not to make any capital out of the
fact that I have put forward such a far-fetched explanation.'[43] For a year or
two his interest flagged, then it was revived when a bricklayer working at
Broadlands justified his late arrival at work by reporting a sighting of a flying
saucer in the park between the house and the town of Romsey. By 1957 he
had been put off by the amount of arrant nonsense published on the subject,
and refused an offer to see the reports of a more ardent student of the subject:
'I must be honest and confess that I no longer take the same interest.'[44] He
never rejected the possibility that the objects existed, however, merely
insisted that if they did they must be susceptible of rational explanation. Few
senior naval officers would have been ready to confront the paranormal with
such equanimity.

He showed the same flexibility of mind in his professional life. In the
manoeuvres of March 1949 Power put him in charge of the Mediterranean
Fleet. His task was to pass through the Strait of Gibraltar against the
opposition of the larger Home Fleet under Vice-Admiral Guy Russell. The
Fleet was spotted by 'enemy' aircraft when still a hundred miles out to sea and
his chances seemed slight. His force approached in two parts, each hugging
the coast and uniting a few miles from Gibraltar. They attempted to infiltrate
the Straits by night, some ships darkened, others burning merchant navigation lights. Success was not total, but greater than had seemed likely
twenty-four hours before.

As they were approaching Gibraltar on the outward journey, Mountbatten called for Charles Cox, the ship's Warrant Telegraphist. 'Good-morning,
Cox,' said the Admiral. 'I've sent for you because I want to break your arm.'

Heavily bandaged, Cox was put ashore with a radio-transmitter concealed in the boot of Mountbatten's car. Not only did he report the movements of the enemy fleet, he even penetrated their headquarters and took notes of their plans. It seems unlikely that his activities made any serious contribution to the outcome of the manoeuvres, but they caused a furore when Mountbatten revealed them at the subsequent post-mortem. The Flag Officer, Gibraltar, said haughtily that in wartime such a ploy would quickly be detected. Mountbatten retorted that the exercise was intended to test readiness for war; 'when he played war, he played with no holds barred'.[45] Next year Charles Lambe reported that the Home Fleet was in such a pother about Mountbatten's activities that a wholly innocent passenger had been refused permission to land in Gibraltar on suspicion of being a spy.

Only in the handling of the ships of his squadron did anyone criticize his performance. Once on a night exercise he gave the order 'Train torpedo tubes to port,' and then circled the Squadron so that all the tubes were pointing in and his ships would have sent themselves to the bottom if they had been fired. A junior officer blurted out: 'The man's mad!' His Captain rebuked the insubordination but privately agreed.[46] The story is reminiscent of the charges levelled at Mountbatten over his handling of the 5th Destroyer Flotilla during the war. They were evidently not taken seriously on high: in June 1949 he was promoted to Vice-Admiral, and in April 1950 followed in his father's footsteps to become Second-in-Command of the Mediterranean Fleet. 'I shall get another £1 a day table money,' he told his mother, '– as this is tax free it is the equivalent to a gross increase of £40 a day.'[47] Nor did Admiral Power express any doubts in his final report.

> Vice-Admiral Mountbatten is most versatile and remarkable in ability and energy alike. He is not a law unto himself as some suppose, but as great a subordinate as he is a leader. Ambitious and perhaps impetuous, but not rash.
>
> The manner in which he has served this fleet . . . after years of unequalled responsibilities . . . has earned everyone's admiration. Ordinary men may climb up with distinction – only extraordinary men can climb down without some loss of distinction – he has achieved the latter.
>
> A tremendous asset to the service to which he is devoted.[48]

Mountbatten would not have contested these conclusions. 'I have, I believe, transformed my Squadron in a quiet way to an utterly different standard to last year,' he told his son-in-law in September 1949.[49] But he had no illusions about the effectiveness of the force he commanded. Two weeks before he wrote this letter he told a friend in the Admiralty that he proposed to draft a report which would set out 'why I regard the modern Cruiser Squadron as so much less efficient and ready for battle than a 1938 Cruiser Squadron'.[50] The report proved to be a sharp indictment of what he described to Patricia as 'the ineptitude of this incompetent but well-meaning Government'. The Conservatives, he felt, would be much more competent but much less well-meaning. 'I wonder which form of Government is the worst. I believe my benevolent autocracy in South East Asia was the best.'[51] But neither Conservatives nor Socialists, he was certain, would be prepared to find sufficient money to put right the weaknesses of which he complained. The Navy would have to put its own house in order.

The apparent efficiency of the Cruiser Squadron, he claimed, was misleading, first because there was undermanning and a chronic shortage of trained personnel, second because much of the equipment was obsolescent if not obsolete. The damage could be mitigated if a more sensible policy were adopted over the frequent changing of personnel between ships and stations. This, however, would not affect the basic problem. 'In the Navy today,' wrote Mountbatten, 'we are trying to do too much with too little' and 'we are developing a Navy which we cannot afford to maintain and which is out of harmony with the requirements of a future war'.[52] It was the same approach as he had advocated for his son-in-law: first define your object, then decide how it was to be achieved. His report was written as Flag Officer Commanding First Cruiser Squadron and addressed to the Commander-in-Chief, but it read like the reflections of a future First Sea Lord. He must have been reasonably confident that in a few years' time it would fall to him to solve the problems which he was now propounding.

He left Malta in May 1950 in the happy certainty that he belonged once more to the Royal Navy. He was sped on his way with the usual festivities, but the farewell which pleased him most came on the polo field. Almost on his last day his team won the Spencer Cup in a thrilling replay. Mountbatten presented the trophy. Then, to his astonishment, thirty-two players dashed out, mounted ponies at the far end of the ground and formed themselves into an escort around Prince Philip's little open car.

> The General was the Commander of the Escort on the left of the car (and saluted with his polo stick like a sword) and Philip was the adjutant on the right. We all thought it was for Lilibet and tried to make her get in, but she had been in the secret for a week and knew it was for us and refused, saying, 'I'm always *in* these processions. This time I'm determined to be outside it and take a film of it.'
>
> So Mummy, Pammy and I got in and to the familiar command of 'Escort Walk-March' the cavalcade moved off. All the spectators in

the polo pavilion stood up and cheered wildly. Then came the order 'Escort Trot' and we moved off at a smart trot till we came to the end of the ground where they formed in two lines and gave us three cheers. Then they rode back, charged across the ground and gave three cheers for Lilibet. We were all *thrilled*.[53]

The logical next step in Mountbatten's career was a seat on the Board of Admiralty. There were five Sea Lords: the First being the professional head of the Navy, the Second in charge of personnel, the Third of the design and building of ships, the Fourth of stores and pay, the Fifth of the naval air service. Mountbatten had set his heart on personnel and was disconcerted when Lord Hall, First Lord of the Admiralty, invited him to join the Board as Fourth Sea Lord.[54] This was certainly the least glamorous of the five functions; whether it was also the least desirable is a matter of opinion: to Hughes Hallett it seemed a perfectly acceptable stepping-stone to higher office; to Admiral Grantham it was probably the least important and certainly the least interesting job on the Board. Mountbatten inclined to the second view. 'I said I served where I was sent and thanked him,' he told Patricia after his interview with Hall, but his chagrin must have been evident. 'What can one do to help the country in looking after Stores, clothes and oil fuel? And Pay would only help if one had a free hand! Either they mean to break me and finish me this time or else they think that because I'm 49 and all other Vice-Admirals are more like 56, that I'm so young I can wait.'[55]

Admiral Power protested robustly to the First Sea Lord about what he felt was a misuse of Mountbatten's talents. The reply was that there was an important job to be done in a field that had been neglected since the war.[56] Mountbatten was unconvinced but acquiescent. 'Well, having blown off steam,' he wrote to his daughter, 'let me tell you that if I am sent as 4th Sea Lord I should go very humbly and loyally and do my best. I accepted to go back and take my chance at carving out a naval career and I have such ludicrous self-confidence that I still think I can and will get to First Sea Lord.' She might discuss the matter with the Duke of Edinburgh, 'but I do NOT want him to get the King to interfere at any price. I must stand on my own two legs.'[57] Patricia returned from abroad a few weeks after her father started work, and said that she hoped the job was not proving too bad. She was not altogether surprised when he looked incredulous: of course it was not too bad, it was fascinating, engrossing, one of the best jobs he had ever had. She must have completely misunderstood his letters.

He took up his office in June 1950 and was shocked by what he found. One hundred and fifty thousand reservists were supposed to be available for

instant mobilization, yet there were only uniforms and kit for 40,000. There
was insufficient mine-sweeping gear even for the existing fleet of mine-
sweepers. There was no reserve of stores, nor any plan to build one up.
Mountbatten contemplated presenting the First Sea Lord with a demand for a
guarantee of sufficient funds to enable him to put his department in order, but
hesitated to say that he would abandon the job if such a guarantee was not
forthcoming. '. . . because what happens then?' he asked Lambe. 'Presumably I am slung out, or alternatively have to resign. . . . Then . . . the fat will be
in the fire, because I could hardly give up my life's career without taking
advantage of a seat in the House of Lords to say exactly what I think about
Naval policy.'[58]

In the end he settled for a policy of gradualism, little by little building up
what he considered the essential minimum of stores and disposing of the
mountains of obsolete equipment which were mouldering in warehouses
around the country. He began work in mid June, took over officially in mid
July, and by the latter date had already visited the depots at Bath, Deptford,
Portsmouth, Rosyth and Rigley. He had visited every office in the Victualling
and Stores Department, including the typing pools. Within another month or
two he had started an enquiry into mechanical accounting, a pre-computer
foray which eventually foundered because it was thought it would make too
many people redundant. His former staff officer from Kandy, Michael
Goodenough, had already formulated plans for streamlining the organization. It was perhaps hardly surprising that, as Mountbatten told Lambe,
'everybody in the Admiralty seems to think that my arrival is bound to produce some terrific stir, and that I am going to do something fairly drastic'. On
the contrary; 'The very last thing I want to do is to create any sort of stir.'[59]

On the whole he managed to accomplish this somewhat uncharacteristic
ambition, but on the question of pay he was forced to play a leading role.
There had been no pay review for any of the Services since just after the war
and Mountbatten found himself negotiating an increase with the Treasury.
The crucial meeting came in August, when he confronted Gaitskell, then
Minister of State at the Treasury, and Shinwell, the Minister of Defence.
Shinwell was sympathetic about the pay for ratings but took the line that the
officers had enough already. Mountbatten retorted that few officers now had
private means and that the Government must be prepared to pay them
enough to live in reasonable comfort. He got his way – 'Victory over Pay!' he
noted triumphantly in his diary – and never forgave Shinwell: 'he is the lowest
form of Labour life and a poor operator', he remarked ten years later.[60]
Shinwell's own recollection of events is, not surprisingly, different. He can
remember no confrontation with Mountbatten over pay – 'Ministers of
Defence don't usually meet those at the bottom level' – and takes full credit

for all the increases that were forced from a reluctant Treasury.[61] Whatever the truth, the problems of pay certainly preoccupied Mountbatten. He maintained that pay should be reconsidered every two years, and was dismayed to find when he returned to the Admiralty in 1955 that there had been no review since the one in which he had participated. He got one under way within a few months.

'As 4th Sea Lord I have such an unimportant job that no one could possibly feel jealous or think I was trying to throw my weight about.'[62] Mountbatten was genuinely anxious to play a humble role, knowing that nothing would do more to harm his prospects of becoming First Sea Lord than a show of conceit or arrogance. Shortly after McGrigor succeeded as First Sea Lord in 1952 he had some cause to rebuke Mountbatten, which he did with gusto. Mountbatten professed himself delighted, 'the best thing that had happened to him in years'.[63] At Board meetings he would lie low and speak only when his own subjects came up. But his restraint was not invariable. Once he wanted approval for a change in the uniform. The Board expressed some doubts and asked him to report back the following week with further details. When the meeting resumed after lunch, however, Mountbatten asked leave to raise the matter again. He had cleared up the details and, furthermore, had lunched with the King. By a remarkable coincidence George VI had raised the very point which was being debated and had said how anxious he was to see the change in the uniform implemented as soon as possible. In view of this. . . .[64] However decorously or demurely Mountbatten might behave, his colleagues were left with the impression that he had a large number of trumps up his sleeve, which he would play only with reluctance but which were always available in case of need.

His readiness to stray beyond his appointed field was illustrated in the furore over Persian oil. A radical Government inspired by Dr Mossadeq in March 1951 threatened to nationalize the Anglo-Iranian Oil Company (A.I.O.C.), which was not only British property but also a principal source of Britain's oil. As Fourth Sea Lord Mountbatten was responsible for naval fuel, but the role he gave himself was much more extensive than that of a mere technician. On 29 March, without any reference to the First Sea Lord, who was not told of his colleague's activities for another three months, he sent Lord Hall a note stressing that the nation's oil supply was in danger. The present policy of emitting vague economic or military threats could only make things worse. 'I suggested that it would be better to appear to go along with the strong nationalistic feelings in Persia, but to divert them to an acceptable course for us.'[65]

When Hall sent for Mountbatten two days later, the Fourth Sea Lord made the same points still more forcibly. Economic pressure, even if it worked, would only drive Mossadeq into the hands of the Communists. Military action would be denounced as aggression in the United Nations and would give Russia an excuse to intervene in north Persia. Britain must not allow itself to be blinded by considerations of prestige but should be prepared to negotiate with the Persians and try not to reverse history but to secure better terms. A diplomatic initiative, if it came quickly, could still change the course of events.

Hall, much struck by these arguments, suggested that Mountbatten should go to Teheran to negotiate with the Persians. Mountbatten was less than enthusiastic about this idea, but agreed to call on Herbert Morrison, the notoriously bellicose Foreign Secretary, to present what Hall agreed should be the Admiralty point of view. The meeting took place on 2 April. Only Mountbatten's record of the conversation exists but it seems that Morrison opened by hoping that the Admiralty were going to propose sending a fleet to the Persian Gulf to cow these insolent natives. When Mountbatten explained how disastrous he felt any such escapade would be, Morrison retorted:

'Oh! All you Admirals and Generals are the same. You are all pacifists. Why don't you want to fight?'

'Because I have children and grandchildren whom I would like to see survive.'

'I don't believe in all that rot about modern scientific inventions wiping out the whole of the human race!'

'I never suggested that the whole human race would be wiped out. Personally I think it is only the inhabitants of the British Isles who will buy it in the next war, as we shall be the main target whatever happens.'

After this exchange Morrison simmered down and carefully noted the main heads of Mountbatten's argument: 'accept nationalisation', 'negotiation'. . . . 'He was very pleasant and receptive, but had to have things explained to him several times. . . . Particularly he did not seem to realise that there was any need for urgency.' Morrison eventually agreed to the setting up of a small committee on which Mountbatten was asked to serve, but did not take the opportunity to send a Minister to Teheran while Persian attitudes were relatively flexible.[66] Mountbatten was still pleading for such a mission towards the end of April – 'I feel that immediate and really strong pressure on the Foreign Office might still retrieve the situation.'[67] – but Hall was not the man to fight the issue in Cabinet and did no more than forward this latest memorandum to the Foreign Secretary.

Mountbatten now cast around for a new initiative, and on 1 June suggested to Attlee that Maulana Azad, the Indian Minister of Education, who was a friend of Mossadeq, could act as honest broker. 'In his view no Persian Government could survive . . . which held back on the principle of nationalisation. But he feels that a workable compromise could still be found.'[68] This idea does not seem to have been followed up; the next serious initiative came from the Americans. In November 1951 the American Secretary of State, Dean Acheson, proposed a settlement which would have conceded the principle of nationalization but still left Britain a stake in Persian oil. A Conservative Government was now in power, and Mountbatten pleaded that the emergence of new Ministers should be made an excuse for a change of heart. He wrote to the new First Lord, Jim Thomas:

> The British policy, as I understand it, seems to rest on two false assumptions:
> (a) That the Persians as a nation, irrespective of what Persian government is in power, would ever go back on nationalisation in principle.
> (b) That the A.I.O.C. (against whom such a hate has been cooked up in Persia) would ever be accepted back in Persia.
> I should have thought that the only wise course was to build the best possible structure we can get on the U.S. proposals, which would at least enable us to get both oil and a large measure of indirect control.[69]

Mountbatten may have been deceived about the readiness of the Persians to negotiate reasonable terms, but a policy of bluster without any serious intent to resort to arms was still less likely to succeed. Mountbatten's conviction that it was better to work with Persian nationalism rather than obstinately to oppose it was consistent with his views on every similar issue. Such views, which he propagated with indiscreet fervour, won him a reputation among the more right-wing as being a friend of revolution, soft on Communism, unsound. This caused him considerable concern. In February 1952 he wrote to Edwina:

> Four different people have come to me in the last two or three days to say that London is buzzing with rumours and talk in the clubs, etc. that I was to be offered an immediate post abroad so as to remove us from being able to influence Lilibet through Philip. My own influence was viewed with apprehension, and there was also the view that I would be passing on extreme left wing views from you! Of course you always tell me that I am very right wing and reactionary compared with you. . . .[70]

The flames of gossip were fanned by the Bulletin of the International Services of Information, edited from Baltimore by a Mr Ulius Amoss, who, under the headlines 'A Red Aura Hangs over the Mountbattens,' published a fine selection of titbits about the Fourth Sea Lord and his family.[71] Peter Murphy, Mountbatten's 'secretary', was a card-carrying Communist, yet Mountbatten told journalists: 'See Murphy if you want my views on the Soviet Union.' Lady Mountbatten was an acknowledged fellow-traveller – 'her close friends include known Communist agitators – and Paul Robeson'. Pamela had publicly stated that although she was not a party member she was a Communist. Mountbatten believed capitalism was on the way out and was preparing the way for some sort of regency when the royal family fell. 'Some rumours go further, and allude to the bizarre possibility of a future Marxist King Louis of England.'

The vision of Mountbatten as Philippe Egalité to George VI's Louis XVI may seem grotesque but it was taken seriously by a surprising number of people who fancied themselves well-informed. 'What a *fantastic* story, and how *wicked*!' wrote Edwina. '. . . You always stress the point about *my* politics!! But I can assure you that whatever *I* may think your attitude is . . . *I* have endless worryings about *your* links with people such as Peter and supposedly Communist sympathisers from many who appear to think I am Right Wing compared to you!!'[72] The press delighted in any gossip which seemed to substantiate the theory of a rift between the courtiers and the Mountbattens. When the *Sunday Pictorial* wrote an article on the subject, Mountbatten was surprised to find that his supposed influence over the young royal couple was treated as of minor importance. It was not till Kingsley Martin wrote to boast that he had succeeded in getting the article toned down that Mountbatten knew why he had escaped so lightly. 'I do not need to tell you that the Duke of Edinburgh has got his head screwed on in very much the right way,' he told Martin, 'and a man of thirty who is on the point of substantive promotion to Commander R.N. on his own merits, certainly stands in no need of advice from anyone, least of all an uncle!'[73]

Mountbatten's reputation suffered from his habit of airing whatever political philosophy was uppermost in his mind without stopping to consider the likely reactions of his audience. At the end of 1951 he dined with Winston Churchill aboard the *Queen Mary* at Southampton. He recorded the conversation in some detail.[74] He questioned the wisdom of linking Britain irrevocably to American foreign policy, especially if it seemed that the course followed by the Americans was likely to lead to war; 'the one thing that could destroy the present relatively happy and peaceful conditions in this country would of course be a war'. Churchill replied that the only security for Britain was to be found in linking its fortunes entirely with the Americans.

He then turned to me and said 'I think you should be careful about your anti-American attitude. The Americans like you. They trust

# Irresistible!

# BUSINESS REPLY MAIL

FIRST CLASS     PERMIT NO. 85407     CHICAGO, IL.

POSTAGE WILL BE PAID BY ADDRESSEE

**Time & Life Building**
**541 North Fairbanks Court**
**Chicago, Illinois 60672-2058**

# TIME

Subscribe now and get TIME delivered to your door at more than 40% OFF the $1.95 cover price! That's just $1.12 an issue. Please send:

☐ **18 months** (78 issues)  ☐ **1 year** (52 issues)  ☐ **9 months** (39 issues)  ☐ **6 months** (26 issues)

☐ Payment enclosed.  ☐ Bill me later.
☐ Bill me in three monthly installments.

Name _____
(please print)

Address _____

City _____ State _____ Zip _____          T61321

**Mail today or call toll free: 1-800-621-8200**
In Illinois: 1-800-972-8302.

Rate good in U.S. only  ©1985 TIME INC.

you. You are one of the few commanders that they would willingly serve under. You will throw all that away if they think you are against them!'

I replied that I was very fond of all my American friends, and that individually I thought they were a charming people; but, taken as a corporate mass, they were immature, and if they were allowed their own way they would probably take a course which would not only destroy this country but would ultimately end in the destruction of their own system. . . .

He then said: 'I am very sorry to hear you express such Left-Wing views. I think you should try and avoid expressing any political opinions. Your one value as a sailor is that you are completely non-political. Take care you remain so!'

I pointed out that I had always been completely non-political. . . . I had never been known to make any political remarks, but that I could not see that expressing the hope that he would be able to guide the Americans in such a way that our own country would not be destroyed could possibly be regarded as Left-Wing.

My impressions of this grand old man are that he is really past his prime. He was very deaf and kept having to have things repeated to him. He quoted poetry at great length. He went through the whole of the verses of 'Rule Britannia' and 'It's All Quiet Along The Potomac'. He was very sentimental and full of good will towards me. He kept telling me what a friend he was of mine and of my family. . . .

I realise that I made myself very unpopular by the views that I expressed that night. But I also believe that he is a big enough man to at least have absorbed the point of view I was putting forward.

To John Colville, Churchill's private secretary, who recorded the dinner in his diary, Mountbatten was talking 'arrant political nonsense; he might have learned by heart a leader from the *New Statesman*. The P.M. laughed at him but did not, so Pug Ismay thought, snub him sufficiently.'[75] There is no doubt that, in orthodox Tory circles, Mountbatten was at this time a suspect figure. He consoled himself with the reflection that in his day Churchill had been still less acceptable. When Labour lost the 1951 election, Mountbatten was unperturbed. He knew that he would find the new First Lord, Jim Thomas, quite as easy to deal with as Lord Hall and saw no reason why the other Ministers should present more of a problem. It seemed to him unlikely that he would ever find himself in conflict with his political masters on any matter for which he had direct responsibility. It was not until the Suez Crisis of 1956 that he was proved wrong.

Though hard economic and strategic facts caused him in time to modify his views, Mountbatten at this point supported an independent foreign policy and the avoidance of measures which would integrate British forces too closely with those of the Americans or, indeed, any non-Commonwealth power. When an American was appointed as the first Supreme Allied Commander in the Atlantic, Mountbatten quoted with approval the indignation of a friend's hairdresser – 'it shows that the people of this country have some pride left and don't want the British Navy under an American'.[76] During the Commonwealth Conference of January 1951 he urged Nehru to press for the adoption of a firm declaration which would make it clear to the Americans 'where the Commonwealth stood, particularly with regard to the admission of China to the United Nations'.[77]

It was his record in India and his continued close association with the Indians that did most to damage his standing in the eyes of the right wing. Ismay warned him that he had many critics. 'First, there are the people that grudge you your meteoric rise. . . . Secondly, there are the people who genuinely and profoundly disagree with the Indian policy. . . . And thirdly there are the people who consider that after partition you were not as unbiased as you should have been.'[78] The moral Ismay drew was that Mountbatten should lie low, and in particular not appear as India's champion when she took action which was disapproved of in Britain. This was more than Mountbatten could manage; he was determined to ensure that India's case was heard in the highest quarters. What was unfortunate was that, while British Ministers constantly heard Mountbatten urging the case for India, they were not aware of the excellent and often unpalatable advice which he was simultaneously giving to the Indians. 'I have no right whatsoever to make any comments, let alone give you any advice now,' he told Nehru[79] shortly after he left India, but he then proceeded to comment and advise with unabated vigour. This was in the context of Kashmir, where Mountbatten repeatedly urged patience and conciliation: 'After all that the . . . leaders of free India have said and stand for . . . can we honestly contemplate that India's first major international act should be a declaration of war?' India must put its faith in the United Nations; 'it is the first time humanity has got together to try and find an alternative to war'.

But it was Hyderabad that proved the greater test. Through the summer months of 1948 Mountbatten had been left in no doubt that military action was in the offing. Hyderabad was controlled by madmen, wrote Nehru; then, six weeks later, 'I have tried my utmost to avoid or delay military action . . . but events are stronger than me'; finally, on 29 August, 'There can be no solution . . . unless some effective punitive measures are taken. . . . If these measures have to be taken, then there is not much point in indefinitely delaying them.'[80] In reply Mountbatten advised restraint. No doubt the Hindu majority in Hyderabad was clamouring for intervention, the fanatical Muslim leadership was missing no chance to provoke the Indian Government, 'But may I say that India does not appear to be quite alive to what the outside world is thinking; and I do not mean reactionary prejudiced opinion, but well-meaning average liberal opinion.'[81] Armed aggression would be seen as such, however good the excuses.

On 13 September armed aggression came. The British, Mountbatten told V. P. Menon, were shocked and disturbed. Now India must behave generously and not as a conqueror. If they did so, 'Gradually we shall get all reasonable people round to see your point of view about Hyderabad; but it will still take time.'[82] He missed no chance of pressing the same views on Nehru: the Nizam must not be deposed, there must be free elections. 'Nehru is spending the weekend with us,' he told Ismay, 'and I shall do everything in my power to ensure that he follows the line which you yourself say you hope against hope he will follow.'[83] At the same time as he lectured Nehru, he prepared the way for him in London. The Indian Prime Minister was due to see the King, and Mountbatten wrote to warn George VI that his 'great friend' was 'shy and reserved and nervous of the Audience'. He had urged him to tell the King the whole Hyderabad story.[84] The meeting was a success and the King wrote to Mountbatten to tell him how impressed he had been by the Indian leader. Nehru, Mountbatten told Rajagopalachari, 'has literally taken, not only everyone that matters in England, but all the Commonwealth Representatives by storm'. The visit had helped enormously to make people forget what Mountbatten described as the 'ridiculous misunderstanding' over Hyderabad – a euphemism that showed how reluctant he was to recognize the outrage with which his fellow countrymen viewed the attack on Hyderabad.[85]

Mountbatten's attitude towards Nehru was an attractive compound of the respectful and the avuncular. In February 1952 he wrote to chide the Prime Minister for his laggardness in selecting a successor and preparing him for the job; '. . . as long ago as 1948 you promised me to find someone who you would train up. . . . Four years have passed since then, and I have yet to hear that you have anybody in sight!' First Nehru should review the politicians, then the younger professors, then the lawyers. 'I would suggest that Rajaji should make a short list of, say, three or four of the most suitable men he found between the ages of, say, 35 and 45, and then bring them along for you to vet.'[86] From anybody else Nehru would have resented this sensible yet somewhat impertinent advice. Mountbatten, in Indian eyes, had earned the right to interfere. His good will was proven, his wisdom respected; Nehru would not necessarily act as he suggested but he would listen with attention.

Mountbatten's close relationship with the Indian Government, Nehru in particular, caused concern in January 1955 when he was on the point of becoming First Sea Lord. Jim Thomas wrote to urge him not to invite Nehru to Broadlands, because of the bad feeling this would cause in Pakistan. 'I know how bloody this letter is, but I am *absolutely* convinced that it is in the best interests of us both and the Navy.' Mountbatten was *absolutely* convinced to the contrary, and, since he had already invited Anthony Eden to Broadlands to meet the Indian Prime Minister, was well placed to maintain his position. Thomas withdrew his objections and Nehru duly came to stay.[87]

Not many Admirals have one actual and one future Prime Minister to stay. For that matter, not many Fourth Sea Lords could give the farewell dinner which the Mountbattens gave for the retiring First Sea Lord, Bruce Fraser, at which the other guests were the Queen, Princess Elizabeth and the Duke of Edinburgh, Princess Margaret, Lord Porchester and Noel Coward – 'we all sang till two', he noted in his diary.[88] Not many Fourth Sea Lords can have been escorted to the airport by the President of Portugal. 'Dr Salazar came to the aeroplane door in the rain to see me off. Great honour.'[89] A typical week involved, beside his regular naval duties, a British Empire Service League lunch in Edinburgh, the opening of the Festival Exhibition, a British League dinner in London, the Land Agents' Society Dinner, the BIRE annual banquet, the opening of a Shipping and Industries Exhibition in Southampton, a mayoral banquet and a Scouts and Girl Guides' Display; eight speeches in all. Mountbatten did his best to pass himself off as an ordinary Admiral. He told Neville that he would be unable to play polo because he would be working till six or seven o'clock every evening, 'and the last thing I want people to do is to think that I am taking my work on the Board of Admiralty lightheartedly. Even more so since I shall be serving in a relatively humble position.'[90] Sometimes he almost convinced himself that he was a simple sailor, but the performance rarely carried conviction.

Considering the distaste with which he had first confronted the post, his time as Fourth Sea Lord was a happy and useful one. He brought to the job energy and enthusiasm to a degree which had rarely been lavished on it and made the supply departments notably more economical and efficient. He learned much, both about the workings of Whitehall and the infrastructure of the Navy, which was to be of great value to him in the future. He enhanced his claim to rise to the top of his profession.

There was one cause of sadness in those years. In the summer of 1950 his eighty-seven-year-old mother fell ill at Broadlands. Firmly, she removed herself to London: 'It is better to die at home,' she said.[91] Her death-bed was marked by the same calm, dignity and good sense which had characterized her life; her only complaint was that she took so long in dying that she inconvenienced other people. At 7.45 a.m. on 24 September she 'just stopped breathing. She looked so sweet and calm.' She was buried next to her husband on the Isle of Wight. 'A sad but beautiful end. Mama would have been so happy to feel the Navy had buried her,' wrote her son in his diary. When he was a boy and young man, she had been the strongest influence in his life; with his marriage his relationship with her had grown far less close but he had never ceased to love and admire her, or to be slightly frightened of her. Since his brother George had died he had been in fact, if not in title, head of his branch of the family, yet always this matriarchal figure loomed in the background. Her disappearance left a void which he had been prepared for, yet which took him unawares. He missed her sorely, and was to do so for many years.

# CHAPTER 39

## *The Mediterranean Fleet*

AFTER A SEAT ON THE BOARD OF ADMIRALTY Mountbatten could expect to command one of the two great fleets: the Home Fleet or the Mediterranean. On the whole he would have preferred the former; he had already served many times in the Mediterranean and a posting to Portsmouth would have been both convenient and educational. Admiral Edelsten, however, was due for a move from Malta and there was no question of missing this opportunity. Edwina was less complaisant, and demanded an assurance that whenever Mountbatten was away from Malta on a cruise she should come along in his despatch vessel, H.M.S. *Surprise*. 'I told her as kindly as I could that I could not give any such undertaking. . . . She is now considering whether to come out at all!!'[1]

St Vincent once remarked that naval command in the Mediterranean called for 'an officer of splendour'.[2] By 1952 some of the splendour had faded; the American Sixth Fleet was the most powerful seaborne force in the area, and with the end of the Indian Empire the significance of the chain of communications that ran through Gibraltar, Malta and the Suez Canal had begun to dwindle. Mountbatten particularly deplored the lack of a battleship in which he could fly his flag: 'We in the Mediterranean are being shown up the whole time by the Sixth Fleet who send their colossal ships following largely in our wake, with powerful press propaganda to show how much superior they are to us.'[3] But the Fleet still consisted of a large aircraft-carrier, three cruisers, three destroyer and frigate squadrons, a submarine squadron and a bevy of mine-sweepers, amphibious warfare ships and other such appendages. Through their control of both ends of the Mediterranean and their central base at Valletta, the British had long ruled the land-locked sea. As Mountbatten loved to remind his American colleagues, the Commander-in-Chief of the Mediterranean Fleet stood in the direct line of descent from Horatio Nelson and drew upon resources of experience and prestige that no other country could match. It was a command of the first importance and one that no man with even a trace of historical imagination could assume without a thrill of pride.

While Mountbatten was making his preparations for departure, George VI died in his sleep. 'Poor sweet Lilibet – now our Queen,' wrote Mountbatten in his diary.[4] He went to the airport to greet her on her return from Africa. Mountbatten established that at the funeral of Edward VII his father had walked immediately behind the gun-carriage and in front of the Royal Standard, and claimed this position for himself. The Earl Marshal refused: 'I am sure that on reflection you will not press for what you have asked, namely, that you should walk, and in fact be the only individual, apart from the Sovereign's Standard, to be between the Queen and her father.' Mountbatten accepted the ruling with good grace, though he noted in a private memorandum that he considered his right to the position had been accepted in principle and that he had only conceded it because of the Queen's unexpected decision to walk behind the gun-carriage herself rather than travel in a carriage.[5] Such questions of precedence never ceased to exercise Mountbatten. A year later, when he was gazetted personal A.D.C. to the Queen, he was demanding to know why his name appeared in *The Times* on a separate line below other members of the royal family. Bad sub-editing, he was told – an explanation he reluctantly accepted.[6]

Mountbatten arrived in Malta in mid May 1952 and took the Fleet to sea for the first time a month later: 'I manoeuvred 3 cruisers and 7 destroyers at high speed. Good fun.'[7] By 11 July he had returned the calls of eighty-five commanding officers, made fifty speeches aboard the ships of the Fleet, taken a different squadron to sea every ten days or so. 'I think that by the end of this year I shall really know the Fleet and I hope that they will know me.'[8] At the first Fleet regatta he was disconcerted to find a lot of indiscipline – 'boats away late, men in water, boats stolen etc.'[9]; his response was to call all his commanding officers aboard his flagship and to order a general drill.

But though he insisted on good order and high standards of turn-out, he was preoccupied by the welfare of the men. He waged a campaign to secure a supply of beer aboard for the Chief Petty Officers: 'If we cannot make a start with the senior ratings having drinks on board then we shall seriously have to consider stopping drinks for the officers.'[10] Those officers for the most part admired his panache, accepted his predilection for dramatic manoeuvres carried out at high speed, recognized that under his command the morale of the men was conspicuously high, but did not feel that he was a great sea-going commander of the calibre of Andrew Cunningham, Somerville or Bruce Fraser.[11]

For the day-to-day work he depended heavily on his Second-in-Command, William Davis. Davis took over in June 1952 and immediately had a long meeting with the Commander-in-Chief. 'He was in splendid heart,' Davis wrote in his diary, 'and made it quite clear he wished me to run the fleet and act as the Sea Commander while he dealt with the hundred and one political, strategical and command questions which were present in abundance.'[12] Davis recommended the appointment of Manley 'Lofty' Power as Chief of Staff. 'Remembering Mountbatten was a bit suspect in the Navy and his professional judgment was at times very suspect, I was sure he needed an officer of outstanding professional ability. Furthermore, one who could by no chance ever have been accused of being one of Dickie's circle!'[13] Power was capable and tough, having won the reputation of being one of the few men who could and did stand up to Andrew Cunningham. He had hardly met Mountbatten and did not much like what he had heard of him – 'I very much did not want this appointment. I was sick of the Mediterranean. I was suspicious of Dickie.'[14] However, the two men met and liked each other: Mountbatten respected Power's competence and independence of mind; Power quickly responded to the Commander-in-Chief's enthusiasm and open-mindedness.

> I got on well with Dickie Mountbatten [he recorded]. We saw eye to eye on most important matters. I found him an endless source of entertainment with his peacock mountebankery which kept popping up at unexpected moments in sharp contrast to his normal sane and statesmanlike person. . . . By the end of my time with Mountbatten I had reached the conclusion that, in spite of several failings, he was a great man and a statesman. He was dynamic, easy to deal with and always open to argument, with a tremendous gift of charm and inspired leadership.[15]

There were plenty of opportunities for the Commander-in-Chief to display his statesmanship. One of the first visits the Fleet paid under his command was to Yugoslavia. 'We spent an amusing day with Tito,' recorded Power. 'At least it was amusing for the Mountbatten family who were accomplished linguists. The only person I got on terms with was a dog.'[16] In honour of Edwina a number of Yugoslav ladies who had never been seen before in a Western embassy emerged to attend a banquet, including one resistance heroine who was reputed to have strangled seven Germans with her own hands.[17] In Brioni Tito invited the party to his villa and returned the compliment by twice visiting H.M.S. *Glasgow*, once for an inspection, the second time to dine.

Mountbatten was an inveterate traveller and was quick to accept when the Emperor Haile Selassie of Ethiopia invited him to visit Addis Ababa. The party prepared themselves by reading Evelyn Waugh's *Black Mischief* and were delighted to find on their arrival that the guard of honour were wearing the thinnest sandals, having evidently followed the example of their fictional originals and eaten their boots. The British Consul told them that Waugh had written the novel to get his own back on the Ambassador's wife, who had refused to receive him since he was staying at the local hotel with Irene Ravensdale. 'Evelyn Waugh's revenge is certainly very amusing,' wrote Mountbatten in his tour diary, 'though the book can only be mentioned to very few high-grade Ethiopians who have a strongly developed sense of humour.' The Emperor had lent them his personal Cadillac and motor-cycle escort, a signal honour but somewhat inconvenient, since every road they travelled on was strewn with the bodies of peasants seeking to present petitions to what they imagined must be their imperial master. 'Another charming habit of Ethiopians who believe themselves to be pursued by evil spirits is to dash across the road in front of the car, timing matters in such a way that they will just not be run over, while the evil spirit is of course cut off by the car.'[18]

More business was discussed when he visited Cairo on a farewell call at the end of 1954. He saw Nasser and had a cordial discussion about Middle Eastern strategy and future Egyptian–British collaboration over defence. He suggested that British officers from the Middle East Planning Staff might visit Cairo in plain clothes from time to time for discreet talks with the newly formed Egyptian Planning Staff. 'This suggestion they gratefully accepted,' reported Mountbatten.[19] Mountbatten never changed the opinion he formed on this visit: that Nasser was radical and strongly nationalistic but by no means ill-disposed to Britain and ready to co-operate if given proper encouragement.

'The Egyptian Ministers were clearly much pleased and impressed by Lord Mountbatten's visit . . . and I am sure we shall reap the fruits of it in the coming months,' was the British Ambassador's conclusion.[20] Not everyone was as enthusiastic about Mountbatten's activities. The First Lord wrote to him in temperate rebuke:

> I know the various visits which you have paid to Mediterranean countries since you became Commander-in-Chief have been extremely useful in many ways, but at the same time I think I ought to remind you that it would be wise to take the greatest care to keep out of political discussions. There is a feeling that in some of your conversations . . . you have approached rather too closely to the dividing line between legitimate naval interests and foreign policy. Both the Prime Minister and Foreign Secretary have lately suggested to me, in a friendly way, that a naval figure of your standing should be particularly careful on this point. . . .
>
> This is not an expression of displeasure but is intended for guidance, as I do not want you to become a controversial figure![21]

Mountbatten was surprised and somewhat injured. He would, he said, 'try and be even more careful in future'. The only political discussion he could remember having was with Field Marshal Papagos in Athens, and that had been at the request of the King of Greece and reported to the British Ambassador. Papagos had complained about the King's hostility and the Queen's malign influence, and Mountbatten had urged him to concentrate on establishing a good relationship with her. No doubt what had happened, suggested the Commander-in-Chief somewhat disingenuously, was that 'a particular British Minister', who had recently visited Malta and expounded his views on the Middle East, had been gratified by their good reception and had subsequently passed off his opinions as emanating from Mountbatten.[22]*

It was while the Fleet was paying its annual visit to Villefranche that a reconciliation of a sort was achieved with Winston Churchill. The Mountbattens dined with him at Beaverbrook's villa at Cap d'Ail, where he was staying. The women left the table at 9.30 p.m. and Churchill and Mountbatten remained alone till 1 a.m. Mountbatten told Patricia: 'With tears in his eyes he kept repeating how much he had loved me, that he had quite forgotten and forgiven me about India, that I had had a wonderful career and was on the threshold of an even finer career, the country needed me, etc. Quite embarrassing.'[23] Time was to show that the Prime Minister had more reservations than he was prepared to own to when in sentimental mood over the brandy, but for the present all was rosy. The next day Churchill attended the *Préfet*'s dinner for the Fleet and was prevailed on to speak. '*Est-ce-que je vous fais de la peine quand j'assassine vos gendres?*' he asked his host.[24]

Lord Beaverbrook's newspapers followed Mountbatten's progresses with avid interest. Potentially damaging was a series of articles by Sefton Delmer, which attacked the Commander-in-Chief's professional skills as well as his social activities. Fortunately, the Admiralty had a spy in the Beaverbrook camp, who not only warned that the articles were coming but secured their eventual suppression on the grounds of their inaccuracy.[25] Fortunately, too, other papers were better disposed. Bill O'Connor – the columnist Cassandra – was sent out by the *Daily Mirror* to investigate morale in the Mediterranean Fleet. At first he refused all invitations to Admiralty House; then, after three or four days, came round to report that Mountbatten was 'O.K. with the sailors' and to accept a celebratory drink.[26]

At one point Mountbatten was particularly incensed by an article in a Beaverbrook paper which he felt went close to accusing him of treason. Lord Kemsley advised him not to sue; Kemsley's elder brother Lord Camrose took

---

* The most recent ministerial visitor had been the Secretary of State for Air, Lord De L'Isle and Dudley, about a month before, who, however, recalls no such conversation.

the opposite line, saying that damages might well be £100,000 and that Beaverbrook would never dare defend the case – 'Incidentally, Camrose pointed out to me that we would not have to pay any tax on £100,000 so it would be worth a couple of million pounds gross to us!'[27] Peter Murphy urged Mountbatten not to go to court. His strongest point in the public's eye was that as a public servant he could *not* answer back – 'you are quids in as the Silent Service, whose honour has been basely attacked by a scurrilous and irresponsible megalomaniac'.[28] Reluctantly Mountbatten accepted the force of the argument and dismissed his dream of a tax-free fortune. 'If I take no action myself,' he told Campbell-Johnson, 'it leaves the onus on H.M.G. to protect me if the attacks become too violent.'[29]

It was as well for Mountbatten that the Beaverbrook journalists did not dwell on his passion for polo. Though never as obsessive on the subject as Roger Keyes, skill in polo was a guarantee of his attention if not his favours and those who did not play grumbled about the list of 'polo-promotions'.[30] The General commanding in Malta had also been a keen polo player and had announced his intention of ensuring that he was succeeded by a similar enthusiast. The General died on the polo field and Mountbatten wrote to a contact in the War Office asking that his friend's wishes should be heeded. Antony Head, once on Mountbatten's staff in Combined Operations and now Secretary of State for War, wrote a magisterial rebuke: 'I am in favour of polo if it can be organised in these impecunious times, but frankly I think that an attempt to influence the ... selection of a General for Malta because of polo-playing qualifications is both improper and anachronistic.' Mountbatten for once had no defence – 'I stand reproved and offer contrite apologies.' The incident did not diminish his zeal, but he displayed it more prudently in future.[31]

Apart from polo, his main diversion was still underwater swimming and spear-fishing. He would habitually stay at sixty to eighty feet and sometimes dive as far as 150 feet. Someone once asked him which he preferred – polo or skin-diving. After a moment's reflection he replied: 'Well, polo, after all, is only a game.'[32] He was in the early fifties, late to embark on so strenuous a sport, let alone practise it with such abandon. When he left for the Red Sea, William Davis told the Captain of his ship that if the Commander-in-Chief got eaten by a shark he had better start packing his bags, because his naval career would be over.[33] But sharks and sting-rays were not the only hazard. Patricia wrote to Edwina to share her fears about Mountbatten's health. 'Can't he be forced to have a thorough check-up, particularly heart? ... I entirely agree the underwater fishing in too-long and too-deep doses is *very* bad.'[34] Mountbatten would coddle himself when ill, but rarely thought to spare himself an exertion that might provoke an illness. Eventually he was persuaded to go to a specialist who had been instructed by Edwina to prohibit any further diving. Not only was this object not achieved, but the next thing Edwina knew was that the specialist was himself attending the diving-school.[35]

In February 1953 Mountbatten was promoted Admiral. The Duke of Edinburgh had been appointed Admiral of the Fleet on his retirement from an active naval career. 'Congratulations on your promotion,' he telegraphed his uncle. 'Keep it up – you may catch up one day!'[36] About this time the Maltese Labour Party under its demagogic leader Dom Mintoff was beginning to clamour for independence and the evacuation of the British naval base. Mountbatten suggested that they should be offered what they wanted provided they could ensure that the standard of living of the Maltese people should not suffer after the Navy left. Since this was clearly impossible, a compromise would be reached by which the British Services would stay on with a guaranteed status within an otherwise independent Malta.[37] This somewhat *simpliste* solution was soon overtaken by a scheme which Mintoff worked out with Mountbatten's enthusiastic support for a union of Malta with Britain. Mintoff took this project to London to drum up support and at first found a backer in Lord Beaverbrook. Then Beaverbrook heard that Mountbatten was also a champion of the plan; his eagerness at once dwindled and, with little other support developing, the union withered before it was properly born.[38]

Mountbatten was one of the few British, certainly the only representative of the Services, who regularly invited Mintoff to his house. Partly this was on the principle that, if it was true that one should know one's enemy, it was doubly true that one should know someone who might prove either enemy or friend; partly because he enjoyed the company of this ebullient and maverick figure. The Mountbattens were notoriously unconventional in their choice of guests, less so in their style of entertaining. Everything was done on the grandest scale. For any large or formal dinners Mountbatten insisted that the silver plates must be used; this could cause inconvenient delay while the plates were washed up between courses and occasionally worse, when the ice-cream melted on the still warm metal. Edwina mocked but did not resist such quirks; she could be ruthless, however, when her own views of propriety were in question. A sad note in his diary recorded that he was suffering from a bad attack of Malta tummy and feeling sick and giddy – 'Doctor put me to bed but Edwina got me up to give Archbishop lunch.'[39]

But the most important visitors were Queen Elizabeth and the Duke of Edinburgh at the end of the Commonwealth Tour of 1954. Mountbatten practised a spectacular manoeuvre to greet the royal couple as they approached in the *Britannia*. The Fleet advanced at twenty-five knots, twice the speed of *Britannia*, then turned inwards and swept past the Royal Yacht, sailing so close that some of the ships splashed *Britannia*'s decks. The exercise was perfectly safe provided that no mistake was made, but even a tiny deviation could have caused a disastrous accident. It never occurred to Mountbatten not to try the manoeuvre, and when one of the navigators later told him that he had aged years during the few moments his ship had taken to pass the yacht, he professed surprise. 'I had not appreciated how worried they had all been, as I wasn't in the least worried.'[40] Certainly he achieved his object of impressing the royal party. 'At no time during this World Tour, either before or afterwards, had quite the same thing been seen,' wrote Conolly Abel-Smith, Captain of the Royal Yacht; 'the dash, timing and setting were things quite different and superior to other occasions. Her Majesty and the Duke of Edinburgh went out of their way to remark on the magnificent exhibition.'[41]

Prince Charles and Princess Anne, aged five and three respectively, had been sent out ten days earlier to spend a few days in Malta before their parents arrived. The Mountbattens had been asked to look after them, and Browning caused some offence when he wrote asking for a programme of excursions to be submitted for the Queen's approval. He was told 'that you would organise the trips, etc, as desirable each day. Really!' wrote Mountbatten to Edwina.[42]

The Prince of Wales's first recollection of his great-uncle is of a tall figure standing on the jetty at Valletta to greet them. Mountbatten, he remembered, was wonderful with children, always tipping them over or throwing them up into the air. He would tell them stories, usually about things he had done rather than fairy tales, and seemed always ready to make time to be with them. It was the beginning of a relationship which was to become progressively more important to both parties.

Another few months and Mountbatten's time in the Mediterranean would be over. 'The job of C.-in-C. Med on its own is a very pleasant and easy one,' Mountbatten told the First Lord. 'The job of CINCAFMED is a complicated, tiring and trying one. The two together . . . are definitely exhausting.'[43] It was his duties as a NATO Commander – Commander-in-Chief, Allied Forces, Mediterranean – which absorbed more and more of his time and energies as his posting to the Mediterranean wore on.


Since Greece and Turkey had joined the North Atlantic Treaty Organization in 1951 it had become obvious that something must be done about the command structure in the Mediterranean. Admiral Carney, the American Commander-in-Chief, with his headquarters at Naples, enjoyed a shadowy suzerainty over a vast area stretching from the Alps to the Caucasus. A school of thought, of which Carney was a vigorous champion, argued that CINC-SOUTH, as he was called, should be in supreme command over the whole Mediterranean. Others, notably the British, considered that a separate command was needed, which should be based on Malta and put under the control of a British admiral. Throughout 1952 the various parties promoted their points of view. Mountbatten was instructed not to put himself into any position 'which might give the impression that Carney was your superior'.[44] The order corresponded satisfactorily with his own predilections but he was nervous lest the British, by hanging back, might miss the opportunity to play a leading role in whatever new organization evolved. When it was suggested that the British should not participate in the 1953 exercises, he protested: 'If we go away and sulk in the corner now, the party will go on and we look like being the only losers. It must also be remembered that Carney is continuing to build up an ever-increasing Empire and if we are not associated with it in any way it would be rather difficult to take over the control if ever I were to be appointed Allied C.-in-C. Mediterranean.'[45]

Through the summer and autumn of 1952 relations between the naval commands grew worse. Mountbatten's irritation became increasingly evident.

> I have been trying ever since I took up my command here to cooperate with you on a fair and reasonable basis, as my predecessor did before me [he wrote to Carney]. He warned me when I came that ever since you had taken up the appointment of CINCSOUTH he had found service co-operation increasingly difficult to achieve, though personal relations remain most harmonious. Frankly I have found the same; I am glad our personal relationships are friendly, and I hope they will always remain so. But in spite of every effort on my part, our professional relationships have become more and more difficult, even though I have conceded a number of points in an effort to achieve some compromise which would enable our mutual plans to progress.[46]

No doubt Carney would have echoed these sentiments with equal certainty that it was he who had made the concessions. The main cause of the conflict was Carney's refusal to allow certain planning tasks – principally connected with submarines and convoys – to be transferred from Naples to Malta. Mountbatten argued that the existing facilities in Malta were far more efficient than those in Naples and that strategically Malta was in the right place: 'I have here . . . an established headquarters (established, incidentally, a century and a half ago), good communications, and a staff experienced in Mediterranean warfare. . . . I fear . . . that your present attitude of reluctance to allow any lead but your own, is in fact impeding the preparation of the Mediterranean for war to a serious extent.'[47] Carney retorted that he was constitutionally unable to delegate functions to a British or any other commander: 'You are only responsible to the Admiralty. I, on the other hand, am not a national commander . . . any change would require a new NATO directive concurred in by all the partners. There, Dickie, is the rub.'[48]

By November 1952 the main protagonists had accepted in principle that a separate command should be set up. The First Sea Lord was despatched to Washington to argue for a British commander responsible directly to SACEUR, the Supreme Allied Command, Europe, who would control all Allied naval forces in the Mediterranean, other than those employed in national coastal waters, and all air forces concerned with maritime war. 'If the United States so require,' read McGrigor's instructions, 'we could accept initially that the U.S. carrier and amphibious forces should come under the operational command of SACEUR, though it should be laid down that he must assign operational control to the Allied Naval C.-in-C.'[49] They were expecting too much; the Americans had no intention of placing their Sixth Fleet under the command of any international organization, even if the Supreme Commander had been an American and not a Briton. That the Allied Commander should be British was, however, conceded without too much difficulty; the fact that the British candidate was Mountbatten, who had a history of international command behind him and was well known to the Americans, must have eased the way for this decision.

Mountbatten professed a notable lack of enthusiasm for the new appointment. 'I am afraid this will mean a big Allied set-up in Malta and will be a great bore for me and a lot of extra work,' he told Robert Neville.[50] His comment to the senior members of his staff on the day the news was received was more revealing of his real feelings. 'We've got it,' he announced exultantly.[51] The best thing was that he was not required to give up his purely British responsibilities, 'so I will at least have the fun of working with the Fleet'.[52] There were many people, including some in Whitehall, who argued that this was wrong. At the first meeting with the various Commanders-in-Chief in January 1953 Mountbatten agreed that the two jobs might have to be separated in time of war, but that in peacetime it would suffice if his Second-in-Command looked after purely British interests. 'He emphasised that he would, of course, not in any case be influenced by British interests in conducting the Allied Command.'[53] This assurance did not satisfy all his colleagues. In particular, the American Admiral Wright 'voiced the most profound suspicions about my relations with the Middle East and about our employment of force to supply the Middle East. He stated that NATO forces could not be used to supply the Middle East, which was a National interest.'[54]

In his first directive Mountbatten announced that an integrated Naval/Air headquarters in Malta would be opened on 15 March 1953.[55] Under CINCAFMED would be French, Italian, Greek and Turkish Admirals, each commanding their national navies, or, in the case of France, their Mediterranean Fleet, and Admiral Wright for the United States. The American Sixth Fleet remained independent, though Mountbatten had certain ill-defined responsibilities for co-ordinating the movements of that Fleet with the air forces allocated to NATO. Each Mediterranean member had been assigned an appropriate zone, and the boundaries of these caused much ill feeling. 'The Italians were quite ridiculously sensitive about the loss of face involved in increasing the French area,' Mountbatten told McGrigor.[56] Nor were the British models of co-operative good behaviour. Mountbatten was charged by NATO with preparing plans to prevent Russian submarines leaving the Black Sea in case of war; the only mines immediately available were British, and the Admiralty agreed to these being earmarked for this purpose; they would not, however, allow Mountbatten as British Commander-in-Chief to tell Mountbatten as CINCAFMED where the mines actually were. 'This somewhat bizarre situation would not, of course, hamper me if war came,' Mountbatten told Churchill, as he would use all the resources at his disposal in the common cause. He compounded the oddity of the situation by reporting to the Prime Minister on CINCAFMED writing paper.[57]

Not the least of the pleasures of his new post was that it involved him in much extra travelling. This was not always as much a pleasure for members of his staff. On a flight from Malta to Rome there was low cloud round the Italian capital. Mountbatten took this as a personal slight and insisted that the plane must land nevertheless. At his first attempt the pilot narrowly missed the control-tower. The Commander-in-Chief disappeared into the cockpit to take personal control. 'Oh dear,' said Edwina apprehensively. 'We'd better all have a brandy and ginger.' In spite of his efforts, the plane was diverted to Naples. Mountbatten insisted that the party must continue immediately by train and not waste time on ceremonial. To his fury he found a guard from the *Carabinieri* awaiting him on his arrival. 'I won't leave the plane till they've gone,' announced Mountbatten. 'Don't be silly,' said Edwina. 'Of course you must go out,' and, grumbling, her husband did as he was told.[58]

The establishment of the new command might have been expected to resolve the difficulties between Carney and Mountbatten; instead it embittered them. At discussions in Paris in March 1953 Mountbatten complained that Carney was trying to set up a rival Allied headquarters in the Mediterranean. Since Carney's strike force comprised only units of the U.S. Sixth Fleet, CINCAFMED could see no reason why he needed any international organization at all.[59] In the end Mountbatten accepted the existence of an Allied naval headquarters in Naples, provided, as he told General Gruenther (who was at that time Chief of Staff to the Supreme Allied Commander), that 'it is quite clear that I am the sole Allied Naval Commander-in-Chief in the Mediterranean and that this new Strike Force Headquarters does not start trying to usurp my functions'.[60]

It was not quite clear to Carney. As late as July 1953, when he was on the point of departure, he was still stating the major point at issue as being 'whether there are one or two NATO naval commanders in the Mediterranean'. His own opinion was that he was as much a NATO commander as Mountbatten, and that CINCAFMED should exercise his co-ordinating powers only 'as required on occasion and in interest of safety'.[61] Rows were frequent and exhausting. 'The only thing which is now assuming really large proportions is our struggle with CINCSOUTH,' reported Mountbatten's Chief-of-Staff on the NATO side, Peter Cazalet. 'Before we can really get things straight I am convinced that a complete show-down between you and him will be necessary.'[62]

At times the ill-feeling became embarrassingly public. A chance meeting between the two men in Athens gave rise to rumours that they had quarrelled because Mountbatten had been persuading the Greeks to allocate units to the Allied fleet without prior consultation with CINCSOUTH. An Associated Press despatch on the subject was picked up by the *Tribune de Nations* and eventually embroidered by Moscow radio. Moscow gleefully reported that Admiral Radford, Chairman of the American Joint Chiefs of Staff, was demanding Mountbatten's dismissal on the grounds that he was 'the chief culprit for strained Anglo-American relations'.[63] Carney professed amusement at the uproar; if we have any further clashes, he asked Mountbatten, 'be sure to let me know'.[64] But though the details might be embellished, the essentials were true; the alliance was being damaged by bad relations between the two commands.

Mountbatten's troubles with Carney in many ways recall his relationship with Somerville in South-East Asia some ten years before. In SEAC the replacement of Somerville revealed that apparently irreconcilable differences were either trivial, had never existed, or had already been *de facto* resolved. So the arrival of Admiral Fechteler brought peace to the Mediterranean. His appointment was viewed with delight in AFMED, since he had been a champion of the command's independent existence from the start.[65] He proved no disappointment. The first meeting was a 'love-feast', Mountbatten told McGrigor.[66] To Gruenther he reported:

Driving him back to the airfield, I said 'In two hours you never said a single word with which I could not go along.' He replied: 'I agreed with every word you said.'

Those two statements sum up our meeting in a nutshell. I let my hair down and told him what had been wrong in the relations between CINCSOUTH and CINCAFMED in the past, and Bill Fechteler kindly told me what it was that Mick Carney objected to. It appears he had got it into his head that I was trying to extend my grasp on forces to which I was not entitled. . . . Nothing could have been further from the truth.

Anyway, we believe that we shall be able to solve all our outstanding difficulties without worrying you.[67]

Whether Carney or Mountbatten was more to blame is impossible to establish. There is rarely a patently right answer to the sort of problem they were confronting. If one of them had been weaker or more easy-going, the matter would have been swiftly resolved by the adoption of the other's solution. If the two men had been more amenable, or less preoccupied by their own status and the status of their commands, there would have been no problems to resolve. But amenability and indifference to status are not often attributes of great leaders of men, and both Carney and Mountbatten were leaders of the first order. Given their temperaments, a clash was as inevitable as it had been between Somerville and Mountbatten. It was fortunate for NATO that, ultimately, not much damage had been done.

Indeed the new command had got off to a good start. By the time Mountbatten left the Mediterranean, AFMED was a going concern. Its headquarters was installed in its new home in Malta, known to the British as Selfridges because of the many flags along the front of the building. Its first commander welded together the various national fleets into a reasonably coherent international force, accustomed to the idea of operating as a unit. He induced the individual Governments, jealous of their independence, to make over to NATO a larger proportion of their naval resources than had at first seemed likely. Above all, he performed the same trick as he had worked in South-East Asia, meshing together individuals from different Services and different countries so that their loyalty was almost as much to the entity which they served as to their own country. Nothing could make a Natonian out of a Frenchman or a Greek, but Mountbatten got closer to it than could have been expected.

0840 Goodbyes in Admiralty House [reads Mountbatten's diary for 10 December 1954].

Band played 'For He's a Jolly Good Fellow'. 0130 V.I.P.s at

Custom House to see me off. R.A.F. guard in street, Army guard on jetty. Galley manned by my six Allied Admirals in Hafmed pulled me to *Surprise*. All points and both Breakwaters manned and cheered. L.C.A.s and barges escorted us out. Very moving. At sea submarines, carriers and the rest manoeuvred, steamed past and cheered. 3 Admirals dipped their flags to me.

International, inter-Service, it was a fitting farewell to Mountbatten's final Malta posting.

Mountbatten told Charles Lambe in November 1953 that he was now committed to spending till March 1955 in the NATO job. The First Lord had recently 'indicated that I was one of the candidates as a successor to Wee Mac [McGrigor] which rather horrified me as it would mean running through my Naval career much faster than I had hoped'.[68] Nobody knew Mountbatten better than Lambe. He replied that he was 'thoroughly amused by your attempt to convince me that you are surprised at the suggestion that you might succeed the Wee Mac! I hope you do.'[69] A year later the wish had come true, but the interim had provided some painful suspense.

Manley Power returned to London in 1954 to find a debate in progress as to who should be the next First Sea Lord. Philip Vian tackled him and, once he had established that he was in the Mountbatten camp, urged him to lobby Andrew Cunningham, who was proving the greatest stumbling-block. With some reluctance Power did so, to be met by blunt refusal. 'Dickie has great gifts but he lacks judgment. It would never do.' Power argued that, if you were looking for a really first-class car, you looked for one with enormous power and flashing acceleration. Brakes could be separately provided. 'That does not detract from the performance of the car.' Cunningham was unconvinced by this somewhat alarming analogy but promised not to close his mind on the subject.[70]

The main rivals for the position were John Denny, Commander-in-Chief of the Home Fleet, dedicated, austere and somewhat humourless, who was said to take the Ordnance Board minutes away with him as light reading; Guy Russell, the Second Sea Lord; and Guy Grantham, the Vice Chief of Naval Staff. The most senior professional opinion was inclined to favour Denny, as being the sounder man and more experienced sailor; the next echelon was almost unanimously for Mountbatten. McGrigor himself was temperamentally more akin to Denny and was disposed at first to offer him the succession; Thomas, the First Lord of the Admiralty, was strongly for Mountbatten but would not have ventured to overrule the Admirals on his Board or the old guard of Admirals of the Fleet whose voice counted for much in such debates.

'I am sure you will be able to help, dear Pug,' Edwina wrote to Ismay in August 1954. 'It would be heartbreaking if Dickie's remarkable personality and outstanding ability was to be wasted in these next *vital* years in a Back yard. . . . I would so like to see him working with Jim [Thomas] as they get on so *very* well.'[71] How active a role Ismay played in answer to this appeal is uncertain, but by mid October he was writing to Cunningham to report that Thomas badly needed support in his campaign to secure Mountbatten's appointment. The First Lord thought Cunningham still supported Denny. 'Obviously he was wrong in this. But does he know it?'[72] Clearly Ismay had already been told that Cunningham had changed his mind. 'It is quite true that well over a year ago when Thomas asked me about it, I gave him my opinion as not Dickie for 1st Sea Lord,' Cunningham replied, 'but the dire need of the Navy for a colourful personality well in the public eye has completely altered my views.'[73] He had written to Thomas to announce his change of heart. McGrigor too had rallied to the Mountbatten camp. The fact was that the Admiralty had lost out to the other Services in every major Whitehall battle since the war. The new First Sea Lord must be someone who could put the Navy's case forcibly and well, and command the ears of those in supreme authority. Whether Denny was or was not a better sailor was irrelevant; the arts of advocacy rather than navigation were going to be needed over the next few years.

On 15 September 1954 McGrigor wrote to tell Mountbatten that he wanted him to take over as First Sea Lord in the spring. He admitted that this had not always been his opinion, but:

> We are having a continual battle for the very existence of the Navy. A continual series of most unscrupulous and ill-informed attacks on it, on the lines that we cannot afford everything, the R.A.F. is first priority, and the Army has so many commitments that it cannot be cut, so the Navy should be reduced to pretty well its flotillas with perhaps some light fleet-carriers and half a dozen cruisers, but no more. . . . It is one long fight in which we just hold our own with no help or support.
>
> I want you to come here with your drive and powers of persuasion, experience and influence, to keep the Navy on its feet in the nuclear age, to give it a new look where necessary, and to keep up the confidence of the Service. I am sure you are the best man to do it, and it is essential for the good of the Navy and of the Country that you should relieve me. . . . It is not that I have not every confidence in a possible alternative, but I am sure that at this time we need your prestige and qualities.[74]

Cunningham's letter was still more flattering: 'The Navy wants badly a man and a leader. To me and I think quite 99% of the Service you are the man who completely fills the bill.'[75] Mountbatten was, if not overwhelmed, at least genuinely touched. 'Well, you can imagine my feelings!' he told Patricia. Really, he went on, he would have preferred a stint with the Home Fleet, but duty must come first.[76] His daughter was undeceived. 'You can't tell me that for all your nonchalant attitude you aren't really delighted. I know you so well! And you can't fool me as easily as you can yourself!'[77] His delight is patent in his letter to his son-in-law:

> Practically all the old Admirals of the Fleet and Admirals senior to me have written the most unexpected letters of support. Six months ago most of them were against me but now they have the wind up about the future of the Navy and think I'm the only chap who can pull the Navy out of the mess.
>
> With that charming modesty that Patricia has admired so much in me for the last 25 years I can tell you that in my opinion *they are absolutely right*!
>
> I hope the mess will have reached its Nadir before I take over – as in Combined Ops, SEAC and India – then one has that comforting feeling that it can't get worse.[78]

But the battle was not yet won. Churchill, who had done so much to promote Mountbatten's interests in the past, now sought to block this new promotion. His motives remain obscure. Some felt it was still his rancour over India which influenced him, others that the memories of Dieppe proved troublesome. Mountbatten 'was not the man his father was', he told his private secretary, John Colville.[79] The Prime Minister was said to feel that his former protégé had grown improperly familiar of late and was piqued by Mountbatten's less than tactful efforts to change the name of the royal house from Windsor to Mountbatten-Windsor.* Against this there was Thomas's assurances that Churchill had shown 'nothing but friendliness to you and admiration of your qualities. His only hesitation was that to appoint you now when you were comparatively young, might bring your career in the Navy to an end too soon.'[80] Perhaps, too, his attitude reflected his urge to interfere with and overrule his First Lords and their Boards. One of Mountbatten's supporters apparently said to him: 'What the Navy wants is a figure and a strong man.' 'Oh, but I don't think I want a strong man in the Navy,' replied the Prime Minister.[81]

Whatever the causes, Churchill obstinately refused to commit himself to

---

* See p. 682 below.

Mountbatten's appointment, even when he was assured that naval opinion was now solidly in its favour. He did not categorically say no, but he would not say yes. Ismay told Royer Dick, then with NATO in Paris, that he was flying back to London to try to induce the Prime Minister to make up his mind on this and other issues.[82] Montgomery was convinced that his was the decisive voice. 'I explained to him that we needed you in Whitehall,' he told Mountbatten, 'to get our affairs properly geared for the future and to ensure the right decisions are taken *now*. He agreed, so all is now well.'[83] Convinced or not, Churchill kept his counsel for a little while more. Then, at a banquet at Buckingham Palace, McGrigor became engaged in a fierce argument with the Prime Minister about his successor as First Sea Lord. Churchill advanced all the old arguments, then, just as the Duke of Edinburgh was approaching, suddenly said: 'All right, I agree.' According to Thomas, he then turned to the Duke and said cheerfully: 'I was just telling Admiral McGrigor that I propose to submit your uncle's name to the Queen as the new First Sea Lord.'[84] Prince Philip's account, written closer to the event, is slightly different. 'You can relax,' he told his uncle. The only remaining obstacle to Mountbatten's appointment had been overcome. 'The old man asked me about it himself at the banquet in front of the First Sea Lord. In fact he said "Are you in favour of Dickie?" So, taken aback, I said "I'm always in favour of Dickie – but what for?"' Churchill made it very clear what he was talking about. 'I hope this eases your mind,' concluded the Duke.[85] It did, but until the official invitation arrived on 21 October Mountbatten did not allow himself to be certain that he had achieved the ambition of his lifetime.

# CHAPTER 40

# *First Sea Lord*

THE FIRST SEA LORD'S OFFICE [wrote Lord Chatfield] is largely that of making final decisions or, in certain matters, recommendations to the First Lord. In all technical matters he is the final arbiter. Not that it is necessary for the other Sea Lords to refer matters, within their separate administrative tasks, to the First Sea Lord. They are independent and . . . responsible to the First Lord alone. But the First Sea Lord is the experienced leader who stands behind them and to whom they will come . . . should they be in doubt or if the problem be of great importance.[1]

Mountbatten would probably not have disputed this job description, yet his practice was to prove less restrained. Leading by standing behind might have suited Chatfield or the Duke of Plaza Toro, but in 1955 some more dramatic initiative was called for if the Navy was not to be gravely weakened. Britain's strained economy, as so often, made cuts in public spending necessary. A Gallup Poll of October 1955 showed that, in the eyes of the public, defence cuts should be the first priority.[2] In the same month Eden promised the Conservative party conference that over the next thirty months Service personnel would fall from 800,000 to 700,000. Among those in power the feeling was strong that the Navy should suffer most. 'I gather the P.M. has lost interest in the Navy and on Service priorities they are number three,' Harold Wernher had warned Mountbatten.[3] 'There is always this argument as to the future role of the R.N. in view of the Atomic Warfare age. Your great contribution can be to put the Navy back on the map.' In this task he had to overcome the opposition of Montgomery, who in a lecture to the Royal United Services Institute attributed to the Navy only a minor role in global war and almost none at any other time. 'At present the Navy is the Cinderella of the fighting services . . . ,' the Vice Chief of Naval Staff gloomily told Mountbatten. 'The thunder has . . . been stolen by the Air Force and to a lesser extent the Army. . . . We have not stated the Navy's case sufficiently firmly in the past nor are we pointing to the future with sufficient confidence. . . . Much work is required to refute the "one big bang and it is all over" theory so cleverly sponsored by Jack Slessor and the U.S. Strategic Air Force.'[4]

To restate and gain acceptance for the role of the Navy was indeed Mountbatten's first responsibility. The Navy had only recently defined its requirements. It needed 'carriers operating the latest aircraft; powerful ships armed with guided weapons; escorts capable . . . of providing protection for our shipping; submarines and amphibious forces; minesweepers to keep the sea-lanes clear for vital supplies. All these ships must be well-equipped and maintained in a high state of readiness.'[5] But this was asking for too much. Even to keep forces at their present level would demand rapidly rising expenditure, yet however the defence budget was divided it was certain that the naval element would be smaller than before. To ask for too much was to risk losing more. The Navy must define its priorities and make them understood; only then could it be sure of obtaining the minimum necessary to remain an effective and balanced fighting force.

James Callaghan, who had worked with Mountbatten as a junior Minister in the Admiralty and was now an Opposition spokesman on defence, wrote to him while he was still at Malta. He stressed the need for a re-examination of the relationship between the Navy and the R.A.F., perhaps even for an eventual merger of the two. 'I can think of no one better able than yourself to put the Navy's position in any negotiations with the R.A.F., and although this may sound a wild and improbable dream, if there was a drastic modification in the relationship between the two Services, I can think of no one I should prefer to see leading them on the professional side.'[6] Mountbatten was as alive as anyone to the utility of keeping in with a prominent member of what must eventually be the party of government, but knew, too, that serving officers should be discreet in their dealings with politicians. 'V. difficult to answer,' he noted on Callaghan's letter, and sent a temporizing reply. But he did not forget its contents. If the best way to save the Navy was to merge it with the R.A.F., he would not exclude the possibility. He was sufficiently sure of his own abilities to be confident that, if the merger came while he was at the helm, the Navy would not end up the junior partner.

The Board of Admiralty worked in different ways according to the temperaments of the First Lord and the First Sea Lord, the political and the professional masters of the Navy. The former had the last word, but he rarely chose to use it in direct defiance of the latter's advice on any technical question. Views as to what constituted a technical question, however, differed from generation to generation. Thomas was amiable, sensible and complaisant; he was therefore held by the Navy to be an excellent First Lord, but was viewed with less enthusiasm by his political colleagues who felt a stronger line should from time to time be taken with the sailors. But though Mountbatten was the dominant personality on the Board, he did not have things all his own way. Second Sea Lord, appointed almost simultaneously, was his old friend Charles Lambe. 'I should want you to do far more than the normal Second Sea Lord from the point of view of giving me "elder Statesman" advice and help and generally to hold my hand,' wrote Mountbatten.[7] He meant it; for thirty years Lambe had been giving him excellent and often unpalatable advice, and though Mountbatten had by no means always taken it he appreciated its wisdom and the affection from which it sprang. He was to have much cause to be grateful to Lambe for his counsel over the next few years.

The other outstanding personality on the Board was very different. John Lang, Secretary to the Admiralty, was dour and hard-working, determined to show that the civil power controlled the Navy. Both by temperament and by professional conviction it was probable that he would clash with Mountbatten and the laws of probability were not disproved. The two men respected and rather grudgingly liked each other; usually they worked out a line acceptable to both of them. Indeed, almost the only example of direct confrontation which Lang could remember arose over an issue no more significant than whether sailors should wear the same caps the whole year round. Mountbatten thought they should, and won. The Admirals on the Board would usually speak with one voice when politicians were present, but Mountbatten orchestrated his effects with unusual care, and in Lang's view influenced the Board as effectively, if not democratically, as any First Sea Lord he had seen in action.[8]

There was, nevertheless, much in the way Mountbatten conducted his business of which Lang disapproved. Why, he asked, was it necessary always for the First Sea Lord to travel with a valet and stenographer? None of his predecessors had done so. Because he was not the same as other First Sea Lords was, in effect, Mountbatten's answer. 'I would like John Lang to have been here to see the pace which Nelson and Evans have been working,' he wrote from the United States.[9] He agitated for a V.I.P. aircraft for the round-the-world trip he planned for the end of 1955. 'I didn't much fancy trying to get myself about without a Staff, by passenger aircraft, the way Rhoddie [McGrigor] seems to do it. But it all costs money, and the Admiralty may not be willing to cough up.'[10] Lavish though his style of travel might be, however, even he was discomfited when he arrived at Rangoon to discover a two-years' supply of lavatory paper concealed amidst the mountain of luggage that accompanied him. It transpired that the cartons had been delivered at his London house the night before the tour began and had been packed by a new and over-diligent valet who assumed that this was the sort of thing First Sea Lords took on their travels.[11]

A more serious criticism of his manner of working was that he delighted in intrigue, sometimes, it seemed, for intrigue's sake. He would never give a straight answer to a straight question, complained Caspar John, Davis's successor as Vice Chief of Naval Staff. John found that he usually agreed with Mountbatten on objectives but rarely on methods; the First Sea Lord was always seeking a way round difficulties and preferred to deal through a man who knew a man who owed him a favour rather than by direct approach.[12] Manley Power, who took over in 1957 as Fifth Sea Lord, was still more emphatic. He hated the 'squalid underhand inter-Service wrangling'. His own inclination was always to go bull-headedly into an argument. 'Dickie however was a born intriguer. If there was a choice between open dealing and a corkscrew approach he always chose the latter!'[13] Field Marshal Templer once exploded across a dinner table: 'Dickie, you're so crooked that if you swallowed a nail you'd shit a corkscrew!' – a remark which Mountbatten remembered and repeated, though characteristically changing the recipient of the insult.[14]

That Mountbatten did enjoy Whitehall intrigue can hardly be denied; that those whom he had tried to out-manoeuvre reacted sometimes with asperity is equally evident; that his tactics were usually successful is most obvious of all. He was an uncommonly skilful performer in committee or private conclave. Unlike McGrigor, he was notably accessible to people of every rank, relished debate, was always ready to listen to opinions contrary to his own and to take account of what he heard. Though he grew noticeably less conscientious at studying the briefs on minor items, Davis noted that 'he never missed a trick on the important issues and had a much better political sense than some members of the Government'.[15] He took endless trouble to carry the Board with him, regularly invited them to a working breakfast once a week at his house in Wilton Crescent, and held preparatory meetings of the naval members before the full Board met to discuss any significant issue.

He tried to extend his own and naval influence throughout Whitehall. He owed his success partly, at least, to his access to centres of power beyond the purview of the normal admiral and his readiness to exploit his contacts to the full. A typical diary entry covering a weekend at Broadlands read: 'Edwina to church. I hung about for Eden who appeared at lunchtime. . . . Valuable talk on future of Navy.'[16] He took great pains, too, to keep the senior Admirals outside London in touch with what was going on, inaugurating a series of newsletters which he sent out at more or less quarterly intervals, dated (irritatingly, except to the naval historian) Armada Day, Jutland Day and so on through the naval calendar. He used the press more effectively than his predecessors, both negatively, by disarming potential trouble-makers through hospitality and discreet briefings, and positively to promote a particular cause. When there was a budgetary threat to the future of the Royal Marine band, for instance, he alerted the editorial director of the *Daily Mirror*, Hugh Cudlipp, a Marine band enthusiast. Cudlipp in his turn enlisted another devotee, the newspaper's popular columnist Cassandra, who launched a press campaign to save the band.[17] As with every flamboyant, determined and, above all, successful figure, Mountbatten's activities took on a different air according to the angle from which they were viewed. To Lang his conduct of Promotion Boards was marked by his emphatic rejection of any candidate he disliked; to John Hamilton he seemed scrupulously fair. In the many discussions of personnel problems that they had together, Hamilton was impressed by Mountbatten's open-mindedness, his concern for the good of the Navy as well as the individual, and his compassion towards those who for one reason or another had had a bad run of luck.[18]

'First day as First Sea Lord. Thrill to sit under Papa's picture,' was his diary entry for 18 April. Even though the view from the window was now blocked by the drab concrete mass of the Citadel, he insisted on moving back to what had been his father's office. It was an overt celebration of the fact that Prince Louis' downfall had been redeemed, any stain on the family honour finally expunged. Due obeisance made to the past, he turned energetically to the future.

He contrived to instil a sense of urgency into the Whitehall machine. If any letter requiring a reply was not dealt with within a week, he ruled, then he personally must be given an explanation. If obeyed literally this order would no doubt have drowned his staff in unwanted paper; as it was, it put everyone in the Admiralty on notice that no unnecessary delay would be tolerated.[19] Before the Navy could take on its new shape it had to shed the encumbrances of the old. The first stage must be a ruthless programme of rationalization and retrenchment. Here Mountbatten's experience as Fourth Sea Lord proved invaluable. His technical knowledge and commonsense, allied with immense authority, made him uniquely able to tackle the vested interests which abound in any ancient institution. Before he visited Bath, heartland of the Controller's Departments, he was given briefs on the fifty or so people he would be meeting and the work they were doing. By the time he arrived he had mastered their contents and was able to discuss the issues with real understanding. 'Here', felt the technical experts, 'was a man who had a grasp of the issues and would see that the necessary decisions were made.'[20]

Mountbatten's most valuable achievement, said Caspar John, was to make the Navy take a look at itself and no longer say: 'If it was good enough for Nelson, it's good enough for me.'[21] For this his first and most valuable instrument was the 'Way Ahead' Committee.

> Our present Navy afloat is largely the result of arbitrary reductions over a long period to meet our financial object [Mountbatten wrote to his close friend and ally, the American Chief of Naval Operations Arleigh Burke]. On the other hand, the effort and expense ashore has not in my opinion been reduced to the same extent as the cutting of the active Fleet: nor have the resources we have been left with after the reduction been reorganised to meet either present conditions or future developments.
>
> We must therefore get our economies more from reorganisation rather than simply by lopping pieces of inflationary growth, of which by this time very little remains.[22]

Only if such economies could be achieved would there be money for the new building programme without which the Navy would fall disastrously behind its allies and rivals.

The most notable feature about the Way Ahead Committee was that it possessed considerable executive powers yet excluded the political masters of the Navy, the First Lord and the Parliamentary Secretary. John Lang vigorously opposed what he saw as a derogation of civil control, but the easy-going Thomas accepted Mountbatten's assurance that discussion would be too technical for him to follow and that he would do better to take a back seat and rubber-stamp the Committee's decisions as they were put before the Board. 'It was largely through the existence of the Way Ahead Committee that I did in fact run the Admiralty over the heads of the First Lord and the Secretary, much to the latter's indignation,' Mountbatten later recorded.[23]

'Got "Where are we going" back on to Board agenda,' wrote Mountbatten in his diary for 16 June, and four days later, 'First meeting of Quo Vadis.' Within six months the Committee was already reporting its first major recommendations; within two years it could fairly claim to have dismantled and reassembled an administrative and logistic structure that had ossified over the previous decade. The Nore Command was abolished and establishments closed in the Chatham area; the dockyards at Sheerness and Portland were greatly curtailed; research and development was concentrated into two major centres – Portsdown for surface and Portland for underwater weapons; Home Air Command was reduced from nineteen stations to eight; the Royal Marine establishments were slimmed and rationalized. Hatchet work of this kind is not achieved without much pain and the loss of valuable shoots among the dead wood. Mountbatten made some enemies but on the whole the work of the Way Ahead Committee was little criticized – a sure indication of how badly its reforms were needed.

To economize on the shore-based establishments was one thing; to rebuild the sea-going Navy quite another. 'Once we can obtain Government agreement to the fact that we are the mobile large scale rocket carriers of the future then everything else will fall into place,' Mountbatten told William Davis.[24] This was to be one of the two main planks of Admiralty policy during the Mountbatten years; the second, the provision of a powerful amphibious striking-force capable of acting in defence of British interests anywhere in the world, was not even to begin to come about until after the Suez Crisis at the end of 1956. Many of the ships in the Reserve were not needed and could anyway not possibly be prepared in time for use in a nuclear war; a weeding-out was set in hand which was to reduce the Reserve Fleet by more than half within a decade.[25] Mountbatten inherited a programme of conventionally armed 5000-ton destroyers and 18,000-ton cruisers carrying Sea Slug missiles – a project described by David Divine as 'perhaps one of the more disastrous judgments of Naval history'.[26] He scrapped the cruiser programme and gave instructions that the destroyers were to be increased in size by 1000 tons to accommodate Sea Slug – the first generation of the guided-missile destroyers which were to provide the backbone of the future Fleet.

He saw more clearly than his predecessors the contribution that the helicopter could make to naval warfare, in particular in the battle against the submarine, where the aircraft could act as a frigate's eyes and ears and pinpoint the submarine's whereabouts before the surface vessel came within torpedo range. At the Farnborough Air Show in the summer of 1955 he was struck by the potentialities of the Skeeta light-weight helicopter and ordered three – against the advice of the Fifth Sea Lord – for testing and development. Within a few years helicopters were automatically included in the armament of every frigate, as well as operating from aircraft-carriers on search and rescue duties and from commando ships in a reconnaissance role.[27]

Manpower was a cause for concern when he took office. Entrants to the regular Navy had fallen by more than a thousand a year since 1951 and a large number of short-service men were on the point of ending their period. In the short term numbers could be made up by recruits doing their national service, but this was no way to run a fully efficient fleet, and there was, anyway, a risk that conscription would be allowed to lapse when the Act expired at the end of 1958. From the Mediterranean Grantham wrote of a growing malaise among the younger officers, whose main preoccupation seemed to be what sort of living they could make in civilian life. Somehow they had to be reassured that the Navy offered them a worthwhile and secure career.[28] Mountbatten fully agreed; indeed, he saw his function as propagandist for the Navy as being aimed as much at his own personnel as at the politicians or the general public. A committee on Manning and Recruitment was set up to look into the reasons for the shortage of manpower. Mountbatten himself believed that a failure in leadership was as important an element as any in the crumbling of morale. He urged 'Encouragement and more official backing for spare time activities, such as sailing, mountaineering, pot-holing, canoeing, underwater fishing etc, which do so much to strengthen character and leadership. I started a scheme on these lines when I was in the Mediterranean Fleet.'[29]

In April 1955 Churchill at last resigned as Prime Minister – 'Tragic to have to do so in a Press Strike,' was Mountbatten's comment.[30] That autumn his successor, Eden, offered Mountbatten the new post as Chairman of the Chiefs of Staff. Mountbatten had only just taken over as First Sea Lord and was determined to see that job through. He also suspected that the post of Chairman would be more easily established if the first incumbent was less notorious a partisan of centralization than himself. He asked to be excused and urged Eden to appoint the Chief of Air Staff, Dickson, instead. Dickson duly became first Chairman at the beginning of 1956. From time to time he was called on to represent the Chiefs of Staff in the Defence Committee of the Cabinet or before the Minister of Defence. Gerald Templer, the Chief of the Imperial General Staff, resisted what he saw as an encroachment on the independence of the three Services; 'Mountbatten never did,' wrote Dickson, 'and he gave me every support throughout this very difficult period.'[31] The battle was to rage until Mountbatten retired ten years later, and, indeed, long after.

Commonwealth co-operation was one of his favourite themes and he never missed a chance to visit one of the Commonwealth countries. His journeys were always strenuous, sometimes excessively so: 'Canada was really rather ridiculous as through lack of adequate supervision on my part they had produced a programme which ran from about 0800 to midnight every day with barely time to pee, let alone wash my hands.'[32]

His relationship with New Zealand was particularly close. On his first visit as First Sea Lord the Prime Minister, Sydney Holland, cancelled a Cabinet meeting to drive out to the airport and meet his plane as he passed through. The object was to persuade Mountbatten to become Governor-General, an offer which Mountbatten had no hesitation in rejecting on the grounds that he had essential work to do in London. 'Last time I went to Australia the Prime Minister, Mr Chifley, offered me the Governor-Generalship of Australia, and Harry Gloucester refused on my behalf,' he told Patricia. 'These offers become embarrassing!'[33] He took no less interest in

New Zealand affairs, however, and wrote to Holland drawing a parallel between that country's role in the southern hemisphere and Britain's in the northern – both small countries in economic difficulties and living by imports and exports. Yet, he pointed out – perhaps somewhat misleadingly – Britain spent 7% of its gross national product on defence; New Zealand only 2.6%.[34]

Rear-Admiral McBeath, the Chief of Naval Staff, was treated and treated him as a particularly trusted colleague. Mountbatten wrote to him of rumours that his 'Army opposite number, Weir, is very pro-American and . . . is anxious for the Services to be supplied from the United States'. He asked for a private report on Weir and was only partially appeased by the favourable reply.[35] McBeath for his part reported with alarming frankness on the problems he was having with the Labour Government that came to power in December 1957. 'Most of the Cabinet seem to be very ordinary average citizens with no particular merit or background.' The Minister of Defence, P. G. Connolly, was 'very rough and unpolished, slovenly in appearance and of the opinion that his knowledge of the Navy makes him an authority. . . . Connolly is very typical of the rest of the Cabinet, though two or three of the sixteen do *look* like gentlemen.'[36]

Mountbatten would not have had much sympathy with this last animadversion. His views on class were a compound of the royal assumption that one subject was very like another, and his mother's egalitarianism. He expected those with whom he dealt to be competent, hoped they would be sympathetic, but cared little about their gentility. If he made any distinction, it was to assume that sailors were likely to be more resourceful and honest than the generality of mankind. To McBeath and his successor he urged moderation. If the Chiefs of Staff held together and insisted on proper consultation over defence matters, all should prove well in the end. 'In any event I sincerely hope matters will not come to such a pass that *you feel you have to ask to be relieved.*'

His visit in 1956 to his old stamping-grounds in South-East Asia gave him greater satisfaction than any other. It started badly, when Pakistani air-controllers refused to allow his aeroplane to cross their air-space. When the Pakistani High Commissioner in Delhi went to the airport to greet Mountbatten, he was abused by the Karachi paper, *Dawn*, for honouring that 'Serpent'. 'A man like Mountbatten whose hand is stained with the blood of thousands of innocent moslems is nothing but the enemy of Pakistan.'[37] Muhammad Ali, the Prime Minister, subsequently apologized when he was in London for the Commonwealth Conference a few months later. Mountbatten coolly told him that if he really wanted to make amends he should write out a statement absolving the former Viceroy from having shown bias during his time in

India. Muhammad Ali, not surprisingly, demurred.[38]

Pakistani slights lent zeal to the Indian welcome. 'Dickie must remember
. . . that important and high as his position is as First Sea Lord, he will be
welcomed here more as an ex-Governor-General,' Nehru told Edwina. 'We
give our ex-Governor-Generals and ex-Presidents a very high status here.'[39]
He was as good as his word. The Mountbattens arrived in Delhi to be greeted
by a cohort of Ministers, Ambassadors and prominent citizens and to drive to
the President's house through crowds shouting 'Lord Mountbatten *ki
jai*! Lady Mountbatten *ki jai*!' A state banquet was given in his honour.
The President, Rajendra Prasad, sat with his staff grouped behind him. To see
the Maharoa Raja of Bundi (an A.D.C.) and the Maharaj Kumar of Jaipur
(adjutant of the bodyguard) standing throughout dinner behind the President's chair seemed to the visitors 'to epitomize the complete passing of the
old order in India'.[40]

From India Mountbatten moved on to Burma, a country for which he felt
almost equal responsibility. In Rangoon he was invested with the order of the
Agga Maha Thiri Thu Dhamma, meaning, more or less, 'Highest and Most
Glorious Commander of the Most Exalted Order of Truth'. The title was the
noblest in the gift of the Burmese people, the President told Mountbatten,
awarded 'in recognition of signal services rendered by you, firstly, in liberat-
ing my country from the Japanese occupation; secondly, in treating my
countrymen kindly, humanely and sympathetically after liberation and,
thirdly, in paving the way for the quick restoration of our birthright'.[41]


Mountbatten returned from his long tour to find himself at the centre of a
squall over the activities of Commander Crabbe. The Russian leaders,
Bulganin and Khrushchev, were visiting Britain and had arrived in a cruiser
which berthed at Portsmouth. A retired R.N.V.R. officer, Lionel Crabbe,
disappeared while diving in Portsmouth harbour, allegedly to inspect the
bottom and propellers of the Russian cruiser. Mountbatten knew nothing of
this till he went to the Admiralty after his return, by which time the press had
got hold of the story and it was clear that a scandal was about to break. He
insisted that the First Lord should be told at once.

This much is undisputed, but the First Sea Lord's recollections of some of
the more picturesque details of the episode are at variance with those of his
V.C.N.S., William Davis.[42] Mountbatten recalls issuing specific instructions
to Davis shortly before he left on his tour that no such operation was to be
mounted, justifying what might have seemed a superfluous precaution on the
grounds that 'it seems to be irresistible for spies to look at ships' bottoms'.
Davis has no recollection of this percipient instruction. Mountbatten recalls

telling Davis to report the matter at once to the First Lord and, when the V.C.N.S. was reluctant, saying: 'It's an order. If you don't go, I shall run you in!' As Davis moved reluctantly towards the door, Mountbatten called out: 'Run, William, run! Pick up at the double!' Davis recalls a less dramatic interview. Mountbatten agreed that there had been no need to warn the First Lord when it still seemed likely that the story would never become public, and demurred only when Davis suggested waiting a few minutes to let John Lang join the party. 'When the First Lord heard about it, the sparks flew,' recorded Mountbatten; 'I thought the First Lord took the information very calmly,' writes Davis.

Neither account was written till long after the affair was over, though Davis kept a diary at the time. Probably his recollections are more nearly accurate. What is undoubtedly true is that Mountbatten would have stopped the operation if he had been in Britain and aware of it. Quite apart from the fact that he believed its risks far outweighed its possible usefulness, he would have deplored anything that might impair the chances of a reconciliation with the Russians. 'If I were Prime Minister,' David Astor remembers Mountbatten saying when the idea of the visit was mooted, 'I'd go to Moscow tomorrow to meet Khrushchev. I'd say "You want to be friends? Let's be friends!" I know they killed all my family but that mustn't stand in the way of getting on with them now.'[43] It was a somewhat over-simplified approach to foreign policy, and Mountbatten would certainly never have advocated putting much faith in similar protestations from the Russians, but he believed that the Russians were reasonable men, as anxious to avoid war as the leaders of the West, and therefore ready to negotiate on issues of importance.

There were some who found it hard to believe in the innocence of the Admiralty over the Crabbe affair. When Mountbatten accompanied his Minister to the House of Commons on 14 May 1956 the Labour M.P. Colonel Wigg gesticulated in his direction and called out: 'The man responsible is the First Sea Lord, he should be thrown out!' Some time later Mountbatten met him and taxed him with making an unfair accusation; Wigg must have known that he was abroad at the time. Wigg was unimpressed. 'Nothing in the Navy happens unless you want it to,' he retorted. 'They wouldn't have dared do it if they thought you would disapprove.'

Though the *Daily Mirror* took up the Crabbe case with some gusto – 'Hugh, are you trying to get me sacked?' Mountbatten asked Cudlipp loudly when he met him at the Albert Hall[44] – the Beaverbrook press let the First Sea Lord off surprisingly lightly. In July, however, the *Daily Express* launched a ferocious attack on the grounds that he had now been a year in office yet had done nothing to check the Navy's wanton extravagance. 'How much longer does Lord Mountbatten expect to keep the nation waiting? . . . Lord Mountbatten should be told to do his part in this economy drive without any further delay. Or to yield the job to someone who can.'[45] The charge was particularly hurtful to Mountbatten, since he knew that he was doing as much as or more than any of his predecessors to curb expenditure without blunting the Navy's capacity to fight a war. The First Lord, now ennobled as Lord Cilcennin, rose in his defence, asking Beaverbrook to remind his editors that 'the responsibility for the work of the Admiralty rests, not with the First Sea Lord, but with the First Lord. . . . The Minister, after all, has the opportunity of defending himself.'[46]

Beaverbrook's hostility to Mountbatten was not waning with the years. Three months before Slim, now Governor-General in Australia, had told Mountbatten that the *Daily Express* had offered a large sum for the serial rights in his forthcoming book on the Burma campaign; they wished, Slim was told, to give him a fair chance to state his side of all the disagreements and disputes he had had with his Supreme Commander. Slim replied that there had been no disputes, he had always got on very well with Mountbatten. At this the *Daily Express* lost interest in the serial and since then 'they have written nothing but foul things about him'.[47]

Cilcennin's attempt to protect his First Sea Lord was one of his last acts in office. As early as February 1956 his removal had been mooted. Mountbatten told Monckton, the Minister of Defence, that 'the present First Lord was extremely popular in the Navy and if his departure looked anything like a dismissal it would grieve the Navy very much'.[48] Whether or not this intervention made any difference, Cilcennin gained another six months as First Lord. By then ill-health and financial difficulties made him not too sorry to depart. By the time his successor, Lord Hailsham, attended his first Board meeting on 3 September the storm was already gaining strength in the eastern Mediterranean. The Suez Crisis had begun.

# CHAPTER 41

## *Suez*

ON 13 JUNE 1956 the last British troops left the area of the Suez Canal which they had garrisoned for so long. The administration of the waterway remained the responsibility of the Anglo-French Suez Canal Company which had originally constructed it. On 23 June Colonel Nasser was elected President of Egypt. One month later Britain joined the United States in withdrawing financial help from the Aswan High Dam. On 26 July Nasser nationalized the Suez Canal Company. From the vantage-point of history this melancholy procession assumes the inevitability of Greek tragedy or a natural disaster, yet at the time there seemed no reason to believe that one step would lead to another, or all lead to catastrophe. To Mountbatten, convinced that Nasser was neither Communist nor a would-be Hitler, but merely a sincere if sometimes misguided patriot, the logic of events seemed peculiarly hard to follow.

On 26 July he was dining at the Savoy with his daughter Patricia. He saw a Ministry of Defence messenger peering around the tables and knew that trouble was in the offing. Fifteen minutes later he was in Downing Street. The Prime Minister was there with various Cabinet Ministers; the French Ambassador and American Chargé d'Affaires were shortly on the scene; Dermot Boyle, the Chief of Air Staff, had been dining at Number Ten, and General Templer soon arrived also. Dickson being ill, Mountbatten was Acting Chairman of the Chiefs of Staff Committee, and it was in that capacity that Eden turned to him after he had finished his exposition of Nasser's behaviour and asked what immediate military action could be taken. Mountbatten replied that the Fleet was assembled at Malta and could sail within a few hours. The Royal Marine commandos could be picked up at Cyprus, and Port Said occupied within three or four days. 'The Prime Minister', Mountbatten recorded drily, 'was delighted – almost too delighted – with this information.'[1]

In a letter written to Michael Howard in 1973 Mountbatten indicates that this was the course he recommended. 'The Royal Marines . . . could then seize Port Said and the first twenty-five miles of the Causeway along the Canal. All this they would hold very easily without a shot being fired with great political

impact. . . . Aircraft-carriers could easily provide the necessary cover. . . .
The meeting was obviously very impressed and rather favourably inclined
towards my idea.' Eden, however, said that he wanted the whole Canal in the
hands of the British. He therefore 'decided not to accept my offer which
would have meant we would have had as much in our hands within three days
as we subsequently ended up with . . . after three months! The only difference
would have been complete surprise and we certainly could have prevented
any movement through the Canal and . . . negotiated from a point of view of
peaceful strength.'[2]

This version of events, in which he advocated a daring *coup de main* with
light forces but was borne down by the caution of the politicians, was much
put around by Mountbatten in the later years of his life but is contradicted by
his own account dictated early in September 1956.[3] According to this, he
went on to argue that, though the 1200 Marines could seize the Causeway,
they would have great difficulty maintaining themselves there in the face of
Egyptian opposition. 'I recommend that unilateral action by the Royal Navy
and the Royal Marines should not be taken.' This seems more probable.
Certainly it corresponds with accepted military doctrine at the time. Templer
strongly opposed putting ashore a lightly armed force that might easily be
confronted by Egyptian tanks, while General Stockwell, eventual commander of the invasion force, commented that the paratroopers were out of
training and the landing-craft for the most part out of commission.[4]

The Chiefs of Staff were despatched to prepare a plan for a full-scale
invasion and by 9.15 the following morning were at work. Mountbatten
now had time to reflect on the action that was being proposed, and the more
that he did so, whether on grounds of expediency or of morality, the more
he became appalled. On 31 July Eden telephoned him about the fate of two
destroyers which had been bought by the Egyptians from the Royal Navy and
were now on the point of sailing for Alexandria. The Prime Minister
considered that these should be impounded; Mountbatten argued that the
most that could properly be done was to ensure that they sailed without
ammunition. Eden reluctantly agreed, then ended the conversation with: 'I
can't tell you how happy I am to have you with me during this time of crisis
and I hope you agree with all I am doing.' Non-committally Mountbatten
replied: 'The Chiefs of Staff of course will do whatever you wish.' He then
drafted a letter to the Prime Minister in which he said that, as a professional
sailor, he could have no view on the political problems involved, but as 'a very
old friend' he felt he must make his feelings known:

> The absolutely paramount consideration is the marshalling of world
> opinion on our side. We have six weeks in which to do this – so has

Nasser. If he is the megalomaniac we are led to believe . . . we should apply economic sanctions and pressure in the ways best calculated to goad him into further high-handed actions, which would antagonise the world at large, and also British opinion. So far, however, he has shown every sign of being anxious to stress the legality of his action. . . .

It seems to me that the surest way to enlist support for our cause is to offer terms to Nasser which it would be patently unreasonable and provocative for him to reject. The offer should be backed by as many of the maritime nations as we can enlist; so that it should be clear to everyone that we are not aiming primarily at re-asserting ourselves in Egypt, but at securing the greatest benefit for all other potential users of the canal. . . .

Meanwhile, a large share of our Psychological Warfare in the next six weeks could be devoted to establishing in everyone's mind the fact that our concentration of force is purely precautionary. Any idea that we had already decided to launch an invasion . . . could only help to tilt world opinion in his favour. . . .

I am convinced that our trump card is the reasonable, constructive offer, backed by as many nations as we can collect and one that the Americans, as well as the countries of Asia . . . could not conceivably condemn as being 'imperialistic'.[5]

Mountbatten showed this draft to the First Lord, who said that, while he agreed entirely with it, he felt that the letter should not be sent – a Chief of Staff had no business giving avowedly political advice to the Prime Minister. Mountbatten then appealed to the Minister of Defence who took the same line. The draft was put aside. But though he temporarily shelved the idea of a direct appeal to Eden, he fought the case among his colleagues. To the Prime Minister he had based his opposition on the claims of *Realpolitik*; to the Chiefs of Staff he was more passionate and less prudent. Some time earlier, in a similar context, Templer had called for 'resolute action' in the military sphere. Mountbatten expostulated:

If we were fighting a visible enemy who was trying to dominate the Middle East by force of arms I should back you to the limit. . . . But there is no such enemy. . . . The Middle East conflict is about ideas, emotions, loyalties. You and I belong to a people which will not have ideas which we don't believe in thrust down our throats by bayonets or other force. Why should we assume that this process will work with other peoples? . . .

You cannot, I suggest, fight ideas with troops and weapons. The ideas and the problems they create are still there when you withdraw the troops. What effect . . . would it have on our troops? Can the British way of life, which you and I believe must be preserved at all costs, survive if we use our young men to repudiate one of its basic principles – the right to self-determination – as permanent occupation troops?[6]

These words summed up his attitude towards intervention at Suez. As the Chiefs of Staff prepared their answer to Eden's problem, Mountbatten hammered away at the fundamental questions which he felt the Prime Minister was ignoring: what were the political implications of the British action and how in the long run were they to be coped with militarily? On 14 August he asked what steps were being taken to ensure that an Egyptian Government might be found which would both accept British actions and have popular support. He told the Chiefs that he feared the Egyptian people were so solidly behind Nasser that it might be impossible to find such a government. A week later he argued that there was a real danger that Operation MUSKETEER, as the planned invasion was codenamed, would cause serious and continuing disorder in the Middle Eastern countries and make necessary the retention of considerable forces in the area for many years if law and order were to be maintained. On 18 September he insisted that the Chiefs of Staff should press the Foreign Office to reconsider their statement that they could not for the present carry out work on a study of long-term commitments in the Middle East. A week later he complained that present plans only covered military operations up to the capitulation of Egypt. What needed urgent consideration was the scale of the continuing commitment which would be required of the United Kingdom in Egypt and the area generally. Finally, on 9 October he pleaded once more that Ministers should be forced to confront the consequences of undertaking Operation MUS-KETEER. This might involve the occupation of Egypt for a considerable period. Any new Government in Egypt could probably remain in power only so long as some form of occupation continued.[7]

The Prime Minister had no wish to have the consequences of the operation put clearly before him and grew more and more indignant as Mountbatten's heresies became the dogma of the Chiefs of Staff. 'I remember one occasion at No 10,' wrote Dickson, 'when Mountbatten asked for an indication of the political objective, and the P.M. flaring up and telling him that he would have no interference from the Chiefs of Staff on political matters.'[8] Even among the Chiefs, however, he was sometimes a lone voice. Dickson agreed with him but was ill and often absent. Boyle was at the most undecided, and Templer deplored his attitude, at one meeting going so far as to accuse him of being 'yellow'.[9]

Within Eden's inner circle Mountbatten found several who seemed to accept his general view yet none who was prepared to stand up to the Prime Minister. He told Krishna Menon that Monckton was the only Minister fully on his side, Butler might also support him when he returned, and 'there would certainly be two or three other Cabinet Ministers with a broad Liberal approach but I had not yet heard anyone in the smaller Cabinet Committee speak out strongly against a plan to invade Egypt'.[10] Cilcennin was opposed to the operation but he was due to retire on 2 September and he warned Mountbatten that all he knew about the views of his successor, Lord Hailsham, suggested that there was not much to be hoped for from that quarter.[11] Macmillan, then Chancellor of the Exchequer, was enigmatic. His original criticism of the Chiefs of Staff's plan was that it did not go nearly far enough: Egypt should be invaded from Libya and troops landed near Alexandria.[12] Subsequently he changed his mind, but Mountbatten never felt he would prove a reliable ally.

Dickson commented that Mountbatten's 'wartime experiences, and his time in India, led him more than the other Chiefs of Staff to think of the political factors'.[13] It was above all the effect that the Suez venture might have on the Commonwealth that preoccupied Mountbatten. Lord Home had told him that in the Canadian view the invasion of Egypt would cause the break-up of the Commonwealth.[14] All his experience led him to believe that this was likely to prove true. Through Edwina he knew only too well what the Indians felt. 'We are greatly troubled over Suez,' Nehru wrote in August. 'The French have been very bad, but what has happened to Anthony? . . . What is the U.K. Govt aiming at? Surely not a war, even a minor one.'[15] Three weeks later Krishna Menon returned from London, reporting on the 'oppressive atmosphere' that reigned there. Mountbatten, he told Nehru, was looking rather haggard. The Indian Prime Minister still could not believe that it would come to war, but doubts were creeping in. 'From every point of view that would be the height of madness. But then are we after all so logical and reasonable. . . . I wonder if H. G. Wells was not right when he said that the world was disintegrating.'[16] Two months later the war was on. 'I would never have conceived of a government of the United Kingdom functioning as the present one has done,' wrote Nehru in despair. 'Whatever the future may bring, I fear that respect for the U.K. has vanished utterly from Asia and Africa.'[17] It was the confirmation of all that Mountbatten had feared.

Yet outwardly he remained a loyal public servant doing his duty and preparing for war. To his wife, indeed, it sometimes seemed that he was too loyal a servant of the Government. 'I'm sorry we seem so often to have got at cross purposes about Egypt,' he told Edwina. 'Basically we feel the same and I am doing all and more than I ought to do as a serving officer to try and work for a peaceful solution.'[18] Though his colleagues on the Chiefs of Staff were clear about his views, he otherwise kept them to himself. Admiral Durnford-Slater, his original choice to be in charge of the operation, was given no inkling that Mountbatten had reservations about the wisdom of the enter-prise; nor was his Naval Assistant, Peter Howes.[19] Still less did the junior officers and men suspect that there were doubts on high.

By the end of August Mountbatten's distress was so great that he drafted a letter of resignation to the Prime Minister. In it he spoke of the risk of provoking a thermo-nuclear war and of Britain's 'retrograde and absolutely indefensible step' in flouting the principles on which the United Nations had been founded. In these circumstances, he felt, he could not remain in office.[20] The letter was never sent; he brooded over it for twenty-four hours, then compromised by submitting his resignation instead to the First Lord. It cannot have seemed likely to him that it would be accepted. 'This is a matter of conscience for you which I admire and on which I would not presume to dictate,' wrote Cilcennin. 'But you must discuss this with the Minister of Defence and we three must be the *only* people who know how your mind is working.'[21] When he met the two Ministers, they both argued that it was unheard-of for a Service chief to resign rather than carry out the orders of his Government in starting a war on which they had decided. 'Indeed, they questioned the propriety of a serving officer refusing to carry out his orders.' When Mountbatten asked why, in that case, the British had been in-strumental in convicting German officers in the war-trials at Nuremberg in spite of their plea that they were merely obeying orders, the Ministers agreed that there might be circumstances in which disobedience would be permiss-ible. But this was not yet the case, nor would it be until it had been shown beyond doubt that Eden's opponents in the Cabinet had failed to get MUSKETEER stopped or at least modified.[22]

Certainly much modification was needed. The directive given to the Chiefs of Staff made it inevitable that an armed amphibious assault in a densely populated area would be preceded by massive bombardment by sea and air. Thousands, possibly tens of thousands, of civilians would be dead before the first British or French troops landed. As the details were worked out, the planners themselves became more and more aghast at what they were proposing. The Minister of Defence; the First Lord; Nigel Birch, the Secretary of State for Air – all agreed that such carnage could not be permitted. Only the Secretary of State for War, Antony Head, believed that such action was preferable to the 'death by a thousand cuts and slow strangulation' which he felt must be Britain's alternative.[23] There were some grounds for fearing that his position might be reinforced when Lord Hailsham took over as First Lord at the beginning of September, but the contrary proved true. After studying the plans for MUSKETEER, Hailsham told Mountbatten that he had been an ardent advocate of force as the ultimate sanction, but that 'he had never envisaged anything as horrible as this and he was in despair as to what to do'.

On 7 September came a confrontation between the Prime Minister, the Chiefs of Staff and General Keightley, Commander-in-Chief designate of the invasion force. 'Vital meeting,' noted Mountbatten in his diary, '. . . at which I spoke up and managed to produce a debate.'[24] For the first time Eden was confronted with the full consequences of MUSKETEER, the destruction and toll in civilian lives, a campaign that could well last two or three months. The Prime Minister insisted that the Egyptians would not fight; Mountbatten was equally insistent that 'every Egyptian must now feel that . . . they were free and liberated, and that their country was worth fighting for'. Against serious resistance it would take twenty-three days even to reach Cairo. 'I don't think I have ever been so eloquent,' Mountbatten recorded subsequently. 'My colleagues on the Chiefs of Staff Committee supported me with a strength I had not expected and certainly General Keightley was a tremendous supporter.'[25]

He won a partial victory. At a Cabinet meeting that afternoon, so Hailsham told the First Sea Lord, Eden put forward all the arguments which Mountbatten had advanced that morning, and the Cabinet ordered the Chiefs of Staff to prepare a modified MUSKETEER which would eliminate the worst features of the original plan. 'I can't thank you enough for what you did today,' Hailsham wrote to him that evening.[26] But what remained was bad enough. Though the plan was modified, it still involved an act of aggression against an independent country which had behaved perhaps unwisely but not, so far as the law officers of the Crown could see, illegally. Nor would the Government face up to the fact that their problems would only be beginning if resistance crumbled and the Canal Zone was reoccupied. Mountbatten would not leave the issue alone. 'I think we will be failing in our duty', he told Dickson on 27 September, 'if we do not make some attempt to look at the overall military commitments wherever they may be arising out of MUSKETEER.'[27] When the Chiefs of Staff met on 25 October to give final approval to their planning paper, it was at Mountbatten's insistence that they included a paragraph arguing that the right policy was to gain Egyptian co-operation by avoiding any occupation of their territory or, at least, by restricting it to the minimum. Sombrely, they listed the forces that they thought would be required if a prolonged occupation proved to be necessary.[28]

The paper was issued as coming from the Egypt Committee. The result was predictable. The Prime Minister flared up at what he held to be interference by the military in a political matter. He gave personal directions that the paper be withdrawn.[29]

> Our reports have been madly vacillating [Mountbatten told Grantham on 26 October]. The heat was first 'on', then 'off' and now very much 'on', as we have definite reports that Israel is mobilising and requisitioning civilian transports. Our estimate is that they are likely to be ready for war about Monday, or possibly Tuesday, but no overt steps may be taken by us at present.[30]

The mild relief that Mountbatten had experienced when MUSKETEER Mark 1 was cancelled had proved fleeting as it became evident that MUSKETEER Mark 2 was to prove little better. The essence of the revised operation was that preliminary bombing of military targets, psychological warfare, and the cutting off of oil supplies would so have weakened the Egyptian will to resist that the Allied landings would be virtually unopposed. By 2 November, four days after the first Israeli attack and two days after the beginning of the air war against Egypt, it was clear that this hope was illusory. Photo-reconnaissance showed that the Egyptians were strongly dug in at Port Said and every report suggested that they intended to resist as fiercely as lay within their power. On the same day the United Nations General Assembly called for a cease-fire. The Anglo-French force was still at sea four days from Port Said and the first parachute drop was within seventy-two hours. Mountbatten decided that there was still time for one last appeal to the Prime Minister.

> I know that you have been fully aware over these past weeks of my great unhappiness at the prospect of our launching military operations against Egypt, and indeed as recently as Thursday of last week . . . you told Edwina and me that you realised how much I hated making the preparations which had been ordered.
>
> It is not the business of a serving officer to question the political decisions of his government; and although I did not believe that a just and lasting settlement of any dispute could be worked out under a threat of military action, I did everything in my power to carry out your orders as in duty bound, loyally and to the full, in making all the necessary naval preparations for building up a position in which we could have negotiated from strength.
>
> Now, however, the decisive step of armed intervention by the British has been taken; bombing has started and the assault convoy is on its way from Malta.

I am writing to appeal to you to accept the resolution of the overwhelming majority of the United Nations to cease military operations and to beg you to turn back the assault convoy before it is too late, as I feel that the actual landing of troops can only spread the war with untold misery and world-wide repercussions.

You can imagine how hard it is for me to break with all service custom and write direct to you in this way, but I feel so desperate about what is happening that my conscience would not allow me to do otherwise.[31]

This time there was to be no question of the First Lord talking him out of his appeal; the first thing Hailsham knew of it was when Mountbatten told him two days later. It would have been astonishing if the Prime Minister had paid any attention to his First Sea Lord's initiative. He telephoned to thank Mountbatten for showing his confidence in writing so frankly, but that was that. 'When I begged him to act on my suggestion and allow me to turn back the Assault Convoy before it was too late, he replied he could not possibly do that and hung up the telephone.'[32] Mountbatten turned to the First Lord. So far civilian casualties had been almost entirely avoided, but they would be inevitable in the case of an opposed landing and it would be the Navy who would be most likely to inflict them.

However repugnant the task the Navy will carry out its orders. Nevertheless as its professional head I must register the strongest possible protest at this use of my service; and would ask you as the responsible Minister to convey that protest to the Prime Minister.

I recognise that a serving officer cannot back his protest by resignation at a time like this, so I must ask you to handle this whole matter on behalf of the Navy. Bearing in mind all the implications I must ask you, after consulting the Prime Minister, to give me an order to stay or to go.[33]

Once again he can have had little doubt about the reception he would receive. Though he wrote ten years later that he fully expected to be released from his job after writing so tough a letter,[34] it must have been evident that the Government could not possibly let him go while the crisis was at its height. Nor did he wish to go. 'Satisfactory letter from 1st Lord,' was his diary comment on Hailsham's response[35] – a reply that stated bluntly that, if anything happened to impair the honour of the Navy, it was for the First Lord to resign. 'In the meantime you are entitled to be protected by a direct order from me. It is that you remain at your post until further orders.'[36] Next day the First Lord wrote again to state that the Prime Minister had confirmed the decision.[37]

Mountbatten's role in the affair was almost over. He had barely received Hailsham's second letter before the news came that the Government had yielded to international pressure and a cease-fire had been ordered. A few weeks later he noted in his diary that Eden had resigned: 'Sad on account of long personal friendship – but alas I've disagreed to his face with all he has done re Egypt.'[38] He never forgave Eden, and as time passed he became increasingly vociferous in making clear his opposition to the Prime Minister's policy. In 1976 Lord Avon, as Eden became in his retirement, read an article in the *Sunday Times Magazine* by Robert Lacey in which the author implied that the Queen had been strongly opposed to the Suez operation but had been unable to prevent it. When challenged, Lacey replied that he had got his information from two very intimate friends of the royal family who were in a position to know the truth. Avon taxed Mountbatten with being one of the sources. 'I did not attempt to deny it,' wrote Mountbatten. 'I said I had been asked officially . . . to see this man to help him, and had answered all his questions.'[39] In a television interview with Ludovic Kennedy, which was suppressed before being shown but published in some detail in *The Times*, Mountbatten stated that nothing else in peacetime had caused him 'so much trouble, so much worry, so much pain and so much grief as the Suez fiasco. One man was responsible, Anthony Eden the Prime Minister.'[40]

That Mountbatten, from the first moment he had a chance to consider the question, was consistently and unequivocally opposed to the attack on Egypt is demonstrably the case. Whether he could or should have done more to stop it is another matter. His critics might argue that, though he wrote a letter of protest to the Prime Minister at the beginning of August, he did not send it. He wrote another three weeks later, but did not send that either. Instead, he allowed himself to be persuaded out of resigning. When he finally did offer his resignation early in November, it was only a few days before the landings at Port Said, and even then he did not demur when ordered to stay at his post. If he had stuck to his guns and threatened to resign unless MUSKETEER was abandoned, is it not possible that Eden would have thought again? And if even a slight chance of this existed, should he not have sacrificed his career for such an end?

The first question, of course, permits of no firm answer. If chance there was, however, it must have been slight indeed. Mountbatten possessed far greater prestige and stature than any other serviceman, but to expect a Prime Minister to change his mind about declaring war at the behest of a sailor arguing not on military but on political and moral grounds would have been fantasy. There was no shortage of admirals willing to take over as First Sea

Lord and any number of politicians who would have seen in a military revolt a reason for suppressing their doubts and rallying behind the civil power. The certainty that Mountbatten was about to resign his post would have given Eden food for thought, but all that is known of his attitude at the time suggests that it would not have changed his mind.

Should Mountbatten still have tried? He did more than anybody else as it was. It was the politicians who might have been expected to resign. Monckton refused to remain as Minister of Defence, but his departure was unobtrusive and he accepted another post within the Cabinet. Cilcennin departed for other reasons. Otherwise no Cabinet Minister stirred, or made any effective effort to alter policy. Mountbatten at least fought the battle within the Chiefs of Staff and induced that singularly conservative body to challenge the Prime Minister on the consequences of his policy. Even if he did not set out his opposition formally to Eden at an early stage, he can have left no doubt in Downing Street about his views. To have resigned on such grounds would have been contrary to every tradition of the public service; the professional head of the Navy might properly throw up his office if in his view the efficiency and well-being of his Service was threatened, but not because the Government decided to wage a war of which he disapproved. Mountbatten could have resigned, but it is unlikely that he would have achieved anything if he had and he would have earned the justified criticism of the Navy by so doing. He could not realistically have been expected to take his opposition farther.

# CHAPTER 42

## The Sandys Years

WHILE THE SUEZ CRISIS WAS BUILDING, Mountbatten was appointed Admiral of the Fleet. This ultimate promotion consoled him for some, at least, of the pains of the present and fortified him for the struggles that lay ahead. Fortification was needed; the *débâcle* at Suez, Macmillan's succession to Eden as Prime Minister and, above all, Duncan Sandys's arrival at the Ministry of Defence were to impose greater strains on the machinery of defence than it had experienced at any time since the war.

An immediate result of the Suez operation was that Mountbatten's hand was strengthened over a project which he had long held dear. He believed that if an old aircraft-carrier could be converted to carry a contingent of Royal Marines, with helicopters and landing-craft, it would provide a valuable addition to Britain's striking force, particularly in the sort of minor, neo-colonial war which he felt was likely to be a feature of the next decades. His colleagues on the Board did not positively dissent but gave the project low priority; it would be a crime, the V.C.N.S. considered, to pay off a precious cruiser with her big guns so as to refurbish an old carrier for the use of marines.[1] Then came Suez. Suddenly seaborne soldiers equipped with helicopters and landing-craft were all the fashion. Two old carriers, *Theseus* and *Albion*, were fortunately available. Carrier-borne helicopters, Mountbatten announced in his quarterly newsletter, 'were for the First Time employed to land a Royal Marine Commando'.[2]

This feature of the operation was conspicuously successful and opposition to the idea melted. By May 1957 plans were being laid for the permanent conversion of carrier to commando-ship; two months later the ship was selected and in January 1960 H.M.S. *Bulwark* was commissioned. She carried six hundred marines and twenty helicopters. H.M.S. *Albion* followed in 1962.[3] 'Not only is the Commando Carrier the most interesting development in Amphibious Warfare since the end of World War II but the ship will have an important role to play in cold and limited wars,' wrote Mountbatten proudly. 'With the ever-growing uncertainty surrounding our overseas bases it is more than ever necessary that the Navy should be capable of transporting a first-class military force to a potential trouble-spot and landing it there by the quickest possible means.'[4]

Other victories were not to be so easily won. The removal of Head and Hailsham, 'and above all the introduction of Duncan Sandys as Minister of Defence will make my fight for the Navy difficult', commented Mountbatten in his diary.[5] The arrival of Sandys was viewed with dismay throughout the Services. He was Churchill's son-in-law and a former Minister of Supply with a reputation for hatchet work. 'He was known as being opinionated and . . . with little underlying realisation of the strategical needs of the country,' wrote Admiral Davis;[6] he aroused 'the strongest feelings of suspicion and resistance', was Dickson's comment.[7] Their dislike was that of the sheep for the shearer, perhaps even the condemned man for the executioner. Sandys had a mandate to rationalize and impose harsh economies; everything they knew about him suggested that he would perform his task without sentiment or respect for sacred cows. Worst of all was that he had come armed with powers that had been formidably if imprecisely strengthened. In future the Minister of Defence would 'have authority to give decisions on all matters of policy affecting the size, shape, organisation and disposition of the Armed Forces, their equipment and supply . . . and their pay and conditions of service'.[8]

The forebodings of the Chiefs of Staff were largely justified. He treated them with scant consideration, brushed their doubts and fears aside and scarcely allowed them to make their voices heard. In July 1957 the Chiefs asked to be present when the Commonwealth Prime Ministers discussed defence. Sandys objected but was overruled by the Prime Minister. When the time came he insisted on doing all the talking himself. 'Let the Chiefs of Staff answer some of these questions,' Macmillan suggested at one point, but Sandys shook his head. Later the Australian Prime Minister, Menzies, asked why the Chiefs had not intervened. 'Because we were given no opportunity,' Mountbatten told him.[9] Relations became so bad that in February 1958 the Chiefs of Staff formally protested that they were not being consulted over important decisions and that a civil organization within the Ministry of Defence was usurping their functions.[10]

'Duncan Sandys is very bad with flu,' Mountbatten told Patricia. 'As Winston once said on hearing that an unpopular member of the Cabinet could not attend because he was ill, "I hope it's nothing trivial"!'[11] But though he would undoubtedly have wished him far away, Mountbatten felt a grudging admiration and even affection for his termagant Minister. He found him obstinate and truculent in the defence of his views, but ready to listen to counter-arguments and, once convinced, stalwart in his support. Both men were members of that conjurors' empyrean the Magic Circle, which provided a real if *recherché* bond, and both shared a radical philosophy about the future of the defence establishment in its broadest terms which seemed heretical to the more conservative officers and civil servants with whom they worked.

If Hailsham had remained as First Lord, Mountbatten would have had a powerful ally in his efforts to preserve the Navy against the depredations of the freebooting Sandys. It was no part of Macmillan's plan, however, that his nominee should meet opposition from his own followers. Hailsham was removed to Education and Lord Selkirk took his place. Selkirk was a generous and honourable man, but ill-equipped to combat the overweening egos of his superior Minister and – theoretically – junior First Sea Lord. He played an inconspicuous role in the debate on the future of the Navy and accepted his lot with grace and good temper. 'I met Selkirk,' Nehru told Edwina, 'and we talked about Dickie, whom he praised for his thoroughness and abundant energy and charm. Indeed, he added, one has to be careful not to be swept away by his charm!'[12]

Sandys arrived with the reputation of being an enemy of the Royal Navy. McGrigor wrote to warn Mountbatten what to expect. Sandys's views, he said, were:

(a) In War very little in the way of a Navy is necessary as everything will be finally decided by the H-bomb.

(b) In peace foreign stations are unnecessary. We can always warn trouble-makers that if they don't stop it the R.A.F. will deal with them.

(c) Cruisers are not needed and should be scrapped.

(d) Aircraft Carriers and Naval Aircraft are unnecessary. The R.A.F. can do it all and it is their job.

(e) Other types of ships should be drastically reduced.

In fact the Navy is no longer needed and it is a luxury the country cannot afford.[13]

Sandys would have denied that he had any such prejudice. He had gone on to tell McGrigor that 'his métier was always to refute the extravagant claims of the Services and others, force them to do with far less than they considered essential, and so effect drastic economies'. He might have suspected that the Navy was more lavish in its provisions than the other Services, but not that the Navy had no role in the post-Suez world. The role needed definition, perhaps retraction, but he was open-minded about what it might be.

He did, however, come to the Ministry of Defence with instructions that the cost of defence must be cut to sustain Britain's tottering economy. He was viewed as a potential enemy by every serving officer. In his first months he spared no pains to reinforce this image. 'We are having a pretty good tussle with Duncan Sandys just now,' Mountbatten wrote in February. 'He is cutting back heavily on the 1957/58 estimates and also on the long term programme. Her Majesty's Government intends to reduce defence expenditure ruthlessly.'[14] The Minister huffed and puffed with such fury that the Chiefs looked nervously not merely to the roof but to the very foundations of their house. The Board of Admiralty talked of resigning *en bloc* 'if some of the more ridiculous cuts such as nearly halving the size of the navy in a year or so were approved'. Mountbatten, noted Davis, was as indignant as anyone at the proposals, 'but he was at great pains to remain firmly perched on the constitutional fence. . . . He strongly deprecated talk of resigning and at this stage I thought he was right.'[15] By June neither he nor Davis was so sure. Mountbatten prepared a draft letter which he proposed to send to all Admirals if the worst happened and the Navy Vote was cut from £329 million to £290 million.

> We have carried out a full and careful investigation in the Admiralty, and it is clear that a cut of this magnitude can only mean chaos followed by loss of morale.
>
> If it comes to a showdown on this matter, I should, of course, make it clear that I could not possibly stay and be responsible for the resulting chaos; but before even contemplating such a drastic step I should like to know how my contemporaries feel about this.
>
> Would you, if you were in my place, take the responsibility for leading the Service in circumstances where the power to prevent the collapse of morale, the crumbling of efficiency and the destruction of prospects was no longer in the hands of the Admiralty?
>
> If you agree that there are circumstances in which it would not be right, or even possible for me to carry on, then the question arises how to indicate this to Ministers.
>
> I would presumably begin by saying that I could not possibly remain to lead the Navy into chaos. But the question arises whether I should add that I could not imagine any other Flag Officer of the requisite experience and calibre who would be prepared to take over in circumstances in which he had no hope of averting the chaos which so clearly would follow such a drastic cut.[16]

Every aid was invoked to deter the axe-man before he struck a fatal blow. To Admiral Denny, now the Chiefs of Staff representative in Washington, Mountbatten wrote to ask whether he thought that NATO could possibly survive if Britain's contribution was so brutally truncated. He hinted broadly that it would be no bad thing if Admiral Radford was warned what was in the wind; he could then pass it on to the President, and the President tackle the Prime Minister. 'It would at least help to set our mind at rest on the likelihood of NATO's being broken up; because if it is, then all our cuts make nonsense, for we shall have to rearm in a big way to try to protect ourselves.'[17] Robert Scott, the Commissioner-General in South-East Asia, was told that if the full cuts went through it would be necessary to close the Hong Kong dockyard, lease the Singapore dockyard to a commercial firm, and withdraw all but two frigates from the permanent force in the area. 'This will be the end of the British Empire in the Far East,' said Scott. Then lobby the Foreign Secretary and Ministry of Defence, came Mountbatten's reply.[18]

In the end, as usually happens, things did not turn out so disastrously. As Sandys no doubt calculated, cuts which would have appeared fearsome when he took office seemed tolerable in comparison with the horrors that had been forecast. In one field, indeed, Sandys retreated most conspicuously. He came to office believing aircraft-carriers to be expensive, vulnerable and largely irrelevant to national needs. Their only useful function was in anti-submarine warfare and for that barely a third of the present force was required. Mountbatten, on the other hand, was convinced that the carrier was an essential support to land forces east of Suez and managed to persuade his colleagues that this was the case. 'C.O.S. meeting on need for Carriers,' he recorded in his diary. 'Strong paper signed by 2 Air Marshals, 1 Field Marshal and self supports carriers and makes history.'[19] Startled by this unanimity in a field in which he had expected the Navy to be isolated, Sandys accepted defeat. 'We have already won one major victory,' Mountbatten told Ralph Edwards. '. . . the Minister had no option but to give way.'[20]

'Duncan Sandys frightened all of us in 1445–1845 meeting. My colleagues stood by me.' Mountbatten's diary entry for 15 February heralded a debate that was to be one of the most intensely fought Whitehall had ever known. The Defence White Paper of 1957[21] ran into thirteen so-called 'final' drafts and ultimately appeared with wording which had been inserted only minutes before it went to press. By its provisions the base at Scapa Flow and four out of ten naval air-stations were closed, the strength of the Reserve cut from 30,000 to 5000, all but one battleship condemned to the scrap-heap. So much was tolerable – had, indeed, largely been foreshadowed by the work of the Way Ahead Committee. But the White Paper also made it painfully clear that Sandys had not yet been convinced the Navy had a major part to play in Britain's future. 'The role of the Navy in Global War is somewhat uncertain,' was a phrase that struck chill into every sailor. As a member of NATO Britain no longer needed a balanced Fleet in the Atlantic or Mediterranean. It seemed that the naval case must rest principally on the value that was assigned to it in waters east of Suez.

For the six months after the White Paper appeared Mountbatten's task became the persuasion of Sandys that the Navy had a role and that it was as or even more important than the other Services. By September a paper had been prepared on the role of the Navy in cold war, limited war, as a deterrent, and in global war. 'I feel it makes the case so convincing that we should have been almost certain of getting the extra 8500 men and the necessary money to cover them,' wrote Mountbatten.[22] But the economic facts made it sure that there must be cuts in all three Services, the best hope was that the Navy would emerge the most lightly scarred. Mountbatten's mood fluctuated from week to week, sometimes from hour to hour. At the end of October he was near despair. 'It is a sad job for Chiefs of Staff to have to participate in planning the rundown of their services . . . ,' he told Nehru. 'The other day a cynic said to me: "You were the last Viceroy of India. You will probably be the last First Sea Lord!" '[23] Within a few days he was his ebullient self again as he detected signs of flexibility in the attitude of the Minister.

Early in November Sandys visited Portsmouth, dined aboard the *Victory* and went on to spend the weekend at Broadlands. 'This will be my first chance of a really quiet spell alone with him,' announced Mountbatten in his newsletter. 'Wish me luck!'[24] This was why even the most hostile admirals had recognized that Mountbatten had something to offer the Navy which nobody else could provide; no other First Sea Lord would have had the style, the status or, for that matter, the country house to entertain the Minister of Defence and deal with him on equal terms. 'We got on very well,' Mountbatten told Patricia, 'too well, I fear.'[25] He underestimated his achievement. No firm bargains were struck but when the weekend was over it was more or less agreed that, if Sandys would accept the larger Navy of 88,000 men, Mountbatten would agree that west of Suez the aircraft-carriers would concentrate on an anti-submarine role. An extra aircraft-carrier was bought for the price of closing some naval air-stations and the commando-carrier got the Minister's blessing. The only serious disagreement came over the aircraft the Navy was to use in future operations. The Navy wanted the NA 39 – the Buccaneer, a fast, low-flying aircraft that would come in to attack below the enemy's radar cover. The Air Force said that this would no doubt do for sailors but that they needed their own aircraft – the heavier, more sophisticated and more expensive TSR 2. Sandys at first insisted that the two Services must use the same aircraft and only after nine months allowed development to proceed on both models.[26] The resultant controversy lingered on for nearly a decade, cost the nation a king's ransom and gave Mountbatten occasion, time and time again, to employ to the full his talents as a fighter in the Whitehall jungle.

Two weeks after the Broadlands Summit, Sandys produced his own paper on the Navy: 'exciting', Mountbatten described it, while to Chatfield he wrote, 'It looks as though Duncan Sandys means to give us a reasonable deal – better than the Army and R.A.F.'[27] The battle was not over but it was going his way. In his last newsletter for 1957 he was able to report that it now seemed reasonably sure they would get the Navy they wanted. They would have to give greater consideration to the Russian submarine threat but the essential balance would be maintained. 'We must . . . do our best to maintain the policy that the Navy is one indivisible whole, flexible and variable as between its different functions, and I hope you will preach this doctrine of VERSATILITY from the house tops.'[28]

In February 1958 came the next round of cuts. Six months before, Mountbatten had feared that they might spell the destruction of the Navy as he knew it; now he could contemplate them with calm, almost with enthusiasm. They would be drastic and painful, he announced in his newsletter, but also 'realistic and imaginative'. The Way Ahead Committee had done its work so well that the weight of the cuts would fall on the shore establishments, while the sea-going ships would maintain or even increase their strength.

'This may be the end of one era,' he declared, 'but it was an era of over-insurance. Let us think of it rather as the beginning of a new era, as a "shot in the arm" for those willing to respond. Let us make sure that we use this volcanic moment to boost our morale and put the Senior Service back into its proper position.'[29]

It was characteristic of Mountbatten that this resounding exhortation was swiftly followed by a paragraph on the re-introduction of gold-laced trousers.


The principles of 'work study' had been adopted by the Navy long before Mountbatten became First Sea Lord, but had not previously been applied with great zeal throughout the Service. To Mountbatten they appeared irresistibly attractive as leading to the efficient, economical and forward-looking Navy which he believed Britain should possess. Whether these particular techniques of job evaluation did in fact invariably conduce to so happy an end may be questionable, but, as Mountbatten wrote in his newsletter, a 'fantastic waste of time' had been accepted without demur, and this was a luxury that could no longer be afforded.[30] It cannot be said that his own practice always accorded with the precepts of his work study experts. When Captain Tighe was sent off to Aden to investigate the workings of the Unified Command he found that his team was notably smaller than that of the Army or the Air Force. Caspar John said that that was as it should be; there must be the strictest economy of personnel and no attempt made to keep up with the military Joneses. Mountbatten blithely countermanded his deputy's instructions; on no account was the naval contingent to be outnumbered by those of the other Services.[31] Try as he might, frugality was not in his nature.

One long-running controversy which reached a climax while Mountbatten was at the Admiralty was the case of Dudley North. In 1940 North had – most sailors felt unfairly – been accused of contributing to the fiasco at Dakar and dismissed. Since then he had made repeated efforts to secure a review of his case and the retirement of Winston Churchill filled him with new hope. Mountbatten knew that Eden would be no more sympathetic than Churchill and was anxious to let this sleeping dog lie. 'I should like to be kind to the old Admiral,' he wrote to John Lang, 'but I think it would be just as well if I made it quite clear that there is no hope of the matter being reopened.'[32] Two years later, however, in February 1957, public interest was revived by the publication of a book dealing with the affair.[33] Mountbatten sounded out Macmillan and found that the change in Prime Minister also meant a change of heart. The Admirals of the Fleet were solemnly empanelled and urged the Prime Minister to order an official inquiry. This was more than he felt able to do, but at least he went some way towards exonerating the Admiral in a statement which he made in the House of Commons. Mountbatten professed dissatisfaction but felt little. He was genuinely sorry for North but knew only relief that the Navy was spared a process which would have involved much dirty linen being washed in public and could hardly have produced any positive result.

Such would have been the preoccupations of any First Sea Lord; Mountbatten inevitably was drawn from time to time on to a wider stage. He did not always welcome such opportunities. In 1948, when de Valera had been visiting Delhi, Mountbatten told him that the only hope for a united Ireland lay in Eire drawing closer to the Commonwealth and accepting a more formal link with the Crown. Evidently the conversation stuck in de Valera's mind for ten years later he asked Mrs Pandit, Nehru's sister, to talk to Mountbatten and try to persuade him to play an active role in bringing about some sort of settlement. Even Mountbatten accepted that this particular minefield was not one into which he would be wise to stray. Mrs Pandit was instructed to reply politely that, whatever Mountbatten might have said as Governor-General, as First Sea Lord he had to keep well away from political entanglements.[34]

He felt no such inhibitions when it came to expressing his opinion on global politics. In particular, he prided himself on his understanding of Asian problems. He was convinced that the Americans were making a disastrous mistake in Vietnam, writing in 1954:

> We missed a wonderful chance of disassociating China from Russia
> when they (the U.S.) failed to follow our lead in 1948, at the time we

made a *de facto* recognition of the Chinese Government. Indeed, in a
rush of enthusiasm, they are under the impression that the European
nations can create a second 'NATO' in South East Asia; whereas to
my mind our only way of success is to get all the Asian nations
organised to guarantee the future of Indo-China. We seem to be the
only people who realise the days of colonialism by European nations
are finished.[35]

Suez shook his faith in the superior wisdom of the British, and one of his
main concerns in the months and years that followed was to restore badly
damaged Anglo-Indian relations. At first he found it an uphill task. In
February 1957 he wrote to Nehru in some dismay:

In the days of Anthony Eden it was very easy to see him at any time
and he was always very happy to listen to my views on India (I only
wish he had been prepared to listen to my views on Egypt as well!). I
hardly know Macmillan; indeed he is the first Prime Minister in the
last 17 years with whom I have not been on intimate terms and so it is
not very easy for me to be as helpful as used to be possible in the past
(perhaps this is why our relations with India are not so good as they
used to be!!!).[36]

He did not for long remain a stranger to the Prime Minister. In June of the
same year Malcolm MacDonald wrote from Delhi to urge him to bring Nehru
and Macmillan together. The first meeting was cool; Nehru was persuaded,
somewhat against his better judgement, to spend a night at Chequers, but the
talk was of generalities rather than the pressing issues of the day. Then
Mountbatten took a hand. He wrote privately to Macmillan asking him to
have another meeting with Nehru and to discuss 'the vital problems such as
Kashmir, the Punjab, Canal waters, India's attitude on Hungary, . . . to the
Commonwealth . . . etc.' The two men met again and it went well. The scars
of Suez were at last covered over, if not healed. Mountbatten did not have the
same success with the Foreign Secretary, Selwyn Lloyd. When Mountbatten
asked Lloyd to meet Nehru privately, the Foreign Secretary complained that
Nehru had referred to him as 'a second-rate man, intellectually unreliable and
morally dishonest; what was the point of seeing a man who thought that
about him?' Mountbatten persisted but it availed little. When they finally did
meet 'it did not work out very well, for Selwyn clearly disagreed on almost
every point that was discussed and I am afraid that they are never likely to
understand each other's point of view'.[37]

Mountbatten was no less ready than in the past to lecture the Indian
leaders whenever he felt it necessary. When Nehru in 1957 flirted with the

Anti-Colonial League, sponsored by Kwame Nkrumah, Prime Minister of Ghana, Mountbatten described the idea as 'deplorable' and warned that if the Indian Prime Minister had anything to do with such a body it would fortify his enemies in Britain and dismay his friends. 'If you can avoid identifying yourself . . . with an organisation which appears to be against our government, it would be far wiser.'[38] Once again the hot-tempered Nehru accepted from Mountbatten criticism and advice that would have enraged him from any other man; almost meekly he replied that he had been misled about the nature of Nkrumah's proposed conference and he had decided not to attend.[39]

The problem of Britain's deterrent was at the heart of Mountbatten's plans for the Navy's future, and an essential element of the plans was the development of nuclear propulsion. Mountbatten described how he sold the idea to the Treasury. Knowing that the Chancellor, Heathcoat Amory, came from an old naval family, he commissioned a twenty-inch model of a nuclear submarine which opened up to display the workings. This he placed in front of the Chancellor's seat at a meeting of the Defence Committee. Heathcoat Amory was fascinated, played with it throughout the discussion of earlier items on the agenda and, when the question of nuclear propulsion came up, merely looked across the table and asked, 'How much?' 'And so we got our first nuclear submarine authorised,' concluded Mountbatten triumphantly.[40] No doubt some such picturesque incident occurred, but the naval team which did the preliminary work on the subject was set up in June 1954, while Mountbatten was still in Malta. Progress was slow, however, and it was Mountbatten's championship of the project which helped it gather momentum. By energy, enthusiasm and skilful lobbying he won the support or, at least, the tolerance of all those who might have been expected to oppose this speculative project – the only certain element of which, indeed, was that the cost would be extravagantly high. Only the Admiralty could afford such a project, said Mountbatten; only a nuclear submarine could provide sufficient military advantage to justify the cost; but this was not the end of the road. 'There are glittering prizes to be won, not least by making our merchant ships less dependent on that controversial commodity, oil.'[41]

Without the help of the Americans the path would have been far more arduous, and it was in securing their co-operation that Mountbatten made his greatest contribution to the project. Arleigh Burke was a staunch ally. At one of their first meetings Burke took Mountbatten to an American football-match. On the way he expounded some of the finer points of the game, only to be corrected by his guest. Mountbatten had studied the rules the night before and knew them thoroughly. Burke was impressed by such professionalism and soon grew to respect his visitor greatly: 'He was a good sailor. He did his best for his country. He had good judgment. He worked hard. I trusted his integrity.'[42]

When Mountbatten visited the United States in October 1955 Burke wanted to give him a trip in America's first and recently launched nuclear submarine, the *Nautilus*, but the plan was blocked by Admiral Hyman Rickover, the all-powerful master of the naval nuclear programme, who claimed that the Agreement on Military Atomic Co-operation was not intended to extend so far.[43] This obstacle was eliminated the following year by a new agreement, but there was still reason to fear that Rickover, who held both the British and the British nuclear programme in supreme contempt, would refuse to give any substantial help. Then in August 1956 Rickover visited London and was introduced to Mountbatten. Their meeting was an immediate success. 'The introvert iconoclast from the Ukraine . . . fell under the spell and aura of Queen Victoria's grandson.'[44] Mountbatten wrote to Denny in Washington to describe the visit: 'He could not possibly have been more friendly to us and I am hoping for great things from our contact.'[45] Great things transpired, and the fact that they did so arose directly from the First Sea Lord's success with the prickly American Admiral. 'Rickover didn't give a damn whether we as a country got the submarine or not, but he did care whether Lord Mountbatten got one or not!' wrote Denys Wyatt, one of the First Sea Lord's staff officers.[46] Rickover's readiness to help the Royal Navy was 'the decisive factor in our co-operation', reported Lord Hood from the Embassy at Washington, and it arose largely 'by the personal efforts of the First Sea Lord'.[47]

At first Mountbatten underestimated his own achievement. Eighteen months before, American help would have been valuable, he told Sandys, but now 'we have had to develop our own ideas' and the need was largely past.[48] He soon changed his mind. When Rickover visited Britain in May 1957 he stated that little progress had been made and when he returned seven months later the estimated completion date was actually farther away than the previous time he had been there. I asked Mountbatten, wrote Rickover, 'whether the British Admiralty wanted to satisfy its pride or whether it desired to build a nuclear submarine as quickly as possible. He replied that he wanted to get a nuclear submarine as quickly as possible.'[49] Within five minutes the deal was done; Britain would acquire a ready-made propulsion-plant from the Americans. The two men went straight into the meeting at which all the most senior members of the British project were assembled. Mountbatten explained at some length why he considered it was essential to buy American. 'This produced a deathly hush of disapproval,' recalled Denning Pearson of

Rolls-Royce,[50] but he and Lord Weeks of Vickers both backed the First Sea Lord's decision. Opposition crumbled. It was a '*tour de force*', remarked Wyatt. 'That evening I took Rickover's Executive Assistant out to dinner and he could scarcely get over his admiration of the handling of the meeting.'[51]

Keeping Rickover interested in the British project without allowing him to take it over became one of Mountbatten's main preoccupations over the following years. 'That stormy petrel of the American Navy, Vice-Admiral Hyman G. Rickover, arrives next Sunday . . . ,' he told Charles Lambe. 'As we virtually owe him the ability to complete *Dreadnought* two or three years ahead of time, with the saving of millions of pounds on R and D, we must all keep in with him.'[52] He asked Lang to ensure that Rickover was given red-carpet treatment when he visited the civil nuclear establishments; he had secured him an interview with the Prime Minister, he reported, but had failed to get him an honorary K.B.E.[53] He drew the line, though, when it came to Rickover's demand that he should personally select all the senior personnel for *Dreadnought*, explaining politely that, since Rickover had selected *him*, he could safely take the rest on trust. Rickover tried to fob off the British with the type of plant used in the U.S.S. *Skate*, but in October 1958 Mountbatten saw a newer version in the *Skipjack*. 'A fantastic peep into the future,' he called it. 'Rickover certainly is an absolute genius.'[54] Rickover showed him over the Atomic Top-Secret Room. 'Admiral,' he said, 'I think your British set-up is lousy. . . . What you want to run a show like this is a real son-of-a-bitch!' He was delighted with Mountbatten's reply: 'That is where you Americans have the edge on us, you have the only real son-of-a-bitch in the business!'[55] He was equally struck by Mountbatten's thoroughness. 'Those with whom he dealt', he told the British Ambassador, Harold Caccia, 'were impressed not only with his enthusiasm but with his detailed knowledge of engineering. They were particularly impressed with the fact that he crawled through all parts of the nuclear submarine he visited, right down to the bottom of the bilges.'[56] After the visit there were no more suggestions that the British might make do with *Skate*.

In October 1957 the U.S.S. *Nautilus* had visited Britain. The Prime Minister was put out because the visit had been arranged without consultation with the civil authorities. A fierce argument was in progress as to whether the American reactor was less of a hazard to human life than the type favoured by the British. Macmillan feared that if the *Nautilus* visited Portsmouth, as had been proposed, it would be used as a piece of propaganda to demonstrate the superior safety of the American design. At first he wanted to ban the visit altogether, then relented, and let the submarine call on the more secluded base at Portland.[57] Mountbatten took Sandys to visit her. The Minister of Defence was enormously impressed, too much so for Mountbatten's peace of mind because, as he told the Commander-in-Chief of the Home Fleet, 'he is a man given to reaching sudden conclusions; and there is a very real danger that he may decide that the nuclear-propelled submarine has made our present Navy completely obsolete'.[58]

Ever since Arleigh Burke had told him in November 1955 that the U.S. Navy was trying to develop a solid-fuel rocket which could be fired from a submerged submarine, Mountbatten had dreamed of the day when Britain's deterrent would depend not on land-based missiles or the R.A.F.'s bombers but on the efforts of the Royal Navy.[59] Burke had pointed out that seventy per cent of the surface of the globe was sea, fifty per cent of the world's population lived within fifty miles of the sea and, of the fifty-five cities with more than one million inhabitants, forty were seaports. How obvious it was, he argued, that the deterrent of the future must come from under-water.[60] 'If the British were to put their share of the deterrent into submarines,' wrote the First Sea Lord in his newsletter, 'there would be no call for the Russians to have to attack our missile sites and bomber fields as an act of self-preservation if they feared a possible attack.'[61]

Mountbatten contrived to place his man in the American team developing the missile and extracted a statement from Burke that he 'hoped it might be possible' for Polaris missiles to be supplied to the Royal Navy.[62] This, however, was far in the future and there would be many problems to surmount, political as well as technical, before nuclear submarines carrying nuclear missiles could sail under a British flag. One problem was the cost. 'If opinion swings towards putting the deterrent at sea,' Mountbatten wrote, 'we want the money for Polaris to be found from the overall Defence Vote.'[63] Another was the likely hostility of the Air Force. 'Both of us', he told Burke, 'believe that this is a weapon which, if entrusted to our Navies, may prove to be the ultimate answer. Just because of this, both of us can expect opposition from those in lighter uniforms.'[64] He set out to prepare the British public for the day when Polaris would be available as a British deterrent. Early in 1958 a series of articles in the press – one at least inspired by Mountbatten – argued that the conventional land-based missile was now obsolescent. 'Anything we can do to stimulate this line of thought is obviously to our advantage,' he told his Admirals. '. . . now that the security cloak around Polaris has been lifted, I am encouraging everyone to introduce this topic into their general conversation.'[65] But about his own role in the matter the security cloak was kept in place. Shortly after he left the Admiralty for the Ministry of Defence, a letter arrived for him from Arleigh Burke which was opened in error and shown to his successor, Lambe. 'As this whole subject of the British contribution to the Deterrent is a pretty hot one politically,' Lambe told Burke, 'I am rather glad that your letter was intercepted in this way, as it could be unfortunate if anyone else in the Ministry of Defence became aware of how closely you and Dickie are working together in this matter.'[66]

The possibility that Britain might one day acquire the Polaris missile did not affect Mountbatten's views about the so-called 'independent' deterrent. Both Americans and Russians had enough nuclear missiles to destroy each other several times over. The Chief of Air Staff felt that the independent British deterrent was all-important in such circumstances and should be augmented even at the expense of the rest of the defence budget. Mountbatten and Templer flatly disagreed: 'We have both stated in our paper that we absolutely oppose the concept of an independent U.K. nuclear deterrent.'[67] Templer retired a few days later and, with Festing feeling his way into his new job, Mountbatten found himself left to fight the battle without help. What was unacceptable, he argued, was to insist that the British deterrent alone should be able to pose 'a threat of unacceptable destruction to Russia'. An independent British force would be 'neither credible as a deterrent, nor necessary as part of the Western deterrent'.[68]

On 28 October 1958 the Chiefs met with the Minister of Defence. Sandys declared that he did not believe there was any question of the United States not being ready to use its strategic weapons, but that, if such circumstances arose, 'it was inconceivable that Britain would hesitate to use her own nuclear retaliatory power'. To Mountbatten it was inconceivable that they would do anything of the sort: 'To use it in retaliation for an attack on Western Europe would surely be to commit national suicide immediately.' Sandys retorted by saying that he did not believe Mountbatten and Festing were really concerned about deterrent policy; what worried them was that the high cost of the deterrent might lead to cuts in conventional arms. It was a month before a record of the meeting was circulated[69] and Mountbatten then commented that it accurately reflected the Minister's summing-up. 'I am sure he will remember', the First Sea Lord added, 'that I said in a polite and quiet voice that I would wish it recorded that I had in no way changed the opinions I had expressed in the paper I had prepared with the C.I.G.S. This remains my position.'[70] Much though he welcomed the advent of the Polaris submarine and the Navy's taking over of the deterrent, it remained his position till the day he died.

In the battles over deterrent policy Mountbatten had been allied with the C.I.G.S. against the Chief of Air Staff; when the reorganization of the machinery of defence was concerned he found himself supporting Dickson against both his colleagues. The matter was initiated by Macmillan, who reckoned that the Minister of Defence had inadequate powers for the task of

co-ordination that was required. By appointing a strong Minister he had
created the opportunity; now new machinery was needed to make it work. As
a first step it was proposed that the Chairman of the Chiefs of Staff
Committee should also act as Chief Staff Officer to the Minister of Defence.
Templer and Boyle, the other two Chiefs of Staff, correctly saw that this was
the first step in the downgrading of the traditional Service ministries in favour
of an aggrandized Ministry of Defence, and opposed the process fiercely.
Mountbatten drew the same conclusions and supported the measure with
equal fervour.[71]

On 22 January 1957 Sandys called his advisers together to discuss the new
proposal. Mountbatten had promised his colleagues that he would not break
the unity of the Chiefs by expressing his disagreement with their line, but his
resigned shrug of the shoulders when Sandys looked enquiringly at him must
have made his feelings clear. Sandys listened to what was said, pointed out
that the Chiefs of Staff already had divided loyalties between their individual
Services and the Committee as a whole and that his proposal would not make
things worse, and stuck to his position. It was agreed that the scheme should
be tried out for six months. 'I was impressed by his willingness to listen to
arguments,' wrote Mountbatten, 'the intelligent questions he asked and his
apparent reasonableness.'[72] It is perhaps not surprising that this tribute was
paid on one of the occasions when Minister and First Sea Lord were of one
mind.

In fact it took a year before Dickson decided that his position was
intolerable. The Chiefs of Staff felt that their role as military advisers to the
Government was being 'ignored and emasculated'; they made their displea-
sure felt by offering Dickson in his new functions only a degree of co-
operation, 'reluctant almost to the point of non-existence'; he had no staff
with which to carry out whatever his job was supposed to be; his humiliation
was becoming apparent abroad as well as in Britain.[73] Coming from a man of
notable moderation, his letter to Sandys was marked by bitterness and anger.
Only towards Mountbatten did he profess any gratitude. 'Without his loyalty
and support,' he wrote later, 'I doubt if the Chiefs of Staff Committee would
have been able to function properly.'[74]

Macmillan's response to this appeal was to propose a greatly strengthened central body, the Chairman of the Chiefs of Staff becoming Chief of
the Defence Staff, with a powerful organization of his own. Reactions were
exactly as might have been predicted. Dickson and Mountbatten, wrote
Macmillan, were 'keen and loyal supporters of reform; but the others were
highly critical'.[75] Except for Mountbatten the Chiefs of Staff, Service
Ministers and Permanent Under-Secretaries rallied solidly against Sandys and
Macmillan. Though the Sea Lords backed Mountbatten, Selkirk and John

Lang both took the other line. On 10 July Mountbatten noted in his diary: 'Saw First Lord to try to get him to admit that his naval advisers were against him, but he wouldn't and on the way to the Cabinet told me not to reveal the split.' The bitterness of the earlier discussions was redoubled – 'very painful', Mountbatten wrote of another meeting. 'Dermot [Boyle] and Gerald [Templer] pathological.'[76] A few days later Dickson, Templer, Boyle and their wives came to stay at Broadlands. 'A lovely reunion of the C.O.S. after the split,' noted Mountbatten in his diary on 12 July, but the reconciliation was wafer-thin. The highest common factor of their deliberations was enshrined in the White Paper of July 1958, but this tepid manifesto left everyone dissatisfied. To Macmillan it was a defeat; 'the atmosphere in which our discussions were conducted had been at certain periods so disagreeable that I felt unwilling to re-open the question'.[77]

One outside power to whom Mountbatten had appealed while the debate was raging was Field Marshal Montgomery, now deputy to the Supreme Allied Commander in Europe. A close alliance between the two men had grown up since Montgomery had recanted his views on the Navy's insignificance in modern warfare. Mountbatten attended all seven of the annual NATO C.P.X.s – Command Post Exercises, which Montgomery stage-managed and starred in – and on the last occasion invested him with the Order of the C.P.X., which he had had struck at Devonport dockyard, and ceremoniously kissed him on both cheeks in front of the delighted NATO dignitaries.[78] Mountbatten recalled that Montgomery appealed to him for help in gaining promotion in the peerage: 'Dickie, you, Alex and I were all Viscounts, now you and Alex are Earls and I am still a Viscount. Do you think you can persuade the Prime Minister to make me an Earl too?'[79] Now it was Mountbatten who asked Montgomery for support over the powers of the new Chief of Defence Staff.[80] Montgomery's reply was a robust affirmation of the Macmillan case in its entirety. Service Ministers should be downgraded while the C.D.S. should be the only five-star officer in the Services, responsible directly to the Minister of Defence and so far independent of the three Chiefs of Staff as not to sign their joint papers but instead to refer them to the Minister under cover of his own recommendations.[81] Mountbatten was in total agreement, but being now himself a five-star Admiral of the Fleet, and knowing that the office of Chief of the Defence Staff would soon be his, he wished to lie as low as possible.

> I think it would be rather embarrassing if on taking up the appointment as C.D.S. in Five Star rank, I were to take any initiative in trying to cut down the promotion chances of my colleagues on the Chiefs of Staff Committee.

The whole matter is, therefore, over to you again, and I think you will have to write to the Prime Minister or go and see him, or both, to pursue this idea.

I feel that your ideas are so sound that they do not require the support of a comparatively junior Five Star officer like me, and I would be grateful if, in returning to the attack, you do not actually quote my views.[82]

Mountbatten can hardly have hoped that his colleagues on the Chiefs of Staff Committee would be in any doubt about his support for the Montgomery line. Where they were unfair was in the motives they attributed to him. Templer and Boyle, wrote Dickson, regarded Mountbatten 'as a traitor and they attributed his attitude to his desire to become a "Supremo" when he succeeded me'. Dickson himself, who maintained that he knew Mountbatten far better than did either of the other two Chiefs of Staff, denied the charge and said that the First Sea Lord supported reform because he believed it to be right in principle.[83] In 1958 Mountbatten knew perfectly well that he would be the first to benefit from the changes, but he had championed them long before his own succession became a certainty and was to go on fighting for them after he had nothing to gain himself. He argued for a powerful Ministry of Defence and Chief of the Defence Staff because he believed it to be right in principle; whether he was correct in this belief is something that will need consideration over the next few chapters.

The post of C.D.S. was formally offered to Mountbatten by the Prime Minister on 22 May 1958. The problem of who should succeed him as First Sea Lord preoccupied him during his last year at the Admiralty. The two front-runners were Charles Lambe, urbane, cultivated and a past-master at Whitehall warfare, and Guy Grantham, an Admiral in the tradition of Cunningham and Somerville. Lambe was Mountbatten's closest friend in the Navy; Grantham he respected but did not greatly like. But that was not all.

Grantham is a fine sea-going sailor, whom I would put in command of a Fleet before Charles Lambe [he told Sandys]. I think he would just win a 'popularity poll' in the Fleet – but that is his limit. The whole Navy would have confidence in Charles Lambe because they would feel he would be able to look after the interests of the Navy in Whitehall.

So far as you and I are concerned, Charles would make the whole difference to the Chiefs of Staff setup – you would have at least two out of four on your side for we have both been honest supporters of yours ever since we understood what you wanted to do.[84]

Mountbatten knew that the battle over the reorganization of defence was certain to be renewed in the next few years, and he wished above all that the First Sea Lord should be an ally in the confrontation that would follow.

Admirals of the Fleet, Commanders-in-Chief and Sea Lords were circularized and only two favoured Grantham.[85] Sandys was ready to support Lambe's appointment. Lord Selkirk alone dissented. The First Lord, who had strongly differed from Mountbatten on reorganization, was loath to approve a selection which would have perpetuated the heresy within the Navy. He liked and respected Lambe but felt that he was too much Mountbatten's man, and that it would be better for the Admiralty to have its new chief 'out of another fishpond'. When he told Mountbatten that this was his opinion, the First Sea Lord took it as a personal affront and stormed from the office.[86] With both Sandys and Mountbatten ranged against him, however, there was little prospect of Selkirk's view prevailing with the Prime Minister; on 22 December 1958 he telephoned to say that Lambe would be the next First Sea Lord.

It remained only to stage-manage the formalities of the hand-over. In sonorous prose John Lang, commanded by 'My Lords Commissioners of the Admiralty', summarized the details of Mountbatten's career and bewailed his passing. During his time as First Sea Lord, read the letter, there had been many important changes in the Navy:

> Your dynamic leadership has given impetus and purposeful direction to this work and, although it has been necessary to reduce the size of the Fleet, your untiring personal efforts have given the Royal Navy confidence in its own future and have done much to bring the nation to realise the vital role which the Navy must continue to play in peace or in war.[87]

Mountbatten's acknowledgement of this eulogy was less conventional. 'I admire the remarkable degree of factual accuracy in this letter,' he wrote blandly, 'but for the sake of the record would like to point out two very minor slips. . . .'[88]

His last weeks in the Navy were hectically crowded. On 19 and 20 April he signed thirteen hundred letters of farewell, the majority with a personal note in manuscript at the end. On 23 April he appeared on B.B.C. and Independent Television. 'I accepted these invitations in spite of personal reluctance,' he wrote in his final newsletter, 'because I felt it was a unique opportunity to put across to vast numbers of people that the Navy has . . . a

bright future.'[89] Reluctant or not, he took considerable pride in his performance. His interviews were seen by ten million people, and he achieved a
'Nielsen Rating' of 86, second only to a broadcast by the Queen. 'As a basis of
comparison,' he told Campbell-Johnson, '. . . the recent broadcast by Lord
Montgomery achieved a rating of 71.'[90] On 30 April he was in Paris, with a
party of friends at the Lido. At midnight he looked at his watch, said with a
touch of sadness, 'I am no longer in the Royal Navy,' and walked over to the
table where Charles Lambe was sitting to hand over the charge which he had
borne with such relish. Old sailors never die and Admirals of the Fleet never
retire, but Mountbatten's career in the Navy was effectively behind him.

# CHAPTER 43

## *Alone*

WITHIN A FEW YEARS Mountbatten lost the three people who were closest to him in his own generation. Charles Lambe was the first to go. His death, in August 1960, cost Mountbatten not just his dearest friend in the Royal Navy and the man on whose wise and frank advice he had come most to rely, but also his only ally among the Chiefs of Staff. The relationship between the new First Sea Lord and his predecessor might easily have been an unhappy one. Mountbatten was not a man who could lightly shrug off responsibilities. Driving down the Mall one day he saw an enormous ensign flying over the Air Ministry buildings. The Admiralty had nothing similar. At once he wrote to Lambe. Would it not be excellent public relations for a flag to be flown from Admiralty Arch? 'I cannot think why I didn't put up this thought while I was at the Admiralty. . . . This note (which is written on a plain piece of paper) comes from a "former Naval person" and there is no connection with the C.D.S.'[1] Such suggestions proliferated. Lambe was said to have had a rubber stamp prepared for Mountbatten's benefit, which read: 'Forgive me for interfering, but. . . .'[2] Yet though sometimes irritated, Lambe was firm enough to maintain his independence and diplomatic enough to do so without friction. The partnership prospered.

It was to be short-lived. Lambe had taken on the job of First Sea Lord with reluctance, partly because he preferred life in the Mediterranean, but also because his health was uncertain and he doubted whether it would stand up to the rigours of Whitehall. His fears proved justified, and a particularly troublesome visit to Australia compounded the damage. He returned exhausted and suffered a crippling heart-attack shortly afterwards. In May 1960 he wrote to Mountbatten to say 'how dreadfully sad I feel at letting *you* down like this. I know how much store you have always set on us working together at the top as colleagues as well as old friends, and I am ashamed that this foolish body of mine should have proved such a weakling. . . . My only consolation is the thought that in Caspar you have a very sane successor who will I am sure do you proud.'[3] He died three months later.

His successor was the son of the painter Augustus John and inheritor of his father's fiery temperament. Caspar John was a man of outstanding talents, who had worked closely with Mountbatten in the past. All had evidently gone well:

> Once in a lifetime [Mountbatten wrote to him] one has the luck to find a second in command whose thoughts and reactions are so completely in tune with your own. . . . What has made our partnership so particularly valuable to me has been the stimulating and fearless advice which you have always given, for my greatest weakness is to let my enthusiasm run away with me and no one has kept my feet more firmly on the ground than you.[4]

But the association proved less happy when John became First Sea Lord. On matters of policy they generally worked harmoniously together, but the close friendship which had made Lambe's occupation so important to Mountbatten was conspicuously lacking. Brusque, outspoken, totally straightforward, John disliked Mountbatten's theatricality and found his tactics often devious if not dishonest. Lambe could the more easily make Mountbatten change his mind because the C.D.S. knew that his advice was not merely sound but based on deep affection; in John the affection was lacking and the advice was therefore less well received.

Peter Murphy did not die till September 1966, but he had been gravely ill for several years and little seen by his friends. Mountbatten had been giving him £600 a year and had organized his treatment during his last illness, but Murphy's ill-health and the demands of Mountbatten's work meant that the two men had met rarely. For Mountbatten, however, Murphy was still one of the very few men with whom he felt totally secure. He did not necessarily accept his friend's advice, but he knew that it was formed with no other consideration than that of his own best interest. A cross between court-jester and grey eminence, Murphy had time and again proved his dedication to the needs of the two Mountbattens. For many years he had been an almost indispensable element of their marriage. Mountbatten spoke to him on the telephone shortly before he lost consciousness for the last time. 'He sounded cheerful but very tired,' he told Robert Neville. 'Apparently he did not suffer, and had been bravely waiting for death; he did not want to survive as a hopeless invalid. I arrived less than 5 minutes after his breathing stopped. He looked very peaceful and serene. . . . He had been one of my great friends for almost 47 years. I shall miss him very much.'[5]

The loss of Murphy and Lambe had been deeply painful to Mountbatten, but the effect on his daily life was as nothing compared to that caused by the death of Edwina during the night of 20–1 February 1960. 'TRAGEDY' was his diary entry, in huge capital letters – a symbol of grief that in some might have seemed melodramatic but came naturally from Mountbatten.

The last few years of their marriage were the most harmonious. Edwina was no less restless, consumed by the daemons of duty and ambition, but she ceased to work off her frustrations on her husband; she became more patient, more affectionate. The Darby-and-Joan relationship of slippers by the fire which Mountbatten was prone to envisage would never have come about, but a new companionship was developing. In retrospect it seems possible that Edwina knew that their marriage did not have long to last and was resolved to make the most of it. In 1956 her doctor, Wilkes Harvey, had told her that unless she dramatically reduced her activities she must expect to be dead within three years. Her response was to take on fresh responsibilities. Harvey told this to Mountbatten and his daughters after Edwina's death: 'He wanted us to know that he considered she had made a brave and considered decision to go on.'[6] She went on, and in January 1960 embarked on a tour on behalf of St John's Ambulance Brigade Overseas which daunted even her by its intensity. 'I am off at dawn filled with trepidation and hardly dare to even *think* about my Tour, as it would be far too exhausting a process,' she told her husband. 'I shall miss you a lot and think of you a great deal.'[7]

Edwina arrived in Jesselton in Borneo on 20 February and at once plunged into a round of inspections. She seemed as enthusiastic and alert as ever, but Miss Burnham, matron at the Queen Elizabeth Hospital, noticed that she sometimes tottered as she walked and stopped frequently to admire the view, obviously too tired to carry on. So struck was Miss Burnham by her weakness that she had a room at the hospital prepared in case Lady Mountbatten had need of it. In London Mountbatten had gone to bed at 1.30 a.m. Two hours later he was woken to be told that the Governor of Borneo was trying to telephone him; the attempt came to nothing and he went back to sleep. Thirty minutes later the telephone rang again. Half asleep, he heard an indistinct voice saying something about Lady Mountbatten. 'Put her through,' he called impatiently. 'Edwina, darling, is that you?' The voice went on and gradually he took in what it was trying to convey. For several months afterwards he would dream that the telephone was ringing and that he was hearing for the first time the news of his wife's death.

Edwina's body was flown back to England. Mountbatten wrote to Nehru to describe her return:

> Patricia, Pammy, their husbands, Edwina's sister Mary and I went to Broadlands, and were there at the front door to receive her body when she came home for the last time. It was quite unbearably moving, the more so as her little sealyham, Snippet, somehow got loose and dashed out of the front door wagging her tail as she always did whenever Edwina came home.[8]

The body was taken to Romsey Abbey where the eight senior members of the estate staff carried her up to the altar. During the thirteen hours that the coffin remained there, fifty-two men of the house and estate stood guard in turn all night. When the time came for the coffin to be taken to sea, where she had asked that she should be buried, she was piped aboard; an honour, Mountbatten told Nehru, 'which I have never before known to be accorded to any woman other than a reigning sovereign'. Among the escorting ships was the Indian frigate *Trishul*, sent on Nehru's express instructions, 'a really charming gesture which made a deep impression on everybody and would have given darling Edwina such particular satisfaction'.[9]

He found some solace in the deep impression which Edwina's death made on the world at large: 'Fantastic B.B.C., TV and newspaper coverage. Hundreds of telegrams and letters from Presidents, Kings, Prime Ministers, Ambassadors, Commanders-in-Chief and organisations and touching ones from friends and humble folk. It is wonderful to see Edwina so widely acclaimed.'[10] But the excitement of the funeral and the publicity soon wore off and dejection took its place. 'Miserable. I never realised how much I loved her and what she meant to me,' he wrote in his diary the day after she died. Such is the common currency of the bereaved, yet Mountbatten more than most was taken by surprise by the discovery of his dependence on his wife. Their frequent separations, their quarrels, the intense demands of his profession, had led him to believe that though he would miss Edwina greatly, he could manage quite satisfactorily by himself. He quickly realized that he was mistaken. Her absence, sometimes almost to be welcomed if it was temporary, became intolerably painful once it was bound to last for ever. He was lonely and bereft.

'I am afraid that Edwina's death has knocked him about very badly,' wrote Ismay.[11] Those who worked with him noticed that he was nervous and, by his own standards, indecisive, finding it difficult to concentrate and drifting off into reveries even in important meetings. He was withdrawn and listless, felt Ian Hogg.[12] He answered every letter of condolence, but found the effort too great to add the personal messages on which he usually prided himself. Noel Coward wrote both to him and to the Duke of Edinburgh. From Prince Philip he received an 'old chum' reply which touched him deeply: 'From Dickie, however, a not very well-phrased, typewritten form letter, which touched me less.'[13] The comment, perhaps, tells more about Coward than Mountbatten, but it is still the only occasion in the latter's life that he would have allowed a formal, typewritten letter to an old friend to go out without a few words of special greeting.

One effect of Edwina's death was financial. Douglas Fairbanks Junior wrote to him about some potentially profitable investments in the Bahamas.

How typically kind and thoughtful of you to write to me about my financial position [replied Mountbatten]. It is really quite simple. Death duties will be charged at 80%, and on the 20% of Edwina's fortune, 7½% goes to each of the girls and 5% to me. I shall have one shilling for every pound she had.

But I have some money of my own, and I have every hope that the Broadlands estate will really pay for itself and run at a small profit. I am hoping to continue to live at Broadlands and while I am in my present job to keep on 2 Wilton Crescent.

I shall not be able to do things on the scale which Edwina and I could do together in her lifetime, but I am not particularly keen on entertaining, or extravagant in my tastes.

It is true that when I finish from this job I might like to take on some business appointments to keep me occupied and to replace the very handsome salary and allowance which I receive in my present job. But that is still quite a way off, I hope.[14]

Despite these brave words, the conviction that he was shortly to become, if he was not already, a poor man nagged perpetually at the back of Mountbatten's mind. Richard Way, then Permanent Under-Secretary at the War Office, was surprised that, only three days after Edwina's death, it was the financial consequences which seemed to preoccupy Mountbatten.[15] This was no more than the freakish symptom of grief in a distracted man, but it sprang from a real concern about the future. The time was to come when it would grow into a constant and pressing worry.

Many people expected him soon to remarry, for convenience or companionship if not for love. There was no shortage of rich and well-connected women who would have been delighted to become the second Countess Mountbatten of Burma. Mountbatten may have played with the idea from time to time, but there is no reason to think that he ever considered it seriously. To find a woman who would match Edwina's qualities would have been difficult if not impossible, and her defects rapidly receded into a background so remote that his daughters sometimes found it necessary to remind him that married life had not been an uninterrupted idyll. He told Patricia that he could not contemplate remarriage, since he might have a son and thus disturb the plans he had made for her succession to his title. Besides, life as a bachelor had its consolations and the quirks and idiosyncrasies which he could now indulge rapidly took on the significance of holy writ. He greeted with tolerant amusement the attempts of journalists or importunate acquaintances to marry him off to a variety of pretenders. When he arrived in Darwin on the anniversary of Edwina's death a representative of the *Sydney*

*Mirror* asked whether it was true that the real reason for his visit was 'romantic'. Mountbatten answered mildly that when he was nineteen years old he had fallen in love with pretty girls in Sydney, Melbourne and Brisbane. When he met them again in 1946, all three were grandmothers. By now they were no doubt great-grandmothers. The time for romance, he implied, was past. The journalist 'had the grace to blush and apologize, but what a question to be asked on this day of all days!'[16]

In fact he continued to rejoice at evidence that the time for romance was *not* past; 'there's life in the old dog yet', was a constant refrain in the next decades. In 1962 he went to Athens for a royal wedding, to find himself hotly pursued by a princess of considerable beauty and forty years his junior. She announced that she was madly in love and determined to marry him, and caused something of a scandal by rearranging the place-cards at the state banquet so that they were sitting side by side. Since this manoeuvre involved displacing the heirs to the thrones of The Netherlands and Denmark, Mountbatten was not unnaturally nervous about the comment that would be caused. But he was also delighted; 'the whole experience was pretty good for the morale of a sixty-two year old widower'.[17]

'I know you think that I ought to be able to live alone and spend my weekends alone, but I feel so terribly lonely without someone,' Mountbatten wrote to Patricia. He listed the little gang of the faithful who rallied round him at Broadlands. 'However it's you and John and the children and Pammy that make me feel happy and contented when you are with me.'[18] Edwina's death had the result of greatly increasing Mountbatten's dependence on his children – dependence not in any practical sense, for he was more than capable of administering his own life and theirs too if given a chance, but in his craving for affection and the company of those he loved. It was a charge they gladly accepted, but Patricia now had several children, a home of her own, a husband whose career involved much travel and who demanded attention at least equal to that given to his much loved father-in-law. Pamela, for her part, had married only a little time before Edwina's death and inevitably was absorbed by her new life and responsibilities.

'Walked with Pammy barefoot on the lawn for one hour hearing about David Hicks. As a result had blood blisters on both feet. Very painful.'[19] The pain had not been caused only by the blisters. Lord Brabourne was Mountbatten's pattern of an ideal son-in-law – aristocratic, resourceful, at home at a shoot at Sandringham or flogging a stretch of some Irish salmon river. Though far from being an English country gentleman himself, nor particularly respectful of such habits and observances, Mountbatten would still have wished the man his daughter married to cover the gamut of bucolic virtues. An interior decorator, however distinguished, the son of a stockbroker, however eminent, was not what he would have chosen as a recruit for his family. Once he was satisfied, however, that Pamela had made up her mind and that the marriage was likely to make her happy, he supported it whole-heartedly. He espoused his son-in-law's career with characteristic fervour, thenceforward cast a censorious eye over the palaces of the grandees that he visited in the farther-flung reaches of the world, and commented that redecoration seemed overdue. There was a talented young Englishman called David Hicks who by a curious coincidence. . . .

The wedding took place with all due pomp at Romsey on 13 January 1960: thirteen hundred guests, John Brabourne as best man, the Duke of Edinburgh to propose the toast and only a blizzard and a failure of the lights to mar the splendour of the occasion. A few days later Lady Mountbatten left on her final journey. 'Mummy radiated a sort of ethereal beauty and happiness and youth which she retained during the remaining four days I saw her,' Mountbatten later wrote to Pamela.[20] He was not alone in testifying that Edwina was vividly radiant at her daughter's wedding.

It is possible that Mountbatten would not have been quite so quickly reconciled to the marriage if it had been Patricia whose future was involved. Some years before, on New Year's Eve, he had tried to set down on paper his feelings for his elder daughter; the letter that ensued illustrates both his almost alarming capacity for self-revelation and the strength of his affection:

It is close on midnight. Most people are out at parties . . . but I have just finished work and my mind, as always, turns to you.

You yourself know pretty well all that you have meant to me for the past thirty years, for I have never disguised my feeling from you, but in the years to come, after Mummy and I have both 'passed on' as the euphemistic term goes, I would have liked to feel that there was some record in the bottom of your 'Black Box' of the part you play in my life.

I have sometimes regretted that you turned into such a very lovely and attractive woman because I would certainly have loved you just as much, and very possibly more, if you had remained the ungainly, lanky creature with odd teeth and slightly receding chin that you presented when you first went to school. Physical attraction (by no means unknown to Freud between parents and children) has hardly ever entered into our very remarkable friendship . . . the attraction which you have had for me from the day I first saw you in April 1924 was an almost mystical feeling that you were really a part of me living on in the world.

I wanted a boy, not a girl, as you well know, but I am certain if you had had a brother he could never have taken your place because from the day I saw you first as a two month old baby and was allowed to help with you, I have never really had eyes for anyone else.

You know how basically fond I am and always have been of Mummy, you know pretty well about my girl friends, but none of them have had that magic 'something' which you have. . . . Of course, the miracle of our relationship is that you make me feel truly unselfish and wanting only your happiness. Why else should I have done so much to induce you to marry John when you were waver-ing? . . .

I have grown so fond of Pammy, few fathers could be fonder of a daughter or miss her more than I miss Pammy now, but the main-spring of my love is that she is *your* sister and *you* love her. Every achievement in life since 1924 has been achieved for you and because of you. When I passed exams or was promoted my heart was glad because you always appeared so pleased. When I went to sea in the war it was *you* I thought of, when I fought in battles I hoped *your* Father would do well enough for *you* to be proud of him.

When I went to Combined Ops, to South East Asia, to India, and found myself up against it, I struggled through – on your account, and yet I hope I never burdened you with the feeling of responsibility which a young girl might have felt at being such an overwhelming influence and such a splendid spur to an otherwise singularly un-ambitious man. . . .

If in years to come history takes the view that I did well in my jobs, the credit must all go to you. There is always one woman in a man's life and darling – she is you. Bless you always.

You'll never really know how much I love you.[21]

There is an element of hyperbole about this letter – only the most credulous would accept in its entirety the picture of the 'singularly un-ambitious' Mountbatten spurred on uniquely by his wish to shine in his daughter's eyes – but the essential sincerity of his protestations needs no underlining.

It was in the first summer after his wife's death that the practice began of devoting every August to a family holiday at Classiebawn Castle, a neo-Gothic mansion in County Sligo, Ireland, its appearance as charmless as its situation is magnificent, which had been built to the orders of Lord Palmer-ston and descended through the Ashleys to Edwina. Mountbatten had first discovered it in 1941 and was immediately enraptured. 'You never told me how stupendously magnificent the surrounding scenery was,' he wrote in excitement to his wife. 'No place had ever thrilled me more and I can't wait to move in.'[22] The enchantment never faded. Always a manufacturer of instant traditions, Mountbatten soon invested his Irish fastness with a range of rituals: shrimping, lobster-potting, mackerel-fishing, building canals and castles in the sand, riding along the beach – all had to be conducted in certain hallowed ways and, so far as weather permitted, at certain times. For children, grandchildren and a band of select and intimate friends, Classiebawn became a retreat where nothing ever changed, youth could be recaptured. For Mountbatten, with his reverence for family ties, it acquired a still more special significance; there was almost no part of his life which he would not have renounced before his August holiday.

In these early days the spectre of violence seemed distant, almost laughable. When a family party left Classiebawn in 1961 and found that a car was following them, they at once assumed that it must contain intrusive journalists. They doubled back, turned abruptly to left and right, and eventually took refuge in a yard at Sligo. Still the car stuck on their tail. Eventually John Brabourne walked over to ask them what they wanted, only to discover that the car was filled with plain-clothes police guards. It was kind of the Irish to bother was the general reaction, but, really, it was a little hard to see what perils they were anticipating.[23]

One of the few drawbacks about Classiebawn was that its situation in the Irish Republic precluded visits by members of the royal family. His links with Britain's royal house became increasingly important to Mountbatten as he grew older. In Whitehall his staff officers would compete to see who could most quickly make him refer to 'my niece, the Queen'; he never hesitated to invoke her name if it would help him secure what he wanted. The royal officials were perpetually infuriated by Mountbatten's habit of circumventing the usual channels and making his own arrangements direct with the Queen or the Duke of Edinburgh, often to the confusion of existing plans. John Hamilton was responsible for liaison between the Admiralty and the Palace and sometimes had cause to refer to projects which Mountbatten had conceived and privately promoted. 'Naval Secretary,' would come the stern reply, 'we are not interested here in what takes place on the Broadlands wavelength.'[24] Mountbatten got particular pleasure from coaching the Queen in her riding. 'I put Lilibet through her paces on Surprise on the lawn,' he noted in his diary, 'standing in the middle as I made her do dressage round me. She seemed to enjoy it as much as I did.' Whether she did or did not, she recognized his skills as a teacher and his eye for detail. Try as he might, however, he could never persuade her of the merits of riding side-saddle, a practice which he felt to be as elegant as it was functional, but which she disliked, refusing to have recourse to it except at the ceremony of Trooping the Colour.

The royal family were alive to the dangers of letting Mountbatten's role become too conspicuous. Prince Philip wrote to say that he would shortly be needing a new private secretary and looked forward to talking over possible candidates with his uncle. 'If you don't mind my saying so,' he went on, 'I should be a bit careful about discussing this problem because I'm sure you realise what fun some people would have if they thought you were involved in "choosing" my staff!'[25] Both Queen and the Duke felt respect for his wisdom and acumen, but tempered their admiration with affectionate amusement. At a tercentenary dinner for the Royal Marines in 1964, Mountbatten scribbled on the back of a menu card a message to the Queen suggesting that she should commemorate the occasion in 'a dramatic manner' by extending to the Marines the naval privilege of drinking the loyal toast seated, ashore as well as afloat. 'This you can safely do and give great pleasure.' The Captain General would have to agree but, since the Captain General was the Duke of Edinburgh who was seated at the same table, such agreement could readily be obtained. The card was passed to the Duke, who added the comment: 'Trust you to think of such a splendid triviality!' But trivial or not, the advice was followed.

Mountbatten would have taken a keen interest in his nephew's children even if they had not been first and second in line to the throne. He thought of Charles and Anne, in 1958 aged nine and seven respectively, almost as much as he did of his own grandchildren, missed no opportunity to be with them and was constantly buying them presents on his trips abroad. 'I had a letter from Dickie in which I read with amazement that two elephants were going to be sent to me by Jaipur and I was to keep them till you came,' Nehru wrote to Edwina. Anxiously the Prime Minister began to enquire about stabling for elephants in New Delhi. 'Later I remembered Dickie telling me about small enamelled elephants which he intended presenting to the Princess Anne. So all was well.'[26] But it was the Prince of Wales who above all engaged Mountbatten's attention. He was aboard *Britannia* when she called at Holyhead in August 1958, and he and Pamela took the children ashore: 'We thus had the unique privilege of bringing the newly created Prince of Wales to Wales for the first time.' He encouraged the Prince to take an interest in his activities and was delighted when the boy responded. 'Work almost all day,' he entered in his diary during a stay at Windsor. 'Charles came for an hour to see what my work consisted of.'[27] His own child-like enthusiasm and capacity for exposition made him an ideal mentor; it was not going to be till after his own retirement that he would be able to address himself full-bloodedly to the

Prince's education, but already he had established a relationship of trust and affection on which he was later to build.

Yet in spite of all that his family and friends could do, Mountbatten remained a lonely man. Loneliness is more a state of mind than a fact. Mountbatten spent little more time by himself than he would have when his wife was alive, but he still felt himself abandoned.

> *Alone.* . . . The word is life endured and known.
> It is the stillness where our spirits walk
> And all but inmost faith is overthrown.[28]

Mountbatten took no pleasure in solitude. The inmost faith was weak within him. Thrust back on his own resources, he became alarmed and melancholy. He sought relief in working even harder than usual. It was fortunate for him that his career had reached a point where the most intense application was needed to keep him abreast of his responsibilities.

# CHAPTER 44

## *The Defence Staff*

MOUNTBATTEN WAS ONLY the second Chief of the Defence Staff, and he was resolved that the office would be vastly different when he left it to what it was when he took it over. What he envisaged was an overhaul of the whole structure of defence in which the machinery in Whitehall would be radically reorganized and the relationship between the three Services reconsidered.

The role of the Minister of Defence was at the heart of his calculations. Of the Minister in 1946 Michael Howard remarked that to describe him as *primus inter pares* 'would seem unduly flattering. Rather he appeared like one of the unhappier Merovingian kings, without even a Mayor of the Palace to preempt his non-existent powers.'[1] Since then things had improved; the Minister's staff was slightly more competent to undertake the duties that theoretically had been assigned to it, the Minister himself had been given shadowy authority to impose a unified policy on the three Service Ministries. The machinery, however, was still woefully weak, and Duncan Sandys's failure to force through any drastic reorganization showed that the power of the great traditional fiefs in Whitehall had hardly been affected. The Chiefs of Staff retained their separate access to the Cabinet and the Prime Minister and continued to sit on the Defence Committee.

No one suffered more from the failure to establish the authority of a strong Ministry of Defence than the unfortunate William Dickson, first Chief of the Defence Staff. Since the reassessment of his role in 1958, his status had been enhanced, but he had not managed to establish himself as the principal, let alone the sole, professional adviser to the Government on matters of defence policy. Whether this was a reflection of Dickson's unassuming personality or of the powers that had been vested in him was something which was about to be tested by the new incumbent.

Mountbatten had been a partisan of some degree of unification between the three Services for twenty years or more. As long ago as 1944 he had given orders for a paper to be prepared on the future of recruitment and training. 'My own feelings are that there should be common entry for all officers for the three Services, and that they should have a year at Dartmouth, a year at Cranwell and a year at Sandhurst in turn. At each of these establishments they would have a common education and a specialist grounding in the particular Service they deal with.' Cadets would usually but not invariably be able to choose their own Service. All staff courses and war courses should be on an inter-Service basis, and staff officers should serve on staff appointments for six months or a year in each of the other two Services.[2]

As if this was not heretical enough, Mountbatten's comments on his staff's first draft can truly be called remarkable, considering that they were written by an aristocrat and an Admiral a year before the end of the war.

> I agree that the officer's home life should, if possible, present an 'example of decent happiness'. But I do not think we can get away with the assertion that this is more likely to result as a consequence of Public School education than of Secondary or Grammar School upbringing. In fact, I think the majority of people would consider that conventional morality, certainly as far as adultery and divorce are concerned, is far more likely to be found in the lower income groups.
>
> I agree that the officer should be capable of being 'socially at ease in any circle'. But this, I think, will increasingly cease to mean that those of a lower income should adapt themselves to the social usages of people of a higher income: presumably the Public Schoolboy will increasingly accommodate himself to the manners and outlook of those whom he has previously considered his inferiors.[3]

Now it seemed that he might practise what he had preached for so long. In the complex of considerations that shaped his views, the most pressing was the wastefulness and inefficiency endemic in the present system. However successful the Services might be in resisting attacks upon their budgets, it was inevitable that the pressure for economies would sometimes prove irresistible. A situation in which Navy, Army and Air Force pursued their separate requirements without reference to the needs or wishes of their sister Services was no longer tolerable. Some standardization was essential, and it would come only if imposed from above. A strong Minister of Defence and Chief of the Defence Staff were thus essential. The fact that he would be the strong Chief of the Defence Staff gave Mountbatten confidence that the scheme would work, but he would have felt it was the proper answer whoever the new incumbent might be.

He started work on 13 July 1959, and officially took over three days later. Duncan Sandys was still Minister of Defence. On the whole Mountbatten was satisfied at the prospect of working with him. He knew that they thought alike on reorganization and had established a relationship based on mutual respect and trust. To the Chiefs of Staff he said with some arrogance that he had moved to a new office not so that it would be easier for him to visit the Minister of Defence but so that the Minister of Defence would find it easier to visit him. These were empty words prompted by his desire to present himself as the defender of the Services against the depredations of politicians.[4] In fact C.D.S. and Minister co-existed on terms of slightly uneasy equality: Mountbatten knew that, in the last resort, any Prime Minister would support his Cabinet colleague against a Service officer, while Sandys was equally clear that, if the C.D.S. opposed his ideas, there would be only the slimmest chance of making them prevail.

Mountbatten's hopes of pushing his ideas on unification through the Chiefs of Staff had been raised by the retirement of Field Marshal Templer. His successor was General Festing, 'my old friend', as Mountbatten described him,[5] and former divisional commander in South-East Asia. Mountbatten admired him and the feeling, on the whole, was mutual. 'He had one of the most efficient brains that I have ever had occasion to work with, but I would not say that it was necessarily without its complications,' wrote Festing. 'I always had a feeling that some of the peculiarities of the British set-up were never fully understood by him. . . . He was a great colleague and an extremely good Chairman of the Chiefs of Staff.'[6] Festing was an admirably robust character, but slightly in awe of his former Supreme Commander. Such feelings, coupled with genuine affection, promised an easier relationship than Mountbatten had enjoyed with his predecessor. More important, Festing did not share Templer's inveterate hostility to any strengthening of the centre at the expense of the three Services; on the contrary, he felt that some such reform was necessary, even desirable.

Sandys himself did not remain as Minister of Defence long enough to benefit by this change of heart. A general election took place in October 1959. Mountbatten was in Washington, dining with the President, the night the results were announced. Eisenhower, he recorded, was 'considerably more excited than I was . . . and could not conceal his pleasure when Gaitskell conceded the election. He said that though he would personally have no difficulty in working with Gaitskell, he could not see Herter working happily with Bevan. But what pleased him most was being able to work once more with his old friend Harold Macmillan, and that he thought his re-election would be a notable contribution to summit negotiations and world peace.'[7] In the reshuffle that followed, Sandys was shifted to the Ministry of Aviation and Harold Watkinson took over Defence. The change in style could hardly have been more pronounced. Watkinson was a businessman who believed in letting the professionals run things while he played an unobtrusive role. He rarely exercised his prerogative of taking the chair at meetings of the Chiefs of

Staff and, according to Mountbatten, only once rejected the C.D.S.'s advice during his two and a half years in office.*

With Festing as C.I.G.S., the unassertive Pike replacing Boyle as Chief of Air Staff, and Charles Lambe at the Admiralty, the Chiefs of Staff at the beginning of 1960 promised to be an altogether more amenable body than any Mountbatten had served with before. He wrote in exultation to Edwina after a dinner for his colleagues had just broken up at his house in Wilton Crescent:

> I cannot tell you how exciting it is working with the Chiefs of Staff now, and these private meetings I told you about are proving a tremendous success. I now add Playfair and Zuckerman to these meetings, so the Minister only gets advice with a single voice through me, instead of the many rival views Duncan used to get. We spoke for nearly four hours tonight deciding how to make the machine work even better and Tom Pike is proving really splendid.[8]

Edward Playfair was the newly appointed Permanent Under-Secretary at the Ministry of Defence, occupant of the office that, under Sandys, had seemed to the Chiefs of Staff to be gaining dangerously in importance. Solly Zuckerman, the Minister's Chief Scientific Adviser and Mountbatten's old ally from Combined Operations, had been lured back from academic life by the promise of fresh worlds to conquer. He complemented Mountbatten admirably. Sceptical, iconoclastic, analytical yet brilliantly perceptive, he both fuelled the C.D.S. with the ideas that were to shape Britain's defence policy over the next five years and acted as a brake on Mountbatten's more impetuous extravagances. The 'Zuk-Batten Axis' dominated its section of Whitehall. Some people have sought to represent Zuckerman as a puppet-master pulling the strings of a personable but vacuous Admiral, others see him as Mountbatten's creature and hatchet-man. One image is as false as the other. Both men were self-willed and inclined to arrogance; each respected the other's intelligence and abilities; each accepted that, if the other disagreed strongly with his ideas, there was at least a case for re-examination. They composed a partnership, the sum of which was greater than the parts.

With such a team around him, Mountbatten could hope that defence reorganization would soon be open for discussion. He got little encouragement from his Minister. The scars left by Duncan Sandys's aborted efforts had not yet fully healed, and Watkinson was not the man to re-open them unless compelled to do so. If the Prime Minister had shown enthusiasm, it would

* On the TSR 2, a very special case. See p. 587 below.

have been different, but Macmillan was not yet ready to confront an issue that had already produced much acrimony and little advance. With unusual patience Mountbatten accepted that the time was not ripe for major changes and instead concentrated on organizational refinements which cumulatively prepared the way for the structural upheaval that was to come.

The most significant reform was indeed initiated almost immediately after he became C.D.S., while Boyle was still Chief of Air Staff and Sandys Minister of Defence. Echoing the views that he had voiced as Supreme Commander some seventeen years before, Mountbatten argued that the C.D.S. would remain largely impotent so long as he was excluded from the planning process. He must have his own Director of Defence Plans, who would not merely sit with the Joint Planning Staff but would be its permanent chairman. He aired this view at one of those celebrated weekend parties for the Chiefs of Staff at Broadlands, which he was convinced provided an opportunity for relaxed and harmonious discussion but which some of his guests found contrived and painful. Certainly there was nothing relaxed or harmonious about Dermot Boyle's response. 'I consider your appointment as Chief of the Defence Staff the greatest disaster that has befallen the British Defence Services within memory,' he stated bluntly.[9] Mountbatten, in his view, was trying to substitute the authority of a single man for the collective responsibility of the Chiefs of Staff. If the Joint Planning Staff, through its chairman, reported directly to the C.D.S., the Chiefs of Staff would be by-passed and find themselves reduced to rubber-stamping decisions reached by the C.D.S. and Minister of Defence in private conclave. 'The reason I was saying he would be a disaster', wrote Boyle many years later, 'was because he was a superb Supremo and we did not want a Supremo as C.D.S.'[10]

If anything encouraged by this opposition, Mountbatten continued to insist that, if the Minister was to be given quick and authoritative advice, it was essential that the C.D.S. should have his own Chief of Defence Plans. As a sop to Boyle he proposed that Air-Commodore Rosier, the Director of Air Plans, should be the first to fill the new role. Boyle was unconvinced, and threatened that, if the proposal were put to the Chiefs of Staff, he would oppose it categorically. In that case, said Mountbatten, he would appeal to the Minister, who would undoubtedly support him. Lambe now intervened and suggested a compromise by which the new system should be tried for a year and renewed only if it was then approved by the Chiefs of Staff. On this understanding Boyle gave way. Rosier was appointed and performed his task with skill and tact, Mountbatten remained on his best behaviour, and after twelve months the Chiefs of Staff gave the system their formal blessing. Boyle, who had by then anyway retired, bore no grudge for his defeat. 'It is a pity that in our work there have been many things on which we have held opposing views', he wrote on his retirement, 'but our differences were open and honest and we both believed what we thought and said. The great thing now, looking back, is that it has made no difference whatever to our friendship, certainly on my part and I hope on yours.'[11]

Another device by which Mountbatten sought to enhance the stature of the C.D.S. was by providing that he alone should hold five-star rank. By March 1960 the Chiefs had agreed in principle that this ultimate promotion should only come when an officer became C.D.S. or when, as Chief of Staff, he was within a few months of retirement.[12] For some reason, however, no firm ruling was made, and by mid 1962 there was still a full house of Field Marshals, Admirals of the Fleet and Marshals of the Royal Air Force at the head of Britain's defence establishment. Mountbatten waited until all his colleagues either already enjoyed five-star rank or were on the point of doing so, then raised the issue again.[13] This time he was successful, though it was still nearly twelve months later and under a new Minister of Defence, Peter Thorneycroft, that it was ruled that only the C.D.S. should in future enjoy five-star rank, the Chiefs of Staff being promoted on their retirement.[14]

On another issue even closer to his heart Mountbatten was less successful. In 1960 he discovered that he no longer featured on the Army and Air Force lists. This was a point on which he had fought strongly in 1945. He had then established that the monarch alone had the authority to withdraw commissions; there was no evidence that King George VI had given such an order; certainly Queen Elizabeth had not done so; why then was he not still a Lieutenant-General and Air Marshal?[15] Personally he thought that, as C.D.S., he should hold five-star rank in all three Services.

Richard Way was required to brief his Minister on the issue.

> The post of Chief of Defence Staff [he subsequently summarized his views as being], with its strongly co-ordinating role for the three Services, was still in its early stages and was still viewed with some jealousy and suspicion. It was occupied by an officer who was probably the most mistrusted of all senior officers in the three Services for his ambition and for his motives. To give him the ranks of Field Marshal and Marshal of the Royal Air Force could not possibly fail to deepen this mistrust and to harm the progress which was being made towards co-operation between the three Services through the office of Chief of the Defence Staff. Moreover, there were no grounds for doing for Mountbatten something which would not be done for his successors. Were they all to hold five-star rank in the three Services?[16]

Way's advice was taken and Ministers urged Mountbatten not to press his claim. The C.D.S. conceded with good grace. At a meeting of the Chiefs of Staff he said that legally his position was unassailable but that, in the circumstances, he did not propose to press to have his name reinserted on the Army and Air Force lists. Festing and Pike endorsed his view of the legal position and welcomed his decision not to insist on something that 'might be misconstrued, especially by certain mischievous elements in the press'.[17] The issue was never raised again.

Meanwhile, he sought to introduce through the back door the integration of the Services that was temporarily denied him in Whitehall. In his final report as Supreme Commander Mountbatten had urged that the territories of the three Commanders-in-Chief in South-East Asia should coincide, and a Supreme Commander with a small staff be established at Singapore. His initiative foundered, largely because of the obdurate resistance of the Royal Navy.[18] Now, sixteen years later, his chance had come to reintroduce the concept. 'It is the opinion of most close observers, with which I concur,' wrote Franklyn Johnson, leading scholar on the subject, 'that the unified commands would probably have been blocked if any C.D.S. except Mountbatten had espoused them. He pressed relentlessly ahead, foreseeing that the successful example of overseas commands could substantially influence centralization in Whitehall.'[19]

The Near East came first, with a headquarters established in Cyprus in 1960; Middle East Command followed in 1961 at Aden.[20] The Far East proved the toughest nut to crack. In March 1959, when he was still First Sea Lord, Mountbatten wrote to Admiral Gladstone in Hong Kong to report that the Prime Minister had resolved to unify the overseas commands. 'I am anxious personally that we should go slowly,' he remarked, somewhat disingenuously, 'but the threat is clearly held out that if we resist unified commands the pressure to unify the Services and in particular the administration in Whitehall, will become much stronger.'[21] The local Commanders-in-Chief were not wholly convinced. The Gan affair of August 1959 fortified both sides in the conviction that they were right. In this bizarre incident news reached the Commanders-in-Chief that there was trouble on the island of Gan in the Addu Atoll, a chain of islands in the Indian Ocean. Almost casually they decided on intervention, on the basis of 'I've got a frigate here,' 'Well, I've got a regiment there.' No unified command, they felt, could have operated more rapidly or efficiently.[22] Unfortunately, they omitted to tell the Ministry of Defence what they had done, with the result that Mountbatten was left in ignorance until the operation was far advanced and had to explain what had happened to an indignant Prime Minister. 'He was furious and said that the only shooting he would permit this August was grouse. . . . I was delighted. This breakdown gave me the excuse to start work on getting a "Unified Commander-in-Chief" appointed over the other three.'[23]

It still proved a protracted task. When Mountbatten visited Singapore in February 1961 General Hull told him that he did not believe there was room for a Supreme Commander in peacetime. 'From then on Mountbatten knew that he had an opponent in me,' commented Hull, a threat which he more than made good when he became Chief of the Imperial General Staff at the end of that year.[24] It was November 1962 before resistance finally crumbled and Admiral Luce was appointed first unified Commander-in-Chief of the new Far East Command.

Britain's retreat from her responsibilities outside Europe came too soon to allow the new system to be thoroughly tested. In 1961 General Qasim, the Iraqi Prime Minister, revived the claim that Kuwait was part of his country and massed troops menacingly on the border. The Minister of Defence agreed that the commando-carrier H.M.S. *Bulwark* could be moved to the area,[25] with the result that, when the Iraqi menace induced the Ruler of Kuwait to appeal for British assistance, a commando regiment and a squadron of tanks were ashore within twenty-four hours and substantial reinforcement a week later. Iraq was deterred; Kuwait's independence strengthened by its admission to the Arab League; the operation had been a model of its kind.[26] How much its success owed to the unified command is another question. Air Marshal Elworthy had recently been moved into the post. He took his orders direct from Mountbatten and passed them on to his Commanders-in-Chief, eliminating much time-wasting co-ordination in Whitehall and on the ground. He himself believes that the unified command worked well and that British intervention would have been less easily managed without this streamlined system.[27] The operation would certainly not have been more successful and might have been a great deal less so.

The same is true of the other occasion on which unified command was tested, the confrontation with Indonesia when it threatened to annex the British territories in Borneo before they could advance to independence. Here, too, was an operation conducted with exemplary skill and economy, but here, too, it is impossible to be sure that things would have run less smoothly if traditional methods of command had been employed. Field Marshal Hull for one would say that co-operation between the Services was already close and would have proved perfectly adequate for the needs of the occasion.[28] Admiral Begg on the other hand, Commander-in-Chief of British forces in the area, believed that the new command structure was an important element in the British success,[29] while General Walker, the Director of Operations in Borneo, took advantage of a visit by the Minister of Defence to 'stress the success of unified command and that this had been established "in the nick of time" '.[30] Neither of these operations did anything to disprove Mountbatten's theories; most people would agree that they provided evidence to support them.

It was not only defence reorganization that embittered Mountbatten's relationship with his colleagues. It was the function of the C.D.S. to be above the inter-Service rivalries that occasionally racked the Chiefs of Staff, in the same way as the Minister of Defence was above the conflicts that divided the Service Ministers. The Minister of Defence, however, was a politician whose first loyalty was to his party and Cabinet colleagues; the C.D.S. had spent all his working life in one of the three bodies between which he was now supposed to arbitrate. In such circumstances total objectivity was too much to hope for but an approximation to it was expected. Dickson had been generally accepted as impartial; Mountbatten was another matter, if only because his temperament and the active role which he pursued made him far more conspicuous than his predecessor.

The main clashes of interest came usually between the Navy and the Air Force. Boyle and Pike were convinced that Mountbatten abused his position to obtain advantage for his beloved Navy. More objectively, the Minister of Defence, Harold Watkinson, felt that the C.D.S. had never really shed his naval aura. Yet Alfred Earle, himself an airman and, as Deputy Chief of Defence Staff, well placed to judge his chief's proclivities, believed that Mountbatten was as nearly impartial on inter-Service issues as it was possible for him to be.[31]

However innocent or guilty Mountbatten may have been, he could have behaved more tactfully. By May 1960 the faithful Brockman was so alarmed at the envenomed atmosphere that he warned the C.D.S. that Pike was disturbed 'because he thinks you have been handling recent meetings in a dictatorial manner'. In general, Brockman went on, 'he is believed to be upset at the part you have played in stating the Navy's case recently'. A C.D.S. must not only be fair, but must be seen to be fair; in this Mountbatten failed. Whether he was indeed unfair is largely a matter of semantics. On two or three of the major issues that divided Navy and Air Force, Mountbatten took the Navy's side, but these were matters which he believed to be of critical importance, far transcending any mere inter-Service squabble. Should he, for instance, have remained neutral in the great battle over the TSR 2 and the Buccaneer?* Mountbatten was convinced that, if the Air Force was allowed to pursue the exaggeratedly expensive TSR 2, they would bankrupt the

* See p. 553 above.

defence budget and still not end up with the aircraft desired. He thought it essential that Navy and Air Force should standardize on the Buccaneer, an aircraft of lesser performance but vastly cheaper, more readily available and already largely proven. This, he felt, was an issue on which an impartial C.D.S. must decide the best course and fight to impose it. To the Air Force, however, he was displaying not impartiality but wanton favouritism – a naval man supporting a naval plane at the expense of the rival Service.

Mountbatten did his best to oppose the TSR 2 without appearing to do so. First he tried to persuade Solly Zuckerman to lobby the Minister of Defence. He drafted a paper which he suggested the Scientific Adviser might send to Watkinson and scribbled in pencil in a covering note: 'This is the first occasion on which your action is absolutely vital to the Country's Defence Policy, and to save the Minister from making a ghastly mistake. You know why I can't help you in Public. It is NOT moral cowardice but fear that my usefulness as Chairman would be seriously impaired. BURN THIS!'[32] Evidently Zuckerman alone did not carry big enough guns to carry the day. Ten days later Mountbatten approached Watkinson direct, in a hand-written letter delivered at the Minister's house:

> In the context of the present Defence Organisation I am afraid I have had to make a choice between giving you what I believe to be correct advice and destroying my value to you as the impartial Chairman of the Chiefs of Staff Committee, in view of my known opposition to the TSR 2 when First Sea Lord.
>
> I have tried to get round this by giving you my extremely strong views in private about the TSR 2–NA 39 controversy; but, as I warned you, I did not intend to repeat these views so emphatically in public as to cause a rupture between C.A.S. and myself.
>
> Nor do I intend to do propaganda with the other two Chiefs of Staff, which could cause bad feeling between them and Tom Pike as well.

Mountbatten then recapitulated the arguments for the NA 39, or Buccaneer, and against the TSR 2. If he had been Chief of Air Staff, he said, he would either have gone for an improved Buccaneer or for some radically new innovation like Barnes Wallis's 'variable geometry' plane.

> So you can see what a difficult decision I have had to make – should I publicly fight the Air Ministry and thus damage the present C.O.S. organisation, or should I let them persist in pushing through a scheme I believe to be a formidable waste of money, and which may never come into service.

What has come out of my dilemma is a firm conviction that by the
end of the year the Prime Minister and you will have to set up an
investigation into the whole organisation of defence. I shall leave it to
my colleagues while I am away to try and work out proposals for
handling this investigation.[33]

Mountbatten's somewhat transparent deviousness gained him little; the
Air Force had no doubt that he was leading the attack upon their favourite
project, and merely added duplicity to the other charges against him. They
took it for granted that, whenever anything went wrong, the C.D.S. was
responsible. Quite often they were right. In March 1962 George Edwards of
the British Aircraft Corporation, the firm building the TSR 2, did an excellent
job selling his aeroplane to Sir Frederick Scherger, the Australian Chief of
Defence Staff. Next year Scherger visited London, saw Mountbatten and
Zuckerman, and left – according to the somewhat *engagé* historian of the
project – with his enthusiasm for the TSR 2 mysteriously diminished.[34] At
lunch with Julian Amery, the Air Minister, Scherger is said to have asked
pointedly 'why Earl Mountbatten was opposed to the project'.[35] Lord
Zuckerman denies that anything he said could have disillusioned Scherger,[36]
and a transcript of Mountbatten's talk with the Australian would probably
prove similarly innocuous. Even when he wanted to, however, the C.D.S. was
inept at concealing his feelings. It would have been surprising if Scherger had
left his office without a clear impression of his dislike for the whole affair.

Mountbatten overplayed his hand. Watkinson, who anyway felt that the
Buccaneer could not match the Air Force's requirements, finally became so
weary of the C.D.S.'s importunities that he ordered him never to mention the
subject again.[37] Mountbatten obeyed. It was not till several years and many
millions of pounds later that the then Minister of Defence, Denis Healey,
finally abandoned the enterprise. 'One of the tragedies of the aerospace
industry is that the R.A.F. didn't buy the Buccaneer and develop it when it
first came out,' wrote Healey, 'but they were determined to have their own
aircraft.'[38] On the whole this judgement has stood the test of time. Mountbatten today seems more nearly right than his Air Force opponents. His tactics,
however, were questionable. He pushed his campaign against the TSR 2 to
the limit of the scrupulous, some would say beyond it. The hostility that he
generated was to cause him serious problems in the following years.

This was by no means the only case in which Mountbatten seemed to the
Air Force to be unacceptably prejudiced. The long-drawn-out battle over the
future of Coastal Command came to a head shortly after Mountbatten
became C.D.S. This had been a hobby-horse of his for many years. In 1953 he
wrote an impassioned plea to Winston Churchill:

No single man in the world today has done so much for any fighting service of any country as you have for the Royal Navy. As Prime Minister you still have it within your power to give the Navy the new lease of life you are so anxious for it to have. You have only to transfer Coastal Command to the Royal Navy. . . . Give us the right to continue to command the seas by giving us the means of doing so.[39]

The appeal went unheard. When Sandys became Minister of Defence, Coastal Command was still within the grip of the Air Force. Mountbatten seems to have reached an informal understanding with the Chief of Air Staff that the issue should not be revived while 'the whole future of the Services was in the melting pot', but at the end of 1958 Sandys nevertheless ordered an enquiry. Mountbatten wrote to Boyle to express his dismay at suggestions that this constituted 'in some way a breach on my part of the undertaking I gave you'.[40] The Minister had acted entirely on his own initiative. Probably Sandys had not needed much prompting, but Mountbatten's diary entry of a few months before – 'We went to David's cocktail party. I saw Duncan and fixed up Coastal Command.'[41] – suggests that his role had not been quite so passive as he suggested to Boyle.

An acrimonious debate now began: 'Critical Coastal Command meeting of M. of D. with C.O.S. at which Dermot insulted Duncan,' was a note in Mountbatten's diary which indicated how high tempers were running.[42] Sandys supported the Navy and the battle seemed won; then George Ward, the Air Minister, threatened resignation if his Service was thus truncated and the issue was pushed no farther. 'Basically Mountbatten's idea about bringing Coastal Command within the Navy and joining up with the Fleet Air Arm was right and would have made for greater efficiency and greater economy,' concluded William Davis, 'but the proposal was timed badly without sufficient political preparation and consequently failed.'[43] The same could not be said of the long debate over Britain's nuclear deterrent, where the Navy's most fundamental victory over the Air Force was to be won.

# CHAPTER 45

## *The Nuclear Deterrent*

IN OCTOBER 1959 Mountbatten visited the American Air Force base at Vandenberg, home of the Inter-Continental Ballistic Missiles. The base stretched along twenty-four miles of the Pacific coast, and was seven or eight miles deep. He had previously had no idea that the Americans were already able to hit Russia with nuclear missiles and was impressed and appalled by what he saw.

> Nothing I had been told prepared me for the staggering shock of seeing a Titan hole. This is 40 feet in diameter and 165 feet deep, big enough to house a 20 storey sky-scraper.
>
> The Titan comes up on a gigantic lift after the heavy doors of the top of the hole have been opened. The whole complex has been designed to stand up to a pressure of 100 pounds per square inch, and they say that nothing but an absolute direct hit from a nuclear weapon can knock it out.
>
> The whole thing has a gruesome and horrific effect which makes one really fear for the sanity of mankind.[1]

Mountbatten's visit to Vandenberg crystallized beliefs about nuclear warfare and the deterrent which had been forming throughout the previous decade. His ideas were pragmatic, reasonable and humanitarian, owing much to the scientific advice of Solly Zuckerman but also reflecting faithfully his own personality. Today, though still not generally accepted by the powers that be, they seem commonplace; in 1960 they were heretical. Nuclear weapons, he accepted, were here to stay. If it had been possible to reverse time and eliminate them from the world's armoury, he would have done so, but it was too late; even if all the nuclear powers agreed to destroy their stockpiles, there would be no guarantee that one of them or some outsider would not secretly slip back into the race. The emphasis must therefore be not on abolition, but on limitation and control.

He was among the first to attack the pernicious doctrine of overkill. If you shot a burglar and injured him fatally, he would argue, there was no point in emptying the rest of the magazine into his body – he can't be deader than dead. To Americans who maintained that it was essential to 'stay ahead' of Russia in the nuclear arms race, he would insist that there was no such concept as 'ahead' in a world where either side could destroy the other. Improvements in the systems of delivery could indeed be valuable; so, possibly, could improved defences; but the accumulation of ever larger nuclear stockpiles, the proliferation of launching-sites, was not merely wasteful but increased rather than reduced the risk of holocaust.

This was the test he applied to every development in the field – did it make more or less likely the ultimate catastrophe of nuclear warfare? He did not believe it was possible that Britain would ever use nuclear weapons except in conjunction with the United States and her other NATO allies. Brockman wrote to him in 1965 in alarm: 'I should like to tell you privately that there has been a little surprise here at your categorical statement in Canberra at your press conference that "we, the British, have not got an independent nuclear deterrent". Some surprise is being expressed that you are "playing politics" in this way.'[2] Mountbatten did not feel that he had been playing politics, merely stating as a self-evident truth that no Prime Minister of a country as vulnerable as Great Britain could conceivably sign the nation's death-warrant by indulging single-handed in nuclear warfare. 'Independence', in terms of nuclear warfare, was a myth.

In 1962 Zuckerman tabled a paper arguing against the multiplicity of tactical nuclear weapons and inferring that Europe should rely on the American strategic deterrent and itself concentrate on building up conventional forces.[3] Mountbatten insisted that this paper should be considered by the Chiefs of Staff and its author given a chance to defend his view, 'for, as matters stood, he was in agreement with Sir Solly Zuckerman's paper'. The response from the Chiefs was predictably unenthusiastic, Hull arguing that the paper was written from 'an emotional and humanitarian point of view rather than from that of pure scientific advice on defence'.[4]

Mountbatten's sense of the imminence of catastrophe was heightened when in March 1961 he visited Omaha, Nebraska, and was briefed on the future of space exploration and its relationship to defence. He was dazzled by the possibilities that seemed to be opening before mankind, but was also well aware of the latent perils. 'If there is general disarmament this will be a wonderful age,' he wrote in his diary, 'but if our ability to control space is solely to be used to increase our destructive capabilities, then I see little chance of the world surviving.'[5] Unusually among military leaders, the desirability – indeed, the necessity – of controlled disarmament was always in his mind. As early as 1955 he had prepared for the Foreign Secretary a memorandum which argued that, since the Russians enjoyed massive superiority in conventional forces but were well behind in nuclear weapons, 'a method must be found to give them an adequate feeling of security to induce them to go ahead on their proposed reduction of conventional forces'. His proposal was that each country should declare the contents of its nuclear stockpile and that subsequent additions should be monitored, the object being that the totals each side of the Iron Curtain should be roughly the same. There should, he concluded, 'be no limitation to the stockpile or to the continued development of the means of delivery since the higher the capacity on both sides the greater the deterrent to war.'[6]

On this last point he had reversed his views long before he became C.D.S., but on the need for disarmament he never wavered. He conducted a running debate with Solly Zuckerman on the subject during his years in office. To build up NATO's conventional forces to a point where they could defeat the Russians without recourse to nuclear weapons was, both men agreed, politically if not economically impossible. Even if it could be done, the gain would be questionable, since the losing side in any great conventional war would resort to its nuclear armoury rather than face defeat. The deterrent was therefore essential. 'I entirely agree that the Russians do not want war,' wrote Mountbatten, 'and are terrified of the possibility of accidental war. This is a state we must preserve, for it is a real deterrent.' But the present policy of accumulating ever more new and 'sophisticated' weapons, quite apart from the risk of proliferation among countries outside the great power blocs, seemed doomed to end in disaster. 'Probably the only real solution is disarmament. . . .'[7]

Behind Mountbatten's thinking lay an inchoate yet by no means unconsidered conviction that weapons alone would not be enough if the West were to defend itself and its values against the threat of Communism. While he was C.D.S. he prepared a memorandum for his staff in which he tried to define the problem as he saw it.

> The basic thing which seems to put the West at a demonstrable disadvantage with the East is the absence of a philosophy, a policy, an ideal, or an aim.
>
> The East have, of course, Communism, and the creed of Karl Marx, which has undoubtedly helped them to make up their minds on policy, and in their determination to see things through. . . .
>
> Can we not find an aim for the West? What can it be?
>
> RELIGION. We can hardly use Christianity as the aim, for not only are there such great differences between Roman Catholics, Protestants, Orthodox etc, but we certainly would like to see countries in which Mohammedanism, Hinduism and Agnosticism are prevalent, join in our common aim.

WESTERN DEMOCRACY. I feel we have already made a mistake in trying to export the Western parliamentary system to countries where the vast majority of the population is illiterate and backward. One man, one vote, is proving nonsense, and we would have to find a more suitable form of democracy if we were going to use this particular aim.

WAY OF LIFE. A decent standard of living, supported by an emergent form of Welfare State. Freedom of speech (not just freedom from arrest, but freedom from losing your job . . .). Equal opportunity (not just on paper, but genuine). World disarmament and a world authority, would appear to be the right sort of aim, but it is difficult to put over.

ANTI-COMMUNISM. This is the poorest of all aims, for it is negative instead of positive, and leaves us permanently on the defensive instead of taking the initiative. Can we not find some common rallying cry to give us some common purpose? I invite thought and suggestions on this subject.[8]

These reflections were neither profound nor coherent. They were, indeed, no more than rough notes designed to stimulate discussion. The point about them is that they show that Mountbatten *wanted* to stimulate discussion. He was concerned about issues which transcended the mere provision of a nation's defence. His views might be criticized, in the words Hull used to criticize Solly Zuckerman, as 'emotional and humanitarian', but there were plenty of hard-headed realists among his colleagues who could be relied on to correct so perilous a bias. It may be doubted whether such preoccupations made him a more efficient Chief of the Defence Staff but they certainly made him a more interesting and, if a moral value-judgement may be forgiven, a better man.

Most people contrive to place a barrier between principle and practice. Mountbatten was particularly deft at this manoeuvre. He professed a belief in egalitarianism and lived his life in an atmosphere of unabashed elitism. He deplored the cult of the individual yet promoted himself vigorously. He was sceptical about the reality of Britain's independent deterrent but determined that it should be maintained in the most efficient manner. As a concomitant of this he was privately, though not yet publicly, resolved that it should be administered by the Royal Navy.

Blue Streak, Britain's ill-fated inter-continental missile, perished a few months after Mountbatten became C.D.S. 'It is going to take a great deal of courage for the Prime Minister to announce in Parliament the abandonment of the Blue Streak program in view of the amount spent on it,' wrote Arleigh Burke in April 1960. 'The rationalisation will doubtless be that the V-Bomber program will still get a long range air-to-surface missile, but a new one called SKYBOLT. This missile is technically feasible provided enough research and development is done on it, but it is a very expensive and vulnerable system. I believe you will find it advisable to shift to Polaris in the end.'[9] No conclusion could have pleased Mountbatten better. If he had believed that Skybolt had a future he might have felt bound to enrage the Air Force still further by campaigning for its abandonment in favour of Polaris. As it was, he could afford to sit back and let the Americans establish that the air-to-surface missile was technically and economically impossible. Then only Polaris would be left to replace the obsolescent bombers. In October 1960 the Minister of Defence became aware that the Skybolt programme was in danger. 'When Harold told me the disquieting news about Skybolt,' wrote Mountbatten in somewhat unconvincing consternation, 'I strongly advised him to use the same money (over £100,000,000) to buy a couple of American-built Polaris submarines.'[10]

The Air Force was not yet defeated. Pandora, a ram-jet, low-flying projectile, was now produced as an alternative. The C.D.S. expressed interest in the idea, but doubted whether it was wise to pin too much faith on a system that was still on the drawing-board. Watkinson said that he had been told that the bomb would cost only £10 million to develop and could be in service by 1965. 'C.D.S. suggested it would be wise to multiply the cost by three and to add 50% on the time-scale.' Anyway, Pandora would have to be fired from the TSR 2, and there was not the faintest prospect of that aircraft becoming operational before 1967 or 1968. The latest information from America, on the other hand, suggested that Polaris submarines would be available within two or three years. 'Polaris would remain valid as a deterrent for twenty or thirty years as he saw no prospect of anti-submarine measures having the breakthrough of a magnitude needed to attack Polaris submarines over the millions of square miles of ocean or under the North Polar ice cap.'[11] Pandora returned to her box and the Minister of Defence agreed, in principle, that if Skybolt was abandoned Polaris seemed the only alternative.

Late in 1962 Skybolt duly foundered. The United States offered to hand over the derelict programme lock, stock and barrel for Britain to develop as it wished. Macmillan flew to Nassau to confer with President Kennedy. Mountbatten was indignant that he was not invited to join the party. 'The Prime Minister would gladly have taken me,' he told a friend, 'if only Jack Kennedy had agreed to bring the Chairman of his Chiefs of Staff.' But Kennedy preferred to discuss the problems without interference from the military and

Macmillan decided that 'I would be too conspicuous and make the public think they had come to talk of war and not peace'.[12] His absence proved unimportant; Zuckerman was of the party and saw that the Prime Minister did not go astray. According to Dermot Boyle, Thorneycroft accompanied Macmillan to Nassau with a brief to secure Skybolt if he possibly could and came back having purchased Polaris, without any reference to the Chiefs of Staff.[13] If the Chiefs did indeed advocate a last attempt to retain Skybolt, their advice can hardly have been unqualified; Caspar John for one would heartily have deplored any such solution. Once again, however, the Air Force were left with the conviction that they had been outmanoeuvred and robbed of their rightful heritage by the machinations of the C.D.S.

It was over the employment of tactical nuclear weapons that Mountbatten seemed to Britain's NATO allies, and, indeed, to some of his own colleagues, most heretical in his thinking. The official doctrine was that, since conventional NATO forces could never match those of the Eastern bloc, the gap must be filled by the provision of short-range, small-yield tactical nuclear weapons which could be employed to stop the advancing enemy. This, it was believed, need not lead to all-out nuclear war. Mountbatten accepted that the existence of the weapons added to the overall efficiency of the deterrent, and also that, once the weapons had been deployed, it would be exceedingly difficult to secure their withdrawal. 'That being so,' he told Zuckerman, 'the important thing is the political and military control of these weapons. We must spare no effort to achieve the best possible system of battlefield surveillance and communications.'[14]

What disturbed him most was the assumption of many military commanders that it would be possible to use tactical nuclear weapons to repel a Russian invasion and then, when these had achieved their purpose, to revert to conventional arms without any Russian retaliation in kind. He attacked this doctrine at a NATO meeting in Paris in 1962. 'I spoke on Tactical Nuclear Weapons. Very controversial,' he noted with some satisfaction.[15] With deceptive simplicity he sketched out a scenario of a possible Russian invasion on a Corps front, that is to say, one defended by some 200 dispersed units of infantry, guns or tanks. To attack on such a front, according to the traditional rule of thumb by which commanders planned in the Second World War, the Russians could be expected to deploy some 600 roughly similar units. Recent war-games played in England had shown that, on an average, the number of tactical nuclear weapons fired would be about the same as the number of dispersed units destroyed. To reduce the Russian attack to a level at which it would stand little chance of penetrating the Western defences, it would be necessary to reduce the ratio of attackers to defenders from three to one to two to one. The Russians must now be expected to retaliate to restore the balance in their favour; given that the defenders would be better deployed than the attackers, it would probably be necessary for them to fire half as many again tactical missiles to achieve their end: three missiles to every two dispersed units. Allowing for a certain number of missiles fired to prevent reinforcements reaching the respective front lines, it was reasonable to expect some 700 nuclear warheads would be exploded in the first few hours of battle. Mountbatten now admitted that he might be over-pessimistic – divide my figures by ten, he generously suggested, assume that only the smallest tactical nuclear weapons were employed. 1.4 megatons' worth of explosives would still have been unleashed on this limited battle-front, more than the Royal Air Force dropped in four years of war, more than 200 Hiroshimas. And what about the resulting radio-activity? What about the risk of escalation? 'My questions are not intended to invalidate the deterrent effect of tactical nuclear weapons,' Mountbatten concluded. 'They are only asked with a view to clearing my own mind on how field warfare would proceed after the use of tactical nuclear weapons.'[16]

'Dynamite,' had been Mountbatten's description of his forthcoming speech. It would 'set the cat among the pigeons' and make his own position difficult 'because any prophet of things going wrong is unpopular'.[17] It did indeed make a considerable impression and cause some disquiet, but it cannot be said that it affected NATO policy. The commitment to tactical nuclear weapons seemed irrevocable; it was no doubt salutary that the planners should be confronted with the consequences of what they proposed, but the facts could not be changed.

Of all the devices for extending the deployment and control of nuclear weapons, the one that most disturbed Mountbatten was the M.L.F. – the Mixed-Manned Multi-Lateral Force. This scheme involved the creation of a fleet of some twenty-five surface vessels, each one armed with Polaris missiles, which would have crews drawn from all the NATO countries, thus in theory satisfying the wish of the Europeans for some control over the strategic deterrent. Mountbatten believed that it would be expensive, wasteful and militarily unworkable; that the multiple control would either be spurious or cripplingly cumbersome; and that the fleet would greatly expand the armoury of strategic weapons at a time when all sane men should be seeking to reduce it. He campaigned against the M.L.F. with intemperate vigour. In Washington in February 1963 he accused an American admiral who supported the project of suppressing his professional judgement at the behest of his political masters, and when he saw the political master in question the following day he told President Kennedy that he was amazed that a former sailor could support such an act of folly.[18] Warned by the Foreign Office not to get involved in political questions, he contented himself with telling the Belgian Prime Minister that the M.L.F. was 'the greatest piece of military nonsense' he had come across in fifty years. 'This seemed to satisfy the Prime Minister.'[19] Lunching at *The Times*, he 'sat between Gavin Astor and William Haley and did propaganda against the M.L.F'.[20] In the end the idea perished. Its demise was speeded by the development of a rival proposal which was suggested to Kennedy at the Nassau Conference in 1963 and subsequently developed by Mountbatten. This was the A.N.F. – the Atlantic Naval Force – a body of dubiously international status which, in certain circumstances, would have assigned to it Britain's Polaris submarines and nuclear bombers and some part of the American deterrent force. Mountbatten had little faith in the project and doubted whether it would ever come to anything, but it was a handy sop to those Americans who were set on the idea of the M.L.F.[21] The A.N.F., commented Franz-Josef Strauss cynically, was 'the only fleet that had not been created that torpedoed another fleet that hadn't sailed'.[22]

The defeat of the M.L.F. was the last contribution to the nuclear debate that Mountbatten made as Chief of the Defence Staff. His opposition to it was based upon the same principles as shaped all his conduct in this field: abhorrence at the possibility of nuclear warfare and resistance to anything that made it seem more likely. It was a battle that he was to continue when out of office; to striking effect, indeed, when he was within a few months of his death.

# CHAPTER 46

# *The C.D.S. Abroad*

THE CHIEF OF THE DEFENCE STAFF is the professional head of the British armed forces. He is a figure of great importance in his own country and, even in the post-Suez world, of considerable consequence elsewhere. When he was also a former Viceroy, a man who enjoyed Supreme Command at a time when his present colleagues were playing relatively humble roles, a cousin of the monarch, his position became still more gloriously rarefied. Technically junior to the Minister of Defence, Mountbatten in the eyes of the public was an immeasurably greater figure. His function and his special attributes guaranteed that he would be able to range the world almost at will, and that wherever he went he would be received with deference and respect.

However much he might wish that Britain's defences could be wholly independent, Mountbatten knew that her security was inextricably bound up with that of the United States and her European allies. Decisions made in Washington could affect the British Services as much as or more than those taken in Whitehall. It was critically important for him that his connections with the American establishment should remain close. When he became C.D.S. this posed no problem. Eisenhower, his old wartime colleague and friend, was still President and the door to the White House was always open. The new Secretary of State also became an ally. 'I was very favourably impressed by Chris Herter, who seemed to think the same as I did on most subjects,' wrote Mountbatten,[1] whose readiness to be impressed by the intelligence of those who agreed with him was frequently apparent. The following year, however, Eisenhower gave way to Kennedy. Mountbatten did not meet him till April 1961 when Kennedy asked him whether he remembered that as a young student before the war he had been a guest at a party in the Brook House penthouse. 'For the sake of Anglo-U.S. amity I lied and said "yes",' wrote Mountbatten. The visit, supposed to be a courtesy call taking five minutes, instead lasted fifty. 'I formed the highest possible impression of Mr Kennedy, who seemed to be realistic and sound on everything we discussed,' recorded Mountbatten in his diary.[2] No doubt the President had thought the same as Mountbatten did on most subjects.

But pleasant and sometimes useful though it was to hobnob with Presidents, most of the C.D.S.'s business was done with his military colleagues. When Wing-Commander Le Hardy, Mountbatten's personal staff officer, went with him to Washington in February 1963 he was struck by the fact that all the Chiefs of Staff except the Chairman, Maxwell Taylor, were old friends.[3] Curtis Le May of the Air Force and the Chief of Army Staff, General Wheeler, had both served in SEAC, while Admiral Anderson had known him even earlier. The talks were far-reaching and, though many points of disagreement were revealed, they were discussed with frankness and good temper. The meetings were 'the most sensational success of all time', Mountbatten reported jubilantly.[4] Certainly they put Anglo-American relations at the top professional level back on to a basis of mutual confidence which they had hardly attained since the end of the war and were never to reach again. Mountbatten himself rarely hesitated to expound his real feelings to his American colleagues, however unpalatable they might be. When Admiral Sharp, newly appointed Commander-in-Chief in the Pacific, in March 1965 told Mountbatten that he had been instructed to prepare a month's intensive bombing of Vietnam and to work out a scheme for possible intervention by U.S. ground forces, the C.D.S. commented bluntly:

> From my experience in South East Asia, unless a truly acceptable national government could be formed, . . . any stooges they tried to keep in power with American bayonets would merely add to the American unpopularity and finally destroy any national following that the stooges might otherwise have acquired.
>
> I told him that although I regarded it of the highest importance to keep South Vietnam outside the 'bamboo curtain' with a progressive national government, I did not think that the plans he had been ordered to draw up were likely to bring this about.[5]

One of the Americans with whom Mountbatten worked most amicably was the Supreme Allied Commander Europe, SACEUR, General Lauris Norstad. On his first visit to Paris after he had become C.D.S., Mountbatten called on Norstad and said that he had a confession to make. When Norstad had been appointed he had doubted whether this young airman could be right for the job. Now he saw he was mistaken. 'I've come to tell you, you are not merely adequate but outstanding.'[6] This was a ploy that Mountbatten had used on other occasions; after Peter Thorneycroft had been Minister of Defence for a few weeks the C.D.S. called on him and announced, 'I have a confession to make. . . .'[7] Nevertheless, it was sincerely meant; Mountbatten thought Norstad misguided on tactical nuclear weapons but believed that in general he did an almost impossible job with exemplary skill. Norstad reciprocated the admiration and at one stage maintained that Mountbatten ought to succeed him as SACEUR. He would have been the first non-American to fill the post, but Norstad believed that he would have been acceptable in Washington if only the Europeans, in particular the French, had been more receptive to the idea.[8]

Mountbatten enjoyed playing the *enfant terrible* at NATO meetings, asking the questions that nobody else had dared articulate. 'I intervened twice – effectively,' he wrote in his diary after the meeting of the Council in December 1960. 'Norstad congratulated me and said it was the first time in the 10 years he had attended the Council that anyone in uniform at the table had spoken.'[9] Nuclear weapons were his favourite theme, but in 1964 he insisted that NATO must be prepared to contemplate a situation in which the threat in Europe remained constant or even diminished, while in the rest of the world it grew inexorably greater. Not merely was there no need to build up forces in Europe, there might well be a case for reducing them. Since the threat in Europe provided the reason for NATO's existence, SACEUR could hardly be expected to welcome such reasoning. There was some relief mixed with the regret when Mountbatten made his final appearance in 1965. His valedictory address was a plea for sanity; for acceptance of the fact that, if nuclear warfare broke out, NATO would have failed and would have no serious part to play in the ensuing carnage; for an end to the accumulation of ever larger nuclear stockpiles and, instead, for the provision of mobile, well-equipped conventional forces capable of dealing with any sudden but limited incursion by a satellite country. His last words were 'a heartfelt tribute to this, the greatest peacetime Alliance the world has ever seen. Its existence has ensured peace and stability. May it continue to do so.'[10]

The pressures of his work with the Defence Staff could never distract Mountbatten for long from the affairs of India. Their armed forces were his especial preoccupation. The Minister of Defence, Krishna Menon, proved a sad source of worry. When he failed to answer four consecutive letters from the C.D.S., Mountbatten wrote to him to remonstrate. 'I can only hope that this does not mean that you have now decided to end the friendship between us which has existed for so many years;' then, with a touch of menace, '. . . if you feel unable to deal with me, I will discuss the question with the Prime Minister.'[11] That particular issue was solved to the C.D.S.'s satisfaction but the following year the High Commissioner, Paul Gore-Booth, was reporting that Menon seemed to take 'an almost sadistic delight' in criticizing and distorting British policies. 'But there is also a streak of sentimental friendship,' he told Mountbatten, 'at least for a Britain represented by a number of elements in which one will have to include (with apologies) the *New Statesman* and yourself.' Above all, from the point of view of the C.D.S., he had the singular merit of preferring to procure arms from Britain rather than the other countries of East and West eager to provide the equipment for the Indian Services.[12]

This optimism proved premature. In June 1962 it became apparent that the Indians were on the point of buying Russian military aircraft. Mountbatten sent for the Indian High Commissioner and lectured him, speaking, as he told Nehru, not as British C.D.S., or even as an Englishman, 'but as the man who was once your chosen Head of State and who still has a very large part of India in his heart'. To accept Russian planes, he argued, would be to sever the 'priceless connections between our countries in defence' and to imperil future American economic aid.[13] In 1956 he had made the same appeal and succeeded; this time he was too late. In spite of his dire predictions, Anglo-Indian relations survived.

They survived, too, his efforts to persuade Nehru to come to some compromise over Kashmir. Mountbatten had satisfied himself that the only solution which could prove acceptable both to India and Pakistan was that Kashmir should be independent and demilitarized. In 1961 he put this idea to Ayub Khan, the President of Pakistan, and was given some cautious encouragement,[14] but it was not till two years later, when he was in Delhi with Duncan Sandys (now Secretary of State for Commonwealth Relations), that he felt the time was right to present the idea to Nehru. Sandys had asked the C.D.S. to prepare the ground for the formal talks that were to start in two days' time, and Mountbatten accepted the invitation with alacrity. He was, he told Nehru, 'one of the very few Englishmen who really recognised that Kashmir had become legally a part of India'. If even he felt the promised plebiscite was nevertheless overdue, how much harsher a view of the situation would be taken by India's critics? When Nehru pleaded how dangerous any change of the present balance in Kashmir might be for the large Muslim minority in India, Mountbatten replied that he was never one to stir up sleeping dogs unnecessarily, but that this dog was already awake and barking. After long debate Nehru agreed that he might at least agree to the appointment of a mediator, but when Mountbatten broached the same idea with the responsible Indian Ministers he was told that Nehru would never be able to get his Cabinet's agreement to anything that might lead to independence for Kashmir. If he tried he would be thrown from power.[15]

Mountbatten was properly sceptical about this, but he could not fail to be struck by other evidence of Nehru's declining powers. In June 1962 Nehru's sister, Mrs Pandit, had written to ask him to plead with her brother to take things more easily and delegate responsibility. What could he do? he asked. In recent years 'the only person who could control him was darling Edwina and she is no longer with us'. 'You have all my loving thoughts and sympathy for your agony in realising that your wonderful brother is ill and losing his grip,' he concluded. 'It must be unbearably painful to you.'[16] On his visits to Delhi in May 1963 and again in January 1964 he was horrified by the incompetence and rampant corruption. 'With Jawarharlal's [sic] illness there is a complete lack of leadership. Everybody is very pessimistic about the future. Several people have said to me "why don't you come back and run the country again?" '[17] From Rangoon he wrote to Nehru to urge him to get rid of day-to-day administrative detail, to appoint additional Ministers, to cut out public meetings and responsibilities. On one small point he *had* persuaded the Prime Minister to delegate responsibility. 'Thank you', he wrote, 'for saying that Richard Attenborough may correspond with Indira in future about the Gandhi film.' Otherwise Nehru seemed resolved to cling to all his powers.

> I got the distinct impression that at the back of your mind was the feeling that you would like to go on working at full pressure and die in harness. That is what Edwina did to the great distress of all who loved her whom she left behind.
>
> But you owe to India whose independence and greatness is due to you, the continuation of your overall leadership for as many more years as possible. So do please do what is best for India.[18]

Nehru died four months later. Mountbatten, accompanied by his daughter Pamela, represented the Queen at the funeral. 'It is most disturbing', he wrote, 'to see an old friend being man-handled, even though it is by Generals and Admirals in being moved from the lying-in-state position to the traditional Indian litter of bamboos and string.'[19] The journey to the Raj ghat was eventful. His Cadillac was mobbed, he was recognized by everyone, and his daughter was not neglected – 'on two or three occasions, men put their heads in at the windows and grinning with pleasure, shouted "Pamela!" ' Mountbatten had advised his driver to keep as close as possible to the police car in front, which he did too literally, running into its rear and puncturing the Cadillac's radiator. The crowd cheerfully pushed the car until Mountbatten and Pamela got out and walked: 'It was a sort of triumphal procession. . . . As we were walking through the crowd, a man called out "Don't go, Lord Mountbatten!" ' Eventually they clambered into the police car and sweltered in a temperature of more than 100°F. When he got to the Raj ghat Mountbatten found that his seat, next to that of the President, was labelled 'The Ex-Governor-General.' He noticed that Dean Rusk, the American Secretary of State, was not to be seen, established that he was somewhere amid the ruck of diplomats, plunged in and brought him over to meet the President. 'I felt that if the most powerful nation on earth could send their representative at breakneck speed halfway around the world, he certainly deserved a seat next to the President.'[20]

The relationship between Britain and India was not happy in the year after Nehru's death, mainly because India did not get the support it felt it deserved over Pakistan's incursions into the Rann of Kutch. Mountbatten had hoped that he might be appointed Colonel of the 61st Cavalry Regiment, but the Chief of Army Staff bluntly told him that there was no way in which he could arrange this under present circumstances. His farewell visit as C.D.S. was marred by this ill-feeling and Mountbatten found that, though individually the Indian leaders were friendly and communicative, at any formal meeting they became cool, even hostile. 'In the past they have always wanted help over arms or aircraft,' he noted sadly, 'but now their line was that they would follow our example and buy the best equipment available, regardless of whether it was made by the British!'[21] It was a sad ending to his official association with the country he loved so much, but he was comforted by the thought that the storm would pass and that, anyway, the welcome that was denied the C.D.S. would be lavished on the ex-Governor-General.

One of the factors which divided Britain and India was the existence of CENTO – the Central Treaty Organization or Baghdad Pact. Mountbatten had always deplored the existence of this body, which he believed was bound to be used by Pakistan as a weapon against India and posed an open invitation to the Russians to intervene in the Middle East.[22] As Chief of the Defence Staff he found himself willy-nilly Britain's representative on the CENTO Military Committee, and had the additional chagrin of being vetoed by the Pakistanis as unacceptable when the Committee was due to meet in Karachi. The reason given was that, if he came, there would be attacks on him in the local newspapers. Fortunately the Cuba crisis provided a convincing excuse for cancelling the visit, but Mountbatten was distressed and annoyed by this evidence of Pakistan's continued animosity. 'Perhaps the saddest aspect of my not going was that I am the first Englishman to be invited by General Ne Win to visit Burma since he took over power. . . . I had also hoped to tell Mrs Bandaranaike a few home truths about what was going wrong in Ceylon.'[23]

Anything that deprived Mountbatten of an excuse to travel was deplored. He was an inveterate globe-trotter, concerned not so much by the things he saw, though he conscientiously ticked off the principal tourist attractions, as by the people that he met. He was insatiably curious about human beings, how they lived, what they thought; and the more alien the individual, the greater his curiosity became. Formidable lion himself, he was no less a lion-hunter; it was enough for a man to be famous, whatever the reason, for Mountbatten to wish to meet him. Barriers of race, colour, religion meant nothing to him; or, perhaps more correctly, the higher the barrier, the greater the attraction. Racial prejudice seemed to him not so much immoral as incomprehensible. South Africa was almost the only country to which he was resolved never to travel. When it seemed possible that it might apply to rejoin the Commonwealth, Mountbatten proposed that every member or would-be member should be required to subscribe to a 'humanity clause'. This would be so drafted as either to force South Africa to change its policy on apartheid or render it ineligible for membership.[24]

Wherever he went, he could be sure of meeting anyone who interested him or whom he felt to be important. Faithfully he recorded in his diary the compliments that each dignitary paid him. In New Zealand the recently retired Prime Minister, Walter Nash, took him aside for a private word. 'He shook me by saying that after much careful thought he had come to the conclusion that I was a greater man than Winston Churchill. This shows that he is getting softening of the brain.'[25] In Singapore he met Lee Kuan Yew. 'I only knew Lee slightly but I have always been deeply impressed by his extreme intelligence, shrewdness and, I suspect, slyness.' The Prime Minister told a group of journalists how as a young man he had stood in the crowd and watched the surrender of the Japanese. But for Mountbatten, he said, Singapore would not now be enjoying its freedom. Not a bad statement, the C.D.S. commented, 'from a man who had been suspected of being a rabid Communist!'[26]

He could rarely resist a chance to meet a celebrity for the first time, even though he knew that his new acquaintance was disliked by the British Government. He attended a royal wedding in Athens and found that the Greek Cypriot leader, Archbishop Makarios, was a fellow guest. At this time the Archbishop was viewed in London as a national enemy. After the ceremony he was standing in such a position that Mountbatten could not avoid shaking hands with him; 'but I certainly did not give him any smile!' he recorded proudly.[27] Yet only nine months later it was all smiles when he visited Nicosia. Makarios received him at the Presidential Palace and Mountbatten congratulated him on his excellent English, claiming to be responsible for its quality. When asked why, he explained that he had provided the frigate that had taken the Archbishop to exile in the Seychelles. Makarios smiled politely, and the C.D.S. went on to say that he had asked the Colonial Office how long the frigate would have to wait there. Why should it wait at all? he was asked. So as to save fuel, because you will never get any settlement in Cyprus till you have brought the exile back again. 'This delighted His Beatitude,' recorded Mountbatten.[28] The visit was a rousing success. 'Makarios and his ministers went out of their way to express great delight at my visit and pressed me to come again, for they said they knew I was a real friend of Cyprus. I suppose there is really only one country in the Common-wealth that does not regard me as a real friend,' concluded Mountbatten wistfully, 'and that is Pakistan.'[29]

His conclusions at the end of each visit were sensible and have generally stood the test of time. In 1963 he paid an extensive visit to Latin America. He was not favourably impressed.

> I have become somewhat worried and frightened for the future, because so few of the South American countries appear to have any stability. Although many of them have great potential wealth, they are so badly organised and run there is still a great gulf between the over-rich and the miserably poor.
>
> Democracy is beginning to work under Betancourt in Venezuela, and is not too bad in Chile; but in Peru and the Argentine the Services step in and take over wherever an election shows a left-wing major-ity. In fact, democracy just isn't working satisfactorily in South America, and if it can't be made to work the whole continent will become ripe for Communism.
>
> I could not put my hand on my heart and recommend any British firm to put any more capital investment into South America, though I certainly think they should sell more goods and send out more technicians and people with brains.[30]

The C.D.S. travelled in considerable style, and usually in a rich glow of publicity. When he visited Latin America the Foreign Office asked him to allow four journalists to be attached to the party. 'In the face of this request I could not refuse, much as I dislike personal publicity.'[31] It was a dislike which Mountbatten was to overcome on many similar occasions. He enjoyed something approaching royal consequence. Sir Julian Gascoigne, the Gov-ernor of Bermuda, was offended to discover that his A.D.C. had been furnished with a list of the C.D.S.'s likes and dislikes and retorted that he was the Queen's representative and not one of Mountbatten's subordinates.[32] Usually, however, his hosts found him amenable. Lady Garran looked after him in Mexico City in 1963. She arranged for oxygen equipment to be placed in his suite at bedtime since, at 7500 feet, many people had trouble sleeping. The C.D.S. brushed the offer aside; *he* never had trouble sleeping. Next day he complained that he had woken at 4 a.m. and had remained awake till breakfast. 'There you are!' said Lady Garran. 'If you had used the oxygen as I told you, you wouldn't have had any problem.' Mountbatten was still sceptical but asked to be shown how the equipment worked. Next morning he announced triumphantly: 'You were quite right!'[33]

His renown as an insatiable worker was sometimes a disadvantage. From

Trinidad he wrote to his sister Louise complaining that he had just passed a 'non-stop fifteen hour day with scarcely time to blow my nose'. To make matters worse, the Governor, Lord Hailes, had talked incessantly about the wonders of the carnival. Mountbatten had been on the point of remarking that he would much have enjoyed a visit to the carnival himself, when Hailes 'took the wind out of my sails by saying "Of course, I knew that you had only come to work." What a lamentable reputation to have. Nearly as bad as Edwina.'[34] But he still managed to find time for riding, underwater fishing and his other pet pursuits, including more esoteric delights such as the party in Hollywood where, after dinner, the guests were tied up in couples and left to see if they could free themselves. Mountbatten had the pleasure of observing the Prime Minister's eminently respectable secretary, Derek Mitchell, lashed inextricably to Claudia Cardinale, while he himself was tied to Shirley Maclaine. 'I must say Shirley is a very sweet and amusing girl and we got on like a house on fire.'[35]

Not everything was such fun. In 1961 in Hong Kong he had 'one of the most painful interviews of my life'. Lee Onn had been a wealthy plantation owner in Malaya who for more than three years had sheltered some 150 Allied troops at extreme risk to himself. At the end of the war Mountbatten had handed him a printed commendation card, promising that, if ever he were in need, the British authorities would be proud to help him. Now Lee Onn, in financial difficulties, was trying to start a taxi-service in Hong Kong but was meeting much obstruction from the authorities. Mountbatten had already taken up the case, warning the Colonial Secretary that 'I considered the British Government had let down Lee Onn, that they had caused my own name to be dishonoured, and that I reserved the right to take appropriate action when I was free to do so on my retirement'. In Hong Kong he saw the Governor, but was told that there was little to be done. He had to admit to Lee Onn that he was unable to help. 'Altogether I find this a most distressing incident.'[36]

Few journeys failed to provoke Mountbatten into sentimental musings about the past. No visit to Delhi was complete without a tour of those places in which he had wooed Edwina, and in Hollywood he paid a visit to 'Pickfair' where he had spent part of his honeymoon. 'It brought back poignant memories of very happy times and I was sad to see Mary Pickford, the one time "world's sweetheart" who must be now in her seventies, had become very plump and dumpy, but still very sweet.' In 1963 it was Malta that provoked nostalgia: 'I have come to the conclusion that I am becoming rather a sentimental old fool, because I was nearly as upset by seeing Malta again as by seeing India. Memories of my childhood in Malta right through to the many commissions I have spent there kept crowding in on me, and every familiar landmark brought back a fresh memory. But the polo ground gave me the sharpest pang because here I have spent many, many happy hours of my life.'[37]

It was during one of his visits to New Zealand that his sister Louise died in Sweden. Mountbatten had been receiving reports of her last illness and had known that she was unlikely to recover consciousness after the thrombosis that had struck her a few days before. Now King Gustaf telephoned and the two men commiserated with each other. 'I must have been nearly as fond of her as he was,' commented Mountbatten.[38] He offered to cancel the rest of the tour and fly back but Gustaf insisted that Louise would have wanted nothing of the sort. Instead, on the day she was buried, Patricia and he went to an old Protestant church just beyond Bali Hai, 'to pay our own private tribute to her'.[39]

But the sharpest pang of all was that which he experienced when he visited Jesselton a year to the day after Edwina died. Mrs Turner, who had been Edwina's hostess, took him up a staircase:

> and then suddenly I was in Edwina's room. Mrs Turner said very softly, 'We will leave you now if we may.' . . . It was a shock to find that the room was exceptionally simple. It had a bare wooden floor with a couple of small rugs, very simple wooden furniture and plain beds. It was nice and clean . . . but somehow the shock of actually being there and finding it all so different was very much more than I could bear and I was grateful to the Turners for leaving me alone with my thoughts for quite a long while.[40]

# CHAPTER 47

## *The Reorganization of Defence*

IN THE LAST YEARS of his professional life, Mountbatten performed a task as complex, as difficult and, in its own way, as important as any he had tackled in the course of his career. The reorganization of Britain's defence machinery lacked the drama of the conquest of South-East Asia or the liberation of India, but it involved the destruction of institutions that had stood the test of centuries, the elimination of innumerable vested interests, a confrontation with entrenched opposition as determined as any he had met at war. That Mountbatten chose to conduct this battle at an age when most men are content to see out their last years before retirement in dignified popularity was remarkable enough; that he saw it through to something close to victory was truly astonishing. Mountbatten's judgement can sometimes be questioned during these last years of service, but his courage, energy and determination were unimpaired.

At first it was by no means sure that he would be in the fight at all. In December 1959 Macmillan had suggested that his term of three years as Chief of the Defence Staff should be prolonged to five to give him more time to carry out the meditated changes. Mountbatten refused; he hoped, anyway, to do the work in his allotted span and believed that only if he then retired to Broadlands was there any chance of Edwina abandoning her suicidal work-load and settling down to keep him company.[1] The excuse was accepted, but a year later the Prime Minister returned to the charge. Edwina was now dead; if Mountbatten retired as planned he would be bored and lonely. By this time it was clear that reorganization was taking far longer to get under way than the C.D.S. had expected.[2] He accepted the extra two years with alacrity, and on 1 February 1961 received the official minute extending his appointment till July 1964.

At one time Macmillan seems to have considered that Mountbatten could best carry out his task if he took over as Minister of Defence. Early in 1963 the C.D.S. told Campbell-Johnson that the Prime Minister had been staying at Broadlands and had put the idea to him.[3] Mountbatten declined on the grounds that he did not wish to become a party politician. Macmillan said that he would present it as a non-party appointment, but Mountbatten felt that a member of a Cabinet must either be consistently loyal to the Government or at odds with his colleagues – and neither option appealed to him. He had said much the same when given a similar invitation in 1949.[4] To be invited to become Minister of Defence in both Labour and Conservative administrations was, however, an unusual distinction, and when *Newsweek* announced a few months later that Mountbatten was a virtual certainty to become Defence Minister in the event of a Labour victory,[5] the C.D.S. could tell himself that he was indeed becoming that chimerical figure, the indispensable man.

There would have been a vacancy as Minister in July 1962. In that month Harold Watkinson told the Chiefs of Staff that he was retiring. 'We are desperately sorry,' wrote Mountbatten in his diary.[6] Dependable, industrious, unassertive, Watkinson had been every serving officer's ideal politician; all he lacked was the zeal and ruthlessness that were needed if major reforms were to be launched. He was one of the victims in a purge which the Prime Minister had just conducted. 'Said sad goodbye to dear Harold Watkinson . . . who has been sacrified in the massacre and gave my new Minister Peter Thorneycroft lunch,' wrote Mountbatten and then, next day: 'C.O.S. and Minister. He is going to be difficult.'[7]

To the military leaders Thorneycroft was best known as the Chancellor of the Exchequer who had resigned because his demands for cuts in Government spending had not been supported by his Cabinet colleagues. This was a doubtful recommendation to a serving officer. Mountbatten described him to Campbell-Johnson a few days after he took office as 'a brand new Minister who doesn't know anything, in fact he has been at the Ministry of Aviation and has seen the wrong side of these matters'. He had come with a mandate to make quick and dramatic decisions, and nothing was so dangerous as a decisive Minister. Worst of all, almost the first thing he had said was that he did not believe in aircraft-carriers – a heresy calculated to shock the former First Sea Lord to the bottom of his supposedly inter-Service heart.[8] But Thorneycroft's vices could also prove virtues. His energy and incisiveness, if put to the task of re-shaping the Ministry of Defence rather than demolishing the Royal Navy, would prove most potent qualities. Within a few weeks of his taking office, the bandwagon of reorganization was on the move again.

The first thing Mountbatten decided to do was to write a paper setting out his personal vision of the future organization of British defence. He instructed his Military Assistant, Commander Kennon, to prepare a first draft. Using this as a brief, he tackled the Minister of Defence and Prime Minister and got their blessing in principle to his continuing with the work.[9] Finally, he retreated to

Classiebawn and set to work creating his own paper, the 'End Product' as he called it, which in twenty-three much amended pages set out his plan for the future of the Ministry of Defence, the Chiefs of Staff, the Service Ministries, research and development, the whole central machine. Only if this could be got right, he was convinced, could the necessary integration of Army, Navy and Air Force take place successfully. He was determined to put in a tough and realistic paper, he said, 'however much Chief of Air Staff, the old Blimps and the Civil Service may hate it. Both the P.M. and the Minister approve my preparing such a paper and no one can expect me to put up a half-baked wishy-washy compromise. I would sooner have a brave, drastic and "correct" paper turned down than a weak compromise accepted.'[10]

The draft completed, his staff were encouraged to criticize it. One of the few people outside his personal entourage who saw it before the Minister was Rob Scott, the Permanent Under-Secretary at the Ministry of Defence. Mountbatten greatly respected Scott's judgement but feared that it might be hostile to his ideas. He even went to the length of having a minute prepared setting out what Scott's views might be. The putative attack was levelled at the role of Chief of the Defence Staff, as envisaged in Mountbatten's paper. This *might* work when Mountbatten himself was C.D.S., Scott was made to say, but 'Bloggins' would have his turn, and then the Minister of Defence would be in trouble if he had to depend on the advice of Bloggins alone without recourse to the Chiefs of Staff. Scott did indeed comment on this point but in the mildest terms: 'The scheme places very great power in the hands of the Secretary of State . . . and of the Chief of the Defence Staff. I think this is probably inevitable, but it will be a point of attack for critics.'[11] His only serious complaint was that the paper was too long and should be cut to five pages – a proposal to which the C.D.S. responded by reducing it from twenty-three pages to twenty-two, though picking out the main points in fourteen pithy paragraphs at the beginning.

'Handed Minister of Defence my great paper on the Reorganisation of Central Defence,' was Mountbatten's diary entry for 10 October 1962.[12] The great paper did indeed propose a revolutionary reshuffle of the powers of those who controlled Britain's armed services. It stopped short of proposing the fusion of the Services themselves but prepared the way for progressive unification by destroying the forces at the top that kept them separate. The heart of Mountbatten's proposal was contained in one sentence, which followed a recital of the wastefulness and inefficiency endemic to the present system: 'I have come to the firm conclusion that nothing short of the abolition of separate Service Departments and the creation of a single Ministry of Defence will get to the root of the problem.' From this the rest followed. The Secretary of State for Defence would be responsible for all aspects of policy, assisted by two functional Ministers (one for personnel, the other for research) and three junior Ministers, each charged with one of the Services. The Defence Staff would work to the C.D.S., not to the Chiefs of Staffs, and the C.D.S. would only be 'advised' by the Chiefs. The Ministry of Aviation would be absorbed into the central machine, under a Minister responsible to the Minister of Defence. It might take several years before the scheme could be carried through in its entirety, admitted Mountbatten, but it should be accepted now as the ultimate goal and every step in future taken in conformity with it.

Thorneycroft was benevolent but cautious. He put the plan to the Prime Minister with the comment that it was a valuable study and the C.D.S. deserved thanks for all the work he had put into it. 'But these are very big issues with far-reaching consequences, and whilst I believe that a very strong case has been made for a review of the present system, I am not at this stage prepared to say that I endorse all his proposals for its reform.' Mountbatten had expected nothing more; changes so radical and so controversial could be made only if the Prime Minister was not merely acquiescent but determined to force them through. Macmillan, not Thorneycroft, must be their champion.

On 2 November the Prime Minister came to Broadlands for a weekend's shooting. During the visit, wrote Mountbatten later, 'we had many hours of intense discussion of my proposals'.[13] In fact, they seem to have talked for something less than an hour, on Friday evening after the Brabournes had gone to bed. The hyperbole was justified however; fifty minutes was enough to convince the Prime Minister. He had picked Mountbatten for this purpose – 'To do all this, to override some of the feelings of old-fashioned officers and critics, we needed a man of authority and drive. And I felt that in Lord Mountbatten we had the man'[14] – and was not about to balk at the very start. The only question was how the next step should be taken. Both men were aware that the opposition in Whitehall was already gathering, as it had done five years before when the Sandys reforms had been largely defeated. How should the new plan be presented? Mountbatten knew that if he appeared as author of the scheme the opposition would be redoubled. He suggested that a former Minister of Defence should head an enquiry. But Selwyn Lloyd and Watkinson were still in politics, Monckton was too old, Sandys unacceptable, Antony Head High Commissioner in Nigeria. Field Marshal Festing then, recently retired from C.I.G.S., 'who knows his stuff and is trusted and respected – a big man'? He did not carry the necessary guns, it was decided.[15] For the moment the question was left open; the Prime Minister summoned a meeting for the following weekend to take the matter farther.

On Sunday, 11 November, Macmillan, Thorneycroft, Mountbatten, Rob Scott, Solly Zuckerman and the Secretary to the Cabinet, Burke Trend, met at Admiralty House, where the Prime Minister was temporarily living. The selection of those who attended made Macmillan's intentions clear – none of the potential opponents was invited. Zuckerman argued the case for reform on economic grounds, Mountbatten said that the first requirement was a common list of generals, admirals and air marshals and a common promotion board under the control of the Ministry of Defence. 'Patronage was the key to loyalty.' In the end Macmillan said that he wished to go ahead: 'He accepted this, the greatest constitutional change in a century as necessary and good,' Mountbatten wrote triumphantly in his diary. It was agreed that a series of similar meetings would be held to draft a statement of aims to put before the Cabinet. The Service Ministers were still to be kept in the dark; even Thorneycroft was not present at every meeting. Macmillan kept the discussion on the level of generalities, Mountbatten was apt to grow impatient and try to drag in precise proposals. Sometimes he would go too far, and hold forth on the wonders of fully integrated Services. The Prime Minister would recoil in dismay from the vision of the armed services welded into an inchoate mass dressed in 'mud-grey uniforms'.[16] Mountbatten in fact had no wish to advance to the 'Canadian solution' of Army, Navy and Air Force united at every level. 'The greatest nonsense of all time,' he described it to Franklyn Johnson. 'Paul Hellyer, the Minister of Defence who did all the mischief, had several talks with me . . . and simply couldn't understand that he would wreck service morale if he put them all in a green uniform and unified their titles.'[17]

On 9 December Macmillan issued a personal minute calling upon the Service Ministers to discuss the necessary reforms.[18] The existing system, he said, was 'basically one in which policy is divorced from administration in ways which lead to diffusion of responsibility, delay in policy-making and its execution, and waste of resources'. In phrases that sometimes strikingly echoed the terms of Mountbatten's earlier paper, he set out the lines along which he felt the situation should be remedied. For the first time Service Ministers and Chiefs of Staff were officially warned what was in the air.

It came as no surprise; indeed, Mountbatten's paper had already been circulated informally to the Chiefs of Staff. Their reaction had been predictable. 'Men are more ready to sacrifice their lives than their livelihood, and to sacrifice their own importance often comes hardest of all,' wrote Liddell Hart.[19] The Chiefs of Staff and Service Ministers were being asked to do exactly that. It would be unjust to suggest that self-interest was a major factor in their thinking; it was the independence of their Service and their institutions that they were protecting and they were convinced that they had sound arguments of national interest on their side. They fought, however, with the ferocity of men who felt themselves directly threatened, and with the bitterness that sprang from the belief that their most dangerous enemy should have been their ally.

The Chiefs of Staff were not as one. Caspar John was enthusiastic for reform but had doubts about the timing. He 'was really on my side and kept in touch with me', wrote Mountbatten.[20] This overstated the First Sea Lord's amenability, but he was certainly a moderating force. There was nothing moderate about the Chief of Air Staff. According to Mountbatten, Pike had summoned his senior officers and told them that the C.D.S. had 'most disloyally written his own personal views on Defence Reorganisation direct to the Prime Minister'. He had proposed the abolition of the Air Ministry and the Air Council. But there was no cause for despair; these monstrous proposals would be fought to the end. 'The independence of the R.A.F. administration would be maintained, whatever C.D.S. might be planning to the contrary.'[21] Pike, therefore, was a root-and-brancher; Hull for the Army was slightly less dogmatic. He disliked and distrusted Mountbatten, had vigorously opposed the imposition of a joint headquarters in Singapore, and was possessed by the fear so commonly voiced at the time that the Ministry of Defence might become like the German O.K.W. – a body responsible for running the war yet fatally out of touch with those who were actually fighting it. But he was aware that the relationship between Minister of Defence, C.D.S. and Chiefs of Staff was not a happy one, and the knowledge that he would in all probability succeed Mountbatten as Chief of the Defence Staff was an incentive to accept some overhaul of the system.

These were differences of emphasis; all three Chiefs of Staff were prepared to commit themselves formally to opposition to the C.D.S.'s original proposals. Behind them was soon arrayed a formidable array of military dignitaries, the most vocal being a former Chief of Air Staff, Sir John Slessor. Slessor wrote to Thorneycroft to urge the fundamental principle that the men who advised the Minister *must* be the professional heads of the Services responsible for operations. 'I am absolutely opposed to anything in the nature of a Supremo. . . . The two Dickies – Dickson and Mountbatten – are excellent chaps and very old friends of mine; it's not the *chap* I'm getting at but the system.'[22] Field Marshal Harding saw Slessor's letter, and wrote to support it.[23] Lord Portal joined in the fray: 'I hear on very good authority that Thorneycroft and Mountbatten are going to set up what resembles Hitler's O.K.W. system.'[24] The flower of Britain's chivalry girded its loins for battle.

The Chiefs' first blow was struck a few days after the Prime Minister had issued his personal memorandum, when they put in a counter-paper.[25] John told the C.D.S. that the original draft had been a violent attack on Mountbatten's ideas, but that he had refused to sign it until it was re-drafted more moderately and addressed itself to the Prime Minister's memorandum.[26] The result was what Mountbatten himself conceded was a 'not unreasonable paper',[27] accepting in principle the unified overseas commands and various other proposals for strengthening the central staff but contesting vigorously the proposals for an aggrandized C.D.S. and down-graded Chiefs of Staff.

Macmillan was anxious to avoid finding himself in the position he had stumbled into four years before, with the Service Ministers and Chiefs of Staff ranged against him and no alternative but to overrule them or abandon the cause of reform. He detected flexibility in the opposition. 'General Hull is ready for some move,' he told the Queen, 'and even the Chief of the Air Staff is now prepared to agree that the Ministry of defence should be strengthened.'[28] But there was a long way to go and progress proved difficult. At the end of December he recorded gloomily that Ministers and Chiefs of Staff were putting up a 'strong reactionary fight'.[29] In the hope of outflanking them, he resolved to revive the idea of an independent enquiry which he had discussed with Mountbatten at Broadlands the month before.

When and by whom the names of Ismay and Jacob were suggested is uncertain. In a memorandum written some time after the event Mountbatten claimed he had put forward the idea to the Prime Minister at the original Broadlands weekend. Macmillan asked whether they could be trusted to come to the right conclusion.

> Ever cheeky I remember replying 'Why do you think I suggested their names?' He laughed and supposed I knew their views and I assured him we could rely on them. The great advantage of my suggestion would be that my name would fade out and the opposition would have far greater difficulty in mustering support to fight the Jacob –Ismay combination.
>
> Macmillan looked at me quizzically and asked whether I was really prepared to let others take the credit for the greatest constitutional political change in this century. I replied that I was not interested who got the credit for this great idea. . . . I was interested in results and not credit. He laughed and agreed.[30]

This reminiscence does not wholly conform with the record Mountbatten dictated only a few days after the Broadlands meeting, which made no mention of Ismay and Jacob,[31] but it seems probable that their names were canvassed. With Ismay's vast experience of the Whitehall machine and reputation for wisdom and shrewdness, he was an obvious candidate, while

Ian Jacob, once one of Ismay's deputies, was a known authority on the organization of defence at the topmost level and joint author of the White Paper which, as early as 1946, had pointed the way towards the eventual amalgamation of the Services under a single Minister.[32]

Ismay proved reluctant. 'It is seventeen years since I had anything to do with defence,' he told Mountbatten, 'and for the last five years I have worked about as hard as an ailing butterfly. I can't suddenly turn myself into a busy bee again.'[33] It took much persuasion and a promise from Jacob that he would bear the brunt of the work to induce Ismay to lend his name to the enterprise.

> The present position is this [Jacob told Ismay]. The Ministers and Dickie Mountbatten and Rob Scott and Zuckerman all feel that the machine is not working properly and that something must be done about it. They have had a number of discussions and two papers have been written, one by Dickie and one by the three Chiefs of Staff, though from what I can hear the latter do not really see eye to eye. Dickie is advocating the eventual creation of a single Ministry of Defence and has worked his scheme out in some detail. The Ministers are, I think, attracted by this scheme but do not want to go ahead without it being much more thoroughly examined.[34]

It took Jacob only six weeks to prepare his report. The feat was remarkable, though the less surprising because he had thought so much about the problems in the past. He had no doubt that the powers of the Ministry of Defence must be greatly strengthened, the other Service Ministries absorbed into it, a common list introduced for the senior ranks. He was equally clear that any further integration of the three Services would at that time be premature. The main area of doubt concerned the relative powers of the Chief of the Defence Staff and the Chiefs of Staff. It was impossible to consider this in the abstract without the problem being bedevilled by the characters of the individuals concerned. The Chiefs of Staff Committee, as at present constituted, could never function satisfactorily, he told Ismay, and one important reason was 'the personality of Mountbatten, who seems to be universally mistrusted in spite of his great qualities'.[35] He was 'utterly at loggerheads' with the three Chiefs of Staff, Jacob said in 1982. 'They seemed to hate him.'[36]

The antipathy between Mountbatten and the Chiefs of Staff so complicated the discussions on defence reorganization that some thought must be given to its causes. Mountbatten himself harboured no dislikes. He had a poor opinion of Hull and Pike as leaders of their Services but found them amiable as acquaintances – indeed, thought of them as friends. As late as April 1964 he was referring to Hull's 'real personal friendliness'.[37] For him, a weekend at Broadlands or after-dinner pleasantries could expunge any bitterness left by clashes in Whitehall; he would have been disconcerted, even distressed, to find that others were less forgiving. In the case of Hull this was particularly remarkable, since the professional relationship between them was so appalling that their A.D.C.s would discuss the situation together in mingled horror and amusement. It was a clash of temperaments between the austere and rigid cavalry officer, rooted in the immutable traditions of the English gentleman, and the brilliant and infinitely flexible cosmopolitan who found his adversary's preoccupations pettifogging and ridiculous. 'What is the difference between Mountbatten and Hull?' Zuckerman was asked. 'Six feet one and a half inches,' he replied – Mountbatten's height. Hull's champions would have answered with equal conviction that the difference was between the honourable and the unscrupulous, the dignified and the flamboyant.

Their widely different natures were demonstrated after Churchill's death, when Mountbatten suggested that he and the three Chiefs of Staff should hold vigil around the catafalque. The idea was adopted and arrangements made; then, at the last minute, the C.D.S. casually remarked, 'I've laid on a photographer.' 'Then I won't be there,' snapped Hull. 'This is not a publicity stunt.' To Mountbatten it was the most reasonable thing on earth that this moving tribute should be recorded and shared with others; to Hull – perhaps in part because of who had proposed it – it seemed unpardonable vulgarity.[38] But he levelled graver charges than that against the C.D.S. He did not believe that his colleague was to be trusted. Once, he claimed, he arrived unexpectedly in the Minister's office to find a surprised Mountbatten already there. 'The C.D.S. has just been telling me that the Chiefs of Staff have agreed to the full carrier programme,' said Watkinson. There must be some misunderstanding, said Hull. The Chiefs' approval had been qualified and for a modified programme only.[39]

Pike, too, maintained that Mountbatten on several occasions reported the conclusions of the Chiefs of Staff to the Minister of Defence in terms contrary to what had in fact been decided. Pike's successor, Sam Elworthy, personally more sympathetic to the C.D.S. than was either Pike or Hull, discovered that Mountbatten had told the Minister that the Chief of Air Staff had agreed to something to which he was in fact strongly opposed. Elworthy, outraged, announced to Hull and Luce that he would shortly be out of a job because he was about to tell the C.D.S. that he was a liar and a cheat. He did so, but all Mountbatten said was, 'Come off it, Sam, old boy.' He refused to deny the charge, or to quarrel; merely repeated: 'Let's forget it.' Afterwards he would sometimes refer to the incident: 'You remember that row of ours? I was in the right, you know. . . .'[40]*

The curious thing about these episodes is that, if deception there was, nothing could have been gained by it. The true conclusions of the Chiefs of Staff on aircraft-carriers would have been recorded; the Minister would in due course have read them; no order for a massive construction programme would have been placed on the basis of Mountbatten's conversation. Trickery of this kind was not merely reprehensible, it was extraordinarily stupid. Yet not even Mountbatten's fiercest critics have ever accused him of stupidity. The only conclusion that makes sense is that the person who was worst deceived was Mountbatten himself. He had always been prone to hear what he wanted to hear; in the last few years of his professional life he began to hear nothing else. He did not dismiss opinions contrary to his own as unimportant or incorrect, he simply did not hear them, or edited them in his mind so that within a few hours they emerged mysteriously close to his own view. It was not so much arrogance as a kind of sickness. In old age he was to embarrass his friends and delight his enemies by his inability to distinguish between what had happened and what he would have liked to have happened. By 1963 the tendency was already apparent. It was a dangerous failing for a man in his position.[41]

This is not the whole story. Even if he had not thus presented his enemies with a stick with which to beat him, they would have done their best to manufacture one. The policies he was pursuing would have made any C.D.S. disliked, and led his colleagues to put the worst interpretations on all his actions. In June 1963 the Minister of Defence summoned the C.D.S., Scott and Scott's designated successor, Henry Hardman, to discuss a further extension of Mountbatten's period in office. With characteristic courage Scott said bluntly that this would be a very unpopular move; it was well known that the C.D.S. was 'widely disliked and distrusted'. Thorneycroft replied that the leadership which had been required over the last year or two would have made anyone unpopular; it might, indeed, be a measure of Mountbatten's success. Hardman contributed with a helpful quote from Napoleon: 'If the King is popular, the reign is a failure.'[42] The prejudices caused by Mountbatten's policies cannot explain all the distrust felt for him, but they certainly did not help secure a charitable judgement on his frailties.

\*

* Mountbatten's own account of the incident was different; in this he was guilty of nothing worse than telling the Minister of Defence that the formal recommendation of the Chiefs of Staff was ill-conceived and much better not carried out.

Ismay and Jacob suggested that the Government could do one of three things. Course A, some modest tinkering with the existing system, was not advanced as a serious recommendation. Course C, a fully integrated and functional Ministry with no room for inter-Service rivalries at the highest level, was put forward as an eventual goal rather than immediately practicable, though every forward step should be taken with it in mind. Course B was a half-way, or perhaps a two-thirds-of-the-way, house, by which the three Service Ministries retained their individuality but were subordinated to the Ministry of Defence. It was this interim course which the Ismay–Jacob report pointed to as the most satisfactory.

The most serious way in which the report differed from Mountbatten's views was over the Chief of the Defence Staff and the Chiefs of Staff. Ismay would not agree with Slessor's view that if the C.D.S. were given all that Mountbatten wanted for him he would be left with great power but little responsibility: 'On the contrary, he will have thrice the power and thrice the responsibility of the existing Chiefs of Staff and he will be the first man to be shot if things go wrong.'[43] But nor would he accept 'Dickie Mountbatten's suggestion that the Chiefs of Staff Committee as now known should disappear, and that practically supreme power should be vested in the C.D.S.'[44] The Chiefs should retain their access to the Prime Minister and Minister of Defence. 'In the light of the parentage of the reforms,' commented Professor Howard, 'it is a little ironical that the position of the Chief of Defence Staff and his relationship to the Chiefs of Staff themselves, should have been changed rather less than any other element in the structure of the Ministry of Defence.'[45]

One item in the report which Mountbatten particularly welcomed was the proposal that the three separate Service Ministries should be physically amalgamated with the Ministry of Defence in one vast new complex. All his instincts told him that from this collocation would grow co-operation and harmony, as well, he hoped, as economies in staffing. The grandiose new headquarters gave him endless opportunities to indulge his passion for detail, as well as for every kind of gadgetry. In the summer of 1963 he sent a work study team to examine how things were done at the Pentagon in Washington. 'As a result,' he declared proudly, 'we shall get not an antiquated British system, but the world's most wonderful Operational Centre, including Computers, polaroid cameras, instant world wide communications with closed-circuit TV etc.'[46]

If Mountbatten was privately disappointed by some parts of the report, he kept it to himself. It was a 'remarkable document', he told Thorneycroft, 'particularly bearing in mind that it had to be prepared in such a very short time'. Provided that it was accepted that the Government should adopt

Course C as the long-term objective, he was whole-heartedly behind it.[47] The following day the Prime Minister asked him how he could profess satisfaction with a report which retained three separate Service Ministers. 'I replied that I only accepted this as an interim solution,' replied Mountbatten. The report had endorsed his conviction that the Ministry of Defence should in the end be organized on functional lines, with one Minister responsible for logistics, another for finance, rather than one for each Service. What was now being taken was a first step in that direction.[48]

Two days after his call on the Prime Minister, Mountbatten left on a grand tour of Latin America. It was a part of the world largely new to him and he greatly looked forward to the visit, but he still had doubts about the timing. Macmillan suggested that he ought to be in England while defence reorganization was debated in the Cabinet and Mountbatten saw some force in the argument. In the end, however, he concluded that he was better out of the way; it was no longer *his* plan and the less he was identified with it, the less fierce the opposition was likely to be. He flew to Mexico on 24 February, leaving as his legacy a firm recommendation that the Government should announce immediately their adoption of Course B in the Ismay–Jacob report, with the aim of moving on to Course C two or three years later.[49] He was in Caracas on 1 March when he received a personal telegram from the Prime Minister telling him that discussion in the Cabinet had gone well and that an announcement would be made in the forthcoming defence debate. 'We are now working out how best to implement the plan . . . ,' Macmillan went on. 'I would like you to know how grateful I am to you for all the hard work you have put into this which is now beginning to bear fruit.'[50] By the time he reached Chile the news had become public.

> The air mail edition of *The Times* of March 5 arrived today, announcing in fairly sensational terms the Government's decision in principle to adopt my suggestion of abolishing the Admiralty, the War Office and the Air Ministry (and, I hope, the Ministry of Aviation) to form a unified Ministry of Defence.
>
> It is highly satisfactory to me that this decision has been taken by the Government on my advice but in my absence in South America.[51]

The battle was far from over. Much detail had still to be settled and the champions of the traditional Ministries were to have many opportunities to fight a rearguard action. Macmillan, however, was indefatigable in pushing things along. 'The main danger lies in the fact that we may be forced by the terrible weight of inertia of the Service Departments into doing nothing,' he told the Minister of Defence in April. 'This will look very bad. The Government will have been made to appear foolish.'[52] A few weeks later Thorney-croft was inspired by a Churchillian trumpet-blast. 'Pray take no notice at all of any obstruction. You should approach this the way Lloyd George used to approach problems with dashing, slashing methods. Anyone who raises any objection can go, including Ministers.'[53] The work on the White Paper continued through the spring and early summer, 'Thorneycroft showing remarkable patience,' the Prime Minister recorded, 'and being splendidly supported by Lord Mountbatten'.[54] The abolition of the Board of Admiralty and the title of First Lord caused Mountbatten especial anguish. When Hull proposed that the title of First Sea Lord for the professional head of the Navy at least should be preserved, the C.D.S. grasped at the compromise. But what about the Second, Third and other Sea Lords? Thorneycroft was prepared to accept the First, but was doubtful about his retinue. 'Do you travel first or second class by rail?' asked Mountbatten. 'Usually first,' replied the Minister. 'Well, you couldn't go first if there were no second, could you?' concluded Mountbatten triumphantly. He won the day and the Second Sea Lord was preserved to justify the title of his superior.[55]

The White Paper on defence organization was finally published in July 1963.[56] In all essentials it was a considered and amplified version of the Ismay–Jacob report. Mountbatten had no doubt that it represented as full a measure of victory as he could have expected. On the whole he had reason to feel exultant. The supreme authority of the Minister of Defence had been asserted. The position of the Chief of the Defence Staff had been strengthened by the creation of a group of integrated organizations covering signals, intelligence and the main operational requirements. The authority of the Permanent Under-Secretary of the Ministry of Defence had been extended to cover all civil servants within the Service Ministries. Best of all, though much remained to be done before Mountbatten's full vision was achieved, it seemed to have been accepted in principle that further progress should soon be made. A new era had opened. 'If Defence by Committee describes the pre-Sandys era,' wrote Michael Hobkirk, 'the 1964 organisation strengthened the tendency to Defence by Discussion, since there was now a strong central staff to devise guide-lines for policy and to attempt by argument and discussion to arrange a rational allocation of defence resources.'[57]

'P.M. gave First Lord, First Sea Lord, me and Minister of Defence drinks to celebrate our victory,' wrote Mountbatten in his diary for 30 July 1963. It was not till eight months later that he was able to attend the Privy Council to see the royal consent given to the bill and Thorneycroft sworn in as first Secretary of State for Defence, but the interval had not been wasted. On 1 April 1964 the three separate Service Ministries closed down and the staffs moved into a single building. The revolution had been as well received publicly as Mountbatten had claimed. Though the *Sunday Times* complained that the reforms did not go far enough and that the Chiefs of Staff should have been denied access to the Prime Minister, and the *Economist* was doubtful whether so vast an administrative machine could easily be controlled by Ministers,[58] the general tone of the press was friendly, even enthusiastic. Even within the ranks of the enemies of reform there was a readiness to stifle doubts and give the new system a chance to work.

Yet doubts there were, and doubts there would remain.[59] Would the new system create an inflated bureaucracy, out of touch with the Services it was supposed to manage? Could a centralized Ministry effectively control so large a body as the three Services combined? – a doubt which, as Professor Howard has pointed out, can be countered on the grounds that the Services in 1963 were smaller in total numbers than the wartime Army.[60] Would the initiative of the upper echelons of commanders be sapped by the rigid hierarchy necessarily imposed in so vast yet centralized an organization? Would the morale of the individual Services suffer from a loss of identity and traditional loyalties? Would the concentration of power in the hands of the C.D.S. and his inner entourage lead to a stifling of debate, the imposition of a 'party line'? Would the denial to the Services of the right to produce the ideal weapon for their particular purposes lead to the adoption of inferior compromises which would suit nobody and cost as much or more than the previous system?

Only time could answer these questions, and Mountbatten could fairly maintain that time was never given a chance to do so properly. What was intended by Mountbatten as a half-way house became something close to a final product. By 1970 the Ministry of Defence employed less people than had worked in the three headquarters that preceded it, yet the Services themselves were by then far smaller. Few would deny that the Ministry became and remained a swollen and wasteful body. To Mountbatten, however, this was not a condemnation of his ideas but proof that they were never executed. Successive Ministers balked at the hurdle of complete functionalization, and thus the vestigial Service Ministries survived alongside the new central bureaucracy. No categorical judgement can be passed on Mountbatten's vision. In an era when small is once more beautiful, when the virtues of merger and centralization are daily in question, it is inevitable that the need for a massive central organization should be viewed with greater scepticism than in the past. Yet it is hard to escape the conviction that, whatever the cost, change had to come. The traditional structure could not have endured much longer and, though a certain amount of value was lost when it was dismant-led, the damage would have been worse if reconstruction had been long delayed.

What is at least certain is that without Mountbatten the state of Britain's defence machinery would today be very different. He could not have done it alone – the championship of the Prime Minister was above all indispensable – but his was the vision, the will, the sustained determination. On this partisans like Zuckerman and critics like Hull are as one. 'No one but Mountbatten could have pushed it through,' said Lord Thorneycroft. 'Mountbatten was the motive force,' said Sir Henry Hardman. 'The measure of his achievement was that nothing happened after his departure,' said Sir Arthur Drew, last Permanent Under-Secretary at the War Office. Mountbatten fought relentlessly, some would say unfairly, for what he believed to be right; he risked popularity, peace of mind, reputation in the battle; and in the end he won.[61]

In spite of Scott's doubts, the Minister decided that Mountbatten should be asked to stay on for a further year after his first extension ran out in July 1964. That would make six years in office – a period which some felt too long for both the incumbent and for the institution that he directed – but Thorneycroft did not yet feel ready to nominate a successor. The two outstanding candidates, he told the Prime Minister, were Hull and Elworthy, but the latter had only just taken over as Chief of Air Staff and had not yet been given a chance to prove himself. The Minister's main consideration was undoubtedly that Mountbatten needed more time to see through the reforms that had been launched: 'An extension would have the advantage that we should be able to make use of Lord Mountbatten's great experience in the first year or so of the reorganised Ministry of Defence.'[62] Mountbatten himself was ready to accept the extra assignment, though he emphasised that this must be the final prolongation and that he would not be distressed if he was given nine rather than twelve more months.

The news that he was to stay on did not give undiluted satisfaction. In the *Sunday Telegraph* Ivan Rowan reported considerable criticism in the military world.[63] For one thing, it was held to be unfair to Hull (who, in spite of the Minister's professed uncertainty, was assumed by everyone to be the natural successor) to keep him waiting for another year and thus either curtail his time at the summit or establish a pattern by which the C.D.S. stayed on after the normal retirement age. For another, there were rumours that Brockman – quintessentially Mountbatten's man – was to be appointed to the key post of Defence Services Secretary, thus ensuring the C.D.S.'s control of all senior promotions in the three Services. But the real cause for disquiet was the fact that Mountbatten was so patently pre-eminent among the Chiefs of Staff, and yet disagreed with them on so many issues, that discussion tended to be unbalanced and opposition overridden. He was, in effect, too big for the job;

a circumstance which, it was felt, both impaired the present running of affairs and would make life uncommonly difficult for his successor.

Mountbatten was aware of these arguments, indeed saw some force in them, but he believed that the contribution he could still make more than outweighed the disadvantages. That there was much work to be done was illustrated by a memorandum which Thorneycroft circulated in June 1964.[64] The first phase of the reorganization, he said, was now complete. 'This has been a vast operation, and considering its size it has been carried out very smoothly and to the great credit of all concerned.' But they should not rest on their laurels. 'The essential point is that we are still behaving as though we were four departments within one building.' Some additional superstructure had been provided, and the result was 'a classic example of the operation of Parkinson's Law'. There must be streamlining, economy, rationalization. Could it be right for the Chiefs of Staff still each to be separately briefed? 'Would it be more sensible to think of a single briefing or presentation to the Chiefs of Staff which has already been argued out towards a defence solution?' (A point against which Mountbatten put three emphatic ticks in the margin.) The planners should be amalgamated and so should the intelligence organizations – 'Can we take a hint from the present Central Briefing Staff of C.D.S.?'

All this could well have been written by Mountbatten himself, indeed some of it probably was. A committee was set up to decide what structural changes within the Ministry of Defence had been proved necessary, and the C.D.S. took advantage of its existence to hammer home his view about the next stage of reorganization. 'The goal must be a completely functional organisation, which, as you recollect, has been my view from the beginning,' he told the chairman of the committee.[65] Thorneycroft was convinced. He was not yet prepared wholly to abolish the link between individual Ministers and the three Services but he accepted that this should be reduced in importance. Ministers should be given more responsibilities across the board; one Minister should be responsible for all financial questions whether concerning Army, Navy or Air Force, another for all logistics.[66]

Everything seemed set fair for a further measure of reform. If Thorneycroft and Mountbatten had remained in partnership, there is little doubt that it would have followed rapidly. Macmillan's successor as Prime Minister, Alec Douglas-Home, would certainly have concurred. But it was not to be. One of the arguments the Prime Minister had used in persuading Mountbatten to stay on after July 1964 was that the Conservatives were likely to lose the forthcoming election and it was essential to have some continuity so as to ensure that the new Government followed the right course. In October Macmillan's prescience was demonstrated. The Conservative Government was decisively defeated. Harold Wilson took office with Denis Healey as his Defence Secretary. The debate would have to be continued with new men, whose priorities and preoccupations would inevitably be different from those of their predecessors.

# CHAPTER 48

# *Farewell to Arms*

MOUNTBATTEN BY 1964 was one of the least political of men. He still conscientiously took, sometimes even read, the *New Statesman*; professed vague, though sincerely held, egalitarian principles; but any true commitment had perished with Edwina. Equally, he had in no way fallen prey to reaction. He knew that the advent of a Labour Government was likely to mean that his income after tax would be reduced; but if this caused him any concern, it was certainly not evident to others. He judged Ministers by their readiness to do what he wanted, above all in the field of national defence. If Wilson and Healey were likely to be amenable on matters such as defence reorganization, aircraft-carriers, the TSR 2, he would welcome their appointment. Since under Douglas-Home it seemed likely that some of the reforming zeal would anyway go out of the Tory Ministry, he viewed the change with equanimity if not enthusiasm.

He was not wholly free from the traditional preoccupations of his caste. In June 1964 he wrote to Lord Porchester about a rumour that a Labour Government would ban shooting if it came to power. It would be useful, Mountbatten considered,

> if you were able to find out how many keepers would be out of a job or whether the figure is really 5000 as you suggest or not. How many game farms would go broke and throw people out of employment. What the prospects would be of reabsorbing keepers into other forms of employment. You might also go into the question of the amount of Americans who come over because there is shooting in England who would not come if there were not enough birds. Finally, what possible harm could this particular activity do to the community?
>
> If they say that shooting is cruel then they should begin by stopping fishing for at least in shooting we don't spend long minutes drawing out the agony of the death of the pheasant and enjoying it the longer it lasts![1]

625

On such an issue 'they' were clearly the socialists, but this was not inevitably or even generally the case. 'They' were the politicians, a body of men towards whom Mountbatten felt the distrust of a serving officer or civil servant, the aloofness of a member of the royal family and the arrogance inspired by many years in high position. Healey was the eighth Minister of Defence with whom Mountbatten had served since he became First Sea Lord, the fourth since he was Chief of the Defence Staff. He used to remark loftily that he had to have a card put on his desk each day to remind him who was the current incumbent. 'I find it very trying to reeducate each Minister of Defence in turn', he told Ismay, 'because they always seem to come in with preconceived ideas of what they want to abolish!'[2]

He might have hoped that the re-education of Denis Healey would prove relatively easy. Healey was only just forty-seven when he took office. He had risen to the rank of major when Mountbatten was Supreme Commander. He seemed deferential and anxious to please: 'The new Secretary of State is very polite, stands up and salutes when M. comes in, calls him "Boss".'[3] Sir Louis Gluckstein remembered an incident in which Mountbatten, while at a British Legion festival in the Albert Hall, was told that the R.A.F. was dragging its feet over a proposed merger of its film corporation with that of the Army. 'A rather red-faced and sheepish Minister of Defence was extracted from his box and invited, pretty peremptorily, to explain the cause of the delay. . . . The Minister was behaving rather like a small boy in the presence of the Headmaster and was almost physically rubbing one leg against the other in his distress.'[4] But if Mountbatten imagined that this deference was more than skin-deep, he was soon disabused. Healey, he was declaring within a few weeks of the change of Government, was 'brilliant, charming and nice', but determined that nobody should say he was run by the C.D.S. Thorneycroft had been accustomed to let Mountbatten virtually draft his own instructions. Mountbatten tried the same procedure on Healey, 'who said he was sorry but he did not like taking other peoples' Minutes as his own'.[5]

It was, however, the Prime Minister rather than the Secretary of State for Defence who provided the first important challenge. Despite his views on arms limitation and control, Mountbatten was opposed to unilateral disarmament. He was dismayed when Wilson seemed to be supporting this course in the electoral campaign of 1964 and pleaded with him not to make a firm statement on the subject. 'Wilson said he was sorry but he was already committed.'[6] Whatever form this discussion took, it does not seem to have discouraged the C.D.S. unduly. Within a few days of Labour's victory Mountbatten was writing to congratulate the new Prime Minister. He took advantage of the opportunity to make a few of his own points:

The third matter which I am sure you will wish to discuss at an early stage is the future of the United Kingdom's nuclear forces. Here again the Chiefs of Staff and I are unanimous in our advice that the only practical defence in military terms against direct attack at home or indirect blackmail abroad, is the possession of our own nuclear retaliatory capacity. . . .

In the West our priority is, and in the foreseeable future must remain, the deterrence of war with Russia. I doubt if there are many who believe that a war with Russia in the West is in the least likely, but this state of affairs is only brought about by the presence in Europe of NATO, backed by the Western strategic nuclear deterrent. The Russians face the NATO force in Europe in sufficient masses for there to be little doubt of the outcome of a conventional military clash. . . . The balance is kept by the nuclear deterrent and the certainty in the mind of the Russians that a strategic exchange can only result in their virtual annihilation.

The part that the British deterrent has to play in this is to dispel in Russian minds the thought that they will escape scot-free if by any chance the Americans decide to hold back release of a strategic nuclear response to an attack. Our own Polaris force will be capable of inflicting on the Russian homeland damage which the most hard-headed gambler could not regard as anything but utterly unacceptable.[7]

It was the classic internationalist case for the national deterrent, designed for the ears of those who felt chauvinism was out of date and would have deplored any direct appeal to patriotic pride or the role of Britain as a great power. Healey needed no convincing; it was the argument he would have expounded himself. The Prime Minister was a less certain factor. At a critical meeting at Chequers in November – christened by the press 'The Weekend of the Crunch' – he chose to remain above the conflict, leaving Chalfont and Wigg to present the case against the British nuclear force.[8] The result was a triumph for Healey and Mountbatten. They won the day not only on the issue of principle. Even if it was conceded that the national force was desirable in principle, there was still room for argument about its proper size. Four Polaris submarines had already been ordered, all, incidentally, called after ships in which Mountbatten had served – *Renown, Repulse, Revenge* and *Resolution*. Even with four submarines, however, it was not possible to guarantee that there would be two permanently on patrol. In that case, asked Wilson, why not settle for three? If one of those three met with an accident, explained the C.D.S., it might not be possible to guarantee that even a single submarine would be on patrol. Wilson professed himself content; the national deterrent force was saved.[9]

Mountbatten returned from Chequers well satisfied by the way the new Government was shaping. 'M. is very impressed with Wilson's intellect, ability, personality and drive,' recorded Campbell-Johnson. 'He is not sure how far he trusts him, but he certainly knows his stuff. All the Labour Ministers have a higher "I.Q." than the Conservatives.'[10] Mountbatten expounded to Wilson his views on global strategy, which assumed stability in the West and dangerous fluidity east of Suez. To protect its interests and perform its responsibilities in that vital area, Britain was heavily dependent on its bases, yet it was by no means certain that it would be able to maintain its presence in Aden and Singapore for many years longer.

> This is why I am continually advocating the acceptance of a policy of mobility East of Suez. We need to have, so far as is practicable, balanced, hard-hitting, self-reliant forces which happily the improved logistic techniques of the future should make feasible. This points to largely amphibious forces backed perhaps by a base in Australia, relying upon whatever facilities may come available to us on an austere basis in the Indian Ocean.[11]

At the heart of such a strategy, he held, must be the aircraft-carrier. The logic of his argument was clearer to him than to either his Service colleagues or the new Ministers. The debate, in its crudest terms, was between those who argued that Britain's commitments east of Suez could best be met by dependence on island bases which were unsinkable and relatively cheap, but subject to political threat, or on carriers, which would be vulnerable and highly expensive, but immune to vicissitudes among the emergent nations. Mountbatten felt inhibited from taking too overt a position in this controversy by his supposedly neutral position as C.D.S. When in 1961 the Chief of Air Staff had attacked the carrier programme, Brockman had warned: 'The handling of this matter is tricky.' If Mountbatten accepted the C.A.S.'s proposals, he would be acting against his own convictions; if he did not, 'the news will soon spread round what has happened and that you are backing the Navy'.[12] On that occasion the Admiralty had rallied to its own defence, and with the redoubtable Caspar John, himself a veteran of the Fleet Air Arm, to defend naval interests, the C.D.S. could afford to remain detached. When John retired in 1963, however, Admiral Luce took his place. Luce had been Mountbatten's choice for the job, but had proved disconcertingly reluctant to fight for the full carrier programme. 'Though loyal, he has not the character or perception,' said Mountbatten; 'the job is above his head.'[13] The C.D.S. did his best to persuade Healey that carriers were indispensable, but the

Secretary of State was unconvinced and had no intention of plucking out of the fire naval chestnuts which the Admiralty was apparently content to leave there. The battle was to continue over many years, but Mountbatten left office sadly disillusioned by Healey's reluctance to come to the Navy's rescue.

This was not the only issue on which the Secretary of State fell short of the C.D.S.'s expectations. In Mountbatten's inaugural letter to Harold Wilson, the first point that he mentioned was the central organization of defence.

> As I am sure you know I submitted a scheme in October 1962 which has resulted in the Organisation which we have at present. My scheme envisaged two stages, of which we have now achieved the first. We cannot, in my opinion, afford to stand pat and must move on to, or at least towards, the ultimate aim of a functional, closely-knit, smoothly working machine. Detailed proposals for this are with the Secretary of State and he will, of course, be keeping you informed and in due course, I hope, seeking your approval to various measures to bring about this end.[14]

Wilson was content to let the Secretary of State make the running. Nor was he going to protest vociferously if the 'detailed proposals' took some time to formulate. It seemed likely that they would. Healey was careful to concede that he saw the need in principle for further reform. Zuckerman wrote in early December to report that he had 'made a special point of seeing the Secretary of State to reassure myself that he was not going back on "reorganisation". I . . . left satisfied that his eyes are set on the same goals as yours and mine, even if he may not make the same steps in reaching them.'[15] The trouble was that, when it came to the point, Healey proved reluctant to take any steps at all. Mountbatten suspected that the Secretary of State had little enthusiasm for a cause which somebody else had made so conspicuously his own. There may be some truth in this, but Healey could legitimately plead that he was overburdened with other, more immediately pressing problems of finance and of the country's future weapons. He did not accept Mountbatten's thesis that such problems would never be answered correctly until the Ministry of Defence had been finally put to rights. Functionalization was no doubt desirable as a long-term objective, but it would not do to push things too far or too fast. For one thing, the integration of British forces with those of NATO made it desirable to take no steps which might prove incompatible with developments in the other countries of the alliance.[16] 'You mustn't take out a man's appendix while he's moving a grand piano,' was Healey's favourite aphorism on the subject.[17] He did take a somewhat grudging step forward by allocating to one of the three Service Ministers responsibility for personnel and logistics, to another research and development and to the third international policy; but the old responsibilities survived unmodified and the result was confusion.[18]

When Ministers are reluctant to make any move but do not wish to appear obstructive, they appoint a committee to consider the question. Some months before, Thorneycroft had set up a committee on functionalization under Sir Ronald Melville, one of the Permanent Under-Secretaries at the Ministry of Defence. Healey now insisted that this committee must report before any new action could be considered. Melville was conservative by nature and celebrated as an enemy of Mountbatten's plans for further reorganization. Mountbatten tackled him head-on. 'You look like an old blimp,' he recollected saying to Sir Ronald, 'so people will believe you if you say Functional Reorganisation is the right thing; they will have confidence in you and you can prove that you're *not* an old blimp!'[19] This somewhat churlish wooing failed to achieve its end. Melville was unconvinced. For his part he remembered the C.D.S. coming into his office and announcing that he had just been talking to the Prime Minister. 'Dickie,' Harold Wilson had said, 'I do hope your new reorganisation of the Ministry of Defence is going to come about.' 'It's not me, Prime Minister,' Mountbatten had replied. 'It's all in the hands of a chap called Ronald Melville.' Melville took the precaution of ringing up the Private Secretary at Number Ten, established that Mountbatten had not spoken to Wilson for a week at least, and concluded that his career was not immediately at risk.[20] He could not achieve much, however. An early draft of the committee's report declared that functionalization would have 'a dangerous effect on the morale and efficiency of the Fighting Services',[21] but all the other members were sympathetic to Mountbatten's ideas and it did not take much pressure from the C.D.S. to ensure that the phrase was re-drafted in more emollient terms. The final conclusions, though not the call for instant action Mountbatten would have welcomed, were still sympathetic towards functionalization as a long-term aim.

Even before the Melville Committee had reported, Healey had launched another enquiry which also seemed likely to support Mountbatten's theories, but at the cost of further delay. A group was despatched to Singapore and Aden to find out how the unified commands were working, and then to consider how far these findings could be applied to developments in Whitehall. Mountbatten at first welcomed the idea but soon despaired of it. Fred Mulley, the Deputy Secretary of State for Defence, was given charge of the enquiry. First he failed to appoint as chairman the civil servant whom Mountbatten favoured but instead selected William Geraghty, whose ignorance of the background inevitably slowed up work on the study. Then he allowed matters to be spun out so that the committee was not able to leave for South-East Asia until the Commander-in-Chief, Sir Varyl Begg, a renowned champion of unification, was on the point of leaving. 'What a nice, but stupid man he is,' wrote Mountbatten indignantly. 'He is thoroughly reactionary, and is clearly trying to organise the Geraghty Working Party to recommend "No change". I do not believe for one moment that Wilson or the Labour Cabinet will be satisfied with a reactionary outlook when everybody knows that the Conservatives would have gone on developing the organisation to suit the unified Commanders-in-Chief.'[22]

Wilson and the Labour Government did not seem unduly disturbed and the last months of Mountbatten's long reign were slipping away. Early in April he twice wrote formally to the Secretary of State to try to persuade him to get things moving again. 'In my view reorganisation is every bit as important as any other matter with which you are dealing,' he protested. 'The Prime Minister has now said twice, in your presence and in mine, that the Labour party are firmly in favour of pressing on with further reorganisation. So long as this reorganisation is left in the hands of the Deputy Secretary of State and he acts on his present lines, then all I can say is that the Prime Minister's wishes will almost certainly be frustrated.' The second letter was never sent, but the two men discussed the matter fully. Mountbatten's points were made in very similar words.[23]

Progress remained imperceptible; indeed, given that the Secretary of State was now committed to awaiting the Geraghty Report, it is hard to see that there was much he could do. Mountbatten, however, was growing desperate. Geraghty was unlikely to present even provisional findings until a few days before the C.D.S. retired and there did not seem much chance that, when they did come, they would provide a clear blueprint for future action. Opinion against further change was stiffening; Mountbatten's designated successor, Richard Hull, who at one time the C.D.S. had believed was not hostile to a measure of functionalization, now seemed to have moved conclusively against it.[24] It was time for a final effort. Mountbatten insisted that Healey and he should appear before the Prime Minister to argue out the issue. 'P.M. saw Healey and me at my request,' was his diary entry for 10 June 1965. 'I reported lack of progress on Defence Reorganisation and got good hearing.'

Mountbatten's account of the interview is different in some respects to Healey's, and is certainly more picturesque. Healey, he said, was reluctant to attend the meeting and had almost to be dragged there. Mountbatten recapitulated the sorry history of the last year. All that was left to hope for was the Geraghty Report, and that was likely to be 'very incomplete and rather half-baked'. In such circumstances he saw no hope for the immediate future. 'People in the Ministry of Defence were just waiting for 16 July, for the day of my departure, not only to prevent any advance in the organisation but to go backwards.' Already junior officers were being drafted in who would look to their individual Service for their future and would therefore weaken the influence of the centre. But in the long term he could not despair: 'What I wanted done was so obviously right that it was bound to come along within the next few years and people would then begin to see that all the reactionaries were wrong.' A contrite Healey now admitted that he had not devoted as much time as he would have liked to reorganization and that he too was disappointed in Mulley's progress. He was ready to put forward immediate plans for the abolition of the three Service Ministers and the substitution of two functional Deputy Secretaries of State. Wilson expressed keen interest and asked for a timetable to be drawn up. Mountbatten pointed out that Healey would have all Chiefs of Staff and his own civil servants against him. The Secretary of State said 'he thought he could manage that and I need not worry that reorganisation would be progressed'.[25]

Denis Healey for his part says that he always intended to attend the meeting and that any persuasion by Mountbatten would therefore have been superfluous. 'I vaguely remember the meeting on 10 June,' he wrote much later. 'As I recall, Dickie made his usual case for functionalizing the Service. Wilson listened patiently but made no comment, and I explained what we were doing. It was a pretty typical meeting of Chiefs of Staff with the Prime Minister!'[26] The difference is more one of emphasis than of substance. Patrick Nairne, who was then Healey's Private Secretary, feels that the Minister's version rings the truer of the two; Harold Wilson, who was of course a party to the discussion, has a recollection of it quite as hazy as Healey's but thinks that Mountbatten's account sounds broadly correct.[27] What is certain is that, however emphatic Healey was about his future plans and however interested the Prime Minister might have been in furthering them, little happened in the next few years to make them become reality. In this at least Mountbatten was right: the forces of reaction and inertia were building up in Whitehall and after his departure they were to reign triumphant.

In one field, however, he could claim substantial progress. Early in February 1965 he wrote a memorandum to Healey about his cherished scheme for the merger of the three intelligence directorates.[28] Kenneth Strong, the first Director-General of Intelligence, had put forward a plan for this, and Mountbatten, about to leave on a tour abroad, was afraid that it would be discussed while he was away and done to death by the Chiefs of Staff. Healey confirmed that he wanted to push on with the merger as quickly as possible.[29] He was as good as his word. In July 1965 the announcement was made. 'This is one scheme which has been very near to my heart from the beginning,' Mountbatten wrote, 'and it would have been a great blow if it had been turned down before I left.'[30] Ten years later he recorded with satisfaction that he had predicted that the merger would enable personnel to be cut from 1100 to 900, and the total cost by twenty per cent. Now he had just been to a briefing where he had been told that the numbers had in fact fallen to 800 and the cost by twenty-five per cent. 'Finally they confirmed that my prophecy . . . that the quality of intelligence would be immensely improved by integration, had been amply fulfilled.'[31]

Despite this victory, Mountbatten left office a disappointed man. 'Suffice it to say', he told the Prime Minister, 'that with the laudable exception of the announcement on Intelligence, no real progress on functionalisation can be said to have taken place.' Since he believed that such progress was essential 'if we are to keep pace with the changing conditions of the world we live in', it followed that he could not count his tenure of office a complete success.[32] In Wilson's farewell interview with the C.D.S., the Prime Minister made appropriate remarks about Mountbatten's contribution to the future of the nation. The C.D.S. promptly countered with a question about what the Government planned to do next about functionalization. 'He told me he was still very keen on the idea,' Mountbatten wrote hopefully in his diary.[33] No doubt he was, but without Mountbatten's vigorous persistence the impetus had gone. The reform of the Ministry of Defence and the upper echelons of the British armed services stopped far short of Mountbatten's visionary scheme. Whether Britain is notably less secure as a result is a question that, with luck, will never need to be answered.


During his last months as C.D.S. Mountbatten's energies were dissipated by a call to unexpected duties. On 18 March 1965 he visited Los Angeles and mentioned to the Consul-General that, when he had arrived there in October 1941, it had been to find all his plans upset by a telegram from Churchill summoning him home to take over Combined Operations. Apologetically the Consul-General replied that history seemed to be repeating itself; Harold Wilson's Principal Private Secretary was arriving the following day to discuss an urgent matter. 'As I am due back in England on Thursday morning,' wrote Mountbatten, 'I simply cannot imagine what horror the Prime Minister has in store for me.'[34]

The horror turned out to be a mission to enquire into immigration from the Commonwealth and to try to persuade the governments concerned to stamp out illegal immigration at source by establishing adequate controls and health checks. The Labour Government was reluctant itself to impose harsher controls, which might be denounced as racist and illiberal, but was equally concerned about the uncontrolled influx of immigrants. It wanted the

Commonwealth governments to rescue them from this dilemma. R. A. Butler was their first choice to undertake the task of persuasion,[35] but when he was found to be unavailable who would be more likely to succeed than the hero of India's liberation, that celebrated progressive, Earl Mountbatten of Burma?

Why Mountbatten took on the task is harder to understand. It offered little chance of glory and much of lost reputation – particularly in countries where he was justifiably proud of his popularity. The tour involved would cut across the elaborate programme of visits he had planned to mark his retirement. The work involved was so different from anything he had done in the past that he could hardly have been blamed for asking to be excused. That he did not says much for the sense of duty – a naval officer goes where he is told – which had governed his life for fifty years. It also, perhaps, bears witness to the frustration which he was enduring in Whitehall. His dissatisfaction with the lack of progress on reorganization, his feeling that all his colleagues were against him and that even his Minister was not prepared to back him, must cumulatively have been deeply depressing. He would never abandon the fight while it was possible for him to continue, but if he were ordered off the field of battle he would obey without too much regret. Certainly he would not have taken on the mission if Healey had not written to urge him to do so. The Prime Minister, wrote Healey,

> thinks it is vitally important to the health of our national life that the very real problems which immigration presents should not become caught up in the day-to-day political battle and should not sour our relations with the rest of the Commonwealth. I certainly cannot disagree with his assessment that there is nobody who is both better qualified to inspire confidence in all political parties in this country, and also equipped with the skill and experience to talk firmly but diplomatically to Commonwealth governments.
>
> There is no time in the months ahead that we can truly spare you; but the Prime Minister has asked me to try and do so, and we can, if necessary, keep in touch with you by telegram on the major issues of the Defence review. I do not believe, therefore, that you need fear that your duty as C.D.S. should prevent you from meeting the Prime Minister's request.[36]

Mountbatten launched his mission in early April with a call on Malta, and in the next twelve weeks visited New Delhi, Lagos, Ottawa, Jamaica, Trinidad and Nicosia. Only in Pakistan did he allow another member of the team to take on the task. From the start it was clear that he planned to go always to the top. In Delhi he refused to begin the talks until the Prime Minister, Shastri, had arrived. He began his speech: 'These talks are being conducted at . . . ,' and Philip Woodfield, Wilson's former Private Secretary who had recently returned to the Home Office, is certain he was about to go on 'at Prime Ministerial level' but recollected himself in time and concluded 'at the highest possible level'. In Delhi he stayed at the former Government House and insisted that the delegation should attend a party there. With relish he demonstrated how a Viceroy conducted his affairs. He acted out a levee: 'You are an Indian Prince entitled to a seventeen-gun salute. You stand here. Then you walk this way. You wait here. . . .' Then he went through a similar ritual, but casting himself as Governor-General and emphasising the measures he would take to do due honour to his Prime Minister.[37]

Woodfield prepared what Mountbatten described as a 'very learned and rather verbose report' of some sixty pages.[38] Mountbatten then settled down in the plane returning from Cyprus and prepared his own personal two-and-a-half-page memorandum for the Prime Minister. This was promptly leaked to the *Evening Standard*, allegedly because an official at Number Ten put the wrong piece of paper inside an envelope. It was sensible, liberal and undramatic. Mountbatten said that he had made three assumptions: that Commonwealth citizens would be treated wherever possible more and never less favourably than aliens; that Britain would always welcome *bona fide* students from the Commonwealth; and that the right of a wife and dependent children to join an immigrant would always be observed. Subject to this he accepted that the number of new immigrants admitted should be at least halved to about 7000 a year. Malta, where the British base was being rapidly run down, should alone qualify for special treatment. He concluded:

> I have warned Prime Ministers of countries I have visited that drastic restrictions will have to be temporarily imposed on the influx of immigrants who wish to make their homes in Britain and I have explained the reasons fully. I believe that these drastic restrictions will be accepted with understanding so long as they only remain in force during the breathing space needed for assimilation. If the full scale of restrictions is continued beyond the time period which Commonwealth countries understand, I consider there will be a real risk that this could do lasting damage to Commonwealth relations.[39]

Whether the restrictions would have been accepted with less understanding if no mission had visited them, or someone less illustrious than Mountbatten had led it, is debatable. Except in Jamaica, the new policy was accepted almost without question, and even there the British proposals were received sympathetically. The fact that the Government had taken the trouble to send out so powerful a team, however, undoubtedly made a good impression on the Commonwealth countries, and Mountbatten's prestige, charm and patent good will must have made the measures that much more palatable. His presence was not essential, but nor were his efforts wasted.

Healey cannot have been wholly sincere when he told Mountbatten that there was 'no time in the months ahead that we can truly spare you'. In no way did he contrive the mission so as to rid himself of an importunate C.D.S., but there were compensations in being deprived of Mountbatten for a large part of his last few months in office. The question of the C.D.S.'s future had preoccupied the Secretary of State from the moment he took office. When Mountbatten had accepted a further prolongation to July 1965 he had stressed that this must be the end of the affair. At the time it had seemed to him that functionalization would by then be so far advanced as to be irreversible and that he could retire in the consciousness of a job well done. Montgomery had different ideas. As early as April 1964 he wrote to Thorneycroft to report a conversation he had had with Mountbatten's most likely successor, Richard Hull. Hull, he said, 'was outspoken in his disapproval of much that you and Dickie have been doing in forming a unified Ministry of Defence. . . . He said some very unpleasant things about Dickie, adding that he mistrusts him and that he would need to be closely watched to ensure that he did no further mischief.' Hull, Montgomery conceded, had been a 'competent operational Commander' but he was also 'reactionary, single Service minded and has no wide progressive outlook or statesmanship'.[40]

Montgomery kept up his campaign to the bitter end. In November he told Zuckerman that he had lectured both the Prime Minister and Denis Healey on the importance of persuading Mountbatten to remain for a further year. Whether he was more anxious to keep Hull out or Mountbatten in is a finely balanced question. 'Dickie doesn't want to stay on,' he admitted. 'I have told him it is his duty to do so, if asked. The question of its being the Army's turn is nonsense. Only one thing counts: who is the best man for the job?'[41] It was already too late; the day Zuckerman received this letter it was announced that Hull would take over as C.D.S. in the middle of 1965.

There had been powerful forces arrayed against Montgomery. Few soldiers would have agreed with him that the 'question of its being the Army's turn' was nonsense. The rotation of the office between the three Services had become enshrined as part of the constitutional package by which Army, Navy and Air Force retained their individuality even though War Office, Admiralty and Air Ministry might largely have vanished. Elworthy, Chief of Air Staff, would not have been gratified by a solution which eliminated Hull's three years as C.D.S. and forced him to accept promotion after only eighteen months or so at the head of his Service. Even the First Sea Lord, when Mountbatten asked his opinion early in 1965, said that a change was necessary.[42] Healey consulted the top forty people in the Services and

Ministry of Defence and all but one – Kenneth Strong – felt that it was time a new C.D.S. was appointed.[43]

Among the politicians, Wilson was ready, even eager, for Mountbatten to remain, believing that the unique authority enjoyed by the C.D.S. should not be wasted.[44] George Brown, the Minister responsible for economic affairs, was also anxious that he should stay, and threatened that the alternative might be a civilian C.D.S.[45] But it was the opinion of the Secretary of State for Defence that mattered, and Healey had made up his mind. A complex of reasons have been put forward for this: that Healey himself wanted to be in sole command of defence, yet could never manage it while Mountbatten was at his side; that it would be a mistake to keep on a man when his closest associates wanted him to go; that the Navy could never be cut down to size while it was sheltered by this powerful protector; that Mountbatten was growing old and tired, dozing at important meetings, rambling when urgent decisions were what was needed. Probably there was something in all of them; together they made an irresistible case.

But even if he had felt otherwise, it is unlikely that Healey would have been able to convince Mountbatten. The C.D.S. was sixty-four, and was beginning to feel his age. His style of life would have exhausted many who were ten or twenty years younger. On Monday, 1 February 1965, to take a date more or less at random, he left Broadlands at 9.10 and was in his office by 10.30. With only brief interruptions for meals, he worked through to 1.30 on Tuesday morning, then woke at 3.30 and worked till 5 a.m. He was in his office by 9.30, had supper at home and worked till 11.30 p.m. On the following day: 'Started work 0545 to catch up.' That night there was an official dinner-party, after which he worked to 3 a.m. On 4 February an Admiral arrived for breakfast at 9.00. He had dinner with a friend but again worked to 3 a.m. The following day work began at 8.30 and went on till 7 p.m. when he left for Broadlands. Even at the weekend he devoted five or six hours a day to his papers. 'Unable to sleep for a couple of hours. Too tired?' he had noted some months earlier.[46] It was not an entry he would have made a decade before. He was exhausted, he was frustrated, he was even slightly bored. The glory had departed. He had always been apt to relieve tension by blasting off in fury at some trusted subordinate, but now the tendency became more marked. He attacked one aide – a man in his late thirties and with a Military Cross – with such ferocity that the unfortunate man broke down and cried. Mountbatten was appalled and devoted himself to cheering up his victim, but, once again, it would not have happened a decade before.[47]

It is certain that he meant what he said when he first insisted that his extension to July 1965 must be the end of the line. He longed to put his papers in order, to spend more time at Broadlands, to attend to the innumerable

organizations to which he had lent his name. If functionalization had gone as
smoothly and rapidly as he had hoped, he would have departed without a
second thought. There is evidence that he did have some such second thought
early in 1965. The pleas of Montgomery, George Brown, Solly Zuckerman,
had some effect. The fact that he asked Luce's opinion on the question
showed that his mind was still open; a letter he wrote to Healey on 6 April, in
which he said that his earlier request to be released in July had been based on
the premise that the subsequent nine months 'would give time for a decision to
be taken . . . on the future organisation of defence', suggested that even then
he might have reconsidered his decision.[48] But he was given no encouragement and with some relief he closed his mind on the question a second time.
He reverted to the point of view that he had set out the previous year:

> As you know, I have already had two extensions from 1962–64 and
> from 1964 to 1965. If it were now announced that I was going to stay
> on still longer even my best friends and supporters, who think I have
> done a good job up to now, would begin to say of me, as I am afraid
> all said of Lord Beatty at the Admiralty, 'Will the Old Man of the Sea
> never go?'
>
> It is not just laziness – although God knows, after twenty-three
> years continuously at the top level I am tired; but my honest belief,
> with my well wishers and supporters in the Ministry of Defence, is
> that to stay on now would be counter-productive.[49]

Healey told Wilson that Mountbatten 'enthusiastically' agreed that Hull
should replace him in July 1965. Enthusiasm is hardly the word to describe
Mountbatten's feelings when he contemplated the nature of his successor, but
he was certainly resigned to his translation. The fire of life had not begun to
sink, but the fires of ambition burnt less hotly and the prize hardly seemed
worth the conflict. He was ready to depart.

He did so with all due ceremony. In June Brockman wrote to arrange for
the C.D.S. to have a farewell audience with the Queen. He received the reply
that there was no precedent for such an audience and that one could therefore
not be arranged. 'How odd!' commented Mountbatten in the margin.[50] The
answer was not one he was likely to accept placidly. It was hardly surprising
that there was no precedent for a C.D.S. being given a farewell audience, he
pointed out, since to all intents and purposes he was the first C.D.S. Needless
to say, he got his way. When he arrived, the Queen greeted him with the news
that she had something for him.

> She then handed me the Military badge of the Order of Merit. This
> really was an absolutely wonderful gesture on her part. The Order of

Merit only has 24 members and usually is given to great authors like Thomas Hardy or poets like Rudyard Kipling or scientists like Rutherford and, as far as I know, has only been given once before to a sailor for work in peacetime and that was the great Admiral Jackie Fisher in the 1900s. In the First World War Beatty and Jellicoe got it, and in the Second World War A. B. C[unningham], Chatfield and Pound. So far as I know I am only the seventh sailor to get it.[51]

His departure took place in the sentimental haze appropriate to such occasions, in which the acrimony of the last few years was shelved if not forgotten. At the last meeting of the Chiefs of Staff which he attended a cake was produced with 'C.D.S. Farewell' inscribed in icing on the top, presentations were made, the First Sea Lord made a speech, champagne was brought in to toast his future. The news that he was leaving the Ministry of Defence for the last time had spread abroad and a group of journalists, well-wishers and curious passers-by had assembled at the door. Mountbatten glanced out of the window as he walked down the stairs. 'Ah. Quite a satisfactory little crowd!' he remarked approvingly.[52]

Like most departing dignitaries, Mountbatten felt the urge to leave posterity an account of his stewardship and his hopes and fears for the future. The Commander-in-Chief of a fleet traditionally wrote a 'Haul-down Despatch' in which he reviewed the state of the forces under his command. He, too, would write a 'Haul-down Despatch', in which he would survey the whole spectrum of Britain's defences and pronounce on what was needed to save the nation. With a brutal frankness that was all the more effective for being rarely employed, Brockman poured cold water on the idea. 'I do not think that much notice will be taken of your views now that you have retired, and nothing is likely to be done on any paper from you except to "take note".'[53]

Mountbatten was swiftly convinced that Brockman was correct. After his retirement he was allowed to keep a skeleton staff for three months to put his papers in order. 'I had hoped', he wrote, 'to trigger off a request from the Prime Minister or the Secretary of State for Defence . . . for my views on concluding 49 years of active service.' No such request was received. He hinted to Sir Burke Trend, Secretary to the Cabinet, that the Prime Minister might like to invite him to write his impressions after six years as Chief of the Defence Staff. The invitation never came. 'Although I was granted personal interviews with the P.M. and Trend, it was clear they did not want my written views on record.'[54] The great despatch remained in Mountbatten's mind. Posterity would have to do the best it could without it.

Mountbatten was yesterday's man. For somebody who had been at the centre of great events for so long, it was a painful realization. His position, his reputation were such that he would never fade away as so many of his peers had done; but the majesty had departed. 'Farewell the plumed troop and the big wars,' he might have cried but certainly did not. '... The royal banner, and all quality, Pride, pomp, and circumstance of glorious war! . . . Farewell! Mountbatten's occupation's gone!'

OPPOSITE *Mountbatten photographed at Classiebawn, with, behind him, the sea in which he was eventually to die.*

LORD KILBRACKEN/CAMERA PRESS

# CHAPTER 49

# *Retirement:*
# *The Public Man*

FOR FIFTY-FIVE YEARS OR MORE Mountbatten had led a structured life, compelled by duty to do certain things in certain places and at certain times. For anyone accustomed to such a discipline the freedom of retirement is awe-inspiring. The more important and exciting the tasks that have been performed, the greater the gaps left by their disappearance. Mountbatten in 1965 was confronted by a void, a void into which there were many time-consuming and engrossing activities to be fitted but few which were imposed on him. He had to make his own future as he had never been called on to do before. The prospect was exhilarating but also daunting.

He was temperamentally ill-equipped for retirement. He was not reflective by nature, found no pleasure in the thought that he could now take things more leisurely, act with greater deliberation. He had lost the habit of reading for pleasure – indeed, he probably contributed more forewords to others' efforts than he read books himself. He rarely looked at pictures except his own or listened to music unless it was to dance to. The traditional pursuits of the English gentleman gave him little satisfaction; he never gardened, was bored by racing, lacked the patience for fishing. He was too old for polo, though he still took a keen interest in the sport. Shooting he relished, but not so much for the pleasure of the activity as for the satisfaction of breaking records; a bag of more than a thousand birds in a day at Broadlands remained his ambition for many years. He despised the cult of the amateur, and few of the pastimes of retirement are suited to a rigorously professional approach.

What does the man of action do when his habitual field of activity is denied him? To look for another field is the obvious solution. Mountbatten was well qualified to do so. His judgement may have been less good than formerly; to some of his colleagues it seemed that he had grown arrogant and unscrupulous; but his energy and drive were unimpaired. His openness of mind and intellectual curiosity were astonishing for a man of sixty-five. He was unshockable, and avid for new experience, alien points of view. He was taken to Joan Littlewood's pacifist polemic, *Oh, What a Lovely War!*: 'It is a magnificent film,' he commented, 'and although it attacks the Generals and indeed officers as a whole, I am personally prepared to accept it.'[1] He was as self-confident as ever, but no less ready to welcome constructive criticism and more apt than sometimes in the past to admit that he could appear absurd. John Wells caricatured him in the B.B.C.'s *Late Show*. Mountbatten wrote to thank the producer for providing a copy of 'this delightfully libellous portrayal of myself. . . . I am glad he recognised that I put guns into the Navy and invented technology, as I feel that this has been insufficiently recognised up to date.'[2]

Even if he had felt inclined to retire into seclusion, the world would hardly have allowed it. He was bombarded with correspondence. 'I do not think you realise what my life consists of,' he wrote protestingly to Solly Zuckerman, who wanted him to take on a new task. 'I have a private staff of four who are kept fully stretched. I often do thirty, forty and sometimes fifty letters a day and often make three or four and sometimes even five speeches a week.'[3] The postbag included many from the lunatics who assail every celebrity: those in love with him and those who thought him in love with them; pretenders to the throne and illegitimate children; a letter signed 'Philip' beginning 'Oh dear uncle, my Lord'; fan-mail in Gujarati and Greek, Turkish and Tamil; offers of secret weapons and predictions about the end of the world. All except the insults were kindly answered. These were the easy ones, however; the majority posed questions about the past or related to the innumerable organizations with which he was associated.

All were welcome. Mountbatten's response to the fear of loneliness and boredom was to hurl himself into a welter of hyper-activity. In the twenty-five days between 28 September and 23 October 1967 he made twenty speeches, including lengthy and supposedly portentous harangues to the British Computer Society Datafair Dinner, a British-Burma Society Dinner, the Annual Dinner of Shipwright Officers and the Biennial Dinner of the Institute of Brewing. He opened a new factory in the Isle of Wight and unveiled a bust of Augustus John at Fordingbridge. In the ten days after 24 April 1968 he made eleven major speeches; at a Burma Reunion, Brighton College of Technology, Lymington Marina. 'I feel I ought to have my head examined!' he commented ruefully.[4]

Retirement could not end his lifetime's service to the Navy. The fact that he was no longer C.D.S. freed him to fight the battle over aircraft-carriers more vigorously. Early in 1966 he offered to challenge in public the proposed cutting of the carrier programme. Luce told him that any such interference would be counter-productive and Zuckerman confirmed that the First Sea Lord was probably right. 'I want you to know that I loyally accept your decision and I will take no steps whatever unless you ask me,' Mountbatten wrote sadly.[5] Within a few weeks, however, the uproar had reached the newspapers and Mountbatten felt that he was liberated from his self-denying ordinance. He decided to make his maiden speech in the House of Lords and select as his subject the vital role of the carrier in sustaining Britain's policy east of Suez. The day before the debate Solly Zuckerman urged him not to do so. An election was pending, the issue was part of the campaign, to speak out now would be to become involved in party politics. Reluctantly Mountbatten yielded. He sent the Prime Minister a copy of the speech he had planned to make. 'I greatly appreciate and applaud your decision,' replied Wilson. 'Knowing how strongly you feel, I know this was not easy, but believe me, to speak now, during an election, might have incalculable consequences.'[6]

Three years later the provocation was renewed. The Government decided to scrap two aircraft-carriers, H.M.S. *Eagle* and *Ark Royal*, long before vertical-take-off aircraft would be available to fill the gap. Mountbatten chose a Foyle's Literary Lunch – for Oliver Warner's biography of Charles Lambe – as the venue for his attack. He sent his speech in advance to the Prime Minister, saying that his conscience still pricked him for not having spoken out in 1966 and that now he proposed to repair the omission.

> Winston Churchill condemned the *Prince of Wales* and *Repulse* when he persuaded the Admiralty to send them to meet the Japanese without the aircraft-carrier which had been planned to accompany them. But at least he did have aircraft-carriers which could later put things right. From 1972 for some years we will be without any form of mobile air power.[7]

Wilson passed the letter to Healey, whose only comment was that £30 million, not £60 million as Mountbatten had stated, had been spent on refitting the carriers.[8] Mountbatten paid no attention; indeed, when he congratulated Heath on his election victory in June 1970, he raised the figure to £66 million. 'Splendid! Well done!!' he wrote. 'I was one of those who kept saying I thought that you would win; I am very glad to have been proved right. My chief desire to see the Conservatives win centred round defence policy which has been disastrous over the last few years. I feel now that the *Eagle* and *Ark Royal* may have a last minute reprieve.'[9] He reinforced the message when he cornered the new Prime Minister at a ball at Windsor Castle and won a promise that the matter would be examined urgently.[10] These carriers could not be saved but time to re-think the policy might be won.

He never lost interest in or touch with naval matters. 'The six First Sea Lords since I was in the chair have all been very welcome callers from time to time,' he told Admiral Pollock in 1971, 'and if I can be of any help to you at all do please let me know.'[11] He agitated for the placing of his protégés in important offices. 'I hope you don't think I am trying to interfere with your free selection, because it is of course yours,' he wrote to Admiral Lewin, prefacing his recommendation of a 'positive genius' for the post of Rear-Admiral of the Secretariat Branch.[12] Sometimes he fell foul of the authorities. When he addressed a Naval Chaplains' Dinner he elected to make a light-hearted speech including various faintly *risqué* stories, such as one about his grandson who had announced that his teacher had told him the trouble with China was over-copulation. The chaplains seemed pleased enough, but the staunchly Roman Catholic Minister for the Navy, Patrick Duffy, was conspicuously not amused, and an embarrassed First Sea Lord was called on to reprimand Mountbatten for the 'frivolity and vulgarity' of his speech.[13]

Retirement also left him more free to propagate his passionately held view on the need for disarmament and arms control. Just before he retired he received from Duncan Sandys a copy of a plan by which non-nuclear countries would be offered some security without the need to build their own nuclear weapons. His advisers thought it a crackpot scheme and urged him not to get mixed up in it, but Mountbatten refused to dismiss any idea which might diminish the risk of nuclear war.

> I need hardly tell you [he replied to Sandys] that I share your concern about the dangers of the further spread of nuclear weapons and, speaking in a personal capacity, I am prepared to go further and say that finding a means of restraining the spread, possibly by bringing the nuclear armouries of East and West under supranational control, is the most urgent problem mankind has known. My first thought, therefore, is more power to your elbow if you manage to get something moving on the lines which you have set out.[14]

In 1970 his long-held fears about the perils of so-called tactical nuclear weapons were made public in a letter to *The Times*, in which he argued that their use could only end 'in escalation to Total, Global, Nuclear Destruction'.[15] He was far from the first person to say as much, but the signature at the end of the letter created a sensation. 'I was very moved by your announcements concerning nuclear bombs!' wrote Charlie Chaplin. 'I think you have won profound acclaim throughout the world. Good luck to you!'[16] But Mountbatten still kept clear of any pressure-group or unilateralist campaign. When the British group of 'Women for World Disarmament' asked him for a message of good will, he refused to provide one: 'I feel my influence will remain more effective if I stick purely to military reasons and do not become involved in propaganda.'[17]

He never wavered in his belief that the main menace to the West lay east of Suez and in Africa. At a briefing for a group of veteran military leaders in

SHAPE in 1974 he attacked NATO's activities as largely irrelevant. The Russian naval threat in the Indian Ocean and South Atlantic had been colossally enlarged. What was NATO doing about that? The Arabs with their oil blackmail were breaking the West financially. What was NATO doing about that? If NATO was to continue to be a going concern it would have to alter its boundaries and ways of thought. 'When I sat down one could have heard a pin drop,' he concluded with satisfaction.[18] But his radicalism had its limits. The idea of a Channel tunnel, which in its ambitious scale and daring technological conception might have been expected to appeal to him, was instead viewed with horror. It laid the country open to blackmail, he urged: 'A bomb in the Tunnel or even a hoax can bring communications with the Continent almost to a halt.'[19]

The Government found Mountbatten's views on defence embarrassingly heretical, and would have silenced him if they could. In other spheres they were eager to employ him. He had barely been in retirement three months before he found himself called on. What had until recently been Southern Rhodesia was in turmoil. The Government of Ian Smith was believed to be on the point of making a Unilateral Declaration of Independence. The Governor, Sir Humphrey Gibbs, was beleaguered and impotent. Wilson believed that U.D.I. would be followed by civil war and the loss of much life. A *deus ex machina* was needed to conjure a settlement from these unpromising ingredients, and the Cabinet had decided that Mountbatten was the nearest to God that could readily be contrived.

> It was not only that his authority and personality would be of vital importance in influencing the opinions of, at any rate, the moderate Rhodesians, and perhaps many others whose loyalty to the Crown might give them pause when presented with illegal independence. There was the further point that Lord Mountbatten's unique record in the history of Indian independence meant that no one could be more fitted for handling a difficult negotiating problem of this kind.[20]

Wilson had already flown to Balmoral to get the Queen's approval to the appointment; now he summoned Mountbatten to Downing Street, smuggling him in through the garden-door so as to avoid the press.

Mountbatten as C.D.S. had already argued strongly against the use of force in Rhodesia, on grounds both military and ethical. To his relief Wilson made no attempt to dispute this, but said that an announcement of U.D.I. seemed imminent. In that case Gibbs would dismiss the Government. Secret sources suggested that Smith would then appoint a regent, possibly the Duke of Montrose. By sending out a new Governor, who was linked to the Queen yet an experienced administrator, this ploy might be frustrated. The only hope Wilson could see for the future was a strong British-sponsored Government which would hold the position for seven to ten years while a crash-programme for educating the Africans was pushed through. Mountbatten could pave the way for such a development.[21]

The putative Governor found the prospect unappealing: 'The horror that the P.M. offered me', he described it to Lord Brabourne.[22] He promised to consider it, however, and did not finally refuse for a few more days. He could, he pleaded, do nothing that Gibbs – 'courageous, sensible, completely loyal to The Queen and utterly dedicated to the good of Rhodesia' – had not already tried. If a replacement were needed, then it should be another local, not an imported Englishman, 'especially one "tainted" with a "pro-colour" reputation'. Wilson had drawn a parallel between Rhodesia and India, but Mountbatten as Viceroy had been only forty-six years old and supported by 'the world's most remarkable woman'.

> Physically and mentally I just couldn't go to Rhodesia without a wife or a known staff and set myself up as a figure for 'Loyalists' to rally round. . . .
>
> Nothing could be worse for the cause you have at heart than to think that a tired-out widower of 65 could recapture the youth, strength and enthusiasm of twenty years ago. I should be grossly misleading you if I encouraged you to think otherwise.
>
> When an old war horse has been turned out to grass at the end of his time, it's no good thinking he is capable of yet one more great cavalry charge.[23]

The idea was dropped, but a month later the old war-horse showed that he was ready to undertake at least a brief final canter. Mountbatten was again summoned to Downing Street and told that the situation in Rhodesia was still deteriorating. The Governor needed moral support. Would Mountbatten fly out for a visit, to invest Gibbs with some high decoration? There was always a chance that, in such circumstances, Smith might agree to re-open negotiations; even if he did not, the hearts of the loyalists would be uplifted. Would he be smuggled in wearing a false beard and dark glasses? asked Mountbatten. That would be undignified, replied the Prime Minister. He would be the Queen's emissary. Mountbatten entered with relish into the project: he would need a Comet transferred specially to the Queen's Flight and painted with her colours, a royal secretary, a large contingent of journalists, an escort of enormous and awe-inspiring guardsmen. If Smith failed to let such a delegation land at Salisbury it would be proof of his disloyalty.[24]

Mountbatten was spending the weekend with the Wernhers at Luton Hoo and discussed the idea with the Queen and the Duke of Edinburgh. 'Well,' commented the Duke, 'you've got General Gordon shut up in Khartoum and at least Wolseley can fly out in an aeroplane this time.'[25] Mountbatten agreed to undertake the task.[26] Now it was the Prime Minister's turn to hang back. The Governor's brother was on his way to Rhodesia; possibly it would be best to await his return. Mountbatten had little doubt that the idea, once allowed to flag, would never be revived. On the whole he was relieved, but also a little wistful; it would, as he remarked at the time, have 'made quite a scene'.[27]

The Labour Government had other, less exotic, ideas for his employment. In August 1966 George Brown suggested that he should join the Foreign Office as Defence Adviser. Mountbatten replied that if Brown really needed advice he should send for Solly Zuckerman; to drag in a superannuated military man had proved a disaster in Washington and would work no better in Whitehall.[28] Then, two months later, Roy Jenkins telephoned him[29] to say that he was concerned about certain sensational escapes from British jails, culminating in that of the spy George Blake, and that he wanted a man of 'public stature' to lead an enquiry into what was going wrong. A military man with excellent credentials both as a hero and a liberal must have seemed the ideal person to soothe the fears of the right without rousing the suspicions of the left. Some people assumed that Jenkins was looking for a splendiferous figurehead, who would lend his name to findings arrived at by others. The Home Secretary knew his man too well for that. Mountbatten made it a condition that he should put in his own personal report, assisted by three assessors. The work would have to be done with exemplary speed, since he was off to the Far East in February 1967. As assessors he wanted a scientist, a retired prison governor and a serving policeman. It was to the last of these that he attached most importance. He told Jenkins that he wanted 'a young and go-ahead man', and was given Robert Mark, just ending his stint as Chief Constable of Leicester. Mark proved, Mountbatten said, an 'absolute ball-of-fire'.[30] For secretary he chose his old ally from the mission on immigration, Philip Woodfield: after the debate in which the inquiry was announced, Alec Douglas-Home took Woodfield aside and said that he thought there would be no trouble from the opposition – 'Just make it quick, that's all!'[31]

Mountbatten made it quick; indeed, half way through the allotted period he announced that he had seen enough and would now dictate his conclusions for others to criticize. His haste did not imply reluctance to pay attention to other people. He seems, on the contrary, to have been a model chairman, always ready to listen, freely admitting his ignorance, yet resolute when he had made up his mind that something was essential. He decided that the prison service needed a professional leader, an Inspector General, and stuck to his view. 'I can tell you, Philip, you're not going to put me off it,' he told Woodfield. He extolled a particular system of promotion as having been a great success in the Navy. Woodfield investigated and found that it had been abandoned years before. Mountbatten was delighted: 'It will be much more obviously *my* system!' he declared. But he did not stick obstinately to ideas that could be proved unsound. One of the three assessors suggested mushroom-shaped prisons, in which a huge accommodation block would fan out from a slender stem. The concept had the visionary splendour of Habbakuk and appealed greatly to Mountbatten. 'No one will be able to get out!' he claimed. 'No one will be able to get in either,' pointed out Woodfield gloomily. The proposal was not pursued.[32]

The Report into Prison Escapes and Security was published in December 1966.[33] It had been leaked extensively the previous month by Chapman Pincher in the *Daily Express*. 'No one can imagine how he got it,' recorded Bousfield disingenuously, 'except that M. did see all the Editors, 32 London Daily and Weekly Editors on one day, and the following day, 20 Provincial Editors.'[34] Though the draft was prepared by Woodfield, the report bears Mountbatten's imprint and reflects his ideas. He took great pride in it and at Christmas sent a copy to each member of the royal family. It was a curious choice for festive literature, but only the Queen Mother is said to have announced firmly that she had no intention of reading it. Most of the recommendations were sensible if undramatic, dealing with such matters as the improvement of the morale of the prison service by quicker promotion and better facilities, and the strengthening of security by electronic devices or the rearrangement of accommodation. His proposal for an Inspector General was one to which he attached great importance – 'The first man appointed to this post will need to be an outstanding individual' – but he accepted that there was little chance that the Home Office would grant any such worthy the degree of independence which he believed was necessary.

The recommendation which he felt to be the most significant and also likely to be achieved was for the construction of a maximum security prison in which 'Category A' prisoners – 'those whose escape would be highly danger-ous to the public or police or to the security of the State' – could be congregated. Such a prison should be situated on an island off the British coast, preferably, suggested Mountbatten, the Isle of Wight. This proposal generated a storm of abuse so violent that it is hard for the outsider to understand. Mountbatten was condemned not merely for what he did suggest, but for the construction of maximum-security wings within existing prisons – an expedient which his plan for one super-prison was intended to render unnecessary. His policy, wrote Tom Clayton, 'may well have reassured the public but it has probably set back the advance to a humane and sensible prison policy some twenty five years'.[35] Leo Abse was more moderate in his assault. 'I bluntly accused him of responsibility for putting back penal reform in this country by a decade,' he wrote. 'To concentrate a group of evil men . . . in a repressive custodial atmosphere was to invite disaster.'[36] The committee set up under Professor Radzinowicz condemned the concept of centralization in favour of dispersion and armed guards – a refinement for which Mountbatten, incidentally, was often blamed though he had in fact opposed their use.

There are strong arguments against a maximum-security jail, as Mountbatten privately admitted to Philip Woodfield, but in advancing the idea he was seeking to achieve the same objective as that aimed at by his critics. He believed that in a single prison with an invulnerable perimeter it would be possible to allow the Category A prisoner far more liberty than was feasible when he was cooped up in a small section of a conventional prison – 'a cage within a cage', as Clayton described it. If the really dangerous men were removed, it would also be possible to ease restrictions and reduce the strain on the staff at the other prisons. He advocated improved security measures, but only as part of a package which, he believed, would liberalize the system as a whole. Yet it is by these measures that his report is remembered; as Dr Pauline Morris has pointed out, his name has become 'synonymous with the imposition of restriction and an almost obsessional concern with security'.[37]

Mountbatten never gave up his battle for the maximum-security prison. In 1972 he was tackling the new Conservative Home Secretary, Robert Carr. He had visited Kumla Prison in Sweden, he said, and had been struck by the way it vindicated his ideas. If the criticism was that Category A prisoners were not necessarily the most likely to escape, then a new sub-category could be introduced for prisoners who needed to be isolated in a special prison even though not *prima facie* a menace to the public or the state.[38] Five years later it was the turn of the Labour incumbent, Merlyn Rees. 'I gave up all responsibility for Prison Security after the Report was dealt with. In theory it has nothing to do with me now, but I cannot let the disastrous policy of dispersal go unchallenged.'[39] His efforts achieved nothing, partly through the force of the counter-arguments, partly because the money was never available. With the death of the maximum-security prison perished the central plank of Mountbatten's policy.

Robert Mark happened to be on his way to Dartmoor when Mitchell, the mad axe-man, escaped. Mark was intercepted at the railway station and warned what had happened. Mountbatten was proudly able to announce: 'I have a man on the spot already investigating the escape.'[40] Mark became his candidate for the first Inspector General, but Mountbatten accepted that the Chief Constable could render still more useful service with the Metropolitan Police: 'I knew from Peter Murphy', he wrote, 'that Scotland Yard . . . [was] riddled with corruption and it would never be put straight by promotion within the family.'[41] He remained loyal to Mark for the rest of his life. When Mark stirred up a furore by his denunciation in a Dimbleby lecture of dishonest lawyers, Mountbatten showed solidarity by inviting him to dinner at Broadlands with the Prince of Wales and urging him to continue to air his views. He was somewhat offended when his protégé resigned over the Police Act. Mark insisted that he was right to do so. 'Send me the papers,' said Mountbatten. Mark sent over a thick dossier. Two weeks later they met again. 'You were quite right,' was Mountbatten's judgement. 'I was wrong. Bloody politicians!'[42]

Mountbatten's selection of the Isle of Wight as the ideal site for a maximum-security prison was not well received in that favoured island, but the proposal did nothing to diminish his popularity there. He had been invited to become Governor in 1965. His uncle, Prince Henry of Battenberg, had been given the post in 1889 and his wife, Princess Beatrice, had succeeded him. She lasted till 1940 and, after an interregnum, the Duke of Wellington took over, doubling the duty with that of Lord-Lieutenant of Hampshire and the Isle of Wight. The Duke's retirement opened the way for splitting the two jobs once more. Mountbatten accepted with alacrity, persuaded the Queen to preside at his installation and applied himself to organizing the festivities. A snag arose when it seemed that the royal car would be unable to pass through the main gate of Carisbrooke Castle where the ceremony was to take place. The Queen must walk, decided Mountbatten. An A.D.C. rehearsed the exercise, slipped on the greasy stones and fell flat on his face. The Queen must drive, amended Mountbatten, the gate must be removed. 'But the gate has not been moved for three hundred years, sir,' pleaded the Ministry of Works representative. 'Time it was!' barked Mountbatten; and it was done.[43] 'This has been a wonderful and exciting day,' he recorded when all was over. 'Not only did I originally think up the idea of having the Installation Ceremony and inviting Lilibet to perform it, but I had more or less devised the ceremony and rehearsed it. . . . It all passed off without a hitch.'[44]

The new Governor took his duties seriously. He visited the Island seven or eight times a year, often staying overnight and travelling to every corner. He was always ready to pull strings to help his new subjects, sometimes to remarkable effect. At Britten-Norman's factory he found that work on their light Islander plane was being held up by protracted deliberations in the Ministry of Aviation. He asked for a demonstration of the plane, was impressed, wrote to Roy Jenkins and soon won a favourable decision. He even consented to wear the Royal Yacht Squadron's buttons and badge, something he had refused to do before because of his old grudge over his black-balling: 'However, now I am Governor of the Isle of Wight, I feel that I mustn't be silly about this.'[45]

The existence of a rival Lord-Lieutenant might have caused embarrassment. Precedence between these two dignitaries had never been decided, and when Lord Ashburton wanted to attend a funeral at Quarr Abbey on the Island the protocol problems seemed insoluble. 'Oh, well, we shall have to arrive in the same car and walk up the aisle hand in hand!' ruled Mountbatten philosophically. Twin thrones were provided at the entrance to the sanctuary and honour was held to have been satisfied.[46] From 1974 the embarrassment could not recur. The Isle of Wight became a shire county with its own Lord-Lieutenant and Mountbatten was the first incumbent.

But it was above all as roving Ambassador that Mountbatten proved most useful in his retirement. His immense prestige, his network of friends and acquaintances, his loyalty coupled with his notorious independence of mind: all made him uniquely useful as a trouble-shooter or the bearer of a message that came better by unofficial means. In October 1975 he mentioned to the Prime Minister that he had been invited to Saudi Arabia but was in two minds whether to accept.

> He said, 'I order you to accept. Nothing could be more important than that you should visit Saudi Arabia at this time. I will tell the Crown Prince when he sees me this afternoon.' Apparently Harold Wilson is relying on the Saudi Arabians to help him out of some of our financial troubles. No wonder he wanted me to go out there.[47]

In January 1966 he was despatched to represent the Queen at the funeral of the Indian Prime Minister Shastri: George Brown, the Foreign Secretary, represented the Government. Mountbatten travelled in great style. 'George Brown only had his Private Secretary with him,' he wrote, 'but then he is not representing the Queen and ceremonial is less important for him.'[48] To support him on this occasion Mountbatten took his daughter Pamela and her husband, Admiral Brockman, two A.D.C.s, a valet and a private secretary. His sense of his own consequence did not diminish with the years. At Athens he was late for an Air France plane and found its doors already shut. The manager protested that he must take another flight. Mountbatten pointed to his buttonhole and said: 'Do you see this? This is the Grand Cross of your Legion of Honour for my services to your country in French Indo-China; if you don't get that door opened up I shall report you personally to the President of France.' The door was opened.[49]

During this visit he had a long conversation with Indira Gandhi, who had recently been appointed the second senior Cabinet Minister after Nanda, the acting Prime Minister. Nanda, Mountbatten thought, was a nice man but unfit to rule the country, if only because he always consulted an astrologer before taking any decision. Morarji Desai was 'extremely able and clever' but an old-style capitalist and out of place in contemporary India. Chavan, the Minister of Defence, had a record of violence which might bar further promotion. 'I had a feeling that this left Indira as a favourite in the field for Prime Minister.'[50] It was an appointment that he welcomed, but he was deeply disappointed when in 1971 the Indian Government deprived the Princes of their privy purses and other privileges. 'What her father would think of her breaking the promise which he and Vallabhbhai Patel gave to the Princes and which was enshrined in the Constitution, I cannot imagine,' he wrote indignantly.[51] He protested to Mrs Gandhi, inveighed against the decision to every Indian he met, and urged Terence Garvey, the newly appointed British High Commissioner, 'to try and keep a friendly eye on the situation when he got out there'.[52]

As the situation in India grew worse Mountbatten became more and more concerned about Mrs Gandhi's behaviour. In 1975 she was found guilty of incorrect election practices. 'She has not of course been corrupt in the ordinary sense of the word,' Mountbatten wrote, 'but she certainly has got a great deal too big for her boots, and is being very tough and difficult with everybody.'[53] One of the victims was the Rajmata of Jaipur, widow of Mountbatten's closest Indian friend, and of whose children he was a trustee. The Rajmata was imprisoned for illegally concealing gold, a charge which, it was said by some, would not have been pursued if she had not also been an active political opponent of the Prime Minister. Mountbatten was indignant on her behalf and did his best to intercede, but to small effect. 'I must say that every time I visit India it tears at my heart-strings,' he wrote after his visit of 1966. Ten years later he found the prospect so depressing that he almost began to wonder whether he could bear to go there at all.

The Russian representative at Shastri's funeral had been the Chairman of the Council of Ministers, Alexei Kosygin. Mountbatten contrived to have a long talk with him, about the war, Stalin, India and other matters.

I then told him of my various ancestral relations who had married Emperors of Russia. He countered by saying that I evidently had a long ancestry of people who didn't have to work, but that he had a long line of ancestors who had had to work hard in St Petersburg. I then told him how lucky he was to have come from a long line of workers, as it was easy for him to work himself, and how much more difficult it had been for me to . . . have to start to learn how to work myself. This went over very big, and he laughed a lot.[54]

The somewhat laboured jocularity bore fruit with an invitation to visit Russia. It was nine years before he took it up, however. The visit got off to a bad start when the Russians refused to let his private aircraft land, on the grounds that they had not had the necessary forty-eight hours' notice. He got his revenge on arrival when he refused a pressing invitation to stay in a guest villa rather than at the British Embassy on the grounds that he, too, had received inadequate notice. He was forgiven and Kosygin received him. He took advantage of the meeting to press on his host the literature of his son-in-law's firm of decorators, and to hope that David Hicks would be allowed to tender for the design of nine new hotels which were shortly to be built in Moscow. The Russians for their part seemed anxious to honour their visitor. Averell Harriman, the U.S. Ambassador-at-Large, told him that the Russian authorities had several times approached him to get advice on the proper form of address. They favoured 'Your Royal Highness' and were most disappointed when told that, as a mere Earl, Mountbatten qualified for no such honorific.

> It was an interesting visit from every point of view, both historically and politically, and I was over-powered by the emotion of going back to a country I had known fairly well as a child, where so many of my closest family had lived in such tremendous splendour, and then been murdered in this ghastly way. I felt it all the way through, and I was quite exhausted when I came back.[55]

Still stronger memories were kindled by his visits to Germany, particularly to the old family homes in Hesse. 'I don't believe even you can fully realise the emotion which a visit to you at Wolfsgarten produces in me,' he wrote to Princess Margaret of Hesse. His recollections went back through many post-war visits, to the days before 1939, to his honeymoon. 'But Nostalgia goes deeper – to my childhood with both my parents and the blissful days before the 1st Great War shattered all that.'[56] As he grew older, Mountbatten found his earliest memories more and more precious and derived ever greater pleasure from sharing them with other people. In 1973 it seemed as if this

most sacred of all his places of pilgrimage might be threatened. The left-wing
Hessian Government was bent on making life impossible for the owners of
private property. They told Princess Margaret that she would have to take
down the wire fence around her park so that anybody might freely wander
through it. She pointed out that the fence was there not to keep the public out
but to keep in the mentally and physically handicapped children to whom
Wolfsgarten was now largely devoted. She won that battle, but the war went
on.

Malta was another evocative port-of-call. He visited Mintoff in 1973 and
congratulated him on extracting so much money from NATO and the British.
Another turn of the screw would have been enough to drive the British away,
however; he urged Mintoff to be careful in further brinkmanship. 'He took all
this quite well,' Mountbatten recorded, 'but explained at some length that if
he hadn't done this he would not have got the money, which may well be
true!'[57] A few years later the British left the island. It was suggested that
Mountbatten should attend the ceremonies, and he proposed to commemorate the occasion by presenting the Maltese Government with an early
painting of the island collected by his father. Then Mintoff insisted that only
the Prime Minister could represent Britain on such an occasion. In the end he
settled for the Lord President of the Council, Michael Foot.

> I am not surprised at Dom Mintoff's behaviour [wrote Mountbatten
> frostily]. To be rather conceited I am afraid I would have been an
> unwelcome person to have at the ceremonies as I think I might have
> re-introduced some note of British traditional splendour and
> friendship, which is not what he really wants. . . .
>
> My coming with a rather fine gift which I would have insisted on
> making to him in public would . . . not suit the plans of the kicking
> out of the British by the all-powerful Maltese Government.
>
> A Minister against whom he can use political arguments is just
> the sort of person he would like to have.[58]

Wherever he went he was ready to tackle any political odd job that
cropped up. In Malaysia he was told that the Australian Rear-Admiral who
commanded the Commonwealth forces in the area had failed to secure an
interview with the Prime Minister, Tun Razak. He at once called on 'my old
friend Tun Razak' and told him what a charming fellow the Australian was.
How extraordinary the two men had not met! This must be put right at once.
And with the Prime Minister's embarrassed acquiescence, Mountbatten
proceeded to fix an appointment.[59] But he was more ready than sometimes in
the past to recognize his limitations. In 1969 he was told that both Gowon
and Ojukwu would be likely to accept his mediation in an attempt to end the

civil war in Nigeria: 'They are both known to have great admiration for you personally and as exemplifying the finest in [the British] military tradition.'[60] Mountbatten declined. He did not think that any outsider should 'barge in and offer to settle a dispute, which nobody else has been able to, between Nigeria and Biafra. Any attempt would lead to crossing wires.'[61]

In the United States he also did his best to avoid controversy. When he appeared on the Johnny Carson show he insisted that he should be asked no questions about Vietnam. After twenty minutes of knockabout, however – 'rather like David Frost, but more hilarious and sexy' – Carson slipped in: 'If you were President of the United States what would you do about Vietnam?' 'I'd tell the English to keep their noses out of it,' Mountbatten briskly responded.[62] But he was not ready to hear his country abused or patronized. In Philadelphia he was told how everyone in America sympathized with the sad plight of Britain. 'I told them we were equally sympathetic for their troubles, Race Riots, Vietnam and their balance of payments. Once more we were comrades in adversity. This seemed to surprise them.' He took advantage of a visit to America to promote Richard Hough's book about his parents,[63] but he could never quite adapt himself to the hit-or-miss technique of some television interviewers on either side of the Atlantic. Barbara Walters led off by saying how terrible it must have been for him to have been driven out of office by anti-Jewish demonstrations. Mountbatten not unreasonably asked what, or indeed whom, she imagined she was talking about, but got no enlightenment. After a few more questions about the cost of the monarchy and what dukes and marquesses did for a living, Mountbatten announced that he now proposed to talk for two or three minutes uninterrupted about the book. 'This I did, and I hope retrieved the position. But what really inane questions and what stupid interviewers!'[64]

He was in Australia shortly after the Governor-General, Sir John Kerr, had dismissed Gough Whitlam and his Labour Government. Mountbatten much admired this controversial action, not because he took exception to Whitlam's policies, but because he felt that Kerr had been courageous and constitutionally correct. He told Kerr that, wherever he had been in Australia, everyone had admired the Governor-General's courage and thought he had done the right thing. 'I told him that it seemed lucky that Gough Whitlam now appeared to have become involved in a 500,000 dollar gift by the Iraqis to the Australian Labour Party, and he said it was indeed a very fortunate development from his point of view.'[65]

In 1973, with some courage, he went to Toronto to address the Dieppe Veterans. He had previously warned his secretary, John Barratt, that he was widely blamed in Canada for having murdered the Canadians at Dieppe. Barratt assumed that this was exaggeration but changed his mind at dinner

when his neighbour assured him that Mountbatten had deliberately withdrawn air support from the operation, had insisted on a frontal attack against
all advice, and had persisted with the raid even though he knew the date and
place had been discovered by the Germans. To judge by the reception given
him after his speech some, at least, of his critics revised their opinion, but the
prejudice lingered on. Mountbatten derived some consolation when after
dinner a 'slinky, sexy, rather attractive young lady' came over to him and
said: 'Lord Mountbatten, this is the thrill of my life. I have always been in love
with you.' He was flattered, but felt things were going too far when his
admirer first put both arms around his neck and then began to fondle him all
over. Embarrassed, he appealed for help. Two neighbours came to the rescue;
one was kicked on the shins, the other struck savagely in the kidneys.
Eventually the lady was carried struggling from the room. Mountbatten
regretted the inconvenience caused to his fellow diners, but: 'It is rather
gratifying at the age of 73!'[66]

# CHAPTER 50

## *Retirement: The Private Man*

For any member of the royal family the boundary between public and private life is hard to draw. Unless alone with his family or closest friends Mountbatten was always on duty. Some of those duties, however, were wished upon him by the Government; others were self-imposed. Into neither category can comfortably be fitted that curious incident, the *coup d'état* that never was.

This affair had its genesis in a visit paid to Broadlands in May 1968 by Hugh Cudlipp, Mountbatten's closest ally among the journalists of the day. The two men talked of what seemed to Mountbatten the dangerous decline in national morale. They speculated as to who might be found with the *élan* to inspire a resurgence in the country's spirits – Mountbatten's contribution being Barbara Castle. Knowing that his employer, Cecil King, chairman of the giant International Publishing Corporation, was keenly concerned about the same subject, Cudlipp fixed up a meeting at Mountbatten's London flat. Mountbatten's son-in-law, Lord Brabourne, who had little respect for King's wisdom or discretion, felt that the meeting would be a fruitful field for mischief and begged his father-in-law to cancel it. Mountbatten said that it was too late for that but agreed to invite Solly Zuckerman along to see fair play.

The record of the meeting as agreed between Mountbatten, Zuckerman and Cudlipp[1] has King inveighing against the fatuity of the Labour Government, sketching out a scenario of disintegrating authority, bloodshed in the streets, intervention by the military, and finally asking Mountbatten whether, in such circumstances, he would be prepared to take over as head of a Government of National Unity. Mountbatten turned to Zuckerman and asked his views. 'This is rank treachery,' said Zuckerman. '. . . I am a public servant and will have nothing to do with it. Nor should you, Dickie.' He then stormed from the flat, to be followed a few minutes later by King and Cudlipp, with Mountbatten courteously but firmly stating that he could not even contemplate such a proposition.

King's record of the meeting is significantly different. The meeting took place at Mountbatten's request. Solly Zuckerman left early, apparently embarrassed by Mountbatten's description of him as one of the greatest brains in the world. Mountbatten then made the running, emphasising the great anxiety felt by the Queen at the parlous state of the nation. When King suggested a time might come when someone would have to head a national government, Mountbatten said nothing to indicate that he would find the role unattractive. There was no talk of treason, no indignant exit by Solly Zuckerman.[2]

When asked why his version was so different to that of the others, King replied tersely: 'Old men forget. It happened thirteen years ago. I had a note of it, and they did not.' Cudlipp charitably suggests that Zuckerman mis-heard King, and read more into his words than was intended, while King mis-heard Zuckerman, and did not take in the fact that he was being accused of treachery. This does not explain how King could claim that Zuckerman was not even present for most of the discussion. It is really a question of whether one old man was more likely to forget than three old men. Mountbatten was not the only person capable of deluding himself, and certainly his comment in his diary for that day – 'Dangerous nonsense!' – seems more applicable to Cudlipp's account of the meeting than to King's. Two years later King wrote to suggest a further meeting. 'I well recall our meeting,' replied Mountbatten, 'but you will remember that at the end I definitely came to the conclusion that there was nothing I could do to help in the matter. I am afraid my views are unaltered.'[3] Mountbatten sent copies of the letters to Solly Zuckerman. 'As you can imagine,' he wrote, 'the last thing I want to do is to continue any conversation with him!'[4]

King may not have wholly misunderstood Mountbatten's reactions. His proposition was at least flattering. As Zuckerman wrote in his diary when the subject was revived some five years later: 'The fact of the matter is . . . that Dickie was really intrigued by Cecil King's suggestion that he should become the boss man of a "government".'[5] To Cudlipp Zuckerman remarked after the meeting: 'I wonder what Dickie would have said if I hadn't been there.'[6] But there is an ocean of difference between playing idly with the idea of taking power if it were offered in an emergency, and plotting actively to attain it. Nobody at the meeting said anything to suggest that a *coup d'état* was necessary or even possible, still less that steps should be taken to make it more likely. A collapse of authority was the danger to be feared, not the end to be sought. Yet when the story broke in 1981 the headlines told of military coups and conspiracies to overthrow the Government.

To judge by the article in the *Sunday Times*,[7] Lady Falkender, Wilson's political secretary, helped to foster the rumours. In an interview with Barrie

Penrose and Roger Courtiour it is stated that she referred to Lord Mountbatten as 'prime mover' in a plan to overthrow the Government by military coup. 'Mountbatten had a map on the wall of his office showing how it could be done.' This interview presumably took place in 1977, since in July of that year those enterprising journalists Penrose and Courtiour appealed for information to Lord Zuckerman. They said that they had been told that at the meeting in Mountbatten's flat military arrangements had been discussed, maps produced and points indicated where machine-guns were to be mounted.[8] Zuckerman replied that this was fantasy, but that was not enough to kill the story, especially since Harold Wilson seems somewhat inadvisedly to have confided to the Press Association that 'two people high up in the press approached Lord Mountbatten to discuss their plan for a coup', but that 'Mountbatten and Sir Solly Zuckerman sent them packing in the best quarter-deck manner'.[9] His remarks, if correctly quoted, were the more curious because Cudlipp's own account had been published in 1976. Indeed, the year before that, when *Private Eye* had first dropped dark hints about the plot, Mountbatten had shown Wilson the correspondence with Cudlipp in which the two men and Zuckerman had established an agreed record of what they remembered having taken place.[10]

The press made merry with the story for a few days but there were not enough straws to make even a modicum of bricks. King was the main victim; Mountbatten was only smeared by implication, since a vague impression was left in the minds of readers that there was no smoke without fire and that he had at least been guilty of indiscretion. Indiscretion was not an offence of which Mountbatten was invariably guiltless, but on this occasion, thanks perhaps to the promptings of Solly Zuckerman, he behaved with impeccable decorum.

Mountbatten's real views were well expounded in a conversation which he had with Harold Wilson late in 1974 while returning with the Prime Minister from Dublin.

> I told him I had been to the Eleven Club to dinner and there had been a general discussion on the state of the country, and everybody said they were looking for a national personality 'in the wings' to come out and lead the country in its crisis. They seemed to think of somebody like Winston Churchill ready to come forward when called. I pointed out to them that Winston Churchill was a Member of Parliament, in fact already had a seat in the Cabinet . . . and it was easy for him to take over when a National Government was formed. I pointed out that there was no such person in the wings now, except Harold Wilson himself, and somewhat to my astonishment they then

came round to thinking that he would in fact be an acceptable leader for the country if he formed a real National Government. This appeared to surprise Harold Wilson, too. I told him that they were all worried that he was trying to do a sort of balancing act between the Left and the Right wings of the Labour Party, whereas what he ought to be doing was keeping together all the people of good faith who wanted to see the monarchy and democracy survive and to prevent the Communists getting control through the trades unions.[11]

This was his constant refrain. Eight months later he was again lecturing the Prime Minister on the need for decisive action – 'all true patriots of any political persuasion would rally round him if he went out "on his charger with a drawn sword, and determined to do battle" against all those who were trying to bring the Government down by unrealistic wage claims or other attitudes'.[12] Mountbatten did hanker after strong leadership and a government of national unity, but he never contemplated this coming about except by constitutional means. His respect for legitimacy was profound, some might even say exaggerated. If he sometimes cherished Walter Mitty dreams of himself leading the country from the Slough of Despond, an essential part of the scenario would always have been monarch and political leaders in unison begging him to come to the rescue. It would have been hard to find a more unlikely participant in a plot to overthrow the rightful government.

He was, anyway, convinced that Wilson was an excellent Prime Minister. When Wilson had taken office again in 1974 he had insisted that it would only be for two years. On 9 December 1975 he reminded the Queen and the Speaker that this was his intention, and in mid March he duly resigned. 'He will be sadly missed, as I think he has done a good job,' noted Mountbatten. 'He certainly has saved the economic situation.'[13] When the Queen appointed Wilson a Knight of the Garter, Mountbatten rejoiced: 'To have a Labour Prime Minister, like her father had Attlee, is an excellent idea to keep a balance between parties and classes.'[14]


Politics however, in any form, played a small part in Mountbatten's life. He was associated with 179 organizations when he retired, ranging alphabetically from the Admiralty Dramatic Society to the Zoological Society. Some were honorary – like his membership of the All England Lawn Tennis and Croquet Club – others purely social, like Buck's or the United Hunts Club. Some represented his private hobbies, like the Magic Circle or the Society of Genealogists. In others he played an important role: the British-Burma Society, the British Commonwealth Ex-Services League, the Royal Life

Saving Society, the Royal Naval Film Corporation. Almost every one of these bodies would have been delighted if he had chosen to devote more of his time to their concerns; many of them begged him to do so. Instead, he made the centre of his interests a school which had no naval or even military connections and about which he had hardly heard before the 1960s.

The first Atlantic College was opened in 1962. It was, in effect, an international sixth-form college in the private sector – that is to say, a school for boys and girls aged between sixteen and eighteen, drawn from all countries, in theory preparing pupils for universities, and dependent for its income on private donations or the fees that pupils paid or which were paid on their behalf. It was modelled on the institutions created by the German pedagogue Kurt Hahn, with an emphasis on open-air pastimes and service to the community. Mountbatten had had a hand in the appointment of the first headmaster, Rear-Admiral Hoare, but had not given it much more thought until Lord Brabourne persuaded him to take on the chairmanship of the council. The ideals on which the school was founded appealed to him, and his imagination was captured by the vision of a chain of schools where young people from every country would grow up together, rising above narrow nationalism to mutual sympathy and understanding. Unabashedly elitist, he dreamt of a world in which leaders fostered by Atlantic Colleges would come to power in a score of countries, creating an international freemasonry based on trust and good will. He agreed to take on the charge, though insisting that the name should be changed to United World Colleges to emphasise its global appeal, and that an international council and secretariat should be set up.

His support for United World Colleges was as whole-hearted as anybody could have hoped for. He travelled endlessly, visiting thirty-six countries on their behalf, and even when engaged on other missions rarely missed a chance to proselytize. Opposition merely added zest to his efforts. When the Prime Minister of Sweden protested that the schools were 'just places for bringing up the children of the elite', Mountbatten retorted that this was true of the Swedish pupils, since the Government there provided no support, but that seventy per cent of the places were financed from scholarships and all the other Scandinavian countries sent pupils on this basis.[15]

When Kenneth Kaunda was in London Mountbatten left home at 6 a.m. so as to be at the Hilton Hotel in time to breakfast with him. He was disconcerted to be told by the Zambian High Commissioner that there would be no chance of a private conversation, since the President would have his Minister of Finance on one side and the British Government's representative, Lady Llewellyn-Davies, on the other. Undismayed, Mountbatten slipped into the dining-room and rearranged the place cards so that he was only one seat away from his prey. As soon as breakfast started, he leant across his neighbour to announce that he had a special message from the Prince of Wales which he had promised to transmit. Realizing that her chances of getting a word in edgeways were anyway slight, Lady Llewellyn-Davies suggested that they changed seats. Mountbatten accepted with alacrity.

> I then had twenty minutes uninterrupted conversation with Kenneth Kaunda and found him really interested in the United World College concept. I gradually worked him up, gave him a brochure and an aide memoire and told him exactly what I wanted him to do. He gave it some thought, then said: 'All right, I'll do everything you say.' We then stood up and dramatically shook hands on it.[16]

The ideal fund-raiser must be persuasive, persistent and shameless, all attributes that Mountbatten enjoyed in ample measure. He also realized that donors expected to get something for their money, and saw to it that they were satisfied — whether it was by a decoration, a weekend at Broadlands, a cup of tea at Buckingham Palace, or just flattery and gratitude. His resource-fulness was endless. Jeffrey Archer in 1969 was recruited as public relations officer to organize a gala evening. He suggested that Frank Sinatra, Bob Hope and Noel Coward should be recruited to entertain. Ridiculous, said Mount-batten; they were all much too old, nobody would come. He telephoned Bernard Delfont to ask what name would do most to help raise half a million pounds in an evening. 'Sinatra,' said Delfont. Convinced, Mountbatten called in his advisers. 'I've just had a wonderful idea . . . ,' he began. All went to plan until forty-eight hours before the concert, when Coward retired to hospital with pleurisy. Archer appealed for help. 'I could get David Frost,' said Mountbatten. '*I* could get David Frost,' retorted Archer. 'With Sinatra and Hope *anyone* could get David Frost. We need someone only *you* could get. Grace Kelly?' Impossible, said Mountbatten; only a few weeks before Prince Rainier had said he would never let his wife go on the stage again. Eventually Mountbatten said that he would try. First Princess Grace and then her husband were won over. It was typical of his flair for publicity that, though Grace Kelly had just spent a week in London without attracting any attention, her arrival for the concert was on the front page of every British and most foreign papers. The United World Colleges got their half million.[17]

He exploited ruthlessly friends and relations in pursuit of his aim. 'I do hope your lunch with Tito went off all right and that you were able to put in a word on behalf of the U.W.C.,' he wrote to the Queen. 'I am very worried to hear that it may be difficult for you to fit in a visit to the U.W.C. activities in the Singapore International School. . . . Could you not just drive through the school? It would be such a shot in the arm, particularly as you are our Patron.'[18] Sometimes the royal worm would turn. Mr Meurig Owen, headmaster of the school at Singapore, was invited aboard the royal yacht. 'Now you can tell Her Majesty all about United World Colleges,' said Mountbatten. 'No need to tell me, Mr Owen,' put in the Queen. 'I've heard it all often before.'[19]

Mountbatten's judgement of the dignitaries he met around the world tended to be based on their reaction to his blandishments. Occasionally other considerations proved even more decisive. After seeing the film *All the President's Men*, he announced sadly that he had really liked Nixon – 'he was always very friendly to me and very sensible about India, and helped me with the U.W.C., but he turned out to be a real crook and what he did was quite unforgivable'.[20]

Without Mountbatten the United World Colleges might never have got off the ground – certainly they would not have prospered as they did. He himself was sometimes disappointed by their slow and uncertain progress, but with schools in Wales, Canada, Italy and Singapore established before his retirement, the United States and Venezuela added through the efforts of the Prince of Wales, and the multi-racial school of Waterford in Swaziland accepted into the family, the second – Mountbatten – phase of their development is today well advanced. The addition of Waterford showed him at his most decisive. When an eloquent plea for its admission was made at the Eighth International Council Meeting, the more cautious members saw a range of difficulties – constitutional, financial and political. Mountbatten felt instinctively that it must be done; if the precedents prevented it, then a new precedent must be set. He spoke emphatically to that effect, took the meeting with him, and the deed was done.[21]

Not everyone would agree that the final result was worth the trouble. He was 'interested in peace, not education', he was apt to say.[22] Ne Win, ruler of Burma, for one, felt that it was not sensible to send Burmese students half way round the world if they were to return handicapped academically.[23] The International Baccalaureate, which is open to scholars at the United World Colleges, is not viewed with great respect by every national educational authority. Solly Zuckerman spent two days at St Donat's, the College in Wales, and was dismayed by what he felt to be inadequacies in the teaching of science and mathematics. 'This must all be very depressing to you,' he wrote to Mountbatten, 'but I see no point in pulling my punches. . . . Frankly I have a fear that from the point of view of education, Atlantic College falls between two stools.'[24] It was indeed depressing, retorted Mountbatten, but not for the suggested reasons. Science-teaching was already good and was rapidly improving. 'It is depressing that one of my greatest friends should have so completely misunderstood what we are doing at St Donat's.'[25]

Which verdict was the more correct will perhaps be shown only when the first generations of students have returned home and established themselves in their national lives. Will they preserve the internationalist ideas which they absorbed at school? If they do, will they be able to spread them effectively among their own people? Will Mountbatten's dream of a world in which the students of the United World Colleges have risen to leadership ever come about? The concept, anyway, is a noble one; successful or not, the experiment is surely worth the effort.

One of the main reasons put forward by Mountbatten's family to support their pleas that he should retire was that nobody else could put his archives in order. Mountbatten, like his parents before him, had hoarded almost every piece of paper that related to his life. From his successive posts he had acquired a treasure-house of documents, many of them of the utmost secrecy. Now he set out to put this formidable collection in good order and to enrich it still further by persuading his friends to return his letters or other relevant records and to write reminiscences of the experiences that they had shared. The destined end-product of this assiduous accumulation was the biography that would one day be prepared, a contingency he always professed to regard as a remote one – 'My family *tell* me someone may one day wish to write my story' – but nevertheless prepared for with exemplary thoroughness. From the early 1940s biographers had indeed been bombarding him with requests that they should be allowed to take him as a subject. His own choice would probably have been C. S. Forester, who was asked by the Ministry of Information in 1944 whether he would undertake the task. 'If ever there is to be a biography written about me (which God forbid),' wrote Mountbatten, 'there is no single writer I would be more willing to have as the author . . . since you undoubtedly succeed in capturing the spirit of the sea better than any other author I have read.'[26]

Forester having died in 1966, a new candidate would have had to be sought. Mountbatten, however, had by then been convinced that it would be better if his biographer were selected only after his death; otherwise, as he was apt to explain with disarmingly honest immodesty, the flattering portrait that would undoubtedly emerge would be attributed by his detractors to the excessive force of his own personality. To this resolution he kept, though he was usually ready to help in any enterprise touching on his career; ranging from the Official War Histories or Franklyn Johnson's scholarly analysis of the evolving machinery of defence to the colourful and somewhat brash *Freedom at Midnight*, an account of the transfer of power in India by Larry Collins and Dominique Lapierre. This last book is remarkable chiefly for the faithfulness with which it portrays the history of the period as Lord Mountbatten would have wished it to be seen. Not surprisingly, he loved it and recommended it to all his friends and relations, even sending the Queen, when she proved dilatory in reading it, a second copy with the key passages carefully side-lined. 'It is very accurate and brings back astonishing memories for me,' he told a friend. 'The book has already sold over half a million copies in the U.S.A., France, Spain and Italy, but is going badly in England where people don't want to read about any success I may have had in India! What old stick-in-the-muds the Conservatives are here!'[27] It is a disquieting reflection for the official biographer that Lord Mountbatten would undoubtedly have wished his story to be told in the manner of Mr Collins and Mr Lapierre.

Mountbatten was not wholly averse to giving his own account of his career, but chose to do so on film rather than on paper. Soon after he retired he was persuaded by John Brabourne to make himself available, together with all his records, for the preparation of a film series about his life. In return he would possess the foreign rights in the resulting films, to be exploited for the benefit of the Broadlands Trust, which was set up for his children and grandchildren.[28] From the first it was his intention that the film should not only be about his life, but that *he* should present and guide it at every stage. When in Malta, he was startled to be asked what part he would be playing in the serial.[29] He could have answered that he, the living Mountbatten, would be presenting himself, the historic Mountbatten, in a series which would be produced and directed by Peter Morley, written by John Terraine, in all which activities he proposed to play an active role. Confusion about the nature of the enterprise nevertheless persisted. In Colombo he attended the premiere of a film starring Raquel Welch. Shortly afterwards there appeared a story in *Weekend* headed 'Supremo to act with Sex bomb'. Mountbatten, it reported, was to 'co-star with the most talked-of woman in the film world, sex symbol Raquel Welch, in a film that is to be produced by a top-ranking organization in Britain. It is expected to be the most authentic war film ever to be made.' Two days later Mountbatten received a telegram from Lord Brabourne: 'As requested have signed contract for you to co-star in "Life and Times of Raquel Welch".'[30]

Mountbatten ranked professionalism high in his list of favoured qualities. In 1973 he watched with fascination Harold Macmillan's 'marvellous interview' on television. 'What a grand old operator he is!'[31] He was resolved to be a grand old operator himself and settled down to learn a new trade. His humility was as commendable as his assiduity; he was endlessly interested in every technical detail and, as in Combined Operations or SEAC, sought enlightenment and instruction from the men who knew, with indifference to the demands of protocol or personal dignity. 'So we discovered', wrote John Terraine, 'how a leader can dismiss despondency, bring encouragement in a black moment, and, by adding a joke or two, restore the pleasure which goes out of work when a situation goes sour.'[32] He had strong opinions but accepted the expert ruling unless he was convinced it was based on defeatism or the wish to avoid trouble. 'I found with Lord Mountbatten', wrote Howard Thomas, 'that in spite of his forceful personality he was susceptible to reasoned resistance, and there were several occasions when he gave in to determined argument.'[33] In Rangoon Mountbatten recorded:

> I had one of my usual small arguments about the script with John Terraine and warned Patricia that he was sure to see me off. Needless to say he did, though I was able to get my own back by pointing out a grammatical mistake which I insisted on correcting, as I had told him I wanted to speak like an educated man! That thrust got home, I hope, because when it comes to the actual text of the script I always feel I have to give way, and I must be honest and admit in the end he is usually right.[34]

Not everything went smoothly. Once, in Malta, Mountbatten found particular difficulty over a certain speech and was filmed seventeen times before the director gave up and shot the scene in two parts. 'I am told that this can happen to the greatest film stars!' Mountbatten consoled himself.[35] At other times the team were in trouble, thoroughly demoralized because of various technical setbacks. 'There is only one common factor running through all this and that appears to me to be the gross over-anxiety of all the staff at Television House to obtain absolute perfection. Evidently they are in such a state about making this the greatest Rediffusion picture ever that they are criticising every little thing done by the team out here.'[36]

Mountbatten's insatiable appetite for nostalgic reminiscences was richly fed by the travels which the filming made necessary. He visited almost every part of the world where he had played a role, renewed innumerable acquaintances, re-fought old battles and re-lived old experiences. There were moments of embarrassment. In Rangoon he found himself required to say that he knew the Burma National Army had aided the Japanese and been responsible for certain atrocities, but felt unable to get out a word until Patricia Brabourne had persuaded the Burmese captain attached to the party to walk with her out of earshot.[37] In Bangkok he wished to be filmed with the King, but the light in the Audience Chamber was inadequate and protocol evidently made it unthinkable that the two men should walk out into the garden. Queen Sirikit tried to make the King relent, but without success. Finally she agreed to come out into the garden by herself. 'Surely you won't wish me to be photographed alone with the Queen?' appealed Mountbatten. Sirikit took her husband by the sleeve and almost dragged him to the door.

'We walked along in front of the Palace, the Queen all radiant smiles and the King with a face like a boot. However, he relented sufficiently to say: "I am afraid my park is not as beautiful as your park at Broadlands," and then suddenly cheered up a bit.'[38]

Fresh problems arose when the films were made. Burke Trend, responsible for clearance on behalf of the British Government, asked to read the scripts instead of just seeing the films. He would be judging them, he rather rashly offered, 'in terms of official propriety (which is a more relevant term than "security" in this context)'. Mountbatten rose in outraged dignity. ' "Propriety" is a new issue,' he replied. '. . . I am sure you will agree that a former Supreme Commander/Viceroy/First Sea Lord/Chief of the Defence Staff must be allowed to decide for himself questions of Propriety and bear any criticism directed against him. I would not wish to shelter behind that form of Government clearance.'[39]

The series opened to immense popular and considerable critical acclaim. It was breaking all records, exulted Mountbatten. 'The very first programme was 2nd in the Top Twenty!'[40] The success was the more remarkable for the somewhat cautious attitude adopted by the television network. In London Howard Thomas put it on at the peak time of 9 p.m., but Lew Grade was less impressed and insisted on 10.30 p.m. for the rest of the country. Mountbatten protested. 'Howard must be mad, putting on your programme against the B.B.C. at nine!' retorted Grade. 'That's when the B.B.C. put on all those sexy plays with bad language. You'll get slaughtered. Now when I put on the programmes . . . there'll be no opposition.' He bet Mountbatten £500 that he would get better ratings than the London-based Thames Television. Howard Thomas reminded him of this when he had lost. 'I know, I've already sent Mountbatten my cheque,' replied Grade. He lit a new cigar and added: 'Cheap at the price, wasn't it?'[41]

Mountbatten was no less active when it came to selling the programmes to foreign countries. When the French complained that the Second World War programmes treated them unfairly he personally negotiated changes to the script and appealed to de Gaulle for support. The support was forthcoming and proved decisive.[42] It seemed that the Germans might reject the programmes on the grounds that the events leading up to the Second World War had been unfairly presented. Mountbatten was distressed. He had successfully changed the script to satisfy the French, he told Princess Margaret of Hesse; would she now ensure that the Germans realized that 'I am willing to change the script to meet any objection'.[43] That difficulty, too, was surmounted without any amendments of principle being introduced. The Americans proved more intractable. Even the support of Henry Ford II – invited to Broadlands for what Howard Thomas cynically surmised might prove to be 'the most expensive outing of his life'[44] – was not enough to convince the sceptical chiefs of the networks that a film about Mountbatten could win the audience that was essential if their advertising revenue was to be sustained. In the end the series was shown on P.B.S., the unsponsored national television programme, where it was conspicuously successful and was shown twice more in the following decade.

The success was deserved. *The Life and Times of Lord Mountbatten* was skilfully written and made, contained a rich harvest of fascinating historical photographs and film, and contrived to be consistently entertaining without vulgarizing the issues with which it dealt. As is almost inevitable in biographies and autobiographies, it understated the importance of the majority of those who took part by its concentration on the central figure, and inevitably, too, it simplified drastically the complex problems with which its hero was involved, but neither of these endemic weaknesses was unduly prominent. There can have been few who learnt nothing from the twelve hours of film.

To read Mountbatten's papers is to be amazed by the multiplicity of his interests and the energy with which he pursued them. One day he was opening a new College of Nautical Studies in Glasgow. He noticed that the tour of inspection omitted the fourth floor, so transferred to another lift and got himself taken there. As he suspected, he found a dozen or so workmen smoking, drinking and waiting for him to go. 'One of them was stretched flat out on his back having drunk too much, and when we arrived they offered us rum. I made the Lord Provost drink some too. I asked them if they were getting time and a half on a Saturday morning . . . and they said that was indeed the case.'[45] In Glasgow again, to launch a ship built for a rich Arab who was discontented by the consistently late delivery of British vessels, he insisted on meeting the shop stewards. Somewhat sheepishly they filed into the managerial quarters – their first visit to what they called 'The Golden Trough' – and drank and chatted with their visitor. He told them how close they were to losing any further orders and extracted a promise that no industrial problems would delay the work in future. It would be naive to imagine that Mountbatten's visit transformed the relationship between workers and employers, but one can still sympathize with his comment: 'What shocking bad man-management. They don't even have representatives of the shop stewards at the celebrations for the launching. No wonder they have industrial troubles!'[46]

Indeed, as he grew older he became increasingly sceptical about the merits of any kind of management, be it industrial or national. When he proposed to visit Spain in 1970 to launch a ship partly financed by his nephew Lord

Milford Haven, the Foreign Office said that they did not wish him to go. He replied that he would cancel the visit only if asked to do so in writing by the Prime Minister. The Foreign Secretary rang up to support his officials. Mountbatten asked how they proposed to stop him going – he would be flying direct from Paris in a private aircraft. It was for the sake of the people of Gibraltar, he was told. They would be discomfited if so notable a public figure appeared to support the country which was blockading them. Mountbatten promptly telegraphed the Governor of Gibraltar, Sir Varyl Begg, who said he had not the slightest objection to the visit. The ship was duly launched.[47]

His delight in stirring things up never faltered. Addressing the Congress of the Veterinary Association, he caused a furore by describing how his polo pony had been successfully treated by his physiotherapist, Charles Strong. This was contrary to all the rules of the profession. 'We have never been so embarrassed as we were today,' the President told the press afterwards. 'It came as a complete surprise. The Veterinary Surgeons Act of 1948 makes it an offence for anyone to treat an animal and be paid for it without first consulting a veterinary surgeon.' It can hardly have come as a surprise to the President, Mountbatten retorted; he had sent in a text of his address several days before.[48]

Whatever he did, he did with zest and in the expectation that there would be fun to be extracted from it. He went with the Queen to the Cup Final to watch his local team, Southampton. He knew little and cared less about football, but it was *his* team and he was nothing if not partisan. When Southampton won, 'The whole place went mad, but the Royal Box sat rather glumly, so I stood up by myself and cheered and waved and shouted.' He was then seventy-five.[49]

Trying to secure honours for his friends was a pastime which he found satisfying and diverting. Time and again he interceded to procure Noel Coward the Order of Merit or a knighthood. 'He is determined that I should have an honour of some sort,' Coward wrote in his diary. 'He's a dear friend, I must say. He seems to mind about me being decorated much more than I do.'[50] In due course Coward was knighted. Mountbatten was quickly in action once more. 'Sir Noel Coward' must be followed by 'Sir Charles Chaplin' – 'I am convinced it would be acclaimed world wide as an imaginative gesture to the greatest figure in cinema history, and he would be thrilled to be recognised as an Englishman.'[51] He continued to champion the cause of Auchinleck, suggesting that he, too, should be given the Order of Merit, a generous gesture in view of his intense pride at being himself one of the few Service recipients of the honour.[52] But he was never averse to adding to his own phenomenal collection. He was particularly pleased when given the Ethiopian Order of the Seal of Solomon, since Eisenhower, de Gaulle and the

Queen were the only other living foreigners to hold the honour. It was all the more gratifying because numbers were limited and Mountbatten's appointment meant that the Duke of Edinburgh would be fobbed off with the second-class Order of Sheba. At the luncheon which followed the Queen's Silver Jubilee service in St Paul's, Harold Macmillan maliciously remarked to a passing courtier: 'I hope you'll give us all a medal. Dickie will be so disappointed if you don't.' When the medal duly arrived, Macmillan observed: 'I'm afraid the fellow must have taken me seriously.'[53]

The honour which probably gave him more pleasure than any other came to him in January 1965, when Antony Head asked him whether he would consider taking over as Colonel of the Life Guards. He was, he told General Laycock, astounded by the suggestion (a remark not wholly consistent with Lord Head's assertion that Mountbatten had hinted broadly that he would like the job).[54] 'Only Angie [Lady Laycock] will fully appreciate my schoolboy delight at this unique honour, because she knows my weakness for uniforms.'[55] 'I am busy fitting my scarlet tunic, my white leather breeches, my very high jackboots, my helmet and my cuirasse,' he told an American friend. 'One of these days you must see me ride behind the Queen at Trooping the Colour . . . as her Gold Stick!'[56] His sisters were pleased but derisive. 'Congratulations on your new appointment. Nothing surprises me any more,' telegraphed the Queen of Sweden; while at tea at Buckingham Palace before the Lifeguards' Ball, Princess Alice noticed that her brother was given a special pot of Indian tea. 'Well, really!' she said. 'He always was a spoilt child. And as for all this fancy dress!'[57]

Mountbatten took his role in the ceremony of Trooping the Colour with becoming seriousness. Two weeks before the event his charger would be brought down to Broadlands and, dressed in helmet, thigh boots and hacking jacket, Mountbatten would ride around the Hampshire lanes, chatting affably with the farmers whom he met upon his way. The tradition was that the Colonels of the Life Guards and Horse Guards alternated as Gold Stick, riding in close attendance on the Queen. His first year it was the turn of the Life Guards; the second year he agreed that the Horse Guards should have the honour; however, since he was also personal A.D.C. to the Queen, he insisted that he must attend the parade as well.[58] His other duties as Colonel were minimal, but he made a point of interviewing every would-be officer, was a frequent visitor at the Life Guards' barracks and studied the particulars of the men he met as diligently as if they had been his crew in *Kelly*.

The farmers around Broadlands did not only know Mountbatten as a curiously dressed eccentric riding the lanes on his ceremonial charger. Putting the estate on an economic basis became one of his most absorbing activities. Typically, he set up a committee to help with its administration. 'Although my idea of having these Estate Committee meetings was unpopular at first, I think everybody now agrees that this is the finest way of administering a large estate,' he wrote hopefully in his diary.[59] Certainly Broadlands prospered, though its success probably owed as much to the financial acumen of John Brabourne as to his father-in-law's committee. Mountbatten was no farmer; until the Queen broke the news to him he did not even know that a cow had to have calves before giving milk. His ignorance, however, did not affect his readiness to have an opinion on any point. He wished to be consulted on everything, from the sale or purchase of a farm to the redecoration of a lavatory. When Charles Smith, the butler, put in hand the latter operation without waiting for his master to return from abroad, Mountbatten was enraged. Smith was berated roundly, but a few days later Mountbatten addressed him: 'Maybe, Charles, I was a bit hasty. I've given it some thought, but I can't think of any design I would have chosen in preference to yours.'[60]

The planting of commemorative trees in the park at Broadlands was hardly an affair for the Estate Committee, but it still caused Mountbatten great concern. Any truly eminent visitor to Broadlands was required to plant a tree, and since eminent visitors came thick and fast, the trees multiplied. When the Dalai Lama visited nearby Petworth, Mountbatten was reluctant to miss so rare an opportunity. He implored the Lama to come to Broadlands for a night, or at least for a meal. The invitations were refused. He offered to fly over in a helicopter and bring the Lama back to Broadlands for half an hour. The answer was the same. Eventually Mountbatten flew to Petworth with two pots, one containing earth, one a tree. The Dalai Lama was required to transplant the tree from one pot to the other. The tree then returned to Broadlands and was interred, with a notice recording that it had been potted by the Dalai Lama.[61] Mountbatten succeeded in having a short conversation with the Lama, in which he urged him to open some line of communication with the Chinese, otherwise he would never get back to Tibet. He was enchanted when the Lama, trying to say that his country had been beggared by the Chinese, said instead that it had been buggered.[62] But though the visit was enjoyable, the operation failed in its main purpose. The tree died.

Such fancies were peripheral, however; his main object was to place Broadlands on a sound financial footing. Partly this was to secure it for his descendants, partly because he himself was acutely conscious of the need for money. From the time of Edwina's death he felt alarm about his own solvency; once his retirement freed him to brood upon the subject it began to bulk large in his mind. The National Electronic Research Council was his brainchild, founded, in his own words, 'to make sure Britain did not neglect the key to the future – electronics'.[63] But he also viewed it as a source of income, shocking some of the senior civil servants by holding out for a salary of £12,000 a year to start from the time he resigned as C.D.S.[64] 'I have a really strong feeling that the industry is looking to you not primarily as Chairman of NERC but as a "pressure group" on the Government,' warned Ronald Brockman. '. . . I honestly cannot believe that they are prepared to pay you the large sum of money mentioned just for being Chairman of NERC.'[65] Mountbatten was, indeed, short of money compared with the affluent days of the 1930s, but he was a great deal richer than most of the people with whom he dealt. His standard of living was not seriously threatened. The elderly are notoriously inclined to believe that they are richer or poorer than they really are. Mountbatten was in the second camp. The fault lay perhaps in his childhood, when his parents had been conspicuously poor relations of the royal family, perhaps in the efforts of Lord Brabourne to impose some sort of order on his father-in-law's finances. Whatever the cause, a belief that he could not afford this or that non-essential shadowed Mountbatten's final years. The worry never swelled to the dimensions of an obsession, but it was apparent enough to cause distress to those who loved him.

ABOVE *Classiebawn. Ben Bullen is hidden by clouds in the background.*
BELOW *Broadlands.*

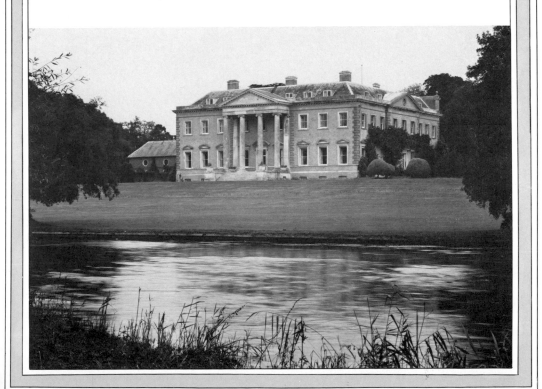

*A ride along the beach at Classiebawn. Mountbatten is flanked by Pamela and Patricia, with Joanna coming up on the right.*

*Mountbatten, in favourite overcoat and hat, instructs the Queen in photography, a science in which he was notoriously unskilled.*

LEFT *With Cary Grant and his favourite actress, Shirley Maclaine.* BELOW *The tree-planting ceremony at Broadlands. The celebrity on this occasion is Yehudi Menuhin.*

*Mountbatten (left) with Patricia at the Calgary Stampede and (below) presenting a cup for polo to his 'honorary grandson', the Prince of Wales.*

LEFT *Mountbatten and John Brabourne each holds his portrait painted by Derek Hill, who sits between them.* BELOW *In helmet, high boots and hacking jacket, practising at Broadlands for the ceremony of Trooping the Colour.*

ABOVE *A family group including Solly Zuckerman aboard* Shadow V. BELOW *Playing trains with grandson Michael-John, who appears to be rather left out of things.*

*Mountbatten talking with his dog.*

# CHAPTER 51

# *The Shop-steward of Royalty*

RETIREMENT IN NO WAY DIMINISHED the satisfaction Mountbatten felt at his relationship with the royal families of Europe, while it gave him more time to foster it. His prestige, his popularity, his vast experience, his wisdom over everybody's problems except his own won him a unique position. He was honorary uncle to the courts of Europe: adviser, matchmaker, honoured guest; sometimes felt to be an infernal nuisance but always respected, listened to and liked.

Because the King was his brother-in-law, it was with Sweden that his links were closest. In Stockholm in 1969 the King's grandson and heir, Carl Gustaf, told Mountbatten that most of his student friends were republicans and he feared for the future of the monarchy. Mountbatten 'tried to buck him up by saying that as he developed and became better known, agitation for a republic would die down', but he did not have much confidence in his own prophecy.[1] When, two years later, Carl Gustaf first took the chair at a Cabinet committee, Mountbatten noted approvingly how much progress he had made, but went on, 'at present there doesn't seem very much hope of his being able to retain the crown after his grandfather's death, but let us hope for the best'.[2]

He did more than hope. Mountbatten convinced himself that the best chance lay in the King abdicating so as to give his grandson a chance to establish himself while the old monarch was still alive. With some courage he tackled his brother-in-law.

> After sleepless nights, thinking over this problem in the light of the long term interests of the Monarchy, I came again and again to the unavoidable question. Have you ever in your heart of hearts given any thought to one way which would be almost certain to solve the problem, although I fear distressing to contemplate?
>
> Only my unbounded admiration and deep devotion to you, and my conviction that your over-riding wish is to see the Monarchy continue gives me the courage to pose the question. Have you ever considered retiring in favour of Carl Gustaf on your 90th birthday [November 1972]? . . .

You can, of course, tell me to go to the Devil and mind my own
business and I will loyally accept your rebuke, but I could not keep
silence merely out of cowardice.[3]

He was not told to go to the Devil, but King Gustaf did not give much
hope of progress.[4] The atmosphere became frostier when Mountbatten
reverted to the topic the following year. Gustaf had unwisely referred to his
father, another nonagenarian monarch, as old and obstinate. Just like you,
retorted Mountbatten: 'You are a very old King and have become just as
obstinate.' Gustaf insisted that the constitution did not allow him to retire
unless mentally incapacitated, and became quite heated, but by the time
Mountbatten left all was forgiven: 'We embraced each other emotionally,
almost tearfully. What a sweet and wonderful person he is.'[5]

It proved to be a final farewell. Gustaf died in September 1973. Mountbatten represented the Queen at the funeral. 'I understand on all hands Carl
Gustaf has done magnificently,' he wrote in his diary. 'It is all very exciting if
the young man has suddenly developed to the point at which he can make the
Monarchy live and able to continue.'[6] But Carl Gustaf was still a bachelor
and Mountbatten was convinced that it was essential he should remedy the
deficiency as soon as possible. Even before Gustaf died, he had tried to
engineer a meeting between the young prince and a Rumanian princess. The
Queen accused him of being no better than a medieval matchmaker. 'I replied
that I was about the only one left, and how did she think kings and crown
princes found the right brides in the old days of many monarchies! Let's hope
I can pull it off!'[7] Carl Gustaf showed no enthusiasm but Mountbatten was
not discomfited. When the young King came to Broadlands he found Lady
Jane Wellesley in attendance, unsuspecting the destiny that her host had
planned for her. 'They appeared to get on very well together and I hoped
something might come of it but, alas, nothing did,'[8] wrote Mountbatten
sadly. Next year he resolved to try again with Lady Leonora Grosvenor, but
she inconsiderately became engaged to Lord Lichfield before the chosen
weekend, so Jane Wellesley was called upon again. This time the King took a
note of her name and address, but Mountbatten was sceptical about his
intentions.

He was proved right when Carl Gustaf told him of his wish to marry a
German commoner, Silvia Sommerlath. He had expected opposition but
instead got strong support. If the Swedes wanted to democratize the royal
family, Mountbatten argued, it was entirely proper for the King to democratize the Queen. The important thing was to do it quickly, preferably before
the forthcoming state visit to Britain. 'He looked very surprised and said he
thought that would be too quick.'[9] Mountbatten's advice was consistent with

his views on royal brides or bridegrooms; blue blood was desirable but a long way behind a range of other qualities.

Greece was another country with which he was closely associated. King Constantine told General Norstad that he looked on Mountbatten as one of his chief advisers, and Norstad replied that he could not have made a better or wiser choice.[10] When the military coup took place in 1967, Mountbatten stoutly insisted that it must have been staged without the King's knowledge and against his will.[11] Next year the King went into exile. Mountbatten wrote to tell him

> . . . how much I personally admire your courage in standing up to the reactionary Colonels and doing your best to rally the country against them. It is a tragedy that your plan went wrong. . . .
>
> I am so glad to hear you are keeping in touch with all the Greek democratic forces, as you have made yourself the focal point of constitutional democracy.
>
> I do not see how you could return on the basis of a bogus constitution, imposed by the Colonels and possibly adopted by a fraudulent plebiscite.[12]

Mountbatten devoted himself to ensuring that King Constantine was kept in touch with the leaders of the West and maintained their support for his cause. He never doubted that the power which could most readily change the future of Greece was the United States. In 1970 he was proselytizing in the White House, urging Nixon and William Rogers to recognize that the Colonels' regime was a greater threat to democracy and the West than the left-wing regime that they feared would replace it. When Rogers suggested that the King should come to terms with the Colonels and return to his throne, Mountbatten argued that he, too, would then be tarred with the fascist brush. 'If they refuse to implement the new Constitution and are eventually thrown out . . . the King will then be thrown out too. And the great danger is that the Communists may then seize power.'[13] He invoked the Communist bogey again three years later when he raised the matter with the Deputy Secretary of State, and Mr Rush said that the main object of the United States was to preserve a stable government. Rush was apparently impressed but 'he seemed a very weak character', noted Mountbatten.[14]

The situation resolved itself a few months later when the military regime crumbled and Karamanlis became President. A plebiscite on Greece's future form of government was held and went against the monarchy by two to one. Mountbatten was saddened but never lost hope. 'I believe that you are necessary for the future stability and well-being of Greece,' he wrote to Constantine. At all costs the King must return to Greece.

> I fear it will be some time before anything can be changed, but I refuse to believe it is possible for a young and attractive couple, with very sweet children, to stay long in a country without becoming known again as you were seven years ago. As people begin to know you and your reasonable attitude I am sure the hostility will change.[15]

He had better luck in Spain. Franco had selected the young Prince Juan Carlos as Spain's King and his own eventual successor. The Prince's father, Don Juan, saw no reason why he should be by-passed. Mountbatten talked to Don Juan at his sister Alice's funeral, invited him to Broadlands and continued the discussion. 'I urged him to execute a legal Instrument of Abdication to be issued by him on the evening before you became King so that the world can see you are the legal King in your own right and not the puppet of a dictator.'[16] When he saw Nixon in Washington he preached the virtues of constitutional monarchy and the need for Franco to hand over the reins before he died: 'Only you, Mr President, are in a powerful enough position to tell him this.'[17] Whether Franco was told or not, Juan Carlos was eventually to emerge as King. Mountbatten watched his progress with avuncular pride. After a few days' stay with Juan Carlos at Zarzuela he wrote to thank him for 'the fabulous caviare', the 'delightful cinema with its shocking Lesbians'; but most of all what thrilled him was 'the tremendous way you have increased your popularity with the people – that is a great personal triumph for both of you'.[18]

Not surprisingly, Mountbatten believed that the best hope for fledgling democracy in Spain was that it should maintain a close relationship with Britain. The existence of Gibraltar made such a rapport difficult to achieve. In the long run Mountbatten felt some sort of internationalization was the only future for Gibraltar, but the immediate object must be to reduce its significance as an irritant. He conferred with Alec Douglas-Home and the British Ambassador at Madrid and told Juan Carlos 'we 3 agreed relations between our countries would greatly improve once the Gibraltar blockade was lifted'.[19] It became his preoccupation to bring Juan Carlos together with British politicians of varying persuasions, though to arrange meetings between prominent socialists and the protégé of Franco called for some diplomatic skills. Evidently he was not wholly satisfied with his efforts, since in 1976 he stage-managed a visit by the King to Sandringham. This, he was sure, 'would get our curious Labour government to see you in the right light, for up to now they don't seem to have understood the tremendous work you are doing in liberalising the constitution'.[20]

*

One royal claimant whose cause he did not espouse was the putative Anastasia. Mountbatten steadfastly refused to countenance the claim of Anna Anderson that she was his cousin, the Russian princess miraculously saved from the massacre at Ekaterinburg. A few of Anastasia's adherents detected something sinister in his attitude, and imagined lost fortunes of which he would have been the beneficiary if none of the Russian royal family had survived. This added unnecessary mystery to what was already mysterious enough. Mountbatten had nothing to gain from the suppression of the truth, if truth it was; indeed, his romantic temperament and strong sense of history would have rejoiced if his cousin had turned out to be still alive. He had been convinced, however, that she was an impostor and he joined with the rest of his family in contesting her claims in the courts. When the B.B.C. proposed to send a representative to interview Frau Anderson, he protested vigorously. 'I can assure you that there is not the remotest doubt that this woman is not my cousin,' he told Ian Jacob, then serving as Director of Overseas Services. 'She was seen by all our closest mutual relations, all of whom declared that there was no resemblance.' Mountbatten recounted all the reasons why Anna Anderson could not really be his cousin, and begged Jacob not to let the B.B.C. abet her backers who 'simply get rich on the royalties of further books, magazine articles, plays etc.' The interview was cancelled; indeed, Jacob was able to tell Mountbatten that a decision to drop it had been made even before his letter was received.[21]

Mountbatten appointed himself as special negotiator between the royal family and the Duke and Duchess of Windsor. The results were not entirely happy. The two men were still able to enjoy each other's company, reminiscing about old times. 'I dined alone with David,' Mountbatten recorded in February 1970. 'Wallis was away "resting" so David and I had a delightful evening entirely to ourselves.'[22] But the old sores had never healed. Repeatedly the Duke would revert to his old complaint that the Duchess had never been created a Royal Highness. 'I explained that it was his own mother's opposition, then followed by his sister's and sister-in-law's . . . which really made it impossible, and I advised him to give up the struggle.'[23] The Duke could never give up. He and his wife, for their part, were irritated by Mountbatten's endless interest in such of their possessions as he felt should properly return to England. 'Who are you going to leave that to? I think that should go to Charles,' was his refrain. 'How dare he!' the Duke once exclaimed indignantly. 'He even tells me what *he* wants left to him!'[24]

The Duke of Windsor died on 28 May 1972. He was buried at Windsor and the Duchess was invited to stay at Buckingham Palace for the funeral.

Mountbatten was asked by the B.B.C. to broadcast a tribute to the former King. At first he refused, saying that he had done nothing similar at the death of George VI, but he was persuaded that it was essential for some member of the family to pay a public tribute and that he was the obvious man. He told the Duchess of his plan and said that he would feel bound to say how much he had disapproved of the abdication. 'You are quite right. I disapproved of it, too,' rejoined the Duchess. 'I spent a long time over a very bad telephone line from France begging him not to abdicate. I went so far as to say if he abdicated I would not marry him!'[25] The tribute was brief and elegantly evasive. 'He was more than my best man, he was my best friend all my life,' said Mountbatten – a piece of hyperbole which can be forgiven in the circumstances. 'What a great debt the people of this country, and indeed the whole Commonwealth, owe him for all he did for us when he was Prince of Wales. Nobody who knew him then can ever forget him.'[26]

Mountbatten was charged with meeting the widow at the airport. He found her extremely nervous at having to confront the whole royal family without her husband's support. She was 'particularly worried about Elizabeth, the Queen Mother, who, she said, never approved of her'. 'Your sister-in-law will receive you with open arms,' Mountbatten reassured her. 'She is so deeply sorry for you in your present grief and remembers what she felt like when her own husband died.'[27] Mountbatten took her to St George's Chapel where the Duke was lying in state.

> At the end she stood again looking at the coffin, and said in the saddest imaginable voice: 'He was my entire life. I can't begin to think what I am going to do without him, he gave up so much for me, and now he has gone. I always hoped that I would die before him.'
>
> Then Charles and I saw her off. She kept on telling me what a charming young man Charles was and what a comfort. Charles certainly was splendid in supporting her.
>
> . . . I must say I am desperately sorry for her – she is so lonely and sad, and yet kept saying how wonderful the family were being to her, and how much better the whole thing had gone than she had expected.[28]

Mountbatten now devoted himself to ensuring that the Duke's estate eventually returned to Britain. When he visited the Duchess during 1973 he found to his dismay that she had dismissed her English solicitor in favour of her French lawyer, Maître Suzanne Blum. Hopefully, Mountbatten volunteered to act as executor of her will and to find another English lawyer associated with the royal family. The Duchess was unenthusiastic about the offers. She seemed cautiously receptive to Mountbatten's suggestion that a foundation should be set up, perhaps with the Prince of Wales as chairman, which would distribute the income from the Duke's estate to suitable charities,[29] and Mountbatten eagerly visited the Duchess in July, hoping to clinch the matter. To his dismay he found Maître Blum on guard. It was a highly unsatisfactory interview. 'She began by saying that she could give me no information as she did not have any authority to disclose the Duchess's testamentary dispositions.' Mountbatten insisted on asking the Duchess herself what her intentions were, but the only reply he got was that she proposed 'to honour her husband's memory'.[30]

Whether Mountbatten or Suzanne Blum was better qualified to interpret the Duchess's true desires is not something which an outsider can readily decide; the lawyer, anyway, was in possession of the field. That she had at least the tacit support of the French Government seems clear; a British lawyer who visited Paris on the same quest found that 'Lord Mountbatten's name always seemed to arouse a degree of apprehension' because it was felt that his influence might prejudice negotiations with the French Treasury.[31] Mountbatten still tried to re-open negotiations but in December 1974 received a rebuff that even he recognized must be final.

> As to the depositions in my will [wrote the Duchess], I confirm to you once more that everything has been taken care of according to David's and my wishes, and I believe that everyone will be satisfied. There is therefore no need of your contacting my advisor in Switzerland. It is always a pleasure to see you, but I must tell you that when you leave me I am always terribly depressed by your reminding me of David's death and my own, and I should be grateful if you would not mention this any more.[32]

Only after the Duchess's death will it be possible to establish whether everyone is indeed satisfied. If the final result is as unappealing to the British as Mountbatten feared, then there will be some grounds for thinking that he contributed to the disaster by pushing for what he wanted with excessive and sometimes tactless zeal. His conduct was, however, inspired only by his devotion to and eagerness to be associated with the British royal family.

So also was the long-drawn-out saga of the name Mountbatten-Windsor. According to Mountbatten, it was the Labour Home Secretary, Chuter Ede, who suggested that Prince Philip, being short of a surname, should take the name Mountbatten.[33] The lawyer and genealogist Edward Iwi, who was Mountbatten's most stalwart ally in this battle, argued from this that the Queen must be the first sovereign of the House of Mountbatten.[34] This pleasing development was, however, short-lived; only two months after her accession the Queen pronounced that the royal House should be that of

Windsor and that her descendants should bear that surname.[35] 'Personally, I think it was Beaverbrook's hatred of me coupled with Winston's disenchantment with what I did in India that brought all this about,' wrote Mountbatten in some dudgeon.[36] It seems in fact to have been Queen Mary who was responsible: her husband, she protested, had founded the House of Windsor *in aeterno*, and no Battenberg marriage could change it.[37] Mountbatten was disconsolate but not defeated. The next round began with Queen Mary safely dead, shortly before Prince Andrew was born in 1960. Dr Bloomer, Bishop of Carlisle, announced that he did not like to think of any child born in wedlock being deprived of the father's family name. The Bishop had been inspired by Mr Iwi to make this pronouncement, and certainly it came as no surprise to Mountbatten.[38] The words fell on carefully prepared ground. On 8 February 1960 the Queen announced in Council that, with certain qualifications, her descendants in future should bear the name 'Mountbatten-Windsor'. She had long wished, said the royal Press Secretary, to associate her husband's name with their descendants.[39] Mountbatten was enraptured. 'Will you tell Jawaharlal all about it in confidence . . . ,' he asked Edwina. 'It would be so nice if he could inspire an enthusiastic reply, saying how pleased the Indians will be to know that the important part Philip is now playing should be recognised in this admirable way.'[40] It seemed that the battle was won. Mountbatten's mind, however, was not entirely at ease. There had been suggestions that members of the royal family bore no surname at all. 'When Anne marries in November,' he wrote to the Prince of Wales in the spring of 1973, 'her marriage certificate will be the first opportunity to settle the Mountbatten-Windsor name for good.' The father's name would undoubtedly be Mountbatten. '. . . if you can make quite sure . . . that her surname is entered as Mountbatten-Windsor it will end all arguments. I hope you can fix this.'[41] It was as Mountbatten-Windsor that Princess Anne was married. Even then constant vigilance was needed to safeguard the position. In 1978 he wrote indignantly to protest that a spokesman for the royal family had been quoted as saying that the sacred surname was 'devised as a matter of convenience and in that sense is unofficial'. He was assured that the spokesman had been misquoted; all he had meant to say was that the hyphenated surname was a convenient way of associating the Duke of Edinburgh's name with the Queen's.[42] Mountbatten was appeased, but ready to spring to arms again as soon as there was a new threat to beat off.

His role as champion of the royal family was not confined to skirmishes with Maître Blum. When James Cameron remarked on Granada Television that Mountbatten in India had done 'an extraordinary job of political manipulation without knowing anything about politics. . . . In fact, he is the only Royal who has ever done a constructive job as far as I know,' Mountbatten took exception to the suggestion that he did not understand politics: 'But what I really objected to was the implied rudeness to the rest of the Royal Family.'[43] His loyalty to the family was unwavering, his influence not so great as he liked to imagine but still considerable. He often urged the Queen towards a course of action: 'Why don't you say such-and-such to the Prime Minister?' 'I should refuse to see so-and-so.' She would listen politely, sometimes take the advice, sometimes not. His grasp of what was practicable or desirable in a constitutional monarchy was not so firm that he could be followed blindly. On personal matters his touch was surer. Prince Philip wanted to shoot on the day after Churchill's death; Mountbatten said he thought it undesirable; Prince Philip was unconvinced; 'Well, I won't anyway,' said Mountbatten, and in the end the shoot was cancelled.

He was not always so successful at swaying his nephew's conduct. The Duke of Windsor wrote to complain that Prince Philip had visited Paris without getting in touch with him. 'Maybe neither he nor I would find an encounter rewarding. Still, as a former King, as well as an uncle by marriage, I consider his recent behaviour to me, in a foreign land, extremely bad manners.' When they had last met, the Duke said, Mountbatten had claimed that he had taught Prince Philip everything 'and had trained him for his present position. There is, however, one elementary subject which I am afraid you must have overlooked in his curriculum, the simple practice of courtesy.' He had never claimed to have taught Prince Philip anything, Mountbatten replied mildly. He had written to the Prince about the Duke of Windsor's complaint and would raise it again when they met at Sandringham.[44] No doubt he did so, but he can have had few illusions about the likely response. Yet Mountbatten's affection for his nephew never lessened. 'I've always been very fond of you from a small boy upwards,' he told him in 1972, 'but I feel that in the last year or two we have grown much closer together. . . . Patricia and Pammy could not be sweeter or more affectionate daughters, but one does miss sons – so I am very lucky to have you and John who are both so affectionate and nice to me.'[45] He genuinely admired the work his nephew was doing and felt that critics like James Cameron were ill-informed and unfair. 'You sometimes seemed rather disappointed, perhaps frustrated would be a better word,' he wrote after a cruise in the Royal Yacht *Britannia* in 1974, 'but I feel you underestimate your effect on the U.K., and especially the Commonwealth. I hear more and more praise and appreciation from people in all walks of life.'[46]

His advice on public relations was particularly cogent. He was concerned by the bad impression which was caused by the ever-increasing cost of the monarchy, especially given the press's interest in the Queen's allegedly enormous private fortune. 'Unless you can get an informed reply published

making just one point, the image of the monarchy will be gravely damaged . . . ,' he told Prince Philip. 'It is true that there is a fortune, which is very
big, but the overwhelming proportion (85%?) is in pictures, *objets d'art*,
furniture etc. in the three State-owned palaces. The Queen can't sell any of
them, they bring in no income.' What was needed was an authoritative article
on the subject in *The Times* which would be picked up by the press of the
world; otherwise people would continue to resent being asked to pay more
and more while the Queen economized on her '£100m fortune'. 'So will you
both please believe a loving old uncle and NOT your constitutional advisers,
and do it.'[47] His advice tended always towards the radical; the scrapping of
traditions unless they were useful or ornamental; the modernization of the
mechanism of the monarchy. He wanted to see more black faces among the
Household Brigade, jokingly suggesting the creation of a regiment to be called
the 'Blackguards'. Pomp and ceremony were to his taste, but the arcane
mystery of the throne held little appeal. Brisk efficiency was what he sought.

He delighted in his membership of the royal family. After a trip in
*Britannia* he wrote that he had loved being aboard a naval vessel again, 'but
what moved me most of all is the increasing kindness of Lilibet and Philip who
treat me more and more as a really intimate member of their immediate
family'.[48] After the Jubilee thanksgiving service he hung back discreetly when
the family went out on to the balcony at Buckingham Palace to acknowledge
the cheering crowd. The Queen insisted that he join the rest of the family.

He relished the royal tours in *Britannia* above all; the jokes and informal-
ity when the ship was at sea, the grandeur and consequence of the state
occasions. He had always been a devotee of funny stories and used to bandy
them over the table with George VI, each provoking the other to fresh
excesses. When the King died, Princess Margaret inherited his mantle. She
shared with Mountbatten a passion for perverted proverbs, such as that
inspired by the team of pelota players who all tried to get out at the same time
through the revolving doors of the hotel in which they were staying. Their
impatience was very properly punished when the door collapsed on top of
them and killed them all. Moral: never put all your Basques into one exit. One
of the royal tours was believed by Mountbatten to have given rise to another
of these monstrosities. A tribal chief had two thrones which had last been
used in the days of King George V. As his grass hut was rather small, he had
them pulled up on ropes into the roof. Unfortunately, when the time came to
use them again, the ropes broke and the thrones crashed down on top of the
chief. As he died, the moral no doubt flashed through his mind: people in
grass houses shouldn't stow thrones.[49]

He was a rewarding guest, even if sometimes he did push rather far his
mania for acquiring and retailing information. Prince Philip told Solly

Zuckerman that he would not bother him with any comments about Easter Island, 'but be warned, Dickie having studied the problem "in depth"is quite ready to explain it to anyone whether they are prepared to listen or not!'[50]

Any expedition was made more pleasurable by the presence of the royal children. Mountbatten admired Princess Anne's toughness and quick wits. He was with the Queen and Prince Philip on a visit to Indonesia when the news came of the attempt to kidnap Princess Anne from her car in The Mall. He congratulated the Prince on the courage she had shown. 'If the man had succeeded in abducting Anne she would have given him a hell of a time while in captivity,' commented her proud father.[51] But, except for their affection for horses, Princess Anne and her great-uncle had little in common. It was her brother, the Prince of Wales, who was to preoccupy Mountbatten as much as any of his own grandchildren in the last decade of his life.

Mountbatten had been one of the panel of sages – the others being the Prime Minister, the Archbishop of Canterbury, the Chairman of the Vice Chancellor's Committee and the Dean of Windsor – who in 1965 were called in to advise on Prince Charles's education and career. The result, with its healthy emphasis on the Royal Navy, was entirely to his liking. It was not till seven years later, however, when the Prince of Wales was posted to Portsmouth, that the two grew really close. Broadlands was near enough to make frequent visits easy and when H.M.S. *Norfolk* was in dry dock there was ample time for leisurely conversations. 'It's lovely having him here,' Mountbatten wrote in his diary, 'we've had so many cosy talks. What a really charming young man he is.'[52] A year later he had graduated to the rank of 'honorary grandson'. 'As you know only too well, to me it has become a second home in so many ways,' wrote the Prince, when he left Broadlands to embark on a six months' cruise, 'and no one could *ever* have had such a splendid honorary grandpapa in the history of avuncular relationships.'[53] Mountbatten found that the Prince's departure left a sad gap; he had grown used to his continual visits and felt lonely and deprived without them. 'I've been thinking of you – far more than I had ever expected to think of a young man – but then I've got to know you so well, I really miss you very much.'[54]

They wrote to each other frequently. The Prince decided that he knew far too little about the history of the Royal Navy: 'I was wondering whether you could recommend me some worthwhile books that might improve my knowledge.'[55] The fact that Mountbatten was a relation but not a parent, his age, his eminence, his tolerance and readiness to examine and accept new ideas, all made it inevitable that the Prince of Wales would take from him advice and warning that he would have rejected from any other quarter. 'I was deeply grateful for our conversation yesterday morning and being able to pick your brains on the subjects was an *immense* help,' wrote the Prince a year before his great-uncle died. 'As I said to you yesterday, I have no idea what we shall do without you when you finally decide to depart. It doesn't bear thinking about, but I only hope I shall have learnt *something* from you in order to carry it on in some way or another.'[56]

The fact that the Prince was more likely to heed Mountbatten's injunctions than those of anybody else was not ignored by the courtiers. His private secretary, David Checketts, appealed for help when he discovered that his employer had become addicted to hot-air ballooning. 'Your influence on the Prince of Wales is enormous,' he wrote, 'and he has an immense admiration and respect of your wise advice and guidance. I would therefore be everlastingly grateful of your valuable help in avoiding or restraining some of the more adventurous and dangerous endeavours of this remarkable young man.'[57] Mountbatten was no stranger to adventurous and dangerous endeavours himself and, given half a chance, would probably have joined the Prince in his balloon. Regretfully, however, he accepted that the heir to the throne already ran more than enough risks in the course of his professional life, and should be discouraged from adding too many extra-curricular hazards. 'I suppose you realise he is contemplating getting the balloon down to Sandringham,' he warned Checketts, 'so you will have to act quickly if you want to do something about it.'[58]

But though the Prince was always ready to listen, and often took his great-uncle's advice, he was far from being a docile worshipper. Mountbatten, for that matter, would not have been at all pleased if he had been. In October 1969 Prince Charles flew in to discuss a speech he was to make the following week for the Gandhi Centenary Tribute. Mountbatten had been through the text the night before and had made a number of suggestions, 'but he very politely pointed out in each case that it was not the way he would have phrased it, and so his speech remained virtually unchanged'. 'I thought it was really splendid,' Mountbatten concluded, though whether he referred to the content of the speech or the Prince of Wales's defence of it is not entirely clear.[59]

If proof were needed that Mountbatten's affection for the Prince of Wales was more than superficial, it lay in the zeal with which he denounced any symptoms of turpitude or self-indulgence. Staying together in the West Indies, Mountbatten sternly warned his great-nephew that 'I thought you were beginning on the downward slope which wrecked your Uncle David's life and led to his disgraceful Abdication and his futile life ever after'. Things got worse when the Prince proposed a sudden change in his plans. Mountbatten was disturbed:

> Of course you were legally right – the U.S. Coastguards could recall a
> crew from Easter weekend leave if you really wanted them. An officer

was on duty and had no claim for the extra 3 days with his fiancée. But how unkind and thoughtless – so typical of how your Uncle David started. When I pointed this out you flared up – so I knew you had seen the point. I spent the night worrying whether you would continue on your Uncle David's sad course or take a pull.[60]

A pull was taken; the coastguard's fiancée was not bereft; Mountbatten, who can never have taken very seriously his analogy with the Duke of Windsor, was left rejoicing. The two men discussed philosophy until far into the night: 'What impressed me most was your desire to be generous, kind-hearted, and to think of others before your own interests.'

The spectre of the Duke of Windsor began also to be invoked every time the question of the Prince of Wales's marriage was discussed. At first Mountbatten had advocated delay. Early in 1974 he wrote:

> I believe, in a case like yours, the man should sow his wild oats and have as many affairs as he can before settling down but for a wife he should choose a suitable, attractive and sweet-charactered girl *before* she met anyone else she might fall for. After all Mummy never seriously thought of anyone else after the Dartmouth encounter when she was 13! I think it is disturbing for women to have experiences if they have to remain on a pedestal after marriage.[61]

The wild oats were presumably sown, but the suitable, attractive and sweet-charactered girl remained unselected at the time Mountbatten died.

Early in 1979 plans were being made for a visit to India by the Prince of Wales. Mountbatten was to accompany him, with his grand-daughter Amanda Knatchbull. Then suddenly all was put in jeopardy. The Duke of Edinburgh argued that the Prince should not pay his first visit to India in the shadow of this legendary figure, who would inevitably claim the limelight. Mountbatten pleaded that he would be able to help the Prince and himself remain silently unobtrusive. The Duke was unconvinced; worse still, Lord Brabourne also thought that the Prince would do better by himself. Mountbatten wrote to his great-nephew to report the conversation:

> From a purely selfish point of view I must confess I would be very, very sad to have to forgo the great happiness of being with two young people I love so much and showing them the country which means so much to me, but if the price of my selfishness were to spoil the visit for you, then that would be a price I could not even contemplate.
>
> So will you please think this over carefully so we can discuss it the next time we meet?[62]

The final solution was a compromise: the party would arrive together but then split up, uniting only for an occasional high spot and two days of holiday. Some of the Prince's advisers were still dubious. 'You think I'll take over the whole show, don't you?' demanded Mountbatten accusingly. It was exactly what they did think. The I.R.A. intervened before they could be proved right or wrong.

# CHAPTER 52

## *The End*

MOUNTBATTEN FOUND IT HARD to believe that he would grow old. In the years after his retirement he accepted that he could no longer play a vigorous game of polo, his reflexes were slower, he was more apt to doze off when bored or tired, but these were trivia; in all essentials he was still able to take on the world and hold his own. So it was when, in July 1970, he carried the Sword of State at the opening of Parliament. A few years before, Montgomery had almost collapsed while performing this picturesquely futile but gruelling ordeal, but it held no terrors for Mountbatten. It was a hot day, the lights needed for the television cameras made matters worse, suddenly 'the ground was starting to come forward in waves, and I realised I was very near fainting'. The Duke of Norfolk, seeing his plight, sent over an usher to lend a hand with the Sword; but Mountbatten braced himself, told his would-be assistant to go to hell, and saw out the ceremony.

> Lilibet was most concerned about my health: she said that she was so horrified to see me swaying in front of her that she tried to read her speech from the Throne more quickly so as to give me a better chance of surviving! She told me that Anne had been sitting with her hands held ready to receive me if I fell.[1]

By the evening he felt fully recovered – so much so that when Lord Carrington came over to enquire after his health he found himself sharply interrogated about the Government's plans for the future of aircraft-carriers.[2] Mountbatten decided to have a medical check-up, however, was referred to the eminent cardiologist Dr Lawson MacDonald, and was told that the arteries of his heart were in a deplorable state, and that he must cancel all his engagements and retire to bed for at least a fortnight. He refused to do anything of the sort until he had delivered the address at the memorial service for his old friend the Maharaja of Jaipur, but once this obligation was satisfied he behaved with exemplary prudence. He cut out all engagements for three months, and agreed to reduce his future commitments – drastically, if not quite by the fifty per cent that the doctor demanded. Within a month he was convinced he had fully recovered. 'Really the incident . . . has not been a bad thing,' he wrote cheerfully, 'because I don't believe I would ever have taken this pull if I had not had this providential warning.'

The pull did not prove permanent. Within a few months his schedule was almost as congested as before. In two days in 1976 he opened a school fête in Romsey, installed a May Queen, attended a *Kelly* reunion dinner, drove to Portsmouth to visit a cadets' school, spent a night at Windsor and made, in all, six speeches. 'This is a strenuous weekend, but it does stir up the old adrenalin. I must say I feel really just as fit as I did when I went as First Sea Lord to the Admiralty twenty-two years ago.'[3] He was interviewed by Eamonn Andrews and asked how long he intended to carry on at this frenetic pace. He replied: 'Anybody who has worked hard all their lives must never stop but go on working if they want to live. So I intend to go on working: I intend to die before I stop.'[4] In part, at least, he ascribed his remarkable health to 'Barbara Cartland's vitamin E capsules, of which I take between three and five every day'.[5] He described these wonder-working pills to Sir Jules Thorn, and said what a remarkable person Barbara Cartland was.

> Jules said she was destroying the National Health Service. . . . I said I could hardly believe this because she wouldn't have time; 'she writes twenty novels a year: she couldn't have time to do all this even if she wanted to'. He said that he was sure Barbara had never written a novel in her life, and it only then transpired . . . he was talking about Barbara Castle.[6]

A friend suggested that he should undergo the fashionable treatment that involved the injection of monkey glands. Mountbatten said that the idea sounded creepy but that he would not rule it out. There was no point in living to extreme old age, however, unless one's comfort was ensured. Would Charles Smith, his butler, take the treatment too? Smith was not tempted by the prospect of immortality, so Mountbatten politely declined. He did, in fact, procure some serum in Paris, which he claimed to be superior to that used by Churchill since it preserved mind as well as body.[7] Whether or not it helped, he seemed astonishingly well-preserved. In October 1976 he made a major speech in Singapore. During a party that followed the Dutch Ambassador congratulated Pamela Hicks on her father's success and asked how old he was. Seventy-six. Well, said the Ambassador thoughtfully, 'he has a great future in front of him'.[8]

Only ten days later the future abruptly retracted. Once more it was the Sword of State that proved his undoing. The Queen insisted that he should have a medical check-up before embarking on this arduous enterprise; he did so with the confidence of a man submitting to a tiresome formality and was disturbed to be told that there had been a 'very disturbing flicker' on his electro-cardiograph. The Sword was not for him. His disappointment turned to mortification when it was given instead to Field Marshal Harding, 'who must be about 80, certainly older than me. He very nearly tripped up twice when his spurs caught the back of his robe. I complained about this afterwards to Lilibet. . . . I warned her I might insist on carrying it if I got an all-clear next year.'[9]

He deluded himself and he knew it. He would not go gentle, would fight every inch of the way, but old age was inexorably advancing. The prospect frightened him. Death he could face with equanimity, but the threat of senility, to be 'an old thing, hanging on and making a nuisance of himself', was another matter. He was haunted by the memory of Peter Murphy who had died of multiple sclerosis, wrecked in mind and body. He was haunted by Churchill, a shattered wraith clinging to power long after all zest had departed. Every lapse of memory, every failure of body, was noted and deplored. In the lift at Broadlands he would stand with his shoulders braced back against the wall, hoping thus to avoid the stoop that he knew was beginning to betray his age.

Thoughts of his funeral had long preoccupied him. As early as 1967, at the funeral of Lord Chatfield, he had been asked what preparations he was making and had answered, in some surprise, that the idea had never entered his head. Slim's funeral three years later renewed the enquiries and this time he was more disposed to listen. In September 1971 the Lord Chamberlain wrote to ask where he wished to be buried; at first he opted to lie with his parents at Whippingham on the Isle of Wight, then changed his mind and decided that Romsey would be more appropriate. But his main concern was the grandiose procession that he foresaw in London. Would the Army and R.A.F. wish to participate, he wondered: 'However, the last thing I wish to do is to pose an unpopular request and as I shall not be there to see it, a private funeral in a motor hearse would be equally acceptable.'[10] Not even he found this humility convincing: with the enthusiasm, persistence and thoroughness that had marked his life, he settled down to ensure that his death was celebrated with suitable pomp and splendour.

How many people could attend a Field Marshal's funeral? he asked the Ministry of Defence.[11] What role would his organization play? he asked the Chairman of the British Legion. Would the King's Troop fire a nineteen-gun salute? he asked the Master-Gunner: 'They did so for Field Marshal Alexander, and in my case as you will remember I was the Honorary Colonel of 289 Airborne R.H.A. Regiment.'[12] Was it true that 2500 naval personnel took part in the funeral of an Admiral of the Fleet? 'Is there any special point about the Royal Marines taking part in larger numbers than usual in view of the fact that I am a Life Colonel Commandant?'[13] It was alarming to reflect that the

Indians might have forgotten him by the time he died; would Admiral Kohli promise to ensure that one of the Chiefs of Staff would fly over as a pall-bearer and a small contingent from each of the Services march in the funeral?[14] Would American forces wish to take part? 'I am sure I do not need to tell you that this is not written with any idea of increasing the size of my own procession but only to make sure that my close association with our American allies is not overlooked.'[15]

The 'Suggestions' for his funeral service could have been composed by no one else. The emphasis was nautical and international. The lesson, Psalm 107, 'They that go down to the sea in ships'; the Prayer of Sir Francis Drake; 'Eternal Father'; 'Jerusalem'; 'I vow to thee my Country' – but it was the optional extras that were so characteristic.

> To keep the Service short it is suggested there be no address, unless the Prime Minister felt he would like to say a word, in which case it is hoped it will be short and mainly confined to Lord Mountbatten's efforts to find peaceful solutions for the emergent nations of South East Asia . . . and to helping India and Pakistan to attain independence. . . . His personal leadership, as long ago as 1945, helped to set the line on which the British Empire changed itself into the Commonwealth of sovereign states. . . .
>
> The Royal Marines Prayer and Life Guards Prayer could be omitted, though this would be a pity since Lord Mountbatten had been Life Colonel Commandant of the Royal Marines and Colonel of the Life Guards since 1965. . . .
>
> The National Anthem. (The additional verse which was sung in Westminster Abbey at the Memorial Service to Lord Hailey should be included.)
>
> > Nor on this land alone –
> > But be God's mercies known
> > From shore to shore.
> > Lord, make the nations see
> > That men should brothers be,
> > And from one family
> > The wide world o'er.

In June 1972 the 'great funeral letter' to the Lord Chamberlain at last went off. 'All this has been gay and very entertaining for me, as you can well imagine,' Mountbatten told John Brabourne.[16] Nothing had been neglected in the preparatory work: should the coffin be lead-lined (difficult for the Grenadier Guards to carry)? What size should the cushions be on which his decorations were carried? Ought the Swedish Order of Seraphim to be included? Might the Burmese Defence Attaché carry the insignia of the Agga Maha Thiri Thu Dhamma on a separate cushion? Mrs Pandit was told that she would be one of the select group accompanying the coffin to Romsey for the interment. Luncheon would be served on the train; he had prepared two menus, one for winter, one for summer. The timing would be precise; as she finished her coffee the train would draw into Romsey station. She forgot wholly about this conversation until the day of the funeral, when she was lunching on the train. As she put down her empty coffee-cup the train drew into Romsey station.[17]

For the old, life sometimes seems a melancholy procession of obituaries and memorial services. Mountbatten helped many old friends on their way. He spent an hour at Malcolm Sargent's deathbed and did more than anyone else to cheer him up, telling him how much he had done in his life and how proud Britain should be of him.[18] Those of his contemporaries who were not dying were in decay. He called on Noel Coward to find the Lunts staying and Charlie Chaplin come over to see him.

> It was really an extraordinary meeting. When I came in Noel leant forward, put both his hands on the arms of his chair and made a motion as though he was going to get up. I asked him not to get up and he replied that he couldn't, anyhow, even if he tried, he was merely trying to look polite; Noel seems in a really bad way. However he was spritely compared with Charlie, who sat on the sofa by me and practically never uttered or moved.
>
> Alfred Lunt was gay, wearing very dark glasses, but I discovered he was completely blind. His wife, Lynn Fontanne, was really the only hale and hearty person, but of course she is getting pretty old, too.[19]

'The secret of good old age', concluded Colonel Aureliano Buendía, 'is simply an honourable pact with solitude.'[20] Such a pact Mountbatten found difficult to conclude. To the outsider it seemed that his life was passed in the most hectic social activity; to him it seemed that he was too often alone. John Barratt, his secretary, was his most constant companion and confidant, and played a part of increasing importance as old age took its toll. A galaxy of young, attractive and devoted women rallied to ride with him, listen to his stories, imbibe his wisdom, notable among them his god-daughter, Sasha Hamilton, who was as dear to him as a member of his closest family. But, at the heart of all such activity, Mountbatten remained a lonely man.

Gradually he began to retreat from the harshest rigours of public life. His greatest renunciation came when he handed over the presidency of the United World Colleges to the Prince of Wales. It was a relief to know that somebody else would now bear the main responsibility but, though his intentions were excellent, he found it hard not to interfere. The Prince had no illusions about his great-uncle's capacity for self-abnegation, and made his position clear:

> I agreed to take over as President from you on the understanding (as I saw it) that you wished to cut down on your commitments, etc. From the way you have been tackling things recently, it looks as though you are still going to do too much as Patron. I hate having to say this, but I believe in being *absolutely* honest with you, and when I take over as President I may easily want to do things in my *own* particular way, and in a way which could conflict with your ideas. So please don't be surprised if, like the other evening at Broadlands, I disagree with your approach or appear to be awkward and argumentative. I am only taking a leaf out of your book after all![21]

Mountbatten took the injunction in good part and honestly intended to abide by it, but those responsible for the day-to-day running of the operation did not find that his interest noticeably diminished in the years before his death.[22]

It was not all renunciation. Opening Broadlands to the public was a new and intriguing occupation. The change was forced upon him for financial reasons and heralded with some gloom, but once embarked on it became almost unmitigated pleasure. Mountbatten took an interest in everything: the siting of the lavatories, the lay-out of the trophy-room, the means of access, the catering. It was his film-making over again; he was always ready to defer to the expert who could prove his case but refused to believe that anything was impossible until it had been examined and tested. His attention to detail was not infallible; the King of Sweden, studying a wall-map illustrating the ramifications of the family, was surprised to find that Copenhagen had become again part of his realm. Such flaws were rare, however. The opening was magnificently stage-managed, with the band of the Royal Marines on the lawn and the Prince of Wales being required to borrow his admission money in front of the massed cameras of television and press. It would have given Mountbatten some satisfaction to know that the sensational nature of his own death was to encourage visitors to such an extent that the late arrival was doomed to wait for hours before he could hope for entrance.

More important, he never relaxed in his campaign to secure control and reduction of the world's nuclear armouries. Early in 1979 he was invited, as a member of the Scientific Council of SIPRI – the Stockholm International Peace Research Institute – to go to Strasbourg to receive an award from the Foundation of France for the greatest contribution to international understanding in the previous year. He decided to make this the occasion for a clarion call for sanity. Solly Zuckerman was recruited to help – 'I now hope you can steam ahead in writing a really tough speech that will shake the conscience of the world.'[23] Every sentence was carefully pondered; Mountbatten had no idea that this was to be his final public pronouncement on the subject – indeed, almost on any subject – but he must have known that his opportunities to sway the world were becoming rarer. This was to be his manifesto, the text by which he hoped he would be remembered.

There was nothing particularly original or dramatic in the Strasbourg speech. It began with a recital of the horrors of nuclear war, the certainty that any use of such weapons would lead to escalation and the end of civilization. A balance of strength between East and West was desirable but this could never be achieved if each side sought perpetually to steal a march on the other. Mutual restraint, better still a reduction of nuclear armouries, was the only way. He reproached the Russians and the Americans for dragging their feet over the disarmament talks; now opposition to any agreement seemed to be growing in certain quarters of the United States. 'What can their motives be?' Many others had said as much; what lent distinction to Mountbatten's speech was that it came from this veteran admiral.

> As a military man who has given half a century of active Service, I say in all sincerity that the nuclear arms race has no military purpose. Wars cannot be fought with nuclear weapons. Their existence only adds to our perils because of the illusions which they have generated.
>
> There are powerful voices around the world who still give evidence to the old Roman precept – if you desire peace, prepare for war. This is absolute nuclear nonsense, and I repeat – it is a disastrous misconception to believe that by increasing the total uncertainty one increases one's own certainty.
>
> It is true that science offers us almost unlimited opportunities but it is up to us, the people, to make the moral and philosophical choices, and since the threat to humanity is the work of human beings, it is up to man to save himself from himself.
>
> The world now stands on the brink of the final Abyss. Let us all resolve to take all possible practicable steps to ensure that we do not, through our own folly, go over the edge.[24]

Mountbatten was disappointed by the attendance at the meeting, and the failure of the world's press to take up his speech. He told Zuckerman that he had over-estimated the power of SIPRI to attract attention. 'It simply was a damp squib and doesn't appear to have been referred to anywhere.'[25] The damp squib did not go out, however, and gradually spluttered into fire.

Particularly after his death it gained new repute. It was published in 1980 by Bertrand Russell House and has been quoted more and more frequently as the years have passed. Mountbatten, indeed, has been invoked as the patron saint of the unilateralists, an honour he would have deplored, since he saw no sense in the renunciation of weapons by a single country – especially the country which he felt was less likely than any other to make use of them. Controlled reduction remained his favoured solution; though he would rather have been classed with the unilateralists – whose hearts at least, he felt, were in the right place – than with those 'out-of-date Service officers', who could not see that the alternative to control must be the end of civilization and whose obtuse short-sightedness he compared with 'the Flat Earth Society who spent so much trouble and money to convince people they could not be living on a sphere'.[26]

He signally failed to convince the Prime Minister of the urgency of his cause. In June he sent her a copy of his speech. Mrs Thatcher's reply bore all the marks of a civil servant's drafting. 'These are very difficult and important issues, and solutions are not easy to find,' she commented sagely. On the one hand, 'I am sure that deterrence must continue to lie at the heart of our defence'; on the other, 'we should be ready to try to achieve arms control measures which are fair to both sides and which can be satisfactorily verified'.[27] The following month he took up the subject again when he sat next to her at dinner. He was relieved to find her preoccupied by Russia's overwhelming naval power, but dismayed by her indifference to the progress of the talks on arms control. 'I have a feeling that you have not yet had a chance to get down to the vital nuclear problem,' he wrote. If the answer to that was wrong, then we 'shall end up in complete devastation of civilisation'. Would she not invite Solly Zuckerman along for a talk?[28] The invitation was forthcoming, but within a few weeks Mountbatten was no longer alive to keep the battle going.

Neither increasing intimations of mortality nor moments of apocalyptic gloom should conceal the fact that Mountbatten was a happy man. 'It is wonderful to have such a delightful family, and all ten of my grandchildren are absolutely enchanting,' he wrote as 1977 began. 'I am indeed a very lucky person.'[29] His happiness centred on his family. He wrote his manifesto of contentment at the end of the Broadlands Christmas, one of the two immutable tribal ceremonies when each year children and grandchildren rallied in force to celebrate together. On Christmas morning adults and children lined up in the hall and the senior staff of household and estate would file past to shake hands and receive their presents. The children abhorred this ritual; Mountbatten delighted in it. There followed a rally in the family pew of Romsey Abbey for the morning Eucharist, a visit to the old people at Edwina Mountbatten House, a massive luncheon for eighteen or more with 'crackers and general excitement', the ceremonial exchange of presents, the Boxing Day shoot.

The other gathering, longer and more relaxed but equally rich in ritual delights, was August at Classiebawn. Mountbatten as *pater familias* was seen in all his splendour in his Irish fastness. Building dams across the mouth of the stream, lobster-potting, prawning, he was always attended by a trail of devoted grandchildren, each performing an allotted task, all delighted to play their part in the unvarying routine, yet none of them even slightly intimidated by this formidable ancestor who ordered them about, bellowed at them, yet patently adored them. Classiebawn was a place for family reunion: a few old friends were asked to stay but only if it was known that they would fit in happily with the established pattern of existence. Once two of Amanda's long-haired boy-friends turned up unexpectedly. Mountbatten did his best to be amiable but the accent of one of them proved impenetrable, while the other appeared not to speak at all. The experiment was not repeated. The tribe was self-sufficient, external stimulus superfluous. 'I simply cannot imagine what all our summer holidays would be like without you at Classiebawn as the focal meeting-point,' Patricia wrote to him, 'certainly nowhere else could so many of us enjoy a traditional Victorian-type family holiday, in a modern setting, or rather a timeless one.'[30] Mountbatten was more happy there than anywhere else on earth.

He did not pay his visits to Ireland without much thought. As early as 1971 twelve policemen were on duty at the castle, 'in case the I.R.A. try to take me as a hostage'.[31] The following year he asked A. P. Hockaday of the Cabinet Office whether it was really sensible for him to go. 'No one can say that there is no risk in any visit to Ireland in present circumstances,' came the reply. 'Nevertheless they [experts from Foreign Office, Home Office and Ministry of Defence] all feel that the risk is one which can reasonably be taken.'[32] When Mountbatten reported that an I.R.A. activist had moved into the village, Hockaday replied consolingly, 'if you had no I.R.A. man on your estate you would probably be the only landowner in the Republic of whom this can be said'.[33]

At a Buckingham Palace garden-party Mountbatten raised the question of security in a group that included the Home Secretary and the Irish Ambassador. 'They seemed to think it was not only safe, but Whitelaw and O'Sullivan strongly recommended me to go.'[34]

So it went on. In 1974 Mountbatten was concerned about the kidnapping of Lord and Lady Donoughmore. Robert Mark established the views of the

Garda and told him that they strongly recommended that the visit should take place. 'We cannot show the white flag to the I.R.A. and although we do not think there is any real danger, we feel obliged to assure you that as many men as are needed will be applied to the task.'[35] Mark told Mountbatten that, speaking personally, he would prefer him not to take the risk, 'or, some might say, offer the challenge', but he could not formally reject the advice of his Irish opposite number.[36] The twelve-man guard of 1972 was raised to fifteen the following year and to twenty-eight in 1974. Each year Mountbatten continued to consult Scotland Yard, but as time passed it seemed more and more of a formality. 'I am writing my usual letter . . . to let you know that I shall be going with my family to my place in Ireland,' he wrote to the new Commissioner in July 1979;[37] he would have been disconcerted and dismayed if the answer had been that his visit would not be welcome.

Curiously enough, the previous year it had been at Broadlands that he had seemed in danger. His distant cousin, Prince Moritz of Hesse Kassel, had been kidnapped in Germany. He had quickly been released, but his abductors had boasted that Lord Mountbatten was another of their targets. The police were not particularly upset, claiming that the concept of kidnapping had not really taken hold in Britain. They were, however, concerned about security at Broadlands. Mountbatten explained that, though he slept alone in the house, he did so behind locked and bolted doors, with an alarm-bell by his side which would sound in the bedrooms of the butler and valet, who lived nearby, and also set off a siren on the roof of the house. The police agreed that this seemed adequate. Prince Moritz, however, whom Mountbatten questioned about every detail of his ordeal, said that one excellent practice was always to go to bed armed, but with a shotgun rather than a revolver. Mountbatten was struck by this piece of wisdom and declared that in future he would always sleep with his Purdeys beside him. 'But, Daddy, who'll load for you?' asked Pamela.[38]

It was in this mood of half-joking resignation that the grown-ups of the party confronted the prospect of kidnapping or other violence at Classiebawn. They knew that the risk existed, that the Irish police could do little to protect them against determined killers who might strike from a distance without concern for the lives of innocent bystanders, but they could not view the possibility with real concern. For so many years now the I.R.A. had forborne to strike; each season Mountbatten became more remote from the power which he had once wielded. 'I hope you are having a decent rest in Ireland and are not working unnecessarily hard,' wrote the Prince of Wales in mid August.[39] Whether necessarily or unnecessarily, Mountbatten was always working hard; but the work was concerned with schools or charities, not national defence, still less the affairs of Ireland. Why kill or kidnap an old man of nearly eighty? The family had noticed that the twenty-nine-foot fishing boat, *Shadow V*, in which they went out most days was left unguarded for long periods; they had even spoken to the police about it; but they did not want to seem importunate. Surely there was no real danger?

At about half past eleven on the morning of 27 August 1979 Mountbatten climbed down into *Shadow V* in the little harbour of Mullaghmore. With him were Lord and Lady Brabourne, Lord Brabourne's mother Doreen, and the Brabournes' fourteen-year-old twin sons, Nicholas and Timothy. An Irish boy from the neighbourhood, Paul Maxwell, came along to help with the boat. A police car had escorted them from the castle to the harbour and proposed to follow them along the coast road, surveying operations from the shore. Until recently a member of the Garda had always come out with them on their expeditions. The last policeman to accompany them, however, had been violently seasick and Mountbatten had suggested that there was no real need for anyone to put to sea.

What had induced the I.R.A. to decide that 1979 was a suitable year in which to kill a distinguished old man and his family may never be known. The fact that the murder was almost simultaneous with the massacre of eighteen paratroopers on the other side of Ireland at Warrenpoint suggests that the decision was taken at a high level. It was, pronounced an I.R.A. bulletin, 'a discriminate operation to bring to the attention of the English people the continuing occupation of our country. We will tear out their sentimental, imperialist heart,' the statement continued. The 'execution' was a way of 'bringing emotionally home to the English ruling-class and its working-class slaves . . . that their government's war on us is going to cost them as well'.[40] The size of the bomb – claimed as fifty pounds and certainly no smaller – makes it evident that the intention was to kill not only Mountbatten but everybody else on board.

As the boat cleared the harbour wall Mountbatten raced the engine furiously. John Brabourne benignly watched his father-in-law as he applied himself to his task with all the concentration he had lavished on the great enterprises of his prime and remarked how much he seemed to be enjoying himself. He was wearing a T-shirt designed to commemorate H.M.S. *Kelly* – bearing the words 'The Fighting Fifth'. It was something his family had never seen him in before. All his other clothes were familiar favourites, twenty years old or more. *Shadow V* slowed down as she approached the first of the lobster-pots which were the object of the expedition. Before Mountbatten had time to cut the engine the bomb, which had been placed beneath his feet, exploded and the boat disintegrated. Probably it was detonated by remote control from the shore, but some sort of timing device may have been used. Paul Maxwell and Nicholas Knatchbull were killed, eighty-three-year-old

Lady Brabourne fatally injured. Timothy was blown some distance from the boat and was picked up with serious injuries but paddling strongly. John and Patricia Brabourne were taken from the water badly hurt, their legs broken, their skin lacerated by splinters of wood and metal. Mountbatten's body was found floating face downwards in the water a few yards away, his limbs remarkably unscathed. He had been killed instantly by the blast. He could never have known what had happened to him, still less to his beloved companions.

To die with no time for fear or regrets, doing what he enjoyed most with the people who were above all precious to him, escaping the horrors of increasing decrepitude or senility, to end not with a whimper but with a bang that reverberated around the world – that truly was the fate Mountbatten would have chosen for himself. But for the tragedy of the other victims, it could be said that he was the most fortunate of men.

The world mourned. Every newspaper headlined the news of his assassination. Letters in their tens of thousands poured in upon the survivors. In Rangoon a book was opened in the Embassy for people to sign in tribute; for four days people queued before it, the line often stretching far out into the garden. In New Delhi every shop and office was closed, a week's state mourning was declared. The rulers of the great nations hastened to express their sympathy. He figured in many dreams. A lady with talents as a medium saw him stumping up and down on the beach at Mullaghmore, trying to take charge of the rescue operation and unable to understand why nobody would pay any attention to him. Two women who had known him well woke to find him sitting on the ends of their beds, wearing blazer and grey flannels, trying to get a message through to the Prince of Wales.

They buried him with all the pomp and ceremony he could have desired. His instructions were faithfully observed, the proper dignitaries were present, the right regiments and institutions played their part, the Burmese Defence Attaché did his bit with the insignia of the Agga Maha Thiri Thu Dhamma. It could not have been better managed if he had been alive to direct it. And as Mrs Pandit finished her cup of coffee, the funeral train glided into Romsey station.

After so long a journey, an author may perhaps be forgiven for airing a few personal impressions. In 1973 Solly Zuckerman told Mountbatten that he was writing a piece about him for publication after his death. Mountbatten professed himself delighted. 'Of course no one knows me better or can expose my weaknesses more effectively,' he replied, 'because there is no good having a picture without the warts.'[41] A picture of Mountbatten without his warts would indeed be unconvincing, for, like everything else about him, his faults were on the grandest scale. His vanity, though child-like, was monstrous, his ambition unbridled. The truth, in his hands, was swiftly converted from what it was to what it should have been. He sought to rewrite history with cavalier indifference to the facts to magnify his own achievements. There was a time when I became so enraged by what I began to feel was his determination to hoodwink me that I found it necessary to place on my desk a notice saying: REMEMBER, IN SPITE OF EVERYTHING, HE WAS A GREAT MAN.

Yet he possessed virtues which outweighed his defects. He was generous and loyal, putting himself to endless trouble for anyone whom he felt had any claim on him, and many who did not. He was warm-hearted, predisposed to like everyone he met, quick-tempered but never bearing grudges. At his most outrageous he was redeemed by an endearing readiness to admit his faults; a half-amused, half-horrified recognition of his capacity for mischief. He was courteous and considerate. His tolerance was extraordinary; his readiness to respect and listen to the views of others was remarkable throughout his life, phenomenal when old age might have been expected to perform its traditional task of narrowing the mind. Those who disliked or distrusted him were usually acquaintances or professional rivals; to his family and close friends he was the wisest, the most honourable of men. I often disapproved of him but never doubted that, subjected to his charm, I would have succumbed and become a disciple.

Even without these attributes he would still have been a GREAT MAN. In what his greatness lay is harder to define. He was not a profound or original thinker and most of his best ideas were taken from other people. What he could do with superlative aplomb was to identify the object at which he was aiming, select the method which was most likely to achieve it, and force it through to its conclusion. A powerful, analytical mind of crystalline clarity, a superabundance of energy, great persuasive powers, endless resilience in the face of setback or disaster rendered him the most formidable of operators. He was infinitely resourceful, quick in his reactions, always ready to cut his losses and start again. He did not know despair. Lee Kuan Yew told Pamela that her father was 'the greatest fixer of all time'; certainly it is hard to conceive a situation in which he would not have been a good man to have on one's side, a dangerous man to have against one. He was an executor of policy rather than an initiator; but whatever the policy, he espoused it with such energy and enthusiasm, made it so completely his own, that it became identified with him and, in the eyes of the outside world as well as his own, his creation.

An indication of his stature lies in the impression he made on others. I have met some who adored him: their adoration flavoured, perhaps, with a trace of amused irritation. I have met some who detested him; their detestation leavened by a grudging respect. I have met nobody who knew him well and yet was indifferent to him. A man of strong reactions himself, he inspired strong reactions in others; he was a leader for whom men would die, who inspired absolute trust and loyalty. Some years ago, writing a biography of Lord Melbourne, I invoked the fearful judgement from the *Revelation of St John the Divine*: 'I know thy works, that thou art neither cold nor hot: I would thou were cold or hot. So because thou art lukewarm and neither hot nor cold, I will spew thee out of my mouth.'

Lukewarm was the last word one could apply to Lord Mountbatten; he was a man of fiery enthusiasm, total commitment, who loved not wisely but too well, who acted first and considered the consequences later. He would have described himself as a moderate; he was the most intemperate of men. He flared brilliantly across the face of the twentieth century; the meteor is extinguished but its glow lingers on in the mind's eye.

# Notes and
# Bibliographical Notes

# Abbreviations Used in Notes

BA     Broadlands Archives
BM     British Museum
CCS    Combined Chiefs of Staff
COS    Chiefs of Staff
EM     Edwina Mountbatten
IO     India Office
LMH    Louis Milford Haven
M      Earl Mountbatten of Burma
NA     National Archives (of Washington)
PRO    Public Record Office
RA     Royal Archives
VMH    Victoria Milford Haven
'Transcripts' refers to transcripts of
tape-recorded interviews between Robin Bousfield
and Lord Mountbatten
'Lady Mountbatten papers' are those of M's
daughter Patricia, now Countess Mountbatten
of Burma

# Notes

## CHAPTER 1

### pages 21–31

1   BA CIII.
2   Princess Marie zu Erbach-Schönberg, *Reminiscences*. London, 1925, p 53.
3   1 August 1877. Hansard. 3rd Series. Vol. 318. 720–1.
4   *Fear God and Dread Nought. The Correspondence of Admiral of the Fleet Lord Fisher of Kilverstone*. Ed. Arthur Marder. London, 1952, Vol. I, p 293.
5   RA GV AA 43/10.
6   21 August 1885. BA S405.
7   Queen Victoria to Crown Princess of Prussia, 25 June 1883. RA Add U32.
8   VMH to M, 14 February 1924. BA S360.
9   Queen Victoria to VMH, 10 June 1900. BA S405.
10  Ibid, 13 July 1900. BA S405.
11  Queen Victoria's Journal, 17 July 1900. RA.
12  15 December 1935. Lady Mountbatten Papers.
13  MS notes made by M on a calendar of his early years. BA.
14  M's notes on calendar, op cit.
15  Ibid.
16  M to LMH, February 1905. BA Vol. IA.
17  J. M. Kenworthy, *Soldiers, Statesmen and Others*. London, 1933, p 39.
18  M's notes on calendar, op cit.
19  Interviews between M and Robin Bousfield. Transcripts, Vol. II, p 2.
20  M's notes on calendar, op cit.
21  M to VMH, 30 October 1912. BA Vol. II.
22  December 1909. BA Vol. IA.
23  12 May 1910. BA Vol. IB.
24  M to VMH, 8 May 1910. BA Vol. I.
25  Ibid.
26  Ibid, 3 July 1910. BA Vol. I.
27  VMH to M, 16 October, 21 November, 3 July 1910. BA S365.
28  August 1910. BA Vol. IA.
29  August 1912. BA Vol. IA.
30  VMH to M, 21 June 1910.
31  Ibid, 16 May 1910. BA S365.
32  M's notes on calendar, op cit.
33  M to VMH, 2 June 1912. BA Vol. II.
34  28 September 1910. BA T78.
35  VMH to M, 19 July 1911. BA S365.
36  25 October 1911. *Fisher Correspondence*, op cit. Vol. II p 397.
37  *John Bull*, 2 November 1911.
38  M to VMH, 8 December 1912. BA Vol. II.

## CHAPTER 2

### pages 32–41

1   Rear-Admiral George Ross. Unpublished autobiography, p 9.
2   E. A. Hughes, *The Royal Naval College, Dartmouth*. London, 1950, p 50.
3   M to VMH, 18 January 1914. BA Vol. IV.
4   M to VMH, 10 May 1913. BA Vol. III.
5   Ibid.
6   Reminiscences of Anthony Combe. BA N100.
7   Interview with Admiral Sir Frederick Parham.
8   M to VMH, 18 May 1913. BA Vol. III.
9   M to VMH, 29 June 1913. BA Vol. III.
10  M to VMH, 12 October 1913. BA Vol. III.
11  Campbell-Johnson narrative. Vol. I, p 37.
12  Interview with Rear-Admiral Ross.
13  M's notes on calendar, op cit.
14  M to VMH, 22 July 1914. BA Vol. IV.
15  M to LMH, 26 July 1914. BA Vol. IB.

16 M to VMH, 18 October 1914. BA Vol. IV.
17 Ibid, 14 August 1914. BA Vol. IV.
18 Percy Christopherson to M, 12 January 1915. BA A7.
19 Hugh-Jones to M, 7 September 1954. BA G21.
20 Bernard Braine to the author, 2 September 1983.
21 M to VMH, 15 January 1915. BA Vol. V.
22 Ibid, 17 January 1915. BA Vol. V.
23 Diary, 8 February 1915.
24 Ibid, February 1915.
25 P. R. Besley to M, 26 June 1915. BA A7.
26 Diary, 8 March 1915.
27 M to VMH, 13 June 1915. BA Vol. V.
28 Diary, 10 June 1915.
29 Ibid, 2 July 1915.
30 Ibid, 7 November and 21 November 1915.
31 Ibid, 29 January 1915.
32 Ibid, April 1915.
33 Campbell-Johnson narrative. Vol. I, p 41.
34 Diary, September 1915.
35 Ibid, 23 July 1915.
36 M to VMH, 3 October 1915. BA Vol. V.
37 LMH to M, 6 October 1915. BA T78.
38 M to VMH, 10 October 1915. BA Vol. V.
39 M to LMH, 23 January 1916. BA Vol. IB.
40 M to Mr Pocock. Published in *Young Elizabethan*. April 1958.
41 M to VMH, 4 June 1916. BA Vol. VI.
42 VMH to M, 26 June 1916. BA S364.

## CHAPTER 3

*pages 42–53*

1 cf Admiral of the Fleet Lord Chatfield, *The Navy and Defence*. London, 1942, pp 171–2.
2 John Wheeler-Bennett, *King George VI*. London, 1958, p 67.
Rear-Admiral G. W. G. Simpson, *Periscope View*. London, 1972, pp 25–6.
3 Reminiscences of Anthony Combe. BA N100.
4 M to Thomas Hussey, 23 January 1975. Hussey papers.
5 Interview with Vice-Admiral Sir Geoffrey Norman.
6 10 December 1916. BA Vol. IB.
7 Tour diaries, 19 August 1976.
8 M to Mr Pocock. Published in *Young Elizabethan*. April 1958.

9 M to VMH, 3 January 1917. BA Vol. VI.
10 Campbell-Johnson narrative. Vol. I, p 119.
11 M to VMH, 16 March 1917. BA Vol. VII.
12 Group Captain T. Hutchinson. Campbell-Johnson narrative. Vol. I, p 49.
13 VMH to Nona Kerr, 11 June 1917. BA S387.
14 Lord Stamfordham to Mr George Barnes, 19 June 1917. RA O 1153 IV 109.
15 M to VMH, 16 March 1917. BA Vol. VII.
16 M to VMH, 30 November 1917. BA Vol. VII.
17 Reminiscences of Lieut. Ernest Frary. BA N100.
18 M to LMH, 4 December 1917. BA Vol. IB.
19 LMH to M, 23 May 1918. BA T78.
20 M to VMH, 31 August and 7 November 1917. BA Vol. VII.
21 *Sea Pie* issue of December 1917; *Royal Magazine* issue of September 1919.
22 J. E. Marshall to M, 24 April 1918. BA A7.
23 M to VMH, 16 March 1919. BA Vol. VII.
24 Ibid, 1 January 1919. BA Vol. VII.
25 Campbell-Johnson narrative. Vol. I, p 54.
26 5 December 1919. BA 05.
27 27 November 1916. Ibid.
28 Campbell-Johnson narrative. Vol. I, p 49.
29 Reminiscences of Thomas Hussey. BA N100.
30 Campbell-Johnson narrative. Vol. I, p 48.
31 M to VMH, 16 July 1919. BA Vol. VII.
32 'The Scholars.' Definitive Edition. London, 1940, p 795.
33 M to Peter Murphy, November 1919. BA S321.
34 Diary, 5 February 1920.
35 Reminiscences of Anthony Combe. BA N100.
36 M to LMH, 16 December 1919. BA Vol. VIIIA.
37 *Demosthenes Demobilised. A Record of Cambridge Union Society Debates 1919–1920*. Cambridge, 1920, pp 39–40.
38 M to LMH, 16 December 1919. BA Vol. VIIIA.
39 *Demosthenes Demobilised*, op cit, p 65.
40 *Demosthenes Demobilised*, op cit, p 76.
41 VMH to M, 1 September 1919. BA S364.
42 M to VMH, 3 July 1919. BA Vol. VII.
43 Ibid.
44 M to VMH, 16 December 1919. BA Vol. VII.

45 December 1919. BA S321.
46 Peter Murphy, 'Reminiscences and Comments concerning Lord Mountbatten.' BA S319.
47 M to LMH, 16 December 1919. BA Vol. VIIIA.
48 Ibid.
49 Issues of 12 October 1979 and 5 December 1980.
50 Tour diaries, 23 October 1975.
51 Interview with Sir Robert Scott.

## CHAPTER 4

### pages 54–65

1 M to VMH, 28 December 1919. BA Vol. VII.
2 Prince of Wales to VMH, undated. BA Vol. VIII.
3 M to VMH, 15 July 1920. BA Vol. VIII.
4 Interview with Sir Alan Lascelles. cf M to VMH, 6 March 1921. BA Vol. VIII.
5 'Unofficial Diary of H.R.H. the Prince of Wales's visit to Australia, New Zealand and the Colonies in the Atlantic and the Pacific. March to October, 1920.' 17 March 1920.
6 Ibid, 19 March 1920.
7 Ibid, 1 April 1920.
8 Ibid, 17 April 1920.
9 Diary of Algernon Willis, 4 September 1920. WLLS 1312.
10 M to VMH, 15 July 1920. BA Vol. VIII.
11 Unofficial Diary, 28 April 1920.
12 Ibid, 11 May 1920.
13 M to VMH, 21 March 1920. BA Vol. VIII.
14 Unofficial Diary, 9 August 1920.
15 Charlotte and Denis Plimner, *A Matter of Expediency. The Jettison of Admiral Sir Dudley North*. London, 1978, p 12.
16 M to VMH, 15 July 1920. BA Vol. VIII.
17 11 June 1920.
18 *Melbourne Herald,* 29 May 1920.
19 Unofficial Diary, 26 May 1920.
20 Ibid, 1 June 1920.
21 Ibid, 21 June 1920.
22 8 July 1920.
23 Unofficial Diary, 5 July 1920.
24 Halsey's submission, No. 120/11 of 9 October 1920; Admiralty M6/4536/20 of 25 October and M 6/4536 of 23 December. BA A10.

25 May 1979. BA N112.
26 M to LMH, 6 April 1920. BA Vol. VIIIA.
27 Report on No. 4 Portsmouth Battalion, 8 June 1921. BA O5.
28 M to Murphy, 23 April 1921. BA S321. M to VMH, 17 April 1921. BA Vol. VIII.
29 31 August 1921. BA S321.
30 11 September 1921. Yates papers.
31 Sir Herbert Russell, *With the Prince in the East*. London, 1922, p 23.
32 The Duke of Windsor, *A King's Story*. New York, 1951, p 173.
33 Unofficial Diary, 13 December 1921 and 13 January 1922.
34 M to EM, 19 January 1922. BA S132.
35 5 November 1921. BA Vol. IX.
36 M to VMH, 11 November 1921. BA Vol. VIII.
37 *A King's Story,* op cit, p 180.
38 M to Prince Albert, 25 January 1922. Precis of letters in BA S93.
39 Unofficial Diary, 1 December 1921.
40 Henry Maule, *Spearhead General. The Epic Story of General Sir Frank Messervy*. London, 1961, p 15.
41 Unofficial Diary, 1 December 1921; 8 December 1921; 16 December 1921; 24 February 1922.
42 Ibid, 7 December 1921; 5 March 1922; 25 November 1921.
43 Ibid, 19 November 1921; 7 December 1921; 3 January 1922.
44 Ibid, 15 January 1922.
45 Ibid, 23 March 1922.
46 Ibid, 12 April 1922.
47 Stephen Roskill, *Naval Policy Between the Wars*. London, 1968, Vol. I, p 531.
48 Unofficial Diary, 22 April 1922.
49 Ibid, 12 May 1922.
50 Ibid, 17 April 1922.

## CHAPTER 5

### pages 66–74

1 15 March 1922. BA S133.
2 Interview with Mary, Lady Delamere.
3 Interview with Captain Andrew Yates.
4 EM to M, 13 September 1921. BA S37. M to EM, 14 September 1921. BA S131.
5 Financial year ending 5 April 1920. BA A10.
6 11 October 1921. BA S37.
7 26 October 1921. BA S131.

8  M to Edwina, 15 January 1922. BA S132.
9  Ibid, 2 January 1922. BA S132.
10  Ibid, 1 January 1922. BA S132.
11  Unofficial Diary, 20 January 1922.
12  M to VMH, 26 February 1922. BA Vol. IX.
13  Unofficial Diary, 17 March 1922.
14  VMH to M, 29 February 1922. BA S360.
15  Interview with General Sir Robert Neville.
16  Prince Albert to M, 18 May 1922. BA S97.
17  1 May 1922. BA S40.
18  Unofficial Diary, 21 June 1922.
19  Diary, 4 August and 8 August 1922.
20  Ibid, 19 August 1922.
21  5 August 1922.
22  Diary, 5 October 1922.
23  14 November 1922.
24  Diary, 19 October 1922.
25  1 November 1922. BA Y20.
26  eg *Arts and Decoration*. New York, February 1923.
27  12 November 1922.
28  *Evening Telegram*. New York, 15 November 1922.
29  *Chicago Evening Post*, 25 October 1922.
30  *New York Times*, 5 October 1922; *The World*, 5 October 1922.
31  *New York Times*, 5 October 1922; *Meriden Daily Journal*, 16 October 1922.
32  *New York Herald*, 5 October 1922.
33  22 February 1922. BA S39.
34  M to Commander Joel, 23 November 1922. BA K157.
35  10 January 1923. BA S135.
36  Roskill, *Naval Policy Between the Wars*, op cit, Vol. I, p 125.
37  Transcripts. Vol. I, pp 49–50.
38  Interview with Lord Chatfield. Campbell-Johnson narrative. Vol. I, p 63.
39  *Naval and Military Record*, 31 December 1922.
40  'The Life and Times of Lord Mountbatten.' Post-production scripts. Programme 3, Reel 1, p 13.

## CHAPTER 6

### pages 75–86

1  30 January 1923. BA S135.
2  M to Commander Joel, 25 January 1923. BA K157.
3  14 January 1923. BA S135.
4  M to Commander Joel, 25 January 1923. BA K157.
5  Campbell-Johnson narrative. Vol. I, p 67.
6  1 August 1924. BA O5.
7  8 February 1924. BA S138.
8  Diary, 22 March 1923.
9  25 February 1923.
10  Diary, 12 March 1923.
11  14 February 1923. BA S42.
12  Diary, 14 March 1923.
13  BA N100.
14  6 January 1973. BA S33.
15  Richard Baker, *The Terror of Tobermory*. London, 1972, p 85.
16  Interview with Vice-Admiral Sir Charles Hughes Hallett.
17  Diary, 11 August 1924.
18  Tour Diaries, 18 July 1976.
19  'Mountbatten and Polo.' Memorandum by General Sir Robert Neville. 1967. BA.
20  Interview with General Sir Robert Neville.
21  Diary, 18 July 1925.
22  1 May 1925–23 September 1925 and 7 April 1926–3 October 1926. BA O5.
23  Lord Chatfield, *The Navy and Defence*. London, 1942, p 223.
24  Jellicoe to Frederick Hamilton, 9 November 1915, cit Roskill, *Naval Policy Between the Wars*, op cit, Vol. I, p 47n.
25  Lambe to his mother, 1928? cit Oliver Warner, *Admiral of the Fleet. The Life of Sir Charles Lambe*. London, 1969, p 43.
26  M to Robert Neville, 1 June 1967. Neville papers.
27  Cecil Aspinall-Oglander, *Roger Keyes*. London, 1951, p 305.
28  Campbell-Johnson narrative. Vol. I, p 80.
29  Diary, 8 October 1927.
30  M to VMH, 7 October 1927. BA Vol. XI.
31  13 October 1926. Yates papers.
32  Interview with Vice-Admiral Sir Charles Norris.
33  *Life of Sir Charles Lambe*, op cit, p 45.
34  11 January 1952 and covering memorandum by M. BA G79.
35  Reminiscences of Vice-Admiral Sir Peter Dawnay. BA N99.
36  Diary, 6 March 1930.
37  1 January 1930. BA O5.
38  Interview with H. A. Brooks. Campbell-Johnson narrative. Vol. I, p 88 and BA A88.
39  Interview with H. A. Brooks. BA A88. Interview between Robin Bousfield and

Rear-Admiral Peter Howes. Transcripts. Vol. I, p 4.
*The Communicator,* Spring 1975.
40  16 November 1923. BA N111.
41  Interview with Commander F. W. B. Edwards.
42  Diary, 12 February and 26 February 1930.
43  Interview with Rear-Admiral Royer Dick.
44  Campbell-Johnson narrative. Vol. I, p 97.
45  31 October 1932; 3 April 1933; 2 August 1933. BA O5.
46  Dawnay Reminiscences, op cit. Interview Royer Dick. Murphy, 'Reminiscences and Comments Concerning Lord Mountbatten,' op cit.
47  Interview with H. A. Brooks. BA A88.
48  Campbell-Johnson narrative. Vol. I, p 90.
49  Interview with H. A. Brooks. BA A88.
50  Interview with Commander F. W. B. Edwards.
51  Interview between M and Robin Bousfield. Transcripts. Vol. I, p 49.
52  Hodges to M, 10 September 1970. BA B29.
53  Lambe to Stewart Perowne, 9 July 1932. BA K54.
54  Prince of Wales to Chatfield, 16 July 1932. Chatfield papers. CHT/2/1.
55  *The Navy and Defence,* op cit, pp 248–9.
56  Prince George to Chatfield, 25 August 1932. CHT/2/1.
57  Captain J. Mansfield Robinson reminiscences. BA N101A.
58  Campbell-Johnson narrative. Vol. I, p 94.
59  Interviews with Royer Dick and Admiral Sir John Hamilton.
60  M to George Milford Haven, 25 October 1932. BA Y20.
61  31 October 1932. BA O5.
62  Murphy, 'Reminiscences and Comments.'

## CHAPTER 7
### pages 87–105

1  9 July 1934. BA Vol. XII.
2  27 February 1934.
3  Unpublished autobiography. National Maritime Museum (uncatalogued).
4  Interview with Mr Thomas Iremonger.
5  Reminiscences of Captain E. G. Roper. BA N100A.

6  Admiral Sir Richard Onslow to Robin Bousfield. Campbell-Johnson narrative. Vol. I, p 105. Murphy, 'Reminiscences and Comments.'
7  9 July 1934. BA Vol. XII.
8  Reminiscences of Commander H. G. Hall. BA N100.
9  16 September 1935. BA A109.
10  14 June 1936. BA O5.
11  Roper Reminiscences, op cit.
12  W 3288/1241/35 of 20 December 1935. BA N111.
13  Interviews with Vice-Admiral Jocelyn Salter, Vice-Admiral Sir Charles Norris, Vice-Admiral Sir Geoffrey Norman, Vice-Admiral Sir Geoffrey Robson, Vice-Admiral Sir Peter Gretton, Captain Andrew Yates.
14  cit Oliver Warner, *Cunningham of Hyndhope.* London, 1967, p 273.
15  Ibid, p 75.
16  1 September 1935. BA Vol. XII.
17  PRO ADM 116/3398. Report dated 24 December 1935.
18  5 February 1936. BA S139.
19  M to VMH, 8 April 1936. BA Vol. XII.
20  27 June 1936. BA O5.
21  28 April 1936.
22  25 January 1936.
23  1 September 1935. BA Vol. XII.
24  The Duchess of Windsor, *The Heart Has Its Reasons.* London, 1956, pp 206–7.
25  30 November 1936. BA S395.
26  Claud Cockburn, *In Time of Trouble.* London, 1956, pp 250–2.
27  7 December 1936. Duke of Windsor papers.
28  Edwina Mountbatten diary, 10 December 1936.
29  Oliver Warner, *Charles Lambe,* op cit, p 69.
30  19 November 1936. BA A48.
31  John Wheeler-Bennett, *King George VI.* London, 1958, pp 293–4.
32  11 December 1936. RA GVI PS.
33  Interview with Lady Alexandra Metcalfe.
34  Duke of Windsor papers.
35  22 January 1936. BA S139.
36  M to Edwina, 5 February 1936. BA S139.
37  Admiral of the Fleet Lord Chatfield, *It Might Happen Again.* London, 1947, p 102.
38  Chatfield papers. 5 May 1936. CHT/4/3.
39  Martin Gilbert, *Winston S. Churchill.* London, 1976, Vol. V, pp 852–3.
40  28 May 1937. BA A110.

41 Stephen Roskill, *Naval Policy Between the Wars*. London, 1976, Vol. II, pp 402–4.
42 Diary, 30 June 1937.
43 Interview with Rear-Admiral W. G. S. Tighe. Campbell-Johnson narrative. Vol. I, pp 122–3.
cf. Vice-Admiral G. M. B. Langley to M, 17 September 1968. BA K283.
44 *The Naval Review*. Vol. 68, No 2 of April 1980, pp 151–4.
45 PRO ADM 1/10291. 14 September 1939.
46 Diary, 2 February 1937.
47 Interview with Commander Du Cane. cf Peter Du Cane, *An Engineer of sorts*. Lymington, 1971, p 40.
48 10 January 1938. BA A53.
49 7 May 1937. BA O5.
50 G. F. Wallace to Rear-Admiral Ross, 5 April 1981. Ross papers.
51 Interview with Lord Adeane.
52 1 May 1939. BA A53.
53 In particular see article by Rear-Admiral Ross, *The Naval Review*. Vol. 69, No 1 of January 1981, pp 19–22.
54 Noel Coward, *Future Indefinite*. London, 1954, p 305.
Cole Lesley, *The Life of Noel Coward*. London, 1977, p. 189.
Coward to M, July 1938. BA A48.
55 cit Oliver Warner, *Cunningham of Hyndhope*. London, 1967, pp 87–8.
56 Diary, 4 April 1939.
57 12 February 1938. BA Vol. XII.
58 Basil Boothroyd, *Philip*. London, 1971, p 54.
59 16 March 1938. Lady Mountbatten papers.
60 10 May 1937. BA A110.
61 Lord Avon to M, 16 July 1964. BA J328.
62 'Life and Times,' op cit. Programme 4. Reel 2, p 15.
63 Eden to M, 22 August 1938. BA A109.
64 9 September 1938. BA A88.
65 Duff Cooper, *Old Men Forget*. London, 1954, p 245.
66 11 April 1938. BA O5.
67 16 February 1939. BA O5.
68 BA N101.

## CHAPTER 8

### *pages 106–118*

1 14 February 1924. BA S138.
2 20 February 1924. BA S395.
3 7 March 1924. BA Vol. X.
4 M to Andrew Yates, 13 October 1926. Yates papers.
cf *Daily Mail*, 1 June 1926.
5 Interview with Lady Alexandra Metcalfe.
6 M to VMH, 10 March 1924. BA Vol. X. VMH to M, 14 March 1924. BA S360.
7 12 July 1975. BA K92.
8 M to George Milford Haven, 25 October 1932. BA Y20.
9 25 February 1923. BA S42.
10 Richard Garrett, *Motoring and the Mighty*. London, 1971, pp 163–4.
11 *The Star*, 18 August 1925.
12 *The Outfitter*, 28 October 1933. *Montreal Star*, 17 May 1925. *London Life*, 7 April 1934.
13 Charles Smith, *Fifty Years with Mountbatten*. London, 1980, p 46.
14 Philip Colville to M, 4 September 1975. BA N100.
15 23 March 1923. BA S34.
16 22 March 1923. BA S34.
17 3 December 1925.
18 Diary, 15 November 1931 and 17 December 1932.
19 20 January 1928. Beaverbrook papers. C/255.
20 3 October 1926.
21 Lord Stamfordham to Lord Birkenhead, 15 July 1926; to Sir Louis Greig, 7 February 1930. RA GV PS6420.
22 May 1931. BA S139.
23 12 January 1927. BA S139.
24 3 September 1928. BA S52.
25 2 September 1933. BA S59.
26 25 April 1929. BA Vol. XI.
27 29 April 1929. BA S55.
28 20 March 1931. BA S57.
29 Edwina Mountbatten diary, 3 July 1932.
30 Richard Hough, *Edwina*. London, 1983, pp 125–27.
31 Edwina Mountbatten diary, 9 July 1932.
32 5 April 1927.
33 16 November 1928. BA Vol. XI.
34 1 January 1936. BA S62.
35 *The Diaries of Sir Robert Bruce Lockhart*. ed. Kenneth Young. London, 1973, p 356.

36 Unofficial diary, 16 April 1922.
37 4 November 1928. BA Vol. XI.

## CHAPTER 9

### *pages 121–133*

1 Campbell-Johnson narrative. Vol. I, p 145.
2 A. P. Cole to Robin Bousfield, 15 May 1962. BA J53.
3 Diary, 20 April 1938.
4 Cole to Bousfield, 24 June 1962. BA J53.
5 BA B1.
6 Kenneth Poolman, *The Kelly*. London, 1954, pp 37–8.
7 6 March 1940. BA S141.
8 Reminiscences of Able-Seaman Sidney Mosses. BA N100 A.
9 Reminiscences of Captain Butler-Bowdon. BA N100.
10 Poolman, *The Kelly*, op cit, pp 60–1.
11 28 August 1939. BA S361.
12 2 September 1939. BA S140.
13 Hansard. House of Commons Vol. 351. Col 1244. 26 September 1939.
14 4 September 1939. BA S140.
15 Stephen Roskill, *Churchill and the Admirals*. London, 1977, p 94.
16 26 August 1940. Lady Mountbatten papers.
17 *The Heart Has Its Reasons*, op cit, pp 322–3.
18 Interview with Captain E. Dunsterville. Butler-Bowdon's reminiscences, op cit, BA N100.
   M to King George VI, 10 November 1939. Transcript. BA S93.
19 23 October 1939. BA S96.
20 Poolman, *The Kelly*, op cit, pp 95–6. Interview with Captain E. Dunsterville.
21 13 November 1939. BA B5.
22 Diary, 12 December 1939.
   Poolman, *The Kelly*, op cit, p 102.
23 Campbell-Johnson narrative. Vol. I, pp 147–8.
24 Poolman, *The Kelly*, op cit, pp 106–7. Butler-Bowdon reminiscences, op cit.
25 Murphy, 'Reminiscences and Comments Concerning Lord Mountbatten,' op cit.
26 Unpublished diary of Vice-Admiral Sir Alistair Ewing. DS/MISC/31, p 163.
27 BA S100.
28 Lieutenant-General Sir Adrian Carton de Wiart, *Happy Odyssey*. London, 1950, p 174.

29 Diary, 2 May 1940.
30 *Happy Odyssey,* op cit, p 174.
31 Diary, 4 May 1940.
32 Mountbatten's Report on Operation. 0320N of 20 May 1940. BA B11b.
   Interviews with Vice-Admiral Sir Geoffrey Robson, Captain E. Dunsterville.
   Record by the Duke of Montrose (Robson papers).
   Poolman, *The Kelly*, op cit, pp 124–33.
   Admiralty WIR No 12 of 31 May 1940.
33 0320N, op cit, para 12.
34 5 June 1973. BA B11b.
35 Transcripts. Vol. I, p 56.
36 Interview with Commander B. P. Skinner.
37 Diary, 15 May 1940.
38 Interview with Vice-Admiral Sir Charles Hughes Hallett.
39 Interview with Captain Stephen Roskill.
40 M to EM, 13 August 1940. BA S141.
41 A. P. Cole to M, 19 September 1940. BA A115.
42 13 August 1940. BA S141.

## CHAPTER 10

### *pages 134–147*

1 8 January 1940. BA A115.
2 15 February 1940. Ibid.
3 23 October 1939. Lady Mountbatten papers.
4 11 November 1939. Ibid.
5 20 June 1940. BA S141.
6 10 October 1940. Lady Mountbatten papers.
7 BA S141.
8 M to Pamela, 5 July 1940. Lady Pamela Hicks papers.
9 13 December 1940. Lady Mountbatten papers.
10 25 November 1940. Ibid.
11 12 April 1941 and 24 April 1941. Ibid.
12 26 March 1941. Lady Pamela Hicks papers.
13 19 April 1941. Lady Mountbatten papers.
14 4 August 1940. Ibid.
15 Commander T. Napier to Mrs Napier, 16 July 1940. Napier papers.
16 Butler-Bowdon's reminiscences, op cit, BA N100.
17 M to George VI, 19 October 1940. (Precis in BA S93.)

18 Diary, 11 October 1940.
M to Patricia, 21 October 1940. Lady Mountbatten papers.
M to Commodore D. M. Maclean, 5 September 1963. BA J297.
19 Diary, 17 and 18 October 1940.
M to George VI, 18 October 1940. (Precis in BA S93.)
Campbell-Johnson narrative. Vol. I, p 179.
20 Diary, 29 November 1940.
Report No 0320U of 3 December 1940. BA B11d.
21 Testimony of Captain Hans Bartel, Wilhelmshaven, 20 March 1947. cf Memorandum by Historical Department, Freiburg. Campbell-Johnson narrative. Vol. I, p 170.
22 Captain Pugsley, *Destroyer Man.* London, 1957, pp 58–60.
23 Campbell-Johnson narrative. Vol. I, pp 169–70.
24 BA B11d.
25 Comments dated 10 September 1966. BA B11e.
26 30 November 1940. BA S14.
27 M to Patricia, 11 December 1940. Lady Mountbatten papers.
28 Diary, 9 December 1940.
29 11 December 1940. Lady Mountbatten papers.
30 M to Patricia, 30 November 1940. Lady Mountbatten papers.
M to George VI, 19 October 1940. (Precis in BA S93.)
31 BA B9.
32 Interview with Admiral Sir Guy Grantham.
33 M to Patricia, 9 January 1941. Lady Mountbatten papers.
34 2 January 1941. BA S142.
35 William Lawlor on B.B.C. North America Service, 8 September 1943.
36 Rear-Admiral G. W. G. Simpson, *Periscope View.* London, 1972, p 139.
37 8 May 1941. Neville papers.
38 16 May 1941. Ibid.
39 Quoted by M in the above letter to T. S. Phillips.
40 18 May 1941. BM Add Mss 52561. 72.
41 9 June 1941. Lady Mountbatten papers.
42 Oliver Warner, *Charles Lambe,* op cit, p 101.
43 Naval Staff History. Second World War. 'Naval Operations in the Battle of Crete.' BR 1736 (2) p 16n.

David A. Thomas, *Crete 1941. The Battle at Sea.* London, 1972, p 164.
44 Butler-Bowdon to M, 5 July 1971. BA B11e.
45 'Kelly's Last Fight' memorandum by M. BA B11.
Interview with Captain Dunsterville. Poolman, *The Kelly,* op cit, pp 196–203. Sidney Mosses's reminiscences. BA N100A.
46 10 June 1941. Lady Mountbatten papers.
47 William Lawlor on B.B.C. North America Service, 8 September 1943.
48 M to the Crown Princess of Sweden. BA B11e.
49 25 May 1941. BA B11e.
50 Oliver Warner, *Cunningham of Hyndhope,* op cit, p 157.
51 11 March 1941. BM Add Mss 52561. 64.
52 Poolman, *The Kelly,* op cit, p 210.
53 M to Patricia, 5 June 1941. Lady Mountbatten papers.

# CHAPTER 11
## *pages 148–159*

1 28 April 1941. Lady Mountbatten papers.
2 5 April 1941. BA S142.
3 *The Killearn Diaries.* ed. Trefor Evans. London, 1972, p 180.
4 M to Pamela, 5 June 1941. Lady Pamela Hicks papers.
5 Oliver Warner, *Charles Lambe,* op cit. p 101.
6 Lord Tedder, *With Prejudice.* London, 1966, p 107.
7 Oliver Warner, *Cunningham of Hyndhope,* op cit, p 157.
8 Rear Admiral A. M. Peters to Hardinge, 21 June 1941. RA GVI PS (Navy) 5378.
9 28 April 1942. BA S14.
10 M to Patricia, 10 October 1972. Lady Mountbatten papers.
11 Unsigned copy of letter (from British Ambassador?) to Brendan Bracken, 27 October 1941. BA A116.
12 10 October 1941. PRO PREM 3 330/2.
13 19 October 1941. BA S142.
14 PRO PREM 3 330/2.
15 15 October 1941. PRO PREM 3 330/2 05723.
16 15 October 1941. *Roosevelt and Churchill. Their Secret Wartime*

*Correspondence.* ed. Frances L. Loewenheim, Harold D. Langley and Manfred Jonas. New York, 1975, p 162.

17 *By Safe Hand. Letters of Sybil and David Eccles, 1939–42.* London, 1983, p 314.

18 *History of the Combined Operations Organisation 1940–1945.* Amphibious Warfare Headquarters. London, 1956, pp 1–11.

19 Bernard Fergusson, *The Watery Maze.* London, 1961, p 41.
Interview between Major-General Macleod and Alan Campbell-Johnson. Campbell-Johnson narrative. Vol. II, p 32.

20 Diary, 16 December 1938.

21 cit Stephen Roskill, *Churchill and the Admirals,* op cit, p 178.

22 1 December 1940. BM Add Mss 52561. 33.

23 *Churchill and the Admirals,* op cit, p 111.

24 Arthur Bryant, *The Turn of the Tide.* London, 1957, pp 255–56n.

25 Admiral Sir William James, *The Portsmouth Letters.* London, 1946, p 92.

26 Pound to Andrew Cunningham, 27 January 1941. BM Add Mss 52561. 48.

27 Cecil Aspinall-Oglander, *Roger Keyes.* London, 1951, pp 408–9.

28 Pound to Andrew Cunningham, 25 November 1941. BM Add Mss 52561. 120.

29 *Roger Keyes,* op cit, p 409.

30 Lord Lovat, *March Past.* London, 1978, p 189.

31 *The Keyes Papers.* ed. Paul Halpern. London, 1981, Vol. III, pp 212–13.

32 Ibid, p 255.

33 Ismay papers. IV/KEY/8/2b.

34 *The Watery Maze,* op cit, pp 87–8.
Campbell-Johnson narrative. Vol. I, p 202.

35 PRO COS (41) 629.

36 11 November 1941. Lady Mountbatten papers.

37 M to Patricia, 26 October 1941 and 5 November 1941. Lady Mountbatten papers.

38 Interview between M and Denis Richards. BA K14.

39 12 November 1941. *The Portsmouth Letters,* op cit, p 141.

40 COS (41) 370 of 28 October 1941.

41 COS (41) 432 of 23 December 1941.

42 Diary, 4 November 1941.

## CHAPTER 12

*pages 160–173*

1 M to Pamela, 11 November 1941. Lady Pamela Hicks papers.
Interview with Vice-Admiral Robson.

2 COS (41) 732 of 9 December 1941.

3 Vice-Admiral John Hughes Hallett. Unpublished memoir. BA B47, p 111.

4 Interview with Arthur Marshall.

5 M to Bernard Fergusson, 29 December 1959. BA J168.

6 Robert Henriques, *From a Biography of Myself.* London, 1969, pp 53–4.

7 Dalton diary, 12 November 1942.

8 Interview with General Sir Robert Neville.

9 Unpublished memoir, op cit, p 120.

10 Diary, 25 March 1943.

11 Peter Murphy, 'Reminiscences and Comments', op cit.
Edwina to M, 15 September 1939. BA S64.

12 Fergusson to M, 25 December 1959. BA J168.

13 Solly Zuckerman, *From Apes to Warlords.* London, 1978, p 151.

14 Ibid, p 180.

15 *The Diaries of Evelyn Waugh.* ed. Michael Davie. London, 1976, p 538.

16 Lord Lovat, *March Past.* op. cit, p 187.

17 Michael Harrison, *Mulberry. The Return in Triumph.* London, 1965, p 146.

18 cit *The Watery Maze,* op cit, p 125.

19 Letter to the author, 14 August 1982.

20 *March Past,* op cit, p 238.

21 Letter from Colonel H. C. Hasler R.M. to the author, 8 February 1982.

22 *The Watery Maze,* op cit, pp 120–1.

23 Interview with Vice-Admiral Robson.

24 *The Watery Maze,* op cit, p 292.

25 J. M. A. Gwyer and J. R. M. Butler, *Grand Strategy.* Vol. III, London, 1964, p 514.

26 M. R. D. Foot. *SOE in France.* London, 1966, pp 182–5.

27 COS (43) 3 (O) of 4 January 1943.

28 COS (42) 140 of 5 May 1942.
cf *History of Combined Operations,* op cit, p 21.

29 *Portsmouth Letters,* op cit, p 156.

30 Diary, 28 March 1942.

31 Interview with Vice-Admiral Sir Charles Norris.

32 C. E. Lucas Phillips, *Cockleshell Heroes.* London, 1956.

cf *History of Combined Operations,* op cit, pp 116–17.

33  PRO PREM 3 376.

34  7 March 1942. Churchill papers. File 119. POUND (S/124). Currently available only in Captain Stephen Roskill's papers.

35  PRO PREM 3 330/2.

36  *The Turn of the Tide,* op cit, pp 691–2.

37  'Life and Times', op cit, Programme 5, Reel 3, p 4.

38  20 March and 3 April 1942. Lady Mountbatten papers.

39  Unpublished diary, 13 April 1942.

40  3 July 1941. *The Noel Coward Diaries.* ed. Graham Payn and Sheridan Morley. London, 1982, p 7.

41  Interview with Lord Miles.

42  Coward to M, 17 September 1941. BA A48.

43  M to Patricia, 3 April 1942. Lady Mountbatten papers.

44  Elliott Roosevelt, *As He Saw It.* New York, 1946, p 58.

45  2 and 17 September 1941.

46  22 December 1941. *Noel Coward Diaries,* op cit, p 15.

47  Noel Coward, *Future Indefinite,* op cit, p 210.

48  M to Coward, 11 September 1953. BA H66.

49  'The Curious Case of Lord Beaverbrook.' BA C20.

# CHAPTER 13

## *pages 174–185*

1  14 July 1941. Lady Pamela Hicks papers.

2  Interview with David Astor.

3  Major-General Sir Kenneth Strong, *Intelligence at the Top.* London, 1968, p 73.

4  *Chips. The Diaries of Sir Henry Channon.* ed. R. Rhodes James. London, 1957, p 328.

5  A. B. Cunningham to J. H. Godfrey, 17 May 1956. BA K129.

6  Ismay to Robin Bousfield, 27 November 1964. BA J184.

7  M to J. H. Godfrey, 9 November 1964. BA J184.

8  *Grand Strategy.* Vol. III, op cit, pp 568–70.

9  COS (42) 9 (0).

10  *The Turn of the Tide,* op cit, p 371.

11  23 August 1977. BA K20B.

12  Unpublished memoir, op cit, p 147.

13  COS (42) 21 (0) of 8 April 1942.

14  H. T. Baillie-Grohman. Unpublished autobiography. Vol. II, p 154.

15  e.g. Habbakuk.

16  Albert Wedemeyer, *Wedemeyer Reports.* New York, 1958, pp 107–8.

17  Interview with General Albert Wedemeyer.

18  COS (42) 24 (0) of 10 April 1942.

19  *History of Combined Operations,* op cit, pp 34 and 53.

20  Dwight D. Eisenhower, *Crusade in Europe.* London, 1948, p 75.

21  *The Papers of Dwight David Eisenhower: The War Years* Vol. 1 ed. Alfred D. Chandler. Baltimore, 1970, pp 320–1.

22  Eisenhower to Marshall, 26 June 1942. Ibid, p 359.

23  Dwight D. Eisenhower, *At Ease. Stories I tell to Friends.* New York, 1967, pp 281–2.

24  NA ABC 385 (1.28.42) Sec I. A.

25  29 July 1942. *Papers,* op cit, p 426.

26  Marshall to Eisenhower, 30 July 1942. Eisenhower to Ismay, 4 August 1942. *Papers,* op cit, pp 440–2.

27  Eisenhower to Ismay, 30 October 1942. *Papers,* op cit, pp 646–7.

28  Dalton diary, 7 September (?) 1942.

29  COS (42) 48 (0) of 1 June 1942.

30  COS (42) 62 (0) of 1 July 1942.

31  28 May 1942. *Grand Strategy,* Vol. III, op cit, p 618.

32  *The Turn of the Tide,* op cit, p 394. Robert E. Sherwood, *The White House Papers of Harry L. Hopkins.* Vol. II. London, 1949, p 559.

33  Interview with Lord Adeane.

34  *Wedemeyer Reports,* op cit, p 136.

35  Unpublished memoir, op cit, p 158.

36  'Points Mentioned by the President to the CCO.' 16 June 1942. BA B13. cf Mountbatten to Roosevelt, 15 June 1942. President's Personal Files. NA Franklin D. Roosevelt Library.

37  Henry L. Stimson and McGeorge Bundy, *On Active Service in Peace and War.* London, 1949, pp 219–20.

## CHAPTER 14

*pages 186–196*

1 Ronald Atkin, *Dieppe, 1942. The Jubilee Disaster*. London, 1980, p 249.
2 DO (42) 10 and COS (4) 103 (0) Final of 18 April 1942.
3 COS (42) 36 (0) of 5 May 1942.
4 COS (42) 48 (0) of 1 June 1942.
5 *Grand Strategy*, Vol. III, op cit, p 621.
6 Colonel C. P. Stacey, *Official History of the Canadian Army in the Second World War*. Vol. I. Ottawa. Fourth Printing (corrected) 1966, pp 340–1.
7 *The Turn of the Tide*, op cit, p 487. cf PRO PREM 3/256. 19 August 1942.
8 COS (42) 211 of 20 July 1942; 213 of 21 July; and 218 of 27 July.
9 *The Turn of the Tide*, op cit, pp 372–3.
10 *The Watery Maze*, op cit, p 169.
11 *Apes to Warlords*, op cit, p 153.
12 PRO DEFE 2/551.
13 Hughes Hallett, Unpublished memoir, op cit, pp 152–4.
   *History of Combined Operations*, op cit, p 38.
14 Hughes Hallett, op cit, p 155.
   *History of Combined Operations*, op cit, p 39.
   PRO DEFE 2/551, p 6.
   *Dieppe*, op cit, p 57.
15 Mountbatten's address to Dieppe veterans, Toronto, 29 September 1973.
16 Unpublished memoir, op cit, Vol. II, p 156.
17 Report by Brigadier L. K. Truscott. PRO DEFE 2/335.
18 Address to Dieppe veterans, op cit.
19 Interview with Viscount Head.
20 PRO DEFE 2/551, p 7.
21 Ibid.
22 Hughes Hallett, Unpublished memoir, op cit, pp 165–6.
   *Dieppe*, op cit, p 32.
   Mountbatten told the story similarly, though addressing Churchill's question to himself.
23 Interview on B.B.C. TV, 19 August 1972.
24 M to Ismay, 29 August 1950. Ismay papers II/3/260/1.
   Ismay to Churchill, 14 August 1950. Ibid, II/3/258.
25 Winston Churchill, *The Second World War*. Vol. IV. London, 1951, pp 458–9.
26 PRO DEFE 2/326.
27 A. B. Austin, *We Landed at Dawn*. London, 1943, p 65.
28 *The Papers of Dwight David Eisenhower*. Vol. III, op. cit, p 1998.
29 14 February 1943. PRO DEFE 2/782a.
30 London, 1976, pp 80–90.
31 *The Second World War*, Vol. IV, op cit, pp 458–9. cf *Grand Strategy*, Vol. III, p 643.
32 Field Marshal Viscount Montgomery, *Memoirs*. London, 1958, pp 75–6.
33 25 February 1959. BA B73.
34 27 February 1959. Ibid.
35 4 March 1959. Ibid.
36 Nigel Hamilton, *Monty. The Making of a General*. London, 1981, pp 547–56.
37 'Military Lessons to be Drawn from the Assault on Dieppe.' SR 830/42 of 1 January 1942.
38 M to Vice-Admiral K. G. B. Dewar, 10 October 1942. DEW/10.
39 Unpublished memoir, op cit, Vol. II, p 156.
40 'Raid on Dieppe (Naval Operations).' Battle Summary No 33. Naval Staff History. BR 1736 (26). Revised 1959. Naval Section, Admiralty.
41 Colonel C. P. Stacey, *Official History of the Canadian Army*, op cit, Vol. I, p 398.
42 Kenneth J. Clifford, *Amphibious Warfare Development in Britain and America from 1920–40*. New York, 1983, p 144.
43 *Memoirs*, op cit, p 77. cf Baillie-Grohman, *RUSI Journal*, May 1953.
44 *Official History of the Candian Army*, op cit, Vol. I, p 399.
45 Churchill to Grigg, 30 August 1942; Grigg to Churchill, 4 September 1942. PRO PREM 3 256.
46 31 August 1942. BA B18.
47 22 December 1942. BA B18.
48 20 April 1959. cit A. J. P. Taylor, *Beaverbrook*. London, 1972, p 638.

Rundstedt's Battle Report of 3 September 1942 and *Abwehr* HQ (Paris) Report of 14 September 1942, cit *Grand Strategy*, Vol. III, p 637.

## CHAPTER 15

*pages 197–215*

1 COS (42) 146 (0) of 13 October 1942.

2   M to Churchill, 15 June 1943. BA N38. '

3   COS (43) 121 (0) of 8 June 1943.

4   Head to Hughes Hallett, 17 December 1942. COHQ SR 1875/42. BA B39.

5   COS (43) 24 (0) of 19 February 1943.

6   *The Turn of the Tide*, op cit, p 596.

7   Robert Adleman and Colonel George Walton, *The Devil's Brigade*. Philadelphia, 1966, p 32.

8   16 February 1943. BA N38.

9   Dalton diary, 8 January 1942.

10  COS (42) 128 of 23 April 1942.

11  *From a Biography of Myself*, op cit, p 132.

12  Ibid, pp 155–7.

13  Unpublished diary, 8 February 1942.

14  7 June 1944. BA S343.

15  7 October 1942. BA B28.

16  8 October 1942. Ibid.

17  *The Watery Maze*, op cit, p 189.

18  Ibid, p 66.

19  *History of Combined Operations*, op cit, pp 44–5.

20  COS (42) 97 (0) of 22 August 1942.

21  Churchill to M, 1 November 1942. PRO PREM 3 260/13.

22  J 0208/1 of 6 November 1942. BA B39.

23  *History of Combined Operations*, op cit, p 46.

24  *The Turn of the Tide*, op cit, p 542.

25  Interview between Major-General Macleod and Alan Campbell-Johnson. Campbell-Johnson narrative. Vol. II, p 33.

26  Robert E. Sherwood, *The White House Papers of Harry L. Hopkins*. Vol. II, op. cit, p 686.

27  Wedemeyer to Handy, 22 January 1943. NA. OPD Exec 3. Item 1a. Paper 5.

28  *The Turn of the Tide*, op cit, p 557.

29  *The White House Papers*, op cit, Vol. II, p 686.
    cf *Grand Strategy*, op cit, Vol. IV, p 265.

30  COS (43) 123 (0) of 11 June 1943.

31  Interview between M and Robin Bousfield. Transcripts. Vol. II, p 36.

32  Diary, 10 July 1943.

33  Anecdote recorded for possible use by Prince of Wales at Alamein Reunion. BA N73.

34  *The Watery Maze*, op cit, p 250.

35  Eisenhower to M, 11 August 1942. *The Papers of Dwight David Eisenhower*, op cit, Vol. I, p 459.

36  CCS 67 of 22 January 1943.

37  *Grand Strategy*, op cit, Vol. IV, p 275.
    *History of Combined Operations*, op cit, pp 58–9.

38  COS (42) 180 of 16 June 1942.

39  26 December 1942. BA S96.

40  M to Churchill, 15 June 1943. BA N38.

41  COS (42) 182 of 18 June 1942.

42  *The Watery Maze*, op cit, p 223.

43  COS (42) 329 of 27 November 1942.

44  PRO PREM 3 260/13.

45  'Life and Times', op cit, Programme 5, Reel 5, Page 1.

46  *Crusade in Europe*, op cit, p 258.

47  *Mulberry*, op cit, p 16 and p 79.

48  30 May 1942. PRO PREM 3/216/1.

49  *Mulberry*, op cit, p 119.

50  27 October 1977. Hussey papers.

51  Hughes Hallett papers. JHH 7/2.

52  *Mulberry*, op cit, p 135.

53  Ibid, pp 138–9.

54  COS (42) 59 (0) of 25 June 1942.

55  *History of Combined Operations*, op cit, p 196.

56  COS (42) 59 (0) of 25 June 1942.

57  Interview between Lloyd and Robin Bousfield. Transcripts. Vol. II, pp 60–1.

58  Ibid. cf Memorandum by Mr G. Whitehead. BA K39.

59  *History of Combined Operations*, op cit, p 195.

60  *From Apes to Warlords*, op cit, p 158.

61  5 December 1942. PRO PREM 3 216/6.

62  10 January 1943. Ibid.

63  COS (43) 51 (0) of 22 March 1943. M to Churchill, 3 May 1943. BA M38. Ernest King and Walter Whitehill, *Fleet Admiral King*. New York, 1952, p 486.

64  NA 165. Anglo British Conversations. 15 September 1943. 825 2.

65  Alexander to Churchill, 7 January 1943. PRO ADM 199/1932.

66  10 June 1943. PREM 3 216/2.

67  14 January 1944. PREM 3 216/4.

68  15 June 1943. Lady Pamela Hicks papers.

69  Interview between Dr Brooks and Robin Bousfield. Campbell-Johnson narrative. Vol. II, p 25.

70  COS (43) 110 (0) of 24 May 1943.

71  Lieutenant-General Sir Frederick Morgan, *Overture to Overlord*. London, 1950, p 181.

72  COS (43) 139 of 3 May 1943. Memo to Churchill of 27 April 1943.

73  Churchill to M, 1 May 1943. *History of Combined Operations*, op cit, p 60.

74  *Overture to Overlord*, op cit, p 143.

75 4 February 1944. BA N77.
76 *Mulberry,* op cit, p 130.
77 *The Watery Maze,* op cit, p 274.
78 *Overture to Overlord,* op cit, p 144.
79 *Mulberry,* op cit, p 130.
80 18 September 1943. BA C50.
81 *History of Combined Operations,* op cit, p 74.
82 6 July 1944. BA C295.
83 14 June 1944. Personal Diary of the Supreme Allied Commander, South-East Asia.

## CHAPTER 16

### *pages 216–226*

1 Diary, 6 August 1943.
2 M to Wildman-Lushington, 9 August 1943. BA C161.
3 *The Turn of the Tide,* op cit, p 713.
4 Churchill to Ismay, 24 July 1943. PRO PREM 3 143/8.
5 M to Wildman-Lushington, 9 August 1943. BA C161.
6 M to Patricia, 2 April 1944. Lady Mountbatten papers.
7 Ismay to M, 14 May 1946. Ismay papers. IV/MOU/4D6.
8 cit Raymond Callahan, *Burma 1942–1945.* London, 1978, p 68.
9 Record of meeting made by M and subsequently confirmed by General Irwin. BA K261.
10 Telegram 6157/COS of 22 July 1943 (DO(43)16).
11 Churchill to Ismay, 26 July 1943. PRO PREM3 143/8.
12 *The Turn of the Tide,* op cit, p 623. COS (43) 121 of 8 June 1943.
13 Leo Amery diaries, 31 May 1943.
14 Ibid, 9 June 1943.
15 Roosevelt to Churchill, 25 June 1943. PRO PREM 3/53/3.
16 Ibid.
   cf Forrest C. Pogue, *George C. Marshall, Organizer of Victory.* New York, 1973, p 259.
17 *Cunningham of Hyndhope,* op cit, p 222.
18 Draft telegram, apparently never sent, from Churchill to Roosevelt. BA C304.
19 Ismay to Churchill, 30 June 1949. Ismay papers. II/3/162/3.
20 Anthony Eden, *The Reckoning.* London, 1965, p 404.
21 Interview with General Sir Ian Jacob. cf Ronald Lewin, *Churchill as Warlord.* London, 1973, p 214.
22 Pound to A. V. Alexander. No 240330. BA C305.
23 *The Turn of the Tide,* op cit, p 693.
24 Concrete No 98 of 11 August 1943. BA C305.
25 Welfare No 64 of 11 August 1943. Ibid.
26 *Fleet Admiral King,* op cit, p 487.
27 Interview with General Wedemeyer.
28 Pound to A. V. Alexander, 25 August 1943. Alexander papers. AVAR/5/8/31.
29 *Washington Despatches 1941–45.* ed. H. G. Nicholas. London, 1981, pp 248–52.
30 Elliott Roosevelt, *As He Saw It.* New York, 1946, pp 71–2.
31 PRO PREM 3/53/4.
32 Interview with General Wedemeyer.
33 Cunningham to Admiral Whitworth, September 1943. Whitworth papers.
34 Somerville to Cunningham, 27 October 1943. BM Add Mss 52563 45.
35 *The War Diaries of Oliver Harvey,* ed. John Harvey. London, 1978, p 286.
36 Campbell-Johnson narrative. Vol. II, pp 22–3.
37 Leo Amery diaries, 31 August 1943.
38 *Mulberry,* op cit, p 176.
39 Campbell-Johnson narrative. Vol. II, p 36.
40 M to Patricia, 18 and 26 August 1943. Lady Mountbatten papers.
   cf M to Lady Milford Haven, 19 August 1943. BA Vol. XIII.
   M to Edwina, 18 August 1943. BA S144.
41 28 August 1943. BA N41.
42 18 August 1943. BA S144.
43 Pound to Churchill, 31 August 1943. PRO PREM 3/53/4.
44 COS (43) 236 of 4 October 1943.
45 7 September 1943. BA S176.
46 Hollis to Ismay, Concrete No 696 of 2 September 1943. PRO PREM 3/53/4.
47 21 August 1943. BA S144.
48 14 November 1943. BA N77.
49 Reminiscences of Air Marshal Sir Victor Goddard. BA N100a.
50 11 September 1943. BA C177.

## CHAPTER 17

### *pages 227–240*

1 5 October 1943. Personal diary of the

Supreme Allied Commander, South-East
Asia.
2  11 October 1943. Ibid.
3  11 October 1943. Ibid.
   M to Prince of Wales, 14 July 1975. BA
   C324.
4  5 November 1943. Personal diary.
5  Roger Parkinson, *The Auk*. London,
   1977, p 245.
6  24 December 1943. BA N78.
7  SACSEA Personalities Report. Paras 118
   and 119. BA C324.
8  *Pownall Diaries*, op cit, pp 110–11.
9  11 November 1943. Auchinleck papers.
   1041.
10 23 December 1943. Ibid. 1045.
11 M to Brooke, 3 February 1944. BA C50.
12 *The Viceroy's Journal*. ed. Penderel
   Moon. London, 1973, p 15.
13 *Grand Strategy*, op cit, Vol. V, p 143.
   cf Eisenhower to M, 14 September 1943.
   *The Papers of Dwight David Eisenhower*,
   op cit, Vol. III, pp 1420–4.
14 Draft of 20 November 1943. BA C229.
15 October 1943. Somerville papers. 208
   3/31.
16 Interview with General Wedemeyer.
17 *The Turn of the Tide*, op cit, p 693.
18 *Pownall Diaries*, op cit, p 117.
19 9 December 1943. Ismay papers. IV/Som
   3a.
20 Ismay to Somerville, 20 December 1943.
   Ismay papers. IV/Som/4c.
21 Wedemeyer to Handy, 13 April 1944.
   NA OPD RG–165 Box No 3.
22 COS (44) 21 (o) of 24 January 1944.
23 3 February 1944. BA S310.
24 M to Brooke, 3 February 1944.
   Brooke to M, 18 February 1944. BA C50.
25 COS (44) 177 (o) of 31 May 1944.
26 1 February 1944. Somerville papers. 208
   3/31.
27 19 January 1944. Ismay papers.
   IV/Som/5/1.
28 Somerville to Cunningham, 9 June 1944.
   BA C88.
29 Ibid, 27 June 1944. Roskill papers. 5/57.
30 Pownall to M, 17 June 1944. BA C229.
31 M to Pownall, 17 and 20 June 1944. BA
   C229.
32 20 June 1944. BA S145.
33 24 June 1944. BA C229.
34 Somerville diary, 7 July 1944. BM Add
   Mss 52564.
35 Lambe to Roskill, undated. BA I16.
36 Philip Mason, *A Shaft of Sunlight*.

London, 1978, pp 177–8.
   Interview with Philip Mason.
37 Somerville diary, 13 July 1944. BM Add
   Mss 52564.
38 COS (44) 211 (o) of 5 August 1944.
39 22 November 1944. BA C250.
40 30 October 1944. BA S310.
41 10 February 1944. BA C88.
42 See pp 294–5 below.
43 Portal to M, 13 March 1959. Roskill
   papers. 5/57.
44 Major-General S. Woodburn Kirby, *The
   War Against Japan*. Vol. III. London,
   1961, pp 47–8.
   *Grand Strategy*, op cit, Vol. V, p 145.
45 BA C324. pp 28–30.
46 *The War Against Japan*, op cit, Vol. III,
   pp 46–7.
   SACSEA Personalities Report, op cit, pp
   14–15.
47 4 March 1944. BA C88.
48 Interview with Vice-Admiral Edden.
49 2 September 1943. BA C93.
50 30 September 1943. Somerville papers.
   208 3/31.
51 PRO WP (43) 414 of 22 September
   1943.
52 27 October 1943. BM Add Mss 52563.
53 COS (43) 277 (o) of 12 November
   1943.
54 17 November 1943. PRO PREM 3 53/7.
55 21 November 1943. cit *Churchill and the
   Admirals*, op cit, pp 251–2.
56 26 June 1944. BA C147.
57 4 December 1943. BM Add Mss 52563.
58 Somerville to Cunningham, 3 January
   1944. BM Add Mss 52563.
   cf Cunningham to Roskill, 20 February
   1957. BA I16.
59 *Pownall Diaries*, op cit, pp 132–3.
   M to Ismay, 17 January 1944. BA C147.
60 M to Ismay, 17 January 1944. BA C147.
61 Lambe to Cunningham, 16 February
   1944. BA S310.
   Cunningham to Somerville, 10 March
   1944. Somerville papers. SMVL 8/2.
   cf Cunningham to M, 10 March 1944.
   BA C99.
62 Interview with Vice-Admiral Edden.
63 Somerville to M. Telegram No 2412/6.
   M to Somerville, 5 March 1944. BA C93.
64 A. W. Laybourne to Roskill, 17 February
   1955. Roskill papers. 5/57.
65 1 March 1944. BA S310.

## CHAPTER 18

### pages 241–249

1 ABC 384. CCS 747/1 of 21 December 1944.
2 COS (43) 115 (0) of 31 May 1943.
3 John Davies, *Dragon by the Tail*. New York, 1972, p 275.
4 Barbara W. Tuchman, *Stilwell and the American Experience in China. 1911–45*. New York, 1970, p 385.
5 Ibid, p 378.
6 Ibid, p 424.
7 26 January 1944. BA C171.
8 Charles F. Romanus and Riley Sunderland, *Stilwell's Mission to China*. Washington, 1966, p 376.
9 OZ 3167 of 12 October 1943. Copy in Alanbrooke papers. Box 004.
10 Personal diary, 16 October 1943.
11 Richard Hough, *Mountbatten. Hero of our Time*. London, 1980, pp 175–6.
12 M to Churchill, 23 October 1943. BA N41.
13 Ibid.
cf 'Report to the Combined Chiefs of Staff by the Supreme Allied Commander South-East Asia 1943–46.' London (HMSO), 1951, p 5.
14 Personal diary, 18 October 1943.
15 *Stilwell's Mission to China*, op cit, p 380. Joseph W. Stilwell, *The Stilwell Papers*. ed. Theodore White. New York, 1948, p 246.
16 Directive from Churchill of 21 October 1943. PRO PREM 3 147/4.
Marshall to Stilwell, 23 October 1943. NA ABC 32201 Sec 1.
G. A. Lincoln to General Hall, 17 November 1943. NA ABC 32201 Sec 1.
17 Personal diary, 19 October 1943.
18 20 October 1943. RA GVI PS 6574.
19 8 November 1943. President's Personal File. NA. Franklin Roosevelt Library.
20 16 November 1943. BA C20.
21 *Pownall Diaries*, op cit, p 116.
22 Edwina to M, 10 November 1943. BA S66.
23 *Stilwell Papers*, op cit, 7 October 1943.
24 SACSEA Personalities Report, op cit, Para 94.
25 1 November 1943. BA C88.
26 *Stilwell Papers*, op cit, 12 January 1944.
27 Ibid, 1 January 1944 to 25 August 1944.
28 *Wedemeyer Reports*, op cit, p 250.

29 Ibid, p 249.
30 3 February 1944. BA C50.
31 Personal diary, 18 September 1945.
32 M to Portal, 22 December 1943. BA C202.
33 1 November 1943. BA C88.
34 *The War Against Japan*, Vol. III, op cit, p 48.
35 Personal diary, 11 December 1943.
36 NA 165 ABC 332 01 of 14 December 1943.
37 Wedemeyer to Handy, 13 April 1944. NA OPD RG–165. Box 3.
38 M to Stratemeyer, 11 December 1943. BA C255.

## CHAPTER 19

### pages 250–259

1 Air Marshal Sir John Baldwin, 'Life and Times', op cit, Programme 6, Reel 4, Page 10.
Personal diary, 22 October 1943.
2 Reminiscences. BA N99.
3 9 November 1943. BA C2.
4 *The War Against Japan*, op cit, Vol. III, pp 34–5.
5 M to Brooke, 3 January 1944. BA C50.
6 Personal diary, 11 September 1944.
7 Ibid, 7 October 1944.
8 3 September 1943. BA S310.
9 Report to the Combined Chiefs of Staff, op cit, pp 16–17.
10 John Connell, *Auchinleck*. London, 1959, p 777.
11 Ministry of Information Far Eastern War Committee. First Quarterly Report. 17 April 1944. PRO HP 950/4.
12 3 October 1943. Beaverbrook papers. C/255.
13 23 September 1943. BA C96.
14 Eden to M, 29 September 1943. BA C96.
15 Churchill to Ismay, 2 October 1943. BA C147.
16 22 November 1943. Auchinleck papers. 1045.
17 Auchinleck to Brooke. Auchinleck papers. 1050.
18 Michael Edwardes, *The Last Years of British India*. London, 1963, p 147.
19 Conversations between Joan Wanklyn, Brigadiers A. J. Woolford and Mead, and Major S. T. Clark. BA K18.

20  Personal diary, 16 December 1943.
21  Ibid, 13 December 1943.
22  Colonel Charles N. Hunter, *Galahad*. San Antonio, Texas, 1963, pp 14–15.
23  Lowell Thomas, *Back to Mandalay*. London, 1952, pp 118–19.
24  20 September 1945. BA C161.
25  Lambe to M. 1 March 1944. BA S310.
26  20 November 1943. BA C229. [draft only].
27  Diary of 11 December 1945. BM Add Mss 52578.
28  Interview with General Sir Hugh Stockwell.
29  Typescript of unpublished autobiography. Joubert papers. AC 71/14. Box 2.
30  SACSEA Personalities Report, op cit, para 67.
    M to Brendan Bracken, May 1944. BA C27.
31  Unpublished autobiography, op cit.
32  COS (44) 177 (o) of 31 May 1944.
33  COS (44) 293 (o) of 31 August 1944.
34  COS (44) 404 (o) of 18 December 1944.
35  M to Bracken, 28 March 1944. Bracken to M, 23 May 1944. BA C27.
36  op cit, para 65.
37  Interview with Vice-Admiral Sir Kaye Edden.
38  M to General H. H. Arnold, 3 January 1944. BA C11.
39  6 February 1945. BA C2.
40  *The Viceroy's Journal*, op cit, p 89.
41  COS (44) 138 (o) of 28 April 1944.
42  COS (44) 204 (o) of 22 June 1944.
43  M to Wildman-Lushington, 12 November 1943. BA C161.
44  Undated. BA S320.
45  Personal diary, 6–11 November 1943.
46  *Stilwell's Mission to China*, op cit, p 383.
47  23 October 1943. BA C50.
48  23 October 1943. PRO PREM 3 70/3.
49  M to Auchinleck, 6 November 1943. BA C137.
50  COS (44) 177 (o) of 31 May 1944.

## CHAPTER 20
### pages 260–267

1  See Chapter 15, p 223 above.
2  Field-Marshal Sir William Slim, *Defeat into Victory*. London, 1956, p 192.
3  *The Second World War*, op cit, Vol. IV, p 119.
4  CPS 83 of 18 August 1943. PRO PREM 3 147/1.
5  13 April 1944. Diaries 1943–6. Library of Congress.
6  JCS 128th Meeting of 23 November 1943. NA ABC 381 (Japan) Sec 6.
7  Arthur Bryant, *Triumph in the West*. London, 1959, p 44.
8  *Churchill and the Admirals*, op cit, p 219.
9  Winston Churchill, *The Second World War*. Vol. V. London, 1952, p 78.
10  7 January 1944. BA S96.
11  COS (Q) 38 of 20 August 1943.
12  M to Brooke, 23 October 1943. Brooke to M, 2 November 1943. BA C50.
13  M to George VI, 7 January 1944. BA S96.
14  *As He Saw It*, op cit, p 144.
15  Fleet Admiral William D. Leahy, *I Was There*, London, 1950, p 236.
16  Personal diary, 21 November 1943.
17  *Triumph in the West*, op cit, p 76.
18  Personal diary, 24 November 1943.
19  Ibid, 27 November 1943.
20  Ibid, 30 November and 1 December 1943.
21  22 December 1943. BA S66.
22  6 December 1943. PRO PREM 3 147/7.
23  Minute of 23 February 1944. PRO ADM 205/35.
24  *The Memoirs of Lord Ismay*. London, 1960, p 336.
    *Triumph in the West*, op cit, p 105.
25  *Triumph in the West*, op cit, p 109.
26  *The Memoirs of Lord Ismay*, op cit, p 342.
27  *The Viceroy's Journal*, op cit, pp 39–40.
28  6 December 1943. BA C50.
29  Ralph Edwards papers. REDW 2/18.
30  COS (43) 313 (o) of 23 December 1943; COS (43) 320 (o) of 29 December 1943; COS (43) 323 (o) of 31 December 1943.
31  *The Watery Maze*, op cit, p 369.
32  25 January 1944. BA C202.
33  3 January 1944. BA S96.
34  3 January 1944. BA C50.
35  COS (44) 48 (o) of 14 February 1944.
36  8 February 1944. BA S145.
37  3 February 1944. BA S310.
38  COS (44) 48 (o) of 14 February 1944; COS (44) 52 (o) of 18 February 1944; COS (44) 54 (o) of 21 February 1944. cf *Triumph in the West*, op cit, pp 147–8.
39  PRO PREM 3 148/4.

40  Charles F. Romanus and Riley Sunderland, *Stilwell's Command Problems*. Washington, 1955, p 161. *Stilwell and the American Experience in China*, op cit, p 428.
41  COS (44) 52 (0) of 18 February 1944.
42  Lambe to M, 1 March 1944. BA S310.
43  *Stilwell's Command Problems*, op cit, p 163.
44  M to Dill, 16 March 1944. BA C88.
45  18 February 1944. Alanbrooke papers. Box 004.
46  Memorandum M 301/4 of 20 March 1944. Alanbrooke papers. Box II.
47  Chiefs of Staff to Churchill of 28 March 1944. Ibid.
48  30 March 1944. Ibid.
49  Dening to M, 15 April 1944. BA C84.

## CHAPTER 21

### pages 268–277

1  4 July 1943. NA SRS 1096. A.I.
2  12 October 1943. NA SRS 1115.
3  *Stilwell's Command Problems*, op cit, p 121n. cf Report to the Combined Chiefs of Staff, op cit, p 40.
4  Marshall to MacArthur, 23 May 1944. NA SRH–034. Ronald Lewin, *Ultra Goes to War*. London, 1978, pp 254–5.
5  Interview with General Wedemeyer.
6  For a lucid analysis of this subject see Ronald Lewin, *The Other Ultra*. London, 1982, p 244.
7  22 January 1944. NA SRS 1221.
8  Personal diary, 14 December 1943.
9  13 December 1943. BA S68.
10  Christison to M, 26 February 1944. BA C49.
11  8 February 1944. Photostat provided by General Mansergh. BA K18.
12  25 February 1944. BA S145.
13  'Life and Times of General Sir Philip Christison, Bart.' Imperial War Museum. p 121.
14  *Pownall Diaries*, op cit, p 128.
15  Reminiscences of General Sir Philip Christison. BA N99a.
16  5 March 1944. BA C247 A.
17  Personal diary, 7 March 1944.

18  SEACOS 112. Copy in NA ABC 686 China.
19  COS (44) 87 (0) of 16 March 1944 and 89 (0) of 17 March 1944.
20  CCS 494/4 of 17 March 1944.
21  *Defeat into Victory*, op cit, p 306.
22  20 and 30 March 1944. BA S145.
23  M to Giffard, 16 March 1944. BA C217.
24  Peirse to Portal, 13 May 1944. BA C217. Somerville diary, 31 May 1944. BM Add Mss 52564.
25  Somerville diary. BM Add Mss 52564.
26  *Pownall Diaries*, op cit, p 151.
27  Peirse to Portal, 13 May 1944. Covering note to letter at n24 above. Peirse papers. AC 71/13. Box 3.
28  6 May 1944. BA S145.
29  Ibid.
30  *The War Against Japan*, Vol. III, op cit, pp 324–5.
31  Memorandum of 5 June 1944, op cit.
32  *Defeat into Victory*, op cit, p 342.
33  Dorman-Smith to Amery, 20 April 1944. 10 Mss Eur E/215/6.
34  Personal diary, 8 April 1944.
35  *The Viceroy's Journal*, op cit, p 65.
36  *Future Indefinite*, op cit, p 304.
37  *Stilwell's Command Problems*, op cit, p 378.
38  *Stilwell and the American Experience in China*, op cit, p 448.
39  19 May 1944. Lady Mountbatten papers.
40  *Pownall Diaries*, op cit, p 126.
41  Derek Tulloch, *Wingate in Peace and War*. London, 1972, pp 152–3.
42  19 March 1944. BA C288.
43  2 April 1944. BA S145. cf M to Churchill, 28 March 1944. BA N41.
44  26 June 1944. BA S145.
45  Report to the Combined Chiefs of Staff, op cit, p 71.
46  SEACOS 152. COS (44) 146 (0) of 5 May 1944.
47  COS (44) 149 (0) of 8 May 1944.
48  COS (44) 171 (0) of 25 May 1944.
49  27 May 1944. Ismay papers. IV/Pow/412.

## CHAPTER 22

### pages 278–292

1  COS (43) 127 (0) of 17 June 1943.
2  COS (43) 129 (0) of 18 June 1943.

3  COS (43) 233 (0) of 1 October 1943.
4  Personal diary, 12–20 November 1943.
5  Somerville to Lady Somerville, 8 October 1943. Somerville papers. 3/31.
6  Ismay to M, 23 November 1943. BA C147.
    Interview with General Wedemeyer.
7  Auchinleck to Ismay, 26 January 1944. Ismay papers IV/Con/I/IE.
8  Ismay to M, 23 November 1943. BA C147.
9  M to Ismay, 27 November 1943. BA C147.
10  Lecture by Admiral Jerram delivered 30 March 1945. BA K58A.
11  19 May 1944. Lady Pamela Hicks papers.
12  Interviews with Mr Philip Mason and Mr Julian Amery.
13  Ralph Arnold, *A Very Quiet War.* London, 1962, p 130.
14  Ismay to Pownall, 27 May 1944. Ismay papers. IV/Pow/4/2a.
15  Diary, 1 June 1944. BM Add Mss 52564.
16  Personal diary, 12–20 November 1943.
17  Layton to Cunningham, 7 February 1944. BM Add Mss 52571.
18  Brooke to M, 18 February 1944. Alanbrooke papers. Box 004.
19  Dening to M, 19 May 1944. BA C84.
20  COS (44) 225 (0) of 6 July 1944 and 236 (0) of 14 July 1944.
21  *Pownall Diaries,* op cit, pp 176–7.
22  25 July 1944. *Auchinleck,* op cit, p 775.
23  *Stilwell and the American Experience in China,* op cit, p 473.
24  Ibid, p 474.
25  Personalities Report, op cit, para 98.
26  COS (44) 262 (0) of 7 August 1944. *Triumph in the West,* op cit, p 248.
27  COS (44) 259 (0) of 4 August 1944 and 261 (0) of 5 August 1944.
    Cunningham Diary, 7 August 1944. BM Add Mss 52577.
28  COS (44) 265 (0) of 8 August 1944 and 269 (0)of 9 August 1944.
    *The Reckoning,* op cit, p 267.
29  COS (44) 403 (0) of 15 December 1944.
30  *The Reckoning,* op cit, p 267.
31  *Triumph in the West,* op cit, p 253.
32  12 June 1944. NA ABC 384 Burma. (8.25.42.) (SCC 6).
33  M to Lambe, 18 July 1944. BA S310.
34  *Pownall Diaries,* op cit, p 187.
35  COS (44) 23 (0) of 2 October 1944.
36  *Triumph in the West,* op cit, p 300.
37  10 October 1944. BA S145.

38  10 October 1944. BA C96.
    cf M to Churchill, 11 October 1944. PRO PREM 3 149/8.
39  Personal diary, 20 October 1944.
40  Personal diary, 21 October 1944.
41  3 August 1944. Alanbrooke papers. 6/X/2/7.
42  16 October 1944. JP (44) 253 (S) Final.
    cf Cunningham diary, 17 October 1944. BM Add Mss 52577.
43  M to Stilwell, 15 July 1944. BA C253.
44  Interview with General Wedemeyer.
45  7 August 1944. BA N41.
46  20 October 1944. Auchinleck papers. 1068.
47  26 October 1944. BA C253.
48  20 November 1944. NA President's Personal Files. Franklin D. Roosevelt Library.
49  M to Carton de Wiart, 14 November 1944. BA C42.
50  *Wedemeyer Reports,* op cit, p 291.
51  20 February 1945. BA C280.
52  cit Richard Humble, *Fraser of North Cape.* London, 1983, p 245.
53  M to Somerville, 22 November 1944. BA C250.
54  Churchill to Alexander, 29 October 1944. PRO PREM 3 164/3.
55  3 January 1945. BM Add Mss 52562.
56  M to Somerville, 2 January 1945. BA C250.
57  26 November 1944. BA C95.
58  Portal to M, 29 October 1943. BA C202.
59  16 August 1944. BA C170.
60  *Pownall Diaries,* op cit, p 168.
61  Charles F. Romanus and Riley Sunderland, *Time Runs Out in CBI.* Washington, 1959, p 88.
    cf M to Montgomery, 20 November 1944. BA N77.
62  20 November 1944. BA N77.
63  31 October 1944. Alanbrooke papers. Box 004.
64  3 November 1944. Ibid.
65  *Pownall Diaries,* op cit, p 193.
66  Personal diary, 15 December 1944.
67  11 March 1945. BA C32.
68  NA President's Personal Files. Franklin D. Roosevelt Library.
69  9 December 1944. Ibid.
70  Somerville to M, 10 November 1944. BA C250.
71  14 December 1944. BA C96.
72  Personal diary, 16 December 1944.
73  Ibid.

74 Report to the Combined Chiefs of Staff, op cit, p 107.
75 SAC 1309 of 22 January 1945. NA President's Personal Files. Franklin D. Roosevelt Library.
76 NA ABC 384 Sec 10.
77 1 December 1944. NA 165 ABC 384 (China) 15, 12, 43.
   Carton de Wiart to M, 30 November 1944. BA C42.
78 *Time Runs Out in CBI*, op cit, pp 225–6.
79 30 March 1945. *The Second World War*. Vol. VI. London, 1954, p 535.
80 Wheeler to Hull, 15 May 1945. cit *Time Runs Out in CBI*, pp 324–5.
81 13 February 1945. NA ABC 384 (Burma) Sec 10.
82 Christison reminiscences. BA N99a. 'Life and Times', op cit, pp 147–8.
83 *Triumph in the West*, op cit, p 382.
84 Memorandum of 9 April 1945. BA C216.
85 Personal diary, 10 April 1945.
86 R.A.F. Museum. AC/76/32. Published in 1972 as *Flying Fever*.
87 Dening to M, 30 March 1945. BA C84.
88 Personal diary, 22 March 1945.
89 Personal diary, 18 April 1945.
90 12 May 1945. Alanbrooke papers.
91 NA. MAGIC Material DIP SRS 1634 of 2 April 1945; SRS 1645 of 11 April 1945; SRS 1647 of 23 April 1945.
92 Report to the Combined Chiefs of Staff, op cit, p 157.
93 8 May 1945. Lady Mountbatten papers.

## CHAPTER 23

### *pages 293–304*

1 Browning to Brooke, 27 March 1945. Alanbrooke papers.
2 cit Nigel Hamilton, *Monty: Master of the Battlefield*. London, 1983, p 804.
3 Browning to Brooke, 27 March 1945. Alanbrooke papers.
4 7 May 1945. BA S146.
5 24 May 1945, Alanbrooke papers. cf M to Brooke, 23 May 1945. BA C50.
6 M to Brooke, 7 June 1945. Leese to M, 8 May 1945. BA C216.
7 Slim papers. SLIM 2/3.
8 23 May 1945. BA C50.
9 94479 CIGS of 18 May 1945. BA C50.
10 Browning to Brooke, 24 May 1945. BA C50.
11 Brooke to M, 19 June 1945. BA C216.
12 cit Ronald Lewin, *Slim the Standardbearer*. London, 1976, p 238.
13 e.g. Reminiscences of General Sir Philip Christison. BA N99a.
14 *Slim the Standardbearer*, op cit, p 128.
15 M to Wedemeyer, 6 May 1945. BA C280. Marshall to Henry Wilson. 5 June 1945. NA ABC 384 (Indo China) 16.12.44.
16 8 May 1945. BA C96.
17 Marshall to Wilson, 5 June 1945. NA ABC 384 (Indo China) 16.12.44.
18 Wedemeyer to M, 14 June 1945. BA C280.
19 Ismay to M, 21 March 1945. Ismay papers. IV/Mou/2Ca.
20 Personal diary, 12 July 1945.
21 Ibid, 13 and 14 July 1945.
22 cit Ronald Lewin, *The Other Ultra*, op cit, p 178.
23 6 April 1945. PRO CCS 802/1.
24 8 May 1945. BA C96.
25 15 May 1945. BM Add Mss 52578.
26 Personalities Report, op cit, para 25.
27 Cunningham diary, 8 August 1945. BM Add Mss 52578.
28 Ibid.
29 Ibid, 9 June 1945. *Triumph in the West*, op cit, p 464.
30 Draft of June 1945. BA C146. Possibly never despatched. Not in Ismay papers.
31 Pownall to M, 1 April 1945. M to Pownall, 25 April 1945. BA C204.
32 Personal diary, 24 July 1945.
33 Ibid.
34 *King George VI*, op cit, p 650.
35 Personal diary, 10 August 1945.
36 Interviews with Admiral Sir John Hamilton and General Sir Ouvry Roberts.
37 Tour diaries, 26 February 1972.
38 For a good description of their activities see Bill Strutton and Michael Pearson, *The Secret Invaders*. London, 1958.
39 Diary of General Sir Ouvry Roberts, 9 September 1945.
40 Interview with General Sir Ouvry Roberts.
41 Personal diary, 14 April 1945.
42 *Triumph in the West*, op cit, p 486.
43 12 August 1945. Ismay papers. IV/Mou/3b.
44 Letter from Russell Braddon to the author.

45  M to MacArthur, 16 August 1945. BA C169.
46  M to Carton de Wiart, 21 August 1945. BA C43.
47  'Life and Times'. Post-production script. Programme 8. Reel 1. Page 4.
48  Blanche d'Alpuget, *Mediator. A Biography of Sir Richard Kirby.* Melbourne, 1977, pp 39–40.
49  Diary of General H. H. Arnold, 24 July 1945. Provided by Mr David Irving.
50  Personal diary, 12 September 1945.

## CHAPTER 24

### pages 305–316

1  8 May 1945. Lady Mountbatten papers.
2  22 August 1944. BA S145.
3  30 August 1944. BA S67.
4  7 May 1945. BA S146.
5  5 May 1944. Lady Mountbatten papers.
6  25 October 1944. BA S17.
7  26 December 1945. BA S146.
8  M to Major-General Dallas Brooks, 23 March 1944. BA C31.
9  Personal diary, 25 December 1943.
10  M to Edwina, 5 May 1944. BA S145.
11  Interview with Mr Alexander Peterson.
12  M to Patricia, 29 March 1942. Lady Mountbatten papers.
13  *King George VI*, op cit, p 749.
14  BA S96.
15  28 August 1944. BA Vol. XIII.
16  9 February 1945. Ibid.
17  6 September 1945. BA S176.
18  14 December 1945. BA S146.
19  M to Edwina, 4 January 1946. BA S146.
20  M to Lady Milford Haven, 23 March 1946. BA Vol. XIII.
21  19 May 1946. BA S93.
22  Portal to M, 13 August 1945. BA C202.
23  M to Portal, 19 August 1945. BA C202.
24  19 August 1945. BA S93.
25  Lascelles to Portal, 31 August 1945. BA S96.
26  3 September 1945. BA S96.
27  Personal diary.
28  Ibid, 7 September 1945.
29  25 September 1945. BA N48.
30  Reminiscences of Sir Brian Kimmins. N99.
31  F. S. V. Donnison, *British Military Administration in the Far East 1943–46.* London, 1956, p 334.
32  Memorandum by Sir Christopher Steel. BA C300.
33  M to Carton de Wiart, 21 August 1945. BA C43.
34  *British Military Administration,* op cit, p 293.
35  Memorandum of 14 April 1944. BA S325. Promulgated in a letter signed by Brigadier E. J. Gibbons, 18 April 1944. Printed in *Burma. The Struggle for Independence.* ed. Hugh Tinker. Vol. I. London, 1983. I have wherever possible given this volume as a reference rather than original manuscript sources.
36  20 March 1944. BA C249.
37  M to Leese. 2 June 1945. *Burma. The Struggle for Independence,* op cit, p 311.
38  20 March 1944. BA C249.
39  11 February 1946. BA S70.
40  Interview with Sir Arthur Drew. Personal diary, 30 September 1945.
41  M to Park, 28 January 1946. BA C196.
42  'Life and Times'. Post-production scripts. Programme 8. Reel 1. Page 7.
43  Interview between Chairman Ne Win and Alan Campbell-Johnson. BA J41.

## CHAPTER 25

### pages 317–323

1  For a good exposition of the background see Hugh Tinker, *The Union of Burma.* Oxford, 1967.
2  Churchill to Amery, PRO PREM 4 50/3. cf Maurice Collis, *Last and First in Burma.* London, 1956, p 14.
3  Dorman-Smith to Amery, May 1944. Dorman-Smith papers. 10 Mss Eur E 215/6.
4  Ibid, 30 October 1944. *Burma. The Struggle for Independence,* op cit, p 105.
5  Personal diary, 25 October 1944.
6  M to Edwina, 7 May 1945. BA S146.
7  2 April 1945. NA MAGIC DIP SRS 1634.
8  16 April 1945. Ibid. SRS 1648.
9  Report to the Combined Chiefs of Staff, op cit, pp 180–1.
10  27 February 1945. *Burma. The Struggle for Independence,* op cit, p 171.
11  1(45)15 of 29 March 1945. PRO CAB 91/5.

12 COSSEA 225 of 30 March 1945. BA
   C248.
   cf M to F. S. V. Donnison, 1 May 1953.
   BA H83.
13 *Defeat into Victory*, op cit, pp 519–20.
14 Dorman-Smith to Amery, 25 July 1945.
   *Burma. The Struggle for Independence*,
   op cit, pp 384–5.
15 Ibid, 25 June 1945. Ibid, p 350.
16 Eden to Churchill, 31 March 1945 and
   Churchill minute of 2 April 1945. PRO
   PREM 3 149/5.
17 Pethick-Lawrence to Attlee, 9 August
   1945. *Burma. The Struggle for
   Independence*, op cit, pp 392–5.
18 M to Chiefs of Staff, 16 May 1945. Ibid,
   p 261.
19 Dorman-Smith to M, 18 May 1945. Ibid,
   p 264.
20 Personal diary, 15 June 1945.
21 Power to Cunningham, 18 June 1945.
   BM Add Mss 52562. 194.
22 Personal diary, 15 June 1945.
23 18 August 1946. Dorman-Smith papers.
   10 Mss Eur E215/15.
24 Dorman-Smith to Amery, 22 July 1945.
   Dorman-Smith papers. 10 Mss Eur
   E215/8.
25 26 August 1945. *Burma. The Struggle for
   Independence*, op cit, p 414.
26 Dorman-Smith to M and to
   Pethick-Lawrence, 27 August 1945.
   *Burma. The Struggle for Independence*,
   op cit, pp 416–20.
27 Interview with U Kyaw Nyein.
28 Maung Maung, *Burma and General Ne
   Win*. Burma, 1969, pp 162–3.
29 Dorman-Smith to Pethick-Lawrence, 10
   September 1945. *Burma. The Struggle for
   Independence*, op cit, pp 465–6.
30 Auchinleck to Wavell, 13 November
   1945. Auchinleck papers. 1112.
31 Unpublished memoir. Dorman-Smith
   papers. 10 Mss Eur. E215/32.
32 Christopher Thorne, *Allies of a Kind*.
   Oxford, 1978, p 685.
33 M to Edwina, 16 January 1946.
   BA S146.
34 Interviews with Chairman Ne Win, U Nu,
   U Maung Maung, U Kyaw Nyein, U
   Myiat Thein.
35 18 August 1945. BA C210.
36 2 April 1946. Dorman-Smith papers. 10
   Mss Eur. E215/10.
37 cit Kenneth Harris, *Attlee*. London, 1982,
   p 359.
38 M to Harold Wilson, 9 July 1968. BA
   K237.
39 5 August 1946. *Burma. The Struggle for
   Independence*, op cit, p 934.

## CHAPTER 26

### pages 324–338

1 *Post Surrender Tasks. Section E of the
   Report to the Combined Chiefs of Staff
   by the Supreme Allied Commander South
   East Asia 1943–45*. London, HMSO,
   1969.
2 Charles Cruickshank, *SOE in the Far
   East*. London, 1983, pp 191–2.
3 *British Military Administration in the Far
   East*, op cit, pp 381–2.
4 M to Oliver Stanley, 29 July 1944. BA
   C252.
5 M to Hall, 4 January 1946. BA C120.
6 Hall to M, 4 February 1946. BA C120.
7 *Post Surrender Tasks*, op cit, para 110.
8 Reminiscences of Sir Ralph Hone. BA
   N99a.
9 cit *Post Surrender Tasks*, op cit, para 113.
10 Personal diary, 29 January 1946.
11 *Post Surrender Tasks*, op cit, para 114.
12 Browning to M, 6 March 1946; M to
   Browning, 9 March 1946. BA C32.
13 Ralph Hone's reminiscences, op cit.
14 Reminiscences of Lieutenant-General Sir
   Denis O'Connor. BA N99a.
15 General J. N. Chaudhuri. *An
   Autobiography*. New Delhi, 1978, p 138.
16 M to Wavell, 31 January 1946. BA C263.
   Sarvepalli Gopal, *Jawaharlal Nehru*. Vol.
   I. London, 1975, p 309.
17 Personal diary, 18 March 1946.
   Gopal, *Nehru*, op cit, p 310.
18 S. K. Chettur, *Malayan Adventure*.
   Bangalore, 1948, p 84.
19 Personal diary, 18 March 1946.
20 Gopal, *Nehru*, op cit, p 310.
21 Interview with U Kyaw Nyein.
22 2 April 1946. Dorman-Smith papers. 10
   Mss Eur. E 215/10.
23 Personal diary, 4 September 1945.
24 *Allies of a Kind*, op cit, p 616.
25 2 February 1945. cit Louis Allen, *The
   End of the War in Asia*. London, 1976,
   pp 34–5.
26 Personal diary, 18 January 1946.

27 Denis O'Connor's reminiscences, op cit.
28 Personal diary, 19 January 1946.
29 25 January 1946. Lady Mountbatten papers.
30 *SOE in the Far East,* op cit, pp 124–5.
31 M to Chiefs of Staff, 14 September 1944. PRO PREM 3 178/3.
32 e.g. M to Eden, 16 August 1944. BA C96.
33 1 January 1945. NA ABC 384 (Indo China). 8.
    cf Louis Allen, 'Studies in the Japanese Occupation of South-East Asia.' *Durham University Journal.* Vol. 64, 1971–2. p 121.
34 Chiefs of Staff to Churchill, 2 August 1944. PRO PREM 3 180/7.
35 M to Sir Hugh Stephenson, 15 June 1968. Brabourne Papers.
36 Louis Allen, *The End of the War in Asia.* op cit, p 118.
37 Ibid. p 113n.
    cf Jean Lacouture, *Ho Chi Minh.* London, 1969, p 83.
38 6 October 1945. BA C281.
    cf Peter M. Dunn, 'Operation Masterdom. The British in Vietnam, 1945–1946.' Unpublished thesis. University of Nevada, 1973, p 71. Copy in BA.
39 9 September 1945. Alanbrooke papers.
40 Philippe Devillers, *Histoire du Vietnam.* Paris, 1952, p 144.
41 Personal diary, 30 November 1945.
42 *Leclerc.* Paris, 1952, p 187.
43 *Post Surrender Tasks,* op cit, para 26.
44 PRO WO 203/4453/HS/SEAC 1567/3. Professor Valentine to M, 13 October 1973 and M to Valentine, 24 October 1973. BA K264.
45 *Post Surrender Tasks,* op cit, paras 28–32.
46 4 October 1945. BA C91
47 cit Peter M. Dunn. 'Operation Masterdom . . .' op cit, pp 77–78.
48 M to Gracey, 31 Oct 1945. Gracey papers. GRACEY 40.
49 'Operation Masterdom . . .', op cit, p 74.
    cf Ellis Hanner, *The Struggle for Indochina, 1940–1953.* Stanford University Press, 1967, p 119.
50 George Rosie, *The British in Vietnam.* London, 1970. See in particular pp 129–40.
51 'Studies in the Japanese Occupation. . . .', op cit, p 127.

52 Tour diaries, 4 June 1972.
53 *Post Surrender Tasks,* op cit, paras 37–42.
    *British Military Administration,* op cit, p 423.
54 *The End of the War in Asia,* op cit, p 83.
55 Laurens van der Post. Unpublished article on publication of *Post Surrender Tasks* (1969). BA K264.
56 Clifford Squire, 'Britain and the Transfer of Power in Indonesia 1945–46.' Unpublished Thesis. BA.
57 Personal diary, 10 October 1945.
58 M to Christison, 13 October 1945. BA C49.
59 Ibid.
60 Christison. 'Life and Times . . .', op cit, p 176.
61 Christison reminiscences, op cit, BA N99a
62 Ibid.
63 12 September 1945. Auchinleck papers. 1193.
64 10 December 1945. NA 165 (ABC) 091 711 Netherlands Sec 3.
65 Pyman diary, 9 October 1945. Pyman papers 5/1.
66 4 October 1945. BA C91.
67 'Britain and the Transfer of Power. . . .', op cit, p 170–1.
68 21 April 1946. BA C29.
69 23 November 1945. BA S325.
70 1–6 December 1945. BA S69.
71 *Triumph in the West,* op cit, p 518.
72 Personal diary, 25 April 1946.
73 7 May 1946. BA S325.
74 30 April 1946. SEACOS 688.
75 BA DH 1051/19 of 7 February 1964. J416.
76 Undated. BA J416.
77 Unpublished article, op cit.
78 *Foreign Relations of the United States.* 1945. Vol. VI, p 1186.
79 Ibid, 1946. Vol. VIII, pp 792–5.
80 International Edition. 27 November 1946. cit Squire, 'Britain and the Transfer of Power . . .", op cit.
81 M to George VI, 2 October 1945. BA S93.
82 Ibid.
83 Ismay to M, 28 December 1945. BA C146.
84 M to Ismay, 22 March 1946. BA C145.
85 14 April 1946. RA GVI PS 6574.
86 Personal diary, 26 May 1946.

# CHAPTER 27

## pages 339–346

1  Copy in BA. C204.
2  See p 336 above.
3  Interview with Lord Thorneycroft.
4  17 November 1945. BA S327.
5  Pyman to Dempsey, 29 October 1945.
   Pyman papers 5/1.
6  Reminiscences of Admiral Sir Rowland
   Jerram. BA N99a.
7  *The Viceroy's Journey,* op cit, p 40.
8  1 December 1944. BM Add Mss 52562.
   155.
9  Personal diary, 26 March 1946.
10  Ibid, 28 March 1946.
11  Ibid, 9 April 1946.
12  Ibid, 30 March 1946.
13  21 and 25 March 1946. BM Add Mss
   52579.
14  11 October 1945.
15  14 April 1946. BA S310.
16  Personal diary, 19 May 1946.
17  Personal diary, 13 December 1946.
18  Interview with Mr A. T. Page.
19  Lambe to M, 6 November 1945; M to
   Lambe, 19 February 1946. BA S310.
20  Interview with Rear-Admiral Royer Dick.
21  Lambe to M, 6 November 1945. BA
   S310.
22  Interview with Admiral Sir Guy
   Grantham.
23  Peter Murphy, 'Reminiscences and
   Comments. . . .', op cit.
24  J. H. Money, 'Some Points regarding
   Lord Mountbatten 1945–1948.'
   Memorandum to author.
25  *Report to the Combined Chiefs of Staff
   by the Supreme Commander, South East
   Asia, 1943–45.* London, 1951.
26  John Shea, *Journal of the Royal Central
   Asian Society,* Vol. XXXVIII, p 200,
   April–June 1951.
27  15 or 16 April 1945. BA S146.

# CHAPTER 28

## pages 349–362

1  Cd 9109 (1918) para 300.
2  cit H. V. Hodson, *The Great Divide.
   Britain–India–Pakistan.* London, 1969,
   p 48.
3  Jawaharlal Nehru, *The Discovery of*

*India.* Calcutta, 1946, p 437.
4  Amery diary, 9 September 1942.
5  *The Viceroy's Journal,* op cit, p 21.
6  Quoted by Olaf Caroe in unpublished
   memoir. Copy in BA.
7  Nehru Memorial Lecture, 24 June 1980.
8  Ibid.
9  15 June 1946. BA E186.
10  cit Ronald Lewin, *The Chief. Field
   Marshal Lord Wavell.* London, 1980, p
   238.
11  Francis Williams, *A Prime Minister
   Remembers.* London, 1961, pp 209–10.
12  CM (46) 104th Conclusions. 10
   December 1946. cit *The Transfer of
   Power in India 1942–1947.* Vol. IX.
   London, 1980, p 320. Throughout the
   following chapters I have given this
   invaluable series as references rather than
   the PRO, India Office Library or the
   Broadlands Archives where the original
   documents are generally to be found.
13  Nehru Memorial Lecture, op cit.
14  cit *A Prime Minister Remembers,* op cit,
   pp 209–10.
   *Attlee,* op cit, p 373.
15  Julian Amery to M, 5 February 1968. NA
   K292.
16  Amery diary, 18 May 1943.
17  Larry Collins and Dominique Lapierre,
   *Freedom at Midnight,* London, 1975, p
   8n.
18  cit *A Prime Minister Remembers,* op cit,
   pp 209–10.
19  Interviews with, *inter alia,* Lady Lambe,
   Vice-Admiral Sir Ronald Brockman,
   Rear-Admiral Royer Dick, General Sir
   Robert Neville.
20  3 January 1947. BA S21.
21  George VI to M, 5 January 1947.
   *Transfer of Power.* Vol. IX, p 454.
22  14 March 1947. BA S21.
23  M to Attlee, 20 December 1946 and 3
   January 1947. *Transfer of Power.* Vol.
   IX, pp 396 and 451.
24  M to Attlee, 3 January 1947. *Transfer of
   Power.* Vol. IX, p 451.
25  *A Prime Minister Remembers,* op cit, p
   208.
26  *Attlee,* op cit, p 374.
27  Attlee to M, 9 and 16 January 1947.
   *Transfer of Power.* Vol. IX, pp 491 and
   505.
28  Wavell to Attlee, 17 February 1947. Ibid,
   p 734.
29  Attlee to M, 18 March 1947. Ibid, p 973.

30  Brockman to M, 26 November 1968, 4 December 1968 and 3 January 1969; M to Brockman, 27 November 1968, 9 December 1968 and 9 January 1969. BA K61.
31  Interview with Lord Listowel.
32  M to Professor Mansergh, 24 April 1979. BA K149B.
33  4 January 1947. *King George VI,* op cit, p 711.
34  3 January 1947. *Transfer of Power.* Vol. IX, p 451.
35  M to Attlee, 11 February 1947. *Transfer of Power.* Vol. IX, p 667.
36  8 January 1947. BA D92.
37  *The Memoirs of Lord Ismay,* op cit, p 407.
38  Ronald Wingate, *Lord Ismay.* London, 1970, pp 137–8.
39  5 January 1947. Ismay papers. III/7/2.
40  M to Attlee, 11 February 1947. *Transfer of Power.* Vol. IX, p 673. Interview with Sir George Abell.
41  M to Attlee, 3 January 1947. Ibid, p 452.
42  Memorandum of 11 February 1947. Ibid, p 674.
43  Alan Campbell-Johnson, *Mission with Mountbatten.* London, 1951, p 22.
44  *The Viceroy's Journal,* op cit, p 419.
45  Interview with Sir George Abell.
46  7 January 1947. *Transfer of Power.* Vol. IX. p 483.
47  6 March 1947. Hansard. Vol. 434. Col 672.
48  Interviews with Sir John Colville and Lord Soames.
49  Debate of 25 and 26 February 1947. Hansard. Vol. 145. Cols 1013–1021.
50  *King George VI,* op cit, p 710.
51  *Transfer of Power.* Vol. IX, pp 972–74.
52  *The Noel Coward Diaries,* op cit, p 83.
53  Interview with Rear-Admiral Howes.
54  19 March 1947. BA E36.

## CHAPTER 29

### pages 363–374

1  13 April 1947. Lady Mountbatten papers.
2  13 May 1947. Ibid.
3  Monckton to Cripps, 1 May 1947. Monckton papers. Box E, f167.
4  Viceroy's Personal Report No 3. 17 April 1947. *Transfer of Power.* Vol. X, p 303.
5  Ibid.
6  Monckton to Cripps, 1 May 1947. Monckton papers. Box E f167.
7  Interview with Sir Ian Scott.
8  13 April 1947. Lady Mountbatten papers.
9  M to Brabourne, 28 April 1947. Brabourne papers.
10  6 April 1947. Lady Mountbatten papers.
11  Interview with Sir George Abell.
12  5 August 1947. Ismay papers. 111/8/13A.
13  Auchinleck to Scoones, 2 March 1947. Auchinleck papers. 1215.
14  Christie diary. 10 Mss Eur D178/3 Part 2.
15  Manmath Nath Das, *Partition and Independence of India.* New Delhi, 1982, p 17.
16  *Transfer of Power.* Vol. X, p 9.
17  Ibid, p 139.
18  Ibid. Vol. IX, p 1010.
19  Viceroy's Interviews Nos 3, 20 and 39. 24 March, 1 and 8 April 1947. *Transfer of Power.* Vol. X, pp 11, 70 and 154.
20  *Mission with Mountbatten,* op cit, p 56.
21  Viceroy's Personal Report No 5. 1 May 1947. *Transfer of Power,* Vol. X, p 540.
22  Ibid, No 2. 9 April 1947. Ibid, p 168.
23  Viceroy's Staff Meeting, 11 April 1947. Ibid, p 190.
24  Viceroy's Interview No 41. 8 April 1947. Ibid, p 160.
25  Chaudhuri Muhammad Ali, *The Emergence of Pakistan.* New York, 1967, p 125.
26  *The Memoirs of Field Marshal Montgomery,* op cit, p 457.
27  Viceroy's Interview No 35. 5 April 1947. *Transfer of Power.* Vol. X, p 138.
28  *Mission with Mountbatten,* op cit, p 52.
29  Uncirculated records of discussion, 6 April 1947. BA D15.
30  Pyarelal, *Mahatma Gandhi: The Last Phase.* Ahmedabad, 1958, p 78.
31  Ibid, pp 104–5.
32  Ibid, p 138.
33  Viceroy's Staff Meeting, 5 April 1947. *Transfer of Power.* Vol. X, p 124. Earlier draft on BA D15.
34  e.g. Leonard Mosley, *The Last Days of the British Raj.* London, 1961, p 95.
35  Viceroy's Interview No 7. 25 March 1947. *Transfer of Power.* Vol. X, p 17.
36  Ibid, No 90. 24 April 1947. Ibid, pp 398–9.

37  28 April 1947. BA D1.
38  Viceroy's Interview No 22. 1 April 1947. *Transfer of Power*. Vol. X, p 74.
39  *Transfer of Power*. Vol. X, pp 75–83.
40  8 April 1947. BA E36.
41  6 April 1947. Lady Mountbatten papers.
42  13 April 1947. Ibid.
43  Ismay to Lady Ismay, 25 March 1947. Ismay papers. III/8/1.
44  Ibid, 28 March 1947. cit *Lord Ismay*, op cit, p 145.
45  Viceroy's Staff Meeting, 29 March 1947. *Transfer of Power*. Vol. X, p 47.
46  13 April 1947. BA Vol. XIV.
47  Viceroy's Staff Meeting, 31 March 1947. *Transfer of Power*. Vol. X, p 49.
48  Viceroy's Personal Report No 1. 2 April 1947. Ibid, p 90.
49  *Sardar Patel*. London, 1970, p 207.
50  Michael Brecher, *Nehru. A Political Biography*. London, 1959, p 375.
51  *Partition and Independence of India,* op cit, p 20.
52  Cripps to Rajkumari Amrit Kaur, 4 March 1947. Amrit Kaur papers, C4.
53  Viceroy's Staff Meeting, 11 April 1947. *Transfer of Power*. Vol. X, p 192.


## CHAPTER 30

### *pages 375–391*

1  Viceroy's Interview No 41. 8 April 1947. *Transfer of Power*. Vol. X, p 158.
2  Viceroy's Personal Report No 3. 17 April 1947. Ibid, pp 297–8.
3  Interviews with Sir Olaf Caroe and Sir George Abell. cf *The Great Divide*, op cit, p 283.
4  *Ismay*, op cit, p 149.
5  20 April 1947. Copy with unpublished memoir, op cit, BA Uncatalogued.
6  1 May 1947. *Transfer of Power*. Vol. X, p 530.
7  Unpublished memoir, op cit.
8  Gopal, *Nehru*, op cit, Vol. I, p 357.
9  M to Caroe, 30 June 1950. Unpublished memoir, op cit.
10  Unpublished memoir, op cit.
11  Viceroy's Personal Report No 3. 17 April 1947. *Transfer of Power*. Vol. X, pp 296–303.
12  23 April 1947. Ismay papers. III 8/5A.
13  Telegram of 1 May 1947. *Transfer of Power*. Vol. X, p 550–3.
14  For a full discussion of this issue see R. J. Moore and H. R. Tinker, *Escape from Empire*. Oxford, 1983, pp 272–74. 'Incident at Simla, May 1947.' *Journal of Commonwealth and Comparative Politics*. Vol. XX, No 2, pp 200–222. July 1982.
15  Miéville to Monckton, 9 May 1947. Monckton papers. Box D 60.
16  2 May 1947. Lady Mountbatten papers.
17  13 May 1947. Ibid.
18  Record of conversation between M and Krishna Menon. Tour diaries, 24 June 1970.
19  11 May 1947. *Transfer of Power*. Vol. X, p 756.
20  Miéville to Monckton, 12 May 1947. Monckton papers. Box D 62.
21  13 May 1947. Lady Mountbatten papers.
22  Miéville to M, 30 April 1947. *Transfer of Power*. Vol. X, p 488.
23  Interview with H. M. Patel.
24  Viceroy's 14th Miscellaneous Meeting, 11 May 1947. *Transfer of Power*. Vol. X, p 762.
25  14 May 1947. 10 Mss Eur D 718/3 Part 2.
26  Y. Krishan, 'Mountbatten and the Partition of India.' *History*. Vol. 68 No 222 of February 1983, p 33.
27  M to Patricia, 13 May 1947. Lady Mountbatten papers.
28  V. P. Menon. *The Transfer of Power in India*. London, 1957, p 358.
29  13 May 1947. Lady Mountbatten papers.
30  *Transfer of Power in India*, op cit, p 358.
31  Nye to M, 2 May 1947. *Transfer of Power*. Vol. X, pp 558–61.
32  *Escape from Empire*, op cit, pp 227–8.
33  Viceroy's Interview No 74. 17 April 1947. *Transfer of Power*. Vol. X, p 312.
34  Ibid, 5 April 1947. Ibid, pp 133–4.
35  *Partition and Independence of India,* op cit, p 265.
36  Viceroy's Interview No 74. 17 April 1947. *Transfer of Power*. Vol. X, pp 312–13.
37  Gopal, *Nehru*, op cit, Vol. I, pp 352–3.
38  V. Shaakar, *My Reminiscences of Sardar Patel*. Delhi, 1974, Vol. I, pp 41–2.
39  Rajendra Prasad to Satish Chandra Mukerji, 5 June 1947. Rajendra Prasad papers.
40  *Transfer of Power*. Vol. X, p 774.
41  Ismay to M, 14 May 1947. *Transfer of Power*. Vol. X, p 822.

42 *Mission with Mountbatten*, op cit, pp 91–2.
43 16 May 1947. *Transfer of Power*. Vol. X, pp 855–6.
44 IB (47) 26 and 27 of 20 and 22 May, and CM (47) 50 of 23 May 1947.
45 *Transfer of Power*. Vol. X, pp 967–8.
46 Viceroy's Interview No 141. 22 May 1947. *Transfer of Power*. Vol. X, pp 944–6.
47 Wedemeyer to M, 30 June 1947. BA E187.
48 *The Memoirs of Lord Ismay*, op cit, p 422.
49 11 June 1947. Lady Mountbatten papers.
50 *Mission with Mountbatten*, op cit, p 108.
51 *Transfer of Power*. Vol. X, pp 115–22. Fuller text in *Time Only to Look Forward: Speeches of Rear-Admiral the Earl Mountbatten of Burma as Viceroy of India and Governor-General of the Dominion of India*. London, 1949, pp 19–48.
52 *Time Only to Look Forward*, op cit, p 43.
53 Viceroy's Interview No 140. 17 May 1947. *Transfer of Power*. Vol. X, p 872.
54 *Freedom at Midnight*, op cit, p 165.
55 'Report on the Last Viceroyalty.' September, 1948. Para 95. BA Uncatalogued.
56 11 June 1947. Lady Mountbatten papers.
57 *Attlee*, op cit, pp 383–4.
58 Viceroy's Personal Report No 16. 8 August 1947. *Transfer of Power*. London, 1983, Vol. XII, p 595.
59 Viceroy's Interview No 143. 4 June 1947. *Transfer of Power*. Vol. XI, pp 131–2.
60 Pyarelal. *Gandhi*, op cit, p 217.
61 *Mission with Mountbatten*, op cit, p 137.
62 Viceroy's Interview No 52. 11 April 1947. *Transfer of Power*. Vol. X, p 201.
63 CAB 134/343. 1B(47) 14th Meeting. 13 March 1947.
64 Major-General Fazal Khan, *The Story of the Pakistan Army*. Karachi, 1963, p 19.
65 Viceroy's Interview No 64. 14 April 1947. *Transfer of Power*. Vol. X, pp 224–6.
66 *Auchinleck*, op cit, p 885.
67 Viceroy's Personal Report No 11. 4 July 1947. *Transfer of Power*. Vol. XI, p 893. cf *The Great Divide*, op cit, p 264.
68 *The Memoirs of Lord Ismay*, op cit, p 415.
69 Viceroy's Personal Report No 16. 8 August 1947. *Transfer of Power*. Vol. XII, p 600.
70 *Mission with Mountbatten*, op cit, p 123.
71 Ismay to Lady Ismay, 24 June 1947. Ismay papers. III/8/11a.
72 Cripps to M, 6 June 1947. BA E46.

## CHAPTER 31

### *pages 392–403*

1 Viceroy's Personal Report No 8. 5 June 1947. *Transfer of Power*. Vol. XI, p 163.
2 Ibid, p 164.
3 27/28 June 1947. *Transfer of Power*. Vol. XI, p 713.
4 *Mission with Mountbatten*, op cit, pp 124–5.
5 Ibid, pp 143–4.
6 Ibid, p 125.
7 25 July 1947. Listowel papers.
8 Viceroy's Personal Report No 13. 19 July 1947. *Transfer of Power*. Vol. XII, p 227.
9 *Mission with Mountbatten*, op cit, p 130.
10 Viceroy's Personal Report No 9. 12 June 1947. *Transfer of Power*. Vol. XI, p 303.
11 Copy in Rajendra Prasad papers. 5-A/47.
12 *Time Only to Look Forward*, op cit, p 38.
13 *The Emergence of Pakistan*, op cit, p 170.
14 Viceroy's Personal Report No 10. 27 June 1947. *Transfer of Power*. Vol. XI, pp 682–3.
15 *The Emergence of Pakistan*, op cit, p 171.
16 21 June 1947. BA D1.
17 Viceroy's Personal Report No 10. 27 June 1947. *Transfer of Power*. Vol. XI, pp 682–5.
18 17 May 1947. *Transfer of Power*. Vol. X, p 869.
19 Viceroy's Interview No 153. 23 June 1947. *Transfer of Power*. Vol. XI, p 580.
20 Viceroy's Personal Report No 11. 4 July 1947. *Transfer of Power*. Vol. XI, pp 898–900.
21 *The Emergence of Pakistan*, op cit, p 177. cf Ian Stephens, *Pakistan*. London, 1963, p 176.
22 Lady Mountbatten papers.
23 *Mission with Mountbatten*, op cit, p 131.
24 Viceroy's 52nd Staff Meeting, 4 July 1947. *Transfer of Power*. Vol. XI, pp 885–6.
25 Viceroy's Interview No 156. 5 July 1947. Ibid, p 935.

26  Viceroy's 53rd Staff Meeting, 7 July 1947. Ibid, p 947.
27  5 July 1947. Lady Mountbatten papers.
28  *Transfer of Power*. Vol. XI, p 922.
29  1B (47) 41st Meeting. Ibid, p 981.
30  cit *The Great Divide*, op cit, pp 335–6.
31  George VI to M, 9 July 1947. BA S95.
32  29 June 1947. Lady Mountbatten papers.
33  24 and 25 July. 10 Mss Eur D718/3 Part 2.
34  *The Partition of India. Policies and Perspectives*. ed. C. H. Philips and Mary Wainwright. London, 1970, p 524.
35  Viceroy's Personal Report No 5. 1 May 1947. *Transfer of Power*. Vol. X, p 539.
36  Jenkins to M, 30 April 1947. *Transfer of Power*. Vol. X, p 506.
37  Viceroy's Personal Report No 10. 27 June 1947. *Transfer of Power*. Vol. XI, p 680.
38  Jenkins to M, 25 June 1947. *Transfer of Power*. Vol. XI, pp 623–7.
39  Viceroy's Miscellaneous Meetings. 14 April 1947. *Transfer of Power*. Vol. X, pp 231–2.
40  CM (47) 50. 23 May 1947. *Transfer of Power*. Vol. X, p 967.
41  Maulana Abdul Kalam Azad, *India Wins Freedom*. London, 1960, p 190.
42  *Mission with Mountbatten*, op cit, pp 148–9, 152.
43  Viceroy's Interview No 146. 10 June 1947. *Transfer of Power*. Vol. XI, p 234.
44  M to Listowel, 27 June 1947. Ibid, p 678.
45  10 August 1947. 10 R/3/1/157.
46  11 August 1947. Ibid.
47  *The Great Divide*, op cit, p 347.

## CHAPTER 32

### pages 404–415

1  CAB 134/343. 1B(47) 26. 20 May 1947.
2  cit *The Great Divide*, op cit, p 29.
3  Viceroy's Interview No 30. 4 April 1947. *Transfer of Power*. Vol. X, p 121.
4  Attlee to M, 18 March 1947. *Transfer of Power*. Vol. IX, p 973.
5  GEN 174/1st Meeting. 13 March 1947. *Transfer of Power*. Vol. IX, p 944.
6  cit *The Last Days of the British Raj*, op cit, p 160.
7  cit H. Tinker, *Experiments with Freedom*. Oxford, 1967, p 121.
8  *The Great Divide*, op cit, p 367.
9  Viceroy's Interview No 146. 10 June 1947. *Transfer of Power*. Vol. XI, p 232.
10  Statement by Sardar Patel. 5 July 1947. *Transfer of Power*. Vol. XI, pp 928–30.
11  3 August 1947. BA S95.
12  Conrad Corfield, 'Some Thoughts on British Policy and the Indian States.' *The Partition of India. Policies and Perspectives*, op cit, p 531.
13  Ibid.
14  *The Last Days of the British Raj*, op cit, p 162.
15  Conrad Corfield, *The Princely India I Knew*. Madras, 1975, p 153.
16  'Some Thoughts on British Policy. . . .', op cit, p 532.
17  10 L/P and S/13/1848.
18  *The Princely India I Knew*, op cit, pp 155–6.
19  Viceroy's 18th Miscellaneous Meeting, 13 June 1947. *Transfer of Power*. Vol. XI, pp 321–2.
20  *The Last Days of the British Raj*, op cit, p 174.
21  Viceroy's Personal Report No 10. 27 June 1947. *Transfer of Power*. Vol. XI, p 687.
22  *The Princely India I Knew*, op cit, p 159.
23  V. P. Menon, *The Integration of the Indian States*. Calcutta, 1956, p 97.
24  cit *The Princely India I Knew*, op cit, pp 183–5.
25  10 Mss Eur D 850/6–7.
26  *The Integration of the Indian States*, op cit, p 108.
27  Text in *Time Only to Look Forward*, op cit, pp 51–6.
28  *Mission with Mountbatten*, op cit, pp 141–2.
29  3 August 1947. Lady Mountbatten papers.
30  Interview with General Sher Ali Pataudi.
31  Viceroy's Personal Report No 16. 8 August 1947. *Transfer of Power*. Vol. XII, p 592.
32  *The Great Divide*, op cit, p 375.
33  Viceroy's Personal Report No 14. 25 July 1947. *Transfer of Power*. Vol. XII, p 336.
34  Viceroy's Personal Report No 17. 16 August 1947. *Transfer of Power*. Vol. XII, p 767.
35  Viceroy's Interview No 162. 12 July 1947. *Transfer of Power*. Vol. XII, p 121.
36  Ismay to Monckton, 14 March 1947. Monckton papers. Box 39. 52.
37  Lord Birkenhead, *Walter Monckton*. London, 1969, p 226.

38  Ibid, p 229.
39  Interview with Sir George Abell.
40  *Mission with Mountbatten*, op cit, p 139.
41  Monckton papers. Box 16.
42  3 August 1947. Ibid, Box 30. 19.
43  Ibid, Box 30. 43.
44  *The Great Divide*, op cit, p 382.
45  Viceroy's Personal Report No 15. 1 August 1947. *Transfer of Power*. Vol. XII, p 450.
46  Lord Birdwood, 'Kashmir.' *International Affairs*. Vol. XXVIII, No 3, July 1952.
47  Karan Singh, *Heir Apparent*. New Delhi, 1982, p 47.
48  Ibid.
49  Viceroy's Personal Report No 10. 27 June 1947. *Transfer of Power*. Vol. XI, p 688.
50  Interview with Dr Karan Singh.
51  *The Great Divide*, op cit, p 384.
52  27 June 1947. Monckton papers. Box 41. 186.
53  *The Emergence of Pakistan*, op cit, p 232.
54  13 August 1947. BA S95.

## CHAPTER 33

### *pages 416–428*

1  2 July 1947. BA DI.
2  16 August 1947. Listowel papers.
3  *Mission with Mountbatten*, op cit, p 152.
4  Sir George Cunningham's diary, 7 November 1947. cit *The Partition of India. . . .*, op cit, p 292.
5  See p 402 above.
6  Christie diary. 12 August 1947. 10 Mss Eur D 718/3 Part 2.
   *The Partition of India. . . .*, op cit, p 23.
7  AICC G33. 1947.
8  Viceroy's Personal Report No 17. 16 August 1947. *Transfer of Power*. Vol. XII, p 761.
9  12 August 1947. 10 Mss Eur D 718/3 Part 2.
   *Mission with Mountbatten*, op cit, p 153.
10  *The Last Days of the British Raj*, op cit, p 229.
11  See, e.g. Major-General Nawabzada Sher Ali Khan Pataudi, *The Story of Soldiering and Politics in India and Pakistan*. Pakistan, 1978.
    *The Emergence of Pakistan*, op cit, pp 215–16.

12  Abell to H. C. Beaumont, 21 July 1947. 10 R/3/1/157.
13  Interview with Sir George Abell.
14  Abell to Stuart Abbott, 8 August 1947. 10 R/3/1/157.
15  Evan Jenkins papers. 10 Mss Eur D807.
16  Kirpal Singh, *The Partition of the Punjab*. Patiala, 1972, pp 78–9.
17  Kanwar Sain, *Reminiscences of an Engineer*. New Delhi, 1978, p 90.
18  10. R L/P and J/ 10/119.
19  A view supported by Dr Karni Singh, eldest son of the then Maharaja.
20  Brecher, *Nehru. A Political Biography*, op cit, p 361.
21  10 Mss Eur D 718/3 Part 2.
22  Interviews with Mr John Christie and Sir George Abell.
23  Interview with Sir Ian Scott.
24  M to Ismay, 12 February 1948. BA E83.
25  26 February 1948. PRO PREM 8/821.
26  10 August 1947. BA D1.
27  Viceroy's Personal Report No 17. 16 August 1947. *Transfer of Power*. Vol. XII, p 770.
    *Mission with Mountbatten*, op cit, p 154.
28  *Mission with Mountbatten*, op cit, p 155.
29  Viceroy's Personal Report No 17. 16 August 1947. *Transfer of Power*. Vol. XII, p 770.
30  Christie diary, 10 August 1947. 10 Mss Eur D 718/3 Part 2.
31  Viceroy's Personal Report No 17. 16 August 1947. *Transfer of Power*. Vol. XII, p 771.
32  *Mission with Mountbatten*, op cit, pp 156–7.
33  Viceroy's 65th Staff Meeting, 28 July 1947. *Transfer of Power*. Vol. XII, p 376.
34  Viceroy's Personal Report No 16. 8 August 1947. Ibid, pp 600–1.
35  *The Great Divide*, op cit, p 389.
    cf Frank Moraes, *Witness to an Era*. London, 1973, p 183.
36  Gopal, *Nehru*, Vol. I, op cit, p 361.
37  Viceroy's Personal Report No 17. 16 August 1947. *Transfer of Power*. Vol. XII, p 772.
38  Ibid, p 773.
39  *Mission with Mountbatten*, op cit, p 168.
40  Viceroy's Personal Report No 17. 16 August 1947. *Transfer of Power*. Vol. XII, p 774.
41  *Time Only to Look Forward*, op cit, p 65.
42  25 August 1947. BA E83.

43 BA S147.
44 18 August 1947. BA S147.
45 15 August 1947. Leo Amery papers.
46 16 August 1947. Ismay papers. III/8/11a.
47 14 August 1947. Lady Mountbatten papers.
48 16 August 1947. BA E196.
49 7 June 1947.

## CHAPTER 34

### *pages 429–441*

1 Viceroy's Personal Report No 17. 16 August 1947. *Transfer of Power.* Vol. XII, p 775.
2 17 August 1947. Auchinleck papers. 1247.
3 Penderel Moon, *Divide and Quit.* London, 1961, p 95.
4 Governor-General's Personal Report No 1. 2 September 1947. BA D86.
5 10 Mss Eur D 718/3 Part 2.
6 *The Transfer of Power in India,* op cit, p 423.
7 *Blitz,* 13 November 1947.
8 M to M. O. Mathai, 14 September 1976. BA K188B.
9 Emergency Committee Paper No 1 (ECP1). 7 September 1947. BA D146.
10 Governor-General's Personal Report No 2. 11 September 1947. BA D86.
11 Ibid.
12 Memo of 7 September 1947. BA D146.
13 M to George VI, 11 September 1947. BA D86.
14 Governor-General's Personal Report No 3. 26 September 1947. BA D86.
15 M to Jinnah, 6 September 1947. BA D146.
16 BA E5.
17 W. H. Morris-Jones, 'The Transfer of Power, 1947.' *Modern Asian Studies.* 16.1 (1982). London, 1982, pp 1–32.
18 *Mission with Mountbatten,* op cit, p 201.
19 Governor-General's Personal Report No 2. 11 September 1947. BA D86.
20 Auchinleck to M, 13 September 1947. Auchinleck papers. 1255.
21 26 August 1947. cit *The Partition of India . . .,* op cit, p 234n.
22 *Mission with Mountbatten,* op cit, p 181.
23 28 September 1947. Lady Mountbatten papers.
24 2 October 1947. Neville papers.
25 *Stern Reckoning.* Delhi, undated, p 299.
26 *Pakistan.* London, 1963, p 83.
27 Trevelyan to M, 28 May 1973. BA K15.
28 *Freedom at Midnight,* op cit, p 342.
29 *Divide and Quit,* op cit, p 283.
30 17 November 1947. Ismay papers. III/8/22b.
31 17 February 1947. *Transfer of Power.* Vol. IX, p 741.
32 *Time Only to Look Forward,* op cit, p 30.
33 *The Transfer of Power in India,* op cit, p 435.
   cf Gopal, *Nehru,* op cit, Vol. I, p 355.
   Brecher, *Nehru,* op cit, p 367.
   Maurice Zimkin, essay in *The Partition of India . . .,* op cit, p 549.
34 11 June 1947. Lady Mountbatten papers.
35 2 October 1947. BA S326.
36 For an interesting re-statement of this argument see I. A. Talbot, 'Mountbatten and the Partition of India.' *History.* Vol. 69, No 225, February 1984, pp 29–35.
37 *Lord Ismay,* op cit, p 167.
38 6 March 1962. BA J238.
39 Interview with Sir George Abell.
40 *The Princely India I Knew,* op cit, p 153.
41 Interview with Sir George Abell.
42 *Divide and Quit,* op cit, pp 277–83.
43 Trevelyan to M, 28 May 1973. BA K215.
44 Interview with H. M. Patel.
45 cit V. B. Kulkarni, *British Dominion in India and After.* Bombay, 1964, p 255.

## CHAPTER 35

### *pages 442–456*

1 Governor-General's Personal Report No 3. 26 September 1947. BA D86.
2 Governor-General's Personal Report No 4. 19 October 1947. BA D86.
3 Ibid.
4 28 September 1947. BA D74.
5 Auchinleck to Nehru, 29 September 1947. BA D74.
6 Governor-General's Interview No 32. 10 October 1947. BA D74.
7 Governor-General's Personal Report No 6. 11 December 1947. BA D78.
8 Governor-General's Interview No 37. 10 October 1947. BA D74.

9 *Memoirs,* op cit, p 433.
10 *The Great Divide,* op cit, p 448.
11 27 June 1948. BA Uncatalogued.
12 *The Integration of the Indian States,* op cit, p 399.
13 Escott Reid, *Envoy to Nehru.* Delhi, 1981, pp 116–17.
14 *The Great Divide,* op cit, p 453.
15 *The Emergence of Pakistan,* op cit, p 293.
16 cit *The Partition of India . . .,* op cit, p 292.
17 Security Council Official Records. Third Year. Nos 1–15, pp 222–3. cit Josef Korbel, *Danger in Kashmir.* Princeton, 1954, p 67–8.
18 Governor-General's Personal Report No 5. 7 November 1947. BA D87.
19 Governor-General's Interview No 43. 29 October 1947. BA D74.
20 Ismay to Lady Ismay, 2 November 1947. Ismay papers. III/8/20Ea.
21 Governor-General's Personal Report No 5. 7 November 1947. BA D87.
22 Ibid.
23 Governor-General's Personal Report No 7. 3 January 1948. BA D88 Appendix II.
24 Ibid. Appendix III.
25 Ibid.
26 Governor-General's Interview No 95. 1 February 1948. BA D76.
27 Governor-General's Interview No 108. 17 February 1948. BA D76.
28 Governor-General's Personal Report No 8. 3 February 1948. BA D88.
29 Governor-General's Interview No 108. 17 February 1948. BA D76.
30 *Ismay,* op cit, p 177.
cf Governor-General's Personal Report No 8. 3 February 1948. BA D88.
31 Governor-General's Personal Report No 9. 19 March 1948. BA D88.
32 Governor-General's Interview No 129. 20 March 1948. BA D77.
33 Governor-General's Interview No 76. 9 January 1948. BA D75.
34 *Envoy to Nehru,* op cit, pp 116–17. B. N. Panday, *Nehru.* London, 1976, p 313.
35 cit *The Great Divide,* op cit, pp 471–2.
36 Governor-General's Personal Report No 5. 11 December 1947. BA D87.
37 *The Integration of the Indian States,* op cit, p 320.
38 29 August 1947. Monckton papers. Box 30. 165.
39 Governor-General's Personal Report No 4. 10 October 1947. BA D86.
40 Ibid.
41 5 December 1947. Lady Mountbatten papers.
42 *The Integration of the Indian States,* op cit, p 330.
43 29 November 1947. BA D180A.
44 18 January 1948. Monckton papers. Box 31. 85.
Governor-General's Personal Report No 8. 3 February 1948. BA D88.
45 *Mission with Mountbatten,* op cit, p 288.
46 cit *Monckton,* op cit, p 243.
47 *Monckton,* op cit, p 245.
48 7 April 1948. Monckton papers. Box 31. 52.
49 Governor-General's Interview No 138. 7 April 1948. BA D87.
M to Birkenhead, cit *Monckton,* op cit, p 246.
50 Governor-General's Interview No 129. 20 March 1948. BA D77.
51 Governor-General's Interview No 176. 25 May 1948. BA D79.
52 7 June 1948. BA D125.
53 Governor-General's Interview No 198. 8 June 1948. BA D80.
54 Draft in BA D180A.
55 5 June 1948. Monckton papers. Box 32. 6.
56 Tahmankar, *Sardar Patel,* op cit, p 230.
57 Interview with H. M. Patel.
58 *Monckton,* op cit, p 250.
59 2 July 1948. Monckton papers. Box 32. 50.

## CHAPTER 36

### *pages 457–469*

1 29 January 1947. BA S176.
2 15 September 1947. BA E23.
3 Driberg to M, 28 July 1947; M to Driberg, 3 August 1947. BA E49.
4 5 October 1947. BA S93.
5 *Mission with Mountbatten,* op cit, p 234.
6 2 November 1947. Ismay papers. III/8/20 H.
7 Diary, 25 April 1948.
8 *Mission with Mountbatten,* op cit, p 296.
9 Tour diaries, 26 July 1969.
10 Diary, 29 August 1947.
11 *Mission with Mountbatten,* op cit, pp 300–5.

12 Ibid, p 351n.
13 Ibid, p 186.
14 22 May 1948. Lady Mountbatten papers.
15 Governor-General's Interview No 61. 3 December 1947. BA D75.
16 *Viceroy's Journal*, op cit, p 437.
17 Governor-General's Interview No 50. 19 November 1947. BA D74.
18 Ibid, No 81. 13 January 1948. BA D76. Governor-General's Personal Report No 7. 3 January 1948. BA D88.
19 *Gandhi: The Last Phase*, Ahmedabad, 1958, p 707.
20 Ibid, p 725.
21 *Mission with Mountbatten*, op cit, p 269.
22 Auchinleck to Scoones, 15 September 1947. Auchinleck papers. 1259.
23 Governor-General's Interview No 33. 2 October 1947. BA D74.
24 Montgomery to M, 24 April 1947; M to Montgomery, 1 May 1947. BA N82.
25 BA N73.
26 1 September 1947. BA N82.
27 Draft in BA N82. No indication whether or not finally sent.
28 12 September 1947. BA E5.
29 26 September 1947. BA E6.
30 26 September 1947. Auchinleck papers. 1261.
31 Auchinleck to Scoones, 5 October 1947. cit *Auchinleck*, op cit, p 925.
32 M to Ismay, 7 October 1947. BA D196.
33 *The Story of the Pakistan Army*, op cit, p 33.
34 *The Spectator*. 12 December 1947, pp 735–6.
35 Governor-General's Personal Report No 6. 11 December 1947. BA D87.
36 Governor-General's Personal Report No 9. 19 March 1948. BA D88.
37 26 September 1947. Auchinleck papers. 1261.
38 Undated memo. Ismay papers. III/7/67/43.
39 2 December 1947. Ismay papers. III/7/9.
40 Christie diary, 23 August and 24 September 1947. 10 Mss Eur D718/3 Part 2.
41 Gopal, *Nehru*, op cit, Vol. 2, p 36.
42 *Mission with Mountbatten*, op cit, p 171.
43 Governor-General's Interview No 169. 10 May 1948. BA D79.
44 Governor-General's Interview No 10. 6 September 1947. BA D73.

45 26 December 1947. *Foreign Relations of the United States*. 1947. Vol. 3 (Washington, 1972), pp 177–8.
46 Governor-General's Interview No 169. 10 May 1948. BA D79.
47 18 April 1948. Gopal, *Nehru*, op cit, Vol. 2, p 47.
48 21 June 1947. BA E141.
49 *Mission with Mountbatten*, op cit, p 262.
50 Hugh Tinker, *Separate and Unequal*. London, 1976, pp 370–1.
51 *Mission with Mountbatten*, op cit, p 291.

# CHAPTER 37

## pages 470–479

1 *Mission with Mountbatten*, op cit, p 271.
2 K. M. Munshi, *The End of an Era*. Bombay, 1957, p 107.
3 *Mission with Mountbatten*, op cit, pp 275–6. *The Great Divide*, op cit, pp 422–3.
4 *Sardar Patel*, op cit, p 250.
5 Ibid.
6 *Gandhi: The Last Phase*, op cit, p 165.
7 *Autobiography*, op cit, p 145.
8 *Mission with Mountbatten*, op cit, p 279.
9 7 February 1948. BA Vol. XIV.
10 14 February 1948. BA E170.
11 Interview between Robin Bousfield and Sir Archibald Nye. 25 April 1948. BA E137.
12 18 March 1948. BA E127.
13 BA S93.
14 Governor-General's Interview No 95. 1 February 1948. BA D76.
15 24 June 1948. BA Uncatalogued.
16 14 April 1948. Ibid.
17 12 March 1957. Ibid.
18 12 June 1948. Lady Mountbatten papers.
19 21 June 1948. BA Uncatalogued.
20 8 February 1952. BA S72.
21 1 February 1953. BA S149.
22 18 January 1948. Monckton papers. Box 31. 85.
23 Governor-General's Interviews No 82 of 13 January and 87 of 22 January 1948. BA D76.
24 Auchinleck to Ismay, 30 January 1948. Ismay papers. IV/CONN/1/2.
25 18 March 1948. Neville papers.
26 Governor-General's Interview No 148. 20 April 1948. BA D78.

27 Governor-General's Interview No 186. 29 May 1948. BA D80.
28 BA D150.
29 *Mission with Mountbatten*, op cit, p 351. *The Great Divide*, op cit, pp 517–18.

## CHAPTER 38
### pages 483–507

1 Reminiscences of Mrs Barbara Cartland. BA N101.
2 17 June 1949. BA S147.
3 22 June 1949. BA S70.
4 28 February 1949. BA Vol. XIV.
5 15 November 1948. Lady Mountbatten papers.
6 9 October 1949. Ibid.
7 11 April 1948. Brabourne papers.
8 4 August 1948. BA N39.
9 10 April 1948. BA S176.
10 9 June 1948. BA S176.
11 3 May 1948. Ismay papers. IV/Mou/6a.
12 George VI to M, 8 June 1948. BA S95.
13 Brockman to Goodenough, 24 May 1948. BA E137.
14 Goodenough to Brockman, 31 May 1948; Brockman to Goodenough, 5 June 1948. BA E137.
15 12 May 1948. BA E137.
16 6 October 1948. BA F47.
17 'Reminiscences and Comments', op cit.
18 Interview with Vice-Admiral Sir Geoffrey Norman.
19 M to Patricia, 3 November 1948. Lady Mountbatten papers.
20 12 February 1948 and 1 March 1948. BA A41.
21 18 January 1948. Monckton papers. Box 31. 85.
22 M to Monckton, 16 July 1948. Monckton papers. Box 32. 63.
23 *Hansard*. Fifth Series. Vol. 469, 7 November 1949, Cols 875–1014.
24 Beaverbrook to Driberg, 1 August 1952. Beaverbrook papers. C/122.
25 Interview between M and Robin Bousfield. Transcripts. Vol. I, p 80.
26 25 November 1948. Neville papers.
27 Brockman to Bousfield, 16 February 1962. BA J53.
28 25 November 1948. Neville papers.
29 11 July 1949. BA S147.
30 M to Patricia, 3 November 1948. Lady Mountbatten papers.

31 10 January 1949. Lady Mountbatten papers.
32 14 July 1949. BA S202. M to Patricia, 14 July 1949. Lady Mountbatten papers.
33 17 January 1950. Sir William Houston-Boswell to F.O. BA F2.
34 14 January 1950. Lady Mountbatten papers. Campbell-Johnson narrative. Vol. II, p 53.
35 M to Patricia, 26 June 1949. Lady Mountbatten papers.
36 3 November 1949. Ibid.
37 21 November 1949. Ibid.
38 8 December and 14 December 1949. Ibid.
39 21 April 1950. Ibid. Interview with Rear-Admiral Howes.
40 Interview with Captain Edward Blundell.
41 M to Patricia, 17 December 1948. Lady Mountbatten papers.
42 3 April 1950. Lady Mountbatten papers.
43 M to Charles Eade, 26 March 1950. BA I172.
44 M to Mr Jack Ibson, 10 April 1957. BA I172.
45 Reminiscences of Mr Charles Cox. BA N101.
46 Interview with Vice-Admiral Sir Kaye Edden.
47 1 April 1950. BA Vol. XIV.
48 15 April 1950. BA O5.
49 19 September 1949. Brabourne papers.
50 M to Max Langley, 5 September 1949. BA F3.
51 12 August 1949. Lady Mountbatten papers.
52 No 405/5/1 of 8 May 1950. BA G1.
53 M to Patricia, 9 May 1950. Lady Mountbatten papers.
54 Hall to M, 15 September 1949. BA F24. This was the formal version of an offer made orally, probably on 31 July.
55 M to Patricia, 12 August 1949. Lady Mountbatten papers.
56 Ibid, 21 September 1949.
57 Ibid, 12 August 1949.
58 22 June 1950. BA S312.
59 Ibid.
60 Interview with Robin Bousfield. Transcripts. Vol. I, p 107.
61 Letter to the author. 16 December 1983.
62 M to Brabourne, 19 September 1949. Brabourne papers.
63 'Reminiscences and Comments', op cit.
64 Interview with Mr James Callaghan.

65 Memorandum of 26 June 1951. BA G46.
66 Record of conversation in BA G46.
67 M to Hall, 25 April 1951. BA G46.
68 1 June 1951. BA G46.
69 13 November 1951. BA G46.
70 28 February 1952. BA S149.
71 Published from 219 W Monument St, Baltimore. Issue of March 1952.
72 10 March 1952. BA S72.
73 21 February 1952. BA H10.
74 30 December 1951. BA G48.
75 30 December 1951. Colville Diary.
76 M to Edwina, 1 March 1951. BA S148.
77 BA G48.
78 1 October 1948. BA F36.
79 15 August 1948. BA F39.
80 3 July 1948, 23 August 1948, 29 August 1948. BA F39.
81 10 September 1948. BA F39.
82 27 September 1948. BA F38.
83 6 October 1948. BA F36.
84 10 October 1948. BA S93.
85 16 October 1948. BA F42.
86 18 February 1952. BA G28.
87 Thomas to M, 17 January 1955; M to Thomas, 18 January 1955. BA I71.
88 19 December 1951.
89 Diary, 21 May 1951.
90 3 October 1950. Neville papers.
91 *Louis and Victoria*, op cit, p 388.

# CHAPTER 39

## pages 508–524

1 M to Brabourne, 18 October 1951.
2 cit *Lambe*, op cit, p 179.
3 M to Grantham, 23 August 1952. BA H218.
4 6 and 7 February 1952.
5 M to Duke of Norfolk, 8 February 1952; Norfolk to M, 9 February 1952. BA G77.
6 Campbell-Johnson narrative. Vol. II, p 74.
7 Diary, 20 June 1952.
8 M to Campbell-Johnson, 11 July 1952. BA H34.
9 Diary, 16 July 1952.
10 M to McGrigor, 1 April 1954. BA H101.
11 Interviews with, *inter alia*, Admiral Sir John Hamilton, Admiral Sir Frederick Parham, Admiral Sir William Davis.
12 Diary of Admiral Sir William Davis, June 1952.
13 Ibid.
14 M. Power. Unpublished memoir, p 92.
15 Ibid, pp 93–6.
16 Ibid, p 93.
17 Campbell-Johnson narrative. Vol. II, p 72.
18 Tour diaries, 6 November 1953.
19 Telegram No 191010Z of 19 November 1954. BA H91.
20 Sir Ralph Murray to F.O. No 245 Saving of 22 November 1954. BA H91.
21 4 September 1952. BA H260.
22 M to Thomas, 10 September 1952. BA H260.
23 19 September 1952. Lady Mountbatten papers.
24 Campbell-Johnson narrative. Vol. II, p 73.
25 Captain A. W. Clarke to Brockman, 1 December 1953. BA H74.
26 M to Hugh Cudlipp, 17 April 1967. BA K305.
27 M to Campbell-Johnson, 9 March 1954. BA H33.
28 10 September 1954. BA S323.
29 17 September 1954. BA H33.
30 Interview with Lady Douglas-Pennant.
31 Head to M, undated; M to Head, 15 November 1953. BA H261.
32 'Reminiscences and Comments', op cit.
33 Interview with Admiral Sir William Davis.
34 Undated. Probably 1953. Lady Mountbatten papers.
35 M to Patricia, 8 June 1954. Lady Mountbatten papers.
36 10 February 1953. BA S180.
37 Campbell-Johnson narrative, Vol. II, p 76.
38 Note by Dom Mintoff of 17 July 1973. BA K25.
39 21 August 1952.
40 Tour diaries, 4 October 1975.
41 Campbell-Johnson narrative. Vol. II, p 80.
42 M to Edwina, 14 March 1954. BA S149.
43 M to Thomas, 26 January 1954. BA H230.
44 McGrigor to M, 9 June 1952. BA H102.
45 M to McGrigor, 9 July 1952. BA H102.
46 Draft of personal letter SP36, possibly never despatched. BA H35.
47 Ibid.
48 Carney to M, 28 July 1952. BA H35.
49 Telegram No 101046Z. 10 November 1952. BA H49.
50 11 December 1952. Neville papers.

51 Interview with Vice-Admiral Sir Ian Hogg.
52 11 December 1952. Neville papers.
53 Minutes of meeting at Naples, 18 January 1953. BA H49.
54 M to McGrigor, 19 January 1953. BA H102.
55 MED 64/2/2. BA H47.
56 24 January 1953. BA H48.
57 23 June 1953. BA N43.
58 Interview with Vice-Admiral Sir Ian Hogg.
59 Discussions at CPX 2. 9–12 March 1953. BA H103.
60 14 March 1953. BA H103.
61 Carney to SACEUR, 9 July 1953. HAFSE/864/53. BA H103.
62 10 June 1953. BA H47.
63 3 November 1953. BA H262.
64 30 June 1953. BA H35.
65 M to Gruenther, 27 June 1953. BA H125.
66 12 September 1953. BA H103.
67 11 September 1953. BA H125.
68 4 November 1953. BA S313.
69 23 November 1953. BA S313.
70 M. Power. Memoir, op cit, p 96.
71 5 August 1954. Ismay papers. IV/Mou/43b.
72 Ismay to Cunningham, 18 October 1954. Ismay papers IV/Mou/46a.
73 Undated. Ismay papers. IV/Mou/47.
74 15 September 1954. BA H266.
75 28 September 1954. BA H266.
76 Undated. Lady Mountbatten papers.
77 27 September 1954. BA S23.
78 6 November 1954. Brabourne papers.
79 Interview with Sir John Colville.
80 Undated. BA H266.
81 William Davis to Brockman, 15 October 1954. BA H266.
82 Interview with Rear-Admiral Royer Dick.
83 22 October 1954. BA H266.
84 Thomas to M, 27 November 1957. BA I30.
85 16 October 1954. BA S181.

# CHAPTER 40

## pages 525–536

1 cit Leslie Gardiner, *The British Admiralty*. Edinburgh, 1968, p 363.
2 C. J. Bartlett, *The Long Retreat*. London, 1972, p 106.
3 3 November 1954. BA S340.
4 31 October 1954. BA H266.
5 Navy Estimates (1955) para 7. B. B. Schofield, *British Sea Power. Naval Policy in the Twentieth Century*. London, 1967, p 222.
6 20 March 1954. BA H31.
7 6 April 1955. BA S314.
8 Interviews with Sir John Lang, Lord Selkirk, and Admiral of the Fleet Sir Caspar John.
9 Tour diaries, 27 August 1959.
10 M to Lambe, 20 January 1955. BA I144.
11 Tour diaries, 24 March 1956.
12 Interview with Admiral of the Fleet Sir Caspar John.
13 M. Power. Memoir, op cit, p 106.
14 M to Dickson, 1 March 1976. BA N99. Interview with Marshal of the Royal Air Force Sir Thomas Pike.
15 Diary of Admiral Sir William Davis, p 783.
16 9 October 1955.
17 Interview with Lord Cudlipp.
18 Interviews with Sir John Lang and Admiral Sir John Hamilton.
19 Interview with Vice-Admiral Sir Ian Hogg.
20 Interview with Admiral Sir John Hamilton.
21 Interview with Admiral of the Fleet Sir Caspar John.
22 29 November 1955. BA I578. cf Quarterly News Letter of 19 August 1955. BA I299.
23 M to Roskill, 11 October 1966. Roskill papers.
24 6 November 1954. BA H266.
25 *The Long Retreat*, op cit, p 114.
26 David Divine, *The Broken Wing*. London, 1966, p 313.
27 Campbell-Johnson narrative. Vol. III, p 3.
28 12 October 1955. BA I188.
29 Quarterly News Letter. Jutland Day, 1956. BA I299.
30 Diary, 5 April 1955.
31 Reminiscences of Sir William Dickson. BA N99.
32 M to Patricia, 30 October 1955. Lady Mountbatten papers.
33 5 April 1956. Lady Mountbatten papers.
34 2 May 1956. BA I303.
35 M to McBeath, 16 December 1957. BA I303.
36 23 January 1958. BA I303.
37 Tour diaries, 18 March 1956.
38 M to Lord Home, 2 July 1956. BA I225.

39  27 October 1955. BA uncatalogued.
40  Tour diaries, 15 March 1956.
41  Ibid, 22 and 23 March 1956.
42  Campbell-Johnson narrative. Vol. III, p 7.
    Sir William Davis to the author, 13 July
    1981.
43  Interview with Mr David Astor.
44  Interview with Lord Cudlipp.
45  2 July 1956.
46  Cilcennin to Beaverbrook, 3 July 1956.
    BA I102.
47  Tour diaries, 11 April 1956.
48  Record of meeting between M and
    Monckton, 24 February 1956. BA I328.

## CHAPTER 41

### *pages 537–547*

1   Personal and Confidential Note dictated
    by First Sea Lord, 7 or 8 September 1956.
    BA N106.
2   12 March 1973. BA N108.
3   See Note 1 above. For a further version of
    the later account, see M's record of a
    conversation with Lord Avon on 13 June
    1976. BA. Tour diaries.
4   Interview with General Sir Hugh
    Stockwell.
5   Draft in BA N106.
6   Undated. BA I283.
7   BA N106.
8   Dickson reminiscences. BA N99.
9   Memorandum on Suez drafted in 1966.
    BA N106.
10  Note of 7 or 8 September 1956. BA
    N106.
11  Campbell-Johnson narrative. Vol. III, p
    13.
12  Memorandum to Minister of Defence of 7
    August 1956. BA N106.
13  Dickson reminiscences. BA N99.
14  Note of 7 or 8 September 1956. BA
    N106.
15  11 August 1956. BA Uncatalogued.
16  2 September 1956. Ibid.
17  4 November 1956. Ibid.
18  5 August 1956. BA S149.
19  Interviews with Admiral Sir Robin
    Durnford-Slater and Rear-Admiral Peter
    Howes.
20  Draft of 20 August 1956. BA N106.
21  21 August 1956. BA N106.
22  Note of 7 or 8 September 1956. BA
    N106.

23  Ibid.
24  Ibid.
25  Memorandum on Suez drafted in 1966.
    BA N106.
26  7 September 1956. BA N106.
27  27 September 1956. BA N106.
28  BA N106.
29  Memorandum on Suez drafted in 1966.
    BA N106.
30  BA N106.
31  2 November 1956. BA N106.
32  Memorandum on Suez drafted in 1966.
    BA N106.
33  4 November 1956. BA N106.
34  Memorandum on Suez drafted in 1966.
    BA N106.
35  5 November 1956.
36  5 November 1956. BA N106.
37  6 November 1956. BA N106.
38  9 January 1957.
39  Tour diaries, 13 June 1976.
40  *The Times,* 5 and 11 November
    1980.

## CHAPTER 42

### *pages 548–566*

1   Campbell-Johnson narrative. Vol. III,
    p 4.
2   26 December 1956. BA I299.
3   Phillip Darby, *British Defence Policy East
    of Suez 1947–1968.* London, 1973, p
    193.
4   Quarterly News Letter. 28 September
    1957. BA I300.
5   14 January 1957.
6   Diary of Admiral Sir William Davis, p
    787.
7   Dickson reminiscences, op cit, BA N99.
8   24 January 1957. *Hansard.* Vol. 563 Col
    396.
9   Memorandum by M of July 1957. BA
    I391.
10  BA J135.
11  28 October 1957. Lady Mountbatten
    papers.
12  13 October 1958. BA Uncatalogued.
13  14 January 1957. BA. I286.
14  M to Ralph Edwards, 25 February 1957.
    BA I276.
15  Diary of Admiral Sir William Davis, p
    798.

16  19 June 1957. BA I300.
17  22 February 1957. BA I41.
18  M to Admiral Scott-Moncrieff, 3 July
    1957. BA I144.
    Interview with Sir Robert Scott.
19  19 February 1957.
20  25 February 1957. BA I276.
21  Cmd: 124.
22  Quarterly News Letter. 28 September
    1957. BA I300.
23  29 October 1957. Copy in Lady
    Mountbatten papers.
24  1 November 1957. BA I300.
25  3 November 1957. Lady Mountbatten
    papers.
26  Quarterly News Letter. 29 September
    1958. BA I301.
27  Diary, 13 November 1957.
    M to Chatfield, 14 November 1957.
    Chatfield papers. CHT/7/9.
28  13 December 1957. BA I300.
29  9 February 1958. BA I301.
30  Quarterly News Letter. 12 April 1957.
    BA I300.
31  Campbell-Johnson narrative. Vol. III, p
    28.
32  Memo of 13 June 1955. BA K208.
33  Noel Monks, *That Day at Gibraltar*.
    London, 1957.
34  Campbell-Johnson narrative. Vol. III, pp
    21–2.
35  M to Davis, 10 May 1954. BA H218.
36  28 February 1957. BA I225.
37  MacDonald to M, 11 June 1957; M to
    MacDonald, 3 and 12 July 1957. BA
    I225.
38  30 May 1957. BA I225.
39  3 June 1957. BA I225.
40  M to Captain P. G. Hammersley, 31 July
    1979. BA K208A.
41  Quarterly News Letter. 14 February
    1957. BA I300.
42  Letter from Burke to the author, 20
    December 1983.
43  'Proceedings of the US Naval Institute.'
    Vol. 107/3/937. March 1981.
44  Ibid.
45  4 September 1956. BA I299.
46  Wyatt to Bousfield. Campbell-Johnson
    narrative. Vol. III, p 31.
47  20 July 1959. Ibid. Vol. III, p 30.
48  24 January 1957. BA I315.
49  Memorandum in Campbell-Johnson
    narrative. Vol. III, p 38.
50  Interview between Bousfield and Sir
    Denning Pearson, 25 July 1961.

51  Wyatt to Bousfield. Campbell-Johnson
    narrative. Vol. III, p 31.
52  29 January 1959. BA I276.
53  15 December 1958. BA I315.
54  Tour diaries, 20 October 1958.
55  Ibid, 17 October 1958.
56  5 November 1958. BA I326.
57  M to Admiral W. J. W. Woods, 2 July
    1957. BA I315.
58  M to Admiral Eccles, 29 October 1957.
    BA I370.
59  M to Rear-Admiral Galantin, 21 January
    1965. BA J40.
60  Quarterly News Letter. 28 September
    1957. BA I300.
61  Ibid, 1 August 1957. BA I300.
62  Ibid.
63  Ibid. 29 September 1958. BA I301.
64  8 May 1958. BA I315.
65  Quarterly News Letter. 9 February 1958.
    BA I301.
66  Lambe to Burke, 11 May 1959. BA S315.
67  Joint memorandum of 22 September
    1958. BA J312.
68  Memorandum of 30 September 1958. BA
    J312.
69  MOM/56. BA J312.
70  28 November 1958. BA J312.
71  Memoranda of 16 and 18 January 1957.
    BA I106.
72  Memorandum of 22 January 1957. BA
    I106.
73  Dickson to Sandys, 2 January 1958. BA
    J135.
74  Dickson reminiscences, op cit. BA N99.
75  Harold Macmillan, *At the End of the
    Day*. London, 1973, p 411.
76  9 July 1958.
77  *At the End of the Day*, op cit, p 412.
78  M to Queen Louise of Sweden, 21 April
    and 4 May 1958. BA S270.
79  Anecdote recorded by M for Prince of
    Wales. BA N73.
80  1 May 1958. BA I64.
81  7 May 1958. BA I64.
82  30 January 1959. BA I325.
83  Dickson reminiscences, op cit. BA N99.
84  5 August 1958. BA S314.
85  Interview with Vice-Admiral Sir Kaye
    Edden.
86  Interview with the Earl of Selkirk.
87  29 May 1959. Campbell-Johnson
    narrative. Vol. III, pp 51–3.
88  2 June 1959. Ibid, p 49.

89  23 April 1959. BA I302.
90  9 July 1959. BA I53.


## CHAPTER 43

### *pages 567–577*

1   20 November 1959. BA S315.
2   Interview with Admiral of the Fleet Sir Edward Ashmore.
3   15 May 1960. BA S315.
4   24 April 1959. BA I150.
5   23 September 1966. Neville papers.
6   Wilkes Harvey to M, 28 March 1961; M to Harvey, 18 April 1961. BA R671.
7   17 January 1960. BA S75.
8   26 February 1960. BA J303.
9   Ibid.
10  Diary, 22 February 1960.
11  Ismay to Vice-Admiral Sir Geoffrey Blake, 3 February 1961. Blake papers. BLE/11.
12  Interview with Vice-Admiral Sir Ian Hogg.
13  *Noel Coward Diaries,* op cit, p 430.
14  31 March 1960. BA J161.
15  Interview with Sir Richard Way.
16  Tour diaries, 20 February 1961.
17  Ibid, 14 May 1962.
18  5 March 1962. Lady Mountbatten papers.
19  Diary, 13 September 1959.
20  21 March 1962. Lady Pamela Hicks papers.
21  31 December 1953. Lady Mountbatten papers.
22  14 February 1941. BA S142.
23  Diary, 6 April 1961.
24  Interview with Admiral Sir John Hamilton.
25  4 February 1957. BA S182.
26  29/30 January 1951. BA. Uncatalogued.
27  2 August 1964.
28  Siegfried Sassoon, *The Heart's Journey.* XII. London, 1928.


## CHAPTER 44

### *pages 578–589*

1   *The Central Organisation of Defence.* RUSI. London, 1970, p 7.

2   SCM/489/44 of 25 September 1944. BA C203.
3   3 January 1946. BA C203.
4   Interview between M and Robin Bousfield. Transcripts. Vol. 1, p 3.
5   Diary, 29 September 1958.
6   Reminiscences of Field-Marshal Sir Francis Festing. BA N99.
7   Tour diaries, 8 October 1959.
8   28 January 1960. BA S150.
9   'Reorganisation of Defence.' Undated memorandum by M. BA K96. p 20.
10  Letter to the author, 20 November 1981.
11  1 January 1960. BA J66.
12  Memorandum of 29 March 1960. BA J360.
13  M to Watkinson, 29 May 1962. BA J360.
14  11 April 1963. BA J360.
15  22 November 1960. BA J196.
16  Memorandum of 11 January 1981. Zuckerman papers.
17  22 November 1960. BA J196.
18  Phillip Darby, *British Defence Policy East of Suez 1947–1968.* London, 1973, p 33.
19  *Defence by Ministry.* London, 1980, p 78.
20  J. H. F. Eberle, 'Defence Organisation–The Future.' *The Management of Defence: Papers presented at the National Defence College, Latimer, in September, 1974.* ed. Laurence Marten. London, 1976, pp 110–11.
21  24 March 1959. BA I144.
22  Interview with Field Marshal Sir Richard Hull.
23  'Reorganisation of Defence', op cit, p 8.
24  Interview with Field Marshal Sir Richard Hull.
25  COS (61) 40. 27 June 1961.
26  *British Defence Policy East of Suez,* op cit, p 255.
27  Interview with Marshal of the Royal Air Force Lord Elworthy.
28  Interview with Field Marshal Sir Richard Hull.
29  Interview with Admiral of the Fleet Sir Varyl Begg.
30  Tom Pocock, *Fighting General.* London, 1973, pp 164 and 182.
31  Interviews with Marshals of the Royal Air Force Sir Dermot Boyle and Sir Thomas Pike, Lord Watkinson, Air Chief Marshal Sir Alfred Earle.
32  3 September 1960. Zuckerman papers.
33  14 September 1960. Ibid.

34 Stephen Hastings, *The Murder of TSR-2*. London, 1966, pp 90–1.
35 Interviews with Mr Julian Amery and Marshal of the Royal Air Force Sir Dermot Boyle.
36 Zuckerman to the author, 5 December 1981.
37 Interview with Lord Watkinson.
38 Bruce Reed and Geoffrey Williams, *Denis Healey and the Policies of Power*. London, 1971, p 177.
39 26 June 1953. BA N43.
40 20 November 1958. BA I326.
41 21 May 1958.
42 7 January 1959.
43 Diary of Admiral Sir William Davis, p 882.

# CHAPTER 45

## *pages 590–597*

1 Tour diaries, 6 October 1959.
2 10 March 1965. BA J72.
3 19 September 1962. Zuckerman papers.
4 18 September 1962. CIGS/PF/499. Zuckerman papers.
5 Tour diaries, 7 March 1961.
6 10 August 1955. BA I120.
7 M to Zuckerman, 12 May 1961. BA J313.
8 Undated memorandum. BA J72.
9 11 April 1960. BA J40.
10 M to Zuckerman, 1 November 1960. BA J311.
11 Record of meeting of 15 November 1960. BA J311.
12 M to Mrs Sybilla O'Donnell. Undated. Mrs S. Clarke papers.
13 Interview with Marshal of the Royal Air Force Sir Dermot Boyle.
14 8 June 1961. Zuckerman papers.
15 Diary, 24 May 1962.
16 Text of talk given at SHAPEX 62, 24 May 1962. BA J401.
17 5 April 1962. Transcripts. Vol. I, p 45.
18 Transcripts, Vol. I, p 86.
19 Tour diaries, 2 October 1964.
20 Diary, 2 July 1964.
21 Transcripts. Vol. I, p 86.
22 *Denis Healey and the Policies of Power*, op cit, p 173.

# CHAPTER 46

## *pages 598–607*

1 Tour diaries, 9 October 1959.
2 Ibid, 11 April 1961.
3 Interview between Alan Campbell-Johnson and Wing Commander A. Le Hardy, 11 February 1963. Transcripts. Vol. I, p 91.
4 Transcripts. Vol. I, p 85.
5 M to Healey, 20 March 1965. BA J215.
6 Interview with General Lauris Norstad.
7 Interview with Lord Thorneycroft.
8 Interview with General Norstad.
9 Diary, 17 December 1960.
10 Annex A to COS/1918/21/6/65. BA J400.
11 8 April 1960. BA J284.
12 2 November 1961. BA J284.
13 M to Nehru, 14 June 1962. BA J302.
14 Record of meeting between M and Field Marshal Ayub Khan, 13 March 1961. BA J324.
15 Record of conversations between M and Nehru, 30 April and 2 May 1963. BA J302.
16 20 June 1962. BA J302.
17 Tour diaries, 2 May 1963 and 27 January 1964.
18 30 January 1964. BA J302.
19 M to Queen Louise of Sweden. Cit Margit Fjellman, *Louise Mountbatten, Queen of Sweden*. London, 1968, pp 198–200.
20 Tour diaries, 28 May 1964.
21 Tour diaries, 6 May 1965.
22 Record of meeting between M and Walter Monckton, 15 February 1956. BA I328.
23 Tour diaries, early November 1962.
24 Record of meeting between M and Field Marshal Ayub Khan, 13 March 1961. BA J324.
25 Tour diaries, 27 February 1961.
26 Ibid, 12 February 1965.
27 Ibid, 16 September 1964.
28 Ibid, 2 June 1965.
29 Ibid, 4 June 1965.
30 Ibid, 22 March 1963.
31 Ibid, 24 February 1963.
32 Interview with Major-General A. P. W. MacLellan.
33 Letter to the author from Sir Peter Garran.
34 8 March 1962. *Louise Mountbatten, Queen of Sweden*, op cit, pp 163–4.

35 Tour diaries, 20 March 1965.
36 Ibid, 18 February 1961.
37 Ibid, 4 May 1963.
38 Ibid, 8 March 1965.
39 Ibid, 13 March 1965.
40 Ibid, 19 February 1961.

## CHAPTER 47
### pages 608–624

1 'Reorganisation of Defence.' Undated memorandum by M. BA K96. p 9.
2 Diary, 30 January 1961.
3 Transcripts. Vol. I, p 80. Macmillan was at Broadlands for the weekend of 2–4 November 1962.
4 See p 489 above for Attlee's invitation.
5 *Newsweek*, 3 June 1963.
6 13 July 1962.
7 Diary, 16 July and 17 July 1962.
8 Transcripts. Vol. I, p 60.
9 2 August 1962. 'Reorganisation of Defence,' op cit, p 10.
10 17 August 1962. BA J117.
11 Scott to M, 18 September 1962. BA J117.
12 Paper dated 9 October 1962. BA J117.
13 'Reorganisation of Defence,' op cit, p 12.
14 'Life and Times.' Programme 11, Reel 6, Pages 2–3.
15 Transcripts. 7 November 1962. Vol. I, pp 69–70.
16 Transcripts. 15 November 1962. Vol. I, p 76. With the exception of Lord Mountbatten I have been able to talk to all the participants at these meetings. Accounts do not tally exactly but there are no serious discrepancies.
17 M to Johnson, 2 February 1974. cit 'Defence by Ministry: the Mountbatten Legacy.' Paper delivered at the international convention of the Inter-University Seminars on the Armed Forces and Society. Chicago, 1983.
18 Prime Minister's Personal Minute No M330/62. BA J102.
19 *Europe in Arms*. London, 1937, pp 189–90.
20 'Reorganisation of Defence,' op cit, p 11.
21 Ibid, p 12.
22 15 December 1962. Ismay papers. III/4/74a.
23 17 December 1962. BA J106.
24 Portal to Ismay, 16 May 1963. Ismay papers. III/4/98.

25 21 December 1962. Ismay papers. III/4/120.
26 Transcripts. 10 January 1963. Vol. I, p 83.
27 'Reorganisation of Defence,' op cit, p 11.
28 Harold Macmillan, *At the End of the Day*, op cit, p 414.
29 Ibid, p 416.
30 'Reorganisation of Defence,' op cit, p 13.
31 Transcripts, 7 November 1962. Vol. I, pp 69–70.
32 Cmd 6923 of 1946.
33 4 January 1963. Ismay papers, III/4/70.
34 3 January 1963. Ibid. III/4/69.
35 18 January 1963. Ibid. III/4/78.
36 Interview with Lieutenant-General Sir Ian Jacob.
37 Transcripts. 15 April 1964. Vol. II, p 2.
38 Interview with Mr Antony Mallaby.
39 Interview with Field Marshal Sir Richard Hull.
40 Interview with Marshal of the Royal Air Force Lord Elworthy.
41 Transcripts. 1 December 1965. Vol. II, p 49.
42 Record of meeting of 13 June 1963. BA J102.
43 Ismay to Jacob, 20 January 1953. Ismay papers. III/4/79.
44 Ismay to Portal, 18 May 1963. Ibid. III/4/99.
45 *The Central Organisation of Defence*, op cit, p 17.
46 Transcripts. 4 July 1963. Vol. I, p 97.
47 21 February 1963. BA J113.
48 Record of meeting on 22 February 1963. BA J113.
49 Memorandum of 21 February 1963. BA J113.
50 282311 of 28 February 1963. BA J106.
51 Tour diaries, 10 March 1963.
52 Macmillan to Thorneycroft, 8 April 1963. *At the End of the Day*, op cit, p 417.
53 29 April 1963. Ibid, p 418.
54 Ibid, p 419.
55 *Defence by Ministry*, op cit, p 119n.
56 Cmnd 2097.
57 *The Management of Defence: Papers presented at the National Defence College, Latimer, in September 1974*, op cit, p 9.
58 7 July and 20 July 1963 respectively.
59 Most ably summarised by Dr Johnson in his *Defence by Ministry*, pp 139–40.

60 *The Central Organisation of Defence,* op cit, p 15.
61 Interviews with Lord Zuckerman, Field Marshal Sir Richard Hull, Lord Thorneycroft, Sir Henry Hardman and Sir Arthur Drew. cf Kenneth Strong. *Intelligence at the Top.* London, 1968, p 225.
62 Thorneycroft to Macmillan, 11 June 1963. BA J72.
63 4 August 1963.
64 18 June 1964. BA J112.
65 4 August 1964. BA J112.
66 Memorandum of 17 September 1964. BA J112.

CHAPTER 48

*pages 625–640*

1 26 June 1964. BA J338.
2 25 July 1962. BA J238.
3 Transcripts. 4 January 1965. Vol. II, p 12.
4 Reminiscences of Sir Louis Gluckstein. BA N99.
5 Transcripts. 20 January 1965. Vol. II, p 14.
6 Transcripts. 4 January 1965. Vol. II, p 8.
7 19 October 1964. BA J61.
8 *Denis Healey and the Policies of Power,* op cit, pp 168–9.
9 Transcripts. 4 January 1965. Vol. II, p 9.
10 Ibid. Vol. II, p 9.
11 M to Wilson, 19 October 1964. BA J61.
12 21 September 1961. BA J56.
13 Transcripts. 1 December 1965. Vol. II, p 48.
14 19 October 1964. BA J61.
15 3 December 1964. BA J112.
16 Interview with Mr Denis Healey.
17 Interview with Sir Patrick Nairne.
18 *The Central Organisation of Defence,* op cit, pp 21–2.
19 Transcripts. 20 January 1965. Vol. II, p 15.
20 Interview with Sir Ronald Melville.
21 Transcripts. 20 January 1965. Vol. II, p 15.
22 M to Sir John Grundy, 13 May 1965. BA J105.
23 1 and 6 April 1965. BA J133.
24 Transcripts. 4 January 1965. Vol. II, pp 12–13.

25 Record of meeting of 10 June 1965. BA J105.
Tour diaries, 14 July 1965.
26 Interview with Mr Healey and letter from Mr Healey to author, 15 July 1981.
27 Interviews with Sir Patrick Nairne and Lord Wilson.
28 2 February 1965. BA J111.
29 Healey to M, 12 April 1965. BA J111.
30 Tour diaries, 14 July 1965. BA J108.
31 Tour diaries, 11 September 1974.
32 17 July 1965. BA J108.
33 Tour diaries, 15 July 1965.
34 Ibid, 18 March 1965.
35 Harold Wilson, *The Labour Government, 1964–70.* London, 1971, p 84.
36 18 March 1965. BA J215.
37 Interview with Sir Philip Woodfield.
38 Transcripts. 9 July 1965. Vol. II, p 39.
39 Minute of 13 June 1965. BA J229.
40 Montgomery to Thorneycroft, 15 April 1964. BA J328.
41 12 November 1964. Zuckerman papers.
42 M to Luce, 3 July 1968; Luce to M, 8 July 1968. BA K176.
43 Interview with Mr Denis Healey.
44 Interview with Lord Wilson.
45 Transcripts. 18 January 1964. Vol. II, pp 2–3.
46 26 July 1964.
47 Interview with Major-General A. P. W. MacLellan.
48 BA J111.
49 M to Montgomery, 27 October 1964. BA N75.
50 Brockman to Rodney Moore, 21 June 1965; Moore to Brockman, 22 June 1965. BA J75.
51 Tour diaries, 15 July 1965.
52 Interview with Sir Patrick Nairne.
53 4 August 1965. BA J74.
54 Memorandum of August 1965. BA J368.

CHAPTER 49

*pages 643–658*

1 M to Lord Brabourne, 7 July 1969. Brabourne papers.
2 M to John Bird, 13 December 1966. BA N88.

3 25 June 1970. Zuckerman papers.
4 Tour diaries, 24 April 1968.
5 M to Luce, 10 February 1966. Zuckerman papers. Transcripts. 13 February 1966. Vol. II, p 52.
6 March 1966. Zuckerman papers. Interviews with Lord Zuckerman and Lord Wilson.
7 M to Wilson, 26 September 1969. Zuckerman papers.
8 Tour diaries, 1 October 1969.
9 19 June 1970. BA K 231A.
10 Tour diaries, 19 June 1970.
11 19 March 1971. BA K115.
12 1 June 1977. BA K115.
13 Tour diaries, 30 July 1976 and memorandum in BA K269A.
14 9 July 1965. BA J685.
15 *The Times,* 20 February 1970.
16 25 February 1970. Zuckerman papers.
17 M to Eileen Bernal, 10 November 1975. Zuckerman papers.
18 Tour diaries, 4 October 1974.
19 M to George Ritchie, 20 June 1973. Brabourne papers.
20 *The Labour Government 1964–70,* op cit, pp 150–1.
21 Record of conversation, 16 October 1965. BA K243.
22 17 October 1965. Brabourne papers.
23 M to Wilson, 20 October 1965. Draft of letter finally sent in shortened form. BA K243.
24 Transcripts. 18 November 1965. Vol. II, p 44.
25 Ibid. 1 December 1965. Vol. II, p 47.
26 M to Wilson, 19 December 1965. Brabourne papers.
27 Transcripts. 1 December 1965. Vol. II, p 48.
28 19–20 August 1966. BA K62.
29 Either on 24 October 1966 (Transcripts. Vol. II, p 57) or 21 October 1966. M to Andrew Yates, 7 January 1977. BA N84.
30 M to Andrew Yates, 7 January 1977. BA N84.
31 Interview with Sir Philip Woodfield.
32 Ibid.
33 Cmnd 3175.
34 *Daily Express,* 24 November 1966. Transcripts. 28 November 1966. Vol. II, p 58.
35 Tom Clayton, *Men in Prison.* London, 1970, p 221.

36 Leo Abse, *Private Member.* London, 1973, pp 133 and 125.
37 Draft article for *The Times,* 8 December 1970. BA N84.
38 M to Sir Philip Allan, 2 September 1972. BA N84.
39 14 November 1977. BA N84.
40 Sir Robert Mark, *In the Office of Constable.* London, 1978, p 76.
41 M to Andrew Yates, 7 January 1977. BA N84.
42 Interview with Sir Robert Mark.
43 Account of M's Governorship supplied to the author by Mr Leslie Baines.
44 Tour diaries, 26 July 1965.
45 Ibid.
46 Account of M's Governorship, op cit.
47 Tour diaries, 22 October 1975.
48 Ibid, 11 January 1966.
49 Ibid, 8 February 1976.
50 Ibid, 13 January 1966.
51 Ibid, 2 February 1971.
52 Ibid, 6 May 1971.
53 Ibid, 18 June 1975.
54 Ibid, 12 January 1966.
55 Ibid, 11 May 1975.
56 30 July 1972. Wolfsgarten papers.
57 Tour diaries, 4 March 1973.
58 M to General Bramall, 13 March 1979. BA K115.
59 Tour diaries, 6 March 1972.
60 Robert Allan to M, 21 November 1969. Zuckerman papers.
61 M to Allan, 1 December 1969. Ibid.
62 Tour diaries, 18 March 1968.
63 *Louis and Victoria,* op cit.
64 Tour diaries, 22 April 1975.
65 Ibid, 26 February 1976.
66 Ibid, 29 September 1973.

# CHAPTER 50

## *pages 659–674*

1 Lord Cudlipp's version of the affair is to be found in his autobiography *Walking on the Water* (London, 1976, pp 324–7) and is brought up to date in his article in *Encounter* of September 1981 (pp 11–21).
2 Cecil King Diary. *Encounter,* September 1981, p 18.
3 King to M, 13 July 1970; M to King, 15 July 1970. BA K162A.

4   15 July 1970. Zuckerman papers.
5   14 November 1975. Zuckerman papers.
6   Interview with Lord Cudlipp.
7   29 March 1981.
8   Zuckerman papers and interview with Lord Zuckerman.
9   *The Times,* 30 March 1981.
10  12 November 1975. BA K162A.
11  Tour diaries, 21 November 1974.
12  Ibid, 8 July 1975.
13  Ibid, 17 March 1976.
14  Ibid, 14 June 1976.
15  Ibid, 9 September 1971.
16  Ibid, 15 May 1978.
    Interview with Sir Ian Gourlay.
17  Interview with Mr Jeffrey Archer.
18  9 November 1971. BA S193.
19  Interview with Mr Robert Blackburn.
20  Tour diaries, 16 May 1976.
21  Interview with Sir Ian Gourlay.
22  Interview with Mr Robert Blackburn.
23  Interview with Chairman Ne Win.
24  10 April 1971. Zuckerman papers.
25  M to Zuckerman, 28 April 1971. Zuckerman papers.
26  5 June 1944. BA C101.
27  M to Sybilla O'Donnell, 11 December 1975. Mrs S. Clarke papers.
28  Howard Thomas, *With an Independent Air.* London, 1977, p 206.
29  Tour diaries, 16 October 1966.
30  Ibid, 2 and 4 February 1967.
31  Ibid, 19 September 1973.
32  John Terraine, *The Life and Times of Lord Mountbatten.* London, 1980, p 193.
33  *With an Independent Air,* op cit, p 214.
34  Tour diaries, 26 February 1967.
35  Ibid, 15 October 1966.
36  Ibid, 1 March 1967.
37  Ibid, 22 February 1967.
38  Ibid, 20 February 1967.
39  Trend to M, 20 May 1968; M to Trend, 29 May 1968. BA K314.
40  M to Mrs Columbus O'Donnell, 13 January 1969. Mrs S. Clarke papers.
41  *With an Independent Air,* op cit, pp 213–15.
42  M to Mrs Sybilla O'Donnell, 17 March 1969. Mrs S. Clarke papers.
    M to Princess Margaret of Hesse, 12 August 1969. Wolfsgarten papers.
43  M to Princess Margaret of Hesse, 12 August 1969. Wolfsgarten papers.
44  *With an Independent Air,* op cit, p 215.
45  Tour diaries, 4 October 1969.

46  Ibid, 18 January 1977.
47  Ibid, June 1970.
48  *Daily Telegraph,* 1 October 1966.
    Sir Charles Strong's reminiscences. BA B205.
49  Tour diaries, 1 May 1976.
50  *Noel Coward Diaries,* op cit, p 634.
51  M to the Queen, 30 November 1971. BA S193.
52  M to Sir Philip Moore, 8 March 1978. BA K7A.
53  Nigel Fisher, *Harold Macmillan.* London, 1982, p 362.
54  Interview with Lord Head.
55  M to Laycock, 1 February 1965. BA J266.
56  M to Mrs Columbus O'Donnell, 7 February 1965. Mrs S. Clarke papers.
57  *Louise Mountbatten, Queen of Sweden,* op cit, p 208.
58  Interview with Lord Adeane.
59  Tour diaries, 25 July 1965.
60  Charles Smith, *Fifty Years with Mountbatten.* London, 1980, p 132.
61  Interviews with Commander Robert De Pass and Lady Alexandra Metcalfe.
62  M to Olaf Caroe, 14 January 1974. BA K281.
63  Jack Kent Hunn, *Not Only Affairs of State.* New Zealand, 1982, p 198.
64  Interview with Sir Henry Hardman.
65  9 March 1965. BA J72.

# CHAPTER 51

*pages 675–688*

1   Tour diaries, 23 March 1969.
2   Ibid, 13 September 1971.
3   10 June 1972. BA S245.
4   Gustaf to M, 6 July 1972. BA S245.
5   M to Prince of Wales, 22 July 1973. BA S33.
    Tour diaries, 11–14 July 1973.
6   Tour diaries, 24 September 1973.
7   M to Prince of Wales, 22 July 1973. BA S33.
8   M to Admiral Stig Ericson, 19 June 1974. BA S239.
9   Ibid, 21 January 1975. BA S239.
10  Interview with General Norstad.
11  M to Constantine, 27 April 1967. BA S203.
12  Ibid, 14 April 1968. BA S203.

13  M to Rogers, 9 November 1970. BA
    K284A.
    Rogers to M, 2 December 1970. BA
    S203.
14  M to Constantine, 27 March 1974. BA
    S202.
15  Ibid, 18 December 1974. BA S202.
16  M to Juan Carlos, 14 December 1969. BA
    S232.
17  M to Rogers, 9 November 1970. BA
    K284A.
18  21 October 1971. BA S232.
19  15 July 1970. BA S232.
20  M to Juan Carlos, 22 November 1976.
    BA S232.
21  M to Jacob, 8 September 1958; Jacob to
    M, 7 October 1958. BA I232.
22  Tour diaries, 22 February 1970.
23  Ibid, 2 March 1970.
24  Interview with Lady Alexandra Metcalfe.
25  Tour diaries, 2 June 1972.
26  Broadcast of 3 June 1972.
27  Tour diaries, 2 June 1972.
28  Ibid, 2 June and 5 June 1972.
29  Ibid, 8 February 1973.
    Record of meeting of June 1973. BA
    S393.
30  Ibid, 27 July 1973.
31  Memorandum of 22 February 1973. BA
    S393.
32  9 December 1974. BA S393.
33  M to Lady Longford, 21 February 1973.
    BA K17.
34  *The Law Journal*, 18 March 1960.
35  Declaration in Council, 9 April 1952.
36  M to Lady Longford, 21 February 1973.
    BA K17.
37  Elizabeth Longford, *Elizabeth R.*
    London, 1983, p 155.
38  M to Lady Longford, 26 June 1973. BA
    K17.
39  *The Law Journal*, 18 March 1960.
40  28 January 1960. BA S150.
41  8 June 1973. BA S33.
42  M to private secretary, 11 January and
    reply on 20 January 1978. BA S194.
43  Tour diaries, 19 July 1972.
44  Duke of Windsor to M, 22 December
    1966; M to Duke of Windsor, 28
    December 1966. BA S395.
45  19 March 1972. BA S185.
46  24 March 1974. BA S185.
47  M to Duke of Edinburgh, 5 June 1971.
    BA S185.
48  Tour diaries, 23 March 1974.
49  Ibid, 25 February 1974.

50  27 February 1971. Zuckerman papers.
51  Tour diaries, 21 March 1974.
52  Ibid, 31 January 1972.
53  19 March 1973. BA S33.
54  28 February 1973. BA S33.
55  29 December 1973. BA S33.
56  27 November 1978. BA S35.
57  19 November 1975. BA S33.
58  24 November 1975. BA S33.
59  Tour diaries, 15 October 1969.
60  21 April 1979. BA S35.
61  14 February 1974. BA S33.
62  27 January 1979. BA S35.

## CHAPTER 52

### *pages 689–702*

1  Tour diaries, 2 July 1970.
2  Interview with Lord Carrington.
3  Tour diaries, 22–23 May 1976.
4  Ibid, 11 March 1976.
5  M to Brabourne, 12 July 1974. Lord
   Brabourne papers.
6  Tour diaries, 13 July 1976.
7  Interview with Major-General A. P. W.
   MacLellan.
8  Tour diaries, 5 October 1976.
9  Ibid, 15 October 1976.
10 Memorandum in BA K381 (i).
11 M to Lieut-Colonel W. Webb-Bowen, 11
   January 1971. BA K381 (i).
12 M to General Sir Robert Mansergh, 19
   November 1969. BA K381 (i).
13 M to Vice-Admiral Sir Andrew Lewis, 18
   January 1971. K381 (i).
14 M to Admiral S. N. Kohli, 23 July 1973.
   BA K381 (2).
15 M to Admiral T. Moorer, 16 July 1971.
   BA K381 (i).
16 7 June 1972. Brabourne papers.
17 Interview with Mrs Pandit.
18 Interview with Miss Sylvia Darley.
19 Tour diaries, 25 September 1971.
20 Gabriel García Márquez, *One Hundred
   Years of Solitude*. London, 1970. Picador
   edition, p 166.
21 15 December 1977. BA S35.
22 Interviews with Sir Ian Gourlay and Mr
   Alexander Peterson.
23 13 March 1979. Zuckerman papers.
24 11 May 1979. Text in *Apocalypse Now?*.
   Bertrand Russell House, Nottingham,
   1980.

25  14 May 1979. Zuckerman papers.
26  M to Prince of Wales, 23 May 1979. BA S35.
27  21 June 1979. BA K231A.
28  27 July 1979. BA K231A.
29  Tour diaries, 31 December 1976.
30  12 September 1971. BA S26.
31  M to the Queen, 25 August 1971. BA S19
32  A. P. Hockaday to M, 10 May 1972. Brabourne papers.
33  Ibid, 17 July 1972. Ibid.

34  Tour diaries, 13 July 1972.
35  12 June 1974. Brabourne papers.
36  7 June 1974. Brabourne papers.
37  M to David McNee, 3 July 1979. Brabourne papers.
38  Interview with Prince Moritz of Hesse-Cassel.
39  13 August 1979. BA S35.
40  *Republican News,* 1 September 1979.
41  30 November 1973. Zuckerman papers.

# Bibliographical Notes

## Manuscript

Incomparably the most important single source for a biography of Lord Mountbatten is the archive at Broadlands (BA). This is organized primarily on chronological principles but there are many exceptions. Correspondence with family and close personal friends has been concentrated in a single section. So, too, have letters which Mountbatten considered to be of particular interest or importance – from and to men such as Churchill, Eisenhower or Montgomery. His letters to his father and mother are not contained in the main sequence but bound in fourteen separate volumes (BA I to XIV). Another section contains reminiscences provided by a wide range of individuals whose lives crossed Mountbatten's at given points (referred to in the notes as 'Reminiscences of. . . .').

There is a multiplicity of diaries. Briefly in 1915 and 1918 and continuously from the early 1920s Mountbatten kept a short daily record of his doings; for the most part this is confined to matters of fact but occasionally opinions and emotions creep in. References to this series appear simply as 'Diary'. In 1920, while with the Prince of Wales on his royal tours, Mountbatten kept informal records described respectively as 'The Unofficial Diary of H.R.H. the Prince of Wales's visit to Australia, New Zealand and the Colonies in the Atlantic and the Pacific. March to October, 1920' and the 'Personal Diary kept by Lieutenant the Lord Louis Mountbatten when accompanying H.R.H. the Prince of Wales on his Tour to India, Japan and the Far East, October 26, 1921–June 21, 1922.' To save unnecessary complication, abbreviated references to both these diaries are to 'Unofficial diary'. As Supreme Commander in South-East Asia, Mountbatten dictated almost every day a long record of his doings for distribution to a short list of recipients. This 'Personal Diary of the Supreme Allied Commander, South-East Asia, 1943–1946' is referred to as 'Personal diary'. Finally, from 1953 onwards he began to keep an extensive record of his various tours abroad. In later years these records increasingly strayed into periods when he was not engaged in travelling but, to follow his own practice, all are referred to as 'Tour diaries'.

Over a period of several years Mr Alan Campbell-Johnson and the late Commander Robin Bousfield worked closely with Lord Mountbatten, collecting material for use by an eventual biographer. Their invaluable labours included many interviews that it would have been impossible for me to repeat due to the death of the chief protagonist, and occasional reference to documents that have subsequently disappeared. References to this series appear as 'Campbell-Johnson narrative'. Distinct from this, Commander Bousfield conducted a large number of interviews with Lord Mountbatten; these are referred to as 'Transcripts'. Mountbatten himself also dictated a series of personal reminiscences, referred to as 'M Reminiscences', and annotated a calendar prepared to list the events of his early life, 'M's notes on calendar'.

Apart from the Broadlands Archives, the most important single source is probably the Public Record Office (PRO), in particular the PREM series and the minutes of the Chiefs of Staff and of the India Committee of the Cabinet. Other useful sources of governmental or quasi-governmental papers are the National Archives in Washington, in particular Anglo-British Conversations (ABC) and Magic material (DIP), and the Nehru Memorial Library in New Delhi (especially the All-India Congress Committee papers).

There are many collections of letters, diaries and relevant papers deposited in public collections, notably those of: Field Marshal Lord Alanbrooke (see also private collections) (Liddell Hart Centre, King's College, London); Mr A. V. Alexander (Churchill College, Cambridge); the Rajkumari Amrit Kaur (Nehru Memorial Library); Field Marshal Sir Claude Auchinleck (Rylands Library, Manchester); Vice-Admiral H. T. Baillie-Grohman (National Maritime Museum, Greenwich); Lord Beaverbrook (House of Lords); Vice-Admiral Sir Geoffrey Blake (National Maritime Museum); Admiral of the Fleet Lord Chatfield (National Maritime Museum); Mr John Christie (India Office Library); Admiral of the Fleet Lord Cunningham (British Library); Mr Hugh Dalton (London School of Economics); Vice-Admiral K. G. B. Dewar (National Maritime Museum); Sir Reginald Dorman-Smith (India Office Library); Admiral Sir Ralph Edwards (Churchill College); Vice-Admiral Sir Alistair Ewing (Imperial War Museum); General Sir Douglas Gracey (Liddell Hart Centre); Vice-Admiral Sir John Hughes Hallett (Imperial War Museum); Field Marshal Lord Ismay (Liddell Hart Centre); Sir Evan Jenkins (India Office Library); Marshal of the Royal Air Force Sir Philip Joubert (R.A.F. Museum, Hendon); Air Chief Marshal Sir Trafford Leigh-Mallory (PRO); Lord Monckton (Bodleian Library, Oxford); Sir Francis Mudie (India Office); Air Chief Marshal Sir Richard Peirse (R.A.F. Museum); Admiral Sir Manley Power (Churchill College); General Sir Harold Pyman (Liddell Hart Centre); President Rajendra Prasad (Indian National Archives); President Roosevelt (President's Personal Files. Franklin D. Roosevelt Library); Captain Stephen Roskill (Churchill College); Field Marshal Lord Slim (Churchill College); Admiral Sir James Somerville (Churchill College); Air Vice Marshal Sir Stanley Vincent (R.A.F. Museum); Admiral Sir William

Whitworth (Imperial War Museum); Admiral Sir Algernon Willis (Churchill College).

Among those collections of papers still in private hands I have consulted those parts of Lord Alanbrooke's papers which have not yet been deposited in the Liddell Hart Centre; the diary of Mr Leo Amery; the papers of Lord Brabourne; Mrs Sybilla Clarke; Admiral Sir William Davis; Mlle Thérèse de Ste Phalle; Princess Margaret of Hesse and the Rhine: Lady Pamela Hicks; Rear-Admiral C. D. Howard-Johnston; Mr Thomas Hussey; Admiral of the Fleet Sir Charles Lambe; the Earl of Listowel; Mr J. H. Money; Lady Mountbatten of Burma; Captain T. Napier; General Sir Robert Neville; Mr Stewart Perowne; the diary of General Sir Ouvry Roberts; the papers of Rear-Admiral George Ross, the Duke of Windsor, Captain Andrew Yates and Lord Zuckerman.

Finally I have been able to read memoirs either published only in part or not at all by Vice-Admiral Baillie-Grohman (National Maritime Museum); Sir Eric Berthoud; Sir Olaf Caroe; General Sir Philip Christison (Imperial War Museum); Sir Conrad Corfield (India Office Library); Vice-Admiral Sir John Hughes Hallett (copy in BA); Marshal of the Royal Air Force Sir Philip Joubert (R.A.F. Museum); Major-General B. D. Kapur and Rear-Admiral George Ross.

## Oral and Correspondence

It has at times seemed to me that there is nobody alive who does not have a view on and some information about Mountbatten. With all those whose names follow I have had communication that has in some way affected the content of this book. A very few who spoke to me asked to remain unmentioned; there must be others whose names should appear here, and to them I apologize. I have not listed separately members of the royal family or of Lord Mountbatten's immediate relations.

Sir George Abell; the Duchess of Abercorn; Mr Edward Adeane; the late Lord Adeane; Mr Joseph Alsop; Mr Julian Amery; Mr Jeffrey Archer; Sir Robert Armstrong; Admiral of the Fleet Sir Edward Ashmore; Mr David Astor; Clarissa, Countess of Avon;

Mr Leslie Baines; Mr John Barratt; Admiral of the Fleet Sir Varyl Begg; Sir Eric Berthoud; Mr Robert Blackburn; Mr Michael Bloch; Maître Suzanne Blum; Captain Edward Blundell; the Rev. Dr Bolt; Mr Clifford Borrett; Marshal of the Royal Air Force Sir Dermot Boyle; Mr Keith Brace; Mr Russell Braddon; Sir Bernard Braine; Rear-Admiral Brian Brayne-Nicholls; Marjorie, Countess of Brecknock; Vice-Admiral Sir Ronald Brockman, Admiral Arleigh Burke;

Mr James Callaghan; Mr Alan Campbell-Johnson; the late Sir Olaf Caroe; Lord Carrington; Mrs Barbara Cartland; the late Lady Casey; Mr Raymond Cazalet; Lord Charteris of Amisfield; Mr George Chowdharay-Best; the late Mr John Christie; Miss Clancy; Mrs Sybilla Clarke; Sir John Colville; Lieutenant-Commander Combe; Mrs Robin Compton; Mr Michael Connolly; Mr J. R. Coolidge; Lord Cudlipp;

Mrs Daly; Miss Sylvia Darley; Admiral Sir William Davis; Sir Patrick Dean; Lady Delamere; Viscount De L'Isle and Dudley; Commander and Mrs Robert De Pass; Mlle Thérèse de Ste Phalle; Rear-Admiral Royer Dick; Lady Douglas-Pennant; Sir Arthur Drew; Commander Peter Du Cane; Captain E. Dunsterville; the late Admiral Sir Robin Durnford-Slater;

Air Chief Marshal Sir Alfred Earle; Vice-Admiral Sir Kaye Edden; Commander F. W. B. Edwards; Mr David Elworthy; Marshal of the Royal Air Force Lord Elworthy;

Lady Falkender;

Mrs Indira Gandhi; Mr Rajiv Gandhi; Sir Peter Garran; Mr Atulya Ghosh; Sir Martin Gilliat; Dr Sarvepalli Gopal; Miss Aideen Gore-Booth; the late Lord Gore-Booth; General Sir Ian Gourlay; Captain E. T. Graham; Admiral Sir Guy Grantham; Vice-Admiral Sir Peter Gretton; Rear-Admiral Gueritz;

Sir Denis Hamilton; Admiral Sir John Hamilton; Sir Henry Hardman; Colonel H. G. Hasler; the late Viscount Head; Mr Denis Healey; Dr A. E. Heenan; Princess Margaret of Hesse and the Rhine; Prince Moritz of Hesse Kassel; Mr Derek Hill; Mrs Michael Hodges; Mr H. V. Hodson; Vice-Admiral Sir Ian Hogg; Lord Home of the Hirsel; Rear-Admiral C. D. Howard-Johnston; the late Rear-Admiral Peter Howes; Vice-Admiral Sir Charles Hughes Hallett; Field Marshal Sir Richard Hull; Mrs Thomas Hussey; Lord Hutchinson;

Mr Thomas Iremonger; Mr David Irving;

Lieutenant-General Sir Ian Jacob; the Rajmata of Jaipur; Mr Roy Jenkins; the late Admiral of the Fleet Sir Caspar John;

Mr Ludovic Kennedy; Daw Khin Kji;

Sir Gilbert Laithwaite; Lady Lambe; Sir John Lang; the late Sir Alan Lascelles; the late Mr Ronald Lewin; the Countess of Lichfield; the Earl of Listowel; Mr David Loman;

Major-General A. P. W. MacLellan; Mr Antony Mallaby; Sir Robert Mark; Mr Arthur Marshall; Mr Philip Mason; Dr Maung Maung; U Maung Maung; Mr Denis McLean; Mr Jagat Mehta; Sir Ronald Melville; Lady Alexandra Metcalfe; Princess Tatiana Metternich; Dr H. G. W. Migeod; Lord Miles; Mr J. H. Money; Mr Anthony Montague Browne; Sir Penderel Moon; Sir Philip Moore; U Myiat Thein;

Sir Patrick Nairne; Mrs Priscilla Napier; General Sir Robert Neville;

Chairman Ne Win; Mr Peter Nicholas; Vice-Admiral Sir Geoffrey Norman; Vice-Admiral Sir Charles Norris; General Lauris Norstad; U Nu; Lady Nye; U Kyaw Nyein;

Lieutenant-General Sir Denis O'Connor; Mr Desmond O'Connor; Mr Vincent Orange;

Mr A. T. Page; Mrs Elizabeth Page; Mrs Vijaya Lakshmi Pandit; Admiral Sir Frederick Parham; General Sher Ali Pataudi; Mr H. M. Patel; Mr Brian Pearce; Mr Stewart Perowne; Mr Alexander Peterson; the late Marshal of the Royal Air Force Sir Thomas Pike; Mrs Emma Pilkington; Sir Raghavan Pillai; Sir Kenneth Ping-fan Fung; Mr John Pownall-Gray;

Mr Siddhartha Ray; Mr G. K. Reddy; Mr Sydney Reynolds; Mr Robert Rhodes-James; General Sir Ouvry Roberts; Captain Alistair Robin; Vice-Admiral Sir Geoffrey Robson; the late Captain Stephen Roskill; Rear-Admiral George Ross; Mrs Walter Rothschild; Madame Ruiller;

Vice-Admiral Jocelyn Salter; Mr Ashoke Kumar Sarkar; Sir Ian Scott; the late Sir Robert Scott; the Earl of Selkirk; Lord Shackleton; Lord Shinwell; Colonel Govind Singh; Dr Karan Singh of Kashmir; Dr Karni Singh of Bikaner; Mr Natwar Singh; Commander B. P. Skinner; Lord Soames; Mr John Somerville; Air Vice-Marshal Sir Deryck Stapleton; General Sir Hugh Stockwell; the late Captain Caspar Swinley;

Mr John Terraine; Lord Thorneycroft; Professor Hugh Tinker; Lord Trend; Mr Hugh Tunney;

Mr Anthony Verrier;

Viscount Watkinson; Sir Richard Way; General Albert Wedemeyer; Lady Jane Wellesley; Mr David Wills; Lord Wilson of Rievaulx; Sir Philip Woodfield; Commissioner Laurence Wren; Sir Woodrow Wyatt;

Captain Andrew Yates;

Lord Zuckerman.

## Printed Sources

It would be profitless to recapitulate all the titles of books referred to in the Notes, but there might be value in a list of those that have been of the greatest help as background to my work.

For Mountbatten's ancestry, childhood and early life Richard Hough's excellent *Louis and Victoria* (London, 1974) provides a useful guide to the available material. For his early life as a sailor, Stephen Roskill's *Naval Policy between the Wars* (2 volumes, London, 1968 and 1976) offers a safe base from which the amateur can operate.

Kenneth Poolman's *The Kelly* (London, 1954) is generally accurate and contains much first-hand reporting not to be found elsewhere.

Mountbatten's career at Combined Operations is well summarized in the official *History of the Combined Operations Organisation, 1940–45* (London, 1956) and, less formally, in Bernard Fergusson's *The Watery Maze* (London, 1961). For this and for Mountbatten's time as Supreme Commander the four relevant volumes of the *Grand Strategy* series (Vol. III, J. M. A. Gwyer and J. R. M. Butler, London, 1964; Vol. IV, Michael Howard, London, 1972; Vol. V, John Ehrman, London, 1956 and Vol. VI, John Ehrman, London, 1956) provide invaluable background.

For this latter period the same is true of the relevant volumes of S. Woodburn Kirby's *The War Against Japan* (Vol. III, London, 1961; Vol. IV, London, 1965; Vol. V, London, 1969). Romanus and Sunderland's *Stilwell's Command Problems* (Washington, 1955), *Time Runs Out in CBI* (Washington, 1959) and *Stilwell's Mission to China* (Washington, 1966) present the American point of view. Christopher Thorne's formidable *Allies of a Kind* (Oxford, 1978) portrays the Anglo-American alliance in Asia and is almost equally valuable for the post-war stage of Mountbatten's period in SEAC. Other particularly useful studies are F. S. V. Donnison's *British Military Administration in the Far East* (London, 1956), Louis Allen's *The End of the War in Asia* (London, 1976) and Hugh Tinker's *The Union of Burma* (Oxford, 1967).

Mountbatten's period in India is majestically documented by Volumes IX to XII of the series *India. The Transfer of Power* (London, 1980, 1981 and 1983). There is much other essential documentation, notably V. P. Menon's *The Transfer of Power in India* (London, 1957) and *The Integration of the Indian States* (Calcutta, 1956) and Alan Campbell-Johnson's contemporary *Mission with Mountbatten* (London, 1951). H. V. Hodson's *The Great Divide* (London, 1969) has stood the test of time remarkably well, though revisionist histories by R. J. Moore, *Escape from Empire* (Oxford, 1983) and Manmath Nath Das, *Partition and Independence of India* (New Delhi, 1982), deserve study.

Books of fundamental importance become more rare in Mountbatten's post-India career. B. B. Schofield's *British Sea Power. Naval Policy in the Twentieth Century* (London, 1967) is useful so far as Mountbatten's periods at the Admiralty are concerned. *Defence by Ministry* by Franklyn Johnson (London, 1980) and *The Central Organisation of Defence* by Michael Howard (London, 1970) provide valuable background to Mountbatten's career as Chief of the Defence Staff.

# Index

# Index

With the exception of the British royal family, crowned heads are listed under the name of their country.
A comma rather than a semi-colon between entries denotes that both entries are covered by the preceding heading. Lord Mountbatten is referred to throughout as M.

A NOTE ON THE TYPE

The text of this book was set in Sabon, a type
face created by Jan Tschichold, the well-
known German typographer. Introduced
in 1967, Sabon was loosely patterned on the
original designs of Claude Garamond
c. 1480-1561.

Composed in Great Britain.
Printed and bound by
Haddon Craftsmen, Inc.
Scranton, Pennsylvania.

Design of display typography,
illustration inserts and binding by
Iris Weinstein and Tasha Hall.

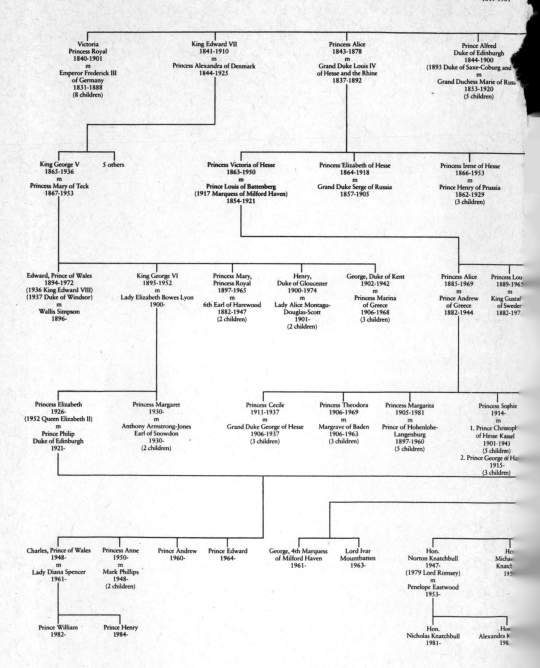

# EARL MOUNTBATTE[N]

QUEEN VICTORI[A]
1819-1901

**Victoria**
**Princess Royal**
1840-1901
m
Emperor Frederick III
of Germany
1831-1888
(8 children)

**King Edward VII**
1841-1910
m
Princess Alexandra of Denmark
1844-1925

**Princess Alice**
1843-1878
m
Grand Duke Louis IV
of Hesse and the Rhine
1837-1892

**Prince Alfred**
**Duke of Edinburgh**
1844-1900
(1893 Duke of Saxe-Coburg and [Gotha])
m
Grand Duchess Marie of Russ[ia]
1853-1920
(5 children)

**King George V**
1865-1936
m
Princess Mary of Teck
1867-1953

**5 others**

**Princess Victoria of Hesse**
1863-1950
m
Prince Louis of Battenberg
(1917 Marquess of Milford Haven)
1854-1921

**Princess Elizabeth of Hesse**
1864-1918
m
Grand Duke Serge of Russia
1857-1905

**Princess Irene of Hesse**
1866-1953
m
Prince Henry of Prussia
1862-1929
(3 children)

**Edward, Prince of Wales**
1894-1972
(1936 King Edward VIII)
(1937 Duke of Windsor)
m
Wallis Simpson
1896-

**King George VI**
1895-1952
m
Lady Elizabeth Bowes Lyon
1900-

**Princess Mary,**
**Princess Royal**
1897-1965
m
6th Earl of Harewood
1882-1947
(2 children)

**Henry,**
**Duke of Gloucester**
1900-1974
m
Lady Alice Montagu-
Douglas-Scott
1901-
(2 children)

**George, Duke of Kent**
1902-1942
m
Princess Marina
of Greece
1906-1968
(3 children)

**Princess Alice**
1885-1969
m
Prince Andrew
of Greece
1882-1944

**Princess Lou[ise]**
1889-1965
m
King Gustaf [VI]
of Sweden
1882-197[3]

**Princess Elizabeth**
1926-
(1952 Queen Elizabeth II)
m
Prince Philip
Duke of Edinburgh
1921-

**Princess Margaret**
1930-
m
Anthony Armstrong-Jones
Earl of Snowdon
1930-
(2 children)

**Princess Cecile**
1911-1937
m
Grand Duke George of Hesse
1906-1937
(3 children)

**Princess Theodora**
1906-1969
m
Margrave of Baden
1906-1963
(3 children)

**Princess Margarita**
1905-1981
m
Prince of Hohenlohe-
Langenburg
1897-1960
(5 children)

**Princess Sophie**
1914-
m
1. Prince Christoph[er]
of Hesse Kassel
1901-1943
(5 children)
2. Prince George of Ha[nover]
1915-
(3 children)

**Charles, Prince of Wales**
1948-
m
Lady Diana Spencer
1961-

**Princess Anne**
1950-
m
Mark Phillips
1948-
(2 children)

**Prince Andrew**
1960-

**Prince Edward**
1964-

**George, 4th Marquess**
**of Milford Haven**
1961-

**Lord Ivar**
**Mountbatten**
1963-

**Hon.**
**Norton Knatchbull**
1947-
(1979 Lord Romsey)
m
Penelope Eastwood
1953-

**Ho[n.]**
Micha[el]
Knatch[bull]
195[-]

**Prince William**
1982-

**Prince Henry**
1984-

**Hon.**
**Nicholas Knatchbull**
1981-

**Ho[n.]**
Alexandra K[natchbull]
198[-]